THOMSON REUTERS™

P9-DEQ-719

NEW! RIA FEDERAL ESTATE AND GIFT TAX HANDBOOK

This new handbook puts up-to-date estate, gift, and generation-skipping transfer tax information at the fingertips of tax professionals, financial planners, estate representatives, and anyone else involved in estate planning or transfer tax return compliance.

The *Handbook* is designed to produce fast, clear answers to a wide range of transfer tax questions and issues. It includes:

- Easily understandable explanations of the latest transfer tax rules and how they affect planning decisions
- Analysis of recent legislative, administrative, and judicial developments affecting transfer taxes
- Tables of rates, exemptions and other key figures, for easy reference
- Sample filled-in estate tax forms based on real world scenarios, to help solve return preparation issues
- A comprehensive topic index to get the user to needed information quickly
- A bound-in quick reference card for handy access to tax rates, exclusions, and other helpful facts and figures

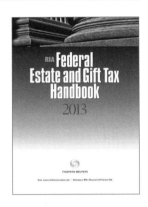

Updated to include coverage of the latest Estate and Gift Tax legislation at the time of publication

AVAILABLE AS AN eBOOK ON
THOMSON REUTERS PROVIEW™

Access trusted Thomson Reuters content from your iPad®, Android® tablet and computer on our revolutionary new eBooks that provide advanced mobility, speed and customization that no other tax and accounting reference providers can match. Our new eBooks allow you to:

- Access your tax and accounting library anytime, anywhere
- Find your answers quickly from the Layered Table of Contents, advanced index tool or full-text search
- Dive deep into your research with fully linked content, history and navigation tools customized to each eBook
- Add personal notes, highlight text and set bookmarks that automatically sync to your other devices and transfer to your next edition – saving you time and ensuring that your work is always with you

ORDER TODAY!
CALL
1.800.950.1216.

FEDERAL ESTATE & GIFT GUIDANCE AT YOUR FINGERTIPS - IN PRINT AND eBOOK.

See back for more details.

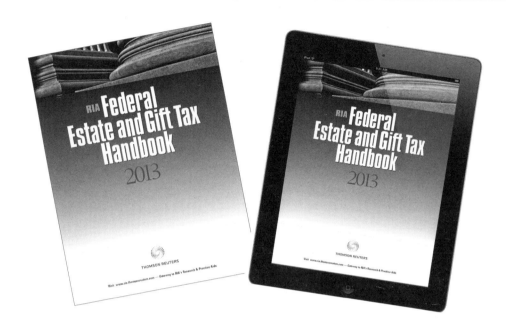

RIA's Complete Analysis of the American Taxpayer Relief Act of 2012 and Earlier Acts of the 112th Congress

With Code and ERISA Sections as
Amended and Committee Reports

Here's your copy of RIA's industry-leading
"Complete Analysis of the American
Taxpayer Relief Act of 2012
and Earlier Acts of the 112th Congress".
We appreciate your patronage.

Here's a list of handy reference numbers:

1-800-950-1216—To place an order for this or other publications
1-800-431-9025—If you have questions about a previously placed
order or a customer service issue
1-800-742-3348—If you have a question about product content

THOMSON REUTERS

This publication is designed to provide accurate and authoritative information in regard to the subject matter covered. It is sold with the understanding that the publisher is not engaged in rendering legal, accounting or other professional service. If legal advice or other expert assistance is required, the services of a competent professional person should be sought.

To ensure compliance with IRS Circular 230 requirements, Thomson Reuters/RIA advises that any discussions of Federal tax issues in its publications and products, or in third-party publications and products on its platforms, are not intended or to be used to avoid any Internal Revenue Code penalty, or to promote, market, or recommend any transaction or subject addressed therein.

RIA's Compete Analysis of the American Taxpayer Relief Act of 2012 and Earlier Acts of the 112th Congress

RIA

Information Products Staff

Helen McFarlane, *Supervisor*

Melissa Acquafredda
Oksana Artemenko
Marie Rivera
Carol Watson
Brett Whitmoyer

Sue Ellen Sobel, *Supervisor*

Alexis Brown
Adel Faltas
Jennifer Huber
Stefan Kunar
Amelia Massiah

Tushar Shetty, *Supervisor*

Raymond AuYeung
Michelle Harmon
Cindy Sotero

Christopher Stryshak, *Supervisor*

John Harrison

Senior Data Support Coordinators

Joan Baselice
Andrew Glicklin
Lisa Sarracino
Jonathan Thayer
Melanie Thomas

Data Analysts

Lisa Alcock
Denise Dockery

Paralegals

Joann Casanova
Catherine Daleo
Monica Grier
Danny Wang

Legal Resource Center & Indexing

Peter Durham, *Manager*

Pierre Calixte
Patricia Link
Theresa Scherne
Michael Stanton
Holly Yue

Janet Mazefsky, *Assistant Manager, Indexing*

Tom Adewolu
Bernie Bayless
George Flynn
Linda Lao
Andrea Leal
Deirdre Simmons
Arlene Verderber

Velma Goodwine-McDermon, *Supervisor*

Charyn Johnson
William Lesesne

Product Development

Nicole Gagnon, *Senior Director, Market Research*

Product Platforms

Kim Chirls, *Lead Project Manager*

End-User Technical Services

Jose Fiol, *Team Lead*

Eric Bauer
Jay Loyola
Tanya

McDonald
Joseph Oliveri

Product Technology

Perry Townes, *Vice President*

Jay Liu, *Director*

Nicole Severson, *Senior Checkpoint Product Manager*

John Melazzo, *Manager*

Laurie Mitchell, *Manager*

Gene Wojna, *Manager*

Jason Shen, *Manager, Technology*

Jason Rapaccuiolo, *Manager, Technology*

Mohammad Nadeem Khan, *Assistant Manager*

Patricia Reilly, *Lead Technical Project Manager*

Shashikanth Ainapur
Sridhar B.
Sunil Bezawada Mohan
Bhairavabhatia
Geoff Braine
Ravindranath Chillagattu
Ram Prasad Chitturi
Resa Cirrincione
Tracey Cruz
Debasis Das
Chris DiGanci

Andy Dreistadt
Peggy Frank
Terri Ganssley
Debashis Ghosh
Vivek Ghosh
Sunil H
Jonathan Henry
Madhu Babu Jellarapu
Sanath Kaspa Gurunadha Sarma Konkapaka
Hena D. Konda
Adithya Koppu
Mallikarjun Kukkadapu
Jay Kwon
Cynthia Lewis
Praveen M.
Praneeth M.
Chris Macano
Venu Masna
Kalyan Maturi
Dave McInerney
Zarina Mohammed
Pamela J. Otruba
Sadguru Palakonda
Amish Parikh
Michelle Paulin
Michael Perrone
Steve Pitamber
Lakshmi Narayana Potnuri
Maria Antony Raja
Abesh Rajasekharan
Randall Rodakowski
Ruth Russell
Madhu Sandepudi
Sirisha Sunkaranam
Sachidananda Swain
Roohi

Tabassum Shafin Thiyam
Vamshi Krishna Thota
Alana Trafford
Vivian Turner
Margaret Taylor Volpe
Connie Wang
Karen Wharton
Steve Wisniewski
Hongtu Zhang

Content Technology

Brian McNamara, *Senior Director*

Alanna Dixon, *Manager*

David Levine, *Architect*

Derek Sanders, *Manager*

Srini Alenoor, *Assistant Manager*

Christopher Grillo, *Project Manager*

Vishal Aruru
David Bantel
Bob Bridier
Satya Devu
John Fletcher K
Gopal Ganta
Nadine Graham
Steven Haber
Prashant Kandukuri
Stephen Karg
Shilesh Karunakaran
Pushpa Malledi
Scott Murphy
Nikitha Naik
Pravallika Parna
William Peake
Phani Kumar Ponugupati
Irina Resnikoff

Swagatika Sahoo
Srinivas Siddavattam
Linda Wiseman

Manufacturing & Fulfillment Services

Rick Bivona, *Director*

Anthony Scribano, *Scheduling and Fulfillment Manager*

Gail Gneiding, *Manufacturing and Outside Composition Manager*

Rachel Hassenbein, *Associate Fulfillment Manager*

John Disposti, *Senior Manufacturing Coordinator*

Greg Miller, *Associate Production Manager*

Bryan Gardner, *Senior Manufacturing Coordinator*

Lourdes Barba
Chris Harrington
Jennifer Kalison

Table of Contents

¶ 1. Organization of the Book

RIA's Complete Analysis of the American Taxpayer Relief Act of 2012 and Earlier Acts of the 112th Congress

This book contains RIA's Complete Analysis of the American Taxpayer Relief Act of 2012 and Earlier Acts of the 112th Congress.

H.R. 8, the American Taxpayer Relief Act of 2012 (PL 112-240, 1/2/2013, referred to in the Analysis as the "2012 Taxpayer Relief Act"), was signed into law by the President on Jan. 2, 2013. The American Taxpayer Relief Act prevents many of the tax hikes that were scheduled to go into effect in 2013 and retains many favorable tax breaks that were scheduled to expire. However, it also increases income taxes for some high-income individuals and slightly increases transfer tax rates.

The Earlier Acts of the 112th Congress, include (1) H.R. 5986, the African Growth and Opportunity Act of 2012 (PL 112-163, 8/10/2012), referred to in the Analysis as the "2012 African Growth Act"; (2) H.R. 4348, the Highway Investment Act of 2012 (PL 112-141, 7/6/2012), referred to in the Analysis as the "2012 Highway Investment Act"; (3) H.R. 3630, the Middle Class Tax Relief and Job Creation Act of 2012 (PL 112-96, 2/22/2012), referred to in the Analysis as the "2012 Middle Class Tax Relief Act"; (4) H.R. 658, the FAA Modernization and Reform Act (PL 112-95, 2/14/2012), referred to in the Analysis as the "2012 FAA Modernization Act"; (5) H.R. 3765, the Temporary Payroll Tax Cut Continuation Act of 2011 (PL 112-78, 12/23/2011), referred to in the Analysis as the "2011 Temporary Payroll Act"; (6) H.R. 674, the Job Creation Act of 2011 (PL 112-56, 11/21/2011), referred to in the Analysis as the "2011 Job Creation Act"; (7) H.R.3080, the United States-Korea Free Trade Agreement Implementation Act (PL 112-41, 10/21/2011) referred to in the Analysis as the "2011 U.S.-Korea Trade Act"; (8) H.R. 2832, the Trade Adjustment Assistance Extension Act.(PL 112-40, 10/21/2011), referred to in the Analysis as the 2011 Trade Extension Act'; (9) H.R. 1473, the Department of Defense and Full-Year Continuing Appropriations Act, 2011 (PL 112-10, 4/15/2011), referred to in the Analysis as the '2011 Appropriations Act'; and (10) H.R. 4, the Comprehensive 1099 Taxpayer Protection and Repayment of Exchange Subsidy Overpayments Act (PL 112-9, 4/14/2011), referred to in the Analysis as the '2011 Taxpayer Protection Act.'

Highlights of the 2012 Taxpayer Relief Act. Highlights of the 2012 Taxpayer Relief Act include (1) the elimination of EGTRRA sunsetting, (2) tax rate increases for higher income taxpayers, (3) capital gain and dividend tax rate increases for higher income taxpayers, (4) the reinstatement of personal exemption phaseouts for higher income taxpayers, (5) the reinstatement of PEASE limitations on itemized deductions of higher income taxpayers, (6) the establishment of permanent AMT relief, (7) retention of the $5 million exemption amount for estate and gift taxes with slight rate increases, (8) 2009 Recovery Act extenders, (9) individual extenders, (10) depreciation changes and extenders, (11) business tax breaks, (12) energy-related tax breaks, and (13) a pension change/revenue raiser that allows for certain retirement plan participants to transfer funds to Roth IRAs.

Elimination of EGTRRA sunsetting. The 2012 Taxpayer Relief Act eliminates the sunsetting provisions in the Economic Growth and Tax Relief Reconciliation Act of 2001 (2001 EGTRRA, PL 107-16, 6/7/2001). The provisions in EGTRRA, other than those made permanent or extended by subsequent legislation, were set to sunset and no longer apply to tax or limitation years beginning after 2010. (EGTRRA § 901, Sec. 901, PL 107-16, 6/7/2001) The Tax Relief, Unemployment Insurance Reauthorization, and Job Creation Act of 2010 (the 2010 Tax Relief Act, PL 111-312, 12/17/2010) extended the EGTRRA provisions for two additional years. Thus, under pre-2012 Taxpayer Relief Act law, beginning in 2013, the EGTRRA sunset would have wiped out a host of favorable tax rules, such as: favorable income tax rate structure for individuals; marriage penalty relief; and liberal education-related deduction rules. The 2012 Taxpayer Relief Act amends EGTRRA so that its provisions are made permanent and no longer automatically sunset in future years.

Tax rate increases for higher income taxpayers. For tax years beginning after 2012, the income tax rates for most individuals will stay at 10%, 15%, 25%, 28%, 33% and 35% (instead of moving to 15%, 28%, 31%, 36% and 39.6% as would have occurred under the EGTRRA sunset). However, a 39.6% rate applying for income above a certain threshold (specifically, income in excess of the "applicable threshold" over the dollar amount at which the 35% bracket begins). The applicable threshold is $450,000 for joint filers and surviving spouses; $425,000 for heads of household; $400,000 for single filers; and $225,000 (one-half of the otherwise applicable amount for joint filers) for married taxpayers filing separately. These dollar amounts are inflation-adjusted for tax years after 2013.

Capital gain and dividend rate increases for higher-income taxpayers. For tax years beginning after 2012, the 2012 Taxpayer Relief Act raises the top rate for capital gains and dividends to 20% (up from 15%) for taxpayers with incomes exceeding $400,000 ($450,000 for married taxpayers). After accounting for the 3.8% surtax under Code Sec. 1411 on investment-type income and gains for tax years beginning after 2012, the overall rate for higher-income taxpayers will be 23.8%. (Under the EGTRRA/Jobs and Growth Act Tax Relief and Reconciliation Act of 2003 (JGTRRA) sunset provisions (EGTRRA § 901 (Sec. 901, PL 107-16, 6/7/2001), and JGTRRA § 107,(Sec. 107, PL 108-27, 5/28/2003) long-term capital gain was to be taxed at a maximum rate of 20%, with an 18% rate for assets held more than five years, and dividends paid to individuals were to be taxed at the same rates that apply to ordinary income.)

For taxpayers whose ordinary income is generally taxed at a rate below 25%, capital gains and dividends will permanently be subject to a 0% rate. (Under the EGTRRA/JGTRRA sunset provisions, long-term capital gain of lower-income taxpayers was to be taxed at a maximum rate of 10%, with an 8% rate for assets held more than five years, and dividends were to be subject to ordinary income rates.) Taxpayers who are subject to a 25%-or-greater rate on ordinary income, but whose income levels fall below the $400,000/$450,000 thresholds, will continue to be subject to a 15% rate on capital gains and dividends. The rate will be 18.8% for those subject to the 3.8% surtax (i.e, those with modified adjusted gross income (MAGI) over $250,000 for joint filers or surviving spouses, $125,000 for a married individual filing a separate return, and $200,000 in any other case).

Reinstatement of personal exemption phaseouts for high income taxpayers. For tax years beginning after 2012, the Personal Exemption Phaseout (PEP), which had previously been suspended, is reinstated with a starting threshold of $300,000 for joint filers and a surviving spouse; $275,000 for heads of household; $250,000 for single filers; and $150,000 (one-half of the otherwise applicable amount for joint filers) for married taxpayers filing separately. Under the phaseout, the total amount of exemptions that can be claimed by a taxpayer subject to the limitation is reduced by 2% for each $2,500 (or portion thereof) by which the taxpayer's AGI exceeds the applicable threshold. These dollar amounts are inflation-adjusted for tax years after 2013.

Reinstatement of Pease limitations for high income taxpayers. For tax years beginning after 2012, the "Pease" limitation on itemized deductions, which had previously been suspended, is reinstated with a starting threshold of $300,000 for joint filers and a surviving spouse, $275,000 for heads of household, $250,000 for single filers, and $150,000 (one-half of the otherwise applicable amount for joint filers) for married taxpayers filing separately. Thus, for taxpayers subject to the 'Pease' limitation, the total amount of their itemized deductions is reduced by 3% of the amount by which the taxpayer's adjusted gross income (AGI) exceeds the threshold amount, with the reduction not to exceed 80% of the otherwise allowable itemized deductions. These dollar amounts are inflation-adjusted for tax years after 2013.

Establishment of permanent AMT relief. The 2012 Taxpayer Relief Act provides permanent alternative minimum tax (AMT) relief. The AMT is the excess, if any, of the tentative minimum tax for the year over the regular tax for the year. In arriving at the tentative minimum tax, an individual begins with taxable income, modifies it with various adjustments and preferences, and then subtracts an exemption amount (which phases out at higher income levels). The result is alternative minimum taxable income (AMTI), which is subject to an AMT rate of 26% or 28%.

Under pre-2012 Taxpayer Relief Act law, the individual AMT exemption amounts for 2012 were to have been $33,750 for unmarried taxpayers, $45,000 for joint filers, and $22,500 for married persons filing separately. Retroactively effective for tax years beginning after 2011, the 2012 Taxpayer Relief Act permanently increases these exemption amounts to $50,600 for unmarried taxpayers, $78,750 for joint filers and $39,375 for married persons filing separately. In addition, for tax years beginning after 2012, it indexes these exemption amounts for inflation.

Under pre-2012 Taxpayer Relief Act law, for 2012, nonrefundable personal credits—other than the adoption credit, the child credit, the savers' credit, the residential energy efficient property credit, the non-depreciable property portions of the alternative motor vehicle credit, the qualified plug-in electric vehicle credit, and the new qualified plug-in electric drive motor vehicle credit—would have been allowed only to the extent that the individual's regular income tax liability exceeded his tentative minimum tax, determined without regard to the minimum tax foreign tax credit. Retroactively effective for tax years beginning after 2011, the 2012 Taxpayer Relief Act permanently allows an individual to offset his entire regular tax liability and AMT liability by the nonrefundable personal credits.

Retention of transfer tax exemption amounts with slight rate increases. The 2012 Taxpayer Relief Act prevents steep increases in estate, gift and generation-skipping transfer (GST) tax that were slated to occur for individuals dying and gifts made after 2012 by permanently keeping the exemption level at $5,000,000 (as indexed for inflation). However, the 2012 Taxpayer Relief Act also permanently increases the top estate, gift and rate from 35% to 40%. The 2012 Taxpayer Relief Act also continues the portability feature that allows the estate of the first spouse to die to transfer his or her unused exclusion to the surviving spouse. All changes are effective for individuals dying and gifts made after 2012.

Extension of certain 2009 Recovery Act provisions. The 2012 Taxpayer Relief Act extends for five years the following items that were originally enacted as part of the American Recovery and Investment Tax Act of 2009 (PL 111-5, 2/17/2009) and that were slated to expire at the end of 2012:

. . . the American Opportunity tax credit, which permits eligible taxpayers to claim a credit equal to 100% of the first $2,000 of qualified tuition and related expenses, and 25% of the next $2,000 of qualified tuition and related expenses (for a maximum tax credit of $2,500 for the first four years of post-secondary education);

. . . eased rules for qualifying for the refundable child credit; and

. . . various earned income tax credit (EITC) changes relating to higher EITC amounts for eligible taxpayers with three or more children, and increases in threshold phaseout amounts for singles, surviving spouses, and heads of households.

Extension of individual tax breaks. The 2012 Taxpayer Relief Act—

... revives for 2012 the deduction for certain expenses of elementary and secondary school teachers, which expired at the end of 2011, and continues it through 2013;

... provides that the exclusion for discharge of qualified principal residence indebtedness, which applied for discharges before Jan. 1, 2013, will continue to apply for discharges before Jan. 1, 2014;

... revives for 2012 the parity for the exclusions for employer-provided mass transit and parking benefits, which applied before 2012, and continues it through 2013;

... revives for 2012 the treatment of mortgage insurance premiums as qualified residence interest, which expired at the end of 2011, and continues it through 2013;

... revives for 2012 the option to deduct State and local general sales taxes, which expired at the end of 2011, and continues it through 2013;

... revives for 2012 the special rule for contributions of capital gain real property made for conservation purposes, which expired at the end of 2011, and continues it through 2013;

... revives for 2012 the above-the-line deduction for qualified tuition and related expenses, which expired at the end of 2011, and continues it through 2013; and

... revives for 2012 the rule allowing tax-free distributions from individual retirement plans for charitable purposes, which expired at the end of 2011, and continues the rule through 2013. Because 2012 has already passed, the 2012 Taxpayer Relief Act provides for a special rule that permits distributions taken in 2012 to be transferred to charities for a limited period in 2013. Another special rule permits certain distributions made in 2013 to be treated as deemed made on Dec. 31, 2012.

Extension and modification of depreciation provisions. The 2012 Taxpayer Relief Act retroactively extends

... 15-year straight line cost recovery for qualified leasehold improvements, qualified restaurant buildings and improvements, and qualified retail improvements;

... 7-year recovery period for motorsports entertainment complexes;

... accelerated depreciation for business property on an Indian reservation;

... increased expensing limitations and treatment of certain real property as Code Sec. 179 property;

... special expensing rules for certain film and television productions; and

... the election to expense mine safety equipment.

The 2012 Taxpayer Relief Act also extends and modifies the 50% bonus depreciation provisions for one year so that it applies to qualified property placed in service before 2014 (before Jan. 1, 2015 for certain aircraft and long-production-period property).

Extension of business tax breaks. The 2012 Taxpayer Relief Act—

... modifies the Code Sec. 41 research credit and retroactively extends it for two years through 2013.

... extends the temporary minimum low-income tax credit rate for nonfederally subsidized new buildings under Code Sec. 42(b)(2)(A) to apply to housing credit dollar amount allocations made before Jan. 1, 2014.

... extends for two years the housing allowance exclusion for determining area median gross income for qualified residential rental project exempt facility bonds.

... retroactively extends the Code Sec. 45A Indian employment tax credit for two years through 2013.

... retroactively extends the Code Sec. 45D new markets tax credits for two years through 2013.

... retroactively extends the Code Sec. 45G railroad track maintenance credit for two years through 2013.

... retroactively extends the Code Sec. 45N mine rescue team training credit for two years through 2013.

... retroactively extends the Code Sec. 45P employer wage credit for employees who are active duty members of the uniformed services for two years through 2013.

... retroactively extends the Code Sec. 51 work opportunity tax credit for two years through 2013.

... retroactively extends Code Sec. 54E qualified zone academy bonds for two years through 2013.

... retroactively extends the enhanced charitable deduction for contributions of food inventory under Code Sec. 174(e) for two years through 2013.

... extends through 2013 the exclusion from a tax-exempt organization's unrelated business taxable income (UBTI) of interest, rent, royalties, and annuities paid to it from a controlled entity under Code Sec. 512(b)(13)(E)(iv).

... extends through 2013 the treatment of certain dividends of regulated investment companies (RICs) as "interest-related dividends."

... extends through 2013 the inclusion of RICs in the definition of a "qualified investment entity" under Code Sec. 897(h)(4).

... extends the subpart F exception for active financing income through tax years beginning before 2014.

... extends through 2013 the look-through treatment for payments between related controlled foreign corporations (CFCs) under the foreign personal holding company rules under Code Sec. 954(c)(6).

... extends the exclusion of 100% of gain on certain small business stock to stock acquired before 2014.

... extends the basis adjustment to stock of S corporations making charitable contributions of property under Code Sec. 1367(a)to apply to tax years beginning in 2013.

... extends through 2013 the reduction in S corporation recognition period for built-in gains tax under Code Sec. 1374(d)(7), replacing the 10-year period with a 5-year period.

... extends various empowerment zone tax incentives, including the designation of an empowerment zone and of additional empowerment zones under Code Sec. 1391(d) (through 2013) and the period for which the percentage exclusion for qualified small business stock of a corporation which is a qualified business entity is 60% under Code Sec. 1202(a)(2) (through 2018).

... extends tax-exempt financing for the New York Liberty Zone under Code Sec. 1400L(d)(2) for bonds issued before 2014.

... extends the temporary increase in the limit on cover over rum excise taxes to Puerto Rico and the Virgin Islands for spirits brought into the U.S. before 2014.

... modifies and extends through 2014 the American Samoa economic development credit.

Extension of energy-related tax breaks. The 2012 Taxpayer Relief Act—

... retroactively extends the nonbusiness energy property credit under Code Sec. 25C for energy-efficient existing homes for two years through 2013. A taxpayer can claim a 10% credit on the cost of: (1) qualified energy efficiency improvements, and (2) residential energy property expenditures, with a lifetime credit limit of $500 ($200 for windows and skylights).

... retroactively extends the alternative fuel vehicle refueling property credit under Code Sec. 30Cfor two years through 2013 so that taxpayers can claim a 30% credit for qualified alternative fuel vehicle refueling property placed in service through 2013, subject to the $30,000 and $1,000 thresholds.

... modifies and retroactively extends the credit for 2- or 3-wheeled plug-in electric vehicles under Code Sec. 30D for two years through 2013.

... modifies and extends the cellulosic biofuel producer credit under Code Sec. 40(b) for one year through 2013.

... retroactively extends the credit for biodiesel and renewable diesel under Code Sec. 40A for two years through 2013.

... extends for one year the production credit for Indian coal facilities placed in service before 2009 under Code Sec. 45(e)(10). The credit applied to coal produced by the taxpayer at an Indian coal production facility during the 8-year period beginning on Jan. 1, 2006, and sold by the taxpayer to an unrelated person during the 8-year period and the tax year.

. . . modifies and extends for one year the credits for facilities producing energy from certain renewable resources underCode Sec. 45. A facility using wind to produce electricity will be a qualified facility if it is placed in service before 2014.

. . . retroactively extends the credit for energy-efficient new homes under Code Sec. 45Lfor two years through 2013.

. . . retroactively extends the credit for energy-efficient appliances under Code Sec. 45Mfor two years through 2013.

. . . modifies and extends for one year the additional depreciation deduction allowance for cellulosic biofuel plant property under Code Sec. 168(l)(2)to include property placed in service before 2014..

. . . retroactively extends for two years through 2013 the special rule for sales or dispositions to implement Federal Energy Regulatory Commission (FERC) or State electric restructuring policy for qualified electric utilities.

. . . retroactively extends for two years through 2013 the alternative fuels excise tax credits under Code Sec. 6426(d)(5) and Code Sec. 6426(e)(3) for sales or use of alternative fuels or alternative fuel mixtures.

Pension change. For transfers after Dec. 31, 2012, in tax years ending after that date, plan provisions in an applicable retirement plan (which includes a qualified Roth contribution program) can allow participants to elect to transfer amounts to designated Roth accounts with the transfer being treated as a taxable qualified rollover contribution under Code Sec. 408A(e).

Highlights of the Earlier Acts of the 112th Congress. Highlights of the Earlier Acts of the 112th Congress include (1) health related provisions, (2) pension provisions, (3) excise provisions, and (4) payroll and other provisions.

Health related provisions. The health related provisions in the Earlier Acts of the 112th Congress include provisions that:

. . . modify AGI for determining eligibility for, and the amount of, the post-2013 premium tax credit to include nontaxable social security income.

. . . apply simplified payback caps on excess advance premium assistance credits to taxpayers below 400% of the poverty line.

. . . repeal the post–2013 rules requiring employers to provide free choice vouchers to employees.

. . . disallow the health coverage tax credit (HCTC) for health insurance costs of trade-displaced workers and PBGC pension recipients after 2013.

. . . reinstate the requirement that IRS make retroactive HCTC payments for coverage months beginning after Nov. 20, 2011.

. . . retroactively increase the HCTC and percentage limit on advance HCTC payments to 72.5% (from 65%) for post-Feb. 2011 coverage months.

. . . extend allowance of HCTC for VEBA coverage.

... retroactively extend HCTC eligibility for individuals not enrolled in training programs to coverage periods beginning after Feb. 12, 2011.

... require HCTC eligibility certificates issued after Nov. 20, 2011 to include information on qualified health insurance and enrollment procedures.

... extend the rule under which a period after a TAA-related loss of health coverage is not counted in determining a HIPAA 63–day lapse in creditable coverage to plan years beginning before Jan. 1, 2014. extend eligibility for COBRA continuation coverage from Nov. 20, 2011 through Jan. 1, 2014 for PBGC recipients and TAA-eligible individuals who lose employment or work hours.

... repeal post-2013 health insurance coverage information reporting and related statement requirements for "offering employers."

Pension provisions. The pension provisions in the Earlier Acts of the 112th Congress include provisions that:

... allow interest rate smoothing over a 25-year period to determine liabilities.

... allow excess pension plan assets to be used to fund retiree group-term life insurance.

... extend rules permitting transfer of excess defined benefit plan assets to retiree health accounts through 2021.

... provide that the additional 10% tax on early withdrawals from qualified retirement plans will not apply to federal phased retirement program payments.

... allow rollovers to traditional IRAs for amounts received from airlines that filed for bankruptcy after Sept. 11, 2001 and before Jan. 1, 2007.

... make certain changes to PBGC premiums for single-employer and multiemployer defined benefit plans.

Excise provisions. The excise provisions in the Earlier Acts of the 112th Congress include provisions that:

... delay reduction of various fuel excise tax rates until after Sept. 30, 2016.

... extend the Leaking Underground Storage Tank (LUST) Trust Fund 0.1-cent-per-gallon tax through Sept. 30, 2016.

... extend the retail truck and manufacturer's tire excise taxes, and certain exemptions, through Sept. 30, 2016.

... apply the floor stock credit, or refund for tire tax and removal-at-terminal fuel tax, to tires or fuel held by dealers on Oct. 1, 2016.

... extend the highway use tax, and certain highway use tax exemptions, through Sept. 30, 2017.

... extend the airport and airway trust fund excise taxes through Sept. 30, 2015.

... eliminate the exemption from air transportation excise taxes for small jet aircraft operated on nonestablished lines.

... impose the 14.1 cents-per-gallon surtax on fuel used in fractional ownership aircraft flights; flights are also taxed as noncommercial aviation, but exempted from air transportation taxes.

Payroll and other provisions. The payroll and other provisions in the Earlier Acts of the 112th Congress include provisions that:

... apply the 10.4% OASDI rate for 2012 to self-employment income up to the $110,100 ceiling.

... apply the reduced 4.2% employee social security tax rate for all of 2012 under the payroll tax holiday.

... allow tax-exempt employers to get FICA tax credit for hiring qualified veterans.

... repeal the expanded information reporting requirement for post-2011 payments of $600 or more to non-tax-exempt corporations.

... repeal the expanded information reporting for post-2011 payments of $600 or more of gross proceeds or amounts in consideration for property.

... retroactively repeal information reporting for certain recipients of rental income for payments of $600 or more to service providers.

... prospectively repeal the mandatory 3% withholding on payments to government contractors.

... extend through 2012modify the work opportunity credit as applied to qualified veterans.

... impose the penalty for lack of transparency in airline passenger tax disclosures.

... the penalty on paid preparers for noncompliance with due diligence rules from $100 to $500.

... allow tax-exempt qualified bonds to be used to finance fixed-wing emergency medical aircraft.

... extend the limitation on the deduction of repurchase premium to debt convertible to parent-subsidiary controlled group stock.

... expand the 100% maximum rate for continuous levy to include governmental payments to vendors from the sale or lease of property.

Analysis of the American Taxpayer Relief Act of 2012 and Earlier Acts of the 112th Congress. This section includes the Analysis of the tax provisions of the 2012 Taxpayer Relief Act, the 2012 African Growth Act, the 2012 Highway Investment Act, the 2012 Middle Class Tax Relief Act, the 2012 FAA Modernization Act, the 2011 Temporary Payroll Act, the 2011 Job Creation Act, the 2011 U.S.-Korea Trade Act, the 2011 Trade Extension Act, the 2011 Appropriations Act and the 2011 Taxpayer Protection Act arranged in topical order. Each analysis paragraph starts with a boldface title. That is followed by a list of the Code sections amended, added, affected, repealed by or related to the change, the Act section that caused the change, and the generally effective date for the change. Each Analysis paragraph discusses the background for the change, the new law change, and the effective date for that change. Analysis paragraphs may include (1) illustrations and observations providing practical insight into the effects of the change, (2) recommendations explaining how to take advantage of opportunities presented by the law change, (3) cautions explaining how to avoid pitfalls created by the law change, and (4) client letters highlighting important law changes. The Analysis is reproduced at ¶ 100 *et seq.* . . . . p. 1

Client Letters. The Analysis includes nine client letters highlighting the tax changes made by the 2012 Taxpayer Relief Act. The Client Letters that highlight the 2010 Tax Relief Act changes begin at ¶ 2001 *et seq.* . . . . . p. 351

Code as Amended. All Code sections that were amended, added, repealed, or redesignated by the tax provisions of the 2012 Taxpayer Relief Act, the 2012 African Growth Act, the 2012 Highway Investment Act, the 2012 Middle Class Tax Relief Act, the 2012 FAA Modernization Act, the 2011 Temporary Payroll Act, the 2011 Job Creation Act, the 2011 U.S.-Korea Trade Act, the 2011 Trade Extension Act, the 2011 Appropriations Act and the 2011 Taxpayer Protection Act appear in Code section order as amended, added, repealed, or redesignated. New matter is shown in italics. Deleted material and effective dates are shown in footnotes. The Code as Amended is reproduced at ¶ 3000 *et seq.* . . . p. 501

ERISA as Amended. All ERISA sections that were amended, added, repealed, or redesignated by the the 2012 Highway Investment Act and the 2011 Trade Extension Act appear in ERISA section order as amended, added, repealed, or redesignated. New matter is shown in italics. Deleted material and effective dates are shown in footnotes. No ERISA changes were made by the 2012 Taxpayer Relief Act, the 2012 African Growth Act, the 2012 Middle Class Tax Relief Act, the 2012 FAA Modernization Act, the 2011 Temporary Payroll Act, the 2011 Job Creation Act, the 2011 U.S.-Korea Trade Act, the 2011 Appropriations Act and the 2011 Taxpayer Protection Act. ERISA as Amended is reproduced at ¶ 3500 *et seq.* . . . . p. 901

Act Sections Not Amending Code. This section reproduces in Act section order, all sections of 2012 Taxpayer Relief Act, the 2012 African Growth Act, the 2012 Highway Investment Act, the 2012 Middle Class Tax Relief Act, the 2012 FAA Modernization Act, the 2011 Temporary Payroll Act, the 2011 Job Creation Act, the 2011 U.S.-Korea Trade Act, the 2011 Trade Extension Act, the 2011 Appropriations Act and the 2011 Taxpayer Protection Act, or portions thereof that are tax or ERISA related but do not amend specific Code or ERISA sections. The Act Sections Not Amending Code are reproduced at ¶ 4000 *et seq.* . . . . p. 1,001

Committee Reports. This section reproduces all relevant parts of Committee Reports and/or Joint Committee on Taxation Explanations that have been issued for the 2012 Taxpayer Relief Act, the 2012 African Growth Act, the 2012 Highway Investment Act, the 2012 Middle Class Tax Relief Act, the 2012 FAA Modernization Act, the 2011 Temporary Payroll Act, the 2011 Job Creation Act, the 2011 U.S.-Korea Trade Act, the 2011 Trade Extension Act, the 2011 Appropriations Act and the 2011 Taxpayer Protection Act.

H Rept No. 112-557 has been issued for the 2012 Highway Investment Act

H Rept No. 112-399 has been issued for the 2012 Middle Class Tax Relief Act.

H Rept No. 112-381 has been issued for the 2012 FAA Modernization Act

H Rept No. 112-253 has been issued for the 2011 Job Creation Act.

H Rept No. 112-239 has been issued for the 2011 U.S.-Korea Trade Act.

H Rept No. 112-15 and JCX-9-11 have been issued for the 2011 Taxpayer Protection Act.

There are no reports for the 2012 Taxpayer Relief Act. However, there is a Senate Finance Committee Staff Summary of the 2012 Taxpayer Relief Act. In addition, on Jan. 8, 2013, the Joint Committee on Taxation issued JCX-2-13R: Overview of the Federal Tax System as in Effect for 2013, which, although not directly related to the 2012 Taxpayer Relief Act, nonetheless provides relevant explanatory material of the state of the tax law immediately after the enactment of the 2012 Taxpayer Relief Act. The Senate Finance Committee Staff Summary and the Joint Committee on Taxation Overview of the Federal Tax System as in Effect for 2013 are reproduced after the Index at the back of the book.

> **observation:** As announced on Jan. 11, 2013 in IR-2013-4, IRS has also issued Rev Proc 2013-15, which provides annual inflation adjustments for the 2013 tax year, including the tax rate schedules, and other tax changes from the 2012 Taxpayer Relief Act.

No reports have been issued for the 2012 African Growth Act, the 2011 Temporary Payroll Act, the 2011 Trade Extension Act, and the 2011 Appropriations Act.

The relevant Committee Reports and explanatory language for the 2012 Highway Investment Act, the 2012 Middle Class Tax Relief Act, the 2012 FAA Modernization Act, the 2011 Job Creation Act, the 2011 U.S.-Korea Trade Act and the 2011 Taxpayer Protections Act are respectively reproduced at ¶ 5401 et seq., ¶ 5501 et seq., ¶ 5601 et seq.; ¶ 5701 et seq.; ¶ 5801 et seq. and ¶ 5901 et seq. . . . . p. 1,301

Act Section Cross Reference Table. Arranged in Act section order, this table shows substantive Code section(s) amended, added, affected, repealed by or related to the 2012 Taxpayer Relief Act, the 2012 African Growth Act, the 2012 Highway Investment Act, the 2012 Middle Class Tax Relief Act, the 2012

FAA Modernization Act, the 2011 Temporary Payroll Act, the 2011 Job Creation Act, the 2011 U.S.-Korea Trade Act, the 2011 Trade Extension Act, the 2011 Appropriations Act and the 2011 Taxpayer Protection Act section, the topic involved, the generally effective date of the amendment, the relevant paragraph number for the Analysis and the paragraph where the relevant Committee Reports are reproduced. The table is reproduced at ¶ 6000. . . . . p. 1,401

Code Section Cross Reference Table. Arranged in Code section order, this table shows the 2012 Taxpayer Relief Act, the 2012 African Growth Act, the 2012 Highway Investment Act, the 2012 Middle Class Tax Relief Act, the 2012 FAA Modernization Act, the 2011 Temporary Payroll Act, the 2011 Job Creation Act, the 2011 U.S.-Korea Trade Act, the 2011 Trade Extension Act, the 2011 Appropriations Act and the 2011 Taxpayer Protection Act section(s) that amend, add, affect, repeal or relate to the Code Section, the topic involved, the generally effective date of the amendment, the relevant paragraph number for the Analysis and the paragraph where the relevant Committee Reports are reproduced. The table is reproduced at ¶ 6001. . . . . p. 1,447

Act Section ERISA Cross Reference Table. Arranged in Act section order, this table shows substantive ERISA section(s) amended, added, affected, repealed by or related to the 2012 Highway Investment Act and 2011 Trade Extension Act section, the topic involved, the generally effective date of the amendment, the relevant paragraph number for the Analysis and the paragraph where the relevant Committee Reports are reproduced. The table is reproduced at ¶ 6002. . . . . p. 1,493

ERISA Section Cross Reference Table. Arranged in ERISA section order, this table shows the 2012 Highway Investment Act and 2011 Trade Extension Act section(s) that amend, add, affect, repeal or relate to the ERISA Section, the topic involved, the generally effective date of the amendment, the relevant paragraph number for the Analysis and the paragraph where the relevant Committee Reports are reproduced. The table is reproduced at ¶ 6003. . . . . p. 1,499

Code Sections Amended by Acts. Arranged in Code section order, this table shows all changes to the Internal Revenue Code made by the 2012 Taxpayer Relief Act, the 2012 African Growth Act, the 2012 Highway Investment Act, the 2012 Middle Class Tax Relief Act, the 2012 FAA Modernization Act, the 2011 Temporary Payroll Act, the 2011 Job Creation Act, the 2011 U.S.-Korea Trade Act, the 2011 Trade Extension Act, the 2011 Appropriations Act and the 2011 Taxpayer Protection Act, including conforming amendments. The table is reproduced at ¶ 6004. . . . . p. 1,505

Act Sections Amending Code. Arranged in Act section order, this table shows all changes to the Internal Revenue Code made by the 2012 Taxpayer Relief Act, the 2012 African Growth Act, the 2012 Highway Investment Act, the 2012 Middle Class Tax Relief Act, the 2012 FAA Modernization Act, the

2011 Temporary Payroll Act, the 2011 Job Creation Act, the 2011 U.S.-Korea Trade Act, the 2011 Trade Extension Act, the 2011 Appropriations Act and the 2011 Taxpayer Protection Act. including conforming amendments. The table is reproduced at ¶ 6005. . . . . p. 1,509

ERISA Sections Amended by Acts. Arranged in ERISA section order, this table shows all changes to ERISA made by the 2012 Highway Investment Act and 2011 Trade Extension Act, including conforming amendments. The table is reproduced at ¶ 6006. . . . . p. 1,513

Act Sections Amending ERISA. Arranged in Act section order, this table shows all changes to ERISA made by the 2012 Highway Investment Act and 2011 Trade Extension Act, including conforming amendments. The table is reproduced at ¶ 6007. . . . . p. 1,515

Federal Tax Coordinator 2d ¶ s Affected by Acts. Arranged in FTC 2d ¶ order, this table shows the FTC 2d paragraphs that have been affected by the 2012 Taxpayer Relief Act, the 2012 African Growth Act, the 2012 Highway Investment Act, the 2012 Middle Class Tax Relief Act, the 2012 FAA Modernization Act, the 2011 Temporary Payroll Act, the 2011 Job Creation Act, the 2011 U.S.-Korea Trade Act, the 2011 Trade Extension Act, the 2011 Appropriations Act and the 2011 Taxpayer Protection Act. The table is reproduced at ¶ 6008. . . . . p. 1,517

United States Tax Reporter ¶ s Affected by Acts. Arranged in USTR ¶ order, this table shows the USTR paragraphs that have been affected by the 2012 Taxpayer Relief Act, the 2012 African Growth Act, the 2012 Highway Investment Act, the 2012 Middle Class Tax Relief Act, the 2012 FAA Modernization Act, the 2011 Temporary Payroll Act, the 2011 Job Creation Act, the 2011 U.S.-Korea Trade Act, the 2011 Trade Extension Act, the 2011 Appropriations Act and the 2011 Taxpayer Protection Act. The table is reproduced at ¶ 6009. . . . . p. 1,521

Tax Desk ¶ s Affected by Acts. Arranged in Tax Desk ¶ order, this table shows the Tax Desk paragraphs that have been affected by the 2012 Taxpayer Relief Act, the 2012 African Growth Act, the 2012 Highway Investment Act, the 2012 Middle Class Tax Relief Act, the 2012 FAA Modernization Act, the 2011 Temporary Payroll Act, the 2011 Job Creation Act, the 2011 U.S.-Korea Trade Act, the 2011 Trade Extension Act, the 2011 Appropriations Act and the 2011 Taxpayer Protection Act. The table is reproduced at ¶ 6010. . . . p. 1,523

Pension Analysis ¶ s Affected by Acts. Arranged in Pension and Benefits Analysis ¶ order, this table shows the Pension and Benefits Analysis paragraphs that have been affected by the 2012 Taxpayer Relief Act, the 2012 African Growth Act, the 2012 Highway Investment Act, the 2012 Middle Class Tax Relief Act, the 2012 FAA Modernization Act, the 2011 Temporary Payroll Act, the 2011 Job Creation Act, the 2011 U.S.-Korea Trade Act, the 2011 Trade

Extension Act, the 2011 Appropriations Act and the 2011 Taxpayer Protection Act. The table is reproduced at ¶ 6011. . . . . p. 1,525

Pension & Benefits Explanations ¶ s Affected by Acts. Arranged in Pension and Benefits Explanations ¶ order, this table shows the Pension and Benefits Explanations paragraphs that have been affected by the 2012 Taxpayer Relief Act, the 2012 African Growth Act, the 2012 Highway Investment Act, the 2012 Middle Class Tax Relief Act, the 2012 FAA Modernization Act, the 2011 Temporary Payroll Act, the 2011 Job Creation Act, the 2011 U.S.-Korea Trade Act, the 2011 Trade Extension Act, the 2011 Appropriations Act and the 2011 Taxpayer Protection Act. The table is reproduced at ¶ 6012. . . . p. 1,527

Benefits Explanations ¶ s Affected by Acts. Arranged in Benefits Explanations ¶ order, this table shows the Benefits Explanations paragraphs that have been affected by the 2012 Taxpayer Relief Act, the 2012 African Growth Act, the 2012 Highway Investment Act, the 2012 Middle Class Tax Relief Act, the 2012 FAA Modernization Act, the 2011 Temporary Payroll Act, the 2011 Job Creation Act, the 2011 U.S.-Korea Trade Act, the 2011 Trade Extension Act, the 2011 Appropriations Act and the 2011 Taxpayer Protection Act. The table is reproduced at ¶ 6013. . . . . p. 1,529

Estate Planning Analysis ¶ s Affected by Acts. Arranged in Estate Planning Analysis ¶ order, this table shows the Estate Planning Analysis paragraphs that have been affected by the 2012 Taxpayer Relief Act, the 2012 African Growth Act, the 2012 Highway Investment Act, the 2012 Middle Class Tax Relief Act, the 2012 FAA Modernization Act, the 2011 Temporary Payroll Act, the 2011 Job Creation Act, the 2011 U.S.-Korea Trade Act, the 2011 Trade Extension Act, the 2011 Appropriations Act and the 2011 Taxpayer Protection Act. The table is reproduced at ¶ 6014. . . . . p. 1,531

Appendix. The Appendix contains (1) the Senate Finance Committee Staff Summary of the 2012 Taxpayer Relief Act, (2) JCX-2-13R, the Joint Committee on Taxation Staff Overview of the Federal Tax System as in Effect for 2013, (3) Rev Proc 2013-15 setting forth inflation adjusted items for 2013, and (4) IR-2013-4 announcing the inflation adjustments for 2013. These documents are reproduced in the Appendix at ¶ 6015. . . . . p. 1,533

Index. A detailed index, which directs the reader to the appropriate Analysis paragraph, is reproduced immediately after the aforementioned Tables for the Complete Analysis. . . . . p. 1,901

¶ 2. Contents

ENERGY PROVISIONS 1000

MISCELLANEOUS PROVISIONS   **1500**

HEALTH RELATED PROVISIONS FROM EARLIER ACTS OF THE 112TH CONGRESS   **1600**

Contents

¶ 100. Noncorporate Income Tax Rates

¶ 101. Individuals' 10%, 25%, 28%, 33%, and 35% tax brackets are made permanent; high-income taxpayers taxed at 39.6% rate after 2012

Code Sec. 1(i)(2), as amended by 2012 Taxpayer Relief Act §101(b)(1)(A)
Code Sec. 1(i)(3), as amended by 2012 Taxpayer Relief Act §101(b)(1)(B)
Code Sec. None, 2012 Taxpayer Relief Act §101(a)(1)
Generally effective: Tax years beginning after Dec. 31, 2012
Committee Reports, None

To compute regular tax liability, an individual uses the appropriate tax rate schedule (or IRS-issued income tax tables for taxable income of less than $100,000). The Code provides four (statutory) tax rate schedules based on filing status, i.e., single, married filing jointly/surviving spouse, married filing separately, and head of household. Each schedule is divided into income ranges ("tax brackets"), which are taxed at progressively higher marginal tax rates as income increases. The same marginal tax rates apply to all individual taxpayers, but the bracket amounts (income ranges) to which the rates apply differ based on the taxpayer's filing status.

The statutory rate schedules are divided into five tax brackets—15%, 28%, 31%, 36%, and 39.6%. But, as described below, other Code provisions modify these statutory rate schedules. Each year IRS adjusts the bracket amounts for each rate schedule for inflation (with certain exceptions, for inflation since 1992), and IRS's inflation-adjusted rate schedules are the ones used to compute tax (not the statutory rate schedules).

EGTRRA/JGTRRA/WFTRA changes. Under the Economic Growth and Tax Relief Reconciliation Act of 2001 ("EGTRRA," Sec. 101, PL 107-16, 6/7/2001), the Jobs and Growth Tax Relief Reconciliation Act of 2003 ("JGTRRA," Sec. 104, PL 108-27, 5/28/2003, and Sec. 105, PL 108-27, 5/28/2003), and the Working Families Tax Relief Act of 2004 ("WFTRA," Sec. 101, PL 108-311, 10/4/2004), the statutory rate schedules were modified to:

- add a new 10% tax bracket for individuals carved out of the existing 15% tax bracket (resulting in six tax brackets for individuals instead of five);

FTC 2d References are to Federal Tax Coordinator 2d
FIN References are to RIA's Analysis of Federal Taxes: Income (print)
USTR References are to United States Tax Reporter: Income
PCA References are to Pension Analysis (print and electronic)
PBE References are to Pension & Benefits Explanations
BCA References are to Benefits Analysis (electronic)
BC References are to Benefits Coordinator (print)
EP References are to Estate Planning Analysis (print and electronic)

- phase-in a reduction of the top four marginal tax rates to 25%, 28%, 33%, and 35%; and

- provide a special inflation adjustment for the 10% bracket (computing inflation since 2002).

IRS also was required to adjust its income tax tables (which are based on the rate schedules) to reflect these EGTRRA changes. (FTC 2d/FIN ¶ A-1100, ¶ A-1101, ¶ A-1102, ¶ A-1103, ¶ A-1104, ¶ A-1113; USTR ¶ 14, ¶ 14.08; TaxDesk ¶ 568,201, ¶ 568,202, ¶ 568,203, ¶ 568,213)

Sunset. Under Sec. 901 of title IX of EGTRRA (Sec. 901, PL 107-16, 6/7/2001), to which the applicable JGTRRA (Sec. 107, PL 108-27, 5/28/2003) and WFTRA provisions (Sec. 105, PL 108-311, 10/4/2004) were made subject, all of the EGTRRA/JGTRRA/WFTRA changes described above were scheduled to expire (sunset) for tax years beginning after Dec. 31, 2010, and the tax rates in effect before the passage of EGTRRA were scheduled to come back into effect, i.e., individuals' taxable income was to be subject again to five tax brackets, taxed at 15%, 28%, 31%, 36%, and 39.6% marginal tax rates.

But Sec. 101(a) of the 2010 Tax Relief Act (Sec. 101(a), PL 111-312, 12/17/2010) modified this EGTRRA sunset provision to make it first apply after Dec. 31, 2012 (instead of after Dec. 31, 2010), i.e., the 10% tax bracket and related special inflation adjustment rules, and the reduced 25%, 28%, 33%, and 35% rates for taxing individuals' taxable income, were extended for two years, through 2012. (FTC 2d/FIN ¶ T-11051, ¶ T-11061, ¶ T-11071; USTR ¶ 79,006.86; TaxDesk ¶ 880,011)

New Law. The 2012 Taxpayer Relief Act repeals title IX of EGTRRA (i.e., the title that includes the above-described EGTRRA sunset). (EGTRRA § 901 (Sec. 901, PL 107-16, 6/7/2001) repealed by (2012 Taxpayer Relief Act §101(a)(1)))

> **RIA** *observation:* The effect of the EGTRRA sunset repeal (with the additional changes described below) is to make permanent the 10%, 25%, 28%, 33%, and 35% marginal tax rates, and the special inflation adjustment rules for the 10% tax bracket.

The 2012 Taxpayer Relief Act specifically provides that the statutory rate schedules for each tax filing status are to be applied (Code Sec. 1(i)(2) as amended by 2012 Taxpayer Relief Act §101(b)(1)(A)) by substituting a 25% (Code Sec. 1(i)(2)(A)), 28% (Code Sec. 1(i)(2)(B)), and 33% rate (Code Sec. 1(i)(2)(C)) for the 28%, 31%, and 36% rates, respectively, listed in those schedules.

In addition, for tax years beginning after Dec. 31, 2012 (Code Sec. 1(i)(3)(A) as amended by 2012 Taxpayer Relief Act §101(b)(1)(B)), the tax rate under the married filing joint/surviving spouse, head-of-household, single, and married filing-separately tax schedules on a taxpayer's taxable income in the highest rate bracket will be:

(1) 35%, to the extent it doesn't exceed an amount equal to the excess of (Code Sec. 1(i)(3)(A)(i)):

(a) the applicable threshold (see below), over (Code Sec. 1(i)(3)(A)(i)(I))

(b) the dollar amount at which that highest bracket begins (Code Sec. 1(i)(3)(A)(i)(II)), *and*

(2) 39.6% on the taxpayer's taxable income that's in excess of the amount to which the 35% rate (described above) applies. (Code Sec. 1(i)(3)(A)(ii))

The applicable threshold for (1)(a) above is (Code Sec. 1(i)(3)(B)):

(i) $450,000 for marrieds-filing-jointly and surviving spouses (Code Sec. 1(i)(3)(B)(i));

(ii) $425,000 for head-of-households (Code Sec. 1(i)(3)(B)(ii));

(iii) $400,000 for singles; and (Code Sec. 1(i)(3)(B)(iii))

(iv) ½ of the marrieds-filing-jointly/surviving spouse threshold amount (after any inflation adjustment of that amount) for married filing separately (Code Sec. 1(i)(3)(B)(iv)) (i.e., for 2013, $225,000).

For tax years beginning after 2013, each of the dollar amounts in (i) through (iii) above will be adjusted for inflation in the same manner as provided under Code Sec. 1(i)(3)(C)(i) (the inflation adjustment for the 10% tax bracket threshold), except that 2012 is substituted for 1992 under Code Sec. 1(f)(3)(B) (Code Sec. 1(i)(3)(C)), i.e., the cost-of-living adjustment will equal the percentage (if any) by which the consumer price index (CPI) for the preceding calendar year exceeds the CPI for 2012, see FTC 2d/FIN ¶ A-1103; TaxDesk ¶ 568,203.

> *observation:* Thus, as a result of all of the 2012 Taxpayer Relief Act changes above, after Dec. 31, 2012 individual taxpayers are subject to seven marginal tax brackets, taxed at 10%, 15%, 25%, 28%, 33%, 35% and 39.6% rates.
>
> And the 39.6% highest tax rate applies only to the amount of taxable income (for 2013) that exceeds $400,000 for singles, $425,000 for heads-of-household, $450,000 for marrieds-filing-jointly, and $225,000 for marrieds filing separately. (For tax years after 2013, these highest bracket threshold amounts are adjusted for inflation, as described above.)

> *observation:* The following 2013 rate schedules were projected by RIA and confirmed by the Joint Committee on Taxation in JCX-2-13R: Overview Of The Federal Tax System As In Effect For 2013 and by

IRS in Rev Proc 2013-15, Sec. 2.01. The schedules take into account the rate changes above, the permanent expansion of the 15% bracket for married joint filers (see ¶ 102), and all applicable inflation adjustments.

PROJECTED 2013 RATE SCHEDULES

FOR SINGLE INDIVIDUALS
(OTHER THAN HEADS OF HOUSEHOLDS AND SURVIVING SPOUSES)

If taxable income is:	The tax would be:
Not over $8,925	10% of taxable income
Over $8,925 but not over $36,250	$892.50 plus 15% of the excess over $8,925
Over $36,250 but not over $87,850	$4,991.25 plus 25% of the excess over $36,250
Over $87,850 but not over $183,250	$17,891.25 plus 28% of the excess over $87,850
Over $183,250 but not over $398,350	$44,603.25 plus 33% of the excess over $183,250
Over $398,350 but not over $400,000	$115,586.25 plus 35% of the excess over $398,350
Over $400,000	$116,163.75 plus 39.6% of the excess over $400,000

FOR HEADS OF HOUSEHOLDS

If taxable income is:	The tax would be:
Not over $12,750	10% of taxable income
Over $12,750 but not over $48,600	$1,275.00 plus 15% of the excess over $12,750
Over $48,600 but not over $125,450	$6,652.50 plus 25% of the excess over $48,600
Over $125,450 but not over $203,150	$25,865.00 plus 28% of the excess over $125,450
Over $203,150 but not over $398,350	$47,621.00 plus 33% of the excess over $203,150
Over $398,350 but not over $425,000	$112,037.00 plus 35% of the excess over $398,350
Over $425,000	$121,364.50 plus 39.6% of the excess over $425,000

FOR MARRIED INDIVIDUALS FILING JOINT RETURNS
AND SURVIVING SPOUSES

If taxable income is:	The tax would be:
Not over $17,850	10% of taxable income
Over $17,850 but not over $72,500	$1,785.00 plus 15% of the excess over $17,850
Over $72,500 but not over $146,400	$9,982.50 plus 25% of the excess over $72,500
Over $146,400 but not over $223,050	$28,457.50 plus 28% of the excess over $146,400
Over $223,050 but not over $398,350	$49,919.50 plus 33% of the excess over $223,050
Over $398,350 but not over $450,000	$107,768.50 plus 35% of the excess over $398,350
Over $450,000	$125,846.00 plus 39.6% of the excess over $450,000

FOR MARRIEDS FILING SEPARATE RETURNS

If taxable income is:	The tax would be:
Not over $8,925	10% of taxable income
Over $8,925 but not over $36,250	$892.50 plus 15% of the excess over $8,925
Over $36,250 but not over $73,200	$4,991.25 plus 25% of the excess over $36,250
Over $73,200 but not over $111,525	$14,228.75 plus 28% of the excess over $73,200
Over $111,525 but not over $199,175	$24,959.75 plus 33% of the excess over $111,525
Over $199,175 but not over $225,000	$53,884.25 plus 35% of the excess over $199,175
Over $225,000	$62,923.00 plus 39.6% of the excess over $225,000

observation: As described above, for tax year 2013, the 35% tax rate bracket for singles applies when taxable income exceeds $398,350. And as described above, the 2012 Taxpayer Relief Act imposes a 39.6% rate (for 2013) on a single individual's taxable income over $400,000. Thus, this change virtually eliminates the 35% bracket for 2013 for single taxpayers, as no more than $1,650 of their taxable income could be taxed at the 35% rate.

observation: In addition to the increased (39.6%) top income rate (above), and an increased (20%) top capital gains and qualified dividends rate (see ¶ 201 and ¶ 202, respectively), the 2012 Taxpayer Relief Act makes a number of other changes that impact the amount of tax certain "high income" taxpayers will pay in 2013. For example, under the 2012 Taxpayer Relief Act, for 2013, both a phase-out of personal exemption amounts and an overall reduction of itemized deductions (the so-called "Pease" limitation) are triggered when taxpayers' adjusted gross income (AGI) exceeds $250,000 for single filers, $275,000 for head-of-households, $300,000 for joint filers, and $150,000 for marrieds-filing-separately (see ¶ 301 and ¶ 302, respectively).

Also beginning in 2013, some new provisions under other laws will impact higher-income taxpayers, including: an additional 0.9% Medicare Hospital Insurance tax (commonly called the "HI" or "Medicare" tax) that applies to wages, or self-employment income, in excess of $250,000 for joint filers, $125,000 for marrieds-filing-separately, and $200,000 in all other cases, e.g., singles (see FTC 2d/FIN ¶s A-6001.2, H-4687; USTR ¶s 14,014, 31,114; TaxDesk ¶s 541,002, 575,501); and a 3.8% net investment income tax (NIIT) on most capital gains and dividends that applies to taxpayers' whose modified adjusted gross income (MAGI) exceeds $250,000 for joint filers and surviving spouses,

$125,000 for marrieds-filing-separately, and $200,000 in all other cases (see FTC 2d/FIN ¶ A-6361; USTR ¶ 14,114.01; TaxDesk ¶ 576,301).

For the 2012 Taxpayer Relief Act's permanent extension of the expanded 15% rate bracket for married joint filers (providing some relief from the "marriage penalty" within the rate structure), see ¶ 102.

For the 2012 Taxpayer Relief Act's permanent extension of reduced rates for kiddie tax and certain withholding (rates tied to the individual rates above), see ¶ 103.

For the 2012 Taxpayer Relief Act changes to the trusts' and estates' income tax rates, see ¶ 104.

For the 2012 Taxpayer Relief Act changes to the capital gains and qualified dividends rates, see ¶ 201 and ¶ 202, respectively.

☐ **Effective:** For tax years beginning after Dec. 31, 2012. (2012 Taxpayer Relief Act §101(a)(3); 2012 Taxpayer Relief Act §101(b)(3))

¶ 102. Expansion of marrieds-filing-jointly 15% rate bracket to provide marriage penalty relief is extended permanently

Code Sec. 1(f)(2)(A), 2012 Taxpayer Relief Act §101(a)(1)
Code Sec. 1(f)(8), 2012 Taxpayer Relief Act §101(a)(1)
Code Sec. None, 2012 Taxpayer Relief Act §101(a)(1)
Generally effective: Tax years beginning after Dec. 31, 2012
Committee Reports, None

A "marriage penalty" exists whenever the tax on a couple's joint return is more than the combined taxes each spouse would pay if they weren't married and if each filed a single or head of household return. The tax is more on a joint return if the couple's taxable income is pushed into a higher marginal tax bracket than would apply if the couple weren't married (so they pay at a higher tax rate on the same total income than they would pay if each were single). And that usually happens where both spouses work and have relatively equal incomes.

EGTRRA/JGTRRA/WFTRA changes. The Economic Growth and Tax Relief Reconciliation Act of 2001 ("EGTRRA," Sec. 302, PL 107-16, 6/7/2001), the Jobs and Growth Tax Relief Reconciliation Act of 2003 ("JGTRRA," Sec. 102, PL 108-27, 5/28/2003), and the Working Families Tax Relief Act of 2004 ("WFTRA," Sec. 101(c), PL 108-311, 10/4/2004) phased-in an increase in the size of the 15% regular income tax rate bracket for a married couple filing a joint return to equal twice the size (200%) of the corresponding rate bracket for an unmarried (single) individual. EGTRRA also provided special inflation adjustment rules relating to this change. Under pre-EGTRRA law, the marrieds-filing-jointly 15% bracket equaled 167% of the singles' bracket, and no special inflation adjustment rule applied. (FTC 2d/FIN ¶ A-1100, ¶ A-1100.1, ¶ A-1103, ¶ A-1114; USTR ¶ 14.08; TaxDesk ¶ 568,203, ¶ 568,214)

Sunset. Under Sec. 901 of title IX of EGTRRA (Sec. 901, PL 107-16, 6/7/2001), to which the applicable JGTRRA (Sec. 107, PL 108-27, 5/28/2003) and WFTRA (Sec. 105, PL 108-311, 10/4/2004) provisions were made subject, the EGTRRA/JGTRRA/WFTRA changes described above were scheduled to expire for tax years beginning after Dec. 31, 2010, and the pre-EGTRRA rules were scheduled to come back into effect, i.e., the married-joint filers bracket was again to equal 167% of the corresponding single filers bracket.

But Sec. 101(a) of the 2010 Tax Relief Act (Sec. 101(a), PL 111-312, 12/17/2010) modified this EGTRRA sunset provision to make it first apply after Dec. 31, 2012 (instead of after Dec. 31, 2010), i.e., the EGTRRA changes above were extended for two years, through 2012. (FTC 2d/FIN ¶ T-11051, ¶ T-11061; USTR ¶ 79,006.86; TaxDesk ¶ 880,011)

New Law. The 2012 Taxpayer Relief Act repeals title IX of EGTRRA (i.e., the title that includes the above-described EGTRRA sunset). (EGTRRA § 901 (Sec. 901, PL 107-16, 6/7/2001) repealed by (2012 Taxpayer Relief Act §101(a)(1))

> *observation:* The effect of the 2012 Taxpayer Relief Act's repeal of the EGTRRA sunset provision is to make permanent the above-described expanded 15% bracket for married joint filers, and the related special inflation adjustment rules.

> *observation:* Because the lowest tax rate bracket (the 10% bracket) for married joint filers is twice the size of the 10% bracket for single filers (see FTC 2d/FIN ¶ A-1104; USTR ¶ 14.08; TaxDesk ¶ 568,204), the tax on a couple's income reported on a joint return, up to the maximum income level under their 15% bracket, equals the tax two single filers—each reporting half that joint income—would pay.

> *observation:* Because all of the tax brackets for joint filers aren't made equal to twice the corresponding single filer tax brackets, however, the marriage penalty effect under the income tax rate schedules (especially for taxpayers in the highest tax brackets, see ¶ 101) isn't eliminated by the above-described changes.

For a projection of the income tax rate schedules for 2013 (taking into account the above-described extension of the expanded 15% tax bracket for joint filers and all applicable inflation adjustments, as well as the other changes to the individual rates made by the 2012 Taxpayer Relief Act), see ¶ 101.

☐ **Effective:** For tax years beginning after Dec. 31, 2012. (2012 Taxpayer Relief Act §101(a)(3))

¶ 103. Reduced rates for kiddie tax and some withholding (each tied to the reduced individual rates) are permanently extended

Code Sec. 1(g)(7)(B)(ii)(II), 2012 Taxpayer Relief Act §101(a)(1)
Code Sec. 3402(p)(1)(B), 2012 Taxpayer Relief Act §101(a)(1)
Code Sec. 3402(p)(2), 2012 Taxpayer Relief Act §101(a)(1)
Code Sec. 3402(q)(1), 2012 Taxpayer Relief Act §101(a)(1)
Code Sec. 3402(r)(3), 2012 Taxpayer Relief Act §101(a)(1)
Code Sec. 3406(a)(1), 2012 Taxpayer Relief Act §101(a)(1)
Code Sec. None, 2012 Taxpayer Relief Act §101(a)(1)
Generally effective: For tax years beginning after Dec. 31, 2012
Committee Reports, None

The "kiddie tax" and certain withholding requirements are tied to the income tax rates imposed on individual taxpayers (under Code Sec. 1).

For the 2012 Taxpayer Relief Act's permanent extension of the reduced Code Sec. 1 individual income tax rates provided (or extended) under the Economic Growth and Tax Relief Reconciliation Act of 2001 ("EGTRRA,") PL 107-16, 6/7/2001, Jobs and Growth Tax Relief Reconciliation Act of 2003 ("JGTRRA," Sec. 104, PL 108-27, 5/28/2003, Sec. 105, PL 108-27, 5/28/2003), Working Families Tax Relief Act of 2004 ("WFTRA," Sec. 101, PL 108-311, 10/4/2004) and 2010 Tax Relief Act (Sec. 101(a), PL 111-312, 12/17/2010), and imposition after 2012 of an additional 39.6% rate bracket—i.e., the imposition after 2012 of 10%, 15%, 25%, 28%, 33%, 35% and 39.6% marginal tax rates—see ¶ 101.

EGTRRA changes. The rates applicable to the following special tax and withholding requirements are tied to the Code Sec. 1 individual income tax rates, and, as described below, EGTRRA Sec. 101(c), PL 107-16, 6/7/2001 specifically conformed most of these rates to the individual tax rate reductions provided under EGTRRA:

Kiddie tax. Under pre-EGTRRA law, a parent who elected to report a child's income on the parent's return had to also include 15% of the lesser of: (a) the inflation-adjusted standard deduction in effect for the tax year allowable to a child who could be claimed as a dependent on the parent's return; or (b) the excess of the child's gross income over that amount. EGTRRA changed the rate applied in this calculation to 10%. (FTC 2d/FIN ¶ A-1325, ¶ A-1330; USTR ¶ 14.11; TaxDesk ¶ 568,405)

Backup withholding rate on reportable payments. Under pre-EGTRRA law, the backup withholding rate payors applied on payments of interest, dividends, and other items was 31%. EGTRRA changed this rate to a rate equal to "the fourth lowest tax rate imposed on single return filers"—i.e., for 2012, 28%. (FTC 2d/FIN ¶ J-9000, ¶ J-9001; USTR ¶ 34,064; TaxDesk ¶ 554,501)

Minimum withholding rates on supplemental wages under flat rate method. If specified conditions are met, an employer may apply an optional flat rate to withhold on an employee's supplemental wages (e.g., bonuses, commissions, overtime pay) paid separately from regular wages that aren't in excess of $1 million. This optional flat rate can't be less than 28%, or the corresponding rate in effect under Code Sec. 1(i)(2) for tax years beginning in the calendar year in which the payment is made—i.e., for 2012, 25%.

For supplemental wage payments by any one employer to an employee during the calendar year that exceed $1 million, the employer must withhold at a mandatory flat rate equal to the maximum rate of tax in effect under Code Sec. 1 for tax years beginning in that calendar year—i.e., for 2012, 35%. (FTC 2d/FIN ¶ H-4530, ¶ H-4541, ¶ H-4542; USTR ¶ 34,024.13; TaxDesk ¶ 538,518, ¶ 538,519)

Voluntary withholding rates on specified federal payments. Under pre-EGTRRA law, the permitted rates for voluntary withholding—withholding requested by the taxpayer—on social security and other specified federal payments were 7%, 15%, 28%, 31%, or any other rate permitted under regs. EGTRRA permitted this voluntary withholding at: (1) 7%; (2) any rate equal to one of the three lowest income tax rates for single filers; or (3) any other rate permitted under regs—i.e., for 2012, at (1) 7%, (2) 10%, 15%, or 25%, or (3) any other rate permitted under regs. (FTC 2d/FIN ¶ H-4475, ¶ H-4483; USTR ¶ 34,024.25; TaxDesk ¶ 538,053)

Voluntary withholding rate on unemployment benefits. Under pre-EGTRRA law, the permitted rate for voluntary withholding on unemployment benefits was 15%. EGTRRA reduced this rate to 10%. (FTC 2d/FIN ¶ H-4475, ¶ H-4483.1; USTR ¶ 34,024.25; TaxDesk ¶ 538,054)

Withholding rate on gambling winnings. Under pre-EGTRRA law, gambling winnings were subject to a 28% withholding rate. EGTRRA changed this rate to a rate equal to the third lowest income tax rate for single filers—i.e., for 2012, 25%. (FTC 2d/FIN ¶ J-8600, ¶ J-8602; USTR ¶ 34,024.26; TaxDesk ¶ 554,001)

Withholding rate on Indian casino profits distributed to tribal members. Under pre-EGTRRA law, the withholding rate used to compute the "annualized tax" withheld on Indian casino profits paid to tribal members was the single filer income tax rates (but not a rate in excess of 31%) that would apply to the payment amount (after certain adjustments). EGTRRA changed the rate limit in this computation to the single filer rates, but not a rate in excess of the fourth lowest income tax rate for single filers—i.e., for 2012, no rate higher than 28%. (FTC 2d/FIN ¶ J-8600, ¶ J-8617; USTR ¶ 34,024.26; TaxDesk ¶ 554,013)

Sunset. Under Sec. 901 of title IX of EGTRRA (Sec. 901, PL 107-16, 6/7/2001), all of the EGTRRA changes described above were scheduled to expire for tax years beginning after Dec. 31, 2010, and the rules in effect before the passage of EGTRRA were due to come back into effect. And, as described at ¶ 101, the EGTRRA/JGTRRA/WFTRA individual tax rate reductions also were scheduled to expire, and the pre-EGTRRA rates again were to apply—i.e., taxable income was to be subject to five tax brackets, taxed at 15%, 28%, 31%, 36%, and 39.6% marginal tax rates.

But Sec. 101(a) of the 2010 Tax Relief Act (Sec. 101(a), PL 111-312, 12/17/2010) modified this EGTRRA sunset provision to make it first apply after Dec. 31, 2012 (instead of after Dec. 31, 2010), i.e., it extended all of the above-described changes to apply through Dec. 31, 2012. (FTC 2d/FIN ¶ T-11051; USTR ¶ 79,006.86; TaxDesk ¶ 880,011)

New Law. The 2012 Taxpayer Relief Act repeals title IX of EGTRRA (i.e., the title that includes the above-described EGTRRA sunset). EGTRRA § 901 (Sec. 901, PL 107-16, 6/7/2001) repealed by (2012 Taxpayer Relief Act §101(a)(1))

> *observation:* The effect of the 2012 Taxpayer Relief Act's repeal of the EGTRRA sunset provision is to make permanent all of the above-described changes. Thus, for tax years after 2012 (see effective date below)—taking into account the 2012 Taxpayer Relief Act changes to the individual tax rates (see ¶ 101):
>
> • *Kiddie tax*—a parent who elected to report a child's income on the parent's return must also include 10% (instead of 15%) of the lesser of: (a) the inflation-adjusted standard deduction in effect for the tax year allowable to a child who can be claimed as a dependent on the parent's return, or (b) the excess of the child's gross income over that amount.
>
> • *Backup withholding rate on reportable payments*—the rate stays at 28% (instead of rising to 31%).
>
> • *Minimum withholding rates on supplemental wages under flat rate method*—the optional flat rate for payments totaling $1 million or less for a calendar year stays at 25% (instead of rising to 28%), and the mandatory flat rate for payments totaling more than $1 million is 39.6% (an increase from 2012, when the highest individual tax rate was 35%).

- *Voluntary withholding rates on specified federal payments*—the rates stay at 7%, 10%, 15%, or 25% (instead of rising to 7%, 15%, 28%, or 31%).

- *Voluntary withholding on unemployment benefits*—the rate stays at 10% (instead of rising to 15%).

- *Withholding on gambling winnings*—the rate stays at 25% (instead of rising to 28%).

- *Withholding on Indian casino profits distributed to tribal members*—limit stays at no single filer rate higher than 28% (instead of no single filer rate higher than 31%).

☐ **Effective:** For tax years beginning after Dec. 31, 2012. (2012 Taxpayer Relief Act §101(a)(3))

¶ 104. 25%, 28%, and 33% trust and estate income tax rates are permanently extended, top rate increases to 39.6% after 2012

Code Sec. 1(i)(2), 2012 Taxpayer Relief Act §101(b)(1)(A)
Code Sec. None, 2012 Taxpayer Relief Act §101(a)(1)
Generally effective: Tax years beginning after Dec. 31, 2012
Committee Reports, None

The income tax liability of trusts and estates is computed using a tax rate schedule applicable only for trusts and estates. That tax rate schedule is divided into five income ranges (tax brackets), which are taxed at progressively higher marginal tax rates as the income brackets increase. Under the statutory rate schedule, those rates are: 15%, 28%, 31%, 36%, and 39.6%. But, as described below, another Code provision modifies the statutory rate schedule. Each year IRS adjusts each bracket (income range) for inflation (computed from 1992), and IRS's inflation-adjusted rate schedule is the one used to compute tax (not the statutory rate schedule).

EGTRRA/JGTRRA changes. The Economic Growth and Tax Relief Reconciliation Act of 2001 ("EGTRRA," Sec. 101, PL 107-16, 6/7/2001), and the Jobs and Growth Tax Relief Reconciliation Act of 2003 ("JGTRRA," Sec. 104, PL 108-27, 5/28/2003), modified the income tax rate schedule for trusts and estates to phase-in a reduction of the top four marginal tax rates to: 25%, 28%, 33%, and 35%. (FTC 2d/FIN ¶ C-1000, ¶ C-1003, ¶ C-1005, ¶ C-7000, ¶ C-7002, ¶ C-7004; USTR ¶ 14.13; TaxDesk ¶ 651,003, ¶ 651,004, ¶ 661,003, ¶ 661,004)

Sunset. Under Sec. 901 of title IX of EGTRRA (Sec. 901, PL 107-16, 6/7/2001), to which the applicable JGTRRA provision is also made subject (Sec.

107, PL 108-27, 5/28/2003), the reduced tax rates described above were due to expire for tax years beginning after Dec. 31, 2010, and the tax rates in effect before the passage of EGTRRA were due to come back into effect, i.e., trusts' and estates' taxable income was again to be taxed at 15%, 28%, 31%, 36%, and 39.6% marginal tax rates.

But Sec. 101(a) of the 2010 Tax Relief Act (Sec. 101(a), PL 111-312, 12/17/2010) modified this EGTRRA sunset provision to make it first apply after Dec. 31, 2012 (instead of after Dec. 31, 2010), i.e., the reduced top four trusts and estates income tax rates (the 25%, 28%, 33%, and 35% rates), were extended for two years, through 2012. (FTC 2d/FIN ¶ T-11051, ¶ T-11061; USTR ¶ 79,006.86; TaxDesk ¶ 880,011)

New Law. The 2012 Taxpayer Relief Act repeals title IX of EGTRRA (i.e., the title that includes the above-described EGTRRA sunset). EGTRRA § 901 (Sec. 901, PL 107-16, 6/7/2001) repealed by (2012 Taxpayer Relief Act §101(a)(1))

But the 2012 Taxpayer Relief Act also changes the rule that modifies the rates to be applied under the statutory trusts and estates income tax rate schedule to specially provide that in applying that statutory rate schedule (Code Sec. 1(i)(2) as amended by 2012 Taxpayer Relief Act §101(b)(1)(A)) a 25% rate is substituted for the 28% rate (Code Sec. 1(i)(2)(A)), a 28% rate is substituted for the 31% rate (Code Sec. 1(i)(2)(B)), and a 33% rate is substituted for the 36% rate. (Code Sec. 1(i)(2)(C))

> **⊘** *observation:* The 2012 Taxpayer Relief Act makes no change to the lowest (15%) or highest (39.6%) trusts' and estates' income tax rates under the statutory rate schedule.
>
> Thus, the effect of the EGTRRA sunset repeal and the other rate changes above is, beginning after 2012, to tax trusts' and estates' income at 15%, 25%, 28%, 33%, and 39.6% marginal tax rates.

> **⊘** *observation:* The projected 2013 trusts and estates income tax rate schedule below (reflecting the changes above, and applicable inflation adjustments) was prepared by RIA and confirmed by IRS in Rev Proc 2013-15, Sec. 2.01:

PROJECTED 2013 RATE SCHEDULE FOR TRUSTS AND ESTATES

If taxable income is:	The tax would be:
Not over $2,450	15% of taxable income
Over $2,450 but not over $5,700	$367.50 plus 25% of the excess over $2,450
Over $5,700 but not over $8,750	$1,180.00 plus 28% of the excess over $5,700
Over $8,750 but not over $11,950	$2,034.00 plus 33% of the excess over $8,750
Over $11,950	$3,090.00 plus 39.6% of the excess over $11,950

☐ **Effective:** Tax years beginning after Dec. 31, 2012. (2012 Taxpayer Relief Act §101(a)(1); 2012 Taxpayer Relief Act §101(b)(3))

¶ 200. Qualified Dividends, Capital Gains and Losses

¶ 201. 0% and 15% capital gain rates are made permanent; 20% rate is added for high-income taxpayers after 2012

Code Sec. 1(h)(1), 2012 Taxpayer Relief Act §102(a)
Code Sec. 1(h)(1)(C), as amended by 2012 Taxpayer Relief Act §102(b)(1)
Code Sec. 1(h)(1)(D), as amended by 2012 Taxpayer Relief Act §102(b)(1)
Code Sec. 1(h)(1)(B), as amended by 2012 Taxpayer Relief Act §102(c)(2)
Generally effective: Tax years beginning after Dec. 31, 2012
Committee Reports, None

Under pre-2012 Taxpayer Relief Act law, the adjusted net capital gain of a noncorporate taxpayer (i.e., an individual, estate, or trust) was taxed at maximum rates of:

. . . 0%, to the extent it would have been taxed at a rate below 25% (i.e., a 10% or 15% rate) if it had been ordinary income, or

. . . 15% on adjusted net capital gain in excess of the amount taxed at 0%. (FTC 2d/FIN ¶ I-5100, ¶ I-5110 *et seq.*; USTR ¶ 14.08; TaxDesk ¶ 223,312)

"Adjusted net capital gain" is net capital gain plus qualified dividend income (see ¶ 202), minus specified types of long-term capital gain that are taxed at a maximum rate of 28% (gain on the sale of most collectibles and the unexcluded part of gain on Code Sec. 1202 small business stock) or 25% (unrecaptured section 1250 gain, i.e., gain attributable to real estate depreciation). (FTC 2d/FIN ¶ I-5110.10; USTR ¶ 14.08; TaxDesk ¶ 223,319.4)

"Net capital gain" is the excess of net long-term capital gains over net short-term capital losses for a tax year. (FTC 2d/FIN ¶ I-5107; USTR ¶ 14.08; TaxDesk ¶ 223,310) Long-term capital gains and losses result from sales or exchanges of capital assets held for more than one year. (FTC 2d/FIN ¶ I-5104; USTR ¶ 12,224.02; TaxDesk ¶ 223,306)

Sunset. Under section 303 of the 2003 Jobs and Growth Act (JGTRRA, Sec. 303, PL 108-27, 5/28/2003), as amended by section 102 of the 2005 Tax

---

FTC 2d References are to Federal Tax Coordinator 2d
FIN References are to RIA's Analysis of Federal Taxes: Income (print)
USTR References are to United States Tax Reporter: Income
PCA References are to Pension Analysis (print and electronic)
PBE References are to Pension & Benefits Explanations
BCA References are to Benefits Analysis (electronic)
BC References are to Benefits Coordinator (print)
EP References are to Estate Planning Analysis (print and electronic)

Increase Prevention Act (TIPRA, Sec. 102, PL 109-222, 5/17/2006) and by section 102 of the 2010 Tax Relief Act (Sec. 102, PL 111-312, 12/17/2010):

. . . the 0% and 15% maximum rates on adjusted net capital gain were due to expire for tax years beginning after Dec. 31, 2012. (FTC 2d/FIN ¶ T-11062; USTR ¶ 79,006.87; TaxDesk ¶ 880,014)

. . . the rates in effect before passage of JGTRRA, which were 8%, 10%, 18%, and 20%, were due to come back into effect. The 8% and 18% rates were to apply to assets held for more than five years. (FTC 2d/FIN ¶ I-5110; USTR ¶ 14.08; TaxDesk ¶ 223,312)

New Law. The 2012 Taxpayer Relief Act removes the JGTRRA sunset provision. Thus, the 0% and 15% capital gain rates under JGTRRA are made permanent. (2003 Jobs and Growth Act § 303 (Sec. 303, PL 108-27, 5/28/2003) repealed by 2012 Taxpayer Relief Act §102(a)) The 2012 Taxpayer Relief Act also adds a new 20% capital gain tax rate for certain high-income taxpayers. (Code Sec. 1(h)(1)(D) as amended by 2012 Taxpayer Relief Act §102(b)(1))

> *observation:* The maximum tax rates on adjusted net capital gain under the 2012 Taxpayer Relief Act, as set forth by the Joint Committee on Taxation in JCX-2-13R: Overview Of The Federal Tax System As In Effect For 2013, are:
>
> . . . 0% on gain that otherwise would be taxed at a 10% or 15% rate.
>
> . . . 15% on gain that otherwise would be taxed at a 25%, 28%, 33%, or 35% rate.
>
> . . . 20% on gain that otherwise would be taxed at a 39.6% rate.

> *observation:* The 39.6% income tax rate applies to taxable income above $450,000 for joint filers and surviving spouses, $425,000 for heads of household, $400,000 for single filers, and $225,000 for married taxpayers filing separately, adjusted for inflation after 2013 (see ¶ 101). Thus, the 20% capital gain rate applies to taxpayers whose income exceeds these thresholds.

Under the 2012 Taxpayer Relief Act, the 15% rate applies to the lesser of: (Code Sec. 1(h)(1)(C))

- the portion of the adjusted net capital gain (or, if less, taxable income) that exceeds the amount that is taxed at a 0% rate, or (Code Sec. 1(h)(1)(C)(i))

- the excess of: (Code Sec. 1(h)(1)(C)(ii))

. . . the amount of taxable income that would otherwise be taxed at a rate below 39.6% (see ¶ 101), over (Code Sec. 1(h)(1)(C)(ii)(I))

. . . the sum of the amounts that are taxed at ordinary income rates or the 0% capital gain rate. (Code Sec. 1(h)(1)(C)(ii)(II))

The 20% rate applies to the adjusted net capital gain (or, if less, taxable income) that exceeds the amount that is taxed at the 0% or 15% rates. (Code Sec. 1(h)(1)(D))

> **⚓ observation:** Because the 3.8% net investment income tax (NIIT) applies to most capital gains starting in 2013 (FTC 2d/FIN ¶ A-6361; USTR ¶ 14,114.01; TaxDesk ¶ 576,301), the overall capital gain rate for some high-income taxpayers will be 23.8% (20% + 3.8%). The NIIT applies to taxpayers whose modified adjusted gross income (MAGI) exceeds $250,000 for joint returns and surviving spouses, $125,000 for separate returns, and $200,000 in all other cases.

> **⚓ observation:** As a result of the repeal of the JGTRRA sunset, sales of assets held more than five years won't be taxed at a lower rate than sales of assets held more than one year.

The 2012 Taxpayer Relief Act removes the reference to the 5% capital gain rate that applied instead of the 0% rate for tax years beginning before 2008. (Code Sec. 1(h)(1)(B) as amended by 2012 Taxpayer Relief Act §102(c)(2))

For application of the capital gain rates to qualified dividend income, see ¶ 202.

For AMT rates on capital gain and qualified dividends, see ¶ 402.

☐ **Effective:** The effect of 2012 Taxpayer Relief Act §102(a) is to remove the sunset that would have been effective for tax years beginning after Dec. 31, 2012. (2012 Taxpayer Relief Act §102(a))

> **⚓ observation:** 2012 Taxpayer Relief Act §102(a), which eliminates the JGTRRA §303 sunset rule, as amended, is effective as if included in the enactment of JGTRRA. JGTRRA was enacted on May 28, 2003, so §102(a) is technically effective as of that date.

The new 20% rate, the new definition of the 15% rate, and the removal of the reference to the pre-2008 5% capital gain rate are effective for tax years beginning after Dec. 31, 2012. (2012 Taxpayer Relief Act §102(d)(1))

¶ 202. Qualified dividends are taxed at 0%, 15%, and 20% rates after 2012

Code Sec. 1(h)(1)(D)(i), 2012 Taxpayer Relief Act §102(a)
Code Sec. 1(h)(3)(B), 2012 Taxpayer Relief Act §102(a)
Code Sec. 1(h)(11), 2012 Taxpayer Relief Act §102(a)
Generally effective: Tax years beginning after Dec. 31, 2012
Committee Reports, None

The qualified dividend income of a noncorporate taxpayer (i.e., an individual, estate, or trust) is effectively treated as, and is taxed at the same rates that apply to, adjusted net capital gain, see ¶ 201. "Qualified dividend income" means dividends received from domestic corporations and qualified foreign corporations, subject to a holding period requirement (see below) and specified exclusions. (FTC 2d/FIN ¶ I-5115 *et seq.*; USTR ¶ 14.085; TaxDesk ¶ 223,345 *et seq.*)

For the definition of a "qualified foreign corporation," see FTC 2d/FIN ¶ I-5115.5; USTR ¶ 14.085. For dividends that are excluded from qualified dividend treatment, see FTC 2d/FIN ¶ I-5115.1; USTR ¶ 14.085; TaxDesk ¶ 223,346.

Holding period. For dividends on stock to qualify as qualified dividend income, the taxpayer must hold the stock for at least 61 days during the 121-day period beginning 60 days before the ex-dividend date. (FTC 2d/FIN ¶ I-5115.2; USTR ¶ 14.085; TaxDesk ¶ 223,347)

Unrecaptured section 1250 gain. The amount of a taxpayer's "unrecaptured section 1250 gain"—that portion of a noncorporate taxpayer's long-term capital gain that is attributable to real estate depreciation (reduced by certain capital losses, see FTC 2d/FIN ¶ I-10401 *et seq.*; USTR ¶ 12504.06; TaxDesk ¶ 223,107 *et seq.*)—that is eligible to be taxed at a maximum 25% rate is limited to the taxpayer's net capital gain determined without regard to the taxpayer's qualified dividend income. (FTC 2d/FIN ¶ I-5110.7; USTR ¶ 14.08; TaxDesk ¶ 223,319.1)

Sunset. Under section 303 of the 2003 Jobs and Growth Act (JGTRRA, Sec. 303, PL 108-27, 5/28/2003), as amended by section 102 of the 2005 Tax Increase Prevention Act (TIPRA, Sec. 102, PL 109-222, 5/17/2006) and by section 102 of the 2010 Tax Relief Act (Sec. 102, PL 111-312, 12/17/2010):

. . . the taxation of qualified dividend income at capital gain rates was due to expire for tax years beginning after Dec. 31, 2012. (FTC 2d/FIN ¶ T-11062; USTR ¶ 79,006.87; TaxDesk ¶ 880,014)

. . . qualified dividend income was then to be taxed at ordinary income rates. (FTC 2d/FIN ¶ I-5115; USTR ¶ 14.08; TaxDesk ¶ 223,345)

Similarly, the following rules were scheduled to expire for tax years beginning after Dec. 31, 2012:

... the holding period rule for determining when dividends on stock qualify as qualified dividend income, and

... the exclusion of qualified dividend income from net capital gain for purposes of computing the limitation on the amount of unrecaptured section 1250 gain that is eligible to be taxed at a maximum 25% rate. (FTC 2d/FIN ¶ T-11062.1; USTR ¶ 79,006.87; TaxDesk ¶ 880,014.1)

New Law. The 2012 Taxpayer Relief Act removes the JGTRRA sunset provision. Thus, the treatment of qualified dividend income as adjusted net capital gain, taxable at the same rates that apply to adjusted net capital gain, is made permanent. (2003 Jobs and Growth Act § 303 (Sec. 303, PL 108-27, 5/28/2003) repealed by 2012 Taxpayer Relief Act §102(a))

> *observation:* The maximum tax rates on adjusted net capital gain under the 2012 Taxpayer Relief Act, as set forth by the Joint Committee on Taxation in JCX-2-13R: Overview Of The Federal Tax System As In Effect For 2013, are:
>
> ... 0% on gain that otherwise would be taxed at a 10% or 15% rate.
>
> ... 15% on gain that otherwise would be taxed at a 25%, 28%, 33%, or 35% rate.
>
> ... 20% on gain that otherwise would be taxed at a 39.6% rate.
>
> Qualified dividends are taxed at the same 0%, 15%, and 20% rates that apply to capital gain.

> *observation:* The 39.6% income tax rate applies to taxable income above $450,000 for joint filers and surviving spouses, $425,000 for heads of household, $400,000 for single filers, and $225,000 for married taxpayers filing separately, adjusted for inflation after 2013 (see ¶ 101). Thus, the 20% rate on qualified dividends and other capital gain applies to taxpayers whose income exceeds these thresholds.

> *observation:* Because the 3.8% net investment income tax (NIIT) applies to dividends starting in 2013 (FTC 2d/FIN ¶ A-6361; USTR ¶ 14,114.01; TaxDesk ¶ 576,301), the overall tax rate on qualified dividends for some high-income taxpayers will be 23.8% (20% + 3.8%). The NIIT applies to taxpayers whose modified adjusted gross income (MAGI) exceeds $250,000 for joint returns and surviving spouses, $125,000 for separate returns, and $200,000 in all other cases.

With the removal of the JGTRRA sunset, the following rules related to qualified dividends, discussed above, have also been made permanent:

... the holding period rule for determining when dividends on stock qualify as qualified dividend income.

... the exclusion of qualified dividend income from net capital gain for purposes of computing the limitation on the amount of unrecaptured section 1250 gain that is eligible to be taxed at a maximum 25% rate. (2003 Jobs and Growth Act § 303 (Sec. 303, PL 108-27, 5/28/2003) repealed by 2012 Taxpayer Relief Act §102(a))

For long-term capital loss treatment on stock to the extent that extraordinary dividends were taxed as capital gain, see ¶ 204.

For passthrough of qualified dividend income by partnerships, see ¶ 205; by RICs and REITs, see ¶ 206; by common trust funds, see ¶ 207.

For the election to include qualified dividends in investment income for purposes of investment interest deduction, see ¶ 208.

For inclusion of qualified dividend income in the prohibition on IRD double benefits, see ¶ 211.

For qualified dividend income treatment of ordinary income on the disposition of Code Sec. 306 stock, see ¶ 212.

☐ **Effective:** The effect of the provision is to remove the sunset that would have been effective for tax years beginning after Dec. 31, 2012. (2012 Taxpayer Relief Act §102(a))

> *observation:* 2012 Taxpayer Relief Act §102(a), which eliminates the JGTRRA §303 sunset rule, as amended, is effective as if included in the enactment of JGTRRA. JGTRRA was enacted on May 28, 2003, so §102(a) is technically effective as of that date.

¶ 203. Accumulated earnings tax rate and personal holding company tax rate of 20% (up from 15%)

Code Sec. 531, as amended by 2012 Taxpayer Relief Act §102(c)(1)(A)
Code Sec. 541, as amended by 2012 Taxpayer Relief Act §102(c)(1)(B)
Code Sec. None, 2012 Taxpayer Relief Act §102(a)
Generally effective: Tax years beginning after Dec. 31, 2012
Committee Reports, None

Under pre-2012 Taxpayer Relief Act law, the tax rate for both the accumulated earnings tax and the undistributed personal holding company tax was 15%. (FTC 2d/FIN ¶ D-2600, ¶ D-2601, ¶ D-3200, ¶ D-3202; USTR ¶ 5324.01, ¶ 5414; TaxDesk ¶ 601,001, ¶ 601,501)

Under §303 of the 2003 Jobs and Growth Act (JGTRRA, Sec. 303, PL 108-27, 5/28/2003) as amended by §102 of the 2005 Tax Increase Prevention and Reconciliation Act (TIPRA, Sec. 102, PL 109-222, 5/17/2006) and the 2010 Job Creation Act (Sec. 102(a), PL 111-312, 12/17/2010), the rules reducing the accumulated earnings tax rate and the undistributed personal holding company tax rate to 15% were due to expire at the end of 2012 (FTC 2d/FIN ¶ T-11060, ¶ T-11062; USTR ¶ 79,006.86), and the rate in effect before passage of the 2003 Jobs and Growth Act (20%) was due to come back into effect. (FTC 2d/FIN ¶ D-2600, ¶ D-2601, ¶ D-3200, ¶ D-3202; USTR ¶ 5324.01, ¶ 5414; TaxDesk ¶ 601,001, ¶ 601,501)

New Law. The 2012 Taxpayer Relief Act removes the JGTRRA sunset provision. This would have made permanent the 15% tax rate on accumulated earnings and undistributed personal holding company income. (2012 Taxpayer Relief Act §102(a)) However, another 2012 Taxpayer Relief Act provision increases the tax rate on accumulated earnings and undistributed personal holding company income to 20%. (Code Sec. 531 as amended by 2012 Taxpayer Relief Act §102(c)(1)(A); Code Sec. 541 as amended by 2012 Taxpayer Relief Act §102(c)(1)(B))

> *observation:* Thus, the accumulated earnings tax rate and undistributed personal holding company income tax rate have been permanently fixed at 20%.

> *observation:* Taxes at a rate of 20% (the top rate generally applicable to dividend income of individuals) may be imposed upon the accumulated earnings or personal holding company income of a corporation. The accumulated earnings tax may be imposed if a corporation retains earnings in excess of reasonable business needs. The personal holding company tax may be imposed upon the excessive passive income of a closely held corporation. The accumulated earnings tax and the personal holding company tax, when they apply, in effect impose the shareholder level tax in addition to the corporate level tax on accumulated earnings or undistributed personal holding company income. (JCX-2-13R, 1/8/2013)

☐ **Effective:** The effect of 2012 Taxpayer Relief Act §102(a) is to remove the sunset that would have been effective for tax years beginning after Dec. 31, 2012. (2012 Taxpayer Relief Act §102(a))

> *observation:* 2012 Taxpayer Relief Act §102(a), which eliminates the JGTRRA §303 sunset rule, as amended, is effective as if included in the enactment of JGTRRA. JGTRRA was enacted on May 28, 2003, so §102(a) is technically effective as of that date.

The increase in the tax rate for accumulated earnings and undistributed personal holding company income to 20% is effective for tax year beginning after Dec. 31, 2012. (2012 Taxpayer Relief Act §102(d)(1))

¶ 204. Long-term capital loss treatment on stock to extent extraordinary dividends were taxed as capital gain is made permanent

Code Sec. 1(h)(11)(D)(ii), 2012 Taxpayer Relief Act §102(a)
Code Sec. None, 2012 Taxpayer Relief Act §102(a)
Generally effective: Tax years beginning after Dec. 31, 2012
Committee Reports, None

If an individual, estate, or trust receives qualified dividend income from one or more extraordinary dividends with respect to a share of stock, any loss on the sale or exchange of that share of stock must be treated as long-term capital loss to the extent of the extraordinary dividends. (FTC 2d/FIN ¶ I-5100, ¶ I-5104.1; USTR ¶ 14.087; TaxDesk ¶ 223,307)

"Qualified dividends" are generally dividends received from domestic corporations and "qualified foreign corporations," subject to holding period requirements and specified exceptions, see ¶ 202. "Extraordinary dividends" are generally dividends greater than 10% (5% for preferred stock) of the holder's adjusted basis in the underlying stock (see FTC 2d/FIN ¶ P-5109; USTR ¶ 10,594; TaxDesk ¶ 216,022).

> **observation:** Under the 2012 Taxpayer Relief Act, capital gain is taxed at 0%, 15%, and 20% rates after 2012, see ¶ 201.

> **observation:** The rule requiring long-term capital loss treatment applies regardless of whether the stock has actually been held for the long-term holding period. So a taxpayer that realizes both qualified dividend income (taxed at long-term capital gain rates) and a loss with respect to the same stock must use the loss to reduce the long-term gain.

> This rule isn't restricted to situations where the taxpayer realizes qualified dividend income and a loss on the underlying stock in the same tax year. Long-term capital loss treatment for a loss on "extraordinary dividend" stock applies, even if the extraordinary dividend, taxed as qualified dividend income, was received in an earlier tax year.

Sunset.   Under section 303 of the 2003 Jobs and Growth Act (JGTRRA, Sec. 303, PL 108-27, 5/28/2003), as amended by section 102 of the 2005 Tax Increase Prevention Act (TIPRA, Sec. 102, PL 109-222, 5/17/2006), as further amended by section 102 of the 2010 Tax Relief Act (PL 111-312, 12/17/2010) the above rule was scheduled to expire for tax years beginning after Dec. 31, 2012. (FTC 2d/FIN ¶ I-5104.1; T-11062; USTR ¶ 14.087; TaxDesk ¶ 880,014)

New Law. The 2012 Taxpayer Relief Act repeals the JGTTRA sunset provision. Thus, the rule providing for long-term capital loss treatment on stock to the extent that extraordinary dividends were taxed as capital gain is made permanent. (2003 Jobs and Growth Act §303 (Sec. 303, PL 108-27, 5/28/2003) repealed by 2012 Taxpayer Relief Act §102(a))

☐ **Effective:** The effect of the provision is to remove the sunset that would have been effective for tax years beginning after Dec. 31, 2012. (2012 Taxpayer Relief Act §102(a))

> **⚫️**observation: 2012 Taxpayer Relief Act § 102(a), which eliminates the JGTRRA §303 sunset rule, as amended, is effective as if included in the enactment of JGTTRA. JGTTRA was enacted on May 28, 2003, so §102(a) is technically effective as of that date.

¶ 205. Passthrough of qualified dividend income by partnerships is made permanent

Code Sec. 702(a)(5), 2012 Taxpayer Relief Act §102(a)
Code Sec. None, 2012 Taxpayer Relief Act §102(a)
Generally effective: Tax years beginning after Dec. 31, 2012
Committee Reports, None

Qualified dividend income received by noncorporate shareholders is taxed at the same maximum rates applicable to adjusted net capital gain, see ¶ 202. For a partnership, each partner's distributive share of qualified dividend income received by the partnership is treated as qualified dividend income in the partner's hands.

> **⚫️**observation: Thus, the qualified character of the dividends passed through to the partners, and the partners' distributive shares of the partnership's qualified dividend income was taxed at the 0% or 15% maximum rates that were applicable to adjusted net capital gain.

Sunset. Under section 303 of the 2003 Jobs and Growth Act (JGTRRA, Sec. 303, PL 108-27, 5/28/2003), as amended by section 102 of the 2005 Tax Increase Prevention Act (TIPRA, Sec. 102, PL 109-222, 5/17/2006), and by the Tax Relief Act of 2010 (Sec. 102(a), PL 111-312, 12/17/2010), the above rule was due to expire for tax years beginning after Dec. 31, 2012, and qualified dividend income was then to be taxed at ordinary income rates. (FTC 2d/FIN ¶ B-1900, ¶ B-1903, ¶ I-5100, ¶ I-5100.1, ¶ T-11060, ¶ T-11062; USTR ¶ 14.085, ¶ 7024.01; TaxDesk ¶ 584,003, ¶ 880,014)

New Law. The 2012 Taxpayer Relief Act removes the sunset provision. (2012 Taxpayer Relief Act §102(a)) Thus, the above passthrough rule for partnership qualified dividend income is made permanent. (2003 Jobs and Growth Act § 303 as repealed by 2012 Taxpayer Relief Act §102(a))

> *observation:* This provision parallels the provision making the rules taxing qualified dividend income at lower maximum rates applicable to adjusted net capital gain permanent, see ¶ 202.

☐ **Effective:** The effect of the provision is to remove the sunset that would have been effective for tax years beginning after Dec. 31, 2012. (2012 Taxpayer Relief Act §102(a))

> *observation:* 2012 Taxpayer Relief Act §102(a), which eliminates the JGTRRA §303 sunset rule, as amended, is effective as if included in the enactment of JGTRRA. JGTRRA was enacted on May 28, 2003, so §102(a) is technically effective as of that date.

¶ 206. Passthrough of qualified dividend income by RICs and REITs is made permanent

Code Sec. 854(a), 2012 Taxpayer Relief Act §102(a)
Code Sec. 854(b)(1)(B), 2012 Taxpayer Relief Act §102(a)
Code Sec. 854(b)(1)(C), 2012 Taxpayer Relief Act §102(a)
Code Sec. 854(b)(4), 2012 Taxpayer Relief Act §102(a)
Code Sec. 857(c)(2), 2012 Taxpayer Relief Act §102(a)
Code Sec. None, 2012 Taxpayer Relief Act §102(a)
Generally effective: Tax years beginning after Dec. 31, 2012
Committee Reports, None

Under pre-2012 Taxpayer Relief Act law, the following rules applied to RICs and REITS.

RICs. Where:

• a dividend (other than a capital gains dividend) is received from a regulated investment company (RIC);

• the RIC satisfies the requirements for allowing a RIC to pass through its income by paying deductible dividends; and

• the qualified dividend income (i.e., income from dividends eligible to be taxed at the 0% or 15% maximum adjusted net capital gains rates, see ¶ 202) of the RIC for the tax year is less than 95% of its gross income;

then in computing qualified dividend income paid out by the RIC, only the portion of the dividend designated by the RIC is taken into account.

The total amount that may be designated as qualified dividend income under these rules cannot exceed the sum of:

... the RIC's qualified dividend income for the tax year, and

... the amount of any earnings and profits that were distributed by the RIC for the tax year and accumulated in a tax year during which the RIC was not subject to the RIC rules.

This means that a RIC may distribute qualified dividend income out of its pre-RIC earnings and profits.

> *observation:* So, where the total qualifying dividends received by a RIC during the tax year are less than 95% of its gross income, the dividends that may be designated by the RIC as eligible for capital gains treatment are limited to the total qualifying dividends received by the RIC plus the amount of any dividends it pays out of pre-RIC earnings and profits.

Because the amount of qualified dividend income that may be paid out by the RIC is based on the RIC's qualified dividend income, rather than the RIC's dividend income, section 402 of the 2004 Working Families Act (Sec. 402, PL 108-311, 10/4/2004) (which enacted the above rules) repealed as unnecessary the special rules regarding dividends from REITs (repealed Code Sec. 854(b)(1)(B)(iii)) and foreign corporations (repealed Code Sec. 854(b)(1)(B)(iv)).

The 2004 Working Families Act similarly amended the rules requiring that a RIC notify its shareholders of the amount of eligible dividends attributable to qualified dividend income.

REITs. Where:

• a dividend (other than a capital gains dividend) is received from a real estate investment trust (REIT), and

• the REIT satisfies the requirements for allowing a REIT to pass through its income by paying deductible dividends,

then in computing qualified dividend income paid out by the REIT, only the portion of the dividend designated as qualified dividends by the REIT is taken into account.

The total amount that may be designated as qualified dividend income under these rules cannot exceed the sum of:

(1) the REIT's qualified dividend income for the tax year;

(2) the excess of:

(a) the sum of (i) REIT taxable income for the preceding tax year over the tax payable by the REIT for that year and (ii) the income subject to tax under the regs under Code Sec. 337(d) (see FTC 2d/FIN ¶ E-6850; USTR ¶ 3374.03) for the preceding tax year, *over*

(b) the sum of the taxes imposed on the REIT for the preceding tax year on these items, and

(3) the amount of any earnings and profits that were distributed by the REIT for the tax year and accumulated in a tax year during which the REIT was not subject to the REIT rules.

This means that a REIT may distribute qualified dividend income out of its pre-REIT earnings and profits.

> *observation:* In other words, a REIT may pay qualifying dividends only to the extent of the sum of (i) the qualifying dividends it receives for the tax year and (ii) the amount of its REIT taxable income and income taxed under the Code Sec. 337(d) regs (minus the tax on these items) for the preceding tax year.

The amount of a REIT distribution that is treated as qualified dividend income cannot exceed the amount so designated by the REIT in a written notice to its shareholders mailed not later than 60 days after the close of its tax year.

Sunset. Under section 303 of the 2003 Jobs and Growth Act (JGTRRA) (Sec. 303, PL 108-27, 5/28/2003), and section 402(b) of the 2004 Working Families Act (Sec. 402(b), PL 108-311, 10/4/2004), the above rules regarding the qualified dividend income of RICs and REITs were due to expire at the end of 2008 (along with the rules taxing qualified dividend income at the 0% or 15% adjusted net capital gain rates, see ¶ 202). The above rules were extended by the Tax Increase Prevention and Reconciliation Act of 2005 (Sec. 102, PL 109-222, 5/17/2006) and by the Tax Relief Act of 2010 (Sec. 102(a), PL 111-312, 12/17/2010), for tax years beginning before Jan. 1, 2012. (FTC 2d/FIN ¶ E-6150, ¶ E-6163.1, ¶ E-6600, ¶ E-6619.1, ¶ T-11060, ¶ T-11062, ¶ T-11062.1; USTR ¶ 14.085, ¶ 8524.02, ¶ 8574.02, ¶ 79,006.87; TaxDesk ¶ 173,002.1, ¶ 173,009, ¶ 880,014, ¶ 880,014.1)

New Law. The 2012 Taxpayer Relief Act removes the sunset provision. (2012 Taxpayer Relief Act §102(a)) Thus, the above rules for the passthrough of qualified dividend income are made permanent. (2003 Jobs and Growth Act § 303 as repealed by 2012 Taxpayer Relief Act §102(a))

> *observation:* This provision parallels the provision making the rules taxing qualified dividend income at lower maximum rates applicable to adjusted net capital gain permanent, see ¶ 202.

☐ **Effective:** The effect of the provision is to remove the sunset that would have been effective for tax years beginning after Dec. 31, 2012. (2012 Taxpayer Relief Act §102(a))

observation: 2012 Taxpayer Relief Act §102(a), which eliminates the JGTRRA §303 sunset rule, as amended, is effective as if included in the enactment of JGTRRA. JGTRRA was enacted on May 28, 2003, so §102(a) is technically effective as of that date.

¶ 207. Passthrough of qualified dividend income by common trust funds is made permanent

Code Sec. 584(c), 2012 Taxpayer Relief Act §102(a)
Generally effective: Tax years beginning after 2012
Committee Reports, None

A Code Sec. 584 common trust fund maintained by a bank isn't subject to tax. Instead, each trust participant includes in income its proportionate share of the common trust fund's short term capital gain or loss, long-term capital gain or loss, and ordinary income, regardless of whether the trust distributes these amounts.

Under the 2003 Jobs and Growth Act, qualified dividend income received by noncorporate shareholders was taxed as a capital gain at a maximum 15% rate. As a conforming change, the 2003 Jobs and Growth Act also provided that each common trust fund participant's proportionate share of the amount treated as qualified dividends received by the fund is treated as qualified dividend income. (Sec. 302(e)(7), PL 108-57, 5/28/2003) (FTC 2d/FIN ¶ E-3600, ¶ E-3602; USTR ¶ 5844; TaxDesk ¶ 657,304)

Sunset after 2012. Under 2003 Jobs and Growth Act Sec. 303 (JGTRRA, Sec. 303, PL 108-27, 5/28/2003), this qualified dividend income passthrough rule was due to expire at the end of 2008 (along with the rules taxing qualified dividend income). The 2005 Tax Increase Prevention and Reconciliation Act extended the qualified dividend income passthrough rule for common trust funds (along with the rules taxing qualified dividend income) through tax years beginning before Jan. 1, 2011. (2003 Jobs and Growth Act § 303 as amended by Sec. 102, PL 109-222, 5/17/2006)

Under the 2010 Tax Relief Act, the JGTRRA sunset was extended from Dec. 31, 2010 to Dec. 31, 2012. (Sec. 102(a), PL 111-312, 12/17/2010) Thus, the existing rules applicable to qualified dividends, including the passthrough of qualified dividends from a common trust fund, were extended for two additional years. (FTC 2d/FIN ¶ T-11062; USTR ¶ 79,006.87; TaxDesk ¶ 880,014)

New Law. Under the 2012 Taxpayer Relief Act, the JGTRRA §303 sunset date is repealed. (Sec. 303, PL 108-27, 5/28/2003 repealed by 2012 Taxpayer Relief Act §102(a))

observation: Thus, the existing rules applicable to the passthrough of qualified dividends from a common trust fund, are made permanent.

For the new 20% capital gains rate applicable to the qualified dividends of certain high-income taxpayers, see ¶ 202.

☐ **Effective:** The effect of the provision is to remove the sunset that would have been effective for tax years beginning after Dec. 31, 2012. (2012 Taxpayer Relief Act §102(a))

> **observation:** 2012 Taxpayer Relief Act §102(a), which eliminates the JGTRRA §303 sunset rule, as amended, is effective as if included in the enactment of JGTRRA. JGTRRA was enacted on May 28, 2003, so §102(a) is technically effective as of that date.

¶ 208. Election to include qualified dividends in investment income for purposes of investment interest deduction is made permanent

Code Sec. 1(h)(2), 2012 Taxpayer Relief Act §102(a)
Code Sec. 1(h)(11)(D)(i), 2012 Taxpayer Relief Act §102(a)
Code Sec. 163(d)(4)(B), 2012 Taxpayer Relief Act §102(a)
Generally effective: Tax years beginning after Dec. 31, 2012
Committee Reports, None

A noncorporate taxpayer's deduction for investment interest expense is limited to the amount of the taxpayer's net investment income, i.e., the excess of investment income over investment expenses for the year. (FTC 2d/FIN ¶ K-5311; USTR ¶ 1634.053; TaxDesk ¶ 315,011) Any investment interest that is disallowed because it exceeds this limit is carried over to the next tax year and treated as investment interest paid or accrued in that year. (FTC 2d/FIN ¶ K-5321; USTR ¶ 1634.053; TaxDesk ¶ 315,021)

Qualified dividend income (dividends taxed at capital gain rates, see ¶ 202) is included in "investment income" for this purpose only to the extent the taxpayer elects to include it. Any amount that the taxpayer elects to treat as investment income isn't treated as qualified dividend income and isn't eligible to be taxed at capital gain rates. (FTC 2d/FIN ¶ I-5115.1, ¶ K-5318.1; USTR ¶ 14.085, ¶ 1634.053; TaxDesk ¶ 223,346, ¶ 315,018.1)

> **observation:** A taxpayer whose investment interest deduction is limited because the interest exceeds the amount of his net investment income can increase the deduction by electing to include all or part of qualified dividend income in investment income. The cost of making the election is that the dividends will be taxed as ordinary income rather than capital gain.

Sunset. Under section 303 of the 2003 Jobs and Growth Act (JGTRRA, Sec. 303, PL 108-27, 5/28/2003), as amended by section 102 of the 2005 Tax

Increase Prevention and Reconciliation Act (TIPRA, Sec. 102, PL 109-222, 5/17/2006) and by section 102 of the 2010 Tax Relief Act (Sec. 102, PL 111-312, 12/17/2010), the above rule was due to expire for tax years beginning after Dec. 31, 2012. (FTC 2d/FIN ¶ K-5318.1FTC 2d ¶ T-11062; USTR ¶ 14.085, ¶ 1634.053; TaxDesk ¶ 880,014)

New Law. The 2012 Taxpayer Relief Act removes the JGTRRA sunset provision. Thus, the election to include qualified dividend income in investment income for purposes of the investment interest deduction is made permanent. (2003 Jobs and Growth Act § 303 (Sec. 303, PL 108-27, 5/28/2003) repealed by 2012 Taxpayer Relief Act §102(a))

> *observation:* This change parallels the change under which the taxation of qualified dividend income at capital gain rates is made permanent, see ¶ 202.

☐ **Effective:** The effect of the provision is to remove the sunset that would have been effective for tax years beginning after Dec. 31, 2012. (2012 Taxpayer Relief Act §102(a))

> *observation:* 2012 Taxpayer Relief Act §102(a), which eliminates the JGTRRA §303 sunset rule, as amended, is effective as if included in the enactment of JGTRRA. JGTRRA was enacted on May 28, 2003, so §102(a) is technically effective as of that date.

¶ 209. 100% gain exclusion for qualified small business stock (QSBS) is retroactively restored and extended through Dec. 31, 2013

Code Sec. 1202(a)(4), as amended by 2012 Taxpayer Relief Act §324(a)(1)
Code Sec. 1202(a)(4), as amended by 2012 Taxpayer Relief Act §324(b)(2)
Code Sec. 1202(a)(3), as amended by 2012 Taxpayer Relief Act §324(b)(1)
Generally effective: Stock acquired after Dec. 31, 2011 and before Jan. 1, 2014
Committee Reports, None

Subject to a per taxpayer limit (see below), noncorporate taxpayers exclude 100% of the gain realized on the sale of "qualified small business stock" (QSBS, see below) held for more than five years and acquired in a temporary period (described below), see FTC 2d/FIN ¶ I-9100.1; USTR ¶ 12,024; TaxDesk ¶ 246,601. Additionally, the excluded portion of the gain from eligible QSBS is excepted from treatment as an alternative minimum tax (AMT) preference item, see FTC 2d/FIN ¶ A-8304.2; USTR ¶ 12,024.05; TaxDesk ¶ 697,004.

> ⓡ *observation:* The effect of the AMT exception is that, subject to the per taxpayer limit and the more-than-five-year holding requirement, no gain from QSBS acquired during the temporary period is taxed for either regular tax *or* AMT purposes.

Under pre-2012 Taxpayer Relief Act law, the temporary period began on Sept. 28, 2010 and ended on Dec. 31, 2011. (FTC 2d/FIN ¶ A-8300, ¶ A-8304, ¶ A-8304.1, ¶ A-8304.2, ¶ I-9100, ¶ I-9100.1, ¶ I-9100.1A, ¶ I-9100.1B, ¶ I-9100.1C; USTR ¶ 574, ¶ 12,024, ¶ 12,024.05; TaxDesk ¶ 246,600, ¶ 246,600.1, ¶ 246,601, ¶ 246,602, ¶ 697,004, ¶ 697,004.1)

For periods before and after the temporary period, the exclusion, instead of being a 100% exclusion, is a partial exclusion, allowed in varying amounts. Thus, for stock acquired before or after the temporary period, the excluded percentage is 50% (60% for certain stock issued by corporations in empowerment zones), but is 75% for any QSBS acquired after Feb. 17, 2009 and before Sept. 28, 2010, see FTC 2d/FIN ¶ I-9100 *et seq.*, USTR ¶ 12,024, TaxDesk ¶ 246,600 *et seq.*

For regular income tax purposes, the portion of the gain that *is* includible in taxable income is taxed at a maximum rate of 28%, see FTC 2d/FIN ¶ I-5110.13; USTR ¶ 14.08; TaxDesk ¶ 223,323. Thus, for regular tax purposes, the gain from QSBS that is subject to the 50% exclusion is taxed at a maximum effective rate of 14%, and the gain from QSBS that is subject to the 75% exclusion is taxed at a maximum effective rate of 7%, see FTC 2d/FIN ¶ I-9100.1 *et seq.*; USTR ¶ 12,024; TaxDesk ¶ 246,600.1 *et seq.* For capital gain rates under the 2012 Taxpayer Relief Act, see ¶ 201.

Also, for periods before and after the temporary period discussed above, a varying percentage of the excluded portion of gain from QSBS *is* treated as a preference item and, thus, is *included* in income. The percentage varies depending on when the stock was acquired and other facts, see FTC 2d/FIN ¶s A-8304, A-8304.1; USTR ¶ 574; TaxDesk ¶s 697,004, 697,004.1. For permanent extension of AMT preference for gain excluded on sales or exchanges of QSBS, see ¶ 405. For AMT rates on capital gain under the 2012 Taxpayer Relief Act, see ¶ 402.

> ⓡ *observation:* Presumably, any gain from the sale or exchange of QSBS included in income could be subject to the 3.8% net investment income tax (NIIT) that applies to most capital gains starting in 2013, see FTC 2d/FIN ¶ A-6361; USTR ¶ 14,114; TaxDesk ¶ 576,301.

Generally, QSBS must be acquired by the taxpayer at original issue and after Aug. 10, 1993, see FTC 2d/FIN ¶ I-9102; USTR ¶ 12,024; TaxDesk ¶ 246,636. Also, QSBS must be issued by a corporation that meets a gross assets limit and certain other requirements, see FTC 2d/FIN ¶ I-9103 *et seq.*; USTR ¶ 12,024.02; TaxDesk ¶ 246,641 *et seq.* Under the per taxpayer limit, the gain excludible by a taxpayer for the QSBS of any one corporation is the greater of: (1) ten times the taxpayer's basis (excluding post-issuance basis increases) in that corporation's QSBS disposed of by the taxpayer in the tax year, or (2) $10 million ($5 million if married filing separately), and the $10 million (or $5 million) amount is reduced by the total amount of eligible gain taken into account by the taxpayer on dispositions of that corporation's QSBS in earlier tax years, see FTC 2d/FIN ¶ I-9112; USTR ¶ 12,024.01; TaxDesk ¶ 246,603.

New Law. The 2012 Taxpayer Relief Act retroactively restores and extends the 100% exclusion for QSBS for two years by changing the date before which eligible QSBS must be acquired from Jan. 1, 2012 to Jan. 1, 2014. (Code Sec. 1202(a)(4) as amended by 2012 Taxpayer Relief Act §324(a)(1))

observation: Thus, subject to the per taxpayer limit (see above) and the more-than-five-year holding requirement (see above), no regular tax or AMT is imposed on the sale or exchange of QSBS acquired after Sept. 27, 2010 and before Jan. 1, 2014.

illustration: On Oct. 1, 2012, T, an individual, acquires at original issuance 100 shares of QSBS at a total cost of $100,000. T sells all of the shares on Oct 2, 2017 for $1.1 million. Assuming that none of the possible income exclusion is barred by the per taxpayer limit (see above), T excludes from gross income all of the $1 million of gain for regular tax and AMT purposes.

observation: If all of T's capital gain is excluded from gross income in the illustration above, the 3.8% NIIT (see above) presumably would not apply.

observation: Unless Congress extends beyond Dec. 31, 2013 the deadline for acquiring QSBS eligible for the 100% gain exclusion, the 50% and 60% gain exclusion rules will again be in effect (see above), and a percentage of the excluded portion of the gain will be treated as a preference item for AMT purposes (see above). Presumably, the 3.8% NIIT would apply to any portion of gain from the sale or exchange of QSBS included in gross income.

Acquisition date defined for QSBS. For any QSBS qualifying for the 100% exclusion, the acquisition date for purposes of Code Sec. 1202(a) is the first day on which the stock was held by the taxpayer determined after the application of the holding period rules provided in Code Sec. 1223 (rules permitting the tacking of holding periods for substituted basis property, see FTC 2d/FIN ¶ I-8960). (Code Sec. 1202(a)(4) as amended by 2012 Taxpayer Relief Act §324(b)(2)) Similarly, for any QSBS qualifying for the 75% exclusion, the acquisition date for purposes of Code Sec. 1202(a) is the first day on which the stock was held by the taxpayer determined after the application of Code Sec. 1223. (Code Sec. 1202(a)(3) as amended by 2012 Taxpayer Relief Act §324(b)(1))

> **✓ observation:** Presumably, these rules would allow a taxpayer to tack the holding period of QSBS disposed of in a rollover transaction under Code Sec. 1045 (see FTC 2d/FIN ¶ I-9201; USTR ¶ 10,454; TaxDesk ¶ 247,201) with the holding period of the replacement stock acquired in the rollover transaction (see FTC 2d/FIN ¶ I-9207; USTR ¶ 12,234.24; TaxDesk ¶ 247,211).

☐ **Effective:** Stock acquired after Dec. 31, 2011 (2012 Taxpayer Relief Act §324(c)(1)) and before Jan. 1, 2014 (Code Sec. 1202(a)(4)) for the extension of the 100% exclusion under 2012 Taxpayer Relief Act §324(a)(1).

The definition of the acquisition date for purposes of QSBS qualifying for the 100% exclusion under 2012 Taxpayer Relief Act §324(b)(2) is effective for stock acquired after Sept. 27, 2010. (2012 Taxpayer Relief Act §324(c)(3))

> **✓ observation:** 2012 Taxpayer Relief Act §324(c)(3) provides that the definition of the acquisition date for QSBS qualifying for the 100% exclusion is effective as if included in §2011(a) of 2010 Small Business Act (Sec. 2011(a), PL 111-240, 9/27/2010). That provision is effective for stock acquired after Sept. 27, 2010 under §2011(c) of 2010 Small Business Act (Sec. 2011(c), PL 111-240, 9/27/2010).

The definition of the acquisition date for purposes of QSBS qualifying for the 75% exclusion under 2012 Taxpayer Relief Act §324(b)(1) is effective for stock acquired after Feb. 17, 2009 and before Sept. 28, 2010. (2012 Taxpayer Relief Act §324(c)(2))

> **✓ observation:** 2012 Taxpayer Relief Act §324(c)(2) provides that the definition of the acquisition date for QSBS qualifying for the 75% exclusion is effective as if included in §1241(a) of 2009 Recovery Act (Sec. 1241(a), PL 111-5, 2/17/2009). That provision is effective for stock acquired after Feb. 17, 2009 under §1241(b) of 2009 Recovery Act (Sec. 1241(b), PL 111-5, 2/17/2009) and before Sept. 28, 2010.

¶ 210. Tax rate on individuals' nonqualifying capital gain withdrawals from CCFs is increased from 15% to 20% after 2012

Code Sec. 7518(g)(6)(A), 2012 Taxpayer Relief Act §102(a)
Code Sec. 7518(g)(6)(A), as amended by 2012 Taxpayer Relief Act §102(c)(1)(D)
Code Sec. None, 2012 Taxpayer Relief Act §102(c)(1)(E)
Generally effective: Tax years beginning after Dec. 31, 2012
Committee Reports, None

Taxable income is reduced by certain amounts deposited for the tax year in a Merchant Marine capital construction fund (CCF)—for the construction or re-construction in the U.S. of American vessels—established by agreement with the Secretary of Transportation or the Secretary of Commerce.

"Nonqualifying withdrawals" from a CCF are taxable, but are taxed sepa-rately from the taxpayer's other income or losses. Under pre-2012 Taxpayer Re-lief Act law, the tax rate on individuals' nonqualifying withdrawals from the capital gain account of a CCF couldn't exceed 15%. (FTC 2d/FIN ¶ J-1360; USTR ¶ 75,184)

Sunset. Under section 303 of the 2003 Jobs and Growth Act (JGTRRA, Sec. 303, PL 108-27, 5/28/2003), as amended by section 102 of the 2005 Tax Increase Prevention Act (TIPRA, Sec. 102, PL 109-222, 5/17/2006) and by sec-tion 102 of the 2010 Tax Relief Act (Sec. 102, PL 111-312, 12/17/2010):

... the 15% maximum tax rate on nonqualifying withdrawals from the capital gain account of a capital construction fund was due to expire for tax years be-ginning after Dec. 31, 2010. (FTC 2d/FIN ¶ T-11062; USTR ¶ 79,006.87; TaxDesk ¶ 880,014)

... the 20% maximum tax rate in effect before passage of JGTRRA was due to come back into effect. (FTC 2d/FIN ¶ J-1360; USTR ¶ 75,184)

New Law. The 2012 Taxpayer Relief Act removes the JGTRRA sunset pro-vision. This would have made permanent the 15% maximum tax rate on non-qualified withdrawals by individuals from the capital gain account of a CCF. (2003 Jobs and Growth Act § 303 (Sec. 303, PL 108-27, 5/28/2003) repealed by 2012 Taxpayer Relief Act §102(a)) However, another 2012 Taxpayer Relief Act provision increases the maximum tax rate from 15% to 20%. (Code Sec. 7518(g)(6)(A) as amended by 2012 Taxpayer Relief Act §102(c)(1)(D))

> **✔ observation:** This increase parallels the increase in the highest capi-tal gain tax rate from 15% to 20% after 2012 (see ¶ 201).

The 2012 Taxpayer Relief Act also makes a conforming change to a related non-Code provision (46 USC §53511(f)(2)), increasing the maximum tax rate on nonqualified withdrawals by individuals from the capital gain account of a CCF from 15% to 20%. (46 USC §53511(f)(2) as amended by 2012 Taxpayer Relief Act §102(c)(1)(E))

☐ **Effective:** The effect of 2012 Taxpayer Relief Act §102(a) is to remove the sunset that would have been effective for tax years beginning after Dec. 31, 2012. (2012 Taxpayer Relief Act §102(a))

> **✔️ observation:** 2012 Taxpayer Relief Act §102(a), which eliminates the JGTRRA §303 sunset rule, as amended, is effective as if included in the enactment of JGTRRA. JGTRRA was enacted on May 28, 2003, so §102(a) is technically effective as of that date.

The increase in the maximum tax rate on nonqualified withdrawals by individuals from the capital gain account of a CCF from 15% to 20% is effective for tax years beginning after Dec. 31, 2012. (2012 Taxpayer Relief Act §102(d)(1))

¶ 211. Inclusion of qualified dividend income in prohibition on IRD double benefit is made permanent

Code Sec. 691(c)(4), 2012 Taxpayer Relief Act §102(a)
Generally effective: Tax years beginning after 2012
Committee Reports, None

Under Code Sec. 691(c)(4), when "income in respect of a decedent" (IRD) includes net capital gain, including qualified dividend income, to prevent the estate or heirs from receiving the double benefit of both lower capital gains rates on the IRD and the ordinary income deduction allowed for estate tax attributable to that IRD, the amount subject to the lower capital gains rates is reduced by the amount of the IRD deduction. FTC 2d/FIN ¶ C-9550, ¶ C-9563; USTR ¶ 6914.07; TaxDesk ¶ 579,012

Sunset after 2012. Under section 303 of the 2003 Jobs and Growth Act (JGTRRA, Sec. 303, PL 108-27, 5/28/2003), the inclusion of qualified dividend income in this rule was scheduled to expire, i.e. sunset, for tax years beginning after Dec. 31, 2010.

The 2010 Tax Relief Act extended the inclusion of qualified dividend income in the Code Sec. 691(c)(4) prohibition on an IRD double benefit so that it applied for tax years beginning before Jan. 1, 2013. (Sec. 102(a), PL 111-312, 12/17/2010) (FTC 2d/FIN ¶ T-11060, ¶ T-11062.1; USTR ¶ 14.085; TaxDesk ¶ 880,014.1)

New Law. Under the 2012 Taxpayer Relief Act, the JGTRRA §303 sunset date is repealed. (Sec. 303, PL 108-27, 5/28/2003 repealed by 2012 Taxpayer Relief Act §102(a))

> **observation:** Thus, the existing rules applicable to the inclusion of qualified dividend income in the Code Sec. 691(c)(4) prohibition on an IRD double benefit are made permanent.

☐ **Effective:** The effect of the provision is to remove the sunset that would have been effective for tax years beginning after Dec. 31, 2012. (2012 Taxpayer Relief Act §102(a))

> **observation:** 2012 Taxpayer Relief Act §102(a), which eliminates the JGTRRA §303 sunset rule, as amended, is effective as if included in the enactment of JGTRRA. JGTRRA was enacted on May 28, 2003, so §102(a) is technically effective as of that date.

¶ 212. Qualified dividend income treatment for ordinary income on disposition of Code Sec. 306 stock made permanent

Code Sec. 306(a)(1)(D), 2012 Taxpayer Relief Act §102(a)
Code Sec. None, 2012 Taxpayer Relief Act §102(a)
Generally effective: Tax years beginning after Dec. 31, 2012
Committee Reports, None

Gain realized by individuals and other noncorporate taxpayers on the disposition of preferred stock that qualifies as Code Sec. 306 stock may be taxable as ordinary income rather than as capital gain. Ordinary income treatment applies to that amount that would have been a dividend if the issuing corporation distributed cash equal to the fair market value of the stock sold. However, to the extent an individual shareholder recognizes ordinary income on the disposition of Code Sec. 306 stock (other than a redemption), that amount may be treated as qualified dividend income, which is taxable at the 0%, 15% or 20% maximum rates that otherwise apply to adjusted net capital gain (see ¶ 202). (FTC 2d/FIN ¶ F-12100, ¶ F-12101; USTR ¶ 3064.02; TaxDesk ¶ 244,401)

Sunset. Under section 303 of the 2003 Jobs and Growth Act (JGTRRA, Sec. 303, PL 108-27, 5/28/2003), as amended by section 102 of the 2005 Tax Increase Prevention Act (TIPRA, Sec. 102, PL 109-222, 5/17/2006), and as further amended by section 102(a) of the 2010 Tax Relief Act (Sec. 102(a), PL 111-312, 12/17/2010) the treatment of gains on the disposition of Code Sec. 306 stock as qualified dividend income was scheduled to expire for payments made in tax years beginning after Dec. 31, 2012. (FTC 2d/FIN ¶ F-12100, ¶ F-12101; USTR ¶ 3064.02, ¶ 79,006.87; TaxDesk ¶ 244,401, ¶ 880,014) The provisions treating qualified dividend income as part of adjusted net capital gain were also scheduled to expire on Dec. 31, 2012 (see ¶ 202).

New Law. The 2012 Taxpayer Relief Act makes permanent the treatment of gains on the disposition of Code Sec. 306 stock as qualified dividend income. (2012 Taxpayer Relief Act §102(a))

For the provision making permanent the treatment of qualified dividend income as part of adjusted net capital gain, see ¶ 202.

☐ **Effective:** The effect of the provision is to remove the sunset that would have been effective for tax years beginning after Dec. 31, 2012. (2012 Taxpayer Relief Act §102(a))

> *observation:* 2012 Taxpayer Relief Act §102(a) which eliminates the JGTRRA §303 sunset rule, as amended, is effective as if included in the enactment of JGTRRA. JGTRRA was enacted on May 28, 2003, so 2012 Taxpayer Relief Act §102(a) is technically effective as of that date.

¶ 300. Individuals Deductions and Other Provisions

¶ 301. Personal exemption phaseout (PEP) applies when AGI exceeds $300,000 (joint returns) and $250,000 (single filers) for tax years beginning after Dec. 31, 2012

Code Sec. 151(d)(3), as amended by 2012 Taxpayer Relief Act §101(b)(2)(B)(i)
Code Sec. 151(d)(4), as amended by 2012 Taxpayer Relief Act §101(b)(2)(B)(ii)
Code Sec. None, 2012 Taxpayer Relief Act §101(a)(1)
Generally effective: Tax years beginning after Dec. 31, 2012
Committee Reports, None

Taxpayers are allowed two types of personal exemptions: the exemption for the taxpayer and the taxpayer's spouse, also referred to as the "personal exemptions," and the exemption for dependents. For 2012, an individual was entitled to a $3,800 (inflation-adjusted) deduction for each personal exemption. (FTC 2d/FIN ¶ A-3500.1; USTR ¶ 1514; TaxDesk ¶ 562,201)

Under the personal exemption phaseout (PEP) rules in effect before the 2001 Economic Growth and Tax Relief Reconciliation Act (EGTRRA), the exemption amount of a taxpayer whose adjusted gross income (AGI) for the tax year exceeded a specified threshold amount was reduced by an applicable percentage. That applicable percentage was two percentage points for every $2,500 (or fraction of $2,500) by which the taxpayer's AGI for the tax year exceeded a threshold amount. The threshold amount varied, depending on the taxpayer's filing status. The inflation-adjusted threshold amounts for tax years beginning in 2009 were, for joint filers: $250,200, with complete phaseout occurring at $372,700; and for singles: $166,800, with complete phaseout occurring at $289,300. (FTC 2d/FIN ¶ A-3500, ¶ A-3502; USTR ¶ 1514; TaxDesk ¶ 564,401)

FTC 2d References are to Federal Tax Coordinator 2d
FIN References are to RIA's Analysis of Federal Taxes: Income (print)
USTR References are to United States Tax Reporter: Income
PCA References are to Pension Analysis (print and electronic)
PBE References are to Pension & Benefits Explanations
BCA References are to Benefits Analysis (electronic)
BC References are to Benefits Coordinator (print)
EP References are to Estate Planning Analysis (print and electronic)

EGTRRA changes. Sec. 102 of EGTRRA (Sec. 102, PL 107-16, 6/7/2001):

- reduced the PEP for tax years beginning after Dec. 31, 2005, and before Jan. 1, 2010, (FTC 2d/FIN ¶ A-3502; USTR ¶ 1514; TaxDesk ¶ 564,401) and

- eliminated the PEP for tax years beginning after Dec. 31, 2009. (FTC 2d/FIN ¶ A-3502; USTR ¶ 1514; TaxDesk ¶ 564,401)

Sunset. Under Sec. 901 of title IX of EGTRRA (Sec. 901, PL 107-16, 6/7/2001) all of the EGTRRA changes described above were scheduled to expire (sunset) for tax years beginning after Dec. 31, 2010. (FTC 2d/FIN ¶ T-11051; USTR ¶ 79,006.86; TaxDesk ¶ 880,011) Under the sunset, the PEP rules would have reverted to pre-EGTRRA law for tax years beginning after 2010. (FTC 2d/FIN ¶ A-3502; USTR ¶ 1514; TaxDesk ¶ 564,401)

But Sec. 101(a) of the 2010 Tax Relief Act (Sec. 101(a), PL 111-312, 12/17/2010) extended the EGTRRA sunset to first apply for "tax years beginning after Dec. 31, 2012." So, the PEP didn't apply for two additional years (through 2012).

> **☝observation:** In other words, by extending the EGTRRA sunset provision as it applied to the EGTRRA changes to the PEP rules, the 2010 Tax Relief Act delayed for two years (until after 2012) elimination of the PEP rules.

New Law. The 2012 Taxpayer Relief Act repeals title IX of EGTRRA (i.e., the title containing the above-described EGTRRA sunset). (EGTRRA § 901 (Sec. 901, PL 107-16, 6/7/2001) repealed by 2012 Taxpayer Relief Act §101(a)(1)) The Act then eliminates Code Sec. 151(d)(3)(F), the EGTRRA-added provision that would have terminated the PEP. (Code Sec. 151(d)(3)(F) as amended by 2012 Taxpayer Relief Act §101(b)(2)(B)(i)(III)) So the PEP is restored. Under the 2012 Taxpayer Relief Act, the AGI amounts at which the PEP applies are higher than under pre-2012 Taxpayer Relief Act law. Specifically, a taxpayer's personal exemption amount is reduced by 2% for each $2,500 ($1,250 for married filing separately), or fraction thereof, by which the taxpayer's AGI for the tax year exceeds the "applicable amount" as in effect under Code Sec. 68(b) (i.e., the applicable threshold amounts under the overall limitation on itemized deductions, as increased by the 2012 Taxpayer Relief Act, see ¶ 302). (Code Sec. 151(d)(3) as amended by 2012 Taxpayer Relief Act §101(b)(2)(B)(i)) The applicable threshold amounts will be adjusted for inflation for tax years beginning in calendar years after 2013. (Code Sec. 151(d)(4) as amended by 2012 Taxpayer Relief Act §101(b)(2)(B)(ii))

> **☝observation:** Thus, the "applicable amounts" for purposes of the PEP rules (i.e., the threshold amounts for the 2013 overall limitation on itemized deductions, see ¶ 302) are: for joint filers or surviving

spouses, $300,000; for heads of household, $275,000; for singles, $250,000; and for marrieds filing separately, $150,000.

observation: According to the Joint Committee on Taxation in JCX-2-13R: Overview Of The Federal Tax System As In Effect For 2013, and IRS in Rev Proc 2013-15, Sec. 2.11, the personal exemption amount for 2013 is $3,900. And, for 2013, a taxpayer's personal exemptions will be completely phased out at incomes of: $372,501 (for singles); $397,501 (for heads of household); $422,501 (for joint filers); and $211,251 (for marrieds filing separately).

sample client letter: For a client letter on the personal exemption phaseout provision in the 2012 Taxpayer Relief Act, see ¶ 2002.

☐ **Effective:** Tax years beginning after Dec. 31, 2012. (2012 Taxpayer Relief Act §101(b)(3))

¶ 302. Overall limitation on itemized deductions is restored, applies when AGI exceeds $300,000 (joint returns) and $250,000 (single filers)

Code Sec. 68(b), as amended by 2012 Taxpayer Relief Act §101(b)(2)(A)(i)
Code Sec. 68(g), as amended by 2012 Taxpayer Relief Act §101(b)(2)(A)(ii)
Code Sec. None, 2012 Taxpayer Relief Act §101(a)(1)
Generally effective: Tax years beginning after Dec. 31, 2012
Committee Reports, None

Individuals who don't elect to itemize their deductions are allowed, instead, to deduct from their adjusted gross income (AGI) an inflation-adjusted basic standard deduction to determine their taxable income. (FTC 2d/FIN ¶ A-2800; USTR ¶ 634; TaxDesk ¶ 562,001)

Under an overall limitation on itemized deductions in effect before the 2001 Economic Growth and Tax Relief Reconciliation Act (EGTRRA (PL 107-16, 6/7/2001)), if an individual's adjusted gross income (AGI) exceeded the "applicable amount," the amount of the itemized deductions otherwise allowed for the tax year was reduced by the lesser of: (i) 3% of the excess of AGI over the applicable amount, or (ii) 80% of the amount of itemized deductions otherwise allowable for the tax year. The inflation-adjusted applicable amounts for any tax year beginning in a calendar year equalled the statutory applicable amount ($100,000 or $50,000, whichever applied, see below), multiplied by the percentage (if any) by which the consumer price index (CPI) for the calendar year preceding the calendar year in which the tax year began exceeded the CPI for calendar year 1990. For 2009, an individual's AGI exceeded the statutory $100,000 "applicable amount," as adjusted for inflation, if it exceeded $166,800. For 2009 for marrieds filing separately, an individual's AGI exceeded the statutory $50,000 "applicable amount," as adjusted for inflation, if it exceeded $83,400. (FTC 2d/FIN ¶ A-2730, ¶ A-2731; USTR ¶ 684; TaxDesk ¶ 561,801)

> **observation:** The above-described reduction in total itemized deductions is referred to as the "overall limitation on itemized deductions," the "3%/80% rule," or the "Pease limitation."

The overall limitation on itemized deductions didn't apply to the itemized deductions for: medical expenses, investment interest, casualty and theft losses, or gambling losses. The limitation didn't apply to trusts or estates. If the limitation applied, it was calculated last, after all other limitations. (FTC 2d/FIN ¶ A-2730, ¶ A-2731; USTR ¶ 684; TaxDesk ¶ 561,801)

EGTRRA changes. Sec. 103 of EGTRRA (Sec. 103, PL 107-16, 6/7/2001):

• reduced the above limitation on itemized deductions for tax years beginning after Dec. 31, 2005, and before Jan. 1, 2010, (FTC 2d/FIN ¶ A-2731; USTR ¶ 684; TaxDesk ¶ 561,801) and

• eliminated the above limitation for tax years beginning after Dec. 31, 2009. (FTC 2d/FIN ¶ A-2731; USTR ¶ 684; TaxDesk ¶ 561,801)

Sunset. Under Sec. 901 of title IX of EGTRRA (Sec. 901, PL 107-16, 6/7/2001) the EGTRRA changes described above were scheduled to expire (sunset) for tax years beginning after Dec. 31, 2010. (FTC 2d/FIN ¶ T-11051; USTR ¶ 79,006.86; TaxDesk ¶ 880,011) Under the sunset, the rules for the overall limitation on itemized deductions would have reverted to pre-EGTRRA law for tax years beginning after 2010. (FTC 2d/FIN ¶ A-2730, ¶ A-2731; USTR ¶ 684; TaxDesk ¶ 561,801)

But the 2010 Tax Relief Act extended the EGTRRA sunset to first apply for "tax years beginning after Dec. 31, 2012." (Sec. 901, PL 107-16, 6/7/2001, as amended by Sec. 101(a)(1), PL 111-312, 12/17/2010) So, under the 2010 Tax Relief Act, the overall limitation on itemized deductions didn't apply for two additional years (2011 and 2012).

> **observation:** In other words, by extending the EGTRRA sunset provision as it applied to the EGTRRA changes to the overall limitation on itemized deductions, the 2010 Taxpayer Relief Act delayed for two years (until after 2012) elimination of the overall limitation on itemized deductions.

New Law. The 2012 Taxpayer Relief Act repeals title IX of EGTRRA (i.e., the title containing the above-described EGTRRA sunset). (EGTRRA § 901 (Sec. 901, PL 107-16, 6/7/2001) repealed by 2012 Taxpayer Relief Act §101(a)(1)) The 2010 Taxpayer Relief Act then eliminates Code Sec. 68(g), the EGTRRA-added provision that would have terminated the overall limitation on itemized deductions. (Code Sec. 68(g) as amended by 2012 Taxpayer Relief Act §101(b)(2)(A)(ii)) So the overall limitation on itemized deductions is restored. In addition, the 2010 Taxpayer Relief Act increases the inflation-adjusted "applicable amounts" that trigger application of the overall limitation to (Code Sec. 68(b) as amended by 2012 Taxpayer Relief Act §101(b)(2)(A)(i)):

(1) $300,000, for a joint return or surviving spouse (as defined in Code Sec. 2(a));(Code Sec. 68(b)(1)(A) as amended by 2012 Taxpayer Relief Act §101(b)(2)(A)(i));

(2) $275,000, for a head of household (as defined in Code Sec. 2(b)) (Code Sec. 68(b)(1)(B) as amended by 2012 Taxpayer Relief Act §101(b)(2)(A)(i));

(3) $250,000, for an individual who isn't married and isn't a surviving spouse or head of household (Code Sec. 68(b)(1)(C) as amended by 2012 Taxpayer Relief Act §101(b)(2)(A)(i)); and

(4) one-half the amount in (1) (after adjustment for inflation, see below) (i.e., to $150,000 for 2013), for a married individual filing separately (Code Sec. 68(b)(1)(D) as amended by 2012 Taxpayer Relief Act §101(b)(2)(A)(i)).

> **🔵 observation:** According to the Joint Committee on Taxation in JCX-2-13R: Overview Of The Federal Tax System As In Effect For 2013, and IRS in Rev Proc 2013-15, Sec. 2.08, under the overall limitation on itemized deductions, the total amount of itemized deductions allowed is reduced by 3 cents for each dollar of AGI (for 2013) in excess of $250,000 (single), $275,000 (head-of-household), $300,000 (married filing jointly) and $150,000 (married filing separately). But a taxpayer can't lose more than 80% of his deductions as a result of the limitation.

The 2010 Taxpayer Relief Act provides that for purposes of the overall limitation, marital status is determined under Code Sec. 7703. (Code Sec. 68(b)(1) as amended by 2012 Taxpayer Relief Act §101(b)(2)(A)(i))

The 2010 Taxpayer Relief Act also amends the inflation adjustment rules. The inflation adjustment, which applies to tax years beginning in calendar years after 2013, is arrived at by multiplying the applicable amounts above by the percentage (if any) by which the consumer price index (CPI) for the calendar year before the calendar year in which the tax year begins exceeds the CPI for calendar year *2012*. If any applicable amount, after being adjusted for inflation, isn't a multiple of $50, that amount must be rounded to the next lowest multiple of $50. (Code Sec. 68(b)(2) as amended by 2012 Taxpayer Relief Act §101(b)(2)(A)(i))

> **observation:** The 2010 Taxpayer Relief Act reinstated the overall limitation on itemized deductions without changing any of the rules of Code Sec. 68 other than the rules on "applicable amounts." So, after 2012, the overall limitation doesn't apply to the itemized deductions for medical expenses, investment interest, casualty and theft losses, or gambling losses. Nor does it apply to trusts or estates. And the overall limitation is calculated last, after all other limitations (such as the 2%-of-AGI floor for miscellaneous itemized deductions).

> **sample client letter:** For a client letter on the overall limitation on itemized deductions provision in the 2012 Taxpayer Relief Act, see ¶ 2002.

☐ **Effective:** Tax years beginning after Dec. 31, 2012. (2012 Taxpayer Relief Act §101(b)(3))

¶ 303. Election to claim itemized deduction for state/local sales taxes is extended through 2013

Code Sec. 164(b)(5)(I), as amended by 2012 Taxpayer Relief Act §205(a)
Generally effective: Tax years beginning after Dec. 31, 2011 and before Jan. 1, 2014
Committee Reports, None

Under pre-2012 Taxpayer Relief Act law, taxpayers could—for tax years beginning after Dec. 31, 2003 and before Jan. 1, 2012—elect to take an itemized deduction for state and local general sales taxes instead of an itemized deduction for state and local income taxes (FTC 2d/FIN ¶ K-4500, ¶ K-4510 *et seq.*; USTR ¶ 1644.03; TaxDesk ¶ 326,019 *et seq.*)

New Law. The 2012 Taxpayer Relief Act replaces "Jan. 1, 2012" with "Jan. 1, 2014." (Code Sec. 164(b)(5)(I) as amended by 2012 Taxpayer Relief Act §205(a))

> **observation:** In other words, the 2012 Taxpayer Relief Act extends for two years (through Dec. 31, 2013) the provision allowing taxpayers to elect to deduct state and local sales taxes in lieu of state and local income taxes. This deduction appeals especially to taxpayers in states that impose a sales tax but not an income tax—Alaska, Florida, Nevada, South Dakota, Texas, Washington, and Wyoming. The deduction may also be advantageous to any taxpayer who paid more in sales taxes than income taxes, such as a taxpayer who might have bought a new

car, boosting the sales tax total, or claimed tax credits, lowering the state income tax paid.

☐ **Effective:** Tax years beginning after Dec. 31, 2011 (2012 Taxpayer Relief Act §205(b)) and before Jan. 1, 2014. (Code Sec. 164(b)(5)(I))

¶ 304. Standard deduction marriage penalty relief is made permanent

Code Sec. 63(c)(2), 2012 Taxpayer Relief Act §101(a)(1)
Code Sec. None, 2012 Taxpayer Relief Act §101(a)(1)
Generally effective: Tax years beginning after Dec. 31, 2012
Committee Reports, None

Individuals who don't elect to itemize their deductions are allowed, instead, to deduct from their adjusted gross income (AGI) an inflation-adjusted basic standard deduction to determine their taxable income. (FTC 2d/FIN ¶ A-2800; USTR ¶ 634; TaxDesk ¶ 562,001) The basic standard deduction for 2012 was $5,950 for unmarrieds, $11,900 for marrieds filing jointly and surviving spouses, $5,950 for marrieds filing separately, and $8,700 for heads of household. (FTC 2d/FIN ¶ A-2800, ¶ A-2803; USTR ¶ 634; TaxDesk ¶ 562,002)

Under the standard deduction rules in effect before the Economic Growth and Tax Relief Reconciliation Act of 2001 (EGTRRA) (PL 107-16, 6/7/2001), the basic standard deduction for married taxpayers filing jointly and qualified surviving spouses was the statutory amount of $5,000, as adjusted annually for inflation; for single taxpayers who weren't surviving spouses or heads of household, it was the statutory amount of $3,000, as adjusted annually for inflation; for marrieds filing separately, it was the statutory amount of $2,500, as adjusted annually for inflation. So, the basic standard deduction amount for joint filers and surviving spouses under the pre-EGTRRA rules was 167% (1.6667 × $3,000 = $5,000) of the basic standard deduction amount for single taxpayers who weren't surviving spouses or heads of household. And the standard deduction for marrieds filing separately was half the joint filer amount. (FTC 2d/FIN ¶ A-2803; USTR ¶ 634; TaxDesk ¶ 562,002)

⚫*observation:* A "marriage penalty" exists when the combined tax liability of a married couple filing a joint return is greater than the sum of the tax liabilities of each individual computed as if they weren't married.

EGTRRA/JGTRRA/WFTRA changes. Sec. 301 of EGTRRA (Sec. 301, PL 107-16, 6/7/2001), as amended by the Jobs Growth and Tax Relief Reconciliation Act of 2003 (JGTRRA, Sec. 103, PL 108-27, 5/28/2003), and the Working Families Tax Relief Act of 2004 (WFTRA, Sec. 101(b), PL 108-311,

10/4/2004), increased the basic standard deduction for joint filers and surviving spouses to 200% of the dollar amount in effect for an unmarried individual or a married taxpayer filing a separate return for the tax year. (FTC 2d/FIN ¶ A-2803; USTR ¶ 634; TaxDesk ¶ 562,002)

> **observation:** The EGTRRA increase in the basic standard deduction amount for joint filers was intended to mitigate the so-called "marriage penalty."

EGTRRA also made the basic standard deduction for marrieds filing separately equal to the basic standard deduction for single filers. (FTC 2d/FIN ¶ A-2803; USTR ¶ 634; TaxDesk ¶ 562,002)

Sunset for tax years beginning after 2012. Under Sec. 901 of title IX of EGTRRA (Sec. 901, PL 107-16, 6/7/2001), to which the applicable JGTRRA (Sec. 107, PL 108-27, 5/28/2003) and WFTRA (Sec. 105, PL 108-311, 10/4/2004) provisions were made subject, all of the EGTRRA changes described above were scheduled to expire (sunset) for tax years beginning after Dec. 31, 2010. (FTC 2d/FIN ¶ T-11051, ¶ T-11061, ¶ T-11071; USTR ¶ 79,006.86; TaxDesk ¶ 880,011)

But the 2010 Tax Relief Act extended the EGTRRA sunset to first apply for "tax years beginning after Dec. 31, 2012." (PL 107-16, 6/7/2001, as amended by Sec. 101(a)(1), PL 111-312, 12/17/2010) So, the basic standard deduction for a married couple filing a joint return was increased to twice the basic standard deduction for an unmarried individual filing a single return through 2012. And the basic standard deduction for marrieds filing separately was made equal to the basic standard deduction for single filers through 2012. (Code Sec. 63(c)(2)(C))

Under pre-2012 Taxpayer Relief Act law, the standard deduction rules would have reverted to pre-EGTRRA law for tax years beginning after 2012. (FTC 2d/FIN ¶ A-2803; USTR ¶ 634; TaxDesk ¶ 562,002)

New Law. The 2012 Taxpayer Relief Act repeals title IX of EGTRRA (i.e., the title containing the above-described EGTRRA sunset). (EGTRRA § 901 (Sec. 901, PL 107-16, 6/7/2001) repealed by (2012 Taxpayer Relief Act §101(a)(1))).

> **observation:** In other words, by deleting the EGTRRA sunset provision as it applies to the EGTRRA/JGTRRA/WFTRA changes to the standard deduction rules, the 2012 Taxpayer Relief Act permanently extends the standard deduction marriage penalty relief that would otherwise have expired after 2012. Thus, the basic standard deduction for a married couple filing a joint return continues to be twice the basic standard deduction for an unmarried individual filing a single return. And,

the basic standard deduction for marrieds filing separately equals the basic standard deduction for single filers.

observation: According to the Joint Committee on Taxation in JCX-2-13R: Overview Of The Federal Tax System As In Effect For 2013, and by IRS in Rev Proc 2013-15, Sec. 2.07, the amount of the standard deduction for 2013 is $6,100 for singles and marrieds filing separately, $8,950 for heads of household, and $12,200 for joint filers and surviving spouses.

☐ **Effective:** Tax years beginning after Dec. 31, 2012 (2012 Taxpayer Relief Act §101(a)(3)).

¶ 305. Interest deduction for mortgage insurance premiums is extended to amounts paid or accrued before 2014

Code Sec. 163(h)(3)(E)(iv), as amended by 2012 Taxpayer Relief Act §204(a)
Generally effective: Amounts paid or accrued after Dec. 31, 2011 and before Jan. 1, 2014
Committee Reports, None

Premiums a taxpayer paid or accrued during the tax year for qualified mortgage insurance (as defined below) in connection with acquisition indebtedness for the taxpayer's qualified residence are treated as qualified residence interest, and so are deductible, see FTC 2d/FIN ¶ K-5493; USTR ¶ 1634.052; TaxDesk ¶ 314,519.1, subject to phaseout rules affecting taxpayers with adjusted gross income (AGI) over $100,000 for the tax year (see FTC 2d/FIN ¶ K-5493.1; USTR ¶ 1634.052; TaxDesk ¶ 314,519.2).

"Qualified mortgage insurance" means:

• mortgage insurance provided by the Department of Veterans Affairs (VA), the Federal Housing Administration (FHA), or the Rural Housing Service (RHS), and

• private mortgage insurance (as defined by Sec. 2 of the Homeowners Protection Act of '98 (12 U.S.C. 4901), as in effect on Dec. 20, 2006). See FTC 2d/FIN ¶ K-5493; USTR ¶ 1634.052; TaxDesk ¶ 314,519.1.

To be deductible qualified residence interest, the amounts must be paid or accrued under a mortgage insurance contract issued after Dec. 31, 2006 (see FTC 2d/FIN ¶ K-5493; USTR ¶ 1634.052; TaxDesk ¶ 314,519.1).

Except for amounts paid for qualified mortgage insurance provided by the VA or the RHS (see above), any amount the taxpayer pays for qualified mortgage insurance that is properly allocable to any mortgage the payment of which extends to periods after the close of the tax year in which that amount is paid is chargeable to a capital account and must be treated as paid in those periods to which it is allocated (see FTC 2d/FIN ¶ K-5493; USTR ¶ 1634.052; TaxDesk ¶ 314,519.1).

> **observation:** Presumably, this means that where, in Year 1, a taxpayer "prepays" the premiums for qualified mortgage insurance for the entire term of the mortgage (for example, 15 or 30 years), only the portion allocable to Year 1 is treated as paid in that year. So, only that portion of the payment is deductible in Year 1 under the above rule. The portions allocable to Year 2, Year 3, etc., are treated as paid in those later years, and so are nondeductible in Year 1 under this rule.

Under pre-2012 Taxpayer Relief Act law, the rules treating qualified mortgage insurance premiums as deductible qualified residence interest didn't apply to:

(1) amounts paid or accrued after Dec. 31, 2011; or

(2) amounts properly allocable to any period after Dec. 31, 2011. (FTC 2d/FIN ¶ K-4570, ¶ K-5493; USTR ¶ 1634.052; TaxDesk ¶ 314,519.1)

New Law. Under the 2012 Taxpayer Relief Act (the "Act"), the rules treating the deduction of qualified mortgage insurance premiums as deductible qualified residence interest don't apply with respect to amounts paid or accrued after Dec. 31, 2013, or properly allocable to any period after that date. (Code Sec. 163(h)(3)(E)(iv) as amended by 2012 Taxpayer Relief Act §204(a))

> **observation:** That is, the Act extends the itemized deduction for private mortgage insurance for two years (only for contracts entered into after Dec. 31, 2006). Specifically, the Act extends the deduction to amounts paid or accrued before Jan. 1, 2014 that aren't allocable to any period after Dec. 31, 2013.

☐ **Effective:** Amounts paid or accrued after Dec. 31, 2011 (2012 Taxpayer Relief Act §204(c)) and before Jan. 1, 2014 (Code Sec. 163(h)(3)(E)(iv)).

¶ 306. Exclusion for debt discharge income from home mortgage forgiveness is extended for one year until the end of 2013

Code Sec. 108(a)(1)(E), as amended by 2012 Taxpayer Relief Act §202(a)
Generally effective: Discharges of indebtedness after Dec. 31, 2012, and
*   before Jan. 1, 2014*
Committee Reports, None

The rule that a discharge of indebtedness gives rise to income includible in gross income—"cancellation of debt (COD) income" or "debt discharge income" (FTC 2d/FIN ¶ J-7001; USTR ¶ 614.114; TaxDesk ¶ 186,001)—is subject to certain exceptions, including exceptions for discharges in Title 11 bankruptcy cases or when the taxpayer is insolvent (the "insolvency exclusion"). For these exceptions, taxpayers generally reduce certain tax attributes, including basis in property, by the amount of the debt discharged. (FTC 2d/FIN ¶ J-7401; USTR ¶ 1084.01; TaxDesk ¶ 188,011)

An exception for home mortgages—the "mortgage forgiveness exclusion"—applies to discharges after Dec. 31, 2006. Any debt discharge income resulting from a discharge (in whole or in part) of "qualified principal residence indebtedness" is excluded from gross income. "Qualified principal residence indebtedness" is acquisition indebtedness (as defined by Code Sec. 163(h)(3)(B) except that the dollar limitation is $2 million) with respect to the taxpayer's principal residence—i.e., the debt must have been used to acquire, construct, or substantially improve the taxpayer's principal residence, or to refinance the debt (but only up to the amount refinanced), and must have been secured by the residence (see FTC 2d/FIN ¶ K-5484; USTR ¶ 1634.052; TaxDesk ¶ 314,515). This exclusion applies where taxpayers restructure their acquisition debt on a principal residence or lose their principal residence in a foreclosure. (FTC 2d/FIN ¶ J-7417; USTR ¶ 1084.01; TaxDesk ¶ 188,029)

The basis of the residence is reduced by the amount excluded under the above-described mortgage forgiveness exclusion, but not below zero. (FTC 2d/FIN ¶ P-3006.2; USTR ¶ 1084.02; TaxDesk ¶ 214,500)

"Principal residence" has the same meaning for this purpose as under the Code Sec. 121 homesale exclusion rules—i.e., the home where the taxpayer ordinarily lives most of the time. The exclusion doesn't apply to debt forgiven on second homes, business property, or rental property. (FTC 2d/FIN ¶ J-7417; USTR ¶ 1084.01; TaxDesk ¶ 188,029)

If only part of the discharged loan is qualified principal residence indebtedness, the mortgage forgiveness exclusion applies only to so much of the amount discharged as exceeds the amount of the loan (as determined immediately before the discharge) that isn't qualified principal residence indebtedness. (FTC 2d/FIN ¶ J-7418; USTR ¶ 1084.01; TaxDesk ¶ 188,030)

The mortgage forgiveness exclusion doesn't apply if the discharge is on account of services performed for the lender or any other factor not directly related to a decline in the residence's value or to the taxpayer's financial condition. (FTC 2d/FIN ¶ J-7419; USTR ¶ 1084.01; TaxDesk ¶ 188,031)

The mortgage forgiveness exclusion also doesn't apply to a taxpayer in a Title 11 bankruptcy case; instead, the general exclusion rules apply. Where an insolvent taxpayer (other than one in a Title 11 bankruptcy) qualifies for the mortgage forgiveness exclusion, the mortgage forgiveness exclusion applies unless the taxpayer elects to apply the insolvency exclusion. (FTC 2d/FIN ¶ J-7420; USTR ¶ 1084.01; TaxDesk ¶ 188,012)

Under pre-2012 Taxpayer Relief Act law, the mortgage forgiveness exclusion applied to indebtedness discharged before Jan. 1, 2013. (FTC 2d/FIN ¶ J-7417; USTR ¶ 1084.01; TaxDesk ¶ 188,029)

New Law. The 2012 Taxpayer Relief Act (Act) extends the mortgage forgiveness exclusion for one year, so that it applies to indebtedness discharged before Jan. 1, 2014. (Code Sec. 108(a)(1)(E) as amended by 2012 Taxpayer Relief Act §202(a))

> *observation:* As described above, an insolvent taxpayer (not in a Title 11 bankruptcy case) whose debt is discharged (in whole or in part) uses the mortgage forgiveness exclusion rules, including the basis reduction requirement for the residence, for any portion of the discharged debt that is "qualified real property indebtedness." That is, if the taxpayer wants to use the insolvency exclusion rules, including the tax attribute reduction requirements, he must elect "out" of the mortgage forgiveness exclusion. By extending the mortgage forgiveness exclusion for one year, the Act also extends for one year the period for which an insolvent taxpayer must affirmatively elect to use the insolvency exclusion.

> Taxpayers usually won't benefit from electing the insolvency exclusion here. The insolvency exclusion requires the taxpayer to make the same basis and tax attribute reductions as are required in a Title 11 bankruptcy case (see FTC 2d/FIN ¶ J-7404; USTR ¶ 1084.01; TaxDesk ¶ 188,016). The mortgage forgiveness exclusion requires the taxpayer to reduce his basis in the residence (see FTC 2d/FIN ¶ P-3006.2; USTR ¶ 1084.02; TaxDesk ¶ 214,500). In addition, the amount of debt discharge income that is excluded from income under the insolvency exclusion is limited to the amount by which the taxpayer is insolvent (see FTC 2d/FIN ¶ J-7403; USTR ¶ 1084.01; TaxDesk ¶ 188,014). This limitation doesn't apply in the case of the mortgage forgiveness exclusion (see FTC 2d/FIN ¶ J-7417; USTR ¶ 1084.01; TaxDesk ¶ 188,029).

observation: Apart from providing the one-year extension, the Act doesn't make any changes to the rules for the mortgage forgiveness exclusion.

☐ **Effective:** Discharges of indebtedness after Dec. 31, 2012 (2012 Taxpayer Relief Act §202(b)), and before Jan. 1, 2014. (Code Sec. 108(a)(1)(E))

¶ 307. Parity extended through 2013 for employer-provided mass transit and parking benefits

Code Sec. 132(f)(2), as amended by 2012 Taxpayer Relief Act §203(a)
Generally effective: For months in 2012 and 2013
Committee Reports, None

For months beginning before Feb. 17, 2009, an employer could exclude from an employee's income a statutory amount of up to $100 a month ($120, as adjusted for inflation for 2009) for qualified transportation fringe benefits that the employer provided through transit passes and vanpooling. The 2009 Recovery Act (Sec. 1151, PL 111-5, 2/17/2009), as extended by the 2010 Tax Relief Act (Sec. 727, PL 111-312, 12/17/2010), temporarily raised the excludable amount to provide parity for these benefits with employer-provided parking benefits, which are excluded up to a statutory amount of $175 a month ($230, as adjusted for inflation for 2011), for months beginning before Jan. 1, 2012.

Thus, for 2011, an employer could exclude from an employee's income up to $230 a month for qualified transportation fringe benefits that the employer provided through transit passes and vanpooling, the same amount that an employer could exclude for qualified transportation fringe benefits that the employer provided through employer-provided parking. Before the 2012 Taxpayer Relief Act, there was no such parity for 2012 and 2013 when the monthly exclusion was only $125 for employer-provided transit and vanpooling benefits, while being $240 (estimated to rise to $245 in 2013) for qualified parking. (FTC 2d/FIN ¶ H-2200, ¶ H-2217; USTR ¶ 1324.08; TaxDesk ¶ 134,591; PBE ¶ 132-4.08; BC ¶ 27,511, ¶ 32,309; BCA ¶ 127,511, ¶ 132,309)

New Law. The 2012 Taxpayer Relief Act extends parity for the entire 2012 and 2013 tax years. Thus, for any month beginning before Jan. 1, 2014 (i.e., in 2012 and 2013), the monthly exclusion limitation for employer-provided transit and vanpooling benefits is the same as for employer-provided parking. (Code Sec. 132(f)(2) as amended by 2012 Taxpayer Relief Act §203(a))

observation: According to an early summary of the provision, as a practical matter, in order for the extension to be effective retroactive to Jan. 1, 2012, monthly expenses for transit and vanpooling incurred by employees before the enactment date could have been reimbursed by employers on a tax-free basis to the extent that these monthly expenses exceeded $125 but were not more than $240. However, the 2012 Tax-payer Relief Act contains no mechanism by which employees and employers can reclaim the 2012 pre-tax benefits they would have obtained if the value of transit passes in excess of $125 a month (and up to $240 a month) had been purchased pre-tax instead of post-tax. It remains to be seen whether Congress or IRS will address this situation.

⚫*observation:* As indicated by IRS in Rev Proc 2013-15, Sec. 2.09, for tax years beginning in 2013, the monthly exclusion limitation for employer-provided transit and vanpooling benefits is $245, the same as for employer-provided parking.

⚫*observation:* For months beginning on or after Jan. 1, 2014, barring another extension, the limit on the excludable amount for employer-provided transit passes and vanpooling benefits will revert to an inflation-adjusted amount, which, but for the change above, would have been $125 in 2012.

☐ **Effective:** For months after Dec. 31, 2011 (2012 Taxpayer Relief Act §203(b)) and before Jan. 1, 2014, i.e., for months in 2012 and 2013. (Code Sec. 132(f)(2)).

¶ 308. Up-to-$250 above-the-line deduction for teachers' out-of-pocket classroom-related expenses is retroactively extended through 2013

Code Sec. 62(a)(2)(D), as amended by 2012 Taxpayer Relief Act §201(a)
Generally effective: Tax years beginning after Dec. 31, 2011 and before Jan. 1, 2014
Committee Reports, None

"Eligible educators"—kindergarten through 12th grade teachers, instructors, counselors, principals, or aides in any elementary or secondary school—are allowed an above-the-line deduction of up to $250 for out-of-pocket expenses they paid in connection with books, supplies (other than nonathletic supplies for courses of instruction in health or physical education), computer equipment (including related software and services), other equipment, and supplementary materials used in the classroom. Under pre-2012 Taxpayer Relief Act law, this deduction for eligible educator expenses was available in tax years beginning during 2002 through 2011. (FTC 2d/FIN ¶ A-2601, ¶ A-2611.2; USTR ¶ 624, ¶ 624.02; TaxDesk ¶ 560,706.1)

New Law. The 2012 Taxpayer Relief Act adds that the deduction for eligible educator expenses is available in tax years beginning during 2012 or 2013. (Code Sec. 62(a)(2)(D) as amended by 2012 Taxpayer Relief Act §201(a))

RIA *observation:* Without the deduction for eligible educator expenses, any unreimbursed expenses that elementary or secondary school teachers might be able to deduct in connection with their teaching activities would be deductible only as unreimbursed employee business expenses—i.e., as miscellaneous itemized deductions subject to the 2%-of-adjusted gross income (AGI) floor on miscellaneous itemized deductions. See FTC 2d/FIN ¶s L-3900 *et seq.,* L-4108; USTR ¶ 1624.067; TaxDesk ¶s 351,500 *et seq.,* 561,604.

☐ **Effective:** Tax years beginning after Dec. 31, 2011 (2012 Taxpayer Relief Act §201(b)) and before Jan. 1, 2014. (Code Sec. 62(a)(2)(D))

¶ 309. Adoption assistance exclusion is made permanent

Code Sec. 137, 2012 Taxpayer Relief Act §101(a)(1)
Code Sec. None, 2012 Taxpayer Relief Act §101(a)(1)
Generally effective: Tax years beginning after 2012
Committee Reports, None

Employees can exclude from gross income the qualified adoption expenses paid or reimbursed by an employer under an employer-provided adoption assistance program. The exclusion is subject to both (1) a dollar limit (under which the total amount of excludible adoption expenses cannot exceed a maximum amount), and (2) an income limit (under which the exclusion is ratably phased out over a certain income range, based on modified adjusted gross income (AGI)).

The 2001 Economic Growth and Tax Relief Reconciliation Act (EGTRRA, PL 107-16, 6/7/2001) made modifications to the adoption assistance exclusion, as described below.

EGTRRA (Sec. 202, PL 107-16, 6/7/2001) modified the exclusion by:

(1) increasing the maximum exclusion from $5,000 ($6,000 for special needs adoptions) to $10,000 (for all adoptions);

(2) allowing the maximum exclusion amount for special needs adoptions, without regard to the amount of adoption expenses actually incurred;

(3) increasing the income phase-out range from a range of $75,000 to $115,000, to a range of $150,000 to $190,000;

(4) providing that the dollar limit and the income limit are to be adjusted for inflation; and

(5) making the exclusion "permanent" (instead of being set to expire after Dec. 31, 2001, as provided under pre-EGTRRA law), but still subject to EGTRRA's sunset provision (Sec. 901, PL 107-16, 6/7/2001) which provided that all changes made by EGTRRA (including the changes to the adoption assis-

tance exclusion described above) were not to apply to tax years beginning after Dec. 31, 2010 (the EGTRRA sunset date).

The 2010 Tax Relief Act (PL 111-312, 12/17/2010) extended the adoption assistance exclusion as expanded by EGTRRA for one year (through 2012). The 2010 Act accomplished this by amending the EGTRRA sunset provision by replacing the Dec. 31, 2010 sunset date with a Dec. 31, 2012 sunset date. Thus, under the 2010 Tax Relief Act, the changes made to the exclusion by EGTRRA (items (1) through (5), above) were extended through 2012. (Sec. 901, PL 107-16, 6/7/2001, as amended by Sec. 101(a)(1), PL 111-312, 12/17/2010)

For tax years beginning in 2012:

. . . the maximum exclusion was $12,170, as adjusted for inflation; and

. . . the phase-out range was $182,520 to $222,520, as adjusted for inflation.

For tax years beginning after Dec. 31, 2012, the adoption assistance exclusion was going to revert to pre-EGTRRA law, which provided that the exclusion was to expire for amounts paid, or expenses incurred, after Dec. 31, 2001. Thus, for tax years beginning after 2012, the exclusion was not going to be available. (FTC 2d/FIN ¶ H-1450, ¶ H-1451, ¶ H-1453; USTR ¶ 1374; TaxDesk ¶ 133,603, ¶ 133,605)

New Law. The 2012 Taxpayer Relief Act repeals title IX of EGTRRA (i.e., the title containing the above-described EGTRRA sunset). (EGTRRA § 901 (Sec. 901, PL 107-16, 6/7/2001) repealed by 2012 Taxpayer Relief Act §101(a)(1))

observation: Thus, the adoption assistance exclusion is made permanent.

observation: As indicated in Rev Proc 2013-15, Sec. 2.10, for tax years beginning in 2013:

. . . the maximum exclusion is $12,970, as adjusted for inflation; and

. . . the phase-out range is $194,580 to $234,580, as adjusted for inflation.

☐ **Effective:** For tax years beginning after Dec. 31, 2012. (2012 Taxpayer Relief Act §101(a)(3))

¶ 310. Tax refunds won't affect eligibility for federal benefit programs

Code Sec. 6409, as amended by 2012 Taxpayer Relief Act §103(d)
Generally effective: Amounts received after Dec. 31, 2012
Committee Reports, None

Under pre-2012 Taxpayer Relief Act law, any refund or advance payment of a refundable credit made to an individual under the Internal Revenue Code isn't taken into account as income, and isn't taken into account as a resource for a period of 12 months from receipt, in determining the eligibility of the recipient or any other individual for benefits or assistance, or the amount or extent of benefits or assistance, under any federal program or any state or local program financed in whole or part with federal funds. This rule overrides any other provision of law.

> **⏺ *observation:*** Thus, the receipt of a tax refund or advance payment of a refundable credit begins a 12-month period during which the refund may not be taken into account as a resource in determining eligibility for federal or federally-assisted programs. The provision would override any state provisions that would take tax refunds and/or advance payments of refundable credits into account in determining eligibility for such programs.

Sunset. This provision was scheduled to expire for amounts received after Dec. 31, 2012.

New Law. The 2012 Taxpayer Relief Act removes the expiration language from Code Sec. 6409, and thus makes permanent the disregard of tax refunds for purposes of determining eligibility for federal benefit programs. (Code Sec. 6409 as amended by 2012 Taxpayer Relief Act §103(d))

☐ **Effective:** The removal of the sunset provision is effective for amounts received after Dec. 31, 2012. (2012 Taxpayer Relief Act §103(e)(2))

¶ 400. Alternative Minimum Tax

¶ 401. AMT exemption amounts are increased to $50,600 for unmarrieds and $78,750 for joint filers for 2012 and are indexed for inflation after 2012

Code Sec. 55(d)(1)(A), as amended by 2012 Taxpayer Relief Act §104(a)(1)(A)

Code Sec. 55(d)(1)(B), as amended by 2012 Taxpayer Relief Act §104(a)(1)(B)

Code Sec. 55(b)(1)(A)(iii), as amended by 2012 Taxpayer Relief Act §104(b)(2)(A)

Code Sec. 55(d)(3), as amended by 2012 Taxpayer Relief Act §104(b)(2)(B)

Code Sec. 55(d)(4), as amended by 2012 Taxpayer Relief Act §104(b)(1)

Generally effective: Tax years beginning after Dec. 31, 2011

Committee Reports, None

In computing the alternative minimum tax (AMT) for individuals, the AMT tax rate is applied against the taxpayer's alternative minimum taxable income (AMTI), as reduced by the taxpayer's exemption amount (which phases out for AMTI above certain threshold levels).

Pre-2012 Taxpayer Relief Act law provided the following statutory AMT exemption amounts for tax years beginning in 2012 (and later years):

... $45,000 for married couples filing jointly and surviving spouses;

... $33,750 for unmarried individuals who aren't surviving spouses; and

... $22,500 (technically, 50% of the joint return/surviving spouse amount) for married individuals filing separate returns.

AMT "patch" provisions (to reduce the number of individuals who otherwise would be subject to the AMT) began with the temporary increases to the AMT exemption amounts provided by the Economic Growth and Tax Relief Reconciliation Act of 2001 (EGTRRA, PL 107-16, 6/7/2001). Additional increases for 2003 and 2004, and temporary increases for 2005, were provided by the Jobs and Growth Tax Relief Reconciliation Act of 2003 (JGTRRA, PL 108-27, 5/28/2003) and the Working Families Tax Relief Act of 2004 (WFTRA, PL 108-311, 10/4/2004), respectively.

FTC 2d References are to Federal Tax Coordinator 2d
FIN References are to RIA's Analysis of Federal Taxes: Income (print)
USTR References are to United States Tax Reporter: Income
PCA References are to Pension Analysis (print and electronic)
PBE References are to Pension & Benefits Explanations
BCA References are to Benefits Analysis (electronic)
BC References are to Benefits Coordinator (print)
EP References are to Estate Planning Analysis (print and electronic)

Later legislation provided similar one- or two-year "patches" for 2006 through 2011. For example, the 2010 Tax Relief Act (2010 TRA, Sec. 201(a), PL 111-312, 12/17/2010) provided the following higher AMT exemption amounts for tax years beginning in 2010:

- $72,450 for married couples filing jointly and surviving spouses;
- $47,450 for unmarried individuals who aren't surviving spouses; and
- $36,225 for married individuals filing separate returns.

For tax years beginning in 2011, the AMT exemption amounts were further increased as follows:

- to $74,450 for married couples filing jointly and surviving spouses;
- to $48,450 for unmarried individuals who aren't surviving spouses; and
- to $37,225 for married individuals filing separate returns.

Under pre-2012 Taxpayer Relief Act law, the temporary increases expired after 2011. This meant that the lower generally applicable statutory AMT exemption amounts were to apply for 2012 and later tax years. (FTC 2d/FIN ¶ A-8160, ¶ A-8162; USTR ¶ 554.01; TaxDesk ¶ 691,302)

New Law. The 2012 Taxpayer Relief Act increases and makes permanent the 2012 AMT exemption amounts and provides for inflation adjustments in later tax years.

Increased AMT exemption amounts. For tax years beginning in 2012, the AMT exemption amounts are:

. . . $78,750 (up from $74,450 in 2011) for married couples filing jointly and surviving spouses (Code Sec. 55(d)(1)(A) as amended by 2012 Taxpayer Relief Act §104(a)(1)(A));

. . . $50,600 (up from $48,450 in 2011) for unmarried individuals who aren't surviving spouses (Code Sec. 55(d)(1)(B) as amended by 2012 Taxpayer Relief Act §104(a)(1)(B)); and

. . . $39,375 (i.e., 50% of the joint return amount) (up from $37,225 in 2011) for married individuals filing separate returns. (Code Sec. 55(d)(1)(C))

For inflation-adjusted 2013 exemption amounts, see below under "Post-2012 AMT amounts adjusted for inflation."

> ⏺ *observation:* The 2012 Taxpayer Relief Act doesn't change the rule that the AMT exemption amount for married individuals filing separately is 50% of the AMT exemption amount for joint filers and surviving spouses (see FTC 2d/FIN ¶ A-8162; USTR ¶ 554.01; TaxDesk ¶ 691,302). Thus, although the 2012 Taxpayer Relief Act doesn't specifically provide increased AMT exemption amounts for married individuals filing separately for 2012, the exemption amount for those indi-

viduals is effectively increased because the joint return/surviving spouse exemption amount is permanently increased for 2012 (and is adjusted for inflation in years after 2012). That is, the AMT exemption amount for married individuals filing separately is increased to $39,375 (50% × $78,750 for 2012). Under pre-2012 Taxpayer Relief Act law, their AMT exemption amount would have dropped to $22,500 in 2012.

For the permanent extension of the rule allowing nonrefundable personal credits to offset AMT (as well as regular tax), see ¶ 403.

The following table shows the impact of 2012 Taxpayer Relief Act §104(a):

AMT Exemption Amount

	Pre-2012 Taxpayer Relief Act			2012 Taxpayer Relief Act		
	Unmarried	Joint	Married Filing Separate	Unmarried	Joint	Married Filing Separate
2010	$47,450	$72,450	$36,225	$47,450	$72,450	$36,225
2011	$48,450	$74,450	$37,225	$48,450	$74,450	$37,225
2012	$33,750	$45,000	$22,500	$50,600	$78,750	$39,375

☑ caution: Congress's intent in permanently increasing the exemption amount is to minimize the "spread" of AMT liability to increasing numbers of taxpayers. However, given the enormous complexity of the AMT, the determination as to whether an individual has AMT liability still must be made on an individual basis.

Kiddie tax AMT exemption amount. For a child subject to the "kiddie tax" (i.e., certain children with unearned income over $1,900 for 2012 ($2,000 for 2013) (see FTC 2d/FIN ¶ A-1300 et seq.; USTR ¶ 14.09; TaxDesk ¶ 568,300 et seq.), the AMT exemption amount can't exceed the sum of the child's earned income plus $6,950 in 2012 ($7,150 in 2013). In addition, the kiddie tax AMT exemption can't be more than the child's regular AMT exemption (the unmarried individual's exemption amount, discussed above). (FTC 2d/FIN ¶ A-8163; USTR ¶ 594; TaxDesk ¶ 691,303)

☑ observation: As stated above, the unmarried individual's AMT exemption amount is $50,600 for tax years beginning in 2012. Thus, a child subject to the kiddie tax is entitled to a maximum AMT exemption of $50,600 in 2012 but only if he has earned income of $43,650 ($43,650 + $6,950 = $50,600) or more before taking the phaseout for unmarried individuals into account.

AMT exemption amount for estates and trusts.

observation: The 2012 Taxpayer Relief Act doesn't change the $22,500 exemption amount for an estate or trust but does adjust it for inflation in years after 2012, as discussed below (see FTC 2d/FIN ¶ A-8164; USTR ¶ 554.01; TaxDesk ¶ 691,304). The 2012 Taxpayer Relief Act also modifies the phase-out of the exemption amount for an estate or trust to account for inflation adjustments in years after 2012, as discussed below.

Phase-out of AMT exemption amount. The 2012 Taxpayer Relief Act provides that, in the case of a married individual filing a separate return, an estate, or a trust, the phase-out of exemption amount is 50% of the dollar amount applicable under Code Sec. 55(d)(3)(A) (i.e., the phase-out of exemption amount for married individuals filing jointly or surviving spouses). (Code Sec. 55(d)(3)(C) as amended by 2012 Taxpayer Relief Act §104(b)(2)(B))

observation: So, in 2012, under the phase-out rules, the AMT exemption amount is reduced by an amount equal to 25% of the amount by which the individual's AMTI exceeds the following threshold amounts: (FTC 2d/FIN ¶ A-8162; USTR ¶ 554.01; TaxDesk ¶ 691,302)

... $150,000 for married couples filing jointly and surviving spouses,

... $112,500 for unmarried individuals who aren't surviving spouses, and

... $75,000 (i.e., 50% of the phase-out amount for joint returns) for married individuals filing separate returns, estates, and trusts.

For inflation-adjusted 2013 threshold amounts, see below under "Post-2012 AMT amounts adjusted for inflation."

observation: Under these rules, the exemption is completely phased-out at an AMTI dollar amount equal to:

Applicable phase-out threshold + (4 × applicable exemption amount).

observation: Thus, the AMT exemption for 2012 completely phases out (i.e., the taxpayer is subject to AMT on *all* of his AMTI), at the following AMTI levels:

... $465,000 ($150,000 + $315,000 [4 × $78,750]) for married couples filing jointly and surviving spouses,

... $314,900 ($112,500 + $202,400 [4 × $50,600]) for unmarried individuals who aren't surviving spouses,

... $232,500 ($75,000 + $157,500 [4 × $39,375]) for married individuals filing separate returns, and

. . . $165,000 ($75,000 + 90,000 [4 × $22,500]) for estates and trusts.

⊘observation: The 2012 Taxpayer Relief Act also changes the phase-out rules for the AMT exemption amount by adjusting the amounts for inflation for tax years after 2012, as discussed below.

Post-2012 AMT amounts adjusted for inflation. For any tax year beginning in a calendar year after 2012, the 2012 Taxpayer Relief Act provides for inflation adjustments for the following AMT amounts:

. . . the exemption amounts provided in Code Sec. 55(d)(1). (Code Sec. 55(d)(4)(B)(ii) as amended by 2012 Taxpayer Relief Act §104(b)(1))

⊘observation: The inflation-adjusted exemption amounts for 2013, as set forth by the Joint Committee on Taxation in JCX-2-13R: Overview Of The Federal Tax System As In Effect For 2013, and by IRS in Rev Proc 2013-15, Sec. 2.06, are:

. . . $80,800 for married individuals filing jointly and surviving spouses;

. . . $51,900 for unmarried individuals who aren't surviving spouses;

. . . $40,400 for married individuals filing separate returns; and

. . . $23,100 for estates and trusts.

. . . the phase-out of exemption amounts provided in Code Sec. 55(d)(3)(A) (for married couples filing jointly and surviving spouses) and Code Sec. 55(d)(3)(B) (for unmarried individuals who aren't surviving spouses). (Code Sec. 55(d)(4)(B)(iii))

⊘observation: The inflation-adjusted phase-out thresholds for 2013, as set forth by the Joint Committee on Taxation in JCX-2-13R: Overview Of The Federal Tax System As In Effect For 2013, and by IRS in Rev Proc 2013-15, Sec. 2.06, are:

. . . $153,900 for married individuals filing jointly and surviving spouses;

. . . $115,400 for unmarried individuals who aren't surviving spouses; and

. . . $76,950 for married individuals filing separate returns, estates, and trusts.

. . . the $175,000 statutory amount contained in Code Sec. 55(b)(1)(A)(i) relating to the computation of an individual's tentative minimum tax. (Code Sec. 55(d)(4)(B)(i)) In the case of a married individual filing a separate return, the amount used to compute the tentative minimum tax will be 50% of the dollar amount otherwise applicable under Code Sec. 55(b)(1)(A)(i). (Code Sec. 55(b)(1)(A)(iii) as amended by 2012 Taxpayer Relief Act §104(b)(2)(A))

The adjustment to each of those amounts for a calendar year is made using the consumer price index computation in Code Sec. 1(f)(3), but substituting calendar year 2011 for calendar year 1992. (Code Sec. 55(d)(4)(A))

The inflation-adjusted amounts are rounded to the nearest multiple of $100. (Code Sec. 55(d)(4)(C))

> *observation:* As indicated by IRS in Rev Proc 2013-15, Sec. 2.06, for tax years beginning in 2013, the $175,000 statutory amount referred to above is increased to $179,500 ($89,750 for marrieds filing separately).

> *sample client letter:* For a client letter on the AMT provisions in the 2012 Taxpayer Relief Act, see ¶ 2003.

☐ **Effective:** Tax years beginning after Dec. 31, 2011. (2012 Taxpayer Relief Act §104(d))

> *observation:* The 2012 Taxpayer Relief Act §104(a) increases the AMT exemption amounts for 2012, and so applies retroactively to tax years beginning after Dec. 31, 2011.

> *recommendation:* Individuals subject to estimated tax in 2012 may have already used the lower AMT exemption amounts that were in effect under pre-2012 Taxpayer Relief Act law to compute their first three installments of estimated tax for 2012 (i.e., the installments due on Apr. 12, June 15, and Sept. 15, 2012). That is, unmarried individuals may have used $33,750 (rather than $50,600), married couples filing jointly and surviving spouses may have used $45,000 (rather than $78,750), and marrieds filing separately may have used $22,500 (rather than $33,375), as their AMT exemption amount for 2012. Individuals in this situation should recompute their required payment for the fourth installment for 2012 (due Jan. 15, 2013), to account for the retroactive increases in the AMT exemption amounts for 2012. (See FTC 2d/FIN ¶ S-5200 *et seq.*; USTR ¶ 66,544; TaxDesk ¶ 571,300 *et seq.*)

¶ 402. AMT rates on capital gain and qualified dividends are 0%, 15%, and 20% after 2012

Code Sec. 55(b)(3), 2012 Taxpayer Relief Act §102(a)
Code Sec. 55(b)(3)(C), as amended by 2012 Taxpayer Relief Act §102(b)(2)
Code Sec. 55(b)(3)(D), as amended by 2012 Taxpayer Relief Act §102(b)(2)
Code Sec. 55(b)(3)(B), as amended by 2012 Taxpayer Relief Act §102(c)(2)
Generally effective: Tax years beginning after Dec. 31, 2012
Committee Reports, None

The starting point for computing the alternative minimum tax (AMT) is taxable income. Various adjustments and preferences are added or subtracted to arrive at alternative minimum taxable income (AMTI).

For noncorporate taxpayers, the "taxable excess" (AMTI minus the AMT exemption amount), is subject to a tentative minimum tax of 26% or 28% (reduced by any AMT foreign tax credit). (FTC 2d/FIN ¶ A-8101; USTR ¶ 554.01; TaxDesk ¶ 691,001)

However, a noncorporate taxpayer's tentative minimum tax is subject to a limit that is intended to insure that the maximum tax rates on capital gain (see ¶ 201) and qualified dividends (see ¶ 202) that apply for regular tax purposes also apply for AMT purposes.

Under pre-2012 Taxpayer Relief Act law, this limit, set forth by Code Sec. 55(b)(3), was the sum of various amounts, including:

(1) 0% of so much of the taxpayer's adjusted net capital gain (or, if less, taxable excess) as didn't exceed the amount on which a 10% or 15% regular tax rate was imposed under Code Sec. 1(h)(1)(B), and

(2) 15% of the adjusted net capital gain (or, if less, taxable excess) in excess of the amount on which tax was determined under paragraph (1) above.

"Adjusted net capital gain" has the same meaning for AMT purposes as it has for purposes of the regular income tax (see ¶ 201), though the amount of gain may differ due to AMT adjustments and preferences. (FTC 2d/FIN ¶ A-8300, ¶ A-8102; USTR ¶ 554.01; TaxDesk ¶ 691,002)

Sunset. Under section 303 of the 2003 Jobs and Growth Act (JGTRRA, Sec. 303, PL 108-27, 5/28/2003), as amended by section 102 of the 2005 Tax Increase Prevention Act (TIPRA, Sec. 102, PL 109-222, 5/17/2006) and by section 102 of the 2010 Tax Relief Act (Sec. 102, PL 111-312, 12/17/2010):

. . . the 0% and 15% AMT rates on adjusted net capital gain (items (1) and (2), above) were due to expire for tax years beginning after Dec. 31, 2012. (FTC 2d/FIN ¶ T-11062; USTR ¶ 79,006.87; TaxDesk ¶ 880,014)

... the rates in effect before passage of JGTRRA, which ranged from 8% to 20%, were due to come back into effect. (FTC 2d/FIN ¶ A-8102; USTR ¶ 554.01; TaxDesk ¶ 691,002)

New Law. The 2012 Taxpayer Relief Act removes the JGTRRA sunset provision. Thus, the 0% and 15% AMT capital gain rates under JGTRRA are made permanent. (2003 Jobs and Growth Act § 303 (Sec. 303, PL 108-27, 5/28/2003) repealed by 2012 Taxpayer Relief Act §102(a)) The 2012 Taxpayer Relief Act also adds a new 20% AMT capital gain tax rate for certain high-income taxpayers. (Code Sec. 55(b)(3)(D) as amended by 2012 Taxpayer Relief Act §102(b)(2))

observation: The maximum AMT tax rates on adjusted net capital gain under the 2012 Taxpayer Relief Act, as set forth by the Joint Committee on Taxation in JCX-2-13R: Overview Of The Federal Tax System As In Effect For 2013, are:

... 0% on gain that otherwise would be taxed at a regular tax 10% or 15% rate.

... 15% on gain that otherwise would be taxed at a regular tax 25%, 28%, 33%, or 35% rate.

... 20% on gain that otherwise would be taxed at a regular tax 39.6% rate.

observation: The 0%, 15%, and 20% AMT capital gain rates also apply to qualified dividends, which are permanently treated as adjusted net capital gain under the 2012 Taxpayer Relief Act (see ¶ 202).

observation: The 39.6% regular income tax rate applies to taxable income above $450,000 for joint filers and surviving spouses, $425,000 for heads of household, $400,000 for single filers, and $225,000 for married taxpayers filing separately, adjusted for inflation after 2013, see ¶ 101. Thus, the 20% AMT rate applies to capital gain and qualified dividends of taxpayers whose income exceeds these thresholds.

Under the 2012 Taxpayer Relief Act, the 15% rate applies to the lesser of: (Code Sec. 55(b)(3)(C))

• the portion of the adjusted net capital gain (or, if less, taxable excess) that exceeds the amount that is taxed at a 0% rate, or (Code Sec. 55(b)(3)(C)(i))

• the excess of:

... the amount of taxable income that would otherwise be taxed at a regular tax rate below 39.6% (see ¶ 101), over

... the sum of the amounts that are taxed at ordinary income rates or the 0% capital gain rate. (Code Sec. 55(b)(3)(C)(ii))

The 20% rate applies to the adjusted net capital gain (or, if less, taxable excess) that exceeds the amount that is taxed at the 0% or 15% rates. (Code Sec. 55(b)(3)(D))

> **☑ observation:** Because the 3.8% net investment income tax (NIIT) applies to capital gains and dividends starting in 2013 (FTC 2d/FIN ¶ A-6361; USTR ¶ 14,114.01; TaxDesk ¶ 576,301), the overall tax rate on those items for some high-income taxpayers will be 23.8% (20% + 3.8%). The NIIT applies to taxpayers whose modified adjusted gross income (MAGI) exceeds $250,000 for joint returns and surviving spouses, $125,000 for separate returns, and $200,000 in all other cases.

The 2012 Taxpayer Relief Act removes the reference to the 5% AMT capital gain rate that applied instead of the 0% rate for tax years beginning before 2008. (Code Sec. 55(b)(3)(B) as amended by 2012 Taxpayer Relief Act §102(c)(2))

☐ **Effective:** The effect of 2012 Taxpayer Relief Act §102(a) is to remove the sunset that would have been effective for tax years beginning after Dec. 31, 2012. (2012 Taxpayer Relief Act §102(a))

> **☑ observation:** 2012 Taxpayer Relief Act §102(a), which eliminates the JGTRRA §303 sunset rule, as amended, is effective as if included in the enactment of JGTRRA. JGTRRA was enacted on May 28, 2003, so §102(a) is technically effective as of that date.

The new 20% rate, the new definition of the 15% rate, and the removal of the reference to the pre-2008 5% AMT capital gain rate are effective for tax years beginning after Dec. 31, 2012. (2012 Taxpayer Relief Act §102(d)(1))

¶ 403. Nonrefundable personal credits can offset AMT and regular tax for all tax years beginning after Dec. 31, 2011

Code Sec. 26(a), as amended by 2012 Taxpayer Relief Act §104(c)(1)
Code Sec. 23(b)(4), 2012 Taxpayer Relief Act §104(c)(2)
Code Sec. 24(b)(3), 2012 Taxpayer Relief Act §104(c)(2)
Code Sec. 25(e)(1)(C), 2012 Taxpayer Relief Act §104(c)(2)
Code Sec. 25A(i)(5), 2012 Taxpayer Relief Act §104(c)(2)
Code Sec. 25B(g), 2012 Taxpayer Relief Act §104(c)(2)
Code Sec. 25D(c), 2012 Taxpayer Relief Act §104(c)(2)
Code Sec. 26(a)(1), 2012 Taxpayer Relief Act §104(c)(2)
Code Sec. 30(c)(2), 2012 Taxpayer Relief Act §104(c)(2)
Code Sec. 30B(g)(2), 2012 Taxpayer Relief Act §104(c)(2)
Code Sec. 30D(c)(2), 2012 Taxpayer Relief Act §104(c)(2)
Code Sec. 904(i), 2012 Taxpayer Relief Act §104(c)(2)
Code Sec. 1400C(d), 2012 Taxpayer Relief Act §104(c)(2)
Generally effective: Tax years beginning after Dec. 31, 2011.
Committee Reports, None

Individuals can qualify for a number of nonrefundable personal tax credits as listed below. Under pre-2012 Taxpayer Relief Act law, these credits were subject to limitations based on tax liability, generally under former Code Sec. 26(a)(2) or former Code Sec. 26(a)(1). For tax years when former Code Sec. 26(a)(2) applied, the credits could be used to offset alternative minimum tax (AMT) as well as regular income tax. For tax years when former Code Sec. 26(a)(2) didn't apply, most of the credits were subject to former Code Sec. 26(a)(1), which didn't allow the AMT offset. Certain "specified personal credits" were excepted from former Code Sec. 26(a)(1) and had their own separate limitations that allowed the AMT offset. (FTC 2d/FIN ¶ A-4900 *et seq.*; USTR ¶ 264; TaxDesk ¶ 569,600 *et seq.*)

The nonrefundable personal credits subject to these limitations were:

(1) the Code Sec. 21 child and dependent care credit (see FTC 2d/FIN ¶ A-4300 *et seq.*; USTR ¶ 214; TaxDesk ¶ 569,300 *et seq.*);

(2) the Code Sec. 22 credit for the elderly and disabled (see FTC 2d/FIN ¶ A-4100 *et seq.*; USTR ¶ 224; TaxDesk ¶ 568,700 *et seq.*);

(3) the Code Sec. 23 adoption expense credit (see FTC 2d/FIN ¶ A-4400; USTR ¶ 234; TaxDesk ¶ 569,500);

(4) the Code Sec. 24 child tax credit (see FTC 2d/FIN ¶ A-4050 *et seq.*; USTR ¶ 214; TaxDesk ¶ 569,100 *et seq.*);

(5) the Code Sec. 25 credit for interest paid or accrued on certain home mortgages of low-income persons (the mortgage credit certificate [MCC] credit), see FTC 2d/FIN ¶ A-4008; USTR ¶ 254.01; TaxDesk ¶ 568,507);

(6) the Code Sec. 25A Lifetime Learning credit (see FTC 2d/FIN ¶ A-4500 *et seq.*; USTR ¶ 25A4; TaxDesk ¶ 568,900 *et seq.*);

(7) the Code Sec. 25A(i) modified Hope credit/American Opportunity Tax Credit (AOTC) (see FTC 2d/FIN ¶ A-4523; USTR ¶ 25A4.03; TaxDesk ¶ 568,923);

(8) the Code Sec. 25B credit for elective deferrals and IRA contributions (the saver's credit) (see FTC 2d/FIN ¶ A-4450 *et seq.*; USTR ¶ 25B4; TaxDesk ¶ 569,200 *et seq.*);

(9) the Code Sec. 25C nonbusiness energy property credit for energy-efficient improvements to a principal residence (see FTC 2d/FIN ¶ A-4750 *et seq.*; USTR ¶ 25C4; TaxDesk ¶ 569,550 *et seq.*);

(10) the Code Sec. 25D residential energy efficient property (REEP) credit for photovoltaic, solar hot water, and fuel cell property added to a residence (see FTC 2d/FIN ¶ A-4780 *et seq.*; USTR ¶ 25D4; TaxDesk ¶ 569,560 *et seq.*);

(11) the nonbusiness portion of the Code Sec. 30 qualified plug-in electric vehicle (QPEV) credit (see FTC 2d/FIN ¶ L-18035 *et seq.*; USTR ¶ 304; TaxDesk ¶ 397,170 *et seq.*);

(12) the nonbusiness portion of the Code Sec. 30B alternative motor vehicle (AMV) credit (see FTC 2d/FIN ¶ L-18020 *et seq.*; USTR ¶ 30B4; TaxDesk ¶ 397,100 *et seq.*);

(13) the nonbusiness portion (i.e., any portion that doesn't relate to depreciable property) of the Code Sec. 30D new qualified plug-in electric drive motor vehicle (NQPEDMV) credit (see FTC 2d/FIN ¶ L-18030 *et seq.*; USTR ¶ 30D4; TaxDesk ¶ 397,130 *et seq.*); and

(14) the Code Sec. 1400C first-time homebuyer credit for the District of Columbia (the "first-time D.C. homebuyer credit," see FTC 2d/FIN ¶ A-4250 *et seq.*; USTR ¶ 1400C4; TaxDesk ¶ 568,800 *et seq.*).

(FTC 2d/FIN ¶ A-4902; USTR ¶ 264; TaxDesk ¶ 569,602)

Under pre-2012 Taxpayer Relief Act law, for tax years beginning before 2012, the nonrefundable personal credits were allowed to the extent of the full amount of the individual's regular tax and AMT under former Code Sec. 26(a)(2). For tax years beginning in 2012 and later (in which former Code Sec. 26(a)(2) didn't apply), the nonrefundable personal tax credits listed above (other than the "specified personal credits" discussed below) were subject to former Code Sec. 26(a)(1). These credits—collectively, the "Code Sec. 26(a)(1) limitation credits"—were allowed to the extent that the total amount of those credits didn't exceed the excess of:

... the taxpayer's regular tax liability (FTC 2d/FIN ¶ A-4905; USTR ¶ 264.01; TaxDesk ¶ 569,604) for the tax year, over

... the taxpayer's tentative minimum tax for the tax year, determined under Code Sec. 55(b)(1) (FTC 2d/FIN ¶ A-8801; USTR ¶ 554.01; TaxDesk ¶ 691,001), but without regard to the AMT foreign tax credit (FTC 2d/FIN ¶ A-8181 *et seq.*; USTR ¶ 594; TaxDesk ¶ 691,401 *et seq.*)

Thus, for tax years beginning in 2012 and later, pre-2012 Taxpayer Relief Act law didn't allow taxpayers to use those credits to offset AMT. (FTC 2d/FIN ¶ A-4900, ¶ A-4901; USTR ¶ 264; TaxDesk ¶ 569,601)

The "specified personal credits" that were excepted from the former Code Sec. 26(a)(1) limitation were:

- the Code Sec. 23 adoption expense credit (item (3) above);
- the Code Sec. 24 child tax credit (item (4) above);
- the Code Sec. 25A(i) modified Hope credit/AOTC (item (7), above),
- the Code Sec. 25B saver's credit (item (8) above);
- the Code Sec. 25D REEP credit (item (10) above); and
- the nonbusiness portions of the Code Sec. 30 QPEV credit, Code Sec. 30B AMV credit, and Code Sec. 30D NQPEDMV credit (items (11)–(13) above). (FTC 2d/FIN ¶ A-4903; USTR ¶ 264; TaxDesk ¶ 569,603)

Under pre-2012 Taxpayer Relief Act law, for tax years beginning after 2011, each of the "specified personal credits" was subject to a separate tax liability limitation (rather than the former Code Sec. 26(a)(1) limitation). The separate tax liability limitation for each credit allowed the particular credit to offset the AMT. (FTC 2d/FIN ¶ A-4050, ¶ A-4054, ¶ A-4400, ¶ A-4405, ¶ A-4450, ¶ A-4455, ¶ A-4500, ¶ A-4525.1, ¶ A-4780, ¶ A-4781.1, ¶ L-18020, ¶ L-18022.1, ¶ L-18030, ¶ L-18034.1, ¶ L-18035, ¶ L-18039.1, ¶ A-8300, ¶ A-8320; USTR ¶ 234, ¶ 244.01, ¶ 25A4.03, ¶ 25B4, ¶ 25D4, ¶ 304.06, ¶ 30B4, ¶ 30D4.07; TaxDesk ¶ 568,925, ¶ 569,104, ¶ 569,205, ¶ 569,505, ¶ 569,561.1, ¶ 397,103, ¶ 397,143, ¶ 397,180)

New Law. The 2012 Taxpayer Relief Act ("the Act") permanently extends the rule of former Code Sec. 26(a)(2) (the "AMT offset rule") and eliminates the rule of former Code Sec. 26(a)(1). (Code Sec. 26(a) as amended by 2012 Taxpayer Relief Act §104(c)(1))

Specifically, for tax years beginning after Dec. 31, 2011, the total amount of nonrefundable personal credits can't exceed the sum of:

... the taxpayer's regular tax liability (FTC 2d/FIN ¶ A-4905; USTR ¶ 264.01; TaxDesk ¶ 569,604) for the tax year, reduced by the foreign tax credit allowable under Code Sec. 27(a), (Code Sec. 26(a)(1) as amended by 2012 Taxpayer Relief Act §104(c)(1)) and

. . . the tax imposed by Code Sec. 55(a) for the tax year—i.e., the AMT (see FTC 2d/FIN ¶ A-8101; USTR ¶ 554.01; TaxDesk ¶ 691,002). (Code Sec. 26(a)(2) as amended by 2012 Taxpayer Relief Act §104(c)(1))

⚫ *observation:* This means that for tax years beginning after 2011 (as was the case in 2000 through 2011), all of the otherwise allowable nonrefundable personal credits—i.e., not just the "specified personal credits"—can be used to reduce AMT (as well as regular tax). This is because the maximum amount of total nonrefundable personal credits that a taxpayer can claim can't exceed the sum of: (1) his regular tax liability (reduced by the foreign tax credit) for the tax year, plus (2) his AMT liability for the tax year. Under this rule, the taxpayer can claim up to the amount of that sum (i.e., regular tax plus AMT) as nonrefundable personal credits.

⚫ *observation:* The Act thus provides a permanent extension for the pre-Act Code Sec. 26(a)(2) AMT offset rule, as part of the permanent extension provided for individual AMT relief. The Act also permanently increases the AMT exemption amounts, see ¶ 401.

⚫ *observation:* A taxpayer is subject to the AMT if his tentative minimum tax liability for the tax year is greater than his regular tax liability for the tax year. The AMT equals the amount of that excess, if any (see FTC 2d/FIN ¶ A-8101; USTR ¶ 554.01; TaxDesk ¶ 691,002).

⚫ *illustration (1):* In 2012, Taxpayer's regular tax is $8,000, and her tentative minimum tax is $7,200. Thus, she is liable for $8,000 regular tax, but no AMT. Taxpayer can claim up to $8,000 of nonrefundable personal credits for 2012. Under pre-Act law, the amount of nonrefundable personal credits Taxpayer could claim for 2012 would have been limited to $800—i.e., the excess of $8,000 regular tax over $7,200 tentative minimum tax.

⚫ *illustration (2):* In 2012, Taxpayer's regular tax is $5,000, and his tentative minimum tax is $5,500. Thus, Taxpayer must pay a regular tax of $5,000, plus an AMT of $500 (excess of $5,500 tentative minimum tax over $5,000 regular tax). Taxpayer can claim up to $5,500 of nonrefundable personal credits for 2012 (the sum of his $5,000 regular tax and $500 AMT). Under pre-Act law, the Taxpayer couldn't have claimed any nonrefundable personal credits for 2012, because his regular tax ($5,000) didn't exceed his tentative minimum tax ($5,500).

⚫ *observation:* Allowing the nonrefundable personal credits to reduce AMT (as well as regular tax) benefits middle income individuals who:

. . . have low taxable income (and thus a low regular tax), e.g., because of a large number of personal exemptions;

. . . are subject to the AMT because personal exemptions (as well as the standard deduction and certain itemized deductions) generally aren't allowed in computing the AMT (see FTC 2d/FIN ¶s A-8305, A-8315; USTR ¶ 564.02; TaxDesk ¶s 697,005, 697,015); and

. . . have substantial nonrefundable personal credits such as the child tax credit.

🔲 *observation:* By permanently extending the AMT offset rule, the Act eliminates the separate limitations that, under pre-Act law, would have applied after 2011 (see discussion below).

How the permanent extension of the AMT offset rule affects other credit limitations and carryover rules.

🔲 *observation:* The pre-2012 Taxpayer Relief Act statutory rules that provided for the limitations on and carryover of certain unused personal credits and the foreign tax credit included two sets of rules: (1) rules for tax years in which the personal credits were allowed against the AMT—i.e., tax years when the former Code Sec. 26(a)(2) AMT offset rule applied, and (2) rules for tax years in which the credits weren't so allowed—i.e., tax years when former Code Sec. 26(a)(1) applied. Thus, permanently extending the AMT offset rule also affects the limitation and carryover rules for certain credits in 2012 and later tax years.

Adoption expense credit (Code Sec. 23). The adoption expense credit was subject to the tax liability limitation prescribed by Code Sec. 23(b)(4) in tax years when the AMT offset rule didn't apply (see FTC 2d/FIN ¶ A-4405; USTR ¶ 234; TaxDesk ¶ 569,505). Because the Act makes permanent the AMT offset rule (under Code Sec. 26(a)), the adoption expense credit is subject to that limitation (Code Sec. 26(a) as amended by 2012 Taxpayer Relief Act §104(c)(1)), and the separate limitation under Code Sec. 23(b)(4) is eliminated. (Code Sec. 23(b)(4) as amended by 2012 Taxpayer Relief Act §104(c)(2)(A))

🔲 *observation:* As noted above, the separate tax liability limitation on the adoption expense credit would have let taxpayers use the credit to offset AMT as well as regular tax. Thus, the permanent extension of the AMT offset rule (which lets *all* the nonrefundable personal credits offset AMT as well as regular tax) doesn't affect the AMT offset allowance for the adoption expense credit in 2012 and later years.

If the adoption expense credit exceeds the "applicable limitation" for the year, the excess is carried over to each of the next five years. (FTC 2d/FIN ¶ A-4406; USTR ¶ 234; TaxDesk ¶ 569,506) The "applicable limitation" is the limitation imposed by Code Sec. 26(a) for the tax year, reduced by the nonrefundable personal credits (other than the adoption expense credit, the REEP credit, and the D.C. first-time homebuyers credit) for the year. (Code Sec. 23(c)(1) as amended by 2012 Taxpayer Relief Act §104(c)(2)(A))

> *observation:* The permanent extension of the AMT offset rule means that limitation (under Code Sec. 26(a)) is the starting point for determining the adoption expense credit carryover.

Child tax credit (Code Sec. 24). The child tax credit was subject to the tax liability limitation prescribed by Code Sec. 24(b)(3) in tax years when the AMT offset rule didn't apply (see FTC 2d/FIN ¶ A-4054; USTR ¶ 244.01; TaxDesk ¶ 569,104). Because the Act makes permanent the AMT offset rule (under Code Sec. 26(a)), the child tax credit is subject to that limitation (Code Sec. 26(a) as amended by 2012 Taxpayer Relief Act §104(c)(1)), and the separate limitation under Code Sec. 24(b)(3) is eliminated. (Code Sec. 24(b)(3) as amended by 2012 Taxpayer Relief Act §104(c)(2)(B))

> *observation:* As noted above, the separate tax liability limitation on the child tax credit would have let taxpayers use the credit to offset AMT as well as regular tax. Thus, the permanent extension of the AMT offset rule (which lets *all* the nonrefundable personal credits offset AMT as well as regular tax) doesn't affect the AMT offset allowance for the child tax credit. However, Code Sec. 24(b)(3) had specific ordering rules that could have reduced the amount of the allowable child tax credit for 2012 and later years.

MCC credit (Code Sec. 25). If the MCC credit for a tax year exceeds the "applicable limitation" for the year, the excess is carried over to each of the next three years. (FTC 2d/FIN ¶ A-4010; USTR ¶ 254.01; TaxDesk ¶ 380,502) The "applicable limitation" is the limitation imposed by Code Sec. 26(a) for the tax year reduced by the nonrefundable personal credits (other than the MCC, the adoption expense credit, the REEP credit, and the D.C. first-time homebuyers credit) for the year. (Code Sec. 25(e)(1)(C) as amended by 2012 Taxpayer Relief Act §104(c)(2)(C))

> *observation:* The permanent extension of the AMT offset rule means that limitation (under Code Sec. 26(a)) is the starting point for determining the MCC credit carryover.

AOTC/modified Hope credit (Code Sec. 25A(i)). The modified AOTC/modified Hope credit was subject to the tax liability limitation prescribed by Code Sec. 25A(i)(5) in tax years when the AMT offset rule didn't apply. (FTC 2d/FIN ¶ A-4525.1; USTR ¶ 25A4.03; TaxDesk ¶ 568,925.1) Because the Act makes permanent the AMT offset rule (under Code Sec. 26(a)), the AOTC/modified Hope credit is subject to that limitation (Code Sec. 26(a) as amended by

2012 Taxpayer Relief Act §104(c)(1)), and the separate limitation under Code Sec. 25A(i)(5) is eliminated. (Code Sec. 25A(i) as amended by 2012 Taxpayer Relief Act §104(c)(2)(D))

> **observation:** The permanent extension of the AMT offset rule means that limitation (under Code Sec. 26(a)) is the starting point for determining the refundable portion of the AOTC/modified Hope credit for 2012 and later years (see FTC 2d/FIN ¶ A-4525.2; USTR ¶ 25A4.03; TaxDesk ¶ 568,925.2).

For the 2012 Taxpayer Relief Act provision extending the AOTC/modified Hope credit, see ¶ 701.

Saver's credit (Code Sec. 25B). The saver's credit was subject to the tax liability limitation prescribed by Code Sec. 25B(g) in tax years when the AMT offset rule didn't apply. (see FTC 2d/FIN ¶ A-4455; USTR ¶ 25B4; TaxDesk ¶ 569,205) Because the Act makes permanent the AMT offset rule (under Code Sec. 26(a)), the saver's credit is subject to that limitation, (Code Sec. 26(a) as amended by 2012 Taxpayer Relief Act §104(c)(1)) and the separate limitation under Code Sec. 25B(g) is eliminated. (Code Sec. 25B(g) as amended by 2012 Taxpayer Relief Act §104(c)(2)(E))

> **observation:** As noted above, the separate tax liability limitation on the saver's credit would have let taxpayers use the credit to offset AMT as well as regular tax. Thus, the permanent extension of the AMT offset rule doesn't change the AMT offset allowance for the saver's credit. However, Code Sec. 25B(g) had specific ordering rules that could have reduced the amount of the allowable saver's credit for 2012 and later years.

Residential energy efficient property (REEP) credit (Code Sec. 25D). If the REEP credit for a tax year exceeds the "applicable limitation" for the year, the excess is carried over to the next tax year. (FTC 2d/FIN ¶ A-4781.1; USTR ¶ 25D4; TaxDesk ¶ 569,561.1) The applicable limitation is the limitation imposed by Code Sec. 26(a) for the tax year reduced by the nonrefundable personal credits (other than the REEP credit) for the year. (Code Sec. 25D(c) as amended by 2012 Taxpayer Relief Act §104(c)(2)(F)) The permanent extension of the AMT offset rule means that the REEP credit is subject to that limitation. (Code Sec. 26(a) as amended by 2012 Taxpayer Relief Act §104(c)(1))

> **observation:** The separate tax liability limitation on the REEP credit would have let taxpayers use the credit to offset AMT as well as regular tax. Thus, the permanent extension of the AMT offset rule doesn't affect the AMT offset allowance for the REEP credit. It also means that the limitation under Code Sec. 26(a) is the starting point for determining the REEP credit carryover.

Qualified plug-in electric vehicle (QPEV) credit (Code Sec. 30). The nonbusiness portion of the QPEV credit was treated as a nonrefundable personal credit subject to the AMT offset rule in tax years when it applied, and to a separate limitation under Code Sec. 30(c)(2) in other years. (FTC 2d/FIN ¶ L-18039.1; USTR ¶ 304.06; TaxDesk ¶ 397,180) Because the Act makes permanent the AMT offset rule (under Code Sec. 26(a)), the nonbusiness portion of the QPEV credit is treated as a nonrefundable personal credit subject to that limitation. (Code Sec. 30(c)(2) as amended by 2012 Taxpayer Relief Act §104(c)(2)(G))

Alternative motor vehicle (AMV) credit (Code Sec. 30B). The nonbusiness portion of the AMV credit was treated as a nonrefundable personal credit subject to the AMT offset rule in tax years when it applied, and to a separate limitation under Code Sec. 30B(g)(2) in other years. (FTC 2d/FIN ¶ L-18022.1; USTR ¶ 30B4; TaxDesk ¶ 397,102.1) Because the Act makes permanent the AMT offset rule (under Code Sec. 26(a)), the nonbusiness portion of the AMV credit is treated as a nonrefundable personal credit subject to that limitation. (Code Sec. 30B(g)(2) as amended by 2012 Taxpayer Relief Act §104(c)(2)(H))

New qualified plug-in electric drive motor vehicle (NQPEDMV) credit (Code Sec. 30D). The nonbusiness portion of the NQPEDMV credit was subject to the tax liability limitation prescribed by Code Sec. 30D(c)(2)(B) in tax years when the AMT offset rule didn't apply (see FTC 2d/FIN ¶ L-18034.1; USTR ¶ 30D4; TaxDesk ¶ 397,143). Because the Act makes permanent the AMT offset rule (under Code Sec. 26(a)), the nonbusiness portion of the NQPEDMV credit is treated as a nonrefundable personal credit subject to that limitation. (Code Sec. 30D(c)(2) as amended by 2012 Taxpayer Relief Act §104(c)(2)(I))

> **observation:** As noted above, the separate tax liability limitations on the nonbusiness portions of the QPEV credit, AMV credit, and NQPEDMV credit would have let taxpayers use the credits to offset AMT as well as regular tax. Thus, the permanent extension of the AMT offset rule doesn't affect the AMT offset allowance for those credits.

D.C. first-time homebuyer credit (Code Sec. 1400C). If the D.C. first-time homebuyer credit exceeds the "applicable limitation" for the tax year, the excess is carried over to the next tax year. (FTC 2d/FIN ¶ A-4255; USTR ¶ 14,00C4; TaxDesk ¶ 568,805) The "applicable limitation" is the limitation imposed under Code Sec. 26(a) for the tax year reduced by the nonrefundable personal credits (other than the D.C. first-time homebuyer credit and the REEP) for the year. (Code Sec. 1400C(d) as amended by 2012 Taxpayer Relief Act §104(c)(2)(L))

> **observation:** The permanent extension of the AMT offset rule means that limitation (under Code Sec. 26(a)) is the starting point for determining the D.C. first-time homebuyer credit carryover.

Foreign tax credit (Code Sec. 904). For tax years to which the AMT offset rule *didn't* apply, former Code Sec. 904(i) reduced the U.S. tax liability against which an individual's foreign tax credit was taken by the sum of the nonrefundable personal credits (other than the specified personal credits) allowable for the year. (FTC 2d/FIN ¶ O-4401; USTR ¶ 9044.01; TaxDesk ¶ 393,001) Because the Act makes permanent the AMT offset rule (under Code Sec. 26(a)), former Code Sec. 904(i) is eliminated as unnecessary. (Code Sec. 904(i) as amended by 2012 Taxpayer Relief Act §104(c)(2)(K))

> 🔧 *observation:* The permanent extension of the AMT offset rule means that the above-described reduction is no longer made in computing the foreign tax credit. Thus, in computing the foreign tax credit for 2012 and later years, an individual doesn't reduce his U.S. tax liability by the personal credits (other than the specified personal credits). This, in turn, results in a larger foreign tax credit for those years.

AMT not offset by qualified alternative vehicle fuel (QAFV) refueling property credit. The Code Sec. 26(a) limitations don't apply to the Code Sec. 30C refueling property credit (see FTC 2d/FIN ¶ L-18040 *et seq.*; USTR ¶ 30C4; TaxDesk ¶ 397,200 *et seq.*). The separate tax liability limitation that applies to this credit doesn't permit the use of the nonbusiness portion of the credit (i.e., any portion that doesn't relate to depreciable property) as an offset against AMT (see FTC 2d/FIN ¶ L-18022; L-18042; USTR ¶ 30B4; 30C4; TaxDesk ¶ 397,102; 397,202).

> 🔧 *observation:* The Act doesn't make any changes to the tax liability limitations applicable to the QAFV refueling property credit generally (see FTC 2d/FIN ¶ L-18042; USTR ¶ 30C4; TaxDesk ¶ 397,202), or otherwise provide for the credit to be used to offset AMT in 2012 and later years (e.g., by making it subject to the AMT offset rule). Thus, as under pre-Act law, the nonbusiness portions of the credit can't be used to reduce AMT. However, the increased AMT exemption amounts that Act §104 provides (see ¶ 401) will allow some previously ineligible taxpayers to claim a larger portion of the credit in those years.

> 🔧 *sample client letter:* For a client letter on the AMT provisions in the 2012 Taxpayer Relief Act, see ¶ 2003.

☐ **Effective:** Tax years beginning after Dec. 31, 2011. (2012 Taxpayer Relief Act §104(d))

> 🔧 *recommendation:* The permanent extension of the AMT offset rule applies retroactively. Individuals subject to estimated tax in 2012 may have already computed their first three installments of estimated tax for 2012 (i.e., the installments due on Apr. 15, June 15, and Sept. 15,

2012) without taking into account the newly-extended AMT offset rule for 2012. Individuals in this situation should recompute their required payment for the fourth installment for 2012 (due Jan. 15, 2013), to account for the retroactive allowance of the AMT offset for 2012. (See FTC 2d/FIN ¶ S-5200 *et seq.*; USTR ¶ 66,544; TaxDesk ¶ 571,300 *et seq.*)

¶ 404. Child tax credit can permanently offset AMT

Code Sec. 24(b)(3), 2012 Taxpayer Relief Act §101(a)(1)
Code Sec. 26(a)(1), 2012 Taxpayer Relief Act §101(a)(1)
Code Sec. None, 2012 Taxpayer Relief Act §101(a)(1)
Generally effective: Tax years beginning after Dec. 31, 2012
Committee Reports, None

Under pre-2012 Taxpayer Relief Act law, qualifying taxpayers could use the Code Sec. 24 child tax credit (CTC) to offset alternative minimum tax (AMT) (as well as regular income tax) as follows:

. . . for tax years beginning before Jan. 1, 2013, the CTC was subject to Code Sec. 26(a)(2)—a temporary limitation on all the nonrefundable personal credits that permitted a general AMT offset,

. . . for tax years beginning after Dec. 31, 2012 (when most credits were subject to the general Code Sec. 26(a)(1) limitation that didn't permit the AMT offset), the CTC was subject to Code Sec. 24(b)(3)—a separate limitation provided under the 2001 Economic Growth and Tax Relief Reconciliation Act (EGTRRA, PL 107-16, 6/7/2001) that permitted the CTC to offset AMT.

The EGTRRA changes (i.e., the separate CTC limitation rules) were originally to be effective for tax years beginning after Dec. 31, 2001 (i.e., after Code Sec. 26(a)(2) was scheduled to expire). However, the 2002 Job Creation and Worker Assistance Act (JCWAA, PL 107-147, 3/9/2002) extended Code Sec. 26(a)(2) through 2003, and the 2004 Working Families Tax Relief Act (WFTRA, PL 108-311, 10/4/2004) extended it through 2005. Later legislation also provided one- and two-year "patches" that extended application of Code Sec. 26(a)(2) through 2012. Thus, under pre-2012 Taxpayer Relief Act law, the effective date for application of the separate limitation on the CTC was effectively postponed to tax years beginning after Dec. 31, 2012. (For the 2012 Taxpayer Relief Act's permanent extension of the AMT offset rule of former Code Sec. 26(a)(2), see ¶ 403.)

Sunset. Under the EGTRRA sunset provision (Sec. 901 of title IX of EGTRRA), to which applicable WFTRA (FTC 2d/FIN ¶ T-11070, ¶ T-11071; USTR ¶ 79,006.88; TaxDesk ¶ 880,015), 2005 Gulf Opportunity Zone Act (GOZA) (FTC 2d/FIN ¶ T-11051.1A), 2008 Energy Act (FTC 2d/FIN

¶ T-11051.2, ¶ T-11051.3, ¶ T-11051.4, ¶ T-11051.5; USTR ¶ 79,006.86; TaxDesk ¶ 880,011.2, ¶ 880,011.3, ¶ 880,011.4, ¶ 880,011.5), and 2009 Recovery Act (ARRA) provisions were subject, the exception to pre-2012 Taxpayer Relief Act Code Sec. 26(a)(1) for the CTC, the CTC's separate limitation rule, and conforming modifications to credit carryover ordering rules, wouldn't apply after the EGTRRA sunset date. (FTC 2d/FIN ¶ A-4050.1) Under pre-2012 Taxpayer Relief Act law, this meant that these provisions wouldn't apply in tax years beginning after Dec. 31, 2012. (FTC 2d/FIN ¶ T-11050, ¶ T-11051; USTR ¶ 79,006.86; TaxDesk ¶ 880,011)

New Law. The 2012 Taxpayer Relief Act repeals title IX of EGTRRA (i.e., the title containing the above-described EGTRRA sunset rule). (Sec. 901, PL 107-16, 6/7/2001 as repealed by 2012 Taxpayer Relief Act §101(a)(1))

> *observation:* Under 2012 Taxpayer Relief Act §104(c), the AMT offset rule under former Code Sec. 26(a)(2) is permanently extended (retroactive to tax years beginning after Dec. 31, 2012) as part of the permanent extension of individual's AMT relief. Thus, that AMT offset rule will apply to the CTC for all tax years beginning after Dec. 31, 2012, and the separate limitation for the CTC under Code Sec. 24(b)(3) is eliminated as unnecessary, see ¶ 403.
>
> Without these changes, the repeal of the sunset would have made permanent the application of the separate CTC limitation rules.

☐ **Effective:** For tax years beginning after Dec. 31, 2012. (2012 Taxpayer Relief Act §101(a)(3))

¶ 405. 7% AMT preference for excluded gain on qualified small business stock is permanently extended

Code Sec. 57(a)(7), 2012 Taxpayer Relief Act §102(a)
Code Sec. None, 2012 Taxpayer Relief Act §102(a)
Generally effective: Tax years beginning after Dec. 31, 2012
Committee Reports, None

Under Code Sec. 1202, a taxpayer who satisfies certain requirements (including a more-than-five-year holding period requirement) can exclude from gross income, for qualified small business stock (QSBS):

... acquired after Sept. 27, 2010, and before Jan. 1, 2012, 100% of the gain realized on the sale or disposition. (FTC 2d/FIN ¶ I-9100.1; USTR ¶ 12,024; TaxDesk ¶ 246,600.1)

... acquired after Feb. 17, 2009, and before Sept. 28, 2010, 75% of the gain realized on the sale or disposition. (FTC 2d/FIN ¶ I-9100.1A; USTR ¶ 12,024; TaxDesk ¶ 246,600.1)

. . . acquired before Feb. 18, 2009, *or* after Dec. 31, 2011, 50% of the gain realized on the sale or disposition (60% for certain gain with respect to QSBS in a qualified business entity). (FTC 2d/FIN ¶ I-9100.1B; I-9100.1C; USTR ¶ 12,024; TaxDesk ¶ 246,601; 246,602)

> *caution:* The 2012 Taxpayer Relief Act retroactively restores and extends the 100% exclusion for QSBS (above) for two years by changing the date before which eligible QSBS must be acquired from Jan. 1, 2012 to Jan. 1, 2014, see ¶ 209.

However, 7% of the amount excluded under Code Sec. 1202 is treated as a preference item for alternative minimum tax (AMT) purposes. (FTC 2d/FIN ¶ A-8300, ¶ A-8304 *et seq.*; USTR ¶ 574; TaxDesk ¶ 697,004)

For the requirements for stock held by a taxpayer to qualify as QSBS, see FTC 2d/FIN ¶ I-9101; USTR ¶ 12,024; TaxDesk ¶ 246,635.

Sunset. Under section 303 of the 2003 Jobs and Growth Act (JGTRRA, Sec. 303, PL 108-27, 5/28/2003), as amended by section 102 of the Tax Increase Prevention and Reconciliation Act of 2005 (TIPRA, Sec. 102, PL 109-222, 5/17/2006), and further amended by section 102 of the Tax Relief Act of 2010 (Sec. 102, PL 111-312, 12/17/2010):

. . . the 7% preference percentage was scheduled to expire for tax years beginning after Dec. 31, 2012. (FTC 2d/FIN ¶ T-11062; USTR ¶ 79,006.87; TaxDesk ¶ 880,014)

. . . the 28% and 42% preference percentages in effect before passage of JGTRRA were scheduled to come back into effect. (FTC 2d/FIN ¶ A-8304; USTR ¶ 574)

New Law. The 2012 Taxpayer Relief Act repeals the JGTRRA sunset provision. Thus, the rule providing for the 7% AMT preference percentage for excluded gain on QSBS is made permanent. (2003 Jobs and Growth Act §303 (Sec. 303, PL 108-27, 5/28/2003) repealed by 2012 Taxpayer Relief Act §102(a))

☐ **Effective:** The effect of the provision is to remove the sunset that would have been effective for tax years beginning after Dec. 31, 2012. (2012 Taxpayer Relief Act §102(a))

> *observation:* 2012 Taxpayer Relief Act §102(a), which eliminates the JGTRRA §303 sunset rule, as amended, is effective as if included in the enactment of JGTRRA. JGTRRA was enacted on May 28, 2003, so §102(a) is technically effective as of that date.

¶ 500. Estate/Transfer Tax

¶ 501. 2012 estate, gift and GST tax rules made permanent, but top rate increases from 35% to 40%

Code Sec. 2001(c), as amended by 2012 Taxpayer Relief Act §101(c)(1)
Code Sec. 2010(c)(4)(B)(i), as amended by 2012 Taxpayer Relief Act §101(c)(2)
Code Sec. None, 2012 Taxpayer Relief Act §101(a)
Generally effective: After 2012
Committee Reports, None

Under the 2001 Economic Growth and Tax Relief Reconciliation Act (EGTRRA), the estate tax was scheduled to be repealed in 2010, and then to return in 2011 with an exemption of $1 million and graduated rates reaching a top rate of 55% on transfers over $3 million. (Sec. 901, PL 107-16, 6/7/2001) The 2010 Tax Relief Act reinstated the estate tax retroactively to the beginning of 2010, *except* where the executor of the estate of a decedent dying in 2010 made an election to opt out of the estate tax and be subject to the modified carryover basis rules instead. (Sec. 301, PL 111-312, 12/17/2010)

Other EGTRRA changes. Title V of EGTRRA (Sec. 501, PL 107-16, 6/7/2001) also:

(1) repealed the state death tax credit for estates of decedents dying after 2004 (after phasing out the credit for estates of decedents dying in 2002, 2003, or 2004) (FTC 2d ¶ R-7200, ¶ R-7200.1; USTR Estate & Gift Taxes ¶ 20,114; TaxDesk ¶ 782,001; EP ¶ 45,151.1), and replaced the credit with a deduction for state death taxes (FTC 2d ¶ R-6900, ¶ R-6901; USTR Estate & Gift Taxes ¶ 20,584; TaxDesk ¶ 779,001; EP ¶ 44,892);

(2) repealed the estate tax deduction for qualified family-owned business interests (QFOBIs), for estates of decedents dying after 2003 (FTC 2d ¶ R-4500, ¶ R-4501; USTR Estate & Gift Taxes ¶ 20,574; TaxDesk ¶ 761,200.1; EP ¶ 43,872);

(3) expanded the availability of the estate tax exclusion for qualified conservation easements by eliminating the requirement that the land be located within a certain distance of a metropolitan area, national park, wilderness area, or Ur-

---

FTC 2d References are to Federal Tax Coordinator 2d
FIN References are to RIA's Analysis of Federal Taxes: Income (print)
USTR References are to United States Tax Reporter: Income
PCA References are to Pension Analysis (print and electronic)
PBE References are to Pension & Benefits Explanations
BCA References are to Benefits Analysis (electronic)
BC References are to Benefits Coordinator (print)
EP References are to Estate Planning Analysis (print and electronic)

ban National Forest (FTC 2d ¶ R-4700, ¶ R-4708; USTR Estate & Gift Taxes ¶ 20,314.13; TaxDesk ¶ 773,408; EP ¶ 43,900.3);

(4) for purposes of the installment payment of the estate tax attributable to a closely-held business interest:

(a) increased, from 15 to 45, the maximum number of partners in a partnership and shareholders in a corporation that may be treated as a closely-held business (FTC 2d ¶ S-6000, ¶ S-6013; USTR Estate & Gift Taxes ¶ 61,664.01; TaxDesk ¶ 784,002; EP ¶ 83,214);

(b) provided that the estate of a decedent with an interest in a qualifying lending and finance business is eligible for installment of the estate tax (FTC 2d ¶ S-6000, ¶ S-6030.1; USTR Estate & Gift Taxes ¶ 61,664.01; EP ¶ 83,231.1); and

(c) clarified that the installment payment provisions require that only the stock of holding companies, not the stock of operating subsidiaries, must be non-readily-tradable to qualify for installment payment (FTC 2d ¶ S-6000, ¶ S-6037; USTR Estate & Gift Taxes ¶ 61,664.01; EP ¶ 83,238);

(5) provided that the generation-skipping transfer (GST) exemption will be allocated automatically to transfers made during life that are indirect skips (FTC 2d ¶ R-9550, ¶ R-9552; USTR Estate & Gift Taxes ¶ 26,324; EP ¶ 46,093);

(6) provided that, under certain circumstances, the GST exemption can be allocated retroactively when there is an unnatural order of death (FTC 2d ¶ R-9550, ¶ R-9554.1; USTR Estate & Gift Taxes ¶ 26,324; EP ¶ 46,095.1);

(7) provided that a trust that is only partially subject to GST tax because its inclusion ratio is less than one can be severed in a "qualified severance" (FTC 2d ¶ R-9500, ¶ R-9522; USTR Estate & Gift Taxes ¶ 26,424.01; EP ¶ 46,053);

(8) provided that, in connection with timely and automatic allocations of the GST exemption, the value of the property for purposes of determining the inclusion ratio is its finally determined gift tax value or estate tax value, depending on the circumstances of the transfer (FTC 2d ¶ R-9570, ¶ R-9584, ¶ R-9586; USTR Estate & Gift Taxes ¶ 26,424; EP ¶ 46,175; 46,177);

(9) authorized and directed IRS to grant extensions of time to make the election to allocate the GST exemption, and to grant exceptions to the time requirement, without regard to whether any period of limitations has expired (FTC 2d ¶ R-9550, ¶ R-9562; USTR Estate & Gift Taxes ¶ 26,424.02; EP ¶ 46,103); and

(10) provided that substantial compliance with the statutory and regulatory requirements for allocating the GST exemption will suffice to establish that the GST exemption was allocated to a particular transfer or a particular trust. (FTC 2d ¶ R-9550, ¶ R-9563; USTR Estate & Gift Taxes ¶ 26,424; EP ¶ 46,104)

2010 Tax Relief Act changes. For estates of decedents dying after 2009, the 2010 Tax Relief Act provided an estate tax exemption of $5 million (indexed for inflation after 2011). The exemption amount was $5,120,000 for

2012, and is $5,250,000 for 2013, based on inflation data as indicated by IRS in Rev Proc 2013-15, Sec. 2.13. Also, under the 2010 Tax Relief Act, the tax was imposed at a top rate of 35% on all transfers exceeding the exemption amount.

For estates of decedents dying after 2010, the 2010 Tax Relief Act made the estate tax exclusion (but not the GST exemption) portable between spouses, by allowing the estate of a surviving spouse to use any unused portion of the deceased spouse's exclusion, in addition to the surviving spouse's own exclusion.

Under pre-2010 Tax Relief Act law, the GST tax was scheduled to be repealed in 2010. The 2010 Tax Relief Act reinstated the GST tax retroactively to the beginning of 2010. For transfers in 2010 only, the tax rate for GST tax purposes was zero. The amount of the GST exemption was the same as the estate tax exemption ($5 million in 2010 and 2011, indexed for inflation after 2011, see above). The GST exemption may have been allocated to a trust created or funded in 2010. Further, the GST tax uses the top estate tax rate to calculate the "applicable rate" on a transfer. Thus, the tax on generation-skipping transfers made in 2011 and 2012 was reduced via the reduction in the top estate tax rate to 35%.

The gift tax was never scheduled to be repealed. For gifts made after 2010, the 2010 Tax Relief Act reunified the gift tax exemption with the estate tax exemption ($5 million, as indexed for inflation, see above). For gifts made after 2010, the 2010 Tax Relief Act reunified the gift and estate tax rate schedule, which imposed tax at a top rate of 35% on all transfers exceeding the exemption amount.

Sunset after 2012. The 2010 Tax Relief Act provided that several estate and gift tax changes that were made by EGTRRA, which had been scheduled to sunset on Dec. 31, 2010, would expired on Dec. 31, 2012 instead. The 2010 Tax Relief Act §304 also provided that the EGTRRA sunset date (as extended to Dec. 31, 2012) applied to the estate, gift, and GST tax changes made by the 2010 Tax Relief Act. This meant that, after 2012, in the absence of further legislation:

- the estate, gift, and GST exemption would have been $1 million (the amount that, under pre-EGTRRA law, had been scheduled to apply in 2006 and later years);

- the maximum estate and gift tax rate would have been 55% on transfers in excess of $3 million; and

- the rules allowing for the portability of the estate tax exclusion between spouses would not have applied.

(FTC 2d ¶ R-1000.1, ¶ R-7006, ¶ R-7101, ¶ R-9551, ¶ Q-8003.1; USTR Estate & Gift Taxes ¶ 20,014, ¶ 22,104, ¶ 26,644; TaxDesk ¶ 744,003.1, ¶ 751,000.1, ¶ 780,506, ¶ 791,004; EP ¶ 43,051.1, ¶ 44,907, ¶ 46,031.1, ¶ 46,092)

New Law. The 2012 Taxpayer Relief Act repeals title IX of EGTRRA (i.e., the title containing the above-described EGTRRA sunset) and the 2010 Tax Relief Act §304 (i.e., the section that subjected the 2010 Tax Relief Act changes to the EGTRRA sunset). (Sec. 901, PL 107-16, 6/7/2001 repealed by 2012 Taxpayer Relief Act §101(a)(1); Sec. 304, PL 111-312, 12/17/2010 repealed by 2012 Taxpayer Relief Act §101(a)(2)).

> *observation:* Thus, except for the changes to the estate and gift tax rates (see below), all of the estate, gift and GST tax rules applicable during the years 2010 to 2012, including all of the EGTRRA changes that were extended by the 2010 Tax Relief Act, are made permanent starting in 2013. This includes the increased and indexed estate, gift and GST tax exemption of $5 million ($5,250,000 in 2013, as indexed for inflation), and the portability rules.

> *observation:* Using the exemption amount, a married couple may transfer a total of $10.5 million in 2013 without incurring any transfer tax.

> *observation:* Since, under the Act, there was no reduction in the amount of the estate and gift tax exemption, there is no need to worry about a possible "clawback." Practitioners had been concerned about the possibility of the exemption amount going from $5 million to $1 million (or to any other number less than $5 million) because there was the potential for the benefit of the exemption to be recaptured as additional estate taxes, i.e., a clawback. The potential for the clawback derives from the fact that the estate and gift taxes are unified, and estate tax computations include the value of taxable gifts made during the decedent's lifetime. Before the Act, it was not clear whether a higher gift tax exemption amount from an earlier year would have been applied to gifts made in those earlier years upon the later calculation of the estate tax. Now, after the Act, it is clear that the full amount of any exemption used for lifetime gifts from 2010 to 2012 will be applied to the future estate tax calculations.

Top tax rate increased to 40%. The Act also provides that the estate and gift tax rates for "tentative tax" amounts over $500,000 are as follows:

for amounts over $500,000 but not over $750,000, the tax is $155,800, plus 37% of the excess over $500,000;

for amounts over $750,000 but not over $1 million, the tax is $248,300, plus 39% of the excess over $750,000; and

for amounts over $1 million, the tax is $345,800, plus 40% of the excess over $1 million. (Code Sec. 2001(c) as amended by 2012 Taxpayer Relief Act §101(c)(1)) *observation:* Thus, under the Act, the top estate and gift tax rate is increased from 35% to 40%. Also, since the GST tax also uses this 40% rate to calculate the tax on transfers, the GST tax rate increases as well.

Technical correction to portability rules. The Act also provides a technical correction to a provision of the portability rules that already had been assumed by IRS in proposed regs to be a drafting error. (Preamble to Reg §20.2010-2T) In Code Sec. 2010(c)(4)(B)(i), the phrase "basic exclusion amount" is replaced by "applicable exclusion amount." (Code Sec. 2010(c)(4)(B)(i) as amended by 2012 Taxpayer Relief Act §101(c)(2))

☐ **Effective:** For estates of decedents dying, generation-skipping transfers, and gifts made after Dec. 31, 2012. (2012 Taxpayer Relief Act §101(a)(3); 2012 Taxpayer Relief Act §101(c)(3)(A)

The technical correction is effective for estates of decedents dying and gifts made after Dec. 31, 2010. 2012 Taxpayer Relief Act §101(c)(3)(B)

observation: The technical correction is effective as if it had been included in 2010 Tax Relief Act §303. Under 2010 Tax Relief Act §303(c)(1), the portability rules were effective for estates of decedents dying and gifts made after Dec. 31, 2010.

¶ 600. Individual Tax Credits

¶ 601. $1,000 per child amount and expanded refundability of child tax credit are permanently extended

Code Sec. 24(a), 2012 Taxpayer Relief Act §101(a)(1)
Code Sec. 24(d)(1), 2012 Taxpayer Relief Act §101(a)(1)
Code Sec. 32(n), 2012 Taxpayer Relief Act §101(a)(1)
Code Sec. None, 2012 Taxpayer Relief Act §101(a)(1)
Generally effective: Tax years beginning after Dec. 31, 2012.
Committee Reports, None

An individual may claim a child tax credit (CTC) for each qualifying child under the age of 17. (FTC 2d/FIN ¶ A-4050 *et seq.*; USTR ¶ 244; TaxDesk ¶ 569,100 *et seq.*)

EGTRRA changes. Sec. 201 of the 2001 Economic Growth and Tax Relief Reconciliation Act (EGTRRA, Sec. 201, PL 107-16, 6/7/2001) as amended by the 2003 Jobs and Growth Tax Relief Reconciliation Act (JGTRRA, Sec. 101(a), PL 108-27, 5/28/2003) and the 2004 Working Families Tax Relief Act (WFTRA, Sec. 101(a), 102(a), PL 108-311, 10/4/2004), modified the CTC as follows:

(1) the per-child amount of the CTC was gradually increased to $1,000 (from $500). (FTC 2d/FIN ¶ A-4051; USTR ¶ 244; TaxDesk ¶ 569,100)

(2) the CTC was made refundable for all taxpayers with qualifying children, regardless of the number of children, to the extent of 15% of the taxpayer's earned income in excess of a threshold amount (the "earned income formula"). The statutory threshold amount of $10,000 was indexed for inflation from 2001 (see ¶ 602 for use of $3,000 threshold). Families with three or more children were allowed to compute their refundable CTC using either (a) the earned income formula or (b) the formula available to them under pre-EGTRRA law—the excess, if any, of the taxpayer's social security taxes over the earned income credit (EIC) for the year. (FTC 2d/FIN ¶ A-4055; USTR ¶ 244.02; TaxDesk ¶ 569,100)

(3) Code Sec. 32(n), which provided that a portion of the CTC was to be treated as a supplemental child credit amount added to the EIC otherwise allowable to the taxpayer, was eliminated. This supplemental child credit was sub-

tracted from the taxpayer's other allowable credits, and had no impact on the total amount of credits allowed to the taxpayer. (FTC 2d/FIN ¶ A-4200)

Sunset. Under Sec. 901 of EGTRRA, to which the applicable JGTRRA (FTC 2d/FIN ¶ T-11061, ¶ T-11060; USTR ¶ 79,006.87; TaxDesk ¶ 880,013) and WFTRA (FTC 2d/FIN ¶ T-11070, ¶ T-11071; USTR ¶ 79,006.88; TaxDesk ¶ 880,015) provisions were made subject, all of these changes were scheduled to expire after the EGTRRA sunset date. The pre-EGTRRA rules—i.e., the $500 per child CTC amount, the credit's refundability only for families with more than two qualifying children and only to the extent the taxpayer's social security taxes exceed the EIC, and the Code Sec. 32(n) supplemental child credit—were scheduled to come back into effect in tax years beginning after the sunset date. (FTC 2d/FIN ¶ T-11050, ¶ T-11051; USTR ¶ 79,006; TaxDesk ¶ 880,011)

Under pre-2012 Taxpayer Relief Act law, the EGTRRA enhancements to the CTC were scheduled to sunset, and the pre-EGTRRA rules were to apply, for tax years beginning after Dec. 31, 2012. (FTC 2d/FIN ¶ A-4050)

New Law. The 2012 Taxpayer Relief Act eliminates the EGTRRA sunset by striking title IX of EGTRRA (i.e., Sec. 901, the sunset provision). Thus, the EGTRRA changes to the CTC that are listed at (1)–(3) (above) are made permanent. (Sec. 901, PL 107-16, 6/7/2001 as amended by 2012 Taxpayer Relief Act §101(a)(1))

> *observation:* As a result of the 2012 Taxpayer Relief Act's repeal of the EGTRRA sunset provision, for tax years after 2012 (see effective date below):
>
> . . . the per-child amount of the CTC is $1,000.
>
> . . . the CTC is refundable for all taxpayers with qualifying children, regardless of the number of children, to the extent of 15% of the taxpayer's earned income in excess of a threshold amount (see ¶ 602).
>
> . . . Code Sec. 32(n), which provided that a portion of the CTC was to be treated as a supplemental child credit amount added to the taxpayer's EIC, is permanently eliminated.

For the extension through 2017 of the $3,000 threshold used to determine the refundable portion of the credit, see ¶ 602.

☐ **Effective:** For tax years beginning after Dec. 31, 2012. (2012 Taxpayer Relief Act §101(a)(3))

¶ 602. Increase in refundable portion of child tax credit is extended through 2017

Code Sec. 24(d)(4), as amended by 2012 Taxpayer Relief Act §103(b)(2)
Generally effective: Tax years beginning after Dec 31, 2012 and before Jan. 1, 2018
Committee Reports, None

An individual can claim a child tax credit (CTC) for each qualifying child under the age of 17. (FTC 2d/FIN ¶ A-4050 *et seq.*; USTR ¶ 244; TaxDesk ¶ 569,100 *et seq.*)

The CTC is partially refundable. For all taxpayers with qualifying children (regardless of the number of qualifying children), the CTC is refundable to the extent of 15% of the taxpayer's earned income in excess of a statutory dollar amount threshold ($10,000 as indexed for inflation). The 2009 Recovery Act (ARRA, Sec. 1003(a), PL 111-5, 2/17/2009) reduced the threshold to *$3,000* (with no indexing for inflation) for tax years beginning in 2009 and 2010. The 2010 Tax Relief Act (2010 TRA, Sec. 103(b)(2), PL 111-312, 12/17/2010) extended the $3,000 threshold for the earned income formula for two years (through 2012). The lower threshold increased the refundable portion of the credit for those years.

Under pre-2012 Taxpayer Relief Act law, the lower $3,000 threshold didn't apply in tax years beginning after 2012. (The earned income formula itself was set to expire after 2012, see ¶ 601.) (FTC 2d/FIN ¶ A-4050, ¶ A-4055; USTR ¶ 244.02; TaxDesk ¶ 569,105)

New Law. The 2012 Taxpayer Relief Act extends the $3,000 threshold for the earned income formula for five years (through 2017) by providing that the $3,000 dollar amount will be in effect for any tax year beginning after 2008 and before 2018. (Code Sec. 24(d)(4) as amended by 2012 Taxpayer Relief Act §103(b)(2)) For the permanent extension of the earned income formula, see ¶ 601.

> **⊘** *observation:* In other words, for tax years beginning in 2013, 2014, 2015, 2016 and 2017, a taxpayer's CTC is refundable to the extent of 15% of the taxpayer's earned income in excess of $3,000. Under pre-2012 Taxpayer Relief Act law, the refundable portion would have been determined using $10,000 as the earnings threshold, resulting in a smaller refundable amount.

The $3,000 earnings threshold won't be indexed for inflation for the five years that it applies (through 2017). (Code Sec. 24(d)(4))

☐ **Effective:** Tax years beginning after Dec. 31, 2012 (2012 Taxpayer Relief Act §103(e)(1)) and, as discussed above, before Jan. 1, 2018. (Code Sec. 24(d)(4))

¶ 603. EGTRRA-expanded dependent care credit permanently extended

Code Sec. 21, 2012 Taxpayer Relief Act §101(a)(1)
Code Sec. None, 2012 Taxpayer Relief Act §101(a)(1)
Generally effective: Tax years beginning after Dec. 31, 2012
Committee Reports, None

Taxpayers who have one or more qualifying individuals (a dependent qualifying child under age 13, or a dependent or spouse who is incapable of self-care and has the same principal place of abode as the taxpayer for more than half the tax year) are allowed a dependent care credit equal to a percentage of the expenses paid for the care of the qualifying individual(s) that enable the taxpayer to be gainfully employed ("eligible expenses").

EGTRRA changes. Sec. 204 of the 2001 Economic Growth and Tax Relief Reconciliation Act (EGTRRA, Sec. 204, PL 106-17, 6/7/2001) increased the dependent care credit's credit percentage, credit base, and maximum credit. The maximum credit is $1,050 (35% of up to $3,000 of eligible expenses) if there is one qualifying individual, and $2,100 (35% of up to $6,000 of eligible expenses) if there are two or more qualifying individuals. The 35% credit rate is reduced, but not below 20%, by one percentage point for each $2,000 (or fraction thereof) of adjusted gross income (AGI) above $15,000. (FTC 2d/FIN ¶ A-4300, ¶ A-4301, ¶ A-4302; USTR ¶ 214, ¶ 214.04; TaxDesk ¶ 569,301, ¶ 569,302)

Sunset. The EGTRRA enhancements to the dependent care credit were subject to the EGTRRA sunset provision (Sec. 901, PL 106-17, 6/17/2001) (see FTC 2d/FIN ¶ T-11051; TaxDesk ¶ 880,011). After the EGTRRA sunset date (Dec. 31, 2010), the credit percentage, credit base, and maximum credit all were scheduled to revert to the lower pre-EGTRRA levels for 2011 and later years. That is, the credit percentage would drop to 30% and begin to phase out at AGI of $10,000. The maximum credit would drop to $720 (30% of up to $2,400 of eligible expenses) for one qualifying individual, and to $1,440 (30% of up to $4,800 of eligible expenses) for two or more. (See FTC 2d/FIN ¶ A-4302)

However, the 2010 Tax Relief Act (Sec. 101(a)(1), PL 111-312, 12/17/2010) provided that the EGTRRA sunset would not take effect until after Dec. 31, 2012 (instead of after Dec. 31, 2010), thus extending the dependent care credit enhancements (above) for two years.

New Law. The 2012 Taxpayer Relief Act repeals title IX of EGTRRA (i.e., the title containing the above-described EGTRRA sunset). (EGTRRA § 901 (Sec. 901, PL 107-16, 6/7/2001) repealed by 2012 Taxpayer Relief Act §101(a)(1)).

> ⊘ *observation:* Thus, the Act makes the EGTRRA enhancements to the dependent care credit "permanent" (i.e., the enhancements remain in force until Congress changes them) by eliminating the EGTRRA sunset provision in its entirety.

☐ **Effective:** Tax years beginning after Dec. 31, 2012. (2012 Taxpayer Relief Act §101(a)(3))

¶ 604. Expanded adoption credit rules (but not refundability) made permanent

Code Sec. 23, 2012 Taxpayer Relief Act §101(a)(1)
Code Sec. None, 2012 Taxpayer Relief Act §101(a)(1)
Generally effective: Tax years beginning after Dec. 31, 2012
Committee Reports, None

Under Code Sec. 23, individuals are allowed a credit against income tax and alternative minimum tax (AMT) for qualified adoption expenses paid or incurred for the adoption of an eligible child. The credit is nonrefundable subject to a limitation based on tax liability. The maximum credit is $12,650 per eligible child for 2012. The credit begins to phase out for taxpayers with modified adjusted gross income (AGI) over $189,710 for 2012 and is fully eliminated at modified AGI of $229,710 for 2012. All these dollar amounts are adjusted annually for inflation. (FTC 2d/FIN ¶ A-4400 *et seq.*; USTR ¶ 234; TaxDesk ¶ 569,500 *et seq.*)

EGTRRA sunset provision. The adoption expense credit rules discussed above reflect changes made to expand the adoption credit that existed before the enactment of the 2001 Economic Growth and Tax Relief Reconciliation Act (EGTRRA). The EGTRRA changes (see below) were subject to the EGTRRA sunset provision, i.e., EGTRRA Sec. 901 (Sec. 901, PL 107-16, 6/7/2001), which made these EGTRRA provisions inapplicable to tax years beginning after Dec. 31, 2010. However, Sec. 10909(c) of the 2010 Patient Protection and Affordable Health Care Act (PPACA, PL 111-148, 3/23/2010) delayed the EGTRRA sunset for the adoption credit changes (including those made under both EGTRRA and PPACA, see below) by one year, until Dec. 31, 2011.

EGTRRA changes. The EGTRRA changes, made in EGTRRA §202 (Sec. 202, PL 107-16, 6/7/2001):

(1) increased the maximum per-child credit from $5,000 ($6,000 for special needs adoptions) to $10,000 for all adoptions;

(2) increased the modified AGI starting point for the credit phase-out from $75,000 to $150,000;

(3) for special needs adoptions, allowed the $10,000 maximum credit regardless of actual expenses, and liberalized certain timing rules;

(4) provided for inflation adjustments to the $10,000/$150,000 statutory dollar amounts;

(5) for non-special needs adoptions, made the credit permanent (as was the case for special needs adoptions) by eliminating the scheduled Dec. 31, 2001 termination date; and

(6) allowed the credit against AMT by making it subject to a separate tax liability limitation instead of Code Sec. 26(a)(1) (which generally prevents the offset of AMT by nonrefundable personal credits).

PPACA changes. The PPACA changes, made in PPACA §10909 (Sec. 10909, PL 111-148, 3/23/2010):

(a) increased the maximum per-child credit from $12,170 to $13,170 (indexed for inflation after 2010);

(b) made the credit refundable (instead of nonrefundable) by redesignating the former Code Sec. 23 adoption credit provisions as Code Sec. 36C;

(c) eliminated the separate tax liability limitation and carryover rules that applied (under former Code Sec. 23) when the credit was nonrefundable; and

(d) deleted references to Code Sec. 23 from the tax liability limitation and carryover rules for certain other credits to account for the adoption credit being changed to a refundable credit.

PPACA 2011 sunset and extension of EGTRRA sunset. The EGTRRA changes expanding the adoption credit rules (items (1) through (6), above), which were subject to the PPACA §10909(c) sunset date (and so were scheduled to sunset in tax years beginning after Dec. 31, 2011, see above), were extended for one year, through 2012 (under Sec. 101(a)(1), PL 111-312, 12/17/2010).

The PPACA sunset provision was *not* similarly extended. Thus, the PPACA changes (items (a) through (d), above) don't apply in tax years beginning after Dec. 31, 2011. As a result, the credit is refundable for only two years (2010 and 2011). (FTC 2d/FIN ¶ T-11050, ¶ T-11054; USTR ¶ 79,006.86; TaxDesk ¶ 880,017)

> **⊘** *observation:* The *Dec. 31, 2011* sunset date for the PPACA changes meant that the changes listed in items (a) through (d), above, didn't ap-

ply for tax years beginning after Dec. 31, 2011. Thus, the adoption credit rules reverted to pre-PPACA law. This means that, in 2012:

... the maximum per-child credit was reduced (in 2012, the credit was $12,650, see above);

... the credit wasn't refundable, and was provided under Code Sec. 23, instead of former Code Sec. 36C;

... the credit was subject to the tax liability limitations (under either Code Sec. 26(a)(2) or Code Sec. 23(b)(4), whichever applied, see ¶ 403) and carryover rules that applied before the PPACA changes were enacted; and

... the references to Code Sec. 23 that were deleted from certain credit provisions (see (d), above) were restored.

Effect of 2012 EGTRRA sunset. The EGTRRA changes (listed in items (1) through (6), above) were scheduled to become inapplicable after the Dec. 31, 2012 sunset date.

observation: The *Dec. 31, 2012* sunset date for the EGTRRA changes meant that the changes listed in items (1) through (6), above, wouldn't have applied for tax years beginning after Dec. 31, 2012. Thus, the adoption credit rules would have reverted to pre-EGTRRA law. This would have meant that, starting in 2013:

• the credit would have been available only for special needs adoptions;

• the maximum per-child credit would have dropped to $6,000, and would have depended on actual expenses;

• the modified AGI starting point for the credit phase-out would have been reduced to $75,000—i.e., the credit would have been eliminated at modified AGI of $115,000;

• absent a further extension of Code Sec. 26(a)(2) (see ¶ 403), the credit wouldn't have been allowed against AMT because it would have been subject to the general Code Sec. 26(a)(1) tax liability limitation.

New Law. The 2012 Taxpayer Relief Act repeals title IX of EGTRRA (i.e., the title containing the above-described EGTRRA sunset). (EGTRRA § 901 (Sec. 901, PL 107-16, 6/7/2001) repealed by (2012 Taxpayer Relief Act §101(a)(1))

observation: As a result of the repeal of the EGTRRA sunset provision, the EGTRRA-expanded adoption expense credit rules are no longer subject to a sunset provision. Thus:

(a) the maximum per-child credit is based on $10,000, as adjusted for inflation ($12,650 for 2012, and $12,970 for 2013 (as indicated in Rev Proc 2013-15, Sec. 2.02));

(b) the modified AGI starting point for the credit phase-out begins at $150,000, as adjusted for inflation ($189,710 for 2012, and $194,580 for 2013 (as indicated in Rev Proc 2013-15, Sec. 2.02));

(c) the credit applies for any eligible child, and not just a child with special needs. A credit for the adoption of a child with special needs is allowed regardless of actual expenses; and

(d) the credit may be taken against AMT.

However, the PPACA changes are not part of the credit. Thus, for example, the credit remains nonrefundable, and continues to be provided in Code Sec. 23.

☐ **Effective:** Tax years beginning after Dec. 31, 2012. (2012 Taxpayer Relief Act §101(a)(1))

¶ 605. EIC simplification made permanent

Code Sec. 32(a)(2)(B), 2012 Taxpayer Relief Act §101(a)(1)
Code Sec. 32(c)(1)(C), 2012 Taxpayer Relief Act §101(a)(1)
Code Sec. 32(c)(2)(A)(i), 2012 Taxpayer Relief Act §101(a)(1)
Code Sec. 32(c), 2012 Taxpayer Relief Act §101(a)(1)
Code Sec. 32(h), 2012 Taxpayer Relief Act §101(a)(1)
Code Sec. None, 2012 Taxpayer Relief Act §101(a)(1)
Generally effective: Tax years beginning after Dec. 31, 2012
Committee Reports, None

Certain low- and moderate-income workers are allowed a refundable credit, the "earned income credit" (EIC). (FTC 2d/FIN ¶ A-4200, ¶ A-4201; USTR ¶ 324.01; TaxDesk ¶ 569,001) Eligibility for the EIC is based, in part, on earned income, adjusted gross income, filing status, and number of qualifying children. The amount of the EIC is based on the presence and number of qualifying children in the taxpayer's family, as well as on adjusted gross income (AGI) and earned income. (FTC 2d/FIN ¶ A-4201, ¶ A-4202, ¶ A-4203, ¶ A-4209, ¶ A-4211, ¶ A-4212, ¶ A-4216, ¶ A-4222; USTR ¶ 324.01, ¶ 324.02, ¶ 324.05; TaxDesk ¶ 569,001, ¶ 569,003, ¶ 569,009, ¶ 569,010, ¶ 569,011, ¶ 569,012, ¶ 569,023) The EIC is computed (subject to a phaseout, discussed below) by multiplying a credit percentage by the taxpayer's earned income. (FTC 2d/FIN ¶ A-4201; USTR ¶ 324.01; TaxDesk ¶ 569,001)

The EIC generally equals a specified percentage of earned income up to a maximum dollar amount. The maximum amount applies over a certain income range and then diminishes to zero over a specified phaseout range. For taxpayers with earned income (or AGI, if greater) in excess of the beginning of the phaseout range, the maximum EIC amount is reduced by the phaseout rate multiplied by the amount of earned income (or AGI, if greater) in excess of the beginning of the phaseout range. For taxpayers with earned income (or AGI, if greater) in excess of the end of the phaseout range, no credit is allowed. (FTC 2d/FIN ¶ A-4201, ¶ A-4202; USTR ¶ 324.01; TaxDesk ¶ 569,001, ¶ 569,002)

EGTRRA/JGTRRA/WFTRA changes. Under the Economic Growth and Tax Relief Reconciliation Act of 2001 ("EGTRRA," Sec. 303, PL 107-16, 6/7/2001), the Jobs and Growth Tax Relief Reconciliation Act ("JGTRRA," PL 108-27, 5/28/2003), and the Working Families Tax Relief Act of 2004 ("WFTRA," PL 108-311, 10/4/2004), the EIC rules were simplified as follows:

. . . the definition of earned income was modified to include only amounts that are includible in gross income for the tax year. So, the definition includes wages, salaries, tips and other employee compensation, if includible in gross income for the tax year, plus net earnings from self-employment. (FTC 2d/FIN ¶ A-4200, ¶ A-4222; USTR ¶ 324.05; TaxDesk ¶ 569,023);

. . . reduction of the EIC for taxpayers subject to the alternative minimum tax (AMT) was eliminated. (FTC 2d/FIN ¶ A-4201; USTR ¶ 324.01);

. . . adjusted gross income (AGI) replaced *modified* adjusted gross income (MAGI) in the phaseout computation rule, i.e., phaseout was made to apply if the taxpayer's AGI, or earned income, if greater, exceeded the phaseout amount. (FTC 2d/FIN ¶ A-4202, ¶ A-4203; USTR ¶ 324.01; TaxDesk ¶ 569,003);

. . . the relationship test was changed to provide that a qualifying child (including a foster child) must reside with the taxpayer for more than six months; descendants of stepchildren were added to the eligible child category; and a brother, sister, stepbrother or stepsister of the taxpayer were reclassified under the general eligible child category, if the taxpayer cared for them as his own. (FTC 2d/FIN ¶ A-4211, ¶ A-4212; USTR ¶ 324.02; TaxDesk ¶ 569,011, ¶ 569,012); and

. . . the tie-breaking rule were simplified for cases where an individual would be a qualifying child with respect to more than one taxpayer, and more than one taxpayer claimed the EIC with respect to that child. (FTC 2d/FIN ¶ A-4216; USTR ¶ 324.02; TaxDesk ¶ 569,016)

Sunset. Under Sec. 901 of EGTRRA (Sec. 901, PL 107-16, 6/7/2001), to which the applicable JGTRRA (Sec. 107, PL 108-27, 5/28/2003) and WFTRA (Sec. 105, PL 108-311, 10/4/2004) provisions were made subject, all of the EGTRRA/JGTRRA/WFTRA changes described above were scheduled to expire for tax years beginning after Dec. 31, 2010 (FTC 2d/FIN ¶ T-11051; USTR ¶ 79,006.86; TaxDesk ¶ 880,011), and the pre-EGTRRA EIC rules were scheduled to come back into effect. (FTC 2d/FIN ¶ A-4202)

However, the 2010 Tax Relief Act (Sec. 101(a)(1), PL 111-312, 12/17/2010) provided that the EGTRRA sunset would not take effect until after Dec. 31, 2012 (instead of after Dec. 31, 2010), thus extending the EIC simplification rules (above) for two years.

New Law. The 2012 Taxpayer Relief Act repeals title IX of EGTRRA (i.e., the title containing the above-described EGTRRA sunset). (EGTRRA § 901 (Sec. 901, PL 107-16, 6/7/2001) repealed by 2012 Taxpayer Relief Act §101(a)(1)).

> *observation:* Thus, the EIC simplification rules discussed above are permanently extended, and continue in force without being subject to sunset provisions.

☐ **Effective:** Tax years beginning after Dec. 31, 2012. (2012 Taxpayer Relief Act §101(a)(3))

¶ 606. $5,000 increase in EIC phaseout threshold for joint filers is extended through 2017

Code Sec. 32(b)(2), 2012 Taxpayer Relief Act §101(a)(1)
Code Sec. 32(j), 2012 Taxpayer Relief Act §101(a)(1)
Code Sec. 32(b)(3), 2012 Taxpayer Relief Act §103(c)(2)
Code Sec. None, 2012 Taxpayer Relief Act §101(a)(1)
Generally effective: Tax years beginning after Dec. 31, 2012
Committee Reports, None

Certain low-income workers are allowed a refundable credit, the earned income credit (EIC), described in detail at ¶ 605. The credit is computed by multiplying the credit percentage by the individual's earned income up to an earned income amount (as adjusted for inflation). The credit percentage and the earned income amount, and therefore the maximum EIC, depend on the number of "qualifying children" the taxpayer has. (FTC 2d/FIN ¶ A-4200, ¶ A-4201; USTR ¶ 324.01; TaxDesk ¶ 569,001) The EIC is phased out for taxpayers whose earned income, or adjusted gross income (AGI), if greater, exceeds a phaseout amount. For joint filers, the EIC is calculated based on the couple's combined income. (FTC 2d/FIN ¶ A-4202; USTR ¶ 324.01; TaxDesk ¶ 569,002)

EGTRRA/ARRA changes. The Economic Growth and Tax Relief Reconciliation Act of 2001 (EGTRRA, Sec. 303, PL 107-16, 6/7/2001) increased the EIC phaseout threshold amount for joint filers to equal $3,000 more than the amount for other filers, and provided for inflation adjustment of that $3,000 amount.

The American Recovery and Reinvestment Act of 2009 ("ARRA," Sec. 1002(a), PL 111-5, 2/17/2009) provided for tax years 2009 and 2010 only, that the EIC phaseout threshold for joint filers was to be increased to equal *$5,000* more than the threshold amount for other filers (as adjusted for inflation). (FTC 2d/FIN ¶ A-4202; USTR ¶ 324.01; TaxDesk ¶ 569,002)

EGTRRA Sunset/ARRA change expiration. Under section 901 of EGTRRA (Sec. 901, PL 107-16, 6/7/2001), the $3,000 increased phaseout amount for joint filers was scheduled to expire for tax years beginning after Dec. 31, 2010. In addition, the $5,000 increase in the phaseout amount under ARRA was also set to expire. The 2010 Tax Relief Act (i) extended the EGTRRA sunset provision to tax years beginning after Dec. 31, 2012, and (ii) modified the EIC rules themselves to provide that the $5,000 (as adjusted for inflation) increase of the phaseout thresholds for joint filers also applies for tax years 2011 and 2012. (FTC 2d/FIN ¶ T-11051; USTR ¶ 79,006.86; TaxDesk ¶ 880,011)

The threshold phaseout amount for 2012, as adjusted for inflation, was $17,090 ($7,700 for taxpayers with no qualifying children). (FTC 2d/FIN ¶ A-4202; USTR ¶ 324.01; TaxDesk ¶ 569,002)

For tax years beginning after Dec. 31, 2012, the same phaseout threshold amount was scheduled to apply for all filers. That is, neither the $3,000 nor the $5,000 increase would have been in effect.

New Law. The 2012 Taxpayer Relief Act repeals title IX of EGTRRA (i.e., the title containing the above-described EGTRRA sunset). (EGTRRA § 901 (Sec. 901, PL 107-16, 6/7/2001) repealed by (2012 Taxpayer Relief Act §101(a)(1)) In addition, the Act extends the $5,000 increase of the phaseout thresholds for joint filers to any tax year beginning before 2018. (Code Sec. 32(b)(3) as amended by 2012 Taxpayer Relief Act §103(c)(2))

> **RIA** *observation:* Thus, the Act permanently extends the EIC phaseout thresholds for joint filers, as had been provided in EGTRRA. The $5,000 inflation-adjusted increase of the phaseout thresholds for joint filers will continue to apply through 2017 tax years. Following the 2017 tax year, the $3,000 increase provided in EGTRRA will apply.

Thus, as in effect for 2013, the credit begins to phase out at an income level of $17,530 ($7,970 for taxpayers with no qualifying children). (JCX-2-13R, Rev Proc 2013-15, Sec. 2.05)

☐ **Effective:** Tax years beginning after Dec. 31, 2012. (2012 Taxpayer Relief Act §101(a)(3); 2012 Taxpayer Relief Act §103(e)(1))

¶ 607. Increased EIC for families with three or more qualifying children is extended for five years

Code Sec. 32(b)(3), as amended by 2012 Taxpayer Relief Act §103(c)(2)
Generally effective: Tax years beginning after Dec. 31, 2012 and before 2018
Committee Reports, None

Certain low-income workers are allowed a refundable earned income credit (EIC), computed (subject to certain limitations) by multiplying a credit percentage by the individual's earned income. The credit percentage depends on the number of "qualifying children" the taxpayer has. Before 2009, the credit percentages were:

... 7.65% for taxpayers with no qualifying children;

... 34% for taxpayers with one qualifying child; and

... 40% for taxpayers with two or more qualifying children.

A temporary provision had increased the credit percentage for families with three or more qualifying children (from 40%) to 45% for tax years 2009 and 2010 only. For tax years after 2010, the pre-2009 40% credit percentage for families with two or more qualifying children was scheduled to again apply for families with three or more qualifying children.

The 2010 Tax Relief Act extended the EIC at a rate of 45% for three or more qualifying children for two years (2011 and 2012). (Sec. 103(c), PL 111-312, 12/17/2010) (FTC 2d/FIN ¶ A-4200, ¶ A-4201; USTR ¶ 324.01; TaxDesk ¶ 569,001)

New Law. The 2012 Taxpayer Relief Act provides that the increased credit percentage of 45% for taxpayers with three or more qualifying children applies to any tax year beginning after 2008 and before 2018. (Code Sec. 32(b)(3) as amended by 2012 Taxpayer Relief Act §103(c)(2))

> *observation:* Thus, the 2012 Taxpayer Relief Act extends the EIC at a rate of 45% for three or more qualifying children for five years (2013 through 2017).

☐ **Effective:** Tax years beginning after Dec. 31, 2012 (2012 Taxpayer Relief Act §103(e)(1)) and before 2018 (Code Sec. 32(b)(3)).

¶ 700. Education Provisions

¶ 701. American Opportunity Tax Credit (AOTC) for higher education expenses is extended five years, through 2017

Code Sec. 25A(i), as amended by 2012 Taxpayer Relief Act §103(a)(1)
Code Sec. None, 2012 Taxpayer Relief Act §103(a)(2)
Generally effective: Tax years beginning after Dec. 31, 2012 and before Jan. 1, 2018
Committee Reports, None

Before 2009. For tax years beginning before 2009, individual taxpayers could claim a nonrefundable personal credit—the Hope credit (a component credit of the "higher education credit," along with the Lifetime Learning Credit)—against income tax of up to $1,800 (for 2008) per eligible student for qualified tuition and related (QT&R, see below) expenses paid for the first two years of the student's post-secondary education in a degree or certificate program. To claim the Hope credit, the student couldn't have completed the first two years of that post-secondary education before the beginning of the tax year for which the credit was claimed (i.e., the credit was allowed only for QT&R expenses paid for the first two years of the post-secondary education). (FTC 2d/FIN ¶ A-4500, ¶ A-4501, ¶ A-4530; USTR ¶ 25A4, ¶ 25A4.03, ¶ 25A4.04; TaxDesk ¶ 568,901, ¶ 568,930)

The pre-2009 Hope credit equalled: (1) 100% of the first $1,200 (an inflation adjusted amount) of QT&R expenses, plus (2) 50% of the next $1,200 (an inflation-adjusted amount) of QT&R expenses paid, for education furnished to an eligible student in an academic period, for a total maximum Hope credit of $1,800. (FTC 2d/FIN ¶ A-4523; USTR ¶ 25A4.03; TaxDesk ¶ 568,923)

And, for each eligible student, the Hope credit couldn't be claimed if the credit had been claimed for that student for any two earlier tax years. (FTC 2d/FIN ¶ A-4533; USTR ¶ 25A4.03, ¶ 25A4.04; TaxDesk ¶ 528,933)

Generally, QT&R expenses for the pre-2009 Hope credit included, with specific exceptions, tuition and fees (excluding nonacademic fees) required for the enrollment or attendance of the taxpayer, his spouse, or tax dependent, at a post-secondary educational institution eligible to participate in the federal stu-

FTC 2d References are to Federal Tax Coordinator 2d
FIN References are to RIA's Analysis of Federal Taxes: Income (print)
USTR References are to United States Tax Reporter: Income
PCA References are to Pension Analysis (print and electronic)
PBE References are to Pension & Benefits Explanations
BCA References are to Benefits Analysis (electronic)
BC References are to Benefits Coordinator (print)
EP References are to Estate Planning Analysis (print and electronic)

dent loan program. (FTC 2d/FIN ¶ A-4537; USTR ¶ 25A4.07; TaxDesk ¶ 568,937)

An otherwise allowable Hope credit is phased out ratably for taxpayers with specified (inflation adjusted) modified adjusted gross income (MAGI) amounts. For 2008, the Hope credit was phased out between $48,000 and $58,000 ($96,000 and $116,000 for joint filers). (FTC 2d/FIN ¶ A-4517; USTR ¶ 25A4.02; TaxDesk ¶ 568,917)

Under pre-2009 rules, the Hope credit was subject to the general Code Sec. 26 tax liability limitation on nonrefundable personal credits. (FTC 2d/FIN ¶ A-4901, ¶ A-4902; USTR ¶ 264; TaxDesk ¶ 569,601, ¶ 569,602)

For 2009 through 2012. The American Recovery and Reinvestment Act of 2009 (the "2009 Recovery Act," Sec. 1004(a), PL 111-5, 2/17/2009) added Code Sec. 25A(i), which increased and expanded the Hope credit and renamed that modified credit the "American Opportunity tax credit" (AOTC). Specifically, the 2009 Recovery Act:

• increased the maximum credit amount to $2,500 per eligible student per year for qualified QT&R expenses. The AOTC equals the sum of (a) 100% of so much of the QT&R expenses paid by the taxpayer during the tax year (for education furnished to the eligible student during any academic period beginning in the tax year) as doesn't exceed $2,000, plus (b) 25% of the QT&R expenses so paid as exceeds $2,000 but doesn't exceed $4,000. (FTC 2d/FIN ¶ A-4523; USTR ¶ 25A4.03; TaxDesk ¶ 568,923);

• expanded the definition of QT&R expenses to include course materials (FTC 2d/FIN ¶ A-4537; USTR ¶ 25A4.07; TaxDesk ¶ 568,937);

• allowed the AOTC for the first four years of the student's post-secondary education in a degree or certificate program, if the student hasn't completed the first four years of post-secondary education before the beginning of the fourth tax year. And, for each eligible student, the AOTC can be claimed for four tax years. (FTC 2d/FIN ¶ A-4530, ¶ A-4533; USTR ¶ 25A4.03, ¶ 25A4.04; TaxDesk ¶ 568,930, ¶ 568,933);

• increased the MAGI range at which the credit is phased-out to between $80,000 and $90,000 ($160,000 and $180,000 for married joint filers) (FTC 2d/FIN ¶ A-4517; USTR ¶ 25A4.02; TaxDesk ¶ 568,917);

• applied a separate tax liability limitation permitting the AOTC credit to be claimed against alternative minimum tax (AMT) liability (FTC 2d/FIN ¶ A-4525.1; USTR ¶ 25A4; TaxDesk ¶ 568,925.1); and

• allowed 40% of the otherwise allowable AOTC to be refundable (unless the taxpayer claiming the credit was a child to whom the Code Sec. 1(g) "kiddie tax" rules apply for the tax year, i.e., generally, any child under age 18 or any child under age 24 who is a student providing less than one-half of his support, who has at least one living parent, and doesn't file a joint return). (FTC 2d/FIN ¶ A-4525.2; USTR ¶ 25A4.03; TaxDesk ¶ 568,925.2)

The 2009 Recovery Act (Sec. 1004(c), PL 111-5, 2/17/2009) also included a special rule for bona fide residents of U.S. possessions. Under that rule, those individuals can't claim the refundable portion of the AOTC in the U.S. Instead, they claim the refundable portion of the credit in the possession in which they reside. But bona fide residents of non-mirror code possessions (for this purpose, Puerto Rico and American Samoa) can claim the refundable portion of the credit only if the possession establishes a plan for permitting the claim under its internal law. (FTC 2d/FIN ¶ A-4525.2; USTR ¶ 25A4.03; TaxDesk ¶ 568,925.2)

Under pre-2012 Taxpayer Relief Act law, both (1) the Code Sec. 25A(i) AOTC, and (2) the 2009 Recovery Act § 1004(c)(1) special rule for bona fide residents of U.S. possessions, only applied for tax years beginning in 2009 through 2012. For tax years beginning after 2012, the pre-2009 Hope credit rules (described above) were to be applied again. (FTC 2d/FIN ¶ A-4523; USTR ¶ 25A4.03; TaxDesk ¶ 568,923)

New Law. The 2012 Taxpayer Relief Act amends both (1) the Code Sec. 25A(i) AOTC, and (2) the 2009 Recovery Act § 1004(c)(1) special rule for bona fide residents of U.S. possessions, to provide that these rules apply for tax years beginning in 2013 through 2017, in addition to tax years beginning in 2009 through 2012. (Code Sec. 25A(i) as amended by 2012 Taxpayer Relief Act §103(a)(1); and Sec. 1004(c)(1), PL 111-5, 2/17/2009 as amended by 2012 Taxpayer Relief Act §103(a)(2), respectively)

> **RIA** *observation:* Thus, the 2012 Taxpayer Relief Act extends for five years (through 2017) both the AOTC and the rules governing treatment of bona fide residents of U.S. possessions.

> **RIA** *observation:* Specifically, as a result of the above extension of the AOTC, for tax years beginning in 2013 through 2017 (for most individuals who are calendar year taxpayers, 2013 through 2017):
>
> • the maximum AOTC credit amount is $2,500 per eligible student per year (computed as described above) for qualified QT&R expenses;
>
> • QT&R expenses include tuition, fees, and course materials;
>
> • the AOTC is allowed for each of the first four years of the student's post-secondary education in a degree or certificate program. And, for each eligible student, the AOTC can be claimed for four tax years;
>
> • the AOTC is phased-out at MAGI between $80,000 and $90,000 (between $160,000 and $180,000 for joint filers);
>
> • the AOTC can be claimed against AMT liability;
>
> • 40% of the otherwise allowable AOTC is refundable (unless the taxpayer claiming the credit is a child under age 18 or a child under

age 24 who is a student providing less than one-half of his support, who has at least one living parent, and doesn't file a joint return); and

• bona fide residents of U.S. possessions can't claim the refundable portion of the AOTC credit in the U.S. Instead, they claim the refundable portion in the possession in which they reside (subject to the limitations described above).

sample client letter: For a client letter on the AOTC provision in the 2012 Taxpayer Relief Act, see ¶ 2006.

□ **Effective:** For tax years beginning after Dec. 31, 2012 (2012 Taxpayer Relief Act §103(e)(1)) and before Jan. 1, 2018 (Code Sec. 25A(i); 2012 Taxpayer Relief Act §103(a)(2))

¶ 702. Qualified tuition deduction is retroactively extended through 2013

Code Sec. 222(e), as amended by 2012 Taxpayer Relief Act §207(a)
Generally effective: Tax years beginning after Dec. 31, 2011 and before Jan. 1, 2014
Committee Reports, None

An individual is allowed an above-the-line deduction for "qualified tuition and related (QT&R) expenses" for higher education paid by the individual during the tax year. These expenses include tuition and fees for the enrollment or attendance of the taxpayer, the taxpayer's spouse, or any dependent for whom the taxpayer can claim a personal exemption, at an eligible institution of higher education for courses of instruction at the institution. Theses expenses must be in connection with enrollment at an institution of higher education during the tax year, or with an academic term beginning during the tax year or during the first three months of the next tax year. The amount of theses expenses must be reduced by tax-free educational assistance and certain exclusions from income under the rules for savings bond interest, Coverdell education savings accounts (ESAs), and qualified tuition programs (QTPs or 529 plans). (See FTC 2d/FIN ¶ A-4470 et seq.; USTR ¶ 2224 et seq.; TaxDesk ¶ 352,000 et seq.)

The maximum deduction is:

. . . $4,000 for an individual whose adjusted gross income (AGI), with certain modifications, doesn't exceed $65,000 ($130,000 for a joint return),

. . . $2,000 for an individual whose modified AGI exceeds $65,000 ($130,000 for a joint return), but doesn't exceed $80,000 ($160,000 for a joint return), or

. . . zero for other taxpayers.

(See FTC 2d/FIN ¶ A-4471; USTR ¶ 2224; TaxDesk ¶ 352,001).

Under pre-2012 Taxpayer Relief Act law, the higher-education expense deduction wasn't available for tax years beginning after Dec. 31, 2011. (FTC 2d/FIN ¶ A-4470, ¶ A-4471; USTR ¶ 2224, ¶ 2224.01; TaxDesk ¶ 352,000, ¶ 352,001)

New Law. The 2012 Taxpayer Relief Act (Act) replaces "Dec. 31, 2011" with "Dec. 31, 2013." Thus, the Act extends the qualified tuition deduction for two years so that it's generally available for tax years beginning before Jan. 1, 2014. (Code Sec. 222(e) as amended by 2012 Taxpayer Relief Act §207(a))

> *observation:* Most individuals are on a calendar year. For these individuals, the qualified tuition expenses must be paid before 2014. But, as noted above, the deduction is for expenses in connection with enrollment at an institution of higher education during the tax year, or with an academic term beginning during the tax year *or* during the first three months of the next tax year. Thus, expenses for an academic term beginning as late as Mar. 31, 2014 may qualify for the deduction, if the taxpayer pays these expenses before 2014.

> *recommendation:* A taxpayer who plans to go to college or graduate school for an academic term beginning in January, February, or March of 2014 (or whose spouse or dependent plans to do so) should consider paying some tuition for that term at the end of 2013—namely, the dollar amount equal to the maximum allowable deduction ($4,000 or $2,000, depending on the taxpayer's modified AGI).

☐ **Effective:** Tax years beginning after Dec. 31, 2011 (2012 Taxpayer Relief Act §207(b)) and before Jan. 1, 2014. (Code Sec. 222(e))

¶ 703. EGTRRA changes to student loan deduction rules are made permanent

Code Sec. 221, 2012 Taxpayer Relief Act §101(a)(1)
Code Sec. 221(b)(2)(B), 2012 Taxpayer Relief Act §101(a)(1)
Code Sec. 221(f), 2012 Taxpayer Relief Act §101(a)(1)
Generally effective: Tax years beginning after Dec. 31, 2012
Committee Reports, None

Individuals can deduct a maximum of $2,500 annually for interest paid on qualified higher education loans (as defined in FTC 2d/FIN ¶ K-5504; USTR ¶ 2214.02; TaxDesk ¶ 314,110). The deduction is claimed as an adjustment to gross income to arrive at adjusted gross income (AGI). For tax years beginning in 2012, the deduction phases out ratably for taxpayers with modified AGI (as defined in FTC 2d/FIN ¶ K-5502.1; USTR ¶ 2214.01; TaxDesk ¶ 314,106) between $60,000 and $75,000 ($120,000 and $150,000 for joint returns). The phaseout amounts and ranges are indexed for inflation. See FTC 2d/FIN ¶ K-5500 *et seq.*; USTR ¶ 2214 *et seq.*; TaxDesk ¶ 314,100 *et seq.*

2001 EGTRRA changes. Sec. 412 of 2001 Economic Growth and Tax Relief Reconciliation Act (2001 EGTRRA, Sec. 412, PL 107-16, 6/7/2001) amended the rules for deducting interest on student loans, effective generally for tax years beginning after 2001, by:

(1) eliminating the 60-month limit on the deduction for interest paid on a qualified education loan (FTC 2d/FIN ¶ K-5500, ¶ K-5501; USTR ¶ 2214), and

(2) increasing the pre-2001 EGTRRA AGI phaseout ranges ($40,000 to $55,000 for taxpayers other than joint filers; $60,000 to $75,000 for a married couple filing jointly) applicable to the student loan interest deduction. The phaseout ranges, as amended by 2001 EGTRRA, were indexed for inflation. (FTC 2d/FIN ¶ K-5502; USTR ¶ 2214; TaxDesk ¶ 314,105)

Sunset after 2012. Under pre-2012 Taxpayer Relief Act law, a sunset provision in 2001 EGTRRA §901 (Sec. 901(a)(1), PL 107-16, 6/7/2001) as amended by 2010 Tax Relief Act §101(a)(1) (Sec. 101(a)(1), PL 111-312, 12/17/2010) provided that all changes made by 2001 EGTRRA didn't apply to tax years beginning after Dec. 31, *2012*. (FTC 2d/FIN ¶ T-11051; USTR ¶ 79,006.86; TaxDesk ¶ 880,011)

New Law. The 2012 Taxpayer Relief Act repeals title IX of EGTRRA (i.e., the title containing the above-described EGTRRA sunset). (EGTRRA § 901 (Sec. 901, PL 107-16, 6/7/2001) repealed by 2012 Taxpayer Relief Act §101(a)(1))

> *observation:* In other words, the 2012 Taxpayer Relief Act repeals the 2001 EGTRRA sunset as it applies to the student loan interest deduction and makes permanent the provisions of the student loan deduction that were added by 2001 EGTRRA. Thus, for tax years beginning after 2012, the 60-month limitation on the student loan interest deduction will not apply. Also, for tax years beginning after 2012, the AGI phaseout ranges will not revert to the AGI phaseout ranges that applied before 2001 EGTRRA.

> *observation:* As indicated by IRS in Rev Proc 2013-15, Sec. 2.12, for tax years beginning in 2013, the deduction phases out ratably for taxpayers with modified AGI between $60,000 and $75,000 ($125,000 and $155,000 for joint returns).

☐ **Effective:** Tax years beginning after Dec. 31, 2012. (2012 Taxpayer Relief Act §101(a)(3))

¶ 704. Increased $2,000 contribution limit and other EGTRRA enhancements to Coverdell ESAs are made permanent

Code Sec. 25A(e), 2012 Taxpayer Relief Act §101(a)(1)
Code Sec. 530(b)(1), 2012 Taxpayer Relief Act §101(a)(1)
Code Sec. 530(b)(1)(A)(iii), 2012 Taxpayer Relief Act §101(a)(1)
Code Sec. 530(b)(2), 2012 Taxpayer Relief Act §101(a)(1)
Code Sec. 530(b)(4), 2012 Taxpayer Relief Act §101(a)(1)
Code Sec. 530(b)(5), 2012 Taxpayer Relief Act §101(a)(1)
Code Sec. 530(c)(1), 2012 Taxpayer Relief Act §101(a)(1)
Code Sec. 530(d)(2), 2012 Taxpayer Relief Act §101(a)(1)
Code Sec. 530(d)(2)(C), 2012 Taxpayer Relief Act §101(a)(1)
Code Sec. 530(d)(2)(D), 2012 Taxpayer Relief Act §101(a)(1)
Code Sec. 530(d)(4)(C)(i), 2012 Taxpayer Relief Act §101(a)(1)
Code Sec. 4973(e)(1)(A), 2012 Taxpayer Relief Act §101(a)(1)
Code Sec. 4973(e)(1)(B), 2012 Taxpayer Relief Act §101(a)(1)
Code Sec. None, 2012 Taxpayer Relief Act §101(a)(1)
Generally effective: For tax years beginning after Dec. 31, 2012
Committee Reports, None

An individual can make a nondeductible cash contribution to a Coverdell education savings account ("Coverdell ESA," or "CESA," formerly called an "education IRA") for qualified education expenses of a beneficiary under the age of 18. A specified aggregate amount can be contributed each year by all contributors for one beneficiary. The amount an individual contributor can contribute is phased out as the contributor's modified adjusted gross income (MAGI) exceeds specified levels. A 6% excise tax applies to excess contributions.

Earnings on the contributions made to a CESA are subject to tax when withdrawn. But distributions from a CESA are excludable from the distributee's (i.e., the student's) gross income to the extent the distributions don't exceed the qualified education expenses incurred by the beneficiary during the tax year the distributions are made. The earnings portion of a CESA distribution not used to pay qualified education expense is includible in a distributee's income, and that amount is subject to a 10% tax that applies in addition to the regular tax.

Tax-free (including free of the 10% tax described above) transfers or rollovers of CESA account balances from a CESA benefiting one beneficiary to a CESA benefitting another beneficiary (and redesignations of named beneficiaries) are permitted if the new beneficiary is a family member of the previous beneficiary and is under age 30. Generally, a balance remaining in a CESA is deemed to be distributed within 30 days after the beneficiary turns 30.

EGTRRA/WFTRA changes. Under the Economic Growth and Tax Relief Reconciliation Act of 2001 ("EGTRRA," Sec. 401, PL 107-16, 6/7/2001), with a technical correction under the Working Families Tax Relief Act of 2004 ("WFTRA," Sec. 404, PL 108-311, 10/4/2004, the CESA rules were modified to:

• increase the limit on CESA aggregate annual contributions (from $500) to $2,000 per beneficiary (FTC 2d/FIN ¶ A-4600, ¶ A-4601, ¶ A-4603; USTR ¶ 5304; TaxDesk ¶ 147,201, ¶ 147,203);

• permit corporations and other entities (in addition to individuals) to make contributions to a CESA, regardless of the corporation's or entity's income (FTC 2d/FIN ¶ A-4602, ¶ A-4604; USTR ¶ 5304; TaxDesk ¶ 147,202, ¶ 147,204);

• increase the MAGI phaseout range for joint filers (from $150,000 through $160,000) to $190,000 through $220,000, i.e., to equal twice the range for single filers (i.e., $95,000 through $110,000), and so eliminate any "marriage penalty" (FTC 2d/FIN ¶ A-4604; USTR ¶ 5304.01; TaxDesk ¶ 147,204);

• permit contributions to a CESA for a tax year to be made until Apr. 15 of the following year (FTC 2d/FIN ¶ A-4606; USTR ¶ 5304.01; TaxDesk ¶ 147,206);

• modify the definition of excess contribution to a CESA for purposes of the 6% excise tax on excess contributions to reflect various other EGTRRA changes (FTC 2d/FIN ¶ A-4607; USTR ¶ 49,734; TaxDesk ¶ 147,207);

• extend the time (to before June 1 of the following tax year) for taxpayers to withdraw excess contributions (and the earnings on them) to avoid imposition of the 6% excise tax (FTC 2d/FIN ¶ A-4608; USTR ¶ 49,734; TaxDesk ¶ 147,208);

• expand the definition of education expenses that can be paid by CESAs to include elementary and secondary school expenses (in addition to qualified higher education expenses) (FTC 2d/FIN ¶ A-4610, ¶ A-4611, ¶ A-4625; USTR ¶ 5304; TaxDesk ¶ 147,210, ¶ 147,211, ¶ 147,225);

• provide for coordination of the Hope and Lifetime Learning credits with the CESA rules to permit a Hope or Lifetime Learning credit to be taken in the same year as a tax-free distribution is taken from a CESA for a designated beneficiary (but for different expenses) (under pre-EGTRRA law, a taxpayer couldn't claim a Hope credit in the same year he claimed an income exclusion from a CESA) (FTC 2d/FIN ¶ A-4613; USTR ¶ 5304.01; TaxDesk ¶ 147,213);

• provide rules coordinating distributions from both a qualified tuition program (QTP, or "529 plan") and a CESA for the same beneficiary for the same tax year (but for different expenses) (FTC 2d/FIN ¶ A-4614; USTR ¶ 5304.01; TaxDesk ¶ 147,214);

• eliminate the age limitations described above for acceptance of CESA contributions, deemed balance distributions, tax-free rollovers to other family-member-beneficiaries, and tax-free change of beneficiaries, for "special needs beneficiaries" (FTC 2d/FIN ¶ A-4601, ¶ A-4615, ¶ A-4616, ¶ A-4617, ¶ A-4619, ¶ A-4620; USTR ¶ 5304, ¶ 5304.01; TaxDesk ¶ 147,201, ¶ 147,215, ¶ 147,216, ¶ 147,217, ¶ 147,219, ¶ 147,220); and

• provide that the 10% additional tax on taxable distributions from a CESA doesn't apply to distributions of contributions to a CESA made by June 1 of the tax year following the tax year in which the contribution was made (FTC 2d/FIN ¶ A-4618; USTR ¶ 5304.01; TaxDesk ¶ 147,218).

Sunset. Under Sec. 901 of EGTRRA (Sec. 901, PL 107-16, 6/7/2001), to which the applicable WFTRA provision (Sec. 404(f), PL 108-311, 10/4/2004) is made subject, all of the EGTRRA/WFTRA changes described above were scheduled to expire for tax years beginning after Dec. 31, 2010. The 2010 Tax Relief Act extended the EGTRRA/WFTRA rules by providing that the EGTRRA sunset wouldn't take effect until after Dec. 31, 2012. (Sec. 901, PL 107-16, 6/7/2001 as amended by 2012 Taxpayer Relief Act §101(a)(1))(FTC 2d/FIN ¶ T-11051, ¶ T-11071; USTR ¶ 79,006.86; TaxDesk ¶ 880,011).

After the sunset date, the CESA rules in effect before the passage of EGTRRA were scheduled to come back into effect.

New Law. The 2012 Taxpayer Relief Act repeals title IX of EGTRRA (i.e., the title containing the above-described EGTRRA sunset). (EGTRRA § 901 (Sec. 901, PL 107-16, 6/7/2001) repealed by (2012 Taxpayer Relief Act §101(a)(1))

> *observation:* As a result of the repeal of the EGTRRA sunset provision, the following rules apply on a permanent basis:
>
> • the limit on CESA aggregate annual contributions is $2,000 per beneficiary (and isn't decreased to $500 per beneficiary);
>
> • corporations and other entities (not just individuals) can make contributions to a CESA, and the corporations and other entitles can do so regardless of their income;
>
> • the MAGI phaseout range for joint filers is 190,000-$220,000 (and doesn't decrease to $150,000-$160,000);
>
> • CESA contributions for a tax year can be made until Apr. 15 of the following year;
>
> • the definition of CESA excess contribution reflects the various other EGTRRA changes to the CESA rules;
>
> • taxpayers have until June 1 of the following tax year to withdraw excess contributions (and the earnings on them) to avoid imposition of the 6% excise tax;

- education expenses that can be paid by CESAs include elementary and secondary school expenses and qualified higher education expenses (rather than only qualified higher education expenses);

- a Hope or Lifetime Learning credit can be taken in the same year as a tax-free distribution is taken from a CESA for a designated beneficiary (but for different expenses);

- the rule coordinating distributions being made from both a QTP and a CESA for the same beneficiary for the same tax year (but for different expenses) applies;

- special needs beneficiaries are exempted from the age limitations for a CESA's acceptance of contributions, deemed balance distributions, tax-free rollovers to other family-member-beneficiaries, and tax-free change of beneficiaries; and

- the 10% additional tax on taxable distributions from a CESA is inapplicable to distributions of contributions to a CESA made by June 1 of the tax year following the tax year in which the contribution was made.

☐ **Effective:** Tax years beginning after Dec. 31, 2012. (2012 Taxpayer Relief Act §101(a)(3))

¶ 705. Exclusion for employer-provided educational assistance, and restoration of the exclusion for graduate-level courses, made permanent

Code Sec. 127, 2012 Taxpayer Relief Act §101(a)(1)
Generally effective: Tax years beginning after 2012
Committee Reports, None

Under Code Sec. 127, an employee's gross income does not include amounts paid or expenses incurred (up to $5,250 annually) by the employer in providing educational assistance to employees under an educational assistance program. An educational assistance program is a separate written plan of the employer for the exclusive benefit of its employees, having the purpose of providing the employees with educational assistance. The courses taken need not be related to the employee's job for the exclusion to apply. To be qualified, the program must not discriminate in favor of highly compensated employees, nor may more than 5% of the amounts paid or incurred by the employer for educational assistance during the year be provided for individuals (and their spouses and dependents) owning more than 5% of the employer. Further, the program cannot provide employees with a choice between educational assistance and other remuneration that would be includible in their gross income. Finally, reasonable notification of the program's availability and terms must be provided to employees.

Before the 2001 Economic Growth and Tax Relief Reconciliation Act (EGTRRA), Congress had periodically waited until the educational assistance exclusion was set to expire before renewing it, and had sometimes allowed it to expire, and then extended it retroactively. The exclusion was set to expire for courses beginning after Dec. 31, 2001. Under EGTRRA (Sec. 411(a), PL 107-16, 6/7/2001), the exclusion was extended "permanently" subject to the EGTRRA sunset, described below. (FTC 2d/FIN ¶ H-2050, ¶ H-2064; USTR ¶ 1274; TaxDesk ¶ 136,525; PBE ¶ 127-4; BC ¶ 19,210; BCA ¶ 119,210)

Also EGTRRA (Sec. 411(b), PL 107-16, 6/7/2001), restored the exclusion for graduate level courses, which had earlier been eliminated. This was also subject to the EGTRRA sunset, described below. (FTC 2d/FIN ¶ H-2065; USTR ¶ 1274.01; TaxDesk ¶ 136,525; PBE ¶ 127-4.01; BC ¶ 19,211; BCA ¶ 119,211)

Sunset after 2012. With certain exceptions not relevant here, all provisions of, and amendments made by, EGTRRA did *not* apply to tax, plan, or limitation years beginning after Dec. 31, 2010. (Sec. 901(a), PL 107-16, 6/7/2001) Under this sunset rule, the Code was to have been applied and administered to tax, plan, or limitation years beginning after Dec. 31, 2010, as if the provisions of, and amendments made by, EGTRRA had never been enacted. (Sec. 901(a), PL 107-16, 6/7/2001) Thus, for tax years beginning after Dec. 31, 2010, the specific exclusion for employer-provided educational assistance would have expired along with the restoration of the exclusion to graduate courses.

The 2010 Tax Relief Act extended the EGTRRA sunset date from Dec. 31, 2010 to Dec. 31, 2012. (EGTRRA §901, amended by Sec. 101(a)(1), PL 111-312, 12/17/2010). Thus, the Code Sec. 127 exclusion, including the assistance for graduate courses, would have expired after 2012. (FTC 2d/FIN ¶ T-11051; USTR ¶ 79,006.86; TaxDesk ¶ 147,105; PBE ¶ 7900-6.86)

New Law. The 2012 Taxpayer Relief Act repeals title IX of EGTRRA (i.e., the title containing the above-described EGTRRA sunset). (Sec. 901, PL 107-16, 6/7/2001 repealed by 2012 Taxpayer Relief Act §101(a)(1)).

⍒*observation:* Thus, the Code Sec. 127 exclusion, including the assistance for graduate courses, is made permanent.

☐ **Effective:** For tax years beginning after Dec. 31, 2012. (2012 Taxpayer Relief Act §101(a)(3))

¶ 706. Income exclusion for awards under the National Health Service Corps and Armed Forces Health Professions programs made permanent

Code Sec. 117(c)(2), 2012 Taxpayer Relief Act §101(a)(1)
Generally effective: For taxable years beginning after Dec. 31, 2012
Committee Reports, None

Gross income doesn't include (i) any amount received as a "qualified scholarship" by an individual who is a candidate for a degree at a primary, secondary, or post-secondary educational institution, or (ii) qualified tuition reductions for certain education provided to employees (and their spouses and dependents) of those educational institutions. But these exclusions don't apply to any amount that a student receives that represents payment for teaching, research, or other services provided by the student, required as a condition for receiving the scholarship or tuition reduction.

Thus, before enactment of the Economic Growth and Tax Relief Reconciliation Act of 2001 (EGTRRA, Sec. 413, PL 107-16, 6/7/2001), there was no exclusion from gross income for health profession scholarship programs which required scholarship recipients to provide medical services as a condition for their awards.

EGTRRA provided that education awards received under specified health scholarship programs may be tax-free qualified scholarships, without regard to any service obligation on the part of the recipient. Specifically, the rule that the exclusions for qualified scholarships and qualified tuition don't apply to amounts received which represent compensation does *not* apply to any amount received by an individual under the following programs:

(1) the National Health Service Corps Scholarship Program (the "NHSC Scholarship Program," under Sec. 338A(g)(1)(A) of the Public Health Services Act), and

(2) the F. Edward Hebert Armed Forces Health Professions Scholarship and Financial Assistance program (the "Armed Forces Scholarship Program," under Subchapter I of Chapter 105 of Title 10 of the U.S. Code). (FTC 2d/FIN ¶ J-1230, ¶ J-1258.1; USTR ¶ 1174.05; TaxDesk ¶ 193,517)

A sunset provision in EGTRRA (Sec. 901, PL 107-16, 6/7/2001) provided that the changes made by 2001 EGTRRA won't apply to tax years beginning after Dec. 31, 2012. ((FTC 2d/FIN ¶ T-11050, ¶ T-11051; USTR ¶ 79,006.86; TaxDesk ¶ 880,011)) Thus, under pre-2012 Taxpayer Relief Act law, the exception from the payment-for-services rule for NHSC Scholarship Program and the Armed Forces Scholarship Program would not have applied for amounts received in tax years beginning after Dec. 31, 2012.

New Law. The 2012 Taxpayer Relief Act repeals title IX of EGTRRA (i.e., the title containing the above-described EGTRRA sunset). (Sec. 901, PL 107-16, 6/7/2001 repealed by 2012 Taxpayer Relief Act §101(a)(1)). Thus, the exclusion from gross income for awards received under the NHSC and Armed Forces Scholarship Programs is made permanent.

> *observation:* This means that after 2012 recipients of scholarships under the NHSC Scholarship Program and the Armed Forces Scholarship Program, whose awards are conditioned on providing medical services, will not have to include the amount of their scholarships in gross income.

☐ **Effective:** For taxable years beginning after Dec. 31, 2012. (2012 Taxpayer Relief Act §101(a)(3))

¶ 800. Depreciation and Expensing

¶ 801. Increased 2010 and 2011 Code 179 dollar limitation and phase-out threshold, and 2010 and 2011 treatment of qualified real property as section 179 property, are extended to 2012 and 2013

Code Sec. 179(b)(1)(B), as amended by 2012 Taxpayer Relief Act §315(a)(1)(A)

Code Sec. 179(b)(1)(C), as amended by 2012 Taxpayer Relief Act §315(a)(1)(B)

Code Sec. 179(b)(1)(D), as amended and redesignated by 2012 Taxpayer Relief Act §315(a)(1)

Code Sec. 179(b)(2)(B), as amended by 2012 Taxpayer Relief Act §315(a)(2)(A)

Code Sec. 179(b)(2)(C), as amended by 2012 Taxpayer Relief Act §315(a)(2)(B)

Code Sec. 179(b)(2)(D), as amended and redesignated by 2012 Taxpayer Relief Act §315(a)(2)

Code Sec. 179(b)(6), as amended by 2012 Taxpayer Relief Act §315(a)(3)

Code Sec. 179(f)(1), as amended by 2012 Taxpayer Relief Act §315(d)(1)

Code Sec. 179(f)(4), as amended by 2012 Taxpayer Relief Act §315(d)(2)(A)

Code Sec. 179(f)(4)(D), as amended by 2012 Taxpayer Relief Act §315(d)(2)(B)(ii)

Generally effective: Tax years beginning after Dec. 31, 2011 and before Jan. 1, 2014

Committee Reports, None

Subject to certain limitations, taxpayers can elect to treat the cost of any section 179 property placed in service during the tax year as an expense which is not chargeable to capital account, and, thus, allowed as a deduction for the tax year in which the section 179 property is placed in service, see FTC 2d/FIN ¶ L-9900 *et seq.*; USTR ¶ 1794 *et seq.*; TaxDesk ¶ 268,400 *et seq.*

Under pre-2012 Taxpayer Relief Act law, the deductible Code Sec. 179 expense could not exceed $125,000, adjusted for inflation to $139,000, in the case

---

FTC 2d References are to Federal Tax Coordinator 2d
FIN References are to RIA's Analysis of Federal Taxes: Income (print)
USTR References are to United States Tax Reporter: Income
PCA References are to Pension Analysis (print and electronic)
PBE References are to Pension & Benefits Explanations
BCA References are to Benefits Analysis (electronic)
BC References are to Benefits Coordinator (print)
EP References are to Estate Planning Analysis (print and electronic)

of a tax year beginning in 2012, and $500,000 not adjusted for inflation (dollar limitation) in the case of a tax year beginning in 2010 or 2011. The maximum deductible expense had to be reduced (i.e., phased out, but not below zero) by the amount by which the cost of section 179 property placed in service during a tax year beginning in 2012 exceeded $500,000, adjusted for inflation to $560,000, and during a tax year beginning in 2010 or 2011, exceeded $2,000,000 not adjusted for inflation (beginning-of-phaseout amount). (FTC 2d/FIN ¶ L-9900, ¶ L-9907, ¶ L-9907.03; USTR ¶ 1794.01; TaxDesk ¶ 268,411, ¶ 268,411.01)

Under pre-2012 Taxpayer Relief Act law, for tax years beginning after 2012, the dollar limitation (discussed above) was to be $25,000 and the beginning-of-phaseout amount (discussed above) was to be $200,000. (FTC 2d/FIN ¶ L-9900, ¶ L-9907; USTR ¶ 1794.01; TaxDesk ¶ 268,411) The $25,000 and $200,000 amounts were not to be adjusted for inflation. (FTC 2d/FIN ¶ L-9900, ¶ L-9907.1; USTR ¶ 1794.01; TaxDesk ¶ 268,411.02)

Under pre-2012 Taxpayer Relief Act law, for a tax year beginning in 2010 or 2011, subject to the $500,000 dollar limitation and $2,000,000 beginning-of-phaseout amount discussed above, "section 179 property" included, at the election of the taxpayer, up to $250,000 of the cost of "qualified real property." (FTC 2d/FIN ¶ L-9900, ¶ L-9901.1; USTR ¶ 1794.01; TaxDesk ¶ 268,401.1)

"Qualified real property" was defined as qualified leasehold property, qualified restaurant property or qualified retail improvement property that was (1) of a character subject to the allowance for depreciation, (2) acquired for use in the active conduct of a trade or business and (2) not excluded under any of the rules that exclude other types of property from being "section 179 property." (FTC 2d/FIN ¶ L-9900, ¶ L-9922.1; USTR ¶ 1794.02; TaxDesk ¶ 268,424.1) For the other types of property qualifying as "section 179 property," see ¶ 803.

With regard to "qualified real property," pre-2012 Taxpayer Relief Act law further provided that under Code Sec. 179(f)(4)(A), notwithstanding the rule that permits an unlimited carryforward of amounts of Code Sec. 179 expensing that were disallowed because of the taxable income limitation in Code Sec. 179(b)(3)(A), no amount attributable to qualified real property could be carried over to a tax year beginning after 2011. Under Code Sec. 179(f)(4)(B), except as provided in Code Sec. 179(f)(4)(C) (discussed immediately below), to the extent that any amount was not allowed to be carried over to a tax year beginning after 2011 due to the qualified real property carryover limitation (discussed immediately above), the Code was applied as if no Code Sec. 179 election had been made for that amount. Under Code Sec. 179(f)(4)(C), if Code Sec. 179(f)(4)(B) applied to any amount (or portion of an amount) which was carried over from a tax year other than the taxpayer's last tax year beginning in 2011 (i.e., from a tax year beginning in 2010), that amount (or portion of an amount) was treated for purposes of the Code as attributable to property placed in service on the first day of the taxpayer's last tax year beginning in 2011. Code Sec. 179(f)(4)(D) provided rules for allocating amounts disallowed under the taxable income limitation in Code Sec. 179(b)(3)(A) between amounts attributable to qualified real property and attributable to other property. (FTC 2d/FIN ¶ L-9900, ¶ L-9917.1; USTR ¶ 1794.01; TaxDesk ¶ 268,420.1)

New Law. The 2012 Taxpayer Relief Act extends the $500,000 limitation and $2,000,000 beginning-of-phaseout amount, so that each apply not only to tax years beginning in 2010 and 2011, but also to tax years beginning in 2012 and 2013. (Code Sec. 179(b)(1)(B) as amended by 2012 Taxpayer Relief Act §315(a)(1)(A); Code Sec. 179(b)(2)(B) as amended by 2012 Taxpayer Relief Act §315(a)(2)(A))

Thus, the 2012 Taxpayer Relief Act removes from Code Sec. 179(b)(1)(C) the rule which provided the $125,000 ($139,000 as adjusted for inflation) dollar limitation for tax years beginning in 2012, see above. (Code Sec. 179(b)(1)(C) as amended by 2012 Taxpayer Relief Act §315(a)(1)(B)) Further, the 2012 Taxpayer Relief Act substitutes for the removed rule the above rule concerning the $25,000 dollar limitation, except that the rule is amended to apply to tax years beginning after 2013, instead of tax years beginning after 2012. (Code Sec. 179(b)(1)(C) as amended and redesignated by 2012 Taxpayer Relief Act §315(a)(1))

Similarly, the 2012 Taxpayer Relief Act removes from Code Sec. 179(b)(2)(C) the rule which provided the $500,000 ($560,000 as adjusted for inflation) beginning-of-phaseout amount for tax years beginning in 2012 (see above). (Code Sec. 179(b)(2)(C) as amended by 2012 Taxpayer Relief Act §315(a)(2)(B)) Further, the 2012 Taxpayer Relief Act substitutes for the removed rule the above rule concerning the $200,000 beginning-of-phaseout amount, except that the rule is amended to apply to tax years beginning after 2013, instead of to tax years beginning after 2012. (Code Sec. 179(b)(2)(C) as amended and redesignated by 2012 Taxpayer Relief Act §315(a)(2))

The 2012 Taxpayer Relief Act also removes the rule that provided an inflation adjustment of the dollar limitation and beginning-of-phase-out amount for tax years beginning in 2012. (Code Sec. 179(b)(6) as amended by 2012 Taxpayer Relief Act §315(a)(3))

> **^{RIA} observation:** All of the changes discussed above and under the heading **2010 and 2011 treatment of qualified real property is extended** below are retroactive so as to apply tax years beginning as early as Jan. 1, 2012. Thus, the $139,000 and $560,000 amounts that were scheduled to apply to tax years beginning in 2012 are now treated as having never come into effect, and taxpayers can deduct as much as $500,000 under Code Sec. 179 for tax years beginning in 2012 (with a beginning-of-phaseout level of $2,000,000, see above).

2010 and 2011 treatment of qualified real property is extended. The 2012 Taxpayer Relief Act also extends the treatment of up to $250,000 of the cost of "qualified real property" as section 179 property, that applies to tax years beginning in 2010 and 2011, to tax years beginning in 2012 and 2013. (Code Sec. 179(f)(1) as amended by 2012 Taxpayer Relief Act §315(d)(1))

Thus, in Code Sec. 179(f)(4)(A), Code Sec. 179(f)(4)(B) and Code Sec. 179(f)(4)(C) (the first three rules discussed above concerning the limited ability to carry forward amounts, disallowed under the taxable income limitation, that are attributable to qualified real property), "2013" is substituted for "2011." (Code Sec. 179(f)(4) as amended by 2012 Taxpayer Relief Act §315(d)(2)(A))

> **observation:** Accordingly, under Code Sec. 179(f)(4)(A), in no circumstances can amounts disallowed under the taxable income limitation (see above) attributable to "qualified real property" be carried forward to a tax year beginning after 2013.

> **observation:** The conforming date change to "2013" from "2011" in Code Sec. 179(f)(4)(B) amends Code Sec. 179(f)(4)(B) to state that the amounts not allowed to be carried forward under the rule in Code Sec. 179(f)(4)(A), and that are therefore subject to the treatment provided in Code Sec. 179(f)(4)(B) (see above), are amounts that aren't allowed to be carried forward to tax years beginning after 2013, not 2011.

> **observation:** The conforming date change to "2013" from "2011" in Code Sec. 179(f)(4)(C) means that the amounts attributable to "qualified real property" that are carried forward to the tax year beginning in 2013, and treated, under Code Sec. 179(f)(4)(C), as being attributable to property placed in service on the first day of tax year 2013, can be amounts carried forward from tax years beginning in 2010, 2011 or 2012.

The 2012 Taxpayer Relief Act amends Code Sec. 179(f)(4)(D) (which, as discussed above, provided rules for allocating amounts disallowed under the taxable income limitation in Code Sec. 179(b)(3)(A) between amounts attributable to qualified real property and attributable to other property) to add a sentence providing that the amount determined under Code Sec. 179(b)(3)(A) for the last tax year beginning in 2013 is determined without regard Code Sec. 179(f)(4)(D) (i.e., without regard to the allocation rules that Code Sec. 179(f)(4)(D) provides). (Code Sec. 179(f)(4)(D) as amended by 2012 Taxpayer Relief Act §315(d)(2)(B)(ii))

☙ *observation:* It appears that the addition of the sentence discussed above to Code Sec. 179(f)(4)(D) is intended to clarify that the taxable income limitation for the taxpayer's last tax year beginning in 2013 is not to be reduced by the additional depreciation deductions for that year attributable to the amounts of expensing for qualified real property that can't be carried over to a tax year beginning after 2013.

☙ *sample client letter:* For a client letter on the depreciation and expensing provisions in the 2012 Taxpayer Relief Act, see ¶ 2007.

For the extension, to tax years beginning in 2013, of the treatment of certain computer software as section 179 property and of the ability to revoke a Code Sec. 179 election without consent, see ¶ 803.

☐ **Effective:** Tax years beginning after Dec. 31, 2011 (2012 Taxpayer Relief Act §315(f))) and before Jan. 1, 2014. (Code Sec. 179(b)(1)(B); Code Sec. 179(b)(2)(B))

¶ 802. Increase in first-year depreciation cap for cars that are "qualified property" is extended through Dec. 31, 2013

Code Sec. 168(k)(2)(A)(iv), as amended by 2012 Taxpayer Relief Act §331(a)
Generally effective: Property placed in service after Dec. 31, 2012 and before Jan. 1, 2014
Committee Reports, None

Code Sec. 280F(a) imposes dollar limits on the depreciation deductions (including deductions under the Code Sec. 179 expensing election) that can be claimed with respect to "passenger automobiles," see FTC 2d/FIN ¶ L-10003; USTR ¶ 280F4; TaxDesk ¶ 267,603. The dollar limits are adjusted annually from a base amount to reflect changes in the automobile component of the Consumer Price Index (CPI). Generally, for passenger automobiles placed in service in 2012, the adjusted first-year limit was $3,160, see FTC 2d/FIN ¶ L-10004; USTR ¶ 280F4; TaxDesk ¶ 267,601. For passenger automobiles built on a truck chassis ("qualifying trucks and vans") a different CPI component is used, and for 2012 the adjusted first-year limit was $3,360, see FTC 2d/FIN ¶ L-10004.4; USTR ¶ 280F4; TaxDesk ¶ 267,602.3.

For any passenger automobile that is "qualified property" and which *isn't* subject to a taxpayer election to *decline* the bonus depreciation and AMT depreciation relief otherwise available for "qualified property" under Code Sec. 168(k) (see ¶ 804), the above rules apply, except that the applicable first-year depreciation limit is increased by $8,000 (not indexed for inflation).

(FTC 2d/FIN ¶ L-10000, ¶ L-10004, ¶ L-10004.1A; USTR ¶ 1684.0281, ¶ 280F4; TaxDesk ¶ 267,602.2)

Under pre-2012 Taxpayer Relief Act law, qualified property didn't include property placed in service after Dec. 31, 2012, except for certain aircraft and certain long-production-period property that had, instead, a Dec. 31, 2013 placed-in-service deadline. (FTC 2d/FIN ¶ L-9310, ¶ L-9312, ¶ L-9316 *et seq.*; USTR ¶ 1684.026, ¶ 1684.027; TaxDesk ¶ 269,342, ¶ 269,346 *et seq.*)

> **observation:** The Dec. 31, 2013 deadline provided under pre-2012 Taxpayer Relief Act law for certain aircraft and long-production period property isn't available for passenger automobiles. Clearly, passenger automobiles couldn't qualify as aircraft. Additionally, passenger automobiles couldn't qualify as long-production-period property because one of the requirements for being long-production-period property was that the property either have at least a 10 year MACRS recovery period or be used in the trade or business of transporting persons or property. However, passenger automobiles have a recovery period of only five years, see FTC 2d/FIN ¶ L-8205; USTR ¶ 1684.01; TaxDesk ¶ 266,205, and a vehicle used in the trade or business of transporting persons or property isn't treated as a passenger automobile, see FTC 2d/FIN ¶ L-10003; USTR ¶ 280F4; TaxDesk ¶ 267,603. Thus, under pre-2012 Taxpayer Relief Act law, passenger automobiles placed in service after Dec. 31, 2012 couldn't be qualified property and, thus, couldn't qualify for the $8,000 increase in the first-year depreciation limit.

New Law. The 2012 Taxpayer Relief Act provides that the placed-in-service deadline for "qualified property" is Dec. 31, 2013 (Dec. 31, 2014 for the aircraft and long-production-period property discussed above). (Code Sec. 168(k)(2)(A)(iv) as amended by 2012 Taxpayer Relief Act §331(a)(1)) For the changed placed-in-service deadline as it applies to the availability of bonus depreciation and AMT depreciation relief for "qualified property," see ¶ 804.

> **observation:** Thus, for a passenger automobile that satisfies the other requirements (see below) for qualified property (and isn't subject to the election to decline bonus depreciation and AMT depreciation relief), the 2012 Taxpayer Relief Act extends the placed-in-service deadline for the $8,000 increase in the first-year depreciation limit from Dec, 31, 2012 to Dec. 31, 2013. The Dec. 31, 2014 deadline that applies to the aircraft and long-production-period property discussed above isn't available for passenger automobiles for the reasons discussed above concerning the Dec. 31, 2013 deadline under pre-2012 Taxpayer Relief Act law.

☞ observation: Property is "qualified property" if it satisfies the definitional requirements and isn't subject to certain ineligibility rules, see ¶ 804. As applied to passenger automobiles, the effect of these requirements and ineligibility rules is that in most instances a passenger automobile that satisfies the Dec. 31, 2013 placed-in-service deadline will be eligible for the $8,000 increase in the first-year depreciation limit if (1) the automobile's original use begins with the taxpayer after Dec. 31, 2007 (2) the automobile is predominantly used by the taxpayer in his business and (3) the automobile is acquired by the taxpayer after Dec. 31, 2007.

☞ illustration (1): On Oct. 15, 2013, T, a calendar year taxpayer, places a new passenger automobile into service in his business. Assume that the vehicle is "qualified property" (and an election to decline bonus depreciation and AMT depreciation relief doesn't apply to the vehicle). T is allowed first-year depreciation for 2013 of no more than $11,160 (the $3,160 amount discussed above—assuming, for illustration purposes, that it remains the same for 2013—plus $8,000).

☞ illustration (2): The facts are the same as in illustration (1) except that the passenger automobile that T places into service is a "qualifying truck or van" (see above). T is allowed first-year depreciation for 2013 of no more than $11,360 (the $3,360 amount discussed above—assuming, for illustration purposes, that it remains the same for 2013— plus $8,000).

☞ illustration (3): The facts are the same as in illustration (1), except that in 2013 T uses the passenger automobile 80% for business and 20% for personal activities. Because the passenger auto depreciation limits are proportionally reduced to the extent that a vehicle isn't exclusively used in business, see FTC 2d/FIN ¶ L-10004; USTR ¶ 280F4; TaxDesk ¶ 267,601, T is allowed first-year depreciation for 2013 of no more than $8,928 (80% × $11,160).

☐ **Effective:** Property placed in service after Dec. 31, 2012 in tax years ending after Dec. 31, 2012 (2012 Taxpayer Relief Act §331(f)) and before Jan. 1, 2014 (Code Sec. 168(k)(2)(A)(iv))

¶ 803. Revocation of Code Sec. 179 election without IRS consent, and eligibility of software for election, are extended to include tax years beginning in 2013

Code Sec. 179(c)(2), as amended by 2012 Taxpayer Relief Act §315(c)
Code Sec. 179(d)(1)(A)(ii), as amended by 2012 Taxpayer Relief Act §315(b)
Generally effective: Tax years beginning after Dec. 31, 2011 and before Jan. 1, 2014
Committee Reports, None

Subject to certain limitations, taxpayers can elect to treat the cost of any section 179 property placed in service during the tax year as an expense which is not chargeable to capital account, and, thus, allowed as a deduction for the tax year in which the section 179 property is placed in service, see FTC 2d/FIN ¶ L-9900 *et seq.*; USTR ¶ 1794 *et seq.*; TaxDesk ¶ 268,400 *et seq.* and the discussion at ¶ 801.

The election must specify the items of qualifying property, and the portion of the cost of each of those items, to which the election applies, see FTC 2d/FIN ¶ L-9932; USTR ¶ 1794.04; TaxDesk ¶ 268,408.

Under pre-2012 Taxpayer Relief Act law, the Code Sec. 179 expense election, and any "specification" contained in the election (i.e., both the selected specific item of section 179 property and the selected dollar amount allocable to the specific item of property), could not be revoked without IRS consent. However, any Code Sec. 179 expense election and any specification (as defined above) could be irrevocably revoked by the taxpayer without IRS consent for any property for any tax year beginning after 2002 and before *2013*. (FTC 2d/FIN ¶ L-9900, ¶ L-9933; USTR ¶ 1794.04; TaxDesk ¶ 268,409)

Under pre-2012 Taxpayer Relief Act law, "qualifying property" for purposes of the Code Sec. 179 expensing election was (1) depreciable tangible personal property purchased for use in the active conduct of a trade or business and (2) if placed in service in a tax year beginning after 2002 and before *2013*, "off-the-shelf" computer software purchased for use in the active conduct of a trade or business. (FTC 2d/FIN ¶ L-9900, ¶ L-9922; USTR ¶ 1794.02; TaxDesk ¶ 268,424)

New Law. Under the 2012 Taxpayer Relief Act, a taxpayer's ability to revoke a Code Sec. 179 election (and any specification contained in an election) without IRS consent (see above) applies to any tax year beginning after 2002 and before *2014*. (Code Sec. 179(c)(2) as amended by 2012 Taxpayer Relief Act §315(c))

The 2012 Taxpayer Relief Act also provides that computer software (as described above) is qualifying property for purposes of the Code Sec. 179 election if it is placed in service in a tax year beginning after 2002 and before *2014*. (Code Sec. 179(d)(1)(A)(ii) as amended by 2012 Taxpayer Relief Act §315(b))

For increases in the amount of the Code Sec. 179 deduction limitation and beginning-of-phaseout amount, and the availability of the Code Sec. 179 election for qualified real property, for tax years beginning in 2012 and 2013, see ¶ 801.

☐ **Effective:** Tax years beginning after Dec. 31, 2011 (2012 Taxpayer Relief Act §315(f))) (see the observation below) and before Jan. 1, 2014. (Code Sec. 179(c)(2); Code Sec. 179(d)(1)(A)(ii))

> ⓇⒾⒶ*observation:* The tax-years-beginning-after-Dec. 31, 2011 effective date in section 315(f) of the 2012 Taxpayer Relief Act (above) applies to section 315 as a whole. However, while that effective date is consistent with the changes made by section 315 that are discussed at ¶ 801 (i.e., changes concerning deduction limitations, beginning-of-phase-out amount and qualifying real property that apply to tax years beginning in both 2012 and 2013), the date is earlier than it needs to be for the changes concerning computer software and election revocation discussed above. That is so because the changes concerning computer software and election revocation affect only tax years beginning in 2013.

¶ 804. Bonus depreciation and AMT depreciation relief are extended one year to apply to property placed in service before Jan. 1, 2014 (Jan. 1, 2015 for certain other property)

Code Sec. 168(k)(2)(A)(iii), as amended by 2012 Taxpayer Relief Act §331(a)(2)
Code Sec. 168(k)(2)(A)(iv), as amended by 2012 Taxpayer Relief Act §331(a)(1)
Code Sec. 168(k)(2)(A)(iv), as amended by 2012 Taxpayer Relief Act §331(a)(2)
Code Sec. 168(k)(2)(B)(ii), as amended by 2012 Taxpayer Relief Act §331(a)(2)
Code Sec. 168(k)(2)(E)(i), as amended by 2012 Taxpayer Relief Act §331(a)(2)
Generally effective: Property placed in service after Dec. 31, 2012 and before Jan. 1, 2014
Committee Reports, None

Under Code Sec. 168(k), a taxpayer that owns "qualified property" (see below) is, generally, allowed 50% depreciation (bonus depreciation) in the year that the property is placed in service (with corresponding reductions in basis and, thus, reductions of the regular depreciation deductions otherwise allowed in the placed-in-service year and in later years), see FTC 2d/FIN ¶ L-9310 *et seq.*; USTR ¶ 1684.025 *et seq.*; TaxDesk ¶ 269,341 *et seq.* However, 100% bonus depreciation, (resulting in temporary 100% expensing) was available, instead of 50% bonus depreciation, for qualifying property that, generally, was placed in service and acquired after Sept. 8, 2010 and before Jan. 1, 2012, see FTC 2d/FIN ¶ L-9311.2; USTR ¶ 1684.0251; TaxDesk ¶ 269,341.2.

Additionally, qualified property is exempt from the alternative minimum tax (AMT) depreciation adjustment, see FTC 2d/FIN ¶ A-8221; USTR ¶ 1684.029; TaxDesk ¶ 696,514, which is the adjustment that requires that certain property depreciated on the 200% declining balance method for regular income tax purposes must be depreciated on the 150% declining balance method for AMT purposes, see FTC 2d/FIN ¶ A-8220; USTR ¶ 564.01; TaxDesk ¶ 696,513.

Also, qualified property is allowed an $8,000 increase in the otherwise-applicable dollar limit on first-year depreciation for passenger cars, see FTC 2d/FIN ¶ L-10004.1A; USTR ¶s 1684.0281, 280F4; TaxDesk ¶ 267,602.2.

The rules discussed above for qualified property don't apply to classes of property for which, under Code Sec. 168(k)(2)(D)(iii), the taxpayer elects to not apply Code Sec. 168(k) (an "election-out"), see FTC 2d/FIN ¶ L-9318; USTR ¶ 1684.0291; TaxDesk ¶ 269,348.

The following are the requirements for qualified property under Code Sec. 168(k)(2):

. . . the property must be of a qualifying type; i.e., generally, most machinery, equipment or other tangible personal property; most computer software; and certain leasehold improvements;

. . . the property must not be property that must be depreciated under the alternative depreciation system;

. . . the property must not be the subject of certain disqualifying transactions involving users other than the taxpayer or persons related to the taxpayer or the other users;

. . . the property's original use generally must begin with the taxpayer after Dec. 31, 2007;

. . . the property must meet a timely-placed-in-service requirement (see below); and

. . . the property must meet a timely acquisition requirement (see below), see FTC 2d/FIN ¶ L-9312 *et seq.*; USTR ¶ 1684.026 *et seq.*; TaxDesk ¶ 269,342 *et seq.*

Under pre-2012 Taxpayer Relief Act law, the timely-placed-in-service requirement was that the property had to be placed in service by the taxpayer before Jan. 1, 2013, except for certain aircraft and certain long-production-period property that had to be placed in service before Jan. 1, 2014. (FTC 2d/FIN ¶ L-9310, ¶ L-9312, ¶ L-9316 *et seq.*; USTR ¶ 1684.026,

¶ 1684.027; TaxDesk ¶ 269,342, ¶ 269,346 *et seq.*) However, long-production-period property could qualify for the Dec. 31, 2013 placed-in-service deadline only to the extent of adjusted basis attributable to manufacture, construction or production before Jan. 1, 2013 (the progress expenditure rule). (FTC 2d/FIN ¶ L-9310, ¶ L-9316.1; USTR ¶ 1684.027; TaxDesk ¶ 269,346.1)

Under pre-2012 Taxpayer Relief Act law, the timely acquisition requirement was satisfied if the property was acquired by the taxpayer either (1) after Dec. 31, 2007 and before Jan. 1, 2013, but only if no written binding contract for the acquisition was in effect before Jan. 1, 2008, or (2) under a written binding contract entered into after Dec. 31, 2007 and before Jan. 1, 2013. For a taxpayer manufacturing, constructing or producing property for its own use, the timely acquisition requirement was treated as met if the taxpayer began the manufacture, construction or production after Dec. 31, 2007 and before Jan. 1, 2013. (FTC 2d/FIN ¶ L-9310, ¶ L-9312, ¶ L-9315 *et seq.*; USTR ¶ 1684.026; TaxDesk ¶ 269,342, ¶ 269,345 *et seq.*)

New Law.

> **⚫/*caution:*** The 2012 Taxpayer Relief Act extends the availability of 50% bonus depreciation, but not the availability of 100% bonus depreciation (see above).

The 2012 Taxpayer Relief Act changes the timely-placed-in-service requirement (above) to provide that qualified property has to be placed in service by the taxpayer before *Jan. 1, 2014*, except that the aircraft and long-production-period property discussed above have to be placed in service before *Jan. 1, 2015*. (Code Sec. 168(k)(2)(A)(iv) as amended by 2012 Taxpayer Relief Act §331(a)(1); Code Sec. 168(k)(2)(A)(iv) as amended by 2012 Taxpayer Relief Act §331(a)(2))

> **⚫/*observation:*** In addition to extending the eligibility period for bonus depreciation, the extension of the placed-in-service deadline for qualified property also extends the eligibility period for obtaining the exemption, discussed above, from the AMT depreciation adjustment. For the extension of eligibility for the $8,000 increase in the first-year depreciation limit for passenger automobiles (above), see ¶ 802.

Also, the 2012 Taxpayer Relief Act changes the progress expenditure rule to provide that long-production-period property can qualify for the Dec. 31, 2014 placed-in-service deadline only to the extent of adjusted basis attributable to manufacture, construction or production before *Jan. 1, 2014*. (Code Sec. 168(k)(2)(B)(ii) as amended by 2012 Taxpayer Relief Act §331(a)(2))

🔖 *observation:* The change to the progress expenditure rule conforms the rule to the changed placed-in-service deadline, discussed above, for long-production-period property.

Changes to the timely-acquisition rules.   Under the 2012 Taxpayer Relief Act, the timely acquisition requirement is satisfied if the property is acquired by the taxpayer either (1) after Dec. 31, 2007 and before *Jan. 1, 2014,* but only if no written binding contract for the acquisition was in effect before Jan. 1, 2008, or (2) under a written binding contract entered into after Dec. 31, 2007 and *before Jan. 1, 2014.* (Code Sec. 168(k)(2)(A)(iii) as amended by 2012 Taxpayer Relief Act §331(a)(2)) For a taxpayer manufacturing, constructing or producing property for its own use, the timely acquisition requirement is treated as met if the taxpayer began the manufacture, construction or production after Dec. 31, 2007 and *before Jan. 1, 2014.* (Code Sec. 168(k)(2)(E)(i) as amended by 2012 Taxpayer Relief Act §331(a)(2))

🔖 *sample client letter:* For a client letter on the depreciation and expensing provisions in the 2012 Taxpayer Relief Act, see ¶ 2007.

☐ **Effective:** Property placed in service after Dec. 31, 2012 in tax years ending after Dec. 31, 2012 (2012 Taxpayer Relief Act §331(f)) and before Jan. 1, 2014 (before Jan. 1, 2015 for the aircraft and long-term production-period property discussed above). (Code Sec. 168(k)(2)(A)(iv))

¶ 805. Additional round of trading bonus and accelerated depreciation for deferred credits is provided

Code Sec. 168(k)(2)(A)(iv), as amended by 2012 Taxpayer Relief Act §331(a)
Code Sec. 168(k)(4)(D)(iii)(II), as amended by 2012 Taxpayer Relief Act §331(c)(1)
Code Sec. 168(k)(4)(J), as amended by 2012 Taxpayer Relief Act §331(c)(2)
Generally effective: Property placed in service after Dec. 31, 2012 and before Jan. 1, 2014
Committee Reports, None

A corporation can, under an election (a Code Sec. 168(k)(4) election) that is made for its first tax year ending after Mar. 31, 2008 and later years (the March 2008 election), for its first tax year ending after Dec. 31, 2008 and later years (the December 2008 election), or for its first tax year ending after Dec. 31, 2010 and later years (the December 2010 election) forego bonus and accelerated depreciation for "eligible qualified property" (see below) in exchange for the present allowance, as refundable tax credits, of otherwise-deferred "pre-2006 credits" (see below). (FTC 2d/FIN ¶ L-15200, ¶ L-15213 *et seq.*; USTR ¶ 1684.0293; TaxDesk ¶ 380,511 *et seq.*)

The deferred "pre-2006 credits" for which bonus and accelerated depreciation can be exchanged are (1) credits for alternative minimum tax (AMT) paid that is attributable to tax years beginning before 2006 and (2) generally only for eligible qualified property placed in service before Jan. 1, 2011, research credits from tax years beginning before 2006. (FTC 2d/FIN ¶ L-15200, ¶ L-15213.3, ¶ L-15216.1; USTR ¶ 1684.0293; TaxDesk ¶ 380,512, ¶ 380,520.1)

The amount of otherwise-deferred pre-2006 credits presently allowed for a tax year is determined by the bonus depreciation amount for the tax year, which is limited to 20% of the difference between (1) depreciation allowed for "eligible qualified property" if bonus depreciation is allowed and (2) depreciation allowed for "eligible qualified property" if bonus depreciation isn't allowed. Additionally, the bonus depreciation amount for a tax year can't exceed the "maximum amount," which is the lesser of $30 million or 6% of the taxpayer's pre-2006 credits (the maximum increase amount) decreased by the bonus depreciation amount for all preceding tax years, see FTC 2d/FIN ¶ L-15213.2; USTR ¶ 1684.0293; TaxDesk ¶ 380,512.

A separate bonus depreciation amount (see above), maximum amount (see above) and maximum increase amount (see above) are computed and applied for eligible qualified property that is extension property (generally, property placed in service during 2009), eligible qualified property that is round 2 extension property (generally, property placed in service after Dec. 31, 2010 and before Jan. 1, 2013) and eligible qualified property that isn't extension property or round 2 extension property, see FTC 2d/FIN ¶s L-15213.2C, L-15216.1; USTR ¶ 1684.0293; TaxDesk ¶s 380,512.2, 380,520.2.

"Eligible qualified property" is, generally, defined by reference to "qualified property" as defined for bonus depreciation purposes, but with differences in some, but not all, relevant dates, see FTC 2d/FIN ¶s L-9312 *et seq.*, L-15213.4; USTR ¶s 1684.026 *et seq.*, 1684.0293; TaxDesk ¶s 268,342 *et seq.*, 380,513.

Under pre-2012 Taxpayer Relief Act law, neither qualified property nor eligible qualified property included property placed in service after Dec. 31, 2012, except for certain aircraft and certain long-production-period property that had, instead, a Dec. 31, 2013 placed-in-service deadline. (FTC 2d/FIN ¶ L-9310, ¶ L-9312, ¶ L-9316 *et seq.*, ¶ L-15200, ¶ L-15213.4; USTR ¶ 1684.026, ¶ 1684.027, ¶ 1684.0293; TaxDesk ¶ 269,342, ¶ 269,346 *et seq.*, ¶ 380,513)

In the "progress expenditure rule" that is related to the placed-in-service rules for certain long-production-period property, long-production-period property could qualify for the Dec. 31, 2013 placed-in-service deadline only to the extent of adjusted basis attributable to manufacture, construction or production before Jan. 1, 2013. (FTC 2d/FIN ¶ L-9310, ¶ L-9316.1, ¶ L-15200, ¶ L-15213.4; USTR ¶ 1684.027, ¶ 1684.0293; TaxDesk ¶ 269,346.1, ¶ 380,513)

New Law. The 2012 Taxpayer Relief Act changes:

(1) the placed-in-service deadline (above) for "qualified property" (above) to Dec. 31, 2013, but, for the aircraft and long-production-period property dis-

cussed above, to Dec. 31, 2014, (Code Sec. 168(k)(2)(A)(iv) as amended by 2012 Taxpayer Relief Act §331(a))

(2) the progress expenditure rule (above) for eligible qualified property (above) to provide that long-production-period property can qualify for the Dec. 31, 2013 placed-in-service deadline to the extent of adjusted basis attributable to manufacture, construction or production before *Jan. 1, 2014.* (Code Sec. 168(k)(4)(D)(iii)(II) as amended by 2012 Taxpayer Relief Act §331(c)(1))

Additionally, the 2012 Taxpayer Relief Act defines "round 3 extension property" as property which is "eligible qualified property" solely because of the extension of the application of the special allowance under Code Sec. 168(k)(1) (i.e., bonus depreciation) under the amendments made by 2012 Taxpayer Relief Act §331(a) (see item (1) above), and the application of that extension to the Code Sec. 168(k)(4) election by 2012 Taxpayer Relief Act §331(c)(1) (see item (2) above). (Code Sec. 168(k)(4)(J)(iv) as amended by 2012 Taxpayer Relief Act §331(c)(2))

> *observation:* One effect of the above changes is to provide an additional round of Code Sec. 168(k)(4) elections to cover property placed in service after Dec. 31, 2012 and before Jan. 1, 2014 (and after Dec. 31, 2013 and before Jan. 1, 2015 for the aircraft discussed above and, to the extent attributable to pre-2014 progress expenditures, the long-production period property discussed above). The change also has the effect of defining round 3 extension property, in substance, as property to which the additional round applies. However, as discussed below under **"Option to decline round 3 extension,"** taxpayers can decline the additional round. For the changed placed-in-service deadlines and progress expenditure rule that apply to the availability of bonus depreciation and AMT depreciation relief for "qualified property," see ¶ 804.

Research credits excluded for round 3 extension property. For round 3 extension property, the Code Sec. 168(k)(4) election is applied without regard to: (Code Sec. 168(k)(4)(J)(i))

. . . the limitation described in Code Sec. 168(k)(4)(B)(i) (the limitation, provided by Code Sec. 38(c) on presently allowable business credits, see FTC 2d/FIN ¶ L-15202; USTR ¶ 384.02; TaxDesk ¶ 380,502) and, (Code Sec. 168(k)(4)(J)(i)(I))

. . . the business credit increase amount under Code Sec. 168(k)(4)(E)(iii) (generally, the amount by which presently allowable research credits are increased by a Code Sec. 168(k)(4) election, see FTC 2d/FIN ¶ L-15213.3; USTR ¶ 1684.0293; TaxDesk ¶ 380,512). (Code Sec. 168(k)(4)(J)(i)(II))

> *observation:* Thus, for round 3 extension property, the "pre-2006 credits" for which bonus and accelerated depreciation can be exchanged don't include the research credits from tax years beginning before 2006

(see above). Instead, the "pre-2006 credits" for which bonus and accelerated depreciation can be exchanged include only the credits for AMT paid that is attributable to tax years beginning before 2006 (see above).

Separate computations for round 3 extension property. If a taxpayer doesn't make the election (discussed below) to decline applying the Code Sec. 168(k)(4) election to round 3 extension property, a bonus depreciation amount (see above), maximum amount (see above) and maximum increase amount (see above) must be computed and applied to eligible qualified property that is round 3 extension property. (Code Sec. 168(k)(4)(J)(ii)(II)) The bonus depreciation amount, maximum amount and maximum increase amount are computed separately with respect to eligible qualified property that isn't round 3 extension property. (Code Sec. 168(k)(4)(J)(ii))

> **observation:** Thus, in computing the maximum amount, the maximum increase amount for round 3 extension property is reduced by bonus depreciation amounts for preceding tax years only with respect to round 3 extension property. Accordingly, a separate computation may permit a taxpayer to be allowed $30 million of refundable credits under the Code Sec. 168(k)(4) election as applicable to round 3 extension property, in addition to any credits that were allowed under pre-2012 Taxpayer Relief Act law. Thus, for some taxpayers, the separate computation might result in a cumulative allowance of as much as $120 million of refundable credits.

Option to decline round 3 extension. A taxpayer that made the Code Sec. 168(k)(4) election for its first tax year ending after Mar. 31, 2008 (the March 2008 election described above), for its first tax year ending after Dec. 31, 2008 (the December 2008 election described above), *or* for its first tax year ending after Dec. 31, 2010 (the December 2010 election described above) is allowed to elect to not have Code Sec. 168(k)(4) apply to "round 3 extension property." (Code Sec. 168(k)(4)(J)(ii); Code Sec. 168(k)(4)(J)(ii)(I))

> **observation:** Thus, a taxpayer that made the March 2008 election, the December 2008 election or the December 2010 election has the option of not applying the election to eligible qualified property placed in service before Jan. 1, 2014 and after Dec. 31, 2012 (before Jan. 1, 2015 and after Dec. 31, 2012 if the property was certain aircraft (see above) or, to the extent attributable to pre-2014 progress expenditures, long-production-period property (see above).

> **observation:** To decide whether to decline the extension of the election, the taxpayer must decide whether the benefits of bonus and accelerated depreciation for "round 3 extension property" outweigh the cost of not being presently allowed the otherwise-deferred credits the present allowance of which would be attributable to bonus depreciation amounts (see above) attributable to the round 3 extension property.

Generally, the decision will, at the least, (1) require predictions of (a) whether, and in what amounts, the taxpayer will have regular tax or AMT liabilities in future years and (b) the taxpayer's marginal tax rates in future years and (2) require that the taxpayer do a "present value" analysis that compares (a) the value of the credits if allowed immediately against the value of the credits if allowed in future years and (b) the value of depreciation deductions allowed under an accelerated method that also includes bonus depreciation against the value of depreciation deductions allowed under a straight-line method with no bonus depreciation.

observation: Code Sec. 168(k)(4)(J)(ii)(I) doesn't specify when or how the make the election not to apply Code Sec. 168(k)(4) to extension property. Presumably, IRS will provide guidance.

Non-previously electing taxpayers. If a taxpayer didn't make the March 2008 election (see above), *nor* the December 2008 election (see above), *nor* the December 2010 election: (Code Sec. 168(k)(4)(J)(iii))

... that taxpayer is allowed to make the Code Sec. 168(k)(4) election for its first tax year ending after Dec. 31, 2012, and each later tax year, and (Code Sec. 168(k)(4)(J)(iii)(I))

... if the taxpayer makes the above election, the election applies only to eligible qualified property that is round 3 extension property. (Code Sec. 168(k)(4)(J)(iii)(II))

☐ **Effective:** Property placed in service after Dec. 31, 2012 in tax years ending after Dec. 31, 2012 (2012 Taxpayer Relief Act §331(f)) and before Jan. 1, 2014 (before Jan. 1, 2015 for the aircraft and long-production-period property discussed above). (Code Sec. 168(k)(2)(A)(iv))

¶ 806. Disregard of certain bonus depreciation in applying the percentage of completion method is allowed for an additional time period

Code Sec. 460(c)(6)(B)(ii), as amended by 2012 Taxpayer Relief Act §331(b)
Generally effective: Property placed in service after Dec. 31, 2012 and before Jan. 1, 2014
Committee Reports, None

Under the percentage of completion method of accounting (PCM) for a long term contract, the taxpayer includes in income the percentage of the total estimated revenue from the contract that corresponds to the "completion percentage." The completion percentage is determined by comparing costs allocated to the contract and incurred before the close of the tax year with the estimated total contract costs. The completion percentage is then multiplied by the total estimated revenue to obtain the cumulative gross receipts. The gross receipts for the current year are then determined by subtracting the cumulative gross receipts for the immediately preceding tax year. Thus, as the taxpayer incurs allocable contract costs, it includes the contract price in gross income, see FTC 2d/FIN ¶ G-3123; USTR ¶ 4604.001; TaxDesk ¶ 445,002.

Costs are allocated to a contract under a regular PCM method or under an alternative simplified method. Under both methods, depreciation, amortization and cost recovery allowances on equipment and facilities used to perform the contract are taken into account as costs under the contract, see FTC 2d/FIN ¶s G-3125.1, G-3138, G-3142, G-3143, G-3245.4; USTR ¶ 4604.001; TaxDesk ¶s 445,016, 445,017, 445,023, 456,004.

> **observation:** Thus, an increased depreciation deduction for a tax year will increase the percentage of completion for that year and the amount of gross receipts for the year.

Under Code Sec. 168(k), a taxpayer that owns "qualified property," see FTC 2d/FIN ¶ L-9312 *et seq.*; USTR ¶ 1684.026 *et seq.*; TaxDesk ¶ 269,342 *et seq.*, is, generally, allowed a 50% depreciation deduction (bonus depreciation) in the year that the property is placed in service (with corresponding reductions in basis and, thus, reductions of the regular depreciation deductions otherwise allowed in the placed-in-service year and in later years), see FTC 2d/FIN ¶ L-9310; USTR ¶ 1684.025; TaxDesk ¶ 269,341.

For purposes of determining the completion percentage (see above), bonus depreciation, with respect to certain qualified property, isn't taken into account. The qualified property to which the exclusion applies is property that (1) has an MACRS recovery period of seven years or less (the recovery period requirement) and (2) is placed in service during a required period (the timing requirement). Under pre-2012 Taxpayer Relief Act law, the required placed-in-service period was after Dec. 31, 2009 and before Jan. 1, 2011 (after Dec. 31, 2009 and before Jan. 1, 2012 for property described in Code Sec. 168(k)(2)(B); i.e., certain property with a long production period, see FTC 2d/FIN ¶ L-9316.1; USTR ¶ 1684.027; TaxDesk ¶ 269,346.1). (FTC 2d/FIN ¶ G-3143; USTR ¶ 4604.001)

New Law. The 2012 Taxpayer Relief Act adds an additional period of time (see below) during which qualified property satisfies the timing requirement discussed above. The additional period is the period after Dec. 31, 2012 and before Jan. 1, 2014 (after Dec. 31, 2012 and before Jan. 1, 2015 for property described in Code Sec. 168(k)(2)(B), see above). (Code Sec. 460(c)(6)(B)(ii) as amended by 2012 Taxpayer Relief Act §331(b))

☐ **Effective:** Property placed in service after Dec. 31, 2012 in tax years ending after Dec. 31, 2012 (2012 Taxpayer Relief Act §331(f)) and before Jan. 1, 2014 (before Jan. 1, 2015 for property described in Code Sec. 168(k)(2)(B), see above). (Code Sec. 460(c)(6)(B)(ii))

¶ 807. 15-year MACRS depreciation for certain building improvements and restaurants is extended to apply to property placed in service before Jan. 1, 2014

Code Sec. 168(e)(3)(E)(iv), as amended by 2012 Taxpayer Relief Act §311(a)

Code Sec. 168(e)(3)(E)(v), as amended by 2012 Taxpayer Relief Act §311(a)

Code Sec. 168(e)(3)(E)(ix), as amended by 2012 Taxpayer Relief Act §311(a)

Generally effective: Property placed in service after Dec. 31, 2011 and before Jan. 1, 2014

Committee Reports, None

The rules that in most situations assign a recovery period (i.e., depreciation period) to the various types of MACRS property are known as the General Depreciation System (GDS), see FTC 2d/FIN ¶ L-8800; USTR ¶ 1684; TaxDesk ¶ 266,201.

Assets that are nonresidential real property—generally, nonresidential buildings and their structural components—are depreciated on the straight-line method, see FTC 2d/FIN ¶ L-8917; USTR ¶ 1684.02; TaxDesk ¶ 267,018, over a 39-year GDS recovery period, see FTC 2d/FIN ¶ L-8210; USTR ¶ 1684.02; TaxDesk ¶ 266,211.

However, under pre-2012 Taxpayer Relief Act law, a building improvement that was "qualified leasehold improvement property" placed in service before Jan. 1, 2012 was depreciated on the straight-line method, see FTC 2d/FIN ¶ L-8917; USTR ¶ 1684.02; TaxDesk ¶ 267,018, over a 15-year GDS recovery period. (FTC 2d/FIN ¶ L-8200, ¶ L-8208, ¶ L-8208.1; USTR ¶ 1684.02; TaxDesk ¶ 266,208, ¶ 266,208.1).

Similarly, a building improvement that was "qualified retail improvement property" placed in service before Jan. 1, 2012 was depreciated on the straight-line method, see FTC 2d/FIN ¶ L-8917; USTR ¶ 1684.02; TaxDesk ¶ 267,018, over a 15-year GDS recovery period. (FTC 2d/FIN ¶ L-8200, ¶ L-8208, ¶ L-8208.5; USTR ¶ 1684.02; TaxDesk ¶ 266,208, ¶ 266,208.5)

Also, a building or a building improvement that was "qualified restaurant property" placed in service before Jan. 1, 2012 was depreciated on the straight-line method, see FTC 2d/FIN ¶ L-8917; USTR ¶ 1684.02; TaxDesk ¶ 267,018, over a 15-year GDS recovery period. (FTC 2d/FIN ¶ L-8200, ¶ L-8208, ¶ L-8208.2; USTR ¶ 1684.02; TaxDesk ¶ 266,208, ¶ 266,208.2)

Taxpayers are sometimes required to, or may elect to, depreciate MACRS property under the alternative depreciation system (ADS) instead of under the GDS, see FTC 2d/FIN ¶ L-9401; USTR ¶ 1684.03; TaxDesk ¶ 267,501. Nonresidential real property is depreciated over a 40-year recovery period for ADS purposes, see FTC 2d/FIN ¶ L-9403; USTR ¶ 1684.03; TaxDesk ¶ 267,503.

However, under pre-2012 Taxpayer Relief Act law, qualified leasehold improvement property, qualified retail improvement property and qualified restaurant property placed in service before Jan. 1, 2012 were depreciated over a 39-year recovery period for ADS purposes. (FTC 2d/FIN ¶ L-9400, ¶ L-9403; USTR ¶ 1684.03; TaxDesk ¶ 267,503)

New Law. The 2012 Taxpayer Relief Act extends the rules discussed above for qualified leasehold improvement property (Code Sec. 168(e)(3)(E)(iv) as amended by 2012 Taxpayer Relief Act §311(a)), qualified retail improvement property (Code Sec. 168(e)(3)(E)(ix)), and qualified restaurant property (Code Sec. 168(e)(3)(E)(v)) for two years by providing that the three types of property must be placed in service by Jan. 1, 2014. (Code Sec. 168(e)(3)(E))

> **⚡observation:** Thus, the 2012 Taxpayer Relief Act retroactively restores and extends for two years the period in which qualifying property can be placed in service to be eligible for the accelerated depreciation rules discussed above.

> **⚡observation:** The 15-year GDS recovery period and 39-year ADS recovery period continue in effect for qualified leasehold improvement property, qualified retail improvement property and qualified restaurant property placed in service before Jan. 1, 2014, but a 39-year GDS recovery period and 40-year ADS recovery period will apply to qualified leasehold improvement property, qualified retail improvement property and qualified restaurant property placed in service after Dec. 31, 2013.

☐ **Effective:** Property placed in service after Dec. 31, 2011 (2012 Taxpayer Relief Act §311(b)) and before Jan. 1, 2014. (Code Sec. 168(e)(3)(E))

¶ 808. Expensing rules for qualified film and television productions are retroactively extended for two years to productions beginning before Jan. 1, 2014

Code Sec. 181(f), as amended by 2012 Taxpayer Relief Act §317(a)
Generally effective: Productions beginning after Dec. 31, 2011 and before
  Jan. 1, 2014
Committee Reports, None

Under pre-2012 Taxpayer Relief Act law, taxpayers could have elected to expense certain costs of qualified film and television productions (see below), rather than capitalizing those costs, for productions beginning before Jan. 1, 2012. (FTC 2d/FIN ¶ L-3140, ¶ L-3141; USTR ¶ 1814; TaxDesk ¶ 269,451) For a production to be a qualified production and therefore eligible for the expensing election, 75% of the total compensation of the production must be "qualified compensation" (defined below). The production is a qualified production if it is property defined in Code Sec. 168(f)(3) (i.e., any motion picture or film or videotape, see FTC 2d/FIN ¶s L-3142, L-8201; USTR ¶s 1684, 1814.07; TaxDesk ¶ 269,452). For a television series, each episode is treated as a separate production and only the first 44 episodes of the series are taken into account for purposes of the expensing election (see FTC 2d/FIN ¶ L-3142; USTR ¶ 1814.07; TaxDesk ¶ 269,452).

Qualified compensation is compensation for services performed in the U.S. by actors, production personnel, directors, and producers (see FTC 2d/FIN ¶ L-3143; USTR ¶ 1814.09; TaxDesk ¶ 269,452).

New Law. The 2012 Taxpayer Relief Act provides that the Code Sec. 181 expensing election does not apply to qualified film and television productions commencing after Dec. 31, 2013. (Code Sec. 181(f) as amended by 2012 Taxpayer Relief Act §317(a))

> *observation:* Thus, the expensing election is retroactively restored and extended for two years and applies to productions beginning before Jan. 1, 2014.

> *illustration (1):* Taxpayer A begins production on a film on Dec. 31, 2013. Under pre-2012 Taxpayer Relief Act law, the expensing election would not have been available. Under 2012 Taxpayer Relief Act law, Taxpayer A can make the election, provided all the requirements are met for a qualified film described above, because production begins before Jan. 1, 2014.

> *observation:* Taxpayer A produces a television series. Since each episode is treated as a separate production, episodes that began production after Dec. 31, 2013 presumably would not be eligible for the expensing election.

> *illustration (2):* Taxpayer B began production of a qualified motion picture during 2012. Because the expensing election is retroactively extended by the 2012 Taxpayer Relief Act, B can make the election. An amended return might have to be filed.

☐ **Effective:** Productions beginning after Dec. 31, 2011 (2012 Taxpayer Relief Act §317(b)) and before Jan. 1, 2014. (Code Sec. 181(f))

¶ 809. 7-year recovery period for motorsports entertainment complexes extended to facilities placed in service through 2013

Code Sec. 168(i)(15)(D), as amended by 2012 Taxpayer Relief Act §312(a)
Generally effective: Property placed in service after Dec. 31, 2011 and
* before Jan. 1, 2014*
Committee Reports, None

Motorsports entertainment complexes placed in service after Oct. 22, 2004 and before Jan. 1, 2012 are treated as 7-year modified accelerated cost recovery system (MACRS) property. They are not assigned to a specific asset class. Rather, the 2004 Jobs Act (Sec. 704, PL 108-357, 10/22/2004) provided for a 7-year modified accelerated cost recovery period for qualifying facilities placed in service before Dec. 31, 2007. The 2008 Emergency Economic Stabilization Act (Sec. 317(b)DivC, PL 110-343, 10/3/2008) retroactively extended the recovery period to property placed in service after Dec. 31, 2007 and before Jan. 1, 2010, and the 2010 Tax Relief Act (Sec. 738(a), PL 111-312, 12/17/2010) further retroactively extended the recovery period to property placed in service after Dec. 31, 2009 and before Jan. 1, 2012. (FTC 2d/FIN ¶ L-8200, ¶ L-8206, ¶ L-8206.3; USTR ¶ 1684.01; TaxDesk ¶ 266,206)

> **🅁🄸🄰** *observation:* MACRS recovery periods vary with types of property. If the statute did not assign a 7-year recovery period to motorsports entertainment complexes, nonresidential real property of a racetrack would be recoverable under the straight-line method over a period of 39 years and land improvements would be recoverable over 15 years. Property put in use by theme and amusement parks is generally assigned a 7-year recovery period within Asset Class 80.0 of Rev Proc 87-56, but the 2004 Jobs Act provided that racetrack facilities placed in service *after Oct. 22, 2004* are not treated as theme and amusement facilities (Sec. 704(c)(2), PL 108-357, 10/22/2004), see FTC 2d/FIN ¶s L-8208, L-8203, L-8210; USTR ¶s 1684.01, 1684.02; TaxDesk ¶s 266,208, 266,211.

A motorsports entertainment complex is a racing track facility permanently situated on land that hosts for admission at least one public racing event for automobiles, trucks, or motorcycles within 36 months after it is placed in service. Eligible property includes certain land improvements and ancillary facilities (e.g., parking lots, sidewalks, fences), support facilities (e.g., food and beverage retailing, souvenir vending), and appurtenances (e.g., ticket booths, grandstands) owned by the taxpayer who owns the complex and provided for the benefit of its customers. Transportation equipment, warehouses, administrative buildings, hotels, and motels are not eligible property, see FTC 2d/FIN ¶ L-8206.3; USTR ¶ 1684.01.

New Law. The 2012 Taxpayer Relief Act retroactively restores the treatment of qualifying property used for land improvement and support facilities at motorsports entertainment complexes as 7-year property for property placed in service in 2012 and extends it to property placed in service before January 1, 2014. (Code Sec. 168(i)(15)(D) as amended by 2012 Taxpayer Relief Act §312(a))

☐ **Effective:** Property placed in service after Dec. 31, 2011 (2012 Taxpayer Relief Act §312(b)) and before Jan. 1, 2014. ((Code Sec. 168(i)(15)(D))

recommendation: Because the 2012 Taxpayer Relief Act applies retroactively to property placed in service after Dec. 31, 2011, taxpayers who filed returns for a fiscal year including part of calendar year 2012 may consider filing an amended return to claim the accelerated depreciation deductions for qualifying assets it placed in service after Dec. 31, 2011.

observation: The recovery period for motorsports facilities placed in service *after* Dec. 31, 2013, remains uncertain. If the statutory treatment as 7-year property expires without extension, the 2004 Jobs Act provision excluding race track facilities from asset class 80.0 classification (see Sec. 704(c)(2), PL 108-357, 10/22/2004), which is not part of the Code and does not contain a termination date, may apply.

¶ 810. Depreciation tax breaks for Indian reservation property are extended to property placed in service through 2013

Code Sec. 168(j)(8), as amended by 2012 Taxpayer Relief Act §313(a)
Generally effective: Property placed in service after Dec. 31, 2011 and
   before Jan. 1, 2014
Committee Reports, None

Under pre-2012 Taxpayer Relief Act law, shortened depreciation recovery periods could be used for qualified Indian reservation property placed in service before Jan. 1, 2012. For example, property normally depreciable over a five-year period could be depreciated over a three-year period if it was qualified Indian reservation property. In addition, the depreciation deduction allowed for regular tax purposes with respect to qualified Indian reservation property was also allowed for purposes of the alternative minimum tax (AMT). (FTC 2d/FIN ¶ L-8800, ¶ L-8806; USTR ¶ 1684.01; TaxDesk ¶ 267,007)

Generally, qualified Indian reservation property is MACRS property used predominantly in the active conduct of a trade or business on an Indian reservation. Qualified Indian reservation property does not include the following otherwise depreciable property:

(1) Property used or located outside the Indian reservation on a regular basis.

(2) Property acquired directly or indirectly by the taxpayer from a person who is related to the taxpayer under at-risk loss-deduction limitation rules.

(3) Property placed in service for purposes of conducting or housing certain gaming activities.

(4) Property depreciable only under the MACRS straight-line Alternative Depreciation System (ADS). But property for which the taxpayer may elect the straight-line ADS, or listed property required to be depreciated under the straight-line ADS because its business use falls to 50% or less for the tax year, is not excluded from the definition of qualified Indian reservation property, see FTC 2d/FIN ¶ L-8807; USTR ¶ 1684.01; TaxDesk ¶ 267,007.

> *observation:* Despite (1) above, certain infrastructure property does qualify even if it is located outside the Indian reservation. This rule applies to infrastructure property (such as roads, power lines, water systems, railroad spurs, communication facilities, etc.) where its purpose is to connect with qualified infrastructure property located within the reservation. This property must also: (a) benefit the tribal infrastructure, (b) be available to the general public, (c) be placed in service in connection with the taxpayer's active conduct of a trade or business within an Indian reservation, and (d) be depreciable under MACRS, see FTC 2d/FIN ¶ L-8808; USTR ¶ 1684.01.

New Law. The 2012 Taxpayer Relief Act extends the above discussed incentive relating to depreciation of qualified Indian reservation property to apply to property placed in service before Jan. 1, 2014. Specifically, the 2012 Taxpayer Relief Act provides that Code Sec. 168(j) (allowing shortened depreciation recovery periods for qualified Indian reservation property) does not apply to property placed in service after Dec. 31, 2013. (Code Sec. 168(j)(8) as amended by 2012 Taxpayer Relief Act §313(a))

☐ **Effective:** Property placed in service after Dec. 31, 2011 (2012 Taxpayer Relief Act §313(b)) and before Jan. 1, 2014. (Code Sec. 168(j))

> *observation:* Thus, qualified Indian reservation property placed in service during 2012 and 2013 is eligible for accelerated depreciation. This accelerated depreciation also applies for purposes of the AMT.

> *recommendation:* Because 2012 Taxpayer Relief Act §313 applies retroactively to property placed in service after Dec. 31, 2011, taxpayers, such as fiscal year corporations that placed property in service in 2012 and already filed returns for a fiscal year that included a period in 2012 for which depreciation was taken on the property, should consider filing an amended return to claim a refund for the amount of the additional tax that may have been paid as a consequence of not initially claiming all the depreciation allowable because of the retroactive 2012 Taxpayer Relief Act change.

¶ 811. Election to expense cost of qualified advanced mine safety equipment property is extended two years to property placed in service through 2013

Code Sec. 179E(g), as amended by 2012 Taxpayer Relief Act §316(a)
Generally effective: Property placed in service after Dec. 31, 2011 and
*   before Jan. 1, 2014*
Committee Reports, None

The law in effect before the 2012 Taxpayer Relief Act provided for an election to expense advanced mine safety equipment, but the election did not apply to property placed in service after Dec. 31, 2011. (FTC 2d/FIN ¶ L-9940, L-9941; USTR ¶ 179E4; TaxDesk ¶ 268,450, 268,451) The taxpayer could elect to treat 50% of the cost of any qualified advanced mine safety equipment property (defined below) as an expense that was not chargeable to capital account. Thus, any cost for which the election was made was allowed as a deduction for the tax year in which the qualified advanced mine safety equipment property was placed in service, see FTC 2d/FIN ¶ L-9941; USTR ¶ 179E4; TaxDesk ¶ 268,451.

Qualified advanced mine safety equipment property is any advanced mine safety equipment property for use in any underground mine located in the U.S. if the original use of the property commences with the taxpayer. Advanced mine safety equipment property is any of the following:

• an emergency communication technology or device which is used to allow a miner to maintain constant communication with an individual who is not in the mine.

• electronic identification and location devices which allow an individual who is not in the mine to track at all times the movements and location of miners working in or at the mine.

• emergency oxygen-generating, self-rescue devices which provide oxygen for at least 90 minutes.

• pre-positioned supplies of oxygen which (in combination with self-rescue devices) can be used to provide each miner on a shift, in the event of an accident or other event which traps the miner in the mine or otherwise necessitates the use of a self-rescue device, the ability to survive for at least 48 hours.

• a comprehensive atmospheric monitoring system which monitors the levels of carbon monoxide, methane, and oxygen that are present in all areas of the mine and which can detect smoke in the case of a fire in the mine, see FTC 2d/FIN ¶s L-9942, L-9943; USTR ¶ 179E4; TaxDesk ¶s 268,452, 268,453.

New Law. The 2012 Taxpayer Relief Act provides that the placed in service date for the above election is extended for two years, to Dec. 31, 2013. The election will not apply to qualified advanced mine safety equipment property placed in service after Dec. 31, 2013. (Code Sec. 179E(g) as amended by 2012 Taxpayer Relief Act §316(a))

> **observation:** Thus, the Code Sec. 179E election will apply to qualified advanced mine safety equipment property placed in service in 2012 and 2013.

☐ **Effective:** Property placed in service after Dec. 31, 2011 (2012 Taxpayer Relief Act §316(b)) and before Jan. 1, 2014. (Code Sec. 179E(g))

> **recommendation:** Because 2012 Taxpayer Relief Act §316 applies retroactively to property placed in service after Dec. 31, 2011, taxpayers, such as fiscal year corporations that paid or incurred amounts for qualified mine safety equipment placed in service in 2012 and already filed returns for a fiscal year that included a period in 2012 for which such amounts could have been expensed under the retroactive change, should consider filing an amended return to claim a refund for the amount of the additional tax that may have been paid as a consequence of not initially expensing amounts eligible under the retroactive 2012 Taxpayer Relief Act change.

¶ 812. MACRS elections must be taken into account under normalization accounting for public utility property

Code Sec. 168(i)(9)(A)(ii), as amended by 2012 Taxpayer Relief Act §331(d)
Generally effective: Property placed in service after Dec. 31, 2012
Committee Reports, None

For most tangible property, the depreciation deduction allowed for the exhaustion of property used in a trade or business, or for the production of income, is determined under the modified accelerated cost recovery system (MACRS) of Code Sec. 168, see FTC 2d/FIN ¶ L-8101; USTR ¶ 1684; TaxDesk ¶ 266,001.

MACRS isn't allowed for public utility property unless a normalization method of accounting is applied to the property, see FTC 2d/FIN ¶ L-8201; USTR ¶ 1684; TaxDesk ¶ 266,008.

Generally, normalization accounting requires the following:

(1) the taxpayer must, in computing its tax expense for establishing its cost of service for ratemaking purposes and reflecting operating results in its regulated books of account, use a method of depreciation for public utility property that is the same as, and a depreciation period for that property that is no shorter than, the method and period used to compute its depreciation expense for those purposes; and

(2) if the amount allowable as a deduction under Code Sec. 168 (i.e., the MACRS rules) for the property differs from the amount that would be allowable as a deduction under Code Sec. 167—the useful life depreciation rules that would apply if Code Sec. 168 doesn't, see FTC 2d/FIN ¶L-11700 *et seq.*; USTR ¶ 1674 *et seq.*; TaxDesk ¶ 264,500 *et seq.*—using the method (including the period, first and last year convention, and salvage value) used to compute regulated tax expense under (1) above, the taxpayer must make adjustments to a reserve to reflect the deferral of taxes resulting from that difference. (FTC 2d/FIN ¶ L-9304; USTR ¶ 1684.01)

New Law. The 2012 Taxpayer Relief Act specifies that the amount allowable as a deduction under Code Sec. 168 (i.e., the MACRS rules) in (2) above is determined "respecting all elections made by the taxpayer under Code Sec. 168." (Code Sec. 168(i)(9)(A)(ii) as amended by 2012 Taxpayer Relief Act §331(d))

> *observation:* According to a summary of the 2102 Taxpayer Relief Act prepared by Senate staff, the above change "clarifies that it is a violation of the normalization rules to assume a bonus depreciation benefit for ratemaking purposes when a utility has elected not to take bonus depreciation."

☐ **Effective:** Property placed in service after Dec. 31, 2012, in tax years ending after Dec. 31, 2012. (2012 Taxpayer Relief Act §331(f))

¶ 900. Business Credits and Deductions

¶ 901. Research credit is retroactively extended, with modifications, to apply to amounts paid or incurred before Jan. 1, 2014

Code Sec. 41(f)(1)(A), as amended by 2012 Taxpayer Relief Act §301(c)(1)
Code Sec. 41(f)(1)(B), as amended by 2012 Taxpayer Relief Act §301(c)(2)
Code Sec. 41(f)(3)(A), as amended by 2012 Taxpayer Relief Act §301(b)(1)
Code Sec. 41(f)(3)(B), as amended by 2012 Taxpayer Relief Act §301(b)(2)
Code Sec. 41(h)(1)(B), as amended by 2012 Taxpayer Relief Act §301(a)(1)
Code Sec. 45C(b)(1)(D), as amended by 2012 Taxpayer Relief Act §301(a)(2)

Generally effective: Amounts paid or incurred after Dec. 31, 2011 (for credit modifications, tax years beginning after Dec. 31, 2011)
Committee Reports, None

Under pre-2012 Taxpayer Relief Act law, a taxpayer was entitled to a research credit for qualifying amounts paid or incurred before Jan. 1, 2012. (FTC 2d/FIN ¶ L-15300, ¶ L-15301 *et seq.*; USTR ¶ 414 *et seq.*; TaxDesk ¶ 384,001 *et seq.*)

The credit was generally equal to 20% of the amount by which the taxpayer's qualified research expenses exceeded a specific base amount unless the taxpayer elected the alternative simplified credit (ASC, see FTC 2d/FIN ¶ L-15302.2; USTR ¶ 414.0107; TaxDesk ¶ 384,003.1), see FTC 2d/FIN ¶ L-15300 *et seq.*; USTR ¶ 414; TaxDesk ¶ 384,001. Additional components of the research credit included the separately computed "university basic research credit," equal to 20% of the basic research payments to qualified research organizations less the "qualified organization base period amount," see FTC 2d/FIN ¶s L-15302, L-15501 *et seq.*; USTR ¶ 414.02; TaxDesk ¶ 384,018, and a separately computed "energy research consortium credit" based on amounts paid or incurred to an energy research consortium. Unlike the other components of the research credit, the energy research consortium credit applied for all qualified expenditures, not just those in excess of a base amount, see FTC 2d/FIN ¶s L-15302, L-15425.4; USTR ¶ 414.031; TaxDesk ¶ 384,014.1.

FTC 2d References are to Federal Tax Coordinator 2d
FIN References are to RIA's Analysis of Federal Taxes: Income (print)
USTR References are to United States Tax Reporter: Income
PCA References are to Pension Analysis (print and electronic)
PBE References are to Pension & Benefits Explanations
BCA References are to Benefits Analysis (electronic)
BC References are to Benefits Coordinator (print)
EP References are to Estate Planning Analysis (print and electronic)

Qualified clinical drug testing expenses are eligible for the orphan drug credit. Expenses eligible for this credit are defined, with certain modifications, by reference to the Code Sec. 41 definition of expenses qualifying for the research credit. For this purpose, under pre-2012 Taxpayer Relief Act law, Code Sec. 41 was considered to remain in effect for periods after Dec. 31, 2011. (FTC 2d/FIN ¶ L-15615, ¶ L-15624; USTR ¶ 45C4)

The Code provides rules that, under regs (that have yet to be issued), apply to the calculation of the research credit, for both the acquiring and disposing taxpayers, where a major portion of a business or of a separate unit of a business is transferred, see FTC 2d/FIN ¶ L-15300, ¶ L-15321 *et seq.*; USTR ¶ 414.04; TaxDesk ¶ 384,006.

The Code also provides rules that, for controlled groups of corporations and, under regs, for commonly controlled businesses, allocate the research credit among the controlled group members and among the commonly controlled businesses. For a controlled group member or commonly controlled business, the allowable credit is its "proportionate [share] of the qualified research expenses, basic research expenses, and amounts paid or incurred to research consortiums giving rise to the credit," see FTC 2d/FIN ¶ L-15300, ¶ L-15316 *et seq.*; USTR ¶ 414.03; TaxDesk ¶ 384,006.

New Law. The 2012 Taxpayer Relief Act extends the research credit for two years by striking the Dec. 31, 2011 expiration date of the pre-2012 Taxpayer Relief Act research credit (including the university basic research credit and the energy research consortium credit), and replacing that date with Dec. 31, *2013.* (Code Sec. 41(h)(1)(B) as amended by 2012 Taxpayer Relief Act §301(a)(1))

> **🅡ⁱᵃ** *recommendation:* Because the extension of the research credit is retroactive (see **"Effective"** below) to include amounts paid or incurred after Dec. 31, 2011, taxpayers, such as fiscal year corporations that already filed returns for a fiscal year that includes part of 2012, or any other taxpayers that have filed returns for tax years ending after Dec. 31, 2011, should consider filing an amended return to claim a refund for the amount of any additional tax paid because amounts now eligible for the credit under the 2012 Taxpayer Relief Act were not previously claimed.

> **🅡ⁱᵃ** *observation:* Unless the research credit is extended further by future legislation, the credit won't apply to amounts paid or incurred after Dec. 31, 2013.

Orphan drug credit. The 2012 Taxpayer Relief Act also makes a conforming change by providing that, for purposes of the definition of "qualified clinical testing expenses," Code Sec. 41 (the research tax credit) is considered to remain in effect for periods after Dec. 31, *2013*. (Code Sec. 45C(b)(1)(D) as amended by 2012 Taxpayer Relief Act §301(a)(2))

Transfer of a business or business unit. The 2012 Taxpayer Relief Act provides the credit calculation rules (discussed below) where a major portion of a business or a separate business unit is acquired or disposed of. (Code Sec. 41(f)(3)(A) as amended by 2012 Taxpayer Relief Act §301(b)(1); Code Sec. 41(f)(3)(B) as amended by 2012 Taxpayer Relief Act §301(b)(2))

> *observation:* The rules discussed below are more detailed than, and have significant differences from, the rules provided under pre-2012 Taxpayer Relief Act law. Among the differences is the provision of specific rules for the year that the major portion of a business or of a separate business unit is transferred. The mandate that regs are to be issued to carry out the rules (see above) is not changed by the 2012 Taxpayer Relief Act.

Under the credit calculation rules discussed above, if a person acquires the major portion of either a trade or business or a separate unit of a trade or business ("acquired business") of another person ("predecessor"), the amount of qualified research expenses (QREs) paid or incurred by the acquiring person during the "measurement period" must be increased by the amount of QREs determined as discussed below. (Code Sec. 41(f)(3)(A)(i)) The "measurement period," with respect to the tax year of the acquiring person for which the credit is determined, is any period of the acquiring person before that tax year that is taken into account for purposes of determining the credit for that tax year. (Code Sec. 41(f)(3)(A)(vi))

The amount of QREs referred to above is: (Code Sec. 41(f)(3)(A)(ii))

. . . for the tax year in which the acquisition is made, the "acquisition year amount" (defined below), and (Code Sec. 41(f)(3)(A)(ii)(I))

. . . for any tax year after the tax year in which the acquisition is made, the QREs paid or incurred by the predecessor with respect to the acquired business during the measurement period. (Code Sec. 41(f)(3)(A)(ii)(II))

The acquisition year amount is the amount equal to: (Code Sec. 41(f)(3)(A)(iv))

(1) the *product of* (Code Sec. 41(f)(3)(A)(iv))

. . . the QREs paid or incurred by the predecessor with respect to the acquired business during the measurement period, and (Code Sec. 41(f)(3)(A)(iv)(I))

. . . the number of days in the period beginning on the date of the acquisition and ending on the last day of the tax year in which the acquisition is made; (Code Sec. 41(f)(3)(A)(iv)(II))

(2) *divided by* the number of days in the acquiring person's tax year. (Code Sec. 41(f)(3)(A)(iv))

If a person acquires an "acquired business" (see above) of a "predecessor" (see above), the gross receipts of the acquiring person for the "measurement period" (see above) must *also* be increased by a required amount. (Code Sec. 41(f)(3)(A)(i)) That amount is the amount that would be determined under the calculation discussed above for QREs, except that "gross receipts" are substituted for QREs. (Code Sec. 41(f)(3)(A)(iii))

Coordinating tax years. If the tax years of an acquiring person and a "predecessor" (see above) don't begin on the same date: (Code Sec. 41(f)(3)(A)(v))

(1) the appropriate tax year of the acquiring person is the tax year referred to in Code Sec. 41(f)(3)(A)(ii) and Code Sec. 41(f)(3)(A)(iv) (i.e. the rules that determine the required increase in QREs, see above, and that are also applied, under Code Sec. 41(f)(3)(A)(iii), above, to determine the required increase in gross receipts), (Code Sec. 41(f)(3)(A)(v)(I))

(2) the QREs paid or incurred by the "predecessor" (see above), and the gross receipts of the predecessor, during each tax year of the predecessor any portion of which is part of the "measurement period" (see above) must be allocated equally among the days of that tax year, (Code Sec. 41(f)(3)(A)(v)(II))

(3) the amount of those QREs taken into account under Code Sec. 41(f)(3)(A)(ii) and Code Sec. 41(f)(3)(A)(iv) (see (1) above) for a tax year of the acquiring person is equal to the total of the expenses attributable, under (2) above, to the days occurring during that tax year, and (Code Sec. 41(f)(3)(A)(v)(III))

(4) the amount of the gross receipts taken into account under (3) above with respect to a tax year of the acquiring person is equal to the total of the gross receipts attributable under (2) above to the days occurring during that tax year. (Code Sec. 41(f)(3)(A)(v)(IV))

Treatment of the predecessor. If the "predecessor" (see above) furnished to the acquiring person the information necessary for the application of the above rules concerning the acquiring person, then, for purposes of applying the research credit for any tax year ending after the disposition, the amount of QREs paid or incurred by, and the gross receipts of, the predecessor during the "measurement period" (see above), determined by substituting "predecessor" for "acquiring person" in the above rules is reduced (Code Sec. 41(f)(3)(B)) *for the tax year in which the disposition is made*: (Code Sec. 41(f)(3)(B)(i))

(1) by an amount equal to the *product of*: (Code Sec. 41(f)(3)(B)(i))

. . . the QREs paid or incurred by, or gross receipts of, the predecessor with respect to the acquired business during the measurement period (as determined under the above rules), and (Code Sec. 41(f)(3)(B)(i)(I))

... the number of days in the period beginning on the date of acquisition (as determined for purposes of Code Sec. 41(f)(3)(A)(iv)(II), see above) and ending on the last day of the tax year of the predecessor in which the disposition is made, (Code Sec. 41(f)(3)(B)(i)(II))

(2) *divided by* the number of days in the tax year of the predecessor. (Code Sec. 41(f)(3)(B)(i))

For any tax year *ending after* the year in which the disposition is made, the amount by which QREs or gross receipts must be reduced for the measuring period is the amount described in Code Sec. 41(f)(3)(B)(i)(I) (see above). (Code Sec. 41(f)(3)(B)(ii)).

Allocations in a controlled group or among commonly controlled businesses. The 2012 Taxpayer Relief Act also modifies the rules for allocating the research credit among members of a controlled group of corporations or among commonly controlled businesses by substituting, for the allocation rules discussed above, allocation rules that provide (1) that the allowable credit for a controlled group member "shall be determined on a proportionate basis to its share of the aggregate of the qualified research expenses, basic research payments, and amounts paid or incurred to energy research consortiums, taken into account by such controlled group" for purposes of the research credit, and (2) that the allowable credit for a commonly controlled business "shall be determined on a proportionate basis to its share of the aggregate of the qualified research expenses, basic research payments, and amounts paid or incurred to energy research consortiums, taken into account by all such persons under common control" for purposes of the research credit. (Code Sec. 41(f)(1)(A) as amended by 2012 Taxpayer Relief Act §301(c)(1); Code Sec. 41(f)(1)(B) as amended by 2012 Taxpayer Relief Act §301(c)(2))

☐ **Effective:** Amounts paid or incurred after Dec. 31, 2011 (2012 Taxpayer Relief Act §301(d)(1)) and before Jan. 1, 2014 (Code Sec. 41(h)(1)(b)); but for the rules discussed under the headings **Transfer of a business or business unit** and **Allocations in a controlled group or among commonly controlled businesses** above, tax years beginning after Dec. 31, 2011. (2012 Taxpayer Relief Act §301(d)(2))

¶ 902. Work opportunity credit is retroactively extended to apply to all individuals who begin work for an employer through Dec. 31, 2013

Code Sec. 51(c)(4)(B), as amended by 2012 Taxpayer Relief Act §309(a)
Generally effective: Individuals who begin work for the employer after Dec. 31, 2011 and before Jan. 1, 2014
Committee Reports, None

A work opportunity tax credit (WOTC) is available on an elective basis to an employer for a percentage of limited amounts of wages paid or incurred by the employer to individuals who belong to a "targeted group," see FTC 2d/FIN ¶ L-17775; USTR ¶ 514; TaxDesk ¶ 380,700.

Under pre-2012 Taxpayer Relief Act law, the WOTC wasn't available for wages paid or incurred by an employer to:

. . . a qualified veteran who began work for the employer after Dec. 31, 2012, or

. . . any other individual who was a member of a targeted group and who began work for the employer after Dec. 31, 2011. (FTC 2d/FIN ¶ L-17775; USTR ¶ 514; TaxDesk ¶ 380,700)

> **⟁observation:** The 2011 Job Creation Act (Sec. 261(d), PL 112-56, 11/21/2011, see analysis at ¶ 1910) extended the availability of the work opportunity credit for a year for wages paid or incurred by an employer to qualified veterans only. This accounted for the different termination dates above for availability of the credit for wages paid to qualified veterans and for wages paid to any other individuals.

New Law. The 2012 Taxpayer Relief Act extends the starting work date for WOTC qualification for one year for qualified veterans and two years in the case of any other individual by providing that the term "wages" (for purposes of determining the amount of the WOTC) doesn't include any amount paid or incurred to an individual who begins work for the employer after Dec. 31, 2013. (Code Sec. 51(c)(4)(B) as amended by 2012 Taxpayer Relief Act §309(a))

> **⟁observation:** Thus, the 2012 Taxpayer Relief Act retroactively restores the WOTC and provides a uniform end date for the availability of the credit regardless of whether it is for wages paid to a qualified veteran or any other individual that belongs to a targeted group.

☐ **Effective:** Individuals who begin work for the employer after Dec. 31, 2011 (2012 Taxpayer Relief Act §309(b)) and before Jan. 1, 2014. (Code Sec. 51(c)(4)(B))

¶ 903. Employer-provided child care credit is extended permanently

Code Sec. 45F, 2012 Taxpayer Relief Act §101(a)(1)
Code Sec. 38(b)(15), 2012 Taxpayer Relief Act §101(a)(1)
Code Sec. 1016(a)(28), 2012 Taxpayer Relief Act §101(a)(1)
Generally effective: Tax years beginning after 2012
Committee Reports, None

Code Sec. 45F provides a credit to employers for certain costs of providing child care assistance to employees. Subject to a $150,000-per-tax-year limit, the credit is available for (1) 25% of certain costs of acquiring, constructing, rehabilitating, expanding or operating a qualified child care facility, (2) 25% of certain costs paid or incurred under a contract with a qualified child care facility, and (3) 10% of certain costs of providing child care resource and referral services for employees. (FTC 2d/FIN ¶ L-17870, ¶ L-17871; USTR ¶ 45F4; TaxDesk ¶ 382,101)

The Code Sec. 45F employer-provided child care credit is treated as part of the Code Sec. 38 general business credit. (FTC 2d/FIN ¶ L-15201; USTR ¶ 384.01; TaxDesk ¶ 380,501) Under Code Sec. 38, certain business incentive credits are combined into one general business credit for purposes of determining each credit's allowance limitation for the tax year.

With respect to a facility for which an employer-provided child care credit was allowed, basis adjustments required under Code Sec. 45F(1) are proper adjustments to the basis of property which must be made under Code Sec. 1016(a). (FTC 2d ¶ P-1710.1; USTR ¶ 10,164; TaxDesk ¶ 213,011.5)

> **Ⓡ observation:** The above rule does not cause downward basis adjustments made under Code Sec. 45F(1)(A) or upward basis adjustments made under Code Sec. 45F(1)(B) to be repeated under Code Sec. 1016(a). Instead, the main effect of the above rule is to make adjustments under Code Sec. 45F(1) subject to Code provisions which refer to Code Sec. 1016 and, thus, require that adjustments made under Code Sec. 1016 be taken into account. For example, Code Sec. 1011 provides that adjustments under Code Sec. 1016 are taken into account in determining the adjusted basis of property for purposes of determining gain or loss upon sale or other disposition of the property.

Code Sec. 45F was enacted by the Economic Growth and Tax Relief Reconciliation Act of 2001 (EGTRRA, Sec. 205, PL 107-16, 6/7/2001).

A sunset provision in EGTRRA (Sec. 901, PL 107-16, 6/7/2001), as amended by Sec. 101(a), PL 111-312, 12/17/2010, provided that all changes made by

EGTRRA wouldn't have applied to tax years beginning after Dec. 31, 2012. ((FTC 2d/FIN ¶ T-11050, ¶ T-11051; USTR ¶ 79,006.86; TaxDesk ¶ 880,011))

> **⚫️observation:** Thus, under pre-2012 Taxpayer Relief Act law, the Code Sec. 45F employer-provided child care credit, and the related Code Sec. 38 and Code Sec. 1016 rules, would not have applied in tax years beginning after Dec. 31, 2012.

New Law. The 2012 Taxpayer Relief Act repeals title IX of EGTRRA (i.e., the title containing the above-described EGTRRA sunset). (EGTRRA § 901 (Sec. 901, PL 107-16, 6/7/2001) repealed by (2012 Taxpayer Relief Act §101(a)(1))

> **⚫️observation:** Thus, the Act permanently extends the Code Sec. 45F employer-provided tax credit, and the related Code Sec. 38 and Code Sec. 1016 rules.

☐ **Effective:** For tax years beginning after Dec. 31, 2012. (2012 Taxpayer Relief Act §101(a)(3))

¶ 904. Differential wage payment credit is retroactively restored and extended to apply to payments made before Jan. 1, 2014

Code Sec. 45P(f), as amended by 2012 Taxpayer Relief Act §308(a)
Generally effective: Payments made after Dec. 31, 2011 and before Jan. 1, 2014
Committee Reports, None

In the case of an employee who is called to active duty to the U.S. uniformed services, some employers voluntarily pay the employee the difference between the compensation that the employer would have paid to the employee during the period of military service and the amount of pay received by the employee from the military. This payment by the employer is often referred to as "differential pay." Under pre-2012 Taxpayer Relief Act law, an eligible small business employer (as defined in FTC 2d/FIN ¶ L-15677; USTR ¶ 45P4; TaxDesk ¶ 384,852) could have taken a credit against its income tax liability for a tax year in an amount equal to 20% of the sum of the eligible differential wage payments (as defined in FTC 2d/FIN ¶ L-15677.2; USTR ¶ 45P4; TaxDesk ¶ 384,854) for each of the taxpayer's qualified employees (as defined in FTC 2d/FIN ¶ L-15677.1; USTR ¶ 45P4; TaxDesk ¶ 384,853) for the tax year. The differential wage payment credit was not available for payments made after Dec. 31, 2011. (FTC 2d/FIN ¶ L-15675, ¶ L-15676; USTR ¶ 45P4; TaxDesk ¶ 384,851)

New Law. The 2012 Taxpayer Relief Act retroactively restores and extends for two years the differential wage payment credit for employees who are active duty members of the uniformed services. Specifically, the differential wage payment credit does not apply to any payments made after Dec. 31, *2013*. (Code Sec. 45P(f) as amended by 2012 Taxpayer Relief Act §308(a))

☐ **Effective:** Payments made after Dec. 31, 2011 (2012 Taxpayer Relief Act §308(b)) and before Jan. 1, 2014. (Code Sec. 45P(f))

> 🅡🅘🅐 *recommendation:* If a fiscal year taxpayer made any differential wage payments to employees in 2012 (i.e., after the credit had expired under pre-2012 Taxpayer Relief Act law) and that taxpayer has already filed its income tax return for that period, the taxpayer may want to consider amending the return to claim the credit with respect to any payments made after 2011.

¶ 905. Mine rescue team training credit is retroactively restored and extended to tax years beginning before Jan. 1, 2014

Code Sec. 45N(e), as amended by 2012 Taxpayer Relief Act §307(a)
Generally effective: Tax years beginning after Dec. 31, 2011 and before Jan. 1, 2014
Committee Reports, None

Under pre-2012 Taxpayer Relief Act law, the mine rescue team training credit, a general business credit, was allowed for amounts paid or incurred for training mine rescue teams, see FTC 2d/FIN ¶ L-18201; USTR ¶ 45N4; TaxDesk ¶ 384,062. The amount of the credit was the lesser of $10,000 or 20% of the amount the employer paid or incurred during the tax year for the training program costs of its qualified mine rescue team employees (as defined at FTC 2d/FIN ¶ L-18202; USTR ¶ 45N4; TaxDesk ¶ 384,063), including wages (defined at FTC 2d/FIN ¶ L-18204; USTR ¶ 45N4; TaxDesk ¶ 384,063) of the employee while attending the program. See FTC 2d/FIN ¶ L-18201; USTR ¶ 45N4; TaxDesk ¶ 384,062.

Under pre-2012 Taxpayer Relief Act law, the mine rescue team training credit did not apply to tax years beginning after Dec. 31, *2011*. (FTC 2d/FIN ¶ L-18200, ¶ L-18205; USTR ¶ 45N4; TaxDesk ¶ 384,062)

New Law. Under the 2012 Taxpayer Relief Act, the mine rescue team training credit does not apply to tax years beginning after Dec. 31, *2013*. (Code Sec. 45N(e) as amended by 2012 Taxpayer Relief Act §307(a))

> 🅡🅘🅐 *observation:* Thus, the mine rescue team training credit is retroactively restored and extended for two years for calendar year 2012 and

2013 taxpayers, and to fiscal year taxpayers with fiscal years beginning as late as Dec. 31, 2013.

☐ **Effective:** Tax years beginning after Dec. 31, 2011 (2012 Taxpayer Relief Act §307(b)) and before Jan. 1, 2014. (Code Sec. 45N(e))

¶ 906. Temporary minimum low-income housing credit rate of 9% applies to new non-federally subsidized buildings with respect to housing credit dollar amount allocations made before Jan. 1, 2014

Code Sec. 42(b)(2), as amended by 2012 Taxpayer Relief Act §302(a)
Generally effective: Jan. 2, 2013
Committee Reports, None

A taxpayer claims the low-income housing credit over a ten-year credit period after each low-income building is placed-in-service. The amount of the credit for any tax year in the credit period is the applicable percentage of the qualified basis of each qualified low-income building. See FTC 2d/FIN ¶s L-15701, L-15702; USTR ¶ 424; TaxDesk ¶ 383,001.

The calculation of the applicable percentage is designed to produce a credit equal to 70% of the present value of the building's qualified basis in the case of newly constructed or substantially rehabilitated housing that is not federally subsidized (the "70% credit"); or 30% of the present value of the building's qualified basis in the case of newly constructed or substantially rehabilitated housing that is federally subsidized, and existing housing that was substantially rehabilitated (the "30% credit"). (FTC 2d/FIN ¶ L-15714; USTR ¶ 424.10; TaxDesk ¶ 383,006)

The credit percentage for a low-income building is set for the earlier of the month the building is placed in service; or at the election of the taxpayer, (a) the month the taxpayer and the housing credit agency enter into a binding agreement with respect to the building for a credit allocation, or (b) in the case of a tax-exempt bond-financed project for which no credit allocation is required, the month in which the tax-exempt bonds are issued. See FTC 2d/FIN ¶ L-15713; USTR ¶ 424.10; TaxDesk ¶ 383,001.

These credit percentages (used for the 70% credit and the 30% credit) are adjusted monthly by IRS on a discounted after-tax basis (assuming a 28% tax rate) based on the average of the applicable federal rates (AFRs) for mid-term and long-term obligations for the month the building is placed in service. The discounting formula assumes that each credit is received on the last day of each year and that the present value is computed on the last day of the first year. In a project consisting of two or more buildings placed in service in different months, a separate credit percentage may apply to each building. See FTC 2d/ FIN ¶ L-15718; USTR ¶ 424.10; TaxDesk ¶ 383,006.

Under pre-2012 Taxpayer Relief Act law, the applicable percentage isn't less than 9% for any new building that is *placed in service* by the taxpayer after July 30, 2008 *and before Dec. 31, 2013*, and that is not federally subsidized for the tax year. (FTC 2d/FIN ¶ L-15700, ¶ L-15714.1; USTR ¶ 424.10; TaxDesk ¶ 383,001)

New Law. The 2012 Taxpayer Relief Act provides that for any new building that is placed in service by the taxpayer after July 30, 2008 *with respect to housing credit dollar amount allocations made before Jan. 1, 2014*, and that is not federally subsidized for the tax year, the applicable percentage isn't less than 9%. (Code Sec. 42(b)(2) as amended by 2012 Taxpayer Relief Act §302(a))

> *observation:* Thus, the 2012 Taxpayer Relief Act substitutes an allocation deadline for the placed-in-service deadline discussed above in determining eligibility of non-federally-subsidized new buildings for a 9%-or-greater applicable percentage.

☐ **Effective:** Jan. 2, 2013. (2012 Taxpayer Relief Act §302(b))

¶ 907. Indian employment credit for wages paid to qualified Native Americans is extended through Dec. 31, 2013

Code Sec. 45A(f), as amended by 2012 Taxpayer Relief Act §304(a)
Generally effective: Tax years starting after Dec. 31, 2011 and before Jan. 1, 2014
Committee Reports, None

The law in effect before the 2012 Taxpayer Relief Act provided for an Indian employment credit as an incentive for businesses to be located on Indian reservations, but it was scheduled to terminate for tax years beginning after Dec. 31, 2011. Employers were eligible for a credit under Code Sec. 45A equal to 20% of the excess, if any, of the sum of qualified wages and qualified employee health insurance costs paid or incurred during the tax year, over the sum of these same costs paid or incurred in calendar year '93. Qualified wages were wages paid by an employer for services performed by a qualified employee. No more than $20,000 of wages per year per qualified employee was eligible for the 20% credit. A qualified employee meant an employee who was a member of an Indian tribe (or the spouse of a member) who performed substantially all of his services for the employer on an Indian reservation and who lived on or near the reservation. No relative or dependent of the employer, or a 5%-or-more owner of the employer was a qualified employee and the employee couldn't have total wages exceeding an inflation-adjusted maximum. (FTC 2d/FIN ¶ L-15670, ¶ L-15671, ¶ L-15673; USTR ¶ 45A4; TaxDesk ¶ 384,039)

New Law. The 2012 Taxpayer Relief Act extends the present-law Indian employment credit for two years. Thus, under the 2012 Taxpayer Relief Act, the credit is allowed for eligible employers through Dec. 31, 2013. (Code Sec. 45A(f) as amended by 2012 Taxpayer Relief Act §304(a))

> **⚓ observation:** The Indian employment credit is combined with other business related credits into one general business credit with a single tax liability limitation, see FTC 2d/FIN ¶ L-15673.5. The Indian employment credit is claimed on Form 8845 and the general business credit is claimed on Form 3800. Taxpayers that are not partnerships, S corporations, cooperatives, estates, or trusts, and whose only source of the Indian employment credit is from those pass-through entities, aren't required to complete or file Form 8845. They can report the Indian employment credit directly on Form 3800.

☐ **Effective:** Tax years beginning after Dec. 31, 2011 (2012 Taxpayer Relief Act §304(b)) and before Jan. 1, 2014. (Code Sec. 45A(f))

¶ 908. Railroad track maintenance credit for qualified expenditures is extended to include qualified expenditures paid or incurred during tax years beginning in 2012 and 2013

Code Sec. 45G(f), as amended by 2012 Taxpayer Relief Act §306(a)
Generally effective: Expenditures paid or incurred during tax years beginning after Dec. 31, 2011 and before Jan. 1 2014
Committee Reports, None

The 2004 Jobs Act (Sec. 245, PL 108-357, 10/22/2004) added a credit under Code Sec. 45G for 50% of the "qualified railroad track maintenance expenditures" (defined below) paid or incurred by an "eligible taxpayer" (defined below) during a tax year, but only for expenditures paid or incurred during tax years beginning after Dec. 31, 2004 and before Jan. 1, 2008. The credit was later extended for tax years beginning before Jan. 1, 2012. (FTC 2d/FIN ¶ L-18050, ¶ L-18051; USTR ¶ 45G4; TaxDesk ¶ 380,501).

The credit for any tax year could not exceed $3,500 multiplied by the sum of:

(1) the number of miles of railroad track owned or leased by the eligible taxpayer as of the close of the tax year; and

(2) the number of miles of railroad track assigned for purposes of Code Sec. 45G(b) to the eligible taxpayer by a Class II or Class III railroad (defined

below) that owns or leases the railroad track as of the close of the tax year, see FTC 2d/FIN ¶ L-18052; USTR ¶ 45G4.

"Eligible taxpayer" means any Class II or Class III railroad, or any person who transports property using the rail facilities of a Class II or Class III railroad or who furnishes railroad-related property or services to a Class II or Class III railroad, but only for miles of railroad track assigned to that person by the Class II or Class III railroad for purposes of Code Sec. 45G(b), see FTC 2d/FIN ¶ L-18055; USTR ¶ 45G4.

The term "qualified railroad track maintenance expenditures," means expenditures (whether or not otherwise chargeable to capital account) for maintaining railroad track (including roadbed, bridges, and related track structures) owned or leased, as of Jan. 1, 2005, by a Class II or Class III railroad, see FTC 2d/FIN ¶ L-18053; USTR ¶ 45G4.

"Class II or Class III railroad" has the same meaning for purposes of the railroad track maintenance credit as it has when used by the Surface Transportation Board, see FTC 2d/FIN ¶ L-18055; USTR ¶ 45G4.

> **⌾** *observation:* Class II railroads are carriers with annual operating revenues of more than $20 million and less than $250 million. They are also referred to as regional railroads. Class III railroads are carriers with operating revenues of $20 million or less, and all switching and terminal companies regardless of operating revenues. Class III railroads are also called short lines. Thus, the railroad track maintenance credit is designed to help all but the largest railroad carriers.

New Law. The 2012 Taxpayer Relief Act extends the railroad track maintenance credit so that it applies to qualified railroad track maintenance expenditures paid or incurred during tax years beginning before Jan. 1, 2014. (Code Sec. 45G(f) as amended by 2012 Taxpayer Relief Act §306(a))

☐ **Effective:** Expenditures paid or incurred during tax years beginning after Dec. 31, 2011, (2012 Taxpayer Relief Act §306(b)) and before Jan. 1 2014. (Code Sec. 45G(f))

> **⌾** *observation:* This means that the extension applies for expenditures paid or incurred in tax years beginning in 2012 and 2013.

¶ 909. Allowance of Code Sec. 199 deduction for Puerto Rico activities is retroactively extended two years to taxpayer's first eight tax years beginning after 2005

Code Sec. 199(d)(8)(C), as amended by 2012 Taxpayer Relief Act §318(a)
Generally effective: Tax years beginning after Dec. 31, 2011 and before Jan. 1, 2014
Committee Reports, None

The domestic production activities deduction is allowed for various trade or business activities. Generally, those activities must be conducted in the U.S. in order to qualify for the deduction, see FTC 2d/FIN ¶ L-4326.1; USTR ¶ 1994.036; TaxDesk ¶ 307,802. For purposes of the rules governing this deduction, the Commonwealth of Puerto Rico ("Puerto Rico") is generally not treated as part of the U.S., see FTC 2d/FIN ¶ L-4336.1; USTR ¶ 1994.050; TaxDesk ¶ 307,820.

Under special rules for determining domestic production gross receipts, however, for any taxpayer with gross receipts from sources within Puerto Rico, the U.S. includes Puerto Rico, but only if all of the taxpayer's Puerto Rico-sourced gross receipts are taxable under the federal income tax for individuals or corporations, see FTC 2d/FIN ¶ L-4336.2; USTR ¶ 1994.050. In computing the 50% wage limitation, the taxpayer is permitted to take into account wages paid to bona fide residents of Puerto Rico for services performed in Puerto Rico, see FTC 2d/FIN ¶ L-4387.4; USTR ¶ 1994.002.

Under pre-2012 Taxpayer Relief Act law, the special rules for Puerto Rico applied only for the first six tax years of a taxpayer beginning after Dec. 31, 2005 and before Jan. 1, 2012. (FTC 2d/FIN ¶ L-4325, ¶ L-4336.2, ¶ L-4387.4; USTR ¶ 1994.002, ¶ 1994.050)

New Law. The 2012 Taxpayer Relief Act amends the rules to provide that the special provision for Puerto Rico activities apply for the first eight tax years of a taxpayer beginning after Dec. 31, 2005 and before Jan. 1, 2014. (Code Sec. 199(d)(8)(C) as amended by 2012 Taxpayer Relief Act §318(a))

> *observation:* Thus, the special rules for Puerto Rico are retroactively extended to apply to tax years beginning in 2012 and 2013.

☐ **Effective:** Tax years beginning after Dec. 31, 2011 (2012 Taxpayer Relief Act §318(b)) and before Jan. 1, 2014. (Code Sec. 199(d)(8)(C))

¶ 1000. Energy Provisions

¶ 1001. Energy efficient appliance credit is extended for certain appliances manufactured in 2012 or 2013

Code Sec. 45M(b)(1)(D), as amended by 2012 Taxpayer Relief Act §409(a)

Code Sec. 45M(b)(1)(E), as amended by 2012 Taxpayer Relief Act §409(a)

Code Sec. 45M(b)(2)(F), as amended by 2012 Taxpayer Relief Act §409(a)

Code Sec. 45M(b)(3)(E), as amended by 2012 Taxpayer Relief Act §409(a)

Code Sec. 45M(b)(3)(F), as amended by 2012 Taxpayer Relief Act §409(a)

Generally effective: Appliances produced after Dec. 31, 2011 and before Jan. 1, 2014

Committee Reports, None

An "energy efficient appliance credit" is awarded, on a per-item-produced basis, to manufacturers of "qualified energy efficient appliances." The credit amount for each type of qualified energy efficient appliance is the "applicable amount" (FTC 2d/FIN ¶s L-17952, L-17953, L-17954; USTR ¶ 45M4; TaxDesk ¶s 569,582, 569,583, 569,584) for that type multiplied by the "eligible production" (see FTC 2d/FIN ¶ L-17955; USTR ¶ 45M4; TaxDesk ¶ 569,585). (FTC 2d/FIN ¶ L-17951; USTR ¶ 45M4; TaxDesk ¶ 569,581). The credit is subject to annual eligible production limits, an annual percentage-of-gross-receipts limit and a cumulative aggregate limit, see FTC 2d/FIN ¶s L-17955, L-17956, L-17957; USTR ¶ 45M4; TaxDesk ¶s 569,585, 569,586, 569,587. The credit is part of the general business credit under Code Sec. 38, see FTC 2d/FIN ¶ L-15202; USTR ¶ 384.01; TaxDesk ¶ 380,501.

Under pre-2012 Taxpayer Relief Act law, the per-item credit amounts ("applicable amounts") available for each of the types of dishwashers, clothes washers and refrigerators manufactured in 2011 were as follows:

. . . for dishwashers, the applicable amounts were:

- $25 for dishwashers manufactured in calendar year 2011 which use no more than 307 kilowatt hours per year and 5.8 gallons per cycle. (5.5 gallons per cycle for dishwashers designed for greater than 12 place settings).

- $50 for dishwashers manufactured in calendar year 2011 which use no more than 295 kilowatt hours per year and 4.25 gallons per cycle (4.75 gallons per cycle for dishwashers designed for greater than 12 place settings).

FTC 2d References are to Federal Tax Coordinator 2d
FIN References are to RIA's Analysis of Federal Taxes: Income (print)
USTR References are to United States Tax Reporter: Income
PCA References are to Pension Analysis (print and electronic)
PBE References are to Pension & Benefits Explanations
BCA References are to Benefits Analysis (electronic)
BC References are to Benefits Coordinator (print)
EP References are to Estate Planning Analysis (print and electronic)

• $75 for dishwashers manufactured in calendar year 2011 which use no more than 280 kilowatt hours per year and 4 gallons per cycle (4.5 gallons per cycle for dishwashers designed for greater than 12 place settings).

Gallons per cycle with respect to a dishwasher is the amount of water required to complete a normal cycle of a dishwasher. (FTC 2d/FIN ¶ L-17952; USTR ¶ 45M4; TaxDesk ¶ 569,582)

. . . for clothes washers, the applicable amounts were:

• $175 for top-loading clothes washers (see FTC 2d/FIN ¶ L-17953; USTR ¶ 45M4; TaxDesk ¶ 569,583) manufactured in calendar year 2011 which meet or exceed a 2.2 modified energy factor (see FTC 2d/FIN ¶ L-17953; USTR ¶ 45M4; TaxDesk ¶ 569,583) and don't exceed a 4.5 water consumption factor (see FTC 2d/FIN ¶ L-17953; USTR ¶ 45M4; TaxDesk ¶ 569,583).

• $225 for clothes washers manufactured in calendar year 2011:

• which are top-loading clothes washers which meet or exceed a 2.4 modified energy factor and don't exceed a 4.2 water consumption factor, or

• which are front-loading clothes washers which meet or exceed a 2.8 modified energy factor and don't exceed a 3.5 water consumption factor. (FTC 2d/FIN ¶ L-17953; USTR ¶ 45M4; TaxDesk ¶ 569,583)

. . . for refrigerators, the applicable amounts were:

• $150 for refrigerators manufactured in calendar year 2011 that consume at least 30% less energy than the 2001 energy conservation standards.

• $200 for refrigerators manufactured in calendar year 2011 that consume at least 35% less energy than the 2001 energy conservation standards. (FTC 2d/FIN ¶ L-17954; USTR ¶ 45M4; TaxDesk ¶ 569,584)

New Law. The 2012 Taxpayer Relief Act extends the credit for certain appliances manufactured in 2012 or 2013. The 2012 Taxpayer Relief Act modifies the credit eligibility standards and credit amounts ("applicable amounts" or "per-item credit amounts") for dishwashers, clothes washers, and refrigerators as follows:

Dishwashers. The applicable amounts (per-item credit amounts) for dishwashers are as follows:

. . . $50 for dishwashers manufactured in calendar year 2011, *2012, or 2013* and which use no more than 295 kilowatt hours per year and 4.25 gallons per cycle (4.75 gallons per cycle for dishwashers designed for greater than 12 place settings). (Code Sec. 45M(b)(1)(D) as amended by 2012 Taxpayer Relief Act §409(a))

. . . $75 for dishwashers manufactured in calendar year 2011, *2012, or 2013* and which use no more than 280 kilowatt hours per year and 4 gallons per cycle (4.5 gallons per cycle for dishwashers designed for greater than 12 place settings). (Code Sec. 45M(b)(1)(E))

Clothes washers. The applicable amounts (per-item credit amounts) for clothes washers are as follows:

... $225 for a clothes washer manufactured in calendar year 2011, *2012, or 2013*: (Code Sec. 45M(b)(2)(F) as amended by 2012 Taxpayer Relief Act §409(a))

- which is a top-loading clothes washer and which meets or exceeds a 2.4 modified energy factor and doesn't exceed a 4.2 water consumption factor, or (Code Sec. 45M(b)(2)(F)(i))

- which is a front-loading clothes washer which meets or exceeds a 2.8 modified energy factor and doesn't exceed a 3.5 water consumption factor. (Code Sec. 45M(b)(2)(F)(ii))

Refrigerators. The applicable amounts (per-item credit amounts) for refrigerators are as follows:

... $150 for a refrigerator manufactured in calendar year 2011, *2012, or 2013* that consumes at least 30% less energy than the 2001 energy conservation standards. (Code Sec. 45M(b)(3)(E) as amended by 2012 Taxpayer Relief Act §409(a))

... $200 for a refrigerator manufactured in calendar year 2011, *2012, or 2013* that consumes at least 35% less energy than the 2001 energy conservation standards. (Code Sec. 45M(b)(3)(F))

Appliances not qualifying for the credit in 2012 or 2013. The 2012 Taxpayer Relief Act specifically provided that the following provisions were not extended:

... Code Sec. 45M(b)(1)(C) ($25 for dishwashers manufactured in calendar year 2011 which use no more than 307 kilowatt hours per year and 5.8 gallons per cycle (5.5 gallons per cycle for dishwashers designed for greater than 12 place settings)).

... Code Sec. 45M(b)(2)(E) ($175 for top-loading clothes washers manufactured in calendar year 2011 which meet or exceed a 2.2 modified energy factor and don't exceed a 4.5 water consumption factor). (2012 Taxpayer Relief Act §409(a); 2012 Taxpayer Relief Act §409(b))

☐ **Effective:** Appliances produced after Dec. 31, 2011 (2012 Taxpayer Relief Act §409(c)) and before Jan. 1, 2014. (Code Sec. 45M(b))

     ✔ᴿᴵᴬ recommendation: If a fiscal year manufacturer produced appliances in 2012 that would qualify for the credit (as retroactively restored and extended by the 2012 Taxpayer Relief Act) and that taxpayer has already filed its income tax return for that period, the taxpayer may want to consider amending the return to claim the credit with respect to any appliances produced in 2012 that meet the requirements described above.

¶ 1002. New energy efficient home credit for eligible contractors is retroactively restored and extended through Dec. 31, 2013

Code Sec. 45L(g), as amended by 2012 Taxpayer Relief Act §408(a)
Generally effective: Homes acquired after Dec. 31, 2011 and before Jan. 1, 2014
Committee Reports, None

Under pre-2012 Taxpayer Relief Act law, an eligible contractor could claim, as part of the general business credit for the tax year (see FTC 2d/FIN ¶ L-15201; USTR ¶ 384.01; TaxDesk ¶ 380,501), a credit for each qualified new energy efficient home that the contractor constructed and which was acquired by a person from the contractor for use as a residence during the tax year, see FTC 2d/FIN ¶ L-17941; USTR ¶ 45L4; TaxDesk ¶ 569,571.

An "eligible contractor" for this purpose was (1) the person who constructed the qualified new energy efficient home, or (2) for a qualified new energy efficient home which was a manufactured home, the manufactured home producer, see FTC 2d/FIN ¶ L-17943; USTR ¶ 45L4; TaxDesk ¶ 569,571.

The credit was either $2,000 (for a 50% reduction in energy usage) or $1,000 (for a 30% reduction in energy usage), see FTC 2d/FIN ¶ L-17942; USTR ¶ 45L4; TaxDesk ¶ 569,572. The credit was only available for qualified new energy efficient homes substantially completed after Dec. 31, 2005, and acquired after Dec. 31, 2005 and before Jan. 1, 2012. Thus, the credit did not apply to any qualified new energy efficient home acquired after *Dec. 31, 2011.* (FTC 2d/FIN ¶ L-17940, L-17941; USTR ¶ 45L4; TaxDesk ¶ 569,571)

New Law. The 2012 Taxpayer Relief Act retroactively restores and extends the new energy efficient home credit for two years, so that it does not apply to qualified new energy efficient homes acquired after *Dec. 31, 2013.* (Code Sec. 45L(g) as amended by 2012 Taxpayer Relief Act §408(a))

For modification of the construction standards used to determine whether a dwelling unit is a qualified new energy efficient home by the 2012 Taxpayer Relief Act, see ¶ 1003.

☐ **Effective:** Homes acquired after Dec. 31, 2011 (2012 Taxpayer Relief Act §408(c)) and before Jan. 1, 2014. (Code Sec. 45L(g))

¶ 1003. Construction standards for the qualified new energy efficient home credit are modified

Code Sec. 45L(c)(1)(A)(i), as amended by 2012 Taxpayer Relief Act §408(b)
Generally effective: Homes acquired after Dec. 31, 2011
Committee Reports, None

Under pre-2012 Taxpayer Relief Act law, an eligible contractor could claim, as part of the general business credit for the tax year (see FTC 2d/FIN ¶ L-15201; USTR ¶ 384.01; TaxDesk ¶ 380,501), a credit for each qualified new energy efficient home that the contractor constructed and which was acquired by a person from the contractor for use as a residence during the tax year, see FTC 2d/FIN ¶ L-17941; USTR ¶ 45L4; TaxDesk ¶ 569,571. The credit was either $2,000 (for a 50% reduction in energy usage) or $1,000 (for a 30% reduction in energy usage), see FTC 2d/FIN ¶ L-17942; USTR ¶ 45L4; TaxDesk ¶ 569,572. For an extension of the credit under the 2012 Taxpayer Relief Act, see ¶ 1002.

An "eligible contractor" for this purpose was (1) the person who constructed the qualified new energy efficient home (defined below), or (2) for a qualified new energy efficient home which was a manufactured home, the manufactured home producer, see FTC 2d/FIN ¶ L-17943; USTR ¶ 45L4; TaxDesk ¶ 569,571.

A qualified new energy efficient home is a dwelling unit:

. . . located in the U.S.,

. . . the construction of which is substantially completed after Aug. 8, 2005, and

. . . which meets the energy saving requirements (described below). See FTC 2d/ FIN ¶ L-17944; USTR ¶ 45L4; TaxDesk ¶ 569,574.

For this purpose, a dwelling unit satisfied the energy saving requirements under pre-2012 Taxpayer Relief Act law if the unit was certified:

(1) to have a level of annual heating and cooling energy consumption which is at least 50% below the annual level of heating and cooling energy consumption of a comparable dwelling unit:

(a) which is constructed in accordance with the standards of chapter 4 of the *2003 International Energy Conservation Code (IECC), as the IECC (including supplements) was in effect on Aug. 8, 2005* (referred to as "construction standards" below),

(b) for which the heating and cooling equipment efficiencies correspond to the minimum allowed under the regs established by the Dept. of Energy (DOE) under the National Appliance Energy Conservation Act of '87 and in effect at the time of construction (referred to as "heating and cooling equipment efficiency standards," and

(2) to have building envelope component improvements account for at least 1/5 of the 50% savings. (FTC 2d/FIN ¶ L-17940, ¶ L-17947; USTR ¶ 45L4; TaxDesk ¶ 569,575)

New Law. The 2012 Taxpayer Relief Act modifies the construction standards (discussed above at (1)(a)) by replacing "2003 International Energy Conservation Code (IECC), as the IECC (including supplements) was in effect on Aug. 8, 2005" with "*2006 International Energy Conservation Code (IECC), as the IECC (including supplements) was in effect on Jan. 1, 2006.*" (Code Sec. 45L(c)(1)(A)(i) as amended by 2012 Taxpayer Relief Act §408(b))

> ⓡ *observation:* Thus, for houses acquired after Dec. 31, 2011 (see below), an eligible contractor uses the construction standards provided in the 2006 IECC, as the IECC (including supplements) was in effect on Jan. 1, 2006, to determine whether a dwelling unit meets the energy savings requirements provided in the definition of a qualified new energy efficient home. The 2012 Taxpayer Relief Act did not change the heating and cooling equipment efficiency standards (see (1)(b) above) and the building envelope requirements (see (2) above) provided in the definition of a qualified new energy efficient home.

☐ **Effective:** Homes acquired after Dec. 31, 2011. (2012 Taxpayer Relief Act §408(c)) and before Jan. 1, 2014. (Code Sec. 45L(g))

¶ 1004. Nonbusiness energy property credit is retroactively reinstated and extended through 2013

Code Sec. 25C(g)(2), as amended by 2012 Taxpayer Relief Act §401(a)
Generally effective: Property placed in service after Dec. 31, 2011 and
  before Jan. 1, 2014
Committee Reports, None

For property placed in service before Jan. 1, 2012, individuals were allowed a nonrefundable personal income tax credit, known as the nonbusiness energy property credit, for certain energy efficient property installed in a dwelling located in the U.S. and owned and used by the taxpayer as the taxpayer's principal residence. (FTC 2d/FIN ¶ A-4750; USTR ¶ 25C4; TaxDesk ¶ 569,551)

For 2011, the credit equaled the sum of: (1) 10% of the amount paid or incurred by the taxpayer for qualified energy efficiency improvements (i.e., energy-efficient building envelope components) installed during the tax year, and (2) up to specific dollar limits, the amount of residential energy property expenditures (i.e., expenditures for advanced main air circulating fans, for qualified natural gas, propane, or oil furnace or hot water boilers, and for "energy-efficient building property," including heat pumps, water heaters, and central air conditioners, paid or incurred by the taxpayer during the tax year. The credit for 2011 was limited to $500 ($200 for windows), minus the credits claimed in previous years. (A more generous version of the credit applied for property placed in service during 2009 and 2010.) (FTC 2d/FIN ¶ A-4750, ¶ A-4751; USTR ¶ 25C4; TaxDesk ¶ 569,551)

New Law. Under the 2012 Taxpayer Relief Act, the nonbusiness energy property credit won't apply for property placed in service after Dec. 31, 2013 (rather than after Dec. 31, 2011). (Code Sec. 25C(g)(2) as amended by 2012 Taxpayer Relief Act §401(a))

> *observation:* So, through 2013, taxpayers can claim a credit of: (1) 10% of the cost of qualified energy efficiency improvements, and (2) amounts paid or incurred, up to the specific dollar limits, for residential energy property expenditures. The lifetime credit limit of $500 ($200 for windows and skylights) applies.

☐ **Effective:** Property placed in service after Dec. 31, 2011 (2012 Taxpayer Relief Act §401(b)) and before Jan. 1, 2014. (Code Sec. 25C(g)(2))

¶ 1005. Credits with respect to facilities producing energy from certain renewable resources are extended and modified

Code Sec. 45(d)(1), as amended by 2012 Taxpayer Relief Act §407(a)(1)
Code Sec. 45(d)(1), as amended by 2012 Taxpayer Relief Act §407(a)(3)(A)(i)
Code Sec. 45(d)(2)(A)(i), as amended by 2012 Taxpayer Relief Act §407(a)(3)(A)(ii)
Code Sec. 45(d)(3)(A)(i)(I), as amended by 2012 Taxpayer Relief Act §407(a)(3)(A)(iii)
Code Sec. 45(d)(6), as amended by 2012 Taxpayer Relief Act §407(a)(3)(A)(iv)
Code Sec. 45(d)(7), as amended by 2012 Taxpayer Relief Act §407(a)(3)(A)(v)
Code Sec. 45(d)(9)(B), as amended by 2012 Taxpayer Relief Act §407(a)(3)(A)(vi)
Code Sec. 45(d)(11)(B), as amended by 2012 Taxpayer Relief Act §407(a)(3)(A)(vii)
Code Sec. 45(d)(2)(A), as amended by 2012 Taxpayer Relief Act §407(a)(3)(B)
Code Sec. 45(d)(3)(A)(ii), as amended by 2012 Taxpayer Relief Act §407(a)(3)(C)
Code Sec. 45(d)(4), as amended by 2012 Taxpayer Relief Act §407(a)(3)(D)(i)
Code Sec. 45(d)(9)(C), as amended by 2012 Taxpayer Relief Act §407(a)(3)(E)(iv)
Generally effective: Jan. 2, 2013
Committee Reports, None

In general, for any tax year, a credit for electricity produced from certain renewable resources is available for electricity produced from qualified energy resources and refined coal and Indian coal produced at a qualified facility during the ten-year period beginning on the date the facility was originally placed in service. The electricity must be sold by the taxpayer to an unrelated person during the tax year. The credit is available at a reduced rate for electricity produced and sold from certain types of qualified facilities (see FTC 2d/FIN ¶ L-17770; USTR ¶ 454.04 *et seq.*; TaxDesk ¶ 384,054.1). For certain types of qualified facilities, taxpayers can elect to receive a grant in lieu of the electricity production credit, but cannot receive both a credit and a grant with respect to the same facility (see FTC 2d/FIN ¶s L-17773.2, L-17773.3; USTR ¶ 454.19; TaxDesk ¶s 384,058.3, 384,058.4) For qualified property that is part of qualified investment credit facilities, taxpayers can make an irrevocable election to take a 30% energy credit under Code Sec. 48 instead of the electricity production credit. (FTC 2d/FIN ¶ L-16401.1 *et seq.*; USTR ¶ 484.01; TaxDesk ¶ 381,601.1 *et seq.*)

Under pre-2012 Taxpayer Relief Act law, a wind facility had to be originally placed in service before Jan. 1, 2013. (FTC 2d/FIN ¶ L-17771.5; USTR ¶ 454.14; TaxDesk ¶ 384,054.1) Closed-loop biomass, open-loop biomass, municipal solid waste (which consisted of landfill gas and trash facilities), hydropower, and marine and hydrokinetic facilities had to be "placed in service" before Jan. 1, 2014. (FTC 2d/FIN ¶ L-17750, ¶ L-17771, ¶ L-17771.1B, ¶ L-17771.2, ¶ L-17771.4, ¶ L-17771.6; USTR ¶ 454.09; TaxDesk ¶ 384,028)

New Law. The 2012 Taxpayer Relief Act modifies the definition of qualified facilities producing electricity from the following qualified energy sources:

- wind (see below);
- closed-loop biomass (see below);
- open-loop biomass (see below);
- geothermal energy (see below);
- municipal solid waste (see below);
- marine and hydrokinetic renewable energy (see below); and
- hydropower (see below).

Wind facilities. The 2012 Taxpayer Relief Act provides that a qualified facility for purposes of producing electricity from wind is a facility owned by the taxpayer that is originally placed in service after Dec. 31, '93 and the construction of which begins *before Jan. 1, 2014.* (Code Sec. 45(d)(1) as amended by 2012 Taxpayer Relief Act §407(a)(1); Code Sec. 45(d)(1) as amended by 2012 Taxpayer Relief Act §407(a)(3)(A)(i))

> **✔ observation:** Thus, the 2012 Taxpayer Relief Act conforms the termination date of the credit for electricity produced from qualified wind facilities to those of the credit for electricity produced from other qualified facilities (described below).

illustration (1): Taxpayer A is the original and only owner of a wind facility that he begins construction on during December 2013. The facility is completed and placed in service and begins producing electricity on Dec. 1, 2014. The facility is a qualified facility for purposes of the electricity production credit because construction began before Jan. 1, 2014.

Closed-loop biomass facilities. The 2012 Taxpayer Relief Act provides that a closed-loop biomass facility, the construction of which begins before Jan. 1, 2014, is a qualified facility. (Code Sec. 45(d)(2)(A)(i) as amended by 2012 Taxpayer Relief Act §407(a)(3)(A)(ii))

For certain biomass facilities that are modified to co-fire with coal, with other biomass, or with both, where the modification is approved by the Biomass Power for Rural Development Programs or is part of a pilot project of the Commodity Credit Corporation (CCC) (see FTC 2d/FIN ¶ L-17771; USTR ¶ 454.09; TaxDesk ¶ 384,054.1), a closed-loop biomass facility is treated as modified before Jan. 1, 2014 if the construction of the modification begins before that date. (Code Sec. 45(d)(2)(A) as amended by 2012 Taxpayer Relief Act §407(a)(3)(B))

observation: Presumably, any modification whose construction begins before Jan. 1, 2014 must still be approved by the Biomass Power for Rural Development Programs or part of a pilot project of the CCC.

illustration (2): Taxpayer B owns a closed-loop biomass facility and modifies it to co-fire with coal and other biomass. Construction is begun on the modification in 2013 and is completed and placed in service on Jan. 1, 2014. The facility meets the requirements of a qualified closed-loop biomass facility. Because construction of the modification for co-firing began before Jan. 1, 2014, the modification is treated as if it was modified before Jan. 1, 2014, even though the modification was completed and placed in service after Dec. 31, 2013. If Taxpayer B had begun construction on Jan. 1, 2014, the modification for co-firing wouldn't be a qualified facility.

Open-loop biomass facilities. For open-loop biomass facilities, the 2012 Taxpayer Relief Act provides that a qualified facility includes a facility the construction of which begins before Jan. 1, 2014. (Code Sec. 45(d)(3)(A)(i)(I) as amended by 2012 Taxpayer Relief Act §407(a)(3)(A)(iii); Code Sec. 45(d)(3)(A)(ii) as amended by 2012 Taxpayer Relief Act §407(a)(3)(C))

Geothermal facilities. For geothermal facilities, the 2012 Taxpayer Relief Act provides that a qualified facility includes a facility using geothermal energy, the construction of which begins before Jan. 1, 2014. (Code Sec. 45(d)(4)(B) as amended by 2012 Taxpayer Relief Act §407(a)(3)(D)(i)) A "geothermal facility" doesn't include any qualified business energy property (described in Code

Sec. 48(a)(3), see FTC 2d/FIN ¶ L-16402; USTR ¶ 484; TaxDesk ¶ 381,602) the basis of which is taken into account for purposes of the energy credit under Code Sec. 48. (Code Sec. 45(d)(4) as amended by 2012 Taxpayer Relief Act §407(a)(3)(D)(i))

Municipal solid waste. For municipal solid waste facilities (including landfill gas and trash facilities), a qualified facility for purposes of the electricity production credit includes a facility the construction of which begins before Jan. 1, 2014. (Code Sec. 45(d)(6) as amended by 2012 Taxpayer Relief Act §407(a)(3)(A)(iv); Code Sec. 45(d)(7) as amended by 2012 Taxpayer Relief Act §407(a)(3)(A)(v)) For the modification of the definition of municipal solid waste, see ¶ 1011.

Marine and hydrokinetic renewable energy facilities. For marine and hydrokinetic renewable energy facilities, the 2012 Taxpayer Relief Act provides that a qualified facility includes a facility the construction of which begins before Jan. 1, 2014. (Code Sec. 45(d)(11)(B) as amended by 2012 Taxpayer Relief Act §407(a)(3)(A)(vii))

Hydropower facilities. For a facility producing qualified hydropower (other than incremental hydropower production), a qualified facility is a facility the construction of which begins before Jan. 1, 2014. (Code Sec. 45(d)(9)(B) as amended by 2012 Taxpayer Relief Act §407(a)(3)(A)(vi); Code Sec. 45(d)(9)(A)(ii) as redesignated by 2012 Taxpayer Relief Act §407(a)(3)(E)(i))

For a facility producing incremental hydropower production, an efficiency improvement or addition to capacity is treated as placed in service before Jan. 1, 2014, if the construction of the improvement or addition begins before Jan. 1, 2014. (Code Sec. 45(d)(9)(C) as amended by 2012 Taxpayer Relief Act §407(a)(3)(E)(iv))

> *observation:* Thus, the 2012 Taxpayer Relief Act allows facilities (in some cases, also modifications, additions, and improvements) generating electricity from certain renewable resources that are under construction before Jan. 1, 2014, to be treated as qualified facilities for purposes of the electricity production credit.

☐ **Effective:** Jan. 2, 2013. (2012 Taxpayer Relief Act §407(d)(1))

¶ 1006. Credit for 2- or 3-wheeled plug-in electric vehicles is retroactively extended two years to apply to vehicles acquired before Jan. 1, 2014

Code Sec. 30D(f)(2), as amended by 2012 Taxpayer Relief Act §403(b)(1)
Code Sec. 30D(f)(7), as amended by 2012 Taxpayer Relief Act §403(b)(2)
Code Sec. 30D(g), as amended by 2012 Taxpayer Relief Act §403(a)
Generally effective: Vehicles acquired after Dec. 31, 2011 and before Jan. 1, 2014
Committee Reports, None

Under pre-2012 Taxpayer Relief Act law, a credit, equal to the lesser of 10% of cost or $2,500, was available for each qualified plug-in electric vehicle acquired before Jan. 1, 2012. (FTC 2d/FIN ¶ L-18035 *et seq.*; USTR ¶ 304 *et seq.*; TaxDesk ¶ 397,170 *et seq.*)

Qualified plug-in electric vehicles included low-speed vehicles and 2- or 3-wheeled vehicles that met the following requirements:

(1) the original use of the vehicle began with the taxpayer;

(2) the vehicle was acquired for use or lease by the taxpayer and not for resale;

(3) the vehicle was made by a "manufacturer", as defined in EPA regs;

(4) the vehicle was manufactured primarily for use on public streets, roads and highways;

(5) the vehicle had a gross vehicle weight rating (GVWR (loaded weight)) of less than 14,000 pounds;

(6) the vehicle was propelled to a significant extent by an electric motor that draws electricity from a battery that had a capacity of at least 2.5 kilowatt hours and was capable of being recharged from an external source of electricity. (FTC 2d/FIN ¶ L-18035, ¶ L-18037; USTR ¶ 304.01; TaxDesk ¶ 397,172)

New Law. The 2012 Taxpayer Relief Act provides a credit for each "qualified 2- or 3-wheeled plug-in electric vehicle" placed in service by the taxpayer during the tax year equal to the lesser of 10% of the vehicle's cost or $2,500. (Code Sec. 30D(g)(1) as amended by 2012 Taxpayer Relief Act §403(a)); (Code Sec. 30(g)(2))

Among the requirements for being a "qualified 2- or 3-wheeled plug-in electric vehicle" is that the vehicle be acquired after Dec. 31, 2011 and before Jan. 1, 2014. (Code Sec. 30(g)(3)(E))

> **⚡ observation:** Thus, the 2012 Taxpayer Relief Act retroactively extends for two years the up-to-$2,500 credit available for 2- or 3-wheeled plug-in electric vehicles to apply to vehicles acquired after Dec. 31, 2011 and as late as Dec. 31, 2013. However, the requirements

for being a vehicle eligible for the credit are slightly modified, see the observations below.

Additionally, a "qualified 2- or 3-wheeled vehicle" is required to be a vehicle that: (Code Sec. 30(g)(3))

(1) has two or three wheels. (Code Sec. 30(g)(3)(A))

(2) meets the requirements of Code Sec. 30D(d)(1)(A) through Code Sec. 30D(d)(1)(C) and Code Sec. 30D(d)(1)(E) (see the observation after this list); (Code Sec. 30(g)(3)(B))

(3) meets the requirements of Code Sec. 30D(d)(1)(F) (but with a battery capacity of not less than 2.5 kilowatt hours, rather than the 4 kilowatt hours stated in Code Sec. 30D(d)(1)(F)(i), see the observation after this list); (Code Sec. 30(g)(3)(B))

(4) is manufactured primarily for use on public streets, roads and highways; and (Code Sec. 30(g)(3)(C))

(5) is capable of achieving a speed of at least 45 miles per hour. (Code Sec. 30(g)(3)(D))

> **observation:** The seven requirements referred to or expressly described in items (1) through (4) above are the same as those that applied to 2- or 3-wheeled vehicles under the pre-2012 Taxpayer Relief Act credit for qualified plug-in vehicles (see above). The 45 mile-per-hour speed requirement (item (5)) is new.

> **observation:** The changes to Code Sec. 30D(d)(f)(2) and Code Sec. 30D(d)(f)(7) discussed below were made because the credit for qualified 2- or 3-wheeled plug-in electric vehicles acquired before Jan. 1, 2012 was provided under Code Sec. 30, but, under the 2012 Taxpayer Relief Act, for vehicles acquired after Dec. 31, 2011, and before Jan. 1, 2014, under Code Sec. 30D (which previously provided a credit only for "qualified plug-in electric drive motor vehicles"). The credit provided under Code Sec. 30 for qualified plug-in electric vehicles that were low-speed vehicles wasn't extended by the 2012 Taxpayer Relief Act.

The rule that requires that, in order to be eligible for the credit under Code Sec. 30D, a qualified plug-in electric drive motor vehicle must comply with certain provisions of the Clean Air Act, certain State laws regarding air quality, and certain Federal motor vehicle safety provisions is expanded to apply to qualified 2- or 3-wheeled plug-in electric vehicles. (Code Sec. 30D(f)(7) as amended by 2012 Taxpayer Relief Act §403(b)(2))

> **observation:** In providing a credit for qualified 2- or 3-wheeled plug-in electric vehicles placed in service before Jan. 1, 2012, Code

Sec. 30 *didn't* include a rule similar to the rule in Code Sec. 30D(d)(f)(7) (above) concerning compliance with various federal and state provisions.

Also, the rule that provides that the amount of any deduction or other credit allowable for a qualified plug-in electric drive motor vehicle must be reduced by the credit allowable under Code Sec. 30D for the vehicle is expanded to apply to qualified 2- or 3-wheeled plug-in electric vehicles. (Code Sec. 30D(f)(2) as amended by 2012 Taxpayer Relief Act §403(b)(1))

> ⓡ*observation:* In providing a credit for qualified 2- or 3-wheeled plug-in electric vehicles acquired before Jan. 1, 2012, Code Sec. 30 *did* include a rule similar to the rule in Code Sec. 30D(d)(f)(2) (above) concerning compliance with various federal and state provisions. Other rules that apply to the credit for qualified 2- or 3-wheeled plug-in electric vehicles, whether placed in service before Jan. 1, 2012 or after Dec. 31, 2011, are rules concerning basis reduction, property used by a tax-exempt entity, property used outside of the U.S., recapture of the credit, and the election not to take the credit, see FTC 2d/FIN ¶ L-18037.1 *et seq.*; USTR ¶ 304.02 *et seq.*; TaxDesk ¶ 397,173 *et seq.* and FTC 2d/FIN ¶ L-18032.2 *et seq.*; USTR ¶ 30D4.04 *et seq.*; TaxDesk ¶ 397,136 *et seq.*

For the provision in the 2012 Taxpayer Relief Act that allows the qualified 2- or 3-wheeled plug-in electric vehicle credit, and other non-refundable credits, to be applied against the alternative minimum tax, see ¶ 403.

☐ **Effective:** Vehicles acquired after Dec. 31, 2011 (2012 Taxpayer Relief Act §403(c)) and before Jan. 1, 2014. (Code Sec. 30(D)(g)(3)(E))

¶ 1007. Period of credit for Indian coal produced by taxpayer at Indian coal facilities extended to eight-year period beginning Jan. 1, 2006

Code Sec. 45(e)(10), as amended by 2012 Taxpayer Relief Act §406(a)
Generally effective: Coal produced after Dec. 31, 2012
Committee Reports, None

Code Sec. 45 provides for a credit for electricity produced from certain qualified sources and sold to an unrelated person during the tax year, see FTC 2d/FIN ¶ L-17750; USTR ¶ 454; TaxDesk ¶ 384,054.

Under pre-2012 Taxpayer Relief Act law, for a producer of "Indian coal" (defined below) the credit otherwise determined under Code Sec. 45 for any tax year was increased by an amount equal to the "applicable dollar amount" (adjusted for inflation) per ton of Indian coal that was produced by the taxpayer at an "Indian coal production facility" (defined below) during the *seven*-year period beginning on Jan. 1, 2006, and sold by the taxpayer to an "unrelated person" during that seven-year period and during the tax year. (FTC 2d/FIN ¶ L-17750, ¶ L-17771.8; USTR ¶ 454)

"Indian coal" is coal which is produced from coal reserves that, on June 14, 2005 were owned by an "Indian tribe," or were held in trust by the U.S. for the benefit of an Indian tribe or its members. An "Indian coal production facility" is a facility that is placed in service before Jan. 1, 2009. An "Indian tribe" is any Indian tribe, band, nation, or other organized group or community which is recognized as eligible for the special programs and services provided by the U.S. to Indians because of their status as Indians. The applicable dollar amount for calendar year 2012 was $2.267 per ton, see FTC 2d/FIN ¶ L-17771.8; USTR ¶ 454.

New Law. The 2012 Taxpayer Relief Act provides that the credit based on the production of Indian coal is available to producers of Indian coal at Indian coal facilities during the *eight*-year period beginning on Jan. 1, 2006. Thus, for a producer of Indian coal the credit otherwise determined under Code Sec. 45 for any tax year is increased by an amount equal to the applicable dollar amount per ton of Indian coal that is produced by the taxpayer at an Indian coal production facility during the eight-year period beginning on Jan. 1, 2006, and sold by the taxpayer to an unrelated person during that eight-year period and during the tax year. (Code Sec. 45(e)(10) as amended by 2012 Taxpayer Relief Act §406(a))

> *observation:* Thus, the period for claiming a credit for sales of Indian coal produced at an Indian coal production facility and sold to an unrelated third party is extended from a seven-year period beginning on Jan. 1, 2006, and ending on Dec. 31, 2012 to an eight-year period beginning on Jan. 1, 2006 and ending on Dec. 31, 2013.

☐ **Effective:** Coal produced after Dec. 31, 2012. (2012 Taxpayer Relief Act §406(b))

> *observation:* Although the credit for Indian coal production is effective after Dec. 31, 2012, the eight-year credit period begins on Jan. 1, 2006, as discussed above.

¶ 1008. Non-hydrogen QAFV refueling property credit is retroactively restored and extended to property placed in service before Jan. 1, 2014

Code Sec. 30C(g)(2), as amended by 2012 Taxpayer Relief Act §402(a)
Generally effective: Property placed in service after Dec. 31, 2011 and
before Jan. 1, 2014
Committee Reports, None

Under pre-2012 Taxpayer Relief Act law, a taxpayer was allowed a credit against income tax for the tax year equal to 30% of the cost of any non-hydrogen qualified alternative fuel vehicle refueling property (non-hydrogen QAFV refueling property) placed in service after Dec. 31, 2010 and before Jan. 1, 2012. The credit, which was allowed for all non-hydrogen QAFV refueling property placed in service by the taxpayer during the tax year, could not exceed $30,000 in the case of depreciable non-hydrogen QAFV refueling property, and $1,000 in any other case. (FTC 2d/FIN ¶ L-18040, ¶ L-18041; USTR ¶ 30C4; TaxDesk ¶ 397,201)

New Law. The 2012 Taxpayer Relief Act provides that the credit does *not* apply to non-hydrogen QAFV refueling property placed in service after Dec. 31, *2013.* (Code Sec. 30C(g)(2) as amended by 2012 Taxpayer Relief Act §402(a))

> **Ⓡ** *observation:* Thus, the 2012 Taxpayer Relief Act retroactively restores and extends for two years the period for which the credit is available with respect to non-hydrogen QAFV refueling property placed in service before Jan. 1, 2014.

☐ **Effective:** Property placed in service after Dec. 31, 2011 (2012 Taxpayer Relief Act §402(b)) and before Jan. 1, 2014. (Code Sec. 30C(g)(2))

¶ 1009. Income and excise tax credits/refunds for biodiesel and renewable diesel are extended retroactively through 2013

Code Sec. 40A(g), as amended by 2012 Taxpayer Relief Act §405(a)
Code Sec. 6426(c)(6), as amended by 2012 Taxpayer Relief Act §405(b)(1)
Code Sec. 6427(e)(6)(B), as amended by 2012 Taxpayer Relief Act
§405(b)(2)
Generally effective: Fuel sold or used after Dec. 31, 2011 and before Jan. 1,
2014
Committee Reports, None

Under pre-2012 Taxpayer Relief Act law, for fuel sold or used before Jan. 1, 2012 (FTC 2d/FIN ¶ L-17570, ¶ L-17571; USTR ¶ 40A4; TaxDesk ¶ 382,401), a credit against income tax (the "biodiesel fuels income tax credit") was allowed for biodiesel fuels, as a component of the general business credit. The credit equals the sum of three component credits:

(1) the biodiesel mixture credit—$1.00 for each gallon of biodiesel used in the production of a qualified biodiesel mixture;

(2) the biodiesel credit—$1.00 for each gallon of biodiesel, not in a mixture, that is: (a) used by the taxpayer as a fuel in a trade or business (and not sold in a retail sale), or (b) sold by the taxpayer at retail to a person and placed in the fuel tank of that person's vehicle; and

(3) the small agri-biodiesel producer credit—10¢ for each gallon of "qualified agri-biodiesel production," up to 15 million, produced by a small producer. (See FTC 2d/FIN ¶ L-17571 *et seq.*; USTR ¶ 40A4; TaxDesk ¶ 382,401 *et seq.*)

Also, for fuel sold or used before Jan. 1, 2012 (FTC 2d ¶ W-1500, ¶ W-1518; USTR Excise Taxes ¶ 64,264), the Code provided an excise tax credit (the "biodiesel mixture excise tax credit") which was applied against a taxpayer's Code Sec. 4081 removal-at-terminal excise tax liability, and equalled $1.00 per gallon of biodiesel used by the taxpayer in producing a biodiesel mixture for sale or use in the taxpayer's trade or business. The above excise tax credit and biodiesel fuels income tax credit were coordinated to bar a taxpayer from claiming both credits for the same biodiesel. (See FTC 2d ¶ W-1518 *et seq.*; USTR Excise Taxes ¶ 64,264.)

In addition, for fuel sold or used before Jan. 1, 2012 (FTC 2d ¶ W-1500, ¶ W-1519; USTR Excise Taxes ¶ 64,274), to the extent the above biodiesel mixture excise tax credit exceeded a taxpayer's Code Sec. 4081 excise tax liability, the taxpayer, subject to certain limitations, was allowed an excise tax refund equal to the amount of that excess credit. (See FTC 2d ¶ W-1519 *et seq.*; USTR Excise Taxes ¶ 64,274.)

The above described income tax credit (other than the small agri-producer credit component), excise tax credit, and excise tax refund were also available for renewable diesel (which is, generally, treated the same as biodiesel under the Code). (See FTC 2d/FIN ¶ L-17585.1 *et seq.*; USTR ¶ 40A4.05; TaxDesk ¶ 382,409 *et seq.*) Under pre-2012 Taxpayer Relief Act law, these renewable diesel fuel incentives expired as described above for biodiesel. (FTC 2d/FIN ¶ L-17585, ¶ L-17585.1; USTR ¶ 40A4.05; TaxDesk ¶ 382,409)

New Law. The 2012 Taxpayer Relief Act retroactively (see below) extends the income and excise tax credit and refund provisions for biodiesel and renewable diesel fuel to make them apply for two additional years (through Dec. 31, 2013) by modifying the termination rules under those provisions to replace references to termination for sales or uses after "Dec. 31, 2011" with references to termination for sales or uses after "Dec. 31, 2013." (Code Sec. 40A(g) as amended by 2012 Taxpayer Relief Act §405(a)) (Code Sec. 6426(c)(6) as amended by 2012 Taxpayer Relief Act §405(b)(1)) (Code Sec. 6427(e)(6)(B) as amended by 2012 Taxpayer Relief Act §405(b)(2))

☐ **Effective:** Fuel sold or used after Dec. 31, 2011 (2012 Taxpayer Relief Act §405(c)) and before Jan. 1 2014. (Code Sec. 40A(g)) (Code Sec. 6426(c)(6)) (Code Sec. 6427(e)(6)(B))

> *observation:* Generally, the biodiesel mixture and renewable diesel mixture excise tax credits must first be taken on Form 720, the quarterly excise tax return, as a credit against any taxable fuel tax liability (for gasoline, diesel fuel and kerosene) reported on Form 720 (see FTC 2d ¶ W-1518). Then, any excess credit amounts may generally be claimed as an excise tax refund on Form 8849 (or, alternatively, as a fuels tax credit against income tax on Form 4136) (see FTC 2d ¶ W-1519). IRS may issue guidance on how to claim this excise tax credit/refund retroactively for 2012.

> *observation:* The biodiesel and renewable diesel fuels income tax credits are computed on Form 8864 (see FTC 2d/FIN ¶ L-17571; TaxDesk ¶ 382,401) and then included on Form 3800 (as part of the general business credit) (see FTC 2d/FIN ¶ L-15200; TaxDesk ¶ 380,500), and both forms must be attached to the taxpayer's tax return, i.e., the Form 1040 or Form 1040NR for individuals, Form 1120 for corporations, or Form 1041 for estates and trusts, for the applicable year. If a taxpayer has already filed 2012 returns, the retroactive extension of these credits (to the beginning of 2012) may require that they file an amended return to claim a credit.

¶ 1010. Alternative fuels and alternative fuel mixture excise tax credit, and alternative fuels excise tax refund rules, are retroactively extended through 2013

Code Sec. 6426(d)(5), as amended by 2012 Taxpayer Relief Act §412(a)
Code Sec. 6426(e)(3), as amended by 2012 Taxpayer Relief Act §412(a)
Code Sec. 6427(e)(6)(C), as amended by 2012 Taxpayer Relief Act §412(b)(1)
Code Sec. 6427(e)(6)(D), as amended by 2012 Taxpayer Relief Act §412(b)(2)
Code Sec. 6427(e)(6)(E), as amended by 2012 Taxpayer Relief Act §412(b)(3)
Generally effective: Fuel sold or used after Dec. 31, 2011 and before Jan. 1, 2014
Committee Reports, None

A 50¢-per-gallon (or gasoline gallon equivalent [GGE], for non-liquid fuel) excise tax credit is allowed against:

. . . Code Sec. 4041 retail fuel excise tax liability—for alternative fuel (defined below) sold for use, or used, by the taxpayer as a fuel in a motor vehicle or motorboat, or in aviation (the "alternative fuel excise tax credit"); and

. . . Code Sec. 4081 removal at terminal excise tax liability—for alternative fuel (defined below) used to produce an alternative fuel mixture (i.e., a mixture of alternative fuel and either gasoline, diesel fuel, or kerosene) for sale or use in a trade or business of the taxpayer (the "alternative fuel mixture excise tax credit").

In addition, to the extent the taxpayer's alternative fuel excise tax credit or alternative fuel mixture excise tax credit exceeds the taxpayer's Code Sec. 4041 or Code Sec. 4081 excise tax liability, respectively, the taxpayer, subject to certain limitations, may claim an excise tax refund (or, in some cases, a credit against income tax) equal to the amount of that excess credit.

The alternative fuels that qualify for the above-described incentives are:

(A) liquefied petroleum gas (LPG);

(B) P Series Fuels (as defined by the Secretary of Energy under 42 USC § 13211);

(C) compressed or liquefied natural gas (CNG or LNG);

(D) liquefied hydrogen;

(E) any liquid fuel that meets specified carbon capture requirements, and is derived from coal (including peat) through the Fisher-Tropsch process;

(F) compressed or liquefied gas derived from biomass (as defined in Code Sec. 45K(c)(3)); and

(G) liquid fuel derived from biomass (as defined in Code Sec. 45K(c)(3), e.g., fish oils and liquids derived from other rendered fats).

Fuel that is ethanol, methanol, biodiesel, renewable diesel fuel, or black liquor, doesn't qualify as an alternative fuel.

Under pre-2012 Taxpayer Relief Act law, the alternative fuel and alternative fuel mixture excise tax credit and refund rules, for all fuels *other than* fuels involving liquefied hydrogen, terminated for any sale or use after Dec. 31, 2011. For any sale or use involving liquefied hydrogen, the credit and refund rules terminate for any sale or use after Sept. 30, 2014. (FTC 2d ¶ W-1500, ¶ W-1518, ¶ W-1519, ¶ W-1519.1, ¶ W-1700, ¶ W-1737.1, ¶ W-1737.2, ¶ W-1737.3; USTR Excise Taxes ¶ 64,264, ¶ 64,274)

New Law. The 2012 Taxpayer Relief Act retroactively extends the alternative fuels and alternative fuel mixture excise tax credits, for fuels other than those involving liquefied hydrogen, for two additional years (through Dec. 31, 2013). It does this by modifying the termination rules under those provisions to replace references to termination for sales or uses after "Dec. 31, 2011" with references to termination for sales or uses after "Dec. 31, 2013." (Code Sec.

6426(d)(5) as amended by 2012 Taxpayer Relief Act §412(a)) (Code Sec. 6426(e)(3) as amended by 2012 Taxpayer Relief Act §412(a))

> **🖎 *observation:*** Thus, the excise tax credits for alternative fuels and alternative fuel mixtures, other than for fuels involving liquefied hydrogen, won't apply to sales and uses after Dec. 31, 2013.

The 2012 Taxpayer Relief Act also retroactively extends for two years (through Dec. 31, 2013) the alternative fuels excise tax refund provision, for fuels other than those involving liquefied hydrogen. But it doesn't also extend the alternative fuel mixture excise tax refund rules. Specifically, the 2012 Taxpayer Relief Act creates separate termination rules for alternative fuels and alternative fuel mixture excise tax refunds (Code Sec. 6427(e)(6)(C) as amended by 2012 Taxpayer Relief Act §412(b)(1)(A); Code Sec. 6427(e)(6)(E) as amended by 2012 Taxpayer Relief Act §412(b)(3)), and under the separate alternative fuels refund termination rule replaces references to termination for sales or uses after "Dec. 31, 2011" with references to termination for sales or uses after "Dec. 31, 2013." (Code Sec. 6427(e)(6)(C) as amended by 2012 Taxpayer Relief Act §412(b)(1)(B)) The separate alternative fuel mixture termination rule, however, provides for termination for any alternative fuel mixtures sold or used after Dec. 31, 2011. (Code Sec. 6427(e)(6)(E))

> **🖎 *observation:*** A summary of the 2012 Taxpayer Relief Act prepared by Senate staff explains the above-described failure to extend the alternative fuel mixture excise tax *refund* rules as follows: "Due to claims of abuse in the alternative mixture tax credit, the Committee adopted an amendment denying taxpayers from claiming the refundable portion of the alternative fuel mixture tax credit."

The 2012 Taxpayer Relief Act also eliminates, effective for fuel sold or used after Dec. 31, 2011 (2012 Taxpayer Relief Act §412(c)), the reference to "alternative fuel mixtures" under the termination rule for refunds for sales or uses of fuels involving liquefied hydrogen. (Code Sec. 6427(e)(6)(D) as amended by 2012 Taxpayer Relief Act §412(b)(2))

> **🖎 *observation:*** This change appears to retroactively bar alternative fuel mixture excise tax refunds for sales or uses of alternative fuel mixtures involving liquefied hydrogen after Dec. 31, 2011. But it's not clear that Congress intended to make this particular change retroactive—as taxpayers may have already received refunds for these fuel mixtures for 2012. That's because, as described above, under pre-2012 Taxpayer Relief Act law, refunds for alternative fuel mixtures involving liquefied hydrogen (unlike for other alternative fuel mixtures) were still permitted after Dec. 31, 2011 (and through Sept. 30, 2014). If this change wasn't, in fact, intended to be retroactive, a technical correction would be required.

observation: The 2012 Taxpayer Relief Act leaves unchanged the termination rule for claims for alternative fuels excise tax credits or refunds for alternative fuels involving liquefied hydrogen. That is, alternative fuels excise tax credits or refunds are first barred for sales and uses of alternative fuels involving liquefied hydrogen after Sept. 30, 2014.

☐ **Effective:** For alternative fuels and alternative fuel mixture excise tax credits and refunds (as described above), for fuel other than those involving liquefied hydrogen, sold or used after Dec. 31, 2011 (2012 Taxpayer Relief Act §412(c)) and before Jan. 1, 2014 (Code Sec. 6426(d)(5), Code Sec. 6426(e)(3), Code Sec. 6427(e)(6)(C)).

¶ 1011. Definition of municipal solid waste does not include paper that is commonly recycled and segregated from other solid waste

Code Sec. 45(c)(6), as amended by 2012 Taxpayer Relief Act §407(a)(2)
Generally effective: Electricity produced and sold after Jan. 2, 2013, in tax years ending after Jan. 2, 2013
Committee Reports, None

For purposes of the electricity production credit, qualified energy resources (see FTC 2d/FIN ¶ L-17770 *et seq.*; USTR ¶ 454 *et seq.*; TaxDesk ¶ 384,541) include electricity produced from municipal solid waste (defined below). Under pre-2012 Taxpayer Relief Act law, "municipal solid waste" means solid waste as defined under section 2(27) of the Solid Waste Disposal Act (42 USC §6903). (FTC 2d/FIN ¶ L-17771.4; USTR ¶ 454.13; TaxDesk ¶ 384,054.1)

observation: The above provision of the Solid Waste Disposal Act defines solid waste as "any garbage, refuse, sludge from a waste treatment plant, water supply treatment plant, or air pollution control facility and other discarded material, including solid, liquid, semisolid, or contained gaseous material resulting from industrial, commercial, mining, and agricultural operations, and from community activities, but does not include solid or dissolved material in domestic sewage, or solid or dissolved materials in irrigation return flows or industrial discharges which are point sources subject to permits under section 1342 of title 33, or source, special nuclear, or byproduct material as defined by the Atomic Energy Act of '54, as amended."

New Law. The 2012 Taxpayer Relief Act provides, as an exception to the pre-2012 Taxpayer Relief Act definition of municipal solid waste, that municipal solid waste for purposes of the electricity production credit does *not* include paper that is commonly recycled and has been segregated from other solid waste as defined under pre-2012 Taxpayer Relief Act law. (Code Sec. 45(c)(6) as amended by 2012 Taxpayer Relief Act §407(a)(2))

☐ **Effective:** Electricity produced and sold after Jan. 2, 2013, in tax years ending after Jan. 2, 2013. (2012 Taxpayer Relief Act §407(d)(2))

¶ 1012. Definition of qualified property for purposes of the election to take a 30% energy credit instead of the electricity production credit is retroactively clarified

Code Sec. 48(a)(5)(D), as amended by 2012 Taxpayer Relief Act §407(c)(1)(C)
Generally effective: Facilities placed in service after Dec. 31, 2008
Committee Reports, None

Under pre-2012 Taxpayer Relief Act law, for purposes of the election to take a 30% energy credit instead of the electricity production credit for qualified property that is part of qualified investment credit facilities, qualified property means (1) tangible personal property, or (2) other tangible property (not including a building or its structural components), for which depreciation (or amortization in lieu of depreciation) is allowable, but only if the property is used as an integral part of the qualified investment credit facility. (FTC 2d/FIN ¶ L-16401.2; USTR ¶ 484; TaxDesk ¶ 381,601.2)

The 2009 Recovery Act, specifically 2009 Recovery Act §1603(a), Division B (Sec. 1603(a), PL 111-5, 2/17/2009), also provided for election of a grant in lieu of the credit. (FTC 2d/FIN ¶ L-16440 *et seq.*; USTR ¶ 484.02; TaxDesk ¶ 381,608 *et seq.*) IRS can't make the grant to a person placing qualified property in service unless the property was placed in service:

. . . during 2009, 2010, or 2011, or

. . . after 2011 and before the "credit termination date" (defined in) for that property, but only if construction of the property began during 2009, 2010, or 2011.

New Law. The 2012 Taxpayer Relief Act further defines qualified property for purposes of the election to take a 30% energy credit instead of the electricity production credit as property that is constructed, reconstructed, erected or acquired by the taxpayer *and* the original use of which commences with the taxpayer. (Code Sec. 48(a)(5)(D) as amended by 2012 Taxpayer Relief Act §407(c)(1)(C))

observation: Thus, qualified property for this purpose is property

(i) which is:

(a) tangible personal property, or

(b) other tangible property (not including a building or its structural components), but only if such property is used as an integral part of the qualified investment credit facility,

(ii) for which depreciation (or amortization in lieu of depreciation) is allowable,

(iii) which is constructed, reconstructed, erected, or acquired by the taxpayer, *and*

(iv) the original use of which commences with the taxpayer.

The election can therefore be made only for property satisfying items (i) through (iv), above.

In addition, the term "placed in service" as used in 2009 Recovery Act §1603(a), Division B, is replaced with "originally placed in service by such person." (2009 Recovery Act §1603(a), Division B (Sec. 1603(a), PL 111-5, 2/17/2009) as amended by 2012 Taxpayer Relief Act §407(c)(2))

> **RIA** *observation:* Thus, IRS can't make the grant to a person placing qualified property in service unless the property was *originally* placed in service *by that person*:
>
> . . . during 2009, 2010, or 2011, or
>
> . . . after 2011 and before the "credit termination date" for that property, but only if construction of the property began during 2009, 2010, or 2011.

☐ **Effective:** Facilities placed in service after Dec. 31, 2008. (2012 Taxpayer Relief Act §407(d)(3))

> **RIA** *observation:* The 2012 Taxpayer Relief Act, specifically 2012 Taxpayer Relief Act § 407(d)(3), provides that the above provisions are effective as if included in the provisions of the 2009 Recovery Act to which the above rules relate.
>
> The amendments to Code Sec. 48(a)(5)(D) relate to 2009 Recovery Act §1102(a), Division B (Sec. 1102(a), PL 111-5, 2/17/2009) which, under 2009 Recovery Act §1102(b), Division B (Sec. 1102(b), PL 111-5, 2/17/2009), is effective for facilities placed in service after Dec. 31, 2008.
>
> The amendments to 2009 Recovery Act §1603(a), Division B (Sec. 1603(a), PL 111-5, 2/17/2009) effectively apply under that section for property placed in service after Dec. 31, 2008.

¶ 1013. Bonus depreciation and AMT depreciation relief for certain biofuel plant property is extended one year through Dec. 31, 2013 and expanded

Code Sec. 168(l), as amended by 2012 Taxpayer Relief Act §410(b)(2)(A)
Code Sec. 168(l)(2)(A), as amended by 2012 Taxpayer Relief Act §410(b)(1)
Code Sec. 168(l)(2)(D), as amended by 2012 Taxpayer Relief Act §410(a)(1)
Generally effective: Property placed in service after Dec. 31, 2012 (after Jan. 2, 2013 for qualified second generation biofuel plant property) and before Jan. 1, 2014
Committee Reports, None

For most tangible property, the depreciation deduction under Code Sec. 167(a) is determined under the modified accelerated cost recovery system (MACRS) provided by Code Sec. 168, see FTC 2d/FIN ¶ L-8101; USTR ¶ 1684; TaxDesk ¶ 266,001.

Certain property depreciated on the 200% declining balance method for regular income tax purposes must be depreciated on the 150% declining balance method for alternative minimum tax purposes (the AMT depreciation adjustment), see FTC 2d/FIN ¶ A-8220; USTR ¶ 564.01; TaxDesk ¶ 696,513.

From time to time, for certain depreciable property, there has been allowed both (1) 50% additional first-year depreciation (50% bonus depreciation) in the year that the property was placed in service (with corresponding reduction in basis), see, for example, FTC 2d/FIN ¶ L-9311; USTR ¶ 1684.025; TaxDesk ¶ 269,341, and (2) exemption from the AMT depreciation adjustment, see FTC 2d/FIN ¶ A-8221; USTR ¶ 1684.029; TaxDesk ¶ 696,514.

One of the types of property for which both 50% bonus depreciation and AMT exemption was available was, as provided in Code Sec. 168(l), "qualified cellulosic biofuel plant property." (FTC 2d/FIN ¶ A-8221, ¶ L-9356; USTR ¶ 1684.08)

"Qualified cellulosic biofuel plant property" was defined, generally, as property of a character subject to the allowance for depreciation:

(1) which was used in the U.S. solely to produce cellulosic biofuel,

(2) the original use of which commenced with the taxpayer,

(3) which was acquired by the taxpayer by purchase, and

(4) which was placed in service by the taxpayer before Jan. 1, 2013. (FTC 2d/FIN ¶ L-9357; USTR ¶ 1684.081)

For purposes of the above rules, "cellulosic biofuel" was defined as any liquid fuel which is produced from any lignocellulosic or hemicellulosic matter that is available on a renewable or recurring basis. (FTC 2d/FIN ¶ L-9357; USTR ¶ 1684.081)

New Law. The 2012 Taxpayer Relief Act substitutes "Jan. 1, 2014" for "Jan. 1, 2013" in Code Sec. 168(l)(2)(D) (see the observation immediately below). (Code Sec. 168(l)(2)(D) as amended by 2012 Taxpayer Relief Act §410(a)(1))

> 🄁 *observation:* As a *technical* matter, the date change from "Jan. 1, 2013" to "Jan. 1, 2014" in Code Sec. 168(l)(2)(D) extends bonus depreciation and AMT depreciation relief for (1) "qualified cellulosic biofuel plant property" placed in service on Jan. 1, 2013 or Jan. 2, 2013 (i.e., the extension is only for two days) and (2) "qualified second generation biofuel plant property" placed in service after Jan. 2, 2013 and before Jan. 1, 2014. This is so because as discussed below, for property placed in service after Jan. 2, 2013 (see **Effective** below), "qualified second generation biofuel plant property" and "second generation biofuel" are substituted for "qualified cellulosic biofuel plant property" and "cellulosic biofuel" in Code Sec. 168(l). However, as a *practical* matter, the date change extends the availability of bonus depreciation and AMT depreciation relief for "qualified cellulosic biofuel plant property" through all of calendar year 2013. This is so, because as discussed below, "second generation biofuel" includes cellulosic biofuel.

The 2012 Taxpayer Relief Act replaces all references in Code Sec. 168(l) to "cellulosic biofuel" with references to "second generation biofuel." (Code Sec. 168(l)(2)(A) as amended by 2012 Taxpayer Relief Act §410(b)(1); Code Sec. 168(l) as amended by 2012 Taxpayer Relief Act §410(b)(2)(A))

> 🄁 *observation:* Thus, "qualified second generation biofuel plant property" and "second generation biofuel" are substituted for "qualified cellulosic biofuel plant property" and "cellulosic biofuel" in Code Sec. 168(l). Accordingly, during the period beginning on Jan. 3, 2013 and running through Dec. 31, 2013, it is "qualified second generation biofuel plant property" (a term that includes qualified cellulosic biofuel plant property, see below) that gets the benefit of bonus depreciation and AMT depreciation relief.

For purposes of Code Sec. 168(l), "second generation biofuel" is defined in Code Sec. 40(b)(6)(E). (Code Sec. 168(l)(2)(A))

> 🄁 *observation:* Under Code Sec. 40(b)(6)(E), as amended by the 2012 Taxpayer Relief Act, "second generation biofuel" is defined, generally, as liquid fuel that (1) is derived by or from any qualified feedstocks and (2) meets the registration requirements for fuels and fuel additives established by the Environmental Protection Agency (EPA) under §211 of the Clean Air Act (42 USC 7545), see ¶ 1016. For this purpose, under Code Sec. 40(b)(6)(F) as amended by the 2012 Taxpayer Relief Act, qualified feedstocks include any lignocellulosic or hemicellulosic matter that is available on a renewable or recurring basis *and* any culti-

vated algae, cyanobacteria and lemna, see ¶ 1016. Thus, the terms "qualified second generation biofuel plant property" and "second generation biofuel" include, but are broader than, "qualified cellulosic biofuel plant property" and "cellulosic biofuel."

☐ **Effective:** Property placed in service after Dec. 31, 2012 (2012 Taxpayer Relief Act §410(a)(2)) (but after Jan. 2, 2013 for the substitution of references to "second generation biofuel" for references to "cellulosic biofuel" (2012 Taxpayer Relief Act §410(b)(3)) and before Jan. 1, 2014. (Code Sec. 168(l)(2)(D))

¶ 1014. Gain deferral election on qualifying electric transmission transactions is retroactively restored and extended to dispositions before Jan. 1, 2014

Code Sec. 451(i)(3), as amended by 2012 Taxpayer Relief Act §411(a)
Generally effective: Dispositions after Dec. 31, 2011 and before Jan. 1, 2014
Committee Reports, None

A taxpayer can elect to recognize gain on certain qualifying electric transmission transactions ratably over an eight-year period to the extent the amount realized is used to purchase exempt utility property within four years of the sale date. (FTC 2d/FIN ¶ I-2620 *et seq.*; USTR ¶ 4514.200; TaxDesk ¶ 222,413)

Under pre-2012 Taxpayer Relief Act law, a qualifying electric transmission transaction is any sale or other disposition by a qualified electric utility to an independent transmission company before Jan. 1, *2012* of (i) property used in the trade or business of providing electric transmission services, or (ii) any stock or partnership interest in an entity whose principal trade or business is the provision of the services. (FTC 2d/FIN ¶ I-2600, ¶ I-2622; USTR ¶ 4514.200; TaxDesk ¶ 222,413)

New Law. The 2012 Taxpayer Relief Act provides that a qualifying electric transmission transaction is any sale or other disposition by a qualified electric utility to an independent transmission company before Jan. 1, *2014*. (Code Sec. 451(i)(3) as amended by 2012 Taxpayer Relief Act §411(a))

> ⊕ *observation:* In other words, the 2012 Taxpayer Relief Act extends the treatment under the deferral election to sales or dispositions by a qualified electric utility that occur before Jan. 1, 2014.

☐ **Effective:** Dispositions after Dec. 31, 2011 (2012 Taxpayer Relief Act §411(b)) and before Jan. 1, 2014. (Code Sec. 451(i)(3))

> ⊕ *recommendation:* If a qualified electric utility realized gain from a qualifying electric transmission transaction after Dec. 31, 2011 that qualifies for deferral under Code Sec. 451(i)(3) (as amended by 2012

Taxpayer Relief Act 411(a)), and the utility has already filed its return for the fiscal year (that includes the portion of 2012 in which the disposition occurred), the qualified electric utility may need to consider filing an amended return to claim the deferral of gain under Code Sec. 451(i)(3).

¶ 1015. Cellulosic biofuel producer credit is retroactively restored and extended through Dec. 31, 2013

Code Sec. 40(b)(6)(H), as amended by 2012 Taxpayer Relief Act §404(a)(1)
Generally effective: Fuel produced after Dec. 31, 2008 and before Jan. 1, 2014
Committee Reports, None

The cellulosic biofuel producer credit is a component of the Code Sec. 40 alcohol fuels credit. This credit is a nonrefundable income tax credit for each gallon of qualified cellulosic fuel production of the producer for the tax year, and is in addition to any credit that may be available under the alcohol fuels credit. Under pre-2012 Taxpayer Relief Act law, the credit applied with respect to qualified cellulosic biofuel production after Dec. 31, 2008 and before Jan. 1, 2013. (FTC 2d/FIN ¶ L-17516.1; USTR ¶ 404.07 *et seq.*; TaxDesk ¶ 382,213)

New Law. The 2012 Taxpayer Relief Act retroactively restores and extends the credit for qualified cellulosic biofuel production after Dec. 31, 2008 and before Jan. 1, *2014.* (Code Sec. 40(b)(6)(H)(i) as amended by 2012 Taxpayer Relief Act §404(a)(1))

If the cellulosic biofuel production credit ceases to apply for any period because of the Jan. 1, 2014 termination date provided in Code Sec. 40(b)(6)(H)(i), rules similar to the rules provided in Code Sec. 40(e)(2) (rules providing that certain alcohol fuels credits can't be carried over to tax years after the expiration of the credit, see FTC 2d/FIN ¶ L-17518; USTR ¶ 404; TaxDesk ¶ 382,210) will apply. (Code Sec. 40(b)(6)(H)(ii) as amended by 2012 Taxpayer Relief Act §404(a)(1))

> *observation:* Since the credit, under 2012 Taxpayer Relief Act law, has a termination date of Jan. 1, 2014, a calendar year taxpayer with unclaimed credits at the end of 2013, won't be able to carry over any unused credit to tax years beginning after Dec. 31, 2016.

☐ **Effective:** Fuel produced after Dec. 31, 2008 (2012 Taxpayer Relief Act §404(a)(3)) and before Jan. 1, 2014. (Code Sec. 40(b)(6)(H)(i))

> *observation:* 2012 Taxpayer Relief Act §404(a)(3) provides that the above provision is effective as if included in §15321(b) of the 2008 Farm Act (Sec. 15321(b), PL 110-246, 5/22/2008). That provision was

effective for fuel produced after Dec. 31, 2008 under §15321(g) of the 2008 Farm Act (Sec. 15321(g), PL 110-246, 5/22/2008).

¶ 1016. Algae is treated as a qualified feedstock for purposes of the cellulose biofuel producer credit

Code Sec. 40(b)(6)(E)(i)(I), as amended by 2012 Taxpayer Relief Act §404(b)(1)
Code Sec. 40(b)(6)(F), as amended by 2012 Taxpayer Relief Act §404(b)(2)
Code Sec. 40(b)(6)(G), as amended by 2012 Taxpayer Relief Act §404(b)(2)
Code Sec. 40(b)(6), as amended by 2012 Taxpayer Relief Act §404(b)(3)(A)(ii)
Code Sec. 4101(a), as amended by 2012 Taxpayer Relief Act §404(b)(3)(C)
Generally effective: Fuels sold or used after Jan. 2, 2013.
Committee Reports, None

The cellulosic biofuel producer credit is a component of the Code Sec. 40 alcohol fuels credit. (see FTC 2d/FIN ¶ L-17500 *et seq.*; USTR ¶ 404 *et seq.*; TaxDesk ¶ 382,200 *et seq.*) This credit is a nonrefundable income tax credit for each gallon of qualified cellulosic fuel production (see FTC 2d/FIN ¶ L-17516.3; USTR ¶ 404.09; TaxDesk ¶ 382,213) of the producer for the tax year, and is in addition to any credit that may be available under the alcohol fuels credit. Thus, the alcohol fuels credit determined under Code Sec. 40 for a tax year is an amount equal to the sum of: (1) the alcohol mixture credit, (2) the alcohol credit, (3) the small ethanol producer credit (for an eligible small ethanol producer), and (4) for alcohol fuels produced after Dec. 31, 2008, the cellulosic biofuel producer credit (for a cellulosic biofuel producer) (see FTC 2d/FIN ¶ L-17502; USTR ¶ 404.01; TaxDesk ¶ 382,202). The term cellulosic biofuel under pre-2012 Taxpayer Relief Act law meant any liquid fuel which is produced from any lignocellulosic or hemicellulosic matter that is available on a renewable or recurring basis, and meets the registration requirements for fuels and fuel additives established by the Environmental Protection Agency (EPA) under §211 of the Clean Air Act (42 USC §7545).

Code Sec. 40 referred to cellulosic biofuel rather than second generation biofuel as discussed below. Persons producing second generation biofuel who registered with IRS under Code Sec. 4101(a) were called cellulosic biofuel producers. (FTC 2d/FIN ¶ L-17516.3, ¶ L-17516.5; USTR ¶ 404.07 *et seq.*; TaxDesk ¶ 382,213)

Under pre-2012 Taxpayer Relief Act law, a taxpayer can't receive a credit for cellulosic biofuel production unless that taxpayer registers with IRS as a producer of cellulosic biofuel. Every person producing cellulosic biofuel must register with IRS as a producer of cellulosic biofuel under Code Sec. 4101. (FTC 2d/FIN ¶ L-17516.8, ¶ W-1527; USTR ¶ 41,014)

observation: Under pre-2012 Taxpayer Relief Act law, algae was not specifically mentioned as a feedstock.

New Law. The 2012 Taxpayer Relief Act provides that the term cellulosic biofuel means any liquid fuel which is derived by, or from, qualified feedstocks. (Code Sec. 40(b)(6)(E)(i)(I) as amended by 2012 Taxpayer Relief Act §404(b)(1)) Qualified feedstock is any lignocellulosic or hemicellulosic matter that is available on a renewable or recurring basis and (Code Sec. 40(b)(6)(F)(i) as amended by 2012 Taxpayer Relief Act §404(b)(2)) any cultivated algae, cyanobacteria or lemna. (Code Sec. 40(b)(6)(F)(ii))

observation: Cyanobacteria is also called blue-green bacteria, blue-green algae, and Cyanophyta, and obtains its energy through photosynthesis. Lemna is a type of free-floating aquatic plant.

Special rules for algae. For fuel that is derived by or from any cultivated algae, cyanobacteria or lemna and that is sold by the taxpayer to another person for refining by that other person into a fuel that meets the requirements for fuels and fuel additives established by the Environmental Protection Agency (EPA) under 42 USC §7545 (i.e., §211 of the Clean Air Act), and the refined fuel is not excluded under Code Sec. 40(b)(6)(E)(iii) (i.e., the fuel is (a) more than 4% by weight any combination of water and sediment, (b) the ash content is more than 1% (determined by weight) or (c) the fuel has an acid number greater than 25), that sale is treated as a sale by the taxpayer to another person. (Code Sec. 40(b)(6)(G)(i)) The fuel is treated as meeting the above requirements of the Clean Air Act, and the refined fuel is not excluded from the definition of cellulosic biofuels in the hands of the taxpayer. (Code Sec. 40(b)(6)(G)(ii)) In addition, that fuel will not be taken into account for purposes of cellulosic biofuel production with respect to the taxpayer or any other person. (Code Sec. 40(b)(6)(G)(iii))

The term "cellulosic biofuel" is replaced with "second generation biofuel" wherever it appears in Code Sec. 40 for purposes of the alcohol fuels credit. (Code Sec. 40 as amended by 2012 Taxpayer Relief Act §404(b)(3)(A))

The term "cellulosic biofuel" is also replaced with "second generation biofuel" in Code Sec. 4101 (pertaining to registration by producers and bond for certain excise taxes). (Code Sec. 4101(a)(1) as amended by 2012 Taxpayer Relief Act §404(b)(3)(C))

observation: Thus, with the addition of algae as a feedstock for purposes of the credit and requirements for producers to register, cellulosic biofuel is referred to as second generation biofuel.

☐ **Effective:** Fuels sold or used after Jan. 2, 2013. (2012 Taxpayer Relief Act §404(b)(4))

¶ 1100. Charitable Contributions

¶ 1101. Rule allowing tax-free IRA distributions of up to $100,000 if donated to charity, is retroactively extended through 2013

Code Sec. 408(d)(8)(F), as amended by 2012 Taxpayer Relief Act §208(a)
Generally effective: For IRA distributions made during 2012 and 2013
Committee Reports, None

The IRA distribution rules allow for the tax-free treatment of distributions from IRAs where the distributions are donated to charity. Specifically, a taxpayer may exclude from gross income so much of the aggregate amount of his "qualified charitable distributions" not exceeding $100,000 in a tax year.

A "qualified charitable distribution" is any otherwise taxable distribution from a traditional IRA or a Roth IRA that is:

(1) made directly by the IRA trustee to a Code Sec. 170(b)(1)(A) charitable organization (other than a Code Sec. 509(a)(3) private foundation or a Code Sec. 4966(d)(2) donor advised fund); and

(2) made on or after the date on which the individual for whose benefit the IRA is maintained (i.e., the IRA owner) has attained age 70½.

For purposes of the required minimum distribution (RMD) rules as they apply to individual retirement accounts and individual retirement annuities, qualified charitable distributions may be taken into account to the same extent that the distribution *would* have been taken into account under the RMD rules had the distribution *not* been directly distributed under the IRA qualified charitable distribution rules. Thus, an IRA owner who makes an IRA qualified charitable distribution in an amount equal to his RMD for the tax year is considered to have satisfied his minimum distribution requirement for that year, even though a charitable entity (and not the IRA owner) is the recipient of the distribution.

Under pre-2012 Taxpayer Relief Act law, the tax-free qualified charitable distribution rules, above, only applied to distributions made in tax years beginning no later than Dec. 31, 2011 (the "termination date"). ((FTC 2d/FIN ¶ H-12200, ¶ H-12253.2; USTR ¶ 4084.03; TaxDesk ¶ 143,003.2; PCA ¶ 35,154.2))

New Law. Under the 2012 Taxpayer Relief Act, the termination date of the tax-free qualified charitable distribution rule is amended by substituting Dec.

31, 2013, for Dec. 31, 2011. (Code Sec. 408(d)(8)(F) as amended by 2012 Taxpayer Relief Act §208(a))

> *observation:* So, the Act extends the tax-free qualified charitable distribution rules for two years (through 2013), and thus the rules may be applied to IRA distributions made in tax years beginning after Dec. 31, 2011 and before Jan. 1, 2014.

> *observation:* Thus, under the 2012 Act, taxpayers age 70½ or older may exclude from gross income up to $100,000 of their qualified charitable distributions for each tax year beginning in 2012 and 2013 (in addition to any qualified charitable distributions they may have made through 2011).

Special election for Dec. 2012 distributions. Under a special rule, for purposes of both (i) the tax-free qualified charitable distribution rules, and (ii) the RMD rules as they apply to IRAs, any portion of an IRA distribution made *to the taxpayer* after Nov. 30, 2012, and before Jan. 1, 2013 (i.e., during Dec. 2012), may be treated as a qualified charitable distribution, if the IRA owner so elects at such time and in such manner as IRS will prescribe, to the extent that the portion is:

(i) transferred in cash after the distribution to an eligible charity before Feb. 1, 2013; and

(ii) part of a distribution that would otherwise satisfy the tax-free qualified charitable distribution rules, but for the fact that the distribution was not transferred directly to an eligible charity. (2012 Taxpayer Relief Act §208(b)(2)(B))

> *observation:* Thus, the special election for Dec. 2012 distributions provides a limited exception to the general rule that charitable transfers must be made by the IRA trustee directly to an eligible charity.

> *illustration:* Peter is an individual who is over age 70½, and the owner of a traditional IRA. On Dec. 12, 2012, Peter received a $75,000 distribution from the IRA.
>
> Under the special rule for Dec. 2012 distributions, Peter can elect to transfer to an eligible charity any amount of cash up to $75,000, and the amount transferred will be treated as a tax-free qualified charitable distribution, as long as Peter makes the charitable transfer no later than Jan. 31, 2013.

Special election for Jan. 2013 distributions. Under another special rule, for purposes of both (i) the tax-free qualified charitable distribution rules, and (ii) the RMD rules as they apply to IRAs, any qualified charitable distribution made after Dec. 31, 2012, and before Feb. 1, 2013 (i.e., during Jan. 2013), will be deemed to have been made on Dec. 31, 2012, if the IRA owner so elects at such time and in such manner as IRS will prescribe. (2012 Taxpayer Relief Act §208(b)(2)(A))

> **observation:** Thus, at the taxpayer's election, a qualified charitable distribution made in Jan. 2013 is permitted to be treated as made in 2012, and thus permitted to (a) count against the 2012 $100,000 limitation on the exclusion, and (b) be used to satisfy the taxpayer's RMD for 2012.

> **observation:** For purposes of the special election for Jan. 2013 distributions, the IRA distribution must be made by the IRA trustee *directly* to the eligible charity, unlike the exception to the direct transfer rule provided under the special election for Dec. 2012 distributions, above.

> **illustration:** John is an individual who is over age 70½, and the owner of a traditional IRA. During 2012, he did not take any distributions from the IRA, even though he was required to take a $100,000 minimum distribution for 2012. On Jan. 18, 2013, John directs the IRA trustee to make a $100,000 charitable transfer.

> Under the special rule for Jan. 2013 distributions, John can elect to treat the $100,000 charitable transfer as having been made on Dec. 31, 2012. If John makes the election (pursuant to rules that IRS is to prescribe), he will be (i) considered to have satisfied his minimum distribution requirement for 2012, and (ii) entitled to make *another* tax-free charitable transfer of up to $100,000 in 2013.

☐ **Effective:** For IRA distributions made in tax years beginning after Dec. 31, 2011 (2012 Taxpayer Relief Act §208(b)(1)), but not after Dec. 31, 2013. (Code Sec. 408(d)(8)(F))

¶ 1102. Special rules are retroactively extended for qualified conservation easements contributed by individuals (including ranchers and farmers) before 2014

Code Sec. 170(b)(1)(E)(vi), as amended by 2012 Taxpayer Relief Act §206(a)
Generally effective: Contributions made in tax years beginning after Dec. 31, 2011 and before Jan. 1, 2014
Committee Reports, None

Contributions by individuals of appreciated capital gain property to 50% charities are deductible up to 30% of the taxpayer's contribution base, unless the taxpayer elects to reduce the amount of the contribution, see FTC 2d/FIN ¶ K-3686; USTR ¶ 1704.11; TaxDesk ¶ 333,013. An individual's "contribution base" for a year is his adjusted gross income (AGI) for the year, but without deducting any net operating loss (NOL) carryback to that year, see FTC 2d/FIN ¶ K-3672; USTR ¶ 1704.05; TaxDesk ¶ 333,002.

"Qualified conservation contributions" made by individuals in tax years beginning after Dec. 31, 2005 are deductible to the extent the aggregate of those contributions don't exceed the excess of 50% of the taxpayer's contribution base over the amount of all other allowable charitable contributions. (FTC 2d/FIN ¶ K-3501, ¶ K-3694.1; USTR ¶ 1704.11, ¶ 1704.45; TaxDesk ¶ 333,021.1, ¶ 331,625)

If the individual is a qualified farmer or rancher for the tax year in which the qualified conservation contribution is made, the contribution is allowed to the extent the aggregate of those contributions don't exceed the excess of 100% (rather than 50%) of the taxpayer's contribution base over the amount of all other allowable charitable contributions. (FTC 2d/FIN ¶ K-3670, ¶ K-3694.2; USTR ¶ 1704.11; TaxDesk ¶ 333,021.2)

The excess of a taxpayer's (or a qualified farmer's or rancher's) qualified conservation contributions over the 50% (or 100%) limitation could be carried over for up to 15 years. (FTC 2d/FIN ¶ K-3701.1, ¶ K-3670; USTR ¶ 1704.13; TaxDesk ¶ 333,302.2) This is in contrast to the general five-year carryover period that applies to an individual's charitable contributions in excess of the percentage ceilings for the year, see FTC 2d/FIN ¶ K-3701; USTR ¶ 1704.13; TaxDesk ¶ 333,301.

Under pre-2012 Taxpayer Relief Act law, the above rules on qualified conservation contributions didn't apply to contributions made in tax years beginning after Dec. 31, 2011. (FTC 2d/FIN ¶ K-3670, ¶ K-3694.1, ¶ K-3694.2, ¶ K-3701.1; USTR ¶ 1704.11; TaxDesk ¶ 333,021.1, ¶ 333,021.2, ¶ 333,302.2)

New Law. The 2012 Taxpayer Relief Act replaces Dec. 31, 2011 with Dec. 31, 2013. (Code Sec. 170(b)(1)(E)(vi) as amended by 2012 Taxpayer Relief Act §206(a))

> *observation:* So, the 2012 Taxpayer Relief Act extends the above rules for two years for contributions made in tax years beginning before 2014.

> *observation:* The 50% limitation (100% for qualified farmers and ranchers) and 15-year carryover continue to apply to qualified conservation contributions made by individuals in tax years beginning in 2012 and 2013.

> *illustration:* In 2013, an individual with a contribution base of $100 makes a qualified conservation contribution of property with a fair market value of $80 and makes other charitable contributions subject to the 50% limitation of $60. The individual is allowed a deduction of $50 in 2013 for the non-conservation contributions (50% of the $100 contribution base) and is allowed to carry over the excess $10 for up to five years. No current deduction is allowed for the qualified conservation

contribution, but the entire $80 qualified conservation contribution may be carried forward for up to 15 years.

⚫ observation: The retroactive extension of these special rules may be of limited use to most individuals for 2012 because, before the enactment of the 2012 Taxpayer Relief Act on Jan. 2, 2012, there had been considerable uncertainty about the chances of extending them.

For the extension of incentives for qualified conservation contributions by corporate farmers and ranchers, see ¶ 1103.

☐ **Effective:** Contributions made in tax years beginning after Dec. 31, 2011 (2012 Taxpayer Relief Act §206(c)) and before Jan. 1, 2014. (Code Sec. 170(b)(1)(E)(vi))

¶ 1103. For qualified conservation easements contributed by corporate farmers or ranchers in tax years beginning before 2014, special rules are retroactively extended

Code Sec. 170(b)(2)(B)(iii), as amended by 2012 Taxpayer Relief Act §206(b)
   Generally effective: Contributions made in tax years beginning after Dec. 31, 2011 and before Jan. 1, 2014
   Committee Reports, None

A corporation's charitable deduction for a tax year generally can't exceed 10% of its (adjusted) taxable income for the year, see FTC 2d/FIN ¶ K-3831; USTR ¶ 1704.14; TaxDesk ¶ 333,022. Contributions in excess of this limitation can be carried over and deducted for five years, to the extent the sum of carryovers and contributions for each of those years doesn't exceed the 10% limitation, see FTC 2d/FIN ¶ K-3833; USTR ¶ 1704.14; TaxDesk ¶ 333,315.

However, qualified conservation contributions (defined below) made by a corporate farmer or rancher in tax years beginning after Dec. 31, 2005 are allowed up to 100% of the taxpayer's taxable income, after taking into account other allowable charitable contributions. To qualify, more than 50% of the corporation's gross income for the tax year has to be from the trade or business of farming, and the corporation's stock must not be readily tradable on an established securities market at any time during the year. (FTC 2d/FIN ¶ K-3830, ¶ K-3831.1; USTR ¶ 1704.14; TaxDesk ¶ 333,022.1) If the aggregate amount of qualified conservation contributions by a corporate farmer or rancher exceeds the 100% limitation, the excess is carried over for 15 years as a qualified conservation contribution to which the 100% limitation applies, see FTC 2d/FIN ¶ K-3833; USTR ¶ 1704.14; TaxDesk ¶ 333,315.

A "qualified conservation contribution" is a contribution of a qualified real property interest to a qualified organization exclusively for conservation purposes, and that also prohibits the donee from making certain transfers, see FTC 2d/FIN ¶ K-3501; USTR ¶ 1704.44; TaxDesk ¶ 331,625.

Under pre-2012 Taxpayer Relief Act law, the above rules didn't apply to contributions made in tax years beginning after Dec. 31, 2011. (FTC 2d/FIN ¶ K-3830, ¶ K-3831.1; USTR ¶ 1704.11; TaxDesk ¶ 333,021.1)

New Law. The 2012 Taxpayer Relief Act replaces Dec. 31, 2011 with Dec. 31, 2013. (Code Sec. 170(b)(2)(B)(iii) as amended by 2012 Taxpayer Relief Act §206(b))

> **⊘ observation:** Thus, the 2012 Taxpayer Relief Act extends the above rules for two years for contributions made in tax years beginning before Jan. 1, 2014.

> **⊘ observation:** The 100% limitation and 15-year carryover apply to qualified conservation contributions made by corporate farmers and ranchers in tax years beginning in 2012 and 2013.

For the extension of incentives for qualified conservation contributions by individuals (including individual farmers and ranchers), see ¶ 1102.

☐ **Effective:** Contributions made in tax years beginning after Dec. 31, 2011 (2012 Taxpayer Relief Act §206(c)) and before Jan. 1, 2014. (Code Sec. 170(b)(2)(B)(iii))

¶ 1104. Above-basis deduction rules are retroactively extended for charitable contributions of food inventory made through 2013

Code Sec. 170(e)(3)(C)(iv), as amended by 2012 Taxpayer Relief Act §314(a)
Generally effective: Contributions made after Dec. 31, 2011 and before Jan. 1, 2014
Committee Reports, None

Deductions for charitable contributions of property are subject to the "ordinary income property rule," which generally limits the amount of the deduction for contributed ordinary income property to the property's basis. FTC 2d/FIN ¶ K-3160 *et seq.*; USTR ¶ 1704.42; TaxDesk ¶ 331,609. However, a C corporation that makes a "qualified contribution" of inventory-type property to a Code Sec. 501(c)(3) charitable organization that will use it for the care of the ill, the needy, or infants is entitled to an enhanced, "above-basis" deduction. See FTC 2d/FIN ¶ K-3201 *et seq.*; USTR ¶ 1704.42; TaxDesk ¶ 331,701 *et seq.*

These qualified contribution rules (the "regular qualified contribution rules") apply to a charitable contribution of food from any trade or business of the taxpayer:

- without regard to whether the contribution is made by a C corporation; but
- only if the food is "apparently wholesome food," i.e., food intended for human consumption that meets all quality and labeling standards imposed by federal, state, and local laws and regulations, even though the food may not be readily marketable due to appearance, age, freshness, grade, size, surplus, or other conditions.

For a taxpayer other than a C corporation, the aggregate amount of contributions of apparently wholesome food that may be taken into account for the tax year under the above rule may not exceed 10% of the taxpayer's aggregate net income for that tax year from all trades or businesses from which those contributions were made for that tax year, computed without regard to the above rule.

Under pre-2012 Taxpayer Relief Act law, the above rules regarding qualified contributions of apparently wholesome food (the "apparently wholesome food contribution rules") expired and weren't applicable to any otherwise qualifying contributions made after Dec. 31, 2011. (FTC 2d/FIN ¶ K-3200, ¶ K-3201.1; USTR ¶ 1704.42; TaxDesk ¶ 331,702)

New Law. Under the 2012 Taxpayer Relief Act, the apparently wholesome food contribution rules won't apply to contributions made after Dec. 31, 2013 (rather than Dec. 31, 2011). (Code Sec. 170(e)(3)(C)(iv) as amended by 2012 Taxpayer Relief Act §314(a))

> **observation:** Under the apparently wholesome food contribution rules, any taxpayer engaged in a trade or business, whether or not a C corporation—including sole proprietorships, S corporations, and partnerships—can claim a qualified contribution deduction for donations of apparently wholesome food inventory. C corporations can deduct contributions of food inventory under the regular qualified contribution rules without regard to the apparently wholesome food contribution rules.

☐ **Effective:** Contributions made after Dec. 31, 2011 (2012 Taxpayer Relief Act §314(b)), and before Jan. 1, 2014. (Code Sec. 170(e)(3)(C)(iv))

¶ 1105. Rule that S corporation's charitable contribution of property reduces shareholder's basis only by contributed property's basis is extended for tax years beginning in 2012 and 2013

Code Sec. 1367(a)(2), as amended by 2012 Taxpayer Relief Act §325(a)
Generally effective: Contributions made in tax years beginning after Dec. 31, 2011 and before Jan. 1, 2014.
Committee Reports, None

The 2006 Pension Protection Act (Sec. 1203, PL 109-280, 8/17/2006) amended the S corporation rules so that the decrease in a shareholder's basis in his S corporation stock by reason of a charitable contribution made by the S corporation equals the shareholder's pro rata share of the adjusted basis of the contributed property. Where this rule applies to limit the decrease in the basis resulting from the charitable contribution, the rule that limits the aggregate amount of losses and deductions that may be taken by the S corporation share-holder to his basis in the S corporation's stock and debt does not apply to the extent of the excess of the shareholder's pro rata share of the charitable contri-bution over the shareholder's pro rata share of the adjusted basis of such prop-erty. These rules were originally effective for contributions made in tax years beginning after Dec. 31, 2005 and before Jan. 1, 2008, but were later extended for tax years beginning in 2008 through 2011. (FTC 2d/FIN ¶ D-1760, ¶ D-1775, ¶ D-1860, ¶ D-1865; USTR ¶ 13,664, ¶ 13,674; TaxDesk ¶ 614,716, ¶ 617,001)

New Law. The 2012 Taxpayer Relief Act extends the rule that the de-crease in a shareholder's basis in his S corporation stock by reason of a charita-ble contribution made by the S corporation equals the shareholder's pro rata share of the adjusted basis of the contributed property for contributions in tax years beginning before Jan. 1, 2014. (Code Sec. 1367(a)(2) as amended by 2012 Taxpayer Relief Act §325(a))

> *observation:* This means that the extension applies to contributions made in tax years beginning in 2012 and 2013.

> *observation:* Because the rule regarding the decrease in the share-holder's basis is extended, the rule not applying the deduction limitation is similarly extended for tax years beginning in 2012 and 2013, see FTC 2d/FIN ¶ D-1775.

☐ **Effective:** Contributions made in tax years beginning after Dec. 31, 2011 (2012 Taxpayer Relief Act §325(b)) and before Jan. 1, 2014. (Code Sec. 1367(a)(2))

¶ 1200. Foreign and Possessions

¶ 1201. Subpart F exception for active financing income extended through tax years beginning before 2014

Code Sec. 953(e)(10), as amended by 2012 Taxpayer Relief Act §322(a)
Code Sec. 954(h)(9), as amended by 2012 Taxpayer Relief Act §322(b)
Generally effective: Tax Years beginning after Dec. 31, 2011 and before
Jan. 1, 2014
Committee Reports, None

Under Subpart F, U.S. persons who are 10% shareholders of a controlled foreign corporation (CFC) are required to include in income their pro rata share of the CFC's insurance income and adjusted net foreign base company income (FBCI) whether or not this income is distributed to the shareholders. Insurance income generally includes income of a CFC attributable to the issuing and reinsuring of any insurance or annuity contract that would be taxed under the Subchapter L insurance company taxation rules if the income were income of a domestic insurance company. FBCI includes foreign personal holding income (FPHCI), foreign base company sales income, foreign base company services income (FBCSI), and foreign base company oil related income. FBCSI income generally includes income from technical, managerial, or other skilled services performed outside the country of organization of the CFC. FPHCI includes dividends, interest, income equivalent to interest, gains from certain property transactions, gains from commodities transactions, foreign currency gains, net income from notional principal contracts, payments in lieu of dividends and payments under personal service contracts. (FTC 2d/FIN ¶s O-2401, O-2471, O-2520, O-2531, O-2651; USTR ¶s 9534.01, 9544.02)

Under pre-2012 Taxpayer Relief Act law, certain income from the active conduct of a banking, financing or similar business, or from the conduct of an insurance business was temporarily excluded from the definition of Subpart F income, but only for tax years of foreign corporations beginning after Dec. 31, '98 and before Jan. 1, 2012, and for tax years of U.S. shareholders with or within which any such tax year of the foreign corporation ended. Thus, for that period, FPHCI did not include qualified banking or financing income of an eligible controlled foreign corporation (CFC). A CFC was a CFC that was predominantly engaged in the active conduct of a banking, financing or similar business, and conducted substantial activity with respect to that business. Quali-

---

FTC 2d References are to Federal Tax Coordinator 2d
FIN References are to RIA's Analysis of Federal Taxes: Income (print)
USTR References are to United States Tax Reporter: Income
PCA References are to Pension Analysis (print and electronic)
PBE References are to Pension & Benefits Explanations
BCA References are to Benefits Analysis (electronic)
BC References are to Benefits Coordinator (print)
EP References are to Estate Planning Analysis (print and electronic)

fied banking or financing income meant income that was from the active conduct of a banking, financing, or similar business by the eligible CFC, or a qualified business unit (QBU) of the eligible CFC, and that was from one or more transactions with customers located outside the U.S. (subject to a requirement that related activities be conducted in the home country) and that was treated as earned by the eligible CFC or QBU in its home country for purposes of the home country's tax laws. (FTC 2d/FIN ¶ O-2500, ¶ O-2584, ¶ O-2585, ¶ O-2589; USTR ¶ 9544.02)

For tax years of foreign corporations beginning after Dec. 31, '98 and before Jan. 1, 2012, and for tax years of U.S. shareholders with or within which any such tax year of the foreign corporation ended, FPHCI did not include any dividends, payments in lieu of dividends, interest, or income equivalent to interest, from any transaction (including any hedging transaction or deposits of collateral or margin excluded from U.S. property under Code Sec. 956(c)(2)(I)) entered into in the ordinary course of the dealer's trade or business as a securities dealer. (FTC 2d/FIN ¶ O-2530, ¶ O-2558; USTR ¶ 9544.02)

For tax years of a foreign corporation that begin after Dec. 31, '98 and before Jan. 1, 2012, and for tax years of U.S. shareholders with or within which any such tax years of foreign corporations ended, exempt insurance income was excluded from insurance income that was treated as subpart F income. Exempt insurance income meant income derived by a qualifying insurance company that was attributable to the issuing (or reinsuring) of an exempt contract by the company or a qualifying insurance company branch of that company and was treated as earned by the company or branch in its home country for purposes of the country's tax law. An exempt contract was an insurance or annuity contract issued or reinsured by a qualifying insurance company or qualifying insurance company branch in connection with property in, liability arising out of activity in, or the lives or health of residents of, a country other than the U.S. However, no contracts of a qualifying insurance company or qualifying insurance company branch were treated as exempt contracts unless the company or branch received more than 30% of its net written premiums from exempt contracts (determined without regard to this rule) which covered applicable home country risks and with respect to which no policyholder, insured, annuitant, or beneficiary was a related person. (FTC 2d/FIN ¶ O-2500, ¶ O-2508, ¶ O-2509; USTR ¶ 9534.01)

For tax years of a foreign corporation that begin after Dec. 31, '98 and before Jan. 1, 2012, and for tax years of U.S. shareholders with or within which any such tax years of foreign corporations ended, qualified insurance income of a qualifying insurance company was excluded from foreign personal holding company income (FPHCI). Qualified insurance income was income of a qualifying insurance company that was:

(1) received from an unrelated person and derived from the investments made by a qualifying insurance company or a qualifying insurance company

branch of its reserves allocable to exempt contracts or of 80% of its unearned premiums from exempt contracts, or

(2) received from an unrelated person and derived from investments made by a qualifying insurance company or a qualifying insurance company branch of an amount of its assets allocable to exempt contracts equal to: (a) in the case of property, casualty, or health insurance contracts, one-third of its premiums earned on these insurance contracts during the taxable year and (b) in the case of life insurance or annuity contracts, 10% of the reserves described in (1) for such contracts. (FTC 2d/FIN ¶ O-2530, ¶ O-2591, ¶ O-2592; USTR ¶ 9544.02)

For tax years of a foreign corporation that begin after Dec. 31, '98 and before Jan. 1, 2012, and for tax years of U.S. shareholders with or within which any such tax years of foreign corporations ended, FBCSI didn't include income covered by the above temporary exceptions for qualified banking and financing income, exempt insurance income, qualified insurance income, and securities dealer income. (FTC 2d/FIN ¶ O-2650, ¶ O-2651; USTR ¶ 9544.035)

New Law. The 2012 Taxpayer Relief Act extends the temporary exclusions described above for an additional two years. The temporary exclusions will apply to tax years of a foreign corporation beginning after Dec. 31, '98 and before Jan. 1, 2014, and to tax years of U.S. shareholders with or within which such tax years of foreign corporations end. ((Code Sec. 953(e)(10) as amended by 2012 Taxpayer Relief Act §322(a)); (Code Sec. 954(h)(9) as amended by 2012 Taxpayer Relief Act §322(b)))

> *observation:* The extension allows banks, finance, insurance and similar companies to defer active financing income offshore for tax years beginning before Jan. 1, 2014.

☐ **Effective:** Tax years of foreign corporations beginning after Dec. 31, 2011 (2012 Taxpayer Relief Act §322(c)) and before Jan. 1, 2014 (Code Sec. 953(e)(10); Code Sec. 954(h)(9)), and tax years of U.S. shareholders with or within which any such tax year of such a foreign corporation ends. (2012 Taxpayer Relief Act §322(c))

¶ 1202. Look-through treatment for payments between related CFCs under foreign personal holding company income rules extended through 2013

Code Sec. 954(c)(6)(C), as amended by 2012 Taxpayer Relief Act §323(a)
Generally effective: Tax years of foreign corporations beginning after Dec. 31, 2011 and before Jan. 1, 2014
Committee Reports, None

Under Subpart F, U.S. persons who are 10% shareholders (U.S. shareholders) of a controlled foreign corporation (CFC) are required to include in income their pro rata share of the CFC's subpart F income whether or not this income is distributed to the shareholders. Subpart F income includes foreign base company income (FBCI), which in turn includes foreign personal holding company income (FPHCI). For subpart F purposes, FPHCI includes dividends, interest, income equivalent to interest, rents and royalties. However, FPHCI does not include dividends and interest from a related corporation organized and operating in the same foreign country in which the CFC is organized, or rents and royalties received by a CFC from a related corporation for the use of property within the country in which the CFC is organized. Interest, rent, and royalty payments do not qualify for this exclusion to the extent that such payments reduce the subpart F income of the payor. FTC 2d/FIN ¶s O-2303, O-2401, O-2424, O-2432, O-2433, O-2439, O-2445; USTR ¶ 9544 9544.02

Under pre-2012 Taxpayer Relief Act law, for tax years beginning after Dec. 31, 2005 and before Jan. 1, 2012, look-through treatment applied to dividends, interest, rents, and royalties received by one CFC from a related CFC and the payments weren't treated as FPHCI to the extent attributable or properly allocable to non-subpart-F income, or income that was not effectively connected with the conduct of a U.S. trade or business of the payor. In making this determination, look-through rules similar to those that a U.S. shareholder uses to allocate interest, rent, royalty and dividend income received from a CFC to separate foreign tax credit baskets applied. Interest included factoring income, which is treated as income equivalent to interest for purposes of determining FPHCI. (FTC 2d/FIN ¶ O-2530, ¶ O-2550, ¶ O-2553, ¶ O-2554, ¶ O-2555; USTR ¶ 9544.02 FTC 2d/FIN ¶s O-2433, O-4346, O-4347, O-4348; USTR ¶ 9044.01)

New Law. The 2012 Taxpayer Relief Act extends retroactively look-through treatment for payments of dividends, interest, rents, and royalties between related CFCs for 2012 and 2013. (Code Sec. 954(c)(6)(C) as amended by 2012 Taxpayer Relief Act §323(a))

☐ **Effective:** Tax years of foreign corporations beginning before Jan. 1, 2014 (Code Sec. 954(c)(6)(C)) and beginning after Dec 31, 2011 and tax years of U.S. shareholders with or within which any tax year of such foreign corporation ends. (2012 Taxpayer Relief Act §323(b))

¶ 1203. IRS may impose 20% withholding rate (up from 15%) on USRPI gains passed through to foreign persons by U.S. partnerships, trusts or estates

Code Sec. 1445(e)(1), as amended by 2012 Taxpayer Relief Act §102(c)(1)(C)

Code Sec. None, 2012 Taxpayer Relief Act §102(a)
Generally effective: Amounts paid after Dec. 31, 2012
Committee Reports, None

A U.S. partnership, trustee of a U.S. trust, or executor of a U.S. estate must deduct and withhold income tax on distributions attributable to the disposition of a U.S. real property interest (USRPI) to the extent it is includible in the income of a foreign partner, foreign beneficiary, or, in the case of a trust, a foreign person under the Code Sec. 671 grantor trust rules. For amounts paid after May 28, 2003, IRS could, by regulation, reduce the amount of income tax required to be withheld on a foreign person's gain from the disposition of an interest in U.S. real property from 35% to 15%. Since IRS did not provide for the 15% rate by regulation, domestic partnerships, estates, and trusts had to withhold tax at 35%. (FTC 2d/FIN ¶ O-13000, ¶ O-13035; USTR ¶ 14,454.02; TaxDesk ¶ 644,019)

Under § 303 of the 2003 Jobs and Growth Act (JGTRRA, Sec. 303, PL 108-27, 5/28/2003), as amended by section 102 of the 2005 Tax Increase Prevention Act (TIPRA, Sec. 102, PL 109-222, 5/17/2006) and section 102(a) of the 2010 Tax Relief Act (Sec. 102(a), PL 111-312, 12/17/2012), IRS's authority to provide for a reduced 15% withholding rate by regulation was scheduled to expire for payments made in tax years beginning after Dec. 31, 2012 (in which case the reduced rate would have reverted to the earlier 20%). (FTC 2d/FIN ¶ O-13000, ¶ O-13035, ¶ O-13035, ¶ T-11062; USTR ¶ 14,454.02; TaxDesk ¶ 644,019, ¶ 880,014)

New Law. The 2012 Taxpayer Relief Act removes the JGTRRA sunset provision. This would have made permanent IRS' ability to promulgate regulations reducing the amount of income tax required to be withheld on a foreign person's gain from the disposition of an interest in U.S. real property from 35% to 15%. (2012 Taxpayer Relief Act §102(a)). However, another 2012 Taxpayer Relief Act provision increases this discretionary rate from 15% to 20%. (Code Sec. 1445(e)(1) as amended by 2012 Taxpayer Relief Act §102(c)(1)(C))

> *observation:* This means that IRS may, to the extent provided in regulations, reduce the withholding rate on distributions from a partnership, trust or estate attributable to the disposition of a USRPI from 35% to 20%.

> *observation:* This increase parallels the increase in the highest capital gain tax rate from 15% to 20% after 2012 (see ¶ 201).

☐ **Effective:** The effect of 2012 Taxpayer Relief Act §102(a) is to remove the sunset that would have been effective for tax years beginning after Dec. 31, 2012. (2012 Taxpayer Relief Act §102(a))

⚡*observation:* 2012 Taxpayer Relief Act §102(a), which eliminates the JGTRRA §303 sunset rule, as amended, is effective as if included in the enactment of JGTRRA. JGTRRA was enacted on May 28, 2003, so §102(a) is technically effective as of that date.

For amounts paid after Dec. 31, 2012 IRS may, to the extent provided in regulations, reduce the withholding rate on distributions from a partnership, trust or estate attributable to the disposition of a USRPI to 20%. (2012 Taxpayer Relief Act §102(d)(2))

¶ 1204. Inclusion of RICs in the definition of qualified investment entity is extended for certain FIRPTA purposes through 2013

Code Sec. 897(h)(4)(A)(ii), as amended by 2012 Taxpayer Relief Act §321(a)
Generally effective: Jan. 1, 2012 through Dec. 31, 2013
Committee Reports, None

Foreign investors are generally not subject to U.S. tax on U.S. source capital gain unless it is effectively connected with a U.S. trade or business, or it is realized by an individual who meets certain presence requirements. Gain from the disposition of a U.S. real property interest (USRPI), however, is treated as income effectively connected with a U.S. trade or business under Foreign Investment in Real Property Tax Act (FIRPTA). This FIRPTA gain is subject to tax and withholding under Code Sec. 897 and Code Sec. 1445. Stock or beneficial interests (other than solely as a creditor) in U.S. real property holding corporations (USRPHCs) are USRPIs. Stock that is regularly traded on an established securities market is a USRPI only when a foreign person holds more than 5% of that class of stock at any time during the five year period ending on the disposition date or the taxpayer's shorter holding period (the "regularly traded exception"). Stock of a domestically controlled qualified investment entity is generally not a USRPI (the "domestically controlled exception").

A look through rule requires that a qualified investment entity must generally withhold U.S. tax on a distribution to a foreign person or to another qualified investment entity to the extent it is attributable to FIRPTA gain (unless it relates to an interest regularly traded on an established U.S. securities market and the distributee held no more than 5% of that class of stock or beneficial interest within the one year period ending on the distribution date).

Since stock of a RIC that is a domestically controlled qualified investment entity is not a USRPI, gain on its disposition is not FIRPTA gain and not subject to tax or withholding. However, a shareholder of a domestically controlled RIC that is a qualified investment entity may nonetheless be treated as receiving FIRPTA gain if the shareholder engages in certain wash sale transactions to avoid receipt of a distribution of FIRPTA gain from the RIC.

A real estate investment trust (REIT) is always a qualified investment entity. A regulated investment company (RIC) is a qualified investment entity if it is a USRPHC or would be a USRPHC if the regularly traded exception and the domestically controlled exception didn't apply. A RIC with USRPIs representing 50% or more of the fair market value of its business and real estate assets is therefore a qualified investment entity even if an exception would otherwise have precluded USRPHC status, in which case it must withhold on distributions of FIRPTA gain even though its shares are not USRPIs. (FTC 2d/FIN ¶ O-10700, ¶ O-10701, ¶ O-10734, ¶ O-10734.1, ¶ O-10734.2, ¶ O-10753, ¶ O-10771, ¶ O-13000, ¶ O-13001; USTR ¶ 8974, ¶ 8974.02, ¶ 14,454; TaxDesk ¶ 643,015, ¶ 643,016)

Under pre-2012 Taxpayer Relief Act law, the inclusion of RICs within the definition of qualified investment entity terminated on Dec. 31, 2011. (FTC 2d/FIN ¶ O-10700, ¶ O-10734; USTR ¶ 8974, ¶ 8974.02; TaxDesk ¶ 643,015, ¶ 643,016)

> **RIA** *observation:* The expiration date did not affect the treatment of RICs as qualified investment entities for distributions to foreign persons that are attributable, directly or indirectly, to distributions it receives from a REIT for purposes of (i) the Code Sec. 897(h)(1) look-through rule, (ii) the Code Sec. 1445(e)(6) withholding rules on look-through distributions, or (iii) the Code Sec. 897(h)(5) wash sale rules). (FTC 2d/FIN ¶ O-10700, ¶ O-10734; USTR ¶ 8974.02)

New Law. The 2012 Taxpayer Relief Act retroactively restores the inclusion of RICs within the definition of qualified investment entities from Jan. 1, 2012 through Jan. 2, 2013 and extends the inclusion of RICs within that definition through Dec. 31, 2013 (Code Sec. 897(h)(4)(A)(ii) as amended by 2012 Taxpayer Relief Act §321(a)) for those situations in which that inclusion would otherwise have expired at the end of 2011.

☐ **Effective:** Jan 1, 2012 (2012 Taxpayer Relief Act §321(b)(1)) through Dec. 31, 2013. (Code Sec. 897(h)(4)(A)(ii))

The retroactive inclusion of RICs within the definition of qualified investment entities does *not* apply to withholding obligations under Code Sec. 1445 on payments made on or before Jan. 2, 2013. (2012 Taxpayer Relief Act §321(b)(1)) If a RIC made a distribution after Dec. 31, 2011 and before Jan. 2, 2013 on which withholding would have been required had the extension been applied retroactively to the withholding requirements, the RIC will not be liable to any distributee for any amount that it withheld and paid to IRS. (2012 Taxpayer Relief Act §321(b)(2))

🟢 observation: Thus, if a RIC withheld on a distribution made before Jan. 2, 2013, the recipient of the reduced amount cannot recover from the RIC any amount that was withheld and paid to IRS by the RIC.

¶ 1205. Withholding tax exemption for RIC interest-related dividends and short-term capital gains dividends paid to foreign persons is extended for tax years beginning in 2012 and 2013

Code Sec. 871(k)(1)(C), as amended by 2012 Taxpayer Relief Act §320(a)
Code Sec. 871(k)(2)(C), as amended by 2012 Taxpayer Relief Act §320(a)
Generally effective: Tax years beginning after Dec. 31, 2011 and before Jan. 1, 2014
Committee Reports, None

The 2004 Jobs Act (Sec. 411, PL 108-357, 10/22/2004) added a provision that allowed a regulated investment company (RIC) to designate and pay (i) interest-related dividends out of interest that would generally not be taxable when received directly by a nonresident alien individual or foreign corporations and (ii) short-term capital gains dividends out of short-term capital gains. RIC dividends designated as interest-related dividends and short-term capital gains dividends were generally not taxable when received by a nonresident alien individual or foreign corporation and were not subject to withholding tax. Originally, this provision didn't apply to dividends for RIC tax years beginning after Dec. 31, 2007, but was extended for dividends for RIC tax years beginning in 2008 through 2011. (FTC 2d/FIN ¶ O-10200, ¶ O-10230.2, ¶ O-10230.3, ¶ O-10230.4; USTR ¶ 8714.02, ¶ 14,414.02, ¶ 14,414.05)

New Law. The 2012 Taxpayer Relief Act extends the withholding exemption for RIC interest-related dividends and short-term capital gains dividends so that it expires for dividends paid by RICs in tax years beginning after Dec. 31, 2013. (Code Sec. 871(k)(1)(C) as amended by 2012 Taxpayer Relief Act §320(a)); (Code Sec. 871(k)(2)(C) as amended by 2012 Taxpayer Relief Act §320(a))

☐ **Effective:** Tax years beginning after Dec. 31, 2011 (2012 Taxpayer Relief Act §320(b)) and before Jan. 1, 2014. (2012 Taxpayer Relief Act §320(a))

🟢 observation: This means that the extension of the exemption applies for dividends paid in tax years beginning in 2012 and 2013.

¶ 1206. Possessions tax credit for American Samoa extended through 2013 with an American Samoa production requirement

Code Sec. 30A, 2012 Taxpayer Relief Act §330
Code Sec. 936, 2012 Taxpayer Relief Act §330
Generally effective: Tax years beginning after Dec. 31, 2011 and before Jan. 1, 2014
Committee Reports, None

Although the Code Sec. 936 possessions tax credit generally expired for tax years beginning after Dec. 31, 2005, the 2006 Tax Relief Act (Sec. 119(d), PL 109-432, 12/20/2006) extended the possessions tax credit for U.S. corporations operating in American Samoa that were existing credit claimants (generally, corporations that qualified for the possessions tax credit on Oct. 13, '95 and had an election to take the credit in effect on that date) and that elected the application of Code Sec. 936 for their last tax year beginning before Jan. 1, 2006 (qualifying domestic corporations). Qualifying domestic corporations were allowed to claim a possessions tax credit under the 2006 Tax Relief Act based on the Code Sec. 936 and Code Sec. 30A rules. Under pre-2012 Taxpayer Relief Act law, this extended credit was allowed for the first six tax years of a corporation that began after Dec. 31, 2005 and before Jan. 1, 2012. (FTC 2d/FIN ¶ O-1500, ¶ O-1500.1; USTR ¶ 9314.06; TaxDesk ¶ 394,500.1)

The amount of the extended credit was equal to 60% of qualified wages and fringe benefit expenses and various percentages of short, medium and long-term depreciable tangible property, see FTC 2d/FIN ¶ O-1500.1; USTR ¶ 9314.06; TaxDesk ¶ 394,500.1.

New Law. The 2012 Taxpayer Relief Act extends the possessions tax credit for American Samoa for tax years that begin before Jan. 1, 2014 in modified form. Thus, a domestic corporation will be treated as a qualified domestic corporation eligible for the credit if, in the case of a taxable year beginning after Dec. 31, 2011, it meets qualified domestic production activities requirements. (Sec. 119(a)(2), PL 109-432, 12/20/2006 as amended by 2012 Taxpayer Relief Act §330(a))

The 2012 Taxpayer Relief Act eliminates the requirement that the corporation be an existing credit claimant for tax years beginning after Dec. 31, 2011. Thus, in the case of a corporation that was an existing credit claimant with respect to American Samoa and elected the application of Code Sec. 936 for its last tax year beginning before Jan. 1, 2006, the credit applies to the first eight taxable years of the corporation beginning after Dec. 31, 2006 and before Jan. 1, 2014. For corporations not meeting those requirements it applies to the first two taxable years of the corporation beginning after Dec. 31, 2011 and before Jan. 1, 2014. (Sec. 119(d), PL 109-432, 12/20/2006 as amended by 2012 Taxpayer Relief Act §330(b) and previous Acts) *observation:* The result is that the existing claimant test is replaced with the domestic production requirement for the two years of the extension period.

The domestic production requirement is met if the corporation has qualified production activities income (under the rules of Code Sec. 199(c)) in American Samoa. Sec. 119(e), PL 109-432, 12/20/2006 as added by 2012 Taxpayer Relief Act §330(a))

observation: The term "qualified production activities income (QPAI)" for any tax year means an amount equal to the excess (if any) of:

(1) the taxpayer's domestic production gross receipts (DPGR, see FTC 2d/FIN ¶ L-4337) for that tax year, over

(2) the sum of the cost of goods sold allocable to those receipts and certain allocable expenses, losses, or deductions, see FTC 2d/FIN ¶ L-4361.

Thus, the Code Sec. 199(c) rules, such as the definition of DPGR (i.e., gross receipts derived from specified production in the U.S.) are applied by substituting American Samoa for the U.S. for purposes of its QPAI eligibility test. The result is that QPAI is based on production in American Samoa rather than production in the U.S. for purposes of the test for eligibility for the extended credit.

observation: It appears that a corporation that has any American Samoa QPAI will be eligible for the credit; the amount of the credit is determined as described above.

☐ **Effective:** Tax years beginning after Dec. 31, 2011 (2012 Taxpayer Relief Act §330(c)) and before Jan. 1, 2014. (Sec. 119(d), PL 109-432, 12/20/2006 as amended by 2012 Taxpayer Relief Act §330(b) and previous Acts)

¶ 1300. Roth Rollovers and Conversions

¶ 1301. Distribution restrictions eased for "in-plan Roth rollovers"

Code Sec. 402A(c)(4)(E), as amended by 2012 Taxpayer Relief Act §902(a)
Generally effective: Transfers to designated Roth accounts made after Dec. 31, 2012
Committee Reports, None

If an "applicable retirement plan" (such as a 401(k) plan or a 403(b) annuity plan) includes a "qualified Roth contribution program," then plan participants may elect to make *either* (i) taxable contributions to a "designated Roth account" in the plan, *or* (ii) tax-free elective or salary reduction contributions to a non-Roth account. A participant who receives a plan distribution from a 401(k) plan or 403(b) plan generally must include in gross income the amount of elective or salary reduction contributions received in the distribution, and the earnings on these contributions. In contrast, after a five-tax-year holding period, a participant may receive from a designated Roth account qualified distributions—of both the elective or salary reduction contributions and the earnings on the elective deferrals—that are completely excludable from gross income. Qualified distributions from a designated Roth account must be made after the participant reaches age 59-1/2, dies, or becomes disabled. (FTC 2d/FIN ¶ H-12290; H-12295; H-12295.1 *et seq.*; USTR ¶ 4014.1745; 402A4; TaxDesk ¶ 283,401 *et seq.*; PCA ¶ 35,251.1 *et seq.*; PBE ¶ 401-4.1745; 402A-4)

The term "applicable retirement plan" refers to:

. . . an employees' trust described in Code Sec. 401(a) which is tax-exempt under Code Sec. 501(a),

. . . a plan under which amounts are contributed by an individual's employer for a Code Sec. 403(b) annuity contract, and

. . . a governmental deferred compensation plan under Code Sec. 457. (FTC 2d/FIN ¶ H-12295.10; USTR ¶ 408A4; PCA ¶ 35,251.10; PBE ¶ 408A-4)

> **observation:** Applicable retirement plans that include a "qualified Roth contribution program" are commonly called Roth 401(k), Roth 403(b), or Roth 457 plans.

FTC 2d References are to Federal Tax Coordinator 2d
FIN References are to RIA's Analysis of Federal Taxes: Income (print)
USTR References are to United States Tax Reporter: Income
PCA References are to Pension Analysis (print and electronic)
PBE References are to Pension & Benefits Explanations
BCA References are to Benefits Analysis (electronic)
BC References are to Benefits Coordinator (print)
EP References are to Estate Planning Analysis (print and electronic)

A "qualified Roth contribution program" is a program that allows a participant to elect to make after-tax "designated Roth contributions" in lieu of all or a portion of the "elective deferrals" that the participant would be otherwise eligible to make under the applicable retirement plan.

To include a "qualified Roth contribution program," a 401(k), 403(b), or 457 plan must:

(1) establish a separate "designated Roth account" for the designated Roth contributions of each employee (and for the earnings allocable to these contributions);

(2) maintain separate recordkeeping for each account; and

(3) not allocate to the designated Roth account:

(a) forfeitures, or

(b) contributions other than designated Roth contributions and Code Sec. 402A(c)(3)(B) rollover contributions. (FTC 2d/FIN ¶ H-12295, ¶ H-12295.3; PCA ¶ 35,251, ¶ 35,251.3)

A participant may receive a distribution of elective contributions under a 401(k) plan, or salary reduction contributions under a 403(b) plan, only after attainment of age 59-1/2, severance from employment, plan termination, hardship, disability, or death. (FTC 2d/FIN ¶ H-8975; H-8978; H-9200; H-9201; H-12479; USTR ¶ 4014.1763; 4034.12; TaxDesk ¶ 284,005; PCA ¶ 28,128; 28,502; 36,080; PBE ¶ 401-4.1763; 403-4.12)

Eligible rollover distributions from eligible retirement plans (i.e., generally, plan distributions other than periodic distributions, minimum required distributions, or hardship distributions) may be contributed, without an annual dollar limit, to a 401(k) plan or a 403(b) plan and certain other plans, if certain requirements are met. Distributions rolled over to an eligible retirement plan generally are not includible in gross income. (FTC 2d/FIN ¶ H-3300 H-3305.1 H-11400 H-11402 H-12400 H-12491; USTR ¶ 4024.04; 4034.03 4574; TaxDesk ¶ 135,714 144,001 284,706; PCA ¶ 32,803 36,092 40,406.1; PBE ¶ 402-4 403-4.03 457-4)

In contrast, for any distribution made with respect to an individual from an eligible retirement plan that is contributed to his Roth IRA in a qualified rollover contribution, the individual must include in gross income any amount that would have been includible in gross income if it were not part of a qualified rollover contribution. The Code Sec. 72(t) 10% early withdrawal tax does *not* apply to the rolled over amounts includible in gross income. (FTC 2d/FIN ¶ H-12290 H-12290.20; USTR ¶ 408A4; TaxDesk ¶ 283,326; PCA ¶ 35,221; PBE ¶ 408A-4)

However, any portion of a distribution from a Roth IRA that: (i) is allocable to a qualified rollover contribution that was made to the Roth IRA from an applicable retirement plan, (ii) is made within the five-tax-year period beginning with the tax year in which the rollover contribution was made, and (iii) was includible in gross income as part of the qualified rollover contribution, *is* subject to the 10% early withdrawal tax, as if the distribution were includible in income. (FTC 2d/FIN ¶ H-12290 H-12290.38; USTR ¶ 408A4; TaxDesk ¶ 283,346; PCA ¶ 35,239; PBE ¶ 408A-4)

In-plan Roth rollovers. The 2010 Small Business Act expanded the types of distributions that could be rolled over into designated Roth accounts by providing for so-called "in-plan Roth rollovers." Specifically, for an applicable retirement plan that maintains a qualified Roth contribution program, a distribution to an individual from (i) the portion of the plan that is *not* a designated Roth account, may be rolled over, in a qualified rollover contribution (within the meaning of Code Sec. 408A(e), i.e., the Roth IRA rules), to (ii) the designated Roth account maintained under the plan for the benefit of the individual to whom the distribution was made. However, the rollover is *not* tax-free, see below. (FTC 2d ¶ H-12295.5D; USTR ¶ 402A4; PCA ¶ 35,251.5D; PBE ¶ 402A-4)

> ⚫*observation:* Thus, an "in-plan Roth rollover" is a taxable distribution from an individual's plan account other than a designated Roth account that is rolled over to his designated Roth account in the same plan.

Before the 2012 Taxpayer Relief Act, to be eligible for rollover to a designated Roth account, a distribution had to be (i) an eligible rollover distribution, (ii) otherwise allowed under the plan, and (iii) allowable in the amount and form elected. For example, an amount in a 401(k) plan account that was subject to distribution restrictions (e.g., because the participant has not reached age 59-1/2) could not have been rolled over to a designated Roth account. However, an employer may expand its distribution options beyond those currently allowed by the plan (e.g., by adding in-service distributions or distributions before normal retirement age) in order to allow employees to make rollover contributions to the designated Roth account through a direct rollover. (FTC 2d ¶ H-12295.5E; USTR ¶ 402A4; PCA ¶ 35,251.5E; PBE ¶ 402A-4)

The tax-free treatment of rollovers that ordinarily applies does *not* apply to in-plan Roth rollovers. Instead, the amount that an individual receives in a distribution from an applicable retirement plan that would be includible in gross income if it were not part of a qualified rollover distribution, *must be* included in his gross income. (FTC 2d ¶ H-12295.5K; USTR ¶ 402A4; PCA ¶ 35,251.5K; PBE ¶ 402A-4)

IRS guidance (Notice 2010-84, Q&A 4, 2010-51 IRB 872) provided that a plan could be amended to allow in-plan Roth rollovers for amounts that were permitted to be distributed under the Code, but that were "not otherwise distributable" to plan participants under a plan's more restrictive provisions.

illustration: Wally, age 60, worked for Hi-Tech Corp., and participated in Hi-Tech's Roth 401(k) plan, which provides for in-plan Roth rollovers. Although Wally had already passed the age (59 ½) at which a plan distribution may be paid or made available to him under the Code, the plan did not allow for distributions while Wally was still employed. Under the in-plan Roth rollover rules, however, the plan could be amended so that the vested balance of Wally's 401(k) plan account—that would not otherwise be distributable to him because of the plan's prohibition on in-service distributions—could be transferred to a designated Roth account in an in-plan Roth rollover.

New Law. The 2012 Taxpayer Relief Act provides that an applicable retirement plan that includes a qualified Roth contribution program may allow an individual to elect to have the plan transfer any amount not otherwise distributable under the plan to a designated Roth account maintained for the individual's benefit. The transfer is treated as an in-plan Roth rollover, which was contributed in a qualified rollover contribution to the designated Roth account. (Code Sec. 402A(c)(4)(E) as amended by 2012 Taxpayer Relief Act §902(a))

observation: Thus, pending further guidance, it appears that amounts that do not otherwise meet the Code-based requirements for being a qualified rollover distribution may be deemed to be qualified rollover distributions when rolled-over to a designated Roth account in an in-plan Roth rollover.

observation: Because the Act does not limit the phrase "any amount not otherwise distributable" to 401(k) elective deferrals, it appears that a plan can elect to apply the new in-plan Roth rollover provisions not only to 401(k) elective deferral accounts, but also to any employer contribution accounts (e.g., matching contribution accounts and/or profit sharing contribution accounts), rollover accounts, and employee after-tax contribution accounts. IRS should clarify this in future guidance.

illustration: Sally, age 40, works for Hi-Tech Corp., and participates in Hi-Tech's Roth 401(k) plan, which provides for in-plan Roth rollovers. Although Sally has not yet reached the age (59 ½) at which a plan distribution may be paid or made available to her, or met the other Code-based requirements for a distribution, under the 2012 Taxpayer Relief Act, Sally may have the balance of her 401(k) plan account that's not otherwise distributable to her (i.e., due to her failure to meet the Code Sec. 401(k)(2)(B)(i) distribution restrictions), transferred to a designated Roth account in an in-plan Roth rollover.

Further, under the Act, solely because of the transfer, a plan will not be treated as violating the provisions of:

. . . Code Sec. 401(k)(2)(B)(i), regarding restrictions on the distribution of employer contributions to a 401(k) plan;

. . . Code Sec. 403(b)(7)(A)(i), regarding restrictions on distributions from custodial accounts for regulated investment company stock;

. . . Code Sec. 403(b)(11), regarding restrictions on distributions from a 403(b) plan;

. . . Code Sec. 457(d)(1)(A), regarding restrictions on distributions from a 457 plan; or

. . . 5 USC §8433, regarding restrictions on distributions from the Federal Government's Thrift Savings plan. (Code Sec. 402A(c)(4)(E))

> *observation:* Pending IRS clarification, it is unclear whether limits and/or conditions can be imposed upon participants and/or their accounts in order to make an in-plan Roth rollover election. To avoid major administrative headaches in implementing the expanded in-plan Roth rollover provisions, plan sponsors should include references to an administrative procedure or policy that imposes reasonable conditions on how and when a participant can make an in-plan Roth direct rollover election. These rules should include the following:
>
> • the timing of in-plan Roth rollovers conversions (e.g., effective only on the first day of the month following the date of a participant's request);
>
> • the frequency of such rollovers (e.g., only once annually per participant);
>
> • the accounts that are eligible for a rollover election (e.g., 401(k) elective deferral accounts, matching contribution accounts, profit sharing contribution accounts, rollover accounts, and/or employee after-tax contribution accounts); and
>
> • whether an eligible account must be 100% vested in order for a rollover election to be made.

> *recommendation:* Until IRS provides further guidance, plan sponsors may consider adding the following language when adapting their plans to accommodate the new in-plan Roth rollover rules:
>
> "If the Plan includes a qualified Roth contribution program, a Participant may elect to transfer any amounts under the Plan to the Participant's designated Roth account under the Plan, subject to an administrative procedure/policy established by the Plan Administrator that may include, subject to future guidance issued by IRS, rules relating to (a) the timing of such transfers, (b) the frequency of such transfers, (c) the accounts with respect to which such a transfer election can be made, and (d) whether a Participant must be fully vested in an eligible ac-

count in order for such a transfer election to be made with respect to such account."

sample client letter: For a client letter on the Roth rollover provision in the 2012 Taxpayer Relief Act, see ¶ 2005.

☐ **Effective:** Transfers to designated Roth accounts made after Dec. 31, 2012, in tax years ending after that date. (2012 Taxpayer Relief Act §902(b))

¶ 1400. Tax Exempt Bonds and Development Incentives

¶ 1401. New markets tax credit is extended through calendar year 2013

Code Sec. 45D(f)(1)(G), as amended by 2012 Taxpayer Relief Act §305(a)
Code Sec. 45D(f)(3), as amended by 2012 Taxpayer Relief Act §305(b)
Generally effective: Calendar years starting after 2011 and before 2014
Committee Reports, None

Under pre-2012 Taxpayer Relief Act law, a new markets tax credit was available through calendar year 2011 for qualified equity investments in a qualified community development entity (CDE), see FTC 2d/FIN ¶ L-17921; USTR ¶ 45D4; TaxDesk ¶ 384,701. A qualified equity investment is an equity investment in a CDE for which the CDE has received an allocation from IRS if:

- the taxpayer acquires the investment at its original issue (directly or through an underwriter) solely in exchange for cash,

- the CDE on its books and records using any reasonable method designates the investment for purposes of the credit as either a qualified equity investment or a non-real estate qualified equity investment, and

- the CDE uses substantially all of the cash to make qualified low-income community investments, see FTC 2d/FIN ¶ L-17924; USTR ¶ 45D4; TaxDesk ¶ 384,704.

A CDE is any domestic corporation or partnership if: (a) the primary mission of the entity is serving, or providing investment capital for, low-income communities or low-income persons; (b) the entity maintains accountability to residents of low-income communities through their representation on any governing board of the entity, or on any advisory board to the entity; and (c) the entity is certified by IRS, for purposes of the credit, as being a qualified CDE, see FTC 2d/FIN ¶ L-17923; USTR ¶ 45D4; TaxDesk ¶ 384,703.

Under pre-2012 Taxpayer Relief Act law, the new markets tax credit was subject to a nationwide credit limitation for each calendar year after 2000 and before 2012. The nationwide maximum annual amounts of qualified equity investments for calendar years 2008 and 2009 were $5 billion. The nationwide

FTC 2d References are to Federal Tax Coordinator 2d
FIN References are to RIA's Analysis of Federal Taxes: Income (print)
USTR References are to United States Tax Reporter: Income
PCA References are to Pension Analysis (print and electronic)
PBE References are to Pension & Benefits Explanations
BCA References are to Benefits Analysis (electronic)
BC References are to Benefits Coordinator (print)
EP References are to Estate Planning Analysis (print and electronic)

maximum annual amounts of qualified equity investments for calendar years 2010 and 2011 were $3.5 billion. (FTC 2d/FIN ¶ L-17920, ¶ L-17927; USTR ¶ 45D4; TaxDesk ¶ 384,711)

If the credit limitation for any calendar year exceeded the aggregate amount allocated for that year, the excess was carried over and the limitation for the next calendar year was increased by the amount of the excess. Under pre-2012 Taxpayer Relief Act law, no amount could be carried over to any calendar year after 2016. (FTC 2d/FIN ¶ L-17920, ¶ L-17927; USTR ¶ 45D4; TaxDesk ¶ 384,711)

New Law. The 2012 Taxpayer Relief Act extends the new markets tax credit for two years, through 2013, subject to a $3.5 billion maximum annual amount. Thus, for each of the 2012 and 2013 calendar years, up to $3.5 billion in qualified equity investments is permitted. (Code Sec. 45D(f)(1)(G) as amended by 2012 Taxpayer Relief Act §305(a))

> *observation:* Thus, the extension for two years does not reinstate the $5 billion limits that applied for 2008 and 2009. Instead it extends the $3.5 billion limits of 2010 and 2011 for calendar years 2012 and 2013.

The 2012 Taxpayer Relief Act also extends the carryover period for unused new markets tax credits for two years through 2018. (Code Sec. 45D(f)(3) as amended by 2012 Taxpayer Relief Act §305(b))

> *observation:* Thus, if the credit limitation for any calendar year exceeds the aggregate amount allocated for that year, the excess will be carried over and the limitation for the next calendar year will be increased by the amount of the excess, but no amount will be carried over to any calendar year after 2018.

> *observation:* The new markets tax credit is combined with other business related credits into one general business credit, see FTC 2d/FIN ¶ L-17921. The new markets tax credit is claimed on Form 8874 and the general business credit is claimed on Form 3800. Taxpayers that are not partnerships or S corporations and whose only source of the new markets tax credit is from those pass-through entities, aren't required to complete or file Form 8874. They can report the new markets tax credit directly on Form 3800.

☐ **Effective:** Calendar years starting after 2011 (2012 Taxpayer Relief Act §305(c)) and before 2014. (Code Sec. 45D(f)(1)(G))

¶ 1402. QZAB program is extended through 2013

Code Sec. 54E(c)(1), as amended by 2012 Taxpayer Relief Act §310(a)
Generally effective: Bonds issued after Dec. 31, 2011 and before Jan. 1, 2014
Committee Reports, None

Qualified zone academy bonds (QZABs) are a type of qualified tax credit bond entitling the holder to a nonrefundable tax credit, see FTC 2d/FIN ¶ L-15580; USTR ¶ 54E4. A QZAB is any bond issued as part of an issue if certain requirements are met. Under one of these requirements, the issuer must designate the bond for purposes of the QZAB rules. See FTC 2d/FIN ¶ L-15582; USTR ¶ 54E4. There is a national bond volume limitation on QZABs for each calendar year. (FTC 2d/FIN ¶ L-15580, ¶ L-15586; USTR ¶ 54E4.01)

Under pre-2012 Taxpayer Relief Act law, a total of $400 million of QZABs could be issued for 2008, a total of $1.4 billion could be issued for each of 2009 and 2010, and a total of $400 million could be issued for 2011; the amount after 2011 was zero, subject to a state's carryover. (FTC 2d/FIN ¶ L-15580, ¶ L-15586; USTR ¶ 54E4.01) IRS allocated these amounts among the states (including the District of Columbia and possessions) based on the percentage of their respective populations of individuals below the poverty line (as defined by the Office of Management and Budget), see FTC 2d/FIN ¶ L-15586; USTR ¶ 54E4.01.

New Law. Under the 2012 Taxpayer Relief Act, the national bond volume limitation under Code Sec. 54E(c)(1) is amended to provide a limitation of $400,000,000 for each of 2012 and 2013. (Code Sec. 54E(c)(1) as amended by 2012 Taxpayer Relief Act §310(a))

> **observation:** The election formerly available to issuers of QZABs and other specified tax credit bonds to claim a refundable tax credit instead of the tax credit allowed to the bondholder (the so-called "direct payment" option, see FTC 2d/FIN ¶ L-15547; USTR ¶ 64,314.02) was repealed for obligations issued after 2010. This repeal is not affected by the 2012 Taxpayer Relief Act.

☐ **Effective:** Bonds issued after Dec. 31, 2011 (2012 Taxpayer Relief Act §310(b)) and before Jan. 1, 2014. (Code Sec. 54E(c)(1))

¶ 1403. Tax-exempt status of public educational facility bonds is made permanent

Code Sec. 142(a)(13), 2012 Taxpayer Relief Act §101(a)
Code Sec. 142(k), 2012 Taxpayer Relief Act §101(a)
Code Sec. None, 2012 Taxpayer Relief Act §101(a)
Generally effective: Tax years beginning after Dec. 31, 2012
Committee Reports, None

State and local bonds issued to provide financing for private purposes—i.e., private activity bonds—are not eligible for the exemption from federal income tax applicable to state and local bonds issued to finance governmental activities unless the bond is one of seven specified types of "qualified bonds" *and* meets certain other requirements. The qualified bond rules permit states or local governments to act as conduits providing tax-exempt financing for private activities.

EGTRRA Changes. Sec. 422 of the 2001 Economic Growth and Tax Relief Reconciliation Act (2001 EGTRRA, Sec. 422, PL 107-16, 6/7/2001) added tax-exempt public educational facility bonds as a category of private activity tax-exempt bonds for tax years beginning after 2001. The legislation also provided for a volume cap for tax-exempt public educational facility bonds. (FTC 2d ¶ J-3164, ¶ J-3150, ¶ J-3200, ¶ J-3242; USTR ¶ 1424.13)

Sunset. Under section 901 of 2001 EGTRRA (Sec. 901, PL 107-16, 6/7/2001), as amended by section 101(a)(1) of the 2010 Tax Relief Act (Sec. 101(a)(1), PL 111-312, 12/17/2010), the above described changes made by 2001 EGTRRA won't apply to tax years beginning after Dec. 31, 2012. Thus, under pre-2012 Taxpayer Relief Act law, the changes made by 2001 EGTRRA were to have reverted to pre-2001 EGTRRA law for tax years beginning after 2012. (FTC 2d ¶ T-11050, ¶ T-11051; USTR ¶ 79,006.86; TaxDesk ¶ 880,011)

> *observation:* Presumably, the sunset provision would have prevented the issuance of new tax-exempt public educational facility bonds after 2012, but would not have caused the interest on previously issued tax-exempt public educational facility bonds to become taxable.

New Law. The 2012 Taxpayer Relief Act makes permanent the tax-exempt status of qualified public educational facility bonds by repealing title IX of EGTRRA (i.e., the title containing the above-described EGTRRA sunset). (EGTRRA § 901 (Sec. 901, PL 107-16, 6/7/2001) repealed by (2012 Taxpayer Relief Act §101(a)(1))

☐ **Effective:** The removal of the sunset provision is effective for tax years beginning after Dec. 31, 2012. (2012 Taxpayer Relief Act §101(a)(3))

¶ 1404. Additional increase in arbitrage rebate exception for government bonds used to finance education facilities made permanent

Code Sec. 148(f)(4)(D)(vii), 2012 Taxpayer Relief Act §101(a)
Code Sec. None, 2012 Taxpayer Relief Act §101
Generally effective: Tax, plan or limitation years beginning after Dec. 31, 2012
Committee Reports, None

State or local bonds are not tax-exempt if they are arbitrage bonds. An arbitrage bond is a bond issued as part of an issue any portion of the proceeds of which is reasonably expected to be used to acquire higher yielding investments or to replace funds which were used to acquire higher yielding investments. A bond won't be treated as an arbitrage bond if the arbitrage profits are rebated to the U.S. (FTC 2d/FIN ¶ J-3405; USTR ¶ 1484.04; TaxDesk ¶ 158,013)

Small issuers are exempted from the arbitrage rebate requirement if they expect to issue no more than $5 million of tax-exempt bonds during a calendar year, the bonds are not private activity bonds, and the issuer is a governmental unit with general taxing powers. (FTC 2d/FIN ¶ J-3462; USTR ¶ 1484.04)

Before the Economic Growth and Tax Relief Reconciliation Act of 2001 (EGTRRA), the $5 million limit for small issuers was increased to $10 million if at least $5 million of the bonds were used to finance public school construction.

EGTRRA increased the additional amount of bonds for public school construction that could be issued without being subject to the arbitrage rebate requirements from $5 million to $10 million. Thus, governmental units could issue up to $15 million of bonds in a calendar year provided that at least $10 million of the bonds were used to finance public school construction expenditures. (FTC 2d/FIN ¶ J-3554, ¶ J-3599.12; USTR ¶ 1484.04; TaxDesk ¶ 158,013)

Under pre-2012 Taxpayer Relief Act law, a sunset provision in Sec. 901 of EGTRRA (Sec. 901, PL 107-16, 6/7/2001) provided that the changes made by EGTRRA wouldn't apply to tax years beginning after Dec. 31, 2012. (FTC 2d/FIN ¶ T-11050, ¶ T-11051; USTR ¶ 79,006.86; TaxDesk ¶ 880,011) In other words, the increased public school bond exemptions would revert to pre-EGTRRA law for tax years beginning after 2012. (Sec. 901(a)(1), PL 107-16, 6/7/2001). (FTC 2d/FIN ¶ T-11050, ¶ T-11051; USTR ¶ 79,006.86)

New Law. The 2012 Taxpayer Relief Act repeals title IX of EGTRRA (i.e., the title that includes the above-described EGTRRA sunset). (Sec. 901, PL 107-16, 6/7/2001 repealed by 2012 Taxpayer Relief Act §101(a)(1)) Thus, the $5 million increase in the amount of bonds for public school construction that can be issued without being subject to the arbitrage rebate requirements has been made permanent.

☐ **Effective:** For tax, plan or limitation years beginning after Dec. 31, 2012 and estates of decedents dying, gifts made or generation skipping transfers made after Dec. 31, 2012. (2012 Taxpayer Relief Act §101(a)(3))

¶ 1405. Period for issuance of qualified New York Liberty Bonds is retroactively restored and extended to bonds issued before Jan. 1, 2014

Code Sec. 1400L(d)(2)(D), as amended by 2012 Taxpayer Relief Act §328(a)

Generally effective: Bonds issued after Dec. 31, 2011 and before Jan. 1, 2014

Committee Reports, None

Subject to exceptions, interest on bonds and other obligations issued by states and localities isn't treated as tax-exempt if the borrowings are "private activity bonds." Generally, private activity bonds are borrowings (1) the proceeds of which, in more than a small percentage, are used in private business and are secured by, or paid back from, private business property or funds, or (2) the proceeds of which, in more than a small percentage, are used to make or finance loans to private persons, see FTC 2d/FIN ¶ J-3101 *et seq.*; USTR ¶ 1414 *et seq.*; TaxDesk ¶ 158,009 *et seq.*

Under pre-2012 Taxpayer Relief Act law, one of the exceptions to the rule of taxability for interest on private activity bonds was for interest on "qualified New York Liberty Bonds," see FTC 2d/FIN ¶ J-3325; USTR ¶ 14,00L4.30; TaxDesk ¶ 696,501.1. Further, the interest was excepted from the rule that treats interest on most tax-exempt bonds as a tax preference item for AMT purposes, see FTC 2d/FIN ¶ A-8201.1; USTR ¶ 14,00L4.30; TaxDesk ¶ 696,501.1.

"Qualified New York Liberty Bonds" are bonds most of the proceeds of which are used for qualified project costs, are issued by New York state (or a political subdivision thereof), are designated as qualified New York Liberty Bonds by the governor (of New York state) or mayor (of New York City), and are issued within a specific time period, see FTC 2d/FIN ¶ J-3326; USTR ¶ 14,00L4.30; TaxDesk ¶ 696,501.1.

Under pre-2012 Taxpayer Relief Act law, qualified New York Liberty Bonds had to be issued after Mar. 9, 2002 and before *Jan. 1, 2012.* (FTC 2d/FIN ¶ J-3325, ¶ J-3326; USTR ¶ 14,00L4.30)

New Law. The 2012 Taxpayer Relief Act provides that "qualified New York Liberty Bonds" must be issued after Mar. 9, 2002 and before *Jan. 1,*

2014. (Code Sec. 1400L(d)(2)(D) as amended by 2012 Taxpayer Relief Act §328(a))

> *RIA* **⌾ *observation:*** Thus, the 2012 Taxpayer Relief Act retroactively restores and extends the period in which qualified New York Liberty Bonds can be issued for two years to Jan. 1, 2014.

☐ **Effective:** Bonds issued after Dec. 31, 2011 (2012 Taxpayer Relief Act §328(b)) and before Jan. 1, 2014. (Code Sec. 1400L(d)(2)(D))

¶ 1406. Round I empowerment zone designation period is retroactively extended through the end of 2013

Code Sec. 1391(d)(1)(A)(i), as amended by 2012 Taxpayer Relief Act §327(a)
Code Sec. 1391(d)(1)(B), 2012 Taxpayer Relief Act §327(c)
Generally effective: Periods after Dec. 31, 2011 and before Jan. 1, 2014
Committee Reports, None

Certain distressed urban and rural areas nominated by state or local governments can be designated as empowerment zones eligible for special tax incentives, see FTC 2d/FIN ¶ J-3375; USTR ¶ 13,914; TaxDesk ¶ 384,020. The tax incentives available within the designated empowerment zones include:

(1) an income tax credit for employers who hire qualifying employees, see FTC 2d/FIN ¶ L-15630 *et seq.*; USTR ¶ 13,964; TaxDesk ¶ 384,020 *et seq.*

(2) accelerated depreciation deductions on qualifying equipment, see FTC 2d/FIN ¶ L-9950 *et seq.*; USTR ¶ 13,97A4; TaxDesk ¶ 268,428

(3) tax-exempt bond financing, see FTC 2d/FIN ¶ J-3350 *et seq.*; USTR ¶ 13,944

(4) deferral of capital gains tax on the sale of qualified assets sold and replaced, see FTC 2d/FIN ¶ I-3430 *et seq.*; USTR ¶ 13,97B4; TaxDesk ¶ 227,350 *et seq.* and

(5) partial exclusion of capital gains tax on certain sales of qualified small business stock, see FTC 2d/FIN ¶ I-5110.13; USTR ¶ 12,024; TaxDesk ¶ 223,323.

Designations are permitted for a total of 40 empowerment zones:

(A) 11 "Round I" empowerment zones subject to certain population limits, see FTC 2d/FIN ¶ J-3377; USTR ¶ 13,914; TaxDesk ¶ 384,020;

(B) 20 "Round II" empowerment zones with eligibility criteria expanded in comparison to the eligibility criteria for Round I empowerment zones, see FTC 2d/FIN ¶ J-3377.1; USTR ¶ 13,914; TaxDesk ¶ 384,020; and

(C) nine "Round III" empowerment zones authorized to allow the designation of a replacement empowerment zone for each empowerment zone that becomes a renewal community (and, thus, qualifies for different tax incentives), see FTC 2d/FIN ¶ J-3377.2; USTR ¶ 13,914; TaxDesk ¶ 384,020.

Designations of Round I empowerment zones remain in effect during each zone's designation period. Under pre-2012 Taxpayer Relief Act law, the designation period for an empowerment zone began on the date of its designation and ended on the earliest of:

(a) Dec. 31, 2011,

(b) the termination date designated by the state and local governments in their nomination of the area, or

(c) the date the appropriate secretary (the Secretary of Housing and Urban Development in the case of an urban area, and the Secretary of Agriculture in the case of a rural area) revoked the designation. (FTC 2d/FIN ¶ J-3382; USTR ¶ 13,914; TaxDesk ¶ 384,020)

New Law. The 2012 Taxpayer Relief Act replaces the Dec. 31, 2011 end date for the period for which a Round I empowerment zone designation is in effect with a Dec. 31, 2013 end date. (Code Sec. 1391(d)(1)(A)(i) as amended by 2012 Taxpayer Relief Act §327(a))

> ✔ *observation:* Thus, the 2012 Taxpayer Relief Act retroactively restores and extends for two years the period for which a Round I empowerment zone designation is in effect.

> ✔ *observation:* Under the 2012 Taxpayer Relief Act, the designation period for a Round I empowerment zone thus begins on the date of its designation and ends on the earliest of:

> (i) Dec. 31, 2013,

> (ii) the termination date designated by the state and local governments in their nomination of the area, or

> (iii) the date the appropriate secretary (the Secretary of Housing and Urban Development in the case of any nominated area that is located in an urban area, and the Secretary of Agriculture in the case of any nominated area that is located in a rural area) revokes the designation.

> ✔ *observation:* By extending for two years the period for which the Round I empowerment zone designation can be in effect, the 2012 Taxpayer Relief Act extends for two years the empowerment zone tax incentives. These incentives include an income tax credit for employers who hire qualifying employees, accelerated depreciation deductions on

qualifying equipment, tax-exempt bond financing, and deferral of capital gains tax on the sale of qualified assets sold and replaced.

Relief for certain termination dates specified in nominations. For an empowerment zone designation the nomination for which included a termination date contemporaneous with the date specified in Code Sec. 1391(d)(1)(A)(i) (as in effect before enactment of the 2012 Taxpayer Relief Act, that is, Dec. 31, 2011), Code Sec. 1391(d)(1)(B) (which refers to the termination date designated by the state and local governments in their nomination as a potential ending date for an empowerment zone designation, see item (ii) above) does not apply to that designation if, after Jan. 2, 2013, the entity which made the nomination amends the nomination to provide for a new termination date, in the manner provided by IRS. (2012 Taxpayer Relief Act §327(c))

> *observation:* Thus, if the nomination for an empowerment zone designation provides for a termination date of Dec. 31, 2011, the designation period for that empowerment zone begins on the date of its designation and ends on the earliest of:
>
> (i) Dec. 31, 2013, or
>
> (ii) the date the appropriate secretary (the Secretary of Housing and Urban Development in the case of any nominated area that is located in an urban area, and the Secretary of Agriculture in the case of any nominated area that is located in a rural area) revokes the designation.
>
> However, if, after Jan. 2, 2013, the entity which made the nomination amends the nomination to provide for a new termination date, in the manner provided by IRS, the designation period for that empowerment zone begins on the date of its designation and ends on the termination date designated by the state and local governments in their nomination of the area or the new termination date set forth in the amended nomination.

For the extension of the partial exclusion of gain from the sale or exchange of certain qualified small business stock in empowerment zone C corporations for two years, through the end of 2018, see ¶ 1407.

☐ **Effective:** Periods after Dec. 31, 2011 (2012 Taxpayer Relief Act §327(d)) and before Jan. 1, 2014. (Code Sec. 1391(d)(1)(A)(i))

¶ 1407. Partial exclusion of gain from the sale or exchange of certain QSBS in empowerment zone C corporations is extended through the end of 2018

Code Sec. 1202(a)(2)(C), as amended by 2012 Taxpayer Relief Act §327(b)
Generally effective: Periods after Dec. 31, 2011 and before Jan. 1, 2019
Committee Reports, None

Certain distressed urban and rural areas nominated by state or local governments can be designated as empowerment zones eligible for special tax incentives, see FTC 2d/FIN ¶ J-3375; USTR ¶ 13,914; TaxDesk ¶ 384,020. One of the tax incentives available in the designated empowerment zones is that, in the case of qualified small business stock (QSBS) in a corporation which is a qualified business entity (defined below), noncorporate taxpayers may exclude 60% (75% for QSBS acquired after Feb. 17, 2009 and before Sept. 28, 2010, and 100% for QSBS acquired after Sept. 27, 2010 and before Jan. 1, 2011, see FTC 2d/FIN ¶ I-9100.1; USTR ¶ 12,024; TaxDesk ¶ 246,600.1) of the gain realized on the sale or exchange of QSBS held for more than five years, if the stock is acquired after Dec. 31, 2010 or before Feb. 18, 2009. A qualified business entity is a corporation that satisfies the requirements of a qualifying business under the empowerment zone rules during substantially all of the taxpayer's holding period, see FTC 2d/FIN ¶ L-9955; USTR ¶ 13,97A4; TaxDesk ¶ 268,431.

Under pre-2012 Taxpayer Relief Act law, the 60%-exclusion rule (75%-exclusion rule for QSBS acquired after Feb. 17, 2009 and before Sept. 28, 2010; 100%-exclusion rule for QSBS acquired after Sept. 27, 2010 and before Jan. 1, 2011) did not apply to gain attributable to periods after *Dec. 31, 2016.* (FTC 2d/FIN ¶ I-9100, ¶ I-9100.1C; USTR ¶ 12,024; TaxDesk ¶ 246,602)

New Law. Under the 2012 Taxpayer Relief Act, the partial exclusion (60%, 75%, or 100%, as indicated above) of gain on the sale of QSBS in a corporation which is a qualified business entity held for more than five years does not apply to gain attributable to periods after *Dec. 31, 2018.* (Code Sec. 1202(a)(2)(C) as amended by 2012 Taxpayer Relief Act §327(b)(1))

> **☑ observation:** Thus, the 2012 Taxpayer Relief Act extends for two years, through Dec. 31, 2018, the period for which the percentage exclusion for QSBS in a corporation which is a qualified business entity acquired on or before Feb. 17, 2009 is 60%.

> **☑ observation:** Gain attributable to periods after Dec. 31, 2018 for QSBS acquired on or before Feb. 17, 2009 or after Dec. 31, 2011 is subject to the general rule which provides for a percentage exclusion of 50%.

For the extension of the empowerment zone designation period through the end of 2013, see ¶ 1406.

For extension of the 100% exclusion for QSBS, see ¶ 209.

☐ **Effective:** Periods after Dec. 31, 2011 (2012 Taxpayer Relief Act §327(d)) and before Jan. 1, 2019. (Code Sec. 1202(a)(2)(C))

¶ 1408. The military housing allowance exclusion for tax-exempt bond financing and the low-income housing credit is extended until 2014

Code Sec. 142(d)(2)(B)(ii), 2012 Taxpayer Relief Act §303(a)
Code Sec. 42(g)(4), 2012 Taxpayer Relief Act §303(a)
Generally effective: Income determinations made after July 30, 2008 and before 2014
Committee Reports, None

For income determinations made after July 30, 2008 and before Jan. 1, 2012, the 2008 Housing Act added Code Sec. 142(d)(2)(B)(ii) which excludes certain basic military housing allowances under 37 USC §403 made with respect to any qualified building from the definition of gross income for purposes of determining area median gross income (AMGI) and for purposes of determining the low income housing credit.

A residential rental project won't qualify for tax-exempt bond financing unless it meets one of the two "set-aside" tests based on the income levels of its residents and AMGI. Code Sec. 142(d)(2)(B) provides the rules for determining income and AMGI for these purposes. (FTC 2d/FIN ¶ J-3200, ¶ J-3210, ¶ J-3216; USTR ¶ 1424.02)

> **🅡🅘🅐** *observation:* 37 USC §403 authorizes payment of a basic allowance for housing (BAH) to members of the U.S. Armed Forces. The BAH is a monthly payment based on civilian rental costs by pay grade, dependency status, and location. So, any amount paid as a BAH to a service member occupying a unit in a "qualified building" (i.e., military housing meeting certain requirements) wasn't included in the member's income for purposes of determining whether the building meets the applicable set-aside test to be a "qualified residential rental project." In other words, the BAH wouldn't cause the building to not qualify for tax-exempt bond financing.

Code Sec. 142(d)(2) also applies under Code Sec. 42(g)(4), with certain modifications, in determining whether a project is a "qualified low-income housing project" and whether a unit is a "low-income unit" for purposes of the low income housing credit (LIHC). Thus, the exclusion from income for BAH under

Code Sec. 142(d)(2)(B)(ii) applies in making LIHC determinations. (FTC 2d/ FIN ¶ L-15800, ¶ L-15804)

Under the 2008 Housing Act, the Code Sec. 142(d)(2)(B)(ii) income exclusion would have expired for tax-exempt bond financing and low-income housing credit determinations made after Dec. 31, 2011. (FTC 2d/FIN ¶ J-3200, ¶ J-3216; USTR ¶ 1424.02)

New Law. The Taxpayer Relief Act amends the 2008 Housing Act (Sec. 3005(b), PL 110-289, 7/30/2008) by retroactively restoring and extending the application of the Code Sec. 142(d)(2(B)(ii) income exclusion for two years until Jan 1, 2014. (2012 Taxpayer Relief Act §303(a))

observation: Thus BAH is disregarded for

(1) income determinations made after July 30, 2008 and before Jan. 1, 2014 for a qualified building for which LIHC dollar amounts were allocated on or before July 30, 2008, or a qualified building placed in service before July 30, 2008, to the extent that the Code Sec. 42(h)(1) LIHC allocation limit does not apply to the building by reason of Code Sec. 42(h)(4), but only for bonds issued before July 30, 2008 and

(2) income determinations made after July 30, 2008 for a qualified building for which LIHC dollar amounts are allocated after July 30, 2008 and before Jan. 1, 2014 or a qualified building placed in service after July 30, 2008 and before Jan. 1, 2014, to the extent that the Code Sec. 42(h)(1) LIHC allocation limit does not apply to the building by reason of Code Sec. 42(h)(4), but only for bonds issued after July 30, 2008 and before Jan. 1, 2014.

☐ **Effective:** For income determinations made after July 30, 2008 (Sec. 3005(b), PL 110-289, 7/30/2008) and before 2014. (2012 Taxpayer Relief Act §303(b))

¶ 1500. Miscellaneous Provisions

¶ 1501. Shortened S Corp built-in gains holding period extended for 2012 and 2013 and application of built-in gains tax clarified

Code Sec. 1374(d)(7), as amended by 2012 Taxpayer Relief Act §326(a)
Code Sec. 1374(d)(2)(B), as amended by 2012 Taxpayer Relief Act §326(b)
Generally effective: Tax years beginning after Dec. 31, 2011
Committee Reports, None

An S corporation is generally not subject to tax, but passes through its items to its shareholders, who pay tax on their pro-rata shares of the S corporation's income. See FTC 2d/FIN ¶ D-1640; USTR ¶ 13,664; TaxDesk ¶ 615,000. Where a corporation that was formed as a C corporation elected to become an S corporation (or where an S corporation received property from a C corporation in a nontaxable carryover basis transfer), the S corporation was taxed at the highest corporate rate (currently 35%) on all gains that were built-in at the time of the election if the gains were recognized during the recognition period, i.e., the first ten S corporation years (or during the ten-period after the transfer). The 2009 Recovery Act (Sec. 1251(a), PL 111-5, 2/17/2009) provided that, for S corporation tax years beginning in 2009 and 2010, no tax was imposed on the net unrecognized built-in gain of an S corporation if the *seventh tax year* in the recognition period preceded the 2009 and 2010 tax years. This rule applied separately for property acquired from C corporations in carryover basis transactions. The 2010 Small Business Act (Sec. 2014(a), PL 111-240, 9/27/2010) added that for S corporation tax years beginning in 2011, no tax was imposed on the net unrecognized built-in gain of an S corporation if the fifth year in the recognition period preceded the 2011 tax year. (FTC 2d/FIN ¶ D-1640, ¶ D-1643, ¶ D-1655; USTR ¶ 13,744.01; TaxDesk ¶ 615,014)

Where the net recognized built-in gains (i.e., the amount by which recognized built-in gains exceeded the recognized built-in losses) for any tax year exceeded the taxable income of the S corporation (as determined for purposes of the built-in gains tax), the built-in gains tax was not imposed. However, the excess net recognized built-in gain was carried forward to the next tax year to be treated as a recognized built-in gain in that next tax year. (FTC 2d/FIN

FTC 2d References are to Federal Tax Coordinator 2d
FIN References are to RIA's Analysis of Federal Taxes: Income (print)
USTR References are to United States Tax Reporter: Income
PCA References are to Pension Analysis (print and electronic)
PBE References are to Pension & Benefits Explanations
BCA References are to Benefits Analysis (electronic)
BC References are to Benefits Coordinator (print)
EP References are to Estate Planning Analysis (print and electronic)

¶ D-1644, ¶ D-1645, ¶ D-1655; USTR ¶ 13,744.01; TaxDesk ¶ 615,003, 615,005)

New Law. The 2012 Taxpayer Relief Act provides that for S corporation tax years beginning in 2012 and 2013, the recognition period is limited to five years. (Code Sec. 1374(d)(7)(C) as amended by 2012 Taxpayer Relief Act §326(a)(2))

> **observation:** Thus, a five-year period applies for the 2011, 2012 and 2013 tax years. Since the ten-year period will apply after the 2013 tax year (unless extended by Congress), sellers should complete the sales in the 2013 tax year.

The 2012 Taxpayer Relief Act also provides that when an asset is sold in an installment sale under Code Sec. 453, the treatment of the payments is determined by the tax year in which the sale is made. (Code Sec. 1374(d)(7)(E) as amended by 2012 Taxpayer Relief Act §326(a)(3))

> **observation:** Thus, if an asset is sold within the recognition period, the gain will be subject to the built-in gains tax, even if the gain is recognized after the recognition period under the installment sale rules.

The 2012 Taxpayer Relief Act amends the rules regarding carryovers of net recognized built-in gain so that net recognized built-in gain is only carried over to years that are within the recognition period. (Code Sec. 1374(d)(2)(B) as amended by 2012 Taxpayer Relief Act §326(b))

> **observation:** Thus, if built-in gain is not taxed during the recognition period because of the taxable income limitation, the built-in gain will not be taxed in a later year.

☐ **Effective:** Tax years beginning after Dec. 31, 2011. (2012 Taxpayer Relief Act §326(c))

¶ 1502. Rule mitigating tax-exempt parent's UBTI "specified payments" received from a controlled entity, is retroactively extended through 2013

Code Sec. 512(b)(13)(E)(iv), as amended by 2012 Taxpayer Relief Act §319(a)
Generally effective: Payments received or accrued in 2012 and 2013
Committee Reports, None

Generally, interest, rents, royalties, and annuities (collectively referred to below as "specified payments") are excluded from the unrelated business taxable income (UBTI) of tax-exempt organizations, for purposes of the tax on UBTI.

However, Code Sec. 512(b)(13) treats otherwise-excluded specified payments as UBTI if the income is received from a taxable or tax-exempt subsidiary that is 50% controlled by the parent tax-exempt organization, to the extent the payment reduces the net unrelated income (or increases any net unrelated loss) of the controlled entity (determined as if the entity were tax-exempt).

A special rule that was enacted as part of the Pension Protection Act of 2006 provided that, for payments made under a binding written contract in effect on Aug. 17, 2006 (or a renewal, on substantially similar terms, of a binding written contract in effect on Aug. 17, 2006):

- the general rule of Code Sec. 512(b)(13) applied only to the portion of payments received or accrued in a tax year that exceeded the amount of the payment that *would have been* paid or accrued if the amount of the payment had been determined under the principles of Code Sec. 482 (i.e., at arm's length); and

- a 20% penalty was imposed on the larger of (i) the excess payment, determined without regard to any amendment or supplement to a tax return, or (ii) the excess payment, determined with regard to all amendments and supplements to a tax return.

Under pre-2012 Taxpayer Relief Act law, the above special rule did not apply to payments received or accrued after Dec. 31, 2011 (the "termination date"). (FTC 2d/FIN ¶ D-6900, ¶ D-6913.2; USTR ¶ 5124)

New Law. Under the 2012 Taxpayer Relief Act, the termination date is amended by substituting Dec. 31, 2013, for Dec. 31, 2011. (Code Sec. 512(b)(13)(E)(iv) as amended by 2012 Taxpayer Relief Act §319(a))

> *observation:* The 2012 Taxpayer Relief Act extends the special rule for two years (through 2013), and thus the rule may be applied to payments received or accrued before Jan. 1, 2014.

☐ **Effective:** Applies to payments received or accrued after Dec. 31, 2011 (2012 Taxpayer Relief Act §319(b)) and before Jan. 1, 2014. (Code Sec. 512(b)(13)(E)(iv))

> *observation:* Thus, the special rule is retroactively restored for payments received or accrued after Dec. 31, 2011 and before Jan. 2, 2013 (the date of enactment of the 2012 Taxpayer Relief Act), since the provision extending the special rule is effective for payments received or accrued after Dec. 31, 2011. The special rule does *not* apply to payments received or accrued after Dec. 31, 2013.

¶ 1503. Favorable income tax treatment for Alaska Native Settlement Trusts and their beneficiaries is made permanent

Code Sec. 646, 2012 Taxpayer Relief Act §101(a)(1)
Code Sec. 6039H, 2012 Taxpayer Relief Act §101(a)(1)
Generally effective: Tax years beginning after 2012
Committee Reports, None

The Alaska Native Claims Settlement Act (ANCSA, 43 U.S.C. §1601 *et seq.*) established Alaska Native Corporations to hold property for Alaska Natives. Alaska Natives are generally the only permitted common shareholders of those corporations under ANCSA, unless an Alaska Native Corporation specifically allows other shareholders under specified procedures.

ANCSA permits an Alaska Native Corporation to transfer money or other property to an Alaska Native Settlement Trust for the benefit of beneficiaries who constitute all or a class of the shareholders of the Alaska Native Corporation, to promote the health, education and welfare of beneficiaries, and to preserve the heritage and culture of Alaska Natives.

Alaska Native Corporations and Settlement Trusts, as well as their shareholders and beneficiaries, are generally subject to tax under the same rules and in the same manner as other taxpayers that are corporations, trusts, shareholders, or beneficiaries. However, the Economic Growth and Tax Relief Reconciliation Act of 2001 (EGTRRA, Sec. 671(a), PL 107-16, 6/7/2001) added Code Sec. 646, which permits an Alaska Native Settlement Trust to elect to pay tax on its income at the lowest rate specified for ordinary income of an individual, rather than the higher tax rates applicable to estates and trusts. In addition, trust beneficiaries are not taxed on distributions of an electing trust's taxable income, and contributions by an Alaska Native Corporation to an electing trust are not deemed distributions to the corporation's shareholders. (FTC 2d/FIN ¶ C-1000, ¶ C-1026; USTR ¶ 6464; EP ¶ 85,027)

Electing trusts may comply with certain streamlined information reporting rules under Code Sec. 6039H (added by EGTRRA, Sec. 671(b), PL 107-16, 6/7/2001), instead of the more onerous requirement of providing annual Form K-1's to beneficiaries and IRS under Code Sec. 6034A. (FTC 2d/FIN ¶ S-2000, ¶ S-2009.5; USTR ¶ 60,39H4)

Sunset after 2012. A sunset provision in Sec. 901 of EGTRRA (Sec. 901, PL 107-16, 6/7/2001) provided that all changes made by EGTRRA were to no longer apply to tax years beginning after Dec. 31, 2010 (the "sunset date").

The 2010 Tax Relief Act (PL 111-312, 12/17/2010) delayed for two years the EGTRRA sunset as it applied to electing Alaska Native Settlement Trusts. Thus, the 2010 Act extended the elective tax treatment for Alaska Native Settlement

Trusts for an additional two years, through Dec. 31, 2012. This meant that both the Code Sec. 646 election and the Code Sec. 6039H streamlined reporting rule could be applied by Alaska Native Settlement Trusts for tax years beginning through Dec. 31, 2012. (Sec. 901, PL 107-16, 6/7/2001, as amended by Sec. 101(a)(1), PL 111-312, 12/17/2010) (FTC 2d/FIN ¶ T-11051; USTR ¶ 79,006.86; TaxDesk ¶ 880,011)

New Law. The 2012 Taxpayer Relief Act repeals title IX of EGTRRA (i.e., the title containing the above-described EGTRRA sunset). (EGTRRA § 901 (Sec. 901, PL 107-16, 6/7/2001) repealed by 2012 Taxpayer Relief Act §101(a)(1))

> *observation:* Thus, both the Code Sec. 646 election and the Code Sec. 6039H streamlined reporting rule, as they apply to Alaska Native Settlement Trusts, are made permanent.

☐ **Effective:** For tax years beginning after Dec. 31, 2012. (2012 Taxpayer Relief Act §101(a)(3))

¶ 1504. Repeal of collapsible corporation provision is made permanent

Code Sec. 341, 2012 Taxpayer Relief Act §102(a)
Code Sec. None, 2012 Taxpayer Relief Act §102(a)
Generally effective: Tax years beginning after Dec. 31, 2012.
Committee Reports, None

Under pre-2010 Tax Relief Act law, the collapsible corporation rules were repealed. (FTC 2d/FIN ¶ F-15000 *et seq.*; USTR ¶ 3414)

Sunset. Under section 303 of the 2003 Jobs and Growth Act (JGTRRA, Sec. 303, PL 108-27, 5/28/2003), as amended by section 102 of the 2005 Tax Increase Prevention Act (TIPRA, Sec. 102, PL 109-222, 5/17/2006), and by the Tax Relief Act of 2010 (Sec. 102(a), PL 111-312, 12/17/2010), the repeal of the collapsible corporation rules was to expire for tax years beginning after Dec. 31, 2012. (FTC 2d/FIN ¶ F-15000 *et seq.*, ¶ F-15001; USTR ¶ 3414)

New Law. The 2012 Taxpayer Relief Act removes the sunset provision. (2012 Taxpayer Relief Act §102(a)) Thus, the repeal of the collapsible corporation rules is made permanent. (2003 Jobs and Growth Act § 303 as repealed by 2012 Taxpayer Relief Act §102(a))

☐ **Effective:** The effect of the provision is to remove the sunset that would have been effective for tax years beginning after Dec. 31, 2012. (2012 Taxpayer Relief Act §102(a))

> *observation:* 2012 Taxpayer Relief Act §102(a), which eliminates the JGTRRA §303 sunset rule, as amended, is effective as if included

in the enactment of JGTRRA. JGTRRA was enacted on May 28, 2003, so §102(a) is technically effective as of that date.

¶ 1505. Provision authorizing IRS to disclose certain returns and return information to certain prison officials is improved and made permanent

Code Sec. 6103(k)(10), as amended by 2012 Taxpayer Relief Act §209(a)
Generally effective: Jan. 2, 2013
Committee Reports, None

IRS was allowed to disclose certain prisoner tax information to specified persons in the Federal Bureau of Prisons and state prison systems (FTC 2d/FIN ¶ S-6360.2; USTR ¶ 61,034.052). Under procedures that IRS chose, IRS could disclose to the *head* of the Federal Bureau of Prisons and the *head* of any state agency charged with the responsibility for prison administration (a state prison agency), return information for individuals incarcerated in federal prison or state prison whom IRS determined may have filed or facilitated the filing of a false return. The disclosure was permitted to the extent that IRS determined that it was necessary to permit effective federal tax administration. The head of the Federal Bureau of Prisons or of any state prison agency could redisclose the information received only to officers or employees of the Federal Bureau of Prisons or of a state prison agency. Any information received under the above rules could be used only for purposes of and to the extent necessary in taking administrative action to prevent the filing of false and fraudulent returns, including administrative actions to address possible violations of administrative rules and regulations of the prison facility. (FTC 2d/FIN ¶ S-6360.2; USTR ¶ 61,034.052)

Under pre-2012 Taxpayer Relief Act law, the above rules with respect to disclosure to certain prison officials terminated after Dec. 31, 2011. The disclosure rules were not in effect from Jan. 1, 2012 through Jan. 1, 2013. (FTC 2d/FIN ¶ S-6360.2; USTR ¶ 61,034.052)

New Law. The 2012 Taxpayer Relief Act allows IRS, under procedures it provides, to disclose any returns and return information with respect to persons incarcerated in the federal or a state prison system to officers and employees of the Federal Bureau of Prisons or any state agency charged with responsibility for prison administration, where IRS determines that the incarcerated person may have filed or facilitated the filing of a false or fraudulent return, to the extent that the disclosure is necessary to permit effective federal tax administration. (Code Sec. 6103(k)(10)(A) as amended by 2012 Taxpayer Relief Act §209(a))

> **observation:** Thus, IRS can make a disclosure to an officer or employee of a federal or state agency charged with administering prisons. The disclosure does not have to be to the head of the agency.

Further, the 2012 Taxpayer Relief Act allows IRS to provide procedures for disclosures described in Code Sec. 6103(k)(10)(A) to be made to contractors responsible for the operation of a federal or state prison on behalf of the Federal Bureau of Prisons or a state agency. (Code Sec. 6103(k)(10)(B))

> *observation:* Thus, disclosures by IRS of returns and return information as discussed above, can also be made to contractors operating privately run prisons under the same conditions as disclosures to federal or state government run prisons.

The 2012 Taxpayer Relief Act adds *any return* (as well as return information) to the restrictions of use of disclosed information. (Code Sec. 6103(k)(10)(C))

> *observation:* IRS under the 2012 Taxpayer Relief Act can now specifically disclose any return, as well as return information to prison officials. The broad term "any return" presumably means returns that may relate to a false or fraudulent filing, such as information returns, returns of the incarcerated taxpayer from earlier years, partnership and S corporation returns, trust and estate income tax returns and any other returns that could be necessary for effective federal tax administration.

Code Sec. 6103(k)(10)(D)(i) contains the restrictions on redisclosure formerly contained in pre-2012 Taxpayer Relief Act Code Sec. 6103(k)(10)(B). An exception on restriction of redisclosure is made for legal representatives described in Code Sec. 6103(k)(10)(D)(ii), below. In addition, the head of the Bureau of Prisons and heads of state agencies, officers, employees, and contractors of those agencies can't disclose information obtained under Code Sec. 6103(k)(10) to anyone except an officer, employee or a contractor of the Bureau of Prisons or a state agency, who is personally and directly engaged in the administration of prison facilities on behalf of the Bureau or agency. (Code Sec. 6103(k)(10)(D)(i))

The 2012 Taxpayer Relief Act provides for disclosure of the returns and return information to duly authorized legal representatives of:

- the Federal Bureau of Prisons;
- a state agency or contractor charged with the responsibility for administration of prisons; or
- the incarcerated individual accused of filing the false or fraudulent return who is a party to an administrative or judicial action or proceeding arising from administrative actions to prevent the filing of false and fraudulent returns, solely in preparation for, or for use in, those actions or proceedings.

(Code Sec. 6103(k)(10)(D)(ii))

> *observation:* The term "duly authorized legal representative" is not defined in Code Sec. 6103(k)(10) or referenced in that section to an-

other part of the Code. Thus, it is unclear whether this term refers solely to licensed attorneys, or other persons having power of attorney for tax or other purposes.

observation: It is also unclear whether a party to an administrative or judicial proceeding refers only to the incarcerated person or also to the federal and state agencies.

☐ **Effective:** Jan. 2, 2013. (2012 Taxpayer Relief Act §209(c))

observation: The 2012 Taxpayer Relief Act makes Code Sec. 6103(k)(10) permanent by eliminating the termination date in pre-2012 Taxpayer Relief Act Code Sec. 6103(k)(10)(D).

¶ 1600. Health Related Provisions from Earlier Acts of the 112th Congress

¶ 1601. Modified AGI for determining eligibility for and amount of post-2013 premium tax credit will include nontaxable social security income

Code Sec. 36B(d)(2)(B)(iii), as amended by 2011 Job Creation Act §401(a)
Generally effective: Nov. 21, 2011
Committee Reports, None

Starting in 2014, Code Sec. 36B will allow a premium tax credit (PTC) to qualifying low-income taxpayers who buy health insurance through a state-run insurance exchange (Exchange) (generally, those with household income at 100%-400% of the federal poverty level (FPL) for the family size involved who aren't eligible for Medicaid, employer-sponsored insurance, or other acceptable coverage). The PTC, which will be refundable and payable in advance directly to the insurer, will subsidize the taxpayer's Exchange purchase of coverage of the taxpayer and qualifying family members under a "qualified health plan." The amount allowed as a credit for a tax year will equal a sliding-scale percentage (ranging from 2% to 9.5%, based on household income relative to the FPL) of the premiums paid for the coverage for the year. (See FTC 2d/FIN ¶ A-4200 *et seq.*; USTR ¶s 36B4, 36B4.01; TaxDesk ¶ 569,450 *et seq.*)

The "household income" used in determining a taxpayer's eligibility for, and the amount allowed as, a PTC means an amount equal to the sum of: (1) the taxpayer's modified adjusted gross income (MAGI), plus (2) the total MAGI of all other individuals taken into account in determining the taxpayer's family size (i.e., all individuals the taxpayer is allowed to claim as dependents), but only if those individuals must file a tax return for the tax year. (See FTC 2d/FIN ¶ A-4247; USTR ¶ 36B4.01; TaxDesk ¶ 569,472)

Under pre-2011 Job Creation Act law, MAGI would have been defined for PTC purposes as adjusted gross income (AGI) increased by: (a) any amount excluded from gross income under Code Sec. 911 (the foreign earned income and foreign housing costs exclusions for U.S. citizens or residents living abroad, see FTC 2d/FIN ¶ O-1100 *et seq.*; USTR ¶ 9114; TaxDesk ¶ 191,000 *et seq.*), plus

---

FTC 2d References are to Federal Tax Coordinator 2d
FIN References are to RIA's Analysis of Federal Taxes: Income (print)
USTR References are to United States Tax Reporter: Income
PCA References are to Pension Analysis (print and electronic)
PBE References are to Pension & Benefits Explanations
BCA References are to Benefits Analysis (electronic)
BC References are to Benefits Coordinator (print)
EP References are to Estate Planning Analysis (print and electronic)

(b) any tax-exempt interest received or accrued during the tax year. (FTC 2d/ FIN ¶ A-4240, ¶ A-4247.1; USTR ¶ 36B4.01; TaxDesk ¶ 569,473)

New Law. The 2011 Job Creation Act (the Act) revises the PTC definition of MAGI so that it will include (in addition to amounts excluded under Code Sec. 911 and tax-exempt interest) an amount equal to the part of the taxpayer's social security benefits that is excluded from gross income under Code Sec. 86 for the tax year. (Code Sec. 36B(d)(2)(B)(iii) as amended by 2011 Job Creation Act §401(a) (Sec. 401(a), PL 112-56, 11/21/2011))

> *observation:* Under Code Sec. 86, a taxpayer may have to include from 50% to 85% of social security benefits in gross income, depending on the amount of the taxpayer's other income and the amount of the benefits themselves. (For married taxpayers filing joint returns, both spouses' incomes and benefits are taken into account.)

The extent to which a taxpayer's benefits are taxable is determined by comparing the taxpayer's "provisional income"—i.e., "modified adjusted gross income (AGI)" as specially defined plus one-half of social security benefits received—against two threshold amounts. The benefits aren't taxable (i.e., 100% excludible) if provisional income doesn't exceed the first threshold ($32,000 for joint returns, $25,000 for single and head of household returns), 50% taxable (i.e., 50% excludible) if provisional income exceeds the first threshold, and 85% taxable (i.e., 15% excludible) if provisional income exceeds the second threshold ($44,000 for joint returns, $34,000 for single and head of household returns). (See FTC 2d/FIN ¶ J-1455 *et seq.*; USTR ¶ 864 *et seq.*; TaxDesk ¶ 146,000 *et seq.*)

As explained above, the starting point for determining a taxpayer's MAGI for PTC purposes is the taxpayer's AGI. To the extent that social security benefits are included in a taxpayer's gross income under Code Sec. 86, they're included in the taxpayer's AGI (and so the taxpayer's MAGI). To the extent that the benefits aren't thus included in gross income, new Code Sec. 36B(d)(2)(B)(iii) requires them to be added back to AGI, and included in MAGI for PTC purposes. In other words, the taxpayer will have to take *all* of those benefits into account in determining his eligibility for, and the amount allowed as, a PTC for the year, even if his income level is too low to require any of the benefits to be subject to income tax.

In other words, a taxpayer's household income for purposes of determining the taxpayer's eligibility for, and the amount allowed as, a PTC will consist of the AGI of the taxpayer and all other individuals for whom the taxpayer will be allowed a dependency deduction and whose income would require them to file a return, as increased by the following amounts that were excluded from the gross income of the taxpayer and those individuals:

(a) amounts excluded under the Code Sec. 911 foreign earned income and foreign housing costs exclusions for U.S. citizens and residents living abroad,

(b) tax-exempt interest, and

(c) social security benefits that weren't taxable because the taxpayer's (or other individual's) income level didn't exceed the applicable threshold amount.

☐ **Effective:** Nov. 21, 2011. (2011 Job Creation Act §401(b))

observation: Although the revised definition of MAGI is effective on Nov. 21, 2011, the PTC itself won't apply until tax years ending after Dec. 31, 2013. This means that the change will apply for tax years ending after Dec. 31, 2013.

¶ 1602. Simplified payback caps on excess advance premium assistance credits apply to taxpayers below 400% of poverty line

Code Sec. 36B(f)(2)(B)(i), as amended by 2011 Taxpayer Protection Act §4(a)
Generally effective: Tax years ending after Dec. 31, 2013
Committee Reports, see ¶ 5903

Starting in 2014, a refundable tax credit—the Code Sec. 36B premium assistance credit—will be available to qualifying low-income taxpayers (generally, those with household income at 100%–400% of the federal poverty line (FPL) who aren't eligible for Medicaid, employer-sponsored insurance, or other acceptable coverage) to subsidize coverage of taxpayers and qualifying family members under a qualified health plan (QHP, see FTC 2d/FIN ¶ A-4241.1; USTR ¶ 36B4.01; TaxDesk ¶ 569,452) purchased on a state-run health insurance exchange (Exchange). The amount allowed as a credit for a tax year will equal a sliding-scale percentage (ranging from 2% to 9.5%, based on household income relative to the FPL) of the premiums paid for the QHP coverage for the year. (See FTC 2d/FIN ¶ A-4240 *et seq.*; USTR ¶s 36B4, 36B4.01; TaxDesk ¶ 569,450 *et seq.*)

observation: The premium assistance credit is sometimes referred to as the "health care affordability tax credit."

The credit generally will be payable in advance directly to the insurer during the year for which the coverage is provided (rather than in the next year when the taxpayer's income tax return is filed). The eligibility for and amount of advance credits will be determined before that year, based on the taxpayer's income from two years earlier. For example, the credit for 2014 coverage will be based on 2012 tax-return information provided during the 2013 open-enrollment period. (See FTC 2d/FIN ¶ H-4891; USTR ¶ 36B4.03; TaxDesk ¶ 138,701)

The advance payments must be reconciled with the taxpayer's allowable premium assistance credit for the tax year (based on actual household income, family size, and premiums paid). If the credit received through advance payment exceeds (or is less than) the amount the taxpayer is entitled to claim as a credit for the year, the difference must be reflected on the taxpayer's income tax return for that year, as an increase (or decrease) in tax liability.

The tax increase (also referred to as a "payback") for an excess advance payment will be limited to a specified "applicable dollar amount" based on the taxpayer's household income relative to the FPL. Pre-2011 Taxpayer Protection Act law provided that the payback would be capped if household income for the credit year was under 500% of FPL, with seven dollar-amount caps ranging from $600 (household income under 200% of FPL) to $3,500 (household income at least 450% but under 500% of FPL). (FTC 2d/FIN ¶ A-4240, ¶ A-4248.1; USTR ¶ 36B4.01; TaxDesk ¶ 569,478)

> 🅦 *observation:* The payback cap rules lessen the tax burden for taxpayers whose income for the coverage year turns out to be more than what they expected when the credit amount was determined. The amount of the required payback is capped at an amount determined under a sliding scale based on the taxpayer's income, with lower limits for taxpayers with lower incomes.

New Law. The 2011 Taxpayer Protection Act (the Act) modifies the "applicable dollar amount" limitation on the tax increase required for excess advance payments of the premium assistance credit, by making the limitation apply to taxpayers whose household income is less than 400% (instead of less than 500%) of the poverty line for the size of the family involved for the tax year (the "applicable poverty line") (Code Sec. 36B(f)(2)(B)(i) as amended by 2011 Taxpayer Protection Act §4(a) (Sec. 4(a), PL 112-9, 4/14/2011)) and revising the "applicable dollar amount" for any excess advance payment. (Com Rept, see ¶ 5903)

Specifically, for a taxpayer (other than a single filer, see below) whose household income is less than 400% of the applicable poverty line, the amount of the tax increase can in no event exceed the applicable dollar amount determined under the following table: (Code Sec. 36B(f)(2)(B)(i))

Limitation on Payback of "Excess" Premium Assistance Credits

Household Income Relative to Federal Poverty Line	Cap on Payback Amount
Less than 200%	$ 600
At least 200% but less than 300%	$1,500
At least 300% but less than 400%	$2,500

For a taxpayer whose tax is determined under Code Sec. 1(c) for the tax year (unmarried individuals who aren't surviving spouses or filing as heads of household (Com Rept, see ¶ 5903)—i.e., single filers), the amount of the increase will equal one-half of the amount shown in the above table. (Code Sec. 36B(f)(2)(B)(i))

⨂ observation: For taxpayers whose household income is less than 400% of the applicable poverty line, the Act preserves the $600–$2,500 payback caps, but flattens out the sliding-scale structure: the dollar-amount caps increase only twice (to $1,500 for household income of at least 200% of FPL and to $2,500 for household income of at least 300% of FPL), rather than four times (to $1,000, $1,500, $2,000, and $2,500 for household income of least 200%, 250%, 300%, and 350%, respectively, of FPL), over the applicable household income ranges.

For taxpayers whose household income is at least 400%, but less than 500% of the applicable poverty line, the Act eliminates the payback caps altogether.

Illustration: Taxpayer A is single and has no dependents. The Exchange in A's rating area projects A's 2014 household income to be $27,925 (250% of the FPL for a family of one, applicable percentage 8.05). A enrolls in a QHP. The annual premium for the applicable benchmark plan is $5,200. A's advance credit payments are $2,952, computed as follows: benchmark plan premium of $5,200 less contribution amount of $2,248 (8.05% × projected household income of $27,925) = $2,952.

A's actual household income for 2014 is $43,560 (390% of the FPL, applicable percentage 9.5). So, A's PTC for 2014 is $1,062: benchmark plan premium of $5,200 less contribution amount of $4,138 (9.5% × household income of $43,560). A has excess advance payments of $1,890 ($2,952 advance payments less $1,062 PTC). Because A's household income is between 300% and 400% of the FPL, A's additional tax liability for 2014 will be $1,250 under the repayment limitation. (Reg §1.36B-4(a)(4), Ex. 2)

Taxpayers with household income at or above 400% of the applicable poverty line must repay the full amount of the credit received through an advance payment. (Com Rept, see ¶ 5903)

> **⊘ observation:** Under Code Sec. 36B(c)(1)(A), taxpayers aren't eligible for the credit if their household income is *more than 400%* of the applicable poverty line (see FTC 2d/FIN ¶ A-4243; USTR ¶ 36B4.01; TaxDesk ¶ 569,454). This means that taxpayers with household income *at 400%* of the applicable poverty line are entitled to some credit (assuming the other requirements are met). While the "full repayment" rule that Code Sec. 36B(f)(2)(B)(i) imposes for taxpayers *at 400%* of the applicable poverty line requires taxpayers at that income level to repay the full amount of any excess advance credits paid on their behalf, it doesn't deprive them of their otherwise allowable credit.

> **⊘ observation:** The Act doesn't change Code Sec. 36B(f)(2)(B)(ii), which provides that the dollar amounts under Code Sec. 36B(f)(2)(B)(i) are to be adjusted for inflation for calendar years beginning after 2014 (see FTC 2d/FIN ¶ A-4248.1; USTR ¶ 36B4.01; TaxDesk ¶ 569,478). Thus, starting in 2015, the applicable dollar amounts shown in the above table will be adjusted for inflation.

☐ **Effective:** Tax years ending after Dec. 31, 2013. (2011 Taxpayer Protection Act §4(b))

¶ 1603. Employers won't have to provide free choice vouchers to employees, as post-2013 rules are repealed

Code Sec. None, 2011 Appropriations Act §1858(a)
Code Sec. 139D, as repealed by 2011 Appropriations Act §1858(b)(2)(A)
Code Sec. 4980H(b)(3), as amended by 2011 Appropriations Act §1858(b)(4)
Code Sec. 36B(c)(2), as amended by 2011 Appropriations Act §1858(b)(1)
Code Sec. 162(a), as amended by 2011 Appropriations Act §1858(b)(3)
Generally effective: For vouchers that would have been provided after 2013
Committee Reports, None

Under the Patient Protection and Affordable Care Act (PPACA; PL 111-148, 3/23/2010), individuals will be required to maintain minimum essential health insurance coverage after 2013. Under pre-2011 Appropriations Act law, PPACA would have required an "offering employer" to provide "free choice vouchers" to each of its "qualified employees" after 2013. (Sec. 10108(a), PL 111-148, 3/23/2010)

Under PPACA, an "offering employer" would have been any employer who would have:

(1) offered "minimum essential coverage" to its employees consisting of coverage through an "eligible employer-sponsored plan;" and

(2) paid any portion of the costs of the plan. (Sec. 10108(b), PL 111-148, 3/23/2010)

A "qualified employee" would have been, with respect to any plan year of an offering employer, any employee:

(A) whose "required contribution" (as determined under Code Sec. 5000A(e)(1)(B)) for minimum essential coverage through an eligible employer-sponsored plan:

(i) would have exceeded 8% of the employee's "household income" for the tax year (as described in section 1412(b)(1)(B) of PPACA), which ended with or within the plan year; and

(ii) would not have exceeded 9.8% of the employee's household income for the tax year;

(B) whose household income for the tax year would not have been greater than 400% of the poverty line for a family of the size involved; and

(C) who would not have participated in a health plan offered by the offering employer. (Sec. 10108(c)(1), PL 111-148, 3/23/2010)

For any calendar years after 2014, the 8% (item (A)(i), above) and 9.8% (item (A)(ii), above) figures would have had to be indexed. HHS would have had to adjust the percentages to reflect the rate of premium growth over the rate of income growth between the preceding calendar year and 2013. (Sec. 10108(c)(2), PL 111-148, 3/23/2010)

The amount of any free choice voucher provided would have been equal to the monthly portion of the cost of the eligible employer-sponsored plan that would have been paid by the employer if the employee were covered under the plan with respect to which the employer paid the largest portion of the employee's premium. The amount would have been equal to the amount the employer would have had to pay for an employee with self-only coverage unless the employee would have elected family coverage, in which case the amount would have had to be the amount the employer would pay for family coverage. (Sec. 10108(d)(1)(A), PL 111-148, 3/23/2010)

The cost of any health plan would have been determined under rules similar to those of section 2204 of the Public Health Service Act (the COBRA continuation premium rules), except that the amount would have been adjusted for age and category of coverage in accordance with regulations to have been established by the Secretary of HHS. (Sec. 10108(d)(1)(B), PL 111-148, 3/23/2010)

An Exchange would have had to credit the amount of any free choice voucher to the monthly premium of any qualified health plan in the Exchange in which the qualified employee was enrolled, and the offering employer would have had to pay any amounts so credited to the Exchange. (Sec. 10108(d)(2), PL 111-148, 3/23/2010)

If the amount of the free choice voucher exceeded the amount of the premium of the qualified health plan in which the qualified employee was enrolled for the month, that excess would have been paid to the employee. (Sec. 10108(d)(3), PL 111-148, 3/23/2010)

Any term used in the free choice voucher provisions discussed above that is also used in Code Sec. 5000A would have had the meaning given that term under Code Sec. 5000A. (Sec. 10108(e), PL 111-148, 3/23/2010)

Related provisions. Under pre-2011 Appropriations Act law, certain Code provisions added or amended by PPACA incorporated or referenced the free choice voucher provisions. Specifically, under pre-2011 Appropriation Act law:

. . . After 2013, gross income would not have included the amount of any free choice voucher provided by an employer to the extent that the amount of the voucher did not exceed the amount paid for a qualified health plan (as defined in section 1301 of PPACA) by the taxpayer. (Former Code Sec. 139D)

. . . The post-2013 excise tax that will be imposed on large employers that do not offer certain minimum health care coverage for all its full-time employees would not have been imposed for any month with respect to any employee to whom the employer provided a free choice voucher for that month. (Former Code Sec. 4980H(b)(3))

. . . The post-2013 premium assistance credit that will be available to qualifying individuals at or below 400% of the poverty line who purchase certain health insurance through an Exchange would not have been allowed for the premiums paid by an employee for coverage during any month for which the employee had a free choice voucher. (Former Code Sec. 36B(c)(2)(D))

. . . An employer's post-2013 payments for free choice vouchers would have been deductible as a compensation expense. (Former Code Sec. 162(a))

New Law. The 2011 Appropriations Act generally repeals the free choice voucher rules discussed above.

Specifically, the 2011 Appropriations Act—

. . . repeals the PPACA free choice voucher provisions enacted by Sec. 10108(a), (b), (c), (d), and (e), PL 111-148, 3/23/2010. (2011 Appropriations Act §1858(a));

. . . repeals the Code Sec. 139D income exclusion rules (2011 Appropriations Act §1858(b)(2)(A));

. . . eliminates the special Code Sec. 4980H(b)(3) rule that would have excused imposition of the excise tax for employers that provided a free choice voucher (2011 Appropriations Act §1858(b)(4));

. . . eliminates the Code Sec. 36B(c)(2)(D) rule that would have excluded any month for which an employee has a free choice voucher from the "coverage months" for which the post-2013 premium assistance credit will be allowed (2011 Appropriations Act §1858(b)(1)); and

. . . eliminates the last sentence of Code Sec. 162(a), which would have treated the amount of a free choice voucher as an amount of compensation for personal services actually rendered, for purposes of the business expense deduction. (2011 Appropriations Act §1858(b)(3))

> *⚓caution:* PPACA (section 9021) also enacted an unrelated Code Sec. 139D which provides rules on Indian health care benefits. The 2011 Appropriations Act repeals only the mistakenly numbered Code Sec. 139D added by PPACA section 10108. The Code Sec. 139D rules on Indian health care benefits are unaffected.

See ¶ 1613 for a discussion of the 2011 Appropriations Act provisions repealing certain health insurance reporting rules that would have been imposed on "offering employers."

☐ **Effective:** For vouchers that would have been provided after Dec. 31, 2013. (2011 Appropriations Act §1858(d))

> *⚓observation:* Technically, 2011 Appropriations Act §1858(d) provides that the amendments discussed above take effect as if included in the provisions of, and the amendments made by, the provisions of PPACA to which they relate. PPACA §10108(f)(3) provided that the rules were to go into effect for vouchers provided after Dec. 31, 2013. Thus, the effect of the repeal of these rules by the 2011 Appropriations Act is that the rules will not come into existence.

¶ 1604. Health coverage tax credit (HCTC) for health insurance costs of trade-displaced workers and PBGC pension recipients won't be allowed after 2013

Code Sec. 35(a), as amended by 2011 Trade Extension Act §241(b)(1)(B)
Generally effective: Coverage months beginning after Feb. 12, 2011
Committee Reports, None

"Eligible individuals"—generally, individuals receiving allowances under certain Trade Adjustment Assistance programs for individuals who have become unemployed as a result of increased imports from, or shifts in production to, foreign countries, as well as certain Pension Benefit Guaranty Corporation (PBGC) pension recipients (FTC 2d/FIN ¶ A-4231.1; USTR ¶ 354; TaxDesk ¶ 569,402)—may claim a refundable health coverage tax credit (HCTC) against income tax for a portion of the premiums paid for qualified health insurance coverage (COBRA continuation coverage, various state-based group coverage options, specified individual health insurance, and VEBA coverage, see FTC 2d/FIN ¶ A-4236; USTR ¶ 354; TaxDesk ¶ 569,405) of the individual and qualifying family members for "eligible coverage months" beginning in the tax year. (FTC 2d/FIN ¶ A-4230 *et seq.*; USTR ¶ 354; TaxDesk ¶ 569,400 *et seq.*)

The HCTC is available for "eligible coverage months." Generally, a month is an "eligible coverage month" if, as of the first day of the month, the taxpayer:

(1) is an eligible individual;

(2) is covered by qualified health insurance, the premium for which is paid by the taxpayer;

(3) doesn't have "other specified coverage;" and

(4) isn't imprisoned under federal, state, or local authority.

The pre-2011 Trade Extension Act law definition of "eligible coverage month" didn't include a sunset date. Any month could be an "eligible coverage month" if the above-listed taxpayer requirements were met. This meant the HCTC itself had no fixed end date and so was permanent. (FTC 2d/FIN ¶ A-4230, ¶ A-4234.1; USTR ¶ 354; TaxDesk ¶ 569,401)

New Law. The 2011 Trade Extension Act (the Act) provides that a month won't be an "eligible coverage month" for HCTC purposes, unless (in addition to the above-listed taxpayer requirements) the month begins before Jan. 1, 2014. (Code Sec. 35(b)(1)(B) as amended by 2011 Trade Extension Act §241(a) (Sec. 241(a), PL 112-40, 10/21/2011))

> ⓡ *caution:* In other words, months beginning after Dec. 31, 2013 (i.e., Jan. 2014 and later months) won't be "eligible coverage months." As the allowance of the HCTC is limited to premiums paid for qualified health insurance coverage for "eligible coverage months" beginning in the tax year, the HCTC won't be allowed for any amounts paid for coverage for Jan. 2014 and later months. That is, Act § 241(a) effectively terminates the HCTC as of Jan. 1, 2014.

> ⓡ *observation:* The termination date for the HCTC coincides with the start of the Code Sec. 36B premium tax credit (PTC) provided by the Patient Protection and Affordable Care Act. Starting in 2014, qualifying low-income taxpayers (generally, those at 100%–400% of the poverty line who aren't eligible for Medicaid, employer-sponsored insurance, or other acceptable coverage) who enroll in a "qualified health plan"

through a state-run insurance exchange will be allowed a PTC for a portion of the premiums paid for that coverage. Like the HCTC, the PTC will be refundable and payable in advance. (FTC 2d/FIN ¶ A-4240 *et seq.*; USTR ¶ 36B4; TaxDesk ¶ 569,450 *et seq.*)

Although the amount of the PTC (2%–9.5% of costs, depending on household income relative to the poverty line) will be significantly lower than the 72.5% HCTC, it will provide some help to taxpayers no longer allowed to claim the HCTC.

☐ **Effective:** Coverage months beginning after Feb. 12, 2011. (2011 Trade Extension Act §241(c)(1))

⚫ *observation:* The effective date provided by Act § 241(c)(1) is the effective date that applies generally to Act § 241. That Act section— which generally modifies certain 2010 Trade Act amendments to the HCTC provisions—includes retroactive extensions of rules that, under pre-Act law, no longer applied for coverage months beginning after Feb. 12, 2011 (see ¶ 1608 and ¶ 1609), as well as retroactive changes to pre-Act rules for those months (see ¶ 1606).

¶ 1605. Requirement that IRS make retroactive HCTC payments is reinstated for coverage months beginning after Nov. 20, 2011

Code Sec. 7527(e), as amended by 2011 Trade Extension Act §241(b)(2)(C)
Code Sec. 7527(e), as amended by 2011 Trade Extension Act §241(b)(2)(D)
Generally effective: Coverage months beginning after Nov. 20, 2011
Committee Reports, None

Taxpayers are allowed a refundable health coverage tax credit (HCTC) for a percentage of the amount paid for qualified health insurance for the individual and qualifying family members for "eligible coverage months" (see ¶ 1604 and FTC 2d/FIN ¶ A-4234.1; USTR ¶ 354; TaxDesk ¶ 569,501) beginning in the tax year. (FTC 2d/FIN ¶ A-4230 *et seq.*; USTR ¶ 354; TaxDesk ¶ 569,400 *et seq.*)

Under IRS's advance HCTC payment program, the credit is paid in advance on a monthly basis directly to the insurance provider. Advance payments are required for individuals who have filed the required certificate ("certified individuals"), but the total advance payments made for an individual during the tax year can't exceed a percentage (i.e., the percentage used in determining the HCTC) of the amount paid by the taxpayer for the coverage. (FTC 2d/FIN ¶ A-4870 *et seq.*; USTR ¶ 75,274; TaxDesk ¶ 569,408 *et seq.*)

Certified individuals are also entitled to *retroactive* payments of the credit—i.e., payments for coverage months before the advance payments begin. Specifically, for certified individuals, IRS must make one or more retroactive payments that, in total, equal a percentage of the premiums for qualified health insurance for eligible coverage months before the first month for which an advance payment is made for the individual. The retroactive payment must be reduced by the amount of any payment made to the taxpayer for the purchase of qualified health insurance under Sec. 173(f) of the Workforce Investment Act of 1998 (PL 105-220, 8/7/1998) ("Sec. 173(f) grants") for a tax year including months for which retroactive payments are required.

Under pre-2011 Trade Extension Act Law, retroactive payments were required only for eligible coverage months beginning before Feb. 13, 2011. Thus, IRS wasn't required to make (or reduce) retroactive payments for later months. Also, the total amount of retroactive payments for any pre-Feb. 13, 2011 eligible coverage months had to equal 80% (the then-in-effect HCTC percentage) of the amount paid by the taxpayer for coverage during those months. (FTC 2d/FIN ¶ A-4870, ¶ A-4873; USTR ¶ 75,274; TaxDesk ¶ 569,410)

New Law. The 2011 Trade Extension Act (the Act) eliminates the "eligible coverage months beginning before Feb. 13, 2011" cut-off date on the period for which IRS is required to make retroactive payments of the HCTC on behalf of certified individuals (Code Sec. 7527(e) as amended by 2011 Trade Extension Act §241(b)(2)(D) (Sec. 241(b)(2)(D), PL 112-40, 10/21/2011)) (but only for coverage months beginning after Nov. 20, 2011, see **Effective** below).

> *caution:* In other words, the Act reinstates the retroactive payment requirement that, under pre-Act law, applied only for eligible coverage months beginning before Feb. 13, 2011 (i.e., Feb. 2011 and earlier months). However, the reinstatement is effective for coverage months beginning after Nov. 20, 2011 (i.e., Dec. 2011 and later months) (see **Effective** below), rather than being retroactive to the pre-Act law termination date. So IRS doesn't have to make retroactive payments for the intervening "eligible coverage months"—i.e., for Mar.–Nov. of 2011.

> *observation:* Act § 241(a) provides that months beginning after Dec. 31, 2013 won't be "eligible coverage months," thereby terminating the HCTC as of that date (see ¶ 1604). So, even though the Act doesn't prescribe a specific termination date for the reinstated retroactive payment requirement, it won't apply for coverage periods after 2013.

The Act also provides that the total amount of retroactive payments for any eligible coverage months must equal 72.5% of the amount paid by the taxpayer for coverage during those months. (Code Sec. 7527(e) as amended by 2011 Trade Extension Act §241(b)(2)(C))

> ⬤ *observation:* The 72.5% figure for the retroactive payments corresponds to increased 72.5% (up from 65%) HCTC percentage that Act § 241(b)(1) provides for eligible coverage months beginning after Feb. 12, 2011, see ¶ 1606.

> ⬤ *observation:* Under these rules, IRS is required to make one or more retroactive payments of the HCTC on behalf of a certified individual for eligible coverage months beginning after Nov. 20, 2011, that are before the first month for which an advance payment is made on behalf of the individual. The total amount of the retroactive payments must equal 72.5% of the premiums for coverage of the taxpayer and qualifying family members under qualified health insurance for those eligible coverage months.

The elimination of the "eligible coverage months beginning before Feb. 13, 2011" cut-off date also applies to the rule requiring retroactive payments to be reduced by the amount of any Sec. 173(f) grant payment made to the taxpayer for a tax year that includes months for which retroactive payments are required. (Code Sec. 7527(e))

> ⬤ *observation:* Act § 241(b)(2)(D) eliminates the "eligible coverage months beginning before Feb. 13, 2011" cut-off date that, under pre-Act law, terminated the period for which Sec. 173(f) grants could be made. This means that Sec. 173(f) grants may be made for Dec. 2011 and later months, requiring a reduction in the retroactive payments of the HCTC.

☐ **Effective:** Coverage months beginning after Nov. 20, 2011 (i.e., after the 30th day after Oct. 21, 2011, the Act's enactment date), for the elimination of the "eligible coverage months beginning before Feb. 13, 2011" cut-off date for the requirement to make (or reduce) retroactive payments. (2011 Trade Extension Act §241(c)(2)(B))

Coverage months beginning after Feb. 13, 2011, for the rule providing that the total amount of retroactive payments must equal 72.5% of premiums paid. (2011 Trade Extension Act §241(c)(1))

¶ 1606. HCTC and percentage limit on advance HCTC payments are retroactively increased to 72.5% (from 65%) for post-Feb. 2011 coverage months

Code Sec. 35(a), as amended by 2011 Trade Extension Act §241(a)
Code Sec. 7527(b), as amended by 2011 Trade Extension Act §241(b)(1)
Generally effective: Coverage months beginning after Feb. 12, 2011
Committee Reports, None

"Eligible individuals" may claim a refundable health coverage tax credit (HCTC) against income tax equal to a percentage of the premiums paid for coverage of the individual and qualifying family members under qualified health insurance (COBRA continuation coverage, various state-based group coverage options, individual health insurance [as specially defined], and VEBA coverage) for "eligible coverage months" beginning in the tax year (the "yearly HCTC"). (FTC 2d/FIN ¶ A-4230 *et seq.*; USTR ¶ 354; TaxDesk ¶ 569,400 *et seq.*)

The HCTC is also payable in advance on a monthly basis directly to the insurance provider (the "monthly HCTC"). However, the amount of advance payments that IRS makes on behalf of any individual during the tax year can't exceed a percentage (i.e., the percentage used in determining the HCTC) of the amount paid by the taxpayer for qualifying health insurance coverage for eligible coverage months beginning in the tax year. (FTC 2d/FIN ¶ A-4870 *et seq.*; USTR ¶ 75,274; TaxDesk ¶ 569,408 *et seq.*)

Under pre-2011 Trade Extension Act law, both the HCTC percentage (FTC 2d/FIN ¶ A-4230, ¶ A-4231; USTR ¶ 354; TaxDesk ¶ 569,401) and the percentage limit on advance payments (FTC 2d/FIN ¶ A-4870, ¶ A-4871; USTR ¶ 75,274; TaxDesk ¶ 569,408) were equal to 65%, reflecting a decrease (from 80%) that went into effect for coverage months beginning after Feb. 12, 2011.

New Law. The 2011 Trade Extension Act (the Act) increases the HCTC percentage to 72.5% (from 65%). The HCTC allowed to an individual for qualified health insurance coverage of the taxpayer and qualifying family members is equal to 72.5% of the amount paid by the taxpayer for that coverage for eligible coverage months beginning in the tax year. (Code Sec. 35(a) as amended by 2011 Trade Extension Act §241(b)(1) (Sec. 241(b)(1), PL 112-40, 10/21/2011))

The 72.5% HCTC percentage applies retroactively to coverage months beginning after Feb. 12, 2011. (2011 Trade Extension Act §241(c)(1))

> *observation:* As Mar. 2011 was the first coverage month that began after Feb. 12, 2011, the increased 72.5% HCTC percentage went into effect for premiums paid for Mar. 2011 coverage.

⚡ *observation:* The Act doesn't change the 80% HCTC percentage for eligible coverage months beginning before Feb. 13, 2011 (i.e., Feb. 2011 and earlier months). The HCTC allowed for qualified health insurance coverage of the taxpayer and qualifying family members for those months is equal to 80% of the amounts paid by the taxpayer for that coverage. This means that taxpayers claiming the HCTC for 2011 must make two sets of calculations:

. . . using 80% as the HCTC percentage, for eligible coverage months beginning before Feb. 13, 2011 (Feb. 2011 and earlier months),

. . . using 72.5% as the HCTC percentage, for eligible coverage months beginning after Feb. 12, 2011 (Mar. 2011 and later months).

The Act provides a corresponding increase in the percentage limit on advance payments (the monthly HCTC). The amount of advance payments that IRS makes on behalf of any individual during the tax year can't exceed 72.5% of the amount paid by the taxpayer for qualifying health insurance coverage for eligible coverage months beginning in that year. (Code Sec. 7527(b) as amended by 2011 Trade Extension Act §241(b)(2)(A))

The 72.5% limit applies retroactively to coverage months beginning after Feb. 12, 2011. (2011 Trade Extension Act §241(c)(1))

⚡ *observation:* The Act doesn't change the 80% limit for eligible coverage months beginning before Feb. 13, 2011. Code Sec. 7527(b) limits the amount of advance payments made "during the tax year" to 72.5% (80% for eligible coverage months beginning before Feb. 13, 2011) of the amount paid by the individual for qualified health insurance for himself and qualifying family members for eligible coverage months beginning in the tax year.

Presumably, the "during the tax year" period is meant to correspond to the applicable 80%/72.5% period. That is, the amount of advance payments made for eligible coverage months beginning before Feb. 13, 2011 can't exceed 80% of the amounts paid by the taxpayer for that coverage, and the amount of advance payments made for eligible coverage months beginning after Feb. 12, 2011 can't exceed 72.5% of the amounts paid by the taxpayer for that coverage.

☐ **Effective:** Coverage months beginning after Feb. 12, 2011. (2011 Trade Extension Act §241(c)(1))

⚡ *observation:* As the increased 72.5% HCTC percentage/percentage limit on advance payments (the monthly HCTC) applies retroactively, it's likely that monthly HCTC payments made before Oct. 21, 2011 (the Act's enactment date) were computed based on the then-in-effect

65% figure. Presumably, taxpayers can make up for any "shortfall" in their monthly HCTC that resulted from using 65% for post-Feb. 12, 2011 months, by claiming the yearly HCTC when they file their 2011 tax return—i.e., by computing the HCTC for those months using 72.5% as the HCTC percentage, and subtracting the amount of the monthly HCTC payments that were computed using 65%.

¶ 1607. Allowance of HCTC for VEBA coverage was extended

Code Sec. 35(e)(1)(K), as amended by 2011 Trade Extension Act §241(b)(3)(B)
Generally effective: Coverage months beginning after Feb. 12, 2011
Committee Reports, None

An individual is allowed a health coverage tax credit (HCTC) for a portion of the amounts the individual pays for qualified health insurance for himself and qualifying family members for "eligible coverage months" (generally, months in which, on the first day, the taxpayer is an "eligible individual" covered by qualified health insurance for which he paid the premium and doesn't have other subsidized coverage) beginning in the tax year. (FTC 2d/FIN ¶ A-4230 *et seq.*; USTR ¶ 354; TaxDesk ¶ 569,400 *et seq.*)

"Qualified health insurance" is continuation coverage under the Consolidated Omnibus Reconciliation Act of 1985 (COBRA), certain state-based coverage, individual health insurance (as specially defined), and voluntary employees' beneficiary association (VEBA) coverage. However, pre-2011 Trade Extension Act law provided that VEBA coverage is qualified health insurance only for "eligible coverage months" beginning before Feb. 13, 2012. This meant that taxpayers with VEBA coverage for later months (i.e., Mar. 2012 and later months) couldn't have claimed the HCTC for those months. (FTC 2d/FIN ¶ A-4230, ¶ A-4236; USTR ¶ 354; TaxDesk ¶ 569,405)

New Law. The 2011 Trade Extension Act (the "Act") eliminates the "for eligible coverage months beginning before Feb. 13, 2012" termination date on the rule providing that coverage under a VEBA is "qualified health insurance" for HCTC purposes. (Code Sec. 35(e)(1)(K) as amended by 2011 Trade Extension Act §241(b)(3)(B) (Sec. 241(b)(3)(B), PL 112-40, 10/21/2011))

> **ⓡ** *observation:* As the HCTC is allowed only for "qualified health insurance," the extension of the rule providing that coverage under a VEBA is qualified health insurance extends the availability of the HCTC for VEBA coverage. That is, any otherwise allowable HCTC will be allowed for VEBA coverage for a month beginning after Feb.

12, 2012 (i.e., Mar. 2012 and later, but see the *RIA Caution* below), as well as for earlier months (i.e., months through Feb. 2012).

⚫ caution: Act § 241(a) provides that months beginning after Dec. 31, 2013 won't be "eligible coverage months," thereby terminating the HCTC as of that date (see ¶ 1604). So the HCTC won't be allowed for coverage under a VEBA—or under any other type of qualified health insurance—for months beginning in 2014 and later.

☐ **Effective:** Coverage months beginning after Feb. 12, 2011. (2011 Trade Extension Act §241(c)(1))

⚫ observation: The effective date provided by Act § 241(c)(1) is the effective date that applies generally to Act § 241. That Act section, which generally modifies certain 2010 Trade Act amendments to the HCTC provisions—includes retroactive extensions of rules that, under pre-Act law, no longer applied for coverage months beginning after Feb. 12, 2011 (see ¶ 1608 and ¶ 1609), as well as retroactive changes to pre-Act rules for those months (see ¶ 1606).

The "after Feb. 12, 2011" effective date doesn't relate to a corresponding pre-Act law termination date for the rule providing that VEBA coverage is qualified health insurance. Under pre-Act law, that rule—as extended by the 2010 Trade Act—applied for eligible coverage months beginning before Feb. 13, *2012.* However, because the other HCTC provisions in the 2010 Trade Act were effective "before Feb. 13, *2011*" the "before Feb. 13, *2012*" effective date for the VEBA coverage rule could have been the result of a drafting error. By removing a termination date from this provision, the Act effectively moots any potential drafting-error issue.

¶ 1608. HCTC eligibility for individuals not enrolled in training programs was extended retroactively to coverage periods beginning after Feb. 12, 2011

Code Sec. 35(c)(2)(B), as amended by 2011 Trade Extension Act §241(b)(3)(A)
Generally effective: Coverage months beginning after Feb. 12, 2011
Committee Reports, None

To qualify for the health coverage tax credit (HCTC, see FTC 2d/FIN ¶ A-4230 *et seq.*; USTR ¶ 354; TaxDesk ¶ 569,400 *et seq.*), a taxpayer must be an eligible individual, which includes an eligible trade adjustment allowance (TAA) recipient.

Under a Code Sec. 35(c)(2)(B) definition that, under pre-2011 Trade Extension Act law, applied only for "eligible coverage months" (see ¶ 1604 and FTC 2d/FIN ¶ A-4234.1; USTR ¶ 354; TaxDesk ¶ 569,501) beginning before Feb. 13, 2011, an individual is an eligible TAA recipient for a month if the individual:

(1) is receiving a TAA under chapter 2 of Title II of the Trade Act of 1974 (the Trade Act, 19 USC § 2201 *et seq.*) for any day of that month. Payment of a TAA is generally conditioned upon the individual enrolling in, or receiving a waiver of, certain training programs (the "training program requirement");

(2) would be eligible to receive a TAA except that the individual is in a break in training that meets certain Trade Act requirements; or

(3) is receiving unemployment compensation (as defined in Code Sec. 85(b), see FTC 2d/FIN ¶ H-3008; USTR ¶ 854.01; TaxDesk ¶ 132,507) for any day of that month and would be eligible to receive a TAA for that month but for a requirement to first exhaust unemployment benefits and the training program requirement described in (1), above.

Under pre-2011 Trade Extension Act law, the Code Sec. 35(c)(2)(B) definition didn't apply for "eligible coverage months" beginning after Feb. 12, 2011. Under the Code Sec. 35(c)(2)(A) definition that would have applied, an individual couldn't have been an eligible TAA recipient for later months (i.e., Mar. 2011 and later) under (2) or (3), above. To be an eligible TAA recipient for those months, an individual would have had to: (a) receive a TAA for any day of that month, or be eligible to receive a TAA but for the requirement to first exhaust unemployment benefits, and (b) with respect to that allowance, be covered under a Trade Act certification. This meant that individuals receiving unemployment compensation couldn't be eligible TAA recipients (and so couldn't claim the HCTC) for eligible coverage months beginning after Feb. 12, 2011 (i.e., Mar. 2011 and later months) if they weren't enrolled in (or excused from) the required training programs. (FTC 2d/FIN ¶ A-4230, ¶ A-4232; USTR ¶ 354; TaxDesk ¶ 569,401)

New Law. The 2011 Trade Extension Act (the "Act") extends the rule allowing individuals not enrolled in (or excused from) training programs to be "eligible TAA recipients" (and, therefore, eligible for the HCTC) by eliminating the "for eligible coverage months beginning before Feb. 13, 2011" termination date from the Code Sec. 35(c)(2)(B) definition of "eligible TAA recipient." An individual is an eligible TAA recipient for a month if he meets the requirements described in (1), (2), or (3), above. (Code Sec. 35(c)(2)(B) as amended by 2011 Trade Extension Act §241(b)(3)(A) (Sec. 241(b)(3)(A), PL 112-40, 10/21/2011))

The elimination of the termination date applies retroactively to coverage months beginning after Feb. 12, 2011. (2011 Trade Extension Act §241(c)(1))

✔️ observation: In other words, an individual who receives unemployment compensation for any day during an eligible coverage month beginning after Feb. 12, 2011 (i.e., Mar. 2011 and later, but see the *RIA Caution* below), as well as for earlier months (i.e., months through Feb. 2011), can be an eligible TAA recipient and, therefore, eligible for the HCTC for that month even if the individual isn't enrolled in (or excused from) a Trade Act training program.

In addition, an individual continues to be treated as an eligible TAA recipient during the first month that the individual would otherwise cease to be an eligible TAA recipient by reason of the above rule. (Code Sec. 35(c)(2)(B))

✔️ caution: Act § 241(a) provides that months beginning after Dec. 31, 2013 won't be "eligible coverage months," thereby terminating the HCTC as of that date (see ¶ 1604). So even if an individual qualifies as an eligible TAA recipient, he won't be able to claim the HCTC.

☐ **Effective:** Coverage months beginning after Feb. 12, 2011. (2011 Trade Extension Act §241(c)(1))

✔️ observation: Before Oct. 21, 2011 (the Act's enactment date), individuals who weren't enrolled in (or excused from) training programs couldn't be eligible TAA recipients entitled to the HCTC (and so weren't entitled to advance HCTC payments—the "monthly HCTC," see FTC 2d/FIN ¶ A-4870 *et seq.*; USTR ¶ 75,274; TaxDesk ¶ 569,408 *et seq.*) for coverage months beginning after Feb. 12, 2011 (i.e., Mar. 2011 and later months).

The retroactive extension provided by the Act entitles these individuals to the HCTC (including the advance HCTC payments) for those months. Presumably, taxpayers can make up for any "shortfall" in their monthly HCTC for Mar.–Oct. 2011, by claiming the yearly HCTC for those months when they file their 2011 tax return.

¶ 1609. Continued HCTC eligibility of family members after certain events was extended retroactively to coverage months beginning after Feb. 12, 2011

Code Sec. 35(g)(9), as amended by 2011 Trade Extension Act §241(b)(3)(C)
Generally effective: Coverage months beginning after Feb. 12, 2011
Committee Reports, None

Taxpayers are allowed a health coverage tax credit (HCTC) for amounts paid for qualified health insurance coverage for the taxpayer and qualifying family members (spouse and dependents) for "eligible coverage months" (generally, months in which, on the first day, the taxpayer is an "eligible individual" covered by qualified health insurance for which he paid the premium and doesn't have other subsidized coverage, see ¶ 1604 and FTC 2d/FIN ¶ A-4234.1; USTR ¶ 354; TaxDesk ¶ 569,501) beginning in the tax year. (FTC 2d/FIN ¶ A-4231; USTR ¶ 354; TaxDesk ¶ 569,401)

Qualifying family members may continue claiming the HCTC for up to 24 months after the eligible individual becomes entitled to Medicare, divorces, or dies. Under pre-2011 Trade Extension Act law, the continued HCTC qualification couldn't extend past eligible coverage months beginning after Feb. 12, 2011. (FTC 2d/FIN ¶ A-4230, ¶ A-4235.3; USTR ¶ 354; TaxDesk ¶ 569,404.1)

New Law. The 2011 Trade Extension Act (the "Act") eliminates the "beginning before Feb. 13, 2011" cut-off date for the 24-month period during which an eligible individual's qualifying family members continue to qualify for the HCTC following the events described above. (Code Sec. 35(g)(9) as amended by 2011 Trade Extension Act §241(b)(3)(C) (Sec. 241(b)(3)(C), PL 112-40, 10/21/2011)) (For further discussion, see below.)

> *caution:* Act § 241(a) provides that months beginning after Dec. 31, 2013 won't be "eligible coverage months," thereby terminating the HCTC as of that date (see ¶ 1604). So if the date on which the eligible individual becomes entitled to Medicare, divorces, or dies is after Dec. 31, 2011 (i.e., less than 24 months before the HCTC termination), the qualifying family member won't be able to claim the HCTC for the full 24-month period.

Eligibility if an individual qualifies for Medicare. In the case of any month that would be an eligible coverage month for an eligible individual except for Code Sec. 35(f)(2)(A) (which disqualifies certain Medicare-eligible individuals from claiming the HCTC), that month is treated as an eligible coverage month for that individual solely to determine the amount of the HCTC under Code Sec. 35 for any of that individual's qualifying family members, and any advance payment of the HCTC under Code Sec. 7527 (see ¶ 1606 and FTC 2d/FIN ¶ H-4871; USTR ¶ 75,274; TaxDesk ¶ 569,408). This treatment applies for only the first 24 months after the eligible individual is first entitled to benefits under Medicare Part A (Hospital Insurance) or is enrolled in Medicare Part B (Medical Insurance). (Code Sec. 35(g)(9)(A))

Eligibility after divorce. In the case of the finalization of a divorce between an eligible individual and the individual's spouse, the spouse is treated as an eligible individual for Code Sec. 35 and Code Sec. 7527 purposes for a period of 24 months beginning with the date the divorce is finalized. However, the only qualifying family members who may be taken into account with respect to the spouse are those family members who were qualifying family members immediately before the divorce was finalized. (Code Sec. 35(g)(9)(B))

> **observation:** Under this rule, if the eligible individual's ex-spouse remarries or is allowed dependency exemptions for additional individuals (e.g., for additional children or elderly parents), the ex-spouse's HCTC can't take premiums paid for those additional individuals into account.

Eligibility after death. If an eligible individual dies (Code Sec. 35(g)(9)(C)), the individual's spouse (determined at the time of death) is treated as an eligible individual for Code Sec. 35 and Code Sec. 7527 purposes for a period of 24 months beginning with the date of death. However, the only qualifying family members who may be taken into account with respect to the spouse are those individuals who were qualifying family members immediately before the death. (Code Sec. 35(g)(9)(C)(i))

> **observation:** Under this rule, if the surviving spouse remarries or is allowed dependency exemptions for additional individuals (e.g., for additional children or elderly parents), the spouse's HCTC can't take premiums paid for those additional individuals into account.

Any individual who was a qualifying family member of the eligible individual immediately before his death is treated as an eligible individual for Code Sec. 35 and Code Sec. 7527 purposes for the 24-month period beginning with the date of death. If Code Sec. 35(g)(4) (which denies the HCTC to dependents, see FTC 2d/FIN ¶ A-4231; USTR ¶ 354; TaxDesk ¶ 569,401) applies, the taxpayer to whom the dependency deduction is allowable is an eligible individual. In determining the amount of the HCTC for that taxpayer, only the qualifying family member may be taken into account. (Code Sec. 35(g)(9)(C)(ii))

> **observation:** In other words, any individual who was a qualifying family member of the decedent immediately before the decedent's death is treated as an eligible individual for 24 months beginning with the date of death, except that in determining the amount of the HCTC, only the qualifying family member may be taken into account. For a dependent, the rule applies to the taxpayer to whom the personal exemption deduction under Code Sec. 151 is allowable.

☐ **Effective:** Coverage months beginning after Feb. 12, 2011. (2011 Trade Extension Act §241(c)(1))

> **observation:** Before Oct. 21, 2011 (the Act's enactment date), the qualifying family member's continued HCTC eligibility didn't apply for eligible coverage months beginning after Feb. 12, 2011. This meant the

qualifying family member couldn't claim the HCTC (and so wasn't entitled to advance HCTC payments—the "monthly HCTC," see FTC 2d/FIN ¶ H-4870 *et seq.*; USTR ¶ 75,274; TaxDesk ¶ 569,408 *et seq.*) for coverage months beginning after Feb. 12, 2011 (i.e., Mar. 2011 and later months).

The retroactive elimination of the Feb. 12, 2011 cut-off date entitles these individuals to the HCTC (including the advance HCTC payments) for those months. Presumably, taxpayers can make up for any "shortfall" in their monthly HCTC for Mar.–Oct. 2011, by claiming the yearly HCTC for those months when they file their 2011 tax return.

¶ 1610. HCTC eligibility certificates issued after Nov. 20, 2011 must include information on qualified health insurance and enrollment procedures

Code Sec. 7527(d)(2), as amended by 2011 Trade Extension Act §241(b)(2)(B)
Generally effective: Certificates issued after Nov. 20, 2011
Committee Reports, None

IRS is required to make advance payment of the health coverage tax credit (HCTC) on behalf of an individual for whom a qualified health insurance cost credit eligibility certificate is in effect. A qualified health insurance cost credit eligibility certificate ("certificate") is a written statement that an individual is an "eligible individual" for HCTC purposes—i.e., an eligible Trade Adjustment Assistance (TAA) recipient, an alternative TAA recipient, or an eligible Pension Benefit Guaranty Corporation (PBGC) pension recipient (see FTC 2d/FIN ¶ A-4231; USTR ¶ 354; TaxDesk ¶ 569,401). The certificate must be provided by the Secretary of Labor or the PBGC, as applicable.

A certificate must provide the information that IRS may require for purposes of the advance payment rules. Pre-2011 Trade Extension Act law provided that certificates issued before Feb. 13, 2011 had to include the following information:

(1) the name, address, and telephone number of the state offices responsible for providing the individual with assistance with enrollment in qualified health insurance,

(2) a list of coverage options that are treated as qualified health insurance by the state in which the individual resides, and

(3) in the case of a TAA-eligible individual, a statement informing him that he has 63 days from the date that is seven days after the issuance of the certificate to enroll in the insurance without a lapse in creditable coverage.

Under pre-2011 Trade Extension Act law, the above-listed information didn't have to be included on certificates issued after Feb. 12, 2011. (FTC 2d/FIN ¶ H-4870, ¶ H-4875; USTR ¶ 75,274; TaxDesk ¶ 569,412)

New Law. The 2011 Trade Extension Act (the "Act") eliminates the "issued before Feb. 12, 2011" limitation on the rule requiring that certificates include the information listed at (1)–(3) above (Code Sec. 7527(d)(2) as amended by 2011 Trade Extension Act §241(b)(2)(B) (Sec. 241(b)(2)(B), PL 112-40, 10/21/2011)) (but only for certificates issued after Nov. 20, 2011, see **Effective** below).

> *observation:* In other words, the written statement that the Secretary of Labor or the PBGC provides to certify an individual's eligibility for advance payments of the HCTC must include the information listed at (1)–(3) above.

☐ **Effective:** Certificates issued after Nov. 20, 2011 (i.e., after the 30th day after Oct. 21, 2011, the Act's enactment date). (2011 Trade Extension Act §241(c)(2)(A))

> *observation:* As stated above, certificates issued before Feb. 13, 2011 had to include the above-listed information. The Act requires the information to be included on certificates issued after Nov. 20, 2011. This means that certificates issued after Feb. 12, 2011 and before Nov. 21, 2011 didn't have to include the information listed at (1)–(3) above.

¶ 1611. Rule under which a period after a TAA-related loss of health coverage is not counted in determining a HIPAA 63-day lapse in creditable coverage—extended to plan years beginning before Jan. 1, 2014

Code Sec. 9801(c)(2)(D), as amended by 2011 Trade Extension Act §242(a)(1)
ERISA § 701(c)(2)(C), as amended by 2011 Trade Extension Act §242(a)(2)
Generally effective: Plan years beginning after Feb. 12, 2011 and before Jan. 1, 2014
Committee Reports, None

Group health plans are subject to certain requirements intended to foster access, portability, and renewability of coverage. These requirements limit preexisting condition exclusions, prohibit the exclusion of certain individuals based on health status, and guarantee the renewability of health insurance coverage. These requirements were added by the Health Insurance Portability and Accountability Act of 1996 ("HIPAA") and so are often referred to as "the HIPAA rules."

Under the HIPAA rules, a group health plan may impose a "preexisting condition exclusion" only if: (1) the exclusion relates to a condition (whether physical or mental), regardless of cause, for which medical advice, diagnosis, care, or treatment was recommended or received within the six-month period ending on the enrollment date; (2) the exclusion does not extend for more than 12 months (18 months in the case of a "late enrollee") after the enrollment date; and (3) the period of any preexisting condition exclusion is reduced by the length of the aggregate of the periods of any "creditable coverage" applicable to the participant or beneficiary as of the enrollment date.

Under the HIPAA rules, days of "creditable coverage" that occur before a 63-day break in creditable coverage need not be counted for purposes of reducing the preexisting condition exclusion period. Thus, under this rule, a significant break in coverage means a 63-day period during all of which the individual was not covered under any creditable coverage. (FTC 2d/FIN ¶ H-1325.5 *et seq.*; USTR ¶ 98,014)

In determining if there has been a 63-day lapse in coverage for a "TAA-eligible individual," the period (i) beginning on the date the individual has a "TAA-related loss of coverage," and (ii) ending on the date which is 7 days after the date of IRS's issuance of a qualified health insurance costs credit eligibility certificate (under Code Sec. 7527) for that individual, is not taken into account.

The terms "TAA-eligible individual" and "TAA-related loss of coverage" have the meanings provided in Code Sec. 4980B(f)(5)(C)(iv). Thus, TAA-eligible individuals generally are those who lost jobs due to increased imports from, or a shift in production to, foreign countries, and thus, are eligible for certain benefits.

Before the 2011 Trade Extension Act, the provision providing for the pre-certification period to be ignored in determining whether a 63-day lapse in creditable coverage had occurred (as described above) was scheduled to apply only for plan years beginning before Feb. 13, 2011. (FTC 2d/FIN ¶ H-1325, ¶ H-1325.6; USTR ¶ 98,014)

New Law.   The 2011 Trade Extension Act extends the time for applying the rule that a specified period is not taken into account in determining whether a 63-day lapse in creditable coverage has occurred (as described above), to plan years beginning: (i) after Feb. 12, 2011, and (ii) before Jan. 1, 2014. (Code Sec. 9801(c)(2)(D) as amended by 2011 Trade Extension Act §242(a)(1) (Sec. 242(a)(1), PL 112-40, 10/21/2011); 2011 Trade Extension Act §242(b)(1))

> *observation:* Thus, for plan years beginning before Jan. 1, 2014, a
> specified period after a TAA-related loss of coverage (i.e., the date of
> the loss of coverage until 7 days after the date of IRS's issuance of a

qualified health insurance costs credit eligibility certificate) will not be taken into account in determining whether a 63-day lapse in creditable coverage has occurred.

> **🔵 observation:** The 2011 Trade Extension Act *retroactively* extended the period during which a specified period after a TAA-related loss of coverage will not be taken into account. Specifically, the extension was enacted on Oct. 21, 2011, and applies for plan years beginning after Feb. 12, 2011 (thus continuing the rule that applied for plan years beginning before Feb. 13, 2011, under pre-2011 Trade Extension Act law).
>
> For calendar year plans, the rule for not counting a period following a TAA-related loss of coverage in determining whether there was a 63-day lapse of creditable coverage, did *not* expire before Oct. 21, 2011 (the date on which the extension was enacted).

However, despite the extension of the rules discussed above, transitional rules provide that, for a particular period, benefits don't have to be redetermined, see below.

Transitional rules. Notwithstanding the rules above, a plan is not required to modify benefit determinations for the period: (i) beginning on Feb. 13, 2011, and (ii) ending on Nov. 20, 2011 (i.e., 30 days after Oct. 21, 2011). A plan will not fail to be "qualified health insurance" (within the meaning of Code Sec. 35(e), for purposes of a tax credit for eligible TAA recipients, based on the amount paid for qualified health insurance) during this period merely due to the failure to modify benefit determinations. (2011 Trade Extension Act §242(b)(2)(A))

> **🔵 observation:** For calendar year plans, this transitional rule ordinarily would have no effect. Benefit determinations presumably will have been made for calendar year plans by applying the rule under which a specified period following a TAA-related loss of coverage is not counted in determining whether a 63-day lapse in creditable coverage has occurred, because that rule did not expire for calendar year plans.

The Secretary of the Treasury (or his designee), in consultation with the Secretary of Health and Human Resources and the Secretary of Labor, may issue regulations or other guidance regarding the scope of the application of the statutory change described above to periods before Nov. 20, 2011—except as provided in the transitional rule above, under which a plan is not required to modify benefit determinations for a specified period. (2011 Trade Extension Act §242(b)(2)(B))

For a TAA-related loss of coverage (as defined in Code Sec. 4980B(f)(5)(C)(iv) of the COBRA rules) that occurs during the period (i) beginning on Feb. 13, 2011, and (ii) ending on Nov. 20, 2011 (i.e., 30 days after Oct. 21, 2011), the 7-day period described in Code Sec. 9801(c)(2)(D) (and the parallel ERISA §701(c)(2)(C) and Sec. 2701(c)(2)(C) of the Public Health Service Act) was extended until Nov. 20, 2011 (i.e., 30 days after Oct. 21, 2011). (2011 Trade Extension Act §242(b)(2)(C))

> **◆/observation:** Thus, in determining if there has been a 63-day lapse in coverage for a "TAA-eligible individual," the period (i) beginning on the date the individual had a "TAA-related loss of coverage," and (ii) ending on Nov. 20, 2011, is not taken into account.

ERISA and PHSA also amended. The Act also amends ERISA and the Public Health Services Act (PHSA) to include provisions parallel to the Code provisions described above. (ERISA §701(c)(2)(C) as amended by 2011 Trade Extension Act §242(a)) ; (PHSA §2701(c)(2)(C), as amended by 2011 Trade Extension Act §242(b))

☐ **Effective:** Plan years beginning: after Feb. 12, 2011 (2011 Trade Extension Act §242(b)(1)) and before Jan. 1, 2014. (Code Sec. 9801(c)(2)(D))

¶ 1612. Eligibility for COBRA continuation coverage extended from Nov. 20, 2011 through Jan. 1, 2014 for PBGC recipients and TAA-eligible individuals who lose employment or work hours

Code Sec. 4980B(f)(2)(B)(i), as amended by 2011 Trade Extension Act §243(a)
ERISA § 602(2)(A), as amended by 2011 Trade Extension Act §243(a)
Generally effective: Coverage periods that would otherwise end on or after Nov. 20, 2011 and through Jan. 1, 2014
Committee Reports, None

COBRA requires that a group health plan must offer continuation coverage to qualified beneficiaries if a qualifying event occurs. An excise tax applies on the group health plan's failure to meet this requirement.

Qualifying events include: the death of the covered employee, termination of the covered employee's employment, divorce or legal separation of the covered employee, and certain bankruptcy proceedings of the employer.

For a termination from employment, COBRA continuation coverage must be extended for a period of not less than 18 months. In certain other cases, coverage must be extended for a period of not less than 36 months.

A plan may require the beneficiary to pay a premium of 102% of the applicable premium for a period of COBRA continuation coverage. (FTC 2d/FIN ¶ H-1296 et seq.; USTR ¶ 49,80B4.07)

For PBGC recipients and TAA-eligible individuals, the maximum COBRA continuation period is extended in certain circumstances.

PBGC recipients. For a covered employee (i) whose qualifying event was termination of employment or a reduction in hours of employment, and (ii) who, as of that qualifying event, has a nonforfeitable right to a benefit any portion of which is to be paid by the Pension Benefit Guarantee Corporation (PBGC) under Title IV of ERISA, the period of COBRA continuation coverage must extend at least to:

(a) the date of death of the covered employee, or

(b) for the covered employee's surviving spouse or dependent children, 24 months after the covered employee's date of death.

TAA-eligible individuals. For a covered employee (i) whose qualifying event was a termination of employment or a reduction in hours of employment, and (ii) who is a TAA-eligible individual as of the date that the COBRA continuation coverage period would otherwise terminate, the period of COBRA continuation coverage will not terminate before the later of:

(a) (i) 18 months after the qualifying event (for a qualifying event that was the termination of employment or reduction of hours of employment of the covered employee), or (ii) 36 months after a qualifying event described in item (a)(i), where another qualifying event occurs within 18 months of the prior qualifying event, or

(b) the date on which the covered employee ceases to be a TAA-eligible individual.

Under pre-2011 Trade Extension Act law, the maximum required COBRA continuation period for PBGC recipients and TAA-eligible individuals (described above) for a qualifying event that was a termination of employment or a reduction in hours could not require any period of coverage to extend beyond Feb. 12, 2011. (FTC 2d/FIN ¶ H-1250, ¶ H-1296.4A, ¶ H-1296.4B; USTR ¶ 49,80B4.07)

New Law. For a qualifying event that consists of the termination of employment or a reduction of hours, the 2011 Trade Extension Act provides that the maximum required COBRA continuation period (as described above) may extend through (i.e., not beyond) Jan. 1, 2014, for PBGC recipients (Code Sec. 4980B(f)(2)(B)(i)(V) as amended by 2011 Trade Extension Act §243(a)(3) (Sec. 243(a)(3), PL 112-40, 10/21/2011)) and TAA-eligible individuals. (Code Sec. 4980B(f)(2)(B)(i)(VI))

The restoration of this COBRA continuation period for PBGC recipients and TAA-eligible individuals does not take effect until Nov. 20, 2011 (i.e., 30 days after Oct. 21, 2011, the effective date for the restoration of this COBRA continuation period), see below.

> **✆** *observation:* Despite the extension of the COBRA continuation period for TAA-eligible individuals and PBGC recipients to Jan. 1, 2014, as expressed in Code Sec. 4980B(f)(2)(B)(i)(V) and VI, the extension actually applies only for a TAA-eligible individual or a PBGC recipient (or the latter's surviving spouse or dependent child) whose COBRA continuation period will expire on or after Nov. 20, 2011, without regard to the extension under the Act (see "effective date," below).
>
> That means that COBRA continuation coverage that ended before Nov. 20, 2011 — including COBRA coverage that ended because of the pre-Act expiration date of Feb. 12, 2011 — was *not* reinstated by the Act, even for an individual who would still be eligible for the special COBRA continuation period under the terms of Code Sec. 4980B(f)(2)(B)(i)(V) and VI (i.e., the individual is still a TAA-eligible individual or a PBGC recipient (or the latter's surviving spouse or dependent child), and it is not yet Jan. 1, 2014).
>
> Also, the extension of the Code Sec. 4980B(f)(2)(B)(i)(V) and VI COBRA continuation coverage for TAA-eligible individuals and PBGC recipients expires on Jan. 1, 2014, *only* for a TAA-eligible individual or a PBGC recipient (or the latter's surviving spouse or dependent child) whose "regular" COBRA continuation period ends (generally, for a qualifying event that is a termination of employment or a reduction in hours, 18 months after the event) on or after Nov. 20, 2011.

ERISA and PHSA. The Act amends ERISA and the Public Health Service Act (PHSA) to extend the COBRA continuation period in the same manner as the Code for TAA-eligible individuals. ERISA also provides a parallel extension for PBGC recipients, but PHSA does not contain such a provision. (ERISA §602(2)(A) as amended by 2011 Trade Extension Act §243(a)) ; (PHSA §2202(2)(A) as amended by 2011 Trade Extension Act §243(a)(5)).

☐ **Effective:** Coverage periods that would otherwise end on or after Nov. 20, 2011 (i.e., 30 days after Oct. 21, 2011) (2011 Trade Extension Act §243(b)) and through Jan. 1, 2014. (Code Sec. 4980B(f)(2)(B)(i))

¶ 1613. Post-2013 health insurance coverage information reporting and related statement requirements for "offering employers" are repealed

Code Sec. 6056(a), as amended by 2011 Appropriations Act §1858(b)(5)(A)
Code Sec. 6056(b)(2)(C)(i), as amended by 2011 Appropriations Act §1858(b)(5)(B)(i)
Code Sec. 6056(b)(2)(C)(v), as amended by 2011 Appropriations Act §1858(b)(5)(B)(iv)
Code Sec. 6056(d)(2), as amended by 2011 Appropriations Act §1858(b)(5)(C)
Code Sec. 6056(e), as amended by 2011 Appropriations Act §1858(b)(5)(C)
Code Sec. 6056(f), as amended by 2011 Appropriations Act §1858(b)(5)(D)
Generally effective: Periods beginning after Dec. 31, 2013
Committee Reports, None

For periods beginning after Dec. 31, 2013, every "applicable large employer" (see FTC 2d/FIN ¶ H-1180; USTR ¶ 49,80H4) required to meet the requirements of Code Sec. 4980H (the excise tax imposed on large employers that don't offer affordable health insurance after 2013, see FTC 2d/FIN ¶ H-1175 *et seq.*; USTR ¶ 4980H4) with respect to its full-time employees during a calendar year will be required (see FTC 2d/FIN ¶ S-3331; USTR ¶ 60,564.01), and, under pre-2011 Appropriations Act law, Code Sec. 6056(a) provided that every offering employer (see below under "Offering employer defined") would have been required (FTC 2d/FIN ¶ S-3330, ¶ S-3331; USTR ¶ 60,564.01), at the time IRS prescribes, to make the return described below.

Under Code Sec. 6056(b), a return satisfies the reporting requirement (discussed above) if the return:

(1) is in the form prescribed by IRS, and

(2) contains—

(A) the name, date, and employer identification number (EIN) of the employer,

(B) a certification as to whether the employer offers to its full-time employees (and their dependents) the opportunity to enroll in minimum essential coverage (see FTC 2d/FIN ¶ A-6405; USTR ¶ 50,00A4; TaxDesk ¶ 576,155) under an eligible employer-sponsored plan (as defined in Code Sec. 5000A(f)(2), see FTC 2d/FIN ¶ A-6406; USTR ¶ 50,00A4; TaxDesk ¶ 576,156),

(C) if the employer certifies that the employer did offer to its full-time employees (and their dependents) the opportunity to so enroll— (see FTC 2d/FIN ¶ S-3331; USTR ¶ 60,564.01)

(i) in the case of an applicable large employer (FTC 2d/FIN ¶ S-3330, ¶ S-3331; USTR ¶ 60,564.01), the length of any waiting period (as defined in Public Health Service Act (PHSA) §2701(b)(4), codified at 42 USC 300gg(b)(4)) with respect to that coverage,

(ii) the months during the calendar year for which coverage under the plan was available (see FTC 2d/FIN ¶ S-3331; USTR ¶ 60,564.01),

(iii) the monthly premium for the lowest-cost option in each of the enroll- ment categories under the plan (FTC 2d/FIN ¶ S-3330, ¶ S-3331; USTR ¶ 60,564.01),

(iv) the employer's share of the total allowed costs of benefits provided under the plan, see FTC 2d/FIN ¶ S-3331; USTR ¶ 60,564.01, and (FTC 2d/ FIN ¶ S-3330, ¶ S-3331; USTR ¶ 60,564.01),

(v) under pre-2011 Appropriations Act law, in the case of an offering em- ployer (see below under "Offering employer defined"), the option for which the employer pays the largest portion of the cost of the plan and the portion of the cost paid by the employer in each of the enrollment categories under that option (FTC 2d/FIN ¶ S-3330, ¶ S-3331; USTR ¶ 60,564.01),

(D) the number of full-time employees for each month during the calendar year,

(E) the name, address, and taxpayer identification number (TIN) of each full-time employee during the calendar year and the months (if any) during which the employee (and any dependents) were covered under the health bene- fits plans, and

(F) other information IRS requires (see FTC 2d/FIN ¶ S-3331; USTR ¶ 60,564.01).

> **observation:** "Total allowed costs of benefits" (as used in (C)(iv), above) isn't defined for this purpose.

> **observation:** It isn't clear which form employers will use to provide the information discussed above, or whether IRS will have to issue a new form for this purpose (see below under "Coordination with other requirements").

IRS will have the authority to review the accuracy of the information pro- vided under Code Sec. 6056(b) (items (A) through (F) listed above), including the applicable large employer's share under Code Sec. 6056(b)(2)(C)(iv) (item (C)(iv) listed above) (see FTC 2d/FIN ¶ S-3331; USTR ¶ 60,564.01).

Employer's required statement to each insured employee. Under Code Sec. 6056(c)(1), every person required to make a return under Code Sec. 6056(a) (discussed above) will be required to furnish to each full-time employee whose name is required to be set forth in the return described in Code Sec. 6056(b)(2)(E) (item (E) listed above) a written statement showing—

(1) the name and address of the person required to make the return and the phone number of the information contact for that person, and

(2) the information required to be shown on the return for that individual.

Code Sec. 6056(c)(2) provides that the written statement required as discussed above will have to be furnished on or before Jan. 31 of the year following the calendar year for which the return under Code Sec. 6056(a) (discussed above) was required to be made (see FTC 2d/FIN ¶ S-3333; USTR ¶ 60,564.03).

Offering employer defined. Under pre-2011 Appropriations Act law, Code Sec. 6056(f)(1)(A) defined the term "offering employer" as any offering employer (as defined in §10108(b) of the Patient Protection and Affordable Care Act (PPACA), Sec. 10108(b), PL 111-148, 3/23/2010) if the required contribution (within the meaning of Code Sec. 5000A(e)(1)(B)(i), see FTC 2d/FIN ¶ A-6410; USTR ¶ 50,00A4; TaxDesk ¶ 576,160) of any employee exceeded 8% of the wages (as defined in Code Sec. 3121(a), see FTC 2d/FIN ¶ H-4621; USTR ¶ 31,114; TaxDesk ¶ 544,001) paid to that employee by that employer. (FTC 2d/FIN ¶ S-3330, ¶ S-3332; USTR ¶ 60,564.02)

> **RIA** *observation:* Thus, under pre-2011 Appropriations Act law, if an employer offered minimum essential coverage (see FTC 2d/FIN ¶ A-6405; USTR ¶ 50,00A4; TaxDesk ¶ 576,155) to its employees consisting of coverage through an eligible employer-sponsored plan, paid any portion of the plan costs, and the portion of the annual premium paid by any individual employee (whether through salary reduction or otherwise) for self-only coverage exceeded 8% of the employee's wages, the employer was an "offering employer" that had to report health insurance coverage information to IRS and provide related statements to each insured employee after 2013.

For repeal of the provisions of PPACA §10108(b), see ¶ 1603.

Under pre-2011 Appropriations Act law, Code Sec. 6056(f)(1)(B) provided that in the case of any calendar year beginning after 2014, the 8% of wages requirement under the definition of an offering employer (discussed above) was to be adjusted for the calendar year to reflect the rate of premium growth between the previous calendar year and 2013 over the rate of income growth for that period.

Any term used in Code Sec. 6056 which is also used in Code Sec. 4980H (the excise tax imposed on large employers that don't offer affordable health insurance after 2013, see FTC 2d/FIN ¶ H-1175 *et seq.*; USTR ¶ 4980H4) will have the meaning given that term by Code Sec. 4980H. (Code Sec. 6056(f)(2)) (FTC 2d/FIN ¶ S-3330, ¶ S-3332; USTR ¶ 60,564.02)

Coordination with other requirements. To the maximum extent feasible, Code Sec. 6056(d) provides that IRS will be able to provide that—

(1) any return or statement required to be provided under Code Sec. 6056 (discussed above) can be provided as part of any return or statement required under Code Sec. 6051 (see FTC 2d/FIN ¶ S-3151; USTR ¶ 60,514; TaxDesk ¶ 812,001) or Code Sec. 6055 (see FTC 2d/FIN ¶ S-3320 *et seq.*; USTR ¶ 60,554 *et seq.*), and (see FTC 2d/FIN ¶ S-3334; USTR ¶ 60,564.04)

(2) for an applicable large employer or, under pre-2011 Appropriations Act law, offering employer (see above under "Offering employer defined"), offering health insurance coverage of a health insurance issuer, the employer can enter into an agreement with the issuer to include information required under Code Sec. 6056 with the return and statement required to be provided by the issuer under Code Sec. 6055 (see FTC 2d/FIN ¶ S-3320 *et seq.*; USTR ¶ 60,554 *et seq.*). (FTC 2d/FIN ¶ S-3330, ¶ S-3334; USTR ¶ 60,564.04)

Coverage provided by governmental units. For any applicable large employer or, under pre-2011 Appropriations Act law, offering employer (see above under "Offering employer defined"), which is a governmental unit or any agency or instrumentality thereof, the person appropriately designated for purposes of Code Sec. 6056 (discussed above) will be required to make the required returns and statements under Code Sec. 6056(e). (FTC 2d/FIN ¶ S-3330, ¶ S-3335; USTR ¶ 60,564.05)

New Law. The 2011 Appropriations Act repeals the above-discussed reporting requirements as those rules apply to offering employers, effective for periods beginning after Dec. 31, 2013. Specifically, the 2011 Appropriations Act removes the phrase "and every offering employer" in the reporting rules provided in Code Sec. 6056(a). (Code Sec. 6056(a) as amended by 2011 Appropriations Act §1858(b)(5)(A) (Sec. 1858(b)(5)(A), PL 112-10, 4/15/2011))

> **◆ observation:** Thus, offering employers will not be subject to the post-2013 health insurance coverage information reporting and related statement requirements that were added by PPACA §1514(a) and §10108(j) (Sec. 1514(a), PL 111-148, 3/23/2010; Sec. 10108(j), PL 111-148, 3/23/2010). Under the 2011 Appropriations Act, these reporting and related statement requirements will only apply to applicable large employers.

Conforming changes. In addition to the change described above, the 2011 Appropriations Act makes the following conforming changes:

• removes "and every offering employer" in Code Sec. 6056(a); (Code Sec. 6056(a) as amended by 2011 Appropriations Act §1858(b)(5)(A))

• removes "in the case of an applicable large employer" from the requirement that an employer disclose information concerning waiting periods provided in Code Sec. 6056(b)(2)(C)(i); (Code Sec. 6056(b)(2)(C)(i) as amended by 2011 Appropriations Act §1858(b)(5)(B)(i))

> *☑ observation:* The change to Code Sec. 6056(b)(2)(C)(i) (discussed immediately above) is a conforming change that reflects the fact that, under the 2011 Appropriations Act, the reporting requirements for offering employers under Code Sec. 6056(a) were repealed. As a result of the repeal, the reference to "applicable large employers" in Code Sec. 6056(b)(2)(C)(i) is unnecessary, since applicable large employers are the only employers subject to the Code Sec. 6056 information reporting and related statement requirements. Thus, applicable large employers continue to be subject to the Code Sec. 6056(b)(2)(C)(i) reporting requirement as they were under pre-2011 Appropriations Act law.

• removes the requirement that an offering employer disclose information relating to the portion of the cost paid by the employer provided in Code Sec. 6056(b)(2)(C)(v); (Code Sec. 6056(b)(2)(C)(v) as amended by 2011 Appropriations Act §1858(b)(5)(B)(iv))

• removes "or offering employer" in Code Sec. 6056(d)(2) (rules permitting information to be provided by the health insurance provider under an agreement with the employer) (Code Sec. 6056(d)(2) as amended by 2011 Appropriations Act §1858(b)(5)(C)) and Code Sec. 6056(e); (Code Sec. 6056(e) as amended by 2011 Appropriations Act §1858(b)(5)(C)) and

• removes the definition of an offering employer provided in pre-2011 Appropriations Act Code Sec. 6056(f)(1)(A) and Code Sec. 6056(f)(1)(B). (Code Sec. 6056(f)(1)(A) as amended by 2011 Appropriations Act §1858(b)(5)(D); Code Sec. 6056(f)(1)(B) as amended by 2011 Appropriations Act §1858(b)(5)(D))

Redesignation. Pre-2011 Appropriations Act Code Sec. 6056(f)(2) (discussed above) has been redesignated as Code Sec. 6056(f). (Code Sec. 6056(f) as redesignated by 2011 Appropriations Act §1858(b)(5)(D))

☐ **Effective:** Periods beginning after Dec. 31, 2013. (2011 Appropriations Act §1858(d))

> *☑ observation:* Section 1858(d) of the 2011 Appropriations Act provides that the amendments made by §1858(b)(5) of the 2011 Appropriations Act (discussed above) take effect as if included in the provisions of, and the amendments made by, the provisions of the PPACA (PL 111-148, 3/23/2010) to which they relate. Section 1858(b)(5) of the 2011 Appropriations Act relates to §1514(a) and §10108(j) of the PPACA (Sec. 1514(a), PL 111-148, 3/23/2010; Sec. 10108(j), PL 111-148, 3/23/2010), both of which are effective for periods beginning

after Dec. 31, 2013 (Sec. 1514(d), PL 111-148, 3/23/2010; Sec. 10108(j)(4), PL 111-148, 3/23/2010). Thus, the amendments made by §1858(b)(5) of the 2011 Appropriations Act are effective for periods beginning after Dec. 31, 2013.

¶ 1700. Pension Provisions from Earlier Acts of the 112th Congress

¶ 1701. Plans can use interest rate smoothing over a 25-year period to determine liabilities

Code Sec. 404(o)(6), as amended by 2012 Highway Investment Act §40211(a)(2)(A)

Code Sec. 417(e)(3)(C), as amended by 2012 Highway Investment Act §40211(a)(2)(C)

Code Sec. 417(e)(3)(D), as amended by 2012 Highway Investment Act §40211(a)(2)(C)

Code Sec. 420(g), as amended by 2012 Highway Investment Act §40211(a)(2)(D)

Code Sec. 430(h)(2)(C)(iv), as amended by 2012 Highway Investment Act §40211(a)(1)

Code Sec. 430(h)(2)(F), as amended by 2012 Highway Investment Act §40211(a)(2)(B)

ERISA § 101(f)(2)(D), as amended by 2012 Highway Investment Act §40211(b)(2)(A)

ERISA § 205(g)(3)(B)(ii), as amended by 2012 Highway Investment Act §40211(b)(3)(B)

ERISA § 205(g)(3)(B)(iii), as amended by 2012 Highway Investment Act §40211(b)(3)(B)

ERISA § 303(h)(2)(C)(iv), as amended by 2012 Highway Investment Act §40211(b)(1)

ERISA § 303(h)(2)(F), as amended by 2012 Highway Investment Act §40211(b)(3)(A)

ERISA § 4006(a)(3)(E)(iv), as amended by 2012 Highway Investment Act §40211(b)(3)(C)

ERISA § 4010(d)(3), as amended by 2012 Highway Investment Act §40211(b)(3)(D)

ERISA § None,2012 Highway Investment Act §40211(b)(2)(B)

Generally effective: Plan years beginning after Dec. 31, 2011

Committee Reports, see ¶ 5402

FTC 2d References are to Federal Tax Coordinator 2d
FIN References are to RIA's Analysis of Federal Taxes: Income (print)
USTR References are to United States Tax Reporter: Income
PCA References are to Pension Analysis (print and electronic)
PBE References are to Pension & Benefits Explanations
BCA References are to Benefits Analysis (electronic)
BC References are to Benefits Coordinator (print)
EP References are to Estate Planning Analysis (print and electronic)

Minimum funding requirements. To qualify for tax advantages, defined benefit plans must meet certain minimum funding requirements that were established to regulate the amount an employer must contribute to a covered plan so that the plan is properly funded. The minimum funding rules require that plans conform to a minimum "funding standard," which is a formula or calculation that determines the minimum contribution the employer must make each year. (FTC 2d/FIN ¶ H-7600; USTR ¶ 4124; PCA ¶ 25,601; PBE ¶ 412-4)

Single-employer plans subject to the minimum funding standards must also meet the Code Sec. 430 minimum required contribution rules. Under these rules, a plan's minimum required contribution generally depends on whether the value of plan assets covers the plan's "funding target." A plan's funding target for a plan year is the present value of all benefits accrued or earned under the plan as of the beginning of the plan year. Typically, if the value of a plan's assets is less than the funding target, then a funding shortfall exists, and the plan's minimum required contribution is the sum of the plan's target normal cost and the shortfall and waiver amortization charges for the plan year. (FTC 2d/FIN ¶ H-7751.1; USTR ¶ 4304.01; PCA ¶ 25,752.1; PBE ¶ 430-4.01)

Code Sec. 430(f) provides that defined benefit plans (other than multiemployer plans) may maintain a "funding standard carryover balance," which is a credit balance from the funding standard account under the pre-2008 rules, and a prefunding balance, which results from making plan contributions greater than those required, either to (i) reduce the amount of the minimum required contribution, or (ii) include in the value of plan assets. (FTC 2d/FIN ¶ H-7754; USTR ¶ 4304.017; PCA ¶ 25,755; PBE ¶ 430-4.017)

The value of plan assets must be reduced by the amount of the prefunding balance and the funding standard carryover balance for purposes of determining (i) the minimum required contribution, (ii) the funding shortfall, and (iii) the funding target attainment percentage. (FTC 2d/FIN ¶ H-7754.3; USTR ¶ 4304.017; PCA ¶ 25,755.3; PBE ¶ 430-4.017)

In determining a plan's funding target and target normal cost for a plan year, the interest rates typically used in calculating the present value of the plan's accrued or earned benefits—the "applicable interest rates"—are based on three segment rates applied to a plan's short-term, mid-term, and long-term liabilities. Thus, the interest rate used in determining the present value of a plan's benefits is, for benefits reasonably determined to be payable:

(1) within 5 years—i.e., during the 5-year period that begins on the first day of the plan year—the first segment rate for the "applicable month;"

(2) after 5 years and within 20 years—i.e., during the 15-year period that begins at the end of the period described in item (1), above—the second segment rate for the "applicable month;" and

(3) after 20 years—i.e., after the end of the period described in item (2), above—the third segment rate for the "applicable month."(FTC 2d/FIN ¶ H-7756; USTR ¶ 4304.01; PCA ¶ 25,757; PBE ¶ 430-4.01)

The "first segment rate" (item (1), above) is, for any month, the single rate of interest that IRS determines for that month on the basis of the corporate bond yield curve for that month, taking into account only that portion of the yield curve which is based on bonds maturing during the five-year period beginning with that month. Thus, the first segment rate is, for any month, the single rate of interest determined by IRS on the basis of the monthly corporate bond yield curves for the 24-month period ending with the month preceding that month, taking into account only the first five years of each of those curves.

The "second segment rate" (item (2), above) is, for any month, the single rate of interest that IRS determines for that month on the basis of the corporate bond yield curve for that month, taking into account only that portion of the yield curve which is based on bonds maturing during the 15-year period beginning at the end of the period described for the first segment rate. Thus, the second segment rate is, for any month, the single rate of interest determined by IRS on the basis of the monthly corporate bond yield curves for the 24-month period ending with the month preceding that month, taking into account only the portion of each of those yield curves corresponding to the 15-year period that follows the end of the 5-year period described for the first segment (above).

The "third segment rate" (item (3), above) is, for any month, the single rate of interest that IRS determines for that month on the basis of the "corporate bond yield curve" for that month, taking into account only that portion of the yield curve which is based on bonds maturing during the periods beginning after the period described for the second segment rate. Thus, the third segment rate is, for any month, the single rate of interest determined by IRS on the basis of the monthly corporate bond yield curves for the 24-month period ending with the month preceding that month, taking into account only the portion of each of those yield curves corresponding to the 40-year period that follows the end of the 15-year period described for the second segment (above). (FTC 2d/FIN ¶ H-7756.1; USTR ¶ 4304.01; PCA ¶ 25,757.1; PBE ¶ 430-4.01)

> *observation:* The averaging of the segment rates over a 24-month period is known as interest rate smoothing. Smoothing helps limit the changes in pension funding due to interest rate volatility.

Each month, IRS publishes the segment rates, which are based on the corporate bond yield curve.

Parallel funding rules apply under ERISA §303(h)(2)(C).

Under Code Sec. 404(o), a limit applies to the amount of an employer's deduction for payments, otherwise deductible, that are made in a tax year (or for a tax year) to a qualified pension plan or to an annuity plan. This limit typically equals the employer's funding obligation for each plan year ending with, or within, the employer's tax year. The deduction limit for a single-employer plan is determined using the same actuarial assumptions that are used for the plan year under Code Sec. 430, including the "applicable interest rates." (FTC 2d/ FIN ¶ H-10101, ¶ H-10106; USTR ¶ 4044.02; PCA ¶ 30,202, ¶ 30,207; PBE ¶ 404-4.02)

The rules for determining present value (requiring the use of the applicable interest rate and the applicable mortality table) apply for the calculation of the present value:

(1) of any benefit under a qualified defined benefit plan (other than a benefit paid in the form of certain "nondecreasing annuities");

(2) of a qualified joint and survivor annuity (QJSA) or a qualified pre-retirement survivor annuity (QPSA) for purposes of the cash-out rules;

(3) of accrued benefits for purposes of determining whether a participant's consent is required before a distribution; and

(4) in determining the maximum benefit that can be provided under a defined benefit plan (under Code Sec. 415(b)(2)(E)(ii)). (FTC 2d/FIN ¶ H-8703)

In determining present value, a defined benefit plan must provide that: (a) the present value of any accrued benefit, and (b) the present value of the amount of any distribution, including a single-sum distribution, must be calculated using: (1) the "applicable mortality table" and (2) the "applicable interest rate." The "applicable interest rate" is the adjusted first, second, and third segment rates applied under rules similar to the rules of Code Sec. 430(h)(2)(C) (dealing with the segment interest rates used in determining a plan's funding target under the minimum funding rules, see above) for the month before the date of the distribution, or other time as IRS may by regs prescribe. (FTC 2d/FIN ¶ H-8701, ¶ H-8703; USTR ¶ 4304.01; PCA ¶ 25,757.1; PBE ¶ 430-4.01)

> **observation:** Because the segment rates (and in turn, the applicable interest rates) are based on corporate bond yields, when the corporate bonds yields fall, the present value of a plan's pension liabilities increases.

> **observation:** Before using corporate bond yields, pension plans were required to use the interest rate on 30-year Treasury bonds (long bonds) to determine present value. However, after the collapse of the dot com stock market boom and the tragic events of Sept. 11, 2001, interest rates on these bonds collapsed as investors sought out these high quality, stable investments. To ease the effects on pension plan funding caused by the low yield on the long bonds, Congress replaced the yield on the long bond with the yield on high quality corporate bonds to de-

termine present value. However, due to the Federal Reserve's actions to keep treasury bond yields low, these corporate bonds, too, now have low yields, which are causing the present value of plans' pension liabilities to increase.

Small plan valuation date. All determinations for a plan year of a single-employer defined benefit plan under the minimum funding standards generally must be made as of the plan's valuation date for the plan year. Thus, the determination of a plan's funding target, target normal cost, and asset value, must be made as of the valuation date for the plan year. A plan's valuation date is the first day of the plan year. However, there is an exception for small plans. If, on each day during the preceding plan year, a plan had 100 or fewer participants, then the plan may designate any day during the plan year as its valuation date for the plan year and succeeding plan years. (FTC 2d/FIN ¶ H-7755; USTR ¶ 4304.01; PCA ¶ 25,756; PBE ¶ 430-4.01)

Transfers of excess pension assets. A defined benefit plan (other than a multiemployer plan) can transfer "excess pension assets" to a retiree health account (a so-called 401(h) account) that is part of the plan to fund health benefits for the plan's retirees. "Excess pension assets" are defined as the excess (if any) of:

(A) the lesser of:

. . . the fair market value of the plan's assets (reduced by the pre-funding balance and the funding standard carryover balance, as determined under Code Sec. 430(f)); or

. . . the value of plan assets as determined under Code Sec. 430(g)(3), after reduction under Code Sec. 430(f), over

(B) 125% of the sum of the funding target and the target normal cost determined under Code Sec. 430 for the plan year. (FTC 2d/FIN ¶ H-8162, ¶ H-8167; USTR ¶ 4204.03; PCA ¶ 26,518; PBE ¶ 420-4.03)

Defined benefit plan funding notice requirements. Defined benefit plans (whether single-employer or multiemployer) are subject to certain plan funding notice requirements, which provide that the administrator of a defined benefit plan must provide a plan funding notice every plan year to (i) PBGC, (ii) each plan participant and beneficiary, (iii) each labor organization representing the participants or beneficiaries; and (iv) for a multiemployer plan only, each employer that has an obligation to contribute to the plan. In Prop. Labor Reg. §2520.101-5, DOL provided model funding notices for use by single and multiemployer defined benefit plans. (PCA ¶ 56,456.2; PBE ¶ ER101-4.022)

In addition to the plan funding notice requirements, contributing sponsors of certain large, underfunded, single-employer defined benefit plans, and members of the contributing sponsor's controlled group, must provide annual information to PBGC (sometimes referred to as a "section 4010 information filing") if the plan is covered by the PBGC termination insurance program. Among other items, this information filing must include the plan's funding target, determined as if the plan has been in at-risk status (a funding target attainment percentage for the preceding plan year of less than 80%, and a funding target attainment percentage for the preceding plan year (using the additional actuarial assumptions for at-risk plans) of less than 70%) for at least five plan years, and the plan's funding target attainment percentage. (PCA ¶ 56,620; PBE ¶ ER4010-4.02)

PBGC variable-rate premiums. To fund its insurance program for single-employer defined benefit plans, Pension Benefit Guaranty Corporation (PBGC) requires single-employer plans to pay both a flat rate premium of $36 per participant, and a variable rate premium of $9 per each $1,000 of unfunded vested benefits (UVBs). A plan's UVBs are the excess of its funding target for the plan year over the fair market value of its assets for the plan year. The interest rate used in valuing benefits for purposes of establishing a plan's funding target is the first, second, or third segment rate for the month preceding the month in which the plan year begins, as determined under ERISA §303(h)(2)(C)—the parallel ERISA provision to Code Sec. 430(h)(2)(C). (PCA ¶ 58,307.1; PBE ¶ ER4006-4.01)

New Law. To address concerns of plan sponsors regarding how low corporate bond interest rates are increasing their plan funding obligations, the 2012 Highway Investment Act provides for use of a 25-year interest rate corridor, over which the plan's applicable interest rate can be determined. Thus, the Act provides that, if the first, second, or third segment rate described in Code Sec. 430(h)(2)(C)(i), Code Sec. 430(h)(2)(C)(ii), or Code Sec. 430(h)(2)(C)(iii) for any applicable month (determined without using the smoothing provision) is less than the "applicable minimum percentage" (see below), or more than the "applicable maximum percentage" (see below), of the average of the first, second, or third segment rates for years in the 25-year period ending on Sept. 30 of the calendar year preceding the calendar year in which the plan year begins, then the segment rate for the applicable month is equal to the applicable minimum percentage or the applicable maximum percentage of the 25-year average, whichever is closest. IRS must determine the average on an annual basis, and may prescribe equivalent rates for years in any such 25-year period for which the first, second, or third segment rates are not available. ((Code Sec. 430(h)(2)(C)(iv)(I) as amended by 2012 Highway Investment Act §40211(a)(1)) (Sec. 40211(a)(1), PL 112-141, 7/6/2012)

> *observation:* Thus, the Act increases the allowable smoothing period from two years (24 months) to 25 years. Under the Act, interest rates that were in effect as far back as the 1980's are taken into account in determining the applicable interest rate. In effect, the Act will raise in-

terest rates for funding purposes which will lower the amount of a plan's minimum required contribution.

⚫ *observation:* The 2012 Highway Investment Act is also called the "Moving Ahead for Progress in the 21st Century" Act, or "MAP-21." Thus, the segment rates, as adjusted for 25-year interest rate smoothing, are referred to as the "MAP-21 segment rates."

The "applicable minimum percentage" and the "applicable maximum percentage" for a plan year beginning in a calendar year is determined in accordance with the following table: (Code Sec. 430(h)(2)(C)(iv)(II))

Applicable Percentages

Calendar Year	Applicable Minimum Percentage	Applicable Maximum Percentage
2012	90%	110%
2013	85%	115%
2014	80%	120%
2015	75%	125%
After 2015	70%	130%

⚫ *observation:* Thus, the MAP-21 segment rates could be 10% lower (or higher) than the 25-year average in 2012, rising to 30% lower (or higher) than the 25-year average for years beginning after 2015.

Similar changes are made to ERISA's parallel provision. (ERISA §303(h)(2)(C)(iv) as amended by 2012 Highway Investment Act §40211((b)(1))

The Act provides that, in applying the limit on an employer's deductible contributions to a plan, the limit is determined without taking into account any adjustment due to the MAP-21 segment rates in Code Sec. 430(h)(2)(C)(iv) (above). (Code Sec. 404(o)(6) as amended by 2012 Highway Investment Act §40211(a)(2)(A))

⚫ *observation:* Thus, under the Act, the deductible contribution limit will be higher than it would otherwise be if the limit were determined using the presumably higher interest rates related to the use of the MAP-21 segment rates.

Similarly, the Act provides that the definitions of "applicable interest rate" in Code Sec. 417(e)(3)(C) and "applicable segment rate" in Code Sec. 417(e)(3)(D) are also applied by not taking into account any adjustment due to the use of the MAP-21 segment rates in Code Sec. 430(h)(2)(C)(iv) (above). (Code Sec. 417(e)(3)(C) as amended by 2012 Highway Investment Act §40211(a)(2)(C); Code Sec. 417(e)(3)(D) as amended by 2012 Highway Investment Act §40211(a)(2)(C))

Similar changes are made to ERISA's parallel provision. (ERISA §205(g)(3)(B)(ii) as amended by 2012 Highway Investment Act §40211(b)(3)(B)) ; (ERISA §205(g)(3)(B)(iii) as amended by 2012 Highway Investment Act §40211(b)(3)(B)))

> *observation:* Thus, present value determinations other than for determining a plan's liabilities, such as calculating the amount of a participant's accrued benefit for purposes of determining the cash-out amount or other lump-sum payable to a participant, won't be affected by a change to the presumably higher interest rates related to the use of the MAP-21 segment rates. Otherwise, use of a higher interest rate for these purposes would result in a lower payout for plan participants.

The Act requires IRS to publish the segment rates for the 25-year period. (Code Sec. 430(h)(2)(F) as amended by 2012 Highway Investment Act §40211(a)(2)(B))

Similar changes are made to ERISA's parallel provision. (ERISA §303(h)(2)(F) as amended by 2012 Highway Investment Act §40211(b)(3)(A))

> *observation:* Thus, as with the segment rates based on current corporate bond yields, IRS will publish the segment rates for the 25-year period.

As required under the Act, IRS has published in Notice 2012-55, 2012-36 IRB 332 the MAP-21 segment rates, beginning with those for September 2011. To determine these rates, IRS used a statistical regression analysis that combined information about the relationship of the spot segment rates, zero-coupon yields for Treasury securities, corporate bond index values, and Constant Maturity Treasury rates to estimate spot segment rates for months back to October 1984. See FTC 2d/FIN ¶ TBL-15311.1.

Transfers to retiree health accounts. For purposes of making a transfer to a retiree health account, the determination of a plan's excess pension assets must be made without regard to the MAP-21 segment rates in Code Sec. 430(h)(2)(C)(iv). (Code Sec. 420(g) as amended by 2012 Highway Investment Act §40211(a)(2)(D))

Plan funding notices. The Act requires plans to disclose the effect of the 25-year smoothing provision on plan funding. Thus, for a single-employer plan for an "applicable plan year" (see below) each plan funding notice required under ERISA §101(f)(1) must include:

(I) a statement that the Act modified the method for determining the interest rates used to calculate the actuarial value of benefits earned under the plan, providing for a 25-year average of interest rates to be taken into account in addition to a two-year average;

(II) a statement that, as a result of the Act, the plan sponsor may contribute less money to the plan when interest rates are at historical lows; and

(III) a table that shows the funding target attainment percentage (as defined in ERISA §303(d)(2)), the funding shortfall (as defined in ERISA §303(c)(4)), and the minimum required contribution (as determined under ERISA §303), for the applicable plan year and each of the two preceding plan years, determined both with and without regard to ERISA §303(h)(2)(C)(iv). (ERISA §101(f)(2)(D)(i) as amended by 2012 Highway Investment Act §40211(b)(2)(A))

> *observation:* Thus, the notices must show plan funding both with and without use of the MAP-21 segment rates (i.e., 25-year smoothing).

"Applicable plan year." For purposes of these changes to the plan funding notice requirements, "applicable plan year" means any plan year beginning after Dec. 31, 2011, and before Jan. 1, 2015, for which:

(i) the ERISA §303(d)(2) funding target is less than 95% of the funding target determined without regard to the MAP-21 segment rates in ERISA §303(h)(2)(C)(iv);

(ii) the plan has a funding shortfall (as defined in ERISA §303(c)(4) and determined without regard to the MAP-21 segment rates in ERISA §303(h)(2)(C)(iv)) greater than $500,000; and

(iii) the plan had 50 participants or more on any day during the preceding plan year. (ERISA §101(f)(2)(D)(ii))

In determining if the 50-participant threshold has been met, the aggregation rule "under the last sentence" of ERISA §303(g)(2)(B) must be applied. (ERISA §101(f)(2)(D)(ii))

> *observation:* Thus, all defined benefit single-employer plans maintained by the same employer (or any member of such employer's controlled group) are treated as one plan, with the participants of that employer or member taken into account.

Further, if a plan met the 50-participant threshold for a "preceding plan year" that began before Jan. 1, 2012, the information required to be provided in tabular form under item (III), above, need not provide information about the effect of the MAP-21 segment rates on the plan's funding target attainment percentage, funding shortfall, and minimum required contribution. (ERISA §101(f)(2)(D)(iii))

Model notice changes. The Act requires DOL to modify the model funding notices to prominently include the information described in items (I) through (III), above. (2012 Highway Investment Act §40211(b)(2)(B))

Section 4010 informational filing. The Act provides that, for purposes of section 4010 informational filing, the segment rates used to determine a plan's funding target and funding target attainment percentage must be determined without taking into account any adjustment using the MAP-21 segment rates in ERISA §302(h)(2)(C)(iv). (ERISA §4010(d)(3) as amended by 2012 Highway Investment Act §40211(b)(3)(D))

The Act further provides that the interest rate used in valuing benefits for purposes of establishing a plan's funding target is the first, second, or third segment rate for the month preceding the month in which the plan year begins, as determined under ERISA §303(h)(2)(C), but without regard to any regs issued by PBGC, and without taking into account the MAP-21 segment rates. (ERISA §4006(a)(3)(E)(iv) as amended by 2012 Highway Investment Act §40211(b)(3)(C))

> **✪** *observation:* Thus, the determination of the amount of a plan's UVBs won't be affected by the 25-year interest rate smoothing under the MAP-21 segment rates, and so the variable rate premium a plan must pay to PBGC won't be affected by the change. Presumably, Congress exempted the determination of UVBs from the smoothing provision over concern that this would reduce PBGC's premium income at a time when PBGC is under extreme financial pressure to meet its obligations to participants of terminating plans.

Special rules on elections. Despite the smoothing amendments' effective date (see below), a plan sponsor may elect not to have the MAP-21 segment rates apply to any plan year beginning before Jan. 1, 2013 either (as specified in the election): (i) for all purposes for which the amendments apply, or (ii) solely for purposes of determining the plan's adjusted funding target attainment percentage (AFTAP) under Code Sec. 436 and ERISA §206(g) for a plan year. A plan won't be treated as failing to meet the requirements of the anti-cutback rules set out in Code Sec. 411(d)(6) and ERISA §204(g) solely by making either election. (2012 Highway Investment Act §40211(c)(2)(A))

IRS has issued detailed guidance in Notice 2012-61, 2012-42 IRB 479 on how the election is made. See FTC 2d/FIN ¶ H-7756.2B; PCA ¶ 25,757.2B.

Opt out of existing elections. If, on July 6, 2012, an election to use alternative interest rates for funding purposes under Code Sec. 430(h)(2)(D)(ii) and ERISA's parallel provision, ERISA §303(h)((2)(D)(ii), then, notwithstanding the requirement that this election can only be revoked with IRS's consent, the plan sponsor may revoke this election without the consent of IRS. The revocation may be made at any time within the first year of the Act's enactment, and the revocation will be effective for the first plan year to which the amendments made by 2012 Highway Investment Act §40211 apply and all later plan years. This opt-out does not preclude a plan sponsor from making a later election in accordance with Code Sec. 430(h)(2)(D)(ii) and ERISA §303(h)((2)(D)(ii). (2012 Highway Investment Act §40211(c)(2)(B))

IRS has issued detailed guidance in Notice 2012-61, 2012-42 IRB 479 on how the revocation election is made. See FTC 2d/FIN ¶ H-7756.4; PCA ¶ 25,757.4.

☐ **Effective:** Plan years beginning after Dec. 31, 2011. (2012 Highway Investment Act §40211(c)(1))

¶ 1702. Excess pension plan assets may be used to fund retiree group-term life insurance

Code Sec. 79(f), as amended by 2012 Highway Investment Act §40242(d)

Code Sec. 420(a), as amended by 2012 Highway Investment Act §40242(a)

Code Sec. 420(b)(2), as amended by 2012 Highway Investment Act §40242(e)(3)

Code Sec. 420(b)(4), as amended by 2012 Highway Investment Act §40242(g)(2)

Code Sec. 420(c)(2)(B), as amended by 2012 Highway Investment Act §40242(g)(4)(A)

Code Sec. 420(c)(3)(A), as amended by 2012 Highway Investment Act §40242(c)(1)

Code Sec. 420(c)(3)(B)(i)(I), as amended by 2012 Highway Investment Act §40242(c)(2)(A)(i)

Code Sec. 420(c)(3)(B)(ii), as amended by 2012 Highway Investment Act §40242(c)(2)(A)(ii)

Code Sec. 420(c)(3)(C), as amended by 2012 Highway Investment Act §40242(c)(2)(B)

Code Sec. 420(d)(1)(A), as amended by 2012 Highway Investment Act §40242(e)(2)

Code Sec. 420(e)(1)(A), as amended by 2012 Highway Investment Act §40242(e)(5)(A)

Code Sec. 420(e)(1)(B), as amended by 2012 Highway Investment Act §40242(e)(6)(A)

Code Sec. 420(e)(1)(C), as amended by 2012 Highway Investment Act §40242(b)(3)(B)(i)

Code Sec. 420(e)(1)(D), as amended by 2012 Highway Investment Act §40242(b)(2)

Code Sec. 420(e)(4), as amended by 2012 Highway Investment Act §40242(b)(1)

Code Sec. 420(f)(2)(D)(i)(II), as amended by 2012 Highway Investment Act §40242(c)(2)(E)

Code Sec. 420(f)(2)(D)(ii), as amended by 2012 Highway Investment Act §40242(c)(2)(F)

Code Sec. 420(f)(6)(B), as amended by 2012 Highway Investment Act §40242(f)

Code Sec. 420(f)(6)(C), as amended by 2012 Highway Investment Act §40242(b)(3)(B)(ii)

Code Sec. 420(f)(6)(D), as amended by 2012 Highway Investment Act §40242(b)(3)(A)

ERISA § 101(e), as amended by 2012 Highway Investment Act §40242(e)(14)

Generally effective: Transfers made after July 6, 2012

Committee Reports, see ¶ 5405

A defined benefit plan can provide health benefits to retired employees through a sub-account maintained under the plan (called a "401(h) account," after the Code section that permits it). Under Code Sec. 420, certain over-funded plans are allowed (in any tax year before 2022, as extended by the 2012 Highway Investment Act, see ¶ 1703) to transfer their excess assets to the 401(h) account for purposes of funding the retiree health benefits provided under the account, as long as the transfer is a "qualified transfer." To be qualified, the transfer must satisfy certain use requirements, vesting requirements, and minimum cost requirements. (FTC 2d/FIN ¶ H-8100, ¶ H-8163; USTR ¶ 4204; PCA ¶ 26,514; PBE ¶ 420-4)

If the transfer meets all of the requirements, including ERISA notice requirements, the transfer does *not* cause the plan to lose its tax qualification, and the employer is *not* subject either to income tax or the reversion excise tax. (FTC 2d/FIN ¶ H-8901; USTR ¶ 49,804; TaxDesk ¶ 286,004; PCA ¶ 27,602; PBE ¶ 4980-4)

Under a special rule for 1990, an employer could make a qualified transfer of excess pension assets to a 401(h) account for the amount of qualified current retiree health liabilities for the tax year before the employer's first tax year beginning after Dec. 31, 1990.

Use requirement. Under the use requirement, any assets transferred to a 401(h) account in a qualified transfer can only be used to pay "qualified current retiree health liabilities" for the taxable year of the transfer. Any transferred assets which are not used in this way (and which thus fail to satisfy the use requirement) must be transferred out of the 401(h) account, and returned to the general assets of the plan. The amount returned is treated as an employer reversion, and is subject to a 20% excise tax under Code Sec. 4980, which penalizes certain reversions of plan assets to the employer.

"Qualified current retiree health liabilities" are the aggregate amounts related to applicable health benefits provided during the tax year, which would have been deductible by the employer for that tax year if (1) the benefits were provided directly by the employer, and (2) the employer used the cash receipts and disbursements method of accounting. Certain amounts previously set aside may be used to reduce the amount of qualified current retiree health liabilities. (FTC 2d/FIN ¶ H-8168; USTR ¶ 4204.01; PCA ¶ 26,519; PBE ¶ 420-4.01)

Minimum cost requirements. To satisfy the minimum cost requirement, a group health plan must provide that either: (1) the "applicable employer cost" for each tax year during the cost maintenance period is no less than the higher of the applicable employer costs for each of the two tax years immediately before the tax year of the qualified transfer; or (2) the minimum cost requirement that applies to a collectively bargained transfer is satisfied.

The "applicable employer cost" for a tax year is: (a) the employer's "qualified current retiree health liabilities" for the tax year, divided by (b) the number of individuals to whom coverage for "applicable health benefits" was provided during the tax year.

An employer may elect to calculate the applicable employer cost separately for those individuals who, at any time during the tax year, are eligible for benefits under title XVIII of the Social Security Act (Medicare), and for those not eligible for Medicare. (FTC 2d/FIN ¶ H-8173; USTR ¶ 4204.02; PCA ¶ 26,524; PBE ¶ 420-4.02)

Qualified future transfers and collectively bargained transfers. In addition to allowing plans to make a qualified transfer to pay for current retiree health liabilities, plans are allowed to make either: (1) a qualified future transfer to fund the expected cost of current and future retiree health liabilities; or (2) a collectively bargained transfer to fund the expected cost of retiree health liabilities under a collective bargaining agreement during the collectively bargained cost maintenance period (generally, the shorter of either: (a) the covered retiree's remaining lifetime, or (b) the coverage period provided by the health plan).

A qualified future transfer and a collectively bargained transfer will generally be treated as a qualified transfer.

Under an election to maintain benefits for future transfers, an employer can elect to satisfy the minimum cost rule (as it applies to qualified transfers) by meeting the minimum benefit requirement rule that was in effect before Dec. 18, 1999, for each relevant year. For transfers before Dec. 18, 1999, transfers of excess pension assets to retiree health accounts had to meet a minimum benefit requirement. Under this requirement, a group health plan or arrangement that provided applicable health benefits had to provide substantially the same level of applicable health benefits for each relevant tax year as the applicable health benefits that were provided by the employer during the tax year immediately preceding the tax year of the qualified transfer.

For collectively bargained transfers, each collectively bargained group health plan under which "collectively bargained health benefits" are provided must provide that the collectively bargained employer cost for each tax year during the collectively bargained cost maintenance period cannot be less than the amount specified by the collective bargaining agreement.

Collectively bargained health benefits are benefits or coverage provided to: (i) retired employees—who immediately before the collectively bargained transfer, are entitled to receive such benefits upon retirement, and are entitled to pension benefits under the plan—and their spouses and dependents; and (ii) if specified by the provisions of the collective bargaining agreement governing the collectively bargained transfer, active employees—who following their retirement, are entitled to receive such benefits, and entitled to pension benefits under the plan—and their spouses and dependents. (FTC 2d/FIN ¶ H-8182; USTR ¶ 4204.04; PCA ¶ 26,533; PBE ¶ 420-4.04)

Deduction limits. No deduction is allowed to the employer for either (1) the qualified transfer of any amount into a Code Sec. 401(h) account (or any re-transfer to the plan of transferred amounts not used to pay for qualified current retiree health liabilities), or (2) qualified current retiree health liabilities paid out of the assets (and income allocable to those assets) transferred in a qualified transfer. (FTC 2d/FIN ¶ H-8180; USTR ¶ 4204.03; PCA ¶ 26,531; PBE ¶ 420-4.03)

Taxation of employees receiving group-term life insurance. Under Code Sec. 79(a), group-term life insurance coverage provided under a policy carried by an employer is includible in the gross income of an employee (including a former employee), but only to the extent that the cost exceeds the sum of the cost of $50,000 of the insurance, plus the amount, if any, paid by the employee toward the purchase of the insurance. Under Code Sec. 79(b)(3) and Code Sec. 72(m)(3), the cost of term life insurance provided through a pension plan is includible in the employee's gross income. (FTC 2d/FIN ¶ H-1518; USTR ¶ 794.03; TaxDesk ¶ 137,007; PBE ¶ 79-4.03)

ERISA notice requirements. ERISA §101(e) provides that, at least 60 days before the date of a qualified transfer, the employer must notify the Dept. of Labor (DOL), IRS, employee representatives, and the plan administrator of the transfer, and the plan administrator must notify each plan participant and beneficiary of the transfer. (PCA ¶ 56,411, ¶ 56,456.1; PBE ¶ ER101-4.01)

Under pre-2012 Highway Investment Act law, there was no provision allowing over-funded plans to transfer excess pension assets to fund retiree group-term life insurance.

New Law. The 2012 Highway Investment Act expands the types of accounts to which excess pension assets may be transferred to include "applicable life insurance accounts," as well as retiree health accounts. Thus, under the Act, a qualified transfer of excess pension assets to either an applicable life insurance account or a retiree health account won't cause adverse tax consequences because of the transfer. (Code Sec. 420(a) as amended by 2012 Highway Investment Act §40242(a) (Sec. 40242(a), PL 112-141, 7/6/2012))

An "applicable life insurance account" is a separate account established and maintained for amounts transferred for qualified current retiree liabilities based on premiums for "applicable life insurance benefits." (Code Sec. 420(e)(4))

Thus, the assets transferred for the purchase of group-term life insurance must be maintained in a separate account within the plan, which must be separate both from the assets in the retiree medical account and from the other assets in the defined benefit plan. (Com Rept, see ¶ 5405)

The term "applicable life insurance benefits" means group-term life insurance coverage provided to retired employees who, immediately before the qualified transfer, are entitled to receive such coverage by reason of retirement, and who are entitled to pension benefits under the plan. However, this rule applies only to the extent that the coverage is provided under a policy for retired employees, and the cost of the coverage is excludable from the retired employee's gross income under Code Sec. 79. (Code Sec. 420(e)(1)(D))

Code Sec. 79(b)(3) and Code Sec. 72(m)(3) won't apply for any cost paid (whether directly or indirectly) with assets held in an applicable life insurance account under a defined benefit plan. (Code Sec. 79(f) as amended by 2012 Highway Investment Act §40242(d)) Thus, the general rule that the cost of group-term life insurance coverage provided under a defined benefit plan is includable in a participant's gross income does not apply to group-term life insurance provided through a retiree life insurance account. Instead, the general rule for determining the amount of employer-provided group-term life insurance that is includible in gross income applies. However, group-term life insurance coverage is permitted to be provided through a retiree life insurance account only to the extent that it is not includible in gross income. Thus, generally, only group-term life insurance not in excess of $50,000 may be purchased with transferred assets. (Com Rept, see ¶ 5405)

The Act makes various conforming changes so that generally, the rules for transfers of excess pension assets to retiree medical accounts to fund retiree health benefits also apply to transfers to retiree life insurance accounts to fund retiree group-term life insurance. The rules are generally applied separately to retiree health benefits and to retiree group-term life insurance. (Com Rept, see ¶ 5405) Highlights of these conforming changes are described below.

Qualified transfers. The one-transfer-a-year rule applies separately to transfers to retiree life insurance accounts and transfers to retiree medical accounts. (Com Rept, see ¶ 5405) If there is a transfer from a defined benefit plan to both a health benefits account and an applicable life insurance account during any tax year, the transfer will be treated as one transfer. (Code Sec. 420(b)(2))

The special rule for 1990 for qualified transfers is obsolete (Com Rept, see ¶ 5405), and is thus repealed. (Code Sec. 420(b)(4) as amended by 2012 Highway Investment Act §40242(g)(2); Code Sec. 420(c)(2)(B) as amended by 2012 Highway Investment Act §40242(g)(4)(A))

Minimum cost requirements. The minimum cost requirements that apply to qualified transfers of excess pension assets to retiree health accounts also apply to each group-term life insurance plan under which applicable life insurance benefits are provided. (Code Sec. 420(c)(3)(A))

For purposes of calculating the applicable employer cost, qualified current retiree health liabilities are determined separately for applicable health benefits and applicable life insurance benefits. (Code Sec. 420(c)(3)(B)(i)(I))

The number of individuals to whom coverage was provided during the tax year is based on the same separate determination as is made under Code Sec. 420(c)(3)(B)(i)(I), above. (Code Sec. 420(c)(3)(B)(ii))

For purposes of the employer's election to compute costs separately, the Act provides that an employer may elect to calculate the applicable employer cost separately:

. . . for applicable health benefits with respect to Medicare eligibility; and

. . . for applicable life insurance benefits with respect to:

   ...individuals age 65 or older at any time during the tax year; and

   ...individuals under age 65 during the tax year. (Code Sec. 420(c)(3)(C))

Collectively bargained transfers. For purposes of determining whether a collectively bargained transfer satisfies the minimum cost requirements, the Act provides that each collectively bargained plan under which collectively bargained health benefits or "collectively bargained life insurance benefits" are provided must provide that the collectively bargained employer cost for each tax year during the collectively bargained cost maintenance period cannot be less than the amount specified by the collective bargaining agreement. (Code Sec. 420(f)(2)(D)(i)(II))

The term "collectively bargained life insurance benefits" means, with respect to any collectively bargained transfer:

(i) applicable life insurance benefits which are provided to retired employees who, immediately before the transfer, are entitled to receive such benefits by reason of retirement; and

(ii) if specified by the provisions of the collective bargaining agreement governing the transfer, applicable life insurance benefits which will be provided at retirement to employees who are not retired employees at the time of the transfer. (Code Sec. 420(f)(6)(D))

Under a conforming amendment, the term "collectively bargained health benefits" is modified to mean health benefits or coverage:

(A) which are provided to retired employees—who immediately before the collectively bargained transfer, are entitled to receive such benefits by reason of retirement, and are entitled to pension benefits under the plan—and their spouses and dependents; and

(B) if specified by the provisions of the collective bargaining agreement governing the collectively bargained transfer, which will be provided at retirement to employees who are not retired employees at the time of the transfer and who are entitled to receive such benefits, and entitled to pension benefits under the plan—and their spouses and dependents. (Code Sec. 420(f)(6)(C))

Also, the definition of "applicable health benefits" is amended to mean health benefits or coverage which are provided to retired employees who, immediately before a qualified transfer, are entitled to receive such benefits by reason of retirement, and who are entitled to pension benefits under the plan—and their spouses and dependents. (Code Sec. 420(e)(1)(C))

For purposes of the election to maintain benefits for future transfers, the Act provides that the election can be made separately for applicable health benefits and applicable life insurance benefits. For an election for applicable life insurance benefits (like an election for applicable health benefits), an employer can elect to satisfy the minimum cost rules (as it applies to qualified transfers) by meeting the minimum benefit requirement rule that was in effect before Dec. 18, 1999, for each relevant year. (Code Sec. 420(f)(2)(D)(ii))

"Qualified current retiree health liabilities." "Qualified current retiree health liabilities" (for purposes of determining (i) the limits on the amount of a qualified transfer, and (ii) the applicable employer cost) must take into account aggregate amounts (including administrative expenses) related to applicable life insurance benefits (as well as applicable health benefits). (Code Sec. 420(e)(1)(A)) In addition, the amount of the reduction of qualified current retiree health liabilities for amounts previously set aside must be determined separately for applicable health benefits and applicable life insurance benefits. (Code Sec. 420(e)(1)(B))

Deduction limits. Under the Act, the disallowance of a deduction for the qualified transfer of any amount into a Code Sec. 401(h) account (or any re-transfer to the plan of transferred amounts not used to pay for qualified current retiree health liabilities) is extended to an applicable life insurance account. (Code Sec. 420(d)(1)(A))

ERISA notice requirements. The Act conforms the ERISA §101(e) participant notice requirements to apply to transfers to retiree group-term life insurance accounts, as well as to retiree health accounts. (ERISA §101(e) as amended by 2012 Highway Investment Act §40242(e)(14))

☐ **Effective:** For transfers made after July 6, 2012 (2012 Highway Investment Act §40242(h)(1)), except that the conforming changes made to the Code Sec. 420(f)(6)(C) definition of "collectively bargained health benefits" and the Code Sec. 420(e)(1)(C) definition of "applicable health benefits" are effective for transfers made after Aug. 17, 2006. (2012 Highway Investment Act §40242(h)(2))

> **✎ observation:** 2012 Highway Investment Act § 40242(h)(2) provides that the amendments related to Code Sec. 420(f)(6)(C) and Code Sec. 420(e)(1)(C) take effect as if included in the provision of the 2006 Pension Protection Act (PPA) to which those Code sections relate. Those Code sections relate to PPA § 841(a) (§ 841(a), PL 109-280, 8/17/2006), which, under PPA § 841(b) (§ 841(b), PL 109-280, 8/17/2006), is effective for transfers made after Aug. 17, 2006.

¶ 1703. Rules permitting transfer of excess defined benefit plan assets to retiree health accounts are extended through 2021

Code Sec. 420(b)(5), as amended by 2012 Highway Investment Act §40241(a)

ERISA § 101(e)(3), as amended by 2012 Highway Investment Act §40241(b)(1)

ERISA § 403(c)(1), as amended by 2012 Highway Investment Act §40241(b)(1)

ERISA § 408(b)(13), as amended by 2012 Highway Investment Act §40241(b)(1)

ERISA § 408(b)(13), as amended by 2012 Highway Investment Act §40241(b)(2)

Generally effective: July 6, 2012
Committee Reports, see ¶ 5405

If certain conditions are met, a qualified pension or annuity plan may provide for the payment of health benefits to retired employees, their spouses, and dependents, from a separate account. Before the enactment of Code Sec. 420, if pension plan assets were transferred to one of these retiree health accounts, the plan lost its qualified status, and transferred amounts were subject to income tax and a reversion excise tax. Code Sec. 420 allows "qualified transfers," "qualified future transfers," and "collectively bargained transfers" of excess pension assets from a defined benefit plan (other than a multiemployer plan) to a retiree health account that is part of the plan. If the transfer meets all of the requirements, including ERISA notice requirements, the transfer does *not* cause the plan to lose its tax qualification, and the employer is *not* subject either to income tax or the reversion excise tax. In addition, under ERISA, the asset transfer is *not* a prohibited transaction or a prohibited reversion. However, before the 2012 Highway Investment Act, the rules permitting the transfer of excess assets from a defined benefit plan to a retiree health account were set to expire on Dec. 31, 2013. (FTC 2d/FIN ¶ H-8163; USTR ¶ 4204; PCA ¶ 26,514, ¶ 60,708; PBE ¶ 420-4, ¶ ER408-4.14)

New Law. Under the 2012 Highway Investment Act, the rules allowing the transfer of excess defined benefit plan assets to retiree health accounts are extended to transfers made through Dec. 31, 2021. (Code Sec. 420(b)(5) as amended by 2012 Highway Investment Act §40241(a) (Sec. 40241(a), PL 112-141, 7/6/2012)); (ERISA §101(e)(3) as amended by 2012 Highway Investment Act §40241(b)(1)) ; (ERISA §403(c)(1) as amended by 2012 Highway Investment Act §40241(b)(1)) ; (ERISA §408(b)(13) as amended by 2012 Highway Investment Act §40241(b)(1)) ; (ERISA §408(b)(13) as amended by 2012 Highway Investment Act §40241(b)(2)) Thus, no transfers are permitted after Dec. 31, 2021. (Com Rept, see ¶ 5405)

For a new rule permitting the transfer of excess pension assets to retiree group-term life insurance accounts, see ¶ 1702.

☐ **Effective:** July 6, 2012. (2012 Highway Investment Act §40241(c))

¶ 1704. Additional 10% tax on early withdrawals from qualified retirement plans will not apply to federal phased retirement program payments

Code Sec. 72(t)(2), as amended by 2012 Highway Investment Act §100121(c)
Generally effective: July 6, 2012
Committee Reports, None

Under Code Sec. 72(t)(1), if any taxpayer takes an "early withdrawal" from a "qualified retirement plan" (as defined under Code Sec. 4974(c)), the taxpayer's income tax for the tax year in which that amount is received is increased by an amount equal to 10% of the portion of that amount which is includible in gross income. However, Code Sec. 72(t)(2) delineates a series of exemptions from this 10% additional tax. (FTC 2d/FIN ¶ H-11100, ¶ H-11102; USTR ¶ 724.22; PCA ¶ 32,203)

New Law. As part of the 2012 Highway Investment Act, the federal civil service retirement program was amended to allow for phased retirement, under which a federal agency may allow a full-time retirement eligible employee to elect to enter phased retirement status in accordance with regulations to be issued by the Office of Personnel Management (OPM). During that status, generally, the employee's work schedule is a percentage of a full-time work schedule, and the employee receives a phased retirement annuity. At full-time retirement, the phased retiree is entitled to a composite retirement annuity that also includes the portion of the employee's retirement annuity attributable to the reduced work schedule.

The 2012 Highway Investment Act provides that payments received through this program, either (1) as a phased retirement annuity (under 5 USC §8366a(a)(5) [sic, 5 USC §8336a(a)(5)] or 5 USC §8412a(a)(5)), or (2) as a composite retirement annuity (under 5 USC §8336a(a)(1) [sic, 5 USC §8366a(a)(1)] or 5 USC §8412a(a)(1)) are exempt from the 10% additional tax on early distributions. (Code Sec. 72(t)(2)(A)(viii) as amended by 2012 Highway Investment Act §100121(c)) (Sec. 100121(c), PL 112-141, 7/6/2012))

☐ **Effective:** July 6, 2012.

> **⊘ observation:** Although the exemption is effective on July 6, 2012, the phased retirement provisions themselves take effect on the effective date of the implementing regulations issued by OPM. (Sec. 100121(d), PL 112-141, 7/6/2012) Thus, for practical purposes, no phased retirement payments will be exempt from the 10% additional tax until after the effective date of the OPM regulations.

¶ 1705. Rollovers to traditional IRAs allowed for amounts received from airlines that filed for bankruptcy after Sept. 11, 2001 and before Jan. 1, 2007

Code Sec. 402, 2012 FAA Modernization Act §1106
Generally effective: For amounts paid before, on, or after Feb. 14, 2012
Committee Reports, see ¶ 5606

The Worker, Retiree, and Employer Recovery Act of 2008 (WRERA, PL 110-458, 12/23/2008) provides that certain payments received by employees of bankrupt airlines can be rolled over to Roth IRAs regardless of contribution limits. Under WRERA Sec. 125, a "qualified airline employee" (see below) who receives an "airline payment amount" (see below) can transfer any portion of that amount to a Roth IRA within 180 days of receipt of the amount. The transfer is treated as a qualified rollover contribution to the Roth IRA, and the modified AGI limits on amounts that can be annually contributed to a Roth IRA don't apply. The portion of the airline payment amount contributed to the Roth IRA is includible in gross income to the extent the payment would be includible in income were it not part of the rollover contribution.

A "qualified airline employee" is an employee or former employee of a commercial passenger airline carrier who is a participant in a defined benefit plan maintained by the carrier, where the plan:

(i) is a Code Sec. 401(a) qualified plan that included a Code Sec. 501(a) tax-exempt trust; and

(ii) was either terminated, or became subject to the restrictions on benefit accruals and benefit increases that applied in accordance with the carrier's election to use an alternative plan funding schedule under Sec. 402(b)(2) or 402(b)(3) of the 2006 Pension Protection Act (PPA, PL 109-280, 8/17/2006).

An "airline payment amount" is any payment of money or other property payable by a commercial passenger airline to a qualified airline employee, where the payment:

(1) has been approved by order of a federal bankruptcy court in a case filed after Sept. 11, 2001, and before Jan. 1, 2007; and

(2) is made for either:

(a) the qualified airline employee's interest in a bankruptcy claim against the airline carrier;

(b) any note of the carrier (or amount paid in lieu of a note being issued); or

(c) any other fixed obligation of the carrier to pay a lump-sum amount.

(FTC 2d/FIN ¶ H-12290.19B; USTR ¶ 408A4; PCA ¶ 35,220B; PBE ¶ 408A-4)

Under WRERA, no provision was made for a contribution to a traditional IRA.

New Law. The 2012 FAA Modernization Act expands the choices for recipients of "airline payment amounts" (defined below) by allowing "qualified airline employees" (defined below) to contribute airline payment amounts to a traditional IRA as well as to a Roth IRA. Further, qualified airline employees who were eligible to make a qualified rollover to a Roth IRA but declined to so do, may now roll over those amounts to a traditional IRA.

Thus, subject to an overall limit (see below), if a qualified airline employee receives any airline payment amount, and transfers any portion of that amount to a "traditional IRA" within 180 days of the payment's receipt (or, if later, within 180 days of Feb. 14, 2012, i.e. by Aug. 12, 2012), then that transferred amount is treated as a Code Sec. 402(c) rollover contribution. A qualified airline employee making this transfer may exclude from gross income the amount transferred, in the tax year in which the airline payment amount was paid to the qualified airline employee by the commercial passenger airline carrier. (2012 FAA Modernization Act §1106(a)(1) (Sec. 1106(a)(1), PL 112-95, 2/14/2012))

For this purpose, a "traditional IRA" is an individual retirement plan (as defined in Code Sec. 7701(a)(37)) that is not a "Roth IRA." (2012 FAA Modernization Act §1106(c)(3)) "Roth IRA" has the same meaning as under Code Sec. 408A(b). (2012 FAA Modernization Act §1106(c)(4))

The Act also provides that a qualified airline employee who has contributed an airline payment amount to a Roth IRA that is treated as a qualified rollover contribution under WRERA Sec. 125 (see background, above) may transfer to a traditional IRA, in a trustee-to-trustee transfer, all or any part of that contribution (together with any net income allocable to that contribution). The transfer to the traditional IRA will be deemed to have been made at the time of the rollover to the Roth IRA, if the transfer is made within 180 days of Feb. 14, 2012, i.e. by Aug. 12, 2012.

A qualified airline employee making this transfer may exclude from gross income the airline payment amount previously rolled over to the Roth IRA, to the extent an amount attributable to the previous rollover was transferred to a traditional IRA, in the tax year in which the airline payment amount was paid to the qualified airline employee by the commercial passenger airline carrier. No amount so transferred to a traditional IRA may be treated as a qualified rollover contribution with respect to a Roth IRA within the five-tax year period beginning with the tax year in which the transfer was made. (2012 FAA Modernization Act §1106(a)(2))

> *observation:* Thus, the converted amount cannot be reconverted to a Roth IRA for five years.

Overall 90% limit on amounts transferred to traditional IRAs. The aggregate amount of airline payment amounts which may be transferred to one or more traditional IRAs for any qualified employee for any tax year cannot exceed the excess (if any) of:

(i) 90% of the aggregate airline payment amounts received by the qualified airline employee during the tax year and all preceding tax years, over

(ii) the aggregate amount of transfers to which the above rules applied for all preceding tax years. (2012 FAA Modernization Act §1106(a)(4)(A))

> *observation:* Thus, a qualified employee cannot transfer more than 90% of the total airline payment amounts received, in any tax year, to a traditional IRA.

For purposes of applying the 90% limit:

(1) any airline payment amount received by the surviving spouse of any qualified employee, and any amount transferred to a traditional IRA by that spouse (see below), is treated as an amount received or transferred by the qualified employee, and

(2) any amount transferred to a traditional IRA which is attributable to net income transferred with an airline payment amount that had previously been rolled over to a Roth IRA, is not taken into account. (2012 FAA Modernization Act §1106(a)(4)(B))

observation: The term "qualified employee" is not defined under the Act. Presumably, the term "qualified employee" has the same definition as "qualified airline employee" (see below), since they seem to be used interchangeably.

Refund opportunity. A qualified airline employee who excludes an amount from gross income in an earlier tax year under the above rules may reflect the exclusion in a claim for refund filed within the period of limitation on credits or refunds under Code Sec. 6511(a) (or, if later, April 15, 2013). (2012 FAA Modernization Act §1106(a)(3))

action alert: A qualified airline employee who wishes to exclude an airline payment amount from gross income as a traditional IRA contribution must file for a refund by Apr. 15, 2013, or within the usual limitation period for refund claims, if that is later.

Surviving spouse may roll over decedent spouse's payments. Under the Act, if a qualified airline employee died after receiving an airline payment amount, or if an airline payment amount was paid to the surviving spouse of a qualified airline employee in respect of the qualified airline employee, the surviving spouse may take all actions permitted under WRERA Sec. 125 (see background, above), or under the rules described above, to the same extent that the qualified airline employee could have done had the qualified airline employee survived. (2012 FAA Modernization Act §1106(d))

observation: Thus, surviving spouses of qualified airline employees are granted the same rollover rights as qualified airline employees.

Airline executives not eligible for rollovers. The above rules do not apply to any transfer by a qualified airline employee (or any transfer authorized by a surviving spouse of the qualified airline employee) if at any time during the tax year of the transfer, or any preceding tax year, the qualified airline employee held a position described in Code Sec. 162(m)(3)(A) or (B) (describing employees whose compensation is subject to the $1 million deduction limit) with the commercial passenger airline carrier from which the airline payment amount was received. (2012 FAA Modernization Act §1106(a)(5))

Effect on employment taxes. For purposes of chapter 21 of the Code (Federal Insurance Contributions Act, FICA) and Social Security Act Sec. 209, an airline payment amount must not fail to be treated as a payment of wages by the commercial passenger airline carrier to the qualified airline employee in the tax year of payment because the amount is excluded from the qualified airline employee's gross income under the 2012 FAA Modernization Act §1106(a) rules above. (2012 FAA Modernization Act §1106(b))

> **⚫ observation:** Thus, Social Security and Medicare taxes must be paid on airline payment amounts that are rolled over to traditional IRAs. Employment taxes should have already been withheld for pre–2012 FAA Modernization Act payments that were either transferred to a Roth IRA or paid directly to the employee. Thus, under the Act, the carrier need not refund any employment taxes already paid.

"Airline payment amount" defined. "Airline payment amount" means any payment of any money or other property which is payable by a commercial passenger airline carrier to a qualified airline employee, where the payment:

(1) has been approved by an order of a federal bankruptcy court in a case filed after September 11, 2001, and before January 1, 2007; and

(2) is made for:

(a) the qualified airline employee's interest in a bankruptcy claim against the carrier;

(b) any note of the carrier (or amount paid in lieu of a note being issued); or

(c) any other fixed obligation of the carrier to pay a lump-sum amount. (2012 FAA Modernization Act §1106(c)(1)(A))

> **⚫ observation:** The definition of "airline payment amount" is the same as its definition under WRERA Sec. 125 (see background, above).

The amount of the airline payment is determined by disregarding any requirement to deduct and withhold employment taxes under Code Sec. 3102(a) and Code Sec. 3402(a). (2012 FAA Modernization Act §1106(c)(1)(A))

However, the Act provides that an airline payment amount does *not* include any amount payable on the basis of the carrier's *future* earnings or profits. (2012 FAA Modernization Act §1106(c)(1)(B))

"Qualified airline employee" defined. A "qualified airline employee" is an employee or former employee of a commercial passenger airline carrier who was a participant in a defined benefit plan maintained by the carrier, where the plan:

(i) is a Code Sec. 401(a) qualified plan that included a Code Sec. 501(a) tax-exempt trust; and

(ii) was either terminated, or became subject to the restrictions on benefit accruals and benefit increases that apply in accordance with the carrier's election to use an alternative plan funding schedule under PPA Sec. 402(b)(2) or 402(b)(3) (see background, above). (2012 FAA Modernization Act §1106(c)(2))

> **⚫ observation:** The definition of "qualified airline employee" is the same as its definition under WRERA Sec. 125 (see background, above).

☐ **Effective:** For transfers made after Feb. 14, 2012, with respect to airline payment amounts paid before, on, or after Feb. 14, 2012. (2012 FAA Modernization Act §1106(e))

¶ 1706. PBGC flat-rate premiums for single-employer defined benefit plans are increased from $35 per participant to $42 for 2013, to $49 for 2014, and indexed for inflation after 2014

ERISA § 4006(a)(3)(A)(i), as amended by 2012 Highway Investment Act §40221(a)(1)
ERISA § 4006(a)(3)(F), as amended by 2012 Highway Investment Act §40221(a)(2)
Generally effective: July 6, 2012
Committee Reports, see ¶ 5403

Defined benefit plans subject to ERISA are covered by the Pension Benefit Guaranty Corporation (PBGC) insurance program. For single-employer plans, PBGC premiums apply at a flat rate per participant for basic benefits (see below), and at a variable rate for unfunded vested benefits (see ¶ 1707). For multiemployer plans, a different flat-rate, per-participant PBGC premium applies, see ¶ 1708.

For 2012, flat-rate premiums for single-employer defined benefit plans apply at a rate of $35 per participant. This rate is based on a $30 amount (specified in ERISA §4006(a)(3)(A)(i)) that was indexed for inflation for plan years that began in post-2006 calendar years (see below). But the premium rate, as adjusted for inflation for a plan year, could not have been less than the premium rate in effect for plan years beginning in the preceding calendar year.

Under pre-2012 Highway Investment Act law, the inflation adjustment of the flat-rate premium for a plan year was the $30 amount described above, multiplied by the ratio of:

(a) the national average wage index (as defined in Social Security Act §209(k)(1)) for the first of the two calendar years preceding the calendar year in which the plan year began, to—

(b) the national average wage index for *2004*. (PCA ¶ 58,304; PBE ¶ ER4006-4.01)

New Law. Under the 2012 Highway Investment Act, the PBGC flat-rate premium for single-employer defined benefit plans will be increased—

• to $42 for each plan participant, for plan years beginning after Dec. 31, 2012 and before Jan. 1, 2014; and

- to $49 for each plan participant, for plan years beginning after Dec. 31, 2013. (ERISA §4006(a)(3)(A)(i) as amended by 2012 Highway Investment Act §40221(a)(1)) (Sec. 40221(a)(1), PL 112-141, 7/6/2012)

Inflation adjustment. The flat-rate premium described above is adjusted for inflation—but not for plan years beginning in 2013 or 2014 (for which the flat-rate premiums are increased as indicated above, without regard to inflation). (ERISA §4006(a)(3)(F) as amended by 2012 Highway Investment Act §40221(a)(2)(B))

For plan years beginning after calendar year 2014, the flat-rate premium rate will be adjusted for inflation by substituting for $49 (i.e., the amount specified in ERISA §4006(a)(3)(A)(i)), an amount determined by multiplying $49 by the ratio of:

(a) the national average wage index (as defined in Social Security Act §209(k)(1)) for the first of the two calendar years preceding the calendar year in which the plan year begins, to—

(b) the national average wage index for 2012. (ERISA §4006(a)(3)(F)(i))

The indexed amount cannot be less than the flat-rate premium rate in effect under ERISA §4006(a)(3)(A)(i) (see above) for plan years beginning in the preceding calendar year (i.e., $49, as adjusted for inflation for the preceding calendar year). (ERISA §4006(a)(3)(F)(ii))

As under pre-2012 Highway Investment Act law, if the amount determined by indexing is not a multiple of $1, then the product must be rounded to the nearest multiple of $1. (PCA ¶ 58,307 et seq.; PBE ¶ ER4006-4.01)

☐ **Effective:** July 6, 2012.

¶ 1707. PBGC variable-rate premiums for single-employer defined benefit plans are indexed for inflation after 2012 plan years; increased by $4 for 2014 and by another $5 for 2015; and capped at $400 per participant, as indexed for inflation

ERISA § 4006(a)(3)(E)(ii), as amended by 2012 Highway Investment Act §40221(b)(1)
ERISA § 4006(a)(8), as amended by 2012 Highway Investment Act §40221(b)(2)
ERISA § 4006(a)(3)(E)(i), as amended by 2012 Highway Investment Act §40221(b)(3)(A)
ERISA § 4006(a)(3)(J), as amended by 2012 Highway Investment Act §40221(b)(3)(B)
Generally effective: July 6, 2012
Committee Reports, see ¶ 5403

Defined benefit plans subject to ERISA are covered by the Pension Benefit Guaranty Corporation (PBGC) insurance program. For single-employer plans, PBGC premiums apply at a flat rate per participant for basic benefits (see ¶ 1706), and at a variable rate for unfunded vested benefits (see below). For multiemployer plans, a flat-rate, per-participant PBGC premium applies, see ¶ 1708.

For 2012, variable-rate premiums for single-employer defined benefit plans apply at a rate of $9 per $1,000 of unfunded vested benefits, divided by the number of participants in the plan as of the close of the preceding plan year. Variable-rate premiums for 2012 are not indexed for inflation. (PCA ¶ 58,305; PBE ¶ ER4006-4.01)

For purposes of determining variable-rate premiums, "unfunded vested benefits" are the excess (if any) of: (1) the plan's funding target for the year, determined under the minimum funding rules, but taking into account only vested benefits, over (2) the fair market value of plan assets. In determining the plan's funding target for this purpose, the interest rates used are segment rates determined as they are under the minimum funding rules, but determined on a monthly basis, rather than using a 24-month average of corporate bond rates. (PCA ¶ 58,307 et seq.; PBE ¶ ER4006-4.01)

New Law. Under the 2012 Highway Investment Act, the variable-rate premium for single-employer defined benefit plans is based on "the applicable dollar amount" (as determined under ERISA §4006(a)(8), see below). (ERISA §4006(a)(3)(E)(ii) as amended by 2012 Highway Investment Act §40221(b)(1)) (Sec. 40221(b)(1), PL 112-141, 7/6/2012)

⚡ *observation:* Thus, under the Act, for any plan year, the variable-rate premium for single-employer defined benefit plans is:

(1) the "applicable dollar amount" for each $1,000 of unfunded vested benefits under the plan as of the close of the preceding plan year, divided by—

(2) the number of participants in the plan as of the close of the preceding plan year.

For the cap of $400 on the per-participant amount of the variable-rate premium, and the indexing of the cap for inflation after 2013, see below.

Applicable dollar amount.   To determine the "applicable dollar amount," the 2012 Highway Investment Act—

• begins with $9 (the same amount as under pre-Act law); (ERISA §4006(a)(8)(A)(i))

• requires an inflation adjustment of the $9 for plan years beginning after 2012 (see below); (ERISA §4006(a)(8)(B)) ;

• for plan years beginning in 2014 and 2015, increases the amount of the preceding year's amount, after making the inflation adjustment for the year, by $4 for plan years beginning in 2014, and by another $5 for plan years beginning in 2015 (see below); and (ERISA §4006(a)(8)(C))

• requires an inflation adjustment of the amounts described in ERISA §4006(a)(8)(A) (described above) for ensuing years. (ERISA §4006(a)(8)(B))

⚡ *observation:* Thus, ERISA §4006(a)(8)(A) provides that $9 is the applicable dollar amount, subject to (i) an inflation adjustment (under ERISA §4006(a)(8)(B)) and (ii) additions for 2014 and 2015 (under ERISA §4006(a)(8)(C)). For plan years beginning after 2012, inflation adjustments for preceding year amounts must be made to determine the amounts under ERISA §4006(a)(8)(A)—which are in turn subject to an inflation adjustment (under ERISA §4006(a)(8)(B)).

2013 and 2014 plan years.   The "applicable dollar amount" is $9 for plan years beginning before 2015—as adjusted for inflation after 2012 plan years, and increased for the 2014 plan year (see below). (ERISA §4006(a)(8)(A)(i) as amended by 2012 Highway Investment Act §40221(b)(2))

⚡ *observation:* For plan years that begin in 2013, the applicable dollar amount is $9, subject to an inflation adjustment (see below).

For plan years that begin in 2014 (i) the $9 applicable dollar amount must be adjusted for inflation, and then (ii) an additional $4 must be added (*after* the inflation adjustment, see below).

2015 plan years and later. For plan years beginning *in* calendar year 2015, the applicable dollar amount is the amount in effect for plan years beginning in 2014, determined after the ERISA §4006(a)(8)(C) increases (described below). (ERISA §4006(a)(8)(A)(ii))

> **observation:** Thus, for plan years beginning in calendar year 2015, the applicable dollar amount is: (i) the applicable dollar amount for plan years beginning in 2014 (which includes the $4 addition, see above), as adjusted for inflation, and (ii) with the addition of $5 (see below).

For plan years beginning *after* calendar year 2015, the applicable dollar amount is the amount in effect for plan years beginning in 2015, determined after the ERISA §4006(a)(8)(C) increases (described below). (ERISA §4006(a)(8)(A)(iii))

> **observation:** Thus, for plan years beginning after calendar year 2015, the applicable dollar amount is the amount for plan years beginning in 2015 (which includes the $4 and the $5 additions, as adjusted for inflation for the preceding year, see above), adjusted for inflation.

Inflation adjustment. For each plan year beginning after 2012, the amount in ERISA §4006(a)(8)(A) (as described above) must be adjusted for inflation. This is done by substituting for that amount, the greater of: (i) the amount in ERISA §4006(a)(8)(A), as indexed for inflation (see below), and (ii) the applicable dollar amount in effect for plan years beginning in the preceding year. (ERISA §4006(a)(8)(B))

The inflation adjustment (item (i), above) is determined by multiplying the amount under ERISA §4006(a)(8)(A) (see above) for plan years beginning in that calendar year, by the ratio of:

(a) the national average wage index (as defined in Social Security Act §209(k)(1)) for the first of the two calendar years preceding the calendar year in which the plan year begins, to—

(b) the national average wage index for the "base year." (ERISA §4006(a)(8)(B)(i))

For purposes of the inflation adjustment, the "base year" (see item (b), above) is:

- 2010, for plan years beginning in calendar year 2013 or 2014;

- 2012, for plan years beginning in calendar year 2015; and

- 2013, for plan years beginning after calendar year 2015. (ERISA §4006(a)(8)(D))

If the amount determined by indexing is not a multiple of $1, then the product must be rounded to the nearest multiple of $1. (ERISA §4006(a)(8)(B))

✔ observation: For plan years beginning after 2012, inflation adjustments for preceding year amounts must be made to determine the amounts under ERISA §4006(a)(8)(A), which—after the additions required for 2014 and 2015 under ERISA §4006(a)(8)(C)—are in turn subject to an inflation adjustment (under ERISA §4006(a)(8)(B)).

For which amounts must be adjusted for inflation, see above.

Additional increases in 2014 and 2015. The applicable dollar amount, *after* application of the adjustment for inflation (see above), must be increased:

(i) by $4, for plan years beginning in calendar year 2014; and

(ii) by another $5, for plan years beginning in calendar year 2015. (ERISA §4006(a)(8)(C)) ; (Com Rept, see ¶ 5403)

These increases are applied to the rate applicable for the *preceding* year (that is, $9 per $1,000 of unfunded vested benefits as of the close of the preceding plan year), as indexed for inflation for the preceding year. (Com Rept, see ¶ 5403)

For the application of the additions to the applicable dollar amount for plan years that begin in calendar years 2013, 2014, 2015, and after 2015, see above.

Cap on per-participant amount of variable-rate premium. The variable-rate premium is determined by dividing the amount determined above (i.e., the applicable dollar amount, as adjusted for inflation, and with the additions described above) by the number of participants in the plan as of the close of the preceding plan year. (ERISA §4006(a)(3)(E)(i)(I) as amended by 2012 Highway Investment Act §40221(b)(3))

For plan years beginning in a calendar year after 2012, the per-participant variable-rate premium (as described above) will not exceed $400. (ERISA §4006(a)(3)(E)(i)(II))

Inflation adjustment of the premium cap. For each plan year beginning in a calendar year after 2013, the $400 cap on the per-participant variable-rate premium must be adjusted for inflation. This is done by substituting for the $400 cap, the greater of: (i) the $400 cap amount, as indexed for inflation (see below), and (ii) the cap amount in effect for the preceding year. (ERISA §4006(a)(3)(J) as amended by 2012 Highway Investment Act §40221(b)(3)(B))

The inflation adjustment (item (i), above) is determined by multiplying the $400 cap by the ratio of:

(a) the national average wage index (as defined in Social Security Act §209(k)(1)) for the first of the two calendar years preceding the calendar year in which the plan year begins, to—

(b) the national average wage index for 2011. (ERISA §4006(a)(3)(J)(i))

If the amount determined by indexing is not a multiple of $1, then the product must be rounded to the nearest multiple of $1. (ERISA §4006(a)(3)(J))

☐ **Effective:** July 6, 2012.

¶ 1708. PBGC premium rates for multiemployer defined benefit plans are raised from $9 per participant to $12 after 2012, indexed for inflation for post-2013 plan years

ERISA § 4006(a)(3)(A)(iv), as amended by 2012 Highway Investment Act §40222(a)(1)

ERISA § 4006(a)(3)(A)(v), as amended by 2012 Highway Investment Act §40222(a)(4)

ERISA § 4006(a)(3)(I), as amended by 2012 Highway Investment Act §40222(b)

Generally effective: July 6, 2012

Committee Reports, see ¶ 5403

For 2012, flat-rate premiums for multiemployer defined benefit plans apply at a rate of $9.00 per participant. Multiemployer flat-rate premium rates are indexed for inflation. (PCA ¶ 58,335; PBE ¶ ER4006-4.02)

PBGC flat-rate premiums for multiemployer are expected to increase to $10 for 2013. (Com Rept, see ¶ 5403)

New Law. For plan years beginning after Dec. 31, 2012, the 2012 Highway Investment Act increases the PBGC flat-rate premium for multiemployer defined benefit plans to $12 for each individual who is a plan participant during the applicable plan year. (ERISA §4006(a)(3)(A)(v) as amended by 2012 Highway Investment Act §40222(a)(4)) (Sec. 40222(a)(4), PL 112-141, 7/6/2012)

Inflation adjustment. For each plan year beginning in a calendar year after 2013, the multiemployer flat-rate premium rate will be adjusted for inflation by substituting for $12 (i.e., the premium rate specified in ERISA §4006(a)(3)(A)(v)), an amount determined by multiplying $12 by the ratio of:

(a) the national average wage index (as defined in Social Security Act §209(k)(1)) for the first of the two calendar years preceding the calendar year in which the plan year begins, to—

(b) the national average wage index for 2011. (ERISA §4006(a)(3)(I) as amended by 2012 Highway Investment Act §40222(b))

> *observation:* Thus, for plan years beginning in 2013, the multiemployer plan premium is $12, and will *not* be adjusted for inflation.

The indexed amount cannot be less than the premium rate in effect under ERISA §4006(a)(3)(A)(v) (see above) for plan years beginning in the preceding calendar year (i.e., $12, as adjusted for inflation for the preceding calendar year). (ERISA §4006(a)(3)(I)(ii))

If the amount determined by indexing is not a multiple of $1, then the product must be rounded to the nearest multiple of $1. (ERISA §4006(a)(3)(I))

☐ **Effective:** July 6, 2012.

¶ 1709. ERISA Adds Rules Governing PBGC Board of Directors' Meetings, Actions, and Minutes of Meetings

ERISA § 4002(d)(2), as amended by 2012 Highway Investment Act §40231(a)(1)
ERISA § 4002(d)(3), as amended by 2012 Highway Investment Act §40231(a)(1)
ERISA § 4002(e)(1), as amended by 2012 Highway Investment Act §40231(a)(2)(B)
ERISA § 4002(e)(2), as amended by 2012 Highway Investment Act §40231(a)(2)(C)
ERISA § 4002(h)(3), as amended by 2012 Highway Investment Act §40231(a)(3)(B)
Generally effective: July 6, 2012
Committee Reports, see ¶ 5404

The Pension Benefit Guaranty Corporation (PBGC) was established under Title IV of ERISA to administer the plan termination insurance program. The PBGC Board of Directors, consisting of the Secretary of Labor, the Secretary of the Treasury, and the Secretary of Commerce, is responsible for establishing and overseeing PBGC's policies. The Board may delegate some (but not all) of its powers to the PBGC Director, whose job it is to administer PBGC, and carry out PBGC's functions in accordance with PBGC's policies.

The Board of Directors takes action at meetings. Before the 2012 Highway Investment Act, regular meetings of the Board of Directors were held as often as required to provide appropriate oversight and guidance to PBGC, but ERISA did not provide a required minimum number of meetings of the Board of Directors each year. A majority of the members of the Board of Directors constituted a quorum, and any act of the majority present at any meeting at which a quorum was present was an act of the Board. But ERISA did not specify the requirements for an act of the Board of Directors, or the requirements for a quorum.

Before the Act, ERISA did not require the Board to meet jointly with the PBGC Advisory Committee.

As under current law, the PBGC General Counsel must act as secretary to the Board of Directors and keep its minutes. But before the Act, there was no requirement to make the minutes available to the public. (PCA ¶ 58,106, ¶ 58,107, ¶ 58,107.1; PBE ¶ ER4002-4)

New Law. The 2012 Highway Investment Act amends ERISA to add rules governing how the PBGC Board of Directors accomplishes its purposes, including rules for taking action, the frequency of Board meetings, and requirements for making the minutes for Board meetings available to the public.

Board actions. Under the Act, ERISA provides that a vote of the majority of the members of the Board of Directors who are present and voting at a meeting at which a quorum is present, is an act of the Board of Directors. (ERISA §4002(d)(2) as amended by 2012 Highway Investment Act §40231(a)(1)(B)) (Sec. 40231(a)(1)(B), PL 112-141, 7/6/2012)

Quorum. Under the Act, a majority of the members of the Board of Directors in office is a quorum for the transaction of business. (ERISA §4002(d)(2))

Voting representatives. Under the Act, each member of the Board of Directors must designate, in writing, an official (not below the level of Assistant Secretary) to serve as the Board member's voting representative. The designation is effective until revoked, or until a date or event specified in the designation. (ERISA §4002(d)(3))

Any voting representative may refer, for Board action, any matter under consideration by the designating Board member. However, a Board member's voting representative (see below) does *not* count towards establishing a quorum. (ERISA §4002(d)(3))

Number of Board meetings. Under the Act, the Board of Directors must meet no less than four times a year, with at least two members present. (ERISA §4002(e)(1) as amended by 2012 Highway Investment Act §40231(a)(2)(B)) At least one meeting during each year must be a joint meeting with the PBGC Advisory Committee. (ERISA §4002(e)(1)) ; (ERISA §4002(h)(3) as amended by 2012 Highway Investment Act §40231(a)(3)(B))

Minutes of Board meetings. Under the Act, the chairman of the Board of Directors must make available to the public the minutes from each meeting of the Board of Directors. (ERISA §4002(e)(2)(A) as amended by 2012 Highway Investment Act §40231(a)(2)(C))

However, the minutes of a meeting of the Board of Directors, or a portion of such a meeting, must not be subject to disclosure to the public if the chairman reasonably determines that the minutes, or a portion of the minutes, contain confidential employer information, including information obtained under ERISA

§4010, information about PBGC's investment activities, or information concerning PBGC's personnel decisions. (ERISA §4002(e)(2)(B))

The minutes of a meeting, or a portion of the minutes, that are exempt from disclosure under the rules above, are exempt from disclosure under 5 USCA §552(b). For purposes of §552, ERISA §4002(e)(2)(C) is considered a statute described in 5 USCA §552(b)(3). (ERISA §4002(e)(2)(C))

☐ **Effective:** July 6, 2012.

¶ 1710. Conflict of interest rules established for PBGC Director and Board of Directors

ERISA § 4002(j), as amended by 2012 Highway Investment Act §40231(b)
Generally effective: July 6, 2012
Committee Reports, see ¶ 5404

Any member of the PBGC Board of Directors *may* disqualify himself from participation in a Board action on any matter, if the Board member has, or may appear to have, a conflict of interest. The Board member must notify the other members of the Board of a disqualification. The disqualified Board member's representative, acting independently from the disqualified member, may vote on the matter in the member's place. However, the disqualified Board member need not, and may not, ratify any action taken on the matter giving rise to his disqualification.

Before the 2012 Highway Investment Act, there was no ERISA requirement that a Board member or the PBGC Director disqualify himself because of a conflict of interest. (PCA ¶ 58,107.1; PBE ¶ ER4002-4)

New Law. Under the 2012 Highway Investment Act, the PBGC Director, and each member of the PBGC Board of Directors, is prohibited from participating in a PBGC decision in which the Director or the Board member has a direct financial interest. Also, the Director must not participate in any activities that would present a conflict of interest, or the appearance of a conflict of interest, without approval of the Board of Directors. (ERISA §4002(j)(1) as amended by 2012 Highway Investment Act §40231(b)) (Sec. 40231(b), PL 112-141, 7/6/2012)

The Board of Directors is required to establish a policy that will help identify potential conflict of interests of the members of the Board of Directors, and mitigate the perceived conflicts of interest of the members of the Board and the Director. (ERISA §4002(j)(2))

☐ **Effective:** July 6, 2012.

¶ 1711. Responsibilities of PBGC Inspector General and General Counsel, and the independence of each office, are established in ERISA

ERISA § 4002(d)(4), as amended by 2012 Highway Investment Act §40231(a)(1)

ERISA § 4002(d)(5), as amended by 2012 Highway Investment Act §40231(a)(1)

ERISA § 4002(d)(6), as amended by 2012 Highway Investment Act §40231(a)(1)

Generally effective: July 6, 2012

Committee Reports, see ¶ 5404

Before the 2012 Highway Investment Act, ERISA did not provide any description of the responsibilities of the office of PBGC General Counsel or PBGC Inspector General. Also, ERISA did not address the question of whether the General Counsel had authority over the Office of Inspector General.

New Law. Under the Act, ERISA describes some of the responsibilities of the PBGC Inspector General and the PBGC General Counsel.

Specifically, under the Act, ERISA provides that the PBGC Inspector General must—

• report to the PBGC Board of Directors;

• not less than twice a year, attend a meeting of the Board of Directors to provide a report on the activities, and findings, of the Inspector General, including with respect to monitoring a review of PBGC's operations. (ERISA §4002(d)(4) as amended by 2012 Highway Investment Act §40231(a)(1)) (Sec. 40231(a)(1), PL 112-141, 7/6/2012)

Under the Act, the PBGC General Counsel—

• serves as the secretary to the Board of Directors;

• advises the Board of Directors, as needed; and

• has overall responsibility for all legal matters affecting PBGC, and provides PBGC with legal advice and opinions on all matters of law affecting PBGC. (ERISA §4002(d)(5))

The authority of the General Counsel does *not* extend to the Office of Inspector General or the independent legal counsel of the Office of Inspector General. (ERISA §4002(d)(5)) Instead, the Office of Inspector General and its legal counsel are independent of management of PBGC and the PBGC General Counsel. (ERISA §4002(d)(6))

☐ **Effective:** July 6, 2012.

¶ 1712. ERISA is amended to establish: the position of PBGC Risk Management Officer, the term and accountability of the PBGC Director, and the PBGC Board of Directors' hiring responsibilities

ERISA § 4002(d)(7), as amended by 2012 Highway Investment Act §40231(a)(1)
ERISA § 4002(k), as amended by 2012 Highway Investment Act §40231(c)
ERISA § 4002(c), as amended by 2012 Highway Investment Act §40231(d)
Generally effective: July 6, 2012
Committee Reports, see ¶ 5404

Before the 2012 Highway Investment Act, ERISA did not address the responsibilities of the PBGC Board of Directors in hiring employees to enable the Board to perform its duties. Nor did ERISA specify the term of the PBGC Director. Also, the office of Risk Management Officer did not exist.

New Law. The 2012 Highway Investment Act amends ERISA to provide for a risk management officer, establish a set term for the PBGC Director, and provide rules for the Board of Directors in hiring employees.

Risk management officer. Specifically, under the Act, the position of "Risk Management Officer" is established within PBGC to—

• evaluate and mitigate the risk that PBGC might experience;

• coordinate PBGC's risk management efforts;

• explain risks and controls to senior management and the PBGC Board of Directors; and

• make recommendations. (ERISA §4002(k) as amended by 2012 Highway Investment Act §40231(c)) (Sec. 40231(c), PL 112-141, 7/6/2012)

PBGC Director's term. Under the Act, the PBGC Director is accountable to the PBGC Board of Directors. The Director serves for a term of five years, unless removed by the U.S. President or the PBGC Board of Directors before the expiration of the five-year term. (ERISA §4002(c) as amended by 2012 Highway Investment Act §40231(d))

Setting terms for employees. Under the Act, to enable the PBGC Board of Directors to perform its duties, the Board may appoint and fix the compensation of employees. The Board must determine the qualifications a duties of the employees, and may fix the compensation of experts and consultants, in accordance with the provisions of 5 USCA §3109. (ERISA §4002(d)(7) as amended by 2012 Highway Investment Act §40231(a)(1))

☐ **Effective:** July 6, 2012.

¶ 1713. PBGC must establish "Participant and Plan Sponsor Advocate" position

ERISA § 4002(h)(1), as amended by 2012 Highway Investment Act §40232(b)
ERISA § 4004, as added by 2012 Highway Investment Act §40232(a)
Generally effective: July 6, 2012
Committee Reports, see ¶ *5404*

Under ERISA §4002(h), an advisory committee was created to advise the Pension Benefit Guaranty Corporation (PBGC) and make recommendations concerning (a) the appointment of trustees in termination proceedings; (b) investment of monies; (c) whether or not plans that have been terminated or are being terminated should be liquidated immediately or continued in operation under a trustee; and (d) any other issues that PBGC raises. (PCA ¶ 58,108; PBE ¶ ER4002-4)

New Law. The 2012 Highway Investment Act creates a new position within PBGC—the "Participant and Plan Sponsor Advocate." The PBGC Advisory Committee is charged with nominating—in consultation with the PBGC Director and participant and plan sponsor advocacy groups—at least two, but no more than three individuals, to serve as the Advocate initially (Com Rept, see ¶ 5404), and in the event of a vacancy or impending vacancy in the office. (ERISA §4002(h)(1) as amended by 2012 Highway Investment Act §40232(b)) (PL 112-141, 7/6/2012) The PBGC's board of directors must select the Advocate from that list of candidates, without regard to the USC Title 5 provisions relating to appointments in the competitive service or Senior Executive Service. (ERISA §4004(a) as added by 2012 Highway Investment Act §40232(a)) (PL 112-141, 7/6/2012)

> *observation:* Although ERISA §4002(h)(1) (above) only refers to the Advisory Committee making *nominations* in the event of a vacancy or impending vacancy in the office, the committee report makes no similar restriction, thus indicating that the first Advocate should also be appointed after being nominated by the advisory committee.

> *observation:* Congress has set no deadline either for the Advisory Committee to nominate candidates for the Advocate position, nor for PBGC to name an individual as the Advocate.

The duties of the Participant and Plan Sponsor Advocate are to:

(1) act as a liaison between PBGC, sponsors of defined benefit pension plans insured by PBGC, and participants in pension plans trusteed by PBGC;

(2) advocate for the full attainment of the rights of participants in plans trusteed by PBGC;

(3) assist pension plan sponsors and participants in resolving disputes with PBGC;

(4) identify areas in which participants and plan sponsors have persistent problems in dealings with PBGC;

(5) to the extent possible, propose changes in PBGC's administrative practices to mitigate problems;

(6) identify potential legislative changes which may be appropriate to mitigate problems; and

(7) refer instances of fraud, waste, and abuse, and violations of law to PBGC's Office of the Inspector General. (ERISA §4004(b))

If the Advocate is removed from office or is transferred to another position or location within PBGC or the Department of Labor, PBGC's board of directors must communicate in writing the reasons for any such removal or transfer to Congress not less than 30 days before the removal or transfer. However, this requirement does not prohibit a personnel action otherwise authorized by law, other than transfer or removal. (ERISA §4004(c))

The annual rate of basic pay for the Advocate must be the same rate as the highest rate of basic pay established for the Senior Executive Service under 5 USC §5382, or, if PBGC's board of directors so determines, at a rate fixed under 5 USC §9503. (ERISA §4004(d))

Advocate's annual report. In addition to the duties outlined above, not later than December 31 of each calendar year, the Advocate must submit to Congress a report of the activities of the Office of the Advocate during the fiscal year ending in that calendar year. The congressional committees that are to receive the annual report are the Senate Health, Education, Labor, and Pensions Committee; the Senate Finance Committee; the House Committee on Education and the Workforce; and the House Ways and Means Committee. (ERISA §4004(e)(1))

Each annual report must:

(a) summarize the assistance requests received from participants and plan sponsors; and describe the activities, and evaluate the effectiveness, of the Advocate during the preceding year;

(b) identify significant problems the Advocate has identified;

(c) include specific legislative and regulatory changes to address the problems; and

(d) identify any actions taken to correct problems identified in any previous report. (ERISA §4004(e)(2))

The Advocate must submit a copy of each annual report to the Secretary of Labor, the PBGC Director, and "any other appropriate official," at the same time the report is submitted to the congressional committees. (ERISA §4004(e)(3))

☐ **Effective:** July 6, 2012

¶ 1714. PBGC must adopt specified quality control procedures

ERISA § None,2012 Highway Investment Act §40233
Generally effective: July 6, 2012
Committee Reports, see ¶ 5404

Under ERISA §4002, the Pension Benefit Guaranty Corporation (PBGC) was established to encourage the continuation and maintenance of voluntary private pension plans for the benefit of participants; provide for the timely and uninterrupted payment of pension benefits to participants and beneficiaries of covered plans; and maintain plan termination insurance premiums established by PBGC at the lowest level consistent with PBGC's obligations. (PCA ¶ 58,101; PBE ¶ ER4002-4)

New Law. As part of the 2012 Highway Investment Act, PBGC is responsible for adopting certain measures to improve quality control. Specifically:

(1) PBGC must contract with a capable agency or organization—an entity independent from PBGC, such as the Social Security Administration—to conduct an annual peer review of PBGC's Single-Employer Pension Insurance Modeling System and PBGC's Multiemployer Pension Insurance Modeling System. PBGC's board of directors must designate the agency or organization with which any such contract is entered into, and the first annual peer reviews must be initiated no later than October 6, 2012. (2012 Highway Investment Act §40233(a))

(2) PBGC must develop written quality review policies and procedures for all modeling and actuarial work performed by PBGC's Policy, Research, and Analysis Department. PBGC must also conduct a record management review of that department to determine what records must be retained as federal records. (2012 Highway Investment Act §40233(b))

(3) Not later than September 6, 2012, PBGC must submit to Congress a report, approved by PBGC's board of directors, setting forth a timetable for addressing the outstanding recommendations of the Office of the Inspector General relating to PBGC's Policy, Research, and Analysis Department, and PBGC's Benefits Administration and Payment Department. (2012 Highway Investment Act §40233(c))

☐ **Effective:** July 6, 2012

¶ 1715. PBGC's authority to borrow up to $100 million from the U.S. Treasury is repealed

ERISA § 4005(c), as amended by 2012 Highway Investment Act §40234(a)
Generally effective: July 6, 2012
Committee Reports, see ¶ 5404

Before the 2012 Highway Investment Act, PBGC had authority under ERISA to issue notes or other obligations to the U.S. Treasury for purposes of borrowing up to $100 million. (PCA ¶ 58,112; PBE ¶ ER4005-4)

New Law. The 2012 Highway Investment Act repeals PBGC's authority to issue notes and other obligations to the U.S. Treasury in order to borrow up to $100 million. (ERISA §4005(c) as amended by 2012 Highway Investment Act §40234(a)) (Sec. 40234(a), PL 112-141, 7/6/2012)

> *observation:* The termination of PBGC's borrowing authority means that PBGC no longer has a line of credit from which to borrow funds, and that it would likely have to seek congressional approval for any future loan, should the need arise.

☐ **Effective:** July 6, 2012.

¶ 1800. Excise Provisions from Earlier Acts of the 112th Congress

¶ 1801. Reduction of various fuel excise tax rates is delayed until after Sept. 30, 2016

Code Sec. 4041(a)(1)(C)(iii)(I), as amended by 2012 Highway Investment Act §40102(a)(1)(A)

Code Sec. 4041(m)(1)(A), as amended by 2012 Highway Investment Act §40102(a)(2)(A)

Code Sec. 4041(m)(1)(B), as amended by 2012 Highway Investment Act §40102(a)(1)(B)

Code Sec. 4081(d)(1), as amended by 2012 Highway Investment Act §40102(a)(1)(C)

Generally effective: July 1, 2012

Committee Reports, see ¶ 5401

Under pre-2012 Highway Investment Act law, the following reductions in excise fuel tax rates were scheduled to take effect after July 6, 2012 (as extended several times, including by the 2011 Transportation Extension Act, Sec. 142, PL 112-30, 9/16/2011, the 2012 Surface Transportation Extension Act, Sec. 402, PL 112-102, 3/30/2012, and the 2012 Temporary Surface Transportation Extension Act, Sec. 402, PL 112-140, 6/29/2012):

. . . the 18.3¢ per gallon taxes on (i) removal at the terminal or refinery, etc. of gasoline (other than aviation gasoline) (FTC 2d ¶ W-1501; USTR Excise Taxes ¶ 40,814), and (ii) retail sale for use, or use before sale, of a liquid alternative fuel, other than liquefied natural gas (LNG), any liquid fuel (other than ethanol and methanol) derived from coal (including peat), and liquid fuel derived from biomass, as a fuel for a motor vehicle or motorboat—to 4.3¢ per gallon (FTC 2d ¶ W-1711; USTR Excise Taxes ¶ 40,414);

. . . the 24.3¢ per gallon taxes on (i) removal at the terminal of diesel fuel and kerosene (FTC 2d ¶ W-1501.1; USTR Excise Taxes ¶ 40,814), and (ii) retail sale, or use before sale, of diesel fuel, kerosene, or other fuels (other than gasoline) for use in a diesel-powered highway motor vehicle—to 4.3¢ per gallon (FTC 2d ¶ W-1707; USTR Excise Taxes ¶ 40,414);

FTC 2d References are to Federal Tax Coordinator 2d
FIN References are to RIA's Analysis of Federal Taxes: Income (print)
USTR References are to United States Tax Reporter: Income
PCA References are to Pension Analysis (print and electronic)
PBE References are to Pension & Benefits Explanations
BCA References are to Benefits Analysis (electronic)
BC References are to Benefits Coordinator (print)
EP References are to Estate Planning Analysis (print and electronic)

. . . the 7.3¢ per gallon tax on the retail sale, or use before sale, of diesel fuel or kerosene for use in certain transit-type buses—to 4.3¢ per gallon (FTC 2d ¶ W-1707; USTR Excise Taxes ¶ 40,414);

. . . the 9.15¢ per gallon tax on the retail sale, or use before sale, of partially exempt methanol fuel—to 2.15¢ per gallon (FTC 2d ¶ W-1726; USTR Excise Taxes ¶ 40,414); and

. . . the 11.3¢ per gallon tax on the retail sale, or use before sale, of partially exempt ethanol fuel—to 4.3¢ per gallon (FTC 2d ¶ W-1726; USTR Excise Taxes ¶ 40,414).

New Law. The 2012 Highway Investment Act delays the rate reductions described above until after Sept. 30, 2016. (Code Sec. 4041(a)(1)(C)(iii)(I) as amended by 2012 Highway Investment Act §40102(a)(1)(A) (PL 112-141, 7/6/ 2012); Code Sec. 4041(m)(1)(A) as amended by 2012 Highway Investment Act §40102(a)(2)(A); Code Sec. 4041(m)(1)(B) as amended by 2012 Highway Investment Act §40102(a)(1)(B); Code Sec. 4081(d)(1) as amended by 2012 Highway Investment Act §40102(a)(1)(C)) That is, the current (higher) rates are extended through Sept. 30, 2016. (Com Rept, see ¶ 5401)

> *illustration (1):* Among the rate extensions, the removal-at-terminal, etc. excise tax on (other-than-aviation) gasoline will be imposed at the rate of 18.3¢ per gallon through Sept. 30, 2016, and at the reduced 4.3¢ per gallon thereafter.

> *observation:* All of the fuels listed above, other than LNG, are also subject to an additional 0.1¢-per-gallon tax that funds the Leaking Underground Storage Tank Trust Fund ("LUST" tax) (see FTC 2d ¶s W-1501, W-1501.1, W-1707, W-1711, W-1726; USTR Excise Taxes ¶s 40,414, 40,814), which also applies (as extended by the 2012 Highway Investment Act, see ¶ 1802) through Sept. 30, 2016.

> *illustration (2):* The above-described gasoline (other than aviation gasoline), for which the 18.3¢ per gallon removal-at-terminal, etc. excise tax is extended through Sept. 30, 2016, will be subject to a *total* federal excise tax of 18.4¢ per gallon through Sept. 30, 2016 (i.e., the 18.3¢ per gallon removal-at-terminal tax, plus the 0.1¢ per gallon LUST tax), and 4.3¢ per gallon (i.e., the reduced removal-at-terminal tax only) thereafter.

> *observation:* A credit or refund is available for floor stocks of taxable fuel (taxed at the full removal-at-terminal tax rates above) held for resale by dealers on Oct. 1, 2016 (the date as of which the above-described tax reduction applies), see ¶ 1804.

☐ **Effective:** July 1, 2012. (2012 Highway Investment Act §40102(f))

> **☯ observation:** The wording of 2012 Highway Investment Act §40102(a) above, extending the various above rates (as well as the LUST tax, see ¶ 1802) through Sept. 30, 2016, doesn't reflect the intervening six-day extension of the taxes (from July 1 through July 6, 2012) under the 2012 Temporary Surface Transportation Extension Act, Sec. 402(a), PL 112-140, 6/29/2012, which was passed as a stop-gap to keep the rates from expiring as enactment of the longer 2012 Highway Investment Act extension was in process. Both of these extensions (the temporary and the long-term) were made effective July 1, 2012 (see Sec. 402(f)(1), PL 112-140, 6/29/2012, and 2012 Highway Investment Act §40102(f), above)), and Congress may need to make a technical correction clarifying the timing of the changes.

¶ 1802. Leaking Underground Storage Tank (LUST) Trust Fund 0.1¢-per-gallon tax is extended through Sept. 30, 2016

Code Sec. 4081(d)(3), as amended by 2012 Highway Investment Act §40102(a)(2)(D)
Generally effective: July 1, 2012
Committee Reports, see ¶ 5401

Gasoline, diesel fuel, and kerosene are subject to a 0.1¢-per-gallon excise tax upon the following events: removal from a terminal or refinery; entry into the U.S.; and sale to any person who isn't properly registered (unless there was an earlier taxable removal or entry of the fuel). The 0.1¢-per-gallon tax (which applies in addition to the regular Code Sec. 4081 removal-at-terminal tax rates) is deposited in the Leaking Underground Storage Tank Trust Fund, and is commonly referred to as the "LUSTTF rate" or the "LUST tax." (FTC 2d ¶ W-1501, ¶ W-1501.1; USTR Excise Taxes ¶ 40,814)

And, a 0.1¢-per-gallon "additional" retail tax applies in addition to the retail-level excise taxes imposed under Code Sec. 4041 on: (i) diesel fuel, kerosene, and other fuels (other than gasoline) sold for use, or used, in diesel-powered highway motor vehicles: (ii) liquid alternative fuels (other than liquefied petroleum gas [LPG] and liquefied natural gas [LNG]) sold for use, or used in, motor vehicles or motor boats; and (iii) kerosene used in aviation where no earlier Code Sec. 4081 removal-at-terminal tax was imposed on the fuel. This additional retail tax is only in effect while the LUST tax remains in effect under the Code Sec. 4081 removal-at-terminal tax rules. (FTC 2d ¶ W-3201; USTR Excise Taxes ¶ 40,424)

Further, a LUST tax applies in addition to the Code Sec. 4042 retail tax on fuels used in vessels used on inland waterways. Like the above-described additional retail tax, this retail LUST tax is only in effect while the LUST tax remains in effect under the Code Sec. 4081 removal-at-terminal tax rules. (FTC 2d ¶ W-3201; USTR Excise Taxes ¶ 40,424)

Under pre-2012 Highway Investment Act law, the LUST tax imposed under Code Sec. 4081 (and so the additional retail tax under Code Sec. 4041, and the retail LUST tax under Code Sec. 4042 tied to that tax) was scheduled to expire after July 6, 2012 (as extended several times, including by the 2011 Transportation Extension Act, Sec. 142, PL 112-30, 9/16/2011, the 2012 Surface Transportation Extension Act, Sec. 402, PL 112-102, 3/30/2012, and the 2012 Temporary Surface Transportation Extension Act, Sec. 402, PL 112-140, 6/29/2012). (FTC 2d ¶ W-1501, ¶ W-1501.1, ¶ W-1720; USTR Excise Taxes ¶ 40,414, ¶ 40,814)

New Law. The 2012 Highway Investment Act extends the 0.1¢-per-gallon LUST tax imposed under the Code Sec. 4081 removal-at-terminal tax rules to apply through Sept. 30, 2016. (Code Sec. 4081(d)(3) as amended by 2012 Highway Investment Act §40102(a)(2)(D) (PL 112-141, 7/6/2012))

> *illustration:* As described at ¶ 1801, the 2012 Highway Investment Act also extends various other excise fuel taxes through Sept. 30, 2016, including, for example, the 24.3¢ per gallon regular removal-at-terminal tax on diesel fuel (the "diesel fuel rate"). So, for diesel fuel removed from a terminal through Sept. 30, 2016, the *total* federal excise tax imposed on the fuel is 24.4¢-per-gallon (the 24.3¢-per-gallon diesel fuel rate, plus the 0.1¢-per-gallon LUST tax).

> *observation:* The above 2012 Highway Investment Act change to Code Sec. 4081(d)(3) (under the removal-at-terminal tax rules) also has the effect of extending through Sept. 30, 2016 the additional 0.1¢-per-gallon retail excise tax imposed under Code Sec. 4041 and the retail LUST tax imposed under Code Sec. 4042, because those retail taxes apply for the same period for which the LUST tax imposed under Code Sec. 4081 remains in effect.

☐ **Effective:** July 1, 2012. (2012 Highway Investment Act §40102(f))

> *observation:* The wording of 2012 Highway Investment Act §40102(a) above, extending the LUST tax rate (as well as various other excise fuel tax rates, see ¶ 1801) through Sept. 30, 2016, doesn't reflect the intervening six-day extension of the taxes (from July 1 through July 6, 2012) under the 2012 Temporary Surface Transportation Extension Act, Sec. 402(a), PL 112-140, 6/29/2012, that was passed as a stop-gap

to keep the LUST tax and the other rates from expiring as enactment of the longer 2012 Highway Investment Act extension was in process. Both of these extensions (the temporary and the long-term) were made effective July 1, 2012 (see Sec. 402(f)(1), PL 112-140, 6/29/2012, and 2012 Highway Investment Act §40102(f), above)), and Congress may need to make a technical correction clarifying the timing of the changes.

¶ 1803. Retail truck and manufacturer's tire excise taxes, and certain exemptions, are extended through Sept. 30, 2016

Code Sec. 4051(c), as amended by 2012 Highway Investment Act §40102(a)(2)(B)

Code Sec. 4071(d), as amended by 2012 Highway Investment Act §40102(a)(2)(C)

Code Sec. 4221(a), as amended by 2012 Highway Investment Act §40102(d)(1)

Generally effective: July 1, 2012

Committee Reports, see ¶ 5401

Under pre-2012 Highway Investment Act law, the following excise taxes, and exemptions from those taxes, were scheduled to expire after July 6, 2012 (as extended several times, including by the 2011 Transportation Extension Act, Sec. 142, PL 112-30, 9/16/2011, the 2012 Surface Transportation Extension Act, Sec. 402, PL 112-102, 3/30/2012, and the 2012 Temporary Surface Transportation Extension Act, Sec. 402, PL 112-140, 6/29/2012):

. . . the 12%-of-purchase-price excise tax imposed on the first retail sale of (i) auto truck chassis and bodies (for vehicles weighing over 33,000 pounds), (ii) truck trailer and semi-trailer chassis and bodies (for vehicles weighing over 26,000 pounds), and (iii) tractors used chiefly for highway transportation in combination with a trailer or semi-trailer (for tractors weighing over 19,500 pounds and in combination with a trailer or semi-trailer having a combined weight of over 33,000 pounds) (FTC 2d ¶ W-3101; USTR Excise Taxes ¶ 40,514);

. . . the excise tax on the manufacturer's, producer's, or importer's sale of taxable (highway-type) tires imposed, at a rate of 9.45¢ (4.725¢ for biasply or super single tires) for each 10 pounds by which the tire's maximum rated load capacity exceeds 3,500 pounds (FTC 2d ¶ W-2601; USTR Excise Taxes ¶ 40,714);

. . . exemption from the above-described taxes for sales to a state or local government for the government's exclusive use (FTC 2d ¶ W-2227; USTR Excise Taxes ¶ 42,214); and

. . . exemption from the above-described taxes for sales to a nonprofit educational organization for its exclusive use. (FTC 2d ¶ W-2240; USTR Excise Taxes ¶ 42,214)

New Law. The 2012 Highway Investment Act extends, through Sept. 30, 2016, application of the above-described retail truck tax (Code Sec. 4051(c) as amended by 2012 Highway Investment Act §40102(a)(2)(B) (PL 112-141, 7/6/2012)), manufacturer's tire tax (Code Sec. 4071(d) as amended by 2012 Highway Investment Act §40102(a)(2)(C)), and the state and local and nonprofit educational organization exemptions from those taxes. (Code Sec. 4221(a) as amended by 2012 Highway Investment Act §40102(d)(1))

> **🅡🅘🅐️ *observation:*** A credit or refund is available for floor stocks of taxed tires held for resale by dealers on Oct. 1, 2016 (the date as of which the tax expires, as described above), see ¶ 1804.

☐ **Effective:** July 1, 2012. (2012 Highway Investment Act §40102(f))

> **🅡🅘🅐️ *observation:*** The wording of 2012 Highway Investment Act §40102(a), and 2012 Highway Investment Act §40102(d)(1), extending the retail truck tax, manufacturers tire tax, and the above-described exemptions from those taxes through Sept. 30, 2016, doesn't reflect the intervening six-day extension of the taxes and exemptions (from July 1 through July 6, 2012) under the 2012 Temporary Surface Transportation Extension Act, Sec. 402(a), PL 112-140, 6/29/2012 and Sec. 402(c), PL 112-140, 6/29/2012, which were passed as a stop-gap to keep the taxes and exemptions from expiring as enactment of the longer 2012 Highway Investment Act extension was in process. Both of these extensions (the temporary and the long-term) were made effective July 1, 2012 (see Sec. 402(f)(1), PL 112-140, 6/29/2012, and 2012 Highway Investment Act §40102(f) above)), and Congress may need to make a technical correction clarifying the timing of the changes.

¶ 1804. Floor stocks credit, or refund for tire tax and removal-at-terminal fuel tax, is to apply to tires or fuel held by dealers on Oct. 1, 2016

Code Sec. 6412(a)(1), as amended by 2012 Highway Investment Act §40102(c)
Generally effective: July 1, 2012
Committee Reports, see ¶ 5401

Under pre-2012 Highway Investment Act law (as modified several times including by the 2011 Transportation Extension Act, Sec. 142, PL 112-30, 9/16/2011, the 2012 Surface Transportation Extension Act, Sec. 402, PL 112-102, 3/

30/2012, and the 2012 Temporary Surface Transportation Extension Act, Sec. 402, PL 112-140, 6/29/2012), the manufacturer, producer, or importer could claim a refund or credit (without interest) where (i) taxable (highway-type) tires that were subject to the manufacturer's excise tax on tires, or (ii) "taxable fuel" (i.e., gasoline, aviation gasoline, diesel fuel, or kerosene) that was subject to the removal-at-terminal tax on taxable fuel:

... was sold by the manufacturer, producer, or importer to a dealer before July 7, 2012, and

... on July 7, 2012 hadn't been used and was held by the dealer for resale.

The credit and refund amount was equal to the difference between the tax paid by the manufacturer, producer, or importer on his sale of the taxable article (i.e., the tire or fuel), and the applicable tax imposed on that article on and after July 7, 2012.

To claim the credit or refund:

(a) the claim had to be filed with IRS before Jan. 6, 2013;

(b) the claim had to be based on a request for tax reduction submitted by the dealer to the manufacturer, producer, or importer before Oct. 7, 2012; and

(c) before Jan. 6, 2013, either: (i) the manufacturer, producer, or importer reimbursed the dealer for the tax reduction on the article; or (ii) the dealer gave the manufacturer, producer, or importer a written consent to allowance of the credit or refund. (FTC 2d ¶ W-1570, ¶ W-1571, ¶ W-2621; USTR ¶ 64,124)

New Law. The 2012 Highway Investment Act makes the floor stocks credit and refund available for the above-described tires and fuel that:

... are sold by the manufacturer, producer, or importer to a dealer before Oct. 1, 2016; and

... on Oct. 1, 2016, haven't been used and are held by the dealer for resale. (Code Sec. 6412(a)(1) as amended by 2012 Highway Investment Act §40102(c)(1) (PL 112-141, 7/6/2012))

The credit or refund will equal the difference between the tax paid by the manufacturer, producer, or importer on his sale of the article, and the applicable tax imposed on those tires or taxable fuel on and after Oct. 1, 2016. (Code Sec. 6412(a)(1))

> *observation:* The floor stocks credit/refund provision is tied to the Sept. 30, 2016 date after which:
>
> (1) the manufacturer's excise tax on tires will terminate; and
>
> (2) the removal-at-terminal fuel excise tax will be reduced from 18.3¢ per gallon to 4.3¢ per gallon for gasoline, and from 24.3¢ per gallon to 4.3¢ for diesel fuel and kerosene.

(as extended under the 2012 Highway Investment Act, see ¶ 1803 and ¶ 1801, respectively).

> **⊘** *illustration:* If gasoline, on which an 18.3¢ per gallon removal-at-terminal tax (see ¶ 1801) was paid, is sold by the manufacturer, producer, or importer (who paid the tax) to a dealer before Oct. 1, 2016, and on Oct. 1, 2016, the gasoline hasn't been used and is held by the dealer for resale, the manufacturer, producer, or importer can claim a credit or refund of 14¢ per gallon, assuming the other requirements for claiming the floor stocks credit/refund (see below) are met. That is, the credit/refund equals the difference between the tax paid on the gasoline (18.3¢ per gallon) and the tax on gasoline that applies on and after Oct. 1, 2016 (i.e., the reduced 4.3¢ per gallon tax, see ¶ 1801).

Under the 2012 Highway Investment Act, to claim the floor stocks credit or refund:

(a) the claim will have to be filed with IRS on or before Mar. 31, 2017 (Code Sec. 6412(a)(1) as amended by 2012 Highway Investment Act §40102(c)(2));

(b) the claim will have to be based on a request for tax reduction submitted by the dealer to the manufacturer, producer, or importer before Jan. 1, 2017 (Code Sec. 6412(a)(1) as amended by 2012 Highway Investment Act §40102(c)(3)); and

(c) on or before Mar. 31, 2017, either: (i) the manufacturer, producer, or importer will have to have reimbursed the dealer for the tax; or (ii) the dealer will have to have given the manufacturer, producer, or importer a written consent to allowance of the credit or refund. (Code Sec. 6412(a)(1))

☐ **Effective:** July 1, 2012. (2012 Highway Investment Act §40102(f))

> **⊘** *observation:* The wording of 2012 Highway Investment Act §40102(c), above, extending the above floor stocks credit/refund rules to apply to floor stocks held on Oct. 1, 2016, doesn't reflect the intervening six-day extension of the rules (to apply to floor stocks held on July 7, 2012 instead of on July 1, 2012) under the 2012 Temporary Surface Transportation Extension Act, Sec. 402(b), PL 112-140, 6/29/2012, that was passed as a stop-gap to keep the rules from expiring as enactment of the longer 2012 Highway Investment Act extension was in process. Both of these extensions (the temporary and the long-term) were made effective July 1, 2012 (see Sec. 402(f)(1), PL 112-140, 6/29/2012, and 2012 Highway Investment Act §40102(f), above)), and Con-

gress may need to make a technical correction clarifying the timing of the changes.

¶ 1805. Highway use tax, and certain highway use tax exemptions, are extended through Sept. 30, 2017

Code Sec. 4481(f), as amended by 2012 Highway Investment Act §40102(b)(1)(A)
Code Sec. 4482(c)(4), as amended by 2012 Highway Investment Act §40102(b)(2)(A)
Code Sec. 4482(c)(4), 2012 Highway Investment Act §40102(b)(2)(B)
Code Sec. 4482(d), as amended by 2012 Highway Investment Act §40102(b)(1)(B)
Code Sec. 4483(i), as amended by 2012 Highway Investment Act §40102(d)(2)
Generally effective: July 1, 2012
Committee Reports, see ¶ 5401

An excise tax based on weight is imposed on the first use on U.S. public highways for each "taxable period" of a highway motor vehicle that has a gross vehicle weight of at least 55,000 pounds. Under pre-2012 Highway Investment Act law (as extended several times, including by the 2011 Transportation Extension Act, Sec. 142, PL 112-30, 9/16/2011, the 2012 Surface Transportation Extension Act, Sec. 402, PL 112-102, 3/30/2012, and the 2012 Temporary Surface Transportation Extension Act, Sec. 402, PL 112-140, 6/29/2012), a taxable period for this purpose was defined as:

(1) any year (specially defined as a July 1-June 30 year), beginning before July 1, 2013; and

(2) the period beginning on July 1, 2013 and ending at the close of Sept. 30, 2013 (to which tax was to apply at 25% of the regular highway use tax rates).

The highway use tax itself was scheduled to expire for use after Sept. 30, 2013.

Exemptions from the highway use tax for use of any highway motor vehicle by any state or political subdivision of a state, and use of certain transit-type buses, were scheduled to expire after July 6, 2012.

(FTC 2d ¶ W-6401, ¶ W-6438, ¶ W-6451; USTR Excise Taxes ¶ 44,814, ¶ 44,814.01)

New Law. The 2012 Highway Investment Act extends application of the highway use tax through Sept. 30, 2017. (Code Sec. 4481(f) as amended by 2012 Highway Investment Act §40102(b)(1)(A) (PL 112-141, 7/6/2012))

To reflect the extension of the tax, the 2012 Highway Investment Act also makes the following changes:

. . . a taxable period is defined as: (1) any year (i.e., a July 1 - June 30 year) beginning before July 1 2017; and (2) the period beginning on July 1, 2017 and ending at the close of Sept. 30, 2017 (Code Sec. 4482(c)(4) as amended by 2012 Highway Investment Act §40102(b)(2)(A)); and

. . . for the period beginning on July 1, 2017 through Sept. 30, 2017, the highway use tax is applied at 25% of the regular (full year) highway use tax rates. (Code Sec. 4482(d) as amended by 2012 Highway Investment Act §40102(b)(1)(B))

Congress says that the above change to the definition of a taxable period also corrects a potential drafting ambiguity regarding the taxable period as reflected in § 142 of the 2011 Transportation Extension Act (Com Rept, see ¶ 5401), and, so, makes the change effective as if included in that prior law provision (2012 Highway Investment Act §40102(b)(2)(B))—i.e., Oct. 1, 2011, see Sec. 142(f), PL 112-30, 9/16/2011.

In addition, the 2012 Highway Investment Act extends through Sept. 30, 2017 application of the exemptions from highway use tax for state use and transit buses. (Code Sec. 4483(i) as amended by 2012 Highway Investment Act §40102(d)(2))

> **observation:** The wording of § 40102(d)(2) of the 2012 Highway Investment Act above, extending the exemptions from highway use tax for state use and transit buses through Sept. 30, 2017, doesn't reflect the intervening six-day extension of the exemptions (from July 1 through July 6, 2012) under the 2012 Temporary Surface Transportation Extension Act (Sec. 402(a), PL 112-140, 6/29/2012), which was passed as a stop-gap to keep the exemptions from expiring as enactment of the longer 2012 Highway Investment Act extension was in process. Both of the extensions (the temporary and the long-term) were made effective July 1, 2012 (see Sec. 402(f)(1), PL 112-140, 6/29/2012, and 2012 Highway Investment Act §40102(f) below), and Congress may need to make a technical correction clarifying the timing of the changes.

☐ **Effective:** July 1, 2012 (2012 Highway Investment Act §40102(f)), except as otherwise described above for the change to the definition of a taxable period.

¶ 1806. Airport and airway trust fund excise taxes are extended through Sept. 30, 2015

Code Sec. 4081(d)(2)(B), as amended by 2012 FAA Modernization Act §1101(a)

Code Sec. 4261(j)(1)(A)(ii), as amended by 2012 FAA Modernization Act §1101(b)(1)

Code Sec. 4261(j), as redesignated by 2012 FAA Modernization Act §1103(c)

Code Sec. 4271(d)(1)(A)(ii), as amended by 2012 FAA Modernization Act §1101(b)(2)

Generally effective: Feb. 18, 2012

Committee Reports, see ¶ 5601

Under pre-2012 FAA Modernization Act law, the following excise taxes that fund the Federal Airport and Airway Trust Fund program were scheduled to expire (as per many earlier extensions, including for 2011-2012 under Sec. 2, PL 112-7, 3/31/2011; Sec. 2, PL 112-16, 5/31/2011; Sec. 2, PL 112-21, 6/29/2011; Sec. 2, PL 112-27, 8/5/2011; Sec. 202, PL 112-30, 9/16/2011; and Sec. 2, PL 112-91, 1/31/2012) after Feb. 17, 2012:

(1) 7.5% tax on amounts paid for domestic air passenger tickets. (FTC 2d ¶ W-5100, ¶ W-5101; USTR Excise Taxes ¶ 42,614.01)

(2) $3.00 tax ($3.80 for 2012 as indexed for inflation) imposed on each domestic segment of taxable air transportation (the "domestic segment tax"). (FTC 2d ¶ W-5100, ¶ W-5101; USTR Excise Taxes ¶ 42,614.01)

(3) $12-per-person tax ($16.70 for 2012 as indexed for inflation) on international departures and arrivals by air (the "international air transportation tax"). (FTC 2d ¶ W-5100, ¶ W-5103; USTR Excise Taxes ¶ 42,614.01) (A reduced international tax rate [$8.40 for 2012] applies for use of international facilities for transportation between the continental U.S. and Alaska and Hawaii, and between Alaska and Hawaii, see FTC 2d ¶ W-5126; USTR Excise Taxes ¶ 42,614.01.)

(4) 6.25% tax on domestic air transportation of property. (FTC 2d ¶ W-5200, ¶ W-5201; USTR Excise Taxes ¶ 42,714)

(5) 17.5¢ per gallon of the 21.8¢-per-gallon tax imposed on kerosene removed from a terminal or refinery directly into the fuel tank of an aircraft for use in noncommercial aviation (resulting in a drop in the tax rate to 4.3¢ per gallon). (FTC 2d ¶ W-1500, ¶ W-1501.1; USTR Excise Taxes ¶ 40,814)

(6) 15¢ per gallon of the 19.3¢-per-gallon tax imposed on aviation gasoline upon its removal from the terminal (resulting in a drop in the tax rate to 4.3¢ per gallon). (FTC 2d ¶ W-1500, ¶ W-1501; USTR Excise Taxes ¶ 40,814)

New Law. The 2012 FAA Modernization Act modifies the Code to extend application of the above-described Airport and Airway Trust Fund excise taxes through Sept. 30, 2015 (Code Sec. 4081(d)(2)(B) as amended by 2012 FAA Modernization Act §1101(a) (PL 112-95, 2/14/2012); Code Sec. 4261(j)(1)(A)(ii) as amended by 2012 FAA Modernization Act §1101(b)(1) Code Sec. 4261(k)(1)(A)(ii) as redesignated by 2012 FAA Modernization Act §1103(c); Code Sec. 4271(d)(1)(A)(ii) as amended by 2012 FAA Modernization Act §1101(b)(2)); (Com Rept, see ¶ 5601) (instead of through Feb. 17, 2012).

> 🅡🅘🅐 *observation:* For each of the air transportation taxes listed at (1)–(4) above, Code Sec. 4261(j)(1) (Code Sec. 4261(k)(1) as redesignated) and Code Sec. 4271(d)(1) provide that they apply to transportation beginning during the period they are in effect under the Code—i.e., after the 2012 FAA Modernization Act extension, through Sept. 30, 2015—*and to amounts paid during that period for transportation beginning after that period.*

This means that amounts paid on or before Sept. 30, 2015 for taxable transportation are subject to the applicable air transportation taxes even if the trip itself will take place after Sept. 30, 2015.

> 🅡🅘🅐 *observation:* For 2013, as adjusted for inflation as provided in Rev Proc 2012-41, Sec. 3.21, 2012-45 IRB 539 (see FTC 2d ¶s W-5101, W-5103, W-5126):

... the domestic segment tax (item (2) above), is $3.90 ; and

... the international air transportation tax (item (3) above), is $17.20, ($8.60 for transportation between the continental U.S. and Alaska and Hawaii, and between Alaska and Hawaii).

> 🅡🅘🅐 *observation:* Because the 0.1¢-per-gallon Leaking Underground Storage Tank trust fund financing rate ("LUST tax") is also imposed on kerosene and aviation gasoline (through Sept. 30, 2016, as extended by the 2012 Highway Investment Act, see ¶ 1802), after the 2012 FAA Modernization Act's extension, the total tax actually imposed on removal at the terminal of these fuels through Sept. 30, 2015 is:

... 21.9¢ per gallon for kerosene used in noncommercial aviation and

... 19.4¢ per gallon for aviation gasoline.

After Sept. 30, 2015, if the taxes aren't again extended, the total tax on all of these fuels will drop to 4.4¢ per gallon through Sept. 30, 2016, and to 4.3¢ per gallon thereafter (if the LUST tax is allowed to expire).

☐ **Effective:** Feb. 18, 2012 (2012 FAA Modernization Act §1101(c)) through Sept. 30, 2015, as described above.

Code Sec. 4261(j) redesignated as Code Sec. 4261(k) after Mar. 31, 2012. (2012 FAA Modernization Act §1103(d)(3))

¶ 1807. Exemption from air transportation excise taxes for small jet aircraft operated on nonestablished lines is eliminated

Code Sec. 4281, as amended by 2012 FAA Modernization Act §1107(a)
Generally effective: For taxable transportation provided after Mar. 31, 2012
Committee Reports, see ¶ 5607

Under pre-2012 FAA Modernization Act law, the exemption for "small aircraft operated on nonestablished lines" provided that aircraft having a maximum certified take-off weight of 6,000 pounds or less (as provided in the type certificate or airworthiness certificate) were exempt from the air transportation excise taxes imposed under Code Sec. 4261 and Code Sec. 4271—i.e., the 7.5% tax on domestic air passenger tickets, the $3.80 for 2012 ($3.90 for 2013) domestic segment tax, the $16.70 for 2012 ($17.20 for 2013) tax on international departures and arrivals by air, and the 6.25% tax on domestic air transportation of property—*unless* the aircraft was operated on an "established line" (defined by regs as a route "operated with some degree of regularity between definite points"). (FTC 2d ¶ W-5100, ¶ W-5139, ¶ W-5140, ¶ W-5200, ¶ W-5204.1; USTR Excise Taxes ¶ 42,814.01)

For purposes of the exemption, an aircraft isn't treated as operated on an established line at any time during which it is operated on a flight the sole purpose of which is sightseeing. That is, all flights on aircraft with a maximum certified take-off weight of 6,000 pounds or less that were operated solely for sightseeing qualified for the exemption. (FTC 2d ¶ W-5139, ¶ W-5140, ¶ W-5140.1; USTR Excise Taxes ¶ 42,814.01)

New Law. For transportation provided after Mar. 31, 2012 (see below), the 2012 FAA Modernization Act modifies the above-described exemption from air transportation excise taxes for small aircraft operated on nonestablished lines to add that the exemption doesn't apply to jet aircraft (Code Sec. 4281 as amended by 2012 FAA Modernization Act §1107(a) (PL 112-95, 2/14/2012)), also described by Congress as "turbine engine powered aircraft." (Com Rept, see ¶ 5607)

> *observation:* So, for transportation provided after Mar. 31, 2012, a small aircraft (i.e., one with a maximum certified take-off weight of 6,000 pounds or less, as provided in the type certificate or airworthiness certificate), doesn't qualify for exemption from the air transportation of

persons and property taxes under Code Sec. 4281 if the aircraft: (1) is operated on established lines; or (2) is a jet aircraft.

Because, under pre-2012 FAA Modernization Act law, any above-described small aircraft (including a jet aircraft) operated on established lines were ineligible for the Code Sec. 4281 exemption (i.e., only qualifying small aircraft operated on nonestablished lines qualified), the effect of the 2012 FAA Modernization Act change is to eliminate the (pre-Mar. 31, 2012) exemption for *small jet aircraft operated on nonestablished lines.*

🅡🅘🅐 *observation:* Under the 2012 FAA Modernization Act, small aircraft flights operated solely for sightseeing continue to be treated as operated on nonestablished lines, and so—unless the aircraft is a jet—continue to qualify for exemption from air transportation of persons and property taxes.

☐ **Effective:** For taxable transportation provided after Mar. 31, 2012. (2012 FAA Modernization Act §1107(b))

¶ 1808. 14.1¢-per-gallon surtax is imposed on fuel used in fractional ownership aircraft flights; flights are also taxed as noncommercial aviation, but exempted from air transportation taxes

Code Sec. 4043, as added by 2012 FAA Modernization Act §1103(a)(1)
Code Sec. 4082(e), as amended by 2012 FAA Modernization Act §1103(a)(2)
Code Sec. 4083(b), as amended by 2012 FAA Modernization Act §1103(b)
Code Sec. 4261(j), as redesignated by 2012 FAA Modernization Act §1103(c)
Code Sec. 4261(j), as amended by 2012 FAA Modernization Act §1103(c)
Generally effective: Taxable transportation provided, and aircraft and fuel used, after Mar. 31, 2012
Committee Reports, see ¶ 5603

Under pre-2012 FAA Modernization Act law, for excise tax purposes, fractional ownership aircraft flights were treated as commercial aviation. (Com Rept, see ¶ 5603) Thus, the flights were subject to the following excise taxes:

(1) the 7.5% tax on amounts paid for domestic air passenger tickets (FTC 2d ¶ W-5100, ¶ W-5101; USTR Excise Taxes ¶ 42,614.01), through Sept. 30, 2015 (as extended by the 2012 FAA Modernization Act, see ¶ 1806);

(2) the $3.00 tax ($3.80 for 2012, $3.90 for 2013, as indexed for inflation) imposed on each domestic segment of taxable air transportation (the "domestic segment tax") (FTC 2d ¶ W-5100, ¶ W-5101; USTR Excise Taxes ¶ 42,614.01), through Sept. 30, 2015 (as extended by the 2012 FAA Modernization Act, see ¶ 1806);

(3) the $12-per-person tax ($16.70 for 2012, $17.20 for 2013, as indexed for inflation) on international departures and arrivals by air (the "international air transportation tax") (FTC 2d ¶ W-5100, ¶ W-5103; USTR Excise Taxes ¶ 42,614.01), through Sept. 30, 2015 (as extended by the 2012 FAA Modernization Act, see ¶ 1806);

(4) the 6.25% tax on domestic air transportation of property (FTC 2d ¶ W-5200, ¶ W-5201; USTR Excise Taxes ¶ 42,714), through Sept. 30, 2015 (as extended by the 2012 FAA Modernization Act, see ¶ 1806); and

(5) a 4.3¢ per gallon tax imposed on kerosene either: (i) on removal from a refinery or terminal directly into the fuel tank of an aircraft for use in commercial aviation (FTC 2d ¶ W-1500, ¶ W-1501.1; USTR Excise Taxes ¶ 40,814), or (ii) if tax wasn't imposed on removal at the refinery or terminal, on the retail sale to an aircraft owner, lessee, or other operator, or on the use by any person, in an aircraft used in commercial aviation—*plus*, the 0.1¢-per-gallon Leaking Underground Storage Tank Trust Fund Financing (LUST) tax rate—for a total tax of 4.4¢ per gallon. (FTC 2d ¶ W-1700, ¶ W-1713; USTR Excise Taxes ¶ 40,414)

For kerosene removed directly into the fuel tank of an aircraft for a use exempt from tax under Code Sec. 4041(c), a reduced tax (the 0.1¢ LUST tax only) applied, and a complete exemption from tax (zero tax) applied for kerosene removed directly into the fuel tank of an aircraft for use in foreign trade. (FTC 2d ¶ W-1515.2C; USTR Excise Taxes ¶ 40,824)

Under pre-2012 FAA Modernization Act law, commercial aviation was defined as any use of aircraft in a business of transporting persons or property for compensation or hire by air, unless properly allocable to any transportation that was exempt from the Code Sec. 4261 and Code Sec. 4271 air transportation of persons and property excise taxes under specified exemptions. (FTC 2d ¶ W-1515.1B; USTR Excise Taxes ¶ 40,814)

Kerosene used in *noncommercial aviation* is subject to a 21.8¢ per gallon fuel removal-at-terminal tax through Sept. 30, 2015 (as extended by the 2012 FAA Modernization Act, see ¶ 1806) (and 4.3¢ per gallon thereafter)—plus the 0.1¢ LUST tax (through Sept. 30, 2016, as extended by the 2012 Highway Investment Act, see ¶ 1802)—for a total tax of 21.9¢ per gallon. (FTC 2d ¶ W-1500, ¶ W-1501.1; USTR Excise Taxes ¶ 40,814)). A back-up tax (also totalling 21.9¢ per gallon, including the LUST tax) applies on the retail sale or use of noncommercial aviation fuel if it wasn't previously taxed. (FTC 2d ¶ W-1700, ¶ W-1713; USTR Excise Taxes ¶ 40,414)

New Law. The 2012 FAA Modernization Act provides an exemption, through Sept. 30, 2015, from the above-described fuel and air transportation of persons and property taxes imposed on commercial aviation, for certain fractional aircraft program flights. Instead, through Sept. 30, 2015, these flights are treated as noncommercial aviation for base fuel tax purposes, and through Sept. 30, 2021, are subject to a new 14.1¢ per gallon fuel surtax. (Com Rept, see ¶ 5603) (See FTC 2d ¶ W-3301 *et seq.*; USTR Excise ¶ 40,434 .) The 2012 FAA Modernization Act accomplishes this as specifically described below.

Fuel surtax imposed on fractional ownership aircraft flights, through Sept. 30, 2021. The 2012 FAA Modernization Act adds to Subchapter B of chapter 31 of the Code (i.e., to the provisions on "Retail Excise Taxes" imposed on "Special Fuels") new Code Sec. 4043 (Code Sec. 4043 as added by 2012 FAA Modernization Act §1103(a)(1) (PL 112-95, 2/14/2012)) which imposes a 14.1¢ per gallon tax (Code Sec. 4043(b)) on any liquid used (during any calendar quarter by any person) in a fractional program aircraft (defined below) as fuel (Code Sec. 4043(a)):

(1) for the transportation of a qualified fractional owner (defined below) under the fractional ownership aircraft program (defined below) of which the aircraft is a part (Code Sec. 4043(a)(1)), or

(2) for use of the aircraft on account of the qualified fractional owner, including use in deadhead service (but see exception below).(Code Sec. 4043(a)(2))

Definitions. For purposes of the fuel surtax (Code Sec. 4043(c)):

. . . A *"fractional program aircraft"* is, for any fractional ownership aircraft program (defined below), any aircraft that (Code Sec. 4043(c)(1))

(a) is listed as a fractional program aircraft in the management specifications issued to the manager of the program by the Federal Aviation Administration (FAA) under subpart K of part 91 of title 14, Code of Federal Regulations (Code Sec. 4043(c)(1)(A)), and

(b) is registered in the U.S. (Code Sec. 4043(c)(1)(B))

. . . A *"fractional ownership aircraft program"* is a program under which (Code Sec. 4043(c)(2)):

(a) a single fractional ownership program manager provides fractional ownership program management services on behalf of the fractional owners (Code Sec. 4043(c)(2)(A));

(b) there are one or more fractional owners (defined below) per fractional program aircraft, with at least one fractional program aircraft having more than one owner (Code Sec. 4043(c)(2)(B));

(c) for at least two fractional program aircraft, none of the ownership interests in the aircraft are (Code Sec. 4043(c)(2)(C)) (i) less than the minimum fractional ownership interest (defined below) (Code Sec. 4043(c)(2)(C)(i)), or (ii) held by the program manager in (a) (Code Sec. 4043(c)(2)(C)(ii)), ;

(d) there exists a dry-lease aircraft exchange arrangement (Code Sec. 4043(c)(2)(D)) (i.e., an agreement, documented by the written program agreements, under which the fractional program aircraft are available, on an as needed basis without crew, to each fractional owner) (Code Sec. 4043(c)(4)) among all of the fractional owners (Code Sec. 4043(c)(2)(D)), and

(e) there are multi-year program agreements covering the fractional ownership, fractional ownership program management services, and dry-lease aircraft exchange aspects of the program. (Code Sec. 4043(c)(2)(E))

. . . A *"qualified fractional owner"* is any *"fractional owner"* (Code Sec. 4043(c)(3)(A)) (i.e., any person owning any interest, including the entire interest, in a fractional program interest) (Code Sec. 4043(c)(3)(D)) that has a minimum fractional ownership interest (defined below) in at least one fractional program aircraft. (Code Sec. 4043(c)(3)(A))

. . . A *"minimum fractional ownership interest"* is, for each type of aircraft (Code Sec. 4043(c)(3)(B)): (a) a fractional ownership interest (defined below) equal to or greater than $1/16$ of at least one subsonic, fixed wing, or powered lift aircraft (Code Sec. 4043(c)(3)(B)(i)), or (b) a fractional ownership interest equal to or greater than $1/32$ of at least one rotorcraft aircraft. (Code Sec. 4043(c)(3)(B)(ii))

. . . A *"fractional ownership interest"* is (Code Sec. 4043(c)(3)(C)) (a) the ownership of an interest in a fractional program aircraft (Code Sec. 4043(c)(3)(C)(i)), (b) the holding of a multi-year leasehold interest in a fractional program aircraft (Code Sec. 4043(c)(3)(C)(ii)), or (c) the holding of a multi-year leasehold interest that's convertible into an ownership interest in a fractional program aircraft. (Code Sec. 4043(c)(3)(C)(iii))

Demonstration, maintenance, or crew training flights exempted from fuel surtax. For purposes of the above-described surtax, a fractional program aircraft won't be considered to be used for the transportation of a qualified fractional owner, or on account of the qualified fractional owner, when it's used for flight demonstration, maintenance, or crew training. (Code Sec. 4043(c)(5))

> *observation:* As described under the special rule below, fuel used in fractional ownership aircraft flights that would otherwise be subject to the Code Sec. 4043 fuel surtax but that's exempted from the tax as demonstration, maintenance, or crew training flights, is taxed as fuel used in noncommercial aviation.

Thus, demonstration, maintenance, and crew training flights by a fractional program aircraft is excluded from the fuel surtax and are subject to only the noncommercial aviation fuel tax (see below). (Com Rept, see ¶ 5603)

Certain deadhead service exempted from fuel surtax. A fractional program aircraft won't be considered to be used on account of a qualified fractional owner when it's used in deadhead service (Code Sec. 4043(c)(6))—i.e., positioning flights (Com Rept, see ¶ 5603)—*and* a person other than a qualified fractional owner is separately charged for the service. (Code Sec. 4043(c)(6))

> *observation:* Because use of a fractional ownership aircraft for above-described deadhead service isn't treated as use on account of a qualified fractional owner, fuel used in this service isn't subject to the Code Sec. 4043 fuel surtax, and, as such, isn't subject to the special rule below treating fractional ownership aircraft flights as noncommercial aviation for fuel excise tax purposes. That is, fuel used in above-described deadhead service is subject to only the fuel excise taxes, and under those rules is taxed at the commercial aviation fuel rates, i.e., 4.4¢-per-gallon.

Congress says that a flight in deadhead service is presumed subject to the fuel surtax unless the costs for the flight are separately billed to a person other than a qualified owner. For example, if costs associated with a positioning flight of a fractional program aircraft are separately billed to a person chartering the aircraft, that positioning flight is treated as commercial aviation. (Com Rept, see ¶ 5603)

Termination of the fuel surtax. The Code Sec. 4043 fuel surtax won't apply for liquids used as a fuel in an aircraft after Sept. 30, 2021. (Code Sec. 4043(d))

Treatment of fractional ownership aircraft flights as noncommercial aviation through Sept. 30, 2015. The 2012 FAA Modernization Act modifies the definition of "commercial aviation" to provide that the term won't include the use of any aircraft before Oct. 1, 2015 if tax is imposed under Code Sec. 4043 (i.e., the above-described fuel surtax) for fuel consumed in the use or if no tax is imposed on that use under Code Sec. 4043 by reason of the Code Sec. 4043(c)(5) exemption from the surtax for demonstration, maintenance, or crew training flights (see above). (Code Sec. 4083(b) as amended by 2012 FAA Modernization Act §1103(b))

> *observation:* Presumably, fractional ownership aircraft flights are treated as noncommercial aviation only through Sept. 30, 2015 because, as described above, after that date, noncommercial aviation fuel and commercial aviation fuel are taxed on removal-at-terminal or the refinery at the same rate (i.e., 4.3¢ per gallon, plus any applicable LUST tax).

☞ *observation:* Under the above rule, through Sept. 30, 2015, fuel used in fractional ownership aircraft flights taxed under Code Sec. 4043, or exempted from that tax as demonstration, maintenance, or crew training flights, is taxed as fuel used in noncommercial aviation (instead of as commercial aviation fuel as described at (5) in the background above) at a total removal-at-terminal fuel tax rate (including the 0.1¢ per gallon LUST tax) of 21.9¢ per gallon.

Thus, through Sept. 30, 2015, fractional ownership aircraft flights will be subject to both the noncommercial aviation fuel tax described above, and the Code Sec. 4043 fuel surtax described above. (Com Rept, see ¶ 5603)

☞ *observation:* Thus, through Sept. 30, 2015, fuel used in fractional ownership aircraft flights (other than demonstration, maintenance, or crew training flights) will be subject to both the 21.9¢-per-gallon noncommercial aviation fuel removal-at-terminal tax (including the LUST tax), and the 14.1¢ per gallon fuel surtax—for a total tax on the fuel of 36¢ per gallon.

For the period Oct. 1, 2015 through Sept. 30, 2021, for which the fuel surtax remains in effect but the fractional ownership aircraft flights are no longer subject to a higher noncommercial aviation fuel tax rate on removal-at-terminal, etc. (or the LUST tax which is currently scheduled to expire after Sept. 30, 2016), fuel used in these flights will be subject to both a 4.4¢ (4.3¢ after Sept. 30, 2016) per-gallon fuel tax on removal at the terminal, and the 14.1¢-per-gallon fuel surtax—for a total tax on the fuel of 18.5¢ per gallon (18.4¢ after Sept. 30, 2016).

After Sept. 30, 2021, fuel used in these flights will be subject only to a 4.3¢ per gallon fuel removal-at-terminal tax rate.

Congress says that it intends no inference from the above rules as to the treatment of fractional ownership aircraft flights as noncommercial aviation under pre-2012 FAA Modernization Act rules. (Com Rept, see ¶ 5603)

The 2012 FAA Modernization Act also provides that the reduced fuel tax rate/complete exemption for kerosene removed directly into an aircraft fuel tank for an exempt use/foreign trade use doesn't apply to kerosene that's subject to the Code Sec. 4043 fuel surtax. (Code Sec. 4082(e) as amended by 2012 FAA Modernization Act §1103(a)(2))

Exemption from air transportation of persons and property taxes for fractional ownership aircraft flights, through Sept. 30, 2015. The 2012 FAA Modernization Act also provides that, through Sept. 30, 2015, no air transportation of persons tax imposed under Code Sec. 4261 or air transportation of property tax imposed under Code Sec. 4271 (i.e., the taxes described at (1) through (4) in the background above) will be imposed on any air transportation if the

Code Sec. 4043 fuel surtax tax is imposed on the fuel used in that transportation. (Code Sec. 4261(j) as amended by 2012 FAA Modernization Act §1103(c))

> *observation:* Presumably, this exemption from air transportation of persons and property taxes applies only through Sept. 30, 2015 because, as described above, those taxes expire after that date and so no special exemption is needed.

☐ **Effective:** Fuel surtax applies for fuel used after Mar. 31, 2012 (2012 FAA Modernization Act §1103(d)(1)), through Sept. 30, 2021 (as described above).

The rule treating fractional ownership aircraft flights as noncommercial aviation applies for aircraft uses after Mar. 31, 2012 (2012 FAA Modernization Act §1103(d)(2)), through Sept. 30, 2015 (as described above).

Exemption from air transportation of persons and property taxes applies to taxable transportation provided after Mar. 31, 2012 (2012 FAA Modernization Act §1103(d)(3)), through Sept. 30, 2015 (as described above).

¶ 1900. Payroll and Other Provisions from Earlier Acts of the 112th Congress

¶ 1901. Reduced 10.4% OASDI rate applied for 2012 to self-employment income up to $110,100 ceiling

Code Sec. 1401(a), 2011 Temporary Payroll Act §101(a)
Code Sec. 1401(a), 2011 Temporary Payroll Act §101(b)
Code Sec. 164(f), 2011 Temporary Payroll Act §101(b)
Code Sec. 1401(a), 2012 Middle Class Tax Relief Act §1001(a)
Code Sec. 164(f), 2012 Middle Class Tax Relief Act §1001(b)
Generally effective: Remuneration received, and tax years beginning, after, Dec. 31, 2011
Committee Reports, see ¶ 5501

Self-employment taxes. The Self-Employment Contributions Act (SECA) imposes two taxes on self-employed individuals—an old-age, survivors, and disability insurance (OASDI) tax, commonly known as social security tax, and a hospital insurance (HI) tax, commonly known as Medicare tax.

These self-employment (SE) taxes apply to self-employment income, which is net earnings from self-employment above a $400 minimum for the tax year. There is an annually-adjusted ceiling on the amount subject to OASDI tax ($110,100 for 2012), which is reduced by any wages received by the individual in the same tax year. There is no ceiling on the HI tax. (FTC 2d/FIN ¶ A-6001; A-6035; USTR ¶ 14,014; 14,024; TaxDesk ¶ 575,501; 576,002)

The HI tax rate is 2.9%. (FTC 2d/FIN ¶ A-6001.2; USTR ¶ 14,014; TaxDesk ¶ 575,501)

The OASDI tax rate under Code Sec. 1401(a) is 12.4%. However, 2010 Tax Relief Act §601 (Sec. 601, PL 111-312, 12/17/2010) temporarily reduced the OASDI rate to 10.4% for tax years beginning in the "payroll tax holiday period."

Under the 2010 Tax Relief Act, the payroll tax holiday period was calendar year 2011. Thus, the self-employment OASDI tax rate was 10.4% for 2011, but was to have reverted to 12.4% for tax years beginning after 2011. (FTC 2d/FIN ¶ A-6000, ¶ A-6001.1; USTR ¶ 14,014; TaxDesk ¶ 575,501)

FTC 2d References are to Federal Tax Coordinator 2d
FIN References are to RIA's Analysis of Federal Taxes: Income (print)
USTR References are to United States Tax Reporter: Income
PCA References are to Pension Analysis (print and electronic)
PBE References are to Pension & Benefits Explanations
BCA References are to Benefits Analysis (electronic)
BC References are to Benefits Coordinator (print)
EP References are to Estate Planning Analysis (print and electronic)

Income tax deduction. An income tax deduction is allowed under Code Sec. 164(f) for a part of SE tax. The deduction is taken above the line, in computing adjusted gross income (AGI).

Generally, the Code Sec. 164(f) deduction is equal to 50% of SE tax for the year. However, for tax years beginning in calendar year 2011, the deduction was equal to the sum of: (1) 59.6% of the OASDI tax paid, *plus* (2) 50% of the HI tax paid. The deduction was to have reverted to 50% of SE tax for 2012.

The increased percentage (59.6% rather than 50% of the OASDI tax paid) was used to allow self-employed taxpayers to deduct the full amount of the employer part of self-employment tax. The total OASDI tax rate for 2011 was 10.4% (see ¶ 1902). Thus, the employer share of total OASDI taxes was 59.6% (6.2 ÷ 10.4) of the OASDI portion of self-employment tax. (FTC 2d/FIN ¶ K-4400, ¶ K-4401; USTR ¶ 1644.07; TaxDesk ¶ 326,002)

SE tax deduction for half of SE taxes. Taxpayers are allowed an SE tax deduction under Code Sec. 1402(a)(12) in computing net earnings from self-employment equal to:

... that taxpayer's net earnings from self-employment, as determined before taking the Code Sec. 1402(a)(12) deduction into account, *multiplied by*

... one-half of the sum of the OASDI tax rate and the HI tax rate.

This deduction, which is in lieu of the Code Sec. 164(f) deduction, is built into the SE tax calculation on Schedule SE (Form 1040). It is taken when the taxpayer's trade or business income is multiplied by .9235 on Schedule SE. ((FTC 2d/FIN ¶ A-6100, ¶ A-6114; USTR ¶ 14,024; TaxDesk ¶ 576,025))

New Law. The reduced OASDI tax rate of 10.4% was extended for 2012. This was done in two stages:

... the 2011 Temporary Payroll Act extended the SE tax payroll tax holiday period (during which the 10.4% rate applied) to include tax years beginning in 2012 (2010 Tax Relief Act § 601(c)(1) (Sec. 601(c)(1), PL 111-312, 12/17/2010) as amended by 2011 Temporary Payroll Act §101(a) (Sec. 101(a), PL 112-78, 12/28/2011)), *but only* for the taxpayer's self-employment income of up to $18,350. (2010 Tax Relief Act § 601(f)(1) (Sec. 601(f)(1), PL 111-312, 12/17/2010) as amended by 2011 Temporary Payroll Act §101(b))

... the 2012 Middle Class Tax Relief Act removed the $18,350 limitation on self-employment income that qualified for the reduced 10.4% OASDI rate for tax years beginning in 2012. (2010 Tax Relief Act § 601(f)(1) (Sec. 601(f)(1), PL 111-312, 12/17/2010) as amended by 2011 Temporary Payroll Act §101(b) and by 2012 Middle Class Tax Relief Act §1001(b) (Sec. 1001(b), PL 112-96, 2/22/2012))

⚫️ *observation:* As a result, the SE tax rate for 2012 was 13.3% (10.4% OASDI tax + 2.9% HI tax) on net earnings from self-employment up to the $110,100 ceiling (reduced by any wages received during the year). On net earnings from self-employment in excess of the $110,100 ceiling, the rate was 2.9%.

⚫️ *illustration (1):* Taxpayer A had $50,000 of net earnings from self-employment (and no wages) in 2012. A's SE tax for 2012 was $6,650 ($5,200 OASDI tax + $1,450 HI tax). That's $1,000 less than it would have been without the rate reduction ($50,000 × .02).

⚫️ *observation:* The maximum reduction in SE tax in 2012 on account of the payroll tax holiday was $2,202 ($110,100 × .02). For a married couple, each with net earnings from self-employment of $110,100 or more, the maximum reduction was $4,404.

⚫️ *illustration (2):* Taxpayer B had $120,000 of net earnings from self-employment (and no wages) in 2012. B's SE tax for 2012 was $14,930.40 ([$110,100 × .133 = $14,643.30] + [$9,900 × .029 = $287.10]). That's $2,202 less than it would have been without the rate reduction.

⚫️ *observation:* The payroll tax holiday expired after calendar year 2012 and wasn't extended for 2013. Thus, net earnings from self-employment for 2013 are subject to a 12.4% OASDI tax rate up to the 2013 ceiling of $113,700, for a maximum OASDI tax of $14,098.80. The maximum OASDI tax for 2012 was $11,450.40 ($110,100 × 10.4%).

Income tax deduction for 2012 equaled 59.6% of OASDI tax plus 50% of HI tax. The 2012 Middle Class Tax Relief Act also extended the special rule for computing the Code Sec. 164(f) deduction. The deduction allowed for tax years beginning in 2012 was equal to the sum of: (1) 59.6% of the OASDI tax paid *plus* (2) 50% of the HI tax paid. (2010 Tax Relief Act § 601(b)(2) (Sec. 601(b)(2), PL 111-312, 12/17/2010))

The 2011 Temporary Payroll Act had applied a more complicated formula to take account of the fact that the 10.4% OASDI rate was to have applied only to the first $18,350 of self-employment income. (2010 Tax Relief Act § 601(b)(2)(A) as amended by 2011 Temporary Payroll Act §101(b)) However, the 2012 Middle Class Tax Relief Act repealed that formula and reinstated the formula set forth in the preceding paragraph. (2010 Tax Relief Act § 601(f)(2) (Sec. 601(f)(2), PL 111-312, 12/17/2010) as amended by 2011 Temporary Payroll Act §101(b) and by 2012 Middle Class Tax Relief Act §1001(b))

SE tax deduction was unchanged. The rate reduction wasn't taken into account for purposes of the Code Sec. 1402(a)(12) SE tax deduction allowed for determining the amount of the net earnings from self-employment for the tax year. (2010 Tax Relief Act § 601(b)(1) (Sec. 601(b)(1), PL 111-312, 12/17/2010))

☐ **Effective:** Remuneration received, and tax years beginning, after Dec. 31, 2011. (2012 Middle Class Tax Relief Act §1001(c); 2011 Temporary Payroll Act §101(e)(1))

¶ 1902. Reduced 4.2% employee social security tax rate applied for 2012 under payroll tax holiday

Code Sec. 3101(a), 2011 Temporary Payroll Act §101(a)
Code Sec. 3121(a)(1), 2011 Temporary Payroll Act §101(c)
Code Sec. 3101(a), 2012 Middle Class Tax Relief Act §1001(a)
Code Sec. 3101(a), 2012 Middle Class Tax Relief Act §1001(b)
Code Sec. 3201(a), 2012 Middle Class Tax Relief Act §1001(a)
Code Sec. 3211(a), 2012 Middle Class Tax Relief Act §1001(a)
Generally effective: Remuneration received, and tax years beginning, after
　　Dec. 31, 2011
Committee Reports, see ¶ 5501

The Federal Insurance Contributions Act (FICA) imposes two taxes on employers and employees—an old-age, survivors, and disability insurance (OASDI) tax, commonly known as social security tax, and a hospital insurance (HI) tax, commonly known as Medicare tax.

The HI tax is computed on all of the employee's wages. The HI tax rate is 1.45%, for both employers and employees.

The OASDI tax is computed on an employee's wages up to a ceiling amount ($110,100 for 2012). The employer OASDI tax rate is 6.2%. The employee OASDI tax rate under Code Sec. 3101(a) is also 6.2%. However, 2010 Tax Relief Act §601 (Sec. 601, PL 111-312, 12/17/2010) temporarily reduced the employee rate to 4.2%, for remuneration received during the "payroll tax holiday period."

Under the 2010 Tax Relief Act, the payroll tax holiday period was calendar year 2011. The employee OASDI tax rate was to have reverted to 6.2% after 2011. (FTC 2d/FIN ¶ H-4685, ¶ H-4687; USTR ¶ 31,114; TaxDesk ¶ 541,002)

New Law. The reduced employee OASDI tax rate of 4.2% was extended for 2012. This was done in two stages:

. . . the 2011 Temporary Payroll Act extended the payroll tax holiday period to include the period beginning Jan. 1, 2012 and ending Feb. 29, 2012. (2010 Tax

Relief Act § 601(c)(2) (Sec. 601(c)(2), PL 111-312, 12/17/2010) as amended by 2011 Temporary Payroll Act §101(a) (Sec. 101(a), PL 112-78, 12/23/2011))

... the 2012 Middle Class Tax Relief Act extended the payroll tax holiday period to include *all* of calendar year 2012 (not just Jan. and Feb.). (2010 Tax Relief Act § 601(c) (Sec. 601(c), PL 111-312, 12/17/2010) as amended by 2012 Middle Class Tax Relief Act §1001(a) (Sec. 1001(a), PL 112-96, 2/22/2012))

⦿ *observation:* For 2012, the FICA tax rate on employees' wages up to the 2012 ceiling of $110,100 was 5.65% (4.2% OASDI tax + 1.45% HI tax). On wages in excess of $110,100, the rate was 1.45%.

⦿ *illustration (1):* Employee A received $50,000 of FICA wages in 2012. A's FICA tax for 2012 was $2,825 ($50,000 × .0565). That's $1,000 more ($50,000 × .02) than it would have been without the 2% payroll tax reduction.

⦿ *observation:* The maximum FICA tax saving for 2012 as a result of the payroll tax holiday was $2,202 ($110,100 × .02).

⦿ *illustration (2):* Employee B received $120,000 of FICA wages in 2012. B's FICA tax for 2012 was $6,364.20 ([$111,100 × .0565 = $6.220.65] + [$9,900 × .0145% = $143.55]). That's $2,202 more than it would have been without the 2% payroll tax reduction.

⦿ *observation:* The payroll tax holiday expired after calendar year 2012 and wasn't extended for 2013. Thus, wages for 2013 are subject to a 6.2% employee OASDI tax rate, up from 4.2% in 2012. Wage earners should expect to see an increase in their FICA withholding starting with the first paycheck of 2013.

A worker who earns $50,000 in wages in 2013 will pay $1,000 more in FICA tax (2% × $50,000) than he would have in 2012. The maximum employee OASDI tax for 2013 is $7,049.40 (6.2% × $113,700 ceiling). For 2012, the maximum tax was $4,624.20 (4.2% × $110,100 ceiling).

For related changes to the self-employment tax OASDI rate for 2012, see ¶ 1901.

How employers implemented payroll tax holiday extension. IRS was directed to notify employers about the payroll tax holiday period in any manner deemed appropriate. (2010 Tax Relief Act § 601(d) (Sec. 601(d), PL 111-312, 12/17/2010)

⦿ *observation:* IRS instructed employers to implement the extension of the payroll tax holiday as soon as possible in 2012, but no later than

Jan. 31, 2012. If any OASDI tax was overwithheld during January, employers were to make an offsetting adjustment in employees' pay as soon as possible, but no later than Mar. 31, 2012. (IRS Pub No. 15 (Circular E) (2012), pp. 1–2; IR 2011-124, 12/23/2011, see FTC 2d/ FIN ¶ H-4701; USTR ¶ 35,014.07)

observation: Employees received the benefit of the reduced 4.2% OASDI rate without taking any action, such as filling out a new W-4 withholding form. The withholding changes were handled by employers and payroll companies. (IR 2012-27, 2/23/2012; IR 2011-124, 12/23/ 2011)

Railroad retirement tax. Under the Railroad Retirement Tax Act ("RRTA"), railroad employers and employees are subject to taxes equivalent to the OASDI and HI taxes under FICA. Employers must generally withhold and remit the employee portion of RRTA taxes to the federal government. (Com Rept, see ¶ 5501)

Under the 2012 Middle Class Tax Relief Act, a 4.2% rate (rather than 6.2%) applied for *all* of 2012 for purposes of:

. . . the Tier I railroad retirement tax on employees under Code Sec. 3201(a) and

. . . the Tier I railroad retirement tax on employee representatives under Code Sec. 3211(a). (2010 Tax Relief Act § 601(c) (Sec. 601(c), PL 111-312, 12/17/ 2010) as amended by 2012 Middle Class Tax Relief Act §1001(a))

Previously, the 2011 Temporary Payroll Act had extended the 4.2% rate only for the period beginning Jan. 1, 2012, and ending Feb. 29, 2012. (2010 Tax Relief Act § 601(c)(1) (Sec. 601(c)(1), PL 111-312, 12/17/2010) as amended by 2011 Temporary Payroll Act §101(a))

No effect on social security benefits.

observation: The reduced OASDI tax rate had no effect on the employee's future social security benefits. (IR 2012-27, 2/23/2012)

No effect on other federal laws. As was the case with the 2011 payroll tax holiday (2010 Tax Relief Act § 601(e)(3)), for purposes of applying any provision of federal law other than the Internal Revenue Code, the employee OASDI tax rate will be determined without regard to the extended payroll tax holiday. (Com Rept, see ¶ 5501)

Recapture tax enacted, then repealed. Under the 2011 Temporary Payroll Act, a recapture tax was to have applied to taxpayers who received more than $18,350 of wages during Jan. and Feb. of 2012. (2010 Tax Relief Act § 601(g)(1) (Sec. 601(g)(1), PL 111-312, 12/17/2010) as amended by 2011 Temporary Payroll Act §101(c))

However, the 2012 Middle Class Tax Relief Act repealed this tax. (2010 Tax Relief Act § 601(g) (Sec. 601(g), PL 111-312, 12/17/2010) as amended by 2011 Temporary Payroll Act §101(c) and by 2012 Middle Class Tax Relief Act §1001(b))

☐ **Effective:** Remuneration received, and tax years beginning, after Dec. 31, 2011. (2012 Middle Class Tax Relief Act §1001(c); 2011 Temporary Payroll Act §101(e)(1))

¶ 1903. To qualify for additional FUTA tax credit, state unemployment programs must charge employers for payments caused by employer's failure to respond

Code Sec. 3303(f), as amended by 2011 Trade Extension Act §252(a)(2)
Generally effective: Erroneous payments established after Oct. 20, 2013
Committee Reports, None

Employers must pay a tax under the Federal Unemployment Tax Act (FUTA) on wages paid to their employees. The FUTA tax rate is 6.0%. The maximum amount of wages subject to FUTA tax is $7,000. (FTC 2d/FIN ¶ H-4801; USTR ¶ 35,014.07; TaxDesk ¶ 550,502)

Normal credit against FUTA tax. A credit is allowed against FUTA tax equal to the employer's contributions to a state unemployment fund for the tax year, up to 5.4% of the wage base.

For states that are eligible for the full 5.4% credit, the net FUTA tax rate is 0.6% (6.0% FUTA tax rate less 5.4% credit). The maximum FUTA tax is $42 per employee, per year (0.6% × $7,000 = $42). (FTC 2d/FIN ¶ H-4802; USTR ¶ 35,014.07; TaxDesk ¶ 550,503)

Additional credit. Taxpayers who pay state unemployment tax at a rate that's lower than the state's highest unemployment tax rate can qualify for an additional credit against FUTA tax.

This credit is equal to the difference between: (a) the lower of the state's maximum unemployment tax rate or 5.4%; and (b) the amount of contributions that the employer was required to make to the state fund. (FTC 2d/FIN ¶ H-4805; TaxDesk ¶ 550,505)

observation: The additional credit allows employers that have good experience ratings, and so have a lower state contribution rate, to avoid paying more FUTA tax than employers with bad ratings.

Even if an employer pays state unemployment tax at a 0% rate, based on its experience, the additional credit would allow the employer to claim the total amount of credit available to taxpayers in the state. Although the employer wouldn't have paid any taxes to apply toward the normal credit, it could claim the full 5.4% credit as an additional credit.

The additional credit is permitted only if the Secretary of Labor certifies that the state unemployment law meets certain requirements. Those requirements relate to the way that the state determines the unemployment tax rates of employers. (FTC 2d/FIN ¶ H-4805; TaxDesk ¶ 550,505)

Under pre-2011 Trade Extension Act law, to qualify for the additional FUTA tax credit, states weren't required to charge employer accounts for payments that were caused by an employer's failure to respond to the state agency's request for information.

New Law. Under the 2011 Trade Extension Act, a state unemployment law won't qualify for the additional credit against FUTA tax unless it provides that an employer's account won't be relieved of charges relating to a payment from the state unemployment fund if the state agency determines that: (Code Sec. 3303(f)(1) as amended by 2011 Trade Extension Act §252(a)(2) (Sec. 252(a)(2), PL 112-40, 10/21/2011))

. . . the payment was made because the employer, or the employer's agent, was at fault for failing to respond timely or adequately to the agency's request for information relating to the compensation claim; and (Code Sec. 3303(f)(1)(A))

. . . the employer or agent has established a pattern of failing to respond timely or adequately to those requests. (Code Sec. 3303(f)(1)(B)

> *observation:* This provision is designated as an offset to the extension of trade adjustment assistance (TAA) in Subtitle A of the 2011 Trade Extension Act. It deals with cases in which unemployment benefits were granted because the employer (or the employer's agent) didn't respond to the state agency's request for information about the benefit claim, such as the circumstances that led to the employee's unemployment.
>
> For example, the agency might ask the employer whether the employee was fired for misconduct, which would disqualify the employee for unemployment benefits. If the employer fails to respond, the employee's benefit claim would be granted.
>
> Under the provision, where a payment was made due to the failure to respond, and the employer (or agent) has an established pattern of similar failures, state law must require that the employer's account be charged for the payment. If a state law doesn't include that requirement, employers in that state won't qualify for the additional credit against FUTA tax.

States can impose stricter standards. The above rule doesn't limit a state's authority to provide that an employer's account not be relieved of charges relating to a payment from the state unemployment fund for reasons other than the above-stated reasons—failure to respond to a state agency's information request combined with an established pattern of those failures. (Code Sec. 3303(f)(2))

For example, a state can provide that an employer's account won't be relieved of charges relating to a payment from the state unemployment fund after the *first* instance of a failure to respond timely or adequately to the state agency's request for information about the claim for compensation. (Code Sec. 3303(f)(2))

☐ **Effective:** The provision applies to erroneous payments established after Oct. 20, 2013, i.e., after the end of the two-year period beginning on Oct. 21, 2011, which was the enactment date of the 2011 Trade Extension Act. (2011 Trade Extension Act §252(b)(1))

But states can amend their laws to apply the provision to erroneous payments established *before* Oct. 21, 2013. (2011 Trade Extension Act §252(b)(2))

¶ 1904. Tax-exempt employers get FICA tax credit for hiring qualified veterans

Code Sec. 3111(e), as amended by 2011 Job Creation Act §261(e)(2)
Generally effective: Individuals who begin work for an employer after Nov. 21, 2011
Committee Reports, None

Work opportunity tax credit. Employers can elect a work opportunity tax credit (WOTC) equal to a percentage of limited amounts of wages paid or incurred by the employer to individuals who belong to a "targeted group," see FTC 2d/FIN ¶ L-17775; USTR ¶ 514; TaxDesk ¶ 380,700.

One such targeted group is "qualified veterans," see FTC 2d/FIN ¶ L-17785.1; USTR ¶ 514.002; TaxDesk ¶ 380,711. The 2011 Job Creation Act extended and enhanced the WOTC for qualified veterans. Under the Act, the WOTC won't be available for qualified veterans who begin work for the employer after Dec. 31, 2012, see ¶ 1910.

Subject to certain special rules, the WOTC allowed is 40% of "qualified first-year wages." However, if an individual has completed less than 400 hours, but at least 120 hours, of service for the employer, the percentage is reduced from 40% to 25%. There are limits on the amount of qualified first-year wages that may be taken into account for any individual. See FTC 2d/FIN ¶ L-17778; USTR ¶ 514; TaxDesk ¶ 380,700.1.

Under pre-2011 Job Creation Act law, the WOTC wasn't available to tax-exempt organizations, other than exempt farmers' cooperatives, see FTC 2d/FIN ¶ L-17789A; USTR ¶ 514; TaxDesk ¶ 380,700.

FICA tax. The Federal Insurance Contributions Act (FICA) imposes two taxes on employers and employees, an old-age, survivors, and disability insurance (OASDI) tax, commonly referred to as social security tax, and a hospital insurance (HI) or Medicare tax. (FTC 2d/FIN ¶ H-4685; USTR ¶ 31,114; TaxDesk ¶ 541,002)

Employers that are exempt from income tax are nonetheless subject to FICA tax, see FTC 2d/FIN ¶ H-4226; H-4552; USTR ¶ 34,014.66; TaxDesk ¶ 534,001; 541,002.

New Law. Under the 2011 Job Creation Act, a qualified tax-exempt organization that hires a qualified veteran for whom the WOTC would be allowable if the employer weren't tax-exempt can claim a credit against the employer's OASDI tax. (Code Sec. 3111(e)(1) as amended by 2011 Job Creation Act §261(e)(2) (Sec. 261(e)(2), PL 112-56, 11/21/2011))

> **observation:** The credit that a tax-exempt employer can claim applies to the four categories of qualified veterans under Code Sec. 51(d)(3)(A) (FTC 2d/FIN ¶ L-17785.1; USTR ¶ 514.002; TaxDesk ¶ 380,711). These include the new categories added by the 2011 Job Creation Act, see ¶ 1910.

For this purpose, a "qualified tax-exempt organization" is an employer described in Code Sec. 501(c)(3) and exempt from tax under Code Sec. 501(a), see FTC 2d/FIN ¶ D-4101; USTR ¶ 5014; TaxDesk ¶ 670,600. (Code Sec. 3111(e)(5)(A)) A "qualified veteran" is defined as under Code Sec. 51(d)(3). (Code Sec. 3111(e)(5)(B))

The credit is allowed against the OASDI tax on wages paid for employment of all employees of the tax-exempt organization during the "applicable period." (Code Sec. 3111(e)(1)) The "applicable period" means, for any qualified veteran, the one-year period beginning with the day that the veteran begins work for the tax-exempt organization. (Code Sec. 3111(e)(4))

For the 2011 Job Creation Act's change amending Code Sec. 52(c)—which disallows the WOTC to tax-exempt organizations—to make an exception for this credit, see ¶ 1910.

Amount of credit. The credit equals the WOTC credit with respect to wages paid to the qualified veteran during the applicable period, calculated as it would be under Code Sec. 51, with the following modifications: (Code Sec. 3111(e)(1))

• The general credit percentage of qualifying first-year wages is 26% (instead of 40%). (Code Sec. 3111(e)(3)(A))

• The credit percentage of qualifying wages for a qualified veteran who has completed less than 400, but at least 120, hours of service for the employer is 16.25% (instead of 25%). ((Code Sec. 3111(e)(3)(B)))

• The tax-exempt organization may only take into account wages paid to a qualified veteran for services in furtherance of the activities related to the purposes or function on which the organization's tax-exemption is based. (Code Sec. 3111(e)(3)(C))

> *Illustration:* In 2012, a tax-exempt organization dedicated to eradicating cancer hires V, a disabled veteran, as a statistical analyst, and pays her $50,000 a year. V was out of work for nine months before being hired by the organization, and so is a qualified veteran under Code Sec. 51(d)(3)(A)(ii)(II).
>
> Under Code Sec. 51(b)(3), as amended by the 2011 Job Creation Act (see ¶ 1910), the amount of the qualified first-year wages that may be taken into account with respect to V can't exceed $24,000 per year. So the organization can reduce its 2012 OASDI bill by $6,240 (.26 × $24,000).

Limit on credit. The credit for hiring qualified veterans can't exceed the OASDI tax otherwise payable for employment of all the tax-exempt organization's employees during the applicable period. (Code Sec. 3111(e)(2))

☐ **Effective:** Individuals who begin work for an employer after Nov. 21, 2011. (2011 Job Creation Act §261(g))

> 🅁🅃🄰 *observation:* Because the tax-exempt organizations' FICA tax credit applies for veterans for whom the WOTC would be allowable if the employer weren't tax-exempt, the expiration of the WOTC for qualified veterans, for veterans who begin work for the employer after Dec. 31, 2012, also applies to the FICA tax credit.

¶ 1905. Expanded information reporting requirement for post-2011 payments of $600 or more to non-tax-exempt corporations is repealed

Code Sec. 6041(i), as amended by 2011 Taxpayer Protection Act §2(a)
Code Sec. 6041(j), as amended by 2011 Taxpayer Protection Act §2(a)
Generally effective: Payments made after Dec. 31, 2011
Committee Reports, see ¶ 5901

All "persons" engaged in a trade or business have to file with IRS an information return for "payments" (described below) made to another person (other than certain payments with respect to which information returns are required under Code Sections other than Code Sec. 6041) in the course of the payor's trade or business (see FTC 2d/FIN ¶ S-3660; USTR ¶ 60,414.02; TaxDesk ¶ 814,005) that constitute fixed or determinable income (see FTC 2d/FIN ¶ S-3662; USTR ¶ 60,414.01; TaxDesk ¶ 814,007) aggregating $600 or more in any tax year. The "payments" subject to this information-return requirement are those for:

- salaries, wages, commissions, fees, and other forms of compensation for services rendered amounting to $600 or more in a tax year; and
- interest, rents, royalties, annuities, pensions, and other gains, profits, and income amounting to $600 or more in a tax year, see FTC 2d/FIN ¶ S-3656; USTR ¶ 60,414; TaxDesk ¶ 814,001.

Under pre-2011 Taxpayer Protection Act law, for purposes of the above information-reporting requirement, "payments" were to include gross proceeds and amounts paid in consideration for property amounting to $600 or more in a tax year, if paid after Dec. 31, 2011, and, with certain exceptions, a person receiving rental income after Dec. 31, 2010 from real estate was considered to be engaged in the trade or business of renting property. (FTC 2d/FIN ¶ S-3655, ¶ S-3656; USTR ¶ 60,414; TaxDesk ¶ 814,001)

For repeal of the requirement to file an information return with IRS for post-2011 payments of $600 or more of gross proceeds or amounts paid in consideration for property, see ¶ 1906.

For repeal of the requirement to file an information return with IRS for post-2010 payments for services by certain recipients of rental income from real estate, see ¶ 1907.

The information return has to set forth the amounts of the gains, profits, and income, and the name and address of the recipient of the payment, see FTC 2d/FIN ¶ S-3656; USTR ¶ 60,414; TaxDesk ¶ 814,001. The payor is also required to provide the payment recipient with an annual statement showing the aggregate payments made and contact information for the payor, see FTC 2d/FIN ¶ S-3659; USTR ¶ 60,414; TaxDesk ¶ 814,003.

While Reg §1.6041-3(p)(1) generally excepts from these information reporting requirements, payments made to corporations and certain other types of entities, see FTC 2d/FIN ¶ S-3676; USTR ¶ 60,414,05; TaxDesk ¶ 814,019, regs or Code provisions require reporting of the following types of payments to corporations:

(1) medical and healthcare payments of at least $600, see FTC 2d/FIN ¶ S-3667; USTR ¶ 60,414.05; TaxDesk ¶ 814,011;

(2) fish purchases totaling at least $600 cash, see FTC 2d/FIN ¶ S-3695.1; USTR ¶ 60,50R.4; TaxDesk ¶ 861,054;

(3) attorney's fees (of any amount), see FTC 2d/FIN ¶ S-3851; USTR ¶ 60,454.06; TaxDesk ¶ 814,087;

(4) gross proceeds paid to an attorney of $600 or more, see FTC 2d/FIN ¶ S-3852; USTR ¶ 60,454.06; TaxDesk ¶ 814,087;

(5) substitute payments in lieu of dividends or tax-exempt interest (of any amount), see FTC 2d/FIN ¶ S-3724; USTR ¶ 60,454; TaxDesk ¶ 814,034; and

(6) payments by a Federal executive agency for services (for contracts exceeding $25,000), see FTC 2d/FIN ¶ S-3682; USTR ¶ 60,50M4.01; TaxDesk ¶ 816,014.

Pre-2011 Taxpayer Protection Act law provided that, for payments made after Dec. 31, 2011, notwithstanding any IRS reg issued before Mar. 23, 2010, for information reporting purposes, "person" was to include any corporation not exempt from tax under Code Sec. 501(a) (see FTC 2d/FIN ¶ D-4001; USTR ¶ 5014; TaxDesk ¶ 670,501). (FTC 2d/FIN ¶ S-3655, ¶ S-3656.A1; USTR ¶ 60,414.035)

> *observation:* Thus, under pre-2011 Taxpayer Protection Act law, for payments made after Dec. 31, 2011, a business was required to file an information return for *all* payments aggregating $600 or more in a tax year to a single payee (other than a payee that is a tax-exempt corporation), notwithstanding any reg promulgated before Mar. 23, 2010 (e.g., Reg §1.6041-3(p)(1)).

Pre-2011 Taxpayer Protection Act law further provided that IRS could prescribe regs and other guidance as appropriate or necessary to carry out the purposes of the information-reporting rules, including rules to prevent duplicative reporting of transactions. (FTC 2d/FIN ¶ S-3655, ¶ S-3656.A2; USTR ¶ 60,414.035)

> *observation:* Patient Protection and Affordable Care Act (PPACA) §9006(a) (Sec. 9006(a), PL 111-148, 3/23/2010) added the expanded reporting requirement to Code Sec. 6041 that was to go into effect for payments after Dec. 31, 2011 (i.e., the above rules, providing a reporting requirement for payments to corporations and additional regulatory authority).

New Law. The 2011 Taxpayer Protection Act repeals the information reporting rules for payments to corporations made after Dec. 31, 2011 in their entirety (Com Rept, see ¶ 5901), by striking Code Sec. 6041(i). (Code Sec. 6041(i) as amended by 2011 Taxpayer Protection Act §2(a) (Sec. 2(a), PL 112-9, 4/14/2011))

> *observation:* Thus, the repeal lifts the administrative burden on payors that were in the process of establishing a program of information reporting for payments of $600 or more to non-tax-exempt corporations.

⊘ *observation:* The information-reporting requirements listed at items (1) through (6) above, have not been repealed, and they remain in effect. The repeal discussed above only applies to the *expanded* information-reporting requirement discussed above.

The 2011 Taxpayer Protection Act repeals IRS's authority (described above) to prescribe regs and other guidance as may be appropriate or necessary to carry out the purposes of the information reporting rules, including rules to prevent duplicative reporting of transactions, in its entirety (Com Rept, see ¶ 5901), by striking Code Sec. 6041(j). (Code Sec. 6041(j) as amended by 2011 Taxpayer Protection Act §2(a)) Thus, the 2011 Taxpayer Protection Act repeals in their entirety the changes to Code Sec. 6041 enacted in PPACA §9006(a) (Sec. 9006(a), PL 111-148, 3/23/2010) that provided rules for payments to corporations and provided additional regulatory authority (Com Rept, see ¶ 5901).

For repeal of the requirement to file an information return with IRS for post-2011 payments of $600 or more of gross proceeds or amounts paid in consideration for property, see ¶ 1906.

For repeal of the requirement to file an information return with IRS for post-2010 payments for services by certain recipients of rental income from real estate, see ¶ 1907.

☐ **Effective:** Payments made after Dec. 31, 2011. (2011 Taxpayer Protection Act §2(c))

¶ 1906. Expanded information reporting for post-2011 payments of $600 or more of gross proceeds or amounts in consideration for property is repealed

Code Sec. 6041(a), as amended by 2011 Taxpayer Protection Act §2(b)(1)
Code Sec. 6041(a), as amended by 2011 Taxpayer Protection Act §2(b)(2)
Generally effective: Payments made after Dec. 31, 2011
Committee Reports, see ¶ 5901

All persons engaged in a trade or business have to file with IRS an information return for "payments" (described below) made to another person (other than certain payments with respect to which information returns are required under Code Sections other than Code Sec. 6041) in the course of the payor's trade or business (see FTC 2d/FIN ¶ S-3660; USTR ¶ 60,414.02; TaxDesk ¶ 814,005) that constitute fixed or determinable income (see FTC 2d/FIN ¶ S-3662; USTR ¶ 60,414.01; TaxDesk ¶ 814,007) aggregating $600 or more in any tax year. The "payments" subject to this information-return requirement are those for:

• salaries, wages, commissions, fees, and other forms of compensation for services rendered amounting to $600 or more in a tax year; and

• interest, rents, royalties, annuities, pensions, and other gains, profits, and income amounting to $600 or more in a tax year, see FTC 2d/FIN ¶ S-3656; USTR ¶ 60,414; TaxDesk ¶ 814,001.

Under pre-2011 Taxpayer Protection Act law, for purposes of the above information-reporting requirement, "payments" were to include gross proceeds and amounts paid in consideration for property amounting to $600 or more in a tax year, if paid after Dec. 31, 2011, and, with certain exceptions, a person receiving rental income after Dec. 31, 2010 from real estate was considered to be engaged in the trade or business of renting property. (FTC 2d/FIN ¶ S-3655, ¶ S-3656; USTR ¶ 60,414; TaxDesk ¶ 814,001)

For repeal of the requirement to file an information return with IRS for post-2010 payments for services by certain recipients of rental income from real estate, see ¶ 1907.

> **🅡🅘🅐 observation:** Patient Protection and Affordable Care Act (PPACA) §9006(b) (Sec. 9006(b), PL 111-148, 3/23/2010) added the expanded reporting requirement to Code Sec. 6041 that was to go into effect for payments after Dec. 31, 2011 (i.e., the above rules, providing an information-reporting requirement for post-2011 payments of $600 or more of gross proceeds or amounts in consideration for property).

The information return has to set forth the amounts of the gains, profits, and income, and the name and address of the recipient of the payment, see FTC 2d/FIN ¶ S-3656; USTR ¶ 60,414; TaxDesk ¶ 814,001. The payor is also required to provide the payment recipient with an annual statement showing the aggregate payments made and contact information for the payor, see FTC 2d/FIN ¶ S-3659; USTR ¶ 60,414; TaxDesk ¶ 814,003.

New Law. The 2011 Taxpayer Protection Act repeals the information reporting rules for payments of $600 or more in a tax year, made after Dec. 31, 2011, of gross proceeds or amounts in consideration for property, in their entirety. (Com Rept, see ¶ 5901) Specifically, it strikes "amounts in consideration for property" (Code Sec. 6041(a) as amended by 2011 Taxpayer Protection Act §2(b)(1) Sec. 2(b)(1), PL 112-9, 4/14/2011)) and "gross proceeds" (Code Sec. 6041(a) as amended by 2011 Taxpayer Protection Act §2(b)(2)) from Code Sec. 6041(a).

> **🅡🅘🅐 observation:** Thus, the 2011 Taxpayer Protection Act repeals in its entirety the expanded reporting requirement for post-2011 payments under PPACA §9006(b) (Sec. 9006(b), PL 111-148, 3/23/2010) with respect to gross proceeds from property.

> **🅡🅘🅐 observation:** The repeal also lifts the administrative burden on payors that were in the process of establishing a program of informa-

tion reporting for payments of $600 or more of gross proceeds or amounts in consideration for property.

For repeal of the requirement to file an information return with IRS for all post-2011 payments of $600 or more to a non-tax-exempt corporation, see ¶ 1905.

For repeal of the requirement to file an information return with IRS for post-2010 payments for services by certain recipients of rental income from real estate, see ¶ 1907.

☐ **Effective:** Payments made after Dec. 31, 2011. (2011 Taxpayer Protection Act §2(c))

¶ 1907. Information reporting for certain recipients of rental income for payments of $600 or more to service providers is retroactively repealed

Code Sec. 6041(h), as repealed by 2011 Taxpayer Protection Act §3(a)
Generally effective: Payments made after Dec. 31, 2010
Committee Reports, see ¶ 5902

All persons engaged in a trade or business have to file with IRS an information return for "payments" (described below) made to another person (other than certain payments with respect to which information returns are required under Code Sections other than Code Sec. 6041) in the course of the payor's trade or business (see FTC 2d/FIN ¶ S-3660; USTR ¶ 60,414.02; TaxDesk ¶ 814,005) that constitute fixed or determinable income (see FTC 2d/FIN ¶ S-3662; USTR ¶ 60,414.01; TaxDesk ¶ 814,007) aggregating $600 or more in any tax year. The "payments" subject to this information-return requirement are those for:

- salaries, wages, commissions, fees, and other forms of compensation for services rendered amounting to $600 or more in a tax year; and

- interest, rents, royalties, annuities, pensions, and other gains, profits, and income amounting to $600 or more in a tax year, see FTC 2d/FIN ¶ S-3656; USTR ¶ 60,414; TaxDesk ¶ 814,001.

Under pre-2011 Taxpayer Protection Act law, for purposes of the above information-reporting requirement, "payments" were to include gross proceeds and amounts paid in consideration for property amounting to $600 or more in a tax year, if paid after Dec. 31, 2011, and, with certain exceptions described below, pre-2011 Taxpayer Protection Act Code Sec. 6041(h)(1) provided that a person receiving rental income after Dec. 31, 2010 from real estate is considered to be engaged in the trade or business of renting property. (FTC 2d/FIN ¶ S-3655, ¶ S-3656; USTR ¶ 60,414; TaxDesk ¶ 814,001)

Thus, the pre-2011 Taxpayer Protection Act law effectively provided that the above information requirement applied for post-2010 payments by a person receiving rental income from real property (such as payments to a service provider, like a plumber, painter or accountant, in the course of earning rental income), except that, under pre-2011 Taxpayer Protection Act Code Sec. 6041(h)(2), this requirement did not apply to:

. . . any individual who received rental income of not more than the minimal amount, as determined under IRS regs;

. . . any individual, including one who is an active member of the uniformed services or an employee of the intelligence community (as defined in Code Sec. 121(d)(9)(C)(iv), see (FTC 2d/FIN ¶ I-4528.4A; USTR ¶ 1214; TaxDesk ¶ 225,708.3A), if substantially all rental income was derived from renting the individual's principal residence (within the meaning of Code Sec. 121, see (FTC 2d/FIN ¶ I-4522; USTR ¶ 1214; TaxDesk ¶ 225,702), on a temporary basis;

. . . any other individual for whom the requirements of Code Sec. 6041 would cause hardship, as determined under IRS regs. (FTC 2d/FIN ¶ S-3656; USTR ¶ 60,414; TaxDesk ¶ 814,000 *et seq.*)

For repeal of the requirement to file an information return with IRS for post-2011 payments of $600 or more of gross proceeds or amounts paid in consideration for property, see ¶ 1905.

New Law. The 2011 Taxpayer Protection Act specifically strikes Code Sec. 6041(h) in its entirety from the Internal Revenue Code. (Code Sec. 6041(h) as amended by 2011 Taxpayer Protection Act §3(a) (Sec. 3(a), PL 112-9, 4/14/ 2011)) Thus, as a consequence of the enactment of 2011 Taxpayer Protection Act §3(a) and 2011 Taxpayer Protection Act §3(b), certain recipients of rental income from real estate who are not otherwise considered to be engaged in a trade or business of renting property are not subject to the same information reporting requirements as taxpayers who are considered to be engaged in a trade or business. As a result, rental income recipients making payments of $600 or more to a service provider (such a plumber, painter, or accountant) in the course of earning rental income are not required to provide an information return (typically Form 1099-MISC) to IRS and to the service provider. (Com Rept, see ¶ 5902)

> *observation:* The 2011 Taxpayer Protection Act retroactively repeals, in its entirely, Code Sec. 6041(h), which had been enacted a little more than six months earlier by the 2010 Small Business Jobs Act (Sec. 2101(a), PL 111-240, 9/27/2010; Sec. 2101(b), PL 111-240, 9/27/2010).

For repeal of the requirement to file an information return with IRS for post-2011 payments of $600 or more of gross proceeds or amounts paid in consideration for property, see ¶ 1905.

For repeal of the reporting requirement for post-2011 payments of $600 or more to non-tax-exempt corporations, see ¶ 1906.

☐ **Effective:** Payments made after Dec. 31, 2010. (2011 Taxpayer Protection Act §3(b))

¶ 1908. Principal administrators of U.S. prisons have to provide IRS with certain information about inmates each year

Code Sec. 6116, as added by 2011 U.S.-Korea Trade Act §502(a)
Generally effective: Oct. 21, 2011
Committee Reports, see ¶ 5802

Under pre-2011 U.S.-Korea Trade Act law, administrators of prisons located in the U.S. weren't required to report information about prisoners to IRS.

New Law. Not later than Sept. 15, 2012, and annually after that date, the head of the Federal Bureau of Prisons and the head of any state agency charged with the responsibility for administration of prisons had to provide to IRS in electronic format a list with the information described below of all the inmates incarcerated within the prison system for any part of the earlier two calendar years or the current calendar year through Aug. 31. (Code Sec. 6116(a) as added by 2011 U.S.-Korea Trade Act §502(a) (Sec. 502(a), PL 112-41, 10/21/2011)) The information provided should assist in detecting and deterring fraudulent tax return filings from inmates, and in identifying those inmates that file fraudulent returns. (Com Rept, see ¶ 5802)

The information with respect to each inmate is: (Code Sec. 6116(b))

. . . first, middle, and last name, (Code Sec. 6116(b)(1))

. . . date of birth, (Code Sec. 6116(b)(2))

. . . institution of current incarceration or, for released inmates, most recent incarceration, (Code Sec. 6116(b)(3))

. . . prison assigned inmate number, (Code Sec. 6116(b)(4))

. . . the date of incarceration, (Code Sec. 6116(b)(5))

. . . the date of release or anticipated date of release, (Code Sec. 6116(b)(6))

. . . the date of work release, (Code Sec. 6116(b)(7))

. . . taxpayer identification number (TIN) and whether the prison has verified the TIN, (Code Sec. 6116(b)(8))

. . . last known address (FTC 2d/FIN ¶ T-2850; USTR ¶ 62,124.03; TaxDesk ¶ 831,007), and (Code Sec. 6116(b)(9))

. . . any additional information requested by IRS. (Code Sec. 6116(b)(10)).

IRS was to determine the electronic format of the information described above. (Code Sec. 6116(c)).

Redesignation.   Pre-2011 U.S.-Korea Trade Act Code Sec. 6116 is redesignated as Code Sec. 6117. (2011 U.S.-Korea Trade Act §502(a))

☐ **Effective:** Oct. 21, 2011. (2011 U.S.-Korea Trade Act §107(b)(1))

¶ 1909. Mandatory 3% withholding on payments to government contractors was repealed prospectively

Code Sec. 3402(t), as amended by 2011 Job Creation Act §102(a)
Generally effective: For payments made after 2011
Committee Reports, see ¶ 5701

Under pre-2011 Job Creation Act law, withholding requirements originally enacted in 2006 would have applied to certain government payments (Com Rept, see ¶ 5701) made after 2012 (see the *RIA observation,* below). Under pre-2011 Job Creation Act law, government entities making certain payments to any person providing property or services would have been required to deduct and withhold income tax from that payment in an amount equal to 3% of the payment. The withholding would have applied regardless of whether the government entity making the payment was the recipient of the property or service. The requirement also would have applied to a payment made in connection with a government voucher or certificate program that functioned as a payment for property or services. (Com Rept, see ¶ 5701)

New Law.   The 2011 Job Creation Act repealed the above 3% withholding requirements (Com Rept, see ¶ 5701) by striking subsection (t) of Code Sec. 3402. (Code Sec. 3402(t) as amended by 2011 Job Creation Act §102(a) (Sec. 102(a), PL 112-56, 11/21/2011)) The withholding requirements were repealed because Congress concluded that the burdens resulting from the requirements were disproportionate when compared to the resulting improvement in tax compliance. (Com Rept, see ¶ 5701)

☐ **Effective:** For payments made after Dec. 31, 2011. (2011 Job Creation Act §102(b))

> **RIA** *observation:* The 2005 Tax Increase Prevention and Reconciliation Act (TIPRA) (Sec. 511(b), PL 109-222, 5/17/2006) imposed the above withholding requirements on payments made after 2010. The 2009 American Recovery and Reinvestment Act (ARRA) (Sec. 1511, PL 111-5, 2/17/2009) delayed the effective date, to apply to payments made after 2011. And regs (TD 9524, 05/06/2011) further postponed the effective date, to apply to payments made after 2012.

As noted above, the 2011 Job Creation Act repealed the withholding requirements effective for payments made after 2011. Even though, under the regs, the withholding requirements weren't scheduled to apply until after 2012, the 2011 Job Creation Act's repeal applied to payments made after 2011 because that was the deferred statutory effective date. In effect, the withholding requirements never came into existence.

¶ 1910. Work opportunity credit as applied to qualified veterans was extended through 2012 and modified

Code Sec. 51(b)(3), as amended by 2011 Job Creation Act §261(a)
Code Sec. 51(c)(4)(B), as amended by 2011 Job Creation Act §261(d)
Code Sec. 51(d)(3)(A), as amended by 2011 Job Creation Act §261(b)(3)
Code Sec. 51(d)(13)(D), as amended by 2011 Job Creation Act §261(c)
Code Sec. 52(c), as amended by 2011 Job Creation Act §261(e)(1)
Code Sec. 51, 2011 Job Creation Act §261(f)
Generally effective: Individuals who begin work for the employer after Nov. 21, 2011 and before Jan. 1, 2013
Committee Reports, None

A work opportunity tax credit (WOTC) is available on an elective basis to employers for certain wages paid to members of one or more of nine "targeted groups," see FTC 2d/FIN ¶s L-17775, L-17776; USTR ¶s 514, 514.002; TaxDesk ¶s 380,700, 308,701.

Under pre-2011 Job Creation Act law, for purposes of the WOTC, wages didn't include any amount paid or incurred to an individual who began work for the employer after Dec. 31, 2011. (FTC 2d ¶ L-17775; USTR ¶ 514; TaxDesk ¶ 380,700)

One of the targeted groups consists of "qualified veterans." A "qualified veteran" is an individual who is a veteran (defined at FTC 2d/FIN ¶ L-17785.1; USTR ¶ 514.002; TaxDesk ¶ 380,711) who, under pre-2011 Job Creation Act law, met one of the following three tests:

(1) the individual had to be a member of a family receiving assistance under a supplemental nutrition assistance program under the 2008 Food and Nutrition Act for at least 3 months, all or part of which were during the 12-month period ending on the hiring date (the nutrition assistance test),

(2) the individual had to be entitled to compensation for a service-connected disability and have a hiring date that wasn't more than one year after having been discharged or released from active duty in the U.S. Armed Forces (the disabled-and-recently-discharged test); or

(3) the individual had to be entitled to compensation for a service-connected disability and have aggregate periods of unemployment during the one-year pe-

riod ending on the hiring date that equaled or exceeded six months (the dis-abled-and-6-months-unemployed test). (FTC 2d ¶ L-17785.1; USTR ¶ 514.002; TaxDesk ¶ 380,711)

Also, generally, to qualify as a member of a targeted group an individual must be certified by a designated local agency (i.e., a state employment security agency) as being a member of a targeted group (the general certification re-quirement), see FTC 2d ¶ L-17784.1; USTR ¶ 514; TaxDesk ¶ 380,708. An em-ployer can choose either of two procedures to satisfy the general certification requirement. Under Code Sec. 51(d)(13)(A)(i), on or before the day on which an eligible individual begins work, the employer must receive a certification from the designated local agency that the individual is a member of a targeted group. Alternatively, Code Sec. 51(d)(13)(A)(ii) requires that (1) the individual complete a pre-screening notice on Form 8850 on or before the day the individ-ual is offered employment and (2) the employer submit the notice to the desig-nated local agency, as part of a written request for certification, not later than 28 days after the individual begins work for the employer, see FTC 2d ¶ L-17784.1; USTR ¶ 514; TaxDesk ¶ 380,708.

Further, the Code specifically states that a designated local agency must cer-tify that a veteran meets the requirements for qualified veteran status (the quali-fied veteran certification requirement), see FTC 2d ¶ L-17785.1; USTR ¶ 514.002; TaxDesk ¶ 380,711.

With some exceptions, the maximum WOTC is $2,400 per employee, i.e., 40% of up to a maximum of $6,000 of qualified first-year wages, see FTC 2d/ FIN ¶ L-17778; USTR ¶ 514; TaxDesk ¶ 380,700.1.

Under one of the exceptions to the $2,400-per-employee maximum, under pre-2011 Job Creation Act law, the maximum credit allowed with respect to a qualified veteran who satisfied the disabled-and-recently discharged test or the disabled-and-6-months-unemployed test was $4,800—i.e., 40% of up to a maxi-mum of $12,000 of qualified first-year wages. (FTC 2d ¶ L-17779.2; USTR ¶ 514; TaxDesk ¶ 380,702.2)

> **🅡🅘🅐** *observation:* The maximum credit for a veteran whose basis for sta-tus as a qualified veteran was satisfaction of the nutrition assistance test (above) was the usually applicable $2,400.

Generally, the WOTC isn't allowed to tax-exempt organizations. Under pre-2011 Job Creation Act law, the only exception to the prohibition for tax-exempt organizations was the allowance of the credit to cooperatives de-scribed in Code Sec. 521 (i.e. farmers' cooperatives, see FTC 2d/FIN ¶ E-1007; USTR ¶ 5214.01). (FTC 2d ¶ L-17789A; USTR ¶ 514; TaxDesk ¶ 380,700)

New Law. The 2011 Job Creation Act extended and modified the WOTC, as applied to qualified veterans, as described below.

Extension of credit. The 2011 Job Creation Act provided that for purposes of the WOTC, wages don't include any amount paid or incurred to an individual who begins work for the employer (1) after Dec. 31, 2012, in the case of a qualified veteran (Code Sec. 51(c)(4)(B)(i) as amended by 2011 Job Creation Act §261(d)) (Sec. 261(d), PL 112-56, 11/21/2011) and (2) after Dec. 31, 2011 in the case of any other individual. (Code Sec. 51(c)(4)(B)(ii))

> ⓇⒾⒶ *observation:* Thus, with respect to hiring qualified veterans, but not with respect to hiring members of other targeted groups, the 2011 Job Creation Act extended the WOTC for one year.

> ⓇⒾⒶ *caution:* As discussed at ¶ 140, the 2012 Taxpayer Relief Act extends the starting work date for WOTC qualification for one year for qualified veterans and two years in the case of any other individual by providing that the term "wages" (for purposes of determining the amount of the WOTC) doesn't include any amount paid or incurred to an individual who begins work for the employer after Dec. 31, 2013.

Expansion of qualified veteran definition. The 2011 Job Creation Act provides that a qualified veteran includes a veteran that is certified by the designated local agency as—

... having aggregate periods of unemployment during the 1-year period ending on the hiring date that equal or exceed 4 weeks (but less than 6 months) (the 4-weeks-unemployed test); or (Code Sec. 51(d)(3)(A)(iii) as amended by 2011 Job Creation Act §261(b)(3))

... having aggregate periods of unemployment during the 1-year period ending on the hiring date which equal or exceed 6 months (the 6-months-unemployed test). (Code Sec. 51(d)(3)(A)(iv))

> ⓇⒾⒶ *observation:* The 4-weeks-unemployed test doesn't make unnecessary the 6-months-unemployed test because the maximum WOTC amount varies depending on which of the two tests a veteran satisfies, see **Maximum credit** below.

> ⓇⒾⒶ *observation:* The 6-months-unemployed test doesn't make unnecessary the disabled-and-6-months-unemployed test (already existing under pre-2011 Job Creation Act law, see above) because the maximum WOTC amount varies depending on which of the two tests a veteran satisfies, see **Maximum credit** below.

> ⓇⒾⒶ *observation:* With the addition, by the 2011 Job Creation Act, of the 4-weeks-unemployed test and the 6-months-unemployed test to the three tests that existed under pre-2011 Job Creation Act law (see

above), there are five alternative grounds for a veteran having the status of a qualified veteran.

Certification safe harbors and alternatives. Notwithstanding Code Sec. 51(d)(13)(A) (which provides the general certification requirement, see above), for purposes of Code Sec. 51(d)(3)(A) (which provides the qualified veteran certification requirement, see above)— (Code Sec. 51(d)(13)(D)(i) as amended by 2011 Job Creation Act §261(c))

. . . a veteran is treated as certified by the designated local agency as having aggregate periods of unemployment meeting the requirements of, as applicable, Code Sec. 51(d)(3)(A)(ii)(II) (the disabled-and-6-months-unemployed test, already existing under pre-2011 Job Creation Act law, see above) or Code Sec. 51(d)(3)(A)(iv) (the 6-months-unemployed test, see above) if the veteran is certified by the agency as being in receipt of unemployment compensation under State or Federal law for not less than six months during the one-year period ending on the hiring date, and (Code Sec. 51(d)(13)(D)(i)(I))

. . . a veteran is treated as certified by the designated local agency as having aggregate periods of unemployment meeting the requirements of Code Sec. 51(d)(3)(A)(iii) (the 4-weeks-unemployed test, see above) if the veteran is certified by the agency as being in receipt of unemployment compensation under State or Federal law for not less than four weeks (but less than six months) during the one-year period ending on the hiring date. (Code Sec. 51(d)(13)(D)(i)(II))

> *observation:* Presumably, the above rules are a safe harbor, and not the exclusive means, for certification of unemployment. For example, other means of certification would seem necessary if the unemployment compensation of a veteran has run out before the one-year period ending with the hiring date.

Additionally, IRS is allowed to provide alternative methods for certification of a veteran as a qualified veteran described in Code Sec. 51(d)(3)(A)(ii)(II) (see Code Sec. 51(d)(13)(D)(i)(I) above), Code Sec. 51(d)(3)(A)(iii) (see Code Sec. 51(d)(13)(D)(i)(II) above) or Code Sec. 51(d)(3)(A)(iv) (see Code Sec. 51(d)(13)(D)(i)(I) above). (Code Sec. 51(d)(13)(D)(ii))

IRS relaxation of certification procedure. After the enactment of the 2011 Job Creation Act, IRS, in Notice 2012-13, Sec. III, 2012-9 IRB 421, provided that an employer who hires a qualified veteran after Nov. 21, 2011 and before May 22, 2012 is considered to satisfy the requirements of Code Sec. 51(d)(13)(A)(ii) (see the background discussion above and the first observation below) if the employer submits, before June 20, 2012, a completed pre-screening notice to the designated local agency to request certification, see FTC 2d/FIN ¶ L-17784.1D; USTR ¶ 514; TaxDesk ¶ 308,708.1B.

observation: Thus, if, for a qualified veteran hired after Nov. 21, 2011 and before May 22, 2012, an employer meets the pre-June 20, 2012 filing deadline provided in Notice 2012-13, the requirements in Code Sec. 51(d)(13)(A)(ii) are deemed satisfied (including, as described in the background discussion above, the 28-day filing deadline).

observation: The certification rule provided by Notice 2012-13 applies to *all* qualified veterans, not *only to* veterans who qualify because of changes provided by the 2011 Job Creation Act (see **Expansion of qualified veteran definition** above).

Maximum credit. Under the 2011 Job Creation Act, the amount of qualified first-year wages that can be taken into account in determining the WOTC in the case of an individual who is a qualified veteran:

(1) by reason of Code Sec. 51(d)(3)(A)(ii)(I) (the disabled-and-recently-discharged test, already existing under pre-2011 Job Creation Act law, see above) is $12,000,

(2) by reason of Code Sec. 51(d)(3)(A)(iv) (the 6-months-unemployed test, see above) is $14,000, and

(3) by reason of Code Sec. 51(d)(3)(A)(ii)(II) (the disabled-and-6-months-unemployed test, already existing under pre-2011 Job Creation Act law, see above) is $24,000. (Code Sec. 51(b)(3) as amended by 2011 Job Creation Act §261(a))

observation: Thus, under the first rule listed above, if the basis for an employee being a qualified veteran is that the employee satisfies the disabled-and-recently-discharged test, the maximum WOTC available to the employer with respect to the qualified veteran is $4,800 (i.e., 40% × $12,000).

Under the second rule listed above, if the basis for an employee being a qualified veteran is that the employee satisfies the 6-months-unemployed test, the maximum WOTC available to the employer with respect to the qualified veteran is $5,600 (i.e., 40% × $14,000).

Under the third rule listed above, if the basis for an employee being a qualified veteran is that the employee satisfies the disabled-and-6-months-unemployed test, the maximum WOTC available to the employer with respect to the qualified veteran is $9,600 (i.e., 40% × $24,000)

observation: The three rules listed above apply instead of the more restrictive $2,400 (40% × $6,000) maximum available with respect to (1) most other targeted groups and (2) employees who are qualified veterans by reason of grounds other than those listed above—i.e., by reason of (A) Code Sec. 51(d)(3)(A)(i) (the nutrition assistance test, already existing under pre-2011 Job Creation Act law, see above) or (B) Code Sec. 51(d)(3)(A)(iii) (the 4-weeks-unemployed test, see above).

observation: The net effects of the three rules listed above are that (1) enhanced maximum credit amounts (i.e., amounts in excess of the usually applicable $2,400) are provided for veterans who are qualified veterans by reason of either of the two new tests provided by the 2011 Job Creation Act (i.e., either the 4-weeks-unemployed test or 6-months-unemployed test discussed above), (2) the enhanced maximum credit amount is raised from $4,800 to $9,600 for veterans who are qualified veterans by reason of the disabled-and-6-months-unemployed test, (3) the enhanced maximum credit amount remains at $4,800 for veterans who are qualified veterans by reason of the disabled-and-recently-discharged test, and (4) the usually applicable $2,400 credit amount remains for veterans who are qualified veterans by reason of the nutrition assistance test.

Use of credit by tax-exempt organizations. Under the 2011 Job Creation Act, the WOTC is available, under Code Sec. 3111(e), against payroll taxes for the employment of qualified veterans by qualified tax-exempt organizations. (Code Sec. 52(c)(2) as amended by 2011 Job Creation Act §261(e)(1)(B)) For detailed discussion of the rule for payroll taxes in Code Sec. 3111(e), see ¶ 580.

observation: Before the 2011 Job Creation Act, Code Sec. 52(c) wasn't divided into paragraphs and contained only the general prohibition on the allowance of the WOTC (see above) and the exception for cooperatives described in Code Sec. 521 (see above). That general rule and exception are included by the 2011 Job Creation Act in new Code Sec. 52(c)(1).

Rules for U.S. possessions. The credit allowed against U.S. income taxes for any tax year under the amendments made by 2011 Job Creation Act §261 to Code Sec. 51 (see above) with respect to any qualified veteran is reduced. The reduction is equal to the amount of any credit, or other tax benefit described in 2011 Job Creation Act §261(f)(1)(B) (see below), imposed by a U.S. possession (defined below) by reason of 2011 Job Creation Act §261(f) (see the second observation below) with respect to that qualified veteran for that tax year. (2011 Job Creation Act §261(f)(2))

⊘ observation: Presumably, the effect of the above rule concerning U.S. possessions is that an employer's WOTC otherwise allowable against U.S income taxes for a qualified veteran who begins work for the employer in calendar year 2012 must be reduced by any WOTC, or equivalent tax benefit, allowed against the taxes of any of the five U.S. possessions listed below.

⊘ observation: It is 2011 Job Creation Act §261(a) through 2011 Job Creation Act §261(e), *not 2011 Job Creation Act §261(f),* that provide for the extension and modification of the WOTC as applied to qualified veterans. Thus, presumably, the reference to "this subsection" in the text of 2011 Job Creation Act §261(f)(2) (reflected as a reference to "2011 Job Creation Act §261(f)" in the paraphrase of 2011 Job Creation Act §261(f)(2) above) should instead be to "this section" (i.e., 2011 Job Creation Act §261).

The U.S. Treasury must pay to each U.S. possession with a mirror code tax system (see below) amounts equal to that possession's loss by reason of the amendments made by 2011 Job Creation Act §261. The U.S. Treasury must determine these amounts based on information provided by the respective possession's government. (2011 Job Creation Act §261(f)(1)(A))

The U.S. Treasury will pay to each U.S. possession that does not have a mirror code tax system (see below) the amount estimated by the U.S. Treasury as being equal to the loss to that possession that would have occurred by reason of the amendments made by 2011 Job Creation Act §261 if a mirror code tax system had been in effect in the possession. This rule does not apply with respect to any U.S. possession unless the possession establishes, to the satisfaction of the U.S. Treasury, that the possession has implemented (or, at the discretion of the U.S Treasury, will implement) an income tax benefit that is substantially equivalent to the income tax credit in effect after the amendments made by 2011 Job Creation Act §261. (2011 Job Creation Act §261(f)(1)(B))

For purposes of the above rules— (2011 Job Creation Act §261(f)(3)(A)), (2011 Job Creation Act §261(f)(3)(B))

. . . U.S. possessions include American Samoa, Guam, the Commonwealth of the Northern Mariana Islands, the Commonwealth of Puerto Rico, and the U.S. Virgin Islands. (2011 Job Creation Act §261(f)(3)(A))

. . . a "mirror code tax system" means, with respect to any U.S. possession, the income tax system of the possession if the income tax liability of the residents of the possession under that system is determined by reference to the income tax laws of the U.S. as if the possession were the U.S. (2011 Job Creation Act §261(f)(3)(B))

observation: Presumably, for purposes of the definition immediately above, (1) Guam, the Commonwealth of the North Mariana Islands and the U.S. Virgin Islands are U.S possessions that have mirror code tax systems and (2) American Samoa and the Commonwealth of Puerto Rico are U.S. possessions that don't have mirror code tax systems, see FTC 2d/FIN ¶ L-15219.1; USTR ¶ 384.05; TaxDesk ¶ 389,524.

☐ **Effective:** Individuals who begin work for the employer after Nov. 21, 2011 (2011 Job Creation Act §261(g)) and before Jan. 1, 2013. (Code Sec. 51(c)(4)(B)(i) as amended by 2011 Job Creation Act §261(d))

¶ 1911. Penalty imposed for lack of transparency in airline passenger tax disclosures

Code Sec. 7275(c), as amended and redesignated by 2012 FAA Modernization Act §1104(a)
Generally effective: Taxable transportation provided after Mar. 31, 2012.
Committee Reports, see ¶ 5604

A ticket for air transportation all of which is "taxable transportation" under Code Sec. 4262 (defined below) must show the total of:

(A) the amount paid for the transportation, and

(B) the Code Sec. 4261(a) domestic percentage tax (described below) and the Code Sec. 4261(b) domestic segment tax (described below) imposed.

The above provision requires that air transportation providers separately state the tax on the passenger tickets. FTC 2d/FIN ¶ W-5148.1; USTR Excise ¶ 72,094.

In the case of air transportation all of which is taxable transportation under Code Sec. 4262 (or would be but for Code Sec. 4262(b) which excludes certain transportation to or across foreign places) advertising by the person furnishing the transportation or offering to arrange it which states the transportation cost must state the cost as the total of:

(1) the total amount to be paid for the transportation and

(2) the taxes under Code Sec. 4261(a) and Code Sec. 4261(b) (the domestic percentage and domestic segment taxes, see (b) above) and Code Sec. 4261(c) (the tax on international departures and arrivals by air, i.e., the "international tax" described below).

Under the above rules, the tax must be included in the advertised price.

If any such advertising, in addition to stating the total price, states the cost of transportation or the taxes separately, then the total price must be stated at least as prominently as the more prominently stated of the transportation cost or tax. Taxes must be described substantially as "user taxes to pay for airport construction and airway safety and operations." Each violation of any of the above provisions is a misdemeanor subject to fine of not more than $100. (FTC 2d/FIN ¶ W-5100, ¶ W-5148.1; USTR Excise Taxes ¶ 72,094)

For purposes of the domestic air passenger excise taxes, "taxable transportation" is defined by Code Sec. 4262, subject to the Code Sec. 4262(b) exception for certain transportation to or across foreign places, as the U.S. leg of certain international flights or transportation by air that begins in either the U.S. or a 225-mile zone and ends in either the U.S. or the 225-mile zone (that portion of Canada and Mexico which isn't more than 225 miles from the nearest point in the continental U.S.). FTC 2d/FIN ¶ W-5113; USTR Excise ¶ 42,614.02.

The Code Sec. 4261(a) domestic percentage tax is a tax equal to 7.5% of the amount paid for taxable transportation of any person. The Code Sec. 4261(b) domestic segment tax is a tax equal to an inflation adjusted dollar amount ($3.80 in 2012, $3.90 in 2013) for each domestic segment of taxable transportation by air of persons. FTC 2d/FIN ¶ W-5101; USTR Excise ¶ 42,614.01.

The Code Sec. 4261(c) international tax is a tax of a flat amount indexed for inflation ($16.70 for 2012, $17.20 for 2013) on any amount paid (whether paid within or without the U.S.) for any transportation of any person by air, if that transportation begins or ends in the U.S. The tax doesn't apply to any transportation all of which either is taxable under the Code Sec. 4261(a) domestic percentage tax or would be taxable under that provision were it not for certain exceptions for small aircraft on nonestablished lines and affiliated group member transportation of other group members. FTC 2d/FIN ¶ W-5103; USTR Excise ¶ 42,614.01.

Under pre-2012 FAA Modernization Act law, there was no prohibition against airlines including other charges in the required passenger taxes disclosure (e.g., fuel surcharges retained by the commercial airline). In practice, some but not all airlines included such other charges in the required passenger taxes disclosure.

New Law. In the case of transportation by air for which disclosure on the ticket or advertising for such transportation of the amounts paid for passenger taxes is required by the rule at (B) above or the rule at (2) above, if such amounts are separately disclosed, it is unlawful for the disclosure of such amounts to include any amounts not attributable to such taxes (i.e., the domestic percentage tax or the domestic segment tax imposed by Code Sec. 4261(a) and Code Sec. 4261(b) (described at (B) above) and the international tax imposed by Code Sec. 4261(c)). (Code Sec. 7275(c)(1) as amended by 2012 FAA Modernization Act §1104(a)(3) (Sec. 1104(a)(3), PL 112-95, 2/14/2012)) *observation:* Thus, the new law ensures that Code Sec. 4261 air transportation taxes can't be confused with other charges for purposes of the disclosure rules.

Nothing in the above changes, will prohibit the inclusion of amounts not attributable to the taxes imposed by Code Sec. 4261(a), Code Sec. 4261(b) or Code Sec. 4261(c) in the disclosure of the amount paid for transportation as required by the rules at (A) or (1) above, or in a separate disclosure of amounts not attributable to such taxes. (Code Sec. 7275(c)(2))

The above change prohibits all transportation providers from including amounts other than the passenger taxes imposed by Code Sec. 4261 in the required disclosure of passenger taxes on tickets and in advertising when the amount of such tax is separately stated. Disclosure elsewhere on tickets and in advertising (e.g., as an amount paid for transportation) of non-tax charges is allowed. (Com Rept, see ¶ 5604)

Each violation of any of the new rules is a misdemeanor subject to fine of not more than $100. (Code Sec. 7275(d) as amended and redesignated by 2012 FAA Modernization Act §1104(a)(1))

☐ **Effective:** Taxable transportation provided after Mar. 31, 2012. (2012 FAA Modernization Act §1104(b))

¶ 1912. Penalty on Paid Preparers for Noncompliance with Due Diligence Rules Increased from $100 to $500

Code Sec. 6695(g), as amended by 2011 U.S.-Korea Trade Act §501(a)
Generally effective: Returns required to be filed after Dec. 31, 2011.
Committee Reports, see ¶ 5801

A person who is a tax return preparer for any return or claim for refund who fails to comply with due diligence requirements imposed by IRS regs with regard to determining the eligibility for, or the amount of, an earned income credit (EIC) must pay a penalty for each failure. Under pre-U.S. Korea Trade Act law, the penalty was $100 for each failure. (FTC 2d/FIN ¶ V-2630, ¶ V-2677.1; USTR ¶ 66,954.01; TaxDesk ¶ 867,017)

To meet the due diligence standard and avoid tax return preparer penalties, a preparer must: (a) complete the computation worksheet in the Form 1040 instructions or otherwise record the tax return preparer's EIC computation, including the method and information used to complete the computation; (b) have no knowledge that any of the information used in determining EIC eligibility and the EIC amount is incorrect (nor any reason to know that this information is incorrect); and (c) retain for three years certain material relating to Form 8867 and the EIC computation. The preparer must also meet a Checklist requirement. Before the regs discussed below were finalized, regs provided that a preparer could meet the Checklist requirement by completing Form 8867, Paid Preparer's Earned Income Credit Checklist, or recording the information required by Form 8867 in its files.

For tax returns and claims for refund for tax years ending after Dec. 30, 2011, final regs require, among other things, that tax return preparers complete Form 8867 and submit it with the return or claim for refund. Tax return preparers who prepare a tax return or claim for refund but don't submit it directly to IRS may satisfy the Form 8867 submission requirement of their due diligence obligation by providing the form to the taxpayer or the signing tax return preparer as appropriate for submission with the return or claim for refund.

The final regs also provide that the due diligence penalty covers firms that employ preparers who fail to meet the due diligence requirements where the firms didn't adopt and follow reasonable compliance procedures or where certain firm officers or managers participated in, or (before the return filing) knew of, the failure. FTC 2d/FIN ¶ S-1106.1; USTR ¶ 66,954.01; TaxDesk ¶ 867,017

New Law. The 2011 U.S.-Korea Trade Act increases from $100 to $500 the penalty for lack of due diligence by a return preparer in determining eligibility for the EIC. (Code Sec. 6695(g) as amended by 2011 U.S.-Korea Trade Act §501(a) (Sec. 501(a), PL 112-41, 10/21/2011))

☐ **Effective:** Returns required to be filed after Dec. 31, 2011. (2011 U.S.-Korea Trade Act §501(b))

> *observation:* The increase in the penalty has an effective date that is similar (but not identical) to the effective date of the final regs that, among other things, require the tax return preparer to provide Form 8867 with any federal return or claim for refund claiming the EIC. The final regs apply to tax returns and claims for refund for tax years ending on or after Dec. 31, 2011 (thus, applying to returns and claims for calendar year 2011 and later calendar years). Thus, returns filed in 2012 were subject not only to higher penalties for failure to meet EIC due diligence requirements, but also to more exacting due diligence requirements.

¶ 1913. Tax-exempt qualified bonds can be used to finance fixed-wing emergency medical aircraft

Code Sec. 147(e), as amended by 2012 FAA Modernization Act §1105(a)
Generally effective: Bonds issued after Feb. 14, 2012
Committee Reports, see ¶ 5605

Interest on bonds issued by state and local governments generally is excluded from gross income for federal income tax purposes. Bonds issued by state and local governments may be classified as either governmental bonds or private activity bonds. The proceeds of governmental bonds are primarily used to finance governmental functions. Private activity bonds are generally bonds in which the state or local government serves as a conduit providing financing to private businesses or individuals. The exclusion from income for state and local bonds doesn't apply to private activity bonds, unless the bonds are issued for certain permitted purposes ("qualified bonds") and other requirements are met. FTC 2d/FIN ¶ J-3101 et seq.; USTR ¶ 1034 et seq.; TaxDesk ¶ 158,001 et seq.

Under pre-2012 FAA Modernization Act law, a private activity bond didn't qualify as a tax-exempt qualified bond if it was issued as part of an issue and any part of the proceeds of the issue was used for an airplane. (FTC 2d/FIN ¶ J-3100, ¶ J-3196; USTR ¶ 1474.01) While no part of qualified bonds could be issued for airplanes under pre-2012 FAA Modernization Act law, IRS didn't treat (in Rev Rul 2003-116) a helicopter as an airplane for purposes of this pro-hibition. (Com Rept, see ¶ 5605) So, under pre-2012 FAA Modernization Act law, a tax-exempt entity could use qualified Code Sec. 501(c) bond proceeds to expand a trauma center it operated and buy a helicopter to provide helicopter service to the trauma center for accident victims and other medical emergencies. FTC 2d/FIN ¶ J-3196; USTR ¶ 1474.01

New Law. Under the 2012 FAA Modernization Act, the prohibition on the use of proceeds for airplanes (Com Rept, see ¶ 5605) doesn't apply to any fixed-wing aircraft equipped for, and exclusively dedicated to providing, acute care emergency services (within the meaning of Code Sec. 4261(g)(2)). (Code Sec. 147(e) as amended by 2012 FAA Modernization Act §1105(a)Sec. 1105(a), PL 112-95, 2/14/2012))

> **⦿** *observation:* Code Sec. 4261(g) specifically provides that no Code Sec. 4261 or Code Sec. 4271 excise taxes are imposed on any air trans-portation for the purposes of providing emergency medical services by (1) helicopter, or (2) a fixed-wing aircraft equipped for and exclusively dedicated on that flight to acute care emergency medical services, see FTC 2d ¶ W-5142 and FTC 2d ¶ W-5204.

> **⦿** *observation:* So, Congress added a specific exception to the general prohibition of Code Sec. 147(e) for any fixed-wing aircraft equipped for, and exclusively dedicated to providing, acute care emergency ser-vices. Presumably, IRS's position in Rev Rul 2003-116 (that a helicop-ter isn't an airplane for Code Sec. 147(e) purposes) remains the same.

☐ **Effective:** For bonds issued after Feb. 14, 2012. (2012 FAA Modernization Act §1105(b))

¶ 1914. Repurchase bond premium deduction limitation extended to debt convertible to controlled group stock

Code Sec. 249(a), as amended by 2012 FAA Modernization Act §1108(a)
Code Sec. 249(b), as amended by 2012 FAA Modernization Act §1108(b)
Generally effective: For repurchases after Feb. 14, 2012
Committee Reports, see ¶ 5608

A corporation that retires debt when the value of the instrument exceeds its adjusted issue price can generally deduct the premium it pays as interest. Code Sec. 249(a), however, limits an issuing corporation's deduction for bond premium paid on the repurchase of certain convertible indebtedness. Under pre-2012 FAA Modernization Act law, the deduction was limited if the debt was convertible into stock of the issuing corporation or into stock of a corporation in control of, or controlled by, the issuing corporation within the meaning of Code Sec. 368(c). (FTC 2d/FIN ¶ K-5682, ¶ K-5683, ¶ K-5749; USTR ¶ 2494) Control is defined in Code Sec. 368(c) as the ownership of stock with at least 80% of the total combined voting power of all classes of stock entitled to vote and at least 80% of the total number of shares of all other classes of stock of the corporation. (FTC 2d ¶ F-5500; USTR ¶ 3684.13; TaxDesk ¶ 236,701)

> **✐ observation:** Thus, only bond premium on the repurchase of debt that was convertible into stock of *(1) the issuer, (2) the parent of the issuer, or (3) a first-tier subsidiary of the issuer* was subject to the limitation. Deductions on the repurchase of stock convertible into another member of the same controlled group, however, were not limited.

Under Code Sec. 249(a), the issuing corporation's deduction is limited to the adjusted issue price plus a normal call premium on equivalent nonconvertible indebtedness. (FTC 2d/FIN ¶ K-5682, ¶ K-5683, ¶ K-5684, ¶ K-5685; USTR ¶ 2494)

> **✐ observation:** The Code Sec. 249(a) limitation is designed to disallow interest deductions for amounts paid that aren't properly characterized as interest. Thus, amounts corresponding to an increase in value of the stock that the holder would receive is treated as attributable to the conversion feature of the security and is nondeductible. But amounts paid in excess of a normal call premium attributable to the cost of borrowing, such as amounts paid above the adjusted issue price that reflect the above-market yield of an instrument or a change in issuer's credit, remain deductible. (FTC 2d/FIN ¶ K-5685; USTR ¶ 2494)

New Law. The 2012 FAA Modernization Act (i) extends the limitation on the deduction for bond premium to repurchases of indebtedness that is convertible into stock of the issuing corporation *or any corporation in the same parent-subsidiary controlled group within the meaning Code Sec. 1563(a)(1)* (Code Sec. 249(a) as amended by 2012 FAA Modernization Act §1108(a) (Sec. 1108(a), PL 112-95, 2/14/2012) and (ii) eliminates the reference to control as defined in Code Sec. 368(c) (Code Sec. 249(b) as amended by 2012 FAA Modernization Act §1108(b)). The provision thus modifies the definition of control for purposes of Code Sec. 249 to incorporate the Code Sec. 1563(a)(1) indirect control relationships discussed at FTC 2d/FIN ¶ E-10601; USTR ¶ 15,634; TaxDesk ¶ 607,501. (Com Rept, see ¶ 5608)

> **ℝℐ𝒜** *observation:* As amended, the Code Sec. 249 limitation applies not only to premium paid for indebtedness that is convertible into stock of the issuer, the parent of the issuer, or a first-tier subsidiary of the issuer, but also to indebtedness that is convertible into stock of a corporation that *indirectly* controls the issuer or that is *indirectly* controlled by the issuer, such as an ultimate parent or second- or lower-tier subsidiary.

☐ **Effective:** For repurchases after Feb. 14, 2012. (2012 FAA Modernization Act §1108(c))

¶ 1915. Certain 2017 estimated taxes for corporations with assets of $1 billion or more increase to 100.25%

Code Sec. 6655, 2012 African Growth Act §4(1)
Code Sec. 6655, 2012 African Growth Act §4(2)
Generally effective: Aug. 10, 2012
Committee Reports, None

Generally, corporations are required to pay estimated income tax for each tax year in 4 equal installments due on the 15th day of the 4th, 6th, 9th, and 12th month of the tax year. (FTC 2d/FIN ¶ S-5320, S-5324.1; USTR ¶ 66,554; TaxDesk ¶ 609,201)

> **ℝℐ𝒜** *illustration (1):* D Corp. uses a tax year beginning on Jan. 1. The due dates for its installments are: Apr. 15, June 15, Sept. 15, and Dec. 15.

If any due date falls on a Saturday, Sunday, or legal holiday, the due date is extended to the next succeeding day which is not a Saturday, Sunday, or legal holiday, see FTC 2d/FIN ¶s T-10791, T-10792; USTR ¶ 75,034; TaxDesk ¶ 570,240.

New Law. The 2012 African Growth Act provides that, in the case of a corporation with assets of at least $1,000,000,000 (determined as of the end of the previous tax year), the amount of any required installment of corporate estimated tax which is otherwise due in July, Aug., or Sept. of *2017* will be 100.25% of that amount. (2012 African Growth Act §4(1) (Sec. 4(1), PL 112-163, 8/10/2012)) The amount of the next required installment after the installment due in July, Aug., or Sept. of 2017 must be appropriately reduced to reflect the amount of the 100.25% increase. (2012 African Growth Act §4(2))

> *illustration (2):* X Corp., a calendar-year taxpayer with assets of $2 billion, calculates its estimated tax payment otherwise due in Sept. 2017 to be $100,000,000. Instead, X must make a payment of $100,250,000 ($100,000,000 × 100.25%) by the due date in Sept. 2017. X calculates its estimated tax payment otherwise due in Dec. 2017 to be $100,000,000. X reduces the estimated tax payment otherwise due in Dec. 2017 by $250,000 ($100,250,000 − $100,000,000). Thus, X must make a payment of $99,750,000 ($100,000,000 − $250,000) by the due date in Dec. 2017.

> *observation:* Corporations with a fiscal year that begins July 1 will not be affected by the above rule, because they do not have any estimated tax payments due in July, Aug., or Sept.

> *illustration (3):* Z Corp. uses a tax year beginning on July 1. For Z's tax year beginning July 1, 2017, the due dates for its installments are: Oct. 16, 2017, Dec. 15, 2017, Mar. 15, 2018, and June 15, 2018.

> *observation:* The federal government's fiscal year begins Oct. 1. Thus, the 2012 African Growth Act effectively moves revenues from one fiscal year to another to meet budgetary requirements.

☐ **Effective:** Aug. 10, 2012. (2012 African Growth Act §4)

¶ 1916. 100% maximum rate for continuous levy expanded to include governmental payments to vendors from the sale or lease of property

Code Sec. 6331(h)(3), as amended by 2011 Job Creation Act §301(a)
Generally effective: Levies issued after Nov. 21, 2011
Committee Reports, None

If any person liable to pay any tax neglects or refuses to pay it within 10 days after notice and demand, IRS is authorized to collect the tax (and any further sum sufficient to cover the expenses of the levy) by levy on all property and rights to property (except property exempt under Code Sec. 6334) belonging to that person or on which there is a lien provided under the collection provisions of the Code for the payment of the tax. FTC 2d/FIN ¶ V-5201; USTR ¶ 63,314.01; TaxDesk ¶ 902,201

The effect of an IRS levy on certain "specified payments" payable to or received by a taxpayer is continuous from the date the levy is first made until the levy is released, if the levy is approved by an appropriate authority. A specified payment for this purpose is:

(1) any federal payment for which eligibility isn't based on a payee's income or assets (or both),

(2) the minimum exempted amount of salary and wages,

(3) worker's compensation payments,

(4) annuity or pension payments under the Railroad Retirement Act and benefits under the Railroad Unemployment Insurance Act,

(5) unemployment benefits,

(6) certain means-tested public assistance payments.

Although specified payments may include unemployment benefits, worker's compensation, certain public assistance payments, and the minimum exempted amount of wages, salary and other income (see (2), (3), (5) and (6) above), the Internal Revenue Manual indicates that IRS does not currently pursue these payments. FTC 2d/FIN ¶s V-5216, V-5217; USTR ¶ 63,314.03; TaxDesk ¶ 902,216

This continuous levy will attach to up to 15% of any specified payment due to the taxpayer. However, under pre-2011 Job Creation Act Law, the 15% maximum rate is increased to 100% in the case of any specified payment that is due to a vendor of goods or services sold or leased to the federal government. At the time the 2011 Job Creation Act was enacted, the Internal Revenue Manual said that "goods" or "services" did not include the sale or lease of real estate or computer software for purposes of continuously levying 100% of the payment. (FTC 2d/FIN ¶ V-5200, ¶ V-5216; USTR ¶ 63,314.03; TaxDesk ¶ 902,216)

Code Sec. 6330, which requires that IRS provide a pre-levy Collection Due Process (CDP) hearing relating to a levy doesn't apply to certain situations, including federal contractor levies. In such cases, the taxpayer must be given the opportunity for a CDP hearing regarding the levy within a reasonable period of time after the levy. FTC 2d/FIN ¶ V-5257; USTR ¶ 63,304; TaxDesk ¶ 902,507

The Federal Payment Levy Program (FPLP) is an automated levy program the IRS has implemented with the Department of the Treasury, Financial Management Service (FMS). The FPLP was developed as the means to administer the continuous levy provision. Thus, no paper levy documents are served to effectuate a levy under this provision. Form 668-A or Form 668-W may not be used as a means to levy under the FPLP statute, Code Sec. 6331(h). The criteria and delegation authority for release of levies does not change for the FPLP. FTC 2d/FIN ¶ V-5217

New Law. The 2011 Job Creation Act adds "property" to the vendor items that can trigger the above 100% rate when sold or leased to the federal government. Thus, the increased 100% rate applies to specified payments due to vendors of property, goods, or services sold or leased to the federal government. (Code Sec. 6331(h)(3) as amended by 2011 Job Creation Act §301(a) (Sec. 301(a), PL 112-56, 11/21/2011))

> *observation:* Thus, the above change expands the 100% rate to cover payments for real estate or other property sold or leased to the federal government, and not included in goods or services.

> *observation:* Regardless of whether IRS pursues payments under categories (2) through (6) above, the 100% rate would seem to have little application to those categories, even after the above change, although it could often be applicable to amounts in category (1).

☐ **Effective:** Levies issued after Nov. 21, 2011. (2011 Job Creation Act §301(b))

¶ 2000. Client Letters

¶ 2001. Overview of the tax provisions in the 2012 American Taxpayer Relief Act

> **To the practitioner:** You can use the following letter to provide clients with an overview of these tax provisions in the 2012 American Taxpayer Relief Act. For analysis of the income tax rates beginning in 2013, see ¶ 101. For analysis of the long-term capital gains rates, see ¶ 201. For analysis of the rates for qualified dividends, see ¶ 202. For analysis of the personal exemption phaseout, see ¶ 301. For analysis of the overall limitation on itemized deductions, see ¶ 302. For analysis of the provision extending the election to take an itemized deduction for state and local general sales taxes in lieu of the itemized deduction for state and local income taxes, see ¶ 303. For analysis of the provision extending the $250 above-the-line deduction for certain expenses of elementary and secondary school teachers, see ¶ 308. For analysis of the increased AMT exemption amounts, see ¶ 401. For analysis of the provision allowing the personal credits against the AMT, see ¶ 403. For analysis of the estate tax changes, see ¶ 501. For analysis of the changes to the $1,000 child tax credit, see ¶ 601. For analysis of the earned income tax credit changes, see ¶ 605. For analysis of the extension of the American Opportunity tax credit, see ¶ 701. For analysis of the provisions affecting the Code Section 179 expensing limits, see ¶ 801. For analysis of the bonus depreciation provision, see ¶ 804. For analysis of the extension of the research credit, see ¶ 901. For analysis of the Roth conversion provision, see ¶ 1301.

Dear Client,

The recently enacted 2012 American Taxpayer Relief Act is a sweeping tax package that includes, among many other items, permanent extension of the Bush-era tax cuts for most taxpayers, revised tax rates on ordinary and capital gain income for high-income individuals, modification of the estate tax, permanent relief from the AMT for individual taxpayers, limits on the deductions and exemptions of high-income individuals, and a host of retro-actively resuscitated and extended tax breaks for individuals and businesses. Here's a look at the key elements of the package:

- *Tax rates.* For tax years beginning after 2012, the 10%, 15%, 25%, 28%, 33% and 35% tax brackets reflecting the Bush tax cuts will remain in place and are made permanent. This means that, for most Americans, the tax rates will stay the same. However, there will be a new 39.6% rate, that will apply for income over: $400,000 (single), $425,000 (head of households), $450,000 (joint filers and qualifying widow(er)s), and

---

FTC 2d References are to Federal Tax Coordinator 2d
FIN References are to RIA's Analysis of Federal Taxes: Income (print)
USTR References are to United States Tax Reporter: Income
PCA References are to Pension Analysis (print and electronic)
PBE References are to Pension & Benefits Explanations
BCA References are to Benefits Analysis (electronic)
BC References are to Benefits Coordinator (print)
EP References are to Estate Planning Analysis (print and electronic)

$225,000 (married filing separately). These dollar amounts will be inflation-adjusted for tax years after 2013.

• *Estate tax.* The new law prevents steep increases in estate, gift and generation-skipping transfer (GST) tax that were slated to occur for individuals dying and gifts made after 2012 by permanently keeping the exemption level at $5,000,000 (as indexed for inflation). However, the new law also permanently increases the top estate, gift, and GST rate from 35% to 40% It also continues the portability feature that allows the estate of the first spouse to die to transfer his or her unused exclusion to the surviving spouse. All changes are effective for individuals dying and gifts made after 2012.

• *Capital gains and qualified dividends rates.* The new law retains the 0% tax rate on long-term capital gains and qualified dividends, modifies the 15% rate, and establishes a new 20% rate. Beginning in 2013, the rate will be 0% if income falls below the 25% tax bracket; 15% if income falls at or above the 25% tax bracket but below the new 39.6% rate; and 20% if income falls in the 39.6% tax bracket. It should be noted that the 20% top rate does not include the new 3.8% surtax on investment-type income and gains for tax years beginning after 2012, which applies on investment income above $200,000 (single) and $250,000 (joint filers). So actually, the top rate for capital gains and dividends beginning in 2013 will be 23.8% if income falls in the 39.6% tax bracket. For lower income levels, the tax will be 0%, 15%, or 18.8%.

• *Personal exemption phaseout.* Beginning in 2013, personal exemptions will be phased out (i.e., reduced) for adjusted gross income over $250,000 (single), $275,000 (head of household) and $300,000 (joint filers). Taxpayers claim exemptions for themselves, their spouses and their dependents. Last year, each exemption was worth $3,800.

• *Itemized deduction limitation.* Beginning in 2013, itemized deductions will be limited for adjusted gross income over $250,000 (single), $275,000 (head of household) and $300,000 (joint filers).

• *AMT relief.* The new law provides permanent alternative minimum tax (AMT) relief. Prior to the Act, the individual AMT exemption amounts for 2012 were to have been $33,750 for unmarried taxpayers, $45,000 for joint filers, and $22,500 for married persons filing separately. Retroactively effective for tax years beginning after 2011, the new law permanently increases these exemption amounts to $50,600 for unmarried taxpayers, $78,750 for joint filers and $39,375 for married persons filing separately. In addition, for tax years beginning after 2012, it indexes these exemption amounts for inflation.

• *Tax credits for low to middle wage earners.* The new law extends for five years the following items that were originally enacted as part of the

2009 stimulus package and were slated to expire at the end of 2012: (1) the American Opportunity tax credit, which provides up to $2,500 in refundable tax credits for undergraduate college education; (2) eased rules for qualifying for the refundable child credit; and (3) various earned income tax credit (EITC) changes.

• *Cost recovery.* The new law extends increased expensing limitations and treatment of certain real property as Code Section 179 property. It also extends the bonus depreciation provisions with respect to property placed in service after Dec. 31, 2012.

• *Tax break extenders.* Many of the "traditional" tax extenders are extended for two years, retroactively to 2012 and through the end of 2013. Among many others, the extended provisions include the election to take an itemized deduction for state and local general sales taxes in lieu of the itemized deduction for state and local income taxes, the $250 above-the-line deduction for certain expenses of elementary and secondary school teachers, and the research credit.

• *Pension provision.* For transfers after Dec. 31, 2012, in tax years ending after that date, a plan provision in an applicable retirement plan (which includes a qualified Roth contribution program) can allow participants to elect to transfer amounts to designated Roth accounts with the transfer being treated as a taxable qualified rollover contribution.

• *Payroll tax cut is no more.* The 2% payroll tax cut was allowed to expire at the end of 2012.

I hope this information is helpful. If you would like more details about these provisions or any other aspect of the new law, please do not hesitate to call.

Very truly yours,

¶ 2002. Limits on deductions and exemptions in the 2012 American Taxpayer Relief Act

> **To the practitioner:** You can use the following letter to provide clients with an overview of these tax provisions in the 2012 American Taxpayer Relief Act. For analysis of the personal exemption phaseout, see ¶ 301. For analysis of the overall limitation on itemized deductions, see ¶ 302.

Dear Client,

Among the tax increases in the recently enacted 2012 American Taxpayer Relief Act are provisions that impose, or in some cases reinstate, caps on tax breaks for top earners. The new rules reinstate the personal exemption phase-out (PEP) and so-called Pease limit on itemized deductions — named after its author, former Ohio Democratic representative Don Pease. Both were created in 1990 in an effort to generate more government revenue without raising the marginal tax rates but were phased out by 2010. Now they are back. Here's how they work:

PEP limitations to apply to "high earners." Taxpayers claim exemptions for themselves, their spouses and their dependents. Last year, each exemption was worth $3,800. Under the new law, for tax years beginning after 2012, the Personal Exemption Phaseout (PEP), which had previously been suspended, is reinstated with a starting threshold for those making $300,000 for joint filers and a surviving spouse; $275,000 for heads of household; $250,000 for single filers; and $150,000 (one-half of the otherwise applicable amounts for joint filers) for married taxpayers filing separately. Under the phaseout, the total amount of exemptions that can be claimed by a taxpayer subject to the limitation is reduced by 2% for each $2,500 (or portion thereof) by which the taxpayer's AGI exceeds the applicable threshold. These dollar amounts are inflation-adjusted for tax years after 2013.

Pease limitations to apply to "high earners." For tax years beginning after 2012, the "Pease" limitation on itemized deductions, such as the ones taken for mortgage interest, charitable giving and state and local taxes paid, which had previously been suspended, is reinstated with a starting threshold for those making $300,000 for joint filers and a surviving spouse; $275,000 for heads of household; $250,000 for single filers; and $150,000 (one-half of

---

FTC 2d References are to Federal Tax Coordinator 2d
FIN References are to RIA's Analysis of Federal Taxes: Income (print)
USTR References are to United States Tax Reporter: Income
PCA References are to Pension Analysis (print and electronic)
PBE References are to Pension & Benefits Explanations
BCA References are to Benefits Analysis (electronic)
BC References are to Benefits Coordinator (print)
EP References are to Estate Planning Analysis (print and electronic)

the otherwise applicable amounts for joint filers) for married taxpayers filing separately. Thus, for taxpayers subject to the "Pease" limitation, the total amount of their itemized deductions is reduced by 3% of the amount by which the taxpayer's adjusted gross income (AGI) exceeds the threshold amount, with the reduction not to exceed 80% of the otherwise allowable itemized deductions. These dollar amounts are inflation-adjusted for tax years after 2013.

I hope this information is helpful. If you would like more details about these provisions or any other aspect of the new law, please do not hesitate to call.

Very truly yours,

¶ 2003. AMT relief in the 2012 American Taxpayer Relief Act

To the practitioner: You can use the following letter to provide clients with an overview of these tax provisions in the 2012 American Taxpayer Relief Act. For analysis of the increased AMT exemption amounts, see ¶ 401. For analysis of the provision allowing the personal credits against the AMT, see ¶ 403.

Dear Client,

I am writing to provide details regarding key provisions in the recently enacted 2012 American Taxpayer Relief Act which provide permanent relief to individual taxpayers from the alternative minimum tax, or AMT. Earlier temporary measures to deal with the unintended creep of the AMT's reach expired at the end of 2011, meaning that millions of additional taxpayers would have faced paying the tax on their 2012 returns without the new relief.

Brief overview of the AMT.

The AMT is a parallel tax system which does not permit several of the deductions permissible under the regular tax system, such as property taxes. Taxpayers who may be subject to the AMT must calculate their tax liability under the regular federal tax system and under the AMT system taking into account certain "preferences" and "adjustments." If their liability is found to be greater under the AMT system, that's what they owe the federal government. Originally enacted to make sure that wealthy Americans did not escape paying taxes, the AMT has started to apply to more middle-income taxpayers, due in part to the fact that the AMT parameters were not indexed for inflation.

In recent years, Congress provided a measure of relief from the AMT by raising the AMT "exemption amounts"—allowances that reduced the amount of alternative minimum taxable income (AMTI), reducing or eliminating AMT liability. (However, these exemption amounts are phased out for taxpayers whose AMTI exceeds specified amounts.) For 2011, the AMT exemption amounts were $74,450 for married couples filing jointly and surviving spouses; $48,450 for single taxpayers; and $37,225 for married taxpayers filing separately. However, for 2012, those amounts were scheduled

---

FTC 2d References are to Federal Tax Coordinator 2d
FIN References are to RIA's Analysis of Federal Taxes: Income (print)
USTR References are to United States Tax Reporter: Income
PCA References are to Pension Analysis (print and electronic)
PBE References are to Pension & Benefits Explanations
BCA References are to Benefits Analysis (electronic)
BC References are to Benefits Coordinator (print)
EP References are to Estate Planning Analysis (print and electronic)

to fall back to the amounts that applied in 2000: $45,000, $33,750, and $22,500, respectively. This would have brought millions of additional middle-income Americans under the AMT system, resulting in higher federal tax bills for many of them, along with higher compliance costs associated with filling out and filing the complicated AMT tax form.

New law provides permanent fix.

To prevent the unintended result of having millions of middle-income taxpayers fall prey to the AMT, Congress has once again applied a "patch" to the problem by extending the 2011 exemption amounts, increased slightly, but this time the patch is intended as a permanent fix. Under the new law, for tax years beginning in 2012, the AMT exemption amounts are increased to: (1) $78,750 in the case of married individuals filing a joint return and surviving spouses; (2) $50,600 in the case of unmarried individuals other than surviving spouses; and (3) $39,375 in the case of married individuals filing a separate return. Most importantly, these amounts will be indexed for inflation after 2012, meaning that the annual "patches" will no longer be needed.

Personal credits may be used to offset AMT.

Another provision in the new law provides AMT relief for taxpayers claiming personal tax credits. The tax liability limitation rules used to provide that certain nonrefundable personal credits (including the dependent care credit and the elderly and disabled credit) were allowed only to the extent that a taxpayer had regular income tax liability in excess of the tentative minimum tax, which had the effect of disallowing these credits against the AMT. Temporary provisions had been enacted which permitted these credits to offset the entire regular and AMT liability through the end of 2011. The new law extends this provision permanently, so that the credits are allowed to offset both regular and AMT tax liability.

I hope this information is helpful. If you would like more details about this or any other aspect of the new law, please do not hesitate to call.

Very truly yours,

¶ 2004. Individual extenders in the 2012 American Taxpayer Relief Act

To the practitioner: You can use the following letter to provide clients with an overview of these tax provisions in the 2012 American Taxpayer Relief Act. For analysis of the provision extending the election to take an itemized deduction for state and local general sales taxes in lieu of the itemized deduction for state and local income taxes, see ¶ 303. For analysis of the provision regarding mortgage insurance premiums, see ¶ 305. For analysis of the provision extending the exclusion for debt discharge income from home mortgage forgiveness, see ¶ 306. For analysis of the provision extending parity for employer-provided mass transit and parking benefits, see ¶ 307. For analysis of the provision extending the $250 above-the-line deduction for certain expenses of elementary and secondary school teachers, see ¶ 308. For analysis of the extension of the qualified tuition deduction, see ¶ 702. For analysis of the extension of the rule allowing tax-free IRA distributions to charity, see ¶ 1101. For analysis of the extension of the special rule for contributions of capital gain real property made for conservation purposes, see ¶ 1102.

Dear Client,

In addition to permanently extending the Bush-era tax cuts for most taxpayers, revising tax rates on ordinary and capital gain income for high-income individuals, modifying the estate tax, providing permanent relief from the AMT, and imposing limits on the deductions and exemptions of high-income individuals, the recently enacted 2012 American Taxpayer Relief Act extends a host of important tax breaks for individuals. I'm writing to give you an overview of these key tax breaks that were extended by the new law. Please call our office for details of how the new changes may affect you.

The new law extends the following items for the period indicated beyond their prior termination date as shown in the listing:

... the deduction for certain expenses of elementary and secondary school teachers, which expired at the end of 2011 and which is now revived for 2012 and continued through 2013;

... the exclusion for discharge of qualified principal residence indebtedness, which applied for discharges before Jan. 1, 2013 and which is now continued to apply for discharges before Jan. 1, 2014;

... parity of the monthly dollar limitation for the exclusions for employer-provided mass transit and vanpooling, with the exclusion for parking

FTC 2d References are to Federal Tax Coordinator 2d
FIN References are to RIA's Analysis of Federal Taxes: Income (print)
USTR References are to United States Tax Reporter: Income
PCA References are to Pension Analysis (print and electronic)
PBE References are to Pension & Benefits Explanations
BCA References are to Benefits Analysis (electronic)
BC References are to Benefits Coordinator (print)
EP References are to Estate Planning Analysis (print and electronic)

benefits, which had applied before 2012 and which is now revived for 2012 and continued through 2013;

. . . the treatment of mortgage insurance premiums as qualified residence interest, which expired at the end of 2011 and which is now revived for 2012 and continued through 2013;

. . . the option to deduct state and local general sales taxes, which expired at the end of 2011 and which is now revived for 2012 and continued through 2013;

. . . the special rule for contributions of capital gain real property made for conservation purposes, which expired at the end of 2011 and which is now revived for 2012 and continued through 2013;

. . . the above-the-line deduction for qualified tuition and related expenses, which expired at the end of 2011 and which is now revived for 2012 and continued through 2013; and

. . . tax-free distributions from individual retirement plans for charitable purposes, which expired at the end of 2011 and which is now revived for 2012 and continued through 2013. Because 2012 has already passed, a special rule permits distributions taken in Dec. 2012 to be transferred to charities for a limited period in 2013. Another special rule permits certain distributions made in Jan. 2013 to be deemed made on Dec. 31, 2012.

I hope this information is helpful. If you would like more details about these changes or any other aspect of the new law, please do not hesitate to call..

Very truly yours,

¶ 2005. Roth conversions for retirement plans in the 2012 American Taxpayer Relief Act

To the practitioner: You can use the following letter to provide clients with an overview of this tax provision in the 2012 American Taxpayer Relief Act. For analysis of the Roth conversion provision, see ¶ 1301.

Dear Client,

I am writing to tell you of an interesting opportunity arising from a provision in the recently enacted 2012 American Taxpayer Relief Act. The new provision permits individuals to convert any portion of their balance in an employer-sponsored tax-deferred retirement plan account into a designated Roth account under that plan.

Designated Roth accounts are a popular retirement plan option because they offer several advantages, namely:

• Earnings within the account are tax-sheltered (as they are with a regular qualified employer plan or IRA).

• Unlike a regular qualified employer plan or IRA, withdrawals from a Roth IRA aren't taxed if some relatively liberal conditions are satisfied.

• Although a designated Roth account is subject to the same lifetime required minimum distributions (RMDs) as are regular qualified employer plans or IRAs, designated Roth account owners can avoid these distributions by rolling them over— tax free— to a Roth IRA, which is not subject to RMDs.

• Beneficiaries of Roth IRAs also enjoy tax-sheltered earnings (as with a regular qualified employer plan or IRA) and tax-free withdrawals (unlike with a regular qualified employer plan or IRA). They do, however, have to commence regular withdrawals from a Roth IRA after the account owner dies.

The catch under the new law conversion provision, and it's a big one, is that the conversion will be fully taxed, assuming the conversion is being made with pre-tax dollars (money that wasn't taxed to an employee when contributed to the qualified employer-sponsored retirement plan) and the

FTC 2d References are to Federal Tax Coordinator 2d
FIN References are to RIA's Analysis of Federal Taxes: Income (print)
USTR References are to United States Tax Reporter: Income
PCA References are to Pension Analysis (print and electronic)
PBE References are to Pension & Benefits Explanations
BCA References are to Benefits Analysis (electronic)
BC References are to Benefits Coordinator (print)
EP References are to Estate Planning Analysis (print and electronic)

earnings on those pre-tax dollars. For example, a taxpayer in the 28% federal tax bracket who converted $100,000 from an employer-sponsored plan funded entirely with untaxed dollars to a designated Roth account would owe $28,000 of tax. So, in deciding whether to pursue a Roth conversion, one would need to weigh the price of paying tax now against the advantages afforded by future tax-free withdrawals and freedom from the RMD rules.

Further, unlike conversions involving Roth IRAs, once done, a conversion to a designated Roth account cannot be undone or recharacterized.

The conversion option for retirement plans would only be available if employer plan sponsors include this feature in the plan. The provision is effective for post-2012 transfers, in tax years ending after Dec. 31, 2012.

I hope this information is helpful. If you would like more details about the new Roth conversion provision or any other aspect of the new legislation, please do not hesitate to call.

Very truly yours,

¶ 2006. Extension of the American Opportunity Tax Credit in the 2012 American Taxpayer Relief Act

> **To the practitioner:** You can use the following letter to provide clients with an overview of this tax provision in the 2012 American Taxpayer Relief Act. For analysis of the extension of the American Opportunity tax credit, see ¶ 701.

Dear Client,

The recently enacted 2012 Taxpayer Relief Act includes a 5-year extension (through 2017) of the American Opportunity tax credit for college costs. Added to the tax code in 2009 as a temporary replacement of the previous Hope tax credit, the American Opportunity tax credit both increased the tax relief available for students from middle-income families and also extended relief for the first time to students from lower-income families. Now that the American Opportunity tax credit has been extended for five years, it might be a good time to review the tax benefits available under that credit, with an eye to how it compares with the Hope credit, which would have been in effect over the next two years had the American Opportunity tax credit not been extended.

• Families with a family member in college can benefit from a tax credit for tuition and fees. From a taxpayer's point of view, a credit is almost always preferable to a deduction, because a credit reduces taxes owed, while a deduction only reduces taxable income. The maximum amount of the American Opportunity tax credit is $2,500 (up from a maximum credit of $1,800 under the Hope credit). The credit is 100% of the first $2,000 of qualifying expenses and 25% of the next $2,000, so the maximum credit of $2,500 is reached when a student has qualifying expenses of $4,000 or more.

• While the Hope credit was only available for the first two years of undergraduate education, the American Opportunity tax credit is available for up to four years.

• Under the Hope credit, qualifying expenses were narrowly defined to include just tuition and fees required for the student's enrollment. Textbooks were excluded, despite their escalating cost in recent years. The

FTC 2d References are to Federal Tax Coordinator 2d
FIN References are to RIA's Analysis of Federal Taxes: Income (print)
USTR References are to United States Tax Reporter: Income
PCA References are to Pension Analysis (print and electronic)
PBE References are to Pension & Benefits Explanations
BCA References are to Benefits Analysis (electronic)
BC References are to Benefits Coordinator (print)
EP References are to Estate Planning Analysis (print and electronic)

American Opportunity tax credit expands the list of qualifying expenses to include textbooks.

• The Hope credit was nonrefundable, i.e., it could reduce your regular tax bill to zero but could not result in a refund. This meant that if a family didn't owe any taxes it couldn't benefit from the credit, which prompted critics to argue that the credit was thus denied to those families most in need of help affording college. The American Opportunity tax credit addresses this criticism by providing that 40% of the credit is refundable. This means that someone who has at least $4,000 in qualified expenses and who would thus qualify for the maximum credit of $2,500, but who has no tax liability to offset that credit against, would qualify for a $1,000 (40% of $2,500) refund from the government.

• The Hope credit was not available to someone with higher than moderate income. Under the credit's "phaseout" provision, taxpayers with adjusted gross income (AGI) over $50,000 (for 2009) saw their credits reduced, and the credit was completely eliminated for AGIs over $60,000 (twice those amounts for joint filers). Under the American Opportunity tax credit, taxpayers with somewhat higher incomes can qualify, as the phaseout of the credit begins at AGI in excess of $80,000 ($160,000 for joint filers).

I hope this information is helpful. If you would like more details about the American Opportunity tax credit or any other aspect of the new law, please do not hesitate to call.

Very truly yours,

¶ 2007. Expensing and additional first-year depreciation in the 2012 American Taxpayer Relief Act

> **To the practitioner:** You can use the following letter to provide clients with an overview of these tax provisions in the 2012 American Taxpayer Relief Act. For analysis of the provisions affecting the Code Section 179 expensing limits, see ¶ 801 and ¶ 803. For analysis of the bonus depreciation provision, see ¶ 804 and ¶ 805.

Dear Client,

The recently enacted 2012 Taxpayer Relief Act includes a wide-ranging assortment of tax changes affecting both individuals and business. On the business side, two of the most significant changes provide incentives to invest in machinery and equipment by allowing for faster cost recovery of business property. Here are the details.

Enhanced small business expensing (Section 179 expensing). Generally, the cost of property placed in service in a trade or business can't be deducted in the year it's placed in service if the property will be useful beyond the year. Instead, the cost is "capitalized" and depreciation deductions are allowed for most property (other than land), but are spread out over a period of years. However, to help small businesses quickly recover the cost of capital outlays, small business taxpayers can elect to write off these expenditures in the year they are made instead of recovering them through depreciation. The expense election is made available, on a tax year by tax year basis, under Section 179 of the Internal Revenue Code, and is often referred to as the "Section 179 election" or the "Code Section 179 election." The new law makes three important changes to the Code Section 179 expense election

First, the new law provides that for tax years beginning in 2012 or 2013, a small business taxpayer will be allowed to write off up to $500,000 of capital expenditures subject to a phaseout (i.e., gradual reduction) once capital expenditures exceed $2,000,000. For tax years beginning after 2013, the maximum expensing amount will drop to $25,000 and the phaseout level will drop to $200,000.

Second, the new law extends the rule which treats off-the-shelf computer software as qualifying property through 2013.

FTC 2d References are to Federal Tax Coordinator 2d
FIN References are to RIA's Analysis of Federal Taxes: Income (print)
USTR References are to United States Tax Reporter: Income
PCA References are to Pension Analysis (print and electronic)
PBE References are to Pension & Benefits Explanations
BCA References are to Benefits Analysis (electronic)
BC References are to Benefits Coordinator (print)
EP References are to Estate Planning Analysis (print and electronic)

Finally, the new law extends through 2013 the provision permitting a taxpayer to amend or irrevocably revoke an election under Section 179 for a tax year without IRS's consent.

Extension of additional first-year depreciation. Businesses are allowed to deduct the cost of capital expenditures over time according to depreciation schedules. In previous legislation, Congress allowed businesses to more rapidly deduct capital expenditures of most new tangible personal property, and certain other new property, by permitting an additional first-year write-off of the cost. For qualified property acquired and placed in service after Dec. 31, 2011 and before Jan. 1, 2013 (before Jan. 1, 2014 for certain longer-lived and transportation property), the additional first-year depreciation was 50% of the cost. The new law extends this additional first-year depreciation for investments placed in service before Jan. 1, 2014 (before Jan. 1, 2015 for certain longer-lived and transportation property).

The new law also extends for one year the election to accelerate the AMT credit instead of claiming additional first-year depreciation.

The new law leaves in place the existing rules as to what kinds of property qualify for additional first-year depreciation. Generally, the property must be (1) depreciable property with a recovery period of 20 years or less; (2) water utility property; (3) computer software; or (4) qualified leasehold improvements. Also the original use of the property must commence with the taxpayer – used machinery doesn't qualify.

I hope this information is helpful. If you would like more details about the new cost recovery provisions or any other aspect of the new legislation, please do not hesitate to call.

Very truly yours,

¶ 2008. Business extenders in the 2012 American Taxpayer Relief Act

To the practitioner: You can use the following letter to provide clients with an overview of these tax provisions in the 2012 American Taxpayer Relief Act. For analysis of the new Code Sec. 179 expensing limits, see ¶ 801. For analysis of the provision allowing 50% bonus depreciation, see ¶ 804. For analysis of the provision extending 15-year MACRS depreciation for certain building improvements and restaurants, see ¶ 807. For analysis of the special expensing rules for certain film and television productions, see ¶ 808. For analysis of the provision extending the 7-year recovery period for motorsports entertainment complexes, see ¶ 809. For analysis of the provisions extending depreciation tax breaks for Indian reservation property, see ¶ 810. For analysis of the extension of the election to expense the cost of advanced mine safety equipment, see ¶ 811. For analysis of the extension of the research credit, see ¶ 901. For analysis of the extension of the work opportunity credit, see ¶ 902. For analysis of the extension of the differential wage payment credit, see ¶ 904. For analysis of the extension of the mine rescue team training credit, see ¶ 905. For analysis of the extension of the temporary minimum low-income tax credit rate for nonfederally subsidized new buildings, see ¶ 906. For analysis of the extension of the Indian employment credit, see ¶ 907. For analysis of the extension of the railroad track maintenance credit, see ¶ 908. For analysis of the extension of the allowance of the Code Sec. 199 deduction for Puerto Rico activities, see ¶ 909. For analysis of the extension of the enhanced charitable deduction for contributions of food inventory, see ¶ 1104. For analysis of the extension of the basis adjustment to stock of S corporations making charitable contributions of property, see ¶ 1105. For analysis of the extension of the Subpart F exception for active financing income, see ¶ 1201. For analysis of the extension of look-through treatment for payments between related CFCs under foreign personal holding company income rules, see ¶ 1202. For analysis of the extension of the provision including RICs in the definition of qualified investment entity for certain FIRPTA purposes, see ¶ 1204. For analysis of the extension of the possessions tax credit for American Samoa, see ¶ 1206. For analysis of the extension of the new markets tax credit, see ¶ 1401. For analysis of the extension of the QZAB program, see ¶ 1402. For analysis of the extension of tax-exempt financing for New York Liberty Zone, see ¶ 1405. For analysis of the extension of various empowerment zone tax incentives, see ¶ 1406. For analysis of the extension of the shortened S Corp built-in gains holding period, see ¶ 1501. For analysis of the extension of the exclusion from a tax exempt organization's unrelated business taxable income (UBTI) of interest, rent, royalties, and annuities paid to it from a controlled entity, see ¶ 1502.

Dear Client,

In addition to permanently extending the Bush-era tax cuts for most taxpayers, revising tax rates on ordinary and capital gain income for high-income individuals, modifying the estate tax, providing permanent relief from the AMT, and imposing limits on the deductions and exemptions of high-income individuals, the recently enacted 2012 American Taxpayer Relief Act extends a host of important tax breaks for businesses. I'm writing

FTC 2d References are to Federal Tax Coordinator 2d
FIN References are to RIA's Analysis of Federal Taxes: Income (print)
USTR References are to United States Tax Reporter: Income
PCA References are to Pension Analysis (print and electronic)
PBE References are to Pension & Benefits Explanations
BCA References are to Benefits Analysis (electronic)
BC References are to Benefits Coordinator (print)
EP References are to Estate Planning Analysis (print and electronic)

to give you an overview of these key tax breaks that were extended by the new law. Please call our office for details of how the new changes may affect you or your business.

Depreciation provisions modified and extended. The following depreciation provisions are retroactively extended by the Act:

. . . 15-year straight line cost recovery for qualified leasehold improvements, qualified restaurant buildings and improvements, and qualified retail improvements;

. . . 7-year recovery period for motorsports entertainment complexes;

. . . accelerated depreciation for business property on an Indian reservation;

. . . increased expensing limitations and treatment of certain real property as Section 179 property;

. . . special expensing rules for certain film and television productions; and

. . . the election to expense mine safety equipment.

The new law also extends the bonus depreciation provisions with respect to property placed in service after Dec. 31, 2012.

Business tax breaks extended. The following business credits and special rules are also extended:

. . . The research credit is modified and retroactively extended for two years through 2013.

. . . The temporary minimum low-income tax credit rate for nonfederally subsidized new buildings is extended to apply to housing credit dollar amount allocations made before Jan. 1, 2014.

. . . The housing allowance exclusion for determining area median gross income for qualified residential rental project exempt facility bonds is extended two years.

. . . The Indian employment tax credit is retroactively extended for two years through 2013.

. . . The new markets tax credit is retroactively extended for two years through 2013.

. . . The railroad track maintenance credit is retroactively extended for two years through 2013.

. . . The mine rescue team training credit is retroactively extended for two years through 2013.

. . . The employer wage credit for employees who are active duty members of the uniformed services is retroactively extended for two years through 2013.

. . . The work opportunity tax credit is retroactively extended for two years through 2013.

. . . The qualified zone academy bond (QZAB) program is retroactively extended for two years through 2013.

. . . The enhanced charitable deduction for contributions of food inventory is retroactively extended for two years through 2013.

. . . The domestic production activities deduction for activities in Puerto Rico is extended to apply for tax years beginning in 2012 and 2013.

. . . Exclusion from a tax-exempt organization's unrelated business taxable income (UBTI) of interest, rent, royalties, and annuities paid to it by a controlled entity is extended through Dec. 31, 2013.

. . . Treatment of certain dividends of regulated investment companies (RICs) as "interest-related dividends" is extended through Dec. 31, 2013.

. . . Inclusion of RICs in the definition of a "qualified investment entity" for certain FIRPTA purposes is retroactively extended through Dec. 31, 2013.

. . . The exception under subpart F for active financing income (i.e., certain income from the active conduct of a banking, financing, insurance or similar business) is extended for two years through 2013.

. . . Look-through treatment for payments between related controlled foreign corporations (CFCs) under the foreign personal holding company rules is extended through Jan. 1, 2014.

. . . Exclusion of 100% of the gain on certain small business stock acquired before Jan. 1, 2014.

. . . The basis adjustment to stock of S corporations making charitable contributions of property is extended to apply for tax years beginning in 2012 and 2013.

. . . The 5-year reduced recognition period for the S corporation built-in gains tax is extended for tax years beginning in 2012 and 2013.

. . . Various empowerment zone tax incentive provisions, including the designation of an empowerment zone and of additional empowerment zones (extended through Dec. 31, 2013) and the period for which the percentage exclusion for qualified small business stock (of a corporation which is a qualified business entity) is 60% (extended through Dec. 31, 2018).

. . . Tax-exempt financing for New York Liberty Zone is extended for bonds issued before Jan. 1 2014.

. . . Temporary increase in limit on cover over rum excise taxes to Puerto Rico and the Virgin Islands is extended for spirits brought into the U.S. before Jan. 1, 2014.

. . . American Samoa credit, as modified, is extended through Jan. 1, 2014.

I hope this information is helpful. If you would like more details about these changes or any other aspect of the new law, please do not hesitate to call..

Very truly yours,

¶ 2009. Energy-related tax breaks extended in the 2012 American Taxpayer Relief Act

> **To the practitioner:** You can use the following letter to provide clients with an overview of these tax provisions in the 2012 American Taxpayer Relief Act. For analysis of the extension of the energy efficient appliance credit, see ¶ 1001. For analysis of the extension of the new energy efficient home credit, see ¶ 1002. For analysis of the extension of the credit for non-business energy property, see ¶ 1004. For analysis of the extension of the credits with respect to facilities producing energy from certain renewable resources, see ¶ 1005. For analysis of the extension of the credit for 2- or 3-wheeled plug-in electric vehicles, see ¶ 1006. For analysis of the extension of the production credit for Indian coal facilities placed in service before 2009, see ¶ 1007. For analysis of the extension of the alternative fuel vehicle refueling property credit, see ¶ 1008. For analysis of the extension of the tax credits/refunds for biodiesel and renewable diesel, see ¶ 1009. For analysis of the extension of the alternative fuels excise tax credits for sale or use of alternative fuels or alternative fuel mixtures, see ¶ 1010. For analysis of the extension of the cellulosic biofuel producer credit, see ¶ 1015.

Dear Client,

In addition to permanently extending the Bush-era tax cuts for most taxpayers, revising tax rates on ordinary and capital gain income for high-income individuals, modifying the estate tax, providing permanent relief from the AMT, and imposing limits on the deductions and exemptions of high-income individuals, the recently enacted 2012 American Taxpayer Relief Act extends a host of important energy-related tax breaks for individuals and businesses. I'm writing to give you an overview of these key tax breaks that were extended by the new law. Please call our office for details of how the new changes may affect you or your business.

The various energy credits extended include:

• The nonbusiness energy property credit for certain energy-efficient property installed in existing homes is retroactively extended for two years through 2013. A taxpayer can claim a credit of: (1) 10% of the amount paid for qualified energy efficiency improvements, and (2) the amount of residential energy property expenditures, with a lifetime credit limit of $500 ($200 for windows and skylights).

• The alternative fuel vehicle refueling property credit (for non-hydrogen qualified alternative fuel vehicle refueling property) is retroactively extended for two years through 2013 so that taxpayers can claim a 30%

FTC 2d References are to Federal Tax Coordinator 2d
FIN References are to RIA's Analysis of Federal Taxes: Income (print)
USTR References are to United States Tax Reporter: Income
PCA References are to Pension Analysis (print and electronic)
PBE References are to Pension & Benefits Explanations
BCA References are to Benefits Analysis (electronic)
BC References are to Benefits Coordinator (print)
EP References are to Estate Planning Analysis (print and electronic)

credit for qualified alternative fuel vehicle refueling property placed in service through Dec. 31, 2013, subject to the $30,000 (depreciable property) and $1,000 (nondepreciable property) limitations.

• The credit for 2- or 3-wheeled plug-in electric vehicles is modified and retroactively extended for two years through 2013.

• The cellulosic biofuel producer credit is modified, retroactively restored, and extended for one year through 2013.

• The income and excise credits for biodiesel and renewable diesel are retroactively extended for two years through 2013.

• The production credit for Indian coal facilities placed in service before 2009 is extended for one year. The credit applies to coal produced by the taxpayer at an Indian coal production facility during the 8-year period beginning on Jan. 1, 2006, and sold by the taxpayer to an unrelated person during such 8-year period and the tax year.

• The credit with respect to facilities producing energy from certain renewable resources is modified to include, as qualified facilities, certain modifications, improvements, or additions to qualified facilities under construction before Jan. 1, 2014. A facility using wind to produce electricity will be a qualified facility if it is placed in service before 2014.

• The credit for energy-efficient new homes is retroactively extended for two years through 2013.

• The credit for energy-efficient appliances is retroactively extended for two years through 2013.

• The additional depreciation deduction allowance for cellulosic biofuel plant property is modified and extended for one year.

• The special rule for sale or disposition to implement federal energy regulatory commission (FERC) or State electric restructuring policy for qualified electric utilities is retroactively extended for two years through 2013.

• The excise tax credits for sale or use of alternative fuels and alternative fuel mixtures are retroactively extended for two years though 2013.

I hope this information is helpful. If you would like more details about these changes or any other aspect of the new law, please do not hesitate to call.

Very truly yours,

[¶ 3000]　Code as Amended

This section reproduces Code as Amended by: ,

the Comprehensive 1099 Taxpayer Protection and Repayment of Exchange Subsidy Overpayments Act, P.L. 112-9, 4/14/2011

the Department of Defense and Full-Year Continuing Appropriations Act, 2011, P.L. 112-10, 4/15/2011

the Trade Adjustment Assistance Extension Act, P.L. 112-40, 10/21/2011

the United States-Korea Free Trade Agreement Implementation Act, P.L. 112-41, 10/21/2011

the Job Creation Act of 2011, P.L. 112-56, 11/21/2011

the Temporary Payroll Tax Cut Continuation Act of 2011, P.L. 112-78, 12/23/2011

the FAA Modernization and Reform Act, P.L. 112-95, 2/14/2012

the Middle Class Tax Relief and Job Creation Act of 2012, P.L. 112-96, 2/22/2012

the Highway Investment Act of 2012, P.L. 112-141, 7/6/2012

the African Growth and Opportunity Act of 2012, P.L. 112-163, 8/10/2012

the American Taxpayer Relief Act of 2012, P.L. 112-240, 1/2/2013

[¶ 3001]　Code Sec. 1.　Tax imposed.

(a)　Married individuals filing joint returns and surviving spouses. There is hereby imposed on the taxable income of—

(1) every married individual (as defined in section 7703) who makes a single return jointly with his spouse under section 6013, and

(2) every surviving spouse (as defined in section 2(a)),

a tax determined in accordance with the following table:

If taxable income is:	The tax is:
Not over $36,900	15% of taxable income.
Over $36,900 but not over $89,150	$5,535, plus 28% of the excess over $36,900.
Over $89,150 but not over $140,000.	$20,165, plus 31% of the excess over $89,150.
Over $140,000 but not over $250,000.	$35,928.50, plus 36% of the excess over $140,000.
Over $250,000	$75,528.50, plus 39.6% of the excess over $250,000.

(b)　Heads of households. There is hereby imposed on the taxable income of every head of a household (as defined in section 2(b)) a tax determined in accordance with the following table:

If taxable income is:	The tax is:
Not over $29,600	15% of taxable income.
Over $29,600 but not over $76,400	$4,440, plus 28% of the excess over $29,600.
Over $76,400 but not over $127,500	$17,544, plus 31% of the excess over $76,400.
Over $127,500 but not over $250,000.	$33,385, plus 36% of the excess over $127,500.
Over $250,000	$77,485, plus 39.6% of the excess over $250,000.

(c)　Unmarried individuals (other than surviving spouses and heads of households). There is hereby imposed on the taxable income of every individual (other than a surviving spouse as defined in section 2(a) or the head of a household as defined in section 2(b)) who is not a married individual (as defined in section 7703) a tax determined in accordance with the following table:

If taxable income is:	The tax is:
Not over $22,100	15% of taxable income.
Over $22,100 but not over $53,500	$3,315, plus 28% of the excess over $22,100.
Over $53,500 but not over $115,000	$12,107, plus 31% of the excess over $53,500.
Over $115,000 but not over $250,000.	$31,172, plus 36% of the excess over $115,000.

Over $250,000	$79,772, plus 39.6% of the excess over $250,000.

(d) Married individuals filing separate returns. There is hereby imposed on the taxable income of every married individual (as defined in section 7703) who does not make a single return jointly with his spouse under section 6013, a tax determined in accordance with the following table:

If taxable income is:	The tax is:
Not over $18,450	15% of taxable income.
Over $18,450 but not over $44,575	$2,767.50, plus 28% of the excess over $18,450.
Over $44,575 but not over $70,000	$10,082.50, plus 31% of the excess over $44,575.
Over $70,000 but not over $125,000.	$17,964.25, plus 36% of the excess over $70,000.
Over $125,000	$37,764.25, plus 39.6% of the excess over $125,000.

(e) Estates and trusts. There is hereby imposed on the taxable income of—

(1) every estate, and

(2) every trust,

taxable under this subsection a tax determined in accordance with the following table:

If taxable income is:	The tax is:
Not over $1,500	15% of taxable income.
Over $1,500 but not over $3,500	$225, plus 28% of the excess over $1,500.
Over $3,500 but not over $5,500	$785, plus 31% of the excess over $3,500.
Over $5,500 but not over $7,500.	$1,405, plus 36% of the excess over $5,500.
Over $7,500	$2,125, plus 39.6% of the excess over $7,500.

(f) Phaseout of marriage penalty in 15-percent bracket; adjustments in tax tables so that inflation will not result in tax increases.

(1) In general. Not later than December 15 of 1993, and each subsequent calendar year, the Secretary shall prescribe tables which shall apply in lieu of the tables contained in subsections (a), (b), (c), (d), and (e) with respect to taxable years beginning in the succeeding calendar year.

(2) Method of prescribing tables. The table which under paragraph (1) is to apply in lieu of the table contained in subsection (a), (b), (c), (d), or (e), as the case may be, with respect to taxable years beginning in any calendar year shall be prescribed—

(A) except as provided in paragraph (8), by increasing the minimum and maximum dollar amounts for each rate bracket for which a tax is imposed under such table by the cost-of-living adjustment for such calendar year,

(B) by not changing the rate applicable to any rate bracket as adjusted under subparagraph (A), and

(C) by adjusting the amounts setting forth the tax to the extent necessary to reflect the adjustments in the rate brackets.

(3) Cost-of-living adjustment. For purposes of paragraph (2), the cost-of-living adjustment for any calendar year is the percentage (if any) by which—

(A) the CPI for the preceding calendar year, exceeds

(B) the CPI for the calendar year 1992.

(4) CPI for any calendar year. For purposes of paragraph (3), the CPI for any calendar year is the average of the Consumer Price Index as of the close of the 12-month period ending on August 31 of such calendar year.

(5) Consumer price index. For purposes of paragraph (4), the term "Consumer Price Index" means the last Consumer Price Index for all-urban consumers published by the Department of Labor. For purposes of the preceding sentence, the revision of the Consumer Price Index which is most consistent with the Consumer Price Index for calendar year 1986 shall be used.

(6) Rounding.

(A) In general. If any increase determined under paragraph (2)(A), section 63(c)(4), section 68(b)(2) or section 151(d)(4) is not a multiple of $50, such increase shall be rounded to the next lowest multiple of $50.

(B) Table for married individuals filing separately. In the case of a married individual filing a separate return, subparagraph (A) (other than with respect to sections 63(c)(4) and 151(d)(4)(A)) shall be applied by substituting "$25" for "$50" each place it appears.

(7) Special rule for certain brackets.

(A) Calendar year 1994. In prescribing the tables under paragraph (1) which apply with respect to taxable years beginning in calendar year 1994, the Secretary shall make no adjustment to the dollar amounts at which the 36 percent rate bracket begins or at which the 39.6 percent rate begins under any table contained in subsection (a), (b), (c), (d), or (e).

(B) Later calendar years. In prescribing tables under paragraph (1) which apply with respect to taxable years beginning in a calendar year after 1994, the cost-of-living adjustment used in making adjustments to the dollar amounts referred to in subparagraph (A) shall be determined under paragraph (3)by substituting "1993" for "1992".

(8) Elimination of marriage penalty in 15-percent bracket. With respect to taxable years beginning after December 31, 2003, in prescribing the tables under paragraph (1)—

(A) the maximum taxable income in the 15-percent rate bracket in the table contained in subsection (a) (and the minimum taxable income in the next higher taxable income bracket in such table) shall be 200 percent of the maximum taxable income in the 15-percent rate bracket in the table contained in subsection (c) (after any other adjustment under this subsection), and

(B) the comparable taxable income amounts in the table contained in subsection (d) shall be $1/2$ of the amounts determined under subparagraph (A).

(g) Certain unearned income of children taxed as if parent's income.

(1) In general. In the case of any child to whom this subsection applies, the tax imposed by this section shall be equal to the greater of—

(A) the tax imposed by this sectionwithout regard to this subsection, or

(B) the sum of—

(i) the tax which would be imposed by this sectionif the taxable income of such child for the taxable year were reduced by the net unearned income of such child, plus

(ii) such child's share of the allocable parental tax.

(2) Child to whom subsection applies. This subsection shall apply to any child for any taxable year if—

(A) such child—

(i) has not attained age 18 before the close of the taxable year, or

(ii) (I) has attained age 18 before the close of the taxable year and meets the age requirements of section 152(c)(3) (determined without regard to subparagraph (B) thereof), and

(II) whose earned income (as defined in section 911(d)(2)) for such taxable year does not exceed one-half of the amount of the individual's support (within the meaning of section 152(c)(1)(D) after the application of section 152(f)(5) (without regard to subparagraph (A) thereof)) for such taxable year.

(B) either parent of such child is alive at the close of the taxable year, and

(C) such child does not file a joint return for the taxable year.

(3) Allocable parental tax. For purposes of this subsection—

(A) In general. The term "allocable parental tax" means the excess of—

(i) the tax which would be imposed by this section on the parent's taxable income if such income included the net unearned income of all children of the parent to whom this subsection applies, over

(ii) the tax imposed by this section on the parent without regard to this subsection.

For purposes of clause (i), net unearned income of all children of the parent shall not be taken into account in computing any exclusion, deduction, or credit of the parent.

(B) Child's share. A child's share of any allocable parental tax of a parent shall be equal to an amount which bears the same ratio to the total allocable parental tax as the child's net unearned income bears to the aggregate net unearned income of all children of such parent to whom this subsection applies.

(C) Special rule where parent has different taxable year. Except as provided in regulations, if the parent does not have the same taxable year as the child, the allocable parental tax shall be determined on the basis of the taxable year of the parent ending in the child's taxable year.

(4) Net unearned income. For purposes of this subsection—

(A) In general. The term "net unearned income" means the excess of—

(i) the portion of the adjusted gross income for the taxable year which is not attributable to earned income (as defined in section 911(d)(2)), over

(ii) the sum of—

(I) the amount in effect for the taxable year under section 63(c)(5)(A) (relating to limitation on standard deduction in the case of certain dependents), plus

(II) the greater of the amount described in subclause (I) or, if the child itemizes his deductions for the taxable year, the amount of the itemized deductions allowed by this chapter for the taxable year which are directly connected with the production of the portion of adjusted gross income referred to in clause (i).

(B) Limitation based on taxable income. The amount of the net unearned income for any taxable year shall not exceed the individual's taxable income for such taxable year.

(C) Treatment of distributions from qualified disability trusts. For purposes of this subsection, in the case of any child who is a beneficiary of a qualified disability trust (as defined in section 642(b)(2)(C)(ii)), any amount included in the income of such child under sections 652 and 662 during a taxable year shall be considered earned income of such child for such taxable year.

(5) Special rules for determining parent to whom subsection applies. For purposes of this subsection, the parent whose taxable income shall be taken into account shall be—

(A) in the case of parents who are not married (within the meaning of section 7703), the custodial parent (within the meaning of section 152(e)) of the child, and

(B) in the case of married individuals filing separately, the individual with the greater taxable income.

(6) Providing of parent's TIN. The parent of any child to whom this subsection applies for any taxable year shall provide the TIN of such parent to such child and such child shall include such TIN on the child's return of tax imposed by this section for such taxable year.

(7) Election to claim certain unearned income of child on parent's return.

(A) In general. If—

(i) any child to whom this subsection applies has gross income for the taxable year only from interest and dividends (including Alaska Permanent Fund dividends),

(ii) such gross income is more than the amount described in paragraph (4)(A)(ii)(I) and less than 10 times the amount so described,

(iii) no estimated tax payments for such year are made in the name and TIN of such child, and no amount has been deducted and withheld under section 3406, and

(iv) the parent of such child (as determined under paragraph (5)) elects the application of subparagraph (B),

such child shall be treated (other than for purposes of this paragraph) as having no gross income for such year and shall not be required to file a return under section 6012.

(B) Income included on parent's return. In the case of a parent making the election under this paragraph—

(i) the gross income of each child to whom such election applies (to the extent the gross income of such child exceeds twice the amount described in paragraph (4)(A)(ii)(I)) shall be included in such parent's gross income for the taxable year,

(ii) the tax imposed by this section for such year with respect to such parent shall be the amount equal to the sum of—

(I) the amount determined under this section after the application of clause (i), plus

(II) for each such child, 10 percent of the lessor amount described in paragraph (4)(A)(ii)(I) or the excess of the gross income of such child over the amount so described, and

(iii) any interest which is an item of tax preference under section 57(a)(5) of the child shall be treated as an item of tax preference of such parent (and not of such child).

(C) Regulations. The Secretary shall prescribe such regulations as may be necessary or appropriate to carry out the purposes of this paragraph.

(h) Maximum capital gains rate.

(1) In general. If a taxpayer has a net capital gain for any taxable year, the tax imposed by this section for such taxable year shall not exceed the sum of—

(A) a tax computed at the rates and in the same manner as if this subsection had not been enacted on the greater of—

(i) taxable income reduced by the net capital gain; or

(ii) the lesser of—

(I) the amount of taxable income taxed at a rate below 25 percent; or

(II) taxable income reduced by the adjusted net capital gain,

(B)[1]*0 percent of so much of the adjusted net capital gain (or, if less, taxable income) as does not exceed the excess (if any) of—*

(i) the amount of taxable income which would (without regard to this paragraph) be taxed at a rate below 25 percent, over

(ii) the taxable income reduced by the adjusted net capital gain;

[2]*(C) 15 percent of the lesser of—*

(i) so much of the adjusted net capital gain (or, if less, taxable income) as exceeds the amount on which a tax is determined under subparagraph (B), or

(ii) the excess of—

(I) the amount of taxable income which would (without regard to this paragraph) be taxed at a rate below 39.6 percent, over

(II) the sum of the amounts on which a tax is determined under subparagraphs (A) and (B),

(D) 20 percent of the adjusted net capital gain (or, if less, taxable income) in excess of the sum of the amounts on which tax is determined under subparagraphs (B) and (C),

(E) 25 percent of the excess (if any) of—

(i) the unrecaptured section 1250 gain (or, if less, the net capital gain (determined without regard to paragraph (11))), over

(ii) the excess (if any) of—

(I) the sum of the amount on which tax is determined under subparagraph (A) plus the net capital gain, over

(II) taxable income; and

(E) 28 percent of the amount of taxable income in excess of the sum of the amounts on which tax is determined under the preceding subparagraphs of this paragraph.

(2) Net capital gain taken into account as investment income. For purposes of this subsection, the net capital gain for any taxable year shall be reduced (but not below zero) by the amount which the taxpayer takes into account as investment income under section 163(d)(4)(B)(iii).

(3) Adjusted net capital gain. For purposes of this subsection, the term "adjusted net capital gain" means the sum of—

(A) net capital gain (determined without regard to paragraph (11)) reduced (but not below zero) by the sum of—

(i) unrecaptured section 1250 gain, and

(ii) 28-percent rate gain, plus

(B) qualified dividend income (as defined in paragraph (11)).

(4) 28 percent rate gain. For purposes of this subsection, the term "28-percent rate gain" means the excess (if any) of—

(A) the sum of—

(i) collectibles gain; and

(ii) section 1202 gain, over

(B) the sum of—

(i) collectibles loss;

(ii) the net short-term capital loss; and

(iii) the amount of long-term capital loss carried under section 1212(b)(1)(B) to the taxable year.

(5) Collectibles gain and loss. For purposes of this subsection—

(A) In general. The terms "collectibles gain" and "collectibles loss" mean gain or loss (respectively) from the sale or exchange of a collectible (as defined in section 408(m) without regard to paragraph (3) thereof) which is a capital asset held for more than 1 year but only to the extent such gain is taken into account in computing gross income and such loss is taken into account in computing taxable income.

(B) Partnerships, etc. For purposes of subparagraph (A), any gain from the sale of an interest in a partnership, S corporation, or trust which is attributable to unrealized appreciation in the value of collectibles shall be treated as gain from the sale or exchange of a collectible. Rules similar to the rules of section 751 shall apply for purposes of the preceding sentence.

(6) Unrecaptured section 1250 gain. For purposes of this subsection—

(A) In general. The term "unrecaptured section 1250 gain" means the excess (if any) of—

(i) the amount of long-term capital gain (not otherwise treated as ordinary income) which would be treated as ordinary income if section 1250(b)(1) included all depreciation and the applicable percentage under section 1250(a) were 100 percent, over

(ii) the excess (if any) of—

(I) the amount described in paragraph (4)(B); over

(II) the amount described in paragraph (4)(A).

(B) Limitation with respect to section 1231 property. The amount described in subparagraph (A)(i) from sales, exchanges, and conversions described in section 1231(a)(3)(A) for any taxable year shall not exceed the net section 1231 gain (as defined in section 1231(c)(3)) for such year.

(7) Section 1202 gain. For purposes of this subsection, the term "section 1202 gain" means the excess of—

(A) the gain which would be excluded from gross income under section 1202 but for the percentage limitation in section 1202(a), over

(B) the gain excluded from gross income under section 1202.

(8) Coordination with recapture of net ordinary losses under section 1231. If any amount is treated as ordinary income under section 1231(c), such amount shall be allocated among the separate categories of net section 1231 gain (as defined in section 1231(c)(3)) in such manner as the Secretary may by forms or regulations prescribe.

(9) Regulations. The Secretary may prescribe such regulations as are appropriate (including regulations requiring reporting) to apply this subsection in the case of sales and exchanges by pass-thru entities and of interests in such entities.

(10) Pass-thru entity defined. For purposes of this subsection, the term "pass-thru entity" means—

(A) a regulated investment company;

(B) a real estate investment trust;

(C) an S corporation;

(D) a partnership;

(E) an estate or trust;

(F) a common trust fund; and

(G) a qualified electing fund (as defined in section 1295).

(11) Dividends taxed as net capital gain.

(A) In general. For purposes of this subsection, the term "net capital gain" means net capital gain (determined without regard to this paragraph) increased by qualified dividend income.

(B) Qualified dividend income. For purposes of this paragraph—

(i) In general. The term "qualified dividend income" means dividends received during the taxable year from—

(I) domestic corporations, and

(II) qualified foreign corporations.

(ii) Certain dividends excluded. Such term shall not include—

(I) any dividend from a corporation which for the taxable year of the corporation in which the distribution is made, or the preceding taxable year, is a corporation exempt from tax under section 501 or 521,

(II) any amount allowed as a deduction under section 591 (relating to deduction for dividends paid by mutual savings banks, etc.), and

(III) any dividend described in section 404(k).

(iii) Coordination with section 246(c). Such term shall not include any dividend on any share of stock—

(I) with respect to which the holding period requirements of section 246(c) are not met (determined by substituting in section 246(c) "60 days" for "45 days" each place it appears and by substituting "121-day period" for "91-day period"), or

(II) to the extent that the taxpayer is under an obligation (whether pursuant to a short sale or otherwise) to make related payments with respect to positions in substantially similar or related property.

(C) Qualified foreign corporations.

(i) In general. Except as otherwise provided in this paragraph, the term "qualified foreign corporation" means any foreign corporation if—

(I) such corporation is incorporated in a possession of the United States, or

(II) such corporation is eligible for benefits of a comprehensive income tax treaty with the United States which the Secretary determines is satisfactory for purposes of this paragraph and which includes an exchange of information program.

(ii) Dividends on stock readily tradable on United States securities market. A foreign corporation not otherwise treated as a qualified foreign corporation under clause (i) shall be so treated with respect to any dividend paid by such corporation if the stock with respect to which such dividend is paid is readily tradable on an established securities market in the United States.

(iii) Exclusion of dividends of certain foreign corporations. Such term shall not include any foreign corporation which for the taxable year of the corporation in which the dividend was paid, or the preceding taxable year, is a passive foreign investment company (as defined in section 1297).

(iv) Coordination with foreign tax credit limitation. Rules similar to the rules of section 904(b)(2)(B) shall apply with respect to the dividend rate differential under this paragraph.

(D) Special rules.

(i) Amounts taken into account as investment income. Qualified dividend income shall not include any amount which the taxpayer takes into account as investment income under section 163(d)(4)(B).

(ii) Extraordinary dividends. If a taxpayer to whom this section applies receives, with respect to any share of stock, qualified dividend income from 1 or more dividends which are extraordinary dividends (within the meaning of section 1059(c)), any loss on the sale or exchange of such share shall, to the extent of such dividends, be treated as long-term capital loss.

(iii) Treatment of dividends from regulated investment companies and real estate investment trusts. A dividend received from a regulated investment company or a real estate investment trust shall be subject to the limitations prescribed in sections 854 and 857.

(i)   Rate reductions after 2000.

(1)   10-percent rate bracket.

(A) In general. In the case of taxable years beginning after December 31, 2000—

(i) the rate of tax under subsections (a), (b), (c), and (d) on taxable income not over the initial bracket amount shall be 10 percent, and

(ii) the 15 percent rate of tax shall apply only to taxable income over the initial bracket amount but not over the maximum dollar amount for the 15-percent rate bracket.

(B) Initial bracket amount. For purposes of this paragraph, the initial bracket amount is—

(i) $14,000 in the case of subsection (a),

(ii) $10,000 in the case of subsection (b), and

(iii) ½ the amount applicable under clause (i) (after adjustment, if any, under subparagraph (C)) in the case of subsections (c) and (d).

(C) Inflation adjustment. In prescribing the tables under subsection (f) which apply with respect to taxable years beginning in calendar years after 2003—

(i) the cost-of-living adjustment shall be determined under subsection (f)(3) by substituting "2002" for "1992" in subparagraph (B) thereof, and

(ii) the adjustments under clause (i) shall not apply to the amount referred to in subparagraph (B)(iii).

If any amount after adjustment under the preceding sentence is not a multiple of $50, such amount shall be rounded to the next lowest multiple of $50.

[3]*(2)   25-, 28-, and 33-percent rate brackets. The tables under subsections (a), (b), (c), (d), and (e) shall be applied—*

(A) by substituting "25%" for "28%" each place it appears (before the application of subparagraph (B)),

(B) by substituting "28%" for "31%" each place it appears, and

(C) by substituting "33%" for "36%" each place it appears.

(3)   Modifications to income tax brackets for high-income taxpayers.

(A) 35-percent rate bracket. In the case of taxable years beginning after December 31, 2012.

(i) the rate of tax under subsections (a), (b), (c), and (d) on a taxpayer's taxable income in the highest rate bracket shall be 35 percent to the extent such income does not exceed an amount equal to the excess of—

(I) the applicable threshold, over

(II) the dollar amount at which such bracket begins, and

(ii) the 39.6 percent rate of tax under such subsections shall apply only to the taxpayer's taxable income in such bracket in excess of the amount to which clause (i) applies.

(B) Applicable threshold. For purposes of this paragraph, the term "applicable threshold" means.

(i) $450,000 in the case of subsection (a),

(ii) $425,000 in the case of subsection (b),

(iii) $400,000 in the case of subsection (c), and

    (iv) 1.2 the amount applicable under clause (i) (after adjustment, if any, under subparagraph (C)) in the case of subsection (d).

    (C) Inflation adjustment. For purposes of this paragraph, with respect to taxable years beginning in calendar years after 2013, each of the dollar amounts under clauses (i), (ii), and (iii) of subparagraph (B) shall be adjusted in the same manner as under paragraph (1)(C)(i), except that subsection (f)(3)(B) shall be applied by substituting "2012" for "1992".

    [4](4) **Adjustment of tables.** The Secretary shall adjust the tables prescribed under subsection (f) to carry out this subsection.

    [For Analysis, see ¶ 101, ¶ 102, ¶ 103, ¶ 104, ¶ 201, ¶ 202 and ¶ 204.]

[Endnote Code Sec. 1]

    Sec. 101(a)(1) of the American Taxpayer Relief Act of 2012, P.L. 112-240, 1/2/2013, deleted Title IX [Sec. 901] of the Economic Growth and Tax Relief Reconciliation Act of 2001, P.L. 107-16, the effect of which is to eliminate the sunset of all provisions enacted by P.L. 107-16.

Effective Date (Sec. 101(a)(3), P.L. 112-240, 1/2/2013) effective for tax. plan, or limitation years beginning after 12/31/2012, and estates of decedents dying, gifts made, or generation skipping transfers after 12/31/2012.

    Following is a description of the amendments made to Code Sec. 1, by P.L. 107-16.

    P.L. 107-16, Sec. 101(a), added subsec. (i)

    P.L. 107-16, Sec. 101(c)(1), substituted

    "10 percent" for

    "15 percent" in subclause (g)(7)(B)(ii)(II)

    P.L. 107-16, Sec. 101(c)(2)(A), substituted

    "25 percent" for

    "28 percent" in subclause (h)(1)(A)(ii)(I) and clause (h)(1)(B)(i)

    P.L. 107-16, Sec. 101(c)(2)(B), deleted para. (h)(13)

    Prior to deletion, para. (h)(13) read as follows:

    "(13) Special rules.

    "(A) Determination of 28-percent rate gain. In applying paragraph (5)—

    "(i) the amount determined under subparagraph (A) of paragraph (5) shall include long-term capital gain (not otherwise described in such subparagraph)—

    "(I) which is properly taken into account for the portion of the taxable year before May 7, 1997; or

    "(II) from property held not more than 18 months which is properly taken into account for the portion of the taxable year after July 28, 1997, and before January 1, 1998;

    "(ii) the amount determined under subparagraph (B) of paragraph (5) shall include long-term capital loss (not otherwise described in such subparagraph)—

    "(I) which is properly taken into account for the portion of the taxable year before May 7, 1997; or

    "(II) from property held not more than 18 months which is properly taken into account for the portion of the taxable year after July 28, 1997, and before January 1, 1998; and

    "(iii) subparagraph (B) of paragraph (5) (as in effect immediately before the enactment of this clause shall apply to amounts properly taken income account before January 1, 1998.

    "(B) Determination of unrecaptured section 1250 gain. The amount determined under paragraph (7)(A)(i) shall not include gain—

    "(i) which is properly taken into account for the portion of the taxable year before May 7, 1997; or

    "(ii) from property held not more than 18 months which is properly taken into account for the portion of the taxable year after July 28, 1997, and before January 1, 1998.

    "(C) Special rules for pass-thru entities. In applying this paragraph with respect to any pass-thru entity, the determination of when gains and loss are properly taken into account shall be made at the entity level.

    "(D) Charitable remainder trusts. Subparagraphs (A) and (B)(ii) shall not apply to any capital gain distribution made by a trust described in section 664."

    P.L. 107-16, Sec. 301(c)(1), substituted

    "(other than with respect to sections 63(c)(4) and 151(d)(4)(A)) shall be applied" for

    "(other than with respect to subsection (c)(4) of section 63 (as it applies to subsections (c)(5)(A) and (f) of such section) and section 151(d)(4)(A)) shall be applied" in subpara. (f)(6)(B).

    P.L. 107-16, Sec. 302(a), added para. (f)(8)

    P.L. 107-16, Sec. 302(b)(1), added

    "except as provided in paragraph (8)," before

    "by increasing" in subpara. (f)(2)(A)

    P.L. 107-16, Sec. 302(b)(2), added

    "Phaseout of marriage penalty in 15-percent bracket;" before

    "Adjustments" in the heading of subsec. (f).

    Sec. 102(a) of the American Taxpayer Relief Act of 2012, P.L. 112-240, 1/2/2013, deleted Sec. 303, P.L. 108-27, the Jobs and Growth Tax Relief Reconciliation Act of 2003, the effect of which is to eliminate the sunset of all provisions enacted by Title III of P.L. 108-27.

    Following is a description of the amendments made to Code Sec. 1 by Title III, P.L. 108-27.

    P.L. 108-27, Sec. 301(a)(1), substituted

"5 percent (0 percent in the case of taxable years beginning after 2007)" for
"10 percent" in subpara. (h)(1)(B)

P.L. 108-27, Sec. 301(a)(2)(A), substituted
"15 percent" for
"20 percent" in subpara. (h)(1)(C)

P.L. 108-27, Sec. 301(b)(1)(A), deleted paras. (h)(2) and (9)P.L. 108-27, Sec. 301(b)(1)(B), redesignated paras. (h)(3)-(8) as (h)(2)-(7)

P.L. 108-27, Sec. 301(b)(1)(C), redesignated paras. (h)(10)-(12) as paras. (h)(8)-(10).

Prior to deletion, para. (h)(2) read as follows:

"(2) Reduced capital gain rates for qualified 5-year gain.

"(A) Reduction in 10-percent rate. In the case of any taxable year beginning after December 31, 2000, the rate under paragraph (1)(B) shall be 8 percent with respect to so much of the amount to which the 10-percent rate would otherwise apply as does not exceed qualified 5-year gain, and 10 percent with respect to the remainder of such amount.

"(B) Reduction in 20-percent rate. The rate under paragraph (1)(C) shall be 18 percent with respect to so much of the amount to which the 20-percent rate would otherwise apply as does not exceed the lesser of—

"(i) the excess of qualified 5-year gain over the amount of such gain taken into account under subparagraph (A) of this paragraph; or

"(ii) the amount of qualified 5-year gain (determined by taking into account only property the holding period for which begins after December 31, 2000), and 20 percent with respect to the remainder of such amount. For purposes of determining under the preceding sentence whether the holding period of property begins after December 31, 2000, the holding period of property acquired pursuant to the exercise of an option (or other right or obligation to acquire property) shall include the period such option (or other right or obligation) was held."

Prior to deletion, para. (h)(9) read as follows:

"(9) Qualified 5-year gain. For purposes of this subsection, the term 'qualified 5-year gain' means the aggregate long-term capital gain from property held for more than 5 years. The determination under the preceding sentence shall be made without regard to collectibles gain, gain described in paragraph (7)(A)(i), and section 1202 gain."

P.L. 108-27, Sec. 302(a), added para. (h)(11)

P.L. 108-27, Sec. 302(e)(1), amended para. (h)(3) redesignated by Sec. 301(b)(1)(B), of this Act, see above], effective for tax. yrs. begin. after 12/31/2002.

Prior to amendment, para. (h)(3) redesignated by Sec. 301(b)(1)(B), of this Act, see above] read as follows:

"(3) Adjusted net capital gain. For purposes of this subsection, the term 'adjusted net capital gain' means net capital gain reduced (but not below zero) by the sum of—

"(A) unrecaptured section 1250 gain; and

"(B) 28 percent rate gain."

Code Sec. 1(h)(1)(B), Code Sec. 1(h)(1)(C), Code Sec. 1(h)(1)(D), Code Sec. 1(h)(1)(E) and Code Sec. 1(h)(1)(F)were amended by Sec. 102(b)(1) and (c)(2) of the American Taxpayer Relief Act of 2012, P.L. 112-240, 1/2/2013, as detailed below:

1. Sec. 102(c)(2) substituted '0 percent' for '5 percent (0 percent in the case of taxable years beginning after 2007)' in subpara. (h)(1)(B)

2. Sec. 102(b)(1) deleted subpara. (h)(1)(C) and added new subparas. (h)(1)(C)-(D)

Prior to deletion, subpara. (h)(1)(C) read as follows:

"(C) 20 percent of the adjusted net capital gain (or, if less, taxable income) in excess of the amount on which a tax is determined under subparagraph (B);"

3. Sec. 102(b)(1) redesignated subpara. (h)(1)(D) as subpara. (h)(1)(E)

4. Sec. 102(b)(1) redesignated subpara. (h)(1)(E) as subpara. (h)(1)(F)

Effective Date (Sec. 102(d)(1), P.L. 112-240, 1/2/2013) effective for tax. yrs. begin. after 12/31/2012.

Code Sec. 1(i)(2), Code Sec. 1(i)(3) and Code Sec. 1(i)(4) were amended by Sec. 101(b)(1)(A)-(B), P.L. 112-240, 1/2/2013, as detailed below:

5. Sec. 101(b)(1)(A) amended para. (i)(2)

Prior to amendment, para. (i)(2) read as follows:

"(2) Reductions in rates after June 30, 2001. In the case of taxable years beginning in a calendar year after 2000, the corresponding percentage specified for such calendar year in the following table shall be substituted for the otherwise applicable tax rate in the tables under subsections (a), (b), (c), (d), and (e).

In the case of taxable years beginning during calendar year:	The corresponding percentages shall be substituted for the following percentages:			
	28%	31%	36%	39.6%
2001	27.5%	30.5%	35.5%	39.1%
2002	27.0%	30.0%	35.0%	38.6%
2003 and thereafter . .	25.0%	28.0%	33.0%	35.0%

6. Sec. 101(b)(1)(B) redesignated para. (i)(3) as para. (i)(4) and added para. (i)(3)

Effective Date (Sec. 101(b)(3), P.L. 112-240, 1/2/2013) effective for tax. yrs. begin. after 12/31/2012.

[¶ 3002]   Code Sec. 15.   Effect of changes.

* * * * * * * * * * * *

[1] *(f) Rate reductions enacted by Economic Growth and Tax Relief Reconciliation Act of 2001. This section shall not apply to any change in rates under subsection (i) of section 1 (relating to rate reductions after 2000).*

[Endnote Code Sec. 15]
  Sec. 101(a)(1) of the American Taxpayer Relief Act of 2012, P.L. 112-240, 1/2/2013, deleted Title IX [Sec. 901] of the Economic Growth and Tax Relief Reconciliation Act of 2001, P.L. 107-16, the effect of which is to eliminate the sunset of all provisions enacted by P.L. 107-16. Following are the amendments made to Code Sec. 15, by P.L. 107-16.
Effective Date (Sec. 101(a)(3), P.L. 112-240, 1/2/2013) effective for tax. plan, or limitation years beginning after 12/31/2012, and estates of decedents dying, gifts made, or generation skipping transfers after 12/31/2012.

  Code Sec. 15(f), in *italics*, was added by Sec. 101(c)(3) of the Economic Growth and Tax Relief Reconciliation Act of 2001, P.L. 107-16, 6/7/2001.
  1. Sec. 101(c)(3), P.L. 107-16 added subsec. (f)
Effective Date (Sec. 101(d)(1), P.L. 107-16, 6/7/2001) effective for tax. yrs. begin. after 12/31/2000.

[¶ 3003]   Code Sec. 21.   Expenses for household and dependent care services necessary for gainful employment.

  (a) Allowance of credit.

    (1) In general. In the case of an individual for which there are 1 or more qualifying individuals (as defined in subsection (b)(1)) with respect to such individual, there shall be allowed as a credit against the tax imposed by this chapter for the taxable year an amount equal to the applicable percentage of the employment-related expenses (as defined in subsection (b)(2)) paid by such individual during the taxable year.

    (2) Applicable percentage defined. For purposes of paragraph (1), the term "applicable percentage" means [1] *35 percent* reduced (but not below 20 percent) by 1 percentage point for each $2,000 (or fraction thereof) by which the taxpayer's adjusted gross income for the taxable year exceeds [2] *$15,000.*

* * * * * * * * * * * *

  (c) Dollar limit on amount creditable. The amount of the employment-related expenses incurred during any taxable year which may be taken into account under subsection (a) shall not exceed—

    (1) [3] *$3,000* if there is 1 qualifying individual with respect to the taxpayer for such taxable year, or

    (2) [4] *$6,000* if there are 2 or more qualifying individuals with respect to the taxpayer for such taxable year.

  The amount determined under paragraph (1) or (2) (whichever is applicable) shall be reduced by the aggregate amount excludable from gross income under section 129 for the taxable year.

* * * * * * * * * * * *

[For Analysis, see ¶ 603.]

[Endnote Code Sec. 21]
  Sec. 101(a)(1) of the American Taxpayer Relief Act of 2012, P.L. 112-240, 1/2/2013, deleted Title IX [Sec. 901] of the Economic Growth and Tax Relief Reconciliation Act of 2001, P.L. 107-16, the effect of which is to eliminate the sunset of all provisions enacted by P.L. 107-16. Following are the amendments made to Code Sec. 21, by P.L. 107-16.
Effective Date (Sec. 101(a)(3), P.L. 112-240, 1/2/2013) effective for taxable, plan, or limitation years beginning after 12/31/2012, and estates of decedents dying, gifts made, or generation skipping transfers after 12/31/2012.

Code Sec. 21(a)(2), Code Sec. 21(c)(1) and Code Sec. 21(c)(2) was added by Sec. 204(a)(1), (a)(2), (b)(1) and (b)(2) of the Economic Growth and Tax Relief Reconciliation Act of 2001, P.L. 107-16, 6/7/2001, as detailed below:

1. Sec. 204(b)(1) substituted "35 percent" for "30 percent" in para. (a)(2)
2. Sec. 204(b)(2) substituted "$15,000" for "$10,000" in para. (a)(2)
3. Sec. 204(a)(2) substituted "$3,000" for "$2,400" in para. (c)(1)
4. Sec. 204(a)(2) substituted "$6,000" for "$4,800" in para. (c)(2)

Effective Date (Sec. 204(c), P.L. 107-16, 6/7/2001) effective for tax. yrs. begin. after 12/31/2002.

[¶ 3004]   Code Sec. 23.   Adoption expenses.

(a) **Allowance of credit.**

(1) **In general.** In the case of an individual, there shall be allowed as a credit against the tax imposed by this chapter the amount of the qualified adoption expenses paid or incurred by the taxpayer.

(2) **Year credit allowed.** The credit under paragraph (1) with respect to any expense shall be allowed—

(A) in the case of any expense paid or incurred before the taxable year in which such adoption becomes final, for the taxable year following the taxable year during which such expense is paid or incurred, and

(B) in the case of an expense paid or incurred during or after the taxable year in which such adoption becomes final, for the taxable year in which such expense is paid or incurred.

(3) **$10,000 credit for adoption of child with special needs regardless of expenses.** In the case of an adoption of a child with special needs which becomes final during a taxable year, the taxpayer shall be treated as having paid during such year qualified adoption expenses with respect to such adoption in an amount equal to the excess (if any) of $10,000 over the aggregate qualified adoption expenses actually paid or incurred by the taxpayer with respect to such adoption during such taxable year and all prior taxable years.

(b) **Limitations.**

(1) **Dollar limitation.** The aggregate amount of qualified adoption expenses which may be taken into account under subsection (a) for all taxable years with respect to the adoption of a child by the taxpayer shall not exceed $10,000.

(2) **Income limitation.**

(A) In general. The amount allowable as a credit under subsection (a) for any taxable year (determined without regard to subsection (c)) shall be reduced (but not below zero) by an amount which bears the same ratio to the amount so allowable (determined without regard to this paragraph but with regard to paragraph (1)) as—

(i) the amount (if any) by which the taxpayer's adjusted gross income exceeds $150,000, bears to

(ii) $40,000.

(B) Determination of adjusted gross income. For purposes of subparagraph (A), adjusted gross income shall be determined without regard to sections 911, 931, and 933.

(3) **Denial of double benefit.**

(A) In general. No credit shall be allowed under subsection (a) for any expense for which a deduction or credit is allowed under any other provision of this chapter.

(B) Grants. No credit shall be allowed under subsection (a) for any expense to the extent that funds for such expense are received under any Federal, State, or local program.

[1]*(4) Repealed.*

(c) **Carryforwards of unused credit.**

[2]*(1) In general. If the credit allowable under subsection (a) for any taxable year exceeds the limitation imposed by section 26(a) for such taxable year reduced by the sum of the credits allowable under this subpart (other than this section and sections 25D and 1400C), such excess shall be carried to the succeeding taxable year and added to the credit allowable under subsection (a) for such taxable year.*

[3]*(2)* **Limitation.** *No credit may be carried forward under this subsection to any taxable year following the fifth taxable year after the taxable year in which the credit arose. For purposes of the preceding sentence, credits shall be treated as used on a first-in first-out basis.*

(d) **Definitions.** For purposes of this section—

(1) **Qualified adoption expenses.** The term "qualified adoption expenses" means reasonable and necessary adoption fees, court costs, attorney fees, and other expenses—

(A) which are directly related to, and the principal purpose of which is for, the legal adoption of an eligible child by the taxpayer,

(B) which are not incurred in violation of State or Federal law or in carrying out any surrogate parenting arrangement,

(C) which are not expenses in connection with the adoption by an individual of a child who is the child of such individual's spouse, and

(D) which are not reimbursed under an employer program or otherwise.

(2) **Eligible child.** The term "eligible child" means any individual who—

(A) has not attained age 18, or

(B) is physically or mentally incapable of caring for himself.

(3) **Child with special needs.** The term "child with special needs" means any child if—

(A) a State has determined that the child cannot or should not be returned to the home of his parents,

(B) such State has determined that there exists with respect to the child a specific factor or condition (such as his ethnic background, age, or membership in a minority or sibling group, or the presence of factors such as medical conditions or physical, mental, or emotional handicaps) because of which it is reasonable to conclude that such child cannot be placed with adoptive parents without providing adoption assistance, and

(C) such child is a citizen or resident of the United States (as defined in section 217(h)(3)).

(e) **Special rules for foreign adoptions.** In the case of an adoption of a child who is not a citizen or resident of the United States (as defined in section 217(h)(3))—

(1) subsection (a) shall not apply to any qualified adoption expense with respect to such adoption unless such adoption becomes final, and

(2) any such expense which is paid or incurred before the taxable year in which such adoption becomes final shall be taken into account under this section as if such expense were paid or incurred during such year.

(f) **Filing requirements.**

(1) **Married couples must file joint returns.** Rules similar to the rules of paragraphs (2), (3), and (4) of section 21(e) shall apply for purposes of this section.

(2) **Taxpayer must include TIN.**

(A) In general. No credit shall be allowed under this section with respect to any eligible child unless the taxpayer includes (if known) the name, age, and TIN of such child on the return of tax for the taxable year.

(B) Other methods. The Secretary may, in lieu of the information referred to in subparagraph (A), require other information meeting the purposes of subparagraph (A), including identification of an agent assisting with the adoption.

(g) **Basis adjustments.** For purposes of this subtitle, if a credit is allowed under this section for any expenditure with respect to any property, the increase in the basis of such property which would (but for this subsection) result from such expenditure shall be reduced by the amount of the credit so allowed.

(h) **Adjustments for inflation.** In the case of a taxable year beginning after December 31, 2002, each of the dollar amounts in subsection (a)(3) and paragraphs (1) and (2)(A)(i) of subsection (b) shall be increased by an amount equal to—

(1) such dollar amount, multiplied by

(2) the cost-of-living adjustment determined under section 1(f)(3) for the calendar year in which the taxable year begins, determined by substituting "calendar year 2001" for "calendar year 1992" in subparagraph (B) thereof.

If any amount as increased under the preceding sentence is not a multiple of $10, such amount shall be rounded to the nearest multiple of $10.

(i) Regulations. The Secretary shall prescribe such regulations as may be appropriate to carry out this section and section 137, including regulations which treat unmarried individuals who pay or incur qualified adoption expenses with respect to the same child as 1 taxpayer for purposes of applying the dollar amounts in subsections (a)(3) and (b)(1) of this section and in section 137(b)(1).

[For Analysis, see ¶ 604.]

[Endnote Code Sec. 23]

Sec. 101(a)(1) of the American Taxpayer Relief Act of 2012, P.L. 112-240, 1/2/2013, deleted Title IX [Sec. 901] of the Economic Growth and Tax Relief Reconciliation Act of 2001, P.L. 107-16, the effect of which is to eliminate the sunset of all provisions enacted by P.L. 107-16. Following is a description of the amendments made to Code Sec. 23, by P.L. 107-16.

Sec. 201(b)(2)(E), P.L. 107-16, substituted "and sections 24 and 1400C" for "and section 1400C" in subsec. (c) [prior to amendment by Sec. 202(f)(2)(A)(i)-(ii), P.L. 107-16, see below].

Sec. 202(a)(1), P.L. 107-16, amended para. (a)(1).

Prior to amendment, para. (a)(1) read as follows:

"(1) In general. In the case of an individual, P.L. 107-16, there shall be allowed as a credit against the tax imposed by this chapter the amount of the qualified adoption expenses paid or incurred by the taxpayer."

Sec. 202(b)(1)(A)(i), P.L. 107-16, substituted "$10,000" for "$5,000" in para. (b)(1)

Sec. 202(b)(1)(A)(ii), P.L. 107-16, deleted "($6,000, in the case of a child with special needs)" after "shall not exceed $5,000" in para. (b)(1)

Sec. 202(b)(1)(A)(iii), P.L. 107-16, substituted "subsection (a)(1)(A)" for "subsection (a)" in para. (b)(1)

Sec. 202(b)(2)(A), P.L. 107-16, substituted "$150,000" for "$75,000" in clause (b)(2)(A)(i)

Sec. 202(c), P.L. 107-16, added a flush sentence at the end of para. (a)(2)

Sec. 202(d)(1), P.L. 107-16, amended para. (d)(2)

Sec. 202(e)(1), P.L. 107-16, redesignated subsec. (h) as subsec. (i)

P.L. 107-16, and added new subsec. (h)

Sec. 202(f)(1), P.L. 107-16, added para. (b)(4)

Sec. 202(f)(2)(A)(i), P.L. 107-16, substituted "subsection (b)(4)" for "section 26(a)" in subsec. (c) [as amended by Sec. 201(b)(2)(E) of this Act, see above]

Sec. 202(f)(2)(A)(ii), P.L. 107-16, deleted "reduced by the sum of the credits allowable under this subpart (other than this section and sections 24 and 1400C)" before ", such excess shall be carried" in subsec. (c) [as amended by Sec. 201(b)(2)(E) of this Act, see above].

Prior to amendment, para. (d)(2) read as follows:

"(2) Eligible child. The term 'eligible child' means any individual—

"(A) who—

"(i) has not attained age 18, or

"(ii) is physically or mentally incapable of caring for himself, and

"(B) in the case of a qualified adoption expenses paid or incurred after December 31, 2001, who is a child with special needs."

Effective Date (Sec. 101(a)(3), P.L. 112-240, 1/2/2013) effective for taxable, plan, or limitation years beginning after 12/31/2012, and estates of decedents dying, gifts made, or generation skipping transfers after 12/31/2012.

Code Sec. 23(b)(4), Code Sec. 23(c)(1), Code Sec. 23(c)(2) and Code Sec. 23(c)(3) were amended by Sec. 104(c)(2)(A)(i)-(iii) of the American Taxpayer Relief Act of 2012, P.L. 112-240, 1/2/2013, as detailed below:

1. Sec. 104(c)(2)(A)(i) deleted para. (b)(4)

Prior to deletion, para. (b)(4) read as follows:

"(4) Limitation based on amount of tax. In the case of a taxable year to which section 26(a)(2) does not apply, the credit allowed under subsection (a) for any taxable year shall not exceed the excess of—

'(A) the sum of the regular tax liability (as defined in section 26(b)) plus the tax imposed by section 55, over

"(B) the sum of the credits allowable under this subpart (other than this section and section 25D) and section 27 for the taxable year."

2. Sec. 104(c)(2)(A)(ii) deleted para. (c)(1)-(2) and added new para. (c)(1)

Prior to deletion, para. (c)(1)-(2) read as follows:

"(1) Rule for years in which all personal credits allowed against regular and alternative minimum tax. In the case of a taxable year to which section 26(a)(2) applies, if the credit allowable under subsection (a) for any taxable year exceeds the limitation imposed by section 26(a)(2) for such taxable year reduced by the sum of the credits allowable under this subpart (other than this section and sections 25D and 1400C), such excess shall be carried to the succeeding taxable year and added to the credit allowable under subsection (a) for such taxable year.

'(2) Rule for other years. In the case of a taxable year to which section 26(a)(2) does not apply, if the credit allowable under subsection (a) for any taxable year exceeds the limitation imposed by subsection (b)(4) for such taxable year, such excess shall be carried to the succeeding taxable year and added to the credit allowable under subsection (a) for such taxable year."

3. Sec. 104(c)(2)(A)(iii) redesignated para. (c)(3) as (c)(2)

Effective Date (Sec. 104(d), P.L. 112-240, 1/2/2013) effective for tax. yrs. begin. after 12/31/2011.

[¶ 3005]   Code Sec. 24.   Child tax credit.

(a) Allowance of credit. There shall be allowed as a credit against the tax imposed by this chapter for the taxable year with respect to each qualifying child of the taxpayer for which the taxpayer is allowed a deduction under section 151 an amount equal to $1,000.

(b) Limitations.

(1) Limitation based on adjusted gross income. The amount of the credit allowable under subsection (a) shall be reduced (but not below zero) by $50 for each $1,000 (or fraction thereof) by which the taxpayer's modified adjusted gross income exceeds the threshold amount. For purposes of the preceding sentence, the term "modified adjusted gross income" means adjusted gross income increased by any amount excluded from gross income under section 911, 931, or 933.

(2) Threshold amount. For purposes of paragraph (1), the term "threshold amount" means—

(A) $110,000 in the case of a joint return,

(B) $75,000 in the case of an individual who is not married, and

(C) $55,000 in the case of a married individual filing a separate return.

For purposes of this paragraph, marital status shall be determined under section 7703.

[1](3) **Repealed.**

(c) Qualifying child. For purposes of this section—

(1) In general. The term "qualifying child" means a qualifying child of the taxpayer (as defined in section 152(c)) who has not attained age 17.

(2) Exception for certain noncitizens. The term "qualifying child" shall not include any individual who would not be a dependent if subparagraph (A) of section 152(b)(3) were applied without regard to all that follows "resident of the United States".

(d) Portion of credit refundable.

(1) In general. The aggregate credits allowed to a taxpayer under subpart C shall be increased by the lesser of—

(A) the credit which would be allowed under this section without regard to this subsection and the limitation under [2]*section 26(a)* or

(B) the amount by which the aggregate amount of credits allowed by this subpart (determined without regard to this subsection) would increase if the limitation imposed by [3]*section 26(a)* were increased by the greater of—

(i) 15 percent of so much of the taxpayer's earned income (within the meaning of section 32) which is taken into account in computing taxable income for the taxable year as exceeds $10,000, or

(ii) in the case of a taxpayer with 3 or more qualifying children, the excess (if any) of—

(I) the taxpayer's social security taxes for the taxable year, over

(II) the credit allowed under section 32 for the taxable year.

The amount of the credit allowed under this subsection shall not be treated as a credit allowed under this subpart and shall reduce the amount of credit otherwise allowable under subsection (a) without regard to [4]*section 26(a)*. For purposes of subparagraph (B), any amount excluded from gross income by reason of section 112 shall be treated as earned income which is taken into account in computing taxable income for the taxable year.

(2) Social security taxes. For purposes of paragraph (1)—

(A) In general. The term "social security taxes" means, with respect to any taxpayer for any taxable year—

(i) the amount of the taxes imposed by sections 3101 and 3201(a) on amounts received by the taxpayer during the calendar year in which the taxable year begins,

(ii) 50 percent of the taxes imposed by section 1401 on the self-employment income of the taxpayer for the taxable year, and

(iii) 50 percent of the taxes imposed by section 3211(a) on amounts received by the taxpayer during the calendar year in which the taxable year begins.

(B) Coordination with special refund of social security taxes. The term "social security taxes" shall not include any taxes to the extent the taxpayer is entitled to a special refund of such taxes under section 6413(c).

(C) Special rule. Any amounts paid pursuant to an agreement under section 3121(l) (relating to agreements entered into by American employers with respect to foreign affiliates) which are equivalent to the taxes referred to in subparagraph (A)(i) shall be treated as taxes referred to in such subparagraph.

(3) **Inflation adjustment.** In the case of any taxable year beginning in a calendar year after 2001, the $10,000 amount contained in paragraph (1)(B) shall be increased by an amount equal to—

(A) such dollar amount, multiplied by

(B) the cost-of-living adjustment determined under section 1(f)(3) for the calendar year in which the taxable year begins, determined by substituting "calendar year 2000" for "calendar year 1992" in subparagraph (B) thereof.

Any increase determined under the preceding sentence shall be rounded to the nearest multiple of $50.

(4) **Special rule for** [5]*for certain years.* Notwithstanding paragraph (3), in the case of any taxable year beginning [6]*after 2008 and before 2018*, the dollar amount in effect for such taxable year under paragraph (1)(B)(i) shall be $3,000.

(e) **Identification requirement.** No credit shall be allowed under this section to a taxpayer with respect to any qualifying child unless the taxpayer includes the name and taxpayer identification number of such qualifying child on the return of tax for the taxable year.

(f) **Taxable year must be full taxable year.** Except in the case of a taxable year closed by reason of the death of the taxpayer, no credit shall be allowable under this section in the case of a taxable year covering a period of less than 12 months.

[For Analysis, see ¶ 404, ¶ 601 and ¶ 602.]

[Endnote Code Sec. 24]

Sec. 101(a)(1) of the American Taxpayer Relief Act of 2012, P.L. 112-240, 1/2/2013, deleted Title IX [Sec. 901] of the Economic Growth and Tax Relief Reconciliation Act of 2001, P.L. 107-16, the effect of which is to eliminate the sunset of all provisions enacted by P.L. 107-16.

Effective Date (Sec. 101(a)(3), P.L. 112-240, 1/2/2013) effective for taxable, plan, or limitation years beginning after 12/31/2012, and estates of decedents dying, gifts made, or generation skipping transfers after 12/31/2012.

Following is a description of the amendments made to Code Sec. 24, by P.L. 107-16.

P.L. 107-16, Sec. 201(a), amended subsec. (a).

Prior to amendment, subsec. (a) read as follows:

"(a) Allowance of credit.

"There shall be allowed as a credit against the tax imposed by this chapter for the taxable year with respect to each qualifying child of the taxpayer an amount equal to $500 ($400 in the case of taxable years beginning in 1998)."

P.L. 107-16, Sec. 201(b)(1), added para. (b)(3)

P.L. 107-16, Sec. 201(b)(2)(A), substituted 'Limitations.' for 'Limitation based on adjusted gross income.' in the heading of subsec. (b)

P.L. 107-16, Sec. 201(b)(2)(B), substituted 'Limitation based on adjusted gross income.' for 'In general.' in the heading of para. (b)(1)

P.L. 107-16, Sec. 201(b)(2)(C)(i), substituted 'subsection (b)(3)' for 'section 26(a)' each place it appeared in subsec. (d) [as amended by Sec. 201(c)(1) of this Act, see below]

P.L. 107-16, Sec. 201(b)(2)(C)(ii), substituted 'amount of credit allowed by this section' for 'aggregate amount of credits allowed by this subpart' [this amendment cannot be made. Subpara. (d)(1)(B) already contains the language 'amount of credit allowed by this section' in subpara. (d)(1)(B) [as amended by Sec. 201(c)(1) of this Act, see below].

P.L. 107-16, Sec. 201(c)(1), substituted 'Portion of credit refundable' for 'Additional credit for families with 3 or more children' in the heading of subsec. (d) and amended para. (d)(1)

P.L. 107-16, Sec. 201(c)(2), added para. (d)(4)

P.L. 107-16, Sec. 201(d)(1), deleted para. (d)(2)

P.L. 107-16, Sec. 201(d)(2), redesignated para. (d)(3) as (d)(2) and (d)(4) [as added by Sec. 201(c)(2) of this Act, see above] as (d)(3).

Prior to amendment, para. (d)(1) read as follows:

"(1) In general. In the case of a taxpayer with three or more qualifying children for any taxable year, the aggregate credits allowed under subpart C shall be increased by the lesser of—

"(A) the credit which would be allowed under this section without regard to this subsection and the limitation under section 26(a); or

"(B) the amount by which the aggregate amount of credits allowed by this subpart (without regard to this subsection) would increase if the limitation imposed by section 26(a) were increased by the excess (if any) of—

"(i) the taxpayer's Social Security taxes for the taxable year, over

"(ii) the credit allowed under section 32 (determined without regard to subsection (n)) for the taxable year.

The amount of the credit allowed under this subsection shall not be treated as a credit allowed under this subpart and shall reduce the amount of credit otherwise allowable under subsection (a) without regard to section 26(a)."

Prior to deletion, para. (d)(2) read as follows:

"(2) Reduction of credit to taxpayer subject to alternative minimum tax. For taxable years beginning after December 31, 2001, the credit determined under this subsection for the taxable year shall be reduced by the excess (if any) of—

"(A) the amount of tax imposed by section 55 (relating to alternative minimum tax) with respect to such taxpayer for such taxable year, over

"(B) the amount of the reduction under section 32(h) with respect to such taxpayer for such taxable year."

P.L. 107-16, Sec. 202(f)(2)(B), substituted 'this section and section 23' for 'this section' in subpara. (b)(3)(B).

Code Sec. 24(b)(3), Code Sec. 24(d)(1)(A) and Code Sec. 24(d)(1)(B) in *italics* were amended by Sec. 104(c)(2)(B)(i), Sec. 104(c)(2)(B)(ii)(I), Sec. 104(c)(2)(B)(ii)(II).

1. deleted para. (b)(3)

Prior to deletion, para. (b)(3) read as follows:

"(3) Limitation based on amount of tax. In the case of a taxable year to which section 26(a)(2) does not apply, the credit allowed under subsection (a) for any taxable year shall not exceed the excess of—

"(A) the sum of the regular tax liability (as defined in section 26(b)) plus the tax imposed by section 55, over

"(B) the sum of the credits allowable under this subpart (other than this section and sections 23, 25A(i), 25B, 25D, 30, 30B, and 30D and section 27 for the taxable year."

2. substituted 'section 26(a)' for 'section 26(a)(2) or subsection (b)(3), as the case may be,' in subpara. (d)(1)(A)

3. substituted 'section 26(a)' for 'section 26(a)(2) or subsection (b)(3), as the case may be,' in subpara. (d)(1)(B)

4 .substituted 'section 26(a)' for 'section 26(a)(2) or subsection (b)(3), as the case may be' in the second to last sentence in para. (d)(1)

Effective Date (Sec. 104(d), P.L. 112-240, 1/2/2013) effective for tax. yrs. begin. after 12/31/2011.

Code Sec. 24(d)(4) in *italics* were amended by Sec. 103(b)(1) and (2), P.L. 112-240, as outlined below:

5. substituted 'for certain years' for '2009, 2010, 2011, and 2012' in heading of para. (d)(4)

6. substituted 'after 2008 and before 2018' for 'in 2009, 2010, 2011, or 2012' in para. (d)(4)

Effective Date (Sec. 103(e)(1), P.L. 112-240, 1/2/2013) effective for tax. yrs. begin. after 12/31/2012.

[¶ 3006]   Code Sec. 25.   Interest on certain home mortgages.

* * * * * * * * * * * *

(e) **Special rules and definitions.** For purposes of this section—

(1) **Carryforward of unused credit.**

(A) In general. If the credit allowable under subsection (a) for any taxable year exceeds the applicable tax limit for such taxable year, such excess shall be a carryover to each of the 3 succeeding taxable years and, subject to the limitations of subparagraph (B), shall be added to the credit allowable by subsection (a) for such succeeding taxable year.

(B) Limitation. The amount of the unused credit which may be taken into account under subparagraph (A) for any taxable year shall not exceed the amount (if any) by which the applicable tax limit for such taxable year exceeds the sum of—

(i) the credit allowable under subsection (a) for such taxable year determined without regard to this paragraph, and

(ii) the amounts which, by reason of this paragraph, are carried to such taxable year and are attributable to taxable years before the unused credit year.

[1](C) Applicable tax limit. For purposes of this paragraph, the term "applicable tax limit" means the limitation imposed by section 26(a) for the taxable year reduced by the sum of the credits allowable under this subpart (other than this section and sections 23, 25D, and 1400C).

* * * * * * * * * * * *

[For Analysis, see ¶ 403.]

[Endnote Code Sec. 25]

Sec. 101(a)(1), P.L. 112-240, 1/2/2013, deleted Title IX [Sec. 901], P.L. 107-16, the effect of which is to eliminate the sunset of all provisions enacted by P.L. 107-16. Sec. 201(b)(2)(F), P.L. 107-15 amended Code Sec. 25 by adding ", 24," after "sections 23" in subpara. (e)(1)(C),

Effective Date (Sec. 101(a)(3), P.L. 112-240, 1/2/2013) effective for tax. plan, or limitation years beginning after 12/31/2012, and estates of decedents dying, gifts made, or generation skipping transfers after 12/31/2012.

Code Sec. 25(e)(1)(C) was amended by Sec. 104(c)(2)(C) of the American Taxpayer Relief Act of 2012, P.L. 112-240, 1/2/2013, as detailed below:

1. Sec. 104(c)(2)(C) amended subpara. (e)(1)(C). Prior to amendment, subpara. (e)(1)(C) read as follows:

"(C) Applicable tax limit. For purposes of this paragraph, the term 'applicable tax limit' means—

"(i) in the case of a taxable year to which section 26(a)(2) applies, the limitation imposed by section 26(a)(2) for the taxable year reduced by the sum of the credits allowable under this subpart (other than this section and 23, 25D, and 1400C), and

"(ii) in the case of a taxable year to which section 26(a)(2) does not apply, the limitation imposed by section 26(a)(1) for the taxable year reduced by the sum of the credits allowable under this subpart (other than this section and sections 23, 24, 25A(i), 25B, 25D, 30, 30B, 30D, and 1400C)."

Effective Date (Sec. 104(d), P.L. 112-240, 1/2/2013) effective for tax. yrs. begin. after 12/31/2011.

[¶ 3007]   Code Sec. 25A.   Hope and Lifetime Learning Credits.

* * * * * * * * * * * *

[1]*(e) Election not to have section apply. A taxpayer may elect not to have this section apply with respect to the qualified tuition and related expenses of an individual for any taxable year.*

* * * * * * * * * * * *

(i) American opportunity tax credit. In the case of any taxable year beginning [2]*after 2008 and before 2018*—

(1) Increase in credit. The Hope Scholarship Credit shall be an amount equal to the sum of—

(A) 100 percent of so much of the qualified tuition and related expenses paid by the taxpayer during the taxable year (for education furnished to the eligible student during any academic period beginning in such taxable year) as does not exceed $2,000, plus

(B) 25 percent of such expenses so paid as exceeds $2,000 but does not exceed $4,000.

(2) Credit allowed for first 4 years of post-secondary education. Subparagraphs (A) and (C) of subsection (b)(2) shall be applied by substituting "4" for "2".

(3) Qualified tuition and related expenses to include required course materials. Subsection (f)(1)(A) shall be applied by substituting "tuition, fees, and course materials" for "tuition and fees".

(4) Increase in AGI limits for Hope Scholarship Credit. In lieu of applying subsection (d) with respect to the Hope Scholarship Credit, such credit (determined without regard to this paragraph) shall be reduced (but not below zero) by the amount which bears the same ratio to such credit (as so determined) as—

(A) the excess of—

(i) the taxpayer's modified adjusted gross income (as defined in subsection (d)(3)) for such taxable year, over

(ii) $80,000 ($160,000 in the case of a joint return), bears to

(B) $10,000 ($20,000 in the case of a joint return).

[3]*(5) Portion of credit made refundable.** 40 percent of so much of the credit allowed under subsection (a) as is attributable to the Hope Scholarship Credit (determined after application of paragraph (4) and without regard to this paragraph and [4]*section 26(a)* shall be treated as a credit allowable under subpart C (and not allowed under subsection (a)). The

preceding sentence shall not apply to any taxpayer for any taxable year if such taxpayer is a child to whom subsection (g) of section 1 applies for such taxable year.

⁵*(6)* **Coordination with midwestern disaster area benefits.** In the case of a taxpayer with respect to whom section 702(a)(1)(B) of the Heartland Disaster Tax Relief Act of 2008 applies for any taxable year, such taxpayer may elect to waive the application of this subsection to such taxpayer for such taxable year.

(j) Regulations. The Secretary may prescribe such regulations as may be necessary or appropriate to carry out this section, including regulations providing for a recapture of the credit allowed under this section in cases where there is a refund in a subsequent taxable year of any amount which was taken into account in determining the amount of such credit.

[For Analysis, see ¶ 403, ¶ 701 and ¶ 704.]

[Endnote Code Sec. 25A]
   Sec. 101(a)(1) of the American Taxpayer Relief Act of 2012, P.L. 112-240, 1/2/2013, deleted Title IX [Sec. 901] of the Economic Growth and Tax Relief Reconciliation Act of 2001, P.L. 107-16, the effect of which is to eliminate the sunset of all provisions enacted by P.L. 107-16.
Effective Date (Sec. 101(a)(3), P.L. 112-240, 1/2/2013) effective for taxable, plan, or limitation years beginning after 12/31/2012, and estates of decedents dying, gifts made, or generation skipping transfers after 12/31/2012.
   Following are the amendments made to Code Sec. 25A, by P.L. 107-16.

   Code Sec. 25A(e), in *italics*, was amended by Sec. 401(g)(2)(A) of the Economic Growth and Tax Relief Reconciliation Act of 2001, P.L. 107-16, 6/7/2001.
   1. Sec. 401(g)(2)(A), P.L. 107-16 amended subsec. (e).
   Prior to amendment, subsec. (e) read as follows: "(e) Election to have section apply.
   "(1) In general. No credit shall be allowed under subsection (a) for a taxable year with respect to the qualified tuition and related expenses of an individual unless the taxpayer elects to have this section apply with respect to such individual for such year.
   "(2) Coordination with exclusions. An election under this subsection shall not take effect with respect to an individual for any taxable year if any portion of any distribution during such taxable year from an education individual retirement account is excluded from gross income under section 530(d)(2)."
Effective Date (Sec. 401(h), P.L. 107-16, 6/7/2001) effective for tax. yrs. begin. after 12/31/2001.

   Code Sec. 25A(i) was amended by Sec. 103(a)(1) of the American Taxpayer Relief Act of 2012, P.L. 112-240, 1/2/2013, as detailed below:
   2. Sec. 103(a)(1) substituted "after 2008 and before 2018" for "in 2009, 2010, 2011, or 2012" in subsec. (i)
Effective Date (Sec. 103(e)(1), P.L. 112-240, 1/2/2013) effective for tax. yrs. begin. after 12/31/2012.

   Code Sec. 25A(i)(5), Code Sec. 25A(i)(6) and Code Sec. 25A(i)(7) were amended by Secs. 104(c)(2)(D)(i)-(ii), P.L. 112-240, 1/2/2013, as detailed below:
   3. Sec. 104(c)(2)(D)(i) deleted para. (i)(5) and redesignated para. (i)(6) as (i)(5)
   Prior to deletion, para. (i)(5) read as follows:
   "(5) Credit allowed against alternative minimum tax. In the case of a taxable year to section 26(a)(2) does not apply, so much of the credit allowed under subsection (a) as is attributable to the Hope Scholarship Credit shall not exceed the excess of—
   "(B) the sum of the regular tax liability (as defined in section 26(b)) plus the tax imposed by section 55, over
   "(B) the sum of the credits allowable under this subpart (other than this subsection and sections 23, 25D, and 30D) and section 27 for the taxable year.
   "Any reference in this section or section 24, 25, 26, 25B, 904, or 1400C to a credit allowable under this subsection shall be treated as a reference to so much of the credit allowable under subsection (a) as is attributable to the Hope Scholarship Credit."
   4. Sec. 104(c)(2)(D)(ii) substituted "section 26(a)" for "section 26(a)(2) or paragraph (5), as the case may be" in para. (i)(5) as redesignated
   5. Sec. 104(c)(2)(D)(i) redesignated para. (i)(7) as (i)(6)
Effective Date (Sec. 104(d)(1), P.L. 112-240, 1/2/2013) effective for tax. yrs. begin. after 12/31/2011.

[¶ 3008]   Code Sec. 25B.   Elective deferrals and IRA contributions by certain individuals.

* * * * * * * * * * * *

[1](g) *Repealed.*
[For Analysis, see ¶ 403.]

[Endnote Code Sec. 25B]
Code Sec. 25B(g) was amended by Sec. 104(c)(2)(E) of the American Taxpayer Relief Act of 2012, P.L. 112-240, 1/2/2013, as detailed below:
1. Sec. 104(c)(2)(E) deleted subsec. (g). Prior to amendment, subsec. (g) read as follows:
"(g) Limitation based on amount of tax. In the case of a taxable year to which section 26(a)(2) does not apply, the credit allowed under subsection (a) for the taxable year shall not exceed the excess of—
"(1) the sum of the regular tax liability (as defined in section 26(b)) plus the tax imposed by section 55, over
"(2) the sum of the credits allowable under this subpart (other than this section and sections 23, 25A(i), 25D, 30, 30B, and 30D) and section 27 for the taxable year."
Effective Date (Sec. 104(d), P.L. 112-240, 1/2/2013) effective for tax. yrs. begin. after 12/31/2011.

[¶ 3009]   Code Sec. 25C.   Nonbusiness energy property.

* * * * * * * * * * * *

(g) Termination. This section shall not apply with respect to any property placed in service—

(1) after December 31, 2007, and before January 1, 2009, or

(2) after [1]*December 31, 2013.*
[For Analysis, see ¶ 403 and ¶ 1004.]

[Endnote Code Sec. 25C]
Code Sec. 25C(g)(2) was amended by Sec. 401(a) of the American Taxpayer Relief Act of 2012, P.L. 112-240, 1/2/2013, as detailed below:
Sec. 401(a) substituted "December 31, 2013" for "December 31, 2011" in para. (g)(2)
Effective Date (Sec. 401(b), P.L. 112-240, 1/2/2013) effective for property placed in service after 12/31/2011.

[¶ 3010]   Code Sec. 25D.   Residential energy efficient property.

* * * * * * * * * * * *

[1]*(c) Carryforward of unused credit.* If the credit allowable under subsection (a) exceeds the limitation imposed by section 26(a) for such taxable year reduced by the sum of the credits allowable under this subpart (other than this section), such excess shall be carried to the suceeding taxable year and added to the credit allowable under subsection (a) for such succeeding taxable year.

* * * * * * * * * * * *

[For Analysis, see ¶ 403.]

[Endnote Code Sec. 25D]
Code Sec. 25D(c) was amended by Sec. 104(c)(2)(F) of the American Taxpayer Relief Act of 2012, P.L. 112-240, 1/2/2013, as detailed below:
1. Sec. 104(c)(2)(F) amended subsec. (c)
Prior to deletion, subsec. (c) read as follows:
"(c) Limitation based on amount of tax; carryforward of unused credit.
"(1) Limitation based on amount of tax. In the case of a taxable year to which section 26(a)(2) does not apply, the credit allowed under subsection (a) for the taxable year shall not exceed the excess of—
"(A) the sum of the regular tax liability (as defined in section 26(b)) plus the tax imposed by section 55, over
"(B) the sum of the credits allowable under this subpart (other than this section) and section 27 for the taxable year.
"(2) Carryforward of unused credit.
"(A) Rule for years in which all personal credits allowed against regular and alternative minimum tax. In the case of a taxable year to which section 26(a)(2) applies, if the credit allowable under subsection (a) exceeds the limitation imposed by section 26(a)(2) for such taxable year reduced by the sum of the credits allowable under this subpart (other than this section), such excess shall be carried to the succeeding taxable year and added to the credit allowable under subsection (a) for such succeeding taxable year.

"(B) Rule for other years. In the case of a taxable year to which section 26(a)(2) does not apply, if the credit allowable under subsection (a) exceeds the limitation imposed by paragraph (1) for such taxable year, such excess shall be carried to the succeeding taxable year and added to the credit allowable under subsection (a) for such succeeding taxable year."

Effective Date (Sec. 104(d), P.L. 112-240, 1/2/2013) effective for tax. yrs. begin. after 12/31/2011.

[¶ 3011]   **Code Sec. 26.**   **Limitation based on tax liability; definition of tax liability.**

[1]*(a)*   *Limitation based on amount of tax. The aggregate amount of credits allowed by this subpart for the taxable year shall not exceed the sum of—*

    (1) the taxpayer's regular tax liability for the taxable year reduced by the foreign tax credit allowable under section 27(a), and

    (2) the tax imposed by section 55(a) for the taxable year.

* * * * * * * * * * * *

[For Analysis, see ¶ 403 and ¶ 404.]

[Endnote Code Sec. 26]

    Sec. 101(a)(1) of the American Taxpayer Relief Act of 2012, P.L. 112-240, 1/2/2013, deleted Title IX [Sec. 901] of the Economic Growth and Tax Relief Reconciliation Act of 2001, P.L. 107-16, the effect of which is to eliminate the sunset of all provisions enacted by P.L. 107-16.

Effective Date (Sec. 101(a)(3), P.L. 112-240, 1/2/2013) effective for taxable, plan, or limitation years beginning after 12/31/2012, and estates of decedents dying, gifts made, or generation skipping transfers after 12/31/2012.

    Following are the amendments made to Code Sec. 26, by

    P.L. 107-16, Sec. 201(b)(2)(D), added "(other than section 24)" after "this subpart" in para. (a)(1), effective for tax. yrs. begin. after 12/31/2001.

    P.L. 107-16, Sec. 202(f)(2)(C), substituted "sections 23 and 24" for "section 24" in para. (a)(1) [as amended by Sec. 201(b)(2)(D) of this Act, see above], effective for tax. yrs. begin. after 12/31/2001.

    Code Sec. 26(a) was amended by Sec. 104(c)(1) of the American Taxpayer Relief Act of 2012, P.L. 112-240, 1/2/2013, as detailed below:

    1. Sec. 104(c)(1) amended subsec. (a)

    Prior to amendment, subsec (a) read as follows:

    "(a) Limitation based on amount of tax.

    "(1) In general. The aggregate amount of credits allowed by this subpart (other than 23, 24 , 25A(i) , 25B , 25D , 30 , 30B , and 30D) for the taxable year shall not exceed the excess (if any) of-

    "(A) the taxpayer's regular tax liability for the taxable year, over

    "(B) the tentative minimum tax for the taxable year (determined without regard to the alternative minimum tax foreign tax credit).

    For purposes of subparagraph (B) , the taxpayer's tentative minimum tax for any taxable year beginning during 1999 shall be treated as being zero.

    "(2) Special rule for taxable years 2000 through 2011. For purposes of any taxable year beginning during 2000, 2001, 2002, 2003, 2004, 2005, 2006, 2007, 2008, or 2009, 2010, or 2011 the aggregate amount of credits allowed by this subpart for the taxable year shall not exceed the sum of-

    "(A) the taxpayer's regular tax liability for the taxable year reduced by the foreign tax credit allowable under section 27(a) , and

    "(B) the tax imposed by section 55(a) for the taxable year.

Effective Date (Sec. 104(d), P.L. 112-240, 1/2/2013) effective for tax. yrs. begin. after 12/31/2011.

[¶ 3012]   **Code Sec. 30.**   **Certain plug-in electric vehicles.**

* * * * * * * * * * * *

   (c)   Application with other credits.

    (1)   Business credit treated as part of general business credit. So much of the credit which would be allowed under subsection (a) for any taxable year (determined without regard to this subsection) that is attributable to property of a character subject to an allowance for depreciation shall be treated as a credit listed in section 38(b) for such taxable year (and not allowed under subsection (a)).

(2)[1] *Personal credit.*

(A) For purposes of this title, the credit allowed under subsection (a) for any taxable year (determined after application of paragraph (1)) shall be treated as a credit allowable under subpart A for such taxable year.

(B) Limitation based on amount of tax. In the case of a taxable year to which section 26(a)(2) does not apply, the credit allowed under subsection (a) for any taxable year (determined after application of paragraph (1)) shall not exceed the excess of—

(i) the sum of the regular tax liability (as defined in section 26(b)) plus the tax imposed by section 55, over

(ii) the sum of the credits allowable under subpart A (other than this section and sections 23, 25D, and 30D) and section 27 for the taxable year.

* * * * * * * * * * * * *

[For Analysis, see ¶ 403.]

[Endnote Code Sec. 30]

Code Sec. 30(c)(2) was amended by Sec. 104(c)(2)(G) of the American Taxpayer Relief Act of 2012, P.L. 112-240, 1/2/2013, as detailed below:

1. Sec. 104(c)(2)(G) amended para. (c)(2)

Prior to amendment, subpara. (c)(4)(B) read as follows:

"Personal credit. In general. For purposes of this title, the credit allowed under subsection (a) for any taxable year (determined after application of paragraph (1)) shall be treated as a credit allowable under subpart A for such taxable year."

Effective Date (Sec. 104(d), P.L. 112-240, 1/2/2013) effective for tax. yrs. begin. after 12/31/2011.

[¶ 3013]   Code Sec. 30A.   Puerto Rico economic activity credit.

(a) Allowance of credit.

(1) In general. Except as otherwise provided in this section, if the conditions of both paragraph (1) and paragraph (2) of subsection (b) are satisfied with respect to a qualified domestic corporation, there shall be allowed as a credit against the tax imposed by this chapter an amount equal to the portion of the tax which is attributable to the taxable income, from sources without the United States, from—

(A) the active conduct of a trade or business within Puerto Rico, or

(B) the sale or exchange of substantially all of the assets used by the taxpayer in the active conduct of such trade or business.

In the case of any taxable year beginning after December 31, 2001, the aggregate amount of taxable income taken into account under the preceding sentence (and in applying subsection (d)) shall not exceed the adjusted base period income of such corporation, as determined in the same manner as under section 936(j).

(2) Qualified domestic corporation. For purposes of paragraph (1), the term "qualified domestic corporation" means a domestic corporation—

(A) which is an existing credit claimant with respect to Puerto Rico, and

(B) with respect to which section 936(a)(4)(B) does not apply for the taxable year.

(3) Separate application. For purposes of determining—

(A) whether a taxpayer is an existing credit claimant with respect to Puerto Rico, and

(B) the amount of the credit allowed under this section,

this section (and so much of section 936 as relates to this section) shall be applied separately with respect to Puerto Rico.

(b) Conditions which must be satisfied. The conditions referred to in subsection (a) are—

(1) 3-year period. If 80 percent or more of the gross income of the qualified domestic corporation for the 3-year period immediately preceding the close of the taxable year (or for such part of such period immediately preceding the close of such taxable year as may be applicable) was derived from sources within a possession (determined without regard to section 904(f)).

(2) Trade or business. If 75 percent or more of the gross income of the qualified domestic corporation for such period or such part thereof was derived from the active conduct of a trade or business within a possession.

(c) Credit not allowed against certain taxes. The credit provided by subsection (a) shall not be allowed against the tax imposed by—

(1) section 59A (relating to environmental tax),

(2) section 531 (relating to the tax on accumulated earnings),

(3) section 541 (relating to personal holding company tax), or

(4) section 1351 (relating to recoveries of foreign expropriation losses).

(d) Limitations on credit for active business income. The amount of the credit determined under subsection (a) for any taxable year shall not exceed the sum of the following amounts:

(1) 60 percent of the sum of—

(A) the aggregate amount of the qualified domestic corporation's qualified possession wages for such taxable year, plus

(B) the allocable employee fringe benefit expenses of the qualified domestic corporation for such taxable year.

(2) The sum of—

(A) 15 percent of the depreciation allowances for the taxable year with respect to short-life qualified tangible property,

(B) 40 percent of the depreciation allowances for the taxable year with respect to medium-life qualified tangible property, and

(C) 65 percent of the depreciation allowances for the taxable year with respect to long-life qualified tangible property.

(3) If the qualified domestic corporation does not have an election to use the method described in section 936(h)(5)(C)(ii)(relating to profit split) in effect for the taxable year, the amount of the qualified possession income taxes for the taxable year allocable to non-sheltered income.

(e) Administrative provisions. For purposes of this title—

(1) the provisions of section 936 (including any applicable election thereunder) shall apply in the same manner as if the credit under this section were a credit under section 936(a)(1)(A) for a domestic corporation to which section 936(a)(4)(A) applies,

(2) the credit under this section shall be treated in the same manner as the credit under section 936, and

(3) a corporation to which this section applies shall be treated in the same manner as if it were a corporation electing the application of section 936.

(f) Denial of double benefit. Any wages or other expenses taken into account in determining the credit under this section may not be taken into account in determining the credit under section 41.

(g) Definitions. For purposes of this section, any term used in this section which is also used in section 936 shall have the same meaning given such term by section 936.

(h) Application of section. This section shall apply to taxable years beginning after December 31, 1995, and before January 1, 2006.

[For Analysis, see ¶ 1206.]

[Endnote Code Sec. 30A]

Sec. 330(a)(1), P.L. 112-240, 1/2/2013, amended Sec. 119(a), P.L. 109-432. Sec. 330(a)(2)), P.L. 112-240, 1/2/2013, added Sec. 119(e), P.L. 109-432. Sec. 330(b)), P.L. 112-240, 1/2/2013, amended Sec. 119(d), P.L. 109-432

Effective Date (Sec. 330(c), P.L. 112-240, 1/2/2013) effective for taxable years beginning after 12/31/2011. For Sec. 119, P.L. 109-432 as amended, see below.

Sec. 119, P.L. 109-432, as amended, reads as follows:

"Sec. 119. American Samoa economic development credit.

"(a) In General. For purposes of section 30A of the Internal Revenue Code of 1986, a domestic corporation shall be treated as a qualified domestic corporation to which such section applies if—

"(1) in the case of a taxable year beginning before January 1, 2012, such corporation—

"(A) is an existing credit claimant with respect to American Samoa, and

"(B) elected the application of section 936 of the Internal Revenue Code of 1986 for its last taxable year beginning before January 1, 2006, and

"(2) in the case of a taxable year beginning after December 31, 2011, such corporation meets the requirements of subsection (e).

"(b) Special rules for application of section. The following rules shall apply in applying section 30A of the Internal Revenue Code of 1986 for purposes of this section:

"(1) Amount of credit. Notwithstanding section 30A(a)(1) of such Code, the amount of the credit determined under section 30A(a)(1) of such Code for any taxable year shall be the amount determined under section 30A(d) of such Code, except that section 30A(d) shall be applied without regard to paragraph (3) thereof.

"(2) Separate application. In applying section 30A(a)(3) of such Code in the case of a corporation treated as a qualified domestic corporation by reason of this section, section 30A of such Code (and so much of section 936 of such Code as relates to such section 30A) shall be applied separately with respect to American Samoa.

"(3) Foreign tax credit allowed. Notwithstanding section 30A(e) of such Code, the provisions of section 936(c) of such Code shall not apply with respect to the credit allowed by reason of this section.

"(c) Definitions. For purposes of this section, any term which is used in this section which is also used in section 30A or 936 of such Code shall have the same meaning given such term by such section 30A or 936.

"(d) Application of section. Notwithstanding section 30A(h) or section 936(j) of such Code, this section (and so much of section 30A and section 936 of such Code as relates to this section) shall apply—

"(1) in the case of a corporation that meets the requirements of subparagraphs (A) and (B) of subsection (a)(1), to the first 8 taxable years of such corporation which begin after December 31, 2006, and before January 1, 2014, and

"(2) in the case of a corporation that does not meet the requirements of subparagraphs (A) and (B) of subsection (a)(1), to the first 2 taxable years of such corporation which begin after December 31, 2011, and before January 1, 2014."

"(e) Qualified production activities income requirement. A corporation meets the requirement of this subsection if such corporation has qualified production activities income, as defined in subsection (c) of section 199 of the Internal Revenue Code of 1986, determined by substituting 'American Samoa' for 'the United States' each place it appears in paragraphs (3), (4), and (6) of such subsection (c), for the taxable year."

Prior to amendment, Sec. 119(a), 109-432 read as follows:

"(a) In General. For purposes of section 30A of the Internal Revenue Code of 1986, a domestic corporation shall be treated as a qualified domestic corporation to which such section applies if such corporation—

"(1) is an existing credit claimant with respect to American Samoa, and

"(2) elected the application of section 936 of the Internal Revenue Code of 1986 for its last taxable year beginning before January 1, 2006.

Prior to amendment, Sec. 119(d), 109-432 read as follows:

"(d) Application of section. Notwithstanding section 30A(h) or section 936(j) of such Code, this section (and so much of section 30A and section 936 of such Code as relates to this section) shall apply to the first 6 taxable years of a corporation to which subsection (a) applies which begin after December 31, 2005, and before January 1, 2012."

[¶ 3014]   Code Sec. 30B.   Alternative motor vehicle credit.

* * * * * * * * * * * *

(g) Application with other credits.

(1) Business credit treated as part of general business credit. So much of the credit which would be allowed under subsection (a) for any taxable year (determined without regard to this subsection) that is attributable to property of a character subject to an allowance for depreciation shall be treated as a credit listed in section 38(b) for such taxable year (and not allowed under subsection (a)).

(2)[1] *Personal credit.*

(A) For purposes of this title, the credit allowed under subsection (a) for any taxable year (determined after application of paragraph (1)) shall be treated as a credit allowable under subpart A for such taxable year.

(B) Limitation based on amount of tax. In the case of a taxable year to which section 26(a)(2) does not apply, the credit allowed under subsection (a) for any taxable year (determined after application of paragraph (1)) shall not exceed the excess of—

(i) the sum of the regular tax liability (as defined in section 26(b)) plus the tax imposed by section 55, over

(ii) the sum of the credits allowable under subpart A (other than this section and sections 23, 25D, 30, and 30D) and section 27 for the taxable year.

* * * * * * * * * * * *

[For Analysis, see ¶ 403.]

[Endnote Code Sec. 30B]
  Code Sec. 30B(g)(2) was amended by Sec. 104(c)(2)(H) of the American Taxpayer Relief Act of 2012, P.L. 112-240, 1/2/2013, as detailed below:
  1. Sec. 104(c)(2)(H) amended para. (g)(2)
  Prior to amendment, para. (g)(2) read as follows:
  "In general. For purposes of this title, the credit allowed under subsection (a) for any taxable year (determined after application of paragraph (1)) shall be treated as a credit allowable under subpart A for such taxable year."
Effective Date (Sec. 104(d), P.L. 112-240, 1/2/2013) effective for taxable years beginning after 12/31/2011.

[¶ 3015]   **Code Sec. 30C.**   **Alternative fuel vehicle refueling property credit.**

* * * * * * * * * * * *

  (g) **Termination.** This section shall not apply to any property placed in service—
    (1) in the case of property relating to hydrogen, after December 31, 2014, and
    (2) in the case of any other property, after [1]*December 31, 2013.*

* * * * * * * * * * * *

[For Analysis, see ¶ 1008.]

[Endnote Code Sec. 30C]
  Code Sec. 30C(g)(2) was amended by Sec. 402(a) of the American Taxpayer Relief Act of 2012, P.L. 112-240, 1/2/2013, as detailed below:
  1. Sec. 402(a) substituted 'December 31, 2013' for 'December 31, 2011' in para. (g)(2)
Effective Date (Sec. 402(b), P.L. 112-240, 1/2/2013) effective for property placed in service after 12/31/2011.

[¶ 3016]   **Code Sec. 30D.**   **New qualified plug-in electric drive motor vehicles.**

* * * * * * * * * * * *

  (c) **Application with other credits.**
    (1) **Business credit treated as part of general business credit.** So much of the credit which would be allowed under subsection (a) for any taxable year (determined without regard to this subsection) that is attributable to property of a character subject to an allowance for depreciation shall be treated as a credit listed in section 38(b) for such taxable year (and not allowed under subsection (a)).
    [1]*(2)* *Personal credit. For purposes of this title, the credit allowed under subsection (a) for any taxable year (determined after application of paragraph (1)) shall be treated as a credit allowable under subpart A for such taxable year.*

* * * * * * * * * * * *

  (f) **Special rules.**
    (1) **Basis reduction.** For purposes of this subtitle, the basis of any property for which a credit is allowable under subsection (a) shall be reduced by the amount of such credit so allowed.
    (2) **No double benefit.** The amount of any deduction or other credit allowable under this chapter for a [2]*vehicle for which a credit is allowable under subsection (a)* shall be reduced by the amount of credit [3]*allowed under such subsection* for such vehicle.
    (3) **Property used by tax-exempt entity.** In the case of a vehicle the use of which is described in paragraph (3) or (4) of section 50(b) and which is not subject to a lease, the person who sold such vehicle to the person or entity using such vehicle shall be treated as the taxpayer that placed such vehicle in service, but only if such person clearly discloses to such person or entity in a document the amount of any credit allowable under subsection (a) with respect to such vehicle (determined without regard to subsection (c)).
    (4) **Property used outside united states not qualified.** No credit shall be allowable under subsection (a) with respect to any property referred to in section 50(b)(1).

(5) Recapture. The Secretary shall, by regulations, provide for recapturing the benefit of any credit allowable under subsection (a) with respect to any property which ceases to be property eligible for such credit.

(6) Election not to take credit. No credit shall be allowed under subsection (a) for any vehicle if the taxpayer elects to not have this section apply to such vehicle.

(7) Interaction with air quality and motor vehicle safety standards. A [4]*vehicle* shall not be considered eligible for a credit under this section unless such vehicle is in compliance with—

(A) the applicable provisions of the Clean Air Act for the applicable make and model year of the vehicle (or applicable air quality provisions of State law in the case of a State which has adopted such provision under a waiver under section 209(b) of the Clean Air Act), and

(B) the motor vehicle safety provisions of sections 30101 through 30169 of title 49, United States Code.

[5]*(g) Credit allowed for 2- and 3-wheeled plug-in electric vehicles.*

(1) In general. In the case of a qualified 2- or 3-wheeled plug-in electric vehicle—

(A) there shall be allowed as a credit against the tax imposed by this chapter for the taxable year an amount equal to the sum of the applicable amount with respect to each such qualified 2- or 3-wheeled plug-in electric vehicle placed in service by the taxpayer during the taxable year, and

(B) the amount of the credit allowed under subparagraph (A) shall be treated as a credit allowed under subsection (a).

(2) Applicable amount. For purposes of paragraph (1), the applicable amount is an amount equal to the lesser of—

(A) 10 percent of the cost of the qualified 2- or 3-wheeled plug-in electric vehicle, or

(B) $2,500.

(3) Qualified 2- or 3-wheeled plug-in electric vehicle. The term "qualified 2- or 3-wheeled plug-in electric vehicle" means any vehicle which—

(A) has 2 or 3 wheels,

(B) meets the requirements of subparagraphs (A), (B), (C), (E), and (F) of subsection (d)(1) (determined by substituting "2.5 kilowatt hours" for "4 kilowatt hours" in subparagraph (F)(i)),

(C) is manufactured primarily for use on public streets, roads, and highways,

(D) is capable of achieving a speed of 45 miles per hour or greater, and

(E) is acquired after December 31, 2011, and before January 1, 2014.

[For Analysis, see ¶ 403 and ¶ 1006.]

[Endnote Code Sec. 30D]

Code Sec. 30D(c)(2) was amended by Sec. 104(c)(2)(I) of the American Taxpayer Relief Act of 2012, P.L. 112-240, 1/2/2013, as detailed below:

1. Sec. 104(c)(2)(I) amended para. (c)(2). Prior to amendment, para. (c)(2) read as follows:

"(2) Personal credit.

"(A) In general. For purposes of this title, the credit allowed under subsection (a) for any taxable year (determined after application of paragraph (1)) shall be treated as a credit allowable under subpart A for such taxable year.

"(B) Limitation based on amount of tax. In the case of a taxable year to which section 26(a)(2) does not apply, the credit allowed under subsection (a) for any taxable year (determined after application of paragraph (1)) shall not exceed the excess of—

"(i) the sum of the regular tax liability (as defined in section 26(b)) plus the tax imposed by section 55, over

"(ii) the sum of the credits allowable under subpart A (other than this section and sections 23 and 25D) and section 27 for the taxable year."

Effective Date (Sec. 104(d), P.L. 112-240, 1/2/2013) effective for tax. yrs. begin. after 12/31/2011.

Code Sec. 30D(f)(2), Code Sec. 30D(f)(7) and Code Sec. 30D(g) were amended by Secs. 403(a), (b)(1)(A)-(B) and (b)(2), P.L. 112-240, 1/2/2013, as detailed below:

2. Sec. 403(b)(1)(A) substituted "vehicle for which a credit is allowable under subsection (a)" for "new qualified plug-in electric drive motor vehicle" in para. (f)(2)

3. Sec. 403(b)(1)(B) substituted "allowed under such subsection" for "allowed under subsection (a)" in para. (f)(2)

4. Sec. 403(b)(2) substituted "vehicle" for "motor vehicle" in para. (f)(7)

5. Sec. 403(a) added subsec. (g)

Effective Date (Sec. 403(c), P.L. 112-240, 1/2/2013) effective for vehicles acquired after 12/31/2011.

[¶ 3017]   Code Sec. 32.   Earned income.

(a) Allowance of credit.

(1) In general. In the case of an eligible individual, there shall be allowed as a credit against the tax imposed by this subtitle for the taxable year an amount equal to the credit percentage of so much of the taxpayer's earned income for the taxable year as does not exceed the earned income amount.

(2) Limitation. The amount of the credit allowable to a taxpayer under paragraph (1) for any taxable year shall not exceed the excess (if any) of—

(A) the credit percentage of the earned income amount, over

(B) the phaseout percentage of so much of the adjusted gross income (or, if greater, the earned income) of the taxpayer for the taxable year as exceeds the phaseout amount.

(b) Percentages and amounts. For purposes of subsection (a)—

(1) Percentages. The credit percentage and the phaseout percentage shall be determined as follows:

(A) In general. In the case of taxable years beginning after 1995:

In the case of an eligible individual with:	The credit percentage is:	The phaseout percentage is:
1 qualifying child	34	15.98
2 or more qualifying children	40	21.06
No qualifying children	7.65	7.65

(B) Transitional percentages for 1995. In the case of taxable years beginning in 1995:

In the case of an eligible individual with:	The credit percentage is:	The phaseout percentage is:
1 qualifying child	34	15.98
2 or more qualifying children	36	20.22
No qualifying children	7.65	7.65

(C) Transitional percentages for 1994. In the case of a taxable year beginning in 1994:

In the case of an eligible individual with:	The credit percentage is:	The phaseout percentage is:
1 qualifying child	26.3	15.98
2 or more qualifying children	30	17.68
No qualifying children	7.65	7.65

(2) Amounts.

(A) In general. Subject to subparagraph (B), the earned income amount and the phaseout amount shall be determined as follows:

In the case of an eligible individual with:	The earned income amount is:	The phaseout amount is:
1 qualifying child	$6,330	$11,610
2 or more qualifying children	$8,890	$11,610
No qualifying children	$4,220	$ 5,280

(B) Joint returns. In the case of a joint return filed by an eligible individual and such individual's spouse, the phaseout amount determined under subparagraph (A) shall be increased by—

(i) $1,000 in the case of taxable years beginning in 2002, 2003, and 2004,

(ii) $2,000 in the case of taxable years beginning in 2005, 2006, and 2007, and

(iii) $3,000 in the case of taxable years beginning after 2007.

(3) Special rules ¹*for certain years.* In the case of any taxable year beginning ²*after 2008 and before 2018*—

(A) Increased credit percentage for 3 or more qualifying children. In the case of a taxpayer with 3 or more qualifying children, the credit percentage is 45 percent.

(B) Reduction of marriage penalty.

(i) In general. The dollar amount in effect under paragraph (2)(B) shall be $5,000.

(ii) Inflation adjustment. In the case of any taxable year beginning in 2010, the $5,000 amount in clause (i) shall be increased by an amount equal to—

(I) such dollar amount, multiplied by

(II) the cost of living adjustment determined under section 1(f)(3) for the calendar year in which the taxable year begins determined by substituting "calendar year 2008" for "calendar year 1992" in subparagraph (B) thereof.

(iii) Rounding. Subparagraph (A) of subsection (j)(2) shall apply after taking into account any increase under clause (ii).

(c) Definitions and special rules. For purposes of this section—

(1) Eligible individual.

(A) In general. The term "eligible individual" means—

(i) any individual who has a qualifying child for the taxable year, or

(ii) any other individual who does not have a qualifying child for the taxable year, if—

(I) such individual's principal place of abode is in the United States for more than one-half of such taxable year,

(II) such individual (or, if the individual is married, either the individual or the individual's spouse) has attained age 25 but not attained age 65 before the close of the taxable year, and

(III) such individual is not a dependent for whom a deduction is allowable under section 151 to another taxpayer for any taxable year beginning in the same calendar year as such taxable year.

For purposes of the preceding sentence, marital status shall be determined under section 7703.

(B) Qualifying child ineligible. If an individual is the qualifying child of a taxpayer for any taxable year of such taxpayer beginning in a calendar year, such individual shall not be treated as an eligible individual for any taxable year of such individual beginning in such calendar year.

(C) Exception for individual claiming benefits under section 911. The term "eligible individual" does not include any individual who claims the benefits of section 911 (relating to citizens or residents living abroad) for the taxable year.

(D) Limitation on eligibility of nonresident aliens. The term "eligible individual" shall not include any individual who is a nonresident alien individual for any portion of the taxable year unless such individual is treated for such taxable year as a resident of the United States for purposes of this chapter by reason of an election under subsection (g) or (h) of section 6013.

(E) Identification number requirement. No credit shall be allowed under this section to an eligible individual who does not include on the return of tax for the taxable year—

(i) such individual's taxpayer identification number, and

(ii) if the individual is married (within the meaning of section 7703), the taxpayer identification number of such individual's spouse.

(F) Individuals who do not include TIN, etc., of any qualifying child. No credit shall be allowed under this section to any eligible individual who has one or more qualifying children if no qualifying child of such individual is taken into account under subsection (b) by reason of paragraph (3)(D).

(2) Earned income.

(A) The term "earned income" means—

(i) wages, salaries, tips, and other employee compensation, but only if such amounts are includible in gross income for the taxable year, plus

(ii) the amount of the taxpayer's net earnings from self-employment for the taxable year (within the meaning of section 1402(a)), but such net earnings shall be determined with regard to the deduction allowed to the taxpayer by section 164(f).

(B) For purposes of subparagraph (A)—

(i) the earned income of an individual shall be computed without regard to any community property laws,

(ii) no amount received as a pension or annuity shall be taken into account,

(iii) no amount to which section 871(a) applies (relating to income of nonresident alien individuals not connected with United States business) shall be taken into account,

(iv) no amount received for services provided by an individual while the individual is an inmate at a penal institution shall be taken into account,

(v) no amount described in subparagraph (A) received for service performed in work activities as defined in paragraph (4) or (7) of section 407(d) of the Social Security Act to which the taxpayer is assigned under any State program under part A of title IV of such Act shall be taken into account, but only to the extent such amount is subsidized under such State program, and

(vi) a taxpayer may elect to treat amounts excluded from gross income by reason of section 112 as earned income.

(3) Qualifying child.

(A) In general. The term "qualifying child" means a qualifying child of the taxpayer (as defined in section 152(c), determined without regard to paragraph (1)(D) thereof and section 152(e)).

(B) Married individual. The term "qualifying child" shall not include an individual who is married as of the close of the taxpayer's taxable year unless the taxpayer is entitled to a deduction under section 151 for such taxable year with respect to such individual (or would be so entitled but for section 152(e)).

(C) Place of abode. For purposes of subparagraph (A), the requirements of section 152(c)(1)(B) shall be met only if the principal place of abode is in the United States.

(D) Identification requirements.

(i) In general. A qualifying child shall not be taken into account under subsection (b) unless the taxpayer includes the name, age, and TIN of the qualifying child on the return of tax for the taxable year.

(ii) Other methods. The Secretary may prescribe other methods for providing the information described in clause (i).

(4) Treatment of military personnel stationed outside the United States. For purposes of paragraphs (1)(A)(ii)(I) and (3)(C), the principal place of abode of a member of the Armed Forces of the United States shall be treated as in the United States during any period during which such member is stationed outside the United States while serving on extended active duty with the Armed Forces of the United States. For purposes of the preceding sentence, the term "extended active duty" means any period of active duty pursuant to a call or order to such duty for a period in excess of 90 days or for an indefinite period.

(d) Married individuals. In the case of an individual who is married (within the meaning of section 7703), this section shall apply only if a joint return is filed for the taxable year under section 6013.

(e) Taxable year must be full taxable year. Except in the case of a taxable year closed by reason of the death of the taxpayer, no credit shall be allowable under this section in the case of a taxable year covering a period of less than 12 months.

(f) Amount of credit to be determined under tables.

(1) In general. The amount of the credit allowed by this section shall be determined under tables prescribed by the Secretary.

(2) Requirements for tables. The tables prescribed under paragraph (1) shall reflect the provisions of subsections (a) and (b) and shall have income brackets of not greater than $50 each—

(A) for earned income between $0 and the amount of earned income at which the credit is phased out under subsection (b), and

(B) for adjusted gross income between the dollar amount at which the phaseout begins under subsection (b) and the amount of adjusted gross income at which the credit is phased out under subsection (b).

(g) Repealed.

(h) Repealed.

(i) Denial of credit for individuals having excessive investment income.

(1) In general. No credit shall be allowed under subsection (a) for the taxable year if the aggregate amount of disqualified income of the taxpayer for the taxable year exceeds $2,200.

(2) Disqualified income. For purposes of paragraph (1), the term "disqualified income" means—

(A) interest or dividends to the extent includible in gross income for the taxable year,

(B) interest received or accrued during the taxable year which is exempt from tax imposed by this chapter,

(C) the excess (if any) of—

(i) gross income from rents or royalties not derived in the ordinary course of a trade or business, over

(ii) the sum of—

(I) the deductions (other than interest) which are clearly and directly allocable to such gross income, plus

(II) interest deductions properly allocable to such gross income,

(D) the capital gain net income (as defined in section 1222) of the taxpayer for such taxable year, and

(E) the excess (if any) of—

(i) the aggregate income from all passive activities for the taxable year (determined without regard to any amount included in earned income under subsection (c)(2) or described in a preceding subparagraph), over

(ii) the aggregate losses from all passive activities for the taxable year (as so determined).

For purposes of subparagraph (E), the term "passive activity" has the meaning given such term by section 469.

(j) Inflation adjustments.

(1) In general. In the case of any taxable year beginning after 1996, each of the dollar amounts in subsections (b)(2) and (i)(1) shall be increased by an amount equal to—

(A) such dollar amount, multiplied by

(B) the cost-of-living adjustment determined under section 1(f)(3) for the calendar year in which the taxable year begins, determined—

(i) in the case of amounts in subsections (b)(2)(A) and (i)(1), by substituting "calendar year 1995" for "calendar year 1992" in subparagraph (B) thereof, and

(ii) in the case of the $3,000 amount in subsection (b)(2)(B)(iii), by substituting "calendar year 2007" for "calendar year 1992" in subparagraph (B) of such section 1.

(2) Rounding.

(A) In general. If any dollar amount in subsection (b)(2)(A) (after being increased under subparagraph (B) thereof), after being increased under paragraph (1), is not a multiple of $10, such dollar amount shall be rounded to the nearest multiple of $10.

(B) Disqualified income threshold amount. If the dollar amount in subsection (i)(1), after being increased under paragraph (1), is not a multiple of $50, such amount shall be rounded to the next lowest multiple of $50.

(k) Restrictions on taxpayers who improperly claimed credit in prior year.

(1) Taxpayers making prior fraudulent or reckless claims.

(A) In general. No credit shall be allowed under this section for any taxable year in the disallowance period.

(B) Disallowance period. For purposes of paragraph (1), the disallowance period is—

(i) the period of 10 taxable years after the most recent taxable year for which there was a final determination that the taxpayer's claim of credit under this section was due to fraud, and

(ii) the period of 2 taxable years after the most recent taxable year for which there was a final determination that the taxpayer's claim of credit under this section was due to reckless or intentional disregard of rules and regulations (but not due to fraud).

(2) Taxpayers making improper prior claims. In the case of a taxpayer who is denied credit under this section for any taxable year as a result of the deficiency procedures under subchapter B of chapter 63, no credit shall be allowed under this section for any subsequent taxable year unless the taxpayer provides such information as the Secretary may require to demonstrate eligibility for such credit.

(l) Coordination with certain means-tested programs. For purposes of—

(1) the United States Housing Act of 1937,

(2) title V of the Housing Act of 1949,

(3) section 101 of the Housing and Urban Development Act of 1965,

(4) sections 221(d)(3), 235, and 236 of the National Housing Act, and

(5) the Food and Nutrition Act of 2008,

any refund made to an individual (or the spouse of an individual) by reason of this section, and any payment made to such individual (or such spouse) by an employer under section 3507, shall not be treated as income (and shall not be taken into account in determining resources for the month of its receipt and the following month).

(m) Identification numbers. Solely for purposes of subsections (c)(1)(E) and (c)(3)(D), a taxpayer identification number means a social security number issued to an individual by the Social Security Administration (other than a social security number issued pursuant to clause (II) (or that portion of clause (III) that relates to clause (II)) of section 205(c)(2)(B)(i) of the Social Security Act).

[For Analysis, see ¶ 601, ¶ 605, ¶ 606 and ¶ 607.]

[Endnote Code Sec. 32]

Sec. 101(a)(1) of the American Taxpayer Relief Act of 2012, P.L. 112-240, 1/2/2013, deleted Title IX [Sec. 901] of the Economic Growth and Tax Relief Reconciliation Act of 2001, P.L. 107-16, the effect of which is to eliminate the sunset of all provisions enacted by P.L. 107-16.

Effective Date (Sec. 101(a)(3), P.L. 112-240, 1/2/2013) effective for taxable, plan, or limitation years beginning after 12/31/2012, and estates of decedents dying, gifts made, or generation skipping transfers after 12/31/2012.

Following is a description of the amendments made to Code Sec. 32, by P.L. 107-16.

P.L. 107-16, Sec. 201(c)(3), deleted subsec. (n), effective for tax. yrs. begin. after 12/31/2000.

Prior to deletion, subsec. (n) read as follows:

"(n) Supplemental child credit.

"(1) In general. In the case of a taxpayer with respect to whom a credit is allowed under section 24(a) for the taxable year, the credit otherwise allowable under this section shall be increased by the lesser of—

"(A) the excess of—

"(i) the credits allowed under subpart A (determined after the application of section 26 and without regard to this subsection), over

"(ii) the credits which would be allowed under subpart A after the application of section 26, determined without regard to section 24 and this subsection; or

"(B) the excess of—

"(i) the sum of the credits allowed under this part (determined without regard to sections 31, 33, and 34 and this subsection), over

"(ii) the sum of the regular tax and the Social Security taxes (as defined in section 24(d)).

The credit determined under this subsection shall be allowed without regard to any other provision of this section , including subsection (d).

"(2) Coordination with other credits. The amount of the credit under this subsection shall reduce the amount of the credits otherwise allowable under subpart A for the taxable year (determined after the application of section 26), but the amount of the credit under this subsection (and such reduction) shall not be taken into account in determining the amount of any other credit allowable under this part."

P.L. 107-16, Sec. 303(a)(1)(A), substituted "Amounts. (A) In general. Subject to subparagraph (B), the earned" for "Amounts. The earned" in para. (b)(2)

P.L.107-16, Sec. 303(a)(1)(B), added subpara. (b)(2)(B)

P.L.107-16, Sec. 303(a)(2), amended subpara. (j)(1)(B)

P.L.107-16, Sec. 303(a)(3), substituted "subsection (b)(2)(A) (after being increased under subparagraph (B) thereof)" for "subsection (b)(2)" in subpara. (j)(2)(A)

P.L.107-16, Sec. 303(b), added ", but only if such amounts are includible in gross income for the taxable year" after "other employee compensation" in clause (c)(2)(A)(i)

P.L.107-16, Sec. 303(c), deleted subsec. (h)

P.L.107-16, Sec. 303(d)(1), deleted "modified" after "much of the" in subpara. (a)(2)(B)

P.L.107-16, Sec. 303(d)(2)(A), deleted para. (c)(5)

P.L.107-16, Sec. 303(d)(2)(B), deleted "modified" before "adjusted" each place it appeared in subpara. (f)(2)(B)

P.L.107-16, Sec. 303(e)(1), amended clause (c)(3)(B)(i)

P.L.107-16, Sec. 303(e)(2)(A), amended clause (c)(3)(B)(iii)

P.L.107-16, Sec. 303(e)(2)(B), deleted "except as provided in subparagraph (B)(iii)," before "who" in clause (c)(3)(A)(ii)

P.L.107-16, Sec. 303(f), amended subpara. (c)(1)(C)

P.L.107-16, Sec. 303(h), substituted "subparagraph (A)(ii)" for "subparagraphs (A)(ii) and (B)(iii)(II)" in subpara. (c)(3)(E), effective for tax. yrs. begin. after 12/31/2001.

Prior to amendment, subpara. (j)(1)(B) read as follows:

"(B) the cost-of-living adjustment determined under section 1(f)(3) for the calendar year in which the taxable year begins, determined by substituting 'calendar year 1995' for 'calendar year 1992' in subparagraph (B) thereof."

Prior to deletion, subsec. (h) read as follows:

"(h) Reduction of credit to taxpayers subject to alternative minimum tax. The credit allowed under this section for the taxable year shall be reduced by the amount of tax imposed by section 55 (relating to alternative minimum tax) with respect to such taxpayer for such taxable year."

Prior to deletion, para. (c)(5) read as follows:

"(5) Modified adjusted gross income.

"(A) In general. The term 'modified adjusted gross income' means adjusted gross income determined without regard to the amounts described in subparagraph (B) and increased by the amounts described in subparagraph (C).

"(B) Certain amounts disregarded. An amount is described in this subparagraph if it is—

"(i) the amount of losses from sales or exchanges of capital assets in excess of gains from such sales or exchanges to the extent such amount does not exceed the amount under section 1211(b)(1),

"(ii) the net loss from estates and trusts,

"(iii) the excess (if any) of amounts described in subsection (i)(2)(C)(ii) over the amounts described in subsection (i)(2)(C)(i) (relating to nonbusiness rents and royalties), or

"(iv) 75 percent of the net loss from the carrying on of trades or businesses, computed separately with respect to—

"(I) trades or businesses (other than farming) conducted as sole proprietorships,

"(II) trades or businesses of farming conducted as sole proprietorships, and

"(III) other trades or businesses.

For purposes of clause (iv), there shall not be taken into account items which are attributable to a trade or business which consists of the performance of services by the taxpayer as an employee.

"(C) Certain amounts included. An amount is described in this subparagraph if it is—

"(i) interest received or accrued during the taxable year which is exempt from tax imposed by this chapter; or

"(ii) amounts received as a pension or annuity, and any distributions or payments received from an individual retirement plan, by the taxpayer during the taxable year to the extent not included in gross income.

Clause (ii) shall not include any amount which is not includible in gross income by reason of a trustee-to-trustee transfer or a rollover distribution."

Prior to amendment, clause (c)(3)(B)(i) read as follows:

"(i) In general. An individual bears a relationship to the taxpayer described in this subparagraph if such individual is—

"(I) a son or daughter of the taxpayer, or a descendant of either,

"(II) a stepson or stepdaughter of the taxpayer, or

"(III) an eligible foster child of the taxpayer."

Prior to amendment, clause (c)(3)(B)(iii) read as follows:

"(iii) Eligible foster child. For purposes of clause (i)(III), the term 'eligible foster child' means an individual not described in clause (i)(I) or (II) who—

"(I) is a brother, sister, stepbrother, or stepsister of the taxpayer (or a descendant of any such relative) or is placed with the taxpayer by an authorized placement agency,

"(II) the taxpayer cares for as the taxpayer's own child, and

"(III) has the same principal place of abode as the taxpayer for the taxpayer's entire taxable year."

Prior to amendment, subpara. (c)(1)(C) read as follows:

"(C) 2 or more eligible individuals. If 2 or more individuals would (but for this subparagraph and after application of subparagraph (B)) be treated as eligible individuals with respect to the same qualifying child for taxable years beginning in the same calendar year, only the individual with the highest modified adjusted gross income for such taxable years shall be treated as an eligible individual with respect to such qualifying child."

Code Sec. 32(b)(3) was amended by Sec. 103(c)(1)-(2) of the American Taxpayer Relief Act of 2012, P.L. 112-240, 1/2/2013, as detailed below:

1. Sec. 103(c)(1) substituted "for certain years" for "2009, 2010, 2011, or 2012" in the heading of para. (b)(3)
2. Sec. 103(c)(2) substituted "after 2008 and before 2018" for "in 2009, 2010, 2011, or 2012" in para. (b)(3)
Effective Date (Sec. 103(e)(1), P.L. 112-240, 1/2/2013) effective for tax. yrs. begin. after 12/31/2012.

[¶ 3018]   Code Sec. 35.   Health insurance costs of eligible individuals.

(a) **In general.** In the case of an individual, there shall be allowed as a credit against the tax imposed by subtitle A an amount equal to [1]*72.5 percent* of the amount paid by the taxpayer for coverage of the taxpayer and qualifying family members under qualified health insurance for eligible coverage months beginning in the taxable year.

(b) **Eligible coverage month.** For purposes of this section—

(1) **In general.** The term "eligible coverage month" means any month if—

(A) as of the first day of such month, the taxpayer—

(i) is an eligible individual,

(ii) is covered by qualified health insurance, the premium for which is paid by the taxpayer,

(iii) does not have other specified coverage, and

(iv) is not imprisoned under Federal, State, or local authority, and

(B) such month begins more than 90 days after the date of the enactment of the Trade Act of 2002 [90 days after 8/6/2002][2], *and before January 1, 2014.*

(2) **Joint returns.** In the case of a joint return, the requirements of paragraph (1)(A) shall be treated as met with respect to any month if at least 1 spouse satisfies such requirements.

(c) **Eligible individual.** For purposes of this section—

(1) **In general.** The term "eligible individual" means—

(A) an eligible TAA recipient,

(B) an eligible alternative TAA recipient, and

(C) an eligible PBGC pension recipient.

(2) **Eligible TAA recipient.**

(A) In general. Except as provided in subparagraph (B), the term "eligible TAA recipient" means, with respect to any month, any individual who is receiving for any day of such month a trade readjustment allowance under chapter 2 of title II of the Trade Act of 1974 or who would be eligible to receive such allowance if section 231 of such Act were applied without regard to subsection (a)(3)(B) of such section. An individual shall continue to be treated as an eligible TAA recipient during the first month that such individual would otherwise cease to be an eligible TAA recipient by reason of the preceding sentence.

(B) Special rule. In the case of any eligible coverage month beginning after the date of the enactment of this paragraph[3], the term "eligible TAA recipient" means, with respect to any month, any individual who—

(i) is receiving for any day of such month a trade readjustment allowance under chapter 2 of title II of the Trade Act of 1974,

(ii) would be eligible to receive such allowance except that such individual is in a break in training provided under a training program approved under section 236 of such Act that exceeds the period specified in section 233(e) of such Act, but is within the period for receiving such allowances provided under section 233(a) of such Act, or

(iii) is receiving unemployment compensation (as defined in section 85(b)) for any day of such month and who would be eligible to receive such allowance for such month if section 231 of such Act were applied without regard to subsections (a)(3)(B) and (a)(5) thereof.

An individual shall continue to be treated as an eligible TAA recipient during the first month that such individual would otherwise cease to be an eligible TAA recipient by reason of the preceding sentence.

(3) Eligible alternative TAA recipient. The term "eligible alternative TAA recipient" means, with respect to any month, any individual who—

(A) is a worker described in section 246(a)(3)(B) of the Trade Act of 1974 who is participating in the program established under section 246(a)(1) of such Act, and

(B) is receiving a benefit for such month under section 246(a)(2) of such Act.

An individual shall continue to be treated as an eligible alternative TAA recipient during the first month that such individual would otherwise cease to be an eligible alternative TAA recipient by reason of the preceding sentence.

(4) Eligible PBGC pension recipient. The term "eligible PBGC pension recipient" means, with respect to any month, any individual who—

(A) has attained age 55 as of the first day of such month, and

(B) is receiving a benefit for such month any portion of which is paid by the Pension Benefit Guaranty Corporation under title IV of the Employee Retirement Income Security Act of 1974.

* * * * * * * * * * * *

(e) Qualified health insurance. For purposes of this section—

(1) In general. The term "qualified health insurance" means any of the following:

(A) Coverage under a COBRA continuation provision (as defined in section 9832(d)(1)).

(B) State-based continuation coverage provided by the State under a State law that requires such coverage.

(C) Coverage offered through a qualified State high risk pool (as defined in section 2744(c)(2) of the Public Health Service Act).

(D) Coverage under a health insurance program offered for State employees.

(E) Coverage under a State-based health insurance program that is comparable to the health insurance program offered for State employees.

(F) Coverage through an arrangement entered into by a State and—

(i) a group health plan (including such a plan which is a multiemployer plan as defined in section 3(37) of the Employee Retirement Income Security Act of 1974),

(ii) an issuer of health insurance coverage,

(iii) an administrator, or

(iv) an employer.

(G) Coverage offered through a State arrangement with a private sector health care coverage purchasing pool.

(H) Coverage under a State-operated health plan that does not receive any Federal financial participation.

(I) Coverage under a group health plan that is available through the employment of the eligible individual's spouse.

(J) In the case of any eligible individual and such individual's qualifying family members, coverage under individual health insurance if the eligible individual was covered under individual health insurance during the entire 30-day period that ends on the date that such individual became separated from the employment which qualified such individual for—

(i) in the case of an eligible TAA recipient, the allowance described in subsection (c)(2),

(ii) in the case of an eligible alternative TAA recipient, the benefit described in subsection (c)(3)(B), or

(iii) in the case of any eligible PBGC pension recipient, the benefit described in subsection (c)(4)(B).

For purposes of this subparagraph, the term "individual health insurance" means any insurance which constitutes medical care offered to individuals other than in connection with a group health plan and does not include Federal or State-based health insurance coverage.

(K) [4]*Coverage* under an employee benefit plan funded by a voluntary employees' beneficiary association (as defined in section 501(c)(9)) established pursuant to an order of a bankruptcy court, or by agreement with an authorized representative, as provided in section 1114 of title 11, United States Code.

(2) Requirements for State-based coverage.

(A) In general. The term "qualified health insurance" does not include any coverage described in subparagraphs (B) through (H) of paragraph (1) unless the State involved has elected to have such coverage treated as qualified health insurance under this section and such coverage meets the following requirements:

(i) Guaranteed issue. Each qualifying individual is guaranteed enrollment if the individual pays the premium for enrollment or provides a qualified health insurance costs credit eligibility certificate described in section 7527 and pays the remainder of such premium.

(ii) No imposition of pre-existing condition exclusion. No pre-existing condition limitations are imposed with respect to any qualifying individual.

(iii) Nondiscriminatory premium. The total premium (as determined without regard to any subsidies) with respect to a qualifying individual may not be greater than the total premium (as so determined) for a similarly situated individual who is not a qualifying individual.

(iv) Same benefits. Benefits under the coverage are the same as (or substantially similar to) the benefits provided to similarly situated individuals who are not qualifying individuals.

(B) Qualifying individual. For purposes of this paragraph, the term "qualifying individual" means—

(i) an eligible individual for whom, as of the date on which the individual seeks to enroll in the coverage described in subparagraphs (B) through (H) of paragraph (1), the aggregate of the periods of creditable coverage (as defined in section 9801(c)) is 3 months or longer and who, with respect to any month, meets the requirements of clauses (iii) and (iv) of subsection (b)(1)(A); and

(ii) the qualifying family members of such eligible individual.

(3) Exception. The term "qualified health insurance" shall not include—

(A) a flexible spending or similar arrangement, and

(B) any insurance if substantially all of its coverage is of excepted benefits described in section 9832(c).

* * * * * * * * * * * *

(g) Special rules.

(1) Coordination with advance payments of credit. With respect to any taxable year, the amount which would (but for this subsection) be allowed as a credit to the taxpayer under subsection (a) shall be reduced (but not below zero) by the aggregate amount paid on behalf of such taxpayer under section 7527 for months beginning in such taxable year.

(2) Coordination with other deductions. Amounts taken into account under subsection (a) shall not be taken into account in determining any deduction allowed under section 162(l) or 213.

(3) Medical and health savings accounts. Amounts distributed from an Archer MSA (as defined in section 220(d)) or from a health savings account (as defined in section 223(d)) shall not be taken into account under subsection (a).

(4) Denial of credit to dependents. No credit shall be allowed under this section to any individual with respect to whom a deduction under section 151 is allowable to another taxpayer for a taxable year beginning in the calendar year in which such individual's taxable year begins.

(5) Both spouses eligible individuals. The spouse of the taxpayer shall not be treated as a qualifying family member for purposes of subsection (a), if—

(A) the taxpayer is married at the close of the taxable year,

(B) the taxpayer and the taxpayer's spouse are both eligible individuals during the taxable year, and

(C) the taxpayer files a separate return for the taxable year.

(6) Marital status; certain married individuals living apart. Rules similar to the rules of paragraphs (3) and (4) of section 21(e) shall apply for purposes of this section.

(7) Insurance which covers other individuals. For purposes of this section, rules similar to the rules of section 213(d)(6) shall apply with respect to any contract for qualified health insurance under which amounts are payable for coverage of an individual other than the taxpayer and qualifying family members.

(8) Treatment of payments. For purposes of this section—

(A) Payments by Secretary. Payments made by the Secretary on behalf of any individual under section 7527 (relating to advance payment of credit for health insurance costs of eligible individuals) shall be treated as having been made by the taxpayer on the first day of the month for which such payment was made.

(B) Payments by taxpayer. Payments made by the taxpayer for eligible coverage months shall be treated as having been made by the taxpayer on the first day of the month for which such payment was made.

(9) COBRA premium assistance. In the case of an assistance eligible individual who receives premium reduction for COBRA continuation coverage under section 3001(a) of title III of division B of the American Recovery and Reinvestment Act of 2009 for any month during the taxable year, such individual shall not be treated as an eligible individual, a certified individual, or a qualifying family member for purposes of this section or section 7527 with respect to such month.

(10) Regulations. The Secretary may prescribe such regulations and other guidance as may be necessary or appropriate to carry out this section, section 6050T, and section 7527.

[For Analysis, see ¶ 1604, ¶ 1606, ¶ 1607, ¶ 1608 and ¶ 1609.]

[Endnote Code Sec. 35]

Code Sec. 35(a), Code Sec. 35(b)(1)(B). Code Sec. 35(c)(2)(B), Code Sec. 35(e)(1)(K) and Code Sec. 35(g)(9) were amended by Sec. 241(a), (b)(1), (d)(3)(A)-(C) of the To extend the Generalized System of Preferences, and for other purposes., P.L. 112-40, 10/21/2011, as detailed below:

1. Sec. 241(b)(1) substituted '72.5 percent' for '65 percent (80 percent in the case of eligible coverage months beginning before February 13, 2011)' in subsec. (a)

2. Sec. 241(a) inserted ', and before January 1, 2014' before the period in subpara. (b)(1)(B)

3. Sec. 241(b)(3)(A) deleted 'and before February 13, 2011' after 'this paragraph' in subpara. (c)(2)(B)

4. Sec. 241(b)(3)(B) substituted 'Coverage' for 'In the case of eligible coverage months beginning before February 13, 2012, coverage' in subpara. (e)(1)(K)

5. Sec. 241(b)(3)(C) deleted 'In the case of eligible coverage months beginning before February 13, 2011—' in para. (g)(9) (as added by Sec. 1899E(a) of the American Recovery and Reinvestment Tax Act of 2009)

Effective Date (Sec. 241(c)(1), P.L. 112-40, 10/21/2011) effective for coverage months beginning before 2/13/2011.

[¶ 3019]　　Code Sec. 36B.　　Refundable credit for coverage under a qualified health plan.

* * * * * * * * * * * *

(c) Definition and rules relating to applicable taxpayers, coverage months, and qualified health plan. For purposes of this section—

(1) Applicable taxpayer.

(A) In general. The term "applicable taxpayer" means, with respect to any taxable year, a taxpayer whose household income for the taxable year equals or exceeds 100 percent but does not exceed 400 percent of an amount equal to the poverty line for a family of the size involved.

(B) Special rule for certain individuals lawfully present in the United States. If—

(i) a taxpayer has a household income which is not greater than 100 percent of an amount equal to the poverty line for a family of the size involved, and

(ii) the taxpayer is an alien lawfully present in the United States, but is not eligible for the medicaid program under title XIX of the Social Security Act by reason of such alien status,

the taxpayer shall, for purposes of the credit under this section, be treated as an applicable taxpayer with a household income which is equal to 100 percent of the poverty line for a family of the size involved.

(C) Married couples must file joint return. If the taxpayer is married (within the meaning of section 7703) at the close of the taxable year, the taxpayer shall be treated as an applicable taxpayer only if the taxpayer and the taxpayer's spouse file a joint return for the taxable year.

(D) Denial of credit to dependents. No credit shall be allowed under this section to any individual with respect to whom a deduction under section 151 is allowable to another taxpayer for a taxable year beginning in the calendar year in which such individual's taxable year begins.

(2) **Coverage month.** For purposes of this subsection—

(A) In general. The term "coverage month" means, with respect to an applicable taxpayer, any month if—

(i) as of the first day of such month the taxpayer, the taxpayer's spouse, or any dependent of the taxpayer is covered by a qualified health plan described in subsection (b)(2)(A) that was enrolled in through an Exchange established by the State under section 1311 of the Patient Protection and Affordable Care Act, and

(ii) the premium for coverage under such plan for such month is paid by the taxpayer (or through advance payment of the credit under subsection (a) under section 1412 of the Patient Protection and Affordable Care Act).

(B) Exception for minimum essential coverage.

(i) In general. The term "coverage month" shall not include any month with respect to an individual if for such month the individual is eligible for minimum essential coverage other than eligibility for coverage described in section 5000A(f)(1)(C) (relating to coverage in the individual market).

(ii) Minimum essential coverage. The term "minimum essential coverage" has the meaning given such term by section 5000A(f).

(C) Special rule for employer-sponsored minimum essential coverage. For purposes of subparagraph (B)—

(i) Coverage must be affordable. Except as provided in clause (iii), an employee shall not be treated as eligible for minimum essential coverage if such coverage—

(I) consists of an eligible employer-sponsored plan (as defined in section 5000A(f)(2)), and

(II) the employee's required contribution (within the meaning of section 5000A(e)(1)(B)) with respect to the plan exceeds 9.5 percent of the applicable taxpayer's household income.

This clause shall also apply to an individual who is eligible to enroll in the plan by reason of a relationship the individual bears to the employee.

(ii) Coverage must provide minimum value. Except as provided in clause (iii), an employee shall not be treated as eligible for minimum essential coverage if such coverage consists of an eligible employer-sponsored plan (as defined in section 5000A(f)(2)) and the plan's share of the total allowed costs of benefits provided under the plan is less than 60 percent of such costs.

(iii) Employee or family must not be covered under employer plan. Clauses (i) and (ii) shall not apply if the employee (or any individual described in the last sentence of clause (i)) is covered under the eligible employer-sponsored plan or the grandfathered health plan.

(iv) Indexing. In the case of plan years beginning in any calendar year after 2014, the Secretary shall adjust the 9.5 percent under clause (i)(II) in the same manner as the percentages are adjusted under subsection (b)(3)(A)(ii).

[1]*(D) Repealed.*

537

(3) Definitions and other rules.

(A) Qualified health plan. The term "qualified health plan" has the meaning given such term by section 1301(a) of the Patient Protection and Affordable Care Act, except that such term shall not include a qualified health plan which is a catastrophic plan described in section 1302(e) of such Act.

(B) Grandfathered health plan. The term "grandfathered health plan" has the meaning given such term by section 1251 of the Patient Protection and Affordable Care Act.

* * * * * * * * * * * *

(d) Terms relating to income and families. For purposes of this section—

(1) Family size. The family size involved with respect to any taxpayer shall be equal to the number of individuals for whom the taxpayer is allowed a deduction under section 151 (relating to allowance of deduction for personal exemptions) for the taxable year.

(2) Household income.

(A) Household income. The term "household income" means, with respect to any taxpayer, an amount equal to the sum of—

(i) the modified adjusted gross income of the taxpayer, plus

(ii) the aggregate modified adjusted gross incomes of all other individuals who—

(I) were taken into account in determining the taxpayer's family size under paragraph (1), and

(II) were required to file a return of tax imposed by section 1 for the taxable year.

(B) Modified adjusted gross income. The term "modified adjusted gross income" means adjusted gross income increased by—

(i) any amount excluded from gross income under section 911,[2]

(ii) any amount of interest received or accrued by the taxpayer during the taxable year which is exempt from tax[3], *and*

[4]*(iii) an amount equal to the portion of the taxpayer's social security benefits (as defined in section 86(d)) which is not included in gross income under section 86 for the taxable year.*

(3) Poverty line.

(A) In general. The term "poverty line" has the meaning given that term in section 2110(c)(5) of the Social Security Act (42 U.S.C. 1397jj(c)(5)).

(B) Poverty line used. In the case of any qualified health plan offered through an Exchange for coverage during a taxable year beginning in a calendar year, the poverty line used shall be the most recently published poverty line as of the 1st day of the regular enrollment period for coverage during such calendar year.

* * * * * * * * * * * *

(f) Reconciliation of credit and advance credit.

(1) In general. The amount of the credit allowed under this section for any taxable year shall be reduced (but not below zero) by the amount of any advance payment of such credit under section 1412 of the Patient Protection and Affordable Care Act.

(2) Excess advance payments.

(A) In general. If the advance payments to a taxpayer under section 1412 of the Patient Protection and Affordable Care Act for a taxable year exceed the credit allowed by this section (determined without regard to paragraph (1)), the tax imposed by this chapter for the taxable year shall be increased by the amount of such excess.

(B) Limitation on increase.

(i) In general. In the case of a taxpayer whose household income is less than 400 percent of the poverty line for the size of the family involved for the taxable year, the amount of the increase under subparagraph (A) shall in no event exceed the applicable dollar amount determined in accordance with the following table (one-half of such amount in the case of a taxpayer whose tax is determined under section 1(c) for the taxable year):

If the household income (expressed as a percent of poverty line) is:	The applicable dollar amount is:
Less than 200%	$600
At least 200% but less than 300%	$1,500
At least 300% but less than 400%	$2,500.

(ii) Indexing of amount. In the case of any calendar year beginning after 2014, each of the dollar amounts in the table contained under clause (i) shall be increased by an amount equal to—

(I) such dollar amount, multiplied by

(II) the cost-of-living adjustment determined under section 1(f)(3) for the calendar year, determined by substituting "calendar year 2013" for "calendar year 1992" in subparagraph (B) thereof.

If the amount of any increase under clause (i) is not a multiple of $50, such increase shall be rounded to the next lowest multiple of $50.

(3) **Information requirement.** Each Exchange (or any person carrying out 1 or more responsibilities of an Exchange under section 1311(f)(3) or 1321(c) of the Patient Protection and Affordable Care Act) shall provide the following information to the Secretary and to the taxpayer with respect to any health plan provided through the Exchange:

(A) The level of coverage described in section 1302(d) of the Patient Protection and Affordable Care Act and the period such coverage was in effect.

(B) The total premium for the coverage without regard to the credit under this section or cost-sharing reductions under section 1402 of such Act.

(C) The aggregate amount of any advance payment of such credit or reductions under section 1412 of such Act.

(D) The name, address, and TIN of the primary insured and the name and TIN of each other individual obtaining coverage under the policy.

(E) Any information provided to the Exchange, including any change of circumstances, necessary to determine eligibility for, and the amount of, such credit.

(F) Information necessary to determine whether a taxpayer has received excess advance payments.

* * * * * * * * * * * *

[For Analysis, see ¶ 1601, ¶ 1602 and ¶ 1603. For Committee Reports, see ¶ 5903.]

[Endnote Code Sec. 36B]

Code Sec. 36B(c)(2)(D) was deleted by Sec. 1858(b)(1), P.L. 112-10.

1. Sec. 1858(b)(1), deleted para. (b)(1)

Prior to deletion, subpara. (c)(2)(D), read as follows:

"(D) Exception for individual receiving free choice vouchers. The term 'coverage month' shall not include any month in which such individual has a free choice voucher provided under section 10108 of the Patient Protection and Affordable Care Act. "

Effective Date (Sec. 1858(d), P.L. 112-10) effective for tax. yrs. begin. after 12/31/2013, as if included in the provisions of Sec. 10108(h) of P.L. 111-148 [see below].

Code Sec. 36B(d)(2)(B)(i)-Code Sec. 36B(d)(2)(B)(iii) were amended by Sec. 401(a) of an Act To amend the Internal Revenue Code of 1986 to repeal the imposition of 3 percent withholding on certain payments made to vendors by government entities, to modify the calculation of modified adjusted gross income for purposes of determining eligibility for certain healthcare-related programs, and for other purposes, P.L. 112-56, 11/21/2011, as detailed below:

2. Sec. 401(a) deleted "and" at the end of clause (d)(2)(B)(i)

3. Sec. 401(a) substituted ", and" for the period at the end of clause (d)(2)(B)(ii)

4. Sec. 401(a) added clause (d)(2)(B)(iii)

Effective Date (Sec. 401(b), P.L. 112-56, 11/21/2011) provides that the amendments made by Sec. 401(a) are effective 11/21/2011, however Code Sec. 36B goes into effect as provided in P.L. 111-148, for tax. yrs. end. after 12/31/2013.

Code Sec. 36B(f)(2)(B)(i) was amended by Sec. 4(a), P.L. 112-9, as outlined below:

Prior to amendment clause (f)(2)(B)(i), read as follows:

"(i) In general.

"In the case of a taxpayer whose household income is less than 500 percent of the poverty line for the size of the family involved for the taxable year, the amount of the increase under subparagraph (A) shall in no event exceed the applicable dollar amount determined in accordance with the following table (one-half of such amount in the case of a taxpayer whose tax is determined under section 1(c) for the taxable year):

If the household income (expressed as a percent of poverty line) is:	The applicable dollar amount is:
Less than 200%	$600
At least 200% but less than 250%	$1,000
At least 250% but less than 300%	$1,500.
At least 300% but less than 350%	$2,000
At least 350% but less than 400%	$2,500.
At least 400% but less than 450%	$3,000.
At least 450% but less than 500%	$3,500.

Effective Date (Sec. 4(b), P.L. 112-10) effective for tax. yrs. ending after 12/31/2013.

[¶ 3020]   Code Sec. 38.   General business credit.

* * * * * * * * * * * *

   (b)   Current year business credit. For purposes of this subpart, the amount of the current year business credit is the sum of the following credits determined for the taxable year:

   (1) the investment credit determined under section 46,

   (2) the work opportunity credit determined under section 51(a),

   (3) the alcohol fuels credit determined under section 40(a),

   (4) the research credit determined under section 41(a),

   (5) the low-income housing credit determined under section 42(a),

   (6) the enhanced oil recovery credit under section 43(a),

   (7) in the case of an eligible small business (as defined in section 44(b)), the disabled access credit determined under section 44(a),

   (8) the renewable electricity production credit under section 45(a),

   (9) the empowerment zone employment credit determined under section 1396(a),

   (10) the Indian employment credit as determined under section 45A(a),

   (11) the employer social security credit determined under section 45B(a),

   (12) the orphan drug credit determined under section 45C(a),

   (13) the new markets tax credit determined under section 45D(a),

   (14) in the case of an eligible employer (as defined in section 45E(c)), the small employer pension plan startup cost credit determined under section 45E(a),

   [1]*(15) the employer-provided child care credit determined under section 45F(a),*

   (16) the railroad track maintenance credit determined under section 45G(a),

   (17) the biodiesel fuels credit determined under section 40A(a),

   (18) the low sulfur diesel fuel production credit determined under section 45H(a),

   (19) the marginal oil and gas well production credit determined under section 45I(a),

   (20) the distilled spirits credit determined under section 5011(a),

   (21) the advanced nuclear power facility production credit determined under section 45J(a),

   (22) the nonconventional source production credit determined under section 45K(a),

   (23) the new energy efficient home credit determined under section 45L(a),

   (24) the energy efficient appliance credit determined under section 45M(a),

   (25) the portion of the alternative motor vehicle credit to which section 30B(g)(1) applies,

   (26) the portion of the alternative fuel vehicle refueling property credit to which section 30C(d)(1) applies,

   (27) the Hurricane Katrina housing credit determined under section 1400P(b),

   (28) the Hurricane Katrina employee retention credit determined under section 1400R(a),

   (29) the Hurricane Rita employee retention credit determined under section 1400R(b),

   (30) the Hurricane Wilma employee retention credit determined under section 1400R(c),

   (31) the mine rescue team training credit determined under section 45N(a),

(32) in the case of an eligible agricultural business (as defined in section 45O(e)), the agricultural chemicals security credit determined under section 45O(a),

(33) the differential wage payment credit determined under section 45P(a),

(34) the carbon dioxide sequestration credit determined under section 45Q(a)

(35) the portion of the new qualified plug-in electric drive motor vehicle credit to which section 30D(c)(1) applies, plus

(36) the small employer health insurance credit determined under section 45R.

* * * * * * * * * * * *

[For Analysis, see ¶ 903.]

[Endnote Code Sec. 38]

Sec. 101(a)(1) of the American Taxpayer Relief Act of 2012, P.L. 112-240, 1/2/2013, deleted Title IX [Sec. 901] of the Economic Growth and Tax Relief Reconciliation Act of 2001, P.L. 107-16, the effect of which is to eliminate the sunset of all provisions enacted by P.L. 107-16. Following are the amendments made to Code Sec. 38, by P.L. 107-16. **Effective Date** (Sec. 101(a)(3), P.L. 112-240, 1/2/2013) effective for taxable, plan, or limitation years beginning after 12/31/2012, and estates of decedents dying, gifts made, or generation skipping transfers after 12/31/2012.

Code Sec. 38(b)(13), Code Sec. 38(b)(14) and Code Sec. 38(b)(15) were amended by Sec. 205(b)(1), P.L. 107-16, 6/7/2001, as outlined below:

Sec. 205(b)(1) deleted "plus" at the end of para. (b)(13) . . .

substitued "plus" for the period at the end of para (b)(14), and

1. added para. (b)(15)

Effective Date (Sec. 205(c), P.L. 107-16, 6/7/2001) effective for tax. yrs. begin. after 12/31/2001.

[¶ 3021]   Code Sec. 40.   Alcohol, etc., used as fuel.

(a) General rule. For purposes of section 38, the alcohol fuels credit determined under this section for the taxable year is an amount equal to the sum of—

(1) the alcohol mixture credit,

(2) the alcohol credit,

(3) in the case of an eligible small ethanol producer, the small ethanol producer credit, plus

(4) the [1]*second generation biofuel* producer credit.

(b) Definition of alcohol mixture credit, alcohol credit, and small ethanol producer credit. For purposes of this section, and except as provided in subsection (h)—

(1) Alcohol mixture credit.

(A) In general. The alcohol mixture credit of any taxpayer for any taxable year is 60 cents for each gallon of alcohol used by the taxpayer in the production of a qualified mixture.

(B) Qualified mixture. The term "qualified mixture" means a mixture of alcohol and gasoline or of alcohol and a special fuel which—

(i) is sold by the taxpayer producing such mixture to any person for use as a fuel, or

(ii) is used as a fuel by the taxpayer producing such mixture.

(C) Sale or use must be in trade or business, etc. Alcohol used in the production of a qualified mixture shall be taken into account—

(i) only if the sale or use described in subparagraph (B) is in a trade or business of the taxpayer, and

(ii) for the taxable year in which such sale or use occurs.

(D) Casual off-farm production not eligible. No credit shall be allowed under this section with respect to any casual off-farm production of a qualified mixture.

(2) Alcohol credit.

(A) In general. The alcohol credit of any taxpayer for any taxable year is 60 cents for each gallon of alcohol which is not in a mixture with gasoline or a special fuel (other than any denaturant) and which during the taxable year—

(i) is used by the taxpayer as a fuel in a trade or business, or

(ii) is sold by the taxpayer at retail to a person and placed in the fuel tank of such person's vehicle.

(B) User credit not to apply to alcohol sold at retail. No credit shall be allowed under subparagraph (A)(i) with respect to any alcohol which was sold in a retail sale described in subparagraph (A)(ii).

(3) Smaller credit for lower proof alcohol. In the case of any alcohol with a proof which is at least 150 but less than 190, paragraphs (1)(A) and (2)(A) shall be applied by substituting "45 cents" for "60 cents".

(4) Small ethanol producer credit.

(A) In general. The small ethanol producer credit of any eligible small ethanol producer for any taxable year is 10 cents for each gallon of qualified ethanol fuel production of such producer.

(B) Qualified ethanol fuel production. For purposes of this paragraph, the term "qualified ethanol fuel production" means any alcohol which is ethanol which is produced by an eligible small ethanol producer, and which during the taxable year—

(i) is sold by such producer to another person—

(I) for use by such other person in the production of a qualified mixture in such other person's trade or business (other than casual off-farm production),

(II) for use by such other person as a fuel in a trade or business, or

(III) who sells such ethanol at retail to another person and places such ethanol in the fuel tank of such other person, or

(ii) is used or sold by such producer for any purpose described in clause (i).

(C) Limitation. The qualified ethanol fuel production of any producer for any taxable year shall not exceed 15,000,000 gallons (determined without regard to any qualified [2]second generation biofuel production).

(D) Additional distillation excluded. The qualified ethanol fuel production of any producer for any taxable year shall not include any alcohol which is purchased by the producer and with respect to which such producer increases the proof of the alcohol by additional distillation.

(5) Adding of denaturants not treated as mixture. The adding of any denaturant to alcohol shall not be treated as the production of a mixture.

(6) [3]*Second generation* **biofuel producer credit.**

(A) In general. The [4]*second generation biofuel* producer credit of any taxpayer is an amount equal to the applicable amount for each gallon of qualified [5]*second generation biofuel* production.

(B) Applicable amount. For purposes of subparagraph (A), the applicable amount means $1.01, except that such amount shall, in the case of [6]*second generation biofuel* which is alcohol, be reduced by the sum of—

(i) the amount of the credit in effect for such alcohol under subsection (b)(1) (without regard to subsection (b)(3)) at the time of the qualified [7]*second generation biofuel* production, plus

(ii) in the case of ethanol, the amount of the credit in effect under subsection (b)(4) at the time of such production.

(C) Qualified [8]*second generation* biofuel production. For purposes of this section, the term "qualified [9]*second generation biofuel* production" means any [10]*second generation biofuel* which is produced by the taxpayer, and which during the taxable year—

(i) is sold by the taxpayer to another person—

(I) for use by such other person in the production of a qualified [11]*second generation biofuel* mixture in such other person's trade or business (other than casual off-farm production),

(II) for use by such other person as a fuel in a trade or business, or

(III) who sells such [12]*second generation biofuel* at retail to another person and places such [13]*second generation biofuel* in the fuel tank of such other person, or

(ii) is used or sold by the taxpayer for any purpose described in clause (i).

The qualified [14]*second generation biofuel* production of any taxpayer for any taxable year shall not include any alcohol which is purchased by the taxpayer and with respect to which such producer increases the proof of the alcohol by additional distillation.

(D) Qualified [15]*second generation* biofuel mixture. For purposes of this paragraph, the term "qualified [16]*second generation biofuel* mixture" means a mixture of [17]*second generation biofuel* and gasoline or of [18]*second generation biofuel* and a special fuel which—

(i) is sold by the person producing such mixture to any person for use as a fuel, or

(ii) is used as a fuel by the person producing such mixture.

(E) [19]*Second generation* biofuel. For purposes of this paragraph—

(i) In general. The term "[20]*second generation biofuel*" means any liquid fuel which—

(I)[21] *is derived by, or from, qualified feedstocks, and*

(II) meets the registration requirements for fuels and fuel additives established by the Environmental Protection Agency under section 211 of the Clean Air Act (42 U.S.C. 7545).

(ii) Exclusion of low-proof alcohol. [22]*The term "second generation biofuel" shall not* include any alcohol with a proof of less than 150. The determination of the proof of any alcohol shall be made without regard to any added denaturants.

(iii) Exclusion of certain fuels. The term "[23]*second generation biofuel*" shall not include any fuel if—

(I) more than 4 percent of such fuel (determined by weight) is any combination of water and sediment

(II) the ash content of such fuel is more than 1 percent (determined by weight), or

(III) such fuel has an acid number greater than 25.

(F)[24] *Qualified feedstock. For purposes of this paragraph, the term "qualified feedstock" means—*

(i) any lignocellulosic or hemicellulosic matter that is available on a renewable or recurring basis, and

(i) any cultivated algae, cyanobacteria, or lemna.

(G)[25] *Special rules for algae. In the case of fuel which is derived by, or from, feed-stock described in subparagraph (F)(ii) and which is sold by the taxpayer to another person for refining by such other person into a fuel which meets the requirements of subparagraph (E)(i)(II) and the refined fuel is not excluded under subparagraph (E)(iii)—*

(i) such sale shall be treated as described in subparagraph (C)(i),

(ii) such fuel shall be treated as meeting the requirements of subparagraph (E)(i)(II) and as not being excluded under subparagraph (E)(iii) in the hands of such taxpayer, and

(iii) except as provided in this subparagraph, such fuel (and any fuel derived from such fuel) shall not be taken into account under subparagraph (C) with respect to the taxpayer or any other person.

[26](H) Allocation of [27]*second generation* biofuel producer credit to patrons of cooperative. Rules similar to the rules under subsection (g)(6) shall apply for purposes of this paragraph.

[28](I) Registration requirement. No credit shall be determined under this paragraph with respect to any taxpayer unless such taxpayer is registered with the Secretary as a producer of [29]*second generation biofuel* under section 4101.

[30](J)[31] *Application of paragraph.*

(i) In general. This paragraph shall apply with respect to qualified [32]second generation biofuel production after December 31, 2008, and before January 1, 2014.

(ii) No carryover to certain years after expiration. If this paragraph ceases to apply for any period by reason of clause (i), rules similar to the rules of subsection (e)(2) shall apply.

* * * * * * * * * * * *

(d) Definitions and special rules. For purposes of this section—

(1) Alcohol defined.

(A) In general. The term "alcohol" includes methanol and ethanol but does not include—

(i) alcohol produced from petroleum, natural gas, or coal (including peat), or

(ii) alcohol with a proof of less than 150.

(B) Determination of proof. The determination of the proof of any alcohol shall be made without regard to any added denaturants.

(2) Special fuel defined. The term "special fuel" includes any liquid fuel (other than gasoline) which is suitable for use in an internal combustion engine.

(3) Mixture or alcohol not used as a fuel, etc.

(A) Mixtures. If—

(i) any credit was determined under this section with respect to alcohol used in the production of any qualified mixture, and

(ii) any person—

(I) separates the alcohol from the mixture, or

(II) without separation, uses the mixture other than as a fuel,

then there is hereby imposed on such person a tax equal to 60 cents a gallon (45 cents in the case of alcohol with a proof less than 190) for each gallon of alcohol in such mixture.

(B) Alcohol. If—

(i) any credit was determined under this section with respect to the retail sale of any alcohol, and

(ii) any person mixes such alcohol or uses such alcohol other than as a fuel,

then there is hereby imposed on such person a tax equal to 60 cents a gallon (45 cents in the case of alcohol with a proof less than 190) for each gallon of such alcohol.

(C) Small ethanol producer credit. If—

(i) any credit was determined under subsection (a)(3), and

(ii) any person does not use such fuel for a purpose described in subsection (b)(4)(B),

then there is hereby imposed on such person a tax equal to 10 cents a gallon for each gallon of such alcohol.

(D) [33]*Second generation* biofuel producer credit. If—

(i) any credit is allowed under subsection (a)(4), and

(ii) any person does not use such fuel for a purpose described in subsection (b)(6)(C),

then there is hereby imposed on such person a tax equal to the applicable amount (as defined in subsection (b)(6)(B)) for each gallon of such [34]*second generation biofuel*.

(E) Applicable laws. All provisions of law, including penalties, shall, insofar as applicable and not inconsistent with this section, apply in respect of any tax imposed under subparagraph (A), (B), (C), or (D) as if such tax were imposed by section 4081 and not by this chapter.

(4) Volume of alcohol. For purposes of determining under subsection (a) the number of gallons of alcohol with respect to which a credit is allowable under subsection (a), the volume of alcohol shall include the volume of any denaturant (including gasoline) which is added under any formulas approved by the Secretary to the extent that such denaturants do not exceed 2 percent of the volume of such alcohol (including denaturants).

(5) Pass-thru in the case of estates and trusts. Under regulations prescribed by the Secretary, rules similar to the rules of subsection (d) of section 52 shall apply.

(6) Special rule for [35]*second generation* **biofuel producer credit.** No [36]*second generation biofuel* producer credit shall be determined under subsection (a) with respect to any [37]*second generation biofuel* unless such [38]*second generation biofuel* is produced in the

United States and used as a fuel in the United States. For purposes of this subsection, the term "United States" includes any possession of the United States.

(7) Limitation to alcohol with connection to the United States. No credit shall be determined under this section with respect to any alcohol which is produced outside the United States for use as a fuel outside the United States. For purposes of this paragraph, the term "United States" includes any possession of the United States.

(e) Termination.

(1) In general. This section shall not apply to any sale or use—

(A) for any period after December 31, 2011, or

(B) for any period before January 1, 2012, during which the rates of tax under section 4081(a)(2)(A) are 4.3 cents per gallon.

(2) No carryovers to certain years after expiration. If this section ceases to apply for any period by reason of paragraph (1)[39], no amount attributable to any sale or use before the first day of such period may be carried under section 39 by reason of this section (treating the amount allowed by reason of this section as the first amount allowed by this subpart) to any taxable year beginning after the 3-taxable-year period beginning with the taxable year in which such first day occurs.

(3) Exception for [40]*second generation* **biofuel producer credit.** Paragraph (1) shall not apply to the portion of the credit allowed under this section by reason of subsection (a)(4).

* * * * * * * * * * * *

[For Analysis, see ¶ 1015 and ¶ 1016.]

[Endnote Code Sec. 40]

Code Sec. 40(a)(4), Code Sec. 40(b)(4)(C), Code Sec. 40(b)(6), Code Sec. 40(b)(6)(A), Code Sec. 40(b)(6)(B), Code Sec. 40(b)(6)(B)(i)(I) Code Sec. 40(b)(6)(C), Code Sec. 40(b)(6)(C)(i)(I), Code Sec. 40(b)(6)(C)(i)(III), Code Sec. 40(b)(6)(D), Code Sec. 40(b)(6)(E), Code Sec. 40(b)(6)(E)(i), Code Sec. 40(b)(6)(E)(i)(I), Code Sec. 40(b)(6)(E)(ii), Code Sec. 40(b)(6)(E)(iii), Code Sec. 40(b)(6)(F), Code Sec. 40(b)(6)(G), Code Sec. 40(b)(6)(H), Code Sec. 40(b)(6)(I), and Code Sec. 40(b)(6)(J) were amended by Sec. 404(b)(1)-(b)(2), (b)(3)(A)(i)-(iii), and (b)(3)(B) of the American Taxpayer Relief Act of 2012, P.L. 112-240, 1/2/2013, as detailed below:

1. Sec. 404(b)(3)(A)(i) substituted "second generation biofuel" for "cellulosic biofuel" in para. (a)(4) [as amended]

2. Sec. 404(b)(3)(A)(i) substituted "second generation biofuel" for "cellulosic biofuel" in subpara. (b)(4)(C) [as amended]

3. Sec. 404(b)(3)(A)(ii) substituted "Second generation" for "Cellulosic" in the heading of para. (b)(6) [as amended]

4. Sec. 404(b)(3)(A)(i) substituted "second generation biofuel" for "cellulosic biofuel" in subpara. (b)(6)(A) [as amended]

5. Sec. 404(b)(3)(A)(i) substituted "second generation biofuel" for "cellulosic biofuel" in subpara. (b)(6)(A) [as amended]

6. Sec. 404(b)(3)(A)(i) substituted "second generation biofuel" for "cellulosic biofuel" in subpara. (b)(6)(B) [as amended]

7. Sec. 404(b)(3)(A)(i) substituted "second generation biofuel" for "cellulosic biofuel" in subclause (b)(6)(B)(i)(I) [as amended]

8. Sec. 404(b)(3)(A)(iii) substituted "second generation" for "cellulosic" in the heading of subpara. (b)(6)(C) [as amended]

9. Sec. 404(b)(3)(A)(i) substituted "second generation biofuel" for "cellulosic biofuel" in subpara. (b)(6)(C) [as amended]

10. Sec. 404(b)(3)(A)(i) substituted "second generation biofuel" for "cellulosic biofuel" in subpara. (b)(6)(C) [as amended]

11. Sec. 404(b)(3)(A)(i) substituted "second generation biofuel" for "cellulosic biofuel" in subclause (b)(6)(C)(i)(I) [as amended]

12. Sec. 404(b)(3)(A)(i) substituted "second generation biofuel" for "cellulosic biofuel" in subclause (b)(6)(C)(i)(III) [as amended]

13. Sec. 404(b)(3)(A)(i) substituted "second generation biofuel" for "cellulosic biofuel" in subclause (b)(6)(C)(i)(III) [as amended]

14. Sec. 404(b)(3)(A)(i) substituted "second generation biofuel" for "cellulosic biofuel" in subpara. (b)(6)(C) [as amended]

15. Sec. 404(b)(3)(A)(iii) substituted "second generation" for "cellulosic" in the heading of subpara. (b)(6)(D) [as amended]

16. Sec. 404(b)(3)(A)(i) substituted "second generation biofuel" for "cellulosic biofuel" in subpara. (b)(6)(D) [as amended]

17. Sec. 404(b)(3)(A)(i) substituted "second generation biofuel" for "cellulosic biofuel" in subpara. (b)(6)(D) [as amended]

18. Sec. 404(b)(3)(A)(i) substituted "second generation biofuel" for "cellulosic biofuel" in subpara. (b)(6)(D) [as amended]

19. Sec. 404(b)(3)(A)(ii) substituted "Second generation" for "Cellulosic" in the heading of para. (b)(6)(E) [as amended]

20. Sec. 404(b)(3)(A)(i) substituted "second generation biofuel" for "cellulosic biofuel" in clause (b)(6)(E)(i) [as amended]

21. Sec. 404(b)(1) amended subclause (b)(6)(E)(i)(I)

Prior to amendment, subclause (b)(6)(E)(i)(I) read as follows:

"(I) is produced from any lignocellulosic or hemicellulosic matter that is available on a renewable or recurring basis, and

22. Sec. 404(b)(3)(B) substituted "The term 'second generation biofuel' shall not" for "Such term shall not" in clause (b)(6)(E)(ii)

23. Sec. 404(b)(3)(A)(i) substituted "second generation biofuel" for "cellulosic biofuel" in clause (b)(6)(E)(iii) [as amended]

24. Sec. 404(b)(2) added a new subpara. (b)(6)(F)

25. Sec. 404(b)(2) added a new subpara. (b)(6)(G)

26. Sec. 404(b)(2) redesignated former subpara. (b)(6)(F) as (b)(6)(H) [as amended]

27. Sec. 404(b)(3)(A)(iii) substituted "second generation" for "cellulosic" in the heading of subpara. (b)(6)(H) [as amended]

28. Sec. 404(b)(2) redesignated former subpara. (b)(6)(G) as (b)(6)(I) [as amended]

29. Sec. 404(b)(3)(A)(i) substituted "second generation biofuel" for "cellulosic biofuel" in subpara. (b)(6)(I) [as amended]

30. Sec. 404(b)(2) redesignated former subpara. (b)(6)(H) as (b)(6)(J) [as amended]

Effective Date [Sec. 404(b)(4), P.L. 112-240, 1/2/2013] effective for fuels sold or used after 1/2/2013.

Code Sec. 40(b)(6)(H) was amended by Sec. 404(a)(1) of the American Taxpayer Relief Act of 2012, P.L. 112-240, 1/2/2013, as detailed below:

31. Sec. 404(a)(1) amended subpara. (b)(6)(H)

Prior to amendment, subpara. (b)(6)(H), read as follows:

"(H) Application of paragraph. This paragraph shall apply with respect to qualified cellulosic biofuel production after December 31, 2008, and before January 1, 2013."

Effective Date [Sec. 404(a)(3), P.L. 112-240, 1/2/2013] effective for fuel produced after 12/31/2008, as if included in Sec. 15321(b) of the Heartland, Habitbtat and Horticulture Act of 2008 [PL110-246].

Code Sec. 40(b)(6)(J)(i), Code Sec. 40(d)(3)(D) and Code Sec. 40(d)(6) were amended by Sec. 404(b)(3)(A)(i)-(iii) of the American Taxpayer Relief Act of 2012, P.L. 112-240, 1/2/2013, as detailed below:

32. Sec. 404(b)(3)(A)(i) substituted "second generation biofuel" for "cellulosic biofuel" in clause (b)(6)(J)(i) [as amended]

33. Sec. 404(b)(3)(A)(ii) substituted "Second generation" for "Cellulosic" in the heading of para. (d)(3)(D) [as amended]

34. Sec. 404(b)(3)(A)(i) substituted "second generation biofuel" for "cellulosic biofuel" in subpara. (d)(3)(D) [as amended]

35. Sec. 404(b)(3)(A)(iii) substituted "second generation" for "cellulosic" in the heading of para. (d)(6) [as amended]

36. Sec. 404(b)(3)(A)(i) substituted "second generation biofuel" for "cellulosic biofuel" in para. (d)(6) [as amended]

37. Sec. 404(b)(3)(A)(i) substituted "second generation biofuel" for "cellulosic biofuel" in para. (d)(6) [as amended]

38. Sec. 404(b)(3)(A)(i) substituted "second generation biofuel" for "cellulosic biofuel" in para. (d)(6) [as amended]

Effective Date [Sec. 404(b)(4), P.L. 112-240, 1/2/2013] effective for fuels sold or used after 1/2/2013.

Code Sec. 40(e)(2) was amended by Sec. 404(a)(2) of the American Taxpayer Relief Act of 2012, P.L. 112-240, 1/2/2013, as detailed below:

39. Sec. 404(a)(2) deleted " or subsection (b)(6)(H)" in para. (e)(2)

Effective Date [Sec. 404(a)(3), P.L. 112-240, 1/2/2013) effective for fuel produced after 12/31/2008, as if included in Sec. 15321(b) of the Heartland, Habitbtat and Horticulture Act of 2008 [PL110-246].

Code Sec. 40(e)(3) was amended by Sec. 404(b)(3)(A)(iii) of the American Taxpayer Relief Act of 2012, P.L. 112-240, 1/2/2013, as detailed below:

40. Sec. 404(b)(3)(A)(iii) substituted "second generation" for "cellulosic" in the heading of para. (e)(3) [as amended]

Effective Date [Sec. 404(b)(4), P.L. 112-240, 1/2/2013] effective for fuels sold or used after 1/2/2013.

[¶ 3022]   Code Sec. 40A.   Biodiesel and renewable diesel used as fuel.

* * * * * * * * * * * *

    (g)   Termination. This section shall not apply to any sale or use after [1]*December 31, 2013.*

[For Analysis, see ¶ 1009.]

[Endnote Code Sec. 40A]
Code Sec. 40A(g) was amended by Sec. 405(a) of the American Taxpayer Relief Act of 2012, P.L. 112-240, 1/2/2013, as detailed below:
1. Sec. 405(a) substituted 'December 31, 2013' for 'December 31, 2011' in subsec. (g)
Effective Date (Sec. 405(c), P.L. 112-240, 1/2/2013) effective for fuel sold or used after 12/31/2011.

[¶ 3023]   **Code Sec. 41.**   **Credit for increasing research activities.**

* * * * * * * * * * * *

(f) **Special rules.** For purposes of this section—

(1) **Aggregation of expenditures.**

(A) Controlled group of corporations. In determining the amount of the credit under this section—

(i) all members of the same controlled group of corporations shall be treated as a single taxpayer, and

(ii) the credit (if any) allowable by this section to each such member [1]*shall be determined on a proportionate basis to its share of the aggregate of the qualified research expenses, basic research payments, and amounts paid or incurred to energy research consortiums, taken into account by such controlled group for purposes of this section.*

(B) Common control. Under regulations prescribed by the Secretary, in determining the amount of the credit under this section—

(i) all trades or businesses (whether or not incorporated) which are under common control shall be treated as a single taxpayer, and

(ii) the credit (if any) allowable by this section to each such person [2]*shall be determined on a proportionate basis to its share of the aggregate of the qualified research expenses, basic research payments, and amounts paid or incurred to energy research consortiums, taken into account by all such persons under common control for purposes of this section.*

The regulations prescribed under this subparagraph shall be based on principles similar to the principles which apply in the case of subparagraph (A).

(2) **Allocations.**

(A) Pass-thru in the case of estates and trusts. Under regulations prescribed by the Secretary, rules similar to the rules of subsection (d) of section 52 shall apply.

(B) Allocation in the case of partnerships. In the case of partnerships, the credit shall be allocated among partners under regulations prescribed by the Secretary.

(3) **Adjustments for certain acquisitions, etc.** Under regulations prescribed by the Secretary—

(A)[3] *Acquisitions.*

(i) In general. If a person acquires the major portion of either a trade or business or a separate unit of a trade or business (hereinafter in this paragraph referred to as the "acquired business") of another person (hereinafter in this paragraph referred to as the "predecessor"), then the amount of qualified research expenses paid or incurred by the acquiring person during the measurement period shall be increased by the amount determined under clause (ii), and the gross receipts of the acquiring person for such period shall be increased by the amount determined under clause (iii).

(ii) amount determined with respect to qualified research expenses. The amount determined under this clause is

(I) for purposes of applying this section for the taxable year in which such acquisition is made, the acquisition year amount, and

(II) for purposes of applying this section for any taxable year after the taxable year in which such acquisition is made, the qualified research expenses paid or incurred by the predecessor with respect to the acquired business during the measurement period.

(iii) Amount determined with respect to gross receipts. The amount determined under this clause is the amount which would be determined under clause (ii) if "the gross receipts of" were substituted for "the qualified research expenses paid or incurred by"each place it appears in clauses (ii) and (iv).

(iv) acquisition year amount. For purposes of clause (ii), the acquisition year amount is the amount equal to the product of

(I) the qualified research expenses paid or incurred by the predecessor with respect to the acquired business during the measurement period, and

(II) the number of days in the period beginning on the date of the acquisition and ending on the last day the taxable year in which the acquisition is made, divided by the number of days in the acquiring person's taxable year.

(v) special rules for coordinating taxable years. In the case of an acquiring person and a predecessor whose taxable years do not begin on the same date

(I) each reference to a taxable year in clauses (ii) and (iv) shall refer to the appropriate taxable year of the acquiring person,

(II) the qualified research expenses paid or incurred by the predecessor, and the gross receipts of the predecessor, during each taxable year of the predecessor any portion of which is part of the measurement period shall be allocated equally among the days of such taxable year,

(III) the amount of such qualified research expenses taken into account under clauses (ii) and (iv) with respect to a taxable year of the acquiring person shall be equal to the total of the expenses attributable under subclause (II) to the days occurring during such taxable year, and

(IV) the amount of such gross receipts taken into account under clause (iii) with respect to a taxable year of the acquiring person shall be equal to the total of the gross receipts attributable under subclause (II) to the days occurring during such taxable year

(vi) measurement period. For purposes of this subparagraph, the term "measurement period" means, with respect to the taxable year of the acquiring person for which the credit is determined, any period of the acquiring person preceding such taxable year which is taken into account for purposes of determining the credit for such year.

(B)[4] *Dispositions.* If the predecessor furnished to the acquiring person such information as is necessary for the application of subparagraph (A), then, for purposes of applying this section for any taxable year ending after such disposition, the amount of qualified research expenses paid or incurred by, and the gross receipts of, the predecessor during the measurement period (as defined in subparagraph (A)(vi), determined by substituting "predecessor" for "acquiring person" each place it appears) shall be reduced by

(i) in the case of the taxable year in which such disposition is made, an amount equal to the product of

(I) the qualified research expenses paid or incurred by, or gross receipts of, the predecessor with respect to the acquired business during the measurement period (as so defined and so determined), and

(II) the number of days in the period beginning on the date of acquisition (as determined for purposes of subparagraph subparagraph (A)(i)(II)) and ending on the last day of the taxable year of the predecessor in which the disposition is made, divided by the number of days in the taxable year of the predecessor, and

(ii) in the case of any taxable year ending after the taxable year in which such disposition is made, the amount described in clause (i)(I).

(C) Certain reimbursements taken into account in determining fixed-base percentage. If during any of the 3 taxable years following the taxable year in which a disposition to which subparagraph (B) applies occurs, the disposing taxpayer (or a person with whom the taxpayer is required to aggregate expenditures under paragraph (1)) reimburses the acquiring person (or a person required to so aggregate expenditures with such person) for research on behalf of the taxpayer, then the amount of qualified research expenses of the taxpayer for the taxable years taken into account in computing the fixed-based percentage shall be increased by the lesser of-

(i) the amount of the decrease under subparagraph (B) which is allocable to taxable years so taken into account, or

(ii) the product of the number of taxable years so taken into account, multiplied by the amount of the reimbursement described in this subparagraph.

(4)   Short taxable years. In the case of any short taxable year, qualified research expenses and gross receipts shall be annualized in such circumstances and under such methods as the Secretary may prescribe by regulation.

(5)   Controlled group of corporations. The term "controlled group of corporations" has the same meaning given to such term by section 1563(a), except that—

(A) "more than 50 percent" shall be substituted for "at least 80 percent" each place it appears in section 1563(a)(1), and

(B) the determination shall be made without regard to subsections (a)(4) and (e)(3)(C) of section 1563.

(6)   Energy research consortium.

(A) In general. The term "energy research consortium" means any organization—

(i) which is—

(I) described in section 501(c)(3) and is exempt from tax under section 501(a) and is organized and operated primarily to conduct energy research, or

(II) organized and operated primarily to conduct energy research in the public interest (within the meaning of section 501(c)(3)),

(ii) which is not a private foundation,

(iii) to which at least 5 unrelated persons paid or incurred during the calendar year in which the taxable year of the organization begins amounts (including as contributions) to such organization for energy research, and

(iv) to which no single person paid or incurred (including as contributions) during such calendar year an amount equal to more than 50 percent of the total amounts received by such organization during such calendar year for energy research.

(B) Treatment of persons. All persons treated as a single employer under subsection (a) or (b) of section 52 shall be treated as related persons for purposes of subparagraph (A)(iii) and as a single person for purposes of subparagraph (A)(iv).

(C) Foreign research. For purposes of subsection (a)(3), amounts paid or incurred for any energy research conducted outside the United States, the Commonwealth of Puerto Rico, or any possession of the United States shall not be taken into account.

(D) Denial of double benefit. Any amount taken into account under subsection (a)(3) shall not be taken into account under paragraph (1) or (2) of subsection (a).

(E) Energy research. The term "energy research" does not include any research which is not qualified research.

* * * * * * * * * * * *

(h)   Termination.

(1)   In general. This section shall not apply to any amount paid or incurred—

(A) after June 30, 1995, and before July 1, 1996, or

(B) after [5]*December 31, 2013*.

(2)   Termination of alternative incremental credit. No election under subsection (c)(4) shall apply to taxable years beginning after December 31, 2008.

(3)   Computation for taxable year in which credit terminates. In the case of any taxable year with respect to which this section applies to a number of days which is less than the total number of days in such taxable year—

(A) the amount determined under subsection (c)(1)(B) with respect to such taxable year shall be the amount which bears the same ratio to such amount (determined without regard to this paragraph) as the number of days in such taxable year to which this section applies bears to the total number of days in such taxable year, and

(B) for purposes of subsection (c)(5), the average qualified research expenses for the preceding 3 taxable years shall be the amount which bears the same ratio to such average qualified research expenses (determined without regard to this paragraph) as the number of days in such taxable year to which this section applies bears to the total number of days in such taxable year.

[For Analysis, see ¶ 901.]

[Endnote Code Sec. 41]

Code Sec. 41(f)(1)(A)(ii), Code Sec. 41(f)(1)(B)(ii), Code Sec. 41(f)(3)(A), Code Sec. 41(f)(3)(B) were amended by Sec. 301(c)(1)-(2), (b)(1)-(2) of the American Taxpayer Relief Act of 2012, P.L. 112-240, 1/2/2013, as detailed below:

1. Sec. 301(c)(1) substituted "shall be its proportionate shares of the qualified research expenses, basic research payments, and amounts paid or incurred to energy research consortiums, giving rise to the credit" for "shall be determined on a proportionate basis to its share of the aggregate of the qualified research expenses, basic research payments, and amounts paid or incurred to energy research consortiums, taken into account by such controlled group for purposes of this section" in clause (f)(1)(A)(ii)

2. Sec. 301(c)(2) substituted "shall be its proportionate shares of the qualified research expenses, basic research payments, and amounts paid or incurred to energy research consortiums, giving rise to the credit" for "shall be determined on a proportionate basis to its share of the aggregate of the qualified research expenses, basic research payments, and amounts paid or incurred to energy research consortiums, taken into account by all such persons under common control for purposes of this section" in clause (f)(1)(B)(ii)

3. Sec. 301(b)(1) amended subpara. (f)(3)(A)

4. Sec. 301(b)(2) amended subpara. (f)(3)(B)

Prior to amendment Subpara. (f)(3)(A), read as follows:

"Acquisitions. If, after December 31, 1983, a taxpayer acquires the major portion of a trade or business of another person (hereinafter in 41(f)(3)this paragraph referred to as the "predecessor") or the major portion of a separate unit of a trade or business of a predecessor, then, for purposes of applying 41 this section for any taxable year ending after such acquisition, the amount of qualified research expenses paid or incurred by the taxpayer during periods before such acquisition shall be increased by so much of such expenses paid or incurred by the predecessor with respect to the acquired trade or business as is attributable to the portion of such trade or business or separate unit acquired by the taxpayer, and the gross receipts of the taxpayer for such periods shall be increased by so much of the gross receipts of such predecessor with respect to the acquired trade or business as is attributable to such portion."

Prior to amendment subpara. (f)(3)(B), read as follows:

"Dispositions. If the predecessor furnished to the acquiring person such information as is necessary for the application of subparagraph (A), then, for purposes of applying this section for any taxable year ending after such disposition, the amount of qualified research expenses paid or incurred by, and the gross receipts of, the predecessor during the measurement period (as defined in subparagraph (A)(vi), determined by substituting "predecessor" for "acquiring person" each place it appears) shall be reduced by (i) in the case of the taxable year in which such disposition is made, an amount equal to the product of (I) the qualified research expenses paid or incurred by, or gross receipts of, the predecessor with respect to the acquired business during the measurement period (as so defined and so determined), and (II) the number of days in the period beginning on the date of acquisition (as determined for purposes of subparagraph (A)(iv)(II)) and ending on the last day of the taxable year of the predecessor in which the disposition is made, divided by the number of days in the taxable year of the predecessor, and (ii) in the case of any taxable year ending after the taxable year in which such disposition is made, the amount described in clause (i)(I). "

Effective Date (Sec. 301(d)(2), P.L. 112-240, 1/2/2013) effective for taxable years beginning after 12/31/2011.

Code Sec. 41(h)(1)(B) was amended by Sec. 301(a)(1), P.L. 112-240, 1/2/2013, as detailed below:

5. Sec. 301(a)(1) substituted "December 31, 2013" for "December 31, 2011" in para (h)(1)(B)

Effective Date (Sec. 301(d)(1), P.L. 112-240, 1/2/2013) effective for amounts paid or incurred after 12/31/2011.

[¶ 3024]   Code Sec. 42.   Low-income housing credit.

* * * * * * * * * * * * *

(b) Applicable percentage: 70 percent present value credit for certain new buildings; 30 percent present value credit for certain other buildings.

(1) Determination of applicable percentage.

(A [sic]) For purposes of this section, the term "applicable percentage" means, with respect to any building, the appropriate percentage prescribed by the Secretary for the earlier of—

(i) the month in which such building is placed in service, or

(ii) at the election of the taxpayer—

(I) the month in which the taxpayer and the housing credit agency enter into an agreement with respect to such building (which is binding on such agency, the taxpayer, and all successors in interest) as to the housing credit dollar amount to be allocated to such building, or

(II) in the case of any building to which subsection (h)(4)(B) applies, the month in which the tax-exempt obligations are issued.

A month may be elected under clause (ii) only if the election is made not later than the 5th day after the close of such month. Such an election, once made, shall be irrevocable.

(B) Method of prescribing percentages. The percentages prescribed by the Secretary for any month shall be percentages which will yield over a 10-year period amounts of credit under subsection (a) which have a present value equal to—

(i) 70 percent of the qualified basis of a new building which is not federally subsidized for the taxable year, and

(ii) 30 percent of the qualified basis of a building not described in clause (i).

(C) Method of discounting. The present value under subparagraph (B) shall be determined—

(i) as of the last day of the 1st year of the 10-year period referred to in subparagraph (B),

(ii) by using a discount rate equal to 72 percent of the average of the annual Federal mid-term rate and the annual Federal long-term rate applicable under section 1274(d)(1) to the month applicable under clause (i) or (ii) of subparagraph (A) and compounded annually, and

(iii) by assuming that the credit allowable under this section for any year is received on the last day of such year.

(2) Temporary minimum credit rate for non-federally subsidized new buildings. In the case of any new building—

(A) which is placed in service by the taxpayer after the date of the enactment of this paragraph [1] *with respect to housing credit dollar amount allocations made before January 1, 2014*, and

(B) which is not federally subsidized for the taxable year,

the applicable percentage shall not be less than 9 percent.

(3) Cross references.

(A) For treatment of certain rehabilitation expenditures as separate new buildings, see subsection (e).

(B) For determination of applicable percentage for increases in qualified basis after the 1st year of the credit period, see subsection (f)(3).

(C) For authority of housing credit agency to limit applicable percentage and qualified basis which may be taken into account under this section with respect to any building, see subsection (h)(7).

* * * * * * * * * * * *

(g) Qualified low-income housing project. For purposes of this section—

* * * * * * * * * * * *

(4) Certain rules made applicable. Paragraphs (2) (other than subparagraph (A) thereof), (3), (4), (5), (6), and (7) of section 142(d), and section 6652(j), shall apply for purposes of determining whether any project is a qualified low-income housing project and whether any unit is a low-income unit; except that, in applying such provisions for such purposes, the term "gross rent" shall have the meaning given such term by paragraph (2)(B) of this subsection

[For Analysis, see ¶ 906 and ¶ 1408.]

[Endnote Code Sec. 42]

Code Sec. 42(b)(2)(A) was amended by Sec. 302(a) of the American Taxpayer Relief Act of 2012, P.L. 112-240, 1/2/2013, as detailed below:

1. Sec. 302(a) substituted "with respect to housing credit dollar 20 amount allocations made before January 1, 2014" for "and before December 31, 2013" in subpara. (b)(2)(A)

Effective Date (Sec. 302(b), P.L. 112-240, 1/2/2013) effective 1/2/2013.

Sec. 303(a), P.L. 112-240, 1/2/2013, substituted "January 1, 2014" for "January 1, 2012" each place it appears in Sec. 3005(b), P.L. 110-289. Sec. 3005(b), P.L. 110-289 reads as follows:

"(b) The amendments made by this section shall apply to—

"(1) determinations made after the date of the enactment of this Act and before January 1, 2014, in the case of any qualified building (as defined in section 142(d)(2)(B)(iii) of the Internal Revenue Code of 1986)—

"(A) with respect to which housing credit dollar amounts have been allocated on or before the date of the enactment of this Act, or

"(B) with respect to buildings placed in service before such date of enactment, to the extent paragraph (1) of section 42(h) of such Code does not apply to such building by reason of paragraph (4) thereof, but only with respect to bonds issued before such date of enactment, and

"(2) determinations made after the date of enactment of this Act, in the case of qualified buildings (as so defined)—

"(A) with respect to which housing credit dollar amounts are allocated after the date of the enactment of this Act and before January 1, 2014, or

"(B) with respect to which buildings placed in service after the date of enactment of this Act and before January 1, 2014, to the extent paragraph (1) of section 42(h) of such Code does not apply to such building by reason of paragraph (4) thereof, but only with respect to bonds issued after such date of enactment and before January 1, 2014."

Effective Date (Sec. 303(b), P.L. 112-240, 1/2/2013) effective as if included in the enactment of Sec. 3005, P.L. 110-289. See above for Sec. 3005(b), P.L. 110-289, as amended.

[¶ 3025]   Code Sec. 45.   Electricity produced from certain renewable resources, etc.

* * * * * * * * * * * *

(c) **Resources.** For purposes of this section—

  (1) **In general.** The term "qualified energy resources" means—

  (A) wind,

  (B) closed-loop biomass,

  (C) open-loop biomass,

  (D) geothermal energy,

  (E) solar energy,

  (F) small irrigation power,

  (G) municipal solid waste,

  (H) qualified hydropower production, and

  (I) marine and hydrokinetic renewable energy.

  (2) **Closed-loop biomass.** The term "closed-loop biomass" means any organic material from a plant which is planted exclusively for purposes of being used at a qualified facility to produce electricity.

  (3) **Open-loop biomass.**

  (A) In general. The term "open-loop biomass" means—

    (i) any agricultural livestock waste nutrients, or

    (ii) any solid, nonhazardous, cellulosic waste material or any lignin material which is derived from—

      (I) any of the following forest-related resources: mill and harvesting residues, precommercial thinnings, slash, and brush,

      (II) solid wood waste materials, including waste pallets, crates, dunnage, manufacturing and construction wood wastes (other than pressure-treated, chemically-treated, or painted wood wastes), and landscape or right-of-way tree trimmings, but not including municipal solid waste, gas derived from the biodegradation of solid waste, or paper which is commonly recycled, or

      (III) agriculture sources, including orchard tree crops, vineyard, grain, legumes, sugar, and other crop by-products or residues.

Such term shall not include closed-loop biomass or biomass burned in conjunction with fossil fuel (cofiring) beyond such fossil fuel required for startup and flame stabilization.

(B) Agricultural livestock waste nutrients.

(i) In general. The term "agricultural livestock waste nutrients" means agricultural livestock manure and litter, including wood shavings, straw, rice hulls, and other bedding material for the disposition of manure.

(ii) Agricultural livestock. The term "agricultural livestock" includes bovine, swine, poultry, and sheep.

(4) Geothermal energy. The term "geothermal energy" means energy derived from a geothermal deposit (within the meaning of section 613(e)(2)).

(5) Small irrigation power. The term "small irrigation power" means power—

(A) generated without any dam or impoundment of water through an irrigation system canal or ditch, and

(B) the nameplate capacity rating of which is not less than 150 kilowatts but is less than 5 megawatts.

(6) Municipal solid waste. The term "municipal solid waste" has the meaning given the term "solid waste" under section 2(27) of the Solid Waste Disposal Act (42 U.S.C. 6903) [1], *except that such term does not include paper which is commonly recycled and which has been segregated from other solid waste (as so defined).*

(7) Refined coal.

(A) In general. The term "refined coal" means a fuel—

(i) which—

(I) is a liquid, gaseous, or solid fuel produced from coal (including lignite) or high carbon fly ash, including such fuel used as a feedstock,

(II) is sold by the taxpayer with the reasonable expectation that it will be used for purpose of producing steam, and

(III) is certified by the taxpayer as resulting (when used in the production of steam) in a qualified emission reduction.

(IV) Repealed

(ii) which is steel industry fuel.

(B) Qualified emission reduction. The term "qualified emission reduction" means a reduction of at least 20 percent of the emissions of nitrogen oxide and at least 40 percent of the emissions of either sulfur dioxide or mercury released when burning the refined coal (excluding any dilution caused by materials combined or added during the production process), as compared to the emissions released when burning the feedstock coal or comparable coal predominantly available in the marketplace as of January 1, 2003.

(C) Steel industry fuel.

(i) In general. The term "steel industry fuel" means a fuel which—

(I) is produced through a process of liquefying coal waste sludge and distributing it on coal, and

(II) is used as a feedstock for the manufacture of coke.

(ii) Coal waste sludge. The term "coal waste sludge" means the tar decanter sludge and related byproducts of the coking process, including such materials that have been stored in ground, in tanks and in lagoons, that have been treated as hazardous wastes under applicable Federal environmental rules absent liquefaction and processing with coal into a feedstock for the manufacture of coke.

(8) Qualified hydropower production.

(A) In general. The term "qualified hydropower production" means—

(i) in the case of any hydroelectric dam which was placed in service on or before the date of the enactment of this paragraph, the incremental hydropower production for the taxable year, and

(ii) in the case of any nonhydroelectric dam described in subparagraph (C), the hydropower production from the facility for the taxable year.

(B) Determination of incremental hydropower production.

(i) In general. For purposes of subparagraph (A), incremental hydropower production for any taxable year shall be equal to the percentage of average annual hydropower production at the facility attributable to the efficiency improvements or additions of capacity placed in service after the date of the enactment of this paragraph, determined by using the same water flow information used to determine an historic average annual hydropower production baseline for such facility. Such percentage and baseline shall be certified by the Federal Energy Regulatory Commission.

(ii) Operational changes disregarded. For purposes of clause (i), the determination of incremental hydropower production shall not be based on any operational changes at such facility not directly associated with the efficiency improvements or additions of capacity.

(C) Nonhydroelectric dam. For purposes of subparagraph (A), a facility is described in this subparagraph if—

(i) the hydroelectric project installed on the nonhydroelectric dam is licensed by the Federal Energy Regulatory Commission and meets all other applicable environmental, licensing, and regulatory requirements,

(ii) the nonhydroelectric dam was placed in service before the date of the enactment of this paragraph and operated for flood control, navigation, or water supply purposes and did not produce hydroelectric power on the date of the enactment of this paragraph, and

(iii) the hydroelectric project is operated so that the water surface elevation at any given location and time that would have occurred in the absence of the hydroelectric project is maintained, subject to any license requirements imposed under applicable law that change the water surface elevation for the purpose of improving environmental quality of the affected waterway.

The Secretary, in consultation with the Federal Energy Regulatory Commission, shall certify if a hydroelectric project licensed at a nonhydroelectric dam meets the criteria in clause (iii). Nothing in this section shall affect the standards under which the Federal Energy Regulatory Commission issues licenses for and regulates hydropower projects under part I of the Federal Power Act.

(9) Indian coal.

(A) In general. The term "Indian coal" means coal which is produced from coal reserves which, on June 14, 2005—

(i) were owned by an Indian tribe, or

(ii) were held in trust by the United States for the benefit of an Indian tribe or its members.

(B) Indian tribe. For purposes of this paragraph, the term "Indian tribe" has the meaning given such term by section 7871(c)(3)(E)(ii).

(10) Marine and hydrokinetic renewable energy.

(A) In general. The term "marine and hydrokinetic renewable energy" means energy derived from—

(i) waves, tides, and currents in oceans, estuaries, and tidal areas,

(ii) free flowing water in rivers, lakes, and streams,

(iii) free flowing water in an irrigation system, canal, or other man-made channel, including projects that utilize non-mechanical structures to accelerate the flow of water for electric power production purposes, or

(iv) differentials in ocean temperature (ocean thermal energy conversion).

(B) Exceptions. Such term shall not include any energy which is derived from any source which utilizes a dam, diversionary structure (except as provided in subparagraph (A)(iii)), or impoundment for electric power production purposes.

(d) Qualified facilities. For purposes of this section—

(1) Wind facility. In the case of a facility using wind to produce electricity, the term "qualified facility" means any facility owned by the taxpayer which is originally placed in service after December 31, 1993, and ²the construction of which begins before ³January 1,

2014. Such term shall not include any facility with respect to which any qualified small wind energy property expenditure (as defined in subsection (d)(4) of section 25D) is taken into account in determining the credit under such section.

(2) Closed-loop biomass facility.

(A) In general. In the case of a facility using closed-loop biomass to produce electricity, the term "qualified facility" means any facility—

(i) owned by the taxpayer which is originally placed in service after December 31, 1992, and before January 1, 2014, or

(ii) owned by the taxpayer which [4]*the construction of which begins before January 1, 2014,* is originally placed in service and modified to use closed-loop biomass to co-fire with coal, with other biomass, or with both, but only if the modification is approved under the Biomass Power for Rural Development Programs or is part of a pilot project of the Commodity Credit Corporation as described in 65 Fed. Reg. 63052.

[5]*For purposes of clause (ii), a facility shall be treated as modified before January 1, 2014, if the construction of such modification begins before such date.*

(B) Expansion of facility. Such term shall include a new unit placed in service after the date of the enactment of this subparagraph in connection with a facility described in subparagraph (A)(i), but only to the extent of the increased amount of electricity produced at the facility by reason of such new unit.

(C) Special rules. In the case of a qualified facility described in subparagraph (A)(ii)—

(i) the 10-year period referred to in subsection (a) shall be treated as beginning no earlier than the date of the enactment of this clause, and

(ii) if the owner of such facility is not the producer of the electricity, the person eligible for the credit allowable under subsection (a) shall be the lessee or the operator of such facility.

(3) Open-loop biomass facilities.

(A) In general. In the case of a facility using open-loop biomass to produce electricity, the term "qualified facility" means any facility owned by the taxpayer which—

(i) in the case of a facility using agricultural livestock waste nutrients—

(I) is originally placed in service after the date of the enactment of this subclause and [6]*the construction of which begins before January 1, 2014,* and

(II) the nameplate capacity rating of which is not less than 150 kilowatts, and

(ii) in the case of any other facility, [7]*the construction of which begins* before January 1, 2014.

(B) Expansion of facility. Such term shall include a new unit placed in service after the date of the enactment of this subparagraph in connection with a facility described in subparagraph (A), but only to the extent of the increased amount of electricity produced at the facility by reason of such new unit.

(C) Credit eligibility. In the case of any facility described in subparagraph (A), if the owner of such facility is not the producer of the electricity, the person eligible for the credit allowable under subsection (a) shall be the lessee or the operator of such facility.

(4) Geothermal or solar energy facility. In the case of a facility using geothermal or solar energy to produce electricity, the term "qualified facility" means any facility owned by the taxpayer which is originally placed in service after the date of the enactment of this paragraph [8]*and which—*

(A) *in the case of a facility using solar energy, is placed in service before January 1, 2006, or*

(B) *in the case of a facility using geothermal energy, the construction of which begins before January 1, 2014.*

Such term shall not include any property described in section 48(a)(3) the basis of which is taken into account by the taxpayer for purposes of determining the energy credit under section 48.

(5) Small irrigation power facility. In the case of a facility using small irrigation power to produce electricity, the term "qualified facility" means any facility owned by the taxpayer which is originally placed in service after the date of the enactment of this paragraph and before October 3, 2008.

(6) Landfill gas facilities. In the case of a facility producing electricity from gas derived from the biodegradation of municipal solid waste, the term "qualified facility" means any facility owned by the taxpayer which is originally placed in service after the date of the enactment of this paragraph and [9]*the construction of which begins before January 1, 2014*

(7) Trash facilities. In the case of a facility (other than a facility described in paragraph (6)) which uses municipal solid waste to produce electricity, the term "qualified facility" means any facility owned by the taxpayer which is originally placed in service after the date of the enactment of this paragraph and [10]*the construction of which begins before January 1, 2014.* Such term shall include a new unit placed in service in connection with a facility placed in service on or before the date of the enactment of this paragraph, but only to the extent of the increased amount of electricity produced at the facility by reason of such new unit.

(8) Refined coal production facility. In the case of a facility that produces refined coal, the term "refined coal production facility" means—

(A) with respect to a facility producing steel industry fuel, any facility (or any modification to a facility) which is placed in service before January 1, 2010, and

(B) with respect to any other facility producing refined coal, any facility placed in service after the date of the enactment of the American Jobs Creation Act of 2004 and before January 1, 2012.

(9) Qualified hydropower facility.

[11]*(A) In general. In the case of a facility* producing qualified hydroelectric production described in subsection (c)(8), the term "qualified facility" means—

[12]*(i) in the case of any facility producing incremental hydropower production, such facility but only to the extent of its incremental hydropower production attributable to efficiency improvements or additions to capacity described in subsection (c)(8)(B) placed in service after the date of the enactment of this paragraph and before January 1, 2014, and*

(ii) any other facility placed in service after the date of the enactment of this paragraph and [13]*the construction of which begins before January 1, 2014.*

[14]*(B) Credit period. In the case of a qualified facility described in subparagraph (A), the 10-year period referred to in subsection (a) shall be treated as beginning on the date the efficiency improvements or additions to capacity are placed in service.*

[15]*(C) Special rule. For purposes of subparagraph (A)(i), an efficiency improvement or addition to capacity shall be treated as placed in service before January 1, 2014, if the construction of such improvement or addition begins before such date.*

(10) Indian coal production facility. In the case of a facility that produces Indian coal, the term "Indian coal production facility" means a facility which is placed in service before January 1, 2009.

(11) Marine and hydrokinetic renewable energy facilities. In the case of a facility producing electricity from marine and hydrokinetic renewable energy, the term "qualified facility" means any facility owned by the taxpayer—

(A) which has a nameplate capacity rating of at least 150 kilowatts, and

(B) which is originally placed in service on or after the date of the enactment of this paragraph and [16]*the construction of which begins before January 1, 2014.*

(e) Definitions and special rules. For purposes of this section—

(1) Only production in the United States taken into account. Sales shall be taken into account under this section only with respect to electricity the production of which is within—

(A) the United States (within the meaning of section 638(1)), or

(B) a possession of the United States (within the meaning of section 638(2)).

(2) Computation of inflation adjustment factor and reference price.

(A) In general. The Secretary shall, not later than April 1 of each calendar year, determine and publish in the Federal Register the inflation adjustment factor and the reference price for such calendar year in accordance with this paragraph.

(B) Inflation adjustment factor. The term "inflation adjustment factor" means, with respect to a calendar year, a fraction the numerator of which is the GDP implicit price deflator for the preceding calendar year and the denominator of which is the GDP implicit price deflator for the calendar year 1992. The term "GDP implicit price deflator" means the most recent revision of the implicit price deflator for the gross domestic product as computed and published by the Department of Commerce before March 15 of the calendar year.

(C) Reference price. The term "reference price" means, with respect to a calendar year, the Secretary's determination of the annual average contract price per kilowatt hour of electricity generated from the same qualified energy resource and sold in the previous year in the United States. For purposes of the preceding sentence, only contracts entered into after December 31, 1989, shall be taken into account.

(3) Production attributable to the taxpayer. In the case of a facility in which more than 1 person has an ownership interest, except to the extent provided in regulations prescribed by the Secretary, production from the facility shall be allocated among such persons in proportion to their respective ownership interests in the gross sales from such facility.

(4) Related persons. Persons shall be treated as related to each other if such persons would be treated as a single employer under the regulations prescribed under section 52(b). In the case of a corporation which is a member of an affiliated group of corporations filing a consolidated return, such corporation shall be treated as selling electricity to an unrelated person if such electricity is sold to such a person by another member of such group.

(5) Pass-thru in the case of estates and trusts. Under regulations prescribed by the Secretary, rules similar to the rules of subsection (d) of section 52 shall apply.

(6) Repealed.

(7) Credit not to apply to electricity sold to utilities under certain contracts.

(A) In general. The credit determined under subsection (a) shall not apply to electricity—

(i) produced at a qualified facility described in subsection (d)(1) which is originally placed in service after June 30, 1999, and

(ii) sold to a utility pursuant to a contract originally entered into before January 1, 1987 (whether or not amended or restated after that date).

(B) Exception. Subparagraph (A) shall not apply if—

(i) the prices for energy and capacity from such facility are established pursuant to an amendment to the contract referred to in subparagraph (A)(ii),

(ii) such amendment provides that the prices set forth in the contract which exceed avoided cost prices determined at the time of delivery shall apply only to annual quantities of electricity (prorated for partial years) which do not exceed the greater of—

(I) the average annual quantity of electricity sold to the utility under the contract during calendar years 1994, 1995, 1996, 1997, and 1998, or

(II) the estimate of the annual electricity production set forth in the contract, or, if there is no such estimate, the greatest annual quantity of electricity sold to the utility under the contract in any of the calendar years 1996, 1997, or 1998, and

(iii) such amendment provides that energy and capacity in excess of the limitation in clause (ii) may be—

(I) sold to the utility only at prices that do not exceed avoided cost prices determined at the time of delivery, or

(II) sold to a third party subject to a mutually agreed upon advance notice to the utility.

557

For purposes of this subparagraph, avoided cost prices shall be determined as provided for in 18 CFR 292.304(d)(1) or any successor regulation.

(8) Refined coal production facilities.

(A) Determination of credit amount. In the case of a producer of refined coal, the credit determined under this section (without regard to this paragraph) for any taxable year shall be increased by an amount equal to $4.375 per ton of qualified refined coal—

(i) produced by the taxpayer at a refined coal production facility during the 10-year period beginning on the date the facility was originally placed in service, and

(ii) sold by the taxpayer—

(I) to an unrelated person, and

(II) during such 10-year period and such taxable year.

(B) Phaseout of credit. The amount of the increase determined under subparagraph (A) shall be reduced by an amount which bears the same ratio to the amount of the increase (determined without regard to this subparagraph) as—

(i) the amount by which the reference price of fuel used as a feedstock (within the meaning of subsection (c)(7)(A)) for the calendar year in which the sale occurs exceeds an amount equal to 1.7 multiplied by the reference price for such fuel in 2002, bears to

(ii) $8.75.

(C) Application of rules. Rules similar to the rules of the subsection (b)(3) and paragraphs (1) through (5) of this subsection shall apply for purposes of determining the amount of any increase under this paragraph.

(D) Special rule for steel industry fuel.

(i) In general. In the case of a taxpayer who produces steel industry fuel—

(I) this paragraph shall be applied separately with respect to steel industry fuel and other refined coal, and

(II) in applying this paragraph to steel industry fuel, the modifications in clause (ii) shall apply.

(ii) Modifications.

(I) Credit amount. Subparagraph (A) shall be applied by substituting "$2 per barrel-of-oil equivalent" for "$4.375 per ton".

(II) Credit period. In lieu of the 10-year period referred to in clauses (i) and (ii)(II) of subparagraph (A), the credit period shall be the period beginning on the later of the date such facility was originally placed in service, the date the modifications described in clause (iii) were placed in service, or October 1, 2008, and ending on the later of December 31, 2009, or the date which is 1 year after the date such facility or the modifications described in clause (iii) were placed in service.

(III) No phaseout. Subparagraph (B) shall not apply.

(iii) Modifications. The modifications described in this clause are modifications to an existing facility which allow such facility to produce steel industry fuel.

(iv) Barrel-of-oil equivalent. For purposes of this subparagraph, a barrel-of-oil equivalent is the amount of steel industry fuel that has a Btu content of 5,800,000 Btus.

(9) Coordination with credit for producing fuel from a nonconventional source.

(A) In general. The term "qualified facility" shall not include any facility which produces electricity from gas derived from the biodegradation of municipal solid waste if such biodegradation occurred in a facility (within the meaning of section 45K) the production from which is allowed as a credit under section 45K for the taxable year or any prior taxable year.

(B) Refined coal facilities.

(i) In general. The term "refined coal production facility" shall not include any facility the production from which is allowed as a credit under section 45K for the taxable year or any prior taxable year (or under section 29, as in effect on the day before the date of enactment of the Energy Tax Incentives Act of 2005, for any prior taxable year).

(ii) Exception for steel industry coal. In the case of a facility producing steel industry fuel, clause (i) shall not apply to so much of the refined coal produced at such facility as is steel industry fuel.

(10) Indian coal production facilities.

(A) Determination of credit amount. In the case of a producer of Indian coal, the credit determined under this section (without regard to this paragraph) for any taxable year shall be increased by an amount equal to the applicable dollar amount per ton of Indian coal—

(i) produced by the taxpayer at an Indian coal production facility during the [17]8-*year period* beginning on January 1, 2006, and

(ii) sold by the taxpayer—

(I) to an unrelated person, and

(II) during such [18]8-*year period* and such taxable year.

(B) Applicable dollar amount.

(i) In general. The term "applicable dollar amount" for any taxable year beginning in a calendar year means—

(I) $1.50 in the case of calendar years 2006 through 2009, and

(II) $2.00 in the case of calendar years beginning after 2009.

(ii) Inflation adjustment. In the case of any calendar year after 2006, each of the dollar amounts under clause (i) shall be equal to the product of such dollar amount and the inflation adjustment factor determined under paragraph (2)(B) for the calendar year, except that such paragraph shall be applied by substituting "2005" for "1992".

(C) Application of rules. Rules similar to the rules of the subsection (b)(3) and paragraphs (1), (3), (4), and (5) of this subsection shall apply for purposes of determining the amount of any increase under this paragraph.

(D) Treatment as specified credit. The increase in the credit determined under subsection (a) by reason of this paragraph with respect to any facility shall be treated as a specified credit for purposes of section 38(c)(4)(A) during the 4-year period beginning on the later of January 1, 2006, or the date on which such facility is placed in service by the taxpayer.

(11) Allocation of credit to patrons of agricultural cooperative.

(A) Election to allocate.

(i) In general. In the case of an eligible cooperative organization, any portion of the credit determined under subsection (a) for the taxable year may, at the election of the organization, be apportioned among patrons of the organization on the basis of the amount of business done by the patrons during the taxable year.

(ii) Form and effect of election. An election under clause (i) for any taxable year shall be made on a timely filed return for such year. Such election, once made, shall be irrevocable for such taxable year. Such election shall not take effect unless the organization designates the apportionment as such in a written notice mailed to its patrons during the payment period described in section 1382(d).

(B) Treatment of organizations and patrons. The amount of the credit apportioned to any patrons under subparagraph (A)—

(i) shall not be included in the amount determined under subsection (a) with respect to the organization for the taxable year, and

(ii) shall be included in the amount determined under subsection (a) for the first taxable year of each patron ending on or after the last day of the payment period (as defined in section 1382(d)) for the taxable year of the organization or, if earlier, for the taxable year of each patron ending on or after the date on which the patron receives notice from the cooperative of the apportionment.

(C) Special rules for decrease in credits for taxable year. If the amount of the credit of a cooperative organization determined under subsection (a) for a taxable year is less than the amount of such credit shown on the return of the cooperative organization for such year, an amount equal to the excess of—

(i) such reduction, over

(ii) the amount not apportioned to such patrons under subparagraph (A) for the taxable year,

shall be treated as an increase in tax imposed by this chapter on the organization. Such increase shall not be treated as tax imposed by this chapter for purposes of determining the amount of any credit under this chapter.

(D) Eligible cooperative defined. For purposes of this section the term "eligible cooperative" means a cooperative organization described in section 1381(a) which is owned more than 50 percent by agricultural producers or by entities owned by agricultural producers. For this purpose an entity owned by an agricultural producer is one that is more than 50 percent owned by agricultural producers.

[For Analysis, see ¶ 1005, ¶ 1007 and ¶ 1011.]

[Endnote Code Sec. 45]

Code Sec. 45(c)(6) was amended by Sec. 407(a)(2) of the American Taxpayer Relief Act of 2012, P.L. 112-240, 1/2/2013, as detailed below:

1. Sec. 407(a)(2) added ", except that such term does not include paper which is commonly recycled and which has been segregated from other solid waste (as so defined)" after "(42 U.S.C. 6903)" in para. (c)(6)

Effective Date (Sec. 407(d)(2), P.L. 112-240, 1/2/2013) effective for electricity produced and sold after 1/2/2013, in tax. yrs. ending after 1/2/2013.

Code Sec. 45(d)(1), Code Sec. 45(d)(2)(A), Code Sec. 45(d)(3)(A), Code Sec. 45(d)(4), Code Sec. 45(d)(6), Code Sec. 45(d)(7), Code Sec. 45(d)(9) and Code Sec. 45(d)(11)(A) were amended by Sec. 406(a), 407(a)(1), 407(a)(3)(A)(i)-(vi) and 407(a)(3)(B)-(E), P.L. 112-240, 1/2/2013, as detailed below:

2. Sec. 407(a)(3)(A)(i) substituted "the construction of which begins before January 1, 2014" for "before January 1, 2014" in para. (d)(1) [previously amended by Sec. 407(a)(1) of this Act, see below]

3. Sec. 407(a)(1) substituted "January 1, 2014" for "January 1, 2013" in para. (d)(1)

4. Sec. 407(a)(3)(A)(ii) substituted "the construction of which begins before January 1, 2014" for "before January 1, 2014" in clause (d)(2)(A)(i)

5. Sec. 407(a)(3)(B) added "For purposes of clause (ii), a facility shall be treated as modified before January 1, 2014, if the construction of such modification begins before such date." as a flush sentence at the end of subpara. (d)(2)(A)

6. Sec. 407(a)(3)(A)(iii) substituted "the construction of which begins before January 1, 2014" for "before January 1, 2014" in subclause (d)(3)(A)(i)(I)

7. Sec. 407(a)(3)(C) substituted "the construction of which begins" for "is originally placed in service" in clause (d)(3)(A)(ii)

8. Sec. 407(a)(3)(D)(i) substituted "and which"

"(A) in the case of a facility using solar energy, is placed in service before January 1, 2006, or

"(B) in the case of a facility using geothermal energy, the construction of which begins before January 1, 2014.

"Such term shall not include any property described in section 48(a)(3) the basis of which is taken into account by the taxpayer for purposes of determining the energy credit under section 48." for "and before January 1, 2014 (January 1, 2006, in the case of a facility using solar energy). Such term shall not include any property described in section 48(a)(3) the basis of which is taken into account by the taxpayer for purposes of determining the energy credit under section 48." in para. (d)(4)

9. Sec. 407(a)(3)(A)(iv) substituted "the construction of which begins before January 1, 2014" for "before January 1, 2014" in para. (d)(6)

10. Sec. 407(a)(3)(A)(v) substituted "the construction of which begins before January 1, 2014" for "before January 1, 2014" in para. (d)(7)

11. Sec. 407(a)(3)(E)(ii) substituted "(A) In general. In the case of a facility" for "In the case of a facility" in para. (d)(9)

12. Sec. 407(a)(3)(E)(i) redesignated subparas. (d)(9)(A)-(B) as clauses (d)(9)(A)(i)-(ii)

13. Sec. 407(a)(3)(A)(vi) substituted "the construction of which begins before January 1, 2014" for "before January 1, 2014" in clause (d)(9)(A)(ii) [redesignated by Sec. 407(a)(3)(E)(i), see above]

14. Sec. 407(a)(3)(E)(iii) redesignated subpara. (d)(9)(C) as subpara. (d)(9)(B)

15. Sec. 407(a)(3)(E)(iv) added new subpara. (d)(9)(C)

16. Sec. 407(a)(3)(A)(vii) substituted "the construction of which begins before January 1, 2014" for "before January 1, 2014" in subpara. (d)(11)(B)

Effective Date (Sec. 407(d)(1), P.L. 112-240, 1/2/2013) effective 1/2/2013.

Code Sec. 45(e)(10)(A) was amended by Sec. 406(a), P.L. 112-240, 1/2/2013, as detailed below:

17. Sec. 406(a) substituted "8-year period" for "7-year period" in clause (e)(10)(A)(i)

18. Sec. 406(a) substituted "8-year period" for "7-year period" in subclause (e)(10)(A)(ii)(II)

Effective Date (Sec. 406(b), P.L. 112-240, 1/2/2013) effective for coal produced after 12/31/2012.

[¶ 3026]   Code Sec. 45A.   Indian employment credit.

* * * * * * * * * * * *

(f) Termination. This section shall not apply to taxable years beginning after [1]*December 31, 2013.*
[For Analysis, see ¶ 907.]

[Endnote Code Sec. 45A]
  Code Sec. 45A(f) was amended by Sec. 304(a) of the American Taxpayer Relief Act of 2012, P.L. 112-240, 1/2/2013, as detailed below:
  1. Sec. 304(a) substituted "December 31, 2013" for "December 31, 2011" in subsec. (f)
Effective Date (Sec. 304(b), P.L. 112-240, 1/2/2013) effective for tax. yrs. begin. after 12/31/2011.

[¶ 3027]   Code Sec. 45C.   Clinical testing expenses for certain drugs for rare diseases or conditions.

* * * * * * * * * * * *

(b) Qualified clinical testing expenses. For purposes of this section—

(1) Qualified clinical testing expenses.

(A) In general. Except as otherwise provided in this paragraph, the term "qualified clinical testing expenses" means the amounts which are paid or incurred by the taxpayer during the taxable year which would be described in subsection (b) of section 41 if such subsection were applied with the modifications set forth in subparagraph (B).

(B) Modifications. For purposes of subparagraph (A), subsection (b) of section 41 shall be applied—

(i) by substituting "clinical testing" for "qualified research" each place it appears in paragraphs (2) and (3) of such subsection, and

(ii) by substituting "100 percent" for "65 percent" in paragraph (3)(A) of such subsection.

(C) Exclusion for amounts funded by grants, etc. The term "qualified clinical testing expenses" shall not include any amount to the extent such amount is funded by any grant, contract, or otherwise by another person (or any governmental entity).

(D) Special rule. For purposes of this paragraph, section 41 shall be deemed to remain in effect for periods after June 30, 1995, and before July 1, 1996, and periods after [1]*December 31, 2013.*

(2) Clinical testing.

(A) In general. The term "clinical testing" means any human clinical testing—

(i) which is carried out under an exemption for a drug being tested for a rare disease or condition under section 505(i) of the Federal Food, Drug, and Cosmetic Act (or regulations issued under such section),

(ii) which occurs—

(I) after the date such drug is designated under section 526 of such Act, and

(II) before the date on which an application with respect to such drug is approved under section 505(b) of such Act or, if the drug is a biological product, before the date on which a license for such drug is issued under section 351 of the Public Health Service Act; and

(iii) which is conducted by or on behalf of the taxpayer to whom the designation under such section 526 applies.

(B) Testing must be related to use for rare disease or condition. Human clinical testing shall be taken into account under subparagraph (A) only to the extent such testing is related to the use of a drug for the rare disease or condition for which it was designated under section 526 of the Federal Food, Drug, and Cosmetic Act.

* * * * * * * * * * * *

[For Analysis, see ¶ 901.]

[Endnote Code Sec. 45C]
    Code Sec. 45C(b)(1)(D) was amended by Sec. 301(a)(2) of the American Taxpayer Relief Act of 2012, P.L. 112-240, 1/2/2013, as detailed below:
    1. Sec. 301(a)(2) substituted "December 31, 2013" for "December 31, 2011" in subpara. (b)(1)(D)
Effective Date (Sec. 301(d)(1), P.L. 112-240, 1/2/2013) effective for amounts paid or incurred after 12/31/2011.

[¶ 3028]   Code Sec. 45D.   New markets tax credit.

* * * * * * * * * * * *

(f)   National limitation on amount of investments designated.

   (1)   In general. There is a new markets tax credit limitation for each calendar year. Such limitation is—

   (A) $1,000,000,000 for 2001,

   (B) $1,500,000,000 for 2002 and 2003,

   (C) $2,000,000,000 for 2004 and 2005,

   (D) $3,500,000,000 for 2006 and 2007,

   (E) $5,000,000,000 for 2008,

   (F) $5,000,000,000 for 2009

   (G) $3,500,000,000 for [1]*2010, 2011, 2012, and 2013.*

   (2)   Allocation of limitation. The limitation under paragraph (1) shall be allocated by the Secretary among qualified community development entities selected by the Secretary. In making allocations under the preceding sentence, the Secretary shall give priority to any entity—

   (A) with a record of having successfully provided capital or technical assistance to disadvantaged businesses or communities, or

   (B) which intends to satisfy the requirement under subsection (b)(1)(B) by making qualified low-income community investments in 1 or more businesses in which persons unrelated to such entity (within the meaning of section 267(b) or 707(b)(1)) hold the majority equity interest.

   (3)   Carryover of unused limitation. If the new markets tax credit limitation for any calendar year exceeds the aggregate amount allocated under paragraph (2) for such year, such limitation for the succeeding calendar year shall be increased by the amount of such excess. No amount may be carried under the preceding sentence to any calendar year after [2]*2018.*

* * * * * * * * * * * *

[For Analysis, see ¶ 1401.]

[Endnote Code Sec. 45D]
    Code Sec. 45D(f)(1)(G) and Code Sec. 45D(f)(3) were amended by Sec. 305(a) and (b) of the American Taxpayer Relief Act of 2012, P.L. 112-240, 1/2/2013, as detailed below:
    1. Sec. 305(a) substituted "2010, 2011, 2012, and 2013" for "2010 and 2011" in subpara. (f)(1)(G)
    2. Sec. 305(b) substituted "2018" for "2016" in para. (f)(3)
Effective Date (Sec. 305(c), P.L. 112-240, 1/2/2013) effective for calendar yrs. begin. after 12/31/2011.

[¶ 3029]   *Code Sec.[1] 45F.   Employer-provided child care credit.*

   (a)   *In general.* *For purposes of section 38, the employer-provided child care credit determined under this section for the taxable year is an amount equal to the sum of—*

   (1) 25 percent of the qualified child care expenditures, and

   (2) 10 percent of the qualified child care resource and referral expenditures,
   of the taxpayer for such taxable year.

(b) **Dollar limitation.** *The credit allowable under subsection (a) for any taxable year shall not exceed $150,000.*

(c) **Definitions.** *For purposes of this section—*

   (1) **Qualified child care expenditure.**

     (A) In general. The term "qualified child care expenditure" means any amount paid or incurred—

       (i) to acquire, construct, rehabilitate, or expand property—

        (I) which is to be used as part of a qualified child care facility of the taxpayer,

        (II) with respect to which a deduction for depreciation (or amortization in lieu of depreciation) is allowable, and

        (III) which does not constitute part of the principal residence (within the meaning of section 121) of the taxpayer or any employee of the taxpayer,

       (ii) for the operating costs of a qualified child care facility of the taxpayer, including costs related to the training of employees, to scholarship programs, and to the providing of increased compensation to employees with higher levels of child care training, or

       (iii) under a contract with a qualified child care facility to provide child care services to employees of the taxpayer.

     (B) Fair market value. The term "qualified child care expenditures" shall not include expenses in excess of the fair market value of such care.

   (2) **Qualified child care facility.**

     (A) In general. The term "qualified child care facility" means a facility—

       (i) the principal use of which is to provide child care assistance, and

       (ii) which meets the requirements of all applicable laws and regulations of the State or local government in which it is located, including the licensing of the facility as a child care facility.

     Clause (i) shall not apply to a facility which is the principal residence (within the meaning of section 121) of the operator of the facility.

     (B) Special rules with respect to a taxpayer. A facility shall not be treated as a qualified child care facility with respect to a taxpayer unless—

       (i) enrollment in the facility is open to employees of the taxpayer during the taxable year,

       (ii) if the facility is the principal trade or business of the taxpayer, at least 30 percent of the enrollees of such facility are dependents of employees of the taxpayer, and

       (iii) the use of such facility (or the eligibility to use such facility) does not discriminate in favor of employees of the taxpayer who are highly compensated employees (within the meaning of section 414(q)).

   (3) **Qualified child care resource and referral expenditure.**

     (A) In general. The term "qualified child care resource and referral expenditure" means any amount paid or incurred under a contract to provide child care resource and referral services to an employee of the taxpayer.

     (B) Nondiscrimination. The services shall not be treated as qualified unless the provision of such services (or the eligibility to use such services) does not discriminate in favor of employees of the taxpayer who are highly compensated employees (within the meaning of section 414(q)).

(d) **Recapture of acquisition and construction credit.**

   (1) **In general.** *If, as of the close of any taxable year, there is a recapture event with respect to any qualified child care facility of the taxpayer, then the tax of the taxpayer under this chapter for such taxable year shall be increased by an amount equal to the product of—*

     (A) the applicable recapture percentage, and

     (B) the aggregate decrease in the credits allowed under section 38 for all prior taxable years which would have resulted if the qualified child care expenditures of the taxpayer described in subsection (c)(1)(A) with respect to such facility had been zero.

563

(2) Applicable recapture percentage.

(A) *In general.* For purposes of this subsection, the applicable recapture percentage shall be determined from the following table:

If the recapture event occurs in:	The applicable recapture percentage is:
Years 1-3	100
Year 4	85
Year 5	70
Year 6	55
Year 7	40
Year 8	25
Years 9 and 10	10
Years 11 and thereafter	0.

(B) *Years.* For purposes of subparagraph (A), year 1 shall begin on the first day of the taxable year in which the qualified child care facility is placed in service by the taxpayer.

(3) Recapture event defined. For purposes of this subsection, the term "recapture event" means—

(A) *Cessation of operation.* The cessation of the operation of the facility as a qualified child care facility.

(B) *Change in ownership.*

(i) *In general.* Except as provided in clause (ii), the disposition of a taxpayer's interest in a qualified child care facility with respect to which the credit described in subsection (a) was allowable.

(ii) *Agreement to assume recapture liability.* Clause (i) shall not apply if the person acquiring such interest in the facility agrees in writing to assume the recapture liability of the person disposing of such interest in effect immediately before such disposition. In the event of such an assumption, the person acquiring the interest in the facility shall be treated as the taxpayer for purposes of assessing any recapture liability (computed as if there had been no change in ownership).

(4) Special rules.

(A) *Tax benefit rule.* The tax for the taxable year shall be increased under paragraph (1) only with respect to credits allowed by reason of this section which were used to reduce tax liability. In the case of credits not so used to reduce tax liability, the carryforwards and carrybacks under section 39 shall be appropriately adjusted.

(B) *No credits against tax.* Any increase in tax under this subsection shall not be treated as a tax imposed by this chapter for purposes of determining the amount of any credit under [1]this chapter or for purposes of section 55.

(C) *No recapture by reason of casualty loss.* The increase in tax under this subsection shall not apply to a cessation of operation of the facility as a qualified child care facility by reason of a casualty loss to the extent such loss is restored by reconstruction or replacement within a reasonable period established by the Secretary.

(e) Special rules. For purposes of this section—

(1) Aggregation rules. All persons which are treated as a single employer under subsections (a) and (b) of section 52 shall be treated as a single taxpayer.

(2) Pass-thru in the case of estates and trusts. Under regulations prescribed by the Secretary, rules similar to the rules of subsection (d) of section 52 shall apply.

(3) Allocation in the case of partnerships. In the case of partnerships, the credit shall be allocated among partners under regulations prescribed by the Secretary.

(f) No double benefit.

(1) Reduction in basis. For purposes of this subtitle—

(A) *In general.* If a credit is determined under this section with respect to any property by reason of expenditures described in subsection (c)(1)(A), the basis of such property shall be reduced by the amount of the credit so determined.

(B) Certain dispositions. If, during any taxable year, there is a recapture amount determined with respect to any property the basis of which was reduced under subparagraph (A), the basis of such property (immediately before the event resulting in such recapture) shall be increased by an amount equal to such recapture amount. For purposes of the preceding sentence, the term "recapture amount" means any increase in tax (or adjustment in carrybacks or carryovers) determined under subsection (d).

(2) **Other deductions and credits.** No deduction or credit shall be allowed under any other provision of this chapter with respect to the amount of the credit determined under this section.

[For Analysis, see ¶ 903.]

[Endnote Code Sec. 45F]
  Sec. 101(a)(1) of the American Taxpayer Relief Act of 2012, P.L. 112-240, 1/2/2013, deleted Title IX [Sec. 901] of the Economic Growth and Tax Relief Reconciliation Act of 2001, P.L. 107-16, the effect of which is to eliminate the sunset of all provisions enacted by P.L. 107-16. Following are the amendments made to Code Sec. 45F by P.L. 107-16.
Effective Date (Sec. 101(a)(3), P.L. 112-240, 1/2/2013) effective for taxable, plan, or limitation years beginning after 12/31/2012, and estates of decedents dying, gifts made, or generation skipping transfers after 12/31/2012.

  Code Sec. 45F was added by Sec. 205(a) of the Economic Growth and Tax Relief Reconciliation Act of 2001, P.L. 107-16, 6/7/2001.
  1. Sec. 205(a), P.L. 107-16 added Code Sec. 45F
Effective Date (Sec. 205(c), P.L. 107-16, 6/7/2001) effective for tax. yrs. begin. after 12/31/2001.

[¶ 3030]   Code Sec. 45G.   Railroad track maintenance credit.

* * * * * * * * * * * *

(f) **Application of section.** This section shall apply to qualified railroad track maintenance expenditures paid or incurred during taxable years beginning after December 31, 2004, and before [1]*January 1, 2014.*

[For Analysis, see ¶ 908.]

[Endnote Code Sec. 45G]
  Code Sec. 45G(f) was amended by Sec. 306(a) of the American Taxpayer Relief Act of 2012, 1/2/2013, as detailed below:
  1. Sec. 306(a) substituted "January 1, 2014" for "January 1, 2012" in subsec. (f)
Effective Date (Sec. 306(b), P.L. 112-240, 1/2/2013) effective for expenditures paid or incurred in tax. yrs. begin. after 12/31/2011.

[¶ 3031]   Code Sec. 45L.   New energy efficient home credit.

* * * * * * * * * * * *

(c) **Energy saving requirements.** A dwelling unit meets the energy saving requirements of this subsection if such unit is—

(1) certified—

(A) to have a level of annual heating and cooling energy consumption which is at least 50 percent below the annual level of heating and cooling energy consumption of a comparable dwelling unit—

(i) which is constructed in accordance with the standards of chapter 4 of the [1]*2006 International Energy Conservation Code, as such Code (including supplements) is in effect on January 1, 2006,* and

(ii) for which the heating and cooling equipment efficiencies correspond to the minimum allowed under the regulations established by the Department of Energy pursuant to the National Appliance Energy Conservation Act of 1987 and in effect at the time of completion of construction, and

(B) to have building envelope component improvements account for at least 1/5 of such 50 percent,

(2) a manufactured home which conforms to Federal Manufactured Home Construction and Safety Standards (part 3280 of title 24, Code of Federal Regulations) and which meets the requirements of paragraph (1), or

(3) a manufactured home which conforms to Federal Manufactured Home Construction and Safety Standards (part 3280 of title 24, Code of Federal Regulations) and which—

(A) meets the requirements of paragraph (1) applied by substituting "30 percent" for "50 percent" both places it appears therein and by substituting "1/3" for "1/5" in subparagraph (B) thereof, or

(B) meets the requirements established by the Administrator of the Environmental Protection Agency under the Energy Star Labeled Homes program.

* * * * * * * * * * * *

(g) Termination. This section shall not apply to any qualified new energy efficient home acquired after [2]*December 31, 2013.*

[For Analysis, see ¶ 1002 and ¶ 1003.]

[Endnote Code Sec. 45L]

Code Sec. 45L(c)(1)(A)(i) and Code Sec. 45L(g) were amended by Secs. 408(a)-(b) of the American Taxpayer Relief Act of 2012, P.L. 112-240, 1/2/2013, as detailed below:

1. Sec. 408(b) substituted "2006 International Energy Conservation Code, as such Code (including supplements) is in effect on January 1, 2006" for "2003 International Energy Conservation Code, as such Code (including supplements) is in effect on the date of the enactment of this section" in clause (c)(1)(A)(i)

2. Sec. 408(a) substituted "December 31, 2013" for "December 31, 2011" in subsec. (g)

Effective Date (Sec. 408(c), P.L. 112-240, 1/2/2013) effective for homes acquired after 12/31/2011.

[¶ 3032]   Code Sec. 45M.   Energy efficient appliance credit.

* * * * * * * * * * * *

(b) Applicable amount. For purposes of subsection (a)—

(1) Dishwashers. The applicable amount is—

(A) $45 in the case of a dishwasher which is manufactured in calendar year 2008 or 2009 and which uses no more than 324 kilowatt hours per year and 5.8 gallons per cycle,

(B) $75 in the case of a dishwasher which is manufactured in calendar year 2008, 2009, or 2010 and which uses no more than 307 kilowatt hours per year and 5.0 gallons per cycle (5.5 gallons per cycle for dishwashers designed for greater than 12 place settings),

(C) $25 in the case of a dishwasher which is manufactured in calendar year 2011 and which uses no more than 307 kilowatt hours per year and 5.0 gallons per cycle (5.5 gallons per cycle for dishwashers designed for greater than 12 place settings),

(D) $50 in the case of a dishwasher which is manufactured in calendar year [1]*2011, 2012, or 2013* and which uses no more than 295 kilowatt hours per year and 4.25 gallons per cycle (4.75 gallons per cycle for dishwashers designed for greater than 12 place settings), and

(E) $75 in the case of a dishwasher which is manufactured in calendar year [2]*2011, 2012, or 2013* and which uses no more than 280 kilowatt hours per year and 4 gallons per cycle (4.5 gallons per cycle for dishwashers designed for greater than 12 place settings).

(2) Clothes washers. The applicable amount is—

(A) $75 in the case of a residential top-loading clothes washer manufactured in calendar year 2008 which meets or exceeds a 1.72 modified energy factor and does not exceed a 8.0 water consumption factor,

(B) $125 in the case of a residential top-loading clothes washer manufactured in calendar year 2008 or 2009 which meets or exceeds a 1.8 modified energy factor and does not exceed a 7.5 water consumption factor,

(C) $150 in the case of a residential or commercial clothes washer manufactured in calendar year 2008, 2009, or 2010 which meets or exceeds 2.0 modified energy factor and does not exceed a 6.0 water consumption factor,

(D) $250 in the case of a residential or commercial clothes washer manufactured in calendar year 2008, 2009, or 2010 which meets or exceeds 2.2 modified energy factor and does not exceed a 4.5 water consumption factor,

(E) $175 in the case of a top-loading clothes washer manufactured in calendar year 2011 which meets or exceeds a 2.2 modified energy factor and does not exceed a 4.5 water consumption factor, and

(F) $225 in the case of a clothes washer manufactured in calendar year [3]*2011, 2012, or 2013*—

(i) which is a top-loading clothes washer and which meets or exceeds a 2.4 modified energy factor and does not exceed a 4.2 water consumption factor, or

(ii) which is a front-loading clothes washer and which meets or exceeds a 2.8 modified energy factor and does not exceed a 3.5 water consumption factor.

(3) Refrigerators. The applicable amount is—

(A) $50 in the case of a refrigerator which is manufactured in calendar year 2008, and consumes at least 20 percent but not more than 22.9 percent less kilowatt hours per year than the 2001 energy conservation standards,

(B) $75 in the case of a refrigerator which is manufactured in calendar year 2008 or 2009, and consumes at least 23 percent but no more than 24.9 percent less kilowatt hours per year than the 2001 energy conservation standards,

(C) $100 in the case of a refrigerator which is manufactured in calendar year 2008, 2009, or 2010, and consumes at least 25 percent but not more than 29.9 percent less kilowatt hours per year than the 2001 energy conservation standards,

(D) $200 in the case of a refrigerator manufactured in calendar year 2008, 2009, or 2010 and which consumes at least 30 percent less energy than the 2001 energy conservation standards,

(E) $150 in the case of a refrigerator manufactured in calendar year [4]*2011, 2012, or 2013* which consumes at least 30 percent less energy than the 2001 energy conservation standards, and

(F) $200 in the case of a refrigerator manufactured in calendar year [5]*2011, 2012, or 2013* which consumes at least 35 percent less energy than the 2001 energy conservation standards.

* * * * * * * * * * * * *

[For Analysis, see ¶ 1001.]

[Endnote Code Sec. 45M]
   Code Sec. 45M(b)(1)(D), Code Sec. 45M(b)(1)(E), Code Sec. 45M(b)(2)(F), Code Sec. 45M(b)(3)(E), Code Sec. 45M(b)(3)(F) were amended by Sec. 409(a) of the American Taxpayer Relief Act of 2012, P.L. 112-240, 1/2/2013, as detailed below:
   1. Sec. 409(a) substituted "2011, 2012, or 2013" for "2011" in subpara. (b)(1)(D).
   2. Sec. 409(a) substituted "2011, 2012, or 2013" for "2011" in subpara. (b)(1)(E).
   3. Sec. 409(a) substituted "2011, 2012, or 2013" for "2011" in subpara. (b)(2)(F).
   4. Sec. 409(a) substituted "2011, 2012, or 2013" for "2011" in subpara. (b)(3)(E).
   5. Sec. 409(a) substituted "2011, 2012, or 2013" for "2011" in subpara. (b)(3)(F).
Effective Date (Sec. 409(c), P.L. 112-240, 1/2/2013) effective for appliances produced after 12/31/2011.

[¶ 3033]   Code Sec. 45N.   Mine rescue team training credit.

* * * * * * * * * * * *

(e) **Termination.** This section shall not apply to taxable years beginning after [1]*December 31, 2013.*

[For Analysis, see ¶ 905.]

[Endnote Code Sec. 45N]

Code Sec. 45N(e) was amended by Sec. 307(a) of the American Taxpayer Relief Act of 2012, P.L. 112-240, 1/2/2013, as detailed below:

1. Sec. 307(a) substituted "December 31, 2013" for "December 31, 2011" in subpara. (e)

Effective Date (Sec. 307(b), P.L. 112-240, 1/2/2013) effective for tax. yrs. begin. after 12/31/2011.

[¶ 3034]   Code Sec. 45P.   Employer wage credit for employees who are active duty members of the uniformed services.

* * * * * * * * * * * *

(f) **Termination.** This section shall not apply to any payments made after [1]*December 31, 2013.*

[For Analysis, see ¶ 904.]

[Endnote Code Sec. 45P]

Code Sec. 45P(f) was amended by Sec. 308(a) of the American Taxpayer Relief Act of 2012, P.L. 112-240, 1/2/2013, as detailed below:

1. Sec. 308(a) substituted "December 31, 2013" for "December 31, 2011" in subsec. (f)

Effective Date (Sec. 308(b), P.L. 112-240, 1/2/2013) effective for payments made after 12/31/2011.

[¶ 3035]   Code Sec. 48.   Energy credit.

(a) **Energy credit.**

(1) **In general.** For purposes of section 46, except as provided in paragraphs (1)(B), and (2)(B), (3)(B), and (4)(B) of subsection (c), the energy credit for any taxable year is the energy percentage of the basis of each energy property placed in service during such taxable year.

(2) **Energy percentage.**

(A) In general. The energy percentage is—

(i) 30 percent in the case of—

(I) qualified fuel cell property,

(II) energy property described in paragraph (3)(A)(i) but only with respect to periods ending before January 1, 2017,

(III) energy property described in paragraph (3)(A)(ii), and

(IV) qualified small wind energy property, and

(ii) in the case of any energy property to which clause (i) does not apply, 10 percent.

(B) Coordination with rehabilitation credit. The energy percentage shall not apply to that portion of the basis of any property which is attributable to qualified rehabilitation expenditures.

(3) **Energy property.** For purposes of this subpart, the term "energy property" means any property—

(A) which is—

(i) equipment which uses solar energy to generate electricity, to heat or cool (or provide hot water for use in) a structure, or to provide solar process heat, excepting property used to generate energy for the purposes of heating a swimming pool,

(ii) equipment which uses solar energy to illuminate the inside of a structure using fiber-optic distributed sunlight but only with respect to periods ending before January 1, 2017,

(iii) equipment used to produce, distribute, or use energy derived from a geothermal deposit (within the meaning of section 613(e)(2)), but only, in the case of electricity generated by geothermal power, up to (but not including) the electrical transmission stage,

(iv) qualified fuel cell property or qualified microturbine property,

(v) combined heat and power system property,

(vi) qualified small wind energy property, or

(vii) equipment which uses the ground or ground water as a thermal energy source to heat a structure or as a thermal energy sink to cool a structure, but only with respect to periods ending before January 1, 2017,

(B)

(i) the construction, reconstruction, or erection of which is completed by the taxpayer, or

(ii) which is acquired by the taxpayer if the original use of such property commences with the taxpayer,

(C) with respect to which depreciation (or amortization in lieu of depreciation) is allowable, and

(D) which meets the performance and quality standards (if any) which—

(i) have been prescribed by the Secretary by regulations (after consultation with the Secretary of Energy), and

(ii) are in effect at the time of the acquisition of the property.

Such term shall not include any property which is part of a facility the production from which is allowed as a credit under section 45 for the taxable year or any prior taxable year.

(4) Special rule for property financed by subsidized energy financing or industrial development bonds.

(A) Reduction of basis. For purposes of applying the energy percentage to any property, if such property is financed in whole or in part by—

(i) subsidized energy financing, or

(ii) the proceeds of a private activity bond (within the meaning of section 141) the interest on which is exempt from tax under section 103,

the amount taken into account as the basis of such property shall not exceed the amount which (but for this subparagraph) would be so taken into account multiplied by the fraction determined under subparagraph (B).

(B) Determination of fraction. For purposes of subparagraph (A), the fraction determined under this subparagraph is 1 reduced by a fraction—

(i) the numerator of which is that portion of the basis of the property which is allocable to such financing or proceeds, and

(ii) the denominator of which is the basis of the property.

(C) Subsidized energy financing. For purposes of subparagraph (A), the term "subsidized energy financing" means financing provided under a Federal, State, or local program a principal purpose of which is to provide subsidized financing for projects designed to conserve or produce energy.

(D) Termination. This paragraph shall not apply to periods after December 31, 2008, under rules similar to the rules of section 48(m) (as in effect on the day before the date of the enactment of the Revenue Reconciliation Act of 1990).

(5) Election to treat qualified facilities as energy property.

(A) In general. In the case of any qualified property which is part of a qualified investment credit facility—

(i) such property shall be treated as energy property for purposes of this section, and

(ii) the energy percentage with respect to such property shall be 30 percent.

(B) Denial of production credit. No credit shall be allowed under section 45 for any taxable year with respect to any qualified investment credit facility.

[1]*(C) Qualified investment credit facility. For purposes of this paragraph, the term "qualified investment credit facility" means any facility—*

(i) which is a qualified facility (within the meaning of section 45) described in paragraph (1), (2), (3), (4), (6), (7), (9), or (11) of section 45(d),

(ii) which is placed in service after 2008 and the construction of which begins before January 1, 2014, and

(iii) with respect to which—

(I) no credit has been allowed under section 45, and

(II) the taxpayer makes an irrevocable election to have this paragraph apply.

(D) Qualified property. For purposes of this paragraph, the term "qualified property" means property—

(i) which is—

(I) tangible personal property, or

(II) other tangible property (not including a building or its structural components), but only if such property is used as an integral part of the qualified investment credit facility, [2]

(ii) with respect to which depreciation (or amortization in lieu of depreciation) is allowable[3],

[4]*(iii) which is constructed, reconstructed, erected, or acquired by the taxpayer, and*

(iv) the original use of which commences with the taxpayer.

* * * * * * * * * * * *

[For Analysis, see ¶ 1012.]

[Endnote Code Sec. 48]

Code Sec. 48(a)(5)(C) was amended by Sec. 407(b) of the American Taxpayer Relief Act of 2012, P.L. 112-240, 1/2/2013, as detailed below:

1. Sec. 407(b) amended subpara. (a)(5)(C)

Prior to amendment, subpara. (a)(5)(C) read as follows:

"(C) Qualified investment credit facility. For purposes of this paragraph, the term 'qualified investment credit facility' means any of the following facilities if no credit has been allowed under section 45 with respect to such facility and the taxpayer makes an irrevocable election to have this paragraph apply to such facility:

"(i) Wind facilities. Any qualified facility (within the meaning of section 45) described in paragraph (1) of section 45(d) if such facility is placed in service in 2009, 2010, 2011, or 2012.

"(ii) Other facilities. Any qualified facility (within the meaning of section 45) described in paragraph (2), (3), (4), (6), (7), (9), or (11) of section 45(d) if such facility is placed in service in 2009, 2010, 2011, 2012, or 2013."

Effective Date (Sec. 407(d)(1), P.L. 112-240, 1/2/2013) effective 1/2/2013.

Code Sec. 48(a)(5)(D)(i)(II) was amended by Sec. 407(c)(1), P.L. 112-240, 1/2/2013, as detailed below:

2. Sec. 407(c)(1)(A) deleted "and" at the end of subclause (a)(5)(D)(i)(II)

3. Sec. 407(c)(1)(B) substituted a comma for the period at the end of clause (a)(5)(D)(ii)

4. Sec. 407(c)(1)(C) added clauses (a)(5)(D)(iii)-(iv)

Effective Date (Sec. 407(d)(3), P.L. 112-240, 1/2/2013) effective for facilities placed in service after 12/31/2008, as if included in the enactment of the provisions of the American Recovery and Reinvestment Act of 2009 [P.L. 111-5, Sec. 1102(a)].

[¶ 3036]   Code Sec. 51.   Amount of credit.

* * * * * * * * * * * *

(b) Qualified wages defined. For purposes of this subpart—

* * * * * * * * * * * *

(3) Limitation on wages per year taken into account. The amount of the qualified first-year wages which may be taken into account with respect to any individual shall not exceed $6,000 per year [1]*($12,000 per year in the case of any individual who is a qualified veteran by reason of subsection (d)(3)(A)(ii)(I), $14,000 per year in the case of any individual who is a qualified veteran by reason of subsection (d)(3)(A)(iv), and $24,000 per* *year in the case of any individual who is a qualified veteran by reason of subsection (d)(3)(A)(ii)(II)).*

* * * * * * * * * * * *

(c) Wages defined. For purposes of this subpart—

(1) In general. Except as otherwise provided in this subsection and subsection (h)(2), the term "wages" has the meaning given to such term by subsection (b) of section 3306 (determined without regard to any dollar limitation contained in such section).

(2) On-the-job training and work supplementation payments.

(A) Exclusion for employers receiving on-the-job training payments. The term "wages" shall not include any amounts paid or incurred by an employer for any period to any individual for whom the employer receives federally funded payments for on-the-job training of such individual for such period.

(B) Reduction for work supplementation payments to employers. The amount of wages which would (but for this subparagraph) be qualified wages under this section for an employer with respect to an individual for a taxable year shall be reduced by an amount equal to the amount of the payments made to such employer (however utilized by such employer) with respect to such individual for such taxable year under a program established under section 482(e) of the Social Security Act.

(3) Payments for services during labor disputes. If—

(A) the principal place of employment of an individual with the employer is at a plant or facility, and

(B) there is a strike or lockout involving employees at such plant or facility,

the term "wages" shall not include any amount paid or incurred by the employer to such individual for services which are the same as, or substantially similar to, those services performed by employees participating in, or affected by, the strike or lockout during the period of such strike or lockout.

(4) Termination. The term "wages" shall not include any amount paid or incurred to an individual who begins work for the employer—

(A) after December 31, 1994, and before October 1, 1996, or [2]

[2]*(B) after December 31, 2013*

(5) Coordination with payroll tax forgiveness. The term "wages" shall not include any amount paid or incurred to a qualified individual (as defined in section 3111(d)(3)) during the 1-year period beginning on the hiring date of such individual by a qualified employer (as defined in section 3111(d)) unless such qualified employer makes an election not to have section 3111(d) apply.

* * * * * * * * * * * *

(d) Members of targeted groups. For purposes of this subpart—

* * * * * * * * * * * *

(3) Qualified veteran.

(A) In general. The term "qualified veteran" means any veteran who is certified by the designated local agency as—

(i) being a member of a family receiving assistance under a supplemental nutrition assistance program under the Food and Nutrition Act of 2008 for at least a 3-month period ending during the 12-month period ending on the hiring date,[3]

(ii) entitled to compensation for a service-connected disability, and—

(I) having a hiring date which is not more that 1 year after having been discharged or released from active duty in the Armed Forces of the United States, or

(II) having aggregate periods of unemployment during the 1-year period ending on the hiring date which equal or exceed 6 months[4]

[5]*(iii) having aggregate periods of unemployment during the 1-year period ending on the hiring date which equal or exceed 4 weeks (but less than 6 months), or*

(iv) having aggregate periods of unemployment during the 1-year period ending on the hiring date which equal or exceed 6 months.

* * * * * * * * * * * *

(13) Special rules for certifications.

(A) In general. An individual shall not be treated as a member of a targeted group unless—

(i) on or before the day on which such individual begins work for the employer, the employer has received a certification from a designated local agency that such individual is a member of a targeted group, or

(ii) (I) on or before the day the individual is offered employment with the employer, a pre-screening notice is completed by the employer with respect to such individual, and

(II) not later than the 28th day after the individual begins work for the employer, the employer submits such notice, signed by the employer and the individual under penalties of perjury, to the designated local agency as part of a written request for such a certification from such agency.

For purposes of this paragraph, the term "pre-screening notice" means a document (in such form as the Secretary shall prescribe) which contains information provided by the individual on the basis of which the employer believes that the individual is a member of a targeted group.

(B) Incorrect certifications. If—

(i) an individual has been certified by a designated local agency as a member of a targeted group, and

(ii) such certification is incorrect because it was based on false information provided by such individual,

the certification shall be revoked and wages paid by the employer after the date on which notice of revocation is received by the employer shall not be treated as qualified wages.

(C) Explanation of denial of request. If a designated local agency denies a request for certification of membership in a targeted group, such agency shall provide to the person making such request a written explanation of the reasons for such denial.

[6]*(D) Credit for unemployed veterans.*

(i) In general. Notwithstanding subparagraph (A), for purposes of paragraph (3)(A)—

(I) a veteran will be treated as certified by the designated local agency as having aggregate periods of unemployment meeting the requirements of clause (ii)(II) or (iv) of such paragraph (whichever is applicable) if such veteran is certified by such agency as being in receipt of unemployment compensation under State or Federal law for not less than 6 months during the 1-year period ending on the hiring date, and

(II) a veteran will be treated as certified by the designated local agency as having aggregate periods of unemployment meeting the requirements of clause (iii) of such paragraph if such veteran is certified by such agency as being in receipt of unemployment compensation under State or Federal law for not less than 4 weeks (but less than 6 months) during the 1-year period ending on the hiring date.

(ii) Regulatory authority. The Secretary may provide alternative methods for certification of a veteran as a qualified veteran described in clause (ii)(II), (iii), or (iv) of paragraph (3)(A), at the Secretary's discretion.

[For Analysis, see ¶ 902 and ¶ 1910.]

[Endnote Code Sec. 51]

Code Sec. 51(b)(3) was amended by Sec. 261(a) of an Act To amend the Internal Revenue Code of 1986 to repeal the imposition of 3 percent withholding on certain payments made to vendors by government entities, to modify the calculation of modified adjusted gross income for purposes of determining eligibility for certain healthcare-related programs, and for other purposes, P.L. 112-56, 11/21/2011, as detailed below:

1. Sec. 261(a) substituted "($12,000 per year in the case of any individual who is a qualified veteran by reason of subsection (d)(3)(A)(ii)(I), $14,000 per year in the case of any individual who is a qualified veteran by reason of subsection (d)(3)(A)(iv), and $24,000 per year in the case of any individual who is a qualified veteran by reason of subsec-

tion (d)(3)(A)(ii)(II))" for "($12,000 per year in the case of any individual who is a qualified veteran by reason of subsection (d)(3)(A)(ii))" in para. (b)(3)
Effective Date (Sec. 261(g), P.L. 112-56, 11/21/2011) effective for individuals who begin work for the employer after 11/21/2011.

Code Sec. 51(c)(4)(B) was amended by Sec. 309(a) of the American Taxpayer Relief Act of 2012, P.L. 112-240, 1/2/2013, as detailed below:
2. Sec. 309(a) substituted 'after December 31, 2013' for 'after' and all that follows in subpara. (c)(4)(B)
Prior to amendment, subpara. (c)(4)(B) read as follows:
"(i) December 31, 2012, in the case of a qualified veteran, and
(ii) December 31, 2011, in the case of any other individual."
Effective Date (Sec. 309(a), P.L. 112-240, 1/2/2013) effective for individuals who begin work for the employer after 12/31/2011.

Code Sec. 51(c)(4)(B), Code Sec. 51(d)(3)(A)(i), Code Sec. 51(d)(3)(A)(ii)(II), Code Sec. 51(d)(3)(A)(iii)-Code Sec. 51(d)(3)(A)(iv) and Code Sec. 51(d)(13)(D) were amended by Sec. 261(b)-(d), P.L. 112-56, 11/21/2011, as detailed below:
Sec. 261(d) amended subpara. (c)(4)(B). Subpara. (c)(4)(B) was further amended by Sec. 309(a), P.L. 112-240, see above.
Prior to amendment by P.L. 112-56, Sec. 51(c)(4)(B) read as follows:
"(B) after December 31, 2011."
3. Sec. 261(b)(1) deleted "or" at the end of clause (d)(3)(A)(i)
4. Sec. 261(b)(2) deleted the period at the end of subclause (d)(3)(A)(ii)(II)
5. Sec. 261(b)(3) added clauses (d)(3)(A)(iii)-(iv)
6. Sec. 261(c) added subpara. (d)(13)(D)
Effective Date (Sec. 261(g), P.L. 112-56, 11/21/2011) effective for individuals who begin work for the employer after 11/21/2011.

[¶ 3037]　　Code Sec. 52.　　Special rules.

* * * * * * * * * * * *

(c)　Tax-exempt organizations.

　[1]*(1)　In general.* No credit shall be allowed under section 38 for any work opportunity credit determined under this subpart to any organization (other than a cooperative described in section 521) which is exempt from income tax under this chapter.

　[2]*(2)　Credit made available to qualified tax-exempt organizations employing qualified veterans. For credit against payroll taxes for employment of qualified veterans by qualified tax-exempt organizations, see section 3111(e).*

* * * * * * * * * * * *

[For Analysis, see ¶ 1910.]

[Endnote Code Sec. 52]
　Code Sec. 52(c)(1) and Code Sec. 52(c)(2) were amended by Sec. 261(e)(1)(A)-(B) of an Act To amend the Internal Revenue Code of 1986 to repeal the imposition of 3 percent withholding on certain payments made to vendors by government entities, to modify the calculation of modified adjusted gross income for purposes of determining eligibility for certain healthcare-related programs, and for other purposes, P.L. 112-56, 11/21/2011, as detailed below:
1. Sec. 261(e)(1)(A) added "(1) In general." before "No credit" in subsec. (c)
2. Sec. 261(e)(1)(B) added para. (c)(2)
Effective Date (Sec. 261(g), P.L. 112-56, 11/21/2011) effective for individuals who begin work for the employer after 11/21/2011.

[¶ 3038]　　Code Sec. 54E.　　Qualified zone academy bonds.

* * * * * * * * * * * *

(c)　Limitation on amount of bonds designated.

　(1)　National limitation. There is a national zone academy bond limitation for each calendar year. Such limitation is $400,000,000 for 2008, $1,400,000,000 for 2009 and 2010, and $400,000,000 for 2011 [1], *2012, and 2013* and, except as provided in paragraph (4), zero thereafter.

(2) Allocation of limitation. The national zone academy bond limitation for a calendar year shall be allocated by the Secretary among the States on the basis of their respective populations of individuals below the poverty line (as defined by the Office of Management and Budget). The limitation amount allocated to a State under the preceding sentence shall be allocated by the State education agency to qualified zone academies within such State.

(3) Designation subject to limitation amount. The maximum aggregate face amount of bonds issued during any calendar year which may be designated under subsection (a) with respect to any qualified zone academy shall not exceed the limitation amount allocated to such academy under paragraph (2) for such calendar year.

(4) Carryover of unused limitation.

(A) In general. If for any calendar year—

(i) the limitation amount for any State, exceeds

(ii) the amount of bonds issued during such year which are designated under subsection (a) with respect to qualified zone academies within such State,

the limitation amount for such State for the following calendar year shall be increased by the amount of such excess.

(B) Limitation on carryover. Any carryforward of a limitation amount may be carried only to the first 2 years following the unused limitation year. For purposes of the preceding sentence, a limitation amount shall be treated as used on a first-in first-out basis.

(C) Coordination with section 1397E. Any carryover determined under section 1397E(e)(4) (relating to carryover of unused limitation) with respect to any State to calendar year 2008 or 2009 shall be treated for purposes of this section as a carryover with respect to such State for such calendar year under subparagraph (A), and the limitation of subparagraph (B) shall apply to such carryover taking into account the calendar years to which such carryover relates.

* * * * * * * * * * * *

[For Analysis, see ¶ 1402.]

[Endnote Code Sec. 54E]

Code Sec. 54E(c)(1) was amended by Sec. 310(a) of the American Taxpayer Relief Act of 2012, P.L. 112-240, 1/2/2013, as detailed below:

1. Sec. 310(a) added ", 2012, and 2013" after "for 2011" in para. (c)(1)

Effective Date (Sec. 310(b), P.L. 112-240, 1/2/2013) effective for obligations issued after 12/31/2011.

[¶ 3039]   Code Sec. 55.   Alternative minimum tax imposed.

(a) General rule. There is hereby imposed (in addition to any other tax imposed by this subtitle) a tax equal to the excess (if any) of—

(1) the tentative minimum tax for the taxable year, over

(2) the regular tax for the taxable year.

(b) Tentative minimum tax. For purposes of this part—

(1) Amount of tentative tax.

(A) Noncorporate taxpayers.

(i) In general. In the case of a taxpayer other than a corporation, the tentative minimum tax for the taxable year is the sum of—

(I) 26 percent of so much of the taxable excess as does not exceed $175,000, plus

(II) 28 percent of so much of the taxable excess as exceeds $175,000.

The amount determined under the preceding sentence shall be reduced by the alternative minimum tax foreign tax credit for the taxable year.

(ii) Taxable excess. For purposes of this subsection, the term "taxable excess" means so much of the alternative minimum taxable income for the taxable year as exceeds the exemption amount.

(iii) Married individual filing separate return. In the case of a married individual filing a separate return, clause (i) shall be applied [1]*by substituting 50 percent of the dollar amount otherwise applicable under subclause (I) and subclause (II) thereof.*For purposes of the preceding sentence, marital status shall be determined under section 7703.

(B) Corporations. In the case of a corporation, the tentative minimum tax for the taxable year is—

(i) 20 percent of so much of the alternative minimum taxable income for the taxable year as exceeds the exemption amount, reduced by

(ii) the alternative minimum tax foreign tax credit for the taxable year.

(2) Alternative minimum taxable income. The term "alternative minimum taxable income" means the taxable income of the taxpayer for the taxable year—

(A) determined with the adjustments provided in section 56 and section 58, and

(B) increased by the amount of the items of tax preference described in section 57.

If a taxpayer is subject to the regular tax, such taxpayer shall be subject to the tax imposed by this section (and, if the regular tax is determined by reference to an amount other than taxable income, such amount shall be treated as the taxable income of such taxpayer for purposes of the preceding sentence).

(3) Maximum rate of tax on net capital gain of noncorporate taxpayers. The amount determined under the first sentence of paragraph (1)(A)(i) shall not exceed the sum of—

(A) the amount determined under such first sentence computed at the rates and in the same manner as if this paragraph had not been enacted on the taxable excess reduced by the lesser of—

(i) the net capital gain; or

(ii) the sum of—

(I) the adjusted net capital gain, plus

(II) the unrecaptured section 1250 gain, plus

(B) [2]*0 percent* of so much of the adjusted net capital gain (or, if less, taxable excess) as does not exceed an amount equal to the excess described in section 1(h)(1)(B), plus

[3]*(C) 15 percent of the lesser of—*

(i) so much of the adjusted net capital gain (or, if less, taxable excess) as exceeds the amount on which tax is determined under subparagraph (B), or

(ii) the excess described in section 1(h)(1)(C)(ii), plus

(D) 20 percent of the adjusted net capital gain (or, if less, taxable excess) in excess of the sum of the amounts on which tax is determined under subparagraphs (B) and (C), plus

[4]*(E)* 25 percent of the amount of taxable excess in excess of the sum of the amounts on which tax is determined under the preceding subparagraphs of this paragraph.

Terms used in this paragraph which are also used in section 1(h) shall have the respective meanings given such terms by section 1(h) but computed with the adjustments under this part.

(4) Maximum rate of tax on qualified timber gain of corporations. In the case of any taxable year to which section 1201(b) applies, the amount determined under clause (i) of subparagraph (B) shall not exceed the sum of—

(A) 20 percent of so much of the taxable excess (if any) as exceeds the qualified timber gain (or, if less, the net capital gain), plus

(B) 15 percent of the taxable excess in excess of the amount on which a tax is determined under subparagraph (A).

Any term used in this paragraph which is also used in section 1201 shall have the meaning given such term by such section, except to the extent such term is subject to adjustment under this part.

(c) Regular tax.

(1) In general. For purposes of this section, the term "regular tax" means the regular tax liability for the taxable year (as defined in section 26(b)) reduced by the foreign tax credit allowable under section 27(a), the section 936 credit allowable under section 27(b), and the Puerto Rico economic activity credit under section 30A. Such term shall not include any increase in tax under section 45(e)(11)(C), 49(b) or 50(a) or subsection (j) or (k) of section 42.

(2) Coordination with income averaging for farmers and fishermen. Solely for purposes of this section, section 1301 (relating to averaging of farm and fishing income) shall not apply in computing the regular tax liability.

(3) Cross references. For provisions providing that certain credits are not allowable against the tax imposed by this section, see [5]*30C(d)(2) and 38(c).*

(d) Exemption amount. For purposes of this section—

(1) Exemption amount for taxpayers other than corporations. In the case of a taxpayer other than a corporation, the term "exemption amount" means—

(A) [6]*$78,750* in the case of—

(i) a joint return, or

(ii) a surviving spouse,

(B) [7]*$50,600* in the case of an individual who—

(i) is not a married individual, and

(ii) is not a surviving spouse,

(C) 50 percent of the dollar amount applicable under [8]*subparagraph (A)* in the case of a married individual who files a separate return, and

(D) $22,500 in the case of an estate or trust.

For purposes of this paragraph, the term "surviving spouse" has the meaning given to such term by section 2(a), and marital status shall be determined under section 7703.

(2) Corporations. In the case of a corporation, the term "exemption amount" means $40,000.

(3) Phase-out of exemption amount. The exemption amount of any taxpayer shall be reduced (but not below zero) by an amount equal to 25 percent of the amount by which the alternative minimum taxable income of the taxpayer exceeds—

(A) $150,000 in the case of a taxpayer described in paragraph (1)(A)[9],

(B) $112,500 in the case of a taxpayer described in paragraph (1)(B), [10]

[11]*(C) 50 percent of the dollar amount applicable under subparagraph (A) in the case of a taxpayer described in subparagraph (C) or (D)of paragraph (1), and*

(D) $150,000 in the case of a taxpayer described in paragraph (2).

In the case of a taxpayer described in paragraph (1)(C), alternative minimum taxable income shall be increased by the lesser of (i) 25 percent of the excess of alternative minimum taxable income (determined without regard to this sentence) over the minimum amount of such income (as so determined) for which the exemption amount under paragraph (1)(C) is zero, or (ii) such exemption amount (determined without regard to this paragraph).

[12]*(4) Inflation adjustment.*

(A) In general. In the case of any taxable year beginning in a calendar year after 2012, the amounts described in subparagraph shall each be increased by an amount equal to—

(i) such dollar amount, multiplied by

(ii) the cost-of-living adjustment determined under section 1(f)(3) for the calendar year in which the taxable year begins, determined by substituting "calendar year 2011" for "calendar year 1992" in subparagraph (B) thereof.

(B) Amounts described. The amounts described in this subparagraph are—

(i) each of the dollar amounts contained in subsection (b)(1)(A)(i),

(ii) each of the dollar amounts contained in paragraph (1), and

(iii) each of the dollar amounts in subparagraphs (A) and (B) of paragraph (3).

(C) Rounding. Any increase determined under subparagraph (A) shall be rounded to the nearest multiple of $100.

* * * * * * * * * * * * *

[For Analysis, see ¶ 401 and ¶ 402.]

[Endnote Code Sec. 55]

Sec. 102(a) of the American Taxpayer Relief Act of 2012, P.L. 112-240, 1/2/2013, deleted Sec. 303, P.L. 108-27, the Jobs and Growth Tax Relief Reconciliation Act of 2003, the effect of which is to eliminate the sunset of all provisions enacted by Title III of P.L. 108-27. Following is a description of the amendments made to Code Sec. 55 by P.L. 108-27.

P.L. 108-27, Sec. 106(a)(1), substituted "$58,000 in the case of taxable years beginning in 2003 and 2004" for "$49,000 in the case of taxable years beginning in 2001, 2002, 2003, and 2004" in subpara. (d)(1)(A)

P.L. 108-27, Sec. 106(a)(2), substituted "$40,250 in the case of taxable years beginning in 2003 and 2004" for "$35,750 in the case of taxable years beginning in 2001, 2002, and 2004" in subpara. (d)(1)(B).

P.L. 108-27, Sec. 301(a)(1), substituted "5 percent (0 percent in the case of taxable years beginning after 2007)" for "10 percent" in subpara. (b)(3)(B)

P.L. 108-27, Sec. 301(a)(2)(B), substituted "15 percent" for "20 percent" in subpara (b)(3)(C)

P.L. 108-27, Sec. 301(b)(2), deleted "In the case of taxable years beginning after December 31, 2000, rules similar to the rules of section 1(h)(2) shall apply for purposes of subparagraphs (B) and (C)." before "Terms used in this paragraph" in para. (b)(3).

Sec. 101(a)(1) of the American Taxpayer Relief Act of 2012, P.L. 112-240, 1/2/2013, deleted Title IX [Sec. 901] of the Economic Growth and Tax Relief Reconciliation Act of 2001, P.L. 107-16, the effect of which is to eliminate the sunset of all provisions enacted by P.L. 107-16.

Effective Date (Sec. 101(a)(3), P.L. 112-240, 1/2/2013) effective for taxable, plan, or limitation years beginning after 12/31/2012, and estates of decedents dying, gifts made, or generation skipping transfers after 12/31/2012.

Following is a description of the amendments made to Code Sec. 55, by P.L. 107-16.

P.L. 107-16, Sec. 701(a)(1), substituted "$45,000 ($49,000 in the case of taxable years beginning in 2001, 2002, 2003, and 2004)" for "$45,000" in subpara. (d)(1)(A)

P.L. 107-16, Sec. 701(a)(2), substituted "$33,750 ($35,750 in the case of taxable years beginning in 2001, 2002, 2003, and 2004)" for "$33,750" in subpara. (d)(1)(B)

P.L. 107-16, Sec. 701(b)(1), deleted "and" at the end of subpara. (d)(1)(B), deleted subpara. (d)(1)(C), and added subparas. (d)(1)(C) and (D)

P.L. 107-16, Sec. 701(b)(2), substituted "subparagraph (C) or (D) of paragraph (1)" for "paragraph (1)(C)" in subpara. (d)(3)(C)

P.L. 107-16, Sec. 701(b)(3)(A), substituted "paragraph (1)(C)" for "paragraph (1)(C)(i)" in the last sentence of para. (d)(3)

P.L. 107-16, Sec. 701(b)(3)(B), substituted "the minimum amount of such income (as so determined) for which the exemption amount under paragraph (1)(C) is zero, or (ii) such exemption amount (determined without regard to this paragraph)" for "$165,000 or (ii) $22,500" in the last sentence of para. (d)(3)

Prior to deletion, subpara. (d)(1)(C) read as follows:

"(C) $22,500 in the case of—

"(i) a married individual who files a separate return, or

"(ii) an estate or trust."

Code Sec. 55(b)(1)(A)(iii) was amended by Sec. 104(b)(2)(A) of the American Taxpayer Relief Act of 2012, P.L. 112-240, 1/2/2013, as detailed below:

1. Sec. 104(b)(2)(A) substituted "by substituting 50 percent of the dollar amount otherwise applicable under subclause (I) and subclause (II) thereof." for "by substituting" and all that follows through "appears." in subpara. (b)(1)(A)(iii)

Effective Date (Sec. 104(d), P.L. 112-240, 1/2/2013) effective for tax. yrs. begin. after 12/31/2011.

Code Sec. 55(b)(3)(B), Code Sec. 55(b)(3)(C), Code Sec. 55(b)(3)(D) and Code Sec. 55(b)(3)(E) wer amended by Secs. 102(b)(2) and (c)(2), 1/2/2013, as detailed below:

2. Sec. 102(c)(2) substituted "0 percent"; for "5 percent (0 percent in the case of taxable years beginning after 2007)" in subpara. (b)(3)(B)

3. Sec. 102(c)(2) deleted subpara. (b)(3)(C) and added new subparas. (b)(3)(C) and (D)

Prior to deletion, subpara. (b)(3)(C) read as follows:

"(C) 15 percent of the adjusted net capital gain (or, if less, taxable excess) in excess of the amount on which tax is determined under subparagraph (B), plus"

4. Sec. 102(c)(2) redesignated subpara. (b)(3)(D) as (b)(3)(E)

Effective Date (Sec. 102(d)(1), P.L. 112-240, 1/2/2013) effective for tax. yrs. begin. after 12/31/2012.

Code Sec. 55(c)(3), Code Sec. 55(d)(1)(A), Code Sec. 55(d)(1)(B), Code Sec. 55(d)(1)(C), Code Sec. 55(d)(3)(A), Code Sec. 55(d)(3)(B), Code Sec. 55(d)(3)(C), Code Sec. 55(d)(1)(D) and Code Sec. 55(d)(4) were amended by Secs. 104(a)(1)(A)-(C), (b)(1), (b)(2)B)(i)-(iii) and (c)(2)(J), 1/2/2013, as detailed below:

5. Sec. 104(c)(2)(J) substituted "30C(d)(2)" for "26(a), 30C(d)(2)," in para. (c)(3)

6. Sec. 104(a)(1)(A) substituted "$78,750" for "$45,000" and all that follows through "2011" in subpara. (d)(1)(A)

7. Sec. 104(a)(1)(B) substituted "$50,600" for "$33,750" and all that follows through "2011" in subpara. (d)(1)(B)

8. Sec. 104(a)(1)(C) substituted "subparagraph (A)" for "paragraph (1)(A)" in subpara. (d)(1)(C)

9. Sec. 104(b)(2)(B)(i) deleted "or (2)" in subpara. (d)(3)(A)

10. Sec. 104(b)(2)(B)(ii) deleted "and" at the end of subpara. (d)(3)(B)

11. Sec. 104(b)(2)(B)(ii) deleted subpara. (d)(3)(C) and added new subparas. (d)(3)(C)-(D)

Prior to deletion, subpara. (d)(3)(C) read as follows:

"(C) $75,000 in the case of a taxpayer described in subparagraph (C) or (D) of paragraph (1)."

12. Sec. 104(b)(1) added para. (d)(4)

Effective Date (Sec. 104(d), P.L. 112-240, 1/2/2013) effective for tax. yrs. begin. after 12/31/2011.

[¶ 3040]   Code Sec. 57.   Items of tax preference.

(a) **General rule.** For purposes of this part, the items of tax preference determined under this section are—

(1) **Depletion.** With respect to each property (as defined in section 614), the excess of the deduction for depletion allowable under section 611 for the taxable year over the adjusted basis of the property at the end of the taxable year (determined without regard to the depletion deduction for the taxable year). Effective with respect to taxable years beginning after December 31, 1992, this paragraph shall not apply to any deduction for depletion computed in accordance with section 613A(c).

(2) **Intangible drilling costs.**

(A) In general. With respect to all oil, gas, and geothermal properties of the taxpayer, the amount (if any) by which the amount of the excess intangible drilling costs arising in the taxable year is greater than 65 percent of the net income of the taxpayer from oil, gas, and geothermal properties for the taxable year.

(B) Excess intangible drilling costs. For purposes of subparagraph (A), the amount of the excess intangible drilling costs arising in the taxable year is the excess of—

(i) the intangible drilling and development costs paid or incurred in connection with oil, gas, and geothermal wells (other than costs incurred in drilling a nonproductive well) allowable under section 263(c) or 291(b) for the taxable year, over

(ii) the amount which would have been allowable for the taxable year if such costs had been capitalized and straight line recovery of intangibles (as defined in subsection (b)) had been used with respect to such costs.

(C) Net income from oil, gas, and geothermal properties. For purposes of subparagraph (A), the amount of the net income of the taxpayer from oil, gas, and geothermal properties for the taxable year is the excess of—

(i) the aggregate amount of gross income (within the meaning of section 613(a)) from all oil, gas, and geothermal properties of the taxpayer received or accrued by the taxpayer during the taxable year, over

(ii) the amount of any deductions allocable to such properties reduced by the excess described in subparagraph (B) for such taxable year.

(D) Paragraph applied separately with respect to geothermal properties and oil and gas properties. This paragraph shall be applied separately with respect to—

(i) all oil and gas properties which are not described in clause (ii), and

(ii) all properties which are geothermal deposits (as defined in section 613(e)(2)).

(E) Exception for independent producers. In the case of any oil or gas well—

(i) In general. In the case of any taxable year beginning after December 31, 1992, this paragraph shall not apply to any taxpayer which is not an integrated oil company (as defined in section 291(b)(4)).

(ii) Limitation on benefit. The reduction in alternative minimum taxable income by reason of clause (i) for any taxable year shall not exceed 40 percent (30 percent in case of taxable years beginning in 1993) of the alternative minimum taxable income for such year determined without regard to clause (i) and the alternative tax net operating loss deduction under section 56(a)(4).

(3) **Repealed.**

(4) **Repealed.**

(5) **Tax-exempt interest.**

(A) In general. Interest on specified private activity bonds reduced by any deduction (not allowable in computing the regular tax) which would have been allowable if such interest were includible in gross income.

(B) Treatment of exempt-interest dividends. Under regulations prescribed by the Secretary, any exempt-interest dividend (as defined in section 852(b)(5)(A)) shall be treated as interest on a specified private activity bond to the extent of its proportionate share of the interest on such bonds received by the company paying such dividend.

(C) Specified private activity bonds.

(i) In general. For purposes of this part, the term "specified private activity bond" means any private activity bond (as defined in section 141) which is issued after August 7, 1986, and the interest on which is not includible in gross income under section 103.

(ii) Exception for qualified 501(c)(3) bonds. For purposes of clause (i), the term "private activity bond" shall not include any qualified 501(c)(3) bond (as defined in section 145).

(iii) Exception for certain housing bonds. For purposes of clause (i), the term "private activity bond" shall not include any bond issued after the date of the enactment of this clause if such bond is—

(I) an exempt facility bond issued as part of an issue 95 percent or more of the net proceeds of which are to be used to provide qualified residential rental projects (as defined in section 142(d)),

(II) a qualified mortgage bond (as defined in section 143(a)), or

(III) a qualified veterans' mortgage bond (as defined in section 143(b)).

The preceding sentence shall not apply to any refunding bond unless such preceding sentence applied to the refunded bond (or in the case of a series of refundings, the original bond).

(iv) Exception for refundings. For purposes of clause (i), the term "private activity bond" shall not include any refunding bond (whether a current or advance refunding) if the refunded bond (or in the case of a series of refundings, the original bond) was issued before August 8, 1986.

(v) Certain bonds issued before September 1, 1986. For purposes of this subparagraph, a bond issued before September 1, 1986, shall be treated as issued before August 8, 1986, unless such bond would be a private activity bond if—

(I) paragraphs (1) and (2) of section 141(b) were applied by substituting "25 percent" for "10 percent" each place it appears,

(II) paragraphs (3), (4), and (5) of section 141(b) did not apply, and

(III) subparagraph (B) of section 141(c)(1) did not apply.

(vi) Exception for bonds issued in 2009 and 2010.

(I) In general. For purposes of clause (i), the term "private activity bond" shall not include any bond issued after December 31, 2008, and before January 1, 2011.

(II) Treatment of refunding bonds. For purposes of subclause (I), a refunding bond (whether a current or advance refunding) shall be treated as issued on the date of the issuance of the refunded bond (or in the case of a series of refundings, the original bond).

(III) Exception for certain refunding bonds. Subclause (II) shall not apply to any refunding bond which is issued to refund any bond which was issued after December 31, 2003, and before January 1, 2009.

(6) Accelerated depreciation or amortization on certain property placed in service before January 1, 1987. The amounts which would be treated as items of tax preference with respect to the taxpayer under paragraphs (2), (3), (4), and (12) of this subsection (as in effect on the day before the date of the enactment [10/22/86] of the Tax Reform Act of 1986). The preceding sentence shall not apply to any property to which section 56(a)(1) or (5) applies.

(7) Exclusion for gains on sale of certain small business stock. An amount equal to [1]7 *percent* of the amount excluded from gross income for the taxable year under section 1202.[2]

* * * * * * * * * * * *

[For Analysis, see ¶ 405.]

[Endnote Code Sec. 57]

Sec. 102(a) of the American Taxpayer Relief Act of 2012, P.L. 112-240, 1/2/2013, deleted Sec. 303, P.L. 108-27, the Jobs and Growth Tax Relief Reconciliation Act of 2003, the effect of which is to eliminate the sunset of all provisions enacted by Title III of P.L. 108-27. Following are the amendments made to Code Sec. 57 by P.L. 108-27.

Matter in *italics* in Code Sec. 57(a)(7) was added by Sec. 301(b)(3)(A) and (B) of the Jobs and Growth Tax Relief Reconciliation Act of 2003, P.L. 108-27, 5/28/2003, which struck out:

1. "42 percent"

2. "In the case of stock the holding period of which begins after December 31, 2000 (determined with the application of the last sentence of section 1(h)(2)(B)), the preceding sentence shall be applied by substituting '28 percent' for '42 percent'."

[¶ 3041]   Code Sec. 62.   Adjusted gross income defined.

(a) **General rule.** For purposes of this subtitle, the term "adjusted gross income" means, in the case of an individual, gross income minus the following deductions:

(1) **Trade and business deductions.** The deductions allowed by this chapter (other than by part VII of this subchapter) which are attributable to a trade or business carried on by the taxpayer, if such trade or business does not consist of the performance of services by the taxpayer as an employee.

(2) **Certain trade and business deductions of employees.**

(A) Reimbursed expenses of employees. The deductions allowed by part VI (section 161 and following) which consist of expenses paid or incurred by the taxpayer, in connection with the performance by him of services as an employee, under a reimbursement or other expense allowance arrangement with his employer. The fact that the reimbursement may be provided by a third party shall not be determinative of whether or not the preceding sentence applies.

(B) Certain expenses of performing artists. The deductions allowed by section 162 which consist of expenses paid or incurred by a qualified performing artist in connection with the performances by him of services in the performing arts as an employee.

(C) Certain expenses of officials. The deductions allowed by section 162 which consist of expenses paid or incurred with respect to services performed by an official as an employee of a State or a political subdivision thereof in a position compensated in whole or in part on a fee basis.

(D) Certain expenses of elementary and secondary school teachers. In the case of taxable years beginning during 2002, 2003, 2004, 2005, 2006, 2007, 2008, 2009, 2010, ¹*2011, 2012, or 2013* the deductions allowed by section 162 which consist of expenses, not in excess of $250, paid or incurred by an eligible educator in connection with books, supplies (other than nonathletic supplies for courses of instruction in health or physical education), computer equipment (including related software and services) and other equipment, and supplementary materials used by the eligible educator in the classroom.

(E) Certain expenses of members of reserve components of the Armed Forces of the United States. The deductions allowed by section 162 which consist of expenses, determined at a rate not in excess of the rates for travel expenses (including per diem in lieu of subsistence) authorized for employees of agencies under subchapter I of chapter 57 of title 5, United States Code, paid or incurred by the taxpayer in connection with the performance of services by such taxpayer as a member of a reserve component of the Armed Forces of the United States for any period during which such individual is more than 100 miles away from home in connection with such services.

(3) **Losses from sale or exchange of property.** The deductions allowed by part VI (Sec. 161 and following) as losses from the sale or exchange of property.

(4) **Deductions attributable to rents and royalties.** The deductions allowed by part VI (Sec. 161 and following), by section 212 (relating to expenses for production of income), and by section 611 (relating to depletion) which are attributable to property held for the production of rents or royalties.

(5) Certain deductions of life tenants and income beneficiaries of property. In the case of a life tenant of property, or an income beneficiary of property held in trust, or an heir, legatee, or devisee of an estate, the deduction for depreciation allowed by section 167 and the deduction allowed by section 611.

(6) Pension, profit-sharing, and annuity plans of self-employed individuals. In the case of an individual who is an employee within the meaning of section 401(c)(1), the deduction allowed by section 404.

(7) Retirement savings. The deduction allowed by section 219 (relating to deduction of certain retirement savings).

(8) Repealed.

(9) Penalties forfeited because of premature withdrawal of funds from time savings accounts or deposits. The deductions allowed by section 165 for losses incurred in any transaction entered into for profit, though not connected with a trade or business, to the extent that such losses include amounts forfeited to a bank, mutual savings bank, savings and loan association, building and loan association, cooperative bank or homestead association as a penalty for premature withdrawal of funds from a time savings account, certificate of deposit, or similar class of deposit.

(10) Alimony. The deduction allowed by section 215.

(11) Reforestation expenses. The deduction allowed by section 194.

(12) Certain required repayments of supplemental unemployment compensation benefits. The deduction allowed by section 165 for the repayment to a trust described in paragraph (9) or (17) of section 501(c) of supplemental unemployment compensation benefits received from such trust if such repayment is required because of the receipt of trade readjustment allowances under section 231 or 232 of the Trade Act of 1974 (19 U.S.C. 2291 and 2292).

(13) Jury duty pay remitted to employer. Any deduction allowable under this chapter by reason of an individual remitting any portion of any jury pay to such individual's employer in exchange for payment by the employer of compensation for the period such individual was performing jury duty. For purposes of the preceding sentence, the term "jury pay" means any payment received by the individual for the discharge of jury duty.

(14) Deduction for clean-fuel vehicles and certain refueling property. The deduction allowed by section 179A.

(15) Moving expenses. The deduction allowed by section 217.

(16) Archer MSAs. The deduction allowed by section 220.

(17) Interest on education loans. The deduction allowed by section 221.

[2]*(18) Higher education expenses. The deduction allowed by section 222.*

(19) Health savings accounts. The deduction allowed by section 223.

(20) Costs involving discrimination suits, etc. Any deduction allowable under this chapter for attorney fees and court costs paid by, or on behalf of, the taxpayer in connection with any action involving a claim of unlawful discrimination (as defined in subsection (e)) or a claim of a violation of subchapter III of chapter 37 of title 31, United States Code or a claim made under section 1862(b)(3)(A) of the Social Security Act (42 U.S.C. 1395y(b)(3)(A)). The preceding sentence shall not apply to any deduction in excess of the amount includible in the taxpayer's gross income for the taxable year on account of a judgment or settlement (whether by suit or agreement and whether as lump sum or periodic payments) resulting from such claim.

(21) Attorneys fees relating to awards to whistleblowers. Any deduction allowable under this chapter for attorney fees and court costs paid by, or on behalf of, the taxpayer in connection with any award under section 7623(b) (relating to awards to whistleblowers). The preceding sentence shall not apply to any deduction in excess of the amount includible in the taxpayer's gross income for the taxable year on account of such award.

Nothing in this section shall permit the same item to be deducted more than once.

* * * * * * * * * * * *

[For Analysis, see ¶ 308.]

[Endnote Code Sec. 62]

Code Sec. 62(a)(2)(D) was amended by Sec. 201(a) of the American Taxpayer Relief Act of 2012, P.L. 112-240, 1/2/2013, as detailed below:

1. Sec. 201(a) substituted "2011, 2012, or 2013" for "or 2011" in subpara. (a)(2)(D)

Effective Date (Sec. 201(b), P.L. 112-240, 1/3/2013) effective for tax. yrs. begin. after 12/31/2011.

Sec. 101(a)(1), P.L. 112-240, 1/2/2013, deleted Title IX [Sec. 901], P.L. 107-16, the effect of which is to eliminate the sunset of all provisions enacted by P.L. 107-16.

Sec. 431(b), P.L. 107-16 added para. (a)(18).

Effective Date (Sec. 101(a)(3), P.L. 112-240, 1/2/2013) effective for tax. plan, or limitation years beginning after 12/31/2012, and estates of decedents dying, gifts made, or generation skipping transfers after 12/31/2012.

[¶ 3042]   Code Sec. 63.   Taxable income defined.

* * * * * * * * * * * *

[1](c) *Standard deduction. For purposes of this subtitle—*

(1) In general. Except as otherwise provided in this subsection, the term "standard deduction" means the sum of—

(A) the basic standard deduction,

(B) the additional standard deduction,

(C) in the case of any taxable year beginning in 2008 or 2009, the real property tax deduction,

(D) the disaster loss deduction, and

(E) the motor vehicle sales tax deduction.

(2) Basic standard deduction. For purposes of paragraph (1), the basic standard deduction is—

(A) 200 percent of the dollar amount in effect under subparagraph (C) for the taxable year in the case of—

(i) a joint return, or

(ii) a surviving spouse (as defined in section 2(a)),

(B) $4,400 in the case of a head of household (as defined in section 2(b)), or

(C) $3,000 in any other case.

(3) Additional standard deduction for aged and blind. For purposes of paragraph (1), the additional standard deduction is the sum of each additional amount to which the taxpayer is entitled under subsection (f).

(4) Adjustments for inflation. In the case of any taxable year beginning in a calendar year after 1988, each dollar amount contained in paragraph (2)(B), (2)(C), or (5) or subsection (f) shall be increased by an amount equal to—

(A) such dollar amount, multiplied by

(B) the cost-of-living adjustment determined under section 1(f)(3) for the calendar year in which the taxable year begins, by substituting for "calendar year 1992" in subparagraph (B) thereof—

(i) "calendar year 1987" in the case of the dollar amounts contained in paragraph (2)(B), (2)(C), or (5)(A) or subsection (f), and

(ii) "calendar year 1997" in the case of the dollar amount contained in paragraph (5)(B).

(5) Limitation on basic standard deduction in the case of certain dependents. In the case of an individual with respect to whom a deduction under section 151 is allowable to another taxpayer for a taxable year beginning in the calendar year in which the individual's taxable year begins, the basic standard deduction applicable to such individual for such individual's taxable year shall not exceed the greater of—

(A) $500, or

(B) the sum of $250 and such individual's earned income.

(6)   Certain individuals, etc., not eligible for standard deduction. In the case of—

   (A) a married individual filing a separate return where either spouse itemizes deductions,

   (B) a nonresident alien individual,

   (C) an individual making a return under section 443(a)(1) for a period of less than 12 months on account of a change in his annual accounting period, or

   (D) an estate or trust, common trust fund, or partnership,

   the standard deduction shall be zero.

(7)   Real property tax deduction. For purposes of paragraph (1), the real property tax deduction is the lesser of—

   (A) the amount allowable as a deduction under this chapter for State and local taxes described in section 164(a)(1), or

   (B) $500 ($1,000 in the case of a joint return).

   Any taxes taken into account under section 62(a) shall not be taken into account under this paragraph.

(8)   Disaster loss deduction. For the purposes of paragraph (1), the term "disaster loss deduction" means the net disaster loss (as defined in section 165(h)(3)(B)).

(9)   Motor vehicle sales tax deduction. For purposes of paragraph (1), the term "motor vehicle sales tax deduction" means the amount allowable as a deduction under section 164(a)(6). Such term shall not include any amount taken into account under section 62(a).

* * * * * * * * * * * *

[For Analysis, see ¶ 304.]

[Endnote Code Sec. 63]

   Sec. 101(a)(1) of the American Taxpayer Relief Act of 2012, P.L. 112-240, 1/2/2013, deleted Title IX [Sec. 901] of the Economic Growth and Tax Relief Reconciliation Act of 2001, P.L. 107-16, the effect of which is to eliminate the sunset of all provisions enacted by P.L. 107-16. Code Sec. 63(c)(2) was amended by Sec. 101(b)(1), P.L. 108-311. Sec. 105, P.L. 108-311, provides that this amendment is subject to the sunset provided in Sec. 901, P.L. 107-16. The deletion of Sec. 901, P.L. 107-16 also eliminates the sunset of the provisions enacted by Sec. 101(b)(1), P.L. 108-311. Following are the amendments made to Code Sec. 63, by P.L. 108-311.

Effective Date (Sec. 101(a)(3), P.L. 112-240, 1/2/2013) effective for taxable, plan, or limitation years beginning after 12/31/2012, and estates of decedents dying, gifts made, or generation skipping transfers after 12/31/2012.

   Code Sec. 63(c)(2) was amended by Sec. 101(b)(1) of the Working Families Tax Relief Act of 2004, P.L. 108-311, 10/4/2004,

   1. Sec. 101(b)(1), P.L. 108-311, amended para. (c)(2). Prior to amendment, para. (c)(2) read as follows:

   "(2) Basic standard deduction. For purposes of paragraph (1), the basic standard deduction is—

   "(A) the applicable percentage of the dollar amount in effect under subparagraph (D) for the taxable year in the case of—

   "(i) a joint return, or

   "(ii) a surviving spouse (as defined in section 2(a)),

   "(B) $4,400 in the case of a head of household (as defined in section 2(b)),

   "(C) one-half of the amount in effect under subparagraph (A) in the case of a married individual filing a separate return, or

   "(D) $3,000 in any other case.

   "If any amount determined under subparagraph (A) is not a multiple of $50, such amount shall be rounded to the next lowest multiple of $50."

Effective Date (Sec. 101(e), P.L. 108-311, 10/4/2004) effective for tax. yrs. begin. after 12/31/2003.

[¶ 3043]   Code Sec. 68.   Overall limitation on itemized deductions.

* * * * * * * * * * * *

¹*(b)   Applicable amount.*

   (1)   In general. For purposes of this section, the term "applicable amount" means—

   (A) $300,000 in the case of a joint return or a surviving spouse (as defined in section 2(a)),

   (B) $275,000 in the case of a head of household (as defined in section 2(b)),

(C) $250,000 in the case of an individual who is not married and who is not a surviving spouse or head of household, and

(D) 1.2 the amount applicable under subparagraph (A) (after adjustment, if any, under paragraph (2)) in the case of a married individual filing a separate return.

For purposes of this paragraph, marital status shall be determined under section 7703.

(2) Inflation adjustment. In the case of any taxable year beginning in calendar years after 2013, each of the dollar amounts under subparagraphs (A), (B), and (C) of paragraph (1) shall be shall be increased by an amount equal to—

(A) such dollar amount, multiplied by

(B) the cost-of-living adjustment determined under section 1(f)(3) for the calendar year in which the taxable year begins, except that section 1(f)(3)(B) shall be applied by substituting "2012" for "1992".

If any amount after adjustment under the preceding sentence is not a multiple of $50, such amount shall be rounded to the next lowest multiple of $50.

* * * * * * * * * * * *

²*(f) Repealed.*

³*(g) Repealed.*
[For Analysis, see ¶ 302.]

[Endnote Code Sec. 68]

Code Sec. 68(b), Code Sec. 68(f), and Code Sec. 68(g) were amended by Sec. 101(b)(2)(A)(i)-(ii) of P.L. 112-240, the American Taxpayer Relief Act of 2012, as detailed below:

1. Sec. 101(b)(2)(A)(i) amended subsec. (b)

Prior to amendment, subsec. (b) read as follows:

"(b) Applicable amount.

"(1) In general. For purposes of this section, the term 'applicable amount' means $100,000 ($50,000 in the case of a separate return by a married individual within the meaning of section 7703).

"(2) Inflation adjustments. In the case of any taxable year beginning in a calendar year after 1991, each dollar amount contained in paragraph (1) shall be increased by an amount equal to—

"(A) such dollar amount, multiplied by

"(B) the cost-of-living adjustment determined under section 1(f)(3) for the calendar year in which the taxable year begins, by substituting 'calendar year 1990' for 'calendar year 1992' in subparagraph (B) thereof."

2. Sec. 101(b)(2)(A)(ii) deleted subsec. (f)

Prior to deletion, subsec. (f) read as follows:

"(f) Phaseout of limitation.

"(1) In general. In the case of taxable years beginning after December 31, 2005, and before January 1, 2010, the reduction under subsection (a) shall be equal to the applicable fraction of the amount which would (but for this subsection) be the amount of such reduction.

"(2) Applicable fraction. For purposes of paragraph (1), the applicable fraction shall be determined in accordance with the following table:

For taxable years beginning in calendar year—	The applicable fraction is—
2006 and 2007	²/₃
2008 and 2009	¹/₃.

3. Sec. 101(b)(2)(A)(ii) deleted subsec. (g)

Prior to deletion, subsec. (g) read as follows:

"(g) Termination. This section shall not apply to any taxable year beginning after December 31, 2009."

Effective Date (Sec. 101(b)(3), P.L. 112-240, 1/2/2013) effective for tax. yrs. begin. after 12/31/2012.

Sec. 101(a)(1), P.L. 112-240, 1/2/2013, deleted Title IX [Sec. 901], P.L. 107-16, the effect of which is to eliminate the sunset of all provisions enacted by P.L. 107-16. Sec. 103(a), P.L. 107-16 amended Code Sec. 68 by adding subsec. (f) and (g)

Effective Date (Sec. 101(a)(3), P.L. 112-240, 1/2/2013) effective for taxable, plan, or limitation years beginning after 12/31/2012, and estates of decedents dying, gifts made, or generation skipping transfers after 12/31/2012.

[¶ 3044]   Code Sec. 72.   Annuities; certain proceeds of endowment and life insurance contracts.

* * * * * * * * * * * *

(t)   10-percent additional tax on early distributions from qualified retirement plans.

(1)   Imposition of additional tax. If any taxpayer receives any amount from a qualified retirement plan (as defined in section 4974(c)), the taxpayer's tax under this chapter for the taxable year in which such amount is received shall be increased by an amount equal to 10 percent of the portion of such amount which is includible in gross income.

(2)   Subsection not to apply to certain distributions. Except as provided in paragraphs (3) and (4), paragraph (1) shall not apply to any of the following distributions:

(A) In general. Distributions which are—

(i) made on or after the date on which the employee attains age 59½,

(ii) made to a beneficiary (or to the estate of the employee) on or after the death of the employee,

(iii) attributable to the employee's being disabled within the meaning of subsection (m)(7),

(iv) part of a series of substantially equal periodic payments (not less frequently than annually) made for the life (or life expectancy) of the employee or the joint lives (or joint life expectancies) of such employee and his designated beneficiary,

(v) made to an employee after separation from service after attainment of age 55,

(vi) dividends paid with respect to stock of a corporation which are described in section 404(k),[1]

(vii) made on account of a levy under section 6331 on the qualified retirement plan[2], *or*

[3]*(viii) payments under a phased retirement annuity under section 8366a(a)(5) or 8412a(a)(5) of title 5, United States Code, or a composite retirement annuity under section 8366a(a)(1) or 8412a(a)(1) of such title.*

(B) Medical expenses. Distributions made to the employee (other than distributions described in subparagraph (A), (C), or (D)) to the extent such distributions do not exceed the amount allowable as a deduction under section 213 to the employee for amounts paid during the taxable year for medical care (determined without regard to whether the employee itemizes deductions for such taxable year).

(C) Payments to alternate payees pursuant to qualified domestic relations orders. Any distribution to an alternate payee pursuant to a qualified domestic relations order (within the meaning of section 414(p)(1)).

(D) Distributions to unemployed individuals for health insurance premiums.

(i) In general. Distributions from an individual retirement plan to an individual after separation from employment—

(I) if such individual has received unemployment compensation for 12 consecutive weeks under any Federal or State unemployment compensation law by reason of such separation,

(II) if such distributions are made during any taxable year during which such unemployment compensation is paid or the succeeding taxable year, and

(III) to the extent such distributions do not exceed the amount paid during the taxable year for insurance described in section 213(d)(1)(D) with respect to the individual and the individual's spouse and dependents (as defined in section 152, determined without regard to subsections (b)(1), (b)(2), and (d)(1)(B) thereof).

(ii) Distributions after reemployment. Clause (i) shall not apply to any distribution made after the individual has been employed for at least 60 days after the separation from employment to which clause (i) applies.

(iii) Self-employed individuals. To the extent provided in regulations, a self-employed individual shall be treated as meeting the requirements of clause (i)(I) if, under Federal or State law, the individual would have received unemployment compensation but for the fact the individual was self-employed.

(E) Distributions from individual retirement plans for higher education expenses. Distributions to an individual from an individual retirement plan to the extent such distributions do not exceed the qualified higher education expenses (as defined in paragraph (7)) of the taxpayer for the taxable year. Distributions shall not be taken into account under the preceding sentence if such distributions are described in subparagraph (A), (C), or (D) or to the extent paragraph (1) does not apply to such distributions by reason of subparagraph (B).

(F) Distributions from certain plans for first home purchases. Distributions to an individual from an individual retirement plan which are qualified first-time homebuyer distributions (as defined in paragraph (8)). Distributions shall not be taken into account under the preceding sentence if such distributions are described in subparagraph (A), (C), (D), or (E) or to the extent paragraph (1) does not apply to such distributions by reason of subparagraph (B).

(G) Distributions from retirement plans to individuals called to active duty.

(i) In general. Any qualified reservist distribution.

(ii) Amount distributed may be repaid. Any individual who receives a qualified reservist distribution may, at any time during the 2-year period beginning on the day after the end of the active duty period, make one or more contributions to an individual retirement plan of such individual in an aggregate amount not to exceed the amount of such distribution. The dollar limitations otherwise applicable to contributions to individual retirement plans shall not apply to any contribution made pursuant to the preceding sentence. No deduction shall be allowed for any contribution pursuant to this clause.

(iii) Qualified reservist distribution. For purposes of this subparagraph, the term "qualified reservist distribution" means any distribution to an individual if—

(I) such distribution is from an individual retirement plan, or from amounts attributable to employer contributions made pursuant to elective deferrals described in subparagraph (A) or (C) of section 402(g)(3) or section 501(c)(18)(D)(iii),

(II) such individual was (by reason of being a member of a reserve component (as defined in section 101 of title 37, United States Code)) ordered or called to active duty for a period in excess of 179 days or for an indefinite period, and

(III) such distribution is made during the period beginning on the date of such order or call and ending at the close of the active duty period.

(iv) Application of subparagraph. This subparagraph applies to individuals ordered or called to active duty after September 11, 2001. In no event shall the 2-year period referred to in clause (ii) end on or before the date which is 2 years after the date of the enactment of this subparagraph.

(3) Limitations.

(A) Certain exceptions not to apply to individual retirement plans. Subparagraphs (A)(v) and (C) of paragraph (2) shall not apply to distributions from an individual retirement plan.

(B) Periodic payments under qualified plans must begin after separation. Paragraph (2)(A)(iv) shall not apply to any amount paid from a trust described in section 401(a) which is exempt from tax under section 501(a) or from a contract described in section 72(e)(5)(D)(ii) unless the series of payments begins after the employee separates from service.

(4) Change in substantially equal payments.

(A) In general. If—

(i) paragraph (1) does not apply to a distribution by reason of paragraph (2)(A)(iv), and

(ii) the series of payments under such paragraph are subsequently modified (other than by reason of death or disability)—

(I) before the close of the 5-year period beginning with the date of the first payment and after the employee attains age 59$\frac{1}{2}$, or

(II) before the employee attains age 59$\frac{1}{2}$,

the taxpayer's tax for the 1st taxable year in which such modification occurs shall be increased by an amount, determined under regulations, equal to the tax which (but for paragraph (2)(A)(iv)) would have been imposed, plus interest for the deferral period.

(B) Deferral period. For purposes of this paragraph, the term "deferral period" means the period beginning with the taxable year in which (without regard to paragraph (2)(A)(iv)) the distribution would have been includible in gross income and ending with the taxable year in which the modification described in subparagraph (A) occurs.

(5) **Employee.** For purposes of this subsection, the term "employee" includes any participant, and in the case of an individual retirement plan, the individual for whose benefit such plan was established.

(6) **Special rules for simple retirement accounts.** In the case of any amount received from a simple retirement account (within the meaning of section 408(p)) during the 2-year period beginning on the date such individual first participated in any qualified salary reduction arrangement maintained by the individual's employer under section 408(p)(2), paragraph (1) shall be applied by substituting "25 percent" for "10 percent".

(7) **Qualified higher education expenses.** For purposes of paragraph (2)(E)—

(A) In general. The term "qualified higher education expenses" means qualified higher education expenses (as defined in section 529(e)(3)) for education furnished to—

(i) the taxpayer,

(ii) the taxpayer's spouse, or

(iii) any child (as defined in section 152(f)(1)) or grandchild of the taxpayer or the taxpayer's spouse,

at an eligible educational institution (as defined in section 529(e)(5)).

(B) Coordination with other benefits. The amount of qualified higher education expenses for any taxable year shall be reduced as provided in section 25A(g)(2).

(8) **Qualified first-time homebuyer distributions.** For purposes of paragraph (2)(F)—

(A) In general. The term "qualified first-time homebuyer distribution" means any payment or distribution received by an individual to the extent such payment or distribution is used by the individual before the close of the 120th day after the day on which such payment or distribution is received to pay qualified acquisition costs with respect to a principal residence of a first-time homebuyer who is such individual, the spouse of such individual, or any child, grandchild, or ancestor of such individual or the individual's spouse.

(B) Lifetime dollar limitation. The aggregate amount of payments or distributions received by an individual which may be treated as qualified first-time homebuyer distributions for any taxable year shall not exceed the excess (if any) of—

(i) $10,000, over

(ii) the aggregate amounts treated as qualified first-time homebuyer distributions with respect to such individual for all prior taxable years.

(C) Qualified acquisition costs. For purposes of this paragraph, the term "qualified acquisition costs" means the costs of acquiring, constructing, or reconstructing a residence. Such term includes any usual or reasonable settlement, financing, or other closing costs.

(D) First-time homebuyer; other definitions. For purposes of this paragraph—

(i) First-time homebuyer. The term "first-time homebuyer" means any individual if—

(I) such individual (and if married, such individual's spouse) had no present ownership interest in a principal residence during the 2-year period ending on the date of acquisition of the principal residence to which this paragraph applies, and

(II) subsection (h) or (k) of section 1034 (as in effect on the day before the date of the enactment of this paragraph) did not suspend the running of any period of time specified in section 1034 (as so in effect) with respect to such individual on the day before the date the distribution is applied pursuant to subparagraph (A).

(ii) Principal residence. The term "principal residence" has the same meaning as when used in section 121.

(iii) Date of acquisition. The term "date of acquisition" means the date—

(I) on which a binding contract to acquire the principal residence to which subparagraph (A) applies is entered into, or

(II) on which construction or reconstruction of such a principal residence is commenced.

(E) Special rule where delay in acquisition. If any distribution from any individual retirement plan fails to meet the requirements of subparagraph (A) solely by reason of a delay or cancellation of the purchase or construction of the residence, the amount of the distribution may be contributed to an individual retirement plan as provided in section 408(d)(3)(A)(i) (determined by substituting "120th day" for "60th day" in such section), except that—

(i) section 408(d)(3)(B) shall not be applied to such contribution, and

(ii) such amount shall not be taken into account in determining whether section 408(d)(3)(B) applies to any other amount.

(9) **Special rule for rollovers to section 457 plans.** For purposes of this subsection, a distribution from an eligible deferred compensation plan (as defined in section 457(b)) of an eligible employer described in section 457(e)(1)(A) shall be treated as a distribution from a qualified retirement plan described in 4974(c)(1) to the extent that such distribution is attributable to an amount transferred to an eligible deferred compensation plan from a qualified retirement plan (as defined in section 4974(c)).

(10) **Distributions to qualified public safety employees in governmental plans.**

(A) In general. In the case of a distribution to a qualified public safety employee from a governmental plan (within the meaning of section 414(d)) which is a defined benefit plan, paragraph (2)(A)(v) shall be applied by substituting "age 50" for "age 55".

(B) Qualified public safety employee. For purposes of this paragraph, the term "qualified public safety employee" means any employee of a State or political subdivision of a State who provides police protection, firefighting services, or emergency medical services for any area within the jurisdiction of such State or political subdivision.

* * * * * * * * * * * *

[For Analysis, see ¶ 1704.]

[Endnote Code Sec. 72]

Code Sec. 72(t)(2)(A)(i), Code Sec. 72(t)(2)(A)(ii) and Code Sec. 72(t)(2)(A)(iii) were amended by Sec. 100121(c) of the Moving Ahead for Progress in the 21st Century Act, P.L. 112-141, 7/6/2012, as detailed below:

1. Sec. 100121(c) deleted "or" at the end of clause (t)(2)(A)(vi)
2. Sec. 100121(c) substituted ", or" for the period at the end of clause (t)(2)(A)(vii)
3. Sec. 100121(c) added clause (t)(2)(A)(viii)

Effective Date Effective 7/6/2012.

[¶ 3045]   Code Sec. 79.   Group-term life insurance purchased for employees.

* * * * * * * * * * * *

[1]*(f) Inflation adjustment.*

(1) In general. In the case of any taxable year beginning after 2012, the $350,000 amount under subsection (a)(1) shall be increased by an amount equal to—

(A) such dollar amount, multiplied by

(B) the cost-of-living adjustment determined under section 1(f)(3) for the calendar year in which the taxable year begins, determined by substituting "2011" for "1992" in subparagraph (B) thereof.

(2) Rounding. If any amount as adjusted under paragraph (1) is not a multiple of $10,000, such amount shall be rounded to the nearest multiple of $10,000.

[For Analysis, see ¶ 1702. For Committee Reports, see ¶ 5405.]

[Endnote Code Sec. 79]
   Code Sec. 79(f) was amended by Sec. 40242(d) of the Moving Ahead for Progress in the 21st Century Act, P.L. 112-141, 7/6/2012, as detailed below:
   1. Sec. 40242(d) added subsec. (f)
Effective Date (Sec. 40242(h)(1), P.L. 112-141, 7/6/2012) effective for transfers made after 7/6/2012.

[¶ 3046]   Code Sec. 108.   Income from discharge of indebtedness.

(a) Exclusion from gross income.

   (1) In general. Gross income does not include any amount which (but for this subsection) would be includible in gross income by reason of the discharge (in whole or in part) of indebtedness of the taxpayer if—

   (A) the discharge occurs in a title 11 case,

   (B) the discharge occurs when the taxpayer is insolvent,

   (C) the indebtedness discharged is qualified farm indebtedness,

   (D) in the case of a taxpayer other than a C corporation, the indebtedness discharged is qualified real property business indebtedness, or

   (E) the indebtedness discharged is qualified principal residence indebtedness which is discharged before [1]*January 1, 2014.*

   (2) Coordination of exclusions.

   (A) Title 11 exclusion takes precedence. Subparagraphs (B), (C) (D), and (E) of paragraph (1) shall not apply to a discharge which occurs in a title 11 case.

   (B) Insolvency exclusion takes precedence over qualified farm exclusion and qualified real property business exclusion. Subparagraphs (C) and (D) of paragraph (1) shall not apply to a discharge to the extent the taxpayer is insolvent.

   (C) Principal residence exclusion takes precedence over insolvency exclusion unless elected otherwise. Paragraph (1)(B) shall not apply to a discharge to which paragraph (1)(E) applies unless the taxpayer elects to apply paragraph (1)(B) in lieu of paragraph (1)(E).

   (3) Insolvency exclusion limited to amount of insolvency. In the case of a discharge to which paragraph (1)(B) applies, the amount excluded under paragraph (1)(B) shall not exceed the amount by which the taxpayer is insolvent.

* * * * * * * * * * * *

[For Analysis, see ¶ 306.]

[Endnote Code Sec. 108]
   Code Sec. 108(a)(1)(E) was amended by Sec. 202(a) of the American Taxpayer Relief Act of 2012, P.L. 112-240, 1/2/2013, as detailed below:
   1. Sec. 202(a) substituted "January 1, 2014" for "January 1, 2013" in subara. (a)(1)(E)
Effective Date (Sec. 202(b), P.L. 112-240, 1/2/2013) effective for indebtedness discharged after 12/31/2012.

[¶ 3047]   Code Sec. 117.   Qualified scholarships.

* * * * * * * * * * * *

(c) Limitation.

   [1]**(1) In general.** *Except as provided in paragraph (2), subsections (a) and (d) shall not apply to that portion of any amount received which represents payment for teaching, research, or other services by the student required as a condition for receiving the qualified scholarship or qualified tuition reduction.*

   [2]**(2) Exceptions.** *Paragraph (1) shall not apply to any amount received by an individual under—*

(A) the National Health Service Corps Scholarship Program under section 338A(g)(1)(A) of the Public Health Service Act, or

(B) the Armed Forces Health Professions Scholarship and Financial Assistance program under subchapter I of chapter 105 of title 10, United States Code.

* * * * * * * * * * * *

[For Analysis, see ¶ 706.]

[Endnote Code Sec. 117]

Sec. 101(a)(1) of the American Taxpayer Relief Act of 2012, P.L. 112-240, 1/2/2013, deleted Title IX [Sec. 901] of the Economic Growth and Tax Relief Reconciliation Act of 2001, P.L. 107-16, the effect of which is to eliminate the sunset of all provisions enacted by P.L. 107-16. Following are the amendments made to Code Sec. 117, by P.L. 107-16. **Effective Date** (Sec. 101(a)(3), P.L. 112-240, 1/2/2013) effective for taxable, plan, or limitation years beginning after 12/31/2012, and estates of decedents dying, gifts made, or generation skipping transfers after 12/31/2012.

Code Sec. 117(c)(1) and Code Sec. 117(c)(2) were amended by Sec. 413(a)(1) and (2) of the Economic Growth and Tax Relief Reconciliation Act of 2001, P.L. 107-16, 6/7/2001, as detailed below:

1. Sec. 413(a)(1) substituted "(1) In general. Except as provided in paragraph (2), subsections (a)" for "Subsections (a)" in subsec. (c)

2. Sec. 413(a)(2) added para. (c)(2)

Effective Date (Sec. 413(b), P.L. 107-16, 6/7/2001) effective for amounts received in tax. yrs. begin. after 12/31/2001.

[¶ 3048]   Code Sec. 127.   Educational assistance programs.

* * * * * * * * * * * *

(c) Definitions; special rules. For purposes of this section—

(1) Educational assistance. The term "educational assistance" means—

(A) the payment, by an employer, of expenses incurred by or on behalf of an employee for education of the employee (including, but not limited to, tuition, fees, and similar payments, books, supplies, and equipment), and

(B) the provision, by an employer, of courses of instruction for such employee (including books, supplies, and equipment),

but does not include payment for, or the provision of, tools or supplies which may be retained by the employee after completion of a course of instruction, or meals, lodging, or transportation. The term "educational assistance" also does not include any payment for, or the provision of any benefits with respect to, any course or other education involving sports, games, or hobbies[1].

(2) Employee. The term "employee" includes, for any year, an individual who is an employee within the meaning of section 401(c)(1) (relating to self-employed individuals).

(3) Employer. An individual who owns the entire interest in an unincorporated trade or business shall be treated as his own employer. A partnership shall be treated as the employer of each partner who is an employee within the meaning of paragraph (2).

(4) Attribution rules.

(A) Ownership of stock. Ownership of stock in a corporation shall be determined in accordance with the rules provided under subsections (d) and (e) of section 1563 (without regard to section 1563(e)(3)(C)).

(B) Interest in unincorporated trade or business. The interest of an employee in a trade or business which is not incorporated shall be determined in accordance with regulations prescribed by the Secretary, which shall be based on principles similar to the principles which apply in the case of subparagraph (A).

(5) Certain tests not applicable. An educational assistance program shall not be held or considered to fail to meet any requirements of subsection (b) merely because—

(A) of utilization rates for the different types of educational assistance made available under the program; or

(B) successful completion, or attaining a particular course grade, is required for or considered in determining reimbursement under the program.

(6)   Relationship to current law. This section shall not be construed to affect the deduction or inclusion in income of amounts (not within the exclusion under this section) which are paid or incurred, or received as reimbursement, for educational expenses under section 117, 162 or 212.

(7)   Disallowance of excluded amounts as credit or deduction. No deduction or credit shall be allowed to the employee under any other section of this chapter for any amount excluded from income by reason of this section.

[2]*(d)*   **Cross reference.** For reporting and recordkeeping requirements, see section 6039D. *[For Analysis, see ¶ 705.]*

[Endnote Code Sec. 127]

Sec. 101(a)(1) of the American Taxpayer Relief Act of 2012, P.L. 112-240, 1/2/2013, deleted Title IX [Sec. 901] of the Economic Growth and Tax Relief Reconciliation Act of 2001, P.L. 107-16, the effect of which is to eliminate the sunset of all provisions enacted by P.L. 107-16. Following are the amendments made to Code Sec. 127, by P.L. 107-16. **Effective Date** (Sec. 101(a)(3), P.L. 112-240, 1/2/2013) effective for taxable, plan, or limitation years beginning after 12/31/2012, and estates of decedents dying, gifts made, or generation skipping transfers after 12/31/2012.

Code Sec. 127(c)(1) and Code Sec. 127(d) were amended by Sec. 411(a) and (b) of the Economic Growth and Tax Relief Reconciliation Act of 2001, P.L. 107-16, 6/7/2001, as outlined below:

1. Sec. 411(b) deleted ", and such term also does not include any payment for, or the provision of any benefits with respect to, any graduate level course of a kind normally taken by an individual pursuing a program leading to a law, business, medical, or other advanced academic or professional degree" after "games, or hobbies" in para. (c)(1)

2. Sec. 411(a) deleted subsec. (d) and redesignated subsec. (e) as subsec. (d). Prior to deletion, subsec. (d) read as follows:

"(d) Termination. This section shall not apply to expenses paid with respect to courses beginning after December 31, 2001.

Effective Date (Sec. 411(d), P.L. 107-16, 6/7/2001) effective for expenses relating to courses begin. after 12/31/2001.

[¶ 3049]   Code Sec. 132.   Certain fringe benefits.

* * * * * * * * * * * *

(f)   Qualified transportation fringe.

(1)   In general. For purposes of this section, the term "qualified transportation fringe" means any of the following provided by an employer to an employee:

(A) Transportation in a commuter highway vehicle if such transportation is in connection with travel between the employee's residence and place of employment.

(B) Any transit pass.

(C) Qualified parking.

(D) Any qualified bicycle commuting reimbursement.

(2)   Limitation on exclusion. The amount of the fringe benefits which are provided by an employer to any employee and which may be excluded from gross income under subsection (a)(5) shall not exceed—

(A) $100 per month in the case of the aggregate of the benefits described in subparagraphs (A) and (B) of paragraph (1),

(B) $175 per month in the case of qualified parking, and

(C) the applicable annual limitation in the case of any qualified bicycle commuting reimbursement.

In the case of any month beginning on or after the date of the enactment of this sentence and before [1]*January 1, 2014*, subparagraph (A) shall be applied as if the dollar amount therein were the same as the dollar amount in effect for such month under subparagraph (B).

(3)   Cash reimbursements. For purposes of this subsection, the term "qualified transportation fringe" includes a cash reimbursement by an employer to an employee for a benefit described in paragraph (1). The preceding sentence shall apply to a cash reimbursement for any transit pass only if a voucher or similar item which may be exchanged only for a transit pass is not readily available for direct distribution by the employer to the employee.

(4) No constructive receipt. No amount shall be included in the gross income of an employee solely because the employee may choose between any qualified transportation fringe (other than a qualified bicycle commuting reimbursement) and compensation which would otherwise be includible in gross income of such employee.

(5) Definitions. For purposes of this subsection—

(A) Transit pass. The term "transit pass" means any pass, token, farecard, voucher, or similar item entitling a person to transportation (or transportation at a reduced price) if such transportation is—

(i) on mass transit facilities (whether or not publicly owned), or

(ii) provided by any person in the business of transporting persons for compensation or hire if such transportation is provided in a vehicle meeting the requirements of subparagraph (B)(i).

(B) Commuter highway vehicle. The term "commuter highway vehicle" means any highway vehicle—

(i) the seating capacity of which is at least 6 adults (not including the driver), and

(ii) at least 80 percent of the mileage use of which can reasonably be expected to be—

(I) for purposes of transporting employees in connection with travel between their residences and their place of employment, and

(II) on trips during which the number of employees transported for such purposes is at least $\frac{1}{2}$ of the adult seating capacity of such vehicle (not including the driver).

(C) Qualified parking. The term "qualified parking" means parking provided to an employee on or near the business premises of the employer or on or near a location from which the employee commutes to work by transportation described in subparagraph (A), in a commuter highway vehicle, or by carpool. Such term shall not include any parking on or near property used by the employee for residential purposes.

(D) Transportation provided by employer. Transportation referred to in paragraph (1)(A) shall be considered to be provided by an employer if such transportation is furnished in a commuter highway vehicle operated by or for the employer.

(E) Employee. For purposes of this subsection, the term "employee" does not include an individual who is an employee within the meaning of section 401(c)(1).

(F) Definitions related to bicycle commuting reimbursement.

(i) Qualified bicycle commuting reimbursement. The term "qualified bicycle commuting reimbursement" means, with respect to any calendar year, any employer reimbursement during the 15-month period beginning with the first day of such calendar year for reasonable expenses incurred by the employee during such calendar year for the purchase of a bicycle and bicycle improvements, repair, and storage, if such bicycle is regularly used for travel between the employee's residence and place of employment.

(ii) Applicable annual limitation. The term "applicable annual limitation" means, with respect to any employee for any calendar year, the product of $20 multiplied by the number of qualified bicycle commuting months during such year.

(iii) Qualified bicycle commuting month. The term "qualified bicycle commuting month" means, with respect to any employee, any month during which such employee—

(I) regularly uses the bicycle for a substantial portion of the travel between the employee's residence and place of employment, and

(II) does not receive any benefit described in subparagraph (A), (B), or (C) of paragraph (1).

(6) Inflation adjustment.

(A) In general. In the case of any taxable year beginning in a calendar year after 1999, the dollar amounts contained in subparagraphs (A) and (B) of paragraph (2) shall be increased by an amount equal to—

(i) such dollar amount, multiplied by

    (ii) the cost-of-living adjustment determined under section 1(f)(3) for the calendar year in which the taxable year begins, by substituting "calendar year 1998" for "calendar year 1992".

    In the case of any taxable year beginning in a calendar year after 2002, clause (ii) shall be applied by substituting "calendar year 2001" for "calendar year 1998" for purposes of adjusting the dollar amount contained in paragraph (2)(A).

    (B) Rounding. If any increase determined under subparagraph (A) is not a multiple of $5, such increase shall be rounded to the next lowest multiple of $5.

    (7) Coordination with other provisions. For purposes of this section, the terms "working condition fringe" and "de minimis fringe" shall not include any qualified transportation fringe (determined without regard to paragraph (2)).

* * * * * * * * * * * *

[For Analysis, see ¶ 307.]

[Endnote Code Sec. 132]

    Code Sec. 132(f)(2) was amended by Sec. 203(a) of the American Taxpayer Relief Act of 2012, P.L. 112-240, 1/2/2013, as detailed below:

    1. Sec. 203(a) substituted "January 1, 2014" for "January 1, 2012" in para. (f)(2)

Effective Date (Sec. 203(b), P.L. 112-240, 1/2/2013) effective for months after 12/31/2011.

[¶ 3050]   **Code Sec. 137.**   **Adoption assistance programs.**

[1]*(a)* *Exclusion.*

    (1) *In general.* *Gross income of an employee does not include amounts paid or expenses incurred by the employer for qualified adoption expenses in connection with the adoption of a child by an employee if such amounts are furnished pursuant to an adoption assistance program.*

    (2) *$10,000 exclusion for adoption of child with special needs regardless of expenses.* *In the case of an adoption of a child with special needs which becomes final during a taxable year, the qualified adoption expenses with respect to such adoption for such year shall be increased by an amount equal to the excess (if any) of $10,000 over the actual aggregate qualified adoption expenses with respect to such adoption during such taxable year and all prior taxable years.*

* * * * * * * * * * * *

[For Analysis, see ¶ 309.]

[Endnote Code Sec. 137]

    Sec. 101(a)(1) of the American Taxpayer Relief Act of 2012, P.L. 112-240, 1/2/2013, deleted Title IX [Sec. 901] of the Economic Growth and Tax Relief Reconciliation Act of 2001, P.L. 107-16, the efet of which is to eliminate the sunset of all provisions enacted by P.L. 107-16. Following are the amendments made to Code Sec. 137, by P.L. 107-16.
Effective Date (Sec. 101(a)(3), P.L. 112-240, 1/2/2013) effective for taxable, plan, or limitation years beginning after 12/31/2012, and estates of decedents dying, gifts made, or generation skipping transfers after 12/31/2012.

    Code Sec. 137(a) was added by Sec. 202(a)(2) of the Economic Growth and Tax Relief Reconciliation Act of 2001, P.L. 107-16, 6/7/2001.
    1. Sec. 202(a)(2) added subsec. (a)
Effective Date (Sec. 202(g)(2), P.L. 107-16, 6/7/2001) effective for tax. yrs. begin. after 12/31/2002.

[¶ 3051]   *Code Sec.*[1] *139D.*   *Free choice vouchers. [Repealed].*

    • *Caution:* Code Sec. 139D following, was added by Sec. 10108(f)(1), P.L. 111-148. Code Sec. 139D as added by P.L. 111-148, Sec. 10108(f)(1) was repealed by Sec. 1858(b)(2)(A), P.L. 112-10.

Gross income shall not include the amount of any free choice voucher provided by an employer under section 10108 of the Patient Protection and Affordable Care Act to the extent that the amount of such voucher does not exceed the amount paid for a qualified health plan (as defined in section 1301 of such Act) by the taxpayer.
[For Analysis, see ¶ 1603.]

[Endnote Code Sec. 139D]

Code Sec. 139D added by Sec. 10108(f)(1), P.L. 111-148, was repealed by Sec. 1858(b)(2)(A), P.L. 112-10, repealed Code Sec. 139D,

Prior to repeal, Code Sec. 139D as added by Sec. 10108(f)(1), P.L. 111-148 reads as follows:

"Sec. 139D. Free choice vouchers

Gross income shall not include the amount of any free choice voucher provided by an employer under section 10108 of the Patient Protection and Affordable Care Act to the extent that the amount of such voucher does not exceed the amount paid for a qualified health plan (as defined in section 1301 of such Act) by the taxpayer.

Effective Date (Sec. 1858(d), P.L. 112-10) effective for vouchers provided after 12/31/2013.

[¶ 3052]   Code Sec. 142.   Exempt facility bond.

(a) **General rule.** For purposes of this part, the term "exempt facility bond" means any bond issued as part of an issue 95 percent or more of the net proceeds of which are to be used to provide—

* * * * * * * * * * * *

(11) high-speed intercity rail facilities,

(12) environmental enhancements of hydro-electric generating facilities,

(13) qualified public educational facilities,

* * * * * * * * * * * *

(d) **Qualified residential rental project.**

* * * * * * * * * * * *

(2) **Definitions and special rules.** For purposes of this subsection—

* * * * * * * * * * * *

(B) Income of individuals; area median gross income.

[1]*(i) In general. The income of individuals and area median gross income shall be determined by the Secretary in a manner consistent with determinations of lower income families and area median gross income under section 8 of the United States Housing Act of 1937 (or, if such program is terminated, under such program as in effect immediately before such termination). Determinations under the preceding sentence shall include adjustments for family size. Subsections (g) and (h) of section 7872 shall not apply in determining the income of individuals under this subparagraph.*

[2]*(ii) Special rule relating to basic housing allowances. For purposes of determining income under this subparagraph, payments under section 403 of title 37, United States Code, as a basic pay allowance for housing shall be disregarded with respect to any qualified building.*

(iii) Qualified building. For purposes of clause (ii), the term "qualified building" means any building located—

(I) in any county in which is located a qualified military installation to which the number of members of the Armed Forces of the United States assigned to units based out of such qualified military installation, as of June 1, 2008, has increased by not less than 20 percent, as compared to such number on December 31, 2005, or

(II) in any county adjacent to a county described in subclause (I).

(iv) Qualified military installation. For purposes of clause (iii), the term "qualified military installation" means any military installation or facility the number of members of the Armed Forces of the United States assigned to which, as of June 1, 2008, is not less than 1,000.

* * * * * * * * * * * *

[3]*(k)   Qualified public educational facilities.*

(1)   In general. For purposes of subsection (a)(13), the term "qualified public educational facility" means any school facility which is—

(A) part of a public elementary school or a public secondary school, and

(B) owned by a private, for-profit corporation pursuant to a public-private partnership agreement with a State or local educational agency described in paragraph (2).

(2)   Public-private partnership agreement described. A public-private partnership agreement is described in this paragraph if it is an agreement—

(A) under which the corporation agrees—

(i) to do 1 or more of the following: construct, rehabilitate, refurbish, or equip a school facility, and

(ii) at the end of the term of the agreement, to transfer the school facility to such agency for no additional consideration, and

(B) the term of which does not exceed the term of the issue to be used to provide the school facility.

(3)   School facility. For purposes of this subsection, the term "school facility" means—

(A) any school building,

(B) any functionally related and subordinate facility and land with respect to such building, including any stadium or other facility primarily used for school events, and

(C) any property, to which section 168 applies (or would apply but for section 179), for use in a facility described in subparagraph (A) or (B).

(4)   Public schools. For purposes of this subsection, the terms "elementary school" and "secondary school" have the meanings given such terms by section 14101 of the Elementary and Secondary Education Act of 1965 (20 U.S.C. 8801), as in effect on the date of the enactment of this subsection.

(5)   Annual aggregate face amount of tax-exempt financing.

(A) In general. An issue shall not be treated as an issue described in subsection (a)(13) if the aggregate face amount of bonds issued by the State pursuant thereto (when added to the aggregate face amount of bonds previously so issued during the calendar year) exceeds an amount equal to the greater of—

(i) $10 multiplied by the State population, or

(ii) $5,000,000.

(B) Allocation rules.

(i) In general. Except as otherwise provided in this subparagraph, the State may allocate the amount described in subparagraph (A) for any calendar year in such manner as the State determines appropriate.

(ii) Rules for carryforward of unused limitation. A State may elect to carry forward an unused limitation for any calendar year for 3 calendar years following the calendar year in which the unused limitation arose under rules similar to the rules of section 146(f), except that the only purpose for which the carryforward may be elected is the issuance of exempt facility bonds described in subsection (a)(13).

* * * * * * * * * * * *

[For Analysis, see ¶ 1905, ¶ 1906 and ¶ 1907. For Committee Reports, see ¶ 5901 and ¶ 5902.] [For Analysis, see ¶ 1403 and ¶ 1408.]

[Endnote Code Sec. 142]

Sec. 101(a)(1) of the American Taxpayer Relief Act of 2012, P.L. 112-240, 1/2/2013, deleted Title IX [Sec. 901] of the Economic Growth and Tax Relief Reconciliation Act of 2001, P.L. 107-16, the effect of which is to eliminate the sunset of all provisions enacted by P.L. 107-16. Following are the amendments made to Code Sec. 142, by P.L. 107-16. **Effective Date** (Sec. 101(a)(3), P.L. 112-240, 1/2/2013) effective for taxable, plan, or limitation years beginning after 12/31/2012, and estates of decedents dying, gifts made, or generation skipping transfers after 12/31/2012.

Sec. 303(a), P.L. 112-240, 1/2/2013, substituted "January 1, 2014" for "January 1, 2012" each place it appears in Sec. 3005(b), P.L. 110-289. Sec. 3005(b), P.L. 110-289 reads as follows:

"(b) The amendments made by this section shall apply to—

"(1) determinations made after the date of the enactment of this Act and before January 1, 2014, in the case of any qualified building (as defined in section 142(d)(2)(B)(iii) of the Internal Revenue Code of 1986)—

"(A) with respect to which housing credit dollar amounts have been allocated on or before the date of the enactment of this Act, or

"(B) with respect to buildings placed in service before such date of enactment, to the extent paragraph (1) of section 42(h) of such Code does not apply to such building by reason of paragraph (4) thereof, but only with respect to bonds issued before such date of enactment, and

"(2) determinations made after the date of enactment of this Act, in the case of qualified buildings (as so defined)—

"(A) with respect to which housing credit dollar amounts are allocated after the date of the enactment of this Act and before January 1, 2014, or

"(B) with respect to which buildings placed in service after the date of enactment of this Act and before January 1, 2014, to the extent paragraph (1) of section 42(h) of such Code does not apply to such building by reason of paragraph (4) thereof, but only with respect to bonds issued after such date of enactment and before January 1, 2014."

Effective Date (Sec. 303(b), P.L. 112-240, 1/2/2013) effective as if included in the enactment of Sec. 3005, P.L. 110-289. See above for Sec. 3005(b), P.L. 110-289, as amended.

Code Sec. 142(a)(11), Code Sec. 142(a)(12) and Code Sec. 142(a)(13) were amended by Sec. 422(a) of the Economic Growth and Tax Relief Reconciliation Act of 2001, P.L. 107-16, 6/7/2001. Code Sec. 142 was further amended by Sec. 11143(a), P.L. 109-59.

Sec. 422(a) deleted "or" at the end of para. (a)(11)

Sec. 422(a) substituted ", or" for the period at the end of para. (a)(12)

Sec. 422(a) added para. (a)(13)

Effective Date (Sec. 422(f), P.L. 107-16, 6/7/2001) effective for bonds issued after 12/31/2001.

Code Sec. 142(d)(2)(B) was amended by Sec. 3005(a)(1)-(2) of the Housing Assistance Tax Act of 2008, P.L. 110-289, 7/30/2008, as detailed below:

1. Sec. 3005(a)(1) substituted "(i) In general. The income" for "The income" in subpara. (d)(2)(B)

2. Sec. 3005(a)(2) added clauses (d)(2)(B)(ii)-(iv)

Effective Date (Sec. 3005(b), P.L. 110-289, 7/30/2008) effective as provided in Sec. 3005(b), P.L.110-289, 7/30/2008, [as amended by Sec. 303(a), P.L. 112-240, see above] which reads as follows:

"(b) The amendments made by this section shall apply to—

"(1) determinations made after the date of the enactment of this Act and before January 1, 2014, in the case of any qualified building (as defined in section 142(d)(2)(B)(iii) of the Internal Revenue Code of 1986)—

"(A) with respect to which housing credit dollar amounts have been allocated on or before the date of the enactment of this Act, or

"(B) with respect to buildings placed in service before such date of enactment, to the extent paragraph (1) of section 42(h) of such Code does not apply to such building by reason of paragraph (4) thereof, but only with respect to bonds issued before such date of enactment, and

"(2) determinations made after the date of enactment of this Act, in the case of qualified buildings (as so defined)—

"(A) with respect to which housing credit dollar amounts are allocated after the date of the enactment of this Act and before January 1, 2014, or

"(B) with respect to which buildings placed in service after the date of enactment of this Act and before January 1, 2014, to the extent paragraph (1) of section 42(h) of such Code does not apply to such building by reason of paragraph (4) thereof, but only with respect to bonds issued after such date of enactment and before January 1, 2014."

Code Sec. 142(k) was amended by Sec. 422(b), P.L. 107-16, 6/7/2001, as detailed below:

3. Sec. 422(b) added subsec. (k)

Effective Date (Sec. 422(f), P.L. 107-16, 6/7/2001) effective for bonds issued after 12/31/2001.

[¶ 3053]   Code Sec. 147.   Other requirements applicable to certain private activity bonds.

* * * * * * * * * * * *

(e) No portion of bonds may be issued for skyboxes, airplanes, gambling establishments, etc. A private activity bond shall not be a qualified bond if issued as part of an issue and any portion of the proceeds of such issue is to be used to provide any airplane, skybox or other private luxury box, health club facility, facility primarily used for gambling, or store the principal business of which is the sale of alcoholic beverages for consumption off premises. [1] *The preceding sentence shall not apply to any fixed-wing aircraft equipped for, and exclusively dedicated to providing, acute care emergency medical services (within the meaning of section 4261(g)(2)).*

* * * * * * * * * * * *

(h) **Certain rules not to apply to** [2]*certain bonds.*

(1) **Mortgage revenue bonds and qualified student loan bonds.** Subsections (a), (b), (c), and (d) shall not apply to any qualified mortgage bond, qualified veterans' mortgage bond, or qualified student loan bond.

(2) **Qualified 501(c)(3) bonds.** Subsections (a), (c), and (d) shall not apply to any qualified 501(c)(3) bond and subsection (e) shall be applied as if it did not contain "health club facility" with respect to such a bond.

[3]*(3) **Exempt facility bonds for qualified public-private schools.** Subsection (c) shall not apply to any exempt facility bond issued as part of an issue described in section 142(a)(13) (relating to qualified public educational facilities).*

[For Analysis, see ¶ 1913. For Committee Reports, see ¶ 5605.]

[Endnote Code Sec. 147]

Code Sec. 147(e) was amended by Sec. 1105(a) of the FAA Modernization and Reform Act of 2012, P.L. 112-95, 2/14/2012, as detailed below:

1. Sec. 1105(a) added "The preceding sentence shall not apply to any fixed-wing aircraft equipped for, and exclusively dedicated to providing, acute care emergency medical services (within the meaning of section 4261(g)(2))." at the end of subsec. (e)

Effective Date (Sec. 1105(b), P.L. 112-95, 2/14/2012) effective for obligations issued after 2/14/2012.

Sec. 101(a)(1) of the American Taxpayer Relief Act of 2012, P.L. 112-240, 1/2/2013, deleted Title IX [Sec. 901] of the Economic Growth and Tax Relief Reconciliation Act of 2001, P.L. 107-16, the effect of which is to eliminate the sunset of all provisions enacted by P.L. 107-16. Following are the amendments made to Code Sec. 147, by P.L. 107-16.
Effective Date (Sec. 101(a)(3), P.L. 112-240, 1/2/2013) effective for taxable, plan, or limitation years beginning after 12/31/2012, and estates of decedents dying, gifts made, or generation skipping transfers after 12/31/2012.

Code Sec. 147(h) was amended by Sec. 422(d) and (e) of the Economic Growth and Tax Relief Reconciliation Act of 2001, P.L. 107-16, 6/7/2001, as detailed below:

2. Sec. 422(e) substituted "certain bonds" for "mortgage revenue bonds, qualified student loan bonds, and qualified 501(c)(3) bonds" in the heading of subsec. (h)

3. Sec. 422(d) added para. (h)(3)

Effective Date (Sec. 422(f), P.L. 107-16, 6/7/2001) effective for bonds issued after 12/31/2001.

[¶ 3054]   **Code Sec. 148.   Arbitrage.**

* * * * * * * * * * * *

(f) **Required rebate to the United States.**

* * * * * * * * * * * *

(4) **Special rules for applying paragraph (2).**

(A) In general. In determining the aggregate amount earned on nonpurpose investments for purposes of paragraph (2)—

(i) any gain or loss on the disposition of a nonpurpose investment shall be taken into account, and

(ii) any amount earned on a bona fide debt service fund shall not be taken into account if the gross earnings on such fund for the bond year is less than $100,000.

In the case of an issue no bond of which is a private activity bond, clause (ii) shall be applied without regard to the dollar limitation therein if the average maturity of the issue (determined in accordance with section 147(b)(2)(A)) is at least 5 years and the rates of interest on bonds which are part of the issue do not vary during the term of the issue.

(B) Temporary investments. Under regulations prescribed by the Secretary—

(i) In general. An issue shall, for purposes of this subsection, be treated as meeting the requirements of paragraph (2) if—

(I) the gross proceeds of such issue are expended for the governmental purposes for which the issue was issued no later than the day which is 6 months after the date of issuance of the issue, and

(II) the requirements of paragraph (2) are met with respect to amounts not required to be spent as provided in subclause (I) (other than earnings on amounts in any bona fide debt service fund).

Gross proceeds which are held in a bona fide debt service fund or a reasonably required reserve or replacement fund, and gross proceeds which arise after such 6 months and which were not reasonably anticipated as of the date of issuance, shall not be considered gross proceeds for purposes of subclause (I) only.

(ii) Additional period for certain bonds.

(I) In general. In the case of an issue described in subclause (II), clause (i) shall be applied by substituting "1 year" for "6 months" each place it appears with respect to the portion of the proceeds of the issue which are not expended in accordance with clause (i) if such portion does not exceed 5 percent of the proceeds of the issue.

(II) Issues to which subclause (I) applies. An issue is described in this subclause if no bond which is part of such issue is a private activity bond (other than a qualified 501(c)(3) bond) or a tax or revenue anticipation bond.

(iii) Safe harbor for determining when proceeds of tax and revenue anticipation bonds are expended.

(I) In general. For purposes of clause (i), in the case of an issue of tax or revenue anticipation bonds, the net proceeds of such issue (including earnings thereon) shall be treated as expended for the governmental purpose of the issue on the 1st day after the date of issuance that the cumulative cash flow deficit to be financed by such issue exceeds 90 percent of the proceeds of such issue.

(II) Cumulative cash flow deficit. For purposes of subclause (I), the term "cumulative cash flow deficit" means, as of the date of computation, the excess of the expenses paid during the period described in subclause (III) which would ordinarily be paid out of or financed by anticipated tax or other revenues over the aggregate amount available (other than from the proceeds of the issue) during such period for the payment of such expenses.

(III) Period involved. For purposes of subclause (II), the period described in this subclause is the period beginning on the date of issuance of the issue and ending on the earlier of the date 6 months after such date of issuance or the date of the computation of cumulative cash flow deficit.

(iv) Payments of principal not to affect requirements. For purposes of this subparagraph, payments of principal on the bonds which are part of an issue shall not be treated as expended for the governmental purposes of the issue.

(C) Exception from rebate for certain proceeds to be used to finance construction expenditures. —

(i) In general. In the case of a construction issue, paragraph (2) shall not apply to the available construction proceeds of such issue if the spending requirements of clause (ii) are met.

(ii) Spending requirements. The spending requirements of this clause are met if at least—

(I) 10 percent of the available construction proceeds of the construction issue are spent for the governmental purposes of the issue within the 6-month period beginning on the date the bonds are issued,

(II) 45 percent of such proceeds are spent for such purposes within the 1-year period beginning on such date,

(III) 75 percent of such proceeds are spent for such purposes within the 18-month period beginning on such date, and

(IV) 100 percent of such proceeds are spent for such purposes within the 2-year period beginning on such date.

(iii) Exception for reasonable retainage. The spending requirement of clause (ii)(IV) shall be treated as met if—

(I) such requirement would be met at the close of such 2-year period but for a reasonable retainage (not exceeding 5 percent of the available construction proceeds of the construction issue), and

(II) 100 percent of the available construction proceeds of the construction issue are spent for the governmental purposes of the issue within the 3-year period beginning on the date the bonds are issued.

(iv) Construction issue. For purposes of this subparagraph, the term "construction issue" means any issue if—

(I) at least 75 percent of the available construction proceeds of such issue are to be used for construction expenditures with respect to property which is to be owned by a governmental unit or a 501(c)(3) organization, and

(II) all of the bonds which are part of such issue are qualified 501(c)(3) bonds, bonds which are not private activity bonds, or private activity bonds issued to finance property to be owned by a governmental unit or a 501(c)(3) organization.

For purposes of this subparagraph, the term "construction" includes reconstruction and rehabilitation, and rules similar to the rules of section 142(b)(1)(B) shall apply.

(v) Portions of issues used for construction. If—

(I) all of the construction expenditures to be financed by an issue are to be financed from a portion thereof, and

(II) the issuer elects to treat such portion as a construction issue for purposes of this subparagraph,

then, for purposes of this subparagraph and subparagraph (B), such portion shall be treated as a separate issue.

(vi) Available construction proceeds. For purposes of this subparagraph—

(I) In general. The term "available construction proceeds" means the amount equal to the issue price (within the meaning of sections 1273 and 1274) of the construction issue, increased by earnings on the issue price, earnings on amounts in any reasonably required reserve or replacement fund not funded from the issue, and earnings on all of the foregoing earnings, and reduced by the amount of the issue price in any reasonably required reserve or replacement fund and the issuance costs financed by the issue.

(II) Earnings on reserve included only for certain periods. The term "available construction proceeds" shall not include amounts earned on any reasonably required reserve or replacement fund after the earlier of the close of the 2-year period described in clause (ii) or the date the construction is substantially completed.

(III) Payments on acquired purpose obligations excluded. The term "available construction proceeds" shall not include payments on any obligation acquired to carry out the governmental purposes of the issue and shall not include earnings on such payments.

(IV) Election to rebate on earnings on reserve. At the election of the issuer, the term "available construction proceeds" shall not include earnings on any reasonably required reserve or replacement fund.

(vii) Election to pay penalty in lieu of rebate.

(I) In general. At the election of the issuer, paragraph (2) shall not apply to available construction proceeds which do not meet the spending requirements of clause (ii) if the issuer pays a penalty, with respect to each 6-month period after the date the bonds were issued, equal to 1 1/2 percent of the amount of the available construction proceeds of the issue which, as of the close of such 6-month period, is not spent as required by clause (ii).

(II) Termination. The penalty imposed by this clause shall cease to apply only as provided in clause (viii) or after the latest maturity date of any bond in the issue (including any refunding bond with respect thereto).

(viii) Election to terminate 1 1/2 percent penalty. At the election of the issuer (made not later than 90 days after the earlier of the end of the initial temporary period or the date the construction is substantially completed), the penalty under clause (vii) shall not apply to any 6-month period after the initial temporary period under subsection (c) if the requirements of subclauses (I), (II), and (III) are met.

(I) 3 Percent Penalty. The requirement of this subclause is met if the issuer pays a penalty equal to 3 percent of the amount of available construction proceeds of the issue which is not spent for the governmental purposes of the issue as of the close of such initial temporary period multiplied by the number of years (including fractions thereof) in the initial temporary period.

(II) Yield restriction at close of temporary period. The requirement of this subclause is met if the amount of the available construction proceeds of the issue which is not spent for the governmental purposes of the issue as of the close of such initial temporary period is invested at a yield not exceeding the yield on the issue or which is invested in any tax-exempt bond which is not investment property.

(III) Redemption of bonds at earliest call date. The requirement of this subclause is met if the amount of the available construction proceeds of the issue which is not spent for the governmental purposes of the issue as of the earliest date on which bonds may be redeemed is used to redeem bonds on such date.

(ix) Election to terminate 1 1/2 percent penalty before end of temporary period. If—

(I) the construction to be financed by a construction issue is substantially completed before the end of the initial temporary period,

(II) the issuer identifies an amount of available construction proceeds which will not be spent for the governmental purposes of the issue,

(III) the issuer has made the election under clause (viii), and

(IV) the issuer makes an election under this clause before the close of the initial temporary period and not later than 90 days after the date the construction is substantially completed,

then clauses (vii) and (viii) shall be applied to the available construction proceeds so identified as if the initial temporary period ended as of the date the election is made.

(x) Failure to pay penalties. In the case of a failure (which is not due to willful neglect) to pay any penalty required to be paid under clause (vii) or (viii) in the amount or at the time prescribed therefor, the Secretary may treat such failure as not occurring if, in addition to paying such penalty, the issuer pays a penalty equal to the sum of—

(I) 50 percent of the amount which was not paid in accordance with clauses (vii) and (viii), plus

(II) interest (at the underpayment rate established under section 6621) on the portion of the amount which was not paid on the date required for the period beginning on such date.

The Secretary may waive all or any portion of the penalty under this clause. Bonds which are part of an issue with respect to which there is a failure to pay the amount required under this clause (and any refunding bond with respect thereto) shall be treated as not being, and as never having been, tax-exempt bonds.

(xi) Election for pooled financing bonds. At the election of the issuer of an issue the proceeds of which are to be used to make or finance loans (other than nonpurpose investments) to 2 or more persons, the periods described in clauses (ii) and (iii) shall begin on—

(I) the date the loan is made, in the case of loans made within the 1-year period after the date the bonds are issued, and

(II) the date following such 1-year period, in the case of loans made after such 1-year period.

If such an election applies to an issue, the requirements of paragraph (2) shall apply to amounts earned before the beginning of the periods determined under the preceding sentence.

(xii) Payments of principal not to affect requirements. For purposes of this subparagraph, payments of principal on the bonds which are part of the construction issue shall not be treated as an expenditure of the available construction proceeds of the issue.

(xiii) Refunding bonds.

(I) In general. Except as provided in this clause, clause (vii)(II), and the last sentence of clause (x), this subparagraph shall not apply to any refunding bond and no proceeds of a refunded bond shall be treated for purposes of this subparagraph as proceeds of a refunding bond.

(II) Determination of construction portion of issue. For purposes of clause (v), any portion of an issue which is used to refund any issue (or portion thereof) shall be treated as a separate issue.

(III) Coordination with rebate requirement on refunding bonds. The requirements of paragraph (2) shall be treated as met with respect to earnings for any period if a penalty is paid under clause (vii) or (viii) with respect to such earnings for such period.

(xiv) Determination of initial temporary period. For purposes of this subparagraph[sic], the end of the initial temporary period shall be determined without regard to section 149(d)(3)(A)(iv).

(xv) Elections. Any election under this subparagraph (other than clauses (viii) and (ix)) shall be made on or before the date the bonds are issued; and, once made, shall be irrevocable.

(xvi) Time for payment of penalties. Any penalty under this subparagraph shall be paid to the United States not later than 90 days after the period to which the penalty relates.

(xvii) Treatment of bona fide debt service funds. If the spending requirements of clause (ii) are met with respect to the available construction proceeds of a construction issue, then paragraph (2) shall not apply to earnings on a bona fide debt service fund for such issue.

(D) Exception for governmental units issuing $5,000,000 or less of bonds.—

(i) In general. An issue shall, for purposes of this subsection, be treated as meeting the requirements of paragraphs (2) and (3) if—

(I) the issue is issued by a governmental unit with general taxing powers,

(II) no bond which is part of such issue is a private activity bond,

(III) 95 percent or more of the net proceeds of such issue are to be used for local governmental activities of the issuer (or of a governmental unit the jurisdiction of which is entirely within the jurisdiction of the issuer), and

(IV) the aggregate face amount of all tax-exempt bonds (other than private activity bonds) issued by such unit during the calendar year in which such issue is issued is not reasonably expected to exceed $5,000,000.

(ii) Aggregation of issuers. For purpose of subclause (IV) of clause (i)—

(I) an issuer and all entities which issue bonds on behalf of such issuer shall be treated as 1 issuer,

(II) all bonds issued by a subordinate entity shall, for purposes of applying such subclause to each other entity to which such entity is subordinate, be treated as issued by such other entity, and

(III) an entity formed (or, to the extent provided by the Secretary, availed of) to avoid the purposes of such subclause (IV) and all other entities benefiting thereby shall be treated as 1 issuer.

(iii) Certain refunding bonds not taken into account in determining small issuer status. There shall not be taken into account under subclause (IV) of clause (i) any bond issued to refund (other than to advance refund) any bond to the extent the amount of the refunding bond does not exceed the outstanding amount of the refunded bond.

(iv) Certain issues issued by subordinate governmental units, etc., exempt from rebate requirement. An issue issued by a subordinate entity of a governmental unit with general taxing powers shall be treated as described in clause (i)(I) if the aggregate face amount of such issue does not exceed the lesser of—

(I) $5,000,000, or

(II) the amount which, when added to the aggregate face amount of other issues issued by such entity, does not exceed the portion of the $5,000,000 limitation under clause (i)(IV) which such governmental unit allocates to such entity.

For purposes of the preceding sentence, an entity which issues bonds on behalf of a governmental unit with general taxing powers shall be treated as a subordinate entity of such unit. An allocation shall be taken into account under subclause (II) only if it is irrevocable and made before the issuance date of such issue and only to the extent that the limitation so allocated bears a reasonable relationship to the benefits received by such governmental unit from issues issued by such entity.

(v) Determination of whether refunding bonds eligible for exception from rebate requirement. If any portion of an issue is issued to refund other bonds, such portion shall be treated as a separate issue which does not meet the requirements of paragraphs (2) and (3) by reason of this subparagraph unless—

(I) the aggregate face amount of such issue does not exceed $5,000,000,

(II) each refunded bond was issued as part of an issue which was treated as meeting the requirements of paragraphs (2) and (3) by reason of this subparagraph,

(III) the average maturity date of the refunding bonds issued as part of such issue is not later than the average maturity date of the bonds to be refunded by such issue, and

(IV) no refunding bond has a maturity date which is later than the date which is 30 years after the date the original bond was issued.

Subclause (III) shall not apply if the average maturity of the issue of which the original bond was a part (and of the issue of which the bonds to be refunded are a part) is 3 years or less. For purposes of this clause, average maturity shall be determined in accordance with section 147(b)(2)(A).

(vi) Refundings of bonds issued under law prior to Tax Reform Act of 1986. If section 141(a) did not apply to any refunded bond, the issue of which such refunded bond was a part shall be treated as meeting the requirements of subclause (II) of clause (v) if—

(I) such issue was issued by a governmental unit with general taxing powers,

(II) no bond issued as part of such issue was an industrial development bond (as defined in section 103(b)(2), but without regard to subparagraph (B) of section 103(b)(3)) or a private loan bond (as defined in section 103(o)(2)(A), but without regard to any exception from such definition other than section 103(o)(2)(C)), and

(III) the aggregate face amount of all tax-exempt bonds (other than bonds described in subclause (II)) issued by such unit during the calendar year in which such issue was issued did not exceed $5,000,000.

References in subclause (II) to section 103 shall be to such section as in effect on the day before the date of the enactment [10/22/86] of the Tax Reform Act of 1986. Rules similar to the rules of clauses (ii) and (iii) shall apply for purposes of subclause (III). For purposes of subclause (II) of clause (i), bonds described in subclause (II) of this clause to which section 141(a) does not apply shall not be treated as private activity bonds.

(vii) Increase in exception for bonds financing public school capital expenditures. Each of the $5,000,000 amounts in the preceding provisions of this subparagraph shall be increased by the lesser of [1]$10,000,000 or so much of the aggregate face amount of the bonds as are attributable to financing the construction (within the meaning of subparagraph (C)(iv)) of public school facilities.

* * * * * * * * * * * *

[For Analysis, see ¶ 1404.]

[Endnote Code Sec. 148]

Sec. 101(a)(1) of the American Taxpayer Relief Act of 2012, P.L. 112-240, 1/2/2013, deleted Title IX [Sec. 901] of the Economic Growth and Tax Relief Reconciliation Act of 2001, P.L. 107-16, the effect of which is to eliminate the sunset of all provisions enacted by P.L. 107-16. Following are the amendments made to Code Sec. 148, by P.L. 107-16. **Effective Date** (Sec. 101(a)(3), P.L. 112-240, 1/2/2013) effective for taxable, plan, or limitation years beginning after 12/31/2012, and estates of decedents dying, gifts made, or generation skipping transfers after 12/31/2012.

Code Sec. 148(f)(4)(D)(vii) was amended by Sec. 421(a) of the Economic Growth and Tax Relief Reconciliation Act of 2001, P.L. 107-16, 6/7/2001, as detailed below:

1. Sec. 421(a) substituted "$10,000,000" for "$5,000,000" the second place it appeared in clause (f)(4)(D)(vii).
Effective Date (Sec. 421(b), P.L. 107-16, 6/7/2001) effective for obligations issued in calendar yrs. begin. after 12/31/2001.

[¶ 3055]   Code Sec. 151.   Allowance of deductions for personal exemptions.

* * * * * * * * * * * *

(d) **Exemption amount.** For purposes of this section—

(1) **In general.** Except as otherwise provided in this subsection, the term "exemption amount" means $2,000.

(2) **Exemption amount disallowed in case of certain dependents.** In the case of an individual with respect to whom a deduction under this section is allowable to another taxpayer for a taxable year beginning in the calendar year in which the individual's taxable year begins, the exemption amount applicable to such individual for such individual's taxable year shall be zero.

(3) **Phaseout.**

(A) In general. In the case of any taxpayer whose adjusted gross income for the taxable year exceeds [1]*the applicable amount in effect under section 68(b)*, the exemption amount shall be reduced by the applicable percentage.

(B) Applicable percentage. For purposes of subparagraph (A), the term "applicable percentage" means 2 percentage points for each $2,500 (or fraction thereof) by which the taxpayer's adjusted gross income for the taxable year exceeds [2]*the applicable amount in effect under section 68(b)*. In the case of a married individual filing a separate return, the preceding sentence shall be applied by substituting "$1,250" for "$2,500". In no event shall the applicable percentage exceed 100 percent.

[3]*(C)* Coordination with other provisions. The provisions of this paragraph shall not apply for purposes of determining whether a deduction under this section with respect to any individual is allowable to another taxpayer for any taxable year.

[4]*(E) Repealed.*

[5]*(F) Repealed.*

[6]*(4)* **Inflation adjustment.** *In the case of any taxable year beginning* in a calendar year after 1989, the dollar amount contained in paragraph (1) shall be increased by an amount equal to—

[7]*(A)* such dollar amount, multiplied by

[8]*(B)* the cost-of-living adjustment determined under section 1(f)(3) for the calendar year in which the taxable year begins, by substituting "calendar year 1988" for "calendar year 1992" in subparagraph (B) thereof.

[9]*(B) Repealed.*

* * * * * * * * * * * *

[For Analysis, see ¶ 301.]

[Endnote Code Sec. 151]

Code Sec. 151(d)(3)(A), Code Sec. 151(d)(3)(B), Code Sec. 151(d)(3)(C), Code Sec. 151(d)(3)(D), Code Sec. 151(d)(3)(E), Code Sec. 151(d)(3)(F), Code Sec. 151(d)(4), Code Sec. 151(d)(4)(A)(i), Code Sec. 151(d)(4)(A)(ii), and Code Sec. 151(d)(4)(B) were amended by Sec. 101(b)(2)(B)(i)(I)-(III), and (b)(2)(B)(ii)(I)-(III) of the American Taxpayer Relief Act of 2012, P.L. 112-240, 1/2/2013, as detailed below:

1. Sec. 101(b)(2)(B)(i)(I) substituted 'the applicable amount in effect under section 68(b)' for 'the threshold amount' in subpara. (d)(3)(A)

2. Sec. 101(b)(2)(B)(i)(I) substituted 'the applicable amount in effect under section 68(b)' for 'the threshold amount' in subpara. (d)(3)(B)

3. Sec. 101(b)(2)(B)(i)(II) deleted subpara. (d)(3)(C), and redesignated subpara. (d)(3)(D) as subpara. (d)(3)(C)

Prior to deletion, subpara. (d)(3)(C) read as follows:

"(C) Threshold amount. For purposes of this paragraph, the term 'threshold amount' means—

"(i) $150,000 in the case of a joint return or a surviving spouse (as defined in section 2(a)),

"(ii) $125,000 in the case of a head of a household (as defined in section 2(b)),

"(iii) $100,000 in the case of an individual who is not married and who is not a surviving spouse or head of a household, and

"(iv) $75,000 in the case of a married individual filing a separate return.

"For purposes of this paragraph, marital status shall be determined under section 7703."

4. Sec. 101(b)(2)(B)(i)(III) deleted subpara. (d)(3)(E)

5. Sec. 101(b)(2)(B)(i)(III) deleted subpara. (d)(3)(F)

Prior to deletion, subparas. (d)(3)(E)-(F) read as follows:

"(E) Reduction of phaseout.

"(i) In general. In the case of taxable years beginning after December 31, 2005, and before January 1, 2010, the reduction under subparagraph (A) shall be equal to the applicable fraction of the amount which would (but for this subparagraph) be the amount of such reduction.

"(ii) Applicable fraction. For purposes of clause (i), the applicable fraction shall be determined in accordance with the following table:

For taxable years beginning in calendar year—	The applicable fraction is—
2006 and 2007	$2/3$
2008 and 2009	$1/3$

"(F) Termination. This paragraph shall not apply to any taxable year beginning after December 31, 2009."

6. Sec. 101(b)(2)(B)(ii)(III) substituted '(4) Inflation adjustment. In the case of 7 any taxable year beginning' for '(4) Inflation adjustments. Adjustment to basic amount of exemption. In the case of any taxable year beginning' in para. (d)(4)

7. Sec. 101(b)(2)(B)(ii)(II) redesignated clause (d)(4)(A)(i) as subpara. (d)(4)(A)

8. Sec. 101(b)(2)(B)(ii)(II) redesignated clause (d)(4)(A)(ii) as subpara. (d)(4)(B)

9. Sec. 101(b)(2)(B)(ii)(I) deleted subpara. (d)(4)(B)

Prior to deletion, subpara. (d)(4)(B) read as follows:

"(B) Adjustment to threshold amounts for years after 1991. In the case of any taxable year beginning in a calendar year after 1991, each dollar amount contained in paragraph (3)(C) shall be increased by an amount equal to—

"(i) such dollar amount, multiplied by

"(ii) the cost-of-living adjustment determined under section 1(f)(3) for the calendar year in which the taxable year begins, by substituting 'calendar year 1990' for 'calendar year 1992' in subparagraph (B) thereof.

Effective Date (Sec. 101(b)(3), P.L. 112-240, 1/2/2013) effective for tax. yrs. begin. after 12/31/2012.

[¶ 3056]   Code Sec. 162.   Trade or business expenses.

(a) **In general.** There shall be allowed as a deduction all the ordinary and necessary expenses paid or incurred during the taxable year in carrying on any trade or business, including—

(1) a reasonable allowance for salaries or other compensation for personal services actually rendered;

(2) traveling expenses (including amounts expended for meals and lodging other than amounts which are lavish or extravagant under the circumstances) while away from home in the pursuit of a trade or business; and

(3) rentals or other payments required to be made as a condition to the continued use or possession, for purposes of the trade or business, of property to which the taxpayer has not taken or is not taking title or in which he has no equity.

For purposes of the preceding sentence, the place of residence of a Member of Congress (including any Delegate and Resident Commissioner) within the State, congressional district, or possession which he represents in Congress shall be considered his home, but amounts expended by such Members within each taxable year for living expenses shall not be deductible for income tax purposes in excess of $3,000. For purposes of paragraph (2), the taxpayer shall not be treated as being temporarily away from home during any period of employment if such period exceeds 1 year. The preceding sentence shall not apply to any Federal employee during any period for which such employee is certified by the Attorney General (or the designee thereof) as traveling on behalf of the United States in temporary duty status to investigate or prosecute, or provide support services for the investigation or prosecution of, a Federal crime. [1]

* * * * * * * * * * *

[For Analysis, see ¶ 1603.]

[Endnote Code Sec. 162]
Code Sec. 162(a) was amended by Sec. 1858(b)(3) of the Department of Defense and Full-Year Continuing Appropriations Act, 2011, P.L. 112-10, 4/15/2011, as detailed below:
1. Sec. 1858(b)(3) deleted 'For purposes of paragraph (1), the amount of a free choice voucher provided under section 10108 of the Patient Protection and Affordable Care Act shall be treated as an amount for compensation for personal services actually rendered.' at the end of subpara. (a)
Effective Date (Sec. 1858(d), P.L. 112-10, 4/15/2011) effective for vouchers provided after 12/31/2013, as if included in the provisions of Sec. 10108(g)(1) of P.L. 111-148.

[¶ 3057]   **Code Sec. 163.**   **Interest.**

* * * * * * * * * * *

(d) Limitation on investment interest.

(1) In general. In the case of a taxpayer other than a corporation, the amount allowed as a deduction under this chapter for investment interest for any taxable year shall not exceed the net investment income of the taxpayer for the taxable year.

(2) Carryforward of disallowed interest. The amount not allowed as a deduction for any taxable year by reason of paragraph (1) shall be treated as investment interest paid or accrued by the taxpayer in the succeeding taxable year.

(3) Investment interest. For purposes of this subsection—

(A) In general. The term "investment interest" means any interest allowable as a deduction under this chapter (determined without regard to paragraph (1)) which is paid or accrued on indebtedness properly allocable to property held for investment.

(B) Exceptions. The term "investment interest" shall not include—

(i) any qualified residence interest (as defined in subsection (h)(3)), or

(ii) any interest which is taken into account under section 469 in computing income or loss from a passive activity of the taxpayer.

(C) Personal property used in short sale. For purposes of this paragraph, the term "interest" includes any amount allowable as a deduction in connection with personal property used in a short sale.

(4) Net investment income. For purposes of this subsection—

(A) In general. The term "net investment income" means the excess of—

(i) investment income, over

(ii) investment expenses.

(B) Investment income. The term "investment income" means the sum of—

(i) gross income from property held for investment (other than any gain taken into account under clause (ii)(I)),

(ii) the excess (if any) of—

(I) the net gain attributable to the disposition of property held for investment, over

(II) the net capital gain determined by only taking into account gains and losses from dispositions of property held for investment, plus

(iii) so much of the net capital gain referred to in clause (ii)(II) (or, if lesser, the net gain referred to in clause (ii)(I)) as the taxpayer elects to take into account under this clause. [1]

Such term shall include qualified dividend income (as defined in section 1(h)(11)(B)) only to the extent the taxpayer elects to treat such income as investment income for purposes of this subsection.

(C) Investment expenses. The term "investment expenses" means the deductions allowed under this chapter (other than for interest) which are directly connected with the production of investment income.

(D) Income and expenses from passive activities. Investment income and investment expenses shall not include any income or expenses taken into account under section 469 in computing income or loss from a passive activity.

(E) Reduction in investment income during phase-in of passive loss rules. Investment income of the taxpayer for any taxable year shall be reduced by the amount of the passive activity loss to which section 469(a) does not apply for such taxable year by reason of section 469(m). The preceding sentence shall not apply to any portion of such passive activity loss which is attributable to a rental real estate activity with respect to which the taxpayer actively participates (within the meaning of section 469(i)(6)) during such taxable year.

(5) Property held for investment. For purposes of this subsection—

(A) In general. The term "property held for investment" shall include—

(i) any property which produces income of a type described in section 469(e)(1), and

(ii) any interest held by a taxpayer in an activity involving the conduct of a trade or business—

(I) which is not a passive activity, and

(II) with respect to which the taxpayer does not materially participate.

(B) Investment expenses. In the case of property described in subparagraph (A)(i), expenses shall be allocated to such property in the same manner as under section 469.

(C) Terms. For purposes of this paragraph, the terms "activity", "passive activity", and "materially participate" have the meanings given such terms by section 469.

(6) Phase-in of disallowance. In the case of any taxable year beginning in calendar years 1987 through 1990—

(A) In general. The amount of interest paid or accrued during any such taxable year which is disallowed under this subsection shall not exceed the sum of—

(i) the amount which would be disallowed under this subsection if—

(I) paragraph (1) were applied by substituting "the sum of the ceiling amount and the net investment income" for "the net investment income", and

(II) paragraphs (4)(E) and (5)(A)(ii) did not apply, and

(ii) the applicable percentage of the excess of—

(I) the amount which (without regard to this paragraph) is not allowable as a deduction under this subsection for the taxable year, over

(II) the amount described in clause (i).

The preceding sentence shall not apply to any interest treated as paid or accrued during the taxable year under paragraph (2).

(B) Applicable percentage. For purposes of this paragraph, the applicable percentage shall be determined in accordance with the following table:

In the case of taxable years beginning in:	The applicable percentage is:
1987	35
1988	60
1989	80
1990	90.

(C) Ceiling amount. For purposes of this paragraph, the term "ceiling amount" means—

(i) $10,000 in the case of a taxpayer not described in clause (ii) or (iii),

(ii) $5,000 in the case of a married individual filing a separate return, and

(iii) zero in the case of a trust.

* * * * * * * * * * * *

(h)   Disallowance of deduction for personal interest.

(1)   In general. In the case of a taxpayer other than a corporation, no deduction shall be allowed under this chapter for personal interest paid or accrued during the taxable year.

(2)   Personal interest. For purposes of this subsection, the term "personal interest" means any interest allowable as a deduction under this chapter other than—

(A) interest paid or accrued on indebtedness properly allocable to a trade or business (other than the trade or business of performing services as an employee),

(B) any investment interest (within the meaning of subsection (d)),

(C) any interest which is taken into account under section 469 in computing income or loss from a passive activity of the taxpayer,

(D) any qualified residence interest (within the meaning of paragraph (3)),

(E) any interest payable under section 6601 on any unpaid portion of the tax imposed by section 2001 for the period during which an extension of time for payment of such tax is in effect under section 6163, and

(F) any interest allowable as a deduction under section 221 (relating to interest on educational loans).

(3)   Qualified residence interest. For purposes of this subsection—

(A) In general. The term "qualified residence interest" means any interest which is paid or accrued during the taxable year on—

(i) acquisition indebtedness with respect to any qualified residence of the taxpayer, or

(ii) home equity indebtedness with respect to any qualified residence of the taxpayer.

For purposes of the preceding sentence, the determination of whether any property is a qualified residence of the taxpayer shall be made as of the time the interest is accrued.

(B) Acquisition indebtedness.

(i) In general. The term "acquisition indebtedness" means any indebtedness which—

(I) is incurred in acquiring, constructing, or substantially improving any qualified residence of the taxpayer, and

(II) is secured by such residence.

Such term also includes any indebtedness secured by such residence resulting from the refinancing of indebtedness meeting the requirements of the preceding sentence (or this sentence); but only to the extent the amount of the indebtedness resulting from such refinancing does not exceed the amount of the refinanced indebtedness.

(ii) $1,000,000 Limitation. The aggregate amount treated as acquisition indebtedness for any period shall not exceed $1,000,000 ($500,000 in the case of a married individual filing a separate return).

(C) Home equity indebtedness.

(i) In general. The term "home equity indebtedness" means any indebtedness (other than acquisition indebtedness) secured by a qualified residence to the extent the aggregate amount of such indebtedness does not exceed—

(I) the fair market value of such qualified residence, reduced by

(II) the amount of acquisition indebtedness with respect to such residence.

(ii) Limitation. The aggregate amount treated as home equity indebtedness for any period shall not exceed $100,000 ($50,000 in the case of a separate return by a married individual).

(D) Treatment of indebtedness incurred on or before October 13, 1987.

(i) In general. In the case of any pre-October 13, 1987, indebtedness—

(I) such indebtedness shall be treated as acquisition indebtedness, and

(II) the limitation of subparagraph (B)(ii) shall not apply.

(ii) Reduction in $1,000,000 limitation. The limitation of subparagraph (B)(ii) shall be reduced (but not below zero) by the aggregate amount of outstanding pre-October 13, 1987, indebtedness.

(iii) Pre-October 13, 1987, indebtedness. The term "pre-October 13, 1987, indebtedness" means—

(I) any indebtedness which was incurred on or before October 13, 1987, and which was secured by a qualified residence on October 13, 1987, and at all times thereafter before the interest is paid or accrued, or

(II) any indebtedness which is secured by the qualified residence and was incurred after October 13, 1987, to refinance indebtedness described in subclause (I) (or refinanced indebtedness meeting the requirements of this subclause) to the extent (immediately after the refinancing) the principal amount of the indebtedness resulting from the refinancing does not exceed the principal amount of the refinanced indebtedness (immediately before the refinancing).

(iv) Limitation on period of refinancing. Subclause (II) of clause (iii) shall not apply to any indebtedness after—

(I) the expiration of the term of the indebtedness described in clause (iii)(I), or

(II) if the principal of the indebtedness described in clause (iii)(I) is not amortized over its term, the expiration of the term of the 1st refinancing of such indebtedness (or if earlier, the date which is 30 years after the date of such 1st refinancing).

(E) Mortgage insurance premiums treated as interest.

(i) In general. Premiums paid or accrued for qualified mortgage insurance by a taxpayer during the taxable year in connection with acquisition indebtedness with respect to a qualified residence of the taxpayer shall be treated for purposes of this section as interest which is qualified residence interest.

(ii) Phaseout. The amount otherwise treated as interest under clause (i) shall be reduced (but not below zero) by 10 percent of such amount for each $1,000 ($500 in the case of a married individual filing a separate return) (or fraction thereof) that the taxpayer's adjusted gross income for the taxable year exceeds $100,000 ($50,000 in the case of a married individual filing a separate return).

(iii) Limitation. Clause (i) shall not apply with respect to any mortgage insurance contracts issued before January 1, 2007.

(iv) Termination. Clause (i) shall not apply to amounts—

(I) paid or accrued after [2]*December 31, 2013*, or

(II) properly allocable to any period after such date.

(4) Other definitions and special rules. For purposes of this subsection—

(A) Qualified residence.

(i) In general. The term "qualified residence" means—

(I) the principal residence (within the meaning of section 121) of the taxpayer, and

(II) 1 other residence of the taxpayer which is selected by the taxpayer for purposes of this subsection for the taxable year and which is used by the taxpayer as a residence (within the meaning of section 280A(d)(1)).

(ii) Married individuals filing separate returns. If a married couple does not file a joint return for the taxable year—

(I) such couple shall be treated as 1 taxpayer for purposes of clause (i), and

(II) each individual shall be entitled to take into account 1 residence unless both individuals consent in writing to 1 individual taking into account the principal residence and 1 other residence.

(iii) Residence not rented. For purposes of clause (i)(II), notwithstanding section 280A(d)(1), if the taxpayer does not rent a dwelling unit at any time during a taxable year, such unit may be treated as a residence for such taxable year.

(B) Special rule for cooperative housing corporations. Any indebtedness secured by stock held by the taxpayer as a tenant-stockholder (as defined in section 216) in a cooperative housing corporation (as so defined) shall be treated as secured by the house or apartment which the taxpayer is entitled to occupy as such a tenant-stockholder. If stock described in the preceding sentence may not be used to secure indebtedness, indebtedness shall be treated as so secured if the taxpayer establishes to the satisfaction of the Secretary that such indebtedness was incurred to acquire such stock.

(C) Unenforceable security interests. Indebtedness shall not fail to be treated as secured by any property solely because, under any applicable State or local homestead or other debtor protection law in effect on August 16, 1986, the security interest is ineffective or the enforceability of the security interest is restricted.

(D) Special rules for estates and trusts. For purposes of determining whether any interest paid or accrued by an estate or trust is qualified residence interest, any residence held by such estate or trust shall be treated as a qualified residence of such estate or trust if such estate or trust establishes that such residence is a qualified residence of a beneficiary who has a present interest in such estate or trust or an interest in the residuary of such estate or trust.

(E) Qualified mortgage insurance. The term "qualified mortgage insurance" means—

(i) mortgage insurance provided by the ³*Department of Veterans Affairs*, the Federal Housing Administration, or the ⁴*Rural Housing Service*, and

(ii) private mortgage insurance (as defined by section 2 of the Homeowners Protection Act of 1998 (12 U.S.C. 4901), as in effect on the date of the enactment of this subparagraph).

(F) Special rules for prepaid qualified mortgage insurance. Any amount paid by the taxpayer for qualified mortgage insurance that is properly allocable to any mortgage the payment of which extends to periods that are after the close of the taxable year in which such amount is paid shall be chargeable to capital account and shall be treated as paid in such periods to which so allocated. No deduction shall be allowed for the unamortized balance of such account if such mortgage is satisfied before the end of its term. The preceding sentences shall not apply to amounts paid for qualified mortgage insurance provided by the Veterans Administration or the Rural Housing Administration.

(5) Phase-in of limitation. In the case of any taxable year beginning in calendar years 1987 through 1990, the amount of interest with respect to which a deduction is disallowed under this subsection shall be equal to the applicable percentage (within the meaning of subsection (d)(6)(B)) of the amount which (but for this paragraph) would have been so disallowed.

* * * * * * * * * * * * *

[For Analysis, see ¶ 208 and ¶ 305.]

[Endnote Code Sec. 163]

Sec. 102(a) of the American Taxpayer Relief Act of 2012, P.L. 112-240, 1/2/2013, deleted Sec. 303, P.L. 108-27, the Jobs and Growth Tax Relief Reconciliation Act of 2003, the effect of which is to eliminate the sunset of all provisions enacted by Title III of P.L. 108-27. Following are the amendments made to Code Sec. 163 by P.L. 108-27.

Code Sec. 163(d)(4)(B) in *italics* was added by Sec. 302(b) of the Jobs and Growth Tax Relief Reconciliation Act of 2003, P.L. 108-27, 5/28/2003.

1. added a flush sentence at the end of subpara. (d)(4)(B)

Effective Date (Sec. 302(f), P.L. 108-27, 5/28/2003) effective for tax. yrs. begin. after 12/31/2002. Secs. 302(f)(2) and 303 of this Act, provide:

Code Sec. 163(h)(3)(E)(iv)(I) and Code Sec. 163(h)(4)(E)(i) were amended by Sec. 204(a)-(b) of the American Taxpayer Relief Act of 2012, P.L. 112-240, 1/2/2013, as detailed below:

2. Sec. 204(a) substituted "December 31, 2013" for "December 31, 2011" in subclause (h)(3)(E)(iv)(I)

3. Sec. 204(b)(1) substituted "Department of Veterans Affairs" for "Veterans Administration" in clause (h)(4)(E)(i)

4. Sec. 204(b)(2) substituted "Rural Housing Service" for "Rural Housing Administration" in clause (h)(4)(E)(i)

Effective Date (Sec. 204(c), P.L. 112-240, 1/2/2013) effective for amounts paid or accrued after 12/31/2011.

[¶ 3058]   Code Sec. 164.   Taxes.

* * * * * * * * * * * * *

(b)   Definitions and special rules. For purposes of this section—

(1)   Personal property taxes. The term "personal property tax" means an ad valorem tax which is imposed on an annual basis in respect of personal property.

(2)   State or local taxes. A State or local tax includes only a tax imposed by a State, a possession of the United States, or a political subdivision of any of the foregoing, or by the District of Columbia.

(3)   Foreign taxes. A foreign tax includes only a tax imposed by the authority of a foreign country.

(4)   Special rules for GST tax.

(A) In general. The GST tax imposed on income distributions is—

(i) the tax imposed by section 2601, and

(ii) any State tax described in section 2604

but only to the extent such tax is imposed on a transfer which is included in the gross income of the distributee and to which section 666 does not apply.

(B) Special rule for tax paid before due date. Any tax referred to in subparagraph (A) imposed with respect to a transfer occurring during the taxable year of the distributee (or, in the case of a taxable termination, the trust) which is paid not later than the time prescribed by law (including extensions) for filing the return with respect to such transfer shall be treated as having been paid on the last day of the taxable year in which the transfer was made.

(5)   General sales taxes. For purposes of subsection (a)—

(A) Election to deduct State and local sales taxes in lieu of State and local income taxes. At the election of the taxpayer for the taxable year, subsection (a) shall be applied—

(i) without regard to the reference to State and local income taxes, and

(ii) as if State and local general sales taxes were referred to in a paragraph thereof.

(B) Definition of general sales tax. The term "general sales tax" means a tax imposed at one rate with respect to the sale at retail of a broad range of classes of items.

(C) Special rules for food, etc. In the case of items of food, clothing, medical supplies, and motor vehicles—

(i) the fact that the tax does not apply with respect to some or all of such items shall not be taken into account in determining whether the tax applies with respect to a broad range of classes of items, and

(ii) the fact that the rate of tax applicable with respect to some or all of such items is lower than the general rate of tax shall not be taken into account in determining whether the tax is imposed at one rate.

(D) Items taxed at different rates. Except in the case of a lower rate of tax applicable with respect to an item described in subparagraph (C), no deduction shall be allowed under this paragraph for any general sales tax imposed with respect to an item at a rate other than the general rate of tax.

(E) Compensating use taxes. A compensating use tax with respect to an item shall be treated as a general sales tax. For purposes of the preceding sentence, the term "compensating use tax" means, with respect to any item, a tax which—

(i) is imposed on the use, storage, or consumption of such item, and

(ii) is complementary to a general sales tax, but only if a deduction is allowable under this paragraph with respect to items sold at retail in the taxing jurisdiction which are similar to such item.

(F) Special rule for motor vehicles. In the case of motor vehicles, if the rate of tax exceeds the general rate, such excess shall be disregarded and the general rate shall be treated as the rate of tax.

(G) Separately stated general sales taxes. If the amount of any general sales tax is separately stated, then, to the extent that the amount so stated is paid by the consumer (other than in connection with the consumer's trade or business) to the seller, such amount shall be treated as a tax imposed on, and paid by, such consumer.

(H) Amount of deduction may be determined under tables.

(i) In general. At the election of the taxpayer for the taxable year, the amount of the deduction allowed under this paragraph for such year shall be—

(I) the amount determined under this paragraph (without regard to this subparagraph) with respect to motor vehicles, boats, and other items specified by the Secretary, and

(II) the amount determined under tables prescribed by the Secretary with respect to items to which subclause (I) does not apply.

(ii) Requirements for tables. The tables prescribed under clause (i)—

(I) shall reflect the provisions of this paragraph,

(II) shall be based on the average consumption by taxpayers on a State-by-State basis (as determined by the Secretary) of items to which clause (i)(I) does not apply, taking into account filing status, number of dependents, adjusted gross income, and rates of State and local general sales taxation, and

(III) need only be determined with respect to adjusted gross incomes up to the applicable amount (as determined under section 68(b)).

(I) Application of paragraph. This paragraph shall apply to taxable years beginning after December 31, 2003, and before [1]*January 1, 2014.*

(6) Qualified motor vehicle taxes.

(A) In general. For purposes of this section, the term "qualified motor vehicle taxes" means any State or local sales or excise tax imposed on the purchase of a qualified motor vehicle.

(B) Limitation based on vehicle price. The amount of any State or local sales or excise tax imposed on the purchase of a qualified motor vehicle taken into account under subparagraph (A) shall not exceed the portion of such tax attributable to so much of the purchase price as does not exceed $49,500.

(C) Income limitation. The amount otherwise taken into account under subparagraph (A) (after the application of subparagraph (B)) for any taxable year shall be reduced (but not below zero) by the amount which bears the same ratio to the amount which is so treated as—

(i) the excess (if any) of—

(I) the taxpayer's modified adjusted gross income for such taxable year, over

(II) $125,000 ($250,000 in the case of a joint return), bears to

(ii) $10,000.

For purposes of the preceding sentence, the term "modified adjusted gross income" means the adjusted gross income of the taxpayer for the taxable year (determined without regard to sections 911, 931, and 933).

(D) Qualified motor vehicle. For purposes of this paragraph—

(i) In general. The term "qualified motor vehicle" means—

(I) a passenger automobile or light truck which is treated as a motor vehicle for purposes of title II of the Clean Air Act, the gross vehicle weight rating of which is not more than 8,500 pounds, and the original use of which commences with the taxpayer,

(II) a motorcycle the gross vehicle weight rating of which is not more than 8,500 pounds and the original use of which commences with the taxpayer, and

(III) a motor home the original use of which commences with the taxpayer.

(ii) Other terms. The terms "motorcycle" and "motor home" have the meanings given such terms under section 571.3 of title 49, Code of Federal Regulations (as in effect on the date of the enactment of this paragraph).

(E) Qualified motor vehicle taxes not included in cost of acquired property. The last sentence of subsection (a) shall not apply to any qualified motor vehicle taxes.

(F) Coordination with general sales tax. This paragraph shall not apply in the case of a taxpayer who makes an election under paragraph (5) for the taxable year.

(G) Termination. This paragraph shall not apply to purchases after December 31, 2009.

* * * * * * * * * * * *

(f) Deduction for one-half of self-employment taxes.

(1) In general. In the case of an individual, in addition to the taxes described in subsection (a), there shall be allowed as a deduction for the taxable year an amount equal to one-half of the taxes imposed by section 1401 (other than the taxes imposed by section 1401(b)(2)) for such taxable year.

(2) Deduction treated as attributable to trade or business. For purposes of this chapter, the deduction allowed by paragraph (1) shall be treated as attributable to a trade or business carried on by the taxpayer which does not consist of the performance of services by the taxpayer as an employee.

* * * * * * * * * * * *

[For Analysis, see ¶ 303 and ¶ 1901. For Committee Reports, see ¶ 5501.]

[Endnote Code Sec. 164]

Code Sec. 164(b)(5)(I) was amended by Sec. 205(a) of the American Taxpayer Relief Act of 2012, P.L. 112-240, 1/2/2013, as detailed below:

1. Sec. 205(a) substituted "January 1, 2014" for "January 1, 2012" in subpara. (b)(5)(I)

Effective Date (Sec. 205(b), P.L. 112-240, 1/2/2013) effective for taxable years beginning after 12/31/2011.

Sec. 601, P.L. 111-312, relating to the temporary employee payroll tax cut, as amended by Sec. 1001(a) and (b), P.L. 112-96 and Sec. 101(a)-(d), P.L. 112-78, reads as follows. For description of those amendments, see below.

"SEC. 601. TEMPORARY EMPLOYEE PAYROLL TAX CUT.

"(a) In general. Notwithstanding any other provision of law, —

"(1) with respect to any taxable year which begins in the payroll tax holiday period, the rate of tax under section 1401(a) of the Internal Revenue Code of 1986 shall be 10.40 percent, and

"(2) with respect to remuneration received during the payroll tax holiday period, the rate of tax under 3101(a) of such Code shall be 4.2 percent (including for purposes of determining the applicable percentage under sections 3201(a) and 3211(a)(1) of such Code).

"(b) Coordination with deductions for employment taxes.

"(1) Deduction in computing net earnings from self-employment. For purposes of applying section 1402(a)(12) of the Internal Revenue Code of 1986, the rate of tax imposed by subsection 1401(a) of such Code shall be determined without regard to the reduction in such rate under this section.

"(2) Individual deduction. In the case of the taxes imposed by section 1401 of such Code for any taxable year which begins in the payroll tax holiday period, the deduction under section 164(f) of such Code with respect to such taxes shall be equal to the sum of —

"(A) 59.6 percent of the portion of such taxes attributable to the tax imposed by section 1401(a) of such Code (determined after the application of this section), plus

"(B) one-half of the portion of such taxes attributable to the tax imposed by section 1401(b) of such Code.

"(c) Payroll Tax Holiday Period. The term 'payroll tax holiday period' means calendar years 2011 and 2012.

"(d) Employer notification. The Secretary of the Treasury shall notify employers of the payroll tax holiday period in any manner the Secretary deems appropriate.

"(e) Transfers of funds.

"(1) Transfers to Federal Old-Age and Survivors Insurance Trust Fund. There are hereby appropriated to the Federal Old-Age and Survivors Trust Fund and the Federal Disability Insurance Trust Fund established under section 201 of the Social Security Act (42 U.S.C. 401) amounts equal to the reduction in revenues to the Treasury by reason of the application of subsection (a). Amounts appropriated by the preceding sentence shall be transferred from the general fund at such times and in such manner as to replicate to the extent possible the transfers which would have occurred to such Trust Fund had such amendments not been enacted.

"(2) Transfers to Social Security Equivalent Benefit Account. There are hereby appropriated to the Social Security Equivalent Benefit Account established under section 15A(a) of the Railroad Retirement Act of 1974 (45 U.S.C. 231n-1(a)) amounts equal to the reduction in revenues to the Treasury by reason of the application of subsection (a)(2). Amounts appropriated by the preceding sentence shall be transferred from the general fund at such times and in such manner as to replicate to the extent possible the transfers which would have occurred to such Account had such amendments not been enacted.

"(3) Coordination with other Federal laws. For purposes of applying any provision of Federal law other than the provisions of the Internal Revenue Code of 1986, the rate of tax in effect under section 3101(a) of such Code shall be determined without regard to the reduction in such rate under this section."

Sec. 1001(a) and (b), P.L. 112-96, amended Sec. 601, P.L. 111-312, 12/17/2010, relating to the temporary employee payroll tax cut, as outlined below:

Sec. 1001(a), amended Sec. 601(c), P.L. 111-312.

Prior to amendment, Sec. 601(c), P.L. 111-312 read as follows:

"(c) Payroll Tax Holiday Period. The term 'payroll tax holiday period' means—

"(1) in the case of the tax described in subsection (a)(1), calendar years 2011 and 2012, and

"(2) in the case of the taxes described in subsection (a)(2), the period beginning January 1, 2011, and ending February 29, 2012."

Sec. 1001(b), deleted Sec. 601(f) and (g) P.L. 111-312.

Prior to deletion, Sec. 601(f) and (g), P.L. 111-312 read as follows:

"(f) Special rules for 2012.

"(1) Limitation on self-employment income. In the case of any taxable year beginning in 2012, subsection (a)(1) shall only apply with respect to so much of the taxpayer's self-employment income (as defined in section 1402(b) of the Internal Revenue Code of 1986) as does not exceed the excess (if any) of—

"(A) $18,350, over

"(B) the amount of wages and compensation received during the portion of the payroll tax holiday period occurring during 2012 subject to tax under section 3101(a) of such Code or section 3201(a) of such Code.

"(2) Coordination with deduction for employment taxes. In the case of a taxable year beginning in 2012, subparagraph (A) of subsection (b)(2) shall be applied as if it read as follows:

"'(A) the sum of—

"'(i) 59.6 percent of the portion of such taxes attributable to the tax imposed by section 1401(a) of such Code (determined after the application of this section) on so much of self-employment income (as defined in section 1402(b) of such Code) as does not exceed the amount of self-employment income described in paragraph (1), plus

"'(ii) one-half of the portion of such taxes attributable to the tax imposed by section 1401(a) of such Code (determined without regard to this section) on self-employment income (as so defined) in excess of such amount, plus'

"(g) Recapture of excess benefit.

"(1) In general. There is hereby imposed on the income of every individual a tax equal to 2 percent of the sum of wages (within the meaning of section 3121(a)(1) of the Internal Revenue Code of 1986) and compensation (to which section 3201(a) of such Code applies) received during the period beginning January 1, 2012, and ending February 29, 2012, to the extent the amount of such sum exceeds $18,350.

"(2) Regulations. The Secretary of the Treasury or the Secretary's delegate shall prescribe such regulations or other guidance as may be necessary or appropriate to carry out this subsection, including guidance for payment by the employee of the tax imposed by paragraph (1)."

Effective Date (Sec. 1001(c), P.L. 112-96) effective for rumeration received, and taxable years beginning after 12/31/2011.

Sec. 101(a), (b) and (c), P.L. 112-78, amended Sec. 601, P.L. 111-312, 12/17/2010, relating to the temporary employee payroll tax cut, as outlined below:

Sec. 101(a), amended Sec. 601(c) of P.L. 111-312

Sec. 101(b), added Sec. 601(f) of P.L. 111-312

Sec. 101(c), added Sec. 601(g) of P.L. 111-312 effective for remuneration received, and tax. yrs. begin., after 12/31/2011.

Prior to amendment, Sec. 601(c) of P.L. 111-312 read as follows:

"(c) Payroll tax holiday period. The term 'payroll tax holiday period' means calendar year 2011."

Effective Date (Sec. 101(e)(1), P.L. 112-78) effective for remuneration received, and taxable years beginning, after 12/31/2011.

Sec. 101(d), P.L. 112-78, amended Sec. 601, P.L. 111-312, 12/17/2010, relating to the temporary employee payroll tax cut, as outlined below:

Sec. 101(d)(1), added "of such Code" after "164(f)" in Sec. 601(b)(2) of P.L. 111-312

Sec. 101(d)(2), added "of such Code" after "1401(a)" in Sec. 601(b)(2)(A) of P.L. 111-312

Sec. 101(d)(3), added "of such Code" after "1401(b)" in Sec. 601(b)(2)(B) of P.L. 111-312, effective as if included in the enactment of Sec. 601 of P.L. 111-312

[¶ 3059]   Code Sec. 168.   Accelerated cost recovery system.

* * * * * * * * * * * *

(e)   **Classification of property.** For purposes of this section—

(1)   **In general.** Except as otherwise provided in this subsection, property shall be classified under the following table:

Property shall be treated as:	If such property has a class life (in years) of:
3-year property	4 or less
5-year property	More than 4 but less than 10
7-year property	10 or more but less than 16
10-year property	16 or more but less than 20
15-year property	20 or more but less than 25
20-year property	25 or more.

(2)   **Residential rental or nonresidential real property.**

(A) Residential rental property.

(i) Residential rental property. The term "residential rental property" means any building or structure if 80 percent or more of the gross rental income from such building or structure for the taxable year is rental income from dwelling units.

(ii) Definitions. For purposes of clause (i)—

(I) the term "dwelling unit" means a house or apartment used to provide living accommodations in a building or structure, but does not include a unit in a hotel, motel, or other establishment more than one-half of the units in which are used on a transient basis, and

(II) if any portion of the building or structure is occupied by the taxpayer, the gross rental income from such building or structure shall include the rental value of the portion so occupied.

(B) Nonresidential real property. The term "nonresidential real property" means section 1250 property which is not—

(i) residential rental property, or

(ii) property with a class life of less than 27.5 years.

(3) Classification of certain property.

(A) 3-year property. The term "3-year property" includes—

(i) any race horse—

(I) which is placed in service before January 1, 2014, and

(II) which is placed in service after December 31, 2013, and which is more than 2 years old at the time such horse is placed in service by such purchaser,

(ii) any horse other than a race horse which is more than 12 years old at the time it is placed in service, and

(iii) any qualified rent-to-own property.

(B) 5-year property. The term "5-year property" includes—

(i) any automobile or light general purpose truck,

(ii) any semi-conductor manufacturing equipment,

(iii) any computer-based telephone central office switching equipment,

(iv) any qualified technological equipment,

(v) any section 1245 property used in connection with research and experimentation,

(vi) any property which—

(I) is described in subparagraph (A) of section 48(a)(3) (or would be so described if "solar or wind energy" were substituted for "solar energy" in clause (i) thereof and the last sentence of such section did not apply to such subparagraph),

(II) is described in paragraph (15) of section 48(l) (as in effect on the day before the date of the enactment [11/5/90] of the Revenue Reconciliation Act of 1990) and is a qualifying small power production facility within the meaning of section 3(17)(C) of the Federal Power Act (16 U.S.C. 796(17)(C)), as in effect on September 1, 1986, or

(III) is described in section 48(l)(3)(A)(ix) (as in effect on the date before the date of the enactment of the Revenue Reconciliation Act of 1990), and

(vii) any machinery or equipment (other than any grain bin, cotton ginning asset, fence, or other land improvement) which is used in a farming business (as defined in section 263A(e)(4)), the original use of which commences with the taxpayer after December 31, 2008, and which is placed in service before January 1, 2010.

Nothing in any provision of law shall be construed to treat property as not being described in clause (vi)(I)(or the corresponding provisions of prior law) by reason of being public utility property (within the meaning of section 48(a)(3)).

(C) 7-year property. The term "7-year property" includes—

(i) any railroad track and

(ii) any motorsports entertainment complex,

(iii) any Alaska natural gas pipeline,

(iv) any natural gas gathering line the original use of which commences with the taxpayer after April 11, 2005, and

(v) any property which—

(I) does not have a class life, and

(II) is not otherwise classified under paragraph (2) or this paragraph.

(D) 10-year property. The term "10-year property" includes—

(i) any single purpose agricultural or horticultural structure (within the meaning of subsection (i)(13)),

(ii) any tree or vine bearing fruit or nuts,

(iii) any qualified smart electric meter, and

(iv) any qualified smart electric grid system.

(E) 15-year property. The term "15-year property" includes—

(i) any municipal wastewater treatment plant,

(ii) any telephone distribution plant and comparable equipment used for 2-way exchange of voice and data communications,

(iii) any section 1250 property which is a retail motor fuels outlet (whether or not food or other convenience items are sold at the outlet),

(iv) any qualified leasehold improvement property placed in service before [1]*January 1, 2014*,

(v) any qualified restaurant property placed in service before [2]*January 1, 2014*,

(vi) initial clearing and grading land improvements with respect to gas utility property,

(vii) any section 1245 property (as defined in section 1245(a)(3)) used in the transmission at 69 or more kilovolts of electricity for sale and the original use of which commences with the taxpayer after April 11, 2005,

(viii) any natural gas distribution line the original use of which commences with the taxpayer after April 11, 2005, and which is placed in service before January 1, 2011, and

(ix) any qualified retail improvement property placed in service after December 31, 2008, and before [3]*January 1, 2014*.

(F) 20-year property. The term "20-year property" means initial clearing and grading land improvements with respect to any electric utility transmission and distribution plant.

(4) Railroad grading or tunnel bore. The term "railroad grading or tunnel bore" means all improvements resulting from excavations (including tunneling), construction of embankments, clearings, diversions of roads and streams, sodding of slopes, and from similar work necessary to provide, construct, reconstruct, alter, protect, improve, replace, or restore a roadbed or right-of-way for railroad track.

(5) Water utility property. The term "water utility property" means property—

(A) which is an integral part of the gathering, treatment, or commercial distribution of water, and which, without regard to this paragraph, would be 20-year property, and

(B) any municipal sewer.

(6) Qualified leasehold improvement property. The term "qualified leasehold improvement property" has the meaning given such term in section 168(k)(3) except that the following special rules shall apply:

(A) Improvements made by lessor. In the case of an improvement made by the person who was the lessor of such improvement when such improvement was placed in service, such improvement shall be qualified leasehold improvement property (if at all) only so long as such improvement is held by such person.

(B) Exception for changes in form of business. Property shall not cease to be qualified leasehold improvement property under subparagraph (A) by reason of—

(i) death,

(ii) a transaction to which section 381(a) applies,

(iii) a mere change in the form of conducting the trade or business so long as the property is retained in such trade or business as qualified leasehold improvement property and the taxpayer retains a substantial interest in such trade or business,

(iv) the acquisition of such property in an exchange described in section 1031, 1033, or 1038 to the extent that the basis of such property includes an amount representing the adjusted basis of other property owned by the taxpayer or a related person, or

(v) the acquisition of such property by the taxpayer in a transaction described in section 332, 351, 361, 721, or 731 (or the acquisition of such property by the taxpayer from the transferee or acquiring corporation in a transaction described in such section), to the extent that the basis of the property in the hands of the taxpayer is determined by reference to its basis in the hands of the transferor or distributor.

(7) Qualified restaurant property.

(A) In general. The term "qualified restaurant property" means any section 1250 property which is—

(i) a building, or

(ii) an improvement to a building,

if more than 50 percent of the building's square footage is devoted to preparation of, and seating for on-premises consumption of, prepared meals.

(B) Exclusion from bonus depreciation. Property described in this paragraphshall not be considered qualified property for purposes of subsection (k).

(8) Qualified retail improvement property.

(A) In general. The term "qualified retail improvement property" means any improvement to an interior portion of a building which is nonresidential real property if—

(i) such portion is open to the general public and is used in the retail trade or business of selling tangible personal property to the general public, and

(ii) such improvement is placed in service more than 3 years after the date the building was first placed in service.

(B) Improvements made by owner. In the case of an improvement made by the owner of such improvement, such improvement shall be qualified retail improvement property (if at all) only so long as such improvement is held by such owner. Rules similar to the rules under paragraph (6)(B) shall apply for purposes of the preceding sentence.

(C) Certain improvements not included. Such term shall not include any improvement for which the expenditure is attributable to—

(i) the enlargement of the building,

(ii) any elevator or escalator,

(iii) any structural component benefitting a common area, or

(iv) the internal structural framework of the building.

(D) Exclusion from bonus depreciation. Property described in this paragraph shall not be considered qualified property for purposes of subsection (k).

(E) Repealed.

* * * * * * * * * * * *

(i) Definitions and special rules. For purposes of this section—

(1) Class life. Except as provided in this section, the term "class life" means the class life (if any) which would be applicable with respect to any property as of January 1, 1986, under subsection (m) of section 167 (determined without regard to paragraph (4) and as if the taxpayer had made an election under such subsection). The Secretary, through an office established in the Treasury, shall monitor and analyze actual experience with respect to all depreciable assets. The reference in this paragraph to subsection (m) of section 167 shall be treated as a reference to such subsection as in effect on the day before the date of the enactment of the Revenue Reconciliation Act of 1990 [11/5/90].

(2) Qualified technological equipment.

(A) In general. The term "qualified technological equipment" means—

(i) any computer or peripheral equipment,

(ii) any high technology telephone station equipment installed on the customer's premises, and

(iii) any high technology medical equipment.

(B) Computer or peripheral equipment defined. For purposes of this paragraph—

(i) In general. The term "computer or peripheral equipment" means—

(I) any computer, and

(II) any related peripheral equipment.

(ii) Computer. The term "computer" means a programmable electronically activated device which—

(I) is capable of accepting information, applying prescribed processes to the information, and supplying the results of these processes with or without human intervention, and

(II) consists of a central processing unit containing extensive storage, logic, arithmetic, and control capabilities.

(iii) Related peripheral equipment. The term "related peripheral equipment" means any auxiliary machine (whether on-line or off-line) which is designed to be placed under the control of the central processing unit of a computer.

(iv) Exceptions. The term "computer or peripheral equipment" shall not include—

(I) any equipment which is an integral part of other property which is not a computer,

(II) typewriters, calculators, adding and accounting machines, copiers, duplicating equipment, and similar equipment, and

(III) equipment of a kind used primarily for amusement or entertainment of the user.

(C) High technology medical equipment. For purposes of this paragraph, the term "high technology medical equipment" means any electronic, electromechanical, or computer-based high technology equipment used in the screening, monitoring, observation, diagnosis, or treatment of patients in a laboratory, medical, or hospital environment.

(3) Lease term.

(A) In general. In determining a lease term—

(i) there shall be taken into account options to renew,

(ii) the term of a lease shall include the term of any service contract or similar arrangement (whether or not treated as a lease under section 7701(e))—

(I) which is part of the same transaction (or series of related transactions) which includes the lease, and

(II) which is with respect to the property subject to the lease or substantially similar property, and

(iii) 2 or more successive leases which are part of the same transaction (or a series of related transactions) with respect to the same or substantially similar property shall be treated as 1 lease.

(B) Special rule for fair rental options on nonresidential real property or residential rental property. For purposes of clause (i) of subparagraph (A), in the case of nonresidential real property or residential rental property, there shall not be taken into account any option to renew at fair market value determined at the time of renewal.

(4) General asset accounts. Under regulations, a taxpayer may maintain 1 or more general asset accounts for any property to which this section applies. Except as provided in regulations, all proceeds realized on any disposition of property in a general asset account shall be included in income as ordinary income.

(5) Changes in use. The Secretary shall, by regulations, provide for the method of determining the deduction allowable under section 167(a) with respect to any tangible property for any taxable year (and the succeeding taxable years) during which such property changes status under this section but continues to be held by the same person.

(6) Treatments of additions or improvements to property. In the case of any addition to (or improvement of) any property—

(A) any deduction under subsection (a) for such addition or improvement shall be computed in the same manner as the deduction for such property would be computed if such property had been placed in service at the same time as such addition or improvement, and

(B) the applicable recovery period for such addition or improvement shall begin on the later of—

(i) the date on which such addition (or improvement) is placed in service, or

(ii) the date on which the property with respect to which such addition (or improvement) was made is placed in service.

(7) Treatment of certain transferees.

(A) In general. In the case of any property transferred in a transaction described in subparagraph (B), the transferee shall be treated as the transferor for purposes of computing the depreciation deduction determined under this section with respect to so much of the basis in the hands of the transferee as does not exceed the adjusted basis in the hands of the transferor. In any case where this section as in effect before the amendments made by section 201 of the Tax Reform Act of 1986 applied to the property in the hands of the transferor, the reference in the preceding sentence to this section shall be treated as a reference to this section as so in effect.

(B) Transactions covered. The transactions described in this subparagraph are—

(i) any transaction described in section 332, 351, 361, 721, or 731, and

(ii) any transaction between members of the same affiliated group during any taxable year for which a consolidated return is made by such group.

Subparagraph (A) shall not apply in the case of a termination of a partnership under section 708(b)(1)(B).

(C) Property reacquired by the taxpayer. Under regulations, property which is disposed of and then reacquired by the taxpayer shall be treated for purposes of computing the deduction allowable under subsection (a) as if such property had not been disposed of.

(8) Treatment of leasehold improvements.

(A) In general. In the case of any building erected (or improvements made) on leased property, if such building or improvement is property to which this section applies, the depreciation deduction shall be determined under the provisions of this section.

(B) Treatment of lessor improvements which are abandoned at termination of lease. An improvement—

(i) which is made by the lessor of leased property for the lessee of such property, and

(ii) which is irrevocably disposed of or abandoned by the lessor at the termination of the lease by such lessee,

shall be treated for purposes of determining gain or loss under this title as disposed of by the lessor when so disposed of or abandoned.

(C) Cross reference. For treatment of qualified long-term real property constructed or improved in connection with cash or rent reduction from lessor to lessee, see section 110(b).

(9) Normalization rules.

(A) In general. In order to use a normalization method of accounting with respect to any public utility property for purposes of subsection (f)(2)—

(i) the taxpayer must, in computing its tax expense for purposes of establishing its cost of service for ratemaking purposes and reflecting operating results in its regulated books of account, use a method of depreciation with respect to such property that is the same as, and a depreciation period for such property that is no shorter than, the method and period used to compute its depreciation expense for such purposes; and

(ii) if the amount allowable as a deduction under this section with respect to such property [4](respecting all elections made by the taxpayer under this section) differs from the amount that would be allowable as a deduction under section 167 using the method (including the period, first and last year convention, and salvage value) used to compute regulated tax expense under clause (i), the taxpayer must make adjustments to a reserve to reflect the deferral of taxes resulting from such difference.

(B) Use of inconsistent estimates and projections, etc.

(i) In general. One way in which the requirements of subparagraph (A) are not met is if the taxpayer, for ratemaking purposes, uses a procedure or adjustment which is inconsistent with the requirements of subparagraph (A).

(ii) Use of inconsistent estimates and projections. The procedures and adjustments which are to be treated as inconsistent for purposes of clause (i) shall include any procedure or adjustment for ratemaking purposes which uses an estimate or projection of the taxpayer's tax expense, depreciation expense, or reserve for deferred taxes under subparagraph (A)(ii) unless such estimate or projection is also used, for ratemaking purposes, with respect to the other 2 such items and with respect to the rate base.

(iii) Regulatory authority. The Secretary may by regulations prescribe procedures and adjustments (in addition to those specified in clause (ii)) which are to be treated as inconsistent for purposes of clause (i).

(C) Public utility property which does not meet normalization rules. In the case of any public utility property to which this section does not apply by reason of subsection (f)(2), the allowance for depreciation under section 167(a) shall be an amount computed using the method and period referred to in subparagraph (A)(i).

(10) **Public utility property.** The term "public utility property" means property used predominantly in the trade or business of the furnishing or sale of—

(A) electrical energy, water, or sewage disposal services,

(B) gas or steam through a local distribution system,

(C) telephone services, or other communication services if furnished or sold by the Communications Satellite Corporation for purposes authorized by the Communications Satellite Act of 1962 (47 U.S.C. 701), or

(D) transportation of gas or steam by pipeline,

if the rates for such furnishing or sale, as the case may be, have been established or approved by a State or political subdivision thereof, by any agency or instrumentality of the United States, or by a public service or public utility commission or other similar body of any State or political subdivision thereof.

(11) **Research and experimentation.** The term "research and experimentation" has the same meaning as the term research and experimental has under section 174.

(12) **Section 1245 and 1250 property.** The terms "section 1245 property" and "section 1250 property" have the meanings given such terms by sections 1245(a)(3) and 1250(c), respectively.

(13) **Single purpose agricultural or horticultural structure.**

(A) In general. The term "single purpose agricultural or horticultural structure" means—

(i) a single purpose livestock structure, and

(ii) a single purpose horticultural structure.

(B) Definitions. For purposes of this paragraph—

(i) Single purpose livestock structure. The term "single purpose livestock structure" means any enclosure or structure specifically designed, constructed, and used—

(I) for housing, raising, and feeding a particular type of livestock and their produce, and

(II) for housing the equipment (including any replacements) necessary for the housing, raising, and feeding referred to in subclause (I).

(ii) Single purpose horticultural structure. The term "single purpose horticultural structure" means—

(I) a greenhouse specifically designed, constructed, and used for the commercial production of plants, and

(II) a structure specifically designed, constructed, and used for the commercial production of mushrooms.

619

(iii) Structures which include work space. An enclosure or structure which provides work space shall be treated as a single purpose agricultural or horticultural structure only if such work space is solely for—

(I) the stocking, caring for, or collecting of livestock or plants (as the case may be) or their produce,

(II) the maintenance of the enclosure or structure, and

(III) the maintenance or replacement of the equipment or stock enclosed or housed therein.

(iv) Livestock. The term "livestock" includes poultry.

(14) Qualified rent-to-own property.

(A) In general. The term "qualified rent-to-own property" means property held by a rent-to-own dealer for purposes of being subject to a rent-to-own contract.

(B) Rent-to-own dealer. The term "rent-to-own dealer" means a person that, in the ordinary course of business, regularly enters into rent-to-own contracts with customers for the use of consumer property, if a substantial portion of those contracts terminate and the property is returned to such person before the receipt of all payments required to transfer ownership of the property from such person to the customer.

(C) Consumer property. The term "consumer property" means tangible personal property of a type generally used within the home for personal use.

(D) Rent-to-own contract. The term "rent-to-own contract" means any lease for the use of consumer property between a rent-to-own dealer and a customer who is an individual which—

(i) is titled "Rent-to-Own Agreement" or "Lease Agreement with Ownership Option," or uses other similar language,

(ii) provides for level (or decreasing where no payment is less than 40 percent of the largest payment), regular periodic payments (for a payment period which is a week or month),

(iii) provides that legal title to such property remains with the rent-to-own dealer until the customer makes all the payments described in clause (ii) or early purchase payments required under the contract to acquire legal title to the item of property,

(iv) provides a beginning date and a maximum period of time for which the contract may be in effect that does not exceed 156 weeks or 36 months from such beginning date (including renewals or options to extend),

(v) provides for payments within the 156-week or 36-month period that, in the aggregate, generally exceed the normal retail price of the consumer property plus interest,

(vi) provides for payments under the contract that, in the aggregate, do not exceed $10,000 per item of consumer property,

(vii) provides that the customer does not have any legal obligation to make all the payments referred to in clause (ii) set forth under the contract, and that at the end of each payment period the customer may either continue to use the consumer property by making the payment for the next payment period or return such property to the rent-to-own dealer in good working order, in which case the customer does not incur any further obligations under the contract and is not entitled to a return of any payments previously made under the contract, and

(viii) provides that the customer has no right to sell, sublease, mortgage, pawn, pledge, encumber, or otherwise dispose of the consumer property until all the payments stated in the contract have been made.

(15) Motorsports entertainment complex.

(A) In general. The term "motorsports entertainment complex" means a racing track facility which—

(i) is permanently situated on land, and

(ii) during the 36-month period following the first day of the month in which the asset is placed in service, hosts 1 or more racing events for automobiles (of any type), trucks, or motorcycles which are open to the public for the price of admission.

(B) Ancillary and support facilities. Such term shall include, if owned by the taxpayer who owns the complex and provided for the benefit of patrons of the complex—

(i) ancillary facilities and land improvements in support of the complex's activities (including parking lots, sidewalks, waterways, bridges, fences, and landscaping),

(ii) support facilities (including food and beverage retailing, souvenir vending, and other nonlodging accommodations), and

(iii) appurtenances associated with such facilities and related attractions and amusements (including ticket booths, race track surfaces, suites and hospitality facilities, grandstands and viewing structures, props, walls, facilities that support the delivery of entertainment services, other special purpose structures, facades, shop interiors, and buildings).

(C) Exception. Such term shall not include any transportation equipment, administrative services assets, warehouses, administrative buildings, hotels, or motels.

(D) Termination. Such term shall not include any property placed in service after [5]*December 31, 2013.*

(16) Alaska natural gas pipeline. The term "Alaska natural gas pipeline" means the natural gas pipeline system located in the State of Alaska which—

(A) has a capacity of more than 500,000,000,000 Btu of natural gas per day, and

(B) is—

(i) placed in service after December 31, 2013, or

(ii) treated as placed in service on January 1, 2014, if the taxpayer who places such system in service before January 1, 2014, elects such treatment.

Such term includes the pipe, trunk lines, related equipment, and appurtenances used to carry natural gas, but does not include any gas processing plant.

(17) Natural gas gathering line. The term "natural gas gathering line" means—

(A) the pipe, equipment, and appurtenances determined to be a gathering line by the Federal Energy Regulatory Commission, and

(B) the pipe, equipment, and appurtenances used to deliver natural gas from the well-head or a commonpoint to the point at which such gas first reaches—

(i) a gas processing plant,

(ii) an interconnection with a transmission pipeline for which a certificate as an interstate transmission pipeline has been issued by the Federal Energy Regulatory Commission,

(iii) an interconnection with an intrastate transmission pipeline, or

(iv) a direct interconnection with a local distribution company, a gas storage facility, or an industrial consumer.

(18) Qualified smart electric meters.

(A) In general. The term "qualified smart electric meter" means any smart electric meter which—

(i) is placed in service by a taxpayer who is a supplier of electric energy or a provider of electric energy services, and

(ii) does not have a class life (determined without regard to subsection (e)) of less than 10 years.

(B) Smart electric meter. For purposes of subparagraph (A), the term "smart electric meter" means any time-based meter and related communication equipment which is capable of being used by the taxpayer as part of a system that—

(i) measures and records electricity usage data on a time-differentiated basis in at least 24 separate time segments per day,

(ii) provides for the exchange of information between supplier or provider and the customer's electric meter in support of time-based rates or other forms of demand response,

(iii) provides data to such supplier or provider so that the supplier or provider can provide energy usage information to customers electronically, and

(iv) provides net metering.

(19) Qualified smart electric grid systems.

(A) In general. The term "qualified smart electric grid system" means any smart grid property which—

(i) is used as part of a system for electric distribution grid communications, monitoring, and management placed in service by a taxpayer who is a supplier of electric energy or a provider of electric energy services, and

(ii) does not have a class life (determined without regard to subsection (e)) of less than 10 years.

(B) Smart grid property. For the purposes of subparagraph (A), the term "smart grid property" means electronics and related equipment that is capable of—

(i) sensing, collecting, and monitoring data of or from all portions of a utility's electric distribution grid,

(ii) providing real-time, two-way communications to monitor or manage such grid, and

(iii) providing real time analysis of and event prediction based upon collected data that can be used to improve electric distribution system reliability, quality, and performance.

(j) Property on Indian reservations.

(1) In general. For purposes of subsection (a), the applicable recovery period for qualified Indian reservation property shall be determined in accordance with the table contained in paragraph (2) in lieu of the table contained in subsection (c).

(2) Applicable recovery period for Indian reservation property. For purposes of paragraph (1)—

In the case of:	The applicable recovery period is:
3-year property	2 years
5-year property	3 years
7-year property	4 years
10-year property	6 years
15-year property	9 years
20-year property	12 years
Nonresidential real property	22 years

(3) Deduction allowed in computing minimum tax. For purposes of determining alternative minimum taxable income under section 55, the deduction under subsection (a) for property to which paragraph (1) applies shall be determined under this section without regard to any adjustment under section 56.

(4) Qualified Indian reservation property defined. For purposes of this subsection—

(A) In general. The term "qualified Indian reservation property" means property which is property described in the table in paragraph (2) and which is—

(i) used by the taxpayer predominantly in the active conduct of a trade or business within an Indian reservation,

(ii) not used or located outside the Indian reservation on a regular basis,

(iii) not acquired (directly or indirectly) by the taxpayer from a person who is related to the taxpayer (within the meaning of section 465(b)(3)(C)), and

(iv) not property (or any portion thereof) placed in service for purposes of conducting or housing class I, II, or III gaming (as defined in section 4 of the Indian Regulatory Act (25 U.S.C. 2703)).

(B) Exception for alternative depreciation property. The term "qualified Indian reservation property" does not include any property to which the alternative depreciation system under subsection (g) applies, determined—

(i) without regard to subsection (g)(7) (relating to election to use alternative depreciation system), and

(ii) after the application of section 280F(b) (relating to listed property with limited business use).

(C) Special rule for reservation infrastructure investment.

(i) In general. Subparagraph (A)(ii) shall not apply to qualified infrastructure property located outside of the Indian reservation if the purpose of such property is to connect with qualified infrastructure property located within the Indian reservation.

(ii) Qualified infrastructure property. For purposes of this subparagraph, the term "qualified infrastructure property" means qualified Indian reservation property (determined without regard to subparagraph (A)(ii)) which—

(I) benefits the tribal infrastructure,

(II) is available to the general public, and

(III) is placed in service in connection with the taxpayer's active conduct of a trade or business within an Indian reservation.

Such term includes, but is not limited to, roads, power lines, water systems, railroad spurs, and communications facilities.

(5) **Real estate rentals.** For purposes of this subsection, the rental to others of real property located within an Indian reservation shall be treated as the active conduct of a trade or business within an Indian reservation.

(6) **Indian reservation defined.** For purposes of this subsection, the term "Indian reservation" means a reservation, as defined in—

(A) section 3(d) of the Indian Financing Act of 1974 (25 U.S.C. 1452(d)), or

(B) section 4(10) of the Indian Child Welfare Act of 1978 (25 U.S.C. 1903(10)).

For purposes of the preceding sentence, such section 3(d) shall be applied by treating the term "former Indian reservations in Oklahoma" as including only lands which are within the jurisdictional area of an Oklahoma Indian tribe (as determined by the Secretary of the Interior) and are recognized by such Secretary as eligible for trust land status under 25 CFR Part 151 (as in effect on the date of the enactment of this sentence).

(7) **Coordination with nonrevenue laws.** Any reference in this subsection to a provision not contained in this title shall be treated for purposes of this subsection as a reference to such provision as in effect on the date of the enactment of this paragraph.

(8) **Termination.** This subsection shall not apply to property placed in service after [6]*December 31, 2013.*

(k)   Special allowance for certain property acquired after December 31, 2007, and before [7]*January 1, 2014.*

(1)   **Additional allowance.** In the case of any qualified property—

(A) the depreciation deduction provided by section 167(a) for the taxable year in which such property is placed in service shall include an allowance equal to 50 percent of the adjusted basis of the qualified property, and

(B) the adjusted basis of the qualified property shall be reduced by the amount of such deduction before computing the amount otherwise allowable as a depreciation deduction under this chapter for such taxable year and any subsequent taxable year.

(2)   **Qualified property.** For purposes of this subsection—

(A) In general. The term "qualified property" means property—

(i)   (I) to which this section applies which has a recovery period of 20 years or less,

(II) which is computer software (as defined in section 167(f)(1)(B)) for which a deduction is allowable under section 167(a) without regard to this subsection,

(III) which is water utility property, or

(IV) which is qualified leasehold improvement property,

(ii) the original use of which commences with the taxpayer after December 31, 2007,

(iii) which is—

(I) acquired by the taxpayer after December 31, 2007, and before [8]*January 1, 2014,* but only if no written binding contract for the acquisition was in effect before January 1, 2008, or

(II) acquired by the taxpayer pursuant to a written binding contract which was entered into after December 31, 2007, and before [9]*January 1, 2014,* and

623

(iv) which is placed in service by the taxpayer before [10]*January 1, 2014*, or, in the case of property described in subparagraph (B) or (C), before [11]*January 1, 2015*.

(B) Certain property having longer production periods treated as qualified property.

(i) In general. The term "qualified property" includes any property if such property—

(I) meets the requirements of clauses (i), (ii), (iii), and (iv) of subparagraph (A),

(II) has a recovery period of at least 10 years or is transportation property,

(III) is subject to section 263A, and

(IV) meets the requirements of clause (iii) of section 263A(f)(1)(B) (determined as if such clauses also apply to property which has a long useful life (within the meaning of section 263A(f))).

(ii) Only [12]*pre-January 1, 2014* basis eligible for additional allowance. In the case of property which is qualified property solely by reason of clause (i), paragraph (1) shall apply only to the extent of the adjusted basis thereof attributable to manufacture, construction, or production before [13]*January 1, 2014*.

(iii) Transportation property. For purposes of this subparagraph, the term "transportation property" means tangible personal property used in the trade or business of transporting persons or property.

(iv) Application of subparagraph. This subparagraph shall not apply to any property which is described in subparagraph (C).

(C) Certain aircraft. The term "qualified property" includes property—

(i) which meets the requirements of clauses (ii) , (iii), and (iv) of subparagraph (A),

(ii) which is an aircraft which is not a transportation property (as defined in subparagraph (B)(iii)) other than for agricultural or firefighting purposes,

(iii) which is purchased and on which such purchaser, at the time of the contract for purchase, has made a nonrefundable deposit of the lesser of—

(I) 10 percent of the cost, or

(II) $100,000, and

(iv) which has—

(I) an estimated production period exceeding 4 months, and

(II) a cost exceeding $200,000.

(D) Exceptions.

(i) Alternative depreciation property. The term "qualified property" shall not include any property to which the alternative depreciation system under subsection (g) applies, determined—

(I) without regard to paragraph (7) of subsection (g) (relating to election to have system apply), and

(II) after application of section 280F(b) (relating to listed property with limited business use).

(ii) Qualified New York Liberty Zone leasehold improvement property. The term "qualified property" shall not include any qualified New York Liberty Zone leasehold improvement property (as defined in section 1400L(c)(2)).

(iii) Election out. If a taxpayer makes an election under this clause with respect to any class of property for any taxable year, this subsection shall not apply to all property in such class placed in service during such taxable year.

(E) Special rules.

(i) Self-constructed property. In the case of a taxpayer manufacturing, constructing, or producing property for the taxpayer's own use, the requirements of clause (iii) of subparagraph (A) shall be treated as met if the taxpayer begins manufacturing, constructing, or producing the property after December 31, 2007, and before [14]*January 1, 2014*.

(ii) Sale-leasebacks. For purposes of clause (iii) and subparagraph (A)(ii), if property is—

(I) originally placed in service after December 31, 2007, by a person, and

(II) sold and leased back by such person within 3 months after the date such property was originally placed in service,

such property shall be treated as originally placed in service not earlier than the date on which such property is used under the leaseback referred to in subclause (II).

(iii) Syndication. For purposes of subparagraph (A)(ii), if—

(I) property is originally placed in service after December 31, 2007, by the lessor of such property,

(II) such property is sold by such lessor or any subsequent purchaser within 3 months after the date such property was originally placed in service (or, in the case of multiple units of property subject to the same lease, within 3 months after the date the final unit is placed in service, so long as the period between the time the first unit is placed in service and the time the last unit is placed in service does not exceed 12 months), and

(III) the user of such property after the last sale during such 3-month period remains the same as when such property was originally placed in service,

such property shall be treated as originally placed in service not earlier than the date of such last sale.

(iv) Limitations related to users and related parties. The term "qualified property" shall not include any property if—

(I) the user of such property (as of the date on which such property is originally placed in service) or a person which is related (within the meaning of section 267(b) or 707(b)) to such user or to the taxpayer had a written binding contract in effect for the acquisition of such property at any time on or before December 31, 2007, or

(II) in the case of property manufactured, constructed, or produced for such user's or person's own use, the manufacture, construction, or production of such property began at any time on or before December 31, 2007.

(F) Coordination with section 280F. For purposes of section 280F—

(i) Automobiles. In the case of a passenger automobile (as defined in section 280F(d)(5)) which is qualified property, the Secretary shall increase the limitation under section 280F(a)(1)(A)(i) by $8,000.

(ii) Listed property. The deduction allowable under paragraph (1) shall be taken into account in computing any recapture amount under section 280F(b)(2).

(G) Deduction allowed in computing minimum tax. For purposes of determining alternative minimum taxable income under section 55, the deduction under subsection (a) for qualified property shall be determined under this section without regard to any adjustment under section 56.

(3) **Qualified leasehold improvement property.** For purposes of this subsection—

(A) In general. The term "qualified leasehold improvement property" means any improvement to an interior portion of a building which is nonresidential real property if—

(i) such improvement is made under or pursuant to a lease (as defined in subsection (h)(7))—

(I) by the lessee (or any sublessee) of such portion, or

(II) by the lessor of such portion,

(ii) such portion is to be occupied exclusively by the lessee (or any sublessee) of such portion, and

(iii) such improvement is placed in service more than 3 years after the date the building was first placed in service.

(B) Certain improvements not included. Such term shall not include any improvement for which the expenditure is attributable to—

(i) the enlargement of the building,

(ii) any elevator or escalator,

(iii) any structural component benefiting a common area, and

(iv) the internal structural framework of the building.

(C) Definitions and special rules. For purposes of this paragraph—

(i) Commitment to lease treated as lease. A commitment to enter into a lease shall be treated as a lease, and the parties to such commitment shall be treated as lessor and lessee, respectively.

(ii) Related persons. A lease between related persons shall not be considered a lease. For purposes of the preceding sentence, the term "related persons" means—

(I) members of an affiliated group (as defined in section 1504), and

(II) persons having a relationship described in subsection (b) of section 267; except that, for purposes of this clause, the phrase "80 percent or more" shall be substituted for the phrase "more than 50 percent" each place it appears in such subsection.

(4) Election to accelerate the AMT and research credits in lieu of bonus depreciation.

(A) In general. If a corporation elects to have this paragraph apply for the first taxable year of the taxpayer ending after March 31, 2008, in the case of such taxable year and each subsequent taxable year—

(i) paragraph (1) shall not apply to any eligible qualified property placed in service by the taxpayer,

(ii) the applicable depreciation method used under this section with respect to such property shall be the straight line method, and

(iii) each of the limitations described in subparagraph (B) for any such taxable year shall be increased by the bonus depreciation amount which is—

(I) determined for such taxable year under subparagraph (C), and

(II) allocated to such limitation under subparagraph (E).

(B) Limitations to be increased. The limitations described in this subparagraph are—

(i) the limitation imposed by section 38(c), and

(ii) the limitation imposed by section 53(c).

(C) Bonus depreciation amount. For purposes of this paragraph—

(i) In general. The bonus depreciation amount for any taxable year is an amount equal to 20 percent of the excess (if any) of—

(I) the aggregate amount of depreciation which would be allowed under this section for eligible qualified property placed in service by the taxpayer during such taxable year if paragraph (1) applied to all such property, over

(II) the aggregate amount of depreciation which would be allowed under this section for eligible qualified property placed in service by the taxpayer during such taxable year if paragraph (1) did not apply to any such property.

The aggregate amounts determined under subclauses (I) and (II) shall be determined without regard to any election made under subsection (b)(2)(C), (b)(3)(D), or (g)(7) and without regard to subparagraph (A)(ii).

(ii) Maximum amount. The bonus depreciation amount for any taxable year shall not exceed the maximum increase amount under clause (iii), reduced (but not below zero) by the sum of the bonus depreciation amounts for all preceding taxable years.

(iii) Maximum increase amount. For purposes of clause (ii), the term "maximum increase amount" means, with respect to any corporation, the lesser of—

(I) $30,000,000, or

(II) 6 percent of the sum of the business credit increase amount, and the AMT credit increase amount, determined with respect to such corporation under subparagraph (E).

(iv) Aggregation rule. All corporations which are treated as a single employer under section 52(a) shall be treated—

(I) as 1 taxpayer for purposes of this paragraph, and

(II) as having elected the application of this paragraph if any such corporation so elects.

(D) Eligible qualified property. For purposes of this paragraph, the term "eligible qualified property" means qualified property under paragraph (2), except that in applying paragraph (2) for purposes of this paragraph—

(i) "March 31, 2008" shall be substituted for "December 31, 2007" each place it appears in subparagraph (A) and clauses (i) and (ii) of subparagraph (E) thereof,

(ii) "April 1, 2008" shall be substituted for "January 1, 2008" in subparagraph (A)(iii)(I) thereof, and

(iii) only adjusted basis attributable to manufacture, construction, or production—

(I) after March 31, 2008, and before January 1, 2010, and

(II) after December 31, 2010, and before January 1, [15]*2014*, shall be taken into account under subparagraph (B)(ii) thereof .

(iv) Repealed.

(v) Repealed.

(E) Allocation of bonus depreciation amounts.

(i) In general. Subject to clauses (ii) and (iii), the taxpayer shall, at such time and in such manner as the Secretary may prescribe, specify the portion (if any) of the bonus depreciation amount for the taxable year which is to be allocated to each of the limitations described in subparagraph (B) for such taxable year.

(ii) Limitation on allocations. The portion of the bonus depreciation amount which may be allocated under clause (i) to the limitations described in subparagraph (B) for any taxable year shall not exceed—

(I) in the case of the limitation described in subparagraph (B)(i), the excess of the business credit increase amount over the bonus depreciation amount allocated to such limitation for all preceding taxable years, and

(II) in the case of the limitation described in subparagraph (B)(ii), the excess of the AMT credit increase amount over the bonus depreciation amount allocated to such limitation for all preceding taxable years.

(iii) Business credit increase amount. For purposes of this paragraph, the term "business credit increase amount" means the amount equal to the portion of the credit allowable under section 38 (determined without regard to subsection (c) thereof) for the first taxable year ending after March 31, 2008, which is allocable to business credit carryforwards to such taxable year which are—

(I) from taxable years beginning before January 1, 2006, and

(II) properly allocable (determined under the rules of section 38(d)) to the research credit determined under section 41(a).

(iv) AMT credit increase amount. For purposes of this paragraph, the term "AMT credit increase amount" means the amount equal to the portion of the minimum tax credit under section 53(b) for the first taxable year ending after March 31, 2008, determined by taking into account only the adjusted minimum tax for taxable years beginning before January 1, 2006. For purposes of the preceding sentence, credits shall be treated as allowed on a first-in, first-out basis.

(F) Credit refundable. For purposes of section 6401(b), the aggregate increase in the credits allowable under part IV of subchapter A for any taxable year resulting from the application of this paragraph shall be treated as allowed under subpart C of such part (and not any other subpart).

(G) Other rules.

(i) Election. Any election under this paragraph (including any allocation under subparagraph (E)) may be revoked only with the consent of the Secretary.

(ii) Partnerships with electing partners. In the case of a corporation making an election under subparagraph (A) and which is a partner in a partnership, for purposes of determining such corporation's distributive share of partnership items under section 702—

(I) paragraph (1) shall not apply to any eligible qualified property, and

(II) the applicable depreciation method used under this section with respect to such property shall be the straight line method.

627

(iii) Special rule for passenger aircraft. In the case of any passenger aircraft, the written binding contract limitation under paragraph (2)(A)(iii)(I) shall not apply for purposes of subparagraphs (C)(i)(I) and (D).

(H) Special rules for extension property.

(i) Taxpayers previously electing acceleration. In the case of a taxpayer who made the election under subparagraph (A) for its first taxable year ending after March 31, 2008—

(I) the taxpayer may elect not to have this paragraph apply to extension property, but

(II) if the taxpayer does not make the election under subclause (I), in applying this paragraph to the taxpayer a separate bonus depreciation amount, maximum amount, and maximum increase amount shall be computed and applied to eligible qualified property which is extension property and to eligible qualified property which is not extension property.

(ii) Taxpayers not previously electing acceleration. In the case of a taxpayer who did not make the election under subparagraph (A) for its first taxable year ending after March 31, 2008—

(I) the taxpayer may elect to have this paragraph apply to its first taxable year ending after December 31, 2008, and each subsequent taxable year, and

(II) if the taxpayer makes the election under subclause (I), this paragraph shall only apply to eligible qualified property which is extension property.

(iii) Extension property. For purposes of this subparagraph, the term "extension property" means property which is eligible qualified property solely by reason of the extension of the application of the special allowance under paragraph (1) pursuant to the amendments made by section 1201(a) of the American Recovery and Reinvestment Tax Act of 2009 (and the application of such extension to this paragraph pursuant to the amendment made by section 1201(b)(1) of such Act).

(I) Special rules for round 2 extension property.

(i) In general. In the case of round 2 extension property, this paragraph shall be applied without regard to—

(I) the limitation described in subparagraph (B)(i) thereof, and

(II) the business credit increase amount under subparagraph (E)(iii) thereof.

(ii) Taxpayers previously electing acceleration. In the case of a tax payer who made the election under subparagraph (A) for its first taxable year ending after March 31, 2008, or a taxpayer who made the election under subparagraph (H)(ii) for its first taxable year ending after December 31, 2008—

(I) the taxpayer may elect not to have this paragraph apply to round 2 extension property, but

(II) if the taxpayer does not make the election under subclause (I), in applying this paragraph to the taxpayer the bonus depreciation amount, maximum amount, and maximum increase amount shall be computed and applied to eligible qualified property which is round 2 extension property.

The amounts described in subclause (II) shall be computed separately from any amounts computed with respect to eligible qualified property which is not round 2 extension property.

(iii) Taxpayers not previously electing acceleration. In the case of a taxpayer who neither made the election under subparagraph (A) for its first taxable year ending after March 31, 2008, nor made the election under subparagraph (H)(ii) for its first taxable year ending after December 31, 2008—

(I) the taxpayer may elect to have this paragraph apply to its first taxable year ending after December 31, 2010, and each subsequent taxable year, and

(II) if the taxpayer makes the election under subclause (I), this paragraph shall only apply to eligible qualified property which is round 2 extension property.

(iv) Round 2 extension property. For purposes of this subparagraph, the term "round 2 extension property" means property which is eligible qualified property solely by reason of the extension of the application of the special allowance under paragraph (1) pursuant to the amendments made by section 401(a) of the Tax Relief, Unemployment Insurance Reauthorization, and Job Creation Act of 2010 (and the application of such extension to this paragraph pursuant to the amendment made by section 401(c)(1) of such Act).

[16](J) *Special rules for round 3 extension property.*

(i) *In general.* In the case of round 3 extension property, this paragraph shall be applied without regard to—

    (I) the limitation described in subparagraph (B)(i) thereof, and

    (II) the business credit increase amount under subparagraph (E)(iii) thereof.

(ii) *Taxpayers previously electing acceleration.* In the case of a taxpayer who made the election under subparagraph (A) for its first taxable year ending after March 31, 2008, a taxpayer who made the election under subparagraph (H)(ii) for its first taxable year ending after December 31, 2008, or a taxpayer who made the election under subparagraph (I)(iii) for its first taxable year ending after December 31, 2010—

    (I) the taxpayer may elect not to have this paragraph apply to round 3 extension property, but

    (II) if the taxpayer does not make the election under subclause (I), in applying this paragraph to the taxpayer the bonus depreciation amount, maximum amount, and maximum increase amount shall be computed and applied to eligible qualified property which is round 3 extension property.

The amounts described in subclause (II) shall be computed separately from any amounts computed with respect to eligible qualified property which is not round 3 extension property.

(iii) *Taxpayers not previously electing acceleration.* In the case of a taxpayer who neither made the election under subparagraph (A) for its first taxable year ending after March 31, 2008, nor made the election under subparagraph (H)(ii) for its first taxable year ending after December 31, 2008, nor made the election under subparagraph (I)(iii) for any taxable year ending after December 31, 2010—

    (I) the taxpayer may elect to have this paragraph apply to its first taxable year ending after December 31, 2012, and each subsequent taxable year, and

    (II) if the taxpayer makes the election under subclause (I), this paragraph shall only apply to eligible qualified property which is round 3 extension property.

(iv) *Round 3 extension property.* For purposes of this subparagraph, the term "round 3 extension property" means property which is eligible qualified property solely by reason of the extension of the application of the special allowance under paragraph (1) pursuant to the amendments made by section 331(a) of the American Taxpayer Relief Act of 2012 (and the application of such extension to this paragraph pursuant to the amendment made by section 331(c)(1) of such Act).

(5) Special rule for property acquired during certain pre-2012 periods. In the case of qualified property acquired by the taxpayer (under rules similar to the rules of clauses (ii) and (iii) of paragraph (2)(A)) after September 8, 2010, and before January 1, 2012, and which is placed in service by the taxpayer before January 1, 2012 (January 1, 2013, in the case of property described in subparagraph (2)(B) or (2)(C)), paragraph (1)(A) shall be applied by substituting "100 percent" for "50 percent".

(l) Special allowance for [17]**second generation biofuel plant property.**

(1) Additional allowance. In the case of any qualified cellulosic biofuel plant property—

    (A) the depreciation deduction provided by section 167(a) for the taxable year in which such property is placed in service shall include an allowance equal to 50 percent of the adjusted basis of such property, and

    (B) the adjusted basis of such property shall be reduced by the amount of such deduction before computing the amount otherwise allowable as a depreciation deduction under this chapter for such taxable year and any subsequent taxable year.

(2)   Qualified [18]*second generation* **biofuel plant property.** The term "qualified [19]*second generation biofuel* plant property" means property of a character subject to the allowance for depreciation—

(A) which is used in the United States [20]*solely to produce second generation biofuel (as defined in section 40(b)(6)(E))*,

(B) the original use of which commences with the taxpayer after the date of the enactment of this subsection,

(C) which is acquired by the taxpayer by purchase (as defined in section 179(d)) after the date of the enactment of this subsection, but only if no written binding contract for the acquisition was in effect on or before the date of the enactment of this subsection, and

(D) which is placed in service by the taxpayer before [21]*January 1, 2014.*

[22]*(3)* **Exceptions.**

(A) Bonus depreciation property under subsection (k). Such term shall not include any property to which section 168(k) applies.

(B) Alternative depreciation property. Such term shall not include any property described in section 168(k)(2)(D)(i).

(C) Tax-exempt bond-financed property. Such term shall not include any property any portion of which is financed with the proceeds of any obligation the interest on which is exempt from tax under section 103.

(D) Election out. If a taxpayer makes an election under this subparagraph with respect to any class of property for any taxable year, this subsection shall not apply to all property in such class placed in service during such taxable year.

(4)   Special rules. For purposes of this subsection, rules similar to the rules of subparagraph (E) of section 168(k)(2) shall apply, except that such subparagraph shall be applied—

(A) by substituting "the date of the enactment of subsection (l)" for "December 31, 2007" each place it appears therein, and

(B) by substituting "qualified [23]*second generation biofuel* plant property" for "qualified property" in clause (iv) thereof.

(5)   Allowance against alternative minimum tax. For purposes of this subsection, rules similar to the rules of section 168(k)(2)(G) shall apply.

(6)   Recapture. For purposes of this subsection, rules similar to the rules under section 179(d)(10) shall apply with respect to any qualified [24]*second generation biofuel* plant property which ceases to be qualified [25]*second generation biofuel* plant property.

(7)   Denial of double benefit. Paragraph (1) shall not apply to any qualified [26]*second generation biofuel* plant property with respect to which an election has been made under section 179C (relating to election to expense certain refineries).

* * * * * * * * * * * * *

(n)   Special allowance for qualified disaster assistance property.

(1)   In general. In the case of any qualified disaster assistance property—

(A) the depreciation deduction provided by section 167(a) for the taxable year in which such property is placed in service shall include an allowance equal to 50 percent of the adjusted basis of the qualified disaster assistance property, and

(B) the adjusted basis of the qualified disaster assistance property shall be reduced by the amount of such deduction before computing the amount otherwise allowable as a depreciation deduction under this chapter for such taxable year and any subsequent taxable year.

(2)   Qualified disaster assistance property. For purposes of this subsection—

(A) In general. The term "qualified disaster assistance property" means any property—

(i)   (I) which is described in subsection (k)(2)(A)(i), or

(II) which is nonresidential real property or residential rental property,

(ii) substantially all of the use of which is—

(I) in a disaster area with respect to a federally declared disaster occurring before January 1, 2010, and

(II) in the active conduct of a trade or business by the taxpayer in such disaster area,

(iii) which—

(I) rehabilitates property damaged, or replaces property destroyed or condemned, as a result of such federally declared disaster, except that, for purposes of this clause, property shall be treated as replacing property destroyed or condemned if, as part of an integrated plan, such property replaces property which is included in a continuous area which includes real property destroyed or condemned, and

(II) is similar in nature to, and located in the same county as, the property being rehabilitated or replaced,

(iv) the original use of which in such disaster area commences with an eligible taxpayer on or after the applicable disaster date,

(v) which is acquired by such eligible taxpayer by purchase (as defined in section 179(d)) on or after the applicable disaster date, but only if no written binding contract for the acquisition was in effect before such date, and

(vi) which is placed in service by such eligible taxpayer on or before the date which is the last day of the third calendar year following the applicable disaster date (the fourth calendar year in the case of nonresidential real property and residential rental property).

(B) Exceptions.

(i) Other bonus depreciation property. The term "qualified disaster assistance property" shall not include—

(I) any property to which subsection (k) (determined without regard to paragraph (4)), (l), or (m) applies,

(II) any property to which section 1400N(d) applies, and

(III) any property described in section 1400N(p)(3).

(ii) Alternative depreciation property. The term "qualified disaster assistance property" shall not include any property to which the alternative depreciation system under subsection (g) applies, determined without regard to paragraph (7) of subsection (g) (relating to election to have system apply).

(iii) Tax-exempt bond financed property. Such term shall not include any property any portion of which is financed with the proceeds of any obligation the interest on which is exempt from tax under section 103.

(iv) Qualified revitalization buildings. Such term shall not include any qualified revitalization building with respect to which the taxpayer has elected the application of paragraph (1) or (2) of section 1400I(a).

(v) Election out. If a taxpayer makes an election under this clause with respect to any class of property for any taxable year, this subsection shall not apply to all property in such class placed in service during such taxable year.

(C) Special rules. For purposes of this subsection, rules similar to the rules of subparagraph (E) of subsection (k)(2) shall apply, except that such subparagraph shall be applied—

(i) by substituting "the applicable disaster date" for "December 31, 2007" each place it appears therein,

(ii) without regard to "and before [27]January 1, 2014" in clause (i) thereof, and

(iii) by substituting "qualified disaster assistance property" for "qualified property" in clause (iv) thereof.

(D) Allowance against alternative minimum tax. For purposes of this subsection, rules similar to the rules of subsection (k)(2)(G) shall apply.

(3) **Other definitions.** For purposes of this subsection—

(A) Applicable disaster date. The term "applicable disaster date" means, with respect to any federally declared disaster, the date on which such federally declared disaster occurs.

(B) Federally declared disaster. The term "federally declared disaster" has the meaning given such term under section 165(h)(3)(C)(i).

(C) Disaster area. The term "disaster area" has the meaning given such term under section 165(h)(3)(C)(ii).

(D) Eligible taxpayer. The term "eligible taxpayer" means a taxpayer who has suffered an economic loss attributable to a federally declared disaster.

(4) **Recapture.** For purposes of this subsection, rules similar to the rules under section 179(d)(10) shall apply with respect to any qualified disaster assistance property which ceases to be qualified disaster assistance property.

[For Analysis, see ¶ 802, ¶ 804, ¶ 805, ¶ 807, ¶ 809, ¶ 810, ¶ 812 and ¶ 1013.]

[Endnote Code Sec. 168]

Code Sec. 168(e)(3)(E)(iv), Code Sec. 168(e)(3)(E)(v), and Code Sec. 168(e)(3)(E)(ix) were amended by Sec. 311(a) of the American Taxpayer Relief Act of 2012, P.L. 112-240, 1/2/2013, as detailed below:

1. Sec. 311(a) substituted "January 1, 2014" for "January 1, 2012" in clause 168(e)(3)(E)(iv)
2. Sec. 311(a) substituted "January 1, 2014" for "January 1, 2012" in clause 168(e)(3)(E)(v)
3. Sec. 311(a) substituted "January 1, 2014" for "January 1, 2012" in clause 168(e)(3)(E)(ix)

Effective Date (Sec. 311(b), P.L. 112-240, 1/2/2013) effective for property placed in service after 12/31/2011.

Code Sec. 168(i)(9)(A)(ii), was amended by Sec. 331(d), P.L. 112-240, 1/2/2013, as detailed below:

4. Sec. 331(d) added "(respecting all elections made by the taxpayer under this section)" after "such property" in clause (i)(9)(A)(ii)

Effective Date (Sec. 331(f), P.L. 112-240, 1/2/2013) effective for property placed in service after 12/31/2012.

Code Sec. 168(i)(15)(D) was amended by Sec. 312(a), P.L. 112-240, 1/2/2013, as detailed below:

5. Sec. 312(a) substituted "December 31, 2013" for "December 31, 2011" in subpara. (i)(15)(D)

Effective Date (Sec. 312(b), P.L. 112-240, 1/2/2013) effective for property placed in service after 12/31/2011.

Code Sec. 168(j)(8) was amended by Sec. 313(a), P.L. 112-240, 1/2/2013, as detailed below:

6. Sec. 313(a) substituted "December 31, 2013" for "December 31, 2011" in para. (j)(8)

Effective Date (Sec. 313(b), P.L. 112-240, 1/2/2013) effective for property placed in service after 12/31/2011.

Code Sec. 168(j)(8), Code Sec. 168(k), Code Sec. 168(k)(2), Code Sec. 168(k)(2)(A)(iv), Code Sec. 168(k)(2)(B)(ii), Code Sec. 168(k)(4)(D)(iii)(II), and Code Sec. 168(k)(4)(J) were amended by Secs. 331(a)(1)-(2), (e)(1)-(2), and (c)(1)-(2), P.L. 112-240, 1/2/2013, as detailed below:

7. Sec. 331(e)(1) substituted "January 1, 2014" for "January 1, 2013" in the heading of subsec. (k)
8. Sec. 331(a)(2) substituted "January 1, 2014" for "January 1, 2013" in subclause (k)(2)(A)(iii)(I)
9. Sec. 331(a)(2) substituted "January 1, 2014" for "January 1, 2013" in subclause (k)(2)(A)(iii)(II)
10. Sec. 331(a)(2) substituted "January 1, 2014" for "January 1, 2013" in clause (k)(2)(A)(iv)
11. Sec. 331(a)(1) substituted "January 1, 2015" for "January 1, 2014" in clause (k)(2)(A)(iv)
12. Sec. 331(e)(2) substituted "pre-January 1, 2014" for "pre-January 1, 2013" in the heading of clause (k)(2)(B)(ii)
13. Sec. 331(a)(2) substituted "January 1, 2014" for "January 1, 2013" in clause (k)(2)(B)(ii)
14. Sec. 331(a)(2) substituted "January 1, 2014" for "January 1, 2013" in clause (k)(2)(E)(i)
15. Sec. 331(c)(1) substituted "2014" for "2013" in subclause (k)(4)(D)(iii)(II)
16. Sec. 331(c)(2) added subpara. (k)(4)(J)

Effective Date (Sec. 331(f), P.L. 112-240, 1/2/2013) effective for property placed in service after 12/31/2012.

Code Sec. 168(l) and Code Sec. 168(l)(2) were amended by Secs. 410(b)(2)(A)-(D), (b)(1), P.L. 112-240, 1/2/2013, as detailed below:

17. Sec. 410(b)(2)(C) substituted "second generation" for "cellulosic" in the heading of subsec. (l)
18. Sec. 410(b)(2)(D) substituted "second generation" for "cellulosic" in the heading of para. (l)(2)
19. Sec. 410(b)(2)(A) substituted "second generation biofuel" for "cellulosic biofuel" each place it appears in the text in subsec. (l) as amended by subsec. (a)
20. Sec. 410(b)(1) substituted "solely to produce second generation biofuel (as defined in section 40(b)(6)(E))" for "solely to produce cellulosic biofuel" in subpara. (l)(2)(A)

Effective Date (Sec. 410(b)(3), P.L. 112-240, 1/2/2013) effective for property placed in service after 12/31/2012.

Code Sec. 168(l)(2)(D) was amended by Sec. 410(a)(1), P.L. 112-240, 1/2/2013, as detailed below:

21. Sec. 410(a)(1) substituted "January 1, 2014" for "January 1, 2013" in subpara. (l)(2)(D)

Effective Date (Sec. 410(a)(2), P.L. 112-240, 1/2/2013) effective for property placed in service after 12/31/2012.

Code Sec. 168(l) [as amended by subsec. (a)], Code Sec. 168(l)(3), Code Sec. 168(l)(4), Code Sec. 168(l)(5), Code Sec. 168(l)(6), Code Sec. 168(l)(7), and Code Sec. 168(l)(8) were amended by Sec. 410(b)(2)(A)-(B), P.L. 112-240, 1/2/2013, as detailed below:

22. Sec. 410(b)(2)(B) deleted para. (l)(3) and redesignated paras. (l)(4)-(8) as paras. (3)-(7)
23. Sec. 410(b)(2)(A) substituted "second generation biofuel" for "cellulosic biofuel" each place it appears in the text in subsec. (l) as amended by subsec. (a)

24. Sec. 410(b)(2)(A) substituted "second generation biofuel" for "cellulosic biofuel" each place it appears in the text in subsec. (l) as amended by subsec. (a)

25. Sec. 410(b)(2)(A) substituted "second generation biofuel" for "cellulosic biofuel" each place it appears in the text in subsec. (l) as amended by subsec. (a)

26. Sec. 410(b)(2)(A) substituted "second generation biofuel" for "cellulosic biofuel" each place it appears in the text in subsec. (l) as amended by subsec. (a)

Effective Date (Sec. 410(b)(3), P.L. 112-240, 1/2/2013) effective for property placed in service after 12/31/2012.

27. Sec. 331(e)(3) substituted "January 1, 2014" for "January 1, 2013" in subpara. (n)(2)(C)

Effective Date (Sec. 331(f), P.L. 112-240, 1/2/2013) effective for property placed in service after 12/31/2012.

[¶ 3060]   Code Sec. 170.   Charitable, etc., contributions and gifts.

* * * * * * * * * * * *

(b)   Percentage limitations.

  (1)   Individuals. In the case of an individual, the deduction provided in subsection (a) shall be limited as provided in the succeeding subparagraphs.

   (A) General rule. Any charitable contribution to—

     (i) a church or a convention or association of churches,

     (ii) an educational organization which normally maintains a regular faculty and curriculum and normally has a regularly enrolled body of pupils or students in attendance at the place where its educational activities are regularly carried on,

     (iii) an organization the principal purpose or functions of which are the providing of medical or hospital care or medical education or medical research, if the organization is a hospital, or if the organization is a medical research organization directly engaged in the continuous active conduct of medical research in conjunction with a hospital, and during the calendar year in which the contribution is made such organization is committed to spend such contributions for such research before January 1 of the fifth calendar year which begins after the date such contribution is made,

     (iv) an organization which normally receives a substantial part of its support (exclusive of income received in the exercise or performance by such organization of its charitable, educational, or other purpose or function constituting the basis for its exemption under section 501(a)) from the United States or any State or political subdivision thereof or from direct or indirect contributions from the general public, and which is organized and operated exclusively to receive, hold, invest, and administer property and to make expenditures to or for the benefit of a college or university which is an organization referred to in clause (ii) of this subparagraph and which is an agency or instrumentality of a State or political subdivision thereof, or which is owned or operated by a State or political subdivision thereof or by an agency or instrumentality of one or more States or political subdivisions,

     (v) a governmental unit referred to in subsection (c)(1),

     (vi) an organization referred to in subsection (c)(2) which normally receives a substantial part of its support (exclusive of income received in the exercise or performance by such organization of its charitable, educational, or other purpose or function constituting the basis for its exemption under section 501(a)) from a governmental unit referred to in subsection (c)(1) or from direct or indirect contributions from the general public,

     (vii) a private foundation described in subparagraph (F), or

     (viii) an organization described in section 509(a)(2) or (3),

   shall be allowed to the extent that the aggregate of such contributions does not exceed 50 percent of the taxpayer's contribution base for the taxable year.

   (B) Other contributions. Any charitable contribution other than a charitable contribution to which subparagraph (A) applies shall be allowed to the extent that the aggregate of such contributions does not exceed the lesser of—

     (i) 30 percent of the taxpayer's contribution base for the taxable year, or

(ii) the excess of 50 percent of the taxpayer's contribution base for the taxable year over the amount of charitable contributions allowable under subparagraph (A) (determined without regard to subparagraph (C)).

If the aggregate of such contributions exceeds the limitation of the preceding sentence, such excess shall be treated (in a manner consistent with the rules of subsection (d)(1)) as a charitable contribution (to which subparagraph (A) does not apply) in each of the 5 succeeding taxable years in order of time.

(C) Special limitation with respect to contributions described in subparagraph (A) of certain capital gain property.

(i) In the case of charitable contributions described in subparagraph (A) of capital gain property to which subsection (e)(1)(B) does not apply, the total amount of contributions of such property which may be taken into account under subsection (a) for any taxable year shall not exceed 30 percent of the taxpayer's contribution base for such year. For purposes of this subsection, contributions of capital gain property to which this subparagraph applies shall be taken into account after all other charitable contributions (other than charitable contributions to which subparagraph (D) applies).

(ii) If charitable contributions described in subparagraph (A) of capital gain property to which clause (i) applies exceeds 30 percent of the taxpayer's contribution base for any taxable year, such excess shall be treated, in a manner consistent with the rules of subsection (d)(1), as a charitable contribution of capital gain property to which clause (i) applies in each of the 5 succeeding taxable years in order of time.

(iii) At the election of the taxpayer (made at such time and in such manner as the Secretary prescribes by regulations), subsection (e)(1) shall apply to all contributions of capital gain property (to which subsection (e)(1)(B) does not otherwise apply) made by the taxpayer during the taxable year. If such an election is made, clauses (i) and (ii) shall not apply to contributions of capital gain property made during the taxable year, and, in applying subsection (d)(1) for such taxable year with respect to contributions of capital gain property made in any prior contribution year for which an election was not made under this clause, such contributions shall be reduced as if subsection (e)(1) had applied to such contributions in the year in which made.

(iv) For purposes of this paragraph, the term "capital gain property" means, with respect to any contribution, any capital asset the sale of which at its fair market value at the time of the contribution would have resulted in gain which would have been long-term capital gain. For purposes of the preceding sentence, any property which is property used in the trade or business (as defined in section 1231(b)) shall be treated as a capital asset.

(D) Special limitation with respect to contributions of capital gain property to organizations not described in subparagraph (A).

(i) In general. In the case of charitable contributions (other than charitable contributions to which subparagraph (A) applies) of capital gain property, the total amount of such contributions of such property taken into account under subsection (a) for any taxable year shall not exceed the lesser of—

(I) 20 percent of the taxpayer's contribution base for the taxable year, or

(II) the excess of 30 percent of the taxpayer's contribution base for the taxable year over the amount of the contributions of capital gain property to which subparagraph (C) applies.

For purposes of this subsection, contributions of capital gain property to which this subparagraph applies shall be taken into account after all other charitable contributions.

(ii) Carryover. If the aggregate amount of contributions described in clause (i) exceeds the limitation of clause (i), such excess shall be treated (in a manner consistent with the rules of subsection (d)(1)) as a charitable contribution of capital gain property to which clause (i) applies in each of the 5 succeeding taxable years in order of time.

(E) Contributions of qualified conservation contributions.

(i) In general. Any qualified conservation contribution (as defined in subsection (h)(1)) shall be allowed to the extent the aggregate of such contributions does not exceed the excess of 50 percent of the taxpayer's contribution base over the amount of all other charitable contributions allowable under this paragraph.

(ii) Carryover. If the aggregate amount of contributions described in clause (i) exceeds the limitation of clause (i), such excess shall be treated (in a manner consistent with the rules of subsection (d)(1)) as a charitable contribution to which clause (i) applies in each of the 15 succeeding years in order of time.

(iii) Coordination with other subparagraphs. For purposes of applying this subsection and subsection (d)(1), contributions described in clause (i) shall not be treated as described in subparagraph (A), (B), (C), or (D) and such subparagraphs shall apply without regard to such contributions.

(iv) Special rule for contribution of property used in agriculture or livestock production.

(I) In general. If the individual is a qualified farmer or rancher for the taxable year for which the contribution is made, clause (i) shall be applied by substituting "100 percent" for "50 percent".

(II) Exception. Subclause (I) shall not apply to any contribution of property made after the date of the enactment of this subparagraph which is used in agriculture or livestock production (or available for such production) unless such contribution is subject to a restriction that such property remain available for such production. This subparagraph shall be applied separately with respect to property to which subclause (I) does not apply by reason of the preceding sentence prior to its application to property to which subclause (I) does apply.

(v) Definition. For purposes of clause (iv), the term "qualified farmer or rancher" means a taxpayer whose gross income from the trade or business of farming (within the meaning of section 2032A(e)(5)) is greater than 50 percent of the taxpayer's gross income for the taxable year.

(vi) Termination. This subparagraph shall not apply to any contribution made in taxable years beginning after [1]December 31, 2013.

(F) Certain private foundations. The private foundations referred to in subparagraph (A)(vii) and subsection (e)(1)(B) are —

(i) a private operating foundation (as defined in section 4942(j)(3)),

(ii) any other private foundation (as defined in section 509(a)) which, not later than the 15th day of the third month after the close of the foundation's taxable year in which contributions are received, makes qualifying distributions (as defined in section 4942(g), without regard to paragraph (3) thereof), which are treated, after the application of section 4942(g)(3), as distributions out of corpus (in accordance with section 4942(h)) in an amount equal to 100 percent of such contributions, and with respect to which the taxpayer obtains adequate records or other sufficient evidence from the foundation showing that the foundation made such qualifying distributions, and

(iii) a private foundation all of the contributions to which are pooled in a common fund and which would be described in section 509(a)(3) but for the right of any substantial contributor (hereafter in this clause called "donor") or his spouse to designate annually the recipients, from among organizations described in paragraph (1) of section 509(a), of the income attributable to the donor's contribution to the fund and to direct (by deed or by will) the payment, to an organization described in such paragraph (1), of the corpus in the common fund attributable to the donor's contribution; but this clause shall apply only if all of the income of the common fund is required to be (and is) distributed to one or more organizations described in such paragraph (1) not later than the 15th day of the third month after the close of the taxable year in which the income is realized by the fund and only if all of the corpus attributable to any donor's contribution to the fund is required to be (and is) distributed to one or more of such organizations not later than one year after his death or after the death of his surviving spouse if she has the right to designate the recipients of such corpus.

(G) Contribution base defined. For purposes of this section, the term "contribution base" means adjusted gross income (computed without regard to any net operating loss carryback to the taxable year under section 172).

(2) **Corporations.** In the case of a corporation—

(A) In general. The total deductions under subsection (a) for any taxable year (other than for contributions to which subparagraph (B) applies) shall not exceed 10 percent of the taxpayer's taxable income.

(B) Qualified conservation contributions by certain corporate farmers and ranchers.

(i) In general. Any qualified conservation contribution (as defined in subsection (h)(1))—

(I) which is made by a corporation which, for the taxable year during which the contribution is made, is a qualified farmer or rancher (as defined in paragraph (1)(E)(v)) and the stock of which is not readily tradable on an established securities market at any time during such year, and

(II) which, in the case of contributions made after the date of the enactment of this subparagraph, is a contribution of property which is used in agriculture or live-stock production (or available for such production) and which is subject to a restriction that such property remain available for such production,

shall be allowed to the extent the aggregate of such contributions does not exceed the excess of the taxpayer's taxable income over the amount of charitable contributions allowable under subparagraph (A).

(ii) Carryover. If the aggregate amount of contributions described in clause (i) exceeds the limitation of clause (i), such excess shall be treated (in a manner consistent with the rules of subsection (d)(2)) as a charitable contribution to which clause (i) applies in each of the 15 succeeding years in order of time.

(iii) Termination. This subparagraph shall not apply to any contribution made in taxable years beginning after [2]December 31, 2013.

(C) Taxable income. For purposes of this paragraph, taxable income shall be computed without regard to—

(i) this section,

(ii) part VIII (except section 248),

(iii) any net operating loss carryback to the taxable year under section 172,

(iv) section 199, and

(v) any capital loss carryback to the taxable year under section 1212(a)(1).

(3) **Temporary suspension of limitations on charitable contributions.** In the case of a qualified farmer or rancher (as defined in paragraph (1)(E)(v)), any charitable contribution of food—

(A) to which subsection (e)(3)(C) applies (without regard to clause (ii) thereof), and

(B) which is made during the period beginning on the date of the enactment of this paragraph and before January 1, 2009,

shall be treated for purposes of paragraph (1)(E) or (2)(B), whichever is applicable, as if it were a qualified conservation contribution which is made by a qualified farmer or rancher and which otherwise meets the requirements of such paragraph.

* * * * * * * * * * * *

(e) **Certain contributions of ordinary income and capital gain property.**

(1) **General rule.** The amount of any charitable contribution of property otherwise taken into account under this section shall be reduced by the sum of—

(A) the amount of gain which would not have been long-term capital gain (determined without regard to section 1221(b)(3)) if the property contributed had been sold by the taxpayer at its fair market value (determined at the time of such contribution), and

(B) in the case of a charitable contribution—

(i) of tangible personal property—

(I) if the use by the donee is unrelated to the purpose or function constituting the basis for its exemption under section 501 (or, in the case of a governmental unit, to any purpose or function described in subsection (c)), or

(II) which is applicable property (as defined in paragraph (7)(C), but without regard to clause (ii) thereof) which is sold, exchanged, or otherwise disposed of by the donee before the last day of the taxable year in which the contribution was made and with respect to which the donee has not made a certification in accordance with paragraph (7)(D),

(ii) to or for the use of a private foundation (as defined in section 509(a)), other than a private foundation described in subsection (b)(1)(F),

(iii) of any patent, copyright (other than a copyright described in section 1221(a)(3) or 1231(b)(1)(C)), trademark, trade name, trade secret, know-how, software (other than software described in section 197(e)(3)(A)(i)), or similar property, or applications or registrations of such property, or

(iv) of any taxidermy property which is contributed by the person who prepared, stuffed, or mounted the property or by any person who paid or incurred the cost of such preparation, stuffing, or mounting,

the amount of gain which would have been long-term capital gain if the property contributed had been sold by the taxpayer at its fair market value (determined at the time of such contribution).

For purposes of applying this paragraph (other than in the case of gain to which section 617(d)(1), 1245(a), 1250(a), 1252(a), or 1254(a) applies), property which is property used in the trade or business (as defined in section 1231(b)) shall be treated as a capital asset. For purposes of applying this paragraph in the case of a charitable contribution of stock in an S corporation, rules similar to the rules of section 751 shall apply in determining whether gain on such stock would have been long-term capital gain if such stock were sold by the taxpayer.

(2) Allocation of basis. For purposes of paragraph (1), in the case of a charitable contribution of less than the taxpayer's entire interest in the property contributed, the taxpayer's adjusted basis in such property shall be allocated between the interest contributed and any interest not contributed in accordance with regulations prescribed by the Secretary.

(3) Special rule for certain contributions of inventory and other property.

(A) Qualified contributions. For purposes of this paragraph, a qualified contribution shall mean a charitable contribution of property described in paragraph (1) or (2) of section 1221(a), by a corporation (other than a corporation which is an S corporation) to an organization which is described in section 501(c)(3) and is exempt under section 501(a) (other than a private foundation, as defined in section 509(a), which is not an operating foundation, as defined in section 4942(j)(3)), but only if—

(i) the use of the property by the donee is related to the purpose or function constituting the basis for its exemption under section 501 and the property is to be used by the donee solely for the care of the ill, the needy, or infants;

(ii) the property is not transferred by the donee in exchange for money, other property, or services;

(iii) the taxpayer receives from the donee a written statement representing that its use and disposition of the property will be in accordance with the provisions of clauses (i) and (ii); and

(iv) in the case where the property is subject to regulation under the Federal Food, Drug, and Cosmetic Act, as amended, such property must fully satisfy the applicable requirements of such Act and regulations promulgated thereunder on the date of transfer and for one hundred and eighty days prior thereto.

(B) Amount of reduction. The reduction under paragraph (1)(A) for any qualified contribution (as defined in subparagraph (A)) shall be no greater than the sum of—

(i) one-half of the amount computed under paragraph (1)(A) (computed without regard to this paragraph), and

(ii) the amount (if any) by which the charitable contribution deduction under this section for any qualified contribution (computed by taking into account the amount determined in clause (i), but without regard to this clause) exceeds twice the basis of such property.

(C) Special rule for contributions of food inventory.

(i) General rule. In the case of a charitable contribution of food from any trade or business of the taxpayer, this paragraph shall be applied—

(I) without regard to whether the contribution is made by a C corporation, and

(II) only to food that is apparently wholesome food.

(ii) Limitation. In the case of a taxpayer other than a C corporation, the aggregate amount of such contributions for any taxable year which may be taken into account under this section shall not exceed 10 percent of the taxpayer's aggregate net income for such taxable year from all trades or businesses from which such contributions were made for such year, computed without regard to this section.

(iii) Apparently wholesome food. For purposes of this subparagraph, the term "apparently wholesome food" has the meaning given to such term by section 22(b)(2) of the Bill Emerson Good Samaritan Food Donation Act (42 U.S.C. 1791(b)(2)), as in effect on the date of the enactment of this subparagraph.

(iv) Termination. This subparagraph shall not apply to contributions made after [3]December 31, 2013.

(D) Special rule for contributions of book inventory to public schools.

(i) Contributions of book inventory. In determining whether a qualified book contribution is a qualified contribution, subparagraph (A) shall be applied without regard to whether the donee is an organization described in the matter preceding clause (i) of subparagraph (A).

(ii) Qualified book contribution. For purposes of this paragraph, the term "qualified book contribution" means a charitable contribution of books to a public school which is an educational organization described in subsection (b)(1)(A)(ii) and which provides elementary education or secondary education (kindergarten through grade 12).

(iii) Certification by donee. Subparagraph (A) shall not apply to any contribution of books unless (in addition to the certifications required by subparagraph (A) (as modified by this subparagraph)), the donee certifies in writing that—

(I) the books are suitable, in terms of currency, content, and quantity, for use in the donee's educational programs, and

(II) the donee will use the books in its educational programs.

(iv) Termination. This subparagraph shall not apply to contributions made after December 31, 2011.

(E) This paragraph shall not apply to so much of the amount of the gain described in paragraph (1)(A) which would be long-term capital gain but for the application of sections 617, 1245, 1250, or 1252.

(4) Special rule for contributions of scientific property used for research.

(A) Limit on reduction. In the case of a qualified research contribution, the reduction under paragraph (1)(A) shall be no greater than the amount determined under paragraph (3)(B).

(B) Qualified research contributions. For purposes of this paragraph, the term "qualified research contribution" means a charitable contribution by a corporation of tangible personal property described in paragraph (1) of section 1221(a), but only if—

(i) the contribution is to an organization described in subparagraph (A) or subparagraph (B) of section 41(e)(6),

(ii) the property is constructed or assembled by the taxpayer,

(iii) the contribution is made not later than 2 years after the date the construction or assembly of the property is substantially completed,

(iv) the original use of the property is by the donee,

(v) the property is scientific equipment or apparatus substantially all of the use of which by the donee is for research or experimentation (within the meaning of section 174), or for research training, in the United States in physical or biological sciences,

(vi) the property is not transferred by the donee in exchange for money, other property, or services, and

(vii) the taxpayer receives from the donee a written statement representing that its use and disposition of the property will be in accordance with the provisions of clauses (v) and (vi).

(C) Construction of property by taxpayer. For purposes of this paragraph, property shall be treated as constructed by the taxpayer only if the cost of the parts used in the construction of such property (other than parts manufactured by the taxpayer or a related person) do not exceed 50 percent of the taxpayer's basis in such property.

(D) Corporation. For purposes of this paragraph, the term "corporation" shall not include—

(i) an S corporation,

(ii) a personal holding company (as defined in section 542), and

(iii) a service organization (as defined in section 414(m)(3)).

(5) Special rule for contributions of stock for which market quotations are readily available.

(A) In general. Subparagraph (B)(ii) of paragraph (1) shall not apply to any contribution of qualified appreciated stock.

(B) Qualified appreciated stock. Except as provided in subparagraph (C), for purposes of this paragraph, the term "qualified appreciated stock" means any stock of a corporation—

(i) for which (as of the date of the contribution) market quotations are readily available on an established securities market, and

(ii) which is capital gain property (as defined in subsection (b)(1)(C)(iv)).

(C) Donor may not contribute more than 10 percent of stock of corporation.

(i) In general. In the case of any donor, the term "qualified appreciated stock" shall not include any stock of a corporation contributed by the donor in a contribution to which paragraph (1)(B)(ii) applies (determined without regard to this paragraph) to the extent that the amount of the stock so contributed (when increased by the aggregate amount of all prior such contributions by the donor of stock in such corporation) exceeds 10 percent (in value) of all of the outstanding stock of such corporation.

(ii) Special rule. For purposes of clause (i), an individual shall be treated as making all contributions made by any member of his family (as defined in section 267(c)(4)).

(6) Special rule for contributions of computer technology and equipment for educational purposes.

(A) Limit on reduction. In the case of a qualified computer contribution, the reduction under paragraph (1)(A) shall be no greater than the amount determined under paragraph (3)(B).

(B) Qualified computer contribution. For purposes of this paragraph, the term "qualified computer contribution" means a charitable contribution by a corporation of any computer technology or equipment, but only if —

(i) the contribution is to—

(I) an educational organization described in subsection (b)(1)(A)(ii),

(II) an entity described in section 501(c)(3) and exempt from tax under section 501(a) other than an entity described in subclause (I)) that is organized primarily for purposes of supporting elementary and secondary education, or

(III) a public library (within the meaning of section 213(1)(A) of the Library Services and Technology Act (20 U.S.C. 9122(1)(A)), as in effect on the date of the enactment [12/21/2000] of the Community Renewal Tax Relief Act of 2000), established and maintained by an entity described in subsection (c)(1),

(ii) the contribution is made not later than 3 years after the date the taxpayer acquired the property (or in the case of property constructed or assembled by the taxpayer, the date the construction or assembling of the property is substantially completed),

(iii) the original use of the property is by the donor or the donee,

(iv) substantially all of the use of the property by the donee is for use within the United States for educational purposes that are related to the purpose or function of the donee,

(v) the property is not transferred by the donee in exchange for money, other property, or services, except for shipping, installation and transfer costs,

(vi) the property will fit productively into the donee's education plan,

(vii) the donee's use and disposition of the property will be in accordance with the provisions of clauses (iv) and (v), and

(viii) the property meets such standards, if any, as the Secretary may prescribe by regulation to assure that the property meets minimum functionality and suitability standards for educational purposes.

(C) Contribution to private foundation. A contribution by a corporation of any computer technology or equipment to a private foundation (as defined in section 509) shall be treated as a qualified computer contribution for purposes of this paragraph if—

(i) the contribution to the private foundation satisfies the requirements of clauses (ii) and (v) of subparagraph (B), and

(ii) within 30 days after such contribution, the private foundation—

(I) contributes the property to a donee described in clause (i) of subparagraph (B) that satisfies the requirements of clauses (iv) through (vii) of subparagraph (B), and

(II) notifies the donor of such contribution.

(D) Donations of property reacquired by manufacturer. In the case of property which is reacquired by the person who constructed or assembled the property—

(i) subparagraph (B)(ii) shall be applied to a contribution of such property by such person by taking into account the date that the original construction or assembly of the property was substantially completed, and

(ii) subparagraph (B)(iii) shall not apply to such contribution.

(E) Special rule relating to construction of property. For the purposes of this paragraph, the rules of paragraph (4)(C) shall apply.

(F) Definitions. For the purposes of this paragraph—

(i) Computer technology or equipment. The term "computer technology or equipment" means computer software (as defined by section 197(e)(3)(B)), computer or peripheral equipment (as defined by section 168(i)(2)(B)), and fiber optic cable related to computer use.

(ii) Corporation. The term "corporation" has the meaning given to such term by paragraph (4)(D).

(G) Termination. This paragraph shall not apply to any contribution made during any taxable year beginning after December 31, 2011.

(7) Recapture of deduction on certain dispositions of exempt use property.

(A) In general. In the case of an applicable disposition of applicable property, there shall be included in the income of the donor of such property for the taxable year of such donor in which the applicable disposition occurs an amount equal to the excess (if any) of—

(i) the amount of the deduction allowed to the donor under this section with respect to such property, over

(ii) the donor's basis in such property at the time such property was contributed.

(B) Applicable disposition. For purposes of this paragraph, the term "applicable disposition" means any sale, exchange, or other disposition by the donee of applicable property—

(i) after the last day of the taxable year of the donor in which such property was contributed, and

(ii) before the last day of the 3-year period beginning on the date of the contribution of such property,

unless the donee makes a certification in accordance with subparagraph (D).

(C) Applicable property. For purposes of this paragraph, the term "applicable property" means charitable deduction property (as defined in section 6050L(a)(2)(A))—

(i) which is tangible personal property the use of which is identified by the donee as related to the purpose or function constituting the basis of the donee's exemption under section 501, and

(ii) for which a deduction in excess of the donor's basis is allowed.

(D) Certification. A certification meets the requirements of this subparagraph if it is a written statement which is signed under penalty of perjury by an officer of the donee organization and—

(i) which—

(I) certifies that the use of the property by the donee was substantial and related to the purpose or function constituting the basis for the donee's exemption under section 501, and

(II) describes how the property was used and how such use furthered such purpose or function, or

(ii) which—

(I) states the intended use of the property by the donee at the time of the contribution, and

(II) certifies that such intended use has become impossible or infeasible to implement.

* * * * * * * * * * * *

[For Analysis, see ¶ 1102, ¶ 1103 and ¶ 1104.]

[Endnote Code Sec. 170]

Code Sec. 170(b)(1)(E)(vi) and Code Sec. 170(b)(2)(B)(iii) were amended by Sec. 206(a)-(b) of the American Taxpayer Relief Act of 2012, P.L. 112-240, 1/2/2013, as detailed below:

1. Sec. 206(a) substituted "December 31, 2013" for "December 31, 2011" in clause (b)(1)(E)(vi)

2. Sec. 206(b) substituted "December 31, 2013" for "December 31, 2011" in clause (b)(2)(B)(iii)

Effective Date (Sec. 206(c), P.L. 112-240, 1/2/2013) effective for contributions made in tax. yrs. begin. after 12/31/2011.

Code Sec. 170(e)(3)(C)(iv) was amended by Sec. 314(a), P.L. 112-240, 1/2/2013, as detailed below:

3. Sec. 314(a) substituted "December 31, 2013" for "December 31, 2011" in clause (e)(3)(C)(iv)

Effective Date (Sec. 314(b), P.L. 112-240, 1/2/2013) effective for contributions made after 12/31/2011.

[¶ 3061]   Code Sec. 179.   Election to expense certain depreciable business assets.

* * * * * * * * * * * *

(b) Limitations.

(1) Dollar limitation. The aggregate cost which may be taken into account under subsection (a) for any taxable year shall not exceed—

(A) $250,000 in the case of taxable years beginning after 2007 and before 2010,

(B) $500,000 in the case of taxable years beginning in [1]*2010, 2011, 2012, or 2013,* and

[2]*(C)* $25,000 in the case of taxable years beginning after [3]*2013.*

(2) Reduction in limitation. The limitation under paragraph (1) for any taxable year shall be reduced (but not below zero) by the amount by which the cost of section 179 property placed in service during such taxable year exceeds—

(A) $800,000 in the case of taxable years beginning after 2007 and before 2010,

(B) $2,000,000 in the case of taxable years beginning in [4]*2010, 2011, 2012, or 2013,* and,

[5]*(C)* $200,000 in the case of taxable years beginning after [6]*2013.*

(3)   Limitation based on income from trade or business.

(A) In general. The amount allowed as a deduction under subsection (a) for any taxable year (determined after the application of paragraphs (1) and (2)) shall not exceed the aggregate amount of taxable income of the taxpayer for such taxable year which is derived from the active conduct by the taxpayer of any trade or business during such taxable year.

(B) Carryover of disallowed deduction. The amount allowable as a deduction under subsection (a) for any taxable year shall be increased by the lesser of—

(i) the aggregate amount disallowed under subparagraph (A) for all prior taxable years (to the extent not previously allowed as a deduction by reason of this subparagraph), or

(ii) the excess (if any) of—

(I) the limitation of paragraphs (1) and (2) (or if lesser, the aggregate amount of taxable income referred to in subparagraph (A)), over

(II) the amount allowable as a deduction under subsection (a) for such taxable year without regard to this subparagraph.

(C) Computation of taxable income. For purposes of this paragraph, taxable income derived from the conduct of a trade or business shall be computed without regard to the deduction allowable under this section.

(4)   Married individuals filing separately. In the case of a husband and wife filing separate returns for the taxable year—

(A) such individuals shall be treated as 1 taxpayer for purposes of paragraphs (1) and (2), and

(B) unless such individuals elect otherwise, 50 percent of the cost which may be taken into account under subsection (a) for such taxable year (before application of paragraph (3)) shall be allocated to each such individual.

(5)   Limitation on cost taken into account for certain passenger vehicles.

(A) In general. The cost of any sport utility vehicle for any taxable year which may be taken into account under this section shall not exceed $25,000.

(B) Sport utility vehicle. For purposes of subparagraph (A)—

(i) In general. The term "sport utility vehicle" means any 4-wheeled vehicle—

(I) which is primarily designed or which can be used to carry passengers over public streets, roads, or highways (except any vehicle operated exclusively on a rail or rails),

(II) which is not subject to section 280F, and

(III) which is rated at not more than 14,000 pounds gross vehicle weight.

(ii) Certain vehicles excluded. Such term does not include any vehicle which—

(I) is designed to have a seating capacity of more than 9 persons behind the driver's seat,

(II) is equipped with a cargo area of at least 6 feet in interior length which is an open area or is designed for use as an open area but is enclosed by a cap and is not readily accessible directly from the passenger compartment, or

(III) has an integral enclosure, fully enclosing the driver compartment and load carrying device, does not have seating rearward of the driver's seat, and has no body section protruding more than 30 inches ahead of the leading edge of the windshield.

[7]*(6)   Repealed.*

(7)   Repealed.

(c)   Election.

(1)   In general. An election under this section for any taxable year shall—

(A) specify the items of section 179 property to which the election applies and the portion of the cost of each of such items which is to be taken into account under subsection (a), and

(B) be made on the taxpayer's return of the tax imposed by this chapter for the taxable year.

Such election shall be made in such manner as the Secretary may by regulations prescribe.

(2) Election irrevocable. Any election made under this section, and any specification contained in any such election, may not be revoked except with the consent of the Secretary. Any such election or specification with respect to any taxable year beginning after 2002 and before [8]*2014* may be revoked by the taxpayer with respect to any property, and such revocation, once made, shall be irrevocable.

(d) Definitions and special rules.

(1) Section 179 property. For purposes of this section, the term "section 179 property" means property—

(A) which is—

(i) tangible property (to which section 168 applies), or

(ii) computer software (as defined in section 197(e)(3)(B)) which is described in section 197(e)(3)(A)(i), to which section 167 applies, and which is placed in service in a taxable year beginning after 2002 and before [9]*2014*,

(B) which is section 1245 property (as defined in section 1245(a)(3)), and

(C) which is acquired by purchase for use in the active conduct of a trade or business.

Such term shall not include any property described in section 50(b) and shall not include air conditioning or heating units.

(2) Purchase defined. For purposes of paragraph (1), the term "purchase" means any acquisition of property, but only if—

(A) the property is not acquired from a person whose relationship to the person acquiring it would result in the disallowance of losses under section 267 or 707(b) (but, in applying section 267(b) and (c) for purposes of this section, paragraph (4) of section 267(c) shall be treated as providing that the family of an individual shall include only his spouse, ancestors, and lineal descendants),

(B) the property is not acquired by one component member of a controlled group from another component member of the same controlled group, and

(C) the basis of the property in the hands of the person acquiring it is not determined—

(i) in whole or in part by reference to the adjusted basis of such property in the hands of the person from whom acquired, or

(ii) under section 1014(a) (relating to property acquired from a decedent).

(3) Cost. For purposes of this section, the cost of property does not include so much of the basis of such property as is determined by reference to the basis of other property held at any time by the person acquiring such property.

(4) Section not to apply to estates and trusts. This section shall not apply to estates and trusts.

(5) Section not to apply to certain non-corporate lessors. This section shall not apply to any section 179 property which is purchased by a person who is not a corporation and with respect to which such person is the lessor unless—

(A) the property subject to the lease has been manufactured or produced by the lessor, or

(B) the term of the lease (taking into account options to renew) is less than 50 percent of the class life of the property (as defined in section 168(i)(1)), and for the period consisting of the first 12 months after the date on which the property is transferred to the lessee the sum of the deductions with respect to such property which are allowable to the lessor solely by reason of section 162 (other than rents and reimbursed amounts with respect to such property) exceeds 15 percent of the rental income produced by such property.

(6) Dollar limitation of controlled group. For purposes of subsection (b) of this section—

(A) all component members of a controlled group shall be treated as one taxpayer, and

(B) the Secretary shall apportion the dollar limitation contained in subsection (b)(1) among the component members of such controlled group in such manner as he shall by regulations prescribe.

(7) Controlled group defined. For purposes of paragraphs (2) and (6), the term "controlled group" has the meaning assigned to it by section 1563(a), except that, for such purposes, the phrase "more than 50 percent" shall be substituted for the phrase "at least 80 percent" each place it appears in section 1563(a)(1).

(8) Treatment of partnerships and S corporations. In the case of a partnership, the limitations of subsection (b) shall apply with respect to the partnership and with respect to each partner. A similar rule shall apply in the case of an S corporation and its shareholders.

(9) Coordination with section 38. No credit shall be allowed under section 38 with respect to any amount for which a deduction is allowed under subsection (a).

(10) Recapture in certain cases. The Secretary shall, by regulations, provide for recapturing the benefit under any deduction allowable under subsection (a) with respect to any property which is not used predominantly in a trade or business at any time.

* * * * * * * * * * * *

(f) Special rules for qualified real property.

(1) In general. If a taxpayer elects the application of this subsection for any taxable year beginning in [10]*2010, 2011, 2012, or 2013*, the term "section 179 property" shall include any qualified real property which is—

(A) of a character subject to an allowance for depreciation,

(B) acquired by purchase for use in the active conduct of a trade or business, and

(C) not described in the last sentence of subsection (d)(1).

(2) Qualified real property. For purposes of this subsection, the term "qualified real property" means—

(A) qualified leasehold improvement property described in section 168(e)(6),

(B) qualified restaurant property described in section 168(e)(7), and

(C) qualified retail improvement property described in section 168(e)(8).

(3) Limitation. For purposes of applying the limitation under subsection (b)(1)(B), not more than $250,000 of the aggregate cost which is taken into account under subsection (a) for any taxable year may be attributable to qualified real property.

(4) Carryover limitation.

(A) In general. Notwithstanding subsection (b)(3)(B), no amount attributable to qualified real property may be carried over to a taxable year beginning after [11]*2013.*

(B) Treatment of disallowed amounts. Except as provided in subparagraph (C), to the extent that any amount is not allowed to be carried over to a taxable year beginning after [12]*2013* by reason of subparagraph (A), this title shall be applied as if no election under this section had been made with respect to such amount.

(C) Amounts carried over from [13]*2010, 2011, and 2012.* If subparagraph (B) applies to any amount (or portion of an amount) which is carried over from a taxable year other than the taxpayer's last taxable year beginning in [14]*2013,* such amount (or portion of an amount) shall be treated for purposes of this title as attributable to property placed in service on the first day of the taxpayer's last taxable year beginning in [15]*2013.* [16]*For the last taxable year beginning in 2013, the amount determined under subsection (b)(3)(A) for such taxable year shall be determined without regard to this paragraph.*

(D) Allocation of amounts. For purposes of applying this paragraph and subsection (b)(3)(B) to any taxable year, the amount which is disallowed under subsection (b)(3)(A) for such taxable year which is attributed to qualified real property shall be the amount which bears the same ratio to the total amount so disallowed as—

(i) the aggregate amount attributable to qualified real property placed in service during such taxable year, increased by the portion of any amount carried over to such taxable year from a prior taxable year which is attributable to such property, bears to

(ii) the total amount of section 179property placed in service during such taxable year, increased by the aggregate amount carried over to such taxable year from any prior taxable year.

For purposes of the preceding sentence, only section 179 property with respect to which an election was made under subsection (c)(1) (determined without regard to subparagraph (B) of this paragraph) shall be taken into account.

[For Analysis, see ¶ 801 and ¶ 803.]

[Endnote Code Sec. 179]
Code Sec. 179(b)(1)(B), Code Sec. 179(b)(1)(C), Code Sec. 179(b)(2)(B), Code Sec. 179(b)(2)(C), Code Sec. 179(b)(6), Code Sec. 179(c)(2), Code Sec. 179(d)(1)(A)(ii), Code Sec. 179(f)(1) and Code Sec. 179(f)(4) were amended by Sec. 315(a)-(d) of the American Taxpayer Relief Act of 2012, P.L. 112-240, 1/2/2013, as detailed below:

1. Sec. 315(a)(1)(A) substituted "2010, 2011, 2012, or 2013, and" for "2010 or 2011," in subpara. (b)(1)(B)

2. Sec. 315(a)(1)(B)-(C) deleted subpara. (b)(1)(C), and redesignated subpara. (b)(1)(D) as subpara. (b)(1)(C). Prior to deletion, subpara. (b)(1)(C) read as follows:
"(C) $125,000 in the case of taxable years beginning in 2012, and"

3. Sec. 315(a)(1)(D) substituted "2013" for "2012" in subpara. (b)(1)(C) [as redesignated by Sec. 315(a)(1)(C), see above]

4. Sec. 315(a)(2)(A) substituted "2010, 2011, 2012, or 2013, and" for "2010 or 2011," in subpara. (b)(2)(B)

5. Sec. 315(a)(2)(B)-(C) deleted subpara. (b)(2)(C), and redesignated subpara. (b)(2)(D) as subpara. (b)(2)(C). Prior to deletion, subpara. (b)(2)(C) read as follows:
"(C) $500,000 in the case of taxable years beginning in 2012, and"

6. Sec. 315(a)(2)(D) substituted "2013" for "2012" in subpara. (b)(2)(C) [as redesignated by Sec. 315(a)(2)(C), see above]

7. Sec. 315(a)(3) deleted para. (b)(6). Prior to deletion, para. (b)(6) read as follows:
"(6) Inflation adjustment.
"(A) In general. In the case of any taxable year beginning in calendar year 2012, the $125,000 and $500,000 amounts in paragraphs (1)(C) and (2)(C) shall each be increased by an amount equal to—
"(i) such dollar amount, multiplied by
"(ii) the cost-of-living adjustment determined under section 1(f)(3) for the calendar year in which the taxable year begins, by substituting "calendar year 2006" for "calendar year 1992" in subparagraph (B) thereof.
"(B) Rounding.
"(i) Dollar limitation. If the amount in paragraph (1) as increased under subparagraph (A) is not a multiple of $1,000, such amount shall be rounded to the nearest multiple of $1,000.
"(ii) Phaseout amount. If the amount in paragraph (2) as increased under subparagraph (A) is not a multiple of $10,000, such amount shall be rounded to the nearest multiple of $10,000."

8. Sec. 315(c) substituted "2014" for "2013" in para. (c)(2)

9. Sec. 315(b) substituted "2014" for "2013" in clause (d)(1)(A)(ii)

10. Sec. 315(d)(1) substituted "2010, 2011, 2012, or 2013" for "2010 or 2011" in para. (f)(1)

11. Sec. 315(d)(2)(A) substituted "2013" for "2011" in subpara. (f)(4)(A)

12. Sec. 315(d)(2)(A) substituted "2013" for "2011" in subpara. (f)(4)(B)

13. Sec. 315(d)(2)(B)(i) substituted "2010, 2011 and 2012" for "2010" in the heading of subpara. (f)(4)(C)

14. Sec. 315(d)(2)(A) substituted "2013" for "2011" in subpara. (f)(4)(C)

15. Sec. 315(d)(2)(A) substituted "2013" for "2011" in subpara. (f)(4)(C)

16. Sec. 315(d)(2)(B)(ii) added "For the last taxable year beginning in 2013, the amount determined under subsection (b)(3)(A) for such taxable year shall be determined without regard to this paragraph." at the end of subpara. (f)(4)(C)

Effective Date (Sec. 315(e), P.L. 112-240, 1/2/2013) effective for tax. yrs. begin. after 12/31/2011.

[¶ 3062]   Code Sec. 179E.   Election to expense advanced mine safety equipment.

(a) Treatment as expenses. A taxpayer may elect to treat 50 percent of the cost of any qualified advanced mine safety equipment property as an expense which is not chargeable to capital account. Any cost so treated shall be allowed as a deduction for the taxable year in which the qualified advanced mine safety equipment property is placed in service.

(b) Election.

(1) In general. An election under this section for any taxable year shall be made on the taxpayer's return of the tax imposed by this chapter for the taxable year. Such election shall specify the advanced mine safety equipment property to which the election applies and shall be made in such manner as the Secretary may by regulations prescribe.

(2)   Election irrevocable. Any election made under this section may not be revoked except with the consent of the Secretary.

(c)   Qualified advanced mine safety equipment property. For purposes of this section, the term "qualified advanced mine safety equipment property" means any advanced mine safety equipment property for use in any underground mine located in the United States—

(1) the original use of which commences with the taxpayer, and

(2) which is placed in service by the taxpayer after the date of the enactment of this section.

(d)   Advanced mine safety equipment property. For purposes of this section, the term "advanced mine safety equipment property" means any of the following:

(1) Emergency communication technology or device which is used to allow a miner to maintain constant communication with an individual who is not in the mine.

(2) Electronic identification and location device which allows an individual who is not in the mine to track at all times the movements and location of miners working in or at the mine.

(3) Emergency oxygen-generating, self-rescue device which provides oxygen for at least 90 minutes.

(4) Pre-positioned supplies of oxygen which (in combination with self-rescue devices) can be used to provide each miner on a shift, in the event of an accident or other event which traps the miner in the mine or otherwise necessitates the use of such a self rescue device, the ability to survive for at least 48 hours.

(5) Comprehensive atmospheric monitoring system which monitors the levels of carbon monoxide, methane, and oxygen that are present in all areas of the mine and which can detect smoke in the case of a fire in a mine.

(e)   Coordination with section 179. No expenditures shall be taken into account under subsection (a) with respect to the portion of the cost of any property specified in an election under section 179.

(f)   Reporting. No deduction shall be allowed under subsection (a) to any taxpayer for any taxable year unless such taxpayer files with the Secretary a report containing such information with respect to the operation of the mines of the taxpayer as the Secretary shall require.

(g)   Termination. This section shall not apply to property placed in service after [1]*December 31, 2013.*

[For Analysis, see ¶ 811.]

[Endnote Code Sec. 179E]

Code Sec. 179E(g) was amended by Sec. 316(a) of the American Taxpayer Relief Act of 2012, P.L. 112-240, 1/2/2013, as detailed below:

1. Sec. 316(a) substituted "December 31, 2013" for "December 31, 2011" in subsec. (g)

Effective Date (Sec. 316(b), P.L. 112-240, 1/2/2013) effective for property placed in service after 12/31/2011.

[¶ 3063]   Code Sec. 181.   Treatment of certain qualified film and television productions.

* * * * * * * * * * * *

(f)   Termination. This section shall not apply to qualified film and television productions commencing after [1]*December 31, 2013.*

[For Analysis, see ¶ 808.]

[Endnote Code Sec. 181]

Code Sec. 181(f) was amended by Sec. 317(a) of the American Taxpayer Relief Act of 2012, P.L. 112-240, 1/2/2013, as detailed below:

1. Sec. 317(a)(1) substituted "December 31, 2013" for "December 31, 2011" in subsec. (f)

Effective Date (Sec. 317(b), P.L. 112-240, 1/2/2013) effective for productions commencing after 12/31/2011.

[¶ 3064]   Code Sec. 199.   Income attributable to domestic production activities.

* * * * * * * * * * * *

(d)   Definitions and special rules.

(1)   Application of section to pass-thru entities.

(A) Partnerships and S corporations. In the case of a partnership or S corporation—

(i) this section shall be applied at the partner or shareholder level,

(ii) each partner or shareholder shall take into account such person's allocable share of each item described in subparagraph (A) or (B) of subsection (c)(1) (determined without regard to whether the items described in such subparagraph (A) exceed the items described in such subparagraph (B)),

(iii) each partner or shareholder shall be treated for purposes of subsection (b) as having W-2 wages for the taxable year in an amount equal to such person's allocable share of the W-2 wages of the partnership or S corporation for the taxable year (as determined under regulations prescribed by the Secretary), and

(iv) in the case of each partner of a partnership, or shareholder of an S corporation, who owns (directly or indirectly) at least 20 percent of the capital interests in such partnership or of the stock of such S corporation—

(I) such partner or shareholder shall be treated as having engaged directly in any film produced by such partnership or S corporation, and

(II) such partnership or S corporation shall be treated as having engaged directly in any film produced by such partner or shareholder.

(B) Trusts and estates. In the case of a trust or estate—

(i) the items referred to in subparagraph (A)(ii) (as determined therein) and the W-2 wages of the trust or estate for the taxable year, shall be apportioned between the beneficiaries and the fiduciary (and among the beneficiaries) under regulations prescribed by the Secretary, and

(ii) for purposes of paragraph (2), adjusted gross income of the trust or estate shall be determined as provided in section 67(e) with the adjustments described in such paragraph.

(C) Regulations. The Secretary may prescribe rules requiring or restricting the allocation of items and wages under this paragraph and may prescribe such reporting requirements as the Secretary determines appropriate.

(2)   Application to individuals. In the case of an individual, subsections (a)(1)(B) and (d)(9)(A)(iii) shall be applied by substituting "adjusted gross income" for "taxable income". For purposes of the preceding sentence, adjusted gross income shall be determined—

(A) after application of sections 86, 135, 137, 219, 221, 222, and 469, and

(B) without regard to this section.

(3)   Agricultural and horticultural cooperatives.

(A) Deduction allowed to patrons. Any person who receives a qualified payment from a specified agricultural or horticultural cooperative shall be allowed for the taxable year in which such payment is received a deduction under subsection (a) equal to the portion of the deduction allowed under subsection (a) to such cooperative which is—

(i) allowed with respect to the portion of the qualified production activities income to which such payment is attributable, and

(ii) identified by such cooperative in a written notice mailed to such person during the payment period described in section 1382(d).

(B) Cooperative denied deduction for portion of qualified payments. The taxable income of a specified agricultural or horticultural cooperative shall not be reduced under

647

section 1382 by reason of that portion of any qualified payment as does not exceed the deduction allowable under subparagraph (A) with respect to such payment.

(C) Taxable income of cooperatives determined without regard to certain deductions. For purposes of this section, the taxable income of a specified agricultural or horticultural cooperative shall be computed without regard to any deduction allowable under subsection (b) or (c) of section 1382 (relating to patronage dividends, per-unit retain allocations, and nonpatronage distributions).

(D) Special rule for marketing cooperatives. For purposes of this section, a specified agricultural or horticultural cooperative described in subparagraph (F)(ii) shall be treated as having manufactured, produced, grown, or extracted in whole or significant part any qualifying production property marketed by the organization which its patrons have so manufactured, produced, grown, or extracted.

(E) Qualified payment. For purposes of this paragraph, the term "qualified payment" means, with respect to any person, any amount which—

(i) is described in paragraph (1) or (3) of section 1385(a),

(ii) is received by such person from a specified agricultural or horticultural cooperative, and

(iii) is attributable to qualified production activities income with respect to which a deduction is allowed to such cooperative under subsection (a).

(F) Specified agricultural or horticultural cooperative. For purposes of this paragraph, the term "specified agricultural or horticultural cooperative" means an organization to which part I of subchapter T applies which is engaged—

(i) in the manufacturing, production, growth, or extraction in whole or significant part of any agricultural or horticultural product, or

(ii) in the marketing of agricultural or horticultural products.

(4) Special rule for affiliated groups.

(A) In general. All members of an expanded affiliated group shall be treated as a single corporation for purposes of this section.

(B) Expanded affiliated group. For purposes of this section, the term "expanded affiliated group" means an affiliated group as defined in section 1504(a), determined—

(i) by substituting "more than 50 percent" for "at least 80 percent" each place it appears, and

(ii) without regard to paragraphs (2) and (4) of section 1504(b).

(C) Allocation of deduction. Except as provided in regulations, the deduction under subsection (a) shall be allocated among the members of the expanded affiliated group in proportion to each member's respective amount (if any) of qualified production activities income.

(5) Trade or business requirement. This section shall be applied by only taking into account items which are attributable to the actual conduct of a trade or business.

(6) Coordination with minimum tax. For purposes of determining alternative minimum taxable income under section 55—

(A) qualified production activities income shall be determined without regard to any adjustments under sections 56 through 59, and

(B) in the case of a corporation, subsection (a)(1)(B) shall be applied by substituting "alternative minimum taxable income" for "taxable income".

(7) Unrelated business taxable income. For purposes of determining the tax imposed by section 511, subsection (a)(1)(B) shall be applied by substituting "unrelated business taxable income" for "taxable income".

(8) Treatment of activities in Puerto Rico.

(A) In general. In the case of any taxpayer with gross receipts for any taxable year from sources within the Commonwealth of Puerto Rico, if all of such receipts are taxable under section 1 or 11 for such taxable year, then for purposes of determining the domestic production gross receipts of such taxpayer for such taxable year under subsection (c)(4), the term "United States" shall include the Common-wealth of Puerto Rico.

(B) Special rule for applying wage limitation. In the case of any taxpayer described in subparagraph (A), for purposes of applying the limitation under subsection (b) for any taxable year, the determination of W-60 wages of such taxpayer shall be made without regard to any exclusion under section 3401(a)(8) for remuneration paid for services performed in Puerto Rico.

(C) Termination. This paragraph shall apply only with respect to the [1]*first 8 taxable years* of the taxpayer beginning after December 31, 2005, and before [2]*January 1, 2014.*

(9) Special rule for taxpayers with oil related qualified production activities income.

(A) In general. If a taxpayer has oil related qualified production activities income for any taxable year beginning after 2009, the amount otherwise allowable as a deduction under subsection (a) shall be reduced by 3 percent of the least of—

(i) the oil related qualified production activities income of the taxpayer for the taxable year,

(ii) the qualified production activities income of the taxpayer for the taxable year, or

(iii) taxable income (determined without regard to this section).

(B) Oil related qualified production activities income. For purposes of this paragraph, the term "oil related qualified production activities income" means for any taxable year the qualified production activities income which is attributable to the production, refining, processing, transportation, or distribution of oil, gas, or any primary product thereof during such taxable year.

(C) Primary product. For purposes of this paragraph, the term "primary product" has the same meaning as when used in section 927(a)(2)(C), as in effect before its repeal.

(10) Regulations. The Secretary shall prescribe such regulations as are necessary to carry out the purposes of this section, including regulations which prevent more than 1 taxpayer from being allowed a deduction under this section with respect to any activity described in subsection (c)(4)(A)(i).

[For Analysis, see ¶ 909.]

[Endnote Code Sec. 199]
 Code Sec. 199(d)(8)(C) was amended by Sec. 318(a)(1)-(2) of the American Taxpayer Relief Act of 2012, P.L. 112-240, 1/2/2013, as detailed below:
 1. Sec. 318(a)(1) substituted "first 8 taxable years" for "first 6 taxable years" in subpara. (d)(8)(C)
 2. Sec. 318(a)(2) substituted "January 1, 2014" for "January 1, 2012" in subpara. (d)(8)(C)
Effective Date (Sec. 318(b), P.L. 112-240, 1/2/2013) effective for tax. yrs. begin. after 12/31/2011.

[¶ 3065] Code Sec. 221. Interest on education loans.

(a) Allowance of deduction. In the case of an individual, there shall be allowed as a deduction for the taxable year an amount equal to the interest paid by the taxpayer during the taxable year on any qualified education loan.

(b) Maximum deduction.

(1) In general. Except as provided in paragraph (2), the deduction allowed by subsection (a) for the taxable year shall not exceed the amount determined in accordance with the following table:

In the case of taxable years beginning in:	The dollar amount is:
1998	$1,000
1999	$1,500
2000	$2,000
2001 or thereafter	$2,500

(2) Limitation based on modified adjusted gross income.

(A) In general. The amount which would (but for this paragraph) be allowable as a deduction under this section shall be reduced (but not below zero) by the amount determined under subparagraph (B).

(B) Amount of reduction. The amount determined under this subparagraph is the amount which bears the same ratio to the amount which would be so taken into account as—

[1](i) the excess of—

(I) the taxpayer's modified adjusted gross income for such taxable year, over

(II) $50,000 ($100,000 in the case of a joint return), bears to

(ii) $15,000 ($30,000 in the case of a joint return).

(C) Modified adjusted gross income. The term "modified adjusted gross income" means adjusted gross income determined—

(i) without regard to this section and sections 199, [2]222, 911, 931, and 933, and

(ii) after application of sections 86, 135, 137, 219, and 469.

* * * * * * * * * * * *

[3](d) **Definitions.** For purposes of this section—

(1) **Qualified education loan.** The term "qualified education loan" means any indebtedness incurred by the taxpayer solely to pay qualified higher education expenses—

(A) which are incurred on behalf of the taxpayer, the taxpayer's spouse, or any dependent of the taxpayer as of the time the indebtedness was incurred,

(B) which are paid or incurred within a reasonable period of time before or after the indebtedness is incurred, and

(C) which are attributable to education furnished during a period during which the recipient was an eligible student.

Such term includes indebtedness used to refinance indebtedness which qualifies as a qualified education loan. The term "qualified education loan" shall not include any indebtedness owed to a person who is related (within the meaning of section 267(b) or 707(b)(1)) to the taxpayer or to any person by reason of a loan under any qualified employer plan (as defined in section 72(p)(4)) or under any contract referred to in section 72(p)(5).

(2) **Qualified higher education expenses.** The term "qualified higher education expenses" means the cost of attendance (as defined in section 472 of the Higher Education Act of 1965, 20 U.S.C. 1087ll, as in effect on the day before the date of the enactment of the Taxpayer Relief Act of 1997) at an eligible educational institution, reduced by the sum of—

(A) the amount excluded from gross income under section 127, 135, 529, or 530 by reason of such expenses, and

(B) the amount of any scholarship, allowance, or payment described in section 25A(g)(2).

For purposes of the preceding sentence, the term "eligible educational institution" has the same meaning given such term by section 25A(f)(2), except that such term shall also include an institution conducting an internship or residency program leading to a degree or certificate awarded by an institution of higher education, a hospital, or a health care facility which offers postgraduate training.

(3) **Eligible student.** The term "eligible student" has the meaning given such term by section 25A(b)(3).

(4) **Dependent.** The term "dependent" has the meaning given such term by section 152 (determined without regard to subsections (b)(1), (b)(2), and (d)(1)(B) thereof).

(e) **Special rules.**

(1) **Denial of double benefit.** No deduction shall be allowed under this section for any amount for which a deduction is allowable under any other provision of this chapter.

(2) Married couples must file joint return. If the taxpayer is married at the close of the taxable year, the deduction shall be allowed under subsection (a) only if the taxpayer and the taxpayer's spouse file a joint return for the taxable year.

(3) Marital status. Marital status shall be determined in accordance with section 7703.

(f) **Inflation adjustments.**

(1) In general. In the case of a taxable year beginning after 2002, the [4]*$50,000 and $100,000 amounts* in subsection (b)(2) shall each be increased by an amount equal to—

(A) such dollar amount, multiplied by

(B) the cost-of-living adjustment determined under section 1(f)(3) for the calendar year in which the taxable year begins, determined by substituting "calendar year 2001" for "calendar year 1992" in subparagraph (B) thereof.

(2) Rounding. If any amount as adjusted under paragraph (1) is not a multiple of $5,000, such amount shall be rounded to the next lowest multiple of $5,000.

[For Analysis, see ¶ 703.]

[Endnote Code Sec. 221]
Sec. 101(a)(1) of the American Taxpayer Relief Act of 2012, P.L. 112-240, 1/2/2013, deleted Title IX [Sec. 901] of the Economic Growth and Tax Relief Reconciliation Act of 2001, P.L. 107-16, the effect of which is to eliminate the sunset of all provisions enacted by P.L. 107-16. Following are the amendments made to Code Sec. 221, by P.L. 107-16, that were subject to the sunset.
Effective Date (Sec. 101(a)(3), P.L. 112-240, 1/2/2013) effective for taxable, plan, or limitation years beginning after 12/31/2012, and estates of decedents dying, gifts made, or generation skipping transfers after 12/31/2012.

Code Sec. 221(b)(2)(B)(i) and Code Sec. 221(b)(2)(B)(ii), in *italics*, were amended Sec. 412(b)(1) of the Economic Growth and Tax Relief Reconciliation Act of 2001, P.L. 107-16, 6/7/2001, as outlined below: out:
1. Sec. 412(b)(1) amended clauses (b)(2)(B)(i) and (ii). Prior to amendment, clauses (b)(2)(B)(i) and (ii) read as follows:
"(i) the excess of—
"(I) the taxpayer's modified adjusted gross income for such taxable year, over
"(II) $40,000 ($60,000 in the case of a joint return), bears to
"(ii) $15,000."
Effective Date (Sec. 412(b)(3), P.L. 107-16, 6/7/2001) effective for tax. yrs. end. after 12/31/2001.

Code Sec. 221(b)(2)(C)(i) was amended by Sec. 431(c)(2), P.L. 107-16, 6/7/2001.
2. added "222" before "911" matter in clause (b)(2)(C)(i)
Effective Date (Sec. 431(d), P.L. 107-16, 6/7/2001) effective for payments made in tax. yrs. begin. after 12/31/2001.

Code Sec. 221(d), Code Sec. 221(e), Code Sec. 221(f) and Code Sec. 221(g) were amended by Sec. 412(a)(1), P.L. 107-16, 6/7/2001, as outlined below
3. Sec. 412(a)(1) deleted subsec. (d) and redesignated subsecs. (e)-(g) as (f)-(d). Prior to deletion, subsec. (d) read as follows:
"(d) Limit on period deduction allowed. A deduction shall be allowed under this section only with respect to interest paid on any qualified education loan during the first 60 months (whether or not consecutive) in which interest payments are required. For purposes of this paragraph, any loan and all refinancings of such loan shall be treated as 1 loan. Such 60 months shall be determined in the manner prescribed by the Secretary in the case of multiple loans which are refinanced by, or serviced as, a single loan and in the case of loans incurred before the date of the enactment of this section.
Effective Date (Sec. 412(a)(3), P.L. 107-16, 6/7/2001) effective with respect to any loan interest paid after 12/31/2001, in tax. yrs. end. after such date. For sunset provision, see Sec. 901 of this Act, reproduced above.

Code Sec. 221(f)(1) was amended by Sec. 412(b)(2), P.L. 107-16, 6/7/2001, as outlined below:
4. Sec. 412(b)(1) substituted "$50,000 and $100,000 amounts" for "$40,000 and $60,000 amounts" in para. (f)(1)
Effective Date (Sec. 412(b)(3), P.L. 107-16, 6/7/2001) effective for tax. yrs. end. after 12/31/2001.

[¶ 3066]   Code Sec. 222.   Qualified tuition and related expenses.

(a) Allowance of deduction. In the case of an individual, there shall be allowed as a deduction an amount equal to the qualified tuition and related expenses paid by the taxpayer during the taxable year.

(b)   Dollar limitations.

(1)   In general. The amount allowed as a deduction under subsection (a) with respect to the taxpayer for any taxable year shall not exceed the applicable dollar limit.

(2)   Applicable dollar limit.

(A) 2002 and 2003. In the case of a taxable year beginning in 2002 or 2003, the applicable dollar limit shall be equal to—

(i) in the case of a taxpayer whose adjusted gross income for the taxable year does not exceed $65,000 ($130,000 in the case of a joint return), $3,000, and—

(ii) in the case of any other taxpayer, zero.

(B) After 2003. In the case of any taxable year beginning after 2003, the applicable dollar amount shall be equal to—

(i) in the case of a taxpayer whose adjusted gross income for the taxable year does not exceed $65,000 ($130,000 in the case of a joint return), $4,000,

(ii) in the case of a taxpayer not described in clause (i) whose adjusted gross income for the taxable year does not exceed $80,000 ($160,000 in the case of a joint return), $2,000, and

(iii) in the case of any other taxpayer, zero.

(C) Adjusted gross income. For purposes of this paragraph, adjusted gross income shall be determined—

(i) without regard to this section and sections 199, 911, 931, and 933, and

(ii) after application of sections 86, 135, 137, 219, 221, and 469.

(c)   No double benefit.

(1)   In general. No deduction shall be allowed under subsection (a) for any expense for which a deduction is allowed to the taxpayer under any other provision of this chapter.

(2)   Coordination with other education incentives.

(A) Denial of deduction if credit elected. No deduction shall be allowed under subsection (a) for a taxable year with respect to the qualified tuition and related expenses with respect to an individual if the taxpayer or any other person elects to have section 25A apply with respect to such individual for such year.

(B) Coordination with exclusions. The total amount of qualified tuition and related expenses shall be reduced by the amount of such expenses taken into account in determining any amount excluded under section 135, 529(c)(1), or 530(d)(2). For purposes of the preceding sentence, the amount taken into account in determining the amount excluded under section 529(c)(1) shall not include that portion of the distribution which represents a return of any contributions to the plan.

(3)   Dependents. No deduction shall be allowed under subsection (a) to any individual with respect to whom a deduction under section 151 is allowable to another taxpayer for a taxable year beginning in the calendar year in which such individual's taxable year begins.

(d)   Definitions and special rules. For purposes of this section—

(1)   Qualified tuition and related expenses. The term "qualified tuition and related expenses" has the meaning given such term by section 25A(f). Such expenses shall be reduced in the same manner as under section 25A(g)(2).

(2)   Identification requirement. No deduction shall be allowed under subsection (a) to a taxpayer with respect to the qualified tuition and related expenses of an individual unless the taxpayer includes the name and taxpayer identification number of the individual on the return of tax for the taxable year.

(3)   Limitation on taxable year of deduction.

(A) In general. A deduction shall be allowed under subsection (a) for qualified tuition and related expenses for any taxable year only to the extent such expenses are in connection with enrollment at an institution of higher education during the taxable year.

(B) Certain prepayments allowed. Subparagraph (A) shall not apply to qualified tuition and related expenses paid during a taxable year if such expenses are in connection with an academic term beginning during such taxable year or during the first 3 months of the next taxable year.

(4)   No deduction for married individuals filing separate returns. If the taxpayer is a married individual (within the meaning of section 7703), this section shall apply only if the taxpayer and the taxpayer's spouse file a joint return for the taxable year.

(5)   Nonresident aliens. If the taxpayer is a nonresident alien individual for any portion of the taxable year, this section shall apply only if such individual is treated as a resident alien of the United States for purposes of this chapter by reason of an election under subsection (g) or (h) of section 6013.

(6)   Regulations. The Secretary may prescribe such regulations as may be necessary or appropriate to carry out this section, including regulations requiring recordkeeping and information reporting.

(e)   Termination. This section shall not apply to taxable years beginning after [1]*December 31, 2013.*
[For Analysis, see ¶ 702.]

[Endnote Code Sec. 222]
    Code Sec. 222(e) was amended by Sec. 207(a) of the American Taxpayer Relief Act of 2012, P.L. 112-240, 1/2/2013, as detailed below:
    1. Sec. 207(a) substituted "December 31, 2013" for "December 31, 2011" in subsec. (e)
Effective Date (Sec. 207(b), P.L. 112-240, 1/2/2013) effective for tax. yrs. begin. after 12/31/2011.

    Sec. 101(a)(1), P.L. 112-240, 1/2/2013, deleted Title IX [Sec. 901], P.L. 107-16, the effect of which is to eliminate the sunset of all provisions enacted by P.L. 107-16. Sec. 431(a), P.L. 107-16 amended Code Sec. 222.
Effective Date (Sec. 101(a)(3), P.L. 112-240, 1/2/2013) effective for tax. plan, or limitation years beginning after 12/31/2012, and estates of decedents dying, gifts made, or generation skipping transfers after 12/31/2012.

[¶ 3067]   Code Sec. 249.   Limitation on deduction of bond premium on repurchase.

(a)   General rule. No deduction shall be allowed to the issuing corporation for any premium paid or incurred upon the repurchase of a bond, debenture, note, or certificate or other evidence of indebtedness which is convertible into the stock of the issuing corporation[1], *or a corporation in the same parent-subsidiary controlled group (within the meaning of section 1563(a)(1)* as the issuing corporation, to the extent the repurchase price exceeds an amount equal to the adjusted issue price plus a normal call premium on bonds or other evidences of indebtedness which are not convertible. The preceding sentence shall not apply to the extent that the corporation can demonstrate to the satisfaction of the Secretary that such excess is attributable to the cost of borrowing and is not attributable to the conversion feature.

[2]*(b)   Adjusted issue price. For purposes of subsection (a), the adjusted issue price is the issue price (as defined in sections 1273(b) and 1274) increased by any amount of discount deducted before repurchase, or, in the case of bonds or other evidences of indebtedness issued after February 28, 1913, decreased by any amount of premium included in gross income before repurchase by the issuing corporation.*[3]
[For Analysis, see ¶ 1914. For Committee Reports, see ¶ 5608.]

[Endnote Code Sec. 249]
    Code Sec. 249(a) and Code Sec. 249(b) was amended by Sec. 1108(a) and 1108(b)(1)-(2) of the FAA Modernization and Reform Act of 2012, P.L. 112-95, 2/14/2012, as detailed below:
    1. Sec. 1108(a) substituted ", or a corporation in the same parent-subsidiary controlled group (within the meaning of section 1563(a)(1) as" for ", or a corporation in control of, or controlled by," in subsec. (a)
    2. Sec. 1108(b)(1) substituted "(b) Adjusted Issue Price. For purposes of subsection (a), the adjusted issue price" for "(b) Special rules. For purposes of subsection (a)— (1) Adjusted issue price. The adjusted issue price in para (b)(1)" in subsec. (b)
    3. Sec. 1108(b)(2) deleted para. (b)(2). Prior to deletion, para. (b)(2) read as follows:
    "(2) Control. The term 'control' has the meaning assigned to such term by section 368(c)."

Effective Date (Sec. 1108(c), P.L. 112-95, 2/14/2012) effective for repurchases after 1/2/2013.

[¶ 3068]   Code Sec. 306.   Dispositions of certain stock.

(a) **General rule.** If a shareholder sells or otherwise disposes of section 306 stock (as defined in subsection (c))—

(1) **Dispositions other than redemptions.** If such disposition is not a redemption (within the meaning of section 317(b))—

(A) The amount realized shall be treated as ordinary income. This subparagraph shall not apply to the extent that—

(i) the amount realized, exceeds

(ii) such stock's ratable share of the amount which would have been a dividend at the time of distribution if (in lieu of section 306 stock) the corporation had distributed money in an amount equal to the fair market value of the stock at the time of distribution.

(B) Any excess of the amount realized over the sum of—

(i) the amount treated under subparagraph (A) as ordinary income, plus

(ii) the adjusted basis of the stock,

shall be treated as gain from the sale of such stock.

(C) No loss shall be recognized.

[1]*(D) Treatment as dividend. For purposes of section 1(h)(11) and such other provisions as the Secretary may specify, any amount treated as ordinary income under this paragraph shall be treated as a dividend received from the corporation.*

(2) **Redemption.** If the disposition is a redemption, the amount realized shall be treated as a distribution of property to which section 301 applies.

* * * * * * * * * * * *

[For Analysis, see ¶ 212.]

[Endnote Code Sec. 306]

Sec. 102(a) of the American Taxpayer Relief Act of 2012, P.L. 112-240, 1/2/2013, deleted Sec. 303, P.L. 108-27, the Jobs and Growth Tax Relief Reconciliation Act of 2003, the effect of which is to eliminate the sunset of all provisions enacted by Title III of P.L. 108-27. Following are the amendments made to Code Sec. 306 by P.L. 108-27.

Code Sec. 306(a)(1)(D), in *italics*, was added by Sec. 302(e)(3) of the Jobs and Growth Tax Relief Reconciliation Act of 2003, P.L. 108-27, 5/28/2003.

1. Sec. 302(e)(3), added subpara. (a)(1)(D)

Effective Date (Sec. 302(f), P.L. 108-27, 5/28/2003) effective for tax. yrs. begin. after 12/31/2002.

[¶ 3069]   Code Sec. 402.   Taxability of beneficiary of employees' trust.

(a) **Taxability of beneficiary of exempt trust.** Except as otherwise provided in this section, any amount actually distributed to any distributee by any employees' trust described in section 401(a) which is exempt from tax under section 501(a) shall be taxable to the distributee, in the taxable year of the distributee in which distributed, under section 72 (relating to annuities).

(b) **Taxability of beneficiary of nonexempt trust.**

(1) **Contributions.** Contributions to an employees' trust made by an employer during a taxable year of the employer which ends with or within a taxable year of the trust for which the trust is not exempt from tax under section 501(a) shall be included in the gross income of the employee in accordance with section 83 (relating to property transferred in connection with performance of services), except that the value of the employee's interest in the trust shall be substituted for the fair market value of the property for purposes of applying such section.

(2) **Distributions.** The amount actually distributed or made available to any distributee by any trust described in paragraph (1) shall be taxable to the distributee, in the taxable

year in which so distributed or made available, under section 72 (relating to annuities), except that distributions of income of such trust before the annuity starting date (as defined in section 72(c)(4)) shall be included in the gross income of the employee without regard to section 72(e)(5) (relating to amounts not received as annuities).

(3) Grantor trusts. A beneficiary of any trust described in paragraph (1) shall not be considered the owner of any portion of such trust under subpart E of part I of subchapter J (relating to grantors and others treated as substantial owners).

(4) Failure to meet requirements of section 410(b).

(A) Highly compensated employees. If 1 of the reasons a trust is not exempt from tax under section 501(a) is the failure of the plan of which it is a part to meet the requirements of section 401(a)(26) or 410(b), then a highly compensated employee shall, in lieu of the amount determined under paragraph (1) or (2) include in gross income for the taxable year with or within which the taxable year of the trust ends an amount equal to the vested accrued benefit of such employee (other than the employee's investment in the contract) as of the close of such taxable year of the trust.

(B) Failure to meet coverage tests. If a trust is not exempt from tax under section 501(a) for any taxable year solely because such trust is part of a plan which fails to meet the requirements of section 401(a)(26) or 410(b), paragraphs (1) and (2) shall not apply by reason of such failure to any employee who was not a highly compensated employee during—

(i) such taxable year, or

(ii) any preceding period for which service was creditable to such employee under the plan.

(C) Highly compensated employee. For purposes of this paragraph, the term "highly compensated employee" has the meaning given such term by section 414(q).

(c) Rules applicable to rollovers from exempt trusts.

(1) Exclusion from income. If—

(A) any portion of the balance to the credit of an employee in a qualified trust is paid to the employee in an eligible rollover distribution,

(B) the distributee transfers any portion of the property received in such distribution to an eligible retirement plan, and

(C) in the case of a distribution of property other than money, the amount so transferred consists of the property distributed,

then such distribution (to the extent so transferred) shall not be includible in gross income for the taxable year in which paid.

(2) Maximum amount which may be rolled over. In the case of any eligible rollover distribution, the maximum amount transferred to which paragraph (1) applies shall not exceed the portion of such distribution which is includible in gross income (determined without regard to paragraph (1)). The preceding sentence shall not apply to such distribution to the extent—

(A) such portion is transferred in a direct trustee-to-trustee transfer to a qualified trust or to an annuity contract described in section 403(b) and such trust or contract provides for separate accounting for amounts so transferred (and earnings thereon), including separately accounting for the portion of such distribution which is includible in gross income and the portion of such distribution which is not so includible, or

(B) such portion is transferred to an eligible retirement plan described in clause (i) or (ii) of paragraph (8)(B).

In the case of a transfer described in subparagraph (A) or (B), the amount transferred shall be treated as consisting first of the portion of such distribution that is includible in gross income (determined without regard to paragraph (1)).

(3) Transfer must be made within 60 days of receipt.

(A) In general. Except as provided in subparagraph (B), paragraph (1) shall not apply to any transfer of a distribution made after the 60th day following the day on which the distributee received the property distributed.

(B) Hardship exception. The Secretary may waive the 60-day requirement under subparagraph (A) where the failure to waive such requirement would be against equity or good conscience, including casualty, disaster, or other events beyond the reasonable control of the individual subject to such requirement.

(4) Eligible rollover distribution. For purposes of this subsection, the term "eligible rollover distribution" means any distribution to an employee of all or any portion of the balance to the credit of the employee in a qualified trust; except that such term shall not include—

(A) any distribution which is one of a series of substantially equal periodic payments (not less frequently than annually) made—

(i) for the life (or life expectancy) of the employee or the joint lives (or joint life expectancies) of the employee and the employee's designated beneficiary, or

(ii) for a specified period of 10 years or more,

(B) any distribution to the extent such distribution is required under section 401(a)(9),

(C) any distribution which is made upon hardship of the employee.

If all or any portion of a distribution during 2009 is treated as an eligible rollover distribution but would not be so treated if the minimum distribution requirements under section 401(a)(9) had applied during 2009, such distribution shall not be treated as an eligible rollover distribution for purposes of section 401(a)(31) or 3405(c) or subsection (f) of this section.

(5) Transfer treated as rollover contribution under section 408. For purposes of this title, a transfer to an eligible retirement plan described in clause (i) or (ii) of paragraph (8)(B) resulting in any portion of a distribution being excluded from gross income under paragraph (1) shall be treated as a rollover contribution described in section 408(d)(3).

(6) Sales of distributed property. For purposes of this subsection—

(A) Transfer of proceeds from sale of distributed property treated as transfer of distributed property. The transfer of an amount equal to any portion of the proceeds from the sale of property received in the distribution shall be treated as the transfer of property received in the distribution.

(B) Proceeds attributable to increase in value. The excess of fair market value of property on sale over its fair market value on distribution shall be treated as property received in the distribution.

(C) Designation where amount of distribution exceeds rollover contribution. In any case where part or all of the distribution consists of property other than money—

(i) the portion of the money or other property which is to be treated as attributable to amounts not included in gross income, and

(ii) the portion of the money or other property which is to be treated as included in the rollover contribution,

shall be determined on a ratable basis unless the taxpayer designates otherwise. Any designation under this subparagraph for a taxable year shall be made not later than the time prescribed by law for filing the return for such taxable year (including extensions thereof). Any such designation, once made, shall be irrevocable.

(D) Nonrecognition of gain or loss. No gain or loss shall be recognized on any sale described in subparagraph (A) to the extent that an amount equal to the proceeds is transferred pursuant to paragraph (1).

(7) Special rule for frozen deposits.

(A) In general. The 60-day period described in paragraph (3) shall not—

(i) include any period during which the amount transferred to the employee is a frozen deposit, or

(ii) end earlier than 10 days after such amount ceases to be a frozen deposit.

(B) Frozen deposits. For purposes of this subparagraph, the term "frozen deposit" means any deposit which may not be withdrawn because of—

(i) the bankruptcy or insolvency of any financial institution, or

(ii) any requirement imposed by the State in which such institution is located by reason of the bankruptcy or insolvency (or threat thereof) of 1 or more financial institutions in such State.

A deposit shall not be treated as a frozen deposit unless on at least 1 day during the 60-day period described in paragraph (3) (without regard to this paragraph) such deposit is described in the preceding sentence.

(8) Definitions. For purposes of this subsection—

(A) Qualified trust. The term "qualified trust" means an employees' trust described in section 401(a) which is exempt from tax under section 501(a).

(B) Eligible retirement plan. The term "eligible retirement plan" means—

(i) an individual retirement account described in section 408(a),

(ii) an individual retirement annuity described in section 408(b) (other than an endowment contract),

(iii) a qualified trust,

(iv) an annuity plan described in section 403(a),

(v) an eligible deferred compensation plan described in section 457(b) which is maintained by an eligible employer described in section 457(e)(1)(A), and

(vi) an annuity contract described in section 403(b).

If any portion of an eligible rollover distribution is attributable to payments or distributions from a designated Roth account (as defined in section 402A), an eligible retirement plan with respect to such portion shall include only another designated Roth account and a Roth IRA.

(9) Rollover where spouse receives distribution after death of employee. If any distribution attributable to an employee is paid to the spouse of the employee after the employee's death, the preceding provisions of this subsection shall apply to such distribution in the same manner as if the spouse were the employee.

(10) Separate accounting. Unless a plan described in clause (v) of paragraph (8)(B) agrees to separately account for amounts rolled into such plan from eligible retirement plans not described in such clause, the plan described in such clause may not accept transfers or rollovers from such retirement plans.

(11) Distributions to inherited individual retirement plan of nonspouse beneficiary.

(A) In general. If, with respect to any portion of a distribution from an eligible retirement plan described in paragraph (8)(B)(iii) of a deceased employee, a direct trustee-to-trustee transfer is made to an individual retirement plan described in clause (i) or (ii) of paragraph (8)(B) established for the purposes of receiving the distribution on behalf of an individual who is a designated beneficiary (as defined by section 401(a)(9)(E)) of the employee and who is not the surviving spouse of the employee—

(i) the transfer shall be treated as an eligible rollover distribution,

(ii) the individual retirement plan shall be treated as an inherited individual retirement account or individual retirement annuity (within the meaning of section 408(d)(3)(C)) for purposes of this title, and

(iii) section 401(a)(9)(B) (other than clause (iv) thereof) shall apply to such plan.

(B) Certain trusts treated as beneficiaries. For purposes of this paragraph, to the extent provided in rules prescribed by the Secretary, a trust maintained for the benefit of one or more designated beneficiaries shall be treated in the same manner as a designated beneficiary.

(d) Taxability of beneficiary of certain foreign situs trusts. For purposes of subsections (a), (b), and (c), a stock bonus, pension, or profit-sharing trust which would qualify for exemption from tax under section 501(a) except for the fact that it is a trust created or organized outside the United States shall be treated as if it were a trust exempt from tax under section 501(a).

(e)　Other rules applicable to exempt trusts.

(1)　Alternate payees.

(A) Alternate payee treated as distributee. For purposes of subsection (a) and section 72, an alternate payee who is the spouse or former spouse of the participant shall be treated as the distributee of any distribution or payment made to the alternate payee under a qualified domestic relations order (as defined in section 414(p)).

(B) Rollovers. If any amount is paid or distributed to an alternate payee who is the spouse or former spouse of the participant by reason of any qualified domestic relations order (within the meaning of section 414(p)), subsection (c) shall apply to such distribution in the same manner as if such alternate payee were the employee.

(2)　Distributions by United States to nonresident aliens. The amount includible under subsection (a) in the gross income of a nonresident alien with respect to a distribution made by the United States in respect of services performed by an employee of the United States shall not exceed an amount which bears the same ratio to the amount includible in gross income without regard to this paragraph as—

(A) the aggregate basic pay paid by the United States to such employee for such services, reduced by the amount of such basic pay which was not includible in gross income by reason of being from sources without the United States, bears to

(B) the aggregate basic pay paid by the United States to such employee for such services.

In the case of distributions under the civil service retirement laws, the term "basic pay" shall have the meaning provided in section 8331(3) of title 5, United States Code.

(3)　Cash or deferred arrangements. For purposes of this title, contributions made by an employer on behalf of an employee to a trust which is a part of a qualified cash or deferred arrangement (as defined in section 401(k)(2)) or which is part of a salary reduction agreement under section 403(b) shall not be treated as distributed or made available to the employee nor as contributions made to the trust by the employee merely because the arrangement includes provisions under which the employee has an election whether the contribution will be made to the trust or received by the employee in cash.

(4)　Net unrealized appreciation.

(A) Amounts attributable to employee contributions. For purposes of subsection (a) and section 72, in the case of a distribution other than a lump sum distribution, the amount actually distributed to any distributee from a trust described in subsection (a) shall not include any net unrealized appreciation in securities of the employer corporation attributable to amounts contributed by the employee (other than deductible employee contributions within the meaning of section 72(o)(5)). This subparagraph shall not apply to a distribution to which subsection (c) applies.

(B) Amounts attributable to employer contributions. For purposes of subsection (a) and section 72, in the case of any lump sum distribution which includes securities of the employer corporation, there shall be excluded from gross income the net unrealized appreciation attributable to that part of the distribution which consists of securities of the employer corporation. In accordance with rules prescribed by the Secretary, a taxpayer may elect, on the return of tax on which a lump sum distribution is required to be included, not to have this subparagraph apply to such distribution.

(C) Determination of amounts and adjustments. For purposes of subparagraphs (A) and (B), net unrealized appreciation and the resulting adjustments to basis shall be determined in accordance with regulations prescribed by the Secretary.

(D) Lump-sum distribution. For purposes of this paragraph—

(i) In general. The term "lump sum distribution" means the distribution or payment within one taxable year of the recipient of the balance to the credit of an employee which becomes payable to the recipient—

(I) on account of the employee's death,

(II) after the employee attains age 59 $1/2$,

(III) on account of the employee's separation from service, or

(IV) after the employee has become disabled (within the meaning of section 72(m)(7)),

from a trust which forms a part of a plan described in section 401(a) and which is exempt from tax under section 501 or from a plan described in section 403(a). Subclause (III) of this clause shall be applied only with respect to an individual who is an employee without regard to section 401(c)(1), and subclause (IV) shall be applied only with respect to an employee within the meaning of section 401(c)(1). For purposes of this clause, a distribution to two or more trusts shall be treated as a distribution to one recipient. For purposes of this paragraph, the balance to the credit of the employee does not include the accumulated deductible employee contributions under the plan (within the meaning of section 72(o)(5)).

(ii) Aggregation of certain trusts and plans. For purposes of determining the balance to the credit of an employee under clause (i)—

(I) all trusts which are part of a plan shall be treated as a single trust, all pension plans maintained by the employer shall be treated as a single plan, all profit-sharing plans maintained by the employer shall be treated as a single plan, and all stock bonus plans maintained by the employer shall be treated as a single plan, and

(II) trusts which are not qualified trusts under section 401(a) and annuity contracts which do not satisfy the requirements of section 404(a)(2) shall not be taken into account.

(iii) Community property laws. The provisions of this paragraph shall be applied without regard to community property laws.

(iv) Amounts subject to penalty. This paragraph shall not apply to amounts described in subparagraph (A) of section 72(m)(5) to the extent that section 72(m)(5) applies to such amounts.

(v) Balance to credit of employee not to include amounts payable under qualified domestic relations order. For purposes of this paragraph, the balance to the credit of an employee shall not include any amount payable to an alternate payee under a qualified domestic relations order (within the meaning of section 414(p)).

(vi) Transfers to cost-of-living arrangement not treated as distribution. For purposes of this paragraph, the balance to the credit of an employee under a defined contribution plan shall not include any amount transferred from such defined contribution plan to a qualified cost-of-living arrangement (within the meaning of section 415(k)(2)) under a defined benefit plan.

(vii) Lump-sum distributions of alternate payees. If any distribution or payment of the balance to the credit of an employee would be treated as a lump-sum distribution, then, for purposes of this paragraph, the payment under a qualified domestic relations order (within the meaning of section 414(p)) of the balance to the credit of an alternate payee who is the spouse or former spouse of the employee shall be treated as a lump-sum distribution. For purposes of this clause, the balance to the credit of the alternate payee shall not include any amount payable to the employee.

(E) Definitions relating to securities. For purposes of this paragraph—

(i) Securities. The term "securities" means only shares of stock and bonds or debentures issued by a corporation with interest coupons or in registered form.

(ii) Securities of the employer. The term "securities of the employer corporation" includes securities of a parent or subsidiary corporation (as defined in subsections (e) and (f) of section 424) of the employer corporation.

(5) **Repealed.**

(6) **Direct trustee-to-trustee transfers.** Any amount transferred in a direct trustee-to-trustee transfer in accordance with section 401(a)(31) shall not be includible in gross income for the taxable year of such transfer.

(f) **Written explanation to recipients of distributions eligible for rollover treatment.**

(1) **In general.** The plan administrator of any plan shall, within a reasonable period of time before making an eligible rollover distribution, provide a written explanation to the recipient—

(A) of the provisions under which the recipient may have the distribution directly transferred to an eligible retirement plan and that the automatic distribution by direct transfer applies to certain distributions in accordance with section 401(a)(31)(B),

(B) of the provision which requires the withholding of tax on the distribution if it is not directly transferred to an eligible retirement plan,

(C) of the provisions under which the distribution will not be subject to tax if transferred to an eligible retirement plan within 60 days after the date on which the recipient received the distribution,

(D) if applicable, of the provisions of subsections (d) and (e) of this section, and

(E) of the provisions under which distributions from the eligible retirement plan receiving the distribution may be subject to restrictions and tax consequences which are different from those applicable to distributions from the plan making such distribution.

(2) Definitions. For purposes of this subsection—

(A) Eligible rollover distribution. The term "eligible rollover distribution" has the same meaning as when used in subsection (c) of this section, paragraph (4) of section 403(a), subparagraph (A) of section 403(b)(8), or subparagraph (A) of section 457(e)(16). Such term shall include any distribution to a designated beneficiary which would be treated as an eligible rollover distribution by reason of subsection (c)(11), or section 403(a)(4)(B), 403(b)(8)(B), or 457(e)(16)(B), if the requirements of subsection (c)(11) were satisfied.

(B) Eligible retirement plan. The term "eligible retirement plan" has the meaning given such term by subsection (c)(8)(B).

(g) Limitation on exclusion for elective deferrals.

(1) In general.

(A) Limitation. Notwithstanding subsections (e)(3) and (h)(1)(B), the elective deferrals of any individual for any taxable year shall be included in such individual's gross income to the extent the amount of such deferrals for the taxable year exceeds the applicable dollar amount. The preceding sentence shall not apply to the portion of such excess as does not exceed the designated Roth contributions of the individual for the taxable year.

(B) Applicable dollar amount. For purposes of subparagraph (A), the applicable dollar amount shall be the amount determined in accordance with the following table:

For taxable years beginning in calendar year:	The applicable dollar amount:
2002	$11,000
2003	$12,000
2004	$13,000
2005	$14,000
2006 or thereafter	$15,000

(C) Catch-up contributions. In addition to subparagraph (A), in the case of an eligible participant (as defined in section 414(v)), gross income shall not include elective deferrals in excess of the applicable dollar amount under subparagraph (B) to the extent that the amount of such elective deferrals does not exceed the applicable dollar amount under section 414(v)(2)(B)(i) for the taxable year (without regard to the treatment of the elective deferrals by an applicable employer plan under section 414(v)).

(2) Distribution of excess deferrals.

(A) In general. If any amount (hereinafter in this paragraph referred to as "excess deferrals") is included in the gross income of an individual under paragraph (1) (or would be included but for the last sentence thereof) for any taxable year—

(i) not later than the 1st March 1 following the close of the taxable year, the individual may allocate the amount of such excess deferrals among the plans under which the deferrals were made and may notify each such plan of the portion allocated to it, and

(ii) not later than the 1st April 15 following the close of the taxable year, each such plan may distribute to the individual the amount allocated to it under clause (i) (and any income allocable to such amount through the end of such taxable year).

The distribution described in clause (ii) may be made notwithstanding any other provision of law.

(B) Treatment of distribution under section 401(k). Except to the extent provided under rules prescribed by the Secretary, notwithstanding the distribution of any portion of an excess deferral from a plan under subparagraph (A)(ii), such portion shall, for purposes of applying section 401(k)(3)(A)(ii), be treated as an employer contribution.

(C) Taxation of distribution. In the case of a distribution to which subparagraph (A) applies—

(i) except as provided in clause (ii), such distribution shall not be included in gross income, and

(ii) any income on the excess deferral shall, for purposes of this chapter, be treated as earned and received in the taxable year in which such income is distributed.

No tax shall be imposed under section 72(t) on any distribution described in the preceding sentence.

(D) Partial distributions. If a plan distributes only a portion of any excess deferral and income allocable thereto, such portion shall be treated as having been distributed ratably from the excess deferral and the income.

(3) **Elective deferrals.** For purposes of this subsection, the term "elective deferrals" means, with respect to any taxable year, the sum of—

(A) any employer contribution under a qualified cash or deferred arrangement (as defined in section 401(k)) to the extent not includible in gross income for the taxable year under subsection (e)(3) (determined without regard to this subsection),

(B) any employer contribution to the extent not includible in gross income for the taxable year under subsection (h)(1)(B) (determined without regard to this subsection),

(C) any employer contribution to purchase an annuity contract under section 403(b) under a salary reduction agreement (within the meaning of section 3121(a)(5)(D)), and

(D) any elective employer contribution under section 408(p)(2)(A)(i).

An employer contribution shall not be treated as an elective deferral described in subparagraph (C) if under the salary reduction agreement such contribution is made pursuant to a one-time irrevocable election made by the employee at the time of initial eligibility to participate in the agreement or is made pursuant to a similar arrangement involving a one-time irrevocable election specified in regulations.

(4) **Cost-of-living adjustment.** In the case of taxable years beginning after December 31, 2006, the Secretary shall adjust the $15,000 amount under paragraph (1)(B) at the same time and in the same manner as under section 415(d), except that the base period shall be the calendar quarter beginning July 1, 2005, and any increase under this paragraph which is not a multiple of $500 shall be rounded to the next lowest multiple of $500.

(5) **Disregard of community property laws.** This subsection shall be applied without regard to community property laws.

(6) **Coordination with section 72.** For purposes of applying section 72, any amount includible in gross income for any taxable year under this subsection but which is not distributed from the plan during such taxable year shall not be treated as investment in the contract.

(7) **Special rule for certain organizations.**

(A) In general. In the case of a qualified employee of a qualified organization, with respect to employer contributions described in paragraph (3)(C) made by such organization, the limitation of paragraph (1) for any taxable year shall be increased by whichever of the following is the least:

(i) $3,000,

(ii) $15,000 reduced by the sum of—

(I) the amounts not included in gross income for prior taxable years by reason of this paragraph, plus

(II) the aggregate amount of designated Roth contributions (as defined in section 402A(c)) permitted for prior taxable years by reason of this paragraph, or

(iii) the excess of $5,000 multiplied by the number of years of service of the employee with the qualified organization over the employer contributions described in paragraph (3) made by the organization on behalf of such employee for prior taxable years (determined in the manner prescribed by the Secretary).

(B) Qualified organization. For purposes of this paragraph, the term "qualified organization" means any educational organization, hospital, home health service agency, health and welfare service agency, church, or convention or association of churches. Such term includes any organization described in section 414(e)(3)(B)(ii). Terms used in this subparagraph shall have the same meaning as when used in section 415(c)(4) (as in effect before the enactment of the Economic Growth and Tax Relief Reconciliation Act of 2001).

(C) Qualified employee. For purposes of this paragraph, the term "qualified employee" means any employee who has completed 15 years of service with the qualified organization.

(D) Years of service. For purposes of this paragraph, the term "years of service" has the meaning given such term by section 403(b).

(8) Matching contributions on behalf of self-employed individuals not treated as elective employer contributions. Except as provided in section 401(k)(3)(D)(ii), any matching contribution described in section 401(m)(4)(A) which is made on behalf of a self-employed individual (as defined in section 401(c)) shall not be treated as an elective employer contribution under a qualified cash or deferred arrangement (as defined in section 401(k)) for purposes of this title.

(h) Special rules for simplified employee pensions. For purposes of this chapter—

(1) In general. Except as provided in paragraph (2), contributions made by an employer on behalf of an employee to an individual retirement plan pursuant to a simplified employee pension (as defined in section 408(k))—

(A) shall not be treated as distributed or made available to the employee or as contributions made by the employee, and

(B) if such contributions are made pursuant to an arrangement under section 408(k)(6) under which an employee may elect to have the employer make contributions to the simplified employee pension on behalf of the employee, shall not be treated as distributed or made available or as contributions made by the employee merely because the simplified employee pension includes provisions for such election.

(2) Limitations on employer contributions. Contributions made by an employer to a simplified employee pension with respect to an employee for any year shall be treated as distributed or made available to such employee and as contributions made by the employee to the extent such contributions exceed the lesser of—

(A) 25 percent of the compensation (within the meaning of section 414(s)) from such employer includible in the employee's gross income for the year (determined without regard to the employer contributions to the simplified employee pension), or

(B) the limitation in effect under section 415(c)(1)(A), reduced in the case of any highly compensated employee (within the meaning of section 414(q)) by the amount taken into account with respect to such employee under section 408(k)(3)(D).

(3) Distributions. Any amount paid or distributed out of an individual retirement plan pursuant to a simplified employee pension shall be included in gross income by the payee or distributee, as the case may be, in accordance with the provisions of section 408(d).

(i) Treatment of self-employed individuals. For purposes of this section, except as otherwise provided in subparagraph (A) of subsection (d)(4), the term "employee" includes a self-employed individual (as defined in section 401(c)(1)(B)) and the employer of such individual shall be the person treated as his employer under section 401(c)(4).

(j) Effect of disposition of stock by plan on net unrealized appreciation.

(1) In general. For purposes of subsection (e)(4), in the case of any transaction to which this subsection applies, the determination of net unrealized appreciation shall be made without regard to such transaction.

(2) Transaction to which subsection applies. This subsection shall apply to any transaction in which—

(A) the plan trustee exchanges the plan's securities of the employer corporation for other such securities, or

(B) the plan trustee disposes of securities of the employer corporation and uses the proceeds of such disposition to acquire securities of the employer corporation within 90 days (or such longer period as the Secretary may prescribe), except that this subparagraph shall not apply to any employee with respect to whom a distribution of money was made during the period after such disposition and before such acquisition.

(k) Treatment of simple retirement accounts. Rules similar to the rules of paragraphs (1) and (3) of subsection (h) shall apply to contributions and distributions with respect to a simple retirement account under section 408(p).

(l) Distributions from governmental plans for health and long-term care insurance.

(1) In general. In the case of an employee who is an eligible retired public safety officer who makes the election described in paragraph (6) with respect to any taxable year of such employee, gross income of such employee for such taxable year does not include any distribution from an eligible retirement plan maintained by the employer described in paragraph (4)(B) to the extent that the aggregate amount of such distributions does not exceed the amount paid by such employee for qualified health insurance premiums for such taxable year.

(2) Limitation. The amount which may be excluded from gross income for the taxable year by reason of paragraph (1) shall not exceed $3,000.

(3) Distributions must otherwise be includible.

(A) In general. An amount shall be treated as a distribution for purposes of paragraph (1) only to the extent that such amount would be includible in gross income without regard to paragraph (1).

(B) Application of section 72. Notwithstanding section 72, in determining the extent to which an amount is treated as a distribution for purposes of subparagraph (A), the aggregate amounts distributed from an eligible retirement plan in a taxable year (up to the amount excluded under paragraph (1)) shall be treated as includible in gross income (without regard to subparagraph (A)) to the extent that such amount does not exceed the aggregate amount which would have been so includible if all amounts to the credit of the eligible public safety officer in all eligible retirement plans maintained by the employer described in paragraph (4)(B) were distributed during such taxable year and all such plans were treated as 1 contract for purposes of determining under section 72 the aggregate amount which would have been so includible. Proper adjustments shall be made in applying section 72 to other distributions in such taxable year and subsequent taxable years.

(4) Definitions. For purposes of this subsection—

(A) Eligible retirement plan. For purposes of paragraph (1), the term "eligible retirement plan" means a governmental plan (within the meaning of section 414(d)) which is described in clause (iii), (iv), (v), or (vi) of subsection (c)(8)(B).

(B) Eligible retired public safety officer. The term "eligible retired public safety officer" means an individual who, by reason of disability or attainment of normal retirement age, is separated from service as a public safety officer with the employer who maintains the eligible retirement plan from which distributions subject to paragraph (1) are made.

(C) Public safety officer. The term "public safety officer" shall have the same meaning given such term by section 1204(9)(A) of the Omnibus Crime Control and Safe Streets Act of 1968 (42 U.S.C. 3796b(9)(A)).

(D) Qualified health insurance premiums. The term "qualified health insurance premiums" means premiums for coverage for the eligible retired public safety officer, his spouse, and dependents (as defined in section 152), by an accident or health plan or qualified long-term care insurance contract (as defined in section 7702B(b)).

(5) **Special rules.** For purposes of this subsection—

(A) Direct payment to insurer required. Paragraph (1) shall only apply to a distribution if payment of the premiums is made directly to the provider of the accident or health plan or qualified long-term care insurance contract by deduction from a distribution from the eligible retirement plan.

(B) Related plans treated as 1. All eligible retirement plans of an employer shall be treated as a single plan.

(6) **Election described.**

(A) In general. For purposes of paragraph (1), an election is described in this paragraph if the election is made by an employee after separation from service with respect to amounts not distributed from an eligible retirement plan to have amounts from such plan distributed in order to pay for qualified health insurance premiums.

(B) Special rule. A plan shall not be treated as violating the requirements of section 401, or as engaging in a prohibited transaction for purposes of section 503(b), merely because it provides for an election with respect to amounts that are otherwise distributable under the plan or merely because of a distribution made pursuant to an election described in subparagraph (A).

(7) **Coordination with medical expense deduction.** The amounts excluded from gross income under paragraph (1) shall not be taken into account under section 213.

(8) **Coordination with deduction for health insurance costs of self-employed individuals.** The amounts excluded from gross income under paragraph (1) shall not be taken into account under section 162(l).

[For Analysis, see ¶ 1705. For Committee Reports, see ¶ 5606.]

[Endnote Code Sec. 402]

Sec. 1106, P.L. 112-95, relating to rollover of amounts received in airline carrier bankruptcy, provides

"Sec. 1106. Rollover of amounts received in airline carrier bankruptcy.

"(a) General Rules

"(1) Rollover of airline payment amount. If a qualified airline employee receives any airline payment amount and transfers any portion of such amount to a traditional IRA within 180 days of receipt of such amount (or, if later, within 180 days of the date of the enactment of this Act), then such amount (to the extent so transferred) shall be treated as a rollover contribution described in section 402(c) of the Internal Revenue Code of 1986. A qualified airline employee making such a transfer may exclude from gross income the amount transferred, in the taxable year in which the airline payment amount was paid to the qualified airline employee by the commercial passenger airline carrier.

"(2) Transfer of amounts attributable to airline payment amount following rollover to Roth IRA. A qualified airline employee who has contributed an airline payment amount to a Roth IRA that is treated as a qualified rollover contribution pursuant to section 125 of the Worker, Retiree, and Employer Recovery Act of 2008, may transfer to a traditional IRA, in a trustee-to-trustee transfer, all or any part of the contribution (together with any net income allocable to such contribution), and the transfer to the traditional IRA will be deemed to have been made at the time of the rollover to the Roth IRA, if such transfer is made within 180 days of the date of the enactment of this Act. A qualified airline employee making such a transfer may exclude from gross income the airline payment amount previously rolled over to the Roth IRA, to the extent an amount attributable to the previous rollover was transferred to a traditional IRA, in the taxable year in which the airline payment amount was paid to the qualified airline employee by the commercial passenger airline carrier. No amount so transferred to a traditional IRA may be treated as a qualified rollover contribution with respect to a Roth IRA within the 5-taxable year period beginning with the taxable year in which such transfer was made.

"(3) Extension of time to file claim for refund. A qualified airline employee who excludes an amount from gross income in a prior taxable year under paragraph (1) or (2) may reflect such exclusion in a claim for refund filed within the period of limitation under section 6511(a) of such Code (or, if later, April 15, 2013).

"(4) Overall limitation on amounts transferred to traditional IRAs.

"(A) In general. The aggregate amount of airline payment amounts which may be transferred to 1 or more traditional IRAs under paragraphs (1) and (2) with respect to any qualified employee for any taxable year shall not exceed the excess (if any) of—

"(i) 90 percent of the aggregate airline payment amounts received by the qualified airline employee during the taxable year and all preceding taxable years, over

"(ii) the aggregate amount of such transfers to which paragraphs (1) and (2) applied for all preceding taxable years.

"(B) Special rules. For purposes of applying the limitation under subparagraph (A)—

"(i) any airline payment amount received by the surviving spouse of any qualified employee, and any amount transferred to a traditional IRA by such spouse under subsection (d), shall be treated as an amount received or transferred by the qualified employee, and

"(ii) any amount transferred to a traditional IRA which is attributable to net income described in paragraph (2) shall not be taken into account.

"(5) Covered executives not eligible to make transfers. Paragraphs (1) and (2) shall not apply to any transfer by a qualified airline employee (or any transfer authorized under subsection (d) by a surviving spouse of the qualified airline employee) if at any time during the taxable year of the transfer or any preceding taxable year the qualified airline employee held a position described in subparagraph (A) or (B) of section 162(m)(3) with the commercial passenger airline carrier from whom the airline payment amount was received.

"(b) Treatment of Airline Payment Amounts and Transfers for Employment Taxes- For purposes of and section 209 of the Social Security Act, an airline payment amount shall not fail to be treated as a payment of wages by the commercial passenger airline carrier to the qualified airline employee in the taxable year of payment because such amount is excluded from the qualified airline employee's gross income under subsection (a).

"(c) Definitions and Special Rules. For purposes of this section —

"(1) Airline payment amount.

"(A) In general. The term 'airline payment amount' means any payment of any money or other property which is payable by a commercial passenger airline carrier to a qualified airline employee —

"(i) under the approval of an order of a Federal bankruptcy court in a case filed after September 11, 2001, and before January 1, 2007, and

"(ii) in respect of the qualified airline employee's interest in a bankruptcy claim against the carrier, any note of the carrier (or amount paid in lieu of a note being issued), or any other fixed obligation of the carrier to pay a lump sum amount. The amount of such payment shall be determined without regard to any requirement to deduct and withhold tax from such payment under sections 3102(a) of the Internal Revenue Code of 1986 and 3402(a) of such Code.

"(B) Exception. An airline payment amount shall not include any amount payable on the basis of the carrier's future earnings or profits.

"(2) Qualified airline employee. The term 'qualified airline employee' means an employee or former employee of a commercial passenger airline carrier who was a participant in a defined benefit plan maintained by the carrier which —

"(A) is a plan described in section 401(a) of the Internal Revenue Code of 1986 which includes a trust exempt from tax under section 501(a) of such Code, and

"(B) was terminated or became subject to the restrictions contained in paragraphs (2) and (3) of section 402(b) of the Pension Protection Act of 2006.

"(3) Traditional ira. The term 'traditional IRA' means an individual retirement plan (as defined in section 7701(a)(37) of the Internal Revenue Code of 1986) which is not a Roth IRA.

"(4) Roth IRA. The term 'Roth IRA' has the meaning given such term by section 408A(b) of such Code .

"(d) Surviving Spouse. If a qualified airline employee died after receiving an airline payment amount, or if an airline payment amount was paid to the surviving spouse of a qualified airline employee in respect of the qualified airline employee, the surviving spouse of the qualified airline employee may take all actions permitted under section 125 of the Worker, Retiree and Employer Recovery Act of 2008, or under this section, to the same extent that the qualified airline employee could have done had the qualified airline employee survived.

"(e) Effective Date. This section shall apply to transfers made after the date of the enactment of this Act with respect to airline payment amounts paid before, on, or after such date."

[¶ 3070]   Code Sec. 402A.   Optional treatment of elective deferrals as Roth contributions.

* * * * * * * * * * * *

(c) **Definitions and rules relating to designated Roth contributions.** For purposes of this section—

(1) **Designated Roth contribution.** The term "designated Roth contribution" means any elective deferral which—

(A) is excludable from gross income of an employee without regard to this section, and

(B) the employee designates (at such time and in such manner as the Secretary may prescribe) as not being so excludable.

(2) **Designation limits.** The amount of elective deferrals which an employee may designate under paragraph (1) shall not exceed the excess (if any) of—

(A) the maximum amount of elective deferrals excludable from gross income of the employee for the taxable year (without regard to this section), over

(B) the aggregate amount of elective deferrals of the employee for the taxable year which the employee does not designate under paragraph (1).

(3) Rollover contributions.

(A) In general. A rollover contribution of any payment or distribution from a designated Roth account which is otherwise allowable under this chapter may be made only if the contribution is to—

(i) another designated Roth account of the individual from whose account the payment or distribution was made, or

(ii) a Roth IRA of such individual.

(B) Coordination with limit. Any rollover contribution to a designated Roth account under subparagraph (A) shall not be taken into account for purposes of paragraph (1).

(4) Taxable rollovers to designated Roth accounts.

(A) In general. Notwithstanding sections 402(c), 403(b)(8), and 457(e)(16), in the case of any distribution to which this paragraph applies—

(i) there shall be included in gross income any amount which would be includible were it not part of a qualified rollover contribution,

(ii) section 72(t) shall not apply, and

(iii) unless the taxpayer elects not to have this clause apply, any amount required to be included in gross income for any taxable year beginning in 2010 by reason of this paragraph shall be so included ratably over the 2-taxable-year period beginning with the first taxable year beginning in 2011.

Any election under clause (iii) for any distributions during a taxable year may not be changed after the due date for such taxable year.

(B) Distributions to which paragraph applies. In the case of an applicable retirement plan which includes a qualified Roth contribution program, this paragraph shall apply to a distribution from such plan other than from a designated Roth account which is contributed in a qualified rollover contribution (within the meaning of section 408A(e)) to the designated Roth account maintained under such plan for the benefit of the individual to whom the distribution is made.

(C) Coordination with limit. Any distribution to which this paragraph applies shall not be taken into account for purposes of paragraph (1).

(D) Other rules. The rules of subparagraphs (D), (E), and (F) of section 408A(d)(3) (as in effect for taxable years beginning after 2009) shall apply for purposes of this paragraph.

[1]*(E) Special rule for certain transfers. In the case of an applicable retirement plan which includes a qualified Roth contribution program—*

(i) the plan may allow an individual to elect to have the plan transfer any amount not otherwise distributable under the plan to a designated Roth account maintained for the benefit of the individual,

(ii) such transfer shall be treated as a distribution to which this paragraph applies which was contributed in a qualified rollover contribution (within the meaning of section 408A(e)) to such account, and

(iii) the plan shall not be treated as violating the provisions of section 401(k)(2)(B)(i), 403(b)(7)(A)(i), 403(b)(11), or 457(d)(1)(A), or of section 8433 of title 5, United States Code, solely by reason of such transfer.

* * * * * * * * * * * *

[For Analysis, see ¶ 1301.]

[Endnote Code Sec. 402A]

Code Sec. 402A(c)(4)(E) was added by Sec. 902(a) of the American Taxpayer Relief Act of 2012, P.L. 112-240, 1/2/2013, as detailed below:

1. Sec. 902(a) added subpara. (c)(4)(E).

Effective Date (Sec. 902(b), P.L. 112-240, 1/2/2013) applies to transfers after 12/31/2012, in taxable years ending after 12/31/2012.

[¶ 3071]   **Code Sec. 404.**   **Deduction for contributions of an employer to an employees' trust or annuity plan and compensation under a deferred-payment plan.**

* * * * * * * * * * * * *

  (o) **Deduction limit for single-employer plans.** For purposes of subsection (a)(1)(A)—

    (1) **In general.** In the case of a defined benefit plan to which subsection (a)(1)(A) applies (other than a multiemployer plan), the amount determined under this subsection for any taxable year shall be equal to the greater of—

      (A) the sum of the amounts determined under paragraph (2) with respect to each plan year ending with or within the taxable year, or

      (B) the sum of the minimum required contributions under section 430 for such plan years.

    (2) **Determination of amount.**

      (A) In general. The amount determined under this paragraph for any plan year shall be equal to the excess (if any) of—

        (i) the sum of—

          (I) the funding target for the plan year,

          (II) the target normal cost for the plan year, and

          (III) the cushion amount for the plan year, over

        (ii) the value (determined under section 430(g)(3)) of the assets of the plan which are held by the plan as of the valuation date for the plan year.

      (B) Special rule for certain employers. If section 430(i) does not apply to a plan for a plan year, the amount determined under subparagraph (A)(i) for the plan year shall in no event be less than the sum of—

        (i) the funding target for the plan year (determined as if section 430(i) applied to the plan), plus

        (ii) the target normal cost for the plan year (as so determined).

    (3) **Cushion amount.** For purposes of paragraph (2)(A)(i)(III)—

      (A) In general. The cushion amount for any plan year is the sum of—

        (i) 50 percent of the funding target for the plan year, and

        (ii) the amount by which the funding target for the plan year would increase if the plan were to take into account—

          (I) increases in compensation which are expected to occur in succeeding plan years, or

          (II) if the plan does not base benefits for service to date on compensation, increases in benefits which are expected to occur in succeeding plan years (determined on the basis of the average annual increase in benefits over the 6 immediately preceding plan years).

      (B) Limitations.

        (i) In general. In making the computation under subparagraph (A)(ii), the plan's actuary shall assume that the limitations under subsection 1 and section 415(b) shall apply.

        (ii) Expected increases. In the case of a plan year during which a plan is covered under section 4021 of the Employee Retirement Income Security Act of 1974, the plan's actuary may, notwithstanding subsection 1, take into account increases in the limitations which are expected to occur in succeeding plan years.

    (4) **Special rules for plans with 100 or fewer participants.**

      (A) In general. For purposes of determining the amount under paragraph (3) for any plan year, in the case of a plan which has 100 or fewer participants for the plan year, the liability of the plan attributable to benefit increases for highly compensated employees (as defined in section 414(q)) resulting from a plan amendment which is made or becomes effective, whichever is later, within the last 2 years shall not be taken into account in determining the target liability.

      (B) Rule for determining number of participants. For purposes of determining the number of plan participants, all defined benefit plans maintained by the same employer (or any member of such employer's controlled group (within the meaning of section 412(d)(3))) shall be treated as one plan, but only participants of such member or employer shall be taken into account.

(5) Special rule for terminating plans. In the case of a plan which, subject to section 4041 of the Employee Retirement Income Security Act of 1974, terminates during the plan year, the amount determined under paragraph (2) shall in no event be less than the amount required to make the plan sufficient for benefit liabilities (within the meaning of section 4041(d) of such Act).

(6) Actuarial assumptions. Any computation under this subsection for any plan year shall use the same actuarial assumptions which are used for the plan year under section 430 [1] *(determined by not taking into account any adjustment under clause (iv) of subsection (h)(2)(C) thereof).*

(7) Definitions. Any term used in this subsection which is also used in section 430 shall have the same meaning given such term by section 430.

[For Analysis, see ¶ 1701. For Committee Reports, see ¶ 5402.]

[Endnote Code Sec. 404]
Code Sec. 404(o)(6) was amended by Sec. 40211(a)(2)(A) of the Moving Ahead for Progress in the 21st Century Act, P.L. 112-141, 12/31/2011, as detailed below:
1. Sec. 40211(a)(2)(A) added "(determined by not taking into account any adjustment under clause (iv) of subsection (h)(2)(C) thereof)" before the period in para. (o)(6)
Effective Date (40211(c), P.L. 112-141, 7/6/2012,) effective for plan yrs. beginning after12/31/2011.

[¶ 3072]   Code Sec. 408.   Individual retirement accounts.

* * * * * * * * * * * *

(d) Tax treatment of distributions.

(1) In general. Except as otherwise provided in this subsection, any amount paid or distributed out of an individual retirement plan shall be included in gross income by the payee or distributee, as the case may be, in the manner provided under section 72.

(2) Special rules for applying section 72. For purposes of applying section 72 to any amount described in paragraph (1)—

(A) all individual retirement plans shall be treated as 1 contract,

(B) all distributions during any taxable year shall be treated as 1 distribution, and

(C) the value of the contract, income on the contract, and investment in the contract shall be computed as of the close of the calendar year in which the taxable year begins.

For purposes of subparagraph (C), the value of the contract shall be increased by the amount of any distributions during the calendar year.

(3) Rollover contribution. An amount is described in this paragraph as a rollover contribution if it meets the requirements of subparagraphs (A) and (B).

(A) In general. Paragraph (1) does not apply to any amount paid or distributed out of an individual retirement account or individual retirement annuity to the individual for whose benefit the account or annuity is maintained if—

(i) the entire amount received (including money and any other property) is paid into an individual retirement account or individual retirement annuity (other than an endowment contract) for the benefit of such individual not later than the 60th day after the day on which he receives the payment or distribution; or

(ii) the entire amount received (including money and any other property) is paid into an eligible retirement plan for the benefit of such individual not later than the 60th day after the date on which the payment or distribution is received, except that the maximum amount which may be paid into such plan may not exceed the portion of the amount received which is includible in gross income (determined without regard to this paragraph).

For purposes of clause (ii), the term "eligible retirement plan" means an eligible retirement plan described in clause (iii), (iv), (v), or (vi) of section 402(c)(8)(B).

(B) Limitation. This paragraph does not apply to any amount described in subparagraph (A)(i) received by an individual from an individual retirement account or individual retirement annuity if at any time during the 1-year period ending on the day of such receipt such individual received any other amount described in that subparagraph from an individual retirement account or an individual retirement annuity which was not includible in his gross income because of the application of this paragraph.

(C) Denial of rollover treatment for inherited accounts, etc.

(i) In general. In the case of an inherited individual retirement account or individual retirement annuity—

(I) this paragraph shall not apply to any amount received by an individual from such an account or annuity (and no amount transferred from such account or annuity to another individual retirement account or annuity shall be excluded from gross income by reason of such transfer), and

(II) such inherited account or annuity shall not be treated as an individual retirement account or annuity for purposes of determining whether any other amount is a rollover contribution.

(ii) Inherited individual retirement account or annuity. An individual retirement account or individual retirement annuity shall be treated as inherited if—

(I) the individual for whose benefit the account or annuity is maintained acquired such account by reason of the death of another individual, and

(II) such individual was not the surviving spouse of such other individual.

(D) Partial rollovers permitted.

(i) In general. If any amount paid or distributed out of an individual retirement account or individual retirement annuity would meet the requirements of subparagraph (A) but for the fact that the entire amount was not paid into an eligible plan as required by clause (i) or (ii) of subparagraph (A), such amount shall be treated as meeting the requirements of subparagraph (A) to the extent it is paid into an eligible plan referred to in such clause not later than the 60th day referred to in such clause.

(ii) Eligible plan. For purposes of clause (i), the term "eligible plan" means any account, annuity, contract, or plan referred to in subparagraph (A).

(E) Denial of rollover treatment for required distributions. This paragraph shall not apply to any amount to the extent such amount is required to be distributed under subsection (a)(6) or (b)(3).

(F) Frozen deposits. For purposes of this paragraph, rules similar to the rules of section 402(c)(7) (relating to frozen deposits) shall apply.

(G) Simple retirement accounts. In the case of any payment or distribution out of a simple retirement account (as defined in subsection (p)) to which section 72(t)(6) applies, this paragraph shall not apply unless such payment or distribution is paid into another simple retirement account.

(H) Application of section 72.

(i) In general. If—

(I) a distribution is made from an individual retirement plan, and

(II) a rollover contribution is made to an eligible retirement plan described in section 402(c)(8)(B)(iii), (iv), (v), or (vi) with respect to all or part of such distribution,

then, notwithstanding paragraph (2), the rules of clause (ii) shall apply for purposes of applying section 72.

(ii) Applicable rules. In the case of a distribution described in clause (i)—

(I) section 72 shall be applied separately to such distribution,

(II) notwithstanding the pro rata allocation of income on, and investment in, the contract to distributions under section 72, the portion of such distribution rolled over to an eligible retirement plan described in clause (i) shall be treated as from income on the contract (to the extent of the aggregate income on the contract from all individual retirement plans of the distributee), and

(III) appropriate adjustments shall be made in applying section 72 to other distributions in such taxable year and subsequent taxable years.

(I) Waiver of 60-day requirement. The Secretary may waive the 60-day requirement under subparagraphs (A) and (D) where the failure to waive such requirement would be against equity or good conscience, including casualty, disaster, or other events beyond the reasonable control of the individual subject to such requirement.

(4)   Contributions returned before due date of return. Paragraph (1) does not apply to the distribution of any contribution paid during a taxable year to an individual retirement account or for an individual retirement annuity if—

(A) such distribution is received on or before the day prescribed by law (including extensions of time) for filing such individual's return for such taxable year,

(B) no deduction is allowed under section 219 with respect to such contribution, and

(C) such distribution is accompanied by the amount of net income attributable to such contribution.

In the case of such a distribution, for purposes of section 61, any net income described in subparagraph (C) shall be deemed to have been earned and receivable in the taxable year in which such contribution is made.

(5)   Distributions of excess contributions after due date for taxable year and certain excess rollover contributions.

(A) In general. In the case of any individual, if the aggregate contributions (other than rollover contributions) paid for any taxable year to an individual retirement account or for an individual retirement annuity do not exceed the dollar amount in effect under section 219(b)(1)(A), paragraph (1) shall not apply to the distribution of any such contribution to the extent that such contribution exceeds the amount allowable as a deduction under section 219 for the taxable year for which the contribution was paid—

(i) if such distribution is received after the date described in paragraph (4),

(ii) but only to the extent that no deduction has been allowed under section 219 with respect to such excess contribution.

If employer contributions on behalf of the individual are paid for the taxable year to a simplified employee pension, the dollar limitation of the preceding sentence shall be increased by the lesser of the amount of such contributions or the dollar limitation in effect under section 415(c)(1)(A) for such taxable year.

(B) Excess rollover contributions attributable to erroneous information. If—

(i) the taxpayer reasonably relies on information supplied pursuant to subtitle F for determining the amount of a rollover contribution, but

(ii) the information was erroneous,

subparagraph (A) shall be applied by increasing the dollar limit set forth therein by that portion of the excess contribution which was attributable to such information.

For purposes of this paragraph, the amount allowable as a deduction under section 219 shall be computed without regard to section 219(g).

(6)   Transfer of account incident to divorce. The transfer of an individual's interest in an individual retirement account or an individual retirement annuity to his spouse or former spouse under a divorce or separation instrument described in subparagraph (A) of section 71(b)(2) is not to be considered a taxable transfer made by such individual notwithstanding any other provision of this subtitle, and such interest at the time of the transfer is to be treated as an individual retirement account of such spouse, and not of such individual. Thereafter such account or annuity for purposes of this subtitle is to be treated as maintained for the benefit of such spouse.

(7)   Special rules for simplified employee pensions or simple retirement accounts.

(A) Transfer or rollover of contributions prohibited until deferral test met. Notwithstanding any other provision of this subsection or section 72(t), paragraph (1) and section 72(t)(1) shall apply to the transfer or distribution from a simplified employee pension of any contribution under a salary reduction arrangement described in subsection (k)(6) (or any income allocable thereto) before a determination as to whether the requirements of subsection (k)(6)(A)(iii) are met with respect to such contribution.

(B) Certain exclusions treated as deductions. For purposes of paragraphs (4) and (5) and section 4973, any amount excludable or excluded from gross income under section 402(h) or 402(k) shall be treated as an amount allowable or allowed as a deduction under section 219.

(8) **Distributions for charitable purposes.**

(A) In general. So much of the aggregate amount of qualified charitable distributions with respect to a taxpayer made during any taxable year which does not exceed $100,000 shall not be includible in gross income of such taxpayer for such taxable year.

(B) Qualified charitable distribution. For purposes of this paragraph, the term "qualified charitable distribution" means any distribution from an individual retirement plan (other than a plan described in subsection (k) or (p))—

(i) which is made directly by the trustee to an organization described in section 170(b)(1)(A) (other than any organization described in section 509(a)(3) or any fund or account described in section 4966(d)(2)), and

(ii) which is made on or after the date that the individual for whose benefit the plan is maintained has attained age 70 $1/2$.

A distribution shall be treated as a qualified charitable distribution only to the extent that the distribution would be includible in gross income without regard to subparagraph (A).

(C) Contributions must be otherwise deductible. For purposes of this paragraph, a distribution to an organization described in subparagraph (B)(i) shall be treated as a qualified charitable distribution only if a deduction for the entire distribution would be allowable under section 170 (determined without regard to subsection (b) thereof and this paragraph).

(D) Application of section 72. Notwithstanding section 72, in determining the extent to which a distribution is a qualified charitable distribution, the entire amount of the distribution shall be treated as includible in gross income without regard to subparagraph (A) to the extent that such amount does not exceed the aggregate amount which would have been so includible if all amounts in all individual retirement plans of the individual were distributed during such taxable year and all such plans were treated as 1 contract for purposes of determining under section 72 the aggregate amount which would have been so includible. Proper adjustments shall be made in applying section 72 to other distributions in such taxable year and subsequent taxable years.

(E) Denial of deduction. Qualified charitable distributions which are not includible in gross income pursuant to subparagraph (A) shall not be taken into account in determining the deduction under section 170.

(F) Termination. This paragraph shall not apply to distributions made in taxable years beginning after [1]December 31, 2013.

(9) **Distribution for health savings account funding.**

(A) In general. In the case of an individual who is an eligible individual (as defined in section 223(c)) and who elects the application of this paragraph for a taxable year, gross income of the individual for the taxable year does not include a qualified HSA funding distribution to the extent such distribution is otherwise includible in gross income.

(B) Qualified HSA funding distribution. For purposes of this paragraph, the term "qualified HSA funding distribution" means a distribution from an individual retirement plan (other than a plan described in subsection (k) or (p)) of the employee to the extent that such distribution is contributed to the health savings account of the individual in a direct trustee-to-trustee transfer.

(C) Limitations.

(i) Maximum dollar limitation. The amount excluded from gross income by subparagraph (A) shall not exceed the excess of—

(I) the annual limitation under section 223(b) computed on the basis of the type of coverage under the high deductible health plan covering the individual at the time of the qualified HSA funding distribution, over

(II) in the case of a distribution described in clause (ii)(II), the amount of the earlier qualified HSA funding distribution.

(ii) One-time transfer.

(I) In general. Except as provided in subclause (II), an individual may make an election under subparagraph (A) only for one qualified HSA funding distribution during the lifetime of the individual. Such an election, once made, shall be irrevocable.

(II) Conversion from self-only to family coverage. If a qualified HSA funding distribution is made during a month in a taxable year during which an individual has self-only coverage under a high deductible health plan as of the first day of the month, the individual may elect to make an additional qualified HSA funding distribution during a subsequent month in such taxable year during which the individual has family coverage under a high deductible health plan as of the first day of the subsequent month.

(D) Failure to maintain high deductible health plan coverage.

(i) In general. If, at any time during the testing period, the individual is not an eligible individual, then the aggregate amount of all contributions to the health savings account of the individual made under subparagraph (A)—

(l) shall be includible in the gross income of the individual for the taxable year in which occurs the first month in the testing period for which such individual is not an eligible individual, and

(ll) the tax imposed by this chapter for any taxable year on the individual shall be increased by 10 percent of the amount which is so includible.

(ii) Exception for disability or death. Subclauses (I) and (II) of clause (i) shall not apply if the individual ceased to be an eligible individual by reason of the death of the individual or the individual becoming disabled (within the meaning of section 72(m)(7)).

(iii) Testing period. The term "testing period" means the period beginning with the month in which the qualified HSA funding distribution is contributed to a health savings account and ending on the last day of the 12th month following such month.

(E) Application of section 72. Notwithstanding section 72, in determining the extent to which an amount is treated as otherwise includible in gross income for purposes of subparagraph (A), the aggregate amount distributed from an individual retirement plan shall be treated as includible in gross income to the extent that such amount does not exceed the aggregate amount which would have been so includible if all amounts from all individual retirement plans were distributed. Proper adjustments shall be made in applying section 72 to other distributions in such taxable year and subsequent taxable years.

* * * * * * * * * * * *

[For Analysis, see ¶ 1101.]

[Endnote Code Sec. 408]

Code Sec. 408(d)(8)(F) was amended by Sec. 208(a) of the American Taxpayer Relief Act of 2012, P.L. 112-240, 1/2/2013, as detailed below:

1. Sec. 208(a) substituted "December 31, 2013" for "December 31, 2011" in subpara. (d)(8)(F)

Effective Date (Sec. 208(b), P.L. 112-240, 1/2/2013) effective for distributions made in tax. yrs. begin. after 12/31/2011.

[¶ 3073]   Code Sec. 417.   Definitions and special rules for purposes of minimum survivor annuity requirements.

* * * * * * * * * * * *

(e) Restrictions on cash-outs.

(1) Plan may require distribution if present value not in excess of dollar limit. A plan may provide that the present value of a qualified joint and survivor annuity or a qualified preretirement survivor annuity will be immediately distributed if such value does not exceed the amount that can be distributed without the participant's consent under section 411(a)(11). No distribution may be made under the preceding sentence after the annuity starting date unless the participant and the spouse of the participant (or where the participant has died, the surviving spouse) consents in writing to such distribution.

(2) **Plan may distribute benefit in excess of dollar limit only with consent.** If—

(A) the present value of the qualified joint and survivor annuity or the qualified preretirement survivor annuity exceeds the amount that can be distributed without the participant's consent under section 411(a)(11), and

(B) the participant and the spouse of the participant (or where the participant has died, the surviving spouse) consent in writing to the distribution,

the plan may immediately distribute the present value of such annuity.

(3) **Determination of present value.**

(A) In general. For purposes of paragraphs (1) and (2), the present value shall not be less than the present value calculated by using the applicable mortality table and the applicable interest rate.

(B) Applicable mortality table. For purposes of subparagraph (A), the term "applicable mortality table" means a mortality table, modified as appropriate by the Secretary, based on the mortality table specified for the plan year under subparagraph (A) of section 430(h)(3) (without regard to subparagraph (C) or (D) of such section).

(C) Applicable interest rate. For purposes of subparagraph (A), the term "applicable interest rate" means the adjusted first, second, and third segment rates applied under rules similar to the rules of [1]*section 430(h)(2)(C) (determined by not taking into account any adjustment under clause (iv) thereof)* for the month before the date of the distribution or such other time as the Secretary may by regulations prescribe.

(D) Applicable segment rates. For purposes of subparagraph (C), the adjusted first, second, and third segment rates are the first, second, and third segment rates which would be determined under [2]*section 430(h)(2)(C) (determined by not taking into account any adjustment under clause (iv) thereof)* if—

(i) section 430(h)(2)(D) were applied by substituting the average yields for the month described in subparagraph (C) for the average yields for the 24-month period described in such section,

(ii) section 430(h)(2)(G)(i)(II) were applied by substituting "section 417(e)(3)(A)(ii)(II)" for "section 412(b)(5)(B)(ii)(II)", and

(iii) the applicable percentage under section 430(h)(2)(G) were determined in accordance with the following table:

In the case of plan years beginning in:	The applicable percentage is:
2008	20 percent
2009	40 percent
2010	60 percent
2011	80 percent.

* * * * * * * * * * * *

[For Analysis, see ¶ 1701. For Committee Reports, see ¶ 5402.]

[Endnote Code Sec. 417]

Code Sec. 417(e)(3)(C) and Code Sec. 417(e)(3)(D) were amended by Secs. 40211(a)(2)(C) of the Moving Ahead for Progress in the 21st Century Act, P.L. 112-141, 7/6/2012, as detailed below:

1. Sec. 40211(a)(2)(C) substituted "section 430(h)(2)(C) (determined by not taking into account any adjustment under clause (iv) thereof)" for "section 430(h)(2)(C)" in subpara. (e)(3)(C)

2. Sec. 40211(a)(2)(C) substituted "section 430(h)(2)(C) (determined by not taking into account any adjustment under clause (iv) thereof)" for "section 430(h)(2)(C)" in subpara. (e)(3)(D)

Effective Date (Sec. 40211(c)(1), P.L. 112-141, 7/6/2012) effective for plan yrs. begin. after 12/31/2011. Sec. 40211(c)(2) of this Act, reads as follows:

"(2) Rules with respect to elections.

"(A) Adjusted funding target attainment percentage. A plan sponsor may elect not to have the amendments made by this section apply to any plan year beginning before January 1, 2013, either (as specified in the election)—

"(i) for all purposes for which such amendments apply, or

"(ii) solely for purposes of determining the adjusted funding target attainment percentage under sections 436 of the Internal Revenue Code of 1986 and 206(g) of the Employee Retirement Income Security Act of 1974 for such plan year.

"A plan shall not be treated as failing to meet the requirements of sections 204(g) of such Act and 411(d)(6) of such Code solely by reason of an election under this paragraph.

"(B) Opt out of existing elections. If, on the date of the enactment of this Act, an election is in effect with respect to any plan under sections 303(h)((2)(D)(ii) of the Employee Retirement Income Security Act of 1974 and 430(h)((2)(D)(ii) of the Internal Revenue Code of 1986, then, notwithstanding the last sentence of each such section, the plan sponsor may revoke such election without the consent of the Secretary of the Treasury. The plan sponsor may make such revocation at any time before the date which is 1 year after such date of enactment and such revocation shall be effective for the 1st plan year to which the amendments made by this section apply and all subsequent plan years. Nothing in this subparagraph shall preclude a plan sponsor from making a subsequent election in accordance with such sections."

[¶ 3074]　　Code Sec. 420.　　Transfers of excess pension assets to retiree health accounts.

(a)　**General rule.** If there is a qualified transfer of any excess pension assets of a defined benefit plan to a health benefits account[1], *or an applicable life insurance account,* which is part of such plan—

(1) a trust which is part of such plan shall not be treated as failing to meet the requirements of subsection (a) or (h) of section 401 solely by reason of such transfer (or any other action authorized under this section),

(2) no amount shall be includible in the gross income of the employer maintaining the plan solely by reason of such transfer,

(3) such transfer shall not be treated—

(A) as an employer reversion for purposes of section 4980, or

(B) as a prohibited transaction for purposes of section 4975, and

(4) the limitations of subsection (d) shall apply to such employer.

(b)　**Qualified transfer.** For purposes of this section

(1)　**In general.** The term "qualified transfer" means a transfer

(A) of excess pension assets of a defined benefit plan to a health benefits account[2], *or an applicable life insurance account,* which is part of such plan[3],

(B) which does not contravene any other provision of law, and

(C) with respect to which the following requirements are met in connection with the plan—

(i) the use requirements of subsection (c)(1),

(ii) the vesting requirements of subsection (c)(2), and

(iii) the minimum cost requirements of subsection (c)(3).

(2)　**Only 1 transfer** [4]*per year.* No more than 1 transfer with respect to any plan during a taxable year may be treated as a qualified transfer for purposes of this section. [5]*If there is a transfer from a defined benefit plan to both a health benefits account and an applicable life insurance account during any taxable year, such transfers shall be treated as 1 transfer for purposes of this paragraph.*[6]

(3)　**Limitation on amount transferred.** The amount of excess pension assets which may be transferred [7]*to an account* in a qualified transfer shall not exceed the amount which is reasonably estimated to be the amount the employer maintaining the plan will pay (whether directly or through reimbursement) out of such account during the taxable year of the transfer for [7A]*qualified current retiree liabilities.*

[8]*(4)*　**Expiration.** No transfer made after [9]*December 31, 2021,* shall be treated as a qualified transfer.

(c)　**Requirements of plans transferring assets.**

(1)　**Use of transferred assets.**

(A) In general. Any assets transferred to a health benefits account[10], *or an applicable life insurance account,* in a qualified transfer (and any income allocable thereto) shall be used only to pay [10A]*qualified current retiree liabilities* (other than liabilities of key employees not taken into account under subsection (e)(1)(D)) for the taxable year of the transfer (whether directly or through reimbursement). In the case of a qualified future transfer or collectively bargained transfer to which subsection (f) applies, any assets so transferred may also be used to pay liabilities described in subsection (f)(2)(C).

(B) Amounts not used to pay for health benefits [11]*or life insurance.*

(i) In general. Any assets transferred to a health benefits account[12], *or an applicable life insurance account,* in a qualified transfer (and any income allocable thereto) which are not used as provided in subparagraph (A) shall be transferred out of the account to the transferor plan.

(ii) Tax treatment of amounts. Any amount transferred out of an account under clause (i)—

(I) shall not be includible in the gross income of the employer for such taxable year, but

(II) shall be treated as an employer reversion for purposes of section 4980 (without regard to subsection (d) thereof).

(C) Ordering rule. For purposes of this section, any amount paid out of a health benefits account[13], *or an applicable life insurance account,* shall be treated as paid first out of the assets and income described in subparagraph (A).

(2) **Requirements relating to pension benefits accruing** [14]***before transfer.*** *The requirements of this paragraph* are met if the plan provides that the accrued pension benefits of any participant or beneficiary under the plan become nonforfeitable in the same manner which would be required if the plan had terminated immediately before the qualified transfer (or in the case of a participant who separated during the 1-year period ending on the date of the transfer, immediately before such separation).[15]

(3) **Minimum cost requirements.**

(A) In general. The requirements of this paragraph are met if each group health plan or arrangement under which applicable health benefits are provided[16], *and each group-term life insurance plan under which applicable life insurance benefits are provided,* provides that the applicable employer cost for each taxable year during the cost maintenance period shall not be less than the higher of the applicable employer costs for each of the 2 taxable years immediately preceding the taxable year of the qualified transfer or, in the case of a transfer which involves a plan maintained by an employer described in subsection (f)(2)(E)(i)(III), if the plan meets the requirements of subsection (f)(2)(D)(i)(II).

(B) Applicable employer cost. For purposes of this paragraph, the term "applicable employer cost" means, with respect to any taxable year, the amount determined by dividing—

(i) the [16A]*qualified current retiree liabilities* of the employer for such taxable year determined—

[17]*(I) separately with respect to applicable health benefits and applicable life insurance benefits,*

[18]*(II)* without regard to any reduction under subsection (e)(1)(B), and

[19]*(III)* in the case of a taxable year in which there was no qualified transfer, in the same manner as if there had been such a transfer at the end of the taxable year, by

(ii) the number of individuals to whom coverage [20]*was provided during such taxable year for the benefits with respect to which the determination under clause (i) is made.*

(C) Election to compute cost separately. An employer may elect to have this paragraph applied separately [21]*for applicable health benefits* with respect to individuals eligible for benefits under title XVIII of the Social Security Act at any time during the taxable year and with respect to individuals not so eligible[22], *and separately for applicable life insurance benefits with respect to individuals age 65 or older at any time during the taxable year and with respect to individuals under age 65 during the taxable year.*

(D) Cost maintenance period. For purposes of this paragraph, the term "cost maintenance period" means the period of 5 taxable years beginning with the taxable year in
which the qualified transfer occurs. If a taxable year is in two or more overlapping cost
maintenance periods, this paragraph shall be applied by taking into account the highest
applicable employer cost required to be provided under subparagraph (A) for such taxable year.

(E) Regulations.

(i) In general. The Secretary shall prescribe such regulations as may be necessary
to prevent an employer who significantly reduces retiree health coverage [23]*or retiree
life insurance coverage, as the case may be,* during the cost maintenance period from
being treated as satisfying the minimum cost requirement of this subsection.

(ii) Insignificant cost reductions [24]*for retiree health coverage* permitted.

(I) In general. An eligible employer shall not be treated as failing to meet the requirements of this paragraph for any taxable year if, in lieu of any reduction of retiree health coverage permitted under the regulations prescribed under clause (i), the
employer reduces applicable employer cost by an amount not in excess of the reduction in costs which would have occurred if the employer had made the maximum permissible reduction in retiree health coverage under such regulations. In applying such regulations to any subsequent taxable year, any reduction in applicable
employer cost under this clause shall be treated as if it were an equivalent reduction
in retiree health coverage.

(II) Eligible employer. For purposes of subclause (I), an employer shall be
treated as an eligible employer for any taxable year if, for the preceding taxable
year, the [25]*qualified current retiree liabilities* of the employer [26]*with respect to applicable health benefits* were at least 5 percent of the gross receipts of the employer. For purposes of this subclause, the rules of paragraphs (2), (3)(B), and
(3)(C) of section 448(c) shall apply in determining the amount of an employer's
gross receipts.

(d)   Limitations on employer. For purposes of this title—

(1)   Deduction limitations. No deduction shall be allowed—

(A) for the transfer of any amount to a health benefits account[27], *or an applicable life
insurance account,*in a qualified transfer (or any retransfer to the plan under subsection
(c)(1)(B)),

(B) for [28]*qualified current retiree liabilities* paid out of the assets (and income) described in subsection (c)(1), or

(C) for any amounts to which subparagraph (B) does not apply and which are paid
for [28A]*qualified current retiree liabilities* for the taxable year to the extent such amounts
are not greater than the excess (if any) of—

(i) the amount determined under subparagraph (A) (and income allocable thereto),
over

(ii) the amount determined under subparagraph (B).

(2)   No contributions allowed. An employer may not contribute[29], any amount to a
health benefits account or welfare benefit fund (as defined in section 419(e)(1)) with respect to [30]*qualified current retiree liabilities* for which transferred assets are required to be
used under subsection (c)(1).

(e)   Definition and special rules. For purposes of this section—

(1)   Qualified current retiree[31] liabilities. For purposes of this section—

(A) In general. The term "[31A]*qualified current retiree liabilities*" means, with respect
to any taxable year, the aggregate amounts (including administrative expenses) which
would have been allowable as a deduction to the employer for such taxable year with respect to applicable health benefits [32]*and applicable life insurance benefits* provided during such taxable year if—

(i) such benefits were provided directly by the employer, and

(ii) the employer used the cash receipts and disbursements method of accounting.

For purposes of the preceding sentence, the rule of section 419(c)(3)(B) shall apply.

(B) Reductions for amounts previously set aside. The amount determined under subparagraph (A) shall be reduced by the amount [33]*(determined separately for applicable health benefits and applicable life insurance benefits)* which bears the same ratio to such amount as—

(i) the value (as of the close of the plan year preceding the year of the qualified transfer) of the assets in all health benefits accounts [34]*or applicable life insurance accounts* or welfare benefit funds (as defined in section 419(e)(1)) set aside to pay for the [35]*qualified current retiree liability*, bears to

(ii) the present value of the [36]*qualified current retiree liabilities* for all plan years (determined without regard to this subparagraph).

(C) Applicable health benefits. The term "applicable health benefits" means health benefits or coverage which are provided to—

(i) retired employees who, immediately before the qualified transfer, are entitled to receive such benefits [37]*by reason of retirement* and who are entitled to pension benefits under the plan, and

(ii) their spouses and dependents.

[38]*(D) Applicable life insurance benefits. The term "applicable life insurance benefits" means group-term life insurance coverage provided to retired employees who, immediately before the qualified transfer, are entitled to receive such coverage by reason of retirement and who are entitled to pension benefits under the plan, but only to the extent that such coverage is provided under a policy for retired employees and the cost of such coverage is excludable from the retired employee's gross income under section 79.*

[39]*(E)* Key employees excluded. If an employee is a key employee (within the meaning of section 416(i)(1)) with respect to any plan year ending in a taxable year, such employee shall not be taken into account in computing [39A]*qualified current retiree liabilities* for such taxable year or in calculating applicable employer cost under subsection (c)(3)(B).

(2) **Excess pension assets.** The term "excess pension assets" means the excess (if any) of—

(A) the lesser of—

(i) the fair market value of the plan's assets (reduced by the prefunding balance and funding standard carryover balance determined under section 430(f)), or

(ii) the value of plan assets as determined under section 430(g)(3) after reduction under section 430(f), over

(B) 125 percent of the sum of the funding target and the target normal cost determined under section 430 for such plan year.

(3) **Health benefits account.** The term "health benefits account" means an account established and maintained under section 401(h).

[40]*(4) Applicable life insurance account. The term "applicable life insurance account" means a separate account established and maintained for amounts transferred under this section for qualified current retiree liabilities based on premiums for applicable life insurance benefits.*

[41]**(5)** Coordination with section 430. In the case of a qualified transfer, any assets so transferred shall not, for purposes of this section and section 430, be treated as assets in the plan.

[42]*(6)* **Application to multiemployer plans.** In the case of a multiemployer plan, this section shall be applied to any such plan—

(A) by treating any reference in this section to an employer as a reference to all employers maintaining the plan (or, if appropriate, the plan sponsor), and

(B) in accordance with such modifications of this section (and the provisions of this title relating to this section) as the Secretary determines appropriate to reflect the fact the plan is not maintained by a single employer.

(f) Qualified transfers to cover future retiree[43] costs and collectively bargained retiree[44] benefits.

(1) In general. An employer maintaining a defined benefit plan (other than a multiemployer plan) may, in lieu of a qualified transfer, elect for any taxable year to have the plan make—

(A) a qualified future transfer, or

(B) a collectively bargained transfer.

Except as provided in this subsection, a qualified future transfer and a collectively bargained transfer shall be treated for purposes of this title and the Employee Retirement Income Security Act of 1974 as if it were a qualified transfer.

(2) Qualified future and collectively bargained transfers. For purposes of this subsection—

(A) In general. The terms "qualified future transfer" and "collectively bargained transfer" mean a transfer which meets all of the requirements for a qualified transfer, except that—

(i) the determination of excess pension assets shall be made under subparagraph (B),

(ii) the limitation on the amount transferred shall be determined under subparagraph (C),

(iii) the minimum cost requirements of subsection (c)(3) shall be modified as provided under subparagraph (D), and

(iv) in the case of a collectively bargained transfer, the requirements of subparagraph (E) shall be met with respect to the transfer.

(B) Excess pension assets.

(i) In general. In determining excess pension assets for purposes of this subsection, subsection (e)(2) shall be applied by substituting "120 percent" for "125 percent".

(ii) Requirement to maintain funded status. If, as of any valuation date of any plan year in the transfer period, the amount determined under subsection (e)(2)(B) (after application of clause (i)) exceeds the amount determined under subsection (e)(2)(A), either—

(I) the employer maintaining the plan shall make contributions to the plan in an amount not less than the amount required to reduce such excess to zero as of such date, or

(II) there is transferred from the health benefits account [45]*or applicable life insurance account, as the case may be,* to the plan an amount not less than the amount required to reduce such excess to zero as of such date.

(C) Limitation on amount transferred. Notwithstanding subsection (b)(3), the amount of the excess pension assets which may be transferred—

(i) in the case of a qualified future transfer shall be equal to the sum of—

(I) if the transfer period includes the taxable year of the transfer, the amount determined under subsection (b)(3) for such taxable year, plus

(II) in the case of all other taxable years in the transfer period, the sum of the [46]*qualified current retiree liabilities* which the plan reasonably estimates, in accordance with guidance issued by the Secretary, will be incurred for each of such years, and

(ii) in the case of a collectively bargained transfer, shall not exceed the amount which is reasonably estimated, in accordance with the provisions of the collective bargaining agreement and generally accepted accounting principles, to be the amount the employer maintaining the plan will pay (whether directly or through reimbursement) out of such account during the collectively bargained cost maintenance period for [47]*collectively bargained retiree liabilities.*

(D) Minimum cost requirements.

(i) In general. The requirements of subsection (c)(3) shall be treated as met if—

(I) in the case of a qualified future transfer, each group health plan or arrangement under which applicable health benefits are provided [48], *and each group-term life insurance plan or arrangement under which applicable life insurance benefits are provided,* provides applicable health benefits [49]*or applicable life insurance bene-*

fits, *as the case may be*, during the period beginning with the first year of the transfer period and ending with the last day of the 4th year following the transfer period such that the annual average amount of the applicable employer cost during such period is not less than the applicable employer cost determined under subsection (c)(3)(A) with respect to the transfer, and

(II) in the case of a collectively bargained transfer, each collectively bargained[50] plan under which collectively bargained health benefits [51]*or collectively bargained life insurance benefits* are provided provides that the collectively bargained employer cost for each taxable year during the collectively bargained cost maintenance period shall not be less than the amount specified by the collective bargaining agreement.

(ii) Election to maintain benefits for future transfers. An employer may elect, in lieu of the requirements of clause (i)(I), to meet the requirements of subsection (c)(3) [52]*with respect to applicable health benefits or applicable life insurance benefits* by meeting the requirements of such subsection (as in effect before the amendments made by section 535 of the Tax Relief Extension Act of 1999) for each of the years described in the period under clause (i)(I). [53]*Such election may be made separately with respect to applicable health benefits and applicable life insurance benefits. In the case of an election with respect to applicable life insurance benefits, the first sentence of this clause shall be applied as if subsection (c)(3) as in effect before the amendments made by such Act applied to such benefits.*

(iii) Collectively bargained employer cost. For purposes of this subparagraph, the term "collectively bargained employer cost" means the average cost per covered individual of providing collectively bargained[54] health benefits[55], *collectively bargained life insurance benefits, or both, as the case may be*, as determined in accordance with the applicable collective bargaining agreement. Such agreement may provide for an appropriate reduction in the collectively bargained employer cost to take into account any portion of the collectively bargained[56] health benefits[57], *collectively bargained life insurance benefits, or both, as the case may be*, that is provided or financed by a government program or other source.

(E) Special rules for collectively bargained transfers.

(i) In general. A collectively bargained transfer shall only include a transfer which—

(I) is made in accordance with a collective bargaining agreement,

(II) before the transfer, the employer designates, in a written notice delivered to each employee organization that is a party to the collective bargaining agreement, as a collectively bargained transfer in accordance with this section, and

(III) involves a [58]*defined benefit* plan maintained by an employer which, in its taxable year ending in 2005, provided health benefits or coverage to retirees and their spouses and dependents under all of the [59]*health* benefit plans maintained by the employer, but only if the aggregate cost (including administrative expenses) of such benefits or coverage which would have been allowable as a deduction to the employer (if such benefits or coverage had been provided directly by the employer and the employer used the cash receipts and disbursements method of accounting) is at least 5 percent of the gross receipts of the employer (determined in accordance with the last sentence of subsection (c)(3)(E)(ii)(II)) for such taxable year, or a plan maintained by a successor to such employer.

(ii) Use of assets. Any assets transferred to a health benefits account[60], *or an applicable life insurance account*, in a collectively bargained transfer (and any income allocable thereto) shall be used only to pay [61]*collectively bargained retiree liabilities* (other than liabilities of key employees not taken into account under paragraph (6)(B)(iii)) for the taxable year of the transfer or for any subsequent taxable year during the collectively bargained cost maintenance period (whether directly or through reimbursement).

(3) Coordination with other transfers. In applying subsection (b)(3) to any subsequent transfer during a taxable year in a transfer period or collectively bargained cost maintenance period, [62]*qualified current retiree liabilities* shall be reduced by any such liabilities taken into account with respect to the qualified future transfer or collectively bargained transfer to which such period relates.

(4) Special deduction rules for collectively bargained transfers. In the case of a collectively bargained transfer—

(A) the limitation under subsection (d)(1)(C) shall not apply, and

(B) notwithstanding subsection (d)(2), an employer may contribute an amount to a health benefits account or welfare benefit fund (as defined in section 419(e)(1)) with respect to collectively bargained retiree liabilities for which transferred assets are required to be used under subsection (c)(1)(B), and the deductibility of any such contribution shall be governed by the limits applicable to the deductibility of contributions to a welfare benefit fund under a collective bargaining agreement (as determined under section 419A(f)(5)(A)) without regard to whether such contributions are made to a health benefits account or welfare benefit fund and without regard to the provisions of section 404 or the other provisions of this section.

The Secretary shall provide rules to ensure that the application of this paragraph does not result in a deduction being allowed more than once for the same contribution or for 2 or more contributions or expenditures relating to the same [63]*collectively bargained retiree liabilities.*

(5) Transfer period. For purposes of this subsection, the term "transfer period" means, with respect to any transfer, a period of consecutive taxable years (not less than 2) specified in the election under paragraph (1) which begins and ends during the 10-taxable-year period beginning with the taxable year of the transfer.

(6) Terms relating to collectively bargained transfers. For purposes of this subsection—

(A) Collectively bargained cost maintenance period. The term "collectively bargained cost maintenance period" means, with respect to each covered retiree and his covered spouse and dependents, the shorter of—

(i) the remaining lifetime of such covered retiree and[64], *in the case of a transfer to a health benefits account,* his covered spouse and dependents, or

(ii) the period of coverage provided by the collectively bargained [65]*plan* (determined as of the date of the collectively bargained transfer) with respect to such covered retiree and[66], *in the case of a transfer to a health benefits account,* his covered spouse and dependents.

(B) Collectively bargained retiree[67] liabilities.

(i) In general. The term "[68]*collectively bargained retiree liabilities*" means the present value, as of the beginning of a taxable year and determined in accordance with the applicable collective bargaining agreement, of all collectively bargained health benefits[69], *and collectively bargained life insurance benefits,* (including administrative expenses) for such taxable year and all subsequent taxable years during the collectively bargained cost maintenance period.

(ii) Reduction for amounts previously set aside. The amount determined under clause (i) shall be reduced by the value (as of the close of the plan year preceding the year of the collectively bargained transfer) of the assets in all health benefits accounts[70], *applicable life insurance accounts,* or welfare benefit funds (as defined in section 419(e)(1)) set aside to pay for the [71]*collectively bargained retiree liabilities.* [72]*The preceding sentence shall be applied separately for collectively bargained health benefits and collectively bargained life insurance benefits.*

(iii) Key employees excluded. If an employee is a key employee (within the meaning of section [73]*416(i)(1)*) with respect to any plan year ending in a taxable year, such employee shall not be taken into account in computing [74]*collectively bargained retiree liabilities* for such taxable year or in calculating collectively bargained employer cost under subsection (c)(3)(C).

(C) Collectively bargained health benefits. The term "collectively bargained health benefits" means health benefits or coverage[75]—

(i) [76]*which are provided to* retired employees who, immediately before the collectively bargained transfer, are entitled to receive such benefits [77]*by reason of retirement* and who are entitled to pension benefits under the plan, and their spouses and dependents, and

(ii) if specified by the provisions of the collective bargaining agreement governing the collectively bargained transfer, [78]*which will be provided at retirement to employees who are not retired employees at the time of the transfer and who* are entitled to receive such benefits and who are entitled to pension benefits under the plan, and their spouses and dependents.

[79]*(D) Collectively bargained life insurance benefits. The term "collectively bargained life insurance benefits" means, with respect to any collectively bargained transfer—*

(i) applicable life insurance benefits which are provided to retired employees who, immediately before the transfer, are entitled to receive such benefits by reason of retirement, and

(ii) if specified by the provisions of the collective bargaining agreement governing the transfer, applicable life insurance benefits which will be provided at retirement to employees who are not retired employees at the time of the transfer.

[80]*(E)* Collectively bargained[81] plan. The term "collectively [82]*bargained* plan" means a group health plan or arrangement for retired employees and their spouses and dependents[83], *or a group-term life insurance plan or arrangement for retired employees,* that is maintained pursuant to 1 or more collective bargaining agreements.

[84]*(g)   Segment rates determined without pension stabilization. For purposes of this section, section 430 shall be applied without regard to subsection (h)(2)(C)(iv) thereof.*

[For Analysis, see ¶ 1701, ¶ 1702 and ¶ 1703. For Committee Reports, see ¶ 5402 and ¶ 5405.]

[Endnote Code Sec. 420]

Code Sec. 420(a), Code Sec. 420(b)(1)(A), Code Sec. 420(b)(2), Code Sec. 420(b)(2)(B), Code Sec. 420(b)(3), Code Sec. 420(b)(4) and Code Sec. 420(b)(5) was amended by Sec. 40242(a), (e)(1)-(2), (3)(A)-(B), (g)(1), (2), and (3)(A)-(B) of the Moving Ahead for Progress in the 21st Century Act, P.L. 112-141, 7/6/2012, as detailed below:

1. Sec. 40242(a) added ", or an applicable life insurance account," after "health benefits account" in subsec. (a)

2. Sec. 40242(e)(2) added ", or an applicable life insurance account," after "a health benefits account" in subpara. (b)(1)(A)

3. Sec. 40242(g)(1) deleted "in a taxable year beginning after December 31, 1990" after "part of such plan," in subpara. (b)(1)(A)

4. Sec. 40242(g)(3)(B) substituted "per year. No more than" for "per year. (A) In general. No more than" in para. (b)(2)

5. Sec. 40242(e)(3)(A) added "If there is a transfer from a defined benefit plan to both a health benefits account and an applicable life insurance account during any taxable year, such transfers shall be treated as 1 transfer for purposes of this paragraph." at the end of subpara. (b)(2) [as amended by Sec. 40242(g)(3)(B), see above]

6. Sec. 40242(e)(3)(A) deleted subpara. (b)(2)(B). Prior to deletion, subpara. (b)(2)(B) read a follows:

"(B) Exception. A transfer described in paragraph (4) shall not be taken into account for purposes of subparagraph (A)."

7. Sec. 40242(e)(3)(B) added "to an account" after "may be transferred" in para. (b)(3)

7A. Sec. 40242(e)(1) substituted "qualified current retiree liabilities" for "qualified current retiree health liabilities" in para. (b)(3)

8. Sec. 40242(g)(2) deleted para. (b)(4), and redesignated para. (b)(5) [as amended by Sec. 40241(a) of this Act, see below] as para. (b)(4)

Prior to deletion, para. (b)(4) read as follows:

"(4) Special rule for 1990.

"(A) In general. Subject to the provisions of subsection (c), a transfer shall be treated as a qualified transfer if such transfer—

"(i) is made after the close of the taxable year preceding the employer's first taxable year beginning after December 31, 1990, and before the earlier of—

"(I) the due date (including extensions) for the filing of the return of tax for such preceding taxable year, or

"(II) the date such return is filed, and

"(ii) does not exceed the expenditures of the employer for qualified current retiree health liabilities for such preceding taxable year.

"(B) Deduction reduced. The amount of the deductions otherwise allowable under this chapter to an employer for the taxable year preceding the employer's first taxable year beginning after December 31, 1990, shall be reduced by the amount of any qualified transfer to which this paragraph applies.

"(C) Coordination with reduction rule. Subsection (e)(1)(B) shall not apply to a transfer described in subparagraph (A)."

Effective Date (Sec. 40242(h)(1), P.L. 112-141, 7/6/2012) effective for transfers made after 7/6/2012.

Code Sec. 420(b)(4) was amended by Sec. 40241(a), P.L. 112-141, 7/6/2012, as detailed below:

9. Sec. 40241(a) substituted "December 31, 2021" for "December 31, 2013" in para. (b)(4) [as redesignated by Sec. 40242(g)(2), see above]

Effective Date (Sec. 40241(c), P.L. 112-141, 7/6/2012) effective 7/6/2012.

Code Sec. 420(b)(1)(A), Code Sec. 420(c)(1)(A), Code Sec. 420(c)(1)(B), Code Sec. 420(c)(1)(B)(i), Code Sec. 420(c)(1)(C), Code Sec. 420(c)(2) Code Sec. 420(c)(2)(B), Code Sec. 420(c)(3)(A), Code Sec. 420(c)(3)(B)(i), Code Sec. 420(c)(3)(B)(i)(I), Code Sec. 420(c)(3)(B)(i)(II), Code Sec. 420(c)(3)(B)(i)(III), Code Sec. 420(c)(3)(C), Code Sec. 420(d)(1)(A), Code Sec. 420(d)(1)(B), Code Sec. 420(d)(1)(C), Code Sec. 420(d)(2), Code Sec. 420(e)(1), Code Sec. 420(e)(1)(A), Code Sec. 420(e)(1)(B), Code Sec. 420(e)(1)(B)(ii) was amended by Sec. 40242(c)(1), (2)(A)(i)-(ii), (B)(i)-(III), (C)(i)-(iii), (e)(1)-6), (g)(4)(A)-(C), (g)(5), P.L. 112-141, 7/6/2012, as detailed below:

10. Sec. 40242(e)(2) added ", or an applicable life insurance account," after "a health benefits account" in subpara. (c)(1)(A)

10A. Sec. 40242(e)(1) substituted "qualified current retiree liabilities" for "qualified current retiree health liabilities" in subpara. (c)(1)(A)

11. Sec. 40242(e)(4) added "or life insurance" after "health benefits" in the heading of subpara. (c)(1)(B)

12. Sec. 40242(e)(2) added ", or an applicable life insurance account," after "a health benefits account" in clause (c)(1)(B)(i)

13. Sec. 40242(e)(2) added ", or an applicable life insurance account," after "a health benefits account" in subpara. (c)(1)(C)

14. Sec. 40242(g)(4)(C) substituted "before transfer. The requirements of this paragraph" for "Before transfer. (A) In general. The requirements of this paragraph" in para. (c)(2)

15. Sec. 40242(g)(4)(A) deleted subpara. (c)(2)(B). Prior to deletion, subpara. (c)(2)(B) read as follows:

"(B) Special rule for 1990. In the case of a qualified transfer described in subsection (b)(4), the requirements of this paragraph are met with respect to any participant who separated from service during the taxable year to which such transfer relates by recomputing such participant's benefits as if subparagraph (A) had applied immediately before such separation."

16. Sec. 40242(c)(1) added ", and each group-term life insurance plan under which applicable life insurance benefits are provided," after "health benefits are provided" in subpara. (c)(3)(A)

16A. Sec. 40242(e)(1) substituted "qualified current retiree liabilities" for "qualified current retiree health liabilities" in clause (c)(3)(B)(i)

17. Sec. 40242(c)(2)(A)(i) added new sbcl. (c)(3)(B)(i)(I)

18. Sec. 40242(c)(2)(A)(i) redesignated sbcl. (c)(3)(B)(i)(I) as sbcl. (c)(3)(B)(i)(II)

19. Sec. 40242(c)(2)(A)(i) redesignated sbcl. (c)(3)(B)(i)(II) as sbcl. (c)(3)(B)(i)(III)

20. Sec. 40242(c)(2)(A)(ii) substituted "was provided during such taxable year for the benefits with respect to which the determination under clause (i) is made." for "for applicable health benefits was provided during such taxable year." in clause (c)(3)(B)(ii)

21. Sec. 40242(c)(2)(B)(i) added "for applicable health benefits" after "applied separately" in subpara. (c)(3)(C)

22. Sec. 40242(c)(2)(B)(ii) inserted ", and separately for applicable life insurance benefits with respect to individuals age 65 or older at any time during the taxable year and with respect to individuals under age 65 during the taxable year" before the period at the end of subpara. (c)(3)(C)

23. Sec. 40242(c)(2)(C)(i) added "or retiree life insurance coverage, as the case may be," after "retiree health coverage" in clause (c)(3)(E)(i)

24. Sec. 40242(c)(2)(C)(ii) added "for retiree health coverage" after "cost reductions" in the heading of clause (c)(3)(E)(ii)

25. Sec. 40242(e)(1) substituted "qualified current retiree liabilities" for "qualified current retiree health liabilities" in sbcl. (c)(3)(E)(ii)(II)

26. Sec. 40242(c)(2)(C)(iii) added "with respect to applicable health benefits" after "liabilities of the employer" in sbcl. (c)(3)(E)(ii)(II)

27. Sec. 40242(e)(2) added ", or an applicable life insurance account," after "a health benefits account" in subpara. (d)(1)(A)

28. Sec. 40242(e)(1) substituted "qualified current retiree liabilities" for "qualified current retiree health liabilities" in subpara. (d)(1)(B)

28A. Sec. 40242(e)(1) substituted "qualified current retiree liabilities" for "qualified current retiree health liabilities" in subpara. (d)(1)(C)

29. Sec. 40242(g)(5) deleted "after December 31, 1990" after "An employer may not contribute" in para. (d)(2)

30. Sec. 40242(e)(1) substituted "qualified current retiree liabilities" for "qualified current retiree health liabilities" in para. (d)(2)

31. Sec. 40242(e)(5)(B) deleted "health" after "current retiree" in the heading of subpara. (e)(1)

31A. Sec. 40242(e)(1) substituted "qualified current retiree liabilities" for "qualified current retiree health liabilities" in subpara. (e)(1)(A)

32. Sec. 40242(e)(5)(A) added "and applicable life insurance benefits" after "applicable health benefits" in subpara. (e)(1)(A)

33. Sec. 40242(e)(6)(A) added "(determined separately for applicable health benefits and applicable life insurance benefits)" after "shall be reduced by the amount" in the matter preceding para. (e)(1)(B)

34. Sec. 40242(e)(6)(B) added "or applicable life insurance accounts" after "health benefit accounts" in clause (e)(1)(B)(i)

35. Sec. 40242(e)(6)(C) substituted "qualified current retiree liability" for "qualified current retiree health liability" in clause (e)(1)(B)(i)

36. Sec. 40242(e)(1) substituted "qualified current retiree liabilities" for "qualified current retiree health liabilities" in clause (e)(1)(B)(ii)

Effective Date (Sec. 40242(h)(1), P.L. 112-141, 7/6/2012) effective for transfers made after 7/6/2012.

Code Sec. 420(e)(1)(C)(i) was amended by Sec. 40242(b)(3)(B)(i), P.L. 112-141, 7/6/2012, as detailed below:

37. Sec. 40242(b)(3)(B)(i) substituted "by reason of retirement" for "upon retirement" in clause (e)(1)(C)(i)

Effective Date (Sec. 40242(h)(2), P.L. 112-141, 7/6/2012) effective for transfers after 8/17/2006, as if included in the amendments made by Sec. 841(a) of the Pension Protection Act of 2006 [P.L. 109-280].

Code Sec. 420(e)(1)(D), Code Sec. 420(e)(1)(E), Code Sec. 420(e)(4), Code Sec. 420(e)(5), Code Sec. 420(e)(6), Code Sec. 420(f), Code Sec. 420(f)(2), Code Sec. 420(f)(2)(B)(ii)(II), Code Sec. 420(f)(2)(D)(i)(I), Code Sec. 420(f)(2)(E)(ii), Code Sec. 420(f)(4), Code Sec. 420(f)(6), Code Sec. 420(f)(6)(A), Code Sec. 420(f)(6)(B) was amended by Sec. 40242(b)(1)-(2), (c)(2)(D), (E), (e)(1)-(2), (7), (8), (10), (11)(A)-(B), (12)(A)-(C), P.L. 112-141, 7/6/2012, as detailed below:

38. Sec. 40242(b)(2) added new subpara. (e)(1)(D)

39. Sec. 40242(b)(2) redesignated subpara. (e)(1)(D) as subpara. (e)(1)(E)

39A. Sec. 40242(e)(1) substituted "qualified current retiree liabilities" for "qualified current retiree health liabilities" in subpara. (e)(1)(E) [as redesignated by Sec. 40242(b)(2) of this Act, see above]

40. Sec. 40242(b)(1) added para. (e)(4)

41. Sec. 40242(b)(1) redesignated para. (e)(4) as para. (e)(5)

42. Sec. 40242(b)(1) redesignated para. (e)(5) as para. (e)(6)

43. Sec. 40242(e)(7) deleted "health" after 'cover future retiree' in the heading of subsec. (f)

44. Sec. 40242(e)(7) deleted "health" after 'collectively bargained retiree' in the heading of subsec. (f)

45. Sec. 40242(e)(8) added "or applicable life insurance account, as the case may be," after "health benefits account" in sbcl. (f)(2)(B)(ii)(II)

46. Sec. 40242(e)(1) substituted "qualified current retiree liabilities" for "qualified current retiree health liabilities" in sbcl. (f)(2)(C)(i)(II)

47. Sec. 40242(c)(2)(D) substituted "collectively bargained retiree liabilities" for "collectively bargained retiree health liabilities" in clause (f)(2)(C)(ii)

48. Sec. 40242(c)(2)(E)(i) added ", and each group-term life insurance plan or arrangement under which applicable life insurance benefits are provided," after "applicable health benefits are provided" in subclause (f)(2)(D)(i)(I)

49. Sec. 40242(c)(2)(E)(ii) added "or applicable life insurance benefits, as the case may be," after "provides applicable health benefits" in subclause (f)(2)(D)(i)(I)

50. Sec. 40242(c)(2)(E)(iii) deleted "group health" after 'each collectively bargained' in sbcl. (f)(2)(D)(i)(II)

51. Sec. 40242(c)(2)(E)(iv) added "or collectively bargained life insurance benefits" after "collectively bargained health benefits" in sbcl. (f)(2)(D)(i)(II)

52. Sec. 40242(c)(2)(F)(i) added "with respect to applicable health benefits or applicable life insurance benefits" after "requirements of subsection (c)(3)" in clause (f)(2)(D)(ii)

53. Sec. 40242(c)(2)(F)(ii) added "Such election may be made separately with respect to applicable health benefits and applicable life insurance benefits. In the case of an election with respect to applicable life insurance benefits, the first sentence of this clause shall be applied as if subsection (c)(3) as in effect before the amendments made by such Act applied to such benefits." at the end of clause (f)(2)(D)(ii)

54. Sec. 40242(c)(2)(G)(i) deleted "retiree" after "providing collectively bargained" in clause (f)(2)(D)(iii)

55. Sec. 40242(c)(2)(G)(ii) inserted ", collectively bargained life insurance benefits, or both, as the case may be," after "health benefits" in clause (f)(2)(D)(iii)

56. Sec. 40242(c)(2)(G)(i) deleted "retiree" after "any portion of the collectively bargained" in clause (f)(2)(D)(iii)

57. Sec. 40242(c)(2)(G)(ii) inserted ", collectively bargained life insurance benefits, or both, as the case may be," after "health benefits" in clause (f)(2)(D)(iii)

58. Sec. 40242(e)(9)(A) added "defined benefit" before "plan maintained by an employer" in sbcl. (f)(2)(E)(i)(III)

59. Sec. 40242(e)(9)(B) added "health" before "benefit plans maintained by the employer" in sbcl. (f)(2)(E)(i)(III)

60. Sec. 40242(e)(2) added ", or an applicable life insurance account," after "a health benefits account" in clause (f)(2)(E)(ii)

61. Sec. 40242(c)(2)(D) substituted "collectively bargained retiree liabilities" for "collectively bargained retiree health liabilities" in clause (f)(2)(E)(ii)

62. Sec. 40242(e)(1) substituted "qualified current retiree liabilities" for "qualified current retiree health liabilities" in para. (f)(3)

63. Sec. 40242(e)(10) substituted "collectively bargained retiree liabilities" for "collectively bargained retiree health liabilities" in para. (f)(4)

64. Sec. 40242(e)(11)(A) added ", in the case of a transfer to a health benefits account," before "his covered spouse and dependents" in clause (f)(6)(A)(i)

65. Sec. 40242(e)(11)(B) substituted "plan" for "health plan" in clause (f)(6)(A)(ii)

66. Sec. 40242(e)(11)(A) added ", in the case of a transfer to a health benefits account," before "his covered spouse and dependents" in clause (f)(6)(A)(ii)

67. Sec. 40242(e)(12)(C) deleted "health" after "Collectively bargained retiree" in the heading of subpara. (f)(6)(B)

68. Sec. 40242(e)(10) substituted "collectively bargained retiree liabilities" for "collectively bargained retiree health liabilities" in clause (f)(6)(B)(i)

69. Sec. 40242(e)(12)(A) added ", and collectively bargained life insurance benefits," after "collectively bargained health benefits" in clause (f)(6)(B)(i)

70. Sec. 40242(e)(12)(B)(ii) added ", applicable life insurance accounts," after "health benefits accounts" in clause (f)(6)(B)(ii)

71. Sec. 40242(e)(10) substituted "collectively bargained retiree liabilities" for "collectively bargained retiree health liabilities" in para. (f)(6)(B)(ii)

72. Sec. 40242(e)(12)(B)(i) added "The preceding sentence shall be applied separately for collectively bargained health benefits and collectively bargained life insurance benefits." at the end of clause (f)(6)(B)(ii)

Effective Date (Sec. 40242(h)(1), P.L. 112-141, 7/6/2012) effective for transfers made after 7/6/2012.

Code Sec. 402(f)(6)(B)(iii) was amended by Sec. 40242(f), P.L. 112-141, 7/6/2012, as detailed below:

73. Sec. 40242(f) substituted "416(i)(1)" for "416(I)(1)" in clause (f)(6)(B)(iii)

Effective Date (Sec. 40242(h)(2), P.L. 112-141, 7/6/2012) effective for transfers after 8/17/2006, as if included in the amendments made by Sec. 841(a) of the Pension Protection Act of 2006 [P.L. 109-280].

Code Sec. 420(f)(6)(B)(iii) was amended by Sec. 40242(e)(10), P.L. 112-141, 7/6/2012, as detailed below:

74. Sec. 40242(e)(10) substituted "collectively bargained retiree liabilities" for "collectively bargained retiree health liabilities" in clause (f)(6)(B)(iii)

Effective Date (Sec. 40242(h)(1), P.L. 112-141, 7/6/2012) effective for transfers made after 7/6/2012.

Code Sec. 420(f)(6)(C), Code Sec. 420(f)(6)(C)(i) and Code Sec. 420(f)(6)(C)(ii) was amended by Sec. 40242(b)(3)(B)(ii)(I)-(IV), P.L. 112-141, 7/6/2012, as detailed below:

75. Sec. 40242(b)(3)(B)(ii)(I) deleted "which are provided to" after "benefits or coverage" in subpara. (f)(6)(C)

76. Sec. 40242(b)(3)(B)(ii)(II) added "which are provided to" before "retired employees" in clause (f)(6)(C)(i)

77. Sec. 40242(b)(3)(B)(ii)(III) substituted "by reason of retirement" for "upon retirement" in clause (f)(6)(C)(i)

78. Sec. 40242(b)(3)(B)(ii)(IV) substituted "which will be provided at retirement to employees who are not retired employees at the time of the transfer and who" for "active employees who, following their retirement," in clause (f)(6)(C)(ii)

Effective Date (Sec. 40242(h)(2), P.L. 112-141, 7/6/2012) effective for transfers after 8/17/2006, as if included in the amendments made by Sec. 841(a) of the Pension Protection Act of 2006 [P.L. 109-280].

Code Sec. 420(f)(6)(D), and Code Sec. 420(f)(6)(E) was amended by Sec. 40242(b)(3)(A), (e)(13)(A)-(C), P.L. 112-141, 7/6/2012, as detailed below:

79. Sec. 40242(b)(3)(A) added subpara. (f)(6)(D)

80. Sec. 40242(b)(3)(A) redesignated subpara. (f)(6)(D) as subpara. (f)(6)(E)

81. Sec. 40242(e)(13)(C) deleted "health" after "Collectively bargained" in the heading of subpara. (f)(6)(E) [as redesignated by Sec. 40242(b)(3)(A), see above]

82. Sec. 40242(e)(13)(A) substituted "bargained" for "bargained health" in subpara. (f)(6)(E) [as redesignated by Sec. 40242(b)(3)(A), see above]

83. Sec. 40242(e)(13)(B) added ", or a group-term life insurance plan or arrangement for retired employees," after "dependents" in subpara. (f)(6)(E) [as redesignated by Sec. 40242(b)(3)(A), see above]

Effective Date (Sec. 40242(h)(1), P.L. 112-141, 7/6/2012) effective for transfers made after 7/6/2012.

Code Sec. 420(g) was added by Sec. 40211(a)(2)(D), P.L. 112-141, 7/6/2012, as detailed below:

84. Sec. 40211(a)(2)(D) added subsec. (g)

Effective Date (Sec. 40211(c), P.L. 112-141, 7/6/2012) effective with respect to plan yrs. begin. after 12/31/2011. Sec. 40211(c)(2) of this Act reads as follows:

"(2) Rules with respect to elections.

"(A) Adjusted funding target attainment percentage. A plan sponsor may elect not to have the amendments made by this section apply to any plan year beginning before January 1, 2013, either (as specified in the election)—

"(i) for all purposes for which such amendments apply, or

"(ii) solely for purposes of determining the adjusted funding target attainment percentage under sections 436 of the Internal Revenue Code of 1986 and 206(g) of the Employee Retirement Income Security Act of 1974 for such plan year.

"A plan shall not be treated as failing to meet the requirements of sections 204(g) of such Act and 411(d)(6) of such Code solely by reason of an election under this paragraph.

"(B) Opt out of existing elections. If, on the date of the enactment of this Act, an election is in effect with respect to any plan under sections 303(h)((2)(D)(ii) of the Employee Retirement Income Security Act of 1974 and 430(h)((2)(D)(ii) of the Internal Revenue Code of 1986, then, notwithstanding the last sentence of each such section, the plan sponsor may revoke such election without the consent of the Secretary of the Treasury. The plan sponsor may make such revocation at any time before the date which is 1 year after such date of enactment and such revocation shall be effective for the 1st plan year to which the amendments made by this section apply and all subsequent plan years.

Nothing in this subparagraph shall preclude a plan sponsor from making a subsequent election in accordance with such sections."

[¶ 3075]   Code Sec. 430.   Minimum funding standards for single-employer defined benefit pension plans.

* * * * * * * * * * * *

(h) Actuarial assumptions and methods.

   (1) In general. Subject to this subsection, the determination of any present value or other computation under this section shall be made on the basis of actuarial assumptions and methods—

     (A) each of which is reasonable (taking into account the experience of the plan and reasonable expectations), and

     (B) which, in combination, offer the actuary's best estimate of anticipated experience under the plan.

   (2) Interest rates.

     (A) Effective interest rate. For purposes of this section, the term "effective interest rate" means, with respect to any plan for any plan year, the single rate of interest which, if used to determine the present value of the plan's accrued or earned benefits referred to in subsection (d)(1), would result in an amount equal to the funding target of the plan for such plan year.

     (B) Interest rates for determining funding target. For purposes of determining the funding target and target normal cost of a plan for any plan year, the interest rate used in determining the present value of the benefits of the plan shall be—

       (i) in the case of benefits reasonably determined to be payable during the 5-year period beginning on the first day of the plan year, the first segment rate with respect to the applicable month,

       (ii) in the case of benefits reasonably determined to be payable during the 15-year period beginning at the end of the period described in clause (i), the second segment rate with respect to the applicable month, and

       (iii) in the case of benefits reasonably determined to be payable after the period described in clause (ii), the third segment rate with respect to the applicable month.

     (C) Segment rates. For purposes of this paragraph—

       (i) First segment rate. The term "first segment rate" means, with respect to any month, the single rate of interest which shall be determined by the Secretary for such month on the basis of the corporate bond yield curve for such month, taking into account only that portion of such yield curve which is based on bonds maturing during the 5-year period commencing with such month.

       (ii) Second segment rate. The term "second segment rate" means, with respect to any month, the single rate of interest which shall be determined by the Secretary for such month on the basis of the corporate bond yield curve for such month, taking into account only that portion of such yield curve which is based on bonds maturing during the 15-year period beginning at the end of the period described in clause (i).

       (iii) Third segment rate. The term "third segment rate" means, with respect to any month, the single rate of interest which shall be determined by the Secretary for such month on the basis of the corporate bond yield curve for such month, taking into account only that portion of such yield curve which is based on bonds maturing during periods beginning after the period described in clause (ii).

       [1](iv) Segment rate stabilization.

         (I) In general. If a segment rate described in clause (i), (ii), or (iii) with respect to any applicable month (determined without regard to this clause) is less than the applicable minimum percentage, or more than the applicable maximum percentage, of the average of the segment rates described in such clause for years in the 25-year period ending with September 30 of the calendar year preceding the calendar year in which the plan year begins, then the segment rate described in such clause with respect to the applicable month shall be equal to the applicable minimum percentage or the applicable maximum percentage of such average, whichever is closest. The Secretary shall determine such average on an annual basis and may prescribe equivalent rates for years in any such 25-year period for which the rates described in any such clause are not available.

(II) *Applicable minimum percentage; applicable maximum percentage.* For purposes of subclause (I), the applicable minimum percentage and the applicable maximum percentage for a plan year beginning in a calendar year shall be determined in accordance with the following table:

(D) Corporate bond yield curve. For purposes of this paragraph—

(i) In general. The term "corporate bond yield curve" means, with respect to any month, a yield curve which is prescribed by the Secretary for such month and which reflects the average, for the 24-month period ending with the month preceding such month, of monthly yields on investment grade corporate bonds with varying maturities and that are in the top 3 quality levels available.

(ii) Election to use yield curve. Solely for purposes of determining the minimum required contribution under this section, the plan sponsor may, in lieu of the segment rates determined under subparagraph (C), elect to use interest rates under the corporate bond yield curve. For purposes of the preceding sentence such curve shall be determined without regard to the 24-month averaging described in clause (i). Such election, once made, may be revoked only with the consent of the Secretary.

(E) Applicable month. For purposes of this paragraph, the term "applicable month" means, with respect to any plan for any plan year, the month which includes the valuation date of such plan for such plan year or, at the election of the plan sponsor, any of the 4 months which precede such month. Any election made under this subparagraph shall apply to the plan year for which the election is made and all succeeding plan years, unless the election is revoked with the consent of the Secretary.

(F) Publication requirements. The Secretary shall publish for each month the corporate bond yield curve (and the corporate bond yield curve reflecting the modification described in section 417(e)(3)(D)(i) for such month) and each of the rates determined under subparagraph (C) [2]*and the averages determined under subparagraph (C)(iv)* for such month. The Secretary shall also publish a description of the methodology used to determine such yield curve and such rates which is sufficiently detailed to enable plans to make reasonable projections regarding the yield curve and such rates for future months based on the plan's projection of future interest rates.

(G) Transition rule.

(i) In general. Notwithstanding the preceding provisions of this paragraph, for plan years beginning in 2008 or 2009, the first, second, or third segment rate for a plan with respect to any month shall be equal to the sum of—

(I) the product of such rate for such month determined without regard to this subparagraph, multiplied by the applicable percentage, and

(II) the product of the rate determined under the rules of section 412(b)(5)(B)(ii)(II) (as in effect for plan years beginning in 2007), multiplied by a percentage equal to 100 percent minus the applicable percentage.

(ii) Applicable percentage. For purposes of clause (i), the applicable percentage is $33^1/_3$ percent for plan years beginning in 2008 and $66^2/_3$ percent for plan years beginning in 2009.

(iii) New plans ineligible. Clause (i) shall not apply to any plan if the first plan year of the plan begins after December 31, 2007.

(iv) Election. The plan sponsor may elect not to have this subparagraph apply. Such election, once made, may be revoked only with the consent of the Secretary.

(3) Mortality tables.

(A) In general. Except as provided in subparagraph (C) or (D), the Secretary shall by regulation prescribe mortality tables to be used in determining any present value or making any computation under this section. Such tables shall be based on the actual experience of pension plans and projected trends in such experience. In prescribing such tables, the Secretary shall take into account results of available independent studies of mortality of individuals covered by pension plans.

(B) Periodic revision. The Secretary shall (at least every 10 years) make revisions in any table in effect under subparagraph (A) to reflect the actual experience of pension plans and projected trends in such experience.

(C) Substitute mortality table.

(i) In general. Upon request by the plan sponsor and approval by the Secretary, a mortality table which meets the requirements of clause (iii) shall be used in determining any present value or making any computation under this section during the period of consecutive plan years (not to exceed 10) specified in the request.

(ii) Early termination of period. Notwithstanding clause (i), a mortality table described in clause (i) shall cease to be in effect as of the earliest of—

(I) the date on which there is a significant change in the participants in the plan by reason of a plan spinoff or merger or otherwise, or

(II) the date on which the plan actuary determines that such table does not meet the requirements of clause (iii).

(iii) Requirements. A mortality table meets the requirements of this clause if—

(I) there is a sufficient number of plan participants, and the pension plans have been maintained for a sufficient period of time, to have credible information necessary for purposes of subclause (II), and

(II) such table reflects the actual experience of the pension plans maintained by the sponsor and projected trends in general mortality experience.

(iv) All plans in controlled group must use separate table. Except as provided by the Secretary, a plan sponsor may not use a mortality table under this subparagraph for any plan maintained by the plan sponsor unless—

(I) a separate mortality table is established and used under this subparagraph for each other plan maintained by the plan sponsor and if the plan sponsor is a member of a controlled group, each member of the controlled group, and

(II) the requirements of clause (iii) are met separately with respect to the table so established for each such plan, determined by only taking into account the participants of such plan, the time such plan has been in existence, and the actual experience of such plan.

(v) Deadline for submission and disposition of application.

(I) Submission. The plan sponsor shall submit a mortality table to the Secretary for approval under this subparagraph at least 7 months before the 1st day of the period described in clause (i).

(II) Disposition. Any mortality table submitted to the Secretary for approval under this subparagraph shall be treated as in effect as of the 1st day of the period described in clause (i) unless the Secretary, during the 180-day period beginning on the date of such submission, disapproves of such table and provides the reasons that such table fails to meet the requirements of clause (iii). The 180-day period shall be extended upon mutual agreement of the Secretary and the plan sponsor.

(D) Separate mortality tables for the disabled. Notwithstanding subparagraph (A)—

(i) In general. The Secretary shall establish mortality tables which may be used (in lieu of the tables under subparagraph (A)) under this subsection for individuals who are entitled to benefits under the plan on account of disability. The Secretary shall establish separate tables for individuals whose disabilities occur in plan years beginning before January 1, 1995, and for individuals whose disabilities occur in plan years beginning on or after such date.

(ii) Special rule for disabilities occurring after 1994. In the case of disabilities occurring in plan years beginning after December 31, 1994, the tables under clause (i) shall apply only with respect to individuals described in such subclause who are disabled within the meaning of title II of the Social Security Act and the regulations thereunder.

(iii) Periodic revision. The Secretary shall (at least every 10 years) make revisions in any table in effect under clause (i) to reflect the actual experience of pension plans and projected trends in such experience.

(4) Probability of benefit payments in the form of lump sums or other optional forms. For purposes of determining any present value or making any computation under this section, there shall be taken into account—

(A) the probability that future benefit payments under the plan will be made in the form of optional forms of benefits provided under the plan (including lump sum distributions, determined on the basis of the plan's experience and other related assumptions), and

(B) any difference in the present value of such future benefit payments resulting from the use of actuarial assumptions, in determining benefit payments in any such optional form of benefits, which are different from those specified in this subsection.

(5) Approval of large changes in actuarial assumptions.

(A) In general. No actuarial assumption used to determine the funding target for a plan to which this paragraph applies may be changed without the approval of the Secretary.

(B) Plans to which paragraph applies. This paragraph shall apply to a plan only if—

(i) the plan is a defined benefit plan (other than a multiemployer plan) to which title IV of the Employee Retirement Income Security Act of 1974 applies,

(ii) the aggregate unfunded vested benefits as of the close of the preceding plan year (as determined under section 4006(a)(3)(E)(iii) of the Employee Retirement Income Security Act of 1974) of such plan and all other plans maintained by the contributing sponsors (as defined in section 4001(a)(13) of such Act) and members of such sponsors' controlled groups (as defined in section 4001(a)(14) of such Act) which are covered by title IV (disregarding plans with no unfunded vested benefits) exceed $50,000,000, and

(iii) the change in assumptions (determined after taking into account any changes in interest rate and mortality table) results in a decrease in the funding shortfall of the plan for the current plan year that exceeds $50,000,000, or that exceeds $5,000,000 and that is 5 percent or more of the funding target of the plan before such change.

* * * * * * * * * * * * *

[For Analysis, see ¶ 1701. For Committee Reports, see ¶ 5402.]

[Endnote Code Sec. 430]

Code Sec. 430(h)(2)(C)(iv) and Code Sec. 430(h)(2)(F) were amended by Secs. 40211(a)(1) and (2)(B) of the Moving Ahead for Progress in the 21st Century Act, P.L. 112-141, 7/6/2012, as detailed below:

1. Sec. 40211(a)(1) added clause (h)(2)(C)(iv)

2. Sec. 40211(a)(2)(B) inserted "and the averages determined under subparagraph (C)(iv)" after "subparagraph (C)" in subpara. (h)(2)(F)

Effective Date (Sec. 40211(c)(1), P.L. 112-141, 7/6/2012) effective with respect to plan yrs. begin. after 12/31/2011. Sec. 40211(c)(2) of this Act, reads as follows:

"(2) Rules with respect to elections.

"(A) Adjusted funding target attainment percentage. A plan sponsor may elect not to have the amendments made by this section apply to any plan year beginning before January 1, 2013, either (as specified in the election)—

"(i) for all purposes for which such amendments apply, or

"(ii) solely for purposes of determining the adjusted funding target attainment percentage under sections 436 of the Internal Revenue Code of 1986 and 206(g) of the Employee Retirement Income Security Act of 1974 for such plan year.

"A plan shall not be treated as failing to meet the requirements of sections 204(g) of such Act and 411(d)(6) of such Code solely by reason of an election under this paragraph.

"(B) Opt out of existing elections. If, on the date of the enactment of this Act, an election is in effect with respect to any plan under sections 303(h)((2)(D)(ii) of the Employee Retirement Income Security Act of 1974 and 430(h)((2)(D)(ii) of the Internal Revenue Code of 1986, then, notwithstanding the last sentence of each such section, the plan sponsor may revoke such election without the consent of the Secretary of the Treasury. The plan sponsor may make such revocation at any time before the date which is 1 year after such date of enactment and such revocation shall be effective for the 1st plan year to which the amendments made by this section apply and all subsequent plan years. Nothing in this subparagraph shall preclude a plan sponsor from making a subsequent election in accordance with such sections."

[¶ 3076]   Code Sec. 451.   General rule for taxable year of inclusion.

* * * * * * * * * * * *

(i) Special rule for sales or dispositions to implement Federal Energy Regulatory Commission or State electric restructuring policy.

(1) In general. In the case of any qualifying electric transmission transaction for which the taxpayer elects the application of this section, qualified gain from such transaction shall be recognized—

(A) in the taxable year which includes the date of such transaction to the extent the amount realized from such transaction exceeds—

(i) the cost of exempt utility property which is purchased by the taxpayer during the 4-year period beginning on such date, reduced (but not below zero) by

(ii) any portion of such cost previously taken into account under this subsection, and

(B) ratably over the 8-taxable year period beginning with the taxable year which includes the date of such transaction, in the case of any such gain not recognized under subparagraph (A).

(2) Qualified gain. For purposes of this subsection, the term "qualified gain" means, with respect to any qualifying electric transmission transaction in any taxable year—

(A) any ordinary income derived from such transaction which would be required to be recognized under section 1245 or 1250 for such taxable year (determined without regard to this subsection), and

(B) any income derived from such transaction in excess of the amount described in subparagraph (A) which is required to be included in gross income for such taxable year (determined without regard to this subsection).

(3) Qualifying electric transmission transaction. For purposes of this subsection, the term "qualifying electric transmission transaction" means any sale or other disposition before January 1, 2008 (before ¹*January 1, 2014,* in the case of a qualified electric utility), of—

(A) property used in the trade or business of providing electric transmission services, or

(B) any stock or partnership interest in a corporation or partnership, as the case may be, whose principal trade or business consists of providing electric transmission services, but only if such sale or disposition is to an independent transmission company.

(4) Independent transmission company. For purposes of this subsection, the term "independent transmission company" means—

(A) an independent transmission provider approved by the Federal Energy Regulatory Commission,

(B) a person—

(i) who the Federal Energy Regulatory Commission determines in its authorization of the transaction under section 203 of the Federal Power Act (16 U.S.C. 824b) or by declaratory order is not a market participant within the meaning of such Commission's rules applicable to independent transmission providers, and

(ii) whose transmission facilities to which the election under this subsection applies are under the operational control of a Federal Energy Regulatory Commission-approved independent transmission provider before the close of the period specified in such authorization, but not later than the date which is 4 years after the close of the taxable year in which the transaction occurs, or

(C) in the case of facilities subject to the jurisdiction of the Public Utility Commission of Texas—

(i) a person which is approved by that Commission as consistent with Texas State law regarding an independent transmission provider, or

(ii) a political subdivision or affiliate thereof whose transmission facilities are under the operational control of a person described in clause (i).

(5)   Exempt utility property. For purposes of this subsection—

(A) In general. The term "exempt utility property" means property used in the trade or business of—

(i) generating, transmitting, distributing, or selling electricity, or

(ii) producing, transmitting, distributing, or selling natural gas.

(B) Nonrecognition of gain by reason of acquisition of stock. Acquisition of control of a corporation shall be taken into account under this subsection with respect to a qualifying electric transmission transaction only if the principal trade or business of such corporation is a trade or business referred to in subparagraph (A).

(C) Exception for property located outside the United States. The term "exempt utility property" shall not include any property which is located outside the United States.

(6)   Qualified electric utility. For purposes of this subsection, the term "qualified electric utility" means a person that, as of the date of the qualifying electric transmission transaction, is vertically integrated, in that it is both—

(A) a transmitting utility (as defined in section 3(23) of the Federal Power Act (16 U.S.C. 796(23))) with respect to the transmission facilities to which the election under this subsection applies, and

(B) an electric utility (as defined in section 3(22) of the Federal Power Act (16 U.S.C. 796(22))).

(7)   Special rule for consolidated groups. In the case of a corporation which is a member of an affiliated group filing a consolidated return, any exempt utility property purchased by another member of such group shall be treated as purchased by such corporation for purposes of applying paragraph (1)(A).

(8)   Time for assessment of deficiencies. If the taxpayer has made the election under paragraph (1) and any gain is recognized by such taxpayer as provided in paragraph (1)(B), then—

(A) the statutory period for the assessment of any deficiency, for any taxable year in which any part of the gain on the transaction is realized, attributable to such gain shall not expire prior to the expiration of 3 years from the date the Secretary is notified by the taxpayer (in such manner as the Secretary may by regulations prescribe) of the purchase of exempt utility property or of an intention not to purchase such property, and

(B) such deficiency may be assessed before the expiration of such 3-year period notwithstanding any law or rule of law which would otherwise prevent such assessment.

(9)   Purchase. For purposes of this subsection, the taxpayer shall be considered to have purchased any property if the unadjusted basis of such property is its cost within the meaning of section 1012.

(10)   Election. An election under paragraph (1) shall be made at such time and in such manner as the Secretary may require and, once made, shall be irrevocable.

(11)   Nonapplication of installment sales treatment. Section 453 shall not apply to any qualifying electric transmission transaction with respect to which an election to apply this subsection is made.

[Endnote Code Sec. 451]

Code Sec. 451(i)(3) was amended by Sec. 411(a) of the American Taxpayer Relief Act of 2012, P.L. 112-240, 1/2/2013, as detailed below:

1. Sec. 451(a) substituted "January 1, 2014" for "January 1, 2012" in para. (i)(3)

Effective Date (Sec. 411(b), P.L. 112-240, 1/2/2013) effective for dispositions after 12/31/2011.

[¶ 3077]   **Code Sec. 460.**   **Special rules for long-term contracts.**

* * * * * * * * * * * *

(c) Allocation of costs to contract.

   (1) Direct and certain indirect costs. In the case of a long-term contract, all costs (including research and experimental costs) which directly benefit, or are incurred by reason of, the long-term contract activities of the taxpayer shall be allocated to such contract in the same manner as costs are allocated to extended period long-term contracts under section 451 and the regulations thereunder.

   (2) Costs identified under cost-plus and certain federal contracts. In the case of a cost-plus long-term contract or a Federal long-term contract, any cost not allocated to such contract under paragraph (1) shall be allocated to such contract if such cost is identified by the taxpayer (or a related person), pursuant to the contract or Federal, State, or local law or regulation, as being attributable to such contract.

   (3) Allocation of production period interest to contract.

     (A) In general. Except as provided in subparagraphs (B) and (C), in the case of a long-term contract, interest costs shall be allocated to the contract in the same manner as interest costs are allocated to property produced by the taxpayer under section 263A(f).

     (B) Production period. In applying section 263A(f) for purposes of subparagraph (A), the production period shall be the period—

       (i) beginning on the later of—

         (I) the contract commencement date, or

         (II) in the case of a taxpayer who uses an accrual method with respect to long-term contracts, the date by which at least 5 percent of the total estimated costs (including design and planning costs) under the contract have been incurred, and

       (ii) ending on the contract completion date.

     (C) Application of de minimis rule. In applying section 263A(f) for purposes of subparagraph (A), paragraph (1)(B)(iii) of such section shall be applied on a contract-by-contract basis; except that, in the case of a taxpayer described in subparagraph (B)(i)(II) of this paragraph, paragraph (1)(B)(iii) of section 263A(f) shall be applied on a property-by-property basis.

   (4) Certain costs not included. This subsection shall not apply to any—

     (A) independent research and development expenses,

     (B) expenses for unsuccessful bids and proposals, and

     (C) marketing, selling, and advertising expenses.

   (5) Independent research and development expenses. For purposes of paragraph (4), the term "independent research and development expenses" means any expenses incurred in the performance of research or development, except that such term shall not include—

     (A) any expenses which are directly attributable to a long-term contract in existence when such expenses are incurred, or

     (B) any expenses under an agreement to perform research or development.

   (6) Special rule for allocation of bonus depreciation with respect to certain property.

     (A) In general. Solely for purposes of determining the percentage of completion under subsection (b)(1)(A), the cost of qualified property shall be taken into account as a cost allocated to the contract as if subsection (k) of section 168 had not been enacted.

     (B) Qualified property. For purposes of this paragraph, the term "qualified property" means property described in section 168(k)(2) which—

       (i) has a recovery period of 7 years or less, and

       (ii) is placed in service after December 31, 2009, and before January 1, 2011 (January 1, 2012, in the case of property described in section 168(k)(2)(B)) [1], *or after December 31, 2012, and before January 1, 2014 (January 1, 2015, in the case of property described in section 168(k)(2)(B)).*

* * * * * * * * * * * *

[For Analysis, see ¶ 806.]

[Endnote Code Sec. 460]
Code Sec. 460(c)(6)(B)(ii) was amended by Sec. 331(b) of the American Taxpayer Relief Act of 2012, P.L. 112-240, 1/2/2013, as detailed below:

1. Sec. 331(b) added ', or after December 31, 2012, and before January 1, 2014 (January 1, 2015, in the case of property described in section 168(k)(2)(B))' before the period in clause (c)(6)(B)(ii)

Effective Date (Sec. 331(f), P.L. 112-240, 1/2/2013) effective for property placed in service after 12/31/2012, in taxable years ending after such date.

[¶ 3078]   Code Sec. 512.   Unrelated business taxable income.

* * * * * * * * * * * *

(b) Modifications. The modifications referred to in subsection (a) are the following:

(1) There shall be excluded all dividends, interest, payments with respect to securities loans (as defined in subsection (a)(5)), amounts received or accrued as consideration for entering into agreements to make loans, and annuities, and all deductions directly connected with such income.

(2) There shall be excluded all royalties (including overriding royalties) whether measured by production or by gross or taxable income from the property, and all deductions directly connected with such income.

(3) In the case of rents—

(A) Except as provided in subparagraph (B), there shall be excluded—

(i) all rents from real property (including property described in section 1245(a)(3)(C)), and

(ii) all rents from personal property (including for purposes of this paragraph as personal property any property described in section 1245(a)(3)(B)) leased with such real property, if the rents attributable to such personal property are an incidental amount of the total rents received or accrued under the lease, determined at the time the personal property is placed in service.

(B) Subparagraph (A) shall not apply—

(i) if more than 50 percent of the total rent received or accrued under the lease is attributable to personal property described in subparagraph (A)(ii), or

(ii) if the determination of the amount of such rent depends in whole or in part on the income or profits derived by any person from the property leased (other than an amount based on a fixed percentage or percentages of receipts or sales).

(C) There shall be excluded all deductions directly connected with rents excluded under subparagraph (A).

(4) Notwithstanding paragraph (1), (2), (3), or (5), in the case of debt-financed property (as defined in section 514) there shall be included, as an item of gross income derived from an unrelated trade or business, the amount ascertained under section 514(a)(1), and there shall be allowed, as a deduction, the amount ascertained under section 514(a)(2).

(5) There shall be excluded all gains or losses from the sale, exchange, or other disposition of property other than—

(A) stock in trade or other property of a kind which would properly be includible in inventory if on hand at the close of the taxable year, or

(B) property held primarily for sale to customers in the ordinary course of the trade or business.

There shall also be excluded all gains or losses recognized, in connection with the organization's investment activities, from the lapse or termination of options to buy or sell securities (as defined in section 1236(c)) or real property and all gains or losses from the forfeiture of good-faith deposits (that are consistent with established business practice) for the purchase, sale, or lease of real property in connection with the organization's investment activities. This paragraph shall not apply with respect to the cutting of timber which is considered, on the application of section 631, as a sale or exchange of such timber.

(6) The net operating loss deduction provided in section 172 shall be allowed, except that—

(A) the net operating loss for any taxable year, the amount of the net operating loss carryback or carryover to any taxable year, and the net operating loss deduction for any taxable year shall be determined under section 172 without taking into account any amount of income or deduction which is excluded under this part in computing the unrelated business taxable income; and

(B) the terms "preceding taxable year" and "preceding taxable years" as used in section 172 shall not include any taxable year for which the organization was not subject to the provisions of this part.

(7) There shall be excluded all income derived from research for (A) the United States, or any of its agencies or instrumentalities, or (B) any State or political subdivision thereof; and there shall be excluded all deductions directly connected with such income.

(8) In the case of a college, university, or hospital, there shall be excluded all income derived from research performed for any person, and all deductions directly connected with such income.

(9) In the case of an organization operated primarily for purposes of carrying on fundamental research the results of which are freely available to the general public, there shall be excluded all income derived from research performed for any person, and all deductions directly connected with such income.

(10) In the case of any organization described in section 511(a), the deduction allowed by section 170 (relating to charitable etc. contributions and gifts) shall be allowed (whether or not directly connected with the carrying on of the trade or business), but shall not exceed 10 percent of the unrelated business taxable income computed without the benefit of this paragraph.

(11) In the case of any trust described in section 511(b), the deduction allowed by section 170 (relating to charitable etc. contributions and gifts) shall be allowed (whether or not directly connected with the carrying on of the trade or business), and for such purpose a distribution made by the trust to a beneficiary described in section 170 shall be considered as a gift or contribution. The deduction allowed by this paragraph shall be allowed with the limitations prescribed in section 170(b)(1)(A) and (B) determined with reference to the unrelated business taxable income computed without the benefit of this paragraph (in lieu of with reference to adjusted gross income).

(12) Except for purposes of computing the net operating loss under section 172 and paragraph (6), there shall be allowed a specific deduction of $1,000. In the case of a diocese, province of a religious order, or a convention or association of churches, there shall also be allowed, with respect to each parish, individual church, district, or other local unit, a specific deduction equal to the lower of—

(A) $1,000, or

(B) the gross income derived from any unrelated trade or business regularly carried on by such local unit.

(13) **Special rules for certain amounts received from controlled entities.**

(A) In general. If an organization (in this paragraph referred to as the "controlling organization") receives or accrues (directly or indirectly) a specified payment from another entity which it controls (in this paragraph referred to as the "controlled entity"), notwithstanding paragraphs (1), (2), and (3), the controlling organization shall include such payment as an item of gross income derived from an unrelated trade or business to the extent such payment reduces the net unrelated income of the controlled entity (or increases any net unrelated loss of the controlled entity). There shall be allowed all deductions of the controlling organization directly connected with amounts treated as derived from an unrelated trade or business under the preceding sentence.

(B) Net unrelated income or loss. For purposes of this paragraph—

(i) Net unrelated income. The term "net unrelated income" means—

(I) in the case of a controlled entity which is not exempt from tax under section 501(a), the portion of such entity's taxable income which would be unrelated business taxable income if such entity were exempt from tax under section 501(a) and had the same exempt purposes as the controlling organization, or

(II) in the case of a controlled entity which is exempt from tax under section 501(a), the amount of the unrelated business taxable income of the controlled entity.

(ii) Net unrelated loss. the term "net unrelated loss" means the net operating loss adjusted under rules similar to the rules of clause (i).

(C) Specified payment. For purposes of this paragraph, the term "specified payment" means any interest, annuity, royalty, or rent.

(D) Definition of control. For purposes of this paragraph—

(i) Control. The term "control" means—

(I) in the case of a corporation, ownership (by vote or value) of more than 50 percent of the stock in such corporation,

(II) in the case of a partnership, ownership of more than 50 percent of the profits interests or capital interests in such partnership, or

(III) in any other case, ownership of more than 50 percent of the beneficial interests in the entity.

(ii) Constructive ownership. Section 318 (relating to constructive ownership of stock) shall apply for purposes of determining ownership of stock in a corporation. Similar principles shall apply for purposes of determining ownership of interests in any other entity.

(E) Paragraph to apply only to certain excess payments.

(i) In general. Subparagraph (A) shall apply only to the portion of a qualifying specified payment received or accrued by the controlling organization that exceeds the amount which would have been paid or accrued if such payment met the requirements prescribed under section 482.

(ii) Addition to tax for valuation misstatements. The tax imposed by this chapter on the controlling organization shall be increased by an amount equal to 20 percent of the larger of—

(I) such excess determined without regard to any amendment or supplement to a return of tax, or

(II) such excess determined with regard to all such amendments and supplements.

(iii) Qualifying specified payment. The term "qualifying specified payment" means a specified payment which is made pursuant to—

(I) a binding written contract in effect on the date of the enactment of this subparagraph, or

(II) a contract which is a renewal, under substantially similar terms, of a contract described in subclause (I).

(iv) Termination. This subparagraph shall not apply to payments received or accrued after [1]December 31, 2013.

(F) Related persons. The Secretary shall prescribe such rules as may be necessary or appropriate to prevent avoidance of the purposes of this paragraph through the use of related persons.

(14) Repealed.

(15) Except as provided in paragraph (4), in the case of a trade or business—

(A) which consists of providing services under license issued by a Federal regulatory agency,

(B) which is carried on by a religious order or by an educational organization described in section 170(b)(1)(A)(ii) maintained by such religious order, and which was so carried on before May 27, 1959, and

(C) less than 10 percent of the net income of which for each taxable year is used for activities which are not related to the purpose constituting the basis for the religious order's exemption,

there shall be excluded all gross income derived from such trade or business and all deductions directly connected with the carrying on of such trade or business, so long as it is established to the satisfaction of the Secretary that the rates or other charges for such services are competitive with rates or other charges charged for similar services by persons not exempt from taxation.

(16) (A) Notwithstanding paragraph (5)(B), there shall be excluded all gains or losses from the sale, exchange, or other disposition of any real property described in subparagraph (B) if—

(i) such property was acquired by the organization from—

(I) a financial institution described in section 581 or 591(a) which is in conservatorship or receivership, or

(II) the conservator or receiver of such an institution (or any government agency or corporation succeeding to the rights or interests of the conservator or receiver),

(ii) such property is designated by the organization within the 9-month period beginning on the date of its acquisition as property held for sale, except that not more than one-half (by value determined as of such date) of property acquired in a single transaction may be so designated,

(iii) such sale, exchange, or disposition occurs before the later of—

(I) the date which is 30 months after the date of the acquisition of such property, or

(II) the date specified by the Secretary in order to assure an orderly disposition of property held by persons described in subparagraph (A), and

(iv) while such property was held by the organization, the aggregate expenditures on improvements and development activities included in the basis of the property are (or were) not in excess of 20 percent of the net selling price of such property.

(B) Property is described in this subparagraph if it is real property which—

(i) was held by the financial institution at the time it entered into conservatorship or receivership, or

(ii) was foreclosure property (as defined in section 514(c)(9)(H)(v)) which secured indebtedness held by the financial institution at such time.

For purposes of this subparagraph, real property includes an interest in a mortgage.

(17) Treatment of certain amounts derived from foreign corporations.

(A) In general. Notwithstanding paragraph (1), any amount included in gross income under section 951(a)(1)(A) shall be included as an item of gross income derived from an unrelated trade or business to the extent the amount so included is attributable to insurance income (as defined in section 953) which, if derived directly by the organization, would be treated as gross income from an unrelated trade or business. There shall be allowed all deductions directly connected with amounts included in gross income under the preceding sentence.

(B) Exception.

(i) In general. Subparagraph (A) shall not apply to income attributable to a policy of insurance or reinsurance with respect to which the person (directly or indirectly) insured is—

(I) such organization,

(II) an affiliate of such organization which is exempt from tax under section 501(a), or

(III) a director or officer of, or an individual who (directly or indirectly) performs services for, such organization or affiliate but only if the insurance covers primarily risks associated with the performance of services in connection with such organization or affiliate.

(ii) Affiliate. For purposes of this subparagraph—

(I) In general. The determination as to whether an entity is an affiliate of an organization shall be made under rules similar to the rules of section 168(h)(4)(B).

(II) Special rule. Two or more organizations (and any affiliates of such organizations) shall be treated as affiliates if such organizations are colleges or universities described in section 170(b)(1)(A)(ii) or organizations described in section 170(b)(1)(A)(iii) and participate in an insurance arrangement that provides for any profits from such arrangement to be returned to the policyholders in their capacity as such.

(C) Regulations. The Secretary shall prescribe such regulations as may be necessary or appropriate to carry out the purposes of this paragraph, including regulations for the application of this paragraph in the case of income paid through 1 or more entities or between 2 or more chains of entities.

(18) Treatment of mutual or cooperative electric companies. In the case of a mutual or cooperative electric company described in section 501(c)(12), there shall be excluded income which is treated as member income under subparagraph (H) thereof.

(19) Treatment of gain or loss on sale or exchange of certain brownfield sites.

(A) In general. Notwithstanding paragraph (5)(B), there shall be excluded any gain or loss from the qualified sale, exchange, or other disposition of any qualifying brownfield property by an eligible taxpayer.

(B) Eligible taxpayer. For purposes of this paragraph—

(i) In general. The term "eligible taxpayer" means, with respect to a property, any organization exempt from tax under section 501(a) which—

(I) acquires from an unrelated person a qualifying brownfield property, and

(II) pays or incurs eligible remediation expenditures with respect to such property in an amount which exceeds the greater of $550,000 or 12 percent of the fair market value of the property at the time such property was acquired by the eligible taxpayer, determined as if there was not a presence of a hazardous substance, pollutant, or contaminant on the property which is complicating the expansion, redevelopment, or reuse of the property.

(ii) Exception. Such term shall not include any organization which is—

(I) potentially liable under section 107 of the Comprehensive Environmental Response, Compensation, and Liability Act of 1980 with respect to the qualifying brownfield property,

(II) affiliated with any other person which is so potentially liable through any direct or indirect familial relationship or any contractual, corporate, or financial relationship (other than a contractual, corporate, or financial relationship which is created by the instruments by which title to any qualifying brownfield property is conveyed or financed or by a contract of sale of goods or services), or

(III) the result of a reorganization of a business entity which was so potentially liable.

(C) Qualifying brownfield property. For purposes of this paragraph—

(i) In general. The term "qualifying brownfield property" means any real property which is certified, before the taxpayer incurs any eligible remediation expenditures (other than to obtain a Phase I environmental site assessment), by an appropriate State agency (within the meaning of section 198(c)(4)) in the State in which such property is located as a brownfield site within the meaning of section 101(39) of the Comprehensive Environmental Response, Compensation, and Liability Act of 1980 (as in effect on the date of the enactment of this paragraph).

(ii) Request for certification. Any request by an eligible taxpayer for a certification described in clause (i) shall include a sworn statement by the eligible taxpayer and supporting documentation of the presence of a hazardous substance, pollutant, or contaminant on the property which is complicating the expansion, redevelopment, or reuse of the property given the property's reasonably anticipated future land uses or capacity for uses of the property (including a Phase I environmental site assessment and, if applicable, evidence of the property's presence on a local, State, or Federal list of brownfields or contaminated property) and other environmental assessments prepared or obtained by the taxpayer.

(D) Qualified sale, exchange, or other disposition. For purposes of this paragraph—

(i) In general. A sale, exchange, or other disposition of property shall be considered as qualified if—

(I) such property is transferred by the eligible taxpayer to an unrelated person, and

(II) within 1 year of such transfer the eligible taxpayer has received a certification from the Environmental Protection Agency or an appropriate State agency (within the meaning of section 198(c)(4)) in the State in which such property is located that, as a result of the eligible taxpayer's remediation actions, such property would not be treated as a qualifying brownfield property in the hands of the transferee.

For purposes of subclause (II), before issuing such certification, the Environmental Protection Agency or appropriate State agency shall respond to comments received pursuant to clause (ii)(V) in the same form and manner as required under section 117(b) of the Comprehensive Environmental Response, Compensation, and Liability Act of 1980 (as in effect on the date of the enactment of this paragraph).

(ii) Request for certification. Any request by an eligible taxpayer for a certification described in clause (i) shall be made not later than the date of the transfer and shall include a sworn statement by the eligible taxpayer certifying the following:

(I) Remedial actions which comply with all applicable or relevant and appropriate requirements (consistent with section 121(d) of the Comprehensive Environmental Response, Compensation, and Liability Act of 1980) have been substantially completed, such that there are no hazardous substances, pollutants, or contaminants which complicate the expansion, redevelopment, or reuse of the property given the property's reasonably anticipated future land uses or capacity for uses of the property.

(II) The reasonably anticipated future land uses or capacity for uses of the property are more economically productive or environmentally beneficial than the uses of the property in existence on the date of the certification described in subparagraph (C)(i). For purposes of the preceding sentence, use of property as a landfill or other hazardous waste facility shall not be considered more economically productive or environmentally beneficial.

(III) A remediation plan has been implemented to bring the property into compliance with all applicable local, State, and Federal environmental laws, regulations, and standards and to ensure that the remediation protects human health and the environment.

(IV) The remediation plan described in subclause (III), including any physical improvements required to remediate the property, is either complete or substantially complete, and, if substantially complete, sufficient monitoring, funding, institutional controls, and financial assurances have been put in place to ensure the complete remediation of the property in accordance with the remediation plan as soon as is reasonably practicable after the sale, exchange, or other disposition of such property.

(V) Public notice and the opportunity for comment on the request for certification was completed before the date of such request. Such notice and opportunity for comment shall be in the same form and manner as required for public participation required under section 117(a) of the Comprehensive Environmental Response, Compensation, and Liability Act of 1980 (as in effect on the date of the enactment of this paragraph). For purposes of this subclause, public notice shall include, at a minimum, publication in a major local newspaper of general circulation.

(iii) Attachment to tax returns. A copy of each of the requests for certification described in clause (ii) of subparagraph (C) and this subparagraph shall be included in

697

the tax return of the eligible taxpayer (and, where applicable, of the qualifying partnership) for the taxable year during which the transfer occurs.

(iv) Substantial completion. For purposes of this subparagraph, a remedial action is substantially complete when any necessary physical construction is complete, all immediate threats have been eliminated, and all long-term threats are under control.

(E) Eligible remediation expenditures. For purposes of this paragraph—

(i) In general. The term "eligible remediation expenditures" means, with respect to any qualifying brownfield property, any amount paid or incurred by the eligible taxpayer to an unrelated third person to obtain a Phase I environmental site assessment of the property, and any amount so paid or incurred after the date of the certification described in subparagraph (C)(i) for goods and services necessary to obtain a certification described in subparagraph (D)(i) with respect to such property, including expenditures—

(I) to manage, remove, control, contain, abate, or otherwise remediate a hazardous substance, pollutant, or contaminant on the property,

(II) to obtain a Phase II environmental site assessment of the property, including any expenditure to monitor, sample, study, assess, or otherwise evaluate the release, threat of release, or presence of a hazardous substance, pollutant, or contaminant on the property,

(III) to obtain environmental regulatory certifications and approvals required to manage the remediation and monitoring of the hazardous substance, pollutant, or contaminant on the property, and

(IV) regardless of whether it is necessary to obtain a certification described in subparagraph (D)(i)(II), to obtain remediation cost-cap or stop-loss coverage, re-opener or regulatory action coverage, or similar coverage under environmental insurance policies, or financial guarantees required to manage such remediation and monitoring.

(ii) Exceptions. Such term shall not include—

(I) any portion of the purchase price paid or incurred by the eligible taxpayer to acquire the qualifying brownfield property,

(II) environmental insurance costs paid or incurred to obtain legal defense coverage, owner/operator liability coverage, lender liability coverage, professional liability coverage, or similar types of coverage,

(III) any amount paid or incurred to the extent such amount is reimbursed, funded, or otherwise subsidized by grants provided by the United States, a State, or a political subdivision of a State for use in connection with the property, proceeds of an issue of State or local government obligations used to provide financing for the property the interest of which is exempt from tax under section 103, or subsidized financing provided (directly or indirectly) under a Federal, State, or local program provided in connection with the property, or

(IV) any expenditure paid or incurred before the date of the enactment of this paragraph.

For purposes of subclause (III), the Secretary may issue guidance regarding the treatment of government-provided funds for purposes of determining eligible remediation expenditures.

(F) Determination of gain or loss. For purposes of this paragraph, the determination of gain or loss shall not include an amount treated as gain which is ordinary income with respect to section 1245 or section 1250 property, including amounts deducted as section 198 expenses which are subject to the recapture rules of section 198(e), if the taxpayer had deducted such amounts in the computation of its unrelated business taxable income.

(G) Special rules for partnerships.

(i) In general. In the case of an eligible taxpayer which is a partner of a qualifying partnership which acquires, remediates, and sells, exchanges, or otherwise disposes of a qualifying brownfield property, this paragraph shall apply to the eligible taxpayer's distributive share of the qualifying partnership's gain or loss from the sale, exchange, or other disposition of such property.

(ii) Qualifying partnership. The term "qualifying partnership" means a partnership which—

(I) has a partnership agreement which satisfies the requirements of section 514(c)(9)(B)(vi) at all times beginning on the date of the first certification received by the partnership under subparagraph (C)(i),

(II) satisfies the requirements of subparagraphs (B)(i), (C), (D), and (E), if "qualified partnership" is substituted for "eligible taxpayer" each place it appears therein (except subparagraph (D)(iii)), and

(III) is not an organization which would be prevented from constituting an eligible taxpayer by reason of subparagraph (B)(ii).

(iii) Requirement that tax-exempt partner be a partner since first certification. This paragraph shall apply with respect to any eligible taxpayer which is a partner of a partnership which acquires, remediates, and sells, exchanges, or otherwise disposes of a qualifying brownfield property only if such eligible taxpayer was a partner of the qualifying partnership at all times beginning on the date of the first certification received by the partnership under subparagraph (C)(i) and ending on the date of the sale, exchange, or other disposition of the property by the partnership.

(iv) Regulations. The Secretary shall prescribe such regulations as are necessary to prevent abuse of the requirements of this subparagraph, including abuse through—

(I) the use of special allocations of gains or losses, or

(II) changes in ownership of partnership interests held by eligible taxpayers.

(H) Special rules for multiple properties.

(i) In general. An eligible taxpayer or a qualifying partnership of which the eligible taxpayer is a partner may make a 1-time election to apply this paragraph to more than 1 qualifying brownfield property by averaging the eligible remediation expenditures for all such properties acquired during the election period. If the eligible taxpayer or qualifying partnership makes such an election, the election shall apply to all qualified sales, exchanges, or other dispositions of qualifying brownfield properties the acquisition and transfer of which occur during the period for which the election remains in effect.

(ii) Election. An election under clause (i) shall be made with the eligible taxpayer's or qualifying partnership's timely filed tax return (including extensions) for the first taxable year for which the taxpayer or qualifying partnership intends to have the election apply. An election under clause (i) is effective for the period—

(I) beginning on the date which is the first day of the taxable year of the return in which the election is included or a later day in such taxable year selected by the eligible taxpayer or qualifying partnership, and

(II) ending on the date which is the earliest of a date of revocation selected by the eligible taxpayer or qualifying partnership, the date which is 8 years after the date described in subclause (I), or, in the case of an election by a qualifying partnership of which the eligible taxpayer is a partner, the date of the termination of the qualifying partnership.

(iii) Revocation. An eligible taxpayer or qualifying partnership may revoke an election under clause (i)(II) by filing a statement of revocation with a timely filed tax return (including extensions). A revocation is effective as of the first day of the taxable year of the return in which the revocation is included or a later day in such taxable year selected by the eligible taxpayer or qualifying partnership. Once an eligible taxpayer or qualifying partnership revokes the election, the eligible taxpayer or qualifying partnership is ineligible to make another election under clause (i) with respect to any qualifying brownfield property subject to the revoked election.

(I) Recapture. If an eligible taxpayer excludes gain or loss from a sale, exchange, or other disposition of property to which an election under subparagraph (H) applies, and such property fails to satisfy the requirements of this paragraph, the unrelated business taxable income of the eligible taxpayer for the taxable year in which such failure occurs shall be determined by including any previously excluded gain or loss from such sale, exchange, or other disposition allocable to such taxpayer, and interest shall be determined at the overpayment rate established under section 6621 on any resulting tax for the period beginning with the due date of the return for the taxable year during which such sale, exchange, or other disposition occurred, and ending on the date of payment of the tax.

(J) Related persons. For purposes of this paragraph, a person shall be treated as related to another person if—

(i) such person bears a relationship to such other person described in section 267(b) (determined without regard to paragraph (9) thereof), or section 707(b)(1), determined by substituting "25 percent" for "50 percent" each place it appears therein, and

(ii) in the case such other person is a nonprofit organization, if such person controls directly or indirectly more than 25 percent of the governing body of such organization.

(K) Termination. Except for purposes of determining the average eligible remediation expenditures for properties acquired during the election period under subparagraph (H), this paragraph shall not apply to any property acquired by the eligible taxpayer or qualifying partnership after December 31, 2009.

* * * * * * * * * * * * *

[For Analysis, see ¶ 1502.]

[Endnote Code Sec. 512]

Code Sec. 512(b)(13)(E)(iv) was amended by Sec. 319(a) of the American Taxpayer Relief Act of 2012, P.L. 112-240, 1/2/2013, as detailed below:

1. Sec. 319(a) substituted "December 31, 2013" for "December 31, 2011" in clause (b)(13)(E)(iv)

Effective Date (Sec. 319(b), P.L. 112-240, 1/2/2013) effective for payments received or accrued after 12/31/2011.

[¶ 3079]   Code Sec. 530.   Coverdell education savings accounts.

(a) **General rule.** A Coverdell education savings account shall be exempt from taxation under this subtitle. Notwithstanding the preceding sentence, the Coverdell education savings account shall be subject to the taxes imposed by section 511 (relating to imposition of tax on unrelated business income of charitable organizations).

(b) **Definitions and special rules.** For purposes of this section—

(1) **Coverdell education savings account.** The term "Coverdell education savings account" means a trust created or organized in the United States exclusively for the purpose of paying the qualified[1] education expenses of an individual who is the designated beneficiary of the trust (and designated as a Coverdell education savings account at the time created or organized), but only if the written governing instrument creating the trust meets the following requirements:

(A) No contribution will be accepted—

(i) unless it is in cash,

(ii) after the date on which such beneficiary attains age 18, or

(iii) except in the case of rollover contributions, if such contribution would result in aggregate contributions for the taxable year exceeding [2]*$2,000.*

(B) The trustee is a bank (as defined in section 408(n)) or another person who demonstrates to the satisfaction of the Secretary that the manner in which that person will administer the trust will be consistent with the requirements of this section or who has so demonstrated with respect to any individual retirement plan.

(C) No part of the trust assets will be invested in life insurance contracts.

(D) The assets of the trust shall not be commingled with other property except in a common trust fund or common investment fund.

(E) Except as provided in subsection (d)(7), any balance to the credit of the designated beneficiary on the date on which the beneficiary attains age 30 shall be distributed within 30 days after such date to the beneficiary or, if the beneficiary dies before attaining age 30, shall be distributed within 30 days after the date of death of such beneficiary.

[3]*The age limitations in subparagraphs (A)(ii) and (E), and paragraphs (5) and (6) of subsection (d), shall not apply to any designated beneficiary with special needs (as determined under regulations prescribed by the Secretary).*

[4]*(2) Qualified education expenses.*

(A) In general. The term "qualified education expenses" means—

(i) qualified higher education expenses (as defined in section 529(e)(3)), and

(ii) qualified elementary and secondary education expenses (as defined in paragraph (3)).

(B) Qualified tuition programs. Such term shall include any contribution to a qualified tuition program (as defined in section 529(b)) on behalf of the designated beneficiary (as defined in section 529(e)(1)); but there shall be no increase in the investment in the contract for purposes of applying section 72 by reason of any portion of such contribution which is not includible in gross income by reason of subsection (d)(2).

(3) Qualified elementary and secondary education expenses.

(A) In general. The term "qualified elementary and secondary education expenses" means—

(i) expenses for tuition, fees, academic tutoring, special needs services in the case of a special needs beneficiary, books, supplies, and other equipment which are incurred in connection with the enrollment or attendance of the designated beneficiary of the trust as an elementary or secondary school student at a public, private, or religious school,

(ii) expenses for room and board, uniforms, transportation, and supplementary items and services (including extended day programs) which are required or provided by a public, private, or religious school in connection with such enrollment or attendance, and

(iii) expenses for the purchase of any computer technology or equipment (as defined in section 170(e)(6)(F)(i)) or Internet access and related services, if such technology, equipment, or services are to be used by the beneficiary and the beneficiary's family during any of the years the beneficiary is in school.

Clause (iii) shall not include expenses for computer software designed for sports, games, or hobbies unless the software is predominantly educational in nature.

(B) School. The term "school" means any school which provides elementary education or secondary education (kindergarten through grade 12), as determined under State law.

(4) Time when contributions deemed made. An individual shall be deemed to have made a contribution to a Coverdell education savings account on the last day of the preceding taxable year if the contribution is made on account of such taxable year and is made not later than the time prescribed by law for filing the return for such taxable year (not including extensions thereof).

(c) Reduction in permitted contributions based on adjusted gross income.

(1) In general. [5]*In the case of a contributor who is an individual, the maximum amount the contributor* could otherwise make to an account under this section shall be reduced by an amount which bears the same ratio to such maximum amount as—

(A) the excess of—

(i) the contributor's modified adjusted gross income for such taxable year, over

(ii) $95,000 ([6]*$190,000* in the case of a joint return), bears to

(B) $15,000 ([7]*$30,000* in the case of a joint return).

(2) Modified adjusted gross income. For purposes of paragraph (1), the term "modified adjusted gross income" means the adjusted gross income of the taxpayer for the taxable year increased by any amount excluded from gross income under section 911, 931, or 933.

(d) Tax treatment of distributions.

(1) In general. Any distribution shall be includible in the gross income of the distributee in the manner as provided in section 72.

(2) Distributions for qualified [8]education expenses.

(A) In general. No amount shall be includible in gross income under paragraph (1) if the qualified [9]education expenses of the designated beneficiary during the taxable year are not less than the aggregate distributions during the taxable year.

(B) Distributions in excess of expenses. If such aggregate distributions exceed such expenses during the taxable year, the amount otherwise includible in gross income under paragraph (1) shall be reduced by the amount which bears the same ratio to the amount which would be includible in gross income under paragraph (1) (without regard to this subparagraph) as the qualified[10] education expenses bear to such aggregate distributions.

[11]*(C) Coordination with hope and lifetime learning credits and qualified tuition programs. For purposes of subparagraph (A)—*

(i) Credit coordination. The total amount of qualified education expenses with respect to an individual for the taxable year shall be reduced—

(I) as provided in section 25A(g)(2), and

(II) by the amount of such expenses which were taken into account in determining the credit allowed to the taxpayer or any other person under section 25A.

(ii) Coordination with qualified tuition programs. If, with respect to an individual for any taxable year—

(I) the aggregate distributions during such year to which subparagraph (A) and section 529(c)(3)(B) apply, exceed

(II) the total amount of qualified education expenses (after the application of clause (i)) for such year,

the taxpayer shall allocate such expenses among such distributions for purposes of determining the amount of the exclusion under subparagraph (A) and section 529(c)(3)(B).

(D) Disallowance of excluded amounts as [12]*deduction, credit, or exclusion.* No deduction, [13]*credit, or exclusion* shall be allowed to the taxpayer under any other section of this chapter for any qualified education expenses to the extent taken into account in determining the amount of the exclusion under this paragraph.

(3) Special rules for applying estate and gift taxes with respect to account. Rules similar to the rules of paragraphs (2), (4), and (5) of section 529(c) shall apply for purposes of this section.

(4) Additional tax for distributions not used for educational expenses.

(A) In general. The tax imposed by this chapter for any taxable year on any taxpayer who receives a payment or distribution from a Coverdell education savings account which is includible in gross income shall be increased by 10 percent of the amount which is so includible.

(B) Exceptions. Subparagraph (A) shall not apply if the payment or distribution is—

(i) made to a beneficiary (or to the estate of the designated beneficiary) on or after the death of the designated beneficiary,

(ii) attributable to the designated beneficiary's being disabled (within the meaning of section 72(m)(7)),

(iii) made on account of a scholarship, allowance, or payment described in section 25A(g)(2) received by the designated beneficiary to the extent the amount of the payment or distribution does not exceed the amount of the scholarship, allowance, or payment,

(iv) made on account of the attendance of the designated beneficiary at the United States Military Academy, the United States Naval Academy, the United States Air Force Academy, the United States Coast Guard Academy, or the United States Merchant Marine Academy, to the extent that the amount of the payment or distribution does not exceed the costs of advanced education (as defined by section 2005(e)(3) of title 10, United States Code, as in effect on the date of the enactment of this section) attributable to such attendance, or

(v) an amount which is includible in gross income solely by application of paragraph (2)(C)(i)(II) for the taxable year.

(C) Contributions returned before [14]*certain date.* Subparagraph (A) shall not apply to the distribution of any contribution made during a taxable year on behalf of the designated beneficiary if—

[15]*(i) such distribution is made before the first day of the sixth month of the taxable year following the taxable year, and*

(ii) such distribution is accompanied by the amount of net income attributable to such excess contribution.

Any net income described in clause (ii) shall be included in gross income for the taxable year in which such excess contribution was made.

(5) Rollover contributions. Paragraph (1) shall not apply to any amount paid or distributed from a Coverdell education savings account to the extent that the amount received is paid, not later than the 60th day after the date of such payment or distribution, into another Coverdell education savings account for the benefit of the same beneficiary or a member of the family (within the meaning of section 529(e)(2)) of such beneficiary who has not attained age 30 as of such date. The preceding sentence shall not apply to any payment or distribution if it applied to any prior payment or distribution during the 12-month period ending on the date of the payment or distribution.

(6) Change in beneficiary. Any change in the beneficiary of a Coverdell education savings account shall not be treated as a distribution for purposes of paragraph (1) if the new beneficiary is a member of the family (as so defined) of the old beneficiary and has not attained age 30 as of the date of such change.

(7) Special rules for death and divorce. Rules similar to the rules of paragraphs (7) and (8) of section 220(f) shall apply. In applying the preceding sentence, members of the family (as so defined) of the designated beneficiary shall be treated in the same manner as the spouse under such paragraph (8).

(8) Deemed distribution on required distribution date. In any case in which a distribution is required under subsection (b)(1)(E), any balance to the credit of a designated beneficiary as of the close of the 30-day period referred to in such subsection for making such distribution shall be deemed distributed at the close of such period.

(9) Military death gratuity.

(A) In general. For purposes of this section, the term "rollover contribution" includes a contribution to a Coverdell education savings account made before the end of the 1-year period beginning on the date on which the contributor receives an amount under section 1477 of title 10, United States Code, or section 1967 of title 38 of such Code, with respect to a person, to the extent that such contribution does not exceed—

(i) the sum of the amounts received during such period by such contributor under such sections with respect to such person, reduced by

(ii) the amounts so received which were contributed to a Roth IRA under section 408A(e)(2) or to another Coverdell education savings account.

(B) Annual limit on number of rollovers not to apply. The last sentence of paragraph (5) shall not apply with respect to amounts treated as a rollover by the subparagraph (A).

(C) Application of section 72. For purposes of applying section 72 in the case of a distribution which is includible in gross income under paragraph (1), the amount treated as a rollover by reason of subparagraph (A) shall be treated as investment in the contract.

(e) Tax treatment of accounts. Rules similar to the rules of paragraphs (2) and (4) of section 408(e) shall apply to any Coverdell education savings account.

(f) Community property laws. This section shall be applied without regard to any community property laws.

(g) **Custodial accounts.** For purposes of this section, a custodial account shall be treated as a trust if the assets of such account are held by a bank (as defined in section 408(n)) or another person who demonstrates, to the satisfaction of the Secretary, that the manner in which he will administer the account will be consistent with the requirements of this section, and if the custodial account would, except for the fact that it is not a trust, constitute an account described in subsection (b)(1). For purposes of this title, in the case of a custodial account treated as a trust by reason of the preceding sentence, the custodian of such account shall be treated as the trustee thereof.

(h) **Reports.** The trustee of a Coverdell education savings account shall make such reports regarding such account to the Secretary and to the beneficiary of the account with respect to contributions, distributions, and such other matters as the Secretary may require. The reports required by this subsection shall be filed at such time and in such manner and furnished to such individuals at such time and in such manner as may be required.

[For Analysis, see ¶ 704.]

[Endnote Code Sec. 530]

Sec. 101(a)(1) of the American Taxpayer Relief Act of 2012, P.L. 112-240, 1/2/2013, deleted Title IX [Sec. 901] of the Economic Growth and Tax Relief Reconciliation Act of 2001, P.L. 107-16, the effect of which is to eliminate the sunset of all provisions enacted by P.L. 107-16.

Effective Date (Sec. 101(a)(3), P.L. 112-240, 1/2/2013) effective for taxable, plan, or limitation years beginning after 12/31/2012, and estates of decedents dying, gifts made, or generation skipping transfers after 12/31/2012.

Code Sec. 530 was amended by Sec. 401 of the Economic Growth and Tax Relief Reconciliation Act of 2001, P.L. 107-16, 6/7/2001, which struck out:

1. Sec. 401(c)(3)(A) deleted "higher" after "qualified" in para. (b)(1)
2. Sec. 401(a)(1), substituted "$2,000" for "$500" in clause (b)(1)(A)(iii)
3. Sec. 401(d) added a flush sentence at the end of para. (b)(1)
4. Sec. 401(c)(1) amended para. (b)(2). Prior to amendment, para. (b)(2) read as follows:

"(2) Qualified higher education expenses.

"(A) In general. The term 'qualified higher education expenses' has the meaning given such term by section 529(e)(3), reduced as provided in section 25A(g)(2).

"(B) Qualified State tuition programs. Such term shall include amounts paid or incurred to purchase tuition credits or certificates, or to make contributions to an account, under a qualified State tuition program (as defined in section 529(b)) for the benefit of the beneficiary of the account."

Sec. 401(c)(2) added para. (b)(4)

Sec. 401(f)(1) added para. (b)(5). Sec. 412(ff)(1), P.L. 109-35 redes. paras. (b)(4)-(5) as paras. (b)(3)-(4)

5. Sec. 401(e) substituted "In the case of a contributor who is an individual, the maximum amount the contributor" for "The maximum amount which a contributor" in para. (c)(1)

6. Sec. 401(b)(1) substituted "$190,000" for "$150,000" in clause (c)(1)(A)(ii)

7. Sec. 401(b)(2) substituted "$30,000" for "$10,000" in subpara. (c)(1)(B)

8. Sec. 401(c)(3)(A) deleted "higher" after "qualified" in the heading of para. (d)(2)

9. Sec. 401(c)(3)(A) deleted "higher" after "qualified" subpara. (d)(2)(A)

10. Sec. 401(c)(3)(A) deleted "higher" after "qualified" subpara. (d)(2)(B)

11. Sec. 401(g)(1) amended subpara. (d)(2)(C). Prior to amendment, subpara. (d)(2)(C) read as follows:

"(C) Election to waive exclusion. A taxpayer may elect to waive the application of this paragraph for any taxable year."

12. Sec. 401(g)(2)(C)(ii) substituted "deduction, credit, or exclusion" for "credit or deduction" in the heading of subpara. (d)(2)(D)

13. Sec. 401(g)(2)(C)(i) substituted ", credit, or exclusion" for "or credit" in subpara. (d)(2)(D)

14. Sec. 401(f)(2)(B) substituted "certain date" for "due date of return" in the heading of subpara. (d)(4)(C)

15. Sec. 401(f)(2)(A), amended clause (d)(4)(C)(i). Prior to amendment, clause (d)(4)(C)(i) read as follows:

"(i) such distribution is made on or before the day prescribed by law (including extensions of time) for filing the beneficiary's return of tax for the taxable year or, if the beneficiary is not required to file such a return, the 15th day of the 4th month of the taxable year following the taxable year; and"

Effective Date (Sec. 401(h), P.L. 107-16, 6/7/2001) effective for tax. yrs. begin. after 12/31/2001.

[¶ 3080]   Code Sec. 531.   Imposition of accumulated earnings tax.

In addition to other taxes imposed by this chapter, there is hereby imposed for each taxable year on the accumulated taxable income (as defined in section 535) of each corporation described in section 532, an accumulated earnings tax equal to [1]*20 percent* of the accumulated taxable income..

[For Analysis, see ¶ 203.]

[Endnote Code Sec. 531]
Sec. 101(a)(1), PL112-240, 1/2/2013, deleted Title IX [Sec. 901], P.L. 107-16, the effect of which is to eliminate the sunset of all provisions enacted by P.L. 107-16.
Effective Date (Sec. 101(a)(3), PL112-240, 1/2/2013) effective for tax. plan, or limitation years beginning after 12/31/2012, and estates of decedents dying, gifts made, or generation skipping transfers after 12/31/2012.
Sec. 101(c)(4), P.L. 107-16 amended Code Sec. 531 by substituting "equal to the product of the highest rate of tax under section 1(c) and the accumulated taxable income." for "equal to 39.6 percent of the accumulated taxable income."

Sec. 102(a), PL112-240, 1/2/2013, deleted Sec. 303, P.L. 108-27, the effect of which is to eliminate the sunset of all provisions enacted by Title III, P.L. 108-27.
Sec. 302(e)(5), P.L. 108-27 amended Code Sec. 531 by substituting "equal to 15 percent of the accumulated taxable income." for "equal to the product of the highest rate of tax under section 1(c) and the accumulated taxable income."
Effective Date 1/2/2013.

Code Sec. 531 was amended by Sec. 102(c)(1)(A) of the American Taxpayer Relief Act of 2012, PL112-240, 1/2/2013, as detailed below:
1. Sec. 102(c)(1)(A) substituted "20 percent" for "15 percent" in Sec. 531
Effective Date (Sec. 102(d)(1), PL112-240, 1/2/2013) effective for tax. yrs. begin. after 12/31/2012.

[¶ 3081]   Code Sec. 541.   Imposition of personal holding company tax.
In addition to other taxes imposed by this chapter, there is hereby imposed for each taxable year on the undistributed personal holding company income (as defined in section 545) of every personal holding company (as defined in section 542) a personal holding company tax equal to [1] *20 percent* of the undistributed personal holding company income.
[For Analysis, see ¶ 203.]

[Endnote Code Sec. 541]
Sec. 101(a)(1), PL112-240, 1/2/2013, deleted Title IX [Sec. 901], P.L. 107-16, the effect of which is to eliminate the sunset of all provisions enacted by P.L. 107-16.
Sec. 101(c)(5), P.L. 107-16 amended Code Sec. 541, by substituting "equal to the product of the highest rate of tax under section 1(c) and the undistributed personal holding company income." for "equal to 39.6 percent of the undistributed personal holding company income."
Effective Date (Sec. 101(a)(3), PL112-240, 1/2/2013) effective for tax. plan, or limitation years beginning after 12/31/2012, and estates of decedents dying, gifts made, or generation skipping transfers after 12/31/2012.

Sec. 102(a), PL112-240, 1/2/2013, deleted Sec. 303, P.L. 108-27, the effect of which is to eliminate the sunset of all provisions enacted by Title III, P.L. 108-27.
Sec. 302(e)(6), P.L. 108-27 amended Code Sec. 541, by substituting "equal to 15 percent of the undistributed personal holding company income." for "equal to the product of the highest rate of tax under section 1(c) and the undistributed personal holding company income."
Effective Date 1/2/2013.

Code Sec. 541 was amended by Sec. 102(c)(1)(B) of the American Taxpayer Relief Act of 2012, PL112-240, 1/2/2013, as detailed below:
1. Sec. 102(c)(1)(B) substituted "20 percent" for "15 percent" in Sec. 541
Effective Date (Sec. 102(d)(1), PL112-240, 1/2/2013) effective for tax. yrs. begin. after 12/31/2012.

[¶ 3082]   Code Sec. 584.   Common trust funds.

* * * * * * * * * * * *

(c) **Income of participants in fund.** Each participant in the common trust fund in computing its taxable income shall include, whether or not distributed and whether or not distributable—

(1) as part of its gains and losses from sales or exchanges of capital assets held for not more than 1 year, its proportionate share of the gains and losses of the common trust fund from sales or exchanges of capital assets held for not more than 1 year,

(2) as part of its gains and losses from sales or exchanges of capital assets held for more than 1 year, its proportionate share of the gains and losses of the common trust fund from sales or exchanges of capital assets held for more than 1 year, and

(3) its proportionate share of the ordinary taxable income or the ordinary net loss of the common trust fund, computed as provided in subsection (d).

[1] *The proportionate share of each participant in the amount of dividends received by the common trust fund and to which section 1(h)(11) applies shall be considered for purposes of such paragraph as having been received by such participant.*

* * * * * * * * * * * *

[For Analysis, see ¶ 207.]

[Endnote Code Sec. 584]

Sec. 102(a) of the American Taxpayer Relief Act of 2012, P.L. 112-240, 1/2/2013, deleted Sec. 303, P.L. 108-27, the Jobs and Growth Tax Relief Reconciliation Act of 2003, the effect of which is to eliminate the sunset of all provisions enacted by Title III of P.L. 108-27 Following are the amendments made to Code Sec. 584 by P.L. 108-27.

Code Sec. 584(c) in *italics* was added by Sec. 302(e)(7) of the Jobs and Growth Tax Relief Reconciliation Act of 2003, P.L. 108-27, 5/28/2003.

1. added flush sentence at the end of subsec. (c)

Effective Date (Sec. 302(f), P.L. 108-27, 5/28/2003) effective for tax. yrs. begin. after 12/31/2002.

[¶ 3083]   Code Sec.[1] 646.   *Tax treatment of electing Alaska Native Settlement Trusts.*

(a) **In general.** *If an election under this section is in effect with respect to any Settlement Trust, the provisions of this section shall apply in determining the income tax treatment of the Settlement Trust and its beneficiaries with respect to the Settlement Trust.*

(b)   **Taxation of income of trust.** *Except as provided in subsection (f)(1)(B)(ii)—*

(1) **In general.** *There is hereby imposed on the taxable income of an electing Settlement Trust, other than its net capital gain, a tax at the lowest rate specified in section 1(c).*

(2) **Capital gain.** *In the case of an electing Settlement Trust with a net capital gain for the taxable year, a tax is hereby imposed on such gain at the rate of tax which would apply to such gain if the taxpayer were subject to a tax on its other taxable income at only the lowest rate specified in section 1(c).*

Any such tax shall be in lieu of the income tax otherwise imposed by this chapter on such income or gain.

(c) **One-time election.**

(1) **In general.** *A Settlement Trust may elect to have the provisions of this section apply to the trust and its beneficiaries.*

(2) **Time and method of election.** *An election under paragraph (1) shall be made by the trustee of such trust —*

(A) *on or before the due date (including extensions) for filing the Settlement Trust's return of tax for the first taxable year of such trust ending after the date of the enactment of this section, and*

(B) *by attaching to such return of tax a statement specifically providing for such election.*

(3) **Period election in effect.** *Except as provided in subsection (f), an election under this subsection—*

(A) *shall apply to the first taxable year described in paragraph (2)(A) and all subsequent taxable years, and*

(B) *may not be revoked once it is made.*

(d) **Contributions to trust.**

(1) **Beneficiaries of electing trust not taxed on contributions.** *In the case of an electing Settlement Trust, no amount shall be includible in the gross income of a beneficiary of such trust by reason of a contribution to such trust.*

(2) **Earnings and profits.** *The earnings and profits of the sponsoring Native Corporation shall not be reduced on account of any contribution to such Settlement Trust.*

(e) Tax treatment of distributions to beneficiaries. Amounts distributed by an electing Settlement Trust during any taxable year shall be considered as having the following characteristics in the hands of the recipient beneficiary:

(1) First, as amounts excludable from gross income for the taxable year to the extent of the taxable income of such trust for such taxable year (decreased by any income tax paid by the trust with respect to the income) plus any amount excluded from gross income of the trust under section 103.

(2) Second, as amounts excludable from gross income to the extent of the amount described in paragraph (1) for all taxable years for which an election is in effect under subsection (c) with respect to the trust, and not previously taken into account under paragraph (1).

(3) Third, as amounts distributed by the sponsoring Native Corporation with respect to its stock (within the meaning of section 301(a)) during such taxable year and taxable to the recipient beneficiary as amounts described in section 301(c)(1), to the extent of current or accumulated earnings and profits of the sponsoring Native Corporation as of the close of such taxable year after proper adjustment is made for all distributions made by the sponsoring Native Corporation during such taxable year.

(4) Fourth, as amounts distributed by the trust in excess of the distributable net income of such trust for such taxable year.

Amounts distributed to which paragraph (3) applies shall not be treated as a corporate distribution subject to section 311(b), and for purposes of determining the amount of a distribution for purposes of paragraph (3) and the basis to the recipients, section 643(e) and not section 301(b) or (d) shall apply.

(f) Special rules where transfer restrictions modified.

(1) Transfer of beneficial interests. If, at any time, a beneficial interest in an electing Settlement Trust may be disposed of to a person in a manner which would not be permitted by section 7(h) of the Alaska Native Claims Settlement Act (43 U.S.C. 1606(h)) if such interest were Settlement Common Stock—

(A) no election may be made under subsection (c) with respect to such trust, and

(B) if such an election is in effect as of such time—

(i) such election shall cease to apply as of the first day of the taxable year in which such disposition is first permitted,

(ii) the provisions of this section shall not apply to such trust for such taxable year and all taxable years thereafter, and

(iii) the distributable net income of such trust shall be increased by the current or accumulated earnings and profits of the sponsoring Native Corporation as of the close of such taxable year after proper adjustment is made for all distributions made by the sponsoring Native Corporation during such taxable year.

In no event shall the increase under clause (iii) exceed the fair market value of the trust's assets as of the date the beneficial interest of the trust first becomes so disposable. The earnings and profits of the sponsoring Native Corporation shall be adjusted as of the last day of such taxable year by the amount of earnings and profits so included in the distributable net income of the trust.

(2) Stock in corporation. If—

(A) stock in the sponsoring Native Corporation may be disposed of to a person in a manner which would not be permitted by section 7(h) of the Alaska Native Claims Settlement Act (43 U.S.C. 1606(h)) if such stock were Settlement Common Stock, and

(B) at any time after such disposition of stock is first permitted, such corporation transfers assets to a Settlement Trust,

paragraph (1)(B) shall be applied to such trust on and after the date of the transfer in the same manner as if the trust permitted dispositions of beneficial interests in the trust in a manner not permitted by such section 7(h).

(3) Certain distributions. For purposes of this section, the surrender of an interest in a Native Corporation or an electing Settlement Trust in order to accomplish the whole or partial redemption of the interest of a shareholder or beneficiary in such corporation or trust, or to accomplish the whole or partial liquidation of such corporation or trust, shall be deemed to be a transfer permitted by section 7(h) of the Alaska Native Claims Settlement Act.

(g)   Taxable income. For purposes of this title, the taxable income of an electing Settlement Trust shall be determined under section 641(b) without regard to any deduction under section 651 or 661.

(h)   Definitions. For purposes of this section—

(1)   Electing Settlement Trust. The term "electing Settlement Trust" means a Settlement Trust which has made the election, effective for a taxable year, described in subsection (c).

(2)   Native Corporation. The term "Native Corporation" has the meaning given such term by section 3(m) of the Alaska Native Claims Settlement Act (43 U.S.C. 1602(m)).

(3)   Settlement Common Stock. The term "Settlement Common Stock" has the meaning given such term by section 3(p) of the Alaska Native Claims Settlement Act (43 U.S.C. 1602(p)).

(4)   Settlement Trust. The term "Settlement Trust" means a trust that constitutes a settlement trust under section 3(t) of the Alaska Native Claims Settlement Act (43 U.S.C. 1602(t)).

(5)   Sponsoring Native Corporation. The term "sponsoring Native Corporation" means the Native Corporation which transfers assets to an electing Settlement Trust.

(i)   Special loss disallowance rule. Any loss that would otherwise be recognized by a shareholder upon a disposition of a share of stock of a sponsoring Native Corporation shall be reduced (but not below zero) by the per share loss adjustment factor. The per share loss adjustment factor shall be the aggregate of all contributions to all electing Settlement Trusts sponsored by such Native Corporation made on or after the first day each trust is treated as an electing Settlement Trust expressed on a per share basis and determined as of the day of each such contribution.

(j)   Cross reference. For information required with respect to electing Settlement Trusts and sponsoring Native Corporations, see section 6039H.

[For Analysis, see ¶ 1503.]

[Endnote Code Sec. 646]

Sec. 101(a)(1) of the American Taxpayer Relief Act of 2012, P.L. 112-240, 1/2/2013, deleted Title IX [Sec. 901] of the Economic Growth and Tax Relief Reconciliation Act of 2001, P.L. 107-16, the effect of which is to eliminate the sunset of all provisions enacted by P.L. 107-16. Following are the amendments made to Code Sec. 646, by P.L. 107-16. **Effective Date** (Sec. 101(a)(3), P.L. 112-240, 1/2/2013) effective for taxable, plan, or limitation years beginning after 12/31/2012, and estates of decedents dying, gifts made, or generation skipping transfers after 12/31/2012.

Code Sec. 646, in *italics*, was added by Sec. 671(a) of the Economic Growth and Tax Relief Reconciliaton Act of 2001, P.L. 107-16, 6/7/2001.

1. added Code Sec. 646

Effective Date (Sec. 671(d), P.L. 107-16, 6/7/2001) effective for tax. yrs. end. after 6/7/2001 and for contributions made to electing Settlement Trusts for such year or any subsequent year.

[¶ 3084]   Code Sec. 691.   Recipients of income in respect of decedents.

* * * * * * * * * * * *

(c)   Deduction for estate tax.

(1)   Allowance of deduction.

(A) General rule. A person who includes an amount in gross income under subsection (a) shall be allowed, for the same taxable year, as a deduction an amount which bears the same ratio to the estate tax attributable to the net value for estate tax purposes of all the items described in subsection (a)(1) as the value for estate tax purposes of the items of gross income or portions thereof in respect of which such person included the amount in gross income (or the amount included in gross income, whichever is lower) bears to the value for estate tax purposes of all the items described in subsection (a)(1).

(B) **Estates and trusts.** In the case of an estate or trust, the amount allowed as a deduction under subparagraph (A) shall be computed by excluding from the gross income of the estate or trust the portion (if any) of the items described in subsection (a)(1) which is properly paid, credited, or to be distributed to the beneficiaries during the taxable year.

(2) **Method of computing deduction.** For purposes of paragraph (1)—

(A) The term "estate tax" means the tax imposed on the estate of the decedent or any prior decedent under section 2001 or 2101, reduced by the credits against such tax.

(B) The net value for estate tax purposes of all the items described in subsection (a)(1) shall be the excess of the value for estate tax purposes of all the items described in subsection (a)(1) over the deductions from the gross estate in respect of claims which represent the deductions and credit described in subsection (b). Such net value shall be determined with respect to the provisions of section 421(c)(2), relating to the deduction for estate tax with respect to stock options to which part II of subchapter D applies.

(C) The estate tax attributable to such net value shall be an amount equal to the excess of the estate tax over the estate tax computed without including in the gross estate such net value.

(3) **Special rule for generation-skipping transfers.** In the case of any tax imposed by chapter 13 on a taxable termination or a direct skip occurring as a result of the death of the transferor, there shall be allowed a deduction (under principles similar to the principles of this subsection) for the portion of such tax attributable to items of gross income of the trust which were not properly includible in the gross income of the trust for periods before the date of such termination.

(4) **Coordination with capital gain provisions.** For purposes of sections 1(h), 1201, 1202, and 1211, the amount[1] taken into account with respect to any item described in subsection (a)(1) shall be reduced (but not below zero) by the amount[1] of the deduction allowable under paragraph (1) of this subsection with respect to such item.

* * * * * * * * * * * *

[For Analysis, see ¶ 211.]

[Endnote Code Sec. 691]

Sec. 102(a) of the American Taxpayer Relief Act of 2012, P.L. 112-240, 1/2/2013, deleted Sec. 303, P.L. 108-27, the Jobs and Growth Tax Relief Reconciliation Act of 2003, the effect of which is to eliminate the sunset of all provisions enacted by Title III of P.L. 108-27. Code Sec. 691(c)(4) was amended by Sec. 402(a)(4), P.L. 402(a)(4), subject to the sunset outlined in Sec. 303, P.L. 108-27.

Sec. 402(a)(4), P.L. 108-311 deleted "of any gain" after "the amount" in para. (c)(4).

[¶ 3085]   Code Sec. 702.   Income and credits of partner.

(a) **General rule.** In determining his income tax, each partner shall take into account separately his distributive share of the partnership's—

(1) gains and losses from sales or exchanges of capital assets held for not more than 1 year,

(2) gains and losses from sales or exchanges of capital assets held for more than 1 year,

(3) gains and losses from sales or exchanges of property described in section 1231 (relating to certain property used in a trade or business and involuntary conversions),

(4) charitable contributions (as defined in section 170(c)),

[1]*(5) dividends with respect to which section 1(h)(11) or part VIII of subchapter B applies,*

(6) taxes, described in section 901, paid or accrued to foreign countries and to possessions of the United States,

(7) other items of income, gain, loss, deduction, or credit, to the extent provided by regulations prescribed by the Secretary, and

(8) taxable income or loss, exclusive of items requiring separate computation under other paragraphs of this subsection.

* * * * * * * * * * * *

[For Analysis, see ¶ 205.]

[Endnote Code Sec. 702]

Sec. 102(a) of the American Taxpayer Relief Act of 2012, P.L. 112-240, 1/2/2013, deleted Sec. 303, P.L. 108-27, the Jobs and Growth Tax Relief Reconciliation Act of 2003, the effect of which is to eliminate the sunset of all provisions enacted by Title III of P.L. 108-27. Following are the amendments made to Code Sec. 702, by P.L. 108-27.

Code Sec. 702(a)(5), in *italics*, was added by Sec. 302(e)(8) of the Jobs and Growth Tax Relief Reconciliation Act of 2003, P.L. 108-27, 5/28/2003, which struck out:

1. "(5) dividends with respect to which there is a deduction under part VIII of subchapter B,"

Effective Date (Sec. 302(f), P.L. 108-27, 5/28/2003) effective for tax. yrs. begin. after 12/31/2002.

[¶ 3086]   Code Sec. 854.   Limitations applicable to dividends received from regulated investment company.

(a)   Capital gain dividend. For purposes of section 1(h)(11) (relating to maximum rate of tax on dividends) and section 243 (relating to deductions for dividends received by corporations), a capital gain dividend (as defined in section 852(b)(3)) received from a regulated investment company shall not be considered as a dividend.

(b)   Other dividends.

(1)   Amount treated as dividend.

(A) Deduction under section 243. In any case in which—

(i) a dividend is received from a regulated investment company (other than a dividend to which subsection (a) applies), and

(ii) such investment company meets the requirements of section 852(a) for the taxable year during which it paid such dividend,

then, in computing any deduction under section 243, there shall be taken into account only that portion of such dividend reported by the regulated investment company as eligible for such deduction in written statements furnished to its shareholders and such dividend shall be treated as received from a corporation which is not a 20-percent owned corporation.

(B) Maximum rate under section 1(h).

(i) In general. In any case in which—

(I) a dividend is received from a regulated investment company (other than a dividend to which subsection (a) applies),

(II) such investment company meets the requirements of section 852(a) for the taxable year during which it paid such dividend, and

(III) the qualified dividend income of such investment company for such taxable year is less than 95 percent of its gross income,

then, in computing qualified dividend income, there shall be taken into account only that portion of such dividend reported by the regulated investment company as qualified dividend income in written statements furnished to its shareholders.

(ii) Gross income. For purposes of clause (i), in the case of 1 or more sales or other dispositions of stock or securities, the term "gross income" includes only the excess of—

(I) the net short-term capital gain from such sales or dispositions, over

(II) the net long-term capital loss from such sales or dispositions.

(C) Limitations.

(i) Subparagraph (A). The aggregate amount which may be reported as dividends under subparagraph (A) shall not exceed the aggregate dividends received by the company for the taxable year.

(ii) Subparagraph (B). The aggregate amount which may be reported as qualified dividend income under subparagraph (B) shall not exceed the sum of—

(I) the qualified dividend income of the company for the taxable year, and

(II) the amount of any earnings and profits which were distributed by the company for such taxable year and accumulated in a taxable year with respect to which this part did not apply.

(2) Aggregate dividends. For purposes of this subsection—

(A) In general. In computing the amount of aggregate dividends received, there shall only be taken into account dividends received from domestic corporations.

(B) Dividends. For purposes of subparagraph (A), the term "dividend" shall not include any distribution from—

(i) a corporation which, for the taxable year of the corporation in which the distribution is made, or for the next preceding taxable year of the corporation, is a corporation exempt from tax under section 501 (relating to certain charitable, etc., organizations) or section 521 (relating to farmers' cooperative associations), or

(ii) a real estate investment trust which, for the taxable year of the trust in which the dividend is paid, qualifies under part II of subchapter M (section 856 and following).

(C) Limitations on dividends from regulated investment companies. In determining the amount of any dividend for purposes of this paragraph, a dividend received from a regulated investment company shall be subject to the limitations prescribed in this section.

(3) Special rule for computing deduction under section 243. For purposes of subparagraph (A) of paragraph (1), an amount shall be treated as a dividend for the purpose of paragraph (1) only if a deduction would have been allowable under section 243 to the regulated investment company determined—

(A) as if section 243 applied to dividends received by a regulated investment company,

(B) after the application of section 246 (but without regard to subsection (b) thereof), and

(C) after the application of section 246A.

(4) Qualified dividend income. For purposes of this subsection, the term "qualified dividend income" has the meaning given such term by section 1(h)(11)(B).

[For Analysis, see ¶ 206.]

[Endnote Code Sec. 854]

Sec. 102(a) of the American Taxpayer Relief Act of 2012, P.L. 112-240, 1/2/2013, deleted Sec. 303, P.L. 108-27, the Jobs and Growth Tax Relief Reconciliation Act of 2003, the effect of which is to eliminate the sunset of all provisions enacted by Title III of P.L. 108-27. Following are the amendments made to Code Sec. 854 by P.L. 108-27.

Code Sec. 854(a), Code Sec. 854(b)(1)(B), Code Sec. 854(b)(1)(C), Code Sec. 854(b)(2) and Code Sec. 854(b)(5) was amended by Sec. 302(c)(1)-(5) of the Jobs and Growth Tax Relief Reconciliation Act of 2003, P.L. 108-27, 5/28/2003. Sec. 854 was further amended by P.L. 111-325 and P.L. 108-311.

1. Sec. 302(c)(1) added "section 1(h)(11) (relating to maximum rate of tax on dividends) and" after "For purposes of" in subsec. (a)

2. Sec. 302(c)(2) added new subpara. (b)(1)(B)

3. Sec. 302(c)(2) redesignated subpara. (b)(1)(B) as (C)

4. Sec. 302(c)(3) substituted "subparagraph (A) or (B)" for "subparagraph (A)" in subpara. (b)(1)(C) [as redesignated by Sec. 302(c)(2) of this Act, see above]

5. Sec. 302(c)(4) added "the maximum rate under section 1(h)(11) and" after "for purposes of" in para. (b)(2)

6. Sec. 302(c)(5) added para. (b)(5)

Effective Date (Sec. 302(f), P.L. 108-27, 5/28/2003) effective for tax. yrs. begin. after 12/31/2002.

[¶ 3087]　　Code Sec.* 857.　　Taxation of real estate investment trusts and their beneficiaries.

¹*(c)　Restrictions applicable to dividends received from real estate investment trusts.*

(1)　Section 243. For purposes of section 243 (relating to deductions for dividends received by corporations), a dividend received from a real estate investment trust which meets the requirements of this part shall not be considered a dividend.

(2) Section (1)(h)(11).

(A) In general. In any case in which—

(i) a dividend is received from a real estate investment trust (other than a capital gain dividend), and

(ii) such trust meets the requirements of section 856(a) for the taxable year during which it paid such dividend,

then, in computing qualified dividend income, there shall be taken into account only that portion of such dividend designated by the real estate investment trust.

(B) Limitation. The aggregate amount which may be designated as qualified dividend income under subparagraph (A) shall not exceed the sum of—

(i) the qualified dividend income of the trust for the taxable year,

(ii) the excess of—

(I) the sum of the real estate investment trust taxable income computed under section 857(b)(2) for the preceding taxable year and the income subject to tax by reason of the application of the regulations under section 337(d) for such preceding taxable year, over

(II) the sum of the taxes imposed on the trust for such preceding taxable year under section 857(b)(1) and by reason of the application of such regulations, and

(iii) the amount of any earnings and profits which were distributed by the trust for such taxable year and accumulated in a taxable year with respect to which this part did not apply.

(C) Notice to shareholders. The amount of any distribution by a real estate investment trust which may be taken into account as qualified dividend income shall not exceed the amount so designated by the trust in a written notice to its shareholders mailed not later than 60 days after the close of its taxable year.

(D) Qualified dividend income. For purposes of this paragraph, the term "qualified dividend income" has the meaning given such term by section 1(h)(11)(B).

* * * * * * * * * * * *

[For Analysis, see ¶ 206.]

[Endnote Code Sec. 857]

Sec. 102(a) of the American Taxpayer Relief Act of 2012, P.L. 112-240, 1/2/2013, deleted Sec. 303, P.L. 108-27, the Jobs and Growth Tax Relief Reconciliation Act of 2003, the effect of which is to eliminate the sunset of all provisions enacted by Title III of P.L. 108-27. Following are the amendments made to Code Sec. 857 by P.L. 108-27.

Code Sec. 857(c), in *italics*, was added by Sec. 302(d) of the Jobs and Growth Tax Relief Reconciliation Act of 2003, P.L. 108-27, 5/28/2003, which struck out:

1. "(c) Restrictions applicable to dividends received from real estate investment trusts. For purposes of section 243 (relating to deductions for dividends received by corporations), a dividend received from a real estate investment trust which meets the requirements of this part shall not be considered as a dividend."

Effective Date (Sec. 302(f), P.L. 108-27, 5/28/2003) effective for tax. yrs. begin. after 12/31/2002.

[¶ 3088]   Code Sec. 871.   Tax on nonresident alien individuals.

* * * * * * * * * * * *

(k) Exemption for certain dividends of regulated investment companies.

(1) Interest-related dividends.

(A) In general. Except as provided in subparagraph (B), no tax shall be imposed under paragraph (1)(A) of subsection (a) on any interest-related dividend received from a regulated investment company which meets the requirements of section 852(a) for the taxable year with respect to which the dividend is paid.

(B) Exceptions. Subparagraph (A) shall not apply—

(i) to any interest-related dividend received from a regulated investment company by a person to the extent such dividend is attributable to interest (other than interest described in subparagraph (E)(i) or (iii)) received by such company on indebtedness issued by such person or by any corporation or partnership with respect to which such person is a 10-percent shareholder,

(ii) to any interest-related dividend with respect to stock of a regulated investment company unless the person who would otherwise be required to deduct and withhold tax from such dividend under chapter 3 receives a statement (which meets requirements similar to the requirements of subsection (h)(5)) that the beneficial owner of such stock is not a United States person, and

(iii) to any interest-related dividend paid to any person within a foreign country (or any interest-related dividend payment addressed to, or for the account of, persons within such foreign country) during any period described in subsection (h)(6) with respect to such country.

Clause (iii) shall not apply to any dividend with respect to any stock which was acquired on or before the date of the publication of the Secretary's determination under subsection (h)(6).

(C) Interest-related dividend. For purposes of this paragraph—

(i) In general. Except as provided in clause (ii), an interest related dividend is any dividend, or part thereof, which is reported by the company as an interest related dividend in written statements furnished to its shareholders.

(ii) Excess reported amounts. If the aggregate reported amount with respect to the company for any taxable year exceeds the qualified net interest income of the company for such taxable year, an interest related dividend is the excess of—

(I) the reported interest related dividend amount, over

(II) the excess reported amount which is allocable to such reported interest related dividend amount.

(iii) Allocation of excess reported amount.

(I) In general. Except as provided in subclause (II), the excess reported amount (if any) which is allocable to the reported interest related dividend amount is that portion of the excess reported amount which bears the same ratio to the excess reported amount as the reported interest related dividend amount bears to the aggregate reported amount.

(II) Special rule for noncalendar year taxpayers. In the case of any taxable year which does not begin and end in the same calendar year, if the post-December reported amount equals or exceeds the excess reported amount for such taxable year, subclause (I) shall be applied by substituting "post-December reported amount" for "aggregate reported amount" and no excess reported amount shall be allocated to any dividend paid on or before December 31 of such taxable year.

(iv) Definitions. For purposes of this subparagraph—

(I) Reported interest related dividend amount. The term "reported interest related dividend amount" means the amount reported to its shareholders under clause (i) as an interest related dividend.

(II) Excess reported amount. The term "excess reported amount" means the excess of the aggregate reported amount over the qualified net interest income of the company for the taxable year.

(III) Aggregate reported amount. The term "aggregate reported amount" means the aggregate amount of dividends reported by the company under clause (i) as interest related dividends for the taxable year (including interest related dividends paid after the close of the taxable year described in section 855).

(IV) Post-december reported amount. The term "post-December reported amount" means the aggregate reported amount determined by taking into account only dividends paid after December 31 of the taxable year.

(v) Termination. The term "interest related dividend" shall not include any dividend with respect to any taxable year of the company beginning after [1]December 31, 2013.

(D) Qualified net interest income. For purposes of subparagraph (C), the term "qualified net interest income" means the qualified interest income of the regulated investment company reduced by the deductions properly allocable to such income.

(E) Qualified interest income. For purposes of subparagraph (D), the term "qualified interest income" means the sum of the following amounts derived by the regulated investment company from sources within the United States:

(i) Any amount includible in gross income as original issue discount (within the meaning of section 1273) on an obligation payable 183 days or less from the date of original issue (without regard to the period held by the company).

(ii) Any interest includible in gross income (including amounts recognized as ordinary income in respect of original issue discount or market discount or acquisition discount under part V of subchapter P and such other amounts as regulations may provide) on an obligation which is in registered form; except that this clause shall not apply to—

(I) any interest on an obligation issued by a corporation or partnership if the regulated investment company is a 10-percent shareholder in such corporation or partnership, and

(ll) any interest which is treated as not being portfolio interest under the rules of subsection (h)(4).

(iii) Any interest referred to in subsection (i)(2)(A) (without regard to the trade or business of the regulated investment company).

(iv) Any interest-related dividend includable in gross income with respect to stock of another regulated investment company.

(F) 10-percent shareholder. For purposes of this paragraph, the term "10-percent shareholder" has the meaning given such term by subsection (h)(3)(B).

(2)   Short-term capital gain dividends.

(A) In general. Except as provided in subparagraph (B), no tax shall be imposed under paragraph (1)(A) of subsection (a) on any short-term capital gain dividend received from a regulated investment company which meets the requirements of section 852(a) for the taxable year with respect to which the dividend is paid.

(B) Exception for aliens taxable under subsection (a)(2). Subparagraph (A) shall not apply in the case of any nonresident alien individual subject to tax under subsection (a)(2).

(C) Short-term capital gain dividend. For purposes of this paragraph—

(i) In general. Except as provided in clause (ii), the term "short-term capital gain dividend" means any dividend, or part thereof, which is reported by the company as a short-term capital gain dividend in written statements furnished to its shareholders.

(ii) Excess reported amounts. If the aggregate reported amount with respect to the company for any taxable year exceeds the qualified short-term gain of the company for such taxable year, the term "shortterm capital gain dividend" means the excess of—

(I) the reported short-term capital gain dividend amount, over

(II) the excess reported amount which is allocable to such reported short-term capital gain dividend amount.

(iii) Allocation of excess reported amount.

(I) In general. Except as provided in subclause (II), the excess reported amount (if any) which is allocable to the reported short-term capital gain dividend amount is that portion of the excess reported amount which bears the same ratio to the excess reported amount as the reported short-term capital gain dividend amount bears to the aggregate reported amount.

(II) Special rule for noncalendar year taxpayers. In the case of any taxable year which does not begin and end in the same calendar year, if the post-December reported amount equals or exceeds the excess reported amount for such taxable year, subclause (I) shall be applied by substituting "post-December reported amount" for "aggregate reported amount" and no excess reported amount shall be allocated to any dividend paid on or before December 31 of such taxable year.

(iv) Definitions. For purposes of this subparagraph—

(I) Reported short-term capital gain dividend amount. The term "reported short-term capital gain dividend amount" means the amount reported to its shareholders under clause (i) as a short-term capital gain dividend.

(II) Excess reported amount. The term "excess reported amount" means the excess of the aggregate reported amount over the qualified short-term gain of the company for the taxable year.

(III) Aggregate reported amount. The term "aggregate reported amount" means the aggregate amount of dividends reported by the company under clause (i) as short-term capital gain dividends for the taxable year (including short-term capital gain dividends paid after the close of the taxable year described in section 855).

(IV) Post-december reported amount. The term "post-December reported amount" means the aggregate reported amount determined by taking into account only dividends paid after December 31 of the taxable year.

(v) Termination. The term "short-term capital gain dividend" shall not include any dividend with respect to'". any taxable year of the company beginning after [2]*December 31, 2013.*

(D) Qualified short-term gain. For purposes of subparagraph (C), the term "qualified short-term gain" means the excess of the net short-term capital gain of the regulated investment company for the taxable year over the net long-term capital loss (if any) of such company for such taxable year. For purposes of this subparagraph, the net short-term capital gain of the regulated investment company shall be computed by treating any short-term capital gain dividend includible in gross income with respect to stock of another regulated investment company as a short-term capital gain.

(E) Certain distributions. In the case of a distribution to which section 897 does not apply by reason of the second sentence of section 897(h)(1), the amount which would be treated as a short-term capital gain dividend to the shareholder (without regard to this subparagraph)—

(i) shall not be treated as a short-term capital gain dividend, and

(ii) shall be included in such shareholder's gross income as a dividend from the regulated investment company.

* * * * * * * * * * * *

[For Analysis, see ¶ 1205.]

[Endnote Code Sec. 871]

Code Sec. 871(k)(1)(C)(v) and Code Sec. 871(k)(2)(C)(v) were amended by Sec. 320(a) of the American Taxpayer Relief Act of 2012, P.L. 112-240, 1/2/2013, as detailed below:

1. Sec. 320(a) substituted "December 31, 2013" for "December 31, 2011" in clause (k)(1)(C)(v)
2. Sec. 320(a) substituted "December 31, 2013" for "December 31, 2011" in clause (k)(2)(C)(v)

Effective Date (Sec. 320(b), P.L. 112-240, 1/2/2013) effective for tax. yrs. begin. after 12/31/2011.

[¶ 3089]   Code Sec. 897.   Disposition of investment in United States real property.

* * * * * * * * * * * *

(h) **Special rules for certain investment entities.** For purposes of this section—

(1) **Look-through of distributions.** Any distribution by a qualified investment entity to a nonresident alien individual, a foreign corporation, or other qualified investment entity shall, to the extent attributable to gain from sales or exchanges by the qualified investment entity of United States real property interests, be treated as gain recognized by such nonresident alien individual, foreign corporation, or other qualified investment entity from the sale or exchange of a United States real property interest. Notwithstanding the preceding sentence, any distribution by a qualified investment entity to a nonresident alien individual

or a foreign corporation with respect to any class of stock which is regularly traded on an established securities market located in the United States shall not be treated as gain recognized from the sale or exchange of a United States real property interest if such individual or corporation did not own more than 5 percent of such class of stock at any time during the 1-year period ending on the date of such distribution.

(2) Sale of stock in domestically controlled entity not taxed. The term "United States real property interest" does not include any interest in a domestically controlled qualified investment entity.

(3) Distributions by domestically controlled qualified investment entities. In the case of a domestically controlled qualified investment entity, rules similar to the rules of subsection (d) shall apply to the foreign ownership percentage of any gain.

(4) Definitions.

(A) Qualified investment entity.

(i) In general. The term "qualified investment entity" means—

(I) any real estate investment trust, and

(II) any regulated investment company which is a United States real property holding corporation or which would be a United States real property holding corporation if the exceptions provided in subsections (c)(3) and (h)(2) did not apply to interests in any real estate investment trust or regulated investment company .

(ii) Termination. Clause (i)(II) shall not apply after [1]December 31, 2013. Notwithstanding the preceding sentence, an entity described in clause (i)(II) shall be treated as a qualified investment entity for purposes of applying paragraphs (1) and (5) and section 1445 with respect to any distribution by the entity to a nonresident alien individual or a foreign corporation which is attributable directly or indirectly to a distribution to the entity from a real estate investment trust.

(B) Domestically controlled. The term "domestically controlled qualified investment entity" means any qualified investment entity in which at all times during the testing period less than 50 percent in value of the stock was held directly or indirectly by foreign persons.

(C) Foreign ownership percentage. The term "foreign ownership percentage" means that percentage of the stock of the qualified investment entity which was held (directly or indirectly) by foreign persons at the time during the testing period during which the direct and indirect ownership of stock by foreign persons was greatest.

(D) Testing period. The term "testing period" means whichever of the following periods is the shortest:

(i) the period beginning on June 19, 1980, and ending on the date of the disposition or of the distribution, as the case may be,

(ii) the 5-year period ending on the date of the disposition or of the distribution, as the case may be, or

(iii) the period during which the qualified investment entity was in existence.

(5) Treatment of certain wash sale transactions.

(A) In general. If an interest in a domestically controlled qualified investment entity is disposed of in an applicable wash sale transaction, the taxpayer shall, for purposes of this section, be treated as having gain from the sale or exchange of a United States real property interest in an amount equal to the portion of the distribution described in subparagraph (B) with respect to such interest which, but for the disposition, would have been treated by the taxpayer as gain from the sale or exchange of a United States real property interest under paragraph (1).

(B) Applicable wash sales transaction. For purposes of this paragraph—

(i) In general. The term "applicable wash sales transaction" means any transaction (or series of transactions) under which a nonresident alien individual, foreign corporation, or qualified investment entity—

(I) disposes of an interest in a domestically controlled qualified investment entity during the 30-day period preceding the ex-dividend date of a distribution which is to be made with respect to the interest and any portion of which, but for the disposition, would have been treated by the taxpayer as gain from the sale or exchange of a United States real property interest under paragraph (1), and

(II) acquires, or enters into a contract or option to acquire, a substantially identical interest in such entity during the 61-day period beginning with the 1st day of the 30-day period described in subclause (I).

For purposes of subclause (II), a nonresident alien individual, foreign corporation, or qualified investment entity shall be treated as having acquired any interest acquired by a person related (within the meaning of section 267(b) or 707(b)(1)) to the individual, corporation, or entity, and any interest which such person has entered into any contract or option to acquire.

(ii) Application to substitute dividend and similar payments. Subparagraph (A) shall apply to—

(I) any substitute dividend payment (within the meaning of section 861), or

(II) any other similar payment specified in regulations which the Secretary determines necessary to prevent avoidance of the purposes of this paragraph.

The portion of any such payment treated by the taxpayer as gain from the sale or exchange of a United States real property interest under subparagraph (A) by reason of this clause shall be equal to the portion of the distribution such payment is in lieu of which would have been so treated but for the transaction giving rise to such payment.

(iii) Exception where distribution actually received. A transaction shall not be treated as an applicable wash sales transaction if the nonresident alien individual, foreign corporation, or qualified investment entity receives the distribution described in clause (i)(I) with respect to either the interest which was disposed of, or acquired, in the transaction.

(iv) Exception for certain publicly traded stock. A transaction shall not be treated as an applicable wash sales transaction if it involves the disposition of any class of stock in a qualified investment entity which is regularly traded on an established securities market within the United States but only if the nonresident alien individual, foreign corporation, or qualified investment entity did not own more than 5 percent of such class of stock at any time during the 1-year period ending on the date of the distribution described in clause (i)(I).

* * * * * * * * * * * *

[For Analysis, see ¶ 1204.]

[Endnote Code Sec. 897]

Code Sec. 897(h)(4)(A)(ii) was amended by Sec. 321(a) of the American Taxpayer Relief Act of 2012, P.L. 112-240, 1/2/2013, as detailed below:

1. Sec. 321(a) substituted "December 31, 2013" for "December 31, 2011" in clause (h)(4)(A)(ii).

Effective Date (Sec. 321(b), P.L. 112-240, 1/2/2013) effective 1/1/2012. Sec. 321(b) of this Act read as follows:

"(b) Effective date.

"(1) In general. The amendment made by subsection (a) shall take effect on January 1, 2012. Notwithstanding the preceding sentence, such amendment shall not apply with respect to the withholding requirement under section 1445 of the Internal Revenue Code of 1986 for any payment made before the date of the enactment of this Act.

"(2) Amounts withheld on or before date of enactment. In the case of a regulated investment company—

"(A) which makes a distribution after December 31, 2011, and before the date of the enactment of this Act; and

"(B) which would (but for the second sentence of paragraph (1)) have been required to withhold with respect to such distribution under section 1445 of such Code,

"such investment company shall not be liable to any person to whom such distribution was made for any amount so withheld and paid over to the Secretary of the Treasury."

[¶ 3090]　　Code Sec. 904.　　Limitation on credit.

* * * * * * * * * * * *

(h)　Source rules in case of United States-owned foreign corporations.

(1)　In general. The following amounts which are derived from a United States-owned foreign corporation and which would be treated as derived from sources outside the United States without regard to this subsection shall, for purposes of this section, be treated as derived from sources within the United States to the extent provided in this subsection:

(A) Any amount included in gross income under—

(i) section 951(a) (relating to amounts included in gross income of United States shareholders), or

(ii) section 1293 (relating to current taxation of income from qualified funds).

(B) Interest.

(C) Dividends.

(2)　Subpart F and passive foreign investment company inclusions. Any amount described in subparagraph (A) of paragraph (1) shall be treated as derived from sources within the United States to the extent such amount is attributable to income of the United States-owned foreign corporation from sources within the United States.

(3)　Certain interest allocable to United States source income. Any interest which—

(A) is paid or accrued by a United States-owned foreign corporation during any taxable year,

(B) is paid or accrued to a United States shareholder (as defined in section 951(b)) or a related person (within the meaning of section 267(b)) to such a shareholder, and

(C) is properly allocable (under regulations prescribed by the Secretary) to income of such foreign corporation for the taxable year from sources within the United States,

shall be treated as derived from sources within the United States.

(4)　Dividends.

(A) In general. The United States source ratio of any dividend paid or accrued by a United States-owned foreign corporation shall be treated as derived from sources within the United States.

(B) United States source ratio. For purposes of subparagraph (A), the term "United States source ratio" means, with respect to any dividend paid out of the earnings and profits for any taxable year, a fraction—

(i) the numerator of which is the portion of the earnings and profits for such taxable year from sources within the United States, and

(ii) the denominator of which is the total amount of earnings and profits for such taxable year.

(5)　Exception where United States-owned foreign corporation has small amount of United States source income. Paragraph (3) shall not apply to interest paid or accrued during any taxable year (and paragraph (4) shall not apply to any dividends paid out of the earnings and profits for such taxable year) if—

(A) the United States-owned foreign corporation has earnings and profits for such taxable year, and

(B) less than 10 percent of such earnings and profits is attributable to sources within the United States.

For purposes of the preceding sentence, earnings and profits shall be determined without any reduction for interest described in paragraph (3) (determined without regard to subparagraph (C) thereof).

(6)　United States-owned foreign corporation. For purposes of this subsection, the term "United States-owned foreign corporation" means any foreign corporation if 50 percent or more of—

(A) the total combined voting power of all classes of stock of such corporation entitled to vote, or

(B) the total value of the stock of such corporation,

is held directly (or indirectly through applying paragraphs (2) and (3) of section 958(a) and paragraph (4) of section 318(a)) by United States persons (as defined in section 7701(a)(30)).

(7) **Dividend.** For purposes of this subsection, the term "dividend" includes any gain treated as ordinary income under section 1246 or as a dividend under section 1248.

(8) **Coordination with subsection (f).** This subsection shall be applied before subsection (f).

(9) **Treatment of certain domestic corporations.** In the case of any dividend treated as not from sources within the United States under section 861(a)(2)(A), the corporation paying such dividend shall be treated for purposes of this subsection as a United States-owned foreign corporation.

(10) **Coordination with treaties.**

(A) In general. If—

(i) any amount derived from a United States-owned foreign corporation would be treated as derived from sources within the United States under this subsection by reason of an item of income of such United States-owned foreign corporation,

(ii) under a treaty obligation of the United States (applied without regard to this subsection and by treating any amount included in gross income under section 951(a)(1) as a dividend), such amount would be treated as arising from sources outside the United States, and

(iii) the taxpayer chooses the benefits of this paragraph,

this subsection shall not apply to such amount to the extent attributable to such item of income (but subsections (a), (b), and (c) of this section and sections 902, 907, and 960 shall be applied separately with respect to such amount to the extent so attributable).

(B) Special rule. Amounts included in gross income under section 951(a)(1) shall be treated as a dividend under subparagraph (A)(ii) only if dividends paid by each corporation (the stock in which is taken into account in determining whether the shareholder is a United States shareholder in the United States-owned foreign corporation), if paid to the United States shareholder, would be treated under a treaty obligation of the United States as arising from sources outside the United States (applied without regard to this subsection).

(11) **Regulations.** The Secretary shall prescribe such regulations as may be necessary or appropriate for purposes of this subsection, including—

(A) regulations for the application of this subsection in the case of interest or dividend payments through 1 or more entities, and

(B) regulations providing that this subsection shall apply to interest paid or accrued to any person (whether or not a United States shareholder).

[1]*(i)* **Limitation on use of deconsolidation to avoid foreign tax credit limitations.** If 2 or more domestic corporations would be members of the same affiliated group if—

(1) section 1504(b) were applied without regard to the exceptions contained therein, and

(2) the constructive ownership rules of section 1563(e) applied for purposes of section 1504(a),

the Secretary may by regulations provide for resourcing the income of any of such corporations or for modifications to the consolidated return regulations to the extent that such resourcing or modifications are necessary to prevent the avoidance of the provisions of this subpart.

(j) Certain individuals exempt.

(1) **In general.** In the case of an individual to whom this subsection applies for any taxable year—

(A) the limitation of subsection (a) shall not apply,

(B) no taxes paid or accrued by the individual during such taxable year may be deemed paid or accrued under subsection (c) in any other taxable year, and

(C) no taxes paid or accrued by the individual during any other taxable year may be deemed paid or accrued under subsection (c) in such taxable year.

(2) Individuals to whom subsection applies. This subsection shall apply to an individual for any taxable year if—

(A) the entire amount of such individual's gross income for the taxable year from sources without the United States consists of qualified passive income,

(B) the amount of the creditable foreign taxes paid or accrued by the individual during the taxable year does not exceed $300 ($600 in the case of a joint return), and

(C) such individual elects to have this subsection apply for the taxable year.

(3) Definitions. For purposes of this subsection—

(A) Qualified passive income. The term "qualified passive income" means any item of gross income if—

(i) such item of income is passive income (as defined in subsection (d)(2)(B) without regard to clause (iii) thereof), and

(ii) such item of income is shown on a payee statement furnished to the individual.

(B) Creditable foreign taxes. The term "creditable foreign taxes" means any taxes for which a credit is allowable under section 901; except that such term shall not include any tax unless such tax is shown on a payee statement furnished to such individual.

(C) Payee statement. The term "payee statement" has the meaning given to such term by section 6724(d)(2).

(D) Estates and trusts not eligible. This subsection shall not apply to any estate or trust.

(k) Cross references.

(1) For increase of limitation under subsection (a) for taxes paid with respect to amounts received which were included in the gross income of the taxpayer for a prior taxable year as a United States shareholder with respect to a controlled foreign corporation, see section 960(b).

(2) For modification of limitation under subsection (a) for purposes of determining the amount of credit which can be taken against the alternative minimum tax, see section 59(a).

[For Analysis, see ¶ 403.]

[Endnote Code Sec. 904]

Sec. 101(a)(1) of the American Taxpayer Relief Act of 2012, P.L. 112-240, 1/2/2013, deleted Title IX [Sec. 901] of the Economic Growth and Tax Relief Reconciliation Act of 2001, P.L. 107-16, the effect of which is to eliminate the sunset of all provisions enacted by P.L. 107-16.

Effective Date (Sec. 101(a)(3), P.L. 112-240, 1/2/2013) effective for taxable, plan, or limitation years beginning after 12/31/2012, and estates of decedents dying, gifts made, or generation skipping transfers after 12/31/2012.

Following is a description of the amendments made to Code Sec. 904, by P.L. 107-16.

P.L. 107-16, Sec. 201(b)(2)(G), added "(other than section 24)" after "chapter" in subsec. (h), effective for tax. yrs. begin. after 12/31/2001.

P.L. 107-16, Sec. 202(f)(2)(C), substituted "sections 23 and 24" for "section 24" in subsec. (h), as amended by Sec. 201(b)(2)(G) of this Act, see above.

Code Sec. 904(i), Code Sec. 904(j) Code Sec. 904(k), and Code Sec. 904(l) were amended by Sec. 104(c)(2)(K) of the American Taxpayer Relief Act of 2012, P.L. 112-240, 1/2/2013, as detailed below:

1. Sec. 104(c)(2)(k) deleted subsec. (i) and redesignated subsecs. (j)-(l) as (i)-(k)

Prior to deletion subsec. (i) read as follows:

"(i) Coordination with nonrefundable personal credits.

"In the case of any taxable year of an individual to which section 26(a)(2) does not apply, for purposes of subsection (a), the tax against which the credit is taken is such tax reduced by the sum of the credits allowable under subpart A of part IV of subchapter A of this chapter (other than sections 23, 24, 25A(i), 25B, 30, 30B, 30D)."

Effective Date (Sec. 104(d), P.L. 112-240, 1/2/2013) effective for tax. yrs. beginn. after 12/31/2011.

[¶ 3091]   Code Sec. 936.   Puerto Rico and possession tax credit.
   (a)   Allowance of credit.
   (1)   In general. Except as otherwise provided in this section, if a domestic corporation elects the application of this section and if the conditions of both subparagraph (A) and subparagraph (B) of paragraph (2) are satisfied, there shall be allowed as a credit against the tax imposed by this chapter an amount equal to the portion of the tax which is attributable to the sum of—
      (A) the taxable income, from sources without the United States, from—
         (i) the active conduct of a trade or business within a possession of the United States, or
         (ii) the sale or exchange of substantially all of the assets used by the taxpayer in the active conduct of such trade or business, and
      (B) the qualified possession source investment income.
   (2)   Conditions which must be satisfied. The conditions referred to in paragraph (1) are:
      (A) 3-year period. If 80 percent or more of the gross income of such domestic corporation for the 3-year period immediately preceding the close of the taxable year (or for such part of such period immediately preceding the close of such taxable year as may be applicable) was derived from sources within a possession of the United States (determined without regard to subsections (f) and (g) of section 904); and
      (B) Trade or business. If 75 percent or more of the gross income of such domestic corporation for such period or such part thereof was derived from the active conduct of a trade or business within a possession of the United States.
   (3)   Credit not allowed against certain taxes. The credit provided by paragraph (1) shall not be allowed against the tax imposed by—
      (A) section 59A (relating to environmental tax),
      (B) section 531 (relating to the tax on accumulated earnings),
      (C) section 541 (relating to personal holding company tax), or
      (D) section 1351 (relating to recoveries of foreign expropriation losses).
   (4)   Limitations on credit for active business income.
      (A) In general. The amount of the credit determined under paragraph (1) for any taxable year with respect to income referred to in subparagraph (A) thereof shall not exceed the sum of the following amounts:
         (i) 60 percent of the sum of—
            (I) the aggregate amount of the possession corporation's qualified possession wages for such taxable year, plus
            (II) the allocable employee fringe benefit expenses of the possession corporation for the taxable year.
         (ii) The sum of—
            (I) 15 percent of the depreciation allowances for the taxable year with respect to short-life qualified tangible property,
            (II) 40 percent of the depreciation allowances for the taxable year with respect to medium-life qualified tangible property, and
            (III) 65 percent of the depreciation allowances for the taxable year with respect to long-life qualified tangible property.
         (iii) If the possession corporation does not have an election to use the method described in subsection (h)(5)(C)(ii) (relating to profit split) in effect for the taxable year, the amount of the qualified possession income taxes for the taxable year allocable to nonsheltered income.
      (B) Election to take reduced credit.
         (i) In general. If an election under this subparagraph applies to a possession corporation for any taxable year—
            (I) subparagraph (A), and the provisions of subsection (i), shall not apply to such possession corporation for such taxable year, and

(II) the credit determined under paragraph (1) for such taxable year with respect to income referred to in subparagraph (A) thereof shall be the applicable percentage of the credit which would otherwise have been determined under such paragraph with respect to such income.

Notwithstanding subclause (I), a possession corporation to which an election under this subparagraph applies shall be entitled to the benefits of subsection (i)(3)(B) for taxes allocable (on a pro rata basis) to taxable income the tax on which is not offset by reason of this subparagraph.

(ii) Applicable percentage. The term "applicable percentage" means the percentage determined in accordance with the following table:

In the case of taxable years beginning in:	The percentage is:
1994	60
1995	55
1996	50
1997	45
1998 and thereafter	40.

(iii) Election.

(I) In general. An election under this subparagraph by any possession corporation may be made only for the corporation's first taxable year beginning after December 31, 1993, for which it is a possession corporation.

(II) Period of election. An election under this subparagraph shall apply to the taxable year for which made and all subsequent taxable years unless revoked.

(III) Affiliated groups. If, for any taxable year, an election is not in effect for any possession corporation which is a member of an affiliated group, any election under this subparagraph for any other member of such group is revoked for such taxable year and all subsequent taxable years. For purposes of this subclause, members of an affiliated group shall be determined without regard to the exceptions contained in section 1504(b) and as if the constructive ownership rules of section 1563(e) applied for purposes of section 1504(a). The Secretary may prescribe regulations to prevent the avoidance of this subclause through deconsolidation or otherwise.

(C) Cross reference. For definitions and special rules applicable to this paragraph, see subsection (i).

(b) Amounts received in United States. In determining taxable income for purposes of subsection (a), there shall not be taken into account as income from sources without the United States any gross income which was received by such domestic corporation within the United States, whether derived from sources within or without the United States. This subsection shall not apply to any amount described in subsection (a)(1)(A)(i) received from a person who is not a related person (within the meaning of subsection (h)(3) but without regard to subparagraphs (D)(ii) and (E)(i) thereof) with respect to the domestic corporation.

(c) Treatment of certain foreign taxes. For purposes of this title, any tax of a foreign country or a possession of the United States which is paid or accrued with respect to taxable income which is taken into account in computing the credit under subsection (a) shall not be treated as income, war profits, or excess profits taxes paid or accrued to a foreign country or possession of the United States, and no deduction shall be allowed under this title with respect to any amounts so paid or accrued.

(d) Definitions and special rules. For purposes of this section—

(1) Possession. The term "possession of the United States" includes the Commonwealth of Puerto Rico, and the Virgin Islands.

(2) Qualified possession source investment income. The term "qualified possession source investment income" means gross income which—

(A) is from sources within a possession of the United States in which a trade or business is actively conducted, and

(B) the taxpayer establishes to the satisfaction of the Secretary is attributable to the investment in such possession (for use therein) of funds derived from the active conduct of a trade or business in such possession, or from such investment,

less the deductions properly apportioned or allocated thereto.

(3) Carryover basis property.

(A) In general. Income from the sale or exchange of any asset the basis of which is determined in whole or in part by reference to its basis in the hands of another person shall not be treated as income described in subparagraph (A) or (B) of subsection (a)(1).

(B) Exception for possessions corporations, etc. For purposes of subparagraph (A), the holding of any asset by another person shall not be taken into account if throughout the period for which such asset was held by such person section 931, this section, or section 957(c) (as in effect on the day before the date of the enactment [10/22/86] of the Tax Reform Act of 1986) applied to such person.

(4) Investment in qualified Caribbean Basin countries.

(A) In general. For purposes of paragraph (2)(B), an investment in a financial institution shall, subject to such conditions as the Secretary may prescribe by regulations, be treated as for use in Puerto Rico to the extent used by such financial institution (or by the Government Development Bank for Puerto Rico or the Puerto Rico Economic Development Bank)—

(i) for investment, consistent with the goals and purposes of the Caribbean Basin Economic Recovery Act, in—

(I) active business assets in a qualified Caribbean Basin country, or

(II) development projects in a qualified Caribbean Basin country, and

(ii) in accordance with a specific authorization granted by the Commissioner of Financial Institutions of Puerto Rico pursuant to regulations issued by such Commissioner.

A similar rule shall apply in the case of a direct investment in the Government Development Bank for Puerto Rico or the Puerto Rico Economic Development Bank.

(B) Qualified Caribbean Basin country. For purposes of this subsection, the term "qualified Caribbean Basin country" means any beneficiary country (within the meaning of section 212(a)(1)(A) of the Caribbean Basin Economic Recovery Act) which meets the requirements of clauses (i) and (ii) of section 274(h)(6)(A) and the Virgin Islands.

(C) Additional requirements. Subparagraph (A) shall not apply to any investment made by a financial institution (or by the Government Development Bank for Puerto Rico or the Puerto Rico Economic Development Bank) unless—

(i) the person in whose trade or business such investment is made (or such other recipient of the investment) and the financial institution or such Bank certify to the Secretary and the Commissioner of Financial Institutions of Puerto Rico that the proceeds of the loan will be promptly used to acquire active business assets or to make other authorized expenditures, and

(ii) the financial institution (or the Government Development Bank for Puerto Rico or the Puerto Rico Economic Development Bank) and the recipient of the investment funds agree to permit the Secretary and the Commissioner of Financial Institutions of Puerto Rico to examine such of their books and records as may be necessary to ensure that the requirements of this paragraph are met.

(D) Requirement for investment in Caribbean Basin countries.

(i) In general. For each calendar year, the government of Puerto Rico shall take such steps as may be necessary to ensure that at least $100,000,000 of qualified Caribbean Basin country investments are made during such calendar year.

(ii) Qualified Caribbean Basin country investment. For purposes of clause (i), the term "qualified Caribbean Basin country investment" means any investment if—

(I) the income from such investment is treated as qualified possession source investment income by reason of subparagraph (A), and

723

(II) such investment is not (directly or indirectly) a refinancing of a prior investment (whether or not such prior investment was a qualified Caribbean Basin country investment).

(e)   Election.

(1)   Period of election. The election provided in subsection (a) shall be made at such time and in such manner as the Secretary may by regulations prescribe. Any such election shall apply to the first taxable year for which such election was made and for which the domestic corporation satisfied the conditions of subparagraphs (A) and (B) of subsection (a)(2) and for each taxable year thereafter until such election is revoked by the domestic corporation under paragraph (2). If any such election is revoked by the domestic corporation under paragraph (2), such domestic corporation may make a subsequent election under subsection (a) for any taxable year thereafter for which such domestic corporation satisfies the conditions of subparagraphs (A) and (B) of subsection (a)(2) and any such subsequent election shall remain in effect until revoked by such domestic corporation under paragraph (2).

(2)   Revocation. An election under subsection (a)—

(A) may be revoked for any taxable year beginning before the expiration of the 9th taxable year following the taxable year for which such election first applies only with the consent of the Secretary; and

(B) may be revoked for any taxable year beginning after the expiration of such 9th taxable year without the consent of the Secretary.

(f)   Limitation on credit for DISC's and FSC's. No credit shall be allowed under this section to a corporation for any taxable year—

(1) for which it is a DISC or former DISC, or

(2) in which it owns at any time stock in a—

(A) DISC or former DISC, or

(B) [1]former FSC.

(g)   Exception to accumulated earnings tax.

(1) For purposes of section 535, the term "accumulated taxable income" shall not include taxable income entitled to the credit under subsection (a).

(2) For purposes of section 537, the term "reasonable needs of the business" includes assets which produce income eligible for the credit under subsection (a).

(h)   Tax treatment of intangible property income.

(1)   In general.

(A) Income attributable to shareholders. The intangible property income of a corporation electing the application of this section for any taxable year shall be included on a pro rata basis in the gross income of all shareholders of such electing corporation at the close of the taxable year of such electing corporation as income from sources within the United States for the taxable year of such shareholder in which or with which the taxable year of such electing corporation ends.

(B) Exclusion from the income of an electing corporation. Any intangible property income of a corporation electing the application of this section which is included in the gross income of a shareholder of such corporation by reason of subparagraph (A) shall be excluded from the gross income of such corporation.

(2)   Foreign shareholders; shareholders not subject to tax.

(A) In general. Paragraph (1)(A) shall not apply with respect to any shareholder—

(i) who is not a United States person, or

(ii) who is not subject to tax under this title on intangible property income which would be allocated to such shareholder (but for this subparagraph).

(B) Treatment of nonallocated intangible property income. For purposes of this subtitle, intangible property income of a corporation electing the application of this section which is not included in the gross income of a shareholder of such corporation by reason of subparagraph (A)—

(i) shall be treated as income from sources within the United States, and

(ii) shall not be taken into account under subsection (a)(2).

724

(3) **Intangible property income.** For purposes of this subsection—

(A) In general. The term "intangible property income" means the gross income of a corporation attributable to any intangible property other than intangible property which has been licensed to such corporation since prior to 1948 and is in use by such corporation on the date of the enactment of this subparagraph.

(B) Intangible property. The term "intangible property" means any—

(i) patent, invention, formula, process, design, pattern, or know-how;

(ii) copyright, literary, musical, or artistic composition;

(iii) trademark, trade name, or brand name;

(iv) franchise, license, or contract;

(v) method, program, system, procedure, campaign, survey, study, forecast, estimate, customer list, or technical data; or

(vi) any similar item,

which has substantial value independent of the services of any individual.

(C) Exclusion of reasonable profit. The term "intangible property income" shall not include any portion of the income from the sale, exchange or other disposition of any product, or from the rendering of services, by a corporation electing the application of this section which is determined by the Secretary to be a reasonable profit on the direct and indirect costs incurred by such electing corporation which are attributable to such income.

(D) Related person.

(i) In general. A person (hereinafter referred to as the "related person") is related to any person if—

(I) the related person bears a relationship to such person specified in section 267(b) or section 707(b)(1), or

(II) the related person and such person are members of the same controlled group of corporations.

(ii) Special rule. For purposes of clause (i), section 267(b) and section 707(b)(1) shall be applied by substituting "10 percent" for "50 percent".

(E) Controlled group of corporations. The term "controlled group of corporations" has the meaning given to such term by section 1563(a), except that—

(i) "more than 10 percent" shall be substituted for "at least 80 percent" and "more than 50 percent" each place either appears in section 1563(a), and

(ii) the determination shall be made without regard to subsections (a)(4), (b)(2), and (e)(3)(C) of section 1563.

(4) **Distributions to meet qualification requirements.**

(A) In general. If the Secretary determines that a corporation does not satisfy a condition specified in subparagraph (A) or (B) of subsection (a)(2) for any taxable year by reason of the exclusion from gross income under paragraph (1)(B), such corporation shall nevertheless be treated as satisfying such condition for such year if it makes a pro rata distribution of property after the close of such taxable year to its shareholders (designated at the time of such distribution as a distribution to meet qualification requirements) with respect to their stock in an amount which is equal to—

(i) if the condition of subsection (a)(2)(A) is not satisfied, that portion of the gross income for the period described in subsection (a)(2)(A)—

(I) which was not derived from sources within a possession, and

(II) which exceeds the amount of such income for such period which would enable such corporation to satisfy the condition of subsection (a)(2)(A),

(ii) if the condition of subsection (a)(2)(B) is not satisfied, that portion of the gross income for such period—

(I) which was not derived from the active conduct of a trade or business within a possession, and

(II) which exceeds the amount of such income for such period which would enable such corporation to satisfy the conditions of subsection (a)(2)(B), or

(iii) if neither of such conditions is satisfied, that portion of the gross income which exceeds the amount of gross income for such period which would enable such corporation to satisfy the conditions of subparagraphs (A) and (B) of subsection (a)(2).

(B) Effectively connected income. In the case of a shareholder who is a nonresident alien individual or a foreign corporation, trust, or estate, any distribution described in subparagraph (A) shall be treated as income which is effectively connected with the conduct of a trade or business conducted through a permanent establishment of such shareholder within the United States.

(C) Distribution denied in case of fraud or willful neglect. Subparagraph (A) shall not apply to a corporation if the determination of the Secretary described in subparagraph (A) contains a finding that the failure of such corporation to satisfy the conditions in subsection (a)(2) was due in whole or in part to fraud with intent to evade tax or willful neglect on the part of such corporation.

(5) Election out.

(A) In general. The rules contained in paragraphs (1) through (4) do not apply for any taxable year if an election pursuant to subparagraph (F) is in effect to use one of the methods specified in subparagraph (C).

(B) Eligibility.

(i) Requirement of significant business presence. An election may be made to use one of the methods specified in subparagraph (C) with respect to a product or type of service only if an electing corporation has a significant business presence in a possession with respect to such product or type of service. An election may remain in effect with respect to such product or type of service for any subsequent taxable year only if such electing corporation maintains a significant business presence in a possession with respect to such product or type of service in such subsequent taxable year. If an election is not in effect for a taxable year because of the preceding sentence, the electing corporation shall be deemed to have revoked the election on the first day of such taxable year.

(ii) Definition. For purposes of this subparagraph, an electing corporation has a "significant business presence" in a possession for a taxable year with respect to a product or type of service if:

(I) the total production costs (other than direct material costs and other than interest excluded by regulations prescribed by the Secretary) incurred by the electing corporation in the possession in producing units of that product sold or otherwise disposed of during the taxable year by the affiliated group to persons who are not members of the affiliated group are not less than 25 percent of the difference between (a) the gross receipts from sales or other dispositions during the taxable year by the affiliated group to persons who are not members of the affiliated group of such units of the product produced, in whole or in part, by the electing corporation in the possession, and (b) the direct material costs of the purchase of materials for such units of that product by all members of the affiliated group from persons who are not members of the affiliated group; or

(II) no less than 65 percent of the direct labor costs of the affiliated group for units of the product produced during the taxable year in whole or in part by the electing corporation or for the type of service rendered by the electing corporation during the taxable year, is incurred by the electing corporation and is compensation for services performed in the possession; or

(III) with respect to purchases and sales by an electing corporation of all goods not produced in whole or in part by any member of the affiliated group and sold by the electing corporation to persons other than members of the affiliated group, no less than 65 percent of the total direct labor costs of the affiliated group in connection with all purchases and sales of such goods sold during the taxable year by such electing corporation is incurred by such electing corporation and is compensation for services performed in the possession.

Notwithstanding satisfaction of one of the foregoing tests, an electing corporation shall not be treated as having a significant business presence in a possession with respect to a product produced in whole or in part by the electing corporation in the possession, for purposes of an election to use the method specified in subparagraph (C)(ii), unless such product is manufactured or produced in the possession by the electing corporation within the meaning of subsection (d)(1)(A) of section 954.

(iii) Special rules.

(I) An electing corporation which produces a product or renders a type of service in a possession on the date of the enactment of this clause is not required to meet the significant business presence test in a possession with respect to such product or type of service for its taxable years beginning before January 1, 1986.

(II) For purposes of this subparagraph, the costs incurred by an electing corporation or any other member of the affiliated group in connection with contract manufacturing by a person other than a member of the affiliated group, or in connection with a similar arrangement thereto, shall be treated as direct labor costs of the affiliated group and shall not be treated as production costs incurred by the electing corporation in the possession or as direct material costs or as compensation for services performed in the possession, except to the extent as may be otherwise provided in regulations prescribed by the Secretary.

(iv) Regulations. The Secretary may prescribe regulations setting forth:

(I) an appropriate transitional (but not in excess of three taxable years) significant business presence test for commencement in a possession of operations with respect to products or types of service after the date of the enactment of this clause and not described in subparagraph (B)(iii)(I),

(II) a significant business presence test for other appropriate cases, consistent with the tests specified in subparagraph (B)(ii),

(III) rules for the definition of a product or type of service, and

(IV) rules for treating components produced in whole or in part by a related person as materials, and the costs (including direct labor costs) related thereto as a cost of materials, where there is an independent resale price for such components or where otherwise consistent with the intent of the substantial business presence tests.

(C) Methods of computation of taxable income. If an election of one of the following methods is in effect pursuant to subparagraph (F) with respect to a product or type of service, an electing corporation shall compute its income derived from the active conduct of a trade or business in a possession with respect to such product or type of service in accordance with the method which is elected.

(i) Cost sharing.

(I) Payment of cost sharing. If an election of this method is in effect, the electing corporation must make a payment for its share of the cost (if any) of product area research which is paid or accrued by the affiliated group during that taxable year. Such share shall not be less than the same proportion of 110 percent of the cost of such product area research which the amount of "possession sales" bears to the amount of "total sales" of the affiliated group. The cost of product area research paid or accrued solely by the electing corporation in a taxable year (excluding amounts paid directly or indirectly to or on behalf of related persons and excluding amounts paid under any cost sharing agreements with related persons) will reduce (but not below zero) the amount of the electing corporation's cost sharing payment under this method for that year. In the case of intangible property described in subsection (h)(3)(B)(i) which the electing corporation is treated as owning under subclause (II), in no event shall the payment required under this subclause be less than the inclusion or payment which would be required under section 367(d)(2)(A)(ii) or section 482 if the electing corporation were a foreign corporation.

(a) Product area research. For purposes of this section, the term "product area research" includes (notwithstanding any provision to the contrary) the research, development and experimental costs, losses, expenses and other related deductions—including amounts paid or accrued for the performance of research or similar activities by another person; qualified research expenses within the meaning of section 41(b); amounts paid or accrued for the use of, or the right to use, research or any of the items specified in subsection (h)(3)(B)(i); and a proper allowance for amounts incurred for the acquisition of any of the items specified in subsection (h)(3)(B)(i)—which are properly apportioned or allocated to the same product area as that in which the electing corporation conducts its activities, and a ratable part of any such costs, losses, expenses and other deductions which cannot definitely be allocated to a particular product area.

(b) Affiliated group. For purposes of this subsection, the term "affiliated group" shall mean the electing corporation and all other organizations, trades or businesses (whether or not incorporated, whether or not organized in the United States, and whether or not affiliated) owned or controlled directly or indirectly by the same interests, within the meaning of section 482.

(c) Possession sales. For purposes of this section, the term "possession sales" means the aggregate sales or other dispositions for the taxable year to persons who are not members of the affiliated group by members of the affiliated group of products produced, in whole or in part, by the electing corporation in the possession which are in the same product area as is used for determining the amount of product area research, and of services rendered, in whole or in part, in the possession in such product area to persons who are not members of the affiliated group.

(d) Total sales. For purposes of this section, the term "total sales" means the aggregate sales or other dispositions for the taxable year to persons who are not members of the affiliated group by members of the affiliated group of all products in the same product area as is used for determining the amount of product area research, and of services rendered in such product area to persons who are not members of the affiliated group.

(e) Product area. For purposes of this section, the term "product area" shall be defined by reference to the three-digit classification of the Standard Industrial Classification code. The Secretary may provide for the aggregation of two or more three-digit classifications where appropriate, and for a classification system other than the Standard Industrial Classification code in appropriate cases.

(II) Effect of election. For purposes of determining the amount of its gross income derived from the active conduct of a trade or business in a possession with respect to a product produced by, or type of service rendered by, the electing corporation for a taxable year, if an election of this method is in effect, the electing corporation shall be treated as the owner (for purposes of obtaining a return thereon) of intangible property described in subsection (h)(3)(B)(i) which is related to the units of the product produced, or type of service rendered, by the electing corporation. Such electing corporation shall not be treated as the owner (for purposes of obtaining a return thereon) of any intangible property described in subsection (h)(3)(B)(ii) through (v) (to the extent not described in subsection (h)(3)(B)(i)) or of any other nonmanufacturing intangible. Notwithstanding the preceding sentence, an electing corporation shall be treated as the owner (for purposes of obtaining a return thereon) of (a) intangible property which was developed solely by such corporation in a possession and is owned by such corporation, (b) intangible property described in subsection (h)(3)(B)(i) acquired by such corporation from a person who was not related to such corporation (or to any person related to such corporation) at the time of, or in connection with, such acquisition, and (c) any intangible property described in subsection (h)(3)(B)(ii) through (v) (to the extent not described in subsection (h)(3)(B)(i)) and other nonmanufacturing intangibles which relate to sales of units of products, or services rendered, to unrelated persons for ultimate consumption or use in the possession in which the electing corporation conducts its trade or business.

(III) Payment provisions.

(a) The cost sharing payment determined under subparagraph (C)(i)(I) for any taxable year shall be made to the person or persons specified in subparagraph (C)(i)(IV)(a) not later than the time prescribed by law for filing the electing corporation's return for such taxable year (including any extensions thereof). If all or part of such payment is not timely made, the amount of the cost sharing payment required to be paid shall be increased by the amount of interest that would have been due under section 6601(a) had the portion of the cost sharing payment that is not timely made been an amount of tax imposed by this title and had the last date prescribed for payment been the due date of the electing corporations return (determined without regard to any extension thereof). The amount by which a cost sharing payment determined under subparagraph (C)(i)(I) is increased by reason of the preceding sentence shall not be treated as a cost sharing payment or as interest. If failure to make timely payment is due in whole or in part to fraud or willful neglect, the electing corporation shall be deemed to have revoked the election made under subparagraph (A) on the first day of the taxable year for which the cost sharing payment was required.

(b) For purposes of this title, any tax of a foreign country or possession of the United States which is paid or accrued with respect to the payment or receipt of a cost sharing payment determined under subparagraph (C)(i)(I) or of an amount of increase referred to in subparagraph (C)(i)(III)(a) shall not be treated as income, war profits, or excess profits taxes paid or accrued to a foreign country or possession of the United States, and no deduction shall be allowed under this title with respect to any amounts of such tax so paid or accrued.

(IV) Special rules.

(a) The amount of the cost sharing payment determined under subparagraph (C)(i)(I), and any increase in the amount thereof in accordance with subparagraph (C)(i)(III)(a), shall not be treated as income of the recipient, but shall reduce the amount of the deductions (and the amount of reductions in earnings and profits) otherwise allowable to the appropriate domestic member or members (other than an electing corporation) of the affiliated group, or, if there is no such domestic member, to the foreign member or members of such affiliated group as the Secretary may provide under regulations.

(b) If an election of this method is in effect, the electing corporation shall determine its intercompany pricing under the appropriate section 482 method, provided, however, that an electing corporation shall not be denied use of the resale price method for purposes of such intercompany pricing merely because the reseller adds more than an insubstantial amount to the value of the product by the use of intangible property.

(c) The amount of qualified research expenses, within the meaning of section 41, of any member of the controlled group of corporations (as defined in section 41(f)) of which the electing corporation is a member shall not be affected by the cost sharing payment required under this method.

(ii) Profit split.

(I) General rule. If an election of this method is in effect, the electing corporation's taxable income derived from the active conduct of a trade or business in a possession with respect to units of a product produced or type of service rendered, in whole or in part, by the electing corporation shall be equal to 50 percent of the combined taxable income of the affiliated group (other than foreign affiliates) derived from covered sales of units of the product produced or type of service rendered, in whole or in part, by the electing corporation in a possession.

(II) Computation of combined taxable income. Combined taxable income shall be computed separately for each product produced or type of service rendered, in

729

whole or in part, by the electing corporation in a possession. Combined taxable income shall be computed (notwithstanding any provision to the contrary) for each such product or type of service rendered by deducting from the gross income of the affiliated group (other than foreign affiliates) derived from covered sales of such product or type of service all expenses, losses, and other deductions properly apportioned or allocated to gross income from such sales or services, and a ratable part of all expenses, losses, or other deductions which cannot definitely be allocated to some item or class of gross income, which are incurred by the affiliated group (other than foreign affiliates). Notwithstanding any other provision to the contrary, in computing the combined taxable income for each such product or type of service rendered, the research, development, and experimental costs, expenses and related deductions for the taxable year which would otherwise be apportioned or allocated to the gross income of the affiliated group (other than foreign affiliates) derived from covered sales of such product produced or type of service rendered, in whole or in part, by the electing corporation in a possession, shall not be less than the same proportion of the amount of the share of product area research determined under subparagraph (C)(i)(I) (without regard to the third and fourth sentences thereof, but substituting "120 percent" for "110 percent" in the second sentence thereof) in the product area which includes such product or type of service, that such gross income from the product or type of service bears to such gross income from all products and types of services, within such product area, produced or rendered, in whole or part, by the electing corporation in a possession.

(III) Division of combined taxable income. 50 percent of the combined taxable income computed as provided in subparagraph (C)(ii)(II) shall be allocated to the electing corporation. Combined taxable income, computed without regard to the last sentence of subparagraph (C)(ii)(II), less the amount allocated to the electing corporation under the preceding sentence, shall be allocated to the appropriate domestic member or members (other than any electing corporation) of the affiliated group and shall be treated as income from sources within the United States, or, if there is no such domestic member, to a foreign member or members of such affiliated group as the Secretary may provide under regulations.

(IV) Covered sales. For purposes of this paragraph, the term "covered sales" means sales by members of the affiliated group (other than foreign affiliates) to persons who are not members of the affiliated group or to foreign affiliates.

(D) Unrelated person. For purposes of this paragraph, the term "unrelated person" means any person other than a person related within the meaning of paragraph (3)(D) to the electing corporation.

(E) Electing corporation. For purposes of this subsection, the term "electing corporation" means a domestic corporation for which an election under this section is in effect.

(F) Time and manner of election; revocation.

(i) In general. An election under subparagraph (A) to use one of the methods under subparagraph (C) shall be made only on or before the due date prescribed by law (including extensions) for filing the tax return of the electing corporation for its first taxable year beginning after December 31, 1982. If an election of one of such methods is made, such election shall be binding on the electing corporation and such method must be used for each taxable year thereafter until such election is revoked by the electing corporation under subparagraph (F)(iii). If any such election is revoked by the electing corporation under subparagraph (F)(iii), such electing corporation may make a subsequent election under subparagraph (A) only with the consent of the Secretary.

(ii) Manner of making election. An election under subparagraph (A) to use one of the methods under subparagraph (C) shall be made by filing a statement to such effect with the return referred to in subparagraph (F)(i) or in such other manner as the Secretary may prescribe by regulations.

(iii) Revocation.

(I) Except as provided in subparagraph (F)(iii)(II), an election may be revoked for any taxable year only with the consent of the Secretary.

(II) An election shall be deemed revoked for the year in which the electing corporation is deemed to have revoked such election under subparagraph (B)(i) or (C)(i)(III)(a).

(iv) Aggregation.

(I) Where more than one electing corporation in the affiliated group produces any product or renders any services in the same product area, all such electing corporations must elect to compute their taxable income under the same method under subparagraph (C).

(II) All electing corporations in the same affiliated group that produce any products or render any services in the same product area may elect, subject to such terms and conditions as the Secretary may prescribe by regulations, to compute their taxable income from export sales under a different method from that used for all other sales and services. For this purpose, export sales means all sales by the electing corporation of products to foreign persons for use or consumption outside the United States and its possessions, provided such products are manufactured or produced in the possession within the meaning of subsection (d)(1)(A) of section 954, and further provided (except to the extent otherwise provided by regulations) the income derived by such foreign person on resale of such products (in the same state or in an altered state) is not included in foreign base company income for purposes of section 954(a).

(III) All members of an affiliated group must consent to an election under this subsection at such time and in such manner as shall be prescribed by the Secretary by regulations.

(6) Treatment of certain sales made after July 1, 1982.

(A) In general. For purposes of this section, in the case of a disposition of intangible property made by a corporation after July 1, 1982, any gain or loss from such disposition shall be treated as gain or loss from sources within the United States to which paragraph (5) does not apply.

(B) Exception. Subparagraph (A) shall not apply to any disposition by a corporation of intangible property if such disposition is to a person who is not a related person to such corporation.

(C) Paragraph does not affect eligibility. This paragraph shall not apply for purposes of determining whether the corporation meets the requirements of subsection (a)(2).

(7) Section 864(e)(1) not to apply. This subsection shall be applied as if section 864(e)(1) (relating to treatment of affiliated groups) had not been enacted.

(8) Regulations. The Secretary shall prescribe such regulations as may be necessary or appropriate to carry out the purposes of this subsection, including rules for the application of this subsection to income from leasing of products to unrelated persons.

(i) Definitions and special rules relating to limitations of subsection (a)(4).

(1) Qualified possession wages. For purposes of this section—

(A) In general. The term "qualified possession wages" means wages paid or incurred by the possession corporation during the taxable year in connection with the active conduct of a trade or business within a possession of the United States to any employee for services performed in such possession, but only if such services are performed while the principal place of employment of such employee is within such possession.

(B) Limitation on amount of wages taken into account.

(i) In general. The amount of wages which may be taken into account under subparagraph (A) with respect to any employee for any taxable year shall not exceed 85 percent of the contribution and benefit base determined under section 230 of the Social Security Act for the calendar year in which such taxable year begins.

(ii) Treatment of part-time employees, etc. If—

(I) any employee is not employed by the possession corporation on a substantially full-time basis at all times during the taxable year, or

(II) the principal place of employment of any employee with the possession corporation is not within a possession at all times during the taxable year,

the limitation applicable under clause (i) with respect to such employee shall be the appropriate portion (as determined by the Secretary) of the limitation which would otherwise be in effect under clause (i).

(C) Treatment of certain employees. The term "qualified possession wages" shall not include any wages paid to employees who are assigned by the employer to perform services for another person, unless the principal trade or business of the employer is to make employees available for temporary periods to other persons in return for compensation. All possession corporations treated as 1 corporation under paragraph (5) shall be treated as 1 employer for purposes of the preceding sentence.

(D) Wages.

(i) In general. Except as provided in clause (ii), the term "wages" has the meaning given to such term by subsection (b) of section 3306 (determined without regard to any dollar limitation contained in such section). For purposes of the preceding sentence, such subsection (b) shall be applied as if the term "United States" included all possession of the United States.

(ii) Special rule for agricultural labor and railway labor. In any case to which subparagraph (A) or (B) of paragraph (1) of section 51(h) applies, the term "wages" has the meaning given to such term by section 51(h)(2).

(2) Allocable employee fringe benefit expenses.

(A) In general. The allocable employee fringe benefit expenses of any possession corporation for any taxable year is an amount which bears the same ratio to the amount determined under subparagraph (B) for such taxable year as—

(i) the aggregate amount of the possession corporation's qualified possession wages for such taxable year, bears to

(ii) the aggregate amount of the wages paid or incurred by such possession corporation during such taxable year.

In no event shall the amount determined under the preceding sentence exceed 15 percent of the amount referred to in clause (i).

(B) Expenses taken into account. For purposes of subparagraph (A), the amount determined under this subparagraph for any taxable year is the aggregate amount allowable as a deduction under this chapter to the possession corporation for such taxable year with respect to—

(i) employer contributions under a stock bonus, pension, profit-sharing, or annuity plan,

(ii) employer-provided coverage under any accident or health plan for employees, and

(iii) the cost of life or disability insurance provided to employees.

Any amount treated as wages under paragraph (1)(D) shall not be taken into account under this subparagraph.

(3) Treatment of possession taxes.

(A) Amount of credit for possession corporations not using profit split.

(i) In general. For purposes of subsection (a)(4)(A)(iii), the amount of the qualified possession income taxes for any taxable year allocable to nonsheltered income shall be an amount which bears the same ratio to the possession income taxes for such taxable years as—

(I) the increase in the tax liability of the possession corporation under this chapter for the taxable year by reason of subsection (a)(4)(A) (without regard to clause (iii) thereof), bears to

(II) the tax liability of the possession corporation under this chapter for the taxable year determined without regard to the credit allowable under this section.

(ii) Limitation on amount of taxes taken into account. Possession income taxes shall not be taken into account under clause (i) for any taxable year to the extent that the amount of such taxes exceeds 9 percent of the amount of the taxable income for such taxable year.

(B) Deduction for possession corporations using profit split. Notwithstanding subsection (c), if a possession corporation is not described in subsection (a)(4)(A)(iii) for the taxable year, such possession corporation shall be allowed a deduction for such taxable year in an amount which bears the same ratio to the possession income taxes for such taxable year as—

(i) the increase in the tax liability of the possession corporation under this chapter for the taxable year by reason of subsection (a)(4)(A), bears to

(ii) the tax liability of the possession corporation under this chapter for the taxable year determined without regard to the credit allowable under this section.

In determining the credit under subsection (a) and in applying the preceding sentence, taxable income shall be determined without regard to the preceding sentence.

(C) Possession income taxes. For purposes of this paragraph, the term "possession income taxes" means any taxes of a possession of the United States which are treated as not being income, war profits, or excess profits taxes paid or accrued to a possession of the United States by reason of subsection (c).

(4) **Depreciation rules.** For purposes of this section—

(A) Depreciation allowances. The term "depreciation allowances" means the depreciation deductions allowable under section 167 to the possession corporation.

(B) Categories of property.

(i) Qualified tangible property. The term "qualified tangible property" means any tangible property used by the possession corporation in a possession of the United States in the active conduct of a trade or business within such possession.

(ii) Short-life qualified tangible property. The term "short-life qualified tangible property" means any qualified tangible property to which section 168 applies and which is 3-year property or 5-year property for purposes of such section.

(iii) Medium-life qualified tangible property. The term "medium-life qualified tangible property" means any qualified tangible property to which section 168 applies and which is a 7-year property or 10-year property for purposes of such section.

(iv) Long-life qualified tangible property. The term "long-life qualified tangible property" means any qualified tangible property to which section 168 applies and which is not described in clause (ii) or (iii).

(v) Transitional rule. In the case of any qualified tangible property to which section 168 (as in effect on the day before the date of the enactment [10/22/86] of the Tax Reform Act of 1986) applies, any reference in this paragraph to section 168 shall be treated as a reference to such section as so in effect.

(5) **Election to compute credit on consolidated basis.**

(A) In general. Any affiliated group may elect to treat all possession corporations which would be members of such group but for section 1504(b)(3) or (4) as 1 corporation for purposes of this section. The credit determined under this section with respect to such 1 corporation shall be allocated among such possession corporations in such manner as the Secretary may prescribe.

(B) Election. An election under subparagraph (A) shall apply to the taxable year for which made and all succeeding taxable years unless revoked with the consent of the Secretary.

(6) **Possession corporation.** The term "possession corporation" means a domestic corporation for which the election provided in subsection (a) is in effect.

(j) **Termination.**

(1) **In general.** Except as otherwise provided in this subsection, this section shall not apply to any taxable year beginning after December 31, 1995.

(2) **Transition rules for active business income credit.** Except as provided in paragraph (3)—

(A) Economic activity credit. In the case of an existing credit claimant—

(i) with respect to a possession other than Puerto Rico, and

(ii) to which subsection (a)(4)(B) does not apply,

the credit determined under subsection (a)(1)(A) shall be allowed for taxable years beginning after December 31, 1995, and before January 1, 2002.

(B) Special rule for reduced credit.

(i) In general. In the case of an existing credit claimant to which subsection (a)(4)(B) applies, the credit determined under subsection (a)(1)(A) shall be allowed for taxable years beginning after December 31, 1995, and before January 1, 1998.

(ii) Election irrevocable after 1997. An election under subsection (a)(4)(B)(iii) which is in effect for the taxpayer's last taxable year beginning before 1997 may not be revoked unless it is revoked for the taxpayer's first taxable year beginning in 1997 and all subsequent taxable years.

(C) Economic activity credit for Puerto Rico. For economic activity credit for Puerto Rico, see section 30A.

(3) Additional restricted credit.

(A) In general. In the case of an existing credit claimant—

(i) the credit under subsection (a)(1)(A) shall be allowed for the period beginning with the first taxable year after the last taxable year to which subparagraph (A) or (B) of paragraph (2), whichever is appropriate, applied and ending with the last taxable year beginning before January 1, 2006, except that

(ii) the aggregate amount of taxable income taken into account under subsection (a)(1)(A) for any such taxable year shall not exceed the adjusted base period income of such claimant.

(B) Coordination with subsection (a)(4). The amount of income described in subsection (a)(1)(A) which is taken into account in applying subsection (a)(4) shall be such income as reduced under this paragraph.

(4) Adjusted base period income. For purposes of paragraph (3)—

(A) In general. The term "adjusted base period income" means the average of the inflation-adjusted possession incomes of the corporation for each base period year.

(B) Inflation-adjusted possession income. For purposes of subparagraph (A), the inflation-adjusted possession income of any corporation for any base period year shall be an amount equal to the sum of—

(i) the possession income of such corporation for such base period year, plus

(ii) such possession income multiplied by the inflation adjustment percentage for such base period year.

(C) Inflation adjustment percentage. For purposes of subparagraph (B), the inflation adjustment percentage for any base period year means the percentage (if any) by which—

(i) the CPI for 1995, exceeds

(ii) the CPI for the calendar year in which the base period year for which the determination is being made ends.

For purposes of the preceding sentence, the CPI for any calendar year is the CPI (as defined in section 1(f)(5)) for such year under section 1(f)(4).

(D) Increase in inflation adjustment percentage for growth during base years. The inflation adjustment percentage (determined under subparagraph (C) without regard to this subparagraph) for each of the 5 taxable years referred to in paragraph (5)(A) shall be increased by—

(i) 5 percentage points in the case of a taxable year ending during the 1-year period ending on October 13, 1995;

(ii) 10.25 percentage points in the case of a taxable year ending during the 1-year period ending on October 13, 1994;

(iii) 15.76 percentage points in the case of a taxable year ending during the 1-year period ending on October 13, 1993;

(iv) 21.55 percentage points in the case of a taxable year ending during the 1-year period ending on October 13, 1992; and

(v) 27.63 percentage points in the case of a taxable year ending during the 1-year period ending on October 13, 1991.

(5)   Base period year. For purposes of this subsection—

(A) In general. The term "base period year" means each of 3 taxable years which are among the 5 most recent taxable years of the corporation ending before October 14, 1995, determined by disregarding—

(i) one taxable year for which the corporation had the largest inflation-adjusted possession income, and

(ii) one taxable year for which the corporation had the smallest inflation-adjusted possession income.

(B) Corporations not having significant possession income throughout 5-year period.

(i) In general. If a corporation does not have significant possession income for each of the most recent 5 taxable years ending before October 14, 1995, then, in lieu of applying subparagraph (A), the term "base period year" means only those taxable years (of such taxable years) for which the corporation has significant possession income; except that, if such corporation has significant possession income for 4 of such 5 taxable years, the rule of subparagraph (A)(ii)shall apply.

(ii) Special rule. If there is no year (of such 5 taxable years) for which a corporation has significant possession income—

(I) the term "base period year" means the first taxable year ending on or after October 14, 1995, but

(II) the amount of possession income for such year which is taken into account under paragraph (4)shall be the amount which would be determined if such year were a short taxable year ending on September 30, 1995.

(iii) Significant possession income. For purposes of this subparagraph, the term "significant possession income" means possession income which exceeds 2 percent of the possession income of the taxpayer for the taxable year (of the period of 6 taxable years ending with the first taxable year ending on or after October 14, 1995) having the greatest possession income.

(C) Election to use one base period year.

(i) In general. At the election of the taxpayer, the term "base period year" means—

(I) only the last taxable year of the corporation ending in calendar year 1992, or

(II) a deemed taxable year which includes the first ten months of calendar year 1995.

(ii) Base period income for 1995. In determining the adjusted base period income of the corporation for the deemed taxable year under clause (i)(II), the possession income shall be annualized and shall be determined without regard to any extraordinary item.

(iii) Election. An election under this subparagraph by any possession corporation may be made only for the corporation's first taxable year beginning after December 31, 1995, for which it is a possession corporation. The rules of subclauses (II) and (III) of subsection (a)(4)(B)(iii) shall apply to the election under this subparagraph.

(D) Acquisitions and dispositions. Rules similar to the rules of subparagraphs (A) and (B) of section 41(f)(3)shall apply for purposes of this subsection.

(6)   Possession income. For purposes of this subsection, the term "possession income" means, with respect to any possession, the income referred to in subsection (a)(1)(A)determined with respect to that possession. In no event shall possession income be treated as being less than zero.

(7)   Short years. If the current year or a base period year is a short taxable year, the application of this subsectionshall be made with such annualizations as the Secretary shall prescribe.

(8)   Special rules for certain possessions.

(A) In general. In the case of an existing credit claimant with respect to an applicable possession, this section (other than the preceding paragraphs of this subsection) shall apply to such claimant with respect to such applicable possession for taxable years beginning after December 31, 1995, and before January 1, 2006.

(B) Applicable possession. For purposes of this paragraph, the term "applicable possession" means Guam, American Samoa, and the Commonwealth of the Northern Mariana Islands.

(9) Existing credit claimant. For purposes of this subsection—

(A) In general. The term "existing credit claimant" means a corporation—

(i) (I) which was actively conducting a trade or business in a possession on October 13, 1995, and

(II) with respect to which an election under this section is in effect for the corporation's taxable year which includes October 13, 1995, or

(ii) which acquired all of the assets of a trade or business of a corporation which—

(I) satisfied the requirements of subclause (I)of clause (i) with respect to such trade or business, and

(II) satisfied the requirements of subclause (II) of clause (i).

(B) New lines of business prohibited. If, after October 13, 1995, a corporation which would (but for this subparagraph) be an existing credit claimant adds a substantial new line of business (other than in an acquisition described in subparagraph (A)(ii)), such corporation shall cease to be treated as an existing credit claimant as of the close of the taxable year ending before the date of such addition.

(C) Binding contract exception. If, on October 13, 1995, and at all times thereafter, there is in effect with respect to a corporation a binding contract for the acquisition of assets to be used in, or for the sale of assets to be produced from, a trade or business, the corporation shall be treated for purposes of this paragraphas actively conducting such trade or business on October 13, 1995. The preceding sentence shall not apply if such trade or business is not actively conducted before January 1, 1996.

(10) Separate application to each possession. For purposes of determining—

(A) whether a taxpayer is an existing credit claimant, and

(B) the amount of the credit allowed under this section,

this subsection (and so much of this section as relates to this subsection) shall be applied separately with respect to each possession.

[For Analysis, see ¶ 1206.]

[Endnote Code Sec. 936]

Sec. 330(a)(1), P.L. 112-240, 1/2/2013, amended Sec. 119(a), P.L. 109-432. Sec. 330(a)(2)), P.L. 112-240, 1/2/2013, added Sec. 119(e), P.L. 109-432. Sec. 330(b)), P.L. 112-240, 1/2/2013, amended Sec. 119(d), P.L. 109-432

Effective Date (Sec. 330(c), P.L. 112-240, 1/2/2013) effective for taxable years beginning after 12/31/2011. For Sec. 119, P.L. 109-432 as amended, see below.

Sec. 119, P.L. 109-432, as amended, reads as follows:

"Sec. 119. American Samoa economic development credit.

"(a) In General. For purposes of section 30A of the Internal Revenue Code of 1986, a domestic corporation shall be treated as a qualified domestic corporation to which such section applies if—

"(1) in the case of a taxable year beginning before January 1, 2012, such corporation—

"(A) is an existing credit claimant with respect to American Samoa, and

"(B) elected the application of section 936 of the Internal Revenue Code of 1986 for its last taxable year beginning before January 1, 2006, and

"(2) in the case of a taxable year beginning after December 31, 2011, such corporation meets the requirements of subsection (e).

"(b) Special rules for application of section. The following rules shall apply in applying section 30A of the Internal Revenue Code of 1986 for purposes of this section:

"(1) Amount of credit. Notwithstanding section 30A(a)(1) of such Code, the amount of the credit determined under section 30A(a)(1) of such Code for any taxable year shall be the amount determined under section 30A(d) of such Code, except that section 30A(d) shall be applied without regard to paragraph (3) thereof.

"(2) Separate application. In applying section 30A(a)(3) of such Code in the case of a corporation treated as a qualified domestic corporation by reason of this section, section 30A of such Code (and so much of section 936 of such Code as relates to such section 30A) shall be applied separately with respect to American Samoa.

"(3) Foreign tax credit allowed. Notwithstanding section 30A(e) of such Code, the provisions of section 936(c) of such Code shall not apply with respect to the credit allowed by reason of this section.

"(c) Definitions. For purposes of this section, any term which is used in this section which is also used in section 30A or 936 of such Code shall have the same meaning given such term by such section 30A or 936.

"(d) Application of section. Notwithstanding section 30A(h) or section 936(j) of such Code, this section (and so much of section 30A and section 936 of such Code as relates to this section) shall apply—

"(1) in the case of a corporation that meets the requirements of subparagraphs (A) and (B) of subsection (a)(1), to the first 8 taxable years of such corporation which begin after December 31, 2006, and before January 1, 2014, and

"(2) in the case of a corporation that does not meet the requirements of subparagraphs (A) and (B) of subsection (a)(1), to the first 2 taxable years of such corporation which begin after December 31, 2011, and before January 1, 2014."

"(e) Qualified production activities income requirement. A corporation meets the requirement of this subsection if such corporation has qualified production activities income, as defined in subsection (c) of section 199 of the Internal Revenue Code of 1986, determined by substituting 'American Samoa' for 'the United States' each place it appears in paragraphs (3), (4), and (6) of such subsection (c), for the taxable year."

Prior to amendment, Sec. 119(a), 109-432 read as follows:

"(a) In General. For purposes of section 30A of the Internal Revenue Code of 1986, a domestic corporation shall be treated as a qualified domestic corporation to which such section applies if such corporation—

"(1) is an existing credit claimant with respect to American Samoa, and

"(2) elected the application of section 936 of the Internal Revenue Code of 1986 for its last taxable year beginning before January 1, 2006.

Prior to amendment, Sec. 119(d), 109-432 read as follows:

"(d) Application of section. Notwithstanding section 30A(h) or section 936(j) of such Code, this section (and so much of section 30A and section 936 of such Code as relates to this section) shall apply to the first 6 taxable years of a corporation to which subsection (a) applies which begin after December 31, 2005, and before January 1, 2012."

[¶ 3092]   Code Sec. 953.   Insurance income.

* * * * * * * * * * * *

(e) **Exempt insurance income.** For purposes of this section—

   (1) **Exempt insurance income defined.**

      (A) In general. The term "exempt insurance income" means income derived by a qualifying insurance company which—

         (i) is attributable to the issuing (or reinsuring) of an exempt contract by such company or a qualifying insurance company branch of such company, and

         (ii) is treated as earned by such company or branch in its home country for purposes of such country's tax laws.

      (B) Exception for certain arrangements. Such term shall not include income attributable to the issuing (or reinsuring) of an exempt contract as the result of any arrangement whereby another corporation receives a substantially equal amount of premiums or other consideration in respect of issuing (or reinsuring) a contract which is not an exempt contract.

      (C) Determinations made separately. For purposes of this subsection and section 954(i), the exempt insurance income and exempt contracts of a qualifying insurance company or any qualifying insurance company branch of such company shall be determined separately for such company and each such branch by taking into account—

         (i) in the case of the qualifying insurance company, only items of income, deduction, gain, or loss, and activities of such company not properly allocable or attributable to any qualifying insurance company branch of such company, and

         (ii) in the case of a qualifying insurance company branch, only items of income, deduction, gain, or loss and activities properly allocable or attributable to such unit.

   (2) **Exempt contract.**

      (A) In general. The term "exempt contract" means an insurance or annuity contract issued or reinsured by a qualifying insurance company or qualifying insurance company branch in connection with property in, liability arising out of activity in, or the lives or health of residents of, a country other than the United States.

      (B) Minimum home country income required.

         (i) In general. No contract of a qualifying insurance company or of a qualifying insurance company branch shall be treated as an exempt contract unless such company or branch derives more than 30 percent of its net written premiums from exempt contracts (determined without regard to this subparagraph)—

(I) which cover applicable home country risks, and

(II) with respect to which no policyholder, insured, annuitant, or beneficiary is a related person (as defined in section 954(d)(3)).

(ii) Applicable home country risks. The term "applicable home country risks" means risks in connection with property in, liability arising out of activity in, or the lives or health of residents of, the home country of the qualifying insurance company or qualifying insurance company branch, as the case may be, issuing or reinsuring the contract covering the risks.

(C) Substantial activity requirements for cross border risks. A contract issued by a qualifying insurance company or qualifying insurance company branch which covers risks other than applicable home country risks (as defined in subparagraph (B)(ii)) shall not be treated as an exempt contract unless such company or branch, as the case may be—

(i) conducts substantial activity with respect to an insurance business in its home country, and

(ii) performs in its home country substantially all of the activities necessary to give rise to the income generated by such contract.

(3) Qualifying insurance company. The term "qualifying insurance company" means any controlled foreign corporation which—

(A) is subject to regulation as an insurance (or reinsurance) company by its home country, and is licensed, authorized, or regulated by the applicable insurance regulatory body for its home country to sell insurance, reinsurance, or annuity contracts to persons other than related persons (within the meaning of section 954(d)(3)) in such home country,

(B) derives more than 50 percent of its aggregate net written premiums from the issuance or reinsurance by such controlled foreign corporation and each of its qualifying insurance company branches of contracts—

(i) covering applicable home country risks (as defined in paragraph (2)) of such corporation or branch, as the case may be, and

(ii) with respect to which no policyholder, insured, annuitant, or beneficiary is a related person (as defined in section 954(d)(3)),

except that in the case of a branch, such premiums shall only be taken into account to the extent such premiums are treated as earned by such branch in its home country for purposes of such country's tax laws, and

(C) is engaged in the insurance business and would be subject to tax under subchapter L if it were a domestic corporation.

(4) Qualifying insurance company branch. The term "qualifying insurance company branch" means a qualified business unit (within the meaning of section 989(a)) of a controlled foreign corporation if—

(A) such unit is licensed, authorized, or regulated by the applicable insurance regulatory body for its home country to sell insurance, reinsurance, or annuity contracts to persons other than related persons (within the meaning of section 954(d)(3)) in such home country, and

(B) such controlled foreign corporation is a qualifying insurance company, determined under paragraph (3) as if such unit were a qualifying insurance company branch.

(5) Life insurance or annuity contract. For purposes of this section and section 954, the determination of whether a contract issued by a controlled foreign corporation or a qualified business unit (within the meaning of section 989(a)) is a life insurance contract or an annuity contract shall be made without regard to sections 72(s), 101(f), 817(h), and 7702 if—

(A) such contract is regulated as a life insurance or annuity contract by the corporation's or unit's home country, and

(B) no policyholder, insured, annuitant, or beneficiary with respect to the contract is a United States person.

(6) Home country. For purposes of this subsection, except as provided in regulations—

(A) Controlled foreign corporation. The term "home country" means, with respect to a controlled foreign corporation, the country in which such corporation is created or organized.

(B) Qualified business unit. The term "home country" means, with respect to a qualified business unit (as defined in section 989(a)), the country in which the principal office of such unit is located and in which such unit is licensed, authorized, or regulated by the applicable insurance regulatory body to sell insurance, reinsurance, or annuity contracts to persons other than related persons (as defined in section 954(d)(3)) in such country.

(7) Anti-abuse rules. For purposes of applying this subsection and section 954(i)—

(A) the rules of section 954(h)(7) (other than subparagraph (B) thereof) shall apply,

(B) there shall be disregarded any item of income, gain, loss, or deduction of, or derived from, an entity which is not engaged in regular and continuous transactions with persons which are not related persons,

(C) there shall be disregarded any change in the method of computing reserves a principal purpose of which is the acceleration or deferral of any item in order to claim the benefits of this subsection or section 954(i),

(D) a contract of insurance or reinsurance shall not be treated as an exempt contract (and premiums from such contract shall not be taken into account for purposes of paragraph (2)(B) or (3)) if—

(i) any policyholder, insured, annuitant, or beneficiary is a resident of the United States and such contract was marketed to such resident and was written to cover a risk outside the United States, or

(ii) the contract covers risks located within and without the United States and the qualifying insurance company or qualifying insurance company branch does not maintain such contemporaneous records, and file such reports, with respect to such contract as the Secretary may require,

(E) the Secretary may prescribe rules for the allocation of contracts (and income from contracts) among 2 or more qualifying insurance company branches of a qualifying insurance company in order to clearly reflect the income of such branches, and

(F) premiums from a contract shall not be taken into account for purposes of paragraph (2)(B) or (3) if such contract reinsures a contract issued or reinsured by a related person (as defined in section 954(d)(3)).

For purposes of subparagraph (D), the determination of where risks are located shall be made under the principles of section 953.

(8) Coordination with subsection (c). In determining insurance income for purposes of subsection (c), exempt insurance income shall not include income derived from exempt contracts which cover risks other than applicable home country risks.

(9) Regulations. The Secretary shall prescribe such regulations as may be necessary or appropriate to carry out the purposes of this subsection and section 954(i).

(10) Application. This subsection and section 954(i) shall apply only to taxable years of a foreign corporation beginning after December 31, 1998, and before [1]*January 1, 2014*, and to taxable years of United States shareholders with or within which any such taxable year of such foreign corporation ends. If this subsection does not apply to a taxable year of a foreign corporation beginning after [2]*December 31, 2013* (and taxable years of United States shareholders ending with or within such taxable year), then, notwithstanding the preceding sentence, subsection (a) shall be applied to such taxable years in the same manner as it would if the taxable year of the foreign corporation began in 1998.

(11) Cross reference. For income exempt from foreign personal holding company income, see section 954(i).

[For Analysis, see ¶ 1201.]

[Endnote Code Sec. 953]
Code Sec. 953(e)(10) was amended by Sec. 322(a)(1)-(2) of the American Taxpayer Relief Act of 2012, P.L. 112-240, 1/2/2013, as detailed below:
  1. Sec. 322(a)(1) substituted 'January 1, 2014' for 'January 1, 2012' in para. (e)(10)
  2. Sec. 322(a)(2) substituted 'December 31, 2013' for 'December 31, 2011' in para. (e)(10)
Effective Date (Sec. 322(c), P.L. 112-240, 1/2/2013) effective for tax. yrs. of foreign corporations begin. after 12/31/ 2011, and to tax. yrs. of United States shareholders with or within which any such tax. yr. of such foreign corporation ends.

[¶ 3093]　　**Code Sec. 954.**　　**Foreign base company income.**

* * * * * * * * * * * *

(c) Foreign personal holding company income.

(1) In general. For purposes of subsection (a)(1), the term "foreign personal holding company income" means the portion of the gross income which consists of:

(A) Dividends, etc. Dividends, interest, royalties, rents, and annuities.

(B) Certain property transactions. The excess of gains over losses from the sale or exchange of property—

(i) which gives rise to income described in subparagraph (A) (after application of paragraph (2)(A)) other than property which gives rise to income not treated as foreign personal holding company income by reason of subsection (h) or (i) for the taxable year,

(ii) which is an interest in a trust, partnership, or REMIC, or

(iii) which does not give rise to any income.

Gains and losses from the sale or exchange of any property which, in the hands of the controlled foreign corporation, is property described in section 1221(a)(1) shall not be taken into account under this subparagraph.

(C) Commodities transactions. The excess of gains over losses from transactions (including futures, forward, and similar transactions) in any commodities. This subparagraph shall not apply to gains or losses which—

(i) arise out of commodity hedging transactions (as defined in paragraph (5)(A)),

(ii) are active business gains or losses from the sale of commodities, but only if substantially all of the controlled foreign corporation's commodities are property described in paragraph (1), (2), or (8) of section 1221(a), or

(iii) are foreign currency gains or losses (as defined in section 988(b)) attributable to any section 988 transactions.

(D) Foreign currency gains. The excess of foreign currency gains over foreign currency losses (as defined in section 988(b)) attributable to any section 988 transactions. This subparagraph shall not apply in the case of any transaction directly related to the business needs of the controlled foreign corporation.

(E) Income equivalent to interest. Any income equivalent to interest, including income from commitment fees (or similar amounts) for loans actually made.

(F) Income from notional principal contracts.

(i) In general. Net income from notional principal contracts.

(ii) Coordination with other categories of foreign personal holding company income.—Any item of income, gain, deduction, or loss from a notional principal contract entered into for purposes of hedging any item described in any preceding subparagraph shall not be taken into account for purposes of this subparagraph but shall be taken into account under such other subparagraph.

(G) Payments in lieu of dividends. Payments in lieu of dividends which are made pursuant to an agreement to which section 1058 applies.

(H) Personal service contracts.

(i) Amounts received under a contract under which the corporation is to furnish personal services if—

(I) some person other than the corporation has the right to designate (by name or by description) the individual who is to perform the services, or

(II) the individual who is to perform the services is designated (by name or by description) in the contract, and

(ii) amounts received from the sale or other disposition of such a contract.

This subparagraph shall apply with respect to amounts received for services under a particular contract only if at some time during the taxable year 25 percent or more in value of the outstanding stock of the corporation is owned, directly or indirectly, by or for the individual who has performed, is to perform, or may be designated (by name or by description) as the one to perform, such services.

(2) Exception for certain amounts.

(A) Rents and royalties derived in active business. Foreign personal holding company income shall not include rents and royalties which are derived in the active conduct of a trade or business and which are received from a person other than a related person (within the meaning of subsection (d)(3)). For purposes of the preceding sentence, rents derived from leasing an aircraft or vessel in foreign commerce shall not fail to be treated as derived in the active conduct of a trade or business if, as determined under regulations prescribed by the Secretary, the active leasing expenses are not less than 10 percent of the profit on the lease.

(B) Certain export financing. Foreign personal holding company income shall not include any interest which is derived in the conduct of a banking business and which is export financing interest (as defined in section 904(d)(2)(G)).

(C) Exception for dealers. Except as provided by regulations, in the case of a regular dealer in property which is property described in paragraph (1)(B), forward contracts, option contracts, or similar financial instruments (including notional principal contracts and all instruments referenced to commodities), there shall not be taken into account in computing foreign personal holding company income—

(i) any item of income, gain, deduction, or loss (other than any item described in subparagraph (A), (E), or (G) of paragraph (1)) from any transaction (including hedging transactions and transactions involving physical settlement) entered into in the ordinary course of such dealer's trade or business as such a dealer, and

(ii) if such dealer is a dealer in securities (within the meaning of section 475), any interest or dividend or equivalent amount described in subparagraph (E) or (G) of paragraph (1) from any transaction (including any hedging transaction or transaction described in section 956(c)(2)(I)) entered into in the ordinary course of such dealer's trade or business as such a dealer in securities, but only if the income from the transaction is attributable to activities of the dealer in the country under the laws of which the dealer is created or organized (or in the case of a qualified business unit described in section 989(a), is attributable to activities of the unit in the country in which the unit both maintains its principal office and conducts substantial business activity).

(3) Certain income received from related persons.

(A) In general. Except as provided in subparagraph (B), the term "foreign personal holding company income" does not include—

(i) dividends and interest received from a related person which (I) is a corporation created or organized under the laws of the same foreign country under the laws of which the controlled foreign corporation is created or organized, and (II) has a substantial part of its assets used in its trade or business located in such same foreign country, and

(ii) rents and royalties received from a corporation which is a related person for the use of, or the privilege of using, property within the country under the laws of which the controlled foreign corporation is created or organized.

To the extent provided in regulations, payments made by a partnership with 1 or more corporate partners shall be treated as made by such corporate partners in proportion to their respective interests in the partnership.

(B) Exception not to apply to items which reduce subpart F income. Subparagraph (A) shall not apply in the case of any interest, rent, or royalty to the extent such interest, rent, or royalty reduces the payor's subpart F income or creates (or increases) a deficit which under section 952(c) may reduce the subpart F income of the payor or another controlled foreign corporation.

(C) Exception for certain dividends. Subparagraph (A)(i) shall not apply to any dividend with respect to any stock which is attributable to earnings and profits of the distributing corporation accumulated during any period during which the person receiving such dividend did not hold such stock either directly, or indirectly through a chain of one or more subsidiaries each of which meets the requirements of subparagraph (A)(i).

(4) Look-thru rule for certain partnership sales.

(A) In general. In the case of any sale by a controlled foreign corporation of an interest in a partnership with respect to which such corporation is a 25-percent owner, such corporation shall be treated for purposes of this subsection as selling the proportionate share of the assets of the partnership attributable to such interest. The Secretary shall prescribe such regulations as may be appropriate to prevent abuse of the purposes of this paragraph, including regulations providing for coordination of this paragraph with the provisions of subchapter K.

(B) 25-percent owner. For purposes of this paragraph, the term "25-percent owner" means a controlled foreign corporation which owns directly 25 percent or more of the capital or profits interest in a partnership. For purposes of the preceding sentence, if a controlled foreign corporation is a shareholder or partner of a corporation or partnership, the controlled foreign corporation shall be treated as owning directly its proportionate share of any such capital or profits interest held directly or indirectly by such corporation or partnership. If a controlled foreign corporation is treated as owning a capital or profits interest in a partnership under constructive ownership rules similar to the rules of section 958(b), the controlled foreign corporation shall be treated as owning such interest directly for purposes of this subparagraph.

(5) Definition and special rules relating to commodity transactions.

(A) Commodity hedging transactions. For purposes of paragraph (1)(C)(i), the term "commodity hedging transaction" means any transaction with respect to a commodity if such transaction—

(i) is a hedging transaction as defined in section 1221(b)(2), determined—

(I) without regard to subparagraph (A)(ii) thereof,

(II) by applying subparagraph (A)(i) thereof by substituting "ordinary property or property described in section 1231(b)" for "ordinary property", and

(III) by substituting "controlled foreign corporation" for "taxpayer" each place it appears, and

(ii) is clearly identified as such in accordance with section 1221(a)(7).

(B) Treatment of dealer activities under paragraph (1)(C). Commodities with respect to which gains and losses are not taken into account under paragraph (2)(C) in computing a controlled foreign corporation's foreign personal holding company income shall not be taken into account in applying the substantially all test under paragraph (1)(C)(ii) to such corporation.

(C) Regulations. The Secretary shall prescribe such regulations as are appropriate to carry out the purposes of paragraph (1)(C) in the case of transactions involving related parties.

(6) Look-thru rule for related controlled foreign corporations.

(A) In general. For purposes of this subsection, dividends, interest, rents, and royalties received or accrued from a controlled foreign corporation which is a related person shall not be treated as foreign personal holding company income to the extent attributable or properly allocable (determined under rules similar to the rules of subparagraphs (C) and

(D) of section 904(d)(3)) to income of the related person which is neither subpart F income nor income treated as effectively connected with the conduct of a trade or business in the United States. For purposes of this subparagraph, interest shall include factoring income which is treated as income equivalent to interest for purposes of paragraph (1)(E). The Secretary shall prescribe such regulations as may be necessary or appropriate to carry out this paragraph, including such regulations as may be necessary or appropriate to prevent the abuse of the purposes of this paragraph.

(B) Exception. Subparagraph (A) shall not apply in the case of any interest, rent, or royalty to the extent such interest, rent, or royalty creates (or increases) a deficit which under section 952(c) may reduce the subpart F income of the payor or another controlled foreign corporation.

(C) Application. Subparagraph (A) shall apply to taxable years of foreign corporations beginning after December 31, 2005, and before [1]*January 1, 2014*, and to taxable years of United States shareholders with or within which such taxable years of foreign corporations end.

* * * * * * * * * * * *

(h) Special rule for income derived in the active conduct of banking, financing, or similar businesses.

(1) In general. For purposes of subsection (c)(1), foreign personal holding company income shall not include qualified banking or financing income of an eligible controlled foreign corporation.

(2) Eligible controlled foreign corporation. For purposes of this subsection—

(A) In general. The term "eligible controlled foreign corporation" means a controlled foreign corporation which—

(i) is predominantly engaged in the active conduct of a banking, financing, or similar business, and

(ii) conducts substantial activity with respect to such business.

(B) Predominantly engaged. A controlled foreign corporation shall be treated as predominantly engaged in the active conduct of a banking, financing, or similar business if—

(i) more than 70 percent of the gross income of the controlled foreign corporation is derived directly from the active and regular conduct of a lending or finance business from transactions with customers which are not related persons,

(ii) it is engaged in the active conduct of a banking business and is an institution licensed to do business as a bank in the United States (or is any other corporation not so licensed which is specified by the Secretary in regulations), or

(iii) it is engaged in the active conduct of a securities business and is registered as a securities broker or dealer under section 15(a) of the Securities Exchange Act of 1934 or is registered as a Government securities broker or dealer under section 15C(a) of such Act (or is any other corporation not so registered which is specified by the Secretary in regulations).

(3) Qualified banking or financing income. For purposes of this subsection—

(A) In general. The term "qualified banking or financing income" means income of an eligible controlled foreign corporation which—

(i) is derived in the active conduct of a banking, financing, or similar business by—

(I) such eligible controlled foreign corporation, or

(II) a qualified business unit of such eligible controlled foreign corporation,

(ii) is derived from one or more transactions—

(I) with customers located in a country other than the United States, and

(II) substantially all of the activities in connection with which are conducted directly by the corporation or unit in its home country, and

(iii) is treated as earned by such corporation or unit in its home country for purposes of such country's tax laws.

(B) Limitation on nonbanking and nonsecurities businesses. No income of an eligible controlled foreign corporation not described in clause (ii) or (iii) of paragraph (2)(B) (or of a qualified business unit of such corporation) shall be treated as qualified banking or financing income unless more than 30 percent of such corporation's or unit's gross income is derived directly from the active and regular conduct of a lending or finance business from transactions with customers which are not related persons and which are located within such corporation's or unit's home country.

(C) Substantial activity requirement for cross border income. The term "qualified banking or financing income" shall not include income derived from 1 or more transactions with customers located in a country other than the home country of the eligible controlled foreign corporation or a qualified business unit of such corporation unless such corporation or unit conducts substantial activity with respect to a banking, financing, or similar business in its home country.

(D) Determinations made separately. For purposes of this paragraph, the qualified banking or financing income of an eligible controlled foreign corporation and each qualified business unit of such corporation shall be determined separately for such corporation and each such unit by taking into account—

(i) in the case of the eligible controlled foreign corporation, only items of income, deduction, gain, or loss and activities of such corporation not properly allocable or attributable to any qualified business unit of such corporation, and

(ii) in the case of a qualified business unit, only items of income, deduction, gain, or loss and activities properly allocable or attributable to such unit.

(E) Direct conduct of activities. For purposes of subparagraph (A)(ii)(II), an activity shall be treated as conducted directly by an eligible controlled foreign corporation or qualified business unit in its home country if the activity is performed by employees of a related person and—

(i) the related person is an eligible controlled foreign corporation the home country of which is the same as the home country of the corporation or unit to which subparagraph (A)(ii)(II) is being applied,

(ii) the activity is performed in the home country of the related person, and

(iii) the related person is compensated on an arm's-length basis for the performance of the activity by its employees and such compensation is treated as earned by such person in its home country for purposes of the home country's tax laws.

(4) Lending or finance business. For purposes of this subsection, the term "lending or finance business" means the business of—

(A) making loans,

(B) purchasing or discounting accounts receivable, notes, or installment obligations,

(C) engaging in leasing (including entering into leases and purchasing, servicing, and disposing of leases and leased assets),

(D) issuing letters of credit or providing guarantees,

(E) providing charge and credit card services, or

(F) rendering services or making facilities available in connection with activities described in subparagraphs (A) through (E) carried on by—

(i) the corporation (or qualified business unit) rendering services or making facilities available, or

(ii) another corporation (or qualified business unit of a corporation) which is a member of the same affiliated group (as defined in section 1504, but determined without regard to section 1504(b)(3)).

(5) Other definitions. For purposes of this subsection—

(A) Customer. The term "customer" means, with respect to any controlled foreign corporation or qualified business unit, any person which has a customer relationship with such corporation or unit and which is acting in its capacity as such.

(B) Home country. Except as provided in regulations—

744

(i) Controlled foreign corporation. The term "home country" means, with respect to any controlled foreign corporation, the country under the laws of which the corporation was created or organized.

(ii) Qualified business unit. The term "home country" means, with respect to any qualified business unit, the country in which such unit maintains its principal office.

(C) Located. The determination of where a customer is located shall be made under rules prescribed by the Secretary.

(D) Qualified business unit. The term "qualified business unit" has the meaning given such term by section 989(a).

(E) Related person. The term "related person" has the meaning given such term by subsection (d)(3).

(6) Coordination with exception for dealers. Paragraph (1) shall not apply to income described in subsection (c)(2)(C)(ii) of a dealer in securities (within the meaning of section 475) which is an eligible controlled foreign corporation described in paragraph (2)(B)(iii).

(7) Anti-abuse rules. For purposes of applying this subsection and subsection (c)(2)(C)(ii)—

(A) there shall be disregarded any item of income, gain, loss, or deduction with respect to any transaction or series of transactions one of the principal purposes of which is qualifying income or gain for the exclusion under this section, including any transaction or series of transactions a principal purpose of which is the acceleration or deferral of any item in order to claim the benefits of such exclusion through the application of this subsection,

(B) there shall be disregarded any item of income, gain, loss, or deduction of an entity which is not engaged in regular and continuous transactions with customers which are not related persons,

(C) there shall be disregarded any item of income, gain, loss, or deduction with respect to any transaction or series of transactions utilizing, or doing business with—

(i) one or more entities in order to satisfy any home country requirement under this subsection, or

(ii) a special purpose entity or arrangement, including a securitization, financing, or similar entity or arrangement,

if one of the principal purposes of such transaction or series of transactions is qualifying income or gain for the exclusion under this subsection, and

(D) a related person, an officer, a director, or an employee with respect to any controlled foreign corporation (or qualified business unit) which would otherwise be treated as a customer of such corporation or unit with respect to any transaction shall not be so treated if a principal purpose of such transaction is to satisfy any requirement of this subsection.

(8) Regulations. The Secretary shall prescribe such regulations as may be necessary or appropriate to carry out the purposes of this subsection, subsection (c)(1)(B)(i), subsection (c)(2)(C)(ii), and the last sentence of subsection (e)(2).

(9) Application. This subsection, subsection (c)(2)(C)(ii), and the last sentence of subsection (e)(2) shall apply only to taxable years of a foreign corporation beginning after December 31, 1998, and before [2]*January 1, 2014*, and to taxable years of United States shareholders with or within which any such taxable year of such foreign corporation ends.

* * * * * * * * * * * *

[For Analysis, see ¶ 1201, ¶ 1202.]

[Endnote Code Sec. 954]

Code Sec. 954(c)(6)(C) was amended by Sec. 323(a) of the American Taxpayer Relief Act of 2012, P.L. 112-240, 1/2/2013, as detailed below:

1. Sec. 323(a) substituted "January 1, 2014" for "January 1, 2012" in subpara. (c)(6)(C).

Effective Date (Sec. 323(b), P.L. 112-240, 1/2/2013) effective for tax. yrs. of foreign corporations begin. after 12/31/2011, and to tax. yrs. of United States shareholders with or within which such tax. yrs. of foreign corporations end.

Code Sec. 954(h)(9) was amended by Sec. 322(b), P.L. 112-240, 1/2/2013, as detailed below:

2. Sec. 322(b) substituted "January 1, 2014" for "January 1, 2012" in para. (h)(9)
Effective Date (Sec. 322(c), P.L. 112-240, 1/2/2013) effective for tax. yrs. of foreign corporations begin. after 12/31/2011, and to tax. yrs. of United States shareholders with or within which any such tax. yr. of such foreign corporation ends.

[¶ 3094]   Code Sec. 1016.   Adjustments to basis.

(a)   **General rule.** Proper adjustment in respect of the property shall in all cases be made—

* * * * * * * * * * * *

(**26**) to the extent provided in sections 23(g) and 137(e),

(**27**) in the case of a residence with respect to which a credit was allowed under section 1400C, to the extent provided in section 1400C(h),

(**28**) in the case of a facility with respect to which a credit was allowed under section 45F, to the extent provided in section 45F(f)(1),

* * * * * * * * * * * *

[For Analysis, see ¶ 903.]

[Endnote Code Sec. 1016]
Sec. 101(a)(1) of the American Taxpayer Relief Act of 2012, P.L. 112-240, 1/2/2013, deleted Title IX [Sec. 901] of the Economic Growth and Tax Relief Reconciliation Act of 2001, P.L. 107-16, the effect of which is to eliminate the sunset of all provisions enacted by P.L. 107-16. Following are the amendments made to Code Sec. 1016, by P.L. 107-16.
Effective Date (Sec. 101(a)(3), P.L. 112-240, 1/2/2013) effective for taxable, plan, or limitation years beginning after 12/31/2012, and estates of decedents dying, gifts made, or generation skipping transfers after 12/31/2012.

Code Sec. 1016(a)(26), Code Sec. 1016(a)(27) and Code Sec. 1016(a)(28) were amended by Sec. 205(b)(3) of the Economic Growth and Tax Relief Reconciliation Act of 2001, P.L. 107-16, 6/7/2001. Code Sec. 1016(a)(26)-(28) was further amended by Sec. 245(c)(2), P.L. 108-357.
1. Sec. 205(b)(3) deleted "and" at the end of para. (a)(26)
2. Sec. 205(b)(3) substituted ", and" for the period at the end of para. (a)(27)
3. Sec. 205(b)(3) added para. (a)(28)
Effective Date (Sec. 205(c), P.L. 107-16, 6/7/2001) effective for tax. yrs. begin. after 12/31/2001.

[¶ 3095]   Code Sec. 1202.   Partial exclusion for gain from certain small business stock.

* * * * * * * * * * * *

(a)   **Exclusion.**

(1)   **In general.** In the case of a taxpayer other than a corporation, gross income shall not include 50 percent of any gain from the sale or exchange of qualified small business stock held for more than 5 years.

(2)   **Empowerment zone businesses.**

(A) In general. In the case of qualified small business stock acquired after the date of the enactment of this paragraph in a corporation which is a qualified business entity (as defined in section 1397C(b)) during substantially all of the taxpayer's holding period for such stock, paragraph (1) shall be applied by substituting "60 percent" for "50 percent".

(B) Certain rules to apply. Rules similar to the rules of paragraphs (5) and (7) of section 1400B(b) shall apply for purposes of this paragraph.

(C) Gain after ¹2018 not qualified. Subparagraph (A) shall not apply to gain attributable to periods after ²December 31, 2018.

(D) Treatment of DC Zone. The District of Columbia Enterprise Zone shall not be treated as an empowerment zone for purposes of this paragraph.

(3) **Special rules for 2009 and certain periods in 2010.** In the case of qualified small business stock acquired after the date of the enactment of this paragraph and on or before the date of the enactment of the Creating Small Business Jobs Act of 2010.

(A) paragraph (1) shall be applied by substituting "75 percent" for "50 percent", and

(B) paragraph (2) shall not apply.

[3]*In the case of any stock which would be described in the preceding sentence (but for this sentence), the acquisition date for purposes of this subsection shall be the first day on which such stock was held by the taxpayer determined after the application of section 1223.*

(4) **100 Percent exclusion for stock acquired during certain periods in 2010** [4], **2011, 2012, and 2013.** In the case of qualified small business stock acquired after the date of the enactment of the Creating Small Business Jobs Act of 2010 and before [5]*January 1, 2014—*

(A) paragraph (1) shall be applied by substituting "100 percent" for "50 percent",

(B) paragraph (2) shall not apply, and

(C) paragraph (7) of section 57(a) shall not apply.

[6]*In the case of any stock which would be described in the preceding sentence (but for this sentence), the acquisition date for purposes of this subsection shall be the first day on which such stock was held by the taxpayer determined after the application of section 1223.*

* * * * * * * * * * * *

[For Analysis, see ¶ 209 and ¶ 1407.]

[Endnote Code Sec. 1202]

Code Sec. 1202(a)(2)(C) was amended by Sec. 327(b)(1)-(2) of the American Taxpayer Relief Act of 2012, P.L. 112-240, 1/2/2013, as detailed below:

1. Sec. 327(b)(2) substituted "2018" for "2016" in the heading of subpara. (a)(2)(C)

2. Sec. 327(b)(1) substituted "December 31, 2018" for "December 31, 2016" in subpara. (a)(2)(C)

Effective Date [Sec. 327(d), P.L. 112-240, 1/2/2013] effective for periods after 12/31/2011.

Code Sec. 1202(a)(3) was amended by Sec. 324(b)(1) of the American Taxpayer Relief Act of 2012, P.L. 112-240, 1/2/2013, as detailed below:

3. Sec. 324(b)(1) added a flush sentence at the end of para. (a)(3)

Effective Date [Sec. 324(c)(2), P.L. 112-240, 1/2/2013] effective for stock acquired after 2/17/2009 [as if included in Sec. 1241(a) of division B of the American Recovery Act and Reinvestment Act of 2009 [P.L.111-5]]

Code Sec. 1202(a)(4) was amended by Sec. 324(a)(1)-(2) of the American Taxpayer Relief Act of 2012, P.L. 112-240, 1/2/2013, as detailed below:

4. Sec. 324(a)(2) substituted ", 2011, 2012, and 2013" for "and 2011" in the heading of para. (a)(4)

5. Sec. 324(a)(1) substituted "January 1, 2014" for "January 1, 2012" in para. (a)(4)

Effective Date [Sec. 324(c)(1), P.L. 112-240, 1/2/2013] effective for stock acquired after 12/31/2011.

Code Sec. 1202(a)(4) was amended by Sec. 324(b)(2) of the American Taxpayer Relief Act of 2012, P.L. 112-240, 1/2/2013, as detailed below:

6. Sec. 324(b)(2) added a flush sentence at the end of para. (a)(4)

Effective Date [Sec. 324(c)(3), P.L. 112-240, 1/2/2013] effective for stock acquired after 9/27/2010 [as if included in Sec. 2011(a) of the Creating Small Business Jobs Act of 2010 [P.L.111-240]]

[¶ 3096]   Code Sec. 1367.   Adjustments to basis of stock of shareholders, etc.

* * * * * * * * * * * *

(a) **General rule.**

(1) **Increases in basis.** The basis of each shareholder's stock in an S corporation shall be increased for any period by the sum of the following items determined with respect to that shareholder for such period:

(A) the items of income described in subparagraph (A) of section 1366(a)(1),

(B) any nonseparately computed income determined under subparagraph (B) of section 1366(a)(1), and

(C) the excess of the deductions for depletion over the basis of the property subject to depletion.

(2) Decreases in basis. The basis of each shareholder's stock in an S corporation shall be decreased for any period (but not below zero) by the sum of the following items determined with respect to the shareholder for such period:

(A) distributions by the corporation which were not includible in the income of the shareholder by reason of section 1368,

(B) the items of loss and deduction described in subparagraph (A) of section 1366(a)(1),

(C) any nonseparately computed loss determined under subparagraph (B) of section 1366(a)(1),

(D) any expense of the corporation not deductible in computing its taxable income and not properly chargeable to capital account, and

(E) the amount of the shareholder's deduction for depletion for any oil and gas property held by the S corporation to the extent such deduction does not exceed the proportionate share of the adjusted basis of such property allocated to such shareholder under section 613A(c)(11)(B).

The decrease under subparagraph (B) by reason of a charitable contribution (as defined in section 170(c)) of property shall be the amount equal to the shareholder's pro rata share of the adjusted basis of such property. The preceding sentence shall not apply to contributions made in taxable years beginning after ¹*December 31, 2013.*

* * * * * * * * * * * *

[For Analysis, see ¶ 1105.]

[Endnote Code Sec. 1367]

Code Sec. 1367(a)(2) was amended by Sec. 325(a) of the American Taxpayer Relief Act of 2012, P.L. 112-240, 1/2/2013, as detailed below:

1. Sec. 325(a) substituted "December 31, 2013" for "December 31, 2011" in para. (a)(2)

Effective Date (Sec. 325(b), P.L. 112-240, 1/2/2013) effective for contributions made in tax. yrs. begin. after 12/31/2011.

[¶ 3097]   Code Sec. 1374.   Tax imposed on certai n built-in gains.

* * * * * * * * * * * *

(d) Definitions and special rules. For purposes of this section—

(1) Net unrealized built-in gain. The term "net unrealized built-in gain" means the amount (if any) by which—

(A) the fair market value of the assets of the S corporation as of the beginning of its 1st taxable year for which an election under section 1362(a) is in effect, exceeds

(B) the aggregate adjusted bases of such assets at such time.

(2) Net recognized built-in gain.

(A) In general. The term "net recognized built-in gain" means, with respect to any taxable year in the recognition period, the lesser of

(i) the amount which would be the taxable income of the S corporation for such taxable year if only recognized built-in gains and recognized built-in losses were taken into account, or

(ii) such corporation's taxable income for such taxable year (determined as provided in section 1375(b)(1)(B)).

(B) Carryover. If, for any taxable year ¹*described in subparagraph (A)*, the amount referred to in clause (i) of subparagraph (A) exceeds the amount referred to in clause (ii) of subparagraph (A), such excess shall be treated as a recognized built-in gain in the succeeding taxable year. The preceding sentence shall apply only in the case of a corporation treated as an S corporation by reason of an election made on or after March 31, 1988.

(3) Recognized built-in gain. The term "recognized built-in gain" means any gain recognized during the recognition period on the disposition of any asset except to the extent that the S corporation establishes that—

(A) such asset was not held by the S corporation as of the beginning of the 1st taxable year for which it was an S corporation, or

(B) such gain exceeds the excess (if any) of—

(i) the fair market value of such asset as of the beginning of such 1st taxable year, over

(ii) the adjusted basis of the asset as of such time.

(4) Recognized built-in losses. The term "recognized built-in loss" means any loss recognized during the recognition period on the disposition of any asset to the extent that the S corporation establishes that—

(A) such asset was held by the S corporation as of the beginning of the 1st taxable year referred to in paragraph (3), and

(B) such loss does not exceed the excess of

(i) the adjusted basis of such asset as of the beginning of such 1st taxable year, over

(ii) the fair market value of such asset as of such time.

(5) Treatment of certain built-in items.

(A) Income items. Any item of income which is properly taken into account during the recognition period but which is attributable to periods before the 1st taxable year for which the corporation was an S corporation shall be treated as a recognized built-in gain for the taxable year in which it is properly taken into account.

(B) Deduction items. Any amount which is allowable as a deduction during the recognition period (determined without regard to any carryover) but which is attributable to periods before the 1st taxable year referred to in subparagraph (A) shall be treated as a recognized built-in loss for the taxable year for which it is allowable as a deduction.

(C) Adjustment to net unrealized built-in gain. The amount of the net unrealized built-in gain shall be properly adjusted for amounts which would be treated as recognized built-in gains or losses under this paragraph if such amounts were properly taken into account (or allowable as a deduction) during the recognition period.

(6) Treatment of certain property. If the adjusted basis of any asset is determined (in whole or in part) by reference to the adjusted basis of any other asset held by the S corporation as of the beginning of the 1st taxable year referred to in paragraph (3)—

(A) such asset shall be treated as held by the S corporation as of the beginning of such 1st taxable year, and

(B) any determination under paragraph (3)(B) or (4)(B) with respect to such asset shall be made by reference to the fair market value and adjusted basis of such other asset as of the beginning of such 1st taxable year.

(7) Recognition period.

(A) In general. The term "recognition period" means the 10-year period beginning with the 1st day of the 1st taxable year for which the corporation was an S corporation.

(B) Special rules for 2009, 2010, and 2011. No tax shall be imposed on the net recognized built-in gain of an S corporation—

(i) in the case of any taxable year beginning in 2009 or 2010, if the 7th taxable year in the recognition period preceded such taxable year, or

(ii) in the case of any taxable year beginning in 2011, if the 5th year in the recognition period preceded such taxable year.

The preceding sentence shall be applied separately with respect to any asset to which paragraph (8) applies.

[2](C) Special rule for 2012 and 2013. For purposes of determining the net recognized built-in gain for taxable years beginning in 2012 or 2013, subparagraphs (A) and (D) shall be applied by substituting "5-year" for "10-year".

[3](D) Special rule for distributions to shareholders. For purposes of applying this section to any amount includible in income by reason of distributions to shareholders pursuant to section 593(e)—

(i) subparagraph (A) shall be applied without regard to the phrase "10-year", and

(i) subparagraph (B) shall not apply.

[4](E) Installment sales. If an S corporation sells an asset and reports the income from the sale using the installment method under section 453, the treatment of all payments received shall be governed by the provisions of this paragraph applicable to the taxable year in which such sale was made.

(8)   Treatment of transfer of assets from C corporation to S corporation.

(A) In general. Except to the extent provided in regulations, if

(i) an S corporation acquires any asset, and

(ii) the S corporation's basis in such asset is determined (in whole or in part) by reference to the basis of such asset (or any other property) in the hands of a C corporation,

then a tax is hereby imposed on any net recognized built-in gain attributable to any such assets for any taxable year beginning in the recognition period. The amount of such tax shall be determined under the rules of this section as modified by subparagraph (B).

(B) Modifications. For purposes of this paragraph, the modifications of this subparagraph are as follows:

(i) In general. The preceding paragraphs of this subsection shall be applied by taking into account the day on which the assets were acquired by the S corporation in lieu of the beginning of the 1st taxable year for which the corporation was an S corporation.

(ii) Subsection (c)(1) not to apply. Subsection (c)(1) shall not apply.

(9)   Reference to 1st taxable year. Any reference in this section to the 1st taxable year for which the corporation was an S corporation shall be treated as a reference to the 1st taxable year for which the corporation was an S corporation pursuant to its most recent election under section 1362.

* * * * * * * * * * * *

[For Analysis, see ¶ 1501.]

[Endnote Code Sec. 1374]

Code Sec. 1374(d)(2)(B), Code Sec. 1374(d)(7)(C), Code Sec. 1374(d)(7)(D) and, Code Sec. 1374(d)(7)(E) were amended by Sec. 326(a)(1)-(3) and (b) of the American Taxpayer Relief Act of 2012, P.L. 112-240, 1/2/2013, as detailed below:

1. Sec. 326(b) added "described in subparagraph (A)" after ", for any taxable year" in subpara. (d)(2)(B)
2. Sec. 326(a)(2) added new subpara. (d)(7)(C)
3. Sec. 326(a)(1) redesignated subpara. (d)(7)(C) as (d)(7)(D)
4. Sec. 326(a)(3) added subpara. (d)(7)(E)

Effective Date (Sec. 326(c), P.L. 112-240, 1/2/2013) effective for tax. yrs. begin. after 12/31/2011.

[¶ 3098]   Code Sec. 1391.   Designation procedure.

* * * * * * * * * * * *

(d)   Period for which designation is in effect.

(1)   In general. Any designation under this section shall remain in effect during the period beginning on the date of the designation and ending on the earliest of—

(A)

(i) in the case of an empowerment zone, [1]*December 31, 2013*, or

(ii) in the case of an enterprise community, the close of the 10th calendar year beginning on or after such date of designation,

(B) the termination date designated by the State and local governments as provided for in their nomination, or

(C) the date the appropriate Secretary revokes the designation.

(2) Revocation of designation. The appropriate Secretary may revoke the designation under this section of an area if such Secretary determines that the local government or the State in which it is located—

(A) has modified the boundaries of the area, or

(B) is not complying substantially with, or fails to make progress in achieving the benchmarks set forth in, the strategic plan under subsection (f)(2).

* * * * * * * * * * * *

[For Analysis, see ¶ 1406.]

[Endnote Code Sec. 1391]
Code Sec. 1391(d)(1)(A)(i) was amended by Sec. 327(a) of the American Taxpayer Relief Act of 2012, P.L. 112-240, 1/2/2013, as detailed below:
1. Sec. 327(a) substituted "December 31, 2013" for "December 31, 2011" in clause (d)(1)(A)(i)
Effective Date (Sec. 327(d), P.L. 112-240, 1/2/2013) effective for periods after 12/31/2011.

[¶ 3099]   Code Sec. 1400C.   First-time homebuyer credit for District of Columbia.

* * * * * * * * * * * *

[1]*(d) Carryforward of unised credit.* If the credit allowable under subsection (a) exceeds the limitation imposed by section 26(a) for such taxable year reduced by the sum of the credits allowable under subpart A of part IV of subchapter A (other than this section and section 25D), such excess shall be carried to the succeeding taxable year and added to the credit allowable under subsection (a)for such taxable year.

* * * * * * * * * * * *

[For Analysis, see ¶ 403.]

[Endnote Code Sec. 1400C]
Sec. 101(a)(1) of the American Taxpayer Relief Act of 2012, P.L. 112-240, 1/2/2013, deleted Title IX [Sec. 901] of the Economic Growth and Tax Relief Reconciliation Act of 2001, P.L. 107-16, the effect of which is to eliminate the sunset of all provisions enacted by P.L. 107-16. Sec. 201(b)(2)(H) and Sec. 201(f)(2)(C) amended subsec. (d). Sec. 402(i)(3)(F), P.L. 109-135 amended subsec. (d). Following are the amendments made to Code Sec. 15, by P.L. 107-16.
Effective Date (Sec. 101(a)(3), P.L. 112-240, 1/2/2013) effective for taxable, plan, or limitation years beginning after 12/31/2012, and estates of decedents dying, gifts made, or generation skipping transfers after 12/31/2012.

Code Sec. 1400C(d) was amended by Sec. 104(c)(2)(L) of the American Taxpayer Relief Act of 2012, P.L. 112-240, 1/2/2013, as detailed below:
1. Sec. 104(c)(2)(L) amended subsec. (d)
Prior to amendment, subsec. (d) read as follows:
"(d) Carryover of credit. If the credit allowable under subsection (a) exceeds the limitation imposed by section 26(a) for such taxable year reduced by the sum of the credits allowable under subpart A of part IV of subchapter A (other than this section), such excess shall be carried to the succeeding taxable year and added to the credit allowable under subsection (a) for such taxable year."
Effective Date (Sec. 104(d), P.L. 112-240, 1/2/2013) effective for tax. yrs. begin. after 12/31/2011.

[¶ 3100]   Code Sec. 1400L.   Tax benefits for New York Liberty Zone.

* * * * * * * * * * * *

(b) Special allowance for certain property acquired after September 10, 2001.

(1) Additional allowance. In the case of any qualified New York Liberty Zone property—

(A) the depreciation deduction provided by section 167(a) for the taxable year in which such property is placed in service shall include an allowance equal to 30 percent of the adjusted basis of such property, and

(B) the adjusted basis of the qualified New York Liberty Zone property shall be reduced by the amount of such deduction before computing the amount otherwise allowable as a depreciation deduction under this chapter for such taxable year and any subsequent taxable year.

(2)　Qualified New York Liberty Zone property. For purposes of this subsection—

(A) In general. The term "qualified New York Liberty Zone property" means property—

(i) (I) which is described in section 168(k)(2)(A)(i), or

(II) which is nonresidential real property, or residential rental property, which is described in subparagraph (B),

(ii) substantially all of the use of which is in the New York Liberty Zone and is in the active conduct of a trade or business by the taxpayer in such Zone,

(iii) the original use of which in the New York Liberty Zone commences with the taxpayer after September 10, 2001,

(iv) which is acquired by the taxpayer by purchase (as defined in section 179(d)) after September 10, 2001, but only if no written binding contract for the acquisition was in effect before September 11, 2001, and

(v) which is placed in service by the taxpayer on or before the termination date.

The term "termination date" means December 31, 2006 (December 31, 2009, in the case of nonresidential real property and residential rental property).

(B) Eligible real property. Nonresidential real property or residential rental property is described in this subparagraph only to the extent it rehabilitates real property damaged, or replaces real property destroyed or condemned, as a result of the September 11, 2001, terrorist attack. For purposes of the preceding sentence, property shall be treated as replacing real property destroyed or condemned if, as part of an integrated plan, such property replaces real property which is included in a continuous area which includes real property destroyed or condemned.

(C) Exceptions.

(i) Bonus depreciation property under section 168(k). Such term shall not include property to which section 168(k) applies.

(ii) Alternative depreciation property. The term "qualified New York Liberty Zone property" shall not include any property described in section 168(k)(2)(D)(i).

(iii) Qualified New York Liberty Zone leasehold improvement property. Such term shall not include any qualified New York Liberty Zone leasehold improvement property.

(iv) Election out. For purposes of this subsection, rules similar to the rules of section 168(k)(2)(D)(iii) shall apply.

(D) Special rules. For purposes of this subsection, rules similar to the rules of section 168(k)(2)(E) shall apply, except that clause (i) thereof shall be applied without regard to "and before ¹*January 1, 2014*", and clause (iv) thereof shall be applied by substituting "qualified New York Liberty Zone property" for "qualified property".

(E) Allowance against alternative minimum tax. For purposes of this subsection, rules similar to the rules of section 168(k)(2)(G) shall apply.

* * * * * * * * * * * *

(d)　Tax-exempt bond financing.

(1)　In general. For purposes of this title, any qualified New York Liberty Bond shall be treated as an exempt facility bond.

(2)　Qualified New York Liberty Bond. For purposes of this subsection, the term "qualified New York Liberty Bond" means any bond issued as part of an issue if—

(A) 95 percent or more of the net proceeds (as defined in section 150(a)(3)) of such issue are to be used for qualified project costs,

(B) such bond is issued by the State of New York or any political subdivision thereof,

(C) the Governor or the Mayor designates such bond for purposes of this section, and

(D) such bond is issued after the date of the enactment of this section and before [2]*January 1, 2014.*

(3) Limitations on amount of bonds.

(A) Aggregate amount designated. The maximum aggregate face amount of bonds which may be designated under this subsection shall not exceed $8,000,000,000, of which not to exceed $4,000,000,000 may be designated by the Governor and not to exceed $4,000,000,000 may be designated by the Mayor.

(B) Specific limitations. The aggregate face amount of bonds issued which are to be used for—

(i) costs for property located outside the New York Liberty Zone shall not exceed $2,000,000,000,

(ii) residential rental property shall not exceed $1,600,000,000, and

(iii) costs with respect to property used for retail sales of tangible property and functionally related and subordinate property shall not exceed $800,000,000.

The limitations under clauses (i), (ii), and (iii) shall be allocated proportionately between the bonds designated by the Governor and the bonds designated by the Mayor in proportion to the respective amounts of bonds designated by each.

(C) Movable property. No bonds shall be issued which are to be used for movable fixtures and equipment.

(4) Qualified project costs. For purposes of this subsection—

(A) In general. The term "qualified project costs" means the cost of acquisition, construction, reconstruction, and renovation of—

(i) nonresidential real property and residential rental property (including fixed tenant improvements associated with such property) located in the New York Liberty Zone, and

(ii) public utility property (as defined in section 168(i)(10)) located in the New York Liberty Zone.

(B) Costs for certain property outside zone included. Such term includes the cost of acquisition, construction, reconstruction, and renovation of nonresidential real property (including fixed tenant improvements associated with such property) located outside the New York Liberty Zone but within the City of New York, New York, if such property is part of a project which consists of at least 100,000 square feet of usable office or other commercial space located in a single building or multiple adjacent buildings.

(5) Special rules. In applying this title to any qualified New York Liberty Bond, the following modifications shall apply:

(A) Section 146 (relating to volume cap) shall not apply.

(B) Section 147(d) (relating to acquisition of existing property not permitted) shall be applied by substituting "50 percent" for "15 percent" each place it appears.

(C) Section 148(f)(4)(C) (relating to exception from rebate for certain proceeds to be used to finance construction expenditures) shall apply to the available construction proceeds of bonds issued under this section.

(D) Repayments of principal on financing provided by the issue—

(i) may not be used to provide financing, and

(ii) must be used not later than the close of the 1st semiannual period beginning after the date of the repayment to redeem bonds which are part of such issue.

The requirement of clause (ii) shall be treated as met with respect to amounts received within 10 years after the date of issuance of the issue (or, in the case of a refunding bond, the date of issuance of the original bond) if such amounts are used by the close of such 10 years to redeem bonds which are part of such issue.

(E) Section 57(a)(5) shall not apply.

(6) Separate issue treatment of portions of an issue. This subsection shall not apply to the portion of an issue which (if issued as a separate issue) would be treated as a qualified bond or as a bond that is not a private activity bond (determined without regard to paragraph (1)), if the issuer elects to so treat such portion.

* * * * * * * * * * * *

[For Analysis, see ¶ 1405.]

[¶ 3101]   Code Sec. 1400N.   Tax benefits for Gulf Opportunity Zone.

* * * * * * * * * * * *

(d)   Special allowance for certain property acquired on or after August 28, 2005.

   (1)   Additional allowance. In the case of any qualified Gulf Opportunity Zone property—

      (A) the depreciation deduction provided by section 167(a) for the taxable year in which such property is placed in service shall include an allowance equal to 50 percent of the adjusted basis of such property, and

      (B) the adjusted basis of the qualified Gulf Opportunity Zone property shall be reduced by the amount of such deduction before computing the amount otherwise allowable as a depreciation deduction under this chapter for such taxable year and any subsequent taxable year.

   (2)   Qualified Gulf Opportunity Zone property. For purposes of this subsection—

      (A) In general. The term "qualified Gulf Opportunity Zone property" means property—

         (i)   (I) which is described in section 168(k)(2)(A)(i), or

            (II) which is nonresidential real property or residential rental property,

         (ii) substantially all of the use of which is in the Gulf Opportunity Zone and is in the active conduct of a trade or business by the taxpayer in such Zone,

         (iii) the original use of which in the Gulf Opportunity Zone commences with the taxpayer on or after August 28, 2005,

         (iv) which is acquired by the taxpayer by purchase (as defined in section 179(d)) on or after August 28, 2005, but only if no written binding contract for the acquisition was in effect before August 28, 2005, and

         (v) which is placed in service by the taxpayer on or before December 31, 2007 (December 31, 2008, in the case of nonresidential real property and residential rental property).

      (B) Exceptions.

         (i) Alternative depreciation property. Such term shall not include any property described in section 168(k)(2)(D)(i).

         (ii) Tax-exempt bond-financed property. Such term shall not include any property any portion of which is financed with the proceeds of any obligation the interest on which is exempt from tax under section 103.

         (iii) Qualified revitalization buildings. Such term shall not include any qualified revitalization building with respect to which the taxpayer has elected the application of paragraph (1) or (2) of section 1400I(a).

         (iv) Election out. If a taxpayer makes an election under this clause with respect to any class of property for any taxable year, this subsection shall not apply to all property in such class placed in service during such taxable year.

(3) **Special rules.** For purposes of this subsection, rules similar to the rules of subparagraph (E) of section 168(k)(2) shall apply, except that such subparagraph shall be applied—

(A) by substituting "August 27, 2005" for "December 31, 2007" each place it appears therein,

(B) without regard to "and before [1]*January 1, 2014*" in clause (i) thereof, and

(C) by substituting "qualified Gulf Opportunity Zone property" for "qualified property" in clause (iv) thereof.

(4) **Allowance against alternative minimum tax.** For purposes of this subsection, rules similar to the rules of section 168(k)(2)(G) shall apply.

(5) **Recapture.** For purposes of this subsection, rules similar to the rules under section 179(d)(10) shall apply with respect to any qualified Gulf Opportunity Zone property which ceases to be qualified Gulf Opportunity Zone property.

(6) **Extension for certain property.**

(A) In general. In the case of any specified Gulf Opportunity Zone extension property, paragraph (2)(A) shall be applied without regard to clause (v) thereof.

(B) Specified Gulf Opportunity Zone extension property. For purposes of this paragraph, the term "specified Gulf Opportunity Zone extension property" means property—

(i) substantially all of the use of which is in one or more specified portions of the GO Zone, and

(ii) which is—

(I) nonresidential real property or residential rental property which is placed in service by the taxpayer on or before December 31, 2011, or

(II) in the case of a taxpayer who places a building described in subclause (I) in service on or before December 31, 2011, property described in section 168(k)(2)(A)(i) if substantially all of the use of such property is in such building and such property is placed in service by the taxpayer not later than 90 days after such building is placed in service.

(C) Specified portions of the GO Zone. For purposes of this paragraph, the term "specified portions of the GO Zone" means those portions of the GO Zone which are in any county or parish which is identified by the Secretary as being a county or parish in which hurricanes occurring during 2005 damaged (in the aggregate) more than 60 percent of the housing units in such county or parish which were occupied (determined according to the 2000 Census).

(D) Only pre-January 1, 2012, basis of real property eligible for additional allowance. In the case of property which is qualified Gulf Opportunity Zone property solely by reason of subparagraph (B)(ii)(I), paragraph (1) shall apply only to the extent of the adjusted basis thereof attributable to manufacture, construction, or production before January 1, 2012.

(E) Exception for bonus depreciation property under section 168(k). The term "specified Gulf Opportunity Zone extension property" shall not include any property to which section 168(k) applies.

* * * * * * * * * * * * *

[Endnote Code Sec. 1400N]

Code Sec. 1400N(d)(3)(B) was amended by Sec. 331(e)(5) of the American Taxpayer Relief Act of 2012, P.L. 112-240, 1/2/2013, as detailed below:

1. Sec. 331(e)(5) substituted "January 1, 2014" for "January 1, 2013" in subpara. (d)(3)(B)

Effective Date (Sec. 331(f), P.L. 112-240, 1/2/2013) effective for property placed in service after 12/31/2012, in tax. yrs. end. after such date.

[¶ 3102]   Code Sec. 1401.   Rate of tax.

(a) **Old-age, survivors, and disability insurance.** In addition to other taxes, there shall be imposed for each taxable year, on the self-employment income of every individual, a tax equal to the following percent of the amount of the self-employment income for such taxable year:

In the case of a taxable year Beginning after:	And before:	Percent:
December 31, 1983	January 1, 1988	11.40
December 31, 1987	January 1, 1990	12.12
December 31, 1989		12.40.

(b) **Hospital insurance.**

(1) **In general.** In addition to the tax imposed by the preceding subsection, there shall be imposed for each taxable year, on the self-employment income of every individual, a tax equal to the following percent of the amount of the self-employment income for such taxable year:

In the case of a taxable year Beginning after:	And before:	Percent:
December 31, 1983	January 1, 1985	2.60
December 31, 1984	January 1, 1986	2.70
December 31, 1985		2.90.

(2) **Additional tax.**

(A) In general. In addition to the tax imposed by paragraph (1) and the preceding subsection, there is hereby imposed on every taxpayer (other than a corporation, estate, or trust) for each taxable year beginning after December 31, 2012, a tax equal to 0.9 percent of the self-employment income for such taxable year which is in excess of—

(i) in the case of a joint return, $250,000,

(ii) in the case of a married taxpayer (as defined in section 7703) filing a separate return, ½ of the dollar amount determined under clause (i), and

(iii) in any other case, $200,000.

(B) Coordination with FICA. The amounts under clause (i), (ii), or (iii) which ever is applicable) of subparagraph (A) shall be reduced (but not below zero) by the amount of wages taken into account in determining the tax imposed under section 3121(b)(2) with respect to the taxpayer.

(c) **Relief from taxes in cases covered by certain international agreements.** During any period in which there is in effect an agreement entered into pursuant to section 233 of the Social Security Act with any foreign country, the self-employment income of an individual shall be exempt from the taxes imposed by this section to the extent that such self-employment income is subject under such agreement exclusively to the laws applicable to the social security system of such foreign country.

[For Analysis, see ¶ 1901. For Committee Reports, see ¶ 5501.]

[Endnote Code Sec. 1401]

Sec. 601, P.L. 111-312, relating to the temporary employee payroll tax cut, as amended by Sec. 1001(a) and (b), P.L. 112-96 and Sec. 101(a)-(d), P.L. 112-78, reads as follows. For description of those amendments, see below.

"SEC. 601. TEMPORARY EMPLOYEE PAYROLL TAX CUT.

"(a) In general. Notwithstanding any other provision of law, —

"(1) with respect to any taxable year which begins in the payroll tax holiday period, the rate of tax under section 1401(a) of the Internal Revenue Code of 1986 shall be 10.40 percent, and

"(2) with respect to remuneration received during the payroll tax holiday period, the rate of tax under 3101(a) of such Code shall be 4.2 percent (including for purposes of determining the applicable percentage under sections 3201(a) and 3211(a)(1) of such Code).

"(b) Coordination with deductions for employment taxes.

"(1) Deduction in computing net earnings from self-employment. For purposes of applying section 1402(a)(12) of the Internal Revenue Code of 1986, the rate of tax imposed by subsection 1401(a) of such Code shall be determined without regard to the reduction in such rate under this section.

"(2) Individual deduction. In the case of the taxes imposed by section 1401 of such Code for any taxable year which begins in the payroll tax holiday period, the deduction under section 164(f) of such Code with respect to such taxes shall be equal to the sum of—

"(A) 59.6 percent of the portion of such taxes attributable to the tax imposed by section 1401(a) of such Code (determined after the application of this section), plus

"(B) one-half of the portion of such taxes attributable to the tax imposed by section 1401(b) of such Code.

"(c) Payroll Tax Holiday Period. The term 'payroll tax holiday period' means calendar years 2011 and 2012.

"(d) Employer notification. The Secretary of the Treasury shall notify employers of the payroll tax holiday period in any manner the Secretary deems appropriate.

"(e) Transfers of funds.

"(1) Transfers to Federal Old-Age and Survivors Insurance Trust Fund. There are hereby appropriated to the Federal Old-Age and Survivors Trust Fund and the Federal Disability Insurance Trust Fund established under section 201 of the Social Security Act (42 U.S.C. 401) amounts equal to the reduction in revenues to the Treasury by reason of the application of subsection (a). Amounts appropriated by the preceding sentence shall be transferred from the general fund at such times and in such manner as to replicate to the extent possible the transfers which would have occurred to such Trust Fund had such amendments not been enacted.

"(2) Transfers to Social Security Equivalent Benefit Account. There are hereby appropriated to the Social Security Equivalent Benefit Account established under section 15A(a) of the Railroad Retirement Act of 1974 (45 U.S.C. 231n-1(a)) amounts equal to the reduction in revenues to the Treasury by reason of the application of subsection (a)(2). Amounts appropriated by the preceding sentence shall be transferred from the general fund at such times and in such manner as to replicate to the extent possible the transfers which would have occurred to such Account had such amendments not been enacted.

"(3) Coordination with other Federal laws. For purposes of applying any provision of Federal law other than the provisions of the Internal Revenue Code of 1986, the rate of tax in effect under section 3101(a) of such Code shall be determined without regard to the reduction in such rate under this section."

Sec. 1001(a) and (b), P.L. 112-96, amended Sec. 601, P.L. 111-312, 12/17/2010, relating to the temporary employee payroll tax cut, as outlined below:

Sec. 1001(a), amended Sec. 601(c), P.L. 111-312.

Prior to amendment, Sec. 601(c), P.L. 111-312 read as follows:

"(c) Payroll Tax Holiday Period. The term 'payroll tax holiday period' means—

"(1) in the case of the tax described in subsection (a)(1), calendar years 2011 and 2012, and

"(2) in the case of the taxes described in subsection (a)(2), the period beginning January 1, 2011, and ending February 29, 2012."

Sec. 1001(b), deleted Sec. 601(f) and (g) P.L. 111-312.

Prior to deletion, Sec. 601(f) and (g), P.L. 111-312 read as follows:

"(f) Special rules for 2012.

"(1) Limitation on self-employment income. In the case of any taxable year beginning in 2012, subsection (a)(1) shall only apply with respect to so much of the taxpayer's self-employment income (as defined in section 1402(b) of the Internal Revenue Code of 1986) as does not exceed the excess (if any) of—

"(A) $18,350, over

"(B) the amount of wages and compensation received during the portion of the payroll tax holiday period occurring during 2012 subject to tax under section 3101(a) of such Code or section 3201(a) of such Code.

"(2) Coordination with deduction for employment taxes. In the case of a taxable year beginning in 2012, subparagraph (A) of subsection (b)(2) shall be applied as if it read as follows:

"'(A) the sum of—

"'(i) 59.6 percent of the portion of such taxes attributable to the tax imposed by section 1401(a) of such Code (determined after the application of this section) on so much of self-employment income (as defined in section 1402(b) of such Code) as does not exceed the amount of self-employment income described in paragraph (1), plus

"(ii) one-half of the portion of such taxes attributable to the tax imposed by section 1401(a) of such Code (determined without regard to this section) on self-employment income (as so defined) in excess of such amount, plus'

"(g) Recapture of excess benefit.

"(1) In general. There is hereby imposed on the income of every individual a tax equal to 2 percent of the sum of wages (within the meaning of section 3121(a)(1) of the Internal Revenue Code of 1986) and compensation (to which section 3201(a) of such Code applies) received during the period beginning January 1, 2012, and ending February 29, 2012, to the extent the amount of such sum exceeds $18,350.

"(2) Regulations. The Secretary of the Treasury or the Secretary's delegate shall prescribe such regulations or other guidance as may be necessary or appropriate to carry out this subsection, including guidance for payment by the employee of the tax imposed by paragraph (1)."

Effective Date (Sec. 1001(c), P.L. 112-96) effective for rumeration received, and taxable years beginning after 12/31/2011.

Sec. 101(a), (b) and (c), P.L. 112-78, amended Sec. 601, P.L. 111-312, 12/17/2010, relating to the temporary employee payroll tax cut, as outlined below:

Sec. 101(a), amended Sec. 601(c) of P.L. 111-312

Sec. 101(b), added Sec. 601(f) of P.L. 111-312

Sec. 101(c), added Sec. 601(g) of P.L. 111-312 effective for remuneration received, and tax. yrs. begin., after 12/31/2011.

Prior to amendment, Sec. 601(c) of P.L. 111-312 read as follows:

"(c) Payroll tax holiday period. The term 'payroll tax holiday period' means calendar year 2011."

Effective Date (Sec. 101(e)(1), P.L. 112-78) effective for remuneration received, and taxable years beginning, after 12/31/2011.

Sec. 101(d), P.L. 112-78, amended Sec. 601, P.L. 111-312, 12/17/2010, relating to the temporary employee payroll tax cut, as outlined below:

Sec. 101(d)(1), added "of such Code" after "164(f)" in Sec. 601(b)(2) of P.L. 111-312

Sec. 101(d)(2), added "of such Code" after "1401(a)" in Sec. 601(b)(2)(A) of P.L. 111-312

Sec. 101(d)(3), added "of such Code" after "1401(b)" in Sec. 601(b)(2)(B) of P.L. 111-312, effective as if included in the enactment of Sec. 601 of P.L. 111-312

[¶ 3103]   Code Sec. 1445.   Withholding of tax on dispositions of United States real property interests.

* * * * * * * * * * * *

(e) **Special rules relating to distributions, etc., by corporations, partnerships, trusts, or estates.**

(1) **Certain domestic partnerships, trusts, and estates.** In the case of any disposition of a United States real property interest as defined in section 897(c) (other than a disposition described in paragraph (4) or 5)) by a domestic partnership, domestic trust, or domestic estate, such partnership, the trustee of such trust, or the executor of such estate (as the case may be) shall be required to deduct and withhold under subsection (a) a tax equal to 35 percent (or, to the extent provided in regulations, [1]*20 percent*) of the gain realized to the extent such gain—

(A) is allocable to a foreign person who is a partner or beneficiary of such partnership, trust, or estate, or

(B) is allocable to a portion of the trust treated as owned by a foreign person under subpart E of part I of subchapter J.

(2) **Certain distributions by foreign corporations.** In the case of any distribution by a foreign corporation on which gain is recognized under subsection (d) or (e) of section 897, the foreign corporation shall deduct and withhold under subsection (a) a tax equal to 35 percent of the amount of gain recognized on such distribution under such subsection.

(3) **Distributions by certain domestic corporations to foreign shareholders.** If a domestic corporation which is or has been a United States real property holding corporation (as defined in section 897(c)(2)) during the applicable period specified in section 897(c)(1)(A)(ii) distributes property to a foreign person in a transaction to which section 302 or part II of subchapter C applies, such corporation shall deduct and withhold under subsection (a) a tax equal to 10 percent of the amount realized by the foreign shareholder. The preceding sentence shall not apply if, as of the date of the distribution, interests in such corporation are not United States real property interests by reason of section 897(c)(1)(B). Rules similar to the rules of the preceding provisions of this paragraph shall apply in the case of any distribution to which section 301 applies and which is not made out of the earnings and profits of such a domestic corporation.

(4) **Taxable distributions by domestic or foreign partnerships, trusts, or estates.** A domestic or foreign partnership, the trustee of a domestic or foreign trust, or the executor of a domestic or foreign estate shall be required to deduct and withhold under subsection (a) a tax equal to 10 percent of the fair market value (as of the time of the taxable distribution) of any United States real property interest distributed to a partner of the partnership or a beneficiary of the trust or estate, as the case may be, who is a foreign person in a transaction which would constitute a taxable distribution under the regulations promulgated by the Secretary pursuant to section 897.

(5) **Rules relating to dispositions of interest in partnerships, trusts, or estates.** To the extent provided in regulations, the transferee of a partnership interest or of a beneficial interest in a trust or estate shall be required to deduct and withhold under subsection (a) a tax equal to 10 percent of the amount realized on the disposition.

(6) Distributions by regulated investment companies and real estate investment trusts. If any portion of a distribution from a qualified investment entity (as defined in section 897(h)(4)) to a nonresident alien individual or a foreign corporation is treated under section 897(h)(1) as gain realized by such individual or corporation from the sale or exchange of a United States real property interest, the qualified investment entity shall deduct and withhold under subsection (a) a tax equal to 35 percent (or, to the extent provided in regulations, [2]*20 percent*) of the amount so treated.

(7) Regulations. The Secretary shall prescribe such regulations as may be necessary to carry out the purposes of this subsection, including regulations providing for exceptions from provisions of this subsection and regulations for the application of this subsection in the case of payments through 1 or more entities.

* * * * * * * * * * * *

[For Analysis, see ¶ 1203.]

[Endnote Code Sec. 1445]
   Code Sec. 1445(e)(1) and Code Sec. 1445(e)(6) were amended by Sec. 102(c)(1)(C) and (3) of the American Taxpayer Relief Act of 2012, P.L. 112-240, 1/2/2013, as detailed below:
   1. Sec. 102(c)(1)(C) substituted '20 percent' for '15 percent' in para. (e)(1)
   2. Sec. 102(c)(3) substituted '20 percent' for '15 percent (20 percent in the case of taxable years beginning after December 31, 2010)' in para. (e)(6)
Effective Date (Sec. 102(d)(2), P.L. 112-240, 1/2/2013) effective for amounts paid on or after 1/1/2013.

   Sec. 102(a), P.L. 112-240, 1/2/2013, deleted Sec. 303, P.L. 108-27, the effect of which is to eliminate the sunset of all provisions enacted by Title III, P.L. 108-27. Sec. 301(a)(2)(C), P.L. 108-27 amended Code Sec. 1445 by substituting "15 percent" for "20 percent" in para. (e)(1).

[¶ 3104]   Code Sec. 2001.   Imposition and rate of tax.

(a) Imposition. A tax is hereby imposed on the transfer of the taxable estate of every decedent who is a citizen or resident of the United States.

(b) Computation of tax. The tax imposed by this section shall be the amount equal to the excess (if any) of—

   (1) a tentative tax computed under subsection (c) on the sum of—

      (A) the amount of the taxable estate, and

      (B) the amount of the adjusted taxable gifts, over

   (2) the aggregate amount of tax which would have been payable under chapter 12 with respect to gifts made by the decedent after December 31, 1976, [1]*if the modifications described in subsection (g) had been applicable at the time of such gifts.*

   For purposes of paragraph (1)(B), the term "adjusted taxable gifts" means the total amount of the taxable gifts (within the meaning of section 2503) made by the decedent after December 31, 1976, other than gifts which are includible in the gross estate of the decedent.

(c) Rate schedule.[2]

If the amount with respect to which the tentative tax to be computed is:	the tentative tax is:
Not over $10,000	18 percent of such amount.
Over $10,000 but not over $20,000	$1,800, plus 20 percent of the excess of such amount over $10,000.
Over $20,000 but not over $40,000	$3,800, plus 22 percent of the excess of such amount over $20,000.
Over $40,000 but not over $60,000	$8,200, plus 24 percent of the excess of such amount over $40,000.
Over $60,000 but not over $80,000	$13,000, plus 26 percent of the excess of such amount over $60,000.
Over $80,000 but not over $100,000	$18,200, plus 28 percent of the excess of such amount over $80,000.

Over $100,000 but not over $150,000	$23,800, plus 30 percent of the excess of such amount over $100,000.
Over $150,000 but not over $250,000	$38,800, plus 32 percent of the excess of such amount over $150,000.
Over $250,000 but not over $500,000	$70,800, plus 34 percent of the excess of such amount over $250,000.
³*Over $500,000 but not over $750,000*	*$155,800, plus 37 percent of the excess of such amount over $500,000.*
Over $750,000 but not over $1,000,000	*$248,300, plus 39 percent of the excess of such amount over $750,000.*
Over $1,000,000	*$345,800, plus 40 percent of the excess of such amount over $1,000,000.*

⁴*(2) Repealed.*

(d)   Adjustment for gift tax paid by spouse. For purposes of subsection (b)(2), if—

(1) the decedent was the donor of any gift one-half of which was considered under section 2513 as made by the decedent's spouse, and

(2) the amount of such gift is includible in the gross estate of the decedent,

any tax payable by the spouse under chapter 12 on such gift (as determined under section 2012(d)) shall be treated as a tax payable with respect to a gift made by the decedent.

(e)   Coordination of sections 2513 and 2035. If—

(1) the decedent's spouse was the donor of any gift one-half of which was considered under section 2513 as made by the decedent, and

(2) the amount of such gift is includible in the gross estate of the decedent's spouse by reason of section 2035,

such gift shall not be included in the adjusted taxable gifts of the decedent for purposes of subsection (b)(1)(B), and the aggregate amount determined under subsection (b)(2) shall be reduced by the amount (if any) determined under subsection (d) which was treated as a tax payable by the decedent's spouse with respect to such gift.

(f)   Valuation of gifts.

(1)   **In general.** If the time has expired under section 6501 within which a tax may be assessed under chapter 12 (or under corresponding provisions of prior laws) on—

(A) the transfer of property by gift made during a preceding calendar period (as defined in section 2502(b)); or

(B) an increase in taxable gifts required under section 2701(d),

the value thereof shall, for purposes of computing the tax under this chapter, be the value as finally determined for purposes of chapter 12.

(2)   **Final determination.** For purposes of paragraph (1), a value shall be treated as finally determined for purposes of chapter 12 if—

(A) the value is shown on a return under such chapter and such value is not contested by the Secretary before the expiration of the time referred to in paragraph (1) with respect to such return;

(B) in a case not described in subparagraph (A), the value is specified by the Secretary and such value is not timely contested by the taxpayer; or

(C) the value is determined by a court or pursuant to a settlement agreement with the Secretary.

For purposes of subparagraph (A), the value of an item shall be treated as shown on a return if the item is disclosed in the return, or in a statement attached to the return, in a manner adequate to apprise the Secretary of the nature of such item.

⁵*(g)   Modifications to gift tax payable to reflect different tax rates. For purposes of applying subsection (b)(2) with respect to 1 or more gifts, the rates of tax under subsection (c) in effect at the decedent's death shall, in lieu of the rates of tax in effect at the time of such gifts, be used both to compute—*

(1) the tax imposed by chapter 12 with respect to such gifts, and

(2) the credit allowed against such tax under section 2505, including in computing—

(A) the applicable credit amount under section 2505(a)(1), and

(B) the sum of the amounts allowed as a credit for all preceding periods under section 2505(a)(2).

[For Analysis, see ¶ 501.]

[Endnote Code Sec. 2001]

Sec. 101(a)(1) of the American Taxpayer Relief Act of 2012, P.L. 112-240, 1/2/2013, deleted Title IX [Sec. 901] of the Economic Growth and Tax Relief Reconciliation Act of 2001, P.L. 107-16, the effect of which is to eliminate the sunset of all provisions enacted by P.L. 107-16. Code Sec. 2001(b)(2), (c) and (g) were amended by Sec. 302(a)(2)(A)-(C) and 302(d)(1)(A)-(B), P.L. 111-312. Sec. 304, P.L. 111-312 provides that this amendment is subject to the sunset provided in Sec. 901, P.L. 107-16. The deletion of Sec. 901, P.L. 107-16 also eliminates the sunset of the provisions enacted by Sec. 304, P.L. 111-312. Following are the amendments made to Code Sec. 2001, by P.L. 111-312. **Effective Date** (Sec. 101(a)(3), P.L. 112-240, 1/2/2013) effective for taxable, plan, or limitation years beginning after 12/31/2012, and estates of decedents dying, gifts made, or generation skipping transfers after 12/31/2012.

Code Sec. 2001(b)(2) and Code Sec. 2001(c) were amended by Sec. 302(d)(1)(A) of the Tax Relief, Unemployment Insurance Reauthorization, and Job Creation Act of 2010, P.L. 111-312, 12/17/2010, as detailed below:

1. Sec. 302(d)(1)(A) substituted "if the modifications described in subsection (g)" for "if the provisions of subsection (c) (as in effect at the decedent's death)" para. (b)(2)

2. Sec. 302(a)(2)(B) deleted "(1) In general." in subsec. (c)

Effective Date (Sec. 302(f), P.L. 111-312, 12/17/2010) effective for estates of decedents dying, generation-skipping transfers, and gifts made, after 12/31/2009.

The table contained in Code Sec. 2001(c) was amended by Sec. 302(d)(1)(A) of the Tax Relief, Unemployment Insurance Reauthorization, and Job Creation Act of 2010, P.L. 111-312, 12/17/2010, and further amended by Sec. 101(c)(1) of the American Taxpayer Relief Act of 2012, P.L. 112-240, 1/2/2013, as detailed below:

3. Sec. 101(c)(1), P.L. 112-240, amended the table in subsec. (c). Prior to this amendment, and following the amendment made by Sec. 302(d)(1)(A), P.L. 111-312, the table in subsec. (c) read as follows:

"If the amount with respect to which the tentative tax to be computed is:	the tentative tax is:
Not over $10,000	18 percent of such amount.
Over $10,000 but not over $20,000	$1,800, plus 20 percent of the excess of such amount over $10,000.
Over $20,000 but not over $40,000	$3,800, plus 22 percent of the excess of such amount over $20,000.
Over $40,000 but not over $60,000	$8,200, plus 24 percent of the excess of such amount over $40,000.
Over $60,000 but not over $80,000	$13,000, plus 26 percent of the excess of such amount over $60,000.
Over $80,000 but not over $100,000	$18,200, plus 28 percent of the excess of such amount over $80,000.
Over $100,000 but not over $150,000	$23,800, plus 30 percent of the excess of such amount over $100,000.
Over $150,000 but not over $250,000	$38,800, plus 32 percent of the excess of such amount over $150,000.
Over $250,000 but not over $500,000	$70,800, plus 34 percent of the excess of such amount over $250,000.
Over $500,000	$155,800, plus 35 percent of the excess of such amount over $500,000."

Effective Date (Sec. 101(c)(3)(A), P.L. 112-240, 1/2/2013) effective for estates of decedents dying, generation-skipping transfers, and gifts made, after 12/31/2012.

Code Sec. 2001(c)(2) and Code Sec. 2001(g) were amended by Sec. 302(a)(2)(C) and 302(d)(1)(B), P.L. 111-312, 12/17/2010, as detailed below:

3. Sec. 302(a)(2)(C) deleted para. (c)(2). Prior to deletion, para. (c)(2) read as follows:

"(2) Phasedown of maximum rate of tax.

"(A) In general. In the case of estates of decedents dying, and gifts made, in calendar years after 2002 and before 2010, the tentative tax under this subsection shall be determined by using a table prescribed by the Secretary (in lieu of using the table contained in paragraph (1)) which is the same as such table; except that —

"(i) the maximum rate of tax for any calendar year shall be determined in the table under subparagraph (B), and

"(ii) the brackets and the amounts setting forth the tax shall be adjusted to the extent necessary to reflect the adjustments under subparagraph (A).

"(B) Maximum rate.

In calendar year:	The maximum rate is:
2003	49 percent
2004	48 percent
2005	47 percent
2006	46 percent
2007, 2008, and 2009	45 percent"

4. Sec. 302(d)(1)(B) added subsec. (g)

Effective Date (Sec. 302(f), P.L. 111-312, 12/17/2010) effective for estates of decedents dying, generation-skipping transfers, and gifts made, after 12/31/2009.

[¶ 3105]   Code Sec. 2010.   Unified credit against estate tax.

* * * * * * * * * * * *

[1]*(c) Applicable credit amount.*

(1) In general. For purposes of this section, the applicable credit amount is the amount of the tentative tax which would be determined under section 2001(c) if the amount with respect to which such tentative tax is to be computed were equal to the applicable exclusion amount.

[2]*(2) Applicable exclusion amount.* For purposes of this subsection, the applicable exclusion amount is the sum of—

(A) the basic exclusion amount, and

(B) in the case of a surviving spouse, the deceased spousal unused exclusion amount.

(3) Basic exclusion amount.

(A) In general. For purposes of this subsection, the basic exclusion amount is $5,000,000.

(B) Inflation adjustment. In the case of any decedent dying in a calendar year after 2011, the dollar amount in subparagraph (A) shall be increased by an amount equal to—

(i) such dollar amount, multiplied by

(ii) the cost-of-living adjustment determined under section 1(f)(3) for such calendar year by substituting "calendar year 2010" for "calendar year 1992" in subparagraph (B) thereof.

If any amount as adjusted under the preceding sentence is not a multiple of $10,000, such amount shall be rounded to the nearest multiple of $10,000.

(4) Deceased spousal unused exclusion amount. For purposes of this subsection, with respect to a surviving spouse of a deceased spouse dying after December 31, 2010, the term "deceased spousal unused exclusion amount" means the lesser of—

(A) the basic exclusion amount, or

(B) the excess of—

(i) the [3]applicable exclusion amount of the last such deceased spouse of such surviving spouse, over

(ii) the amount with respect to which the tentative tax is determined under section 2001(b)(1) on the estate of such deceased spouse.

(5) Special rules.

(A) Election required. A deceased spousal unused exclusion amount may not be taken into account by a surviving spouse under paragraph (2) unless the executor of the estate of the deceased spouse files an estate tax return on which such amount is computed and makes an election on such return that such amount may be so taken into account. Such election, once made, shall be irrevocable. No election may be made under this subparagraph if such return is filed after the time prescribed by law (including extensions) for filing such return.

(B) Examination of prior returns after expiration of period of limitations with respect to deceased spousal unused exclusion amount. Notwithstanding any period of limitation in section 6501, after the time has expired under section 6501 within which a tax may be assessed under chapter 11 or 12 with respect to a deceased spousal unused exclusion amount, the Secretary may examine a return of the deceased spouse to make determinations with respect to such amount for purposes of carrying out this subsection.

(6) **Regulations.** The Secretary shall prescribe such regulations as may be necessary or appropriate to carry out this subsection.

* * * * * * * * * * * *

[For Analysis, see ¶ 501.]

[Endnote Code Sec. 2010]

Sec. 101(a)(1) of the American Taxpayer Relief Act of 2012, HR8, 1/2/2013, deleted Title IX [Sec. 901] of the Economic Growth and Tax Relief Reconciliation Act of 2001, P.L. 107-16, the effect of which is to eliminate the sunset of all provisions enacted by P.L. 107-16. Code Sec. 2010(c) was amended by Sec. 302(a)(1) and 303(a), P.L. 111-312. Sec. 304, P.L. 111-312 provides that this amendment is subject to the sunset provided in Sec. 901, P.L. 107-16. The deletion of Sec. 901, P.L. 107-16 also eliminates the sunset of the provisions enacted by Sec. 304, P.L. 111-312. Following are the amendments made to Code Sec. 2010, by P.L. 111-312.

Effective Date (Sec. 101(a)(3), P.L. 112-240, 1/2/2013) effective for taxable, plan, or limitation years beginning after 12/31/2012, and estates of decedents dying, gifts made, or generation skipping transfers after 12/31/2012.

Code Sec. 2010(c) was amended by Sec. 302(a)(1) of the Tax Relief, Unemployment Insurance Reauthorization, and Job Creation Act of 2010, P.L. 111-312, 12/17/2010, as detailed below:

1. Sec. 302(a)(1) amended subsec. (c)

Prior to amendment, subsec. (c) read as follows:

"(c) Applicable credit amount.

"For purposes of this section, the applicable credit amount is the amount of the tentative tax which would be determined under the rate schedule set forth in section 2001(c) if the amount with respect to which such tentative tax is to be computed were the applicable exclusion amount determined in accordance with the following table:

"In the case of estates of decedents dying during:	The applicable exclusion amount is:
2002 and 2003	$1,000,000
2004 and 2005	$1,500,000
2006, 2007, and 2008	$2,000,000
2009	$3,500,000.

Effective Date (Sec. 302(f), P.L. 111-312, 12/17/2010) effective for estates of decedents dying, generation-skipping transfers, and gifts made, after 12/31/2009.

Code Sec. 2010(c)(2), Code Sec. 2010(c)(3), Code Sec. 2010(c)(4), Code Sec. 2010(c)(5) and Code Sec. 2010(c)(6) were amended by Sec. 303(a), P.L. 111-312, 12/17/2010, as detailed below:

2. Sec. 303(a) deleted para. (c)(2) [as added by Sec. 302(a), see above] and added paras. (c)(2)-(6)

Prior to deletion, para. (c)(2) read as follows:

"(2) Applicable exclusion amount.

"(A) In general. For purposes of this subsection, the applicable exclusion amount is $5,000,000.

"(B) Inflation adjustment. In the case of any decedent dying in a calendar year after 2011, the dollar amount in subparagraph

"(A) shall be increased by an amount equal to—

"(i) such dollar amount, multiplied by

"(ii) the cost-of-living adjustment determined under section 1(f)(3) for such calendar year by substituting "calendar year 2010" for "calendar year 1992" in subparagraph (B) thereof.

"If any amount as adjusted under the preceding sentence is not a multiple of $10,000, such amount shall be rounded to the nearest multiple of $10,000."

Effective Date (Sec. 303(c)(1), P.L. 111-312, 12/17/2010) effective for estates of decedents dying and gifts made after 12/31/2010 [as if included in Sec. 303 of P.L. 111-312, 12/17/2010]

Code Sec. 2010(c)(4)(B)(i) was amended by Sec. 101(c)(2) of the American Taxpayer Relief Act of 2012, 1/2/2013, as detailed below:

3. Sec. 101(c)(2) substituted "applicable exclusive amount" for "basic exclusion amount" in clause (c)(4)(B)(i)

Effective Date (Sec. 101(c)(3)(B), HR8, 1/2/2013) effective for any generation-skipping transfer made after 12/31/2009, and before 1/1/2011 [as if included in Sec. 303 of P.L. 111-312, 12/17/2010]

[¶ 3106]   **Code Sec. 3101.**   **Rate of tax.**

(a)   **Old-age, survivors, and disability insurance.** In addition to other taxes, there is hereby imposed on the income of every individual a tax equal to the following percentages of the wages (as defined in section 3121(a)) received by him with respect to employment (as defined in section 3121(b))—

In cases of wages received during:	The rate shall be:
1984, 1985, 1986, or 1987	5.7 percent
1988 or 1989	6.06 percent
1990 or thereafter	6.2 percent.

(b) Hospital insurance.

(1) In general. In addition to the tax imposed by the preceding subsection, there is hereby imposed on the income of every individual a tax equal to 1.45 percent of the wages (as defined in section 3121(a)) received by him with respect to employment (as defined in section 3121(b)).

(2) Additional tax. In addition to the tax imposed by paragraph (1) and the preceding sub-section, there is hereby imposed on every taxpayer (other than a corporation, estate, or trust) a tax equal to 0.9 percent of wages which are received with respect to employment (as defined in section 3121(b)) during any taxable year beginning after December 31, 2012, and which are in excess of—

(A) in the case of a joint return, $250,000,

(B) in the case of a married taxpayer (as defined in section 7703) filing a separate return, $\frac{1}{2}$ of the dollar amount determined under subparagraph (A), and

(C) in any other case, $200,000.

(c) Relief from taxes in cases covered by certain international agreements. During any period in which there is in effect an agreement entered into pursuant to section 233 of the Social Security Act with any foreign country, wages received by or paid to an individual shall be exempt from the taxes imposed by this section to the extent that such wages are subject under such agreement exclusively to the laws applicable to the social security system of such foreign country.

[For Analysis, see ¶ 1902. For Committee Reports, see ¶ 5501.]

[Endnote Code Sec. 3101]

Sec. 601, P.L. 111-312, relating to the temporary employee payroll tax cut, as amended by Sec. 1001(a) and (b), P.L. 112-96 and Sec. 101(a)-(d), P.L. 112-78, reads as follows. For description of those amendments, see below.

"SEC. 601. TEMPORARY EMPLOYEE PAYROLL TAX CUT.

"(a) In general. Notwithstanding any other provision of law, —

"(1) with respect to any taxable year which begins in the payroll tax holiday period, the rate of tax under section 1401(a) of the Internal Revenue Code of 1986 shall be 10.40 percent, and

"(2) with respect to remuneration received during the payroll tax holiday period, the rate of tax under 3101(a) of such Code shall be 4.2 percent (including for purposes of determining the applicable percentage under sections 3201(a) and 3211(a)(1) of such Code).

"(b) Coordination with deductions for employment taxes.

"(1) Deduction in computing net earnings from self-employment. For purposes of applying section 1402(a)(12) of the Internal Revenue Code of 1986, the rate of tax imposed by subsection 1401(a) of such Code shall be determined without regard to the reduction in such rate under this section.

"(2) Individual deduction. In the case of the taxes imposed by section 1401 of such Code for any taxable year which begins in the payroll tax holiday period, the deduction under section 164(f) of such Code with respect to such taxes shall be equal to the sum of—

"(A) 59.6 percent of the portion of such taxes attributable to the tax imposed by section 1401(a) of such Code (determined after the application of this section), plus

"(B) one-half of the portion of such taxes attributable to the tax imposed by section 1401(b) of such Code.

"(c) Payroll Tax Holiday Period. The term 'payroll tax holiday period' means calendar years 2011 and 2012.

"(d) Employer notification. The Secretary of the Treasury shall notify employers of the payroll tax holiday period in any manner the Secretary deems appropriate.

"(e) Transfers of funds.

"(1) Transfers to Federal Old-Age and Survivors Insurance Trust Fund. There are hereby appropriated to the Federal Old-Age and Survivors Trust Fund and the Federal Disability Insurance Trust Fund established under section 201 of the Social Security Act (42 U.S.C. 401) amounts equal to the reduction in revenues to the Treasury by reason of the application of subsection (a). Amounts appropriated by the preceding sentence shall be transferred from the general fund at such times and in such manner as to replicate to the extent possible the transfers which would have occurred to such Trust Fund had such amendments not been enacted.

"(2) Transfers to Social Security Equivalent Benefit Account. There are hereby appropriated to the Social Security Equivalent Benefit Account established under section 15A(a) of the Railroad Retirement Act of 1974 (45 U.S.C.

231n-1(a)) amounts equal to the reduction in revenues to the Treasury by reason of the application of subsection (a)(2). Amounts appropriated by the preceding sentence shall be transferred from the general fund at such times and in such manner as to replicate to the extent possible the transfers which would have occurred to such Account had such amendments not been enacted.

"(3) Coordination with other Federal laws. For purposes of applying any provision of Federal law other than the provisions of the Internal Revenue Code of 1986, the rate of tax in effect under section 3101(a) of such Code shall be determined without regard to the reduction in such rate under this section."

Sec. 1001(a) and (b), P.L. 112-96, amended Sec. 601, P.L. 111-312, 12/17/2010, relating to the temporary employee payroll tax cut, as outlined below:

Sec. 1001(a), amended Sec. 601(c), P.L. 111-312.

Prior to amendment, Sec. 601(c), P.L. 111-312 read as follows:

"(c) Payroll Tax Holiday Period. The term 'payroll tax holiday period' means—

"(1) in the case of the tax described in subsection (a)(1), calendar years 2011 and 2012, and

"(2) in the case of the taxes described in subsection (a)(2), the period beginning January 1, 2011, and ending February 29, 2012."

Sec. 1001(b), deleted Sec. 601(f) and (g) P.L. 111-312.

Prior to deletion, Sec. 601(f) and (g), P.L. 111-312 read as follows:

"(f) Special rules for 2012.

"(1) Limitation on self-employment income. In the case of any taxable year beginning in 2012, subsection (a)(1) shall only apply with respect to so much of the taxpayer's self-employment income (as defined in section 1402(b) of the Internal Revenue Code of 1986) as does not exceed the excess (if any) of—

"(A) $18,350, over

"(B) the amount of wages and compensation received during the portion of the payroll tax holiday period occurring during 2012 subject to tax under section 3101(a) of such Code or section 3201(a) of such Code.

"(2) Coordination with deduction for employment taxes. In the case of a taxable year beginning in 2012, subparagraph (A) of subsection (b)(2) shall be applied as if it read as follows:

"'(A) the sum of—

"'(i) 59.6 percent of the portion of such taxes attributable to the tax imposed by section 1401(a) of such Code (determined after the application of this section) on so much of self-employment income (as defined in section 1402(b) of such Code) as does not exceed the amount of self-employment income described in paragraph (1), plus

"(ii) one-half of the portion of such taxes attributable to the tax imposed by section 1401(a) of such Code (determined without regard to this section) on self-employment income (as so defined) in excess of such amount, plus'

"(g) Recapture of excess benefit.

"(1) In general. There is hereby imposed on the income of every individual a tax equal to 2 percent of the sum of wages (within the meaning of section 3121(a)(1) of the Internal Revenue Code of 1986) and compensation (to which section 3201(a) of such Code applies) received during the period beginning January 1, 2012, and ending February 29, 2012, to the extent the amount of such sum exceeds $18,350.

"(2) Regulations. The Secretary of the Treasury or the Secretary's delegate shall prescribe such regulations or other guidance as may be necessary or appropriate to carry out this subsection, including guidance for payment by the employee of the tax imposed by paragraph (1)."

Effective Date (Sec. 1001(c), P.L. 112-96) effective for rumeration received, and taxable years beginning after 12/31/2011.

Sec. 101(a), (b) and (c), P.L. 112-78, amended Sec. 601, P.L. 111-312, 12/17/2010, relating to the temporary employee payroll tax cut, as outlined below:

Sec. 101(a), amended Sec. 601(c) of P.L. 111-312

Sec. 101(b), added Sec. 601(f) of P.L. 111-312

Sec. 101(c), added Sec. 601(g) of P.L. 111-312 effective for remuneration received, and tax. yrs. begin., after 12/31/2011.

Prior to amendment, Sec. 601(c) of P.L. 111-312 read as follows:

"(c) Payroll tax holiday period. The term 'payroll tax holiday period' means calendar year 2011."

Effective Date (Sec. 101(e)(1), P.L. 112-78) effective for remuneration received, and taxable years beginning, after 12/31/2011.

Sec. 101(d), P.L. 112-78, amended Sec. 601, P.L. 111-312, 12/17/2010, relating to the temporary employee payroll tax cut, as outlined below:

Sec. 101(d)(1), added "of such Code" after "164(f)" in Sec. 601(b)(2) of P.L. 111-312

Sec. 101(d)(2), added "of such Code" after "1401(a)" in Sec. 601(b)(2)(A) of P.L. 111-312

Sec. 101(d)(3), added "of such Code" after "1401(b)" in Sec. 601(b)(2)(B) of P.L. 111-312, effective as if included in the enactment of Sec. 601 of P.L. 111-312

[¶ 3107]   **Code Sec. 3111.**   **Rate of tax.**

* * * * * * * * * * * *

[1](e) *Credit for employment of qualified veterans.*

(1) In general. If a qualified tax-exempt organization hires a qualified veteran with respect to whom a credit would be allowable under section 38 by reason of section 51 if the organization were not a qualified tax-exempt organization, then there shall be allowed as a credit against the tax imposed by subsection (a) on wages paid with respect to employment of all employees of the organization during the applicable period an amount equal to the credit determined under section 51 (after application of the modifications under paragraph (3)) with respect to wages paid to such qualified veteran during such period.

(2) Overall limitation. The aggregate amount allowed as a credit under this subsection for all qualified veterans for any period with respect to which tax is imposed under subsection (a) shall not exceed the amount of the tax imposed by subsection (a) on wages paid with respect to employment of all employees of the organization during such period.

(3) Modifications. For purposes of paragraph (1), section 51 shall be applied—

(A) by substituting "26 percent" for "40 percent" in subsection (a) thereof,

(B) by substituting "16.25 percent" for "25 percent" in subsection (i)(3)(A) thereof, and

(C) by only taking into account wages paid to a qualified veteran for services in furtherance of the activities related to the purpose or function constituting the basis of the organization's exemption under section 501.

(4) Applicable period. The term "applicable period" means, with respect to any qualified veteran, the 1-year period beginning with the day such qualified veteran begins work for the organization.

(5) Definitions. For purposes of this subsection—

(A) the term "qualified tax-exempt organization" means an employer that is an organization described in section 501(c) and exempt from taxation under section 501(a), and

(B) the term "qualified veteran" has meaning given such term by section 51(d)(3).
[For Analysis, see ¶ 1904.]

[Endnote Code Sec. 3111]
Code Sec. 3111(e) was added by Sec. 261(e)(2) of an Act To amend the Internal Revenue Code of 1986 to repeal the imposition of 3 percent withholding on certain payments made to vendors by government entities, to modify the calculation of modified adjusted gross income for purposes of determining eligibility for certain healthcare-related programs, and for other purposes, P.L. 112-56, 11/21/2011, as detailed below:
1. Sec. 261(e)(2) added subsec. (e)
Effective Date (Sec. 261(g), P.L. 112-56, 11/21/2011) effective for individuals who begin work for the employer after 11/21/2011.

[¶ 3108]   Code Sec. 3121.   Definitions.

(a) Wages. For purposes of this chapter, the term "wages" means all remuneration for employment, including the cash value of all remuneration (including benefits) paid in any medium other than cash; except that such term shall not include—

(1) in the case of the taxes imposed by sections 3101(a) and 3111(a) that part of the remuneration which, after remuneration (other than remuneration referred to in the succeeding paragraphs of this subsection) equal to the contribution and benefit base (as determined under section 230 of the Social Security Act) with respect to employment has been paid to an individual by an employer during the calendar year with respect to which such contribution and benefit base is effective, is paid to such individual by such employer during such calendar year. If an employer (hereinafter referred to as successor employer) during any calendar year acquires substantially all the property used in a trade or business of another employer (hereinafter referred to as a predecessor), or used in a separate unit of a trade or business of a predecessor, and immediately after the acquisition employs in his trade or business an individual who immediately prior to the acquisition was employed in the trade or business of such predecessor, then, for the purpose of determining whether the

successor employer has paid remuneration (other than remuneration referred to in the succeeding paragraphs of this subsection) with respect to employment equal to the contribution and benefit base (as determined under section 230 of the Social Security Act) to such individual during such calendar year, any remuneration (other than remuneration referred to in the succeeding paragraphs of this subsection) with respect to employment paid (or considered under this paragraph as having been paid) to such individual by such predecessor during such calendar year and prior to such acquisition shall be considered as having been paid by such successor employer;

(2) the amount of any payment (including any amount paid by an employer for insurance or annuities, or into a fund, to provide for any such payment) made to, or on behalf of, an employee or any of his dependents under a plan or system established by an employer which makes provision for his employees generally (or for his employees generally and their dependents) or for a class or classes of his employees (or for a class or classes of his employees and their dependents), on account of—

(A) sickness or accident disability (but, in the case of payments made to an employee or any of his dependents, this subparagraph shall exclude from the term "wages" only payments which are received under a workmen's compensation law), or

(B) medical or hospitalization expenses in connection with sickness or accident disability, or

(C) death, except that this paragraph does not apply to a payment for group-term life insurance to the extent that such payment is includible in the gross income of the employee;

(3) **Repealed.**

(4) any payment on account of sickness or accident disability, or medical or hospitalization expenses in connection with sickness or accident disability, made by an employer to, or on behalf of, an employee after the expiration of 6 calendar months following the last calendar month in which the employee worked for such employer;

(5) any payment made to, or on behalf of, an employee or his beneficiary—

(A) from or to a trust described in section 401(a) which is exempt from tax under section 501(a) at the time of such payment unless such payment is made to an employee of the trust as remuneration for services rendered as such employee and not as a beneficiary of the trust,

(B) under or to an annuity plan which, at the time of such payment, is a plan described in section 403(a),

(C) under a simplified employee pension (as defined in section 408(k)(1)), other than any contributions described in section 408(k)(6),

(D) under or to an annuity contract described in section 403(b), other than a payment for the purchase of such contract which is made by reason of a salary reduction agreement (whether evidenced by a written instrument or otherwise),

(E) under or to an exempt governmental deferred compensation plan (as defined in subsection (v)(3)),

(F) to supplement pension benefits under a plan or trust described in any of the foregoing provisions of this paragraph to take into account some portion or all of the increase in the cost of living (as determined by the Secretary of Labor) since retirement but only if such supplemental payments are under a plan which is treated as a welfare plan under section 3(2)(B)(ii) of the Employee Retirement Income Security Act of 1974,

(G) under a cafeteria plan (within the meaning of section 125) if such payment would not be treated as wages without regard to such plan and it is reasonable to believe that (if section 125 applied for purposes of this section) section 125 would not treat any wages as constructively received,

(H) under an arrangement to which section 408(p) applies, other than any elective contributions under paragraph (2)(A)(i) thereof, or

(I) under a plan described in section 457(e)(11)(A)(ii) and maintained by an eligible employer (as defined in section 457(e)(1));

(6) the payment by an employer (without deduction from the remuneration of the employee)—

(A) of the tax imposed upon an employee under section 3101, or

(B) of any payment required from an employee under a State unemployment compensation law,

with respect to remuneration paid to an employee for domestic service in a private home of the employer or for agricultural labor;

(7) (A) remuneration paid in any medium other than cash to an employee for service not in the course of the employer's trade or business or for domestic service in a private home of the employer;

(B) cash remuneration paid by an employer in any calendar year to an employee for domestic service in a private home of the employer (including domestic service on a farm operated for profit), if the cash remuneration paid in such year by the employer to the employee for such service is less than the applicable dollar threshold (as defined in subsection (x)) for such year;

(C) cash remuneration paid by an employer in any calendar year to an employee for service not in the course of the employer's trade or business, if the cash remuneration paid in such year by the employer to the employee for such service is less than $100. As used in this subparagraph, the term "service not in the course of the employer's trade or business" does not include domestic service in a private home of the employer and does not include service described in subsection (g)(5);

(8) (A) remuneration paid in any medium other than cash for agricultural labor;

(B) cash remuneration paid by an employer in any calendar year to an employee for agricultural labor unless—

(i) the cash remuneration paid in such year by the employer to the employee for such labor is $150 or more, or

(ii) the employer's expenditures for agricultural labor in such year equal or exceed $2,500,

except that clause (ii) shall not apply in determining whether remuneration paid to an employee constitutes "wages" under this section if such employee (I) is employed as a hand harvest laborer and is paid on a piece rate basis in an operation which has been, and is customarily and generally recognized as having been, paid on a piece rate basis in the region of employment, (II) commutes daily from his permanent residence to the farm on which he is so employed, and (III) has been employed in agriculture less than 13 weeks during the preceding calendar year;

(9) Repealed.

(10) remuneration paid by an employer in any calendar year to an employee for service described in subsection (d)(3)(C) (relating to home workers), if the cash remuneration paid in such year by the employer to the employee for such service is less than $100;

(11) remuneration paid to or on behalf of an employee if (and to the extent that) at the time of the payment of such remuneration it is reasonable to believe that a corresponding deduction is allowable under section 217 (determined without regard to section 274(n));

(12) (A) tips paid in any medium other than cash;

(B) cash tips received by an employee in any calendar month in the course of his employment by an employer unless the amount of such cash tips is $20 or more;

(13) any payment or series of payments by an employer to an employee or any of his dependents which is paid—

(A) upon or after the termination of an employee's employment relationship because of (i) death, or (ii) retirement for disability, and

(B) under a plan established by the employer which makes provision for his employees generally or a class or classes of his employees (or for such employees or class or classes of employees and their dependents),

other than any such payment or series of payments which would have been paid if the employee's employment relationship had not been so terminated;

(14) any payment made by an employer to a survivor or the estate of a former employee after the calendar year in which such employee died;

(15) any payment made by an employer to an employee, if at the time such payment is made such employee is entitled to disability insurance benefits under section 223(a) of the Social Security Act and such entitlement commenced prior to the calendar year in which such payment is made, and if such employee did not perform any services for such employer during the period for which such payment is made;

(16) remuneration paid by an organization exempt from income tax under section 501(a) (other than an organization described in section 401(a)) or under section 521 in any calendar year to an employee for service rendered in the employ of such organization, if the remuneration paid in such year by the organization to the employee for such service is less than $100;

(17) any contribution, payment, or service provided by an employer which may be excluded from the gross income of an employee, his spouse, or his dependents, under the provisions of section 120 (relating to amounts received under qualified group legal services plans);

(18) any payment made, or benefit furnished, to or for the benefit of an employee if at the time of such payment or such furnishing it is reasonable to believe that the employee will be able to exclude such payment or benefit from income under section 127, 129, 134(b)(4), or 134(b)(5);

(19) the value of any meals or lodging furnished by or on behalf of the employer if at the time of such furnishing it is reasonable to believe that the employee will be able to exclude such items from income under section 119;

(20) any benefit provided to or on behalf of an employee if at the time such benefit is provided it is reasonable to believe that the employee will be able to exclude such benefit from income under section 74(c), 108(f)(4), 117, or 132;

(21) in the case of a member of an Indian tribe, any remuneration on which no tax is imposed by this chapter by reason of section 7873 (relating to income derived by Indians from exercise of fishing rights);

(22) remuneration on account of—

(A) a transfer of a share of stock to any individual pursuant to an exercise of an incentive stock option (as defined in section 422(b)) or under an employee stock purchase plan (as defined in section 423(b)), or

(B) any disposition by the individual of such stock; or

(23) any benefit or payment which is excludable from the gross income of the employee under section 139B(b).

Nothing in the regulations prescribed for purposes of chapter 24 (relating to income tax withholding) which provides an exclusion from "wages" as used in such chapter shall be construed to require a similar exclusion from "wages" in the regulations prescribed for purposes of this chapter.

Except as otherwise provided in regulations prescribed by the Secretary, any third party which makes a payment included in wages solely by reason of the parenthetical matter contained in subparagraph (A) of paragraph (2) shall be treated for purposes of this chapter and chapter 22 as the employer with respect to such wages.

(b) Employment. For purposes of this chapter, the term "employment" means any service, of whatever nature, performed (A) by an employee for the person employing him, irrespective of the citizenship or residence of either, (i) within the United States, or (ii) on or in connection with an American vessel or American aircraft under a contract of service which is entered into within the United States or during the performance of which and while the employee is employed on the vessel or aircraft it touches at a port in the United States, if the employee is employed on and in connection with such vessel or aircraft when outside the United States, or (B) outside the United States by a citizen or resident of the United States as an employee for an American employer (as defined in subsection (h)), or (C) if it is service, regardless of where or by whom performed, which is designated as employment or recognized as equivalent to employment under an agreement entered into under section 233 of the Social Security Act; except that such term shall not include—

(1) service performed by foreign agricultural workers lawfully admitted to the United States from the Bahamas, Jamaica, and the other British West Indies, or from any other foreign country or possession thereof, on a temporary basis to perform agricultural labor;

(2) domestic service performed in a local college club, or local chapter of a college fraternity or sorority, by a student who is enrolled and is regularly attending classes at a school, college, or university;

(3) (A) service performed by a child under the age of 18 in the employ of his father or mother;

(B) service not in the course of the employer's trade or business, or domestic service in a private home of the employer, performed by an individual under the age of 21 in the employ of his father or mother, or performed by an individual in the employ of his spouse or son or daughter; except that the provisions of this subparagraph shall not be applicable to such domestic service performed by an individual in the employ of his son or daughter if—

(i) the employer is a surviving spouse or a divorced individual and has not remarried, or has a spouse living in the home who has a mental or physical condition which results in such spouse's being incapable of caring for a son, daughter, stepson, or stepdaughter (referred to in clause (ii)) for at least 4 continuous weeks in the calendar quarter in which the service is rendered, and

(ii) a son, daughter, stepson, or stepdaughter of such employer is living in the home, and

(iii) the son, daughter, stepson, or stepdaughter (referred to in clause (ii)) has not attained age 18 or has a mental or physical condition which requires the personal care and supervision of an adult for at least 4 continuous weeks in the calendar quarter in which the service is rendered;

(4) service performed by an individual on or in connection with a vessel not an American vessel, or on or in connection with an aircraft not an American aircraft, if (A) the individual is employed on and in connection with such vessel or aircraft, when outside the United States and (B)(i) such individual is not a citizen of the United States or (ii) the employer is not an American employer;

(5) service performed in the employ of the United States or any instrumentality of the United States, if such service—

(A) would be excluded from the term "employment" for purposes of this title if the provisions of paragraphs (5) and (6) of this subsection as in effect in January 1983 had remained in effect, and

(B) is performed by an individual who—

(i) has been continuously performing service described in subparagraph (A) since December 31, 1983, and for purposes of this clause—

(I) if an individual performing service described in subparagraph (A) returns to the performance of such service after being separated therefrom for a period of less than 366 consecutive days, regardless of whether the period began before, on, or after December 31, 1983, then such service shall be considered continuous,

(II) if an individual performing service described in subparagraph (A) returns to the performance of such service after being detailed or transferred to an international organization as described under section 3343 of subchapter III of chapter 33 of title 5, United States Code, or under section 3581 of chapter 35 of such title, then the service performed for that organization shall be considered service described in subparagraph (A),

(III) if an individual performing service described in subparagraph (A) is reemployed or reinstated after being separated from such service for the purpose of accepting employment with the American Institute in Taiwan as provided under section 3310 of chapter 48 of title 22, United States Code, then the service performed for that Institute shall be considered service described in subparagraph (A),

(IV) if an individual performing service described in subparagraph (A) returns to the performance of such service after performing service as a member of a uniformed service (including, for purposes of this clause, service in the National Guard and temporary service in the Coast Guard Reserve) and after exercising restoration or reemployment rights as provided under chapter 43 of title 38, United States Code, then the service so performed as a member of a uniformed service shall be considered service described in subparagraph (A), and

(V) if an individual performing service described in subparagraph (A) returns to the performance of such service after employment (by a tribal organization) to which section 105(e)(2) of the Indian Self-Determination Act applies, then the service performed for that tribal organization shall be considered service described in subparagraph (A); or

(ii) is receiving an annuity from the Civil Service Retirement and Disability Fund, or benefits (for service as an employee) under another retirement system established by a law of the United States for employees of the Federal Government (other than for members of the uniformed service);

except that this paragraph shall not apply with respect to any such service performed on or after any date on which such individual performs—

(C) service performed as the President or Vice President of the United States,

(D) service performed—

(i) in a position placed in the Executive Schedule under sections 5312 through 5317 of title 5, United States Code,

(ii) as a noncareer appointee in the Senior Executive Service or a noncareer member of the Senior Foreign Service, or

(iii) in a position to which the individual is appointed by the President (or his designee) or the Vice President under section 105(a)(1), 106(a)(1), or 107(a)(1) or (b)(1) of title 3, United States Code, if the maximum rate of basic pay for such position is at or above the rate for level V of the Executive Schedule,

(E) service performed as the Chief Justice of the United States, an Associate Justice of the Supreme Court, a judge of a United States court of appeals, a judge of a United States district court (including the district court of a territory), a judge of the United States Claims Court [United States Court of Federal Claims, see §902(b), P.L. 102-572], a judge of the United States Court of International Trade, a judge of the United States Tax Court, a United States magistrate, or a referee in bankruptcy or United States bankruptcy judge,

(F) service performed as a Member, Delegate, or Resident Commissioner of or to the Congress,

(G) any other service in the legislative branch of the Federal Government if such service—

(i) is performed by an individual who was not subject to subchapter III of chapter 83 of title 5, United States Code, or to another retirement system established by a law of the United States for employees of the Federal Government (other than for members of the uniformed services), on December 31, 1983, or

(ii) is performed by an individual who has, at any time after December 31, 1983, received a lump-sum payment under section 8342(a) of title 5, United States Code, or under the corresponding provision of the law establishing the other retirement system described in clause (i), or

(iii) is performed by an individual after such individual has otherwise ceased to be subject to subchapter III of chapter 83 of title 5, United States Code (without having an application pending for coverage under such subchapter), while performing service in the legislative branch (determined without regard to the provisions of subparagraph (B) relating to continuity of employment), for any period of time after December 31, 1983,

and for purposes of this subparagraph (G) an individual is subject to such subchapter III or to any such other retirement system at any time only if (a) such individual's pay is subject to deductions, contributions, or similar payments (concurrent with the service being performed at that time) under section 8334(a) of such title 5 or the corresponding provision of the law establishing such other system, or (in a case to which section 8332(k)(1) of such title applies) such individual is making payments of amounts equivalent to such deductions, contributions, or similar payments while on leave without pay, or (b) such individual is receiving an annuity from the Civil Service Retirement and Disability Fund, or is receiving benefits (for service as an employee) under another retirement system established by a law of the United States for employees of the Federal Government (other than for members of the uniformed services), or

(H) service performed by an individual—

(i) on or after the effective date of an election by such individual, under section 301 of the Federal Employees' Retirement System Act of 1986, section 307 of the Central Intelligence Agency Retirement Act (50 U.S.C. 2157), or the Federal Employees' Retirement System Open Enrollment Act of 1997 to become subject to the Federal Employees' Retirement System provided in chapter 84 of title 5, United States Code, or

(ii) on or after the effective date of an election by such individual, under regulations issued under section 860 of the Foreign Service Act of 1980, to become subject to the Foreign Service Pension System provided in subchapter II of chapter 8 of title I of such Act;

(6) service performed in the employ of the United States or any instrumentality of the United States if such service is performed—

(A) in a penal institution of the United States by an inmate thereof;

(B) by any individual as an employee included under section 5351(2) of title 5, United States Code (relating to certain interns, student nurses, and other student employees of hospitals of the Federal Government), other than as a medical or dental intern or a medical or dental resident in training; or

(C) by any individual as an employee serving on a temporary basis in case of fire, storm, earthquake, flood, or other similar emergency;

(7) service performed in the employ of a State, or any political subdivision thereof, or any instrumentality of any one or more of the foregoing which is wholly owned thereby, except that this paragraph shall not apply in the case of—

(A) service which, under subsection (j), constitutes covered transportation service,

(B) service in the employ of the Government of Guam or the Government of American Samoa or any political subdivision thereof, or of any instrumentality of any one or more of the foregoing which is wholly owned thereby, performed by an officer or employee thereof (including a member of the legislature of any such Government or political subdivision), and, for purposes of this title with respect to the taxes imposed by this chapter—

(i) any person whose service as such an officer or employee is not covered by a retirement system established by a law of the United States shall not, with respect to such service, be regarded as an employee of the United States or any agency or instrumentality thereof, and

(ii) the remuneration for service described in clause (i) (including fees paid to a public official) shall be deemed to have been paid by the Government of Guam or the Government of American Samoa or by a political subdivision thereof or an instrumentality of any one or more of the foregoing which is wholly owned thereby, whichever is appropriate,

(C) service performed in the employ of the District of Columbia or any instrumentality which is wholly owned thereby, if such service is not covered by a retirement system established by a law of the United States (other than the Federal Employees Retirement System provided in chapter 84 of title 5, United States Code); except that the provisions of this subparagraph shall not be applicable to service performed—

(i) in a hospital or penal institution by a patient or inmate thereof;

(ii) by any individual as an employee included under section 5351(2) of title 5, United States Code (relating to certain interns, student nurses, and other student employees of hospitals of the District of Columbia Government), other than as a medical or dental intern or as a medical or dental resident in training;

(iii) by any individual as an employee serving on a temporary basis in case of fire, storm, snow, earthquake, flood or other similar emergency; or

(iv) by a member of a board, committee, or council of the District of Columbia, paid on a per diem, meeting, or other fee basis,

(D) service performed in the employ of the Government of Guam (or any instrumentality which is wholly owned by such Government) by an employee properly classified as a temporary or intermittent employee, if such service is not covered by a retirement system established by a law of Guam; except that (i) the provisions of this subparagraph shall not be applicable to services performed by an elected official or a member of the legislature or in a hospital or penal institution by a patient or inmate thereof, and (ii) for purposes of this subparagraph, clauses (i) and (ii) of subparagraph (B) shall apply,

(E) service included under an agreement entered into pursuant to section 218 of the Social Security Act, or

(F) service in the employ of a State (other than the District of Columbia, Guam, or American Samoa), of any political subdivision thereof, or of any instrumentality of any one or more of the foregoing which is wholly owned thereby, by an individual who is not a member of a retirement system of such State, political subdivision, or instrumentality, except that the provisions of this subparagraph shall not be applicable to service performed—

(i) by an individual who is employed to relieve such individual from unemployment;

(ii) in a hospital, home, or other institution by a patient or inmate thereof;

(iii) by any individual as an employee serving on a temporary basis in case of fire, storm, snow, earthquake, flood, or other similar emergency;

(iv) by an election official or election worker if the remuneration paid in a calendar year for such service is less than $1,000 with respect to service performed during any calendar year commencing on or after January 1, 1995, ending on or before December 31, 1999, and the adjusted amount determined under section 218(c)(8)(B) of the Social Security Act for any calendar year commencing on or after January 1, 2000, with respect to service performed during such calendar year; or

(v) by an employee in a position compensated solely on a fee basis which is treated pursuant to section 1402(c)(2)(E) as a trade or business for purposes of inclusion of such fees in net earnings from self-employment;

for purposes of this subparagraph, except as provided in regulations prescribed by the Secretary, the term "retirement system" has the meaning given such term by section 218(b)(4) of the Social Security Act;

(8) (A) service performed by a duly ordained, commissioned, or licensed minister of a church in the exercise of his ministry or by a member of a religious order in the exercise of duties required by such order, except that this subparagraph shall not apply to service performed by a member of such an order in the exercise of such duties, if an election of coverage under subsection (r) is in effect with respect to such order, or with respect to the autonomous subdivision thereof to which such member belongs;

(B) service performed in the employ of a church or qualified church-controlled organization if such church or organization has in effect an election under subsection (w), other than service in an unrelated trade or business (within the meaning of section 513(a));

(9) service performed by an individual as an employee or employee representative as defined in section 3231;

(10) service performed in the employ of—

(A) a school, college, or university, or

(B) an organization described in section 509(a)(3) if the organization is organized, and at all times thereafter is operated, exclusively for the benefit of, to perform the functions of, or to carry out the purposes of a school, college, or university and is operated, supervised, or controlled by or in connection with such school, college, or university, unless it is a school, college, or university of a State or a political subdivision thereof and the services performed in its employ by a student referred to in section 218(c)(5) of the Social Security Act are covered under the agreement between the Commissioner of Social Security and such State entered into pursuant to section 218 of such Act;

if such service is performed by a student who is enrolled and regularly attending classes at such school, college, or university;

(11) service performed in the employ of a foreign government (including service as a consular or other officer or employee or a nondiplomatic representative);

(12) service performed in the employ of an instrumentality wholly owned by a foreign government—

(A) if the service is of a character similar to that performed in foreign countries by employees of the United States Government or of an instrumentality thereof; and

(B) if the Secretary of State shall certify to the Secretary of the Treasury that the foreign government, with respect to whose instrumentality and employees thereof exemption is claimed, grants an equivalent exemption with respect to similar service performed in the foreign country by employees of the United States Government and of instrumentalities thereof;

(13) service performed as a student nurse in the employ of a hospital or a nurses' training school by an individual who is enrolled and is regularly attending classes in a nurses' training school chartered or approved pursuant to State law;

(14)   (A) service performed by an individual under the age of 18 in the delivery or distribution of newspapers or shopping news, not including delivery or distribution to any point for subsequent delivery or distribution;

(B) service performed by an individual in, and at the time of, the sale of newspapers or magazines to ultimate consumers, under an arrangement under which the newspapers or magazines are to be sold by him at a fixed price, his compensation being based on the retention of the excess of such price over the amount at which the newspapers or magazines are charged to him, whether or not he is guaranteed a minimum amount of compensation for such service, or is entitled to be credited with the unsold newspapers or magazines turned back;

(15) service performed in the employ of an international organization, except service which constitutes "employment" under subsection (y);

(16) service performed by an individual under an arrangement with the owner or tenant of land pursuant to which—

(A) such individual undertakes to produce agricultural or horticultural commodities (including livestock, bees, poultry, and fur-bearing animals and wildlife) on such land,

(B) the agricultural or horticultural commodities produced by such individual, or the proceeds therefrom, are to be divided between such individual and such owner or tenant, and

(C) the amount of such individual's share depends on the amount of the agricultural or horticultural commodities produced;

(17) service in the employ of any organization which is performed (A) in any year during any part of which such organization is registered, or there is in effect a final order of the Subversive Activities Control Board requiring such organization to register, under the Internal Security Act of 1950, as amended, as a Communist-action organization, a Communist-front organization, or a Communist-infiltrated organization, and (B) after June 30, 1956;

(18) service performed in Guam by a resident of the Republic of the Philippines while in Guam on a temporary basis as a nonimmigrant alien admitted to Guam pursuant to section 101(a)(15)(H)(ii) of the Immigration and Nationality Act (8 U.S.C. 1101(a)(15)(H)(ii));

(19) service which is performed by a nonresident alien individual for the period he is temporarily present in the United States as a nonimmigrant under subparagraph (F), (J), (M), or (Q) of section 101(a)(15) of the Immigration and Nationality Act, as amended, and which is performed to carry out the purpose specified in subparagraph (F), (J), (M), or (Q), as the case may be;

(20) service (other than service described in paragraph (3)(A)) performed by an individual on a boat engaged in catching fish or other forms of aquatic animal life under an arrangement with the owner or operator of such boat pursuant to which—

(A) such individual does not receive any cash remuneration other than as provided in subparagraph (B) and other than cash remuneration—

(i) which does not exceed $100 per trip;

(ii) which is contingent on a minimum catch; and

(iii) which is paid solely for additional dues (such as mate, engineer, or cook) for which additional cash remuneration is traditional in the industry,

(B) such individual receives a share of the boat's (or the boats' in the case of a fishing operation involving more than one boat) catch of fish or other forms of aquatic animal life or a share of the proceeds from the sale of such catch, and

(C) the amount of such individual's share depends on the amount of the boat's (or the boats' in the case of a fishing operation involving more than one boat) catch of fish or other forms of aquatic animal life,

but only if the operating crew of such boat (or each boat from which the individual receives a share in the case of a fishing operation involving more than one boat) is normally made up of fewer than 10 individuals; or

(21) domestic service in a private home of the employer which—

(A) is performed in any year by an individual under the age of 18 during any portion of such year; and

(B) is not the principal occupation of such employee.

For purposes of paragraph (20), the operating crew of a boat shall be treated as normally made up of fewer than 10 individuals if the average size of the operating crew on trips made during the preceding 4 calendar quarters consisted of fewer than 10 individuals.

(c) **Included and excluded service.** For purposes of this chapter, if the services performed during one-half or more of any pay period by an employee for the person employing him constitute employment, all the services of such employee for such period shall be deemed to be employment; but if the services performed during more than one-half of any such pay period by an employee for the person employing him do not constitute employment, then none of the services of such employee for such period shall be deemed to be employment. As used in this subsection, the term "pay period" means a period (of not more than 31 consecutive days) for which a payment of remuneration is ordinarily made to the employee by the person employing him. This subsection shall not be applicable with respect to services performed in a pay period by an employee for the person employing him, where any of such service is excepted by subsection (b)(9).

(d) **Employee.** For purposes of this chapter, the term "employee" means—

(1) any officer of a corporation; or

(2) any individual who, under the usual common law rules applicable in determining the employer-employee relationship, has the status of an employee; or

(3) any individual (other than an individual who is an employee under paragraph (1) or (2)) who performs services for remuneration for any person—

(A) as an agent-driver or commission-driver engaged in distributing meat products, vegetable products, fruit products, bakery products, beverages (other than milk), or laundry or dry-cleaning services, for his principal;

(B) as a full-time life insurance salesman;

(C) as a home worker performing work, according to specifications furnished by the person for whom the services are performed, on materials or goods furnished by such person which are required to be returned to such person or a person designated by him; or

(D) as a traveling or city salesman, other than as an agent-driver or commission-driver, engaged upon a full-time basis in the solicitation on behalf of, and the transmission to, his principal (except for side-line sales activities on behalf of some other person) of orders from wholesalers, retailers, contractors, or operators of hotels, restaurants, or other similar establishments for merchandise for resale or supplies for use in their business operations;

if the contract of service contemplates that substantially all of such services are to be performed personally by such individual; except that an individual shall not be included in the term "employee" under the provisions of this paragraph if such individual has a substantial investment in facilities used in connection with the performance of such services (other than in facilities for transportation), or if the services are in the nature of a single transaction not part of a continuing relationship with the person for whom the services are performed; or

(4) any individual who performs services that are included under an agreement entered into pursuant to section 218 of the Social Security Act.

(e) **State, United States, and citizen.** For purposes of this chapter—

(1) **State.** The term "State" includes the District of Columbia, the Commonwealth of Puerto Rico, the Virgin Islands, Guam, and American Samoa.

(2) **United States.** The term "United States" when used in a geographical sense includes the Commonwealth of Puerto Rico, the Virgin Islands, Guam, and American Samoa.

An individual who is a citizen of the Commonwealth of Puerto Rico (but not otherwise a citizen of the United States) shall be considered, for purposes of this section, as a citizen of the United States.

(f) **American vessel and aircraft.** For purposes of this chapter, the term "American vessel" means any vessel documented or numbered under the laws of the United States; and includes any vessel which is neither documented or numbered under the laws of the United States nor documented under the laws of any foreign country, if its crew is employed solely by one or more citizens or residents of the United States or corporations organized under the laws of the United States or of any State; and the term "American aircraft" means an aircraft registered under the laws of the United States.

(g) **Agricultural labor.** For purposes of this chapter, the term "agricultural labor" includes all service performed—

(1) on a farm, in the employ of any person, in connection with cultivating the soil, or in connection with raising or harvesting any agricultural or horticultural commodity, including the raising, shearing, feeding, caring for, training, and management of livestock, bees, poultry, and fur-bearing animals and wildlife;

(2) in the employ of the owner or tenant or other operator of a farm, in connection with the operation, management, conservation, improvement, or maintenance of such farm and its tools and equipment, or in salvaging timber or clearing land of brush and other debris left by a hurricane, if the major part of such service is performed on a farm;

(3) in connection with the production or harvesting of any commodity defined as an agricultural commodity in section 15(g) of the Agricultural Marketing Act, as amended (12 U.S.C. 1141j), or in connection with the ginning of cotton, or in connection with the operation or maintenance of ditches, canals, reservoirs, or waterways, not owned or operated for profit, used exclusively for supplying and storing water for farming purposes;

(4) (A) in the employ of the operator of a farm in handling, planting, drying, packing, packaging, processing, freezing, grading, storing, or delivering to storage or to market or to a carrier for transportation to market, in its unmanufactured state, any agricultural or horticultural commodity; but only if such operator produced more than one-half of the commodity with respect to which such service is performed;

(B) in the employ of a group of operators of farms (other than a cooperative organization) in the performance of service described in subparagraph (A), but only if such operators produced all of the commodity with respect to which such service is performed. For purposes of this subparagraph, any unincorporated group of operators shall be deemed a cooperative organization if the number of operators comprising such group is more than 20 at any time during the calendar year in which such service is performed;

(C) the provisions of subparagraphs (A) and (B) shall not be deemed to be applicable with respect to service performed in connection with commercial canning or commercial freezing or in connection with any agricultural or horticultural commodity after its delivery to a terminal market for distribution for consumption; or

(5) on a farm operated for profit if such service is not in the course of the employer's trade or business .

As used in this subsection, the term "farm" includes stock, dairy, poultry, fruit, fur-bearing animal, and truck farms, plantations, ranches, nurseries, ranges, greenhouses or other similar structures used primarily for the raising of agricultural or horticultural commodities, and orchards.

(h)   American employer. For purposes of this chapter, the term "American employer" means an employer which is—

(1) the United States or any instrumentality thereof,

(2) an individual who is a resident of the United States,

(3) a partnership, if two-thirds or more of the partners are residents of the United States,

(4) a trust, if all of the trustees are residents of the United States, or

(5) a corporation organized under the laws of the United States or of any State.

(i)   Computation of wages in certain cases.

(1)   Domestic service. For purposes of this chapter, in the case of domestic service described in subsection (a)(7)(B), any payment of cash remuneration for such service which is more or less than a whole-dollar amount shall, under such conditions and to such extent as may be prescribed by regulations made under this chapter, be computed to the nearest dollar. For the purpose of the computation to the nearest dollar, the payment of a fractional part of a dollar shall be disregarded unless it amounts to one-half dollar or more, in which case it shall be increased to $1. The amount of any payment of cash remuneration so computed to the nearest dollar shall, in lieu of the amount actually paid, be deemed to constitute the amount of cash remuneration for purposes of subsection (a)(7)(B).

(2)   Service in the uniformed services. For purposes of this chapter, in the case of an individual performing service, as a member of a uniformed service, to which the provisions of subsection (m)(1) are applicable, the term "wages" shall, subject to the provisions of subsection (a)(1) of this section, include as such individual's remuneration for such service only (A) his basic pay as described in chapter 3 and section 1009 of title 37, United States Code, in the case of an individual performing service to which subparagraph (A) of such subsection (m)(1) applies, or (B) his compensation for such service as determined under section 206(a) of title 37, United States Code, in the case of an individual performing service to which subparagraph (B) of such subsection (m)(1) applies.

(3)   Peace Corps volunteer service. For purposes of this chapter, in the case of an individual performing service, as a volunteer or volunteer leader within the meaning of the Peace Corps Act, to which the provisions of section 3121(p) are applicable, the term "wages" shall, subject to the provisions of subsection (a)(1) of this section, include as such individual's remuneration for such service only amounts paid pursuant to section 5(c) or 6(1) of the Peace Corps Act.

(4)   Service performed by certain members of religious orders. For purposes of this chapter, in any case where an individual is a member of a religious order (as defined in subsection (r)(2)) performing service in the exercise of duties required by such order, and an election of coverage under subsection (r) is in effect with respect to such order or with respect to the autonomous subdivision thereof to which such member belongs, the term "wages" shall, subject to the provisions of subsection (a)(1), include as such individual's remuneration for such service the fair market value of any board, lodging, clothing, and other perquisites furnished to such member by such order or subdivision thereof or by any other person or organization pursuant to an agreement with such order or subdivision, except that the amount included as such individual's remuneration under this paragraph shall not be less than $100 a month.

(5)   Service performed by certain retired justices and judges. For purposes of this chapter, in the case of an individual performing service under the provisions of section 294 of title 28, United States Code (relating to assignment of retired justices and judges to active duty), the term "wages" shall not include any payment under section 371(b) of such title 28 which is received during the period of such service.

(j)   Covered transportation service. For purposes of this chapter—

(1)   Existing transportation systems—General rule. Except as provided in paragraph (2), all service performed in the employ of a State or political subdivision in connection with its operation of a public transportation system shall constitute covered transportation service if any part of the transportation system was acquired from private ownership after 1936 and prior to 1951.

(2)   Existing transportation systems—Cases in which no transportation employees, or only certain employees, are covered. Service performed in the employ of a State or political subdivision in connection with the operation of its public transportation system shall not constitute covered transportation service if—

(A) any part of the transportation system was acquired from private ownership after 1936 and prior to 1951, and substantially all service in connection with the operation of the transportation system was, on December 31, 1950, covered under a general retirement system providing benefits which, by reason of a provision of the State constitution dealing specifically with retirement systems of the State or political subdivisions thereof, cannot be diminished or impaired; or

(B) no part of the transportation system operated by the State or political subdivision on December 31, 1950, was acquired from private ownership after 1936 and prior to 1951;

except that if such State or political subdivision makes an acquisition after 1950 from private ownership of any part of its transportation system, then, in the case of any employee who—

(C) became an employee of such State or political subdivision in connection with and at the time of its acquisition after 1950 of such part, and

(D) prior to such acquisition rendered service in employment (including as employment service covered by an agreement under section 218 of the Social Security Act) in connection with the operation of such part of the transportation system acquired by the State or political subdivision,

the service of such employee in connection with the operation of the transportation system shall constitute covered transportation service, commencing with the first day of the third calendar quarter following the calendar quarter in which the acquisition of such part took place, unless on such first day such service of such employee is covered by a general retirement system which does not, with respect to such employee, contain special provisions applicable only to employees described in subparagraph (C).

(3)   Transportation systems acquired after 1950. All service performed in the employ of a State or political subdivision thereof in connection with its operation of a public transportation system shall constitute covered transportation service if the transportation system was not operated by the State or political subdivision prior to 1951 and, at the time of its first acquisition (after 1950) from private ownership of any part of its transportation system, the State or political subdivision did not have a general retirement system covering substantially all service performed in connection with the operation of the transportation system.

(4)   Definitions. For purposes of this subsection—

(A) The term "general retirement system" means any pension, annuity, retirement, or similar fund or system established by a State or by a political subdivision thereof for employees of the State, political subdivision, or both; but such term shall not include such a fund or system which covers only service performed in positions connected with the operation of its public transportation system.

(B) A transportation system or a part thereof shall be considered to have been acquired by a State or political subdivision from private ownership if prior to the acquisition service performed by employees in connection with the operation of the system or part thereof acquired constituted employment under this chapter or subchapter A of chapter 9 of the Internal Revenue Code of 1939 or was covered by an agreement made pursuant to section 218 of the Social Security Act and some of such employees became employees of the State or political subdivision in connection with and at the time of such acquisition.

(C) The term "political subdivision" includes an instrumentality of—

(i) a State,

(ii) one or more political subdivisions of a State, or

(iii) a State and one or more of its political subdivisions.

(k) Repealed.

(l) Agreements entered into by American employers with respect to foreign affiliates.

(1) Agreement with respect to certain employees of foreign affiliate. The Secretary shall, at the American employer's request, enter into an agreement (in such manner and form as may be prescribed by the Secretary) with any American employer (as defined in subsection (h)) who desires to have the insurance system established by title II of the Social Security Act extended to service performed outside the United States in the employ of any 1 or more of such employer's foreign affiliates (as defined in paragraph (6)) by all employees who are citizens or residents of the United States, except that the agreement shall not apply to any service performed by, or remuneration paid to, an employee if such service or remuneration would be excluded from the term "employment" or "wages", as defined in this section, had the service been performed in the United States. Such agreement may be amended at any time so as to be made applicable, in the same manner and under the same conditions, with respect to any other foreign affiliate of such American employer. Such agreement shall be applicable with respect to citizens or residents of the United States who, on or after the effective date of the agreement, are employees of and perform services outside the United States for any foreign affiliate specified in the agreement. Such agreement shall provide—

(A) that the American employer shall pay to the Secretary, at such time or times as the Secretary may by regulations prescribe, amounts equivalent to the sum of the taxes which would be imposed by sections 3101 and 3111 (including amounts equivalent to the interest, additions to the taxes, additional amounts, and penalties which would be applicable) with respect to the remuneration which would be wages if the services covered by the agreement constituted employment as defined in this section; and

(B) that the American employer will comply with such regulations relating to payments and reports as the Secretary may prescribe to carry out the purposes of this subsection.

(2) Effective period of agreement. An agreement entered into pursuant to paragraph (1) shall be in effect for the period beginning with the first day of the calendar quarter in which such agreement is entered into or the first day of the succeeding calendar quarter, as may be specified in the agreement; except that in case such agreement is amended to include the services performed for any other affiliate and such amendment is executed after the first month following the first calendar quarter for which the agreement is in effect, the agreement shall be in effect with respect to service performed for such other affiliate only after the calendar quarter in which such amendment is executed. Notwithstanding any other provision of this subsection, the period for which any such agreement is effective with respect to any foreign entity shall terminate at the end of any calendar quarter in which the foreign entity, at any time in such quarter, ceases to be a foreign affiliate as defined in paragraph (6).

(3) No termination of agreement. No agreement under this subsection may be terminated, either in its entirety or with respect to any foreign affiliate, on or after June 15, 1989.

(4) **Deposits in trust funds.** For purposes of section 201 of the Social Security Act, relating to appropriations to the Federal Old-Age and Survivors Insurance Trust Fund and the Federal Disability Insurance Trust Fund, such remuneration—

(A) paid for services covered by an agreement entered into pursuant to paragraph (1) as would be wages if the services constituted employment, and

(B) as is reported to the Secretary pursuant to the provisions of such agreement or of the regulations issued under this subsection,

shall be considered wages subject to the taxes imposed by this chapter.

(5) **Overpayments and underpayments.**

(A) If more or less than the correct amount due under an agreement entered into pursuant to this subsection is paid with respect to any payment of remuneration, proper adjustments with respect to the amounts due under such agreement shall be made, without interest, in such manner and at such times as may be required by regulations prescribed by the Secretary.

(B) If an overpayment cannot be adjusted under subparagraph (A), the amount thereof shall be paid by the Secretary, through the Fiscal Service of the Treasury Department, but only if a claim for such overpayment is filed with the Secretary within two years from the time such overpayment was made.

(6) **Foreign affiliate defined.** For purposes of this subsection and section 210(a) of the Social Security Act—

(A) In general. A foreign affiliate of an American employer is any foreign entity in which such American employer has not less than a 10-percent interest.

(B) Determination of 10-percent interest. For purposes of subparagraph (A), an American employer has a 10-percent interest in any entity if such employer has such an interest directly (or through one or more entities)—

(i) in the case of a corporation, in the voting stock thereof, and

(ii) in the case of any other entity, in the profits thereof.

(7) **American employer as separate entity.** Each American employer which enters into an agreement pursuant to paragraph (1) of this subsection shall, for purposes of this subsection and section 6413(c)(2)(C), relating to special refunds in the case of employees of certain foreign entities, be considered an employer in its capacity as a party to such agreement separate and distinct from its identity as a person employing individuals on its own account.

(8) **Regulations.** Regulations of the Secretary to carry out the purposes of this subsection shall be designed to make the requirements imposed on American employers with respect to services covered by an agreement entered into pursuant to this subsection the same, so far as practicable, as those imposed upon employers pursuant to this title with respect to the taxes imposed by this chapter.

(m) **Service in the uniformed services.** For purposes of this chapter—

(1) **Inclusion of service.** The term "employment" shall, notwithstanding the provisions of subsection (b) of this section, include—

(A) service performed by an individual as a member of a uniformed service on active duty, but such term shall not include any such service which is performed while on leave without pay, and

(B) service performed by an individual as a member of a uniformed service on inactive duty training.

(2) **Active duty.** The term "active duty" means "active duty" as described in paragraph (21) of section 101 of title 38, United States Code, except that it shall also include "active duty for training" as described in paragraph (22) of such section.

(3) **Inactive duty training.** The term "inactive duty training" means "inactive duty training" as described in paragraph (23) of such section 101.

(n) **Member of a uniformed service.** For purposes of this chapter, the term "member of a uniformed service" means any person appointed, enlisted, or inducted in a component of the Army, Navy, Air Force, Marine Corps, or Coast Guard (including a reserve component as defined in section 101(27) of title 38, United States Code), or in one of those services without specification of component, or as a commissioned officer of the Coast and Geodetic Survey, the National Oceanic and Atmospheric Administration Corps, or the Regular or Reserve Corps of the Public Health Service, and any person serving in the Army or Air Force under call or conscription. The term includes—

    (1) a retired member of any of those services;

    (2) a member of the Fleet Reserve or Fleet Marine Corps Reserve;

    (3) a cadet at the United States Military Academy, a midshipman at the United States Naval Academy, and a cadet at the United States Coast Guard Academy or United States Air Force Academy;

    (4) a member of the Reserve Officers' Training Corps, the Naval Reserve Officers' Training Corps, or the Air Force Reserve Officers' Training Corps, when ordered to annual training duty for fourteen days or more, and while performing authorized travel to and from that duty; and

    (5) any person while en route to or from, or at, a place for final acceptance or for entry upon active duty in the military, naval, or air service—

      (A) who has been provisionally accepted for such duty; or

      (B) who, under the Military Selective Service Act, has been selected for active military, naval, or air service;

    and has been ordered or directed to proceed to such place.

The term does not include a temporary member of the Coast Guard Reserve.

    (o) Crew leader. For purposes of this chapter, the term "crew leader" means an individual who furnishes individuals to perform agricultural labor for another person, if such individual pays (either on his own behalf or on behalf of such person) the individuals so furnished by him for the agricultural labor performed by them and if such individual has not entered into a written agreement with such person whereby such individual has been designated as an employee of such person; and such individuals furnished by the crew leader to perform agricultural labor for another person shall be deemed to be the employees of such crew leader. For purposes of this chapter and chapter 2, a crew leader shall, with respect to service performed in furnishing individuals to perform agricultural labor for another person and service performed as a member of the crew, be deemed not to be an employee of such other person.

    (p) Peace Corps volunteer service. For purposes of this chapter, the term "employment" shall, notwithstanding the provisions of subsection (b) of this section, include service performed by an individual as a volunteer or volunteer leader within the meaning of the Peace Corps Act.

    (q) Tips included for both employee and employer taxes. For purposes of this chapter, tips received by an employee in the course of his employment shall be considered remuneration for such employment (and deemed to have been paid by the employer for purposes of subsections (a) and (b) of section 3111). Such remuneration shall be deemed to be paid at the time a written statement including such tips is furnished to the employer pursuant to section 6053(a) or (if no statement including such tips is so furnished) at the time received; except that, in determining the employer's liability in connection with the taxes imposed by section 3111 with respect to such tips in any case where no statement including such tips was so furnished (or to the extent that the statement so furnished was inaccurate or incomplete), such remuneration shall be deemed for purposes of subtitle F to be paid on the date on which notice and demand for such taxes is made to the employer by the Secretary.

    (r) Election of coverage by religious orders.

    (1) Certificate of election by order. A religious order whose members are required to take a vow of poverty, or any autonomous subdivision of such order, may file a certificate (in such form and manner, and with such official, as may be prescribed by regulations under this chapter) electing to have the insurance system established by title II of the Social Security Act extended to services performed by its members in the exercise of duties required by such order or such subdivision thereof. Such certificate of election shall provide that—

      (A) such election of coverage by such order or subdivision shall be irrevocable;

(B) such election shall apply to all current and future members of such order, or in the case of a subdivision thereof to all current and future members of such order who belong to such subdivision;

(C) all services performed by a member of such an order or subdivision in the exercise of duties required by such order or subdivision shall be deemed to have been performed by such member as an employee of such order or subdivision; and

(D) the wages of each member, upon which such order or subdivision shall pay the taxes imposed by sections 3101 and 3111, will be determined as provided in subsection (i)(4).

(2) Definition of member. For purposes of this subsection, a member of a religious order means any individual who is subject to a vow of poverty as a member of such order and who performs tasks usually required (and to the extent usually required) of an active member of such order and who is not considered retired because of old age or total disability.

(3) Effective date for election.

(A) A certificate of election of coverage shall be in effect, for purposes of subsection (b)(8) and for purposes of section 210(a)(8) of the Social Security Act, for the period beginning with whichever of the following may be designated by the order or subdivision thereof:

(i) the first day of the calendar quarter in which the certificate is filed,

(ii) the first day of the calendar quarter succeeding such quarter, or

(iii) the first day of any calendar quarter preceding the calendar quarter in which the certificate is filed, except that such date may not be earlier than the first day of the twentieth calendar quarter preceding the quarter in which such certificate is filed.

Whenever a date is designated under clause (iii), the election shall apply to services performed before the quarter in which the certificate is filed only if the member performing such services was a member at the time such services were performed and is living on the first day of the quarter in which such certificate is filed.

(B) If a certificate of election filed pursuant to this subsection is effective for one or more calendar quarters prior to the quarter in which such certificate is filed, then—

(i) for purposes of computing interest and for purposes of section 6651 (relating to addition to tax for failure to file tax return), the due date for the return and payment of the tax for such prior calendar quarters resulting from the filing of such certificate shall be the last day of the calendar month following the calendar quarter in which the certificate is filed; and

(ii) the statutory period for the assessment of such tax shall not expire before the expiration of 3 years from such due date.

(s) Concurrent employment by two or more employers. For purposes of sections 3102, 3111, and 3121(a)(1), if two or more related corporations concurrently employ the same individual and compensate such individual through a common paymaster which is one of such corporations, each such corporation shall be considered to have paid as remuneration to such individual only the amounts actually disbursed by it to such individual and shall not be considered to have paid as remuneration to such individual amounts actually disbursed to such individual by another of such corporations.

(t) Repealed.

(u) Application of hospital insurance tax to federal, state, and local employment.

(1) Federal employment. For purposes of the taxes imposed by sections 3101(b) and 3111(b), subsection (b) shall be applied without regard to paragraph (5) thereof.

(2) State and local employment. For purposes of the taxes imposed by sections 3101(b) and 3111(b)—

(A) In general. Except as provided in subparagraphs (B) and (C), subsection (b) shall be applied without regard to paragraph (7) thereof.

(B) Exception for certain services. Service shall not be treated as employment by reason of subparagraph (A) if—

(i) the service is included under an agreement under section 218 of the Social Security Act, or

(ii) the service is performed—

(I) by an individual who is employed by a State or political subdivision thereof to relieve him from unemployment,

(II) in a hospital, home, or other institution by a patient or inmate thereof as an employee of a State or political subdivision thereof or of the District of Columbia,

(III) by an individual, as an employee of a State or political subdivision thereof or of the District of Columbia, serving on a temporary basis in case of fire, storm, snow, earthquake, flood or other similar emergency,

(IV) by any individual as an employee included under section 5351(2) of title 5, United States Code (relating to certain interns, student nurses, and other student employees of hospitals of the District of Columbia Government), other than as a medical or dental intern or a medical or dental resident in training,

(V) by an election official or election worker if the remuneration paid in a calendar year for such service is less than $1,000 with respect to service performed during any calendar year commencing on or after January 1, 1995, ending on or before December 31, 1999, and the adjusted amount determined under section 218(c)(8)(B) of the Social Security Act for any calendar year commencing on or after January 1, 2000, with respect to service performed during such calendar year, or

(VI) by an individual in a position described in section 1402(c)(2)(E).

As used in this subparagraph, the terms "State" and "political subdivision" have the meanings given those terms in section 218(b) of the Social Security Act.

(C) Exception for current employment which continues. Service performed for an employer shall not be treated as employment by reason of subparagraph (A) if—

(i) such service would be excluded from the term "employment" for purposes of this chapter if subparagraph (A) did not apply;

(ii) such service is performed by an individual—

(I) who was performing substantial and regular service for remuneration for that employer before April 1, 1986,

(II) who is a bona fide employee of that employer on March 31, 1986, and

(III) whose employment relationship with that employer was not entered into for purposes of meeting the requirements of this subparagraph; and

(iii) the employment relationship with that employer has not been terminated after March 31, 1986.

(D) Treatment of agencies and instrumentalities. For purposes of subparagraph (C), under regulations—

(i) All agencies and instrumentalities of a State (as defined in section 218(b) of the Social Security Act) or of the District of Columbia shall be treated as a single employer.

(ii) All agencies and instrumentalities of a political subdivision of a State (as so defined) shall be treated as a single employer and shall not be treated as described in clause (i).

(3) **Medicare qualified government employment.** For purposes of this chapter, the term "medicare qualified government employment" means service which—

(A) is employment (as defined in subsection (b)) with the application of paragraphs (1) and (2), but

(B) would not be employment (as so defined) without the application of such paragraphs.

(v) **Treatment of certain deferred compensation and salary reduction arrangements.**

(1) **Certain employer contributions treated as wages.** Nothing in any paragraph of subsection (a) (other than paragraph (1)) shall exclude from the term "wages" —

(A) any employer contribution under a qualified cash or deferred arrangement (as defined in section 401(k)) to the extent not included in gross income by reason of section

402(e)(3) or consisting of designated Roth contributions (as defined in section 402A(c)), or

(B) any amount treated as an employer contribution under section 414(h)(2) where the pickup referred to in such section is pursuant to a salary reduction agreement (whether evidenced by a written instrument or otherwise).

(2) Treatment of certain nonqualified deferred compensation plans.

(A) In general. Any amount deferred under a nonqualified deferred compensation plan shall be taken into account for purposes of this chapter as of the later of—

(i) when the services are performed, or

(ii) when there is no substantial risk of forfeiture of the rights to such amount.

The preceding sentence shall not apply to any excess parachute payment (as defined in section 280G(b)) or to any specified stock compensation (as defined in section 4985) on which tax is imposed by section 4985.

(B) Taxed only once. Any amount taken into account as wages by reason of subparagraph (A) (and the income attributable thereto) shall not thereafter be treated as wages for purposes of this chapter.

(C) Nonqualified deferred compensation plan. For purposes of this paragraph, the term "nonqualified deferred compensation plan" means any plan or other arrangement for deferral of compensation other than a plan described in subsection (a)(5).

(3) Exempt governmental deferred compensation plan. For purposes of subsection (a)(5), the term "exempt governmental deferred compensation plan" means any plan providing for deferral of compensation established and maintained for its employees by the United States, by a State or political subdivision thereof, or by an agency or instrumentality of any of the foregoing. Such term shall not include—

(A) any plan to which section 83, 402(b), 403(c), 457(a), or 457(f)(1) applies,

(B) any annuity contract described in section 403(b), and

(C) the Thrift Savings Fund (within the meaning of subchapter III of chapter 84 of title 5, United States Code).

(w) Exemption of churches and qualified church-controlled organizations.

(1) General rule. Any church or qualified church-controlled organization (as defined in paragraph (3)) may make an election within the time period described in paragraph (2), in accordance with such procedures as the Secretary determines to be appropriate, that services performed in the employ of such church or organization shall be excluded from employment for purposes of title II of the Social Security Act and this chapter. An election may be made under this subsection only if the church or qualified church-controlled organization states that such church or organization is opposed for religious reasons to the payment of the tax imposed under section 3111.

(2) Timing and duration of election. An election under this subsection must be made prior to the first date, more than 90 days after July 18, 1984, on which a quarterly employment tax return for the tax imposed under section 3111 is due, or would be due but for the election, from such church or organization. An election under this subsection shall apply to current and future employees, and shall apply to service performed after December 31, 1983. The election may be revoked by the church or organization under regulations prescribed by the Secretary. The election shall be revoked by the Secretary if such church or organization fails to furnish the information required under section 6051 to the Secretary for a period of 2 years or more with respect to remuneration paid for such services by such church or organization, and, upon request by the Secretary, fails to furnish all such previously unfurnished information for the period covered by the election. Any revocation under the preceding sentence shall apply retroactively to the beginning of the 2-year period for which the information was not furnished.

(3) Definitions.

(A) For purposes of this subsection, the term "church" means a church, a convention or association of churches, or an elementary or secondary school which is controlled, operated, or principally supported by a church or by a convention or association of churches.

(B) For purposes of this subsection, the term "qualified church-controlled organization" means any church-controlled tax-exempt organization described in section 501(c)(3), other than an organization which—

(i) offers goods, services, or facilities for sale, other than on an incidental basis, to the general public, other than goods, services, or facilities which are sold at a nominal charge which is substantially less than the cost of providing such goods, services, or facilities; and

(ii) normally receives more than 25 percent of its support from either (I) governmental sources, or (II) receipts from admissions, sales of merchandise, performance of services, or furnishing of facilities, in activities which are not unrelated trades or businesses, or both.

(x) **Applicable dollar threshold.** For purposes of subsection (a)(7)(B), the term "applicable dollar threshold" means $1,000. In the case of calendar years after 1995, the Commissioner of Social Security shall adjust such $1,000 amount at the same time and in the same manner as under section 215(a)(1)(B)(ii) of the Social Security Act with respect to the amounts referred to in section 215(a)(1)(B)(i) of such Act, except that, for purposes of this paragraph, 1993 shall be substituted for the calendar year referred to in section 215(a)(1)(B)(ii)(II) of such Act. If any amount as adjusted under the preceding sentence is not a multiple of $100, such amount shall be rounded to the next lowest multiple of $100.

(y) **Service in the employ of international organizations by certain transferred Federal employees.**

(1) **In general.** For purposes of this chapter, service performed in the employ of an international organization by an individual pursuant to a transfer of such individual to such international organization pursuant to section 3582 of title 5, United States Code, shall constitute "employment" if—

(A) immediately before such transfer, such individual performed service with a Federal agency which constituted "employment" under subsection (b) for purposes of the taxes imposed by sections 3101(a) and 3111(a), and

(B) such individual would be entitled, upon separation from such international organization and proper application, to reemployment with such Federal agency under such section 3582.

(2) **Definitions.** For purposes of this subsection—

(A) Federal agency. The term "Federal agency" means an agency, as defined in section 3581(1) of title 5, United States Code.

(B) International organization. The term "international organization" has the meaning provided such term by section 3581(3) of title 5, United States Code.

(z) **Treatment of Certain Foreign Persons as American Employers.**

(1) **In general.** If any employee of a foreign person is performing services in connection with a contract between the United States Government (or any instrumentality thereof) and any member of any domestically controlled group of entities which includes such foreign person, such foreign person shall be treated for purposes of this chapter as an American employer with respect to such services performed by such employee.

(2) **Domestically controlled group of entities.** For purposes of this subsection—

(A) In general. The term "domestically controlled group of entities" means a controlled group of entities the common parent of which is a domestic corporation.

(B) Controlled group of entities. The term "controlled group of entities" means a controlled group of corporations as defined in section 1563(a)(1), except that—

(i) "more than 50 percent" shall be substituted for "at least 80 percent" each place it appears therein, and

(ii) the determination shall be made without regard to subsections (a)(4) and (b)(2) of section 1563.

A partnership or any other entity (other than a corporation) shall be treated as a member of a controlled group of entities if such entity is controlled (within the meaning of section 954(d)(3)) by members of such group (including any entity treated as a member of such group by reason of this sentence).

(3) Liability of common parent. In the case of a foreign person who is a member of any domestically controlled group of entities, the common parent of such group shall be jointly and severally liable for any tax under this chapter for which such foreign person is liable by reason of this subsection, and for any penalty imposed on such person by this title with respect to any failure to pay such tax or to file any return or statement with respect to such tax or wages subject to such tax. No deduction shall be allowed under this title for any liability imposed by the preceding sentence.

(4) Provisions preventing double taxation.

(A) Agreements. Paragraph (1) shall not apply to any services which are covered by an agreement under subsection (l).

(B) Equivalent foreign taxation. Paragraph (1) shall not apply to any services if the employer establishes to the satisfaction of the Secretary that the remuneration paid by such employer for such services is subject to a tax imposed by a foreign country which is substantially equivalent to the taxes imposed by this chapter.

(5) Cross reference. For relief from taxes in cases covered by certain international agreements, see sections 3101(c) and 3111(c).

[For Analysis, see ¶ 1902. For Committee Reports, see ¶ 5501.]

[Endnote Code Sec. 3121]

Sec. 601, P.L. 111-312, relating to the temporary employee payroll tax cut, as amended by Sec. 1001(a) and (b), P.L. 112-96 and Sec. 101(a)-(d), P.L. 112-78, reads as follows. For description of those amendments, see below.

"SEC. 601. TEMPORARY EMPLOYEE PAYROLL TAX CUT.

"(a) In general. Notwithstanding any other provision of law, —

"(1) with respect to any taxable year which begins in the payroll tax holiday period, the rate of tax under section 1401(a) of the Internal Revenue Code of 1986 shall be 10.40 percent, and

"(2) with respect to remuneration received during the payroll tax holiday period, the rate of tax under 3101(a) of such Code shall be 4.2 percent (including for purposes of determining the applicable percentage under sections 3201(a) and 3211(a)(1) of such Code).

"(b) Coordination with deductions for employment taxes.

"(1) Deduction in computing net earnings from self-employment. For purposes of applying section 1402(a)(12) of the Internal Revenue Code of 1986, the rate of tax imposed by subsection 1401(a) of such Code shall be determined without regard to the reduction in such rate under this section.

"(2) Individual deduction. In the case of the taxes imposed by section 1401 of such Code for any taxable year which begins in the payroll tax holiday period, the deduction under section 164(f) of such Code with respect to such taxes shall be equal to the sum of—

"(A) 59.6 percent of the portion of such taxes attributable to the tax imposed by section 1401(a) of such Code (determined after the application of this section), plus

"(B) one-half of the portion of such taxes attributable to the tax imposed by section 1401(b) of such Code.

"(c) Payroll Tax Holiday Period. The term 'payroll tax holiday period' means calendar years 2011 and 2012.

"(d) Employer notification. The Secretary of the Treasury shall notify employers of the payroll tax holiday period in any manner the Secretary deems appropriate.

"(e) Transfers of funds.

"(1) Transfers to Federal Old-Age and Survivors Insurance Trust Fund. There are hereby appropriated to the Federal Old-Age and Survivors Trust Fund and the Federal Disability Insurance Trust Fund established under section 201 of the Social Security Act (42 U.S.C. 401) amounts equal to the reduction in revenues to the Treasury by reason of the application of subsection (a). Amounts appropriated by the preceding sentence shall be transferred from the general fund at such times and in such manner as to replicate to the extent possible the transfers which would have occurred to such Trust Fund had such amendments not been enacted.

"(2) Transfers to Social Security Equivalent Benefit Account. There are hereby appropriated to the Social Security Equivalent Benefit Account established under section 15A(a) of the Railroad Retirement Act of 1974 (45 U.S.C. 231n-1(a)) amounts equal to the reduction in revenues to the Treasury by reason of the application of subsection (a)(2). Amounts appropriated by the preceding sentence shall be transferred from the general fund at such times and in such manner as to replicate to the extent possible the transfers which would have occurred to such Account had such amendments not been enacted.

"(3) Coordination with other Federal laws. For purposes of applying any provision of Federal law other than the provisions of the Internal Revenue Code of 1986, the rate of tax in effect under section 3101(a) of such Code shall be determined without regard to the reduction in such rate under this section."

Sec. 1001(a) and (b), P.L. 112-96, amended Sec. 601, P.L. 111-312, 12/17/2010, relating to the temporary employee payroll tax cut, as outlined below:

Sec. 1001(a), amended Sec. 601(c), P.L. 111-312.

Prior to amendment, Sec. 601(c), P.L. 111-312 read as follows:

"(c) Payroll Tax Holiday Period. The term 'payroll tax holiday period' means—

"(1) in the case of the tax described in subsection (a)(1), calendar years 2011 and 2012, and

"(2) in the case of the taxes described in subsection (a)(2), the period beginning January 1, 2011, and ending February 29, 2012."

Sec. 1001(b), deleted Sec. 601(f) and (g) P.L. 111-312.

Prior to deletion, Sec. 601(f) and (g), P.L. 111-312 read as follows:

"(f) Special rules for 2012.

"(1) Limitation on self-employment income. In the case of any taxable year beginning in 2012, subsection (a)(1) shall only apply with respect to so much of the taxpayer's self-employment income (as defined in section 1402(b) of the Internal Revenue Code of 1986) as does not exceed the excess (if any) of—

"(A) $18,350, over

"(B) the amount of wages and compensation received during the portion of the payroll tax holiday period occurring during 2012 subject to tax under section 3101(a) of such Code or section 3201(a) of such Code.

"(2) Coordination with deduction for employment taxes. In the case of a taxable year beginning in 2012, subparagraph (A) of subsection (b)(2) shall be applied as if it read as follows:

"'(A) the sum of—

"'(i) 59.6 percent of the portion of such taxes attributable to the tax imposed by section 1401(a) of such Code (determined after the application of this section) on so much of self-employment income (as defined in section 1402(b) of such Code) as does not exceed the amount of self-employment income described in paragraph (1), plus

"(ii) one-half of the portion of such taxes attributable to the tax imposed by section 1401(a) of such Code (determined without regard to this section) on self-employment income (as so defined) in excess of such amount, plus'

"(g) Recapture of excess benefit.

"(1) In general. There is hereby imposed on the income of every individual a tax equal to 2 percent of the sum of wages (within the meaning of section 3121(a)(1) of the Internal Revenue Code of 1986) and compensation (to which section 3201(a) of such Code applies) received during the period beginning January 1, 2012, and ending February 29, 2012, to the extent the amount of such sum exceeds $18,350.

"(2) Regulations. The Secretary of the Treasury or the Secretary's delegate shall prescribe such regulations or other guidance as may be necessary or appropriate to carry out this subsection, including guidance for payment by the employee of the tax imposed by paragraph (1)."

Effective Date (Sec. 1001(c), P.L. 112-96) effective for rumeration received, and taxable years beginning after 12/31/2011.

Sec. 101(a), (b) and (c), P.L. 112-78, amended Sec. 601, P.L. 111-312, 12/17/2010, relating to the temporary employee payroll tax cut, as outlined below:

Sec. 101(a), amended Sec. 601(c) of P.L. 111-312

Sec. 101(b), added Sec. 601(f) of P.L. 111-312

Sec. 101(c), added Sec. 601(g) of P.L. 111-312 effective for remuneration received, and tax. yrs. begin., after 12/31/2011.

Prior to amendment, Sec. 601(c) of P.L. 111-312 read as follows:

"(c) Payroll tax holiday period. The term 'payroll tax holiday period' means calendar year 2011."

Effective Date (Sec. 101(e)(1), P.L. 112-78) effective for remuneration received, and taxable years beginning, after 12/31/2011.

Sec. 101(d), P.L. 112-78, amended Sec. 601, P.L. 111-312, 12/17/2010, relating to the temporary employee payroll tax cut, as outlined below:

Sec. 101(d)(1), added "of such Code" after "164(f)" in Sec. 601(b)(2) of P.L. 111-312

Sec. 101(d)(2), added "of such Code" after "1401(a)" in Sec. 601(b)(2)(A) of P.L. 111-312

Sec. 101(d)(3), added "of such Code" after "1401(b)" in Sec. 601(b)(2)(B) of P.L. 111-312, effective as if included in the enactment of Sec. 601 of P.L. 111-312

[¶ 3109]   Code Sec. 3201.   Rate of tax.

(a) **Tier 1 tax.** In addition to other taxes, there is hereby imposed on the income of each employee a tax equal to the applicable percentage of the compensation received during any calendar year by such employee for services rendered by such employee. For purposes of the preceding sentence, the term "applicable percentage" means the percentage equal to the sum of the rates of tax in effect under subsections (a) and (b) of section 3101 for the calendar year.

(b) **Tier 2 tax.**

(1) **In general.** In addition to other taxes, there is hereby imposed on the income of each employee a tax equal to the applicable percentage of the compensation received during any calendar year by such employee for services rendered by such employee.

(2) **Applicable percentage.** For purposes of paragraph (1), the term "applicable percentage" means—

(A) 4.90 percent in the case of compensation received during 2002 or 2003, and

(B) in the case of compensation received during any calendar year after 2003, the percentage determined under section 3241 for such calendar year.

(c) **Cross reference.** For application of different contribution bases with respect to the taxes imposed by subsections (a) and (b), see section 3231(e)(2).

[For Analysis, see ¶ 1902. For Committee Reports, see ¶ 5501.]

[Endnote Code Sec. 3201]

Sec. 601, P.L. 111-312, relating to the temporary employee payroll tax cut, as amended by Sec. 1001(a) and (b), P.L. 112-96 and Sec. 101(a)-(d), P.L. 112-78, reads as follows. For description of those amendments, see below.

"SEC. 601. TEMPORARY EMPLOYEE PAYROLL TAX CUT.

"(a) In general. Notwithstanding any other provision of law, —

"(1) with respect to any taxable year which begins in the payroll tax holiday period, the rate of tax under section 1401(a) of the Internal Revenue Code of 1986 shall be 10.40 percent, and

"(2) with respect to remuneration received during the payroll tax holiday period, the rate of tax under 3101(a) of such Code shall be 4.2 percent (including for purposes of determining the applicable percentage under sections 3201(a) and 3211(a)(1) of such Code).

"(b) Coordination with deductions for employment taxes.

"(1) Deduction in computing net earnings from self-employment. For purposes of applying section 1402(a)(12) of the Internal Revenue Code of 1986, the rate of tax imposed by subsection 1401(a) of such Code shall be determined without regard to the reduction in such rate under this section.

"(2) Individual deduction. In the case of the taxes imposed by section 1401 of such Code for any taxable year which begins in the payroll tax holiday period, the deduction under section 164(f) of such Code with respect to such taxes shall be equal to the sum of —

"(A) 59.6 percent of the portion of such taxes attributable to the tax imposed by section 1401(a) of such Code (determined after the application of this section), plus

"(B) one-half of the portion of such taxes attributable to the tax imposed by section 1401(b) of such Code.

"(c) Payroll Tax Holiday Period. The term 'payroll tax holiday period' means calendar years 2011 and 2012.

"(d) Employer notification. The Secretary of the Treasury shall notify employers of the payroll tax holiday period in any manner the Secretary deems appropriate.

"(e) Transfers of funds.

"(1) Transfers to Federal Old-Age and Survivors Insurance Trust Fund. There are hereby appropriated to the Federal Old-Age and Survivors Trust Fund and the Federal Disability Insurance Trust Fund established under section 201 of the Social Security Act (42 U.S.C. 401) amounts equal to the reduction in revenues to the Treasury by reason of the application of subsection (a). Amounts appropriated by the preceding sentence shall be transferred from the general fund at such times and in such manner as to replicate to the extent possible the transfers which would have occurred to such Trust Fund had such amendments not been enacted.

"(2) Transfers to Social Security Equivalent Benefit Account. There are hereby appropriated to the Social Security Equivalent Benefit Account established under section 15A(a) of the Railroad Retirement Act of 1974 (45 U.S.C. 231n-1(a)) amounts equal to the reduction in revenues to the Treasury by reason of the application of subsection (a)(2). Amounts appropriated by the preceding sentence shall be transferred from the general fund at such times and in such manner as to replicate to the extent possible the transfers which would have occurred to such Account had such amendments not been enacted.

"(3) Coordination with other Federal laws. For purposes of applying any provision of Federal law other than the provisions of the Internal Revenue Code of 1986, the rate of tax in effect under section 3101(a) of such Code shall be determined without regard to the reduction in such rate under this section."

Sec. 1001(a) and (b), P.L. 112-96, amended Sec. 601, P.L. 111-312, 12/17/2010, relating to the temporary employee payroll tax cut, as outlined below:

Sec. 1001(a), amended Sec. 601(c), P.L. 111-312.

Prior to amendment, Sec. 601(c), P.L. 111-312 read as follows:

"(c) Payroll Tax Holiday Period. The term 'payroll tax holiday period' means —

"(1) in the case of the tax described in subsection (a)(1), calendar years 2011 and 2012, and

"(2) in the case of the taxes described in subsection (a)(2), the period beginning January 1, 2011, and ending February 29, 2012."

Sec. 1001(b), deleted Sec. 601(f) and (g) P.L. 111-312.

Prior to deletion, Sec. 601(f) and (g), P.L. 111-312 read as follows:

"(f) Special rules for 2012.

"(1) Limitation on self-employment income. In the case of any taxable year beginning in 2012, subsection (a)(1) shall only apply with respect to so much of the taxpayer's self-employment income (as defined in section 1402(b) of the Internal Revenue Code of 1986) as does not exceed the excess (if any) of —

"(A) $18,350, over

"(B) the amount of wages and compensation received during the portion of the payroll tax holiday period occurring during 2012 subject to tax under section 3101(a) of such Code or section 3201(a) of such Code.

"(2) Coordination with deduction for employment taxes. In the case of a taxable year beginning in 2012, subparagraph (A) of subsection (b)(2) shall be applied as if it read as follows:

"'(A) the sum of—

"'(i) 59.6 percent of the portion of such taxes attributable to the tax imposed by section 1401(a) of such Code (determined after the application of this section) on so much of self-employment income (as defined in section 1402(b) of such Code) as does not exceed the amount of self-employment income described in paragraph (1), plus

"(ii) one-half of the portion of such taxes attributable to the tax imposed by section 1401(a) of such Code (determined without regard to this section) on self-employment income (as so defined) in excess of such amount, plus'

"(g) Recapture of excess benefit.

"(1) In general. There is hereby imposed on the income of every individual a tax equal to 2 percent of the sum of wages (within the meaning of section 3121(a)(1) of the Internal Revenue Code of 1986) and compensation (to which section 3201(a) of such Code applies) received during the period beginning January 1, 2012, and ending February 29, 2012, to the extent the amount of such sum exceeds $18,350.

"(2) Regulations. The Secretary of the Treasury or the Secretary's delegate shall prescribe such regulations or other guidance as may be necessary or appropriate to carry out this subsection, including guidance for payment by the employee of the tax imposed by paragraph (1)."

Effective Date (Sec. 1001(c), P.L. 112-96) effective for rumeration received, and taxable years beginning after 12/31/2011.

Sec. 101(a), (b) and (c), P.L. 112-78, amended Sec. 601, P.L. 111-312, 12/17/2010, relating to the temporary employee payroll tax cut, as outlined below:

Sec. 101(a), amended Sec. 601(e) of P.L. 111-312

Sec. 101(b), added Sec. 601(f) of P.L. 111-312

Sec. 101(c), added Sec. 601(g) of P.L. 111-312 effective for remuneration received, and tax. yrs. begin., after 12/31/2011.

Prior to amendment, Sec. 601(c) of P.L. 111-312 read as follows:

"(c) Payroll tax holiday period. The term 'payroll tax holiday period' means calendar year 2011."

Effective Date (Sec. 101(e)(1), P.L. 112-78) effective for remuneration received, and taxable years beginning, after 12/31/2011.

Sec. 101(d), P.L. 112-78, amended Sec. 601, P.L. 111-312, 12/17/2010, relating to the temporary employee payroll tax cut, as outlined below:

Sec. 101(d)(1), added "of such Code" after "164(f)" in Sec. 601(b)(2) of P.L. 111-312

Sec. 101(d)(2), added "of such Code" after "1401(a)" in Sec. 601(b)(2)(A) of P.L. 111-312

Sec. 101(d)(3), added "of such Code" after "1401(b)" in Sec. 601(b)(2)(B) of P.L. 111-312, effective as if included in the enactment of Sec. 601 of P.L. 111-312

[¶ 3110]   Code Sec. 3211.   Rate of tax.

(a) **Tier 1 tax.** In addition to other taxes, there is hereby imposed on the income of each employee representative a tax equal to the applicable percentage of the compensation received during any calendar year by such employee representative for services rendered by such employee representative. For purposes of the preceding sentence, the term "applicable percentage" means the percentage equal to the sum of the rates of tax in effect under subsections (a) and (b) of section 3101 and subsections (a) and (b) of section 3111 for the calendar year.

(b) **Tier 2 tax.**

(1) **In general.** In addition to other taxes, there is hereby imposed on the income of each employee representative a tax equal to the applicable percentage of the compensation received during any calendar year by such employee representatives for services rendered by such employee representative.

(2) **Applicable percentage.** For purposes of paragraph (1), the term "applicable percentage" means —

(A) 14.75 percent in the case of compensation received during 2002,

(B) 14.20 percent in the case of compensation received during 2003, and

(C) in the case of compensation received during any calendar year after 2003, the percentage determined under section 3241 for such calendar year.

(c) **Cross reference.** For application of different contribution bases with respect to the taxes imposed by subsections (a) and (b), see section 3231(e)(2).

[For Analysis, see ¶ 1902. For Committee Reports, see ¶ 5501.]

[Endnote Code Sec. 3211]

Sec. 601, P.L. 111-312, relating to the temporary employee payroll tax cut, as amended by Sec. 1001(a) and (b), P.L. 112-96 and Sec. 101(a)-(d), P.L. 112-78, reads as follows. For description of those amendments, see below.

"SEC. 601. TEMPORARY EMPLOYEE PAYROLL TAX CUT.

"(a) In general. Notwithstanding any other provision of law, —

"(1) with respect to any taxable year which begins in the payroll tax holiday period, the rate of tax under section 1401(a) of the Internal Revenue Code of 1986 shall be 10.40 percent, and

"(2) with respect to remuneration received during the payroll tax holiday period, the rate of tax under 3101(a) of such Code shall be 4.2 percent (including for purposes of determining the applicable percentage under sections 3201(a) and 3211(a)(1) of such Code).

"(b) Coordination with deductions for employment taxes.

"(1) Deduction in computing net earnings from self-employment. For purposes of applying section 1402(a)(12) of the Internal Revenue Code of 1986, the rate of tax imposed by subsection 1401(a) of such Code shall be determined without regard to the reduction in such rate under this section.

"(2) Individual deduction. In the case of the taxes imposed by section 1401 of such Code for any taxable year which begins in the payroll tax holiday period, the deduction under section 164(f) of such Code with respect to such taxes shall be equal to the sum of—

"(A) 59.6 percent of the portion of such taxes attributable to the tax imposed by section 1401(a) of such Code (determined after the application of this section), plus

"(B) one-half of the portion of such taxes attributable to the tax imposed by section 1401(b) of such Code.

"(c) Payroll Tax Holiday Period. The term 'payroll tax holiday period' means calendar years 2011 and 2012.

"(d) Employer notification. The Secretary of the Treasury shall notify employers of the payroll tax holiday period in any manner the Secretary deems appropriate.

"(e) Transfers of funds.

"(1) Transfers to Federal Old-Age and Survivors Insurance Trust Fund. There are hereby appropriated to the Federal Old-Age and Survivors Trust Fund and the Federal Disability Insurance Trust Fund established under section 201 of the Social Security Act (42 U.S.C. 401) amounts equal to the reduction in revenues to the Treasury by reason of the application of subsection (a). Amounts appropriated by the preceding sentence shall be transferred from the general fund at such times and in such manner as to replicate to the extent possible the transfers which would have occurred to such Trust Fund had such amendments not been enacted.

"(2) Transfers to Social Security Equivalent Benefit Account. There are hereby appropriated to the Social Security Equivalent Benefit Account established under section 15A(a) of the Railroad Retirement Act of 1974 (45 U.S.C. 231n-1(a)) amounts equal to the reduction in revenues to the Treasury by reason of the application of subsection (a)(2). Amounts appropriated by the preceding sentence shall be transferred from the general fund at such times and in such manner as to replicate to the extent possible the transfers which would have occurred to such Account had such amendments not been enacted.

"(3) Coordination with other Federal laws. For purposes of applying any provision of Federal law other than the provisions of the Internal Revenue Code of 1986, the rate of tax in effect under section 3101(a) of such Code shall be determined without regard to the reduction in such rate under this section."

Sec. 1001(a) and (b), P.L. 112-96, amended Sec. 601, P.L. 111-312, 12/17/2010, relating to the temporary employee payroll tax cut, as outlined below:

Sec. 1001(a), amended Sec. 601(c), P.L. 111-312.

Prior to amendment, Sec. 601(c), P.L. 111-312 read as follows:

"(c) Payroll Tax Holiday Period. The term 'payroll tax holiday period' means—

"(1) in the case of the tax described in subsection (a)(1), calendar years 2011 and 2012, and

"(2) in the case of the taxes described in subsection (a)(2), the period beginning January 1, 2011, and ending February 29, 2012."

Sec. 1001(b), deleted Sec. 601(f) and (g) P.L. 111-312.

Prior to deletion, Sec. 601(f) and (g), P.L. 111-312 read as follows:

"(f) Special rules for 2012.

"(1) Limitation on self-employment income. In the case of any taxable year beginning in 2012, subsection (a)(1) shall only apply with respect to so much of the taxpayer's self-employment income (as defined in section 1402(b) of the Internal Revenue Code of 1986) as does not exceed the excess (if any) of—

"(A) $18,350, over

"(B) the amount of wages and compensation received during the portion of the payroll tax holiday period occurring during 2012 subject to tax under section 3101(a) of such Code or section 3201(a) of such Code.

"(2) Coordination with deduction for employment taxes. In the case of a taxable year beginning in 2012, subparagraph (A) of subsection (b)(2) shall be applied as if it read as follows:

"'(A) the sum of—

"'(i) 59.6 percent of the portion of such taxes attributable to the tax imposed by section 1401(a) of such Code (determined after the application of this section) on so much of self-employment income (as defined in section 1402(b) of such Code) as does not exceed the amount of self-employment income described in paragraph (1), plus

"(ii) one-half of the portion of such taxes attributable to the tax imposed by section 1401(a) of such Code (determined without regard to this section) on self-employment income (as so defined) in excess of such amount, plus'

"(g) Recapture of excess benefit.

"(1) In general. There is hereby imposed on the income of every individual a tax equal to 2 percent of the sum of wages (within the meaning of section 3121(a)(1) of the Internal Revenue Code of 1986) and compensation (to which section 3201(a) of such Code applies) received during the period beginning January 1, 2012, and ending February 29, 2012, to the extent the amount of such sum exceeds $18,350.

"(2) Regulations. The Secretary of the Treasury or the Secretary's delegate shall prescribe such regulations or other guidance as may be necessary or appropriate to carry out this subsection, including guidance for payment by the employee of the tax imposed by paragraph (1)."

Effective Date (Sec. 1001(c), P.L. 112-96) effective for rumeration received, and taxable years beginning after 12/31/2011.

Sec. 101(a), (b) and (c), P.L. 112-78, amended Sec. 601, P.L. 111-312, 12/17/2010, relating to the temporary employee payroll tax cut, as outlined below:

Sec. 101(a), amended Sec. 601(c) of P.L. 111-312

Sec. 101(b), added Sec. 601(f) of P.L. 111-312

Sec. 101(c), added Sec. 601(g) of P.L. 111-312 effective for remuneration received, and tax. yrs. begin., after 12/31/2011.

Prior to amendment, Sec. 601(c) of P.L. 111-312 read as follows:

"(c) Payroll tax holiday period. The term 'payroll tax holiday period' means calendar year 2011."

Effective Date (Sec. 101(e)(1), P.L. 112-78) effective for remuneration received, and taxable years beginning, after 12/31/2011.

———————

Sec. 101(d), P.L. 112-78, amended Sec. 601, P.L. 111-312, 12/17/2010, relating to the temporary employee payroll tax cut, as outlined below:

Sec. 101(d)(1), added "of such Code" after "164(f)" in Sec. 601(b)(2) of P.L. 111-312

Sec. 101(d)(2), added "of such Code" after "1401(a)" in Sec. 601(b)(2)(A) of P.L. 111-312

Sec. 101(d)(3), added "of such Code" after "1401(b)" in Sec. 601(b)(2)(B) of P.L. 111-312, effective as if included in the enactment of Sec. 601 of P.L. 111-312

[¶ 3111]   Code Sec. 3303.   Conditions of additional credit allowance.

* * * * * * * * * * * *

[1]*(f) Prohibition on noncharging due to employer fault.*

(1) In general. A State law shall be treated as meeting the requirements of subsection (a)(1) only if such law provides that an employer's account shall not be relieved of charges relating to a payment from the State unemployment fund if the State agency determines that—

(A) the payment was made because the employer, or an agent of the employer, was at fault for failing to respond timely or adequately to the request of the agency for information relating to the claim for compensation; and

(B) the employer or agent has established a pattern of failing to respond timely or adequately to such requests.

(2) State authority to impose stricter standards. Nothing in paragraph (1) shall limit the authority of a State to provide that an employer's account not be relieved of charges relating to a payment from the State unemployment fund for reasons other than the reasons described in subparagraphs (A) and (B) of such paragraph, such as after the first instance of a failure to respond timely or adequately to requests described in paragraph (1)(A).

[2]*(g) Repealed.*
[For Analysis, see ¶ 1903.]

[Endnote Code Sec. 3303]

Code Sec. 3303(f) and Code Sec. 3303(g) was amended by Sec. 252(a)(1) and (2) of Trade Adjustment Assistance Extension Act of 2011, P.L. 112-40, 10/21/2011, as detailed below:

1. Sec. 252(a)(2) amended subsec. (f)

Prior to amendment, subsec. (f) read as follows:

"(f) Transition. To facilitate the orderly transition to coverage of service to which section 3309(a)(1)(A) applies, a State law may provide that an organization (or group of organizations) which elects before April 1, 1972, to make payments (in lieu of contributions) into the State unemployment fund as provided in section 3309(a)(2), and which had paid contributions into such fund under the State law with respect to such service performed in its employ before January 1, 1969, is not required to make any such payments (in lieu of contributions) on account of compensation paid after its election as heretofore described which is attributable under the State law to service performed in its employ, until the total of such compensation equals the amount—

"(1) by which the contributions paid by such organization (or group) with respect to a period before the election provided by section 3309(a)(2), exceed

"(2) the unemployment compensation for the same period which was charged to the experience-rating account of such organization (or group) or paid under the State law on the basis of wages paid by it or service performed in its employ, whichever is appropriate."

2. Sec. 252(a)(1) repealed subsec. (g)

Prior to repeal, subsec. (g) read as follows:

"(g) Transitional rule for Unemployment Compensation Amendments of 1976. To facilitate the orderly transition to coverage of service to which section 3309(a)(1)(A) applies by reason of the enactment of the Unemployment Compensation Amendments of 1976, a State law may provide that an organization (or group of organizations) which elects, when such election first becomes available under the State law with respect to such service, to make payments (in lieu of contributions) into the State unemployment fund as provided in section 3309(a)(2), and which had paid contributions into such fund under the State law with respect to such service performed in its employ before the date of the enactment of this subsection, is not required to make any such payment (in lieu of contributions) on account of compensation paid after its election as heretofore described which is attributable under the State law to such service performed in its employ, until the total of such compensation equals the amount—

"(1) by which the contributions paid by such organization (or group) on the basis of wages for such service with respect to a period before the election provided by section 3309(a)(2), exceed

"(2) the unemployment compensation for the same period which was charged to the experience-rating account of such organization (or group) or paid under the State law on the basis of such service performed in its employ or wages paid for such service, whichever is appropriate."

Effective Date (Sec. 252(b), P.L. 112-40, 10/21/2011) effective for erroneous payments established after the end of the 2-year period beginning on 10/21/2011, except as provided in Sec. 252(b)(2) of this Act, which reads as follows:

"(2) Authority. A State may amend its State law to apply such amendments to erroneous payments established prior to the end of the period described in paragraph (1)."

[¶ 3112]   Code Sec. 3402.   Income tax collected at source.

* * * * * * * * * * * *

(p) Voluntary withholding agreements.

(1) Certain federal payments.

(A) In general. If, at the time a specified Federal payment is made to any person, a request by such person is in effect that such payment be subject to withholding under this chapter, then for purposes of this chapter and so much of subtitle F as relates to this chapter, such payment shall be treated as if it were a payment of wages by an employer to an employee.

(B) Amount withheld. The amount to be deducted and withheld under this chapter from any payment to which any request under subparagraph (A) applies shall be an amount equal to the percentage of such payment specified in such request. Such a request shall apply to any payment only if the percentage specified is [1] *7 percent, any percentage applicable to any of the 3 lowest income brackets in the table under section 1(c),* or such other percentage as is permitted under regulations prescribed by the Secretary.

(C) Specified federal payments. For purposes of this paragraph, the term "specified Federal payment" means—

(i) any payment of a social security benefit (as defined in section 86(d)),

(ii) any payment referred to in the second sentence of section 451(d) which is treated as insurance proceeds,

(iii) any amount which is includible in gross income under section 77(a), and

(iv) any other payment made pursuant to Federal law which is specified by the Secretary for purposes of this paragraph.

(D) Requests for withholding. Rules similar to the rules that apply to annuities under subsection (o)(4) shall apply to requests under this paragraph and paragraph (2).

(2) Voluntary withholding on unemployment benefits. If, at the time a payment of unemployment compensation (as defined in section 85(b)) is made to any person, a request by such person is in effect that such payment be subject to withholding under this chapter, then for purposes of this chapter and so much of subtitle F as relates to this chapter, such payment shall be treated as if it were a payment of wages by an employer to an employee. The amount to be deducted and withheld under this chapter from any payment to which any request under this paragraph applies shall be an amount equal to [2] *10 percent* of such payment.

* * * * * * * * * * * *

(q)   Extension of withholding to certain gambling winnings.

(1)   General rule. Every person, including the Government of the United States, a State, or a political subdivision thereof, or any instrumentalities of the foregoing, making any payment of winnings which are subject to withholding shall deduct and withhold from such payment a tax in an amount [3]*equal to the product of the third lowest rate of tax applicable under section 1(c) and such payment.*

* * * * * * * * * * * *

(r)   Extension of withholding to certain taxable payments of Indian casino profits.

* * * * * * * * * * * *

(3)   Annualized tax. For purposes of paragraph (1), the term "annualized tax" means, with respect to any payment, the amount of tax which would be imposed by section 1(c) (determined without regard to any rate of tax in excess of [4]*the fourth lowest rate of tax applicable under section 1(c)*) on an amount of taxable income equal to the excess of—

(A) the annualized amount of such payment, over

(B) the amount determined under paragraph (2).

[5]*(t)   Repealed.*

[For Analysis, see ¶ 103 and ¶ 1909. For Committee Reports, see ¶ 5701.]

[Endnote Code Sec. 3402]

Sec. 101(a)(1) of the American Taxpayer Relief Act of 2012, P.L. 112-240, 1/2/2013, deleted Title IX [Sec. 901] of the Economic Growth and Tax Relief Reconciliation Act of 2001, P.L. 107-16, the effect of which is to eliminate the sunset of all provisions enacted by P.L. 107-16. Following are the amendments made to Code Sec. 3402, by P.L. 107-16.

Effective Date (Sec. 101(a)(3), P.L. 112-240, 1/2/2013) effective for taxable, plan, or limitation years beginning after 12/31/2012, and estates of decedents dying, gifts made, or generation skipping transfers after 12/31/2012.

Matter in *italics* in Code Sec. 3402(p)(1)(B), Code Sec. 3402(p)(2), Code Sec. 3402(q)(1) and Code Sec. 3402(r)(3) was added by Sec. 101(c)(6)-(9) of the Economic Growth and Tax Relief Reconciliation Act of 2001, P.L. 107-16, 6/7/2001, which struck out:

1. "7, 15, 28, or 31 percent"
2. "15 percent"
3. "equal to 28 percent of such payment"
4. "31 percent"

Effective Date (Sec. 101(d)(2), P.L. 107-16, 6/7/2001) effective for "amounts paid after the 60th day after 6/7/2001. References to income brackets and rates of tax in such paragraphs shall be applied without regard to section 1(i)(1)(D) of the Internal Revenue Code of 1986."

Code Sec. 3402(t) was deleted by Sec. 102(a) of an Act To amend the Internal Revenue Code of 1986 to repeal the imposition of 3 percent withholding on certain payments made to vendors by government entities, to modify the calculation of modified adjusted gross income for purposes of determining eligibility for certain healthcare-related programs, and for other purposes, P.L. 112-56, 11/21/2011, as detailed below:

1. Sec. 102(a) deleted subsec. (t)

Prior to deletion, subsec. (t) read as follows:

"(t) Extension of withholding to certain payments made by government entities.

"(1) General rule. The Government of the United States, every State, every political subdivision thereof, and every instrumentality of the foregoing (including multi-State agencies) making any payment to any person providing any property or services (including any payment made in connection with a government voucher or certificate program which functions as a payment for property or services) shall deduct and withhold from such payment a tax in an amount equal to 3 percent of such payment.

"(2) Property and services subject to withholding. Paragraph (1) shall not apply to any payment—

"(A) except as provided in subparagraph (B), which is subject to withholding under any other provision of this chapter or chapter 3,

"(B) which is subject to withholding under section 3406 and from which amounts are being withheld under such section,

"(C) of interest,

"(D) for real property,

"(E) to any governmental entity subject to the requirements of paragraph (1), any tax-exempt entity, or any foreign government,

"(F) made pursuant to a classified or confidential contract described in section 6050M(e)(3),

"(G) made by a political subdivision of a State (or any instrumentality thereof) which makes less than $100,000,000 of such payments annually,

"(H) which is in connection with a public assistance or public welfare program for which eligibility is determined by a needs or income test, and

"(I) to any government employee not otherwise excludable with respect to their services as an employee.

"(3) Coordination with other sections.

"For purposes of sections 3403 and 3404 and for purposes of so much of subtitle F (except section 7205) as relates to this chapter, payments to any person for property or services which are subject to withholding shall be treated as if such payments were wages paid by an employer to an employee."

Effective Date (Sec. 102(b), P.L. 112-56, 11/21/2011) effective for payments made after 12/31/2011.

[¶ 3113]   Code Sec. 3406.   Backup withholding.

(a) Requirement to deduct and withhold.

(1) In general. In the case of any reportable payment, if—

(A) the payee fails to furnish his TIN to the payor in the manner required,

(B) the Secretary notifies the payor that the TIN furnished by the payee is incorrect,

(C) there has been a notified payee under-reporting described in subsection (c), or

(D) there has been a payee certification failure described in subsection (d), then the payor shall deduct and withhold from such payment a tax [1]*equal to the product of the fourth lowest rate of tax applicable under section 1(c) and such payment.*

(2) Subparagraphs (C) and (D) of paragraph (1) apply only to interest and dividend payments. Subparagraphs (C) and (D) of paragraph (1) shall apply only to reportable interest or dividend payments.

* * * * * * * * * * * *

[For Analysis, see ¶ 103.]

[Endnote Code Sec. 3406]

Sec. 101(a)(1) of the American Taxpayer Relief Act of 2012, P.L. 112-240, 1/2/2013, deleted Title IX [Sec. 901] of the Economic Growth and Tax Relief Reconciliation Act of 2001, P.L. 107-16, the effect of which is to eliminate the sunset of all provisions enacted by P.L. 107-16. Following are the amendments made to Code Sec. 15, by P.L. 107-16.
Effective Date (Sec. 101(a)(3), P.L. 112-240, 1/2/2013) effective for taxable, plan, or limitation years beginning after 12/31/2012, and estates of decedents dying, gifts made, or generation skipping transfers after 12/31/2012.

Code Sec. 3406(a)(1)(D) in *italics* was added by Sec. 101(c)(10) of the Economic Growth and Tax Relief Reconciliation Act of 2001, P.L. 107-16, 6/7/2001, as outlined below:
1. Sec. 101(c)(10) substituted "equal to the product of the fourth lowest rate of tax applicable under section 1(c) and such payment" for "equal to 31 percent of such payment" in subpara. (a)(1)(D)
Effective Date (Sec. 101(d)(2), P.L. 107-16, 6/7/2001) effective for amounts paid after the 60th day after 6/7/2001.

[¶ 3114]   Code Sec. 4041.   Imposition of tax.

(a) Diesel fuel and special motor fuels.

(1) Tax on diesel fuel and kerosene in certain cases.

(A) In general. There is hereby imposed a tax on any liquid other than gasoline (as defined in section 4083)—

(i) sold by any person to an owner, lessee, or other operator of a diesel-powered highway vehicle or a diesel-powered train for use as a fuel in such vehicle or train, or

(ii) used by any person as a fuel in a diesel-powered highway vehicle or a diesel-powered train unless there was a taxable sale of such fuel under clause (i).

(B) Exemption for previously taxed fuel. No tax shall be imposed by this paragraph on the sale or use of any liquid if tax was imposed on such liquid under section 4081 (other than such tax at the Leaking Underground Storage Tank Trust Fund financing rate) and the tax thereon was not credited or refunded.

(C) Rate of tax.

(i) In general. Except as otherwise provided in this subparagraph, the rate of the tax imposed by this paragraph shall be the rate of tax specified in section 4081(a)(2)(A) on diesel fuel which is in effect at the time of such sale or use.

(ii) Rate of tax on trains. In the case of any sale for use, or use, of diesel fuel in a train, the rate of tax imposed by this paragraph shall be—

(I) 3.3 cents per gallon after December 31, 2004, and before July 1, 2005,

(II) 2.3 cents per gallon after June 30, 2005, and before January 1, 2007, and

(III) 0 after December 31, 2006.

(iii) Rate of tax on certain buses.

(I) In general. Except as provided in subclause (II), in the case of fuel sold for use or used in a use described in section 6427(b)(1) (after the application of section 6427(b)(3)), the rate of tax imposed by this paragraph shall be 7.3 cents per gallon (4.3 cents per gallon after [1]*September 30, 2016*).

(II) School bus and intracity transportation. No tax shall be imposed by this paragraph on any sale for use, or use, described in subparagraph (B) or (C) of section 6427(b)(2).

(2) Alternative fuels.

(A) In general. There is hereby imposed a tax on any liquid (other than gas oil, fuel oil, or any product taxable under section 4081 (other than such tax at the Leaking Underground Storage Tank Trust Fund financing rate))—

(i) sold by any person to an owner, lessee, or other operator of a motor vehicle or motorboat for use as a fuel in such motor vehicle or motorboat, or

(ii) used by any person as a fuel in a motor vehicle or motorboat unless there was a taxable sale of such liquid under clause (i).

(B) Rate of tax. The rate of the tax imposed by this paragraph shall be—

(i) except as otherwise provided in this subparagraph, the rate of tax specified in section 4081(a)(2)(A)(i) which is in effect at the time of such sale or use, and

(ii) in the case of liquefied natural gas, any liquid fuel (other than ethanol and methanol) derived from coal (including peat), and liquid hydrocarbons derived from biomass (as defined in section 45K(c)(3)), 24.3 cents per gallon.

(3) Compressed natural gas.

(A) In general. There is hereby imposed a tax on compressed natural gas—

(i) sold by any person to an owner, lessee, or other operator of a motor vehicle or motorboat for use as a fuel in such motor vehicle or motorboat, or

(ii) used by any person as a fuel in a motor vehicle or motorboat unless there was a taxable sale of such gas under clause (i).

The rate of the tax imposed by this paragraph shall be 18.3 cents per energy equivalent of a gallon of gasoline.

(B) Bus uses. No tax shall be imposed by this paragraph on any sale for use, or use, described in subparagraph (B) or (C) of section 6427(b)(2) (relating to school bus and intracity transportation).

(C) Administrative provisions. For purposes of applying this title with respect to the taxes imposed by this subsection, references to any liquid subject to tax under this subsection shall be treated as including references to compressed natural gas subject to tax under this paragraph, and references to gallons shall be treated as including references to energy equivalent of a gallon of gasoline with respect to such gas.

* * * * * * * * * * * *

(m) Certain alcohol fuels.

(1) In general. In the case of the sale or use of any partially exempt methanol or ethanol fuel the rate of the tax imposed by subsection (a)(2) shall be—

(A) after September 30, 1997, and before [2]*October 1, 2016*—

(i) in the case of fuel none of the alcohol in which consists of ethanol, 9.15 cents per gallon, and

(ii) in any other case, 11.3 cents per gallon, and

(B) after [3]*September 30, 2016*—

(i) in the case of fuel none of the alcohol in which consists of ethanol, 2.15 cents per gallon, and

(ii) in any other case, 4.3 cents per gallon.

795

(2)   Partially exempt methanol or ethanol fuel. The term "partially exempt methanol or ethanol fuel" means any liquid at least 85 percent of which consists of methanol, ethanol, or other alcohol produced from natural gas.

[For Analysis, see ¶ 1801. For Committee Reports, see ¶ 5401.]

[Endnote Code Sec. 4041]

Code Sec. 4041(a)(1)(C)(iii)(I), Code Sec. 4041(m)(1)(A) and Code Sec. 4041(m)(1)(B), was amended by Sec. 40102(a)(1)(A)-(B) and (a)(2)(A) of the Moving Ahead for Progress in the 21st Century Act, P.L. 112-141, 7/6/2012 , after it was amended by Sec. 402(a)(1)(A)-(B), (2)(A) of the Temporary Surface Transportation Extension Act of 2012, P.L. 112-140, 6/29/2012, as detailed below:

1. Sec. 40102(a)(1)(A) of P.L. 112-141 substituted 'September 30, 2016' for 'June 30, 2012'[sic July 6, 2012] in subclause (a)(1)(C)(iii)(I). [Ed Note: The amendment made by Sec. 40102(a)(1)(A) of P.L. 112-141 did not take into account the previous amendment made by Sec. 402(a)(1)(A) of P.L. 112-140, which substituted 'July 6, 2012' for 'June 30,2012' in subpara. (a)(1)(A)]

2. Sec 40102(a)(2)(A) substituted 'October 1, 2016' for 'July 1, 2012' [sic July 7, 2012] in subpara. (m)(1)(A). [Ed Note: The amendment made by Sec. 40102(a)(2)(A) of P.L. 112-141 did not take into account the previous amendment made by Sec. 402(a)(2)(A) of P.L. 112-140, which substituted 'July 7, 2012' for 'July 1, 2012' in subpara. (m)(1)(A)]

3. Sec. 40102(a)(1)(B) substituted 'September 30, 2016' for 'June 30, 2012' [sic July 6, 2012] in subpara. (m)(1)(B). [Ed Note: The amendment made by Sec. 40102(a)(1)(B) of P.L. 112-141 did not take into account the previous amendment made by Sec. 402(a)(1)(B) of P.L. 112-140, which substituted 'July 6, 2012' for 'June 30, 2012' in subpara. (m)(1)(B)]

Effective Date (Sec. 40102(f), P.L. 112-141, 7/6/2012 and Sec. 402(f)(1), P.L. 112-140, 6/29/2012) effective 7/1/2012.

[¶ 3115]   Code Sec.[1] 4043.   *Surtax on fuel used in aircraft part of a fractional ownership program.*

(a)   In general. There is hereby imposed a tax on any liquid used (during any calendar quarter by any person) in a fractional program aircraft as fuel—

(1) for the transportation of a qualified fractional owner with respect to the fractional ownership aircraft program of which such aircraft is a part, or

(2) with respect to the use of such aircraft on account of such a qualified fractional owner, including use in deadhead service.

(b)   Amount of tax. The rate of tax imposed by subsection (a) is 14.1 cents per gallon.

(c)   Definitions and special rules. For purposes of this section—

(1)   Fractional program aircraft. The term "fractional program aircraft" means, with respect to any fractional ownership aircraft program, any aircraft which—

(A) is listed as a fractional program aircraft in the management specifications issued to the manager of such program by the Federal Aviation Administration under subpart K of part 91 of title 14, Code of Federal Regulations, and

(B) is registered in the United States.

(2)   Fractional ownership aircraft program. The term "fractional ownership aircraft program" means a program under which—

(A) a single fractional ownership program manager provides fractional ownership program management services on behalf of the fractional owners,

(B) there are 1 or more fractional owners per fractional program aircraft, with at least 1 fractional program aircraft having more than 1 owner,

(C) with respect to at least 2 fractional program aircraft, none of the ownership interests in such aircraft are—

(i) less than the minimum fractional ownership interest, or

(ii) held by the program manager referred to in subparagraph (A),

(D) there exists a dry-lease aircraft exchange arrangement among all of the fractional owners, and

(E) there are multi-year program agreements covering the fractional ownership, fractional ownership program management services, and dry-lease aircraft exchange aspects of the program.

(3) Definitions related to fractional ownership interests.

(A) Qualified fractional owner. The term "qualified fractional owner" means any fractional owner which has a minimum fractional ownership interest in at least one fractional program aircraft.

(B) Minimum fractional ownership interest. The term "minimum fractional ownership interest" means, with respect to each type of aircraft—

(i) a fractional ownership interest equal to or greater than $1/16$ of at least 1 subsonic, fixed wing, or powered lift aircraft, or

(ii) a fractional ownership interest equal to or greater than $1/32$ of at least 1 rotorcraft aircraft.

(C) Fractional ownership interest. The term "fractional ownership interest" means—

(i) the ownership of an interest in a fractional program aircraft,

(ii) the holding of a multi-year leasehold interest in a fractional program aircraft, or

(iii) the holding of a multi-year leasehold interest which is convertible into an ownership interest in a fractional program aircraft.

(D) Fractional owner. The term "fractional owner" means any person owning any interest (including the entire interest) in a fractional program aircraft.

(4) Dry-lease aircraft exchange. The term "dry-lease aircraft exchange" means an agreement, documented by the written program agreements, under which the fractional program aircraft are available, on an as needed basis without crew, to each fractional owner.

(5) Special rule relating to use of fractional program aircraft for flight demonstration, maintenance, or training. For purposes of subsection (a), a fractional program aircraft shall not be considered to be used for the transportation of a qualified fractional owner, or on account of such qualified fractional owner, when it is used for flight demonstration, maintenance, or crew training.

(6) Special rule relating to deadhead service. A fractional program aircraft shall not be considered to be used on account of a qualified fractional owner when it is used in deadhead service and a person other than a qualified fractional owner is separately charged for such service.

(d) Termination. This section shall not apply to liquids used as a fuel in an aircraft after September 30, 2021.

[For Analysis, see ¶ 1808. For Committee Reports, see ¶ 5603.]

[Endnote Code Sec. 4043]

Code Sec. 4043 was added by Sec. 1103(a)(1) of the FAA Modernization and Reform Act of 2012, P.L. 112-95, 2/14/2012, as detailed below:

1. Sec. 1103(a)(1) added Code Sec. 4043

Effective Date (Sec. 1103(c), P.L. 112-95, 2/14/2012) effective for fuel used after 3/31/2012.

[¶ 3116]   Code Sec. 4051.   Imposition of tax on heavy trucks and trailers sold at retail.

* * * * * * * * * * * *

(c) Termination. On and after [1]*October 1, 2016,* the taxes imposed by this section shall not apply.

* * * * * * * * * * * *

[For Analysis, see ¶ 1803. For Committee Reports, see ¶ 5401.]

[Endnote Code Sec. 4051]

Code Sec. 4051(c) was amended by Sec. 40102(a)(2)(B) of the Moving Ahead for Progress in the 21st Century Act, P.L. 112-141, 7/6/2012, after it was amended by Sec. 402(a)(2)(B) of the Temporary Surface Transportation Extension Act of 2012, P.L. 112-140, 6/29/2012, as detailed below:

1. Sec. 40102(a)(2)(B) substituted "October 1, 2016" for "July 1, 2012 [sic July 7, 2012]" in subsec. (c). [Ed Note: The amendment made by Sec. 40102(a)(2)(B) of P.L. 112-141 did not take into account the previous amendment made by Sec. 402(a)(2)(B) of P.L. 112-140, which substituted "July 7, 2012" for "July 1, 2012" in subsec. (c)]

Effective Date (Sec. 40102(f), P.L. 112-141, 7/6/2012 and Sec. 402(f)(1), P.L. 112-120, 6/29/2012) effective 7/1/2012.

[¶ 3117]   Code Sec. 4071.   Imposition of tax.

* * * * * * * * * * * *

(d) **Termination.** On and after [1]*October 1, 2016*, the taxes imposed by subsection (a) shall not apply.

[For Analysis, see ¶ 1803. For Committee Reports, see ¶ 5401.]

[Endnote Code Sec. 4071]
    Code Sec. 4071(d) was amended by Sec. 40102(a)(2)(C) of the Moving Ahead for Progress in the 21st Century Act, P.L. 112-141, 7/6/2012, after it was amended by Sec. 402 (a)(2)(C) of the Temporary Surface Transportation Extension Act of 2012, P.L. 112-140, 6/26/2012, as detailed below:
    1. Sec. 40102(a)(2)(C) substituted "October 1, 2016" for "July 1, 2012 [sic July 7, 2012]" in subsec. (d). [Ed Note: The amendment made by Sec. 40102(a)(2)(C) of P.L. 112-141 did not take into account the previous amendment made by Sec. 402(a)(2)(C) of P.L. 112-140, which substituted "July 7, 2012" for "July 1, 2012" in subsec. (d)]
Effective Date (Sec. 40102(f), P.L. 112-141, 7/6/2012 and Sec. 402(f)(1), P.L. 112-120, 6/29/2012) effective 7/1/2012.

[¶ 3118]   Code Sec. 4081.   Imposition of tax.

* * * * * * * * * * * *

(d) **Termination.**

(1) **In general.** The rates of tax specified in clauses (i) and (iii) of subsection (a)(2)(A) shall be 4.3 cents per gallon after [1]*September 30, 2016*.

(2) **Aviation fuels.** The rates of tax specified in subsections (a)(2)(A)(ii) and (a)(2)(C)(ii) shall be 4.3 cents per gallon—

(A) after December 31, 1996, and before the date which is 7 days after the date of the enactment [2/28/97] of the Airport and Airway Trust Fund Tax Reinstatement Act of 1997, and

(B) after September 30, 2015.

(3) **Leaking Underground Storage Tank Trust Fund financing rate.** The Leaking Underground Storage Tank Trust Fund financing rate under subsection (a)(2) shall apply after September 30, 1997, and before [2]*October 1, 2016*.

(e) **Refunds in certain cases.** Under regulations prescribed by the Secretary, if any person who paid the tax imposed by this section with respect to any taxable fuel establishes to the satisfaction of the Secretary that a prior tax was paid (and not credited or refunded) with respect to such taxable fuel, then an amount equal to the tax paid by such person shall be allowed as a refund (without interest) to such person in the same manner as if it were an overpayment of tax imposed by this section.

[For Analysis, see ¶ 1801, ¶ 1802 and ¶ 1806. For Committee Reports, see ¶ 5401 and ¶ 5601.]

[Endnote Code Sec. 4081]
    Code Sec. 4081(d)(1) and Code Sec. 4081(d)(3) was amended by Sec. 40102(a)(1)(C) and (a)(2)(D) of the Moving Ahead for Progress in the 21st Century Act, P.L. 112-141, 7/6/2012 , after it was amended by Sec. 402(a)(1)(C) and (a)(2)(D) of the Temporary Surface Transportation Extension Act of 2012, P.L. 112-140, 6/29/2012, as detailed below:
    1. Sec. 40102(a)(2)(C) of P.L. 112-141 substituted 'September 30, 2016' for 'June 30, 2012 [sic July 6, 2012]' in para. (d)(1). [Ed Note: The amendment made by Sec. 40102(a)(2)(C) of P.L. 112-141 did not take into account the previous amendment made by Sec. 402(a)(1)(C) of P.L. 112-140, which substituted 'July 6, 2012' for 'June 30,2012' in para (d)(1)]
    2. Sec. 40102(a)(2)(D) of P.L. 112-141 substituted 'October 1, 2016' for 'July 1, 2012 [sic July 7, 2012]' in para. (d)(3). [Ed Note: The amendment made by Sec. 40102(a)(2)(D) of P.L. 112-141 did not take into account the previous amendment made by Sec. 402(a)(2)(D) of P.L. 112-140, which substituted "July 7, 2012" for "July 1, 2012" in para. (d)(3)]

Effective Date (Sec. 40102(f), P.L. 112-141, 7/6/2012 and Sec. 402(f)(1), P.L. 112-120, 6/29/2012) effective 7/1/2012.

[¶ 3119]   **Code Sec. 4082.**   **Exemptions for diesel fuel and kerosene.**

* * * * * * * * * * * *

(e) **Kerosene removed into an aircraft.** In the case of kerosene [1]*(other than kerosene with respect to which tax is imposed under section 4043)* which is exempt from the tax imposed by section 4041(c) (other than by reason of a prior imposition of tax) and which is removed from any refinery or terminal directly into the fuel tank of an aircraft—

(1) the rate of tax under section 4081(a)(2)(A)(iii) shall be zero, and

(2) if such aircraft is employed in foreign trade or trade between the United States and any of its possessions, the increase in such rate under section 4081(a)(2)(B) shall be zero.
For purposes of this subsection, any removal described in section 4081(a)(3)(A) shall be treated as a removal from a terminal but only if such terminal is located within a secure area of an airport.

(f) **Exception for leaking Underground Storage Tank Trust Fund financing rate.**

(1) **In general.** Subsection (a) shall not apply to the tax imposed under section 4081 at the Leaking Underground Storage Tank Trust Fund financing rate.

(2) **Exception for export, etc.** Paragraph (1) shall not apply with respect to any fuel if the Secretary determines that such fuel is destined for export or for use by the purchaser as supplies for vessels (within the meaning of section 4221(d)(3)) employed in foreign trade or trade between the United States and any of its possessions.

(g) **Regulations.** The Secretary shall prescribe such regulations as may be necessary to carry out this section, including regulations requiring the conspicuous labeling of retail diesel fuel and kerosene pumps and other delivery facilities to assure that persons are aware of which fuel is available only for nontaxable uses.

(h) **Cross reference.** For tax on train and certain bus uses of fuel purchased tax-free, see subsections (a)(1) and (d)(3) of section 4041.
[For Analysis, see ¶ 1808. For Committee Reports, see ¶ 5603.]

[Endnote Code Sec. 4082]
  Code Sec. 4082(e) was amended by Sec. 1103(a)(2) of the FAA Modernization and Reform Act of 2012, P.L. 112-95, 2/14/2012, as detailed below:
  1. Sec. 1103(a)(2) added "(other than kerosene with respect to which tax is imposed under section 4043)" after "In the case of kerosene" in subsec. (e)
Effective Date (Sec. 1103(d)(1), P.L. 112-95, 2/14/2012) effective for fuel used after 3/31/2012.

[¶ 3120]   **Code Sec. 4083.**   **Definitions; special rule; administrative authority.**

* * * * * * * * * * * *

(b) **Commercial aviation.** For purposes of this subpart, the term "commercial aviation" means any use of an aircraft in a business of transporting persons or property for compensation or hire by air, unless properly allocable to any transportation exempt from the taxes imposed by sections 4261 and 4271 by reason of section 4281 or 4282 or by reason of subsection (h) or (i) of section 4261. [1]*Such term shall not include the use of any aircraft before October 1, 2015, if tax is imposed under section 4043 with respect to the fuel consumed in such use or if no tax is imposed on such use under section 4043 by reason of subsection (c)(5) thereof.*

* * * * * * * * * * * *

[For Analysis, see ¶ 1808. For Committee Reports, see ¶ 5603.]

[Endnote Code Sec. 4083]

Code Sec. 4083(b) was amended by Sec. 1103(b) of the FAA Modernization and Reform Act of 2012, P.L. 112-95, 2/14/2012, as detailed below:

1. Sec. 1103(b) added "Such term shall not include the use of any aircraft before October 1, 2015, if tax is imposed under section 4043 with respect to the fuel consumed in such use or if no tax is imposed on such use under section 4043 by reason of subsection (c)(5) thereof." at the end of subsec. (b)

Effective Date (Sec. 1103(d)(2), P.L. 112-95, 2/14/2012) effective for uses of aircraft after 3/31/2012.

[¶ 3121]   **Code Sec. 4101.**   **Registration and bond.**

(a) Registration.

(1) In general. Every person required by the Secretary to register under this section with respect to the tax imposed by section 4041(a) or 4081, every person producing or importing biodiesel (as defined in section 40A(d)(1)) or alcohol (as defined in section 6426(b)(4)(A)), and every person producing [1]*second generation biofuel* (as defined in section 40(b)(6)(E)) shall register with the Secretary at such time, in such form and manner, and subject to such terms and conditions, as the Secretary may by regulations prescribe. A registration under this section may be used only in accordance with regulations prescribed under this section.

(2) Registration of persons within foreign trade zones, etc. The Secretary shall require registration by any person which—

(A) operates a terminal or refinery within a foreign trade zone or within a customs bonded storage facility, or

(B) holds an inventory position with respect to a taxable fuel in such a terminal.

(3) Display of registration. Every operator of a vessel required by the Secretary to register under this section shall display proof of registration through an identification device prescribed by the Secretary on each vessel used by such operator to transport any taxable fuel.

(4) Registration of persons extending credit on certain exempt sales of fuel. The Secretary shall require registration by any person which—

(A) extends credit by credit card to any ultimate purchaser described in subparagraph (C) or (D) of section 6416(b)(2) for the purchase of taxable fuel upon which tax has been imposed under section 4041 or 4081, and

(B) does not collect the amount of such tax from such ultimate purchaser.

(5) Reregistration in event of change in ownership. Under regulations prescribed by the Secretary, a person (other than a corporation the stock of which is regularly traded on an established securities market) shall be required to reregister under this section if after a transaction (or series of related transactions) more than 50 percent of ownership interests in, or assets of, such person are held by persons other than persons (or persons related thereto) who held more than 50 percent of such interests or assets before the transaction (or series of related transactions).

[For Analysis, see ¶ 1016.]

* * * * * * * * * * * * *

[Endnote Code Sec. 4101]

Code Sec. 4101(a)(1) was amended by Sec. 404(b)(3)(C) of the American Taxpayer Relief Act of 2012, 1/2/2013, as detailed below:

1. Sec. 404(b)(3)(C) substituted "second generation biofuel" for "cellulosic biofuel" in para. (a)(1)

Effective Date (Sec. 404(b)(4), P.L. 112-240, 1/2/2013) effective for fuels sold or used after 1/2/2013.

[¶ 3122]   Code Sec. 4221.   Certain tax-free sales.

(a)   **General rule.** Under regulations prescribed by the Secretary, no tax shall be imposed under this chapter (other than under section 4121 or 4081) on the sale by the manufacturer (or under subchapter A or C of chapter 31 on the first retail sale) of an article—

(1) for use by the purchaser for further manufacture, or for resale by the purchaser to a second purchaser for use by such second purchaser in further manufacture,

(2) for export, or for resale by the purchaser to a second purchaser for export,

(3) for use by the purchaser as supplies for vessels or aircraft,

(4) to a State or local government for the exclusive use of a State or local government,

(5) to a nonprofit educational organization for its exclusive use, or

(6) to a qualified blood collector organization (as defined in section 7701(a)(49)) for such organization's exclusive use in the collection, storage, or transportation of blood,

but only if such exportation or use is to occur before any other use. Paragraphs (4), (5), and (6) shall not apply to the tax imposed by section 4064. In the case of taxes imposed by section 4051, or 4071, paragraphs (4) and (5) shall not apply on and after [1]*October 1, 2016.* In the case of the tax imposed by section 4131, paragraphs (3), (4), and (5) shall not apply and paragraph (2) shall apply only if the use of the exported vaccine meets such requirements as the Secretary may by regulations prescribe. In the case of taxes imposed by subchapter A of chapter 31, paragraphs (1), (3), (4), and (5) shall not apply. In the case of taxes imposed by subchapter C or D, paragraph (6) shall not apply. In the case of the tax imposed by section 4191, paragraphs (3), (4), (5), and (6) shall not apply.

* * * * * * * * * * * *

[For Analysis, see ¶ 1803. For Committee Reports, see ¶ 5401.]

[Endnote Code Sec. 4221]

Code Sec. 4221(a) was amended by Sec. 40102(d)(1) of the Moving Ahead for Progress in the 21st Century Act, P.L. 112-141, 7/6/2012, after it was amended by Sec. 402(c) of the Temporary Surface Transportation Extension Act of 2012, P.L. 112-140, 6/29/2012, as detailed below:

1. Sec. 40102(d)(1) substituted "October 1, 2016" for "July 1, 2012 [sic July 7, 2012]" in subsec. (a). [Ed Note: The amendment made by Sec. 40102(d)(1) of P.L. 112-141 did not take into account the previous amendment made by Sec. 402(c) of P.L. 112-140, which substituted "July 7, 2012" for "July 1, 2012" in subsec. (a)]

Effective Date (Sec. 40102(f), P.L. 112-141, 7/6/2012 and Sec. 402(f)(1), P.L. 112-120, 6/29/2012) effective 7/1/2012.

[¶ 3123]   Code Sec. 4261.   Imposition of tax.

* * * * * * * * * * * *

[1]*(j)   **Exemption for aircraft in fractional ownership aircraft programs.** No tax shall be imposed by this section or section 4271 on any air transportation if tax is imposed under section 4043 with respect to the fuel used in such transportation. This subsection shall not apply after September 30, 2015.*

[2]*(k)*   **Application of taxes.**

(1)   **In general.** The taxes imposed by this section shall apply to—

(A) transportation beginning during the period—

(i) beginning on the 7th day after the date of the enactment of the Airport and Airway Trust Fund Tax Reinstatement Act of 1997, and

(ii) ending on [3]*September 30, 2015,* and

(B) amounts paid during such period for transportation beginning after such period.

(2)   **Refunds.** If, as of the date any transportation begins, the taxes imposed by this section would not have applied to such transportation if paid for on such date, any tax paid under paragraph (1)(B) with respect to such transportation shall be treated as overpayment.

[For Analysis, see ¶ 1806 and ¶ 1808. For Committee Reports, see ¶ 5601 and ¶ 5603.]

[Endnote Code Sec. 4261]

Code Sec. 4261(j)-Code Sec. 4261(k) was amended by Sec. 1101(b)(1) and Sec. 1103(c) of the FAA Modernization and Reform Act of 2012, P.L. 112-95, 2/14/2012, as detailed below:

1. Sec. 1103(c) added new subsec. (j)
2. Sec. 1103(c) redesignated subsec. (j) as subsec. (k)

Effective Date (Sec. 1103(d)(3), P.L. 112-95, 2/14/2012) effective for tax. transportation provided after 3/31/2012.

3. Sec. 1101(b)(1) substituted "September 30, 2015" for "February 17, 2012" in clause (j)(1)(A)(ii) [sic (k)(1)(A)(ii) as so redesignated]

Effective Date (Sec. 1101(c), P.L. 112-95, 2/14/2012) effective 2/18/2012.

[¶ 3124]   Code Sec. 4271.   Imposition of tax.

* * * * * * * * * * * *

(d)   Application of tax.

(1)   In general. The tax imposed by subsection (a) shall apply to—

(A) transportation beginning during the period—

(i) beginning on the 7th day after the date of the enactment [2/28/97] of the Airport and Airway Trust Fund Tax Reinstatement Act of 1997, and

(ii) ending on [1]*September 30, 2015*, and

(B) amounts paid during such period for transportation beginning after such period.

(2)   Refunds. If, as of the date any transportation begins, the taxes imposed by this section would not have applied to such transportation if paid for on such date, any tax paid under paragraph (1)(B) with respect to such transportation shall be treated as an overpayment.

[For Analysis, see ¶ 1806. For Committee Reports, see ¶ 5601.]

[Endnote Code Sec. 4271]

Code Sec. 4271(d)(1)(A)(ii) was amended by Sec. 1101(b)(2) of the FAA Modernization and Reform Act of 2012, P.L. 112-95, 2/14/2012, as detailed below:

1. Sec. 1101(b)(2) substituted "September 30, 2015" for "February 17, 2012" in clause (d)(1)(A)(ii)

Effective Date (Sec. 1101(c), P.L. 112-95, 2/14/2012) effective 2/18/2012.

[¶ 3125]   Code Sec. 4281.   Small aircraft on nonestablished lines.

The taxes imposed by sections 4261 and 4271 shall not apply to transportation by an aircraft having a maximum certificated takeoff weight of 6,000 pounds or less, except when such aircraft is operated on an established line [1]*or when such aircraft is a jet aircraft*. For purposes of the preceding sentence, the term "maximum certificated takeoff weight" means the maximum such weight contained in the type certificate or airworthiness certificate. For purposes of this section, an aircraft shall not be considered as operated on an established line at any time during which such aircraft is being operated on a flight the sole purpose of which is sightseeing.

[For Analysis, see ¶ 1807. For Committee Reports, see ¶ 5607.]

[Endnote Code Sec. 4281]

Code Sec. 4281 was amended by Sec. 1107(a) of the FAA Modernization and Reform Act of 2012, P.L. 112-95, 2/14/2012, as detailed below:

1. Sec. 1107(a) added "or when such aircraft is a jet aircraft" after "an established line" in the first sentence of Code Sec. 4281

Effective Date (Sec. 1107(b), P.L. 112-95, 2/14/2012) effective for taxable transportation provided after 3/31/2012.

[¶ 3126]   Code Sec. 4481.   Imposition of tax.

* * * * * * * * * * * *

(f)   Period tax in effect. The tax imposed by this section shall apply only to use before October 1, ¹*2017.*

[For Analysis, see ¶ 1805. For Committee Reports, see ¶ 5401.]

[Endnote Code Sec. 4481]
   Code Sec. 4481(f) was amended by Sec. 40102(b)(1)(A) of the Moving Ahead for Progress in the 21st Century Act, P.L. 112-141, 7/6/2012, as detailed below:
   1. Sec. 40102(b)(1)(A) substituted "2017" for "2013" in subsec. (f)
Effective Date (Sec. 40102(f), P.L. 112-141, 7/6/2012) effective 7/1/2012.

[¶ 3127]   Code Sec. 4482.   Definitions.

* * * * * * * * * * * *

(c)   Other definitions and special rule. For purposes of this subchapter—
   (1)   State. The term "State" means a State and the District of Columbia.
   (2)   Year. The term "year" means the one-year period beginning on July 1.
   (3)   Use. The term "use" means use in the United States on the public highways.
   (4)   Taxable period. The term "taxable period' means any year beginning before July 1, 2017, and the period which begins on July 1, 2017, and ends at the close of September 30, 2017.
   (5)   Customary use. A semitrailer or trailer shall be treated as customarily used in connection with a highway motor vehicle if such vehicle is equipped to tow such semitrailer or trailer.
(d)   Special rule for taxable period in which termination date occurs. In the case of the taxable period which ends on September 30, ²*2017,* the amount of the tax imposed by section 4481 with respect to any highway motor vehicle shall be determined by reducing each dollar amount in the table contained in section 4481(a) by 75 percent.

[For Analysis, see ¶ 1805. For Committee Reports, see ¶ 5401.]

[Endnote Code Sec. 4482]
   Code Sec. 4482(c)(4) was amended by Sec. 40102(b)(2)(A) of the Moving Ahead for Progress in the 21st Century Act, P.L. 112-141, 7/6/2016, after it was amended by Sec. 402(e) of the Temporary Surface Transportation Extension Act of 2012, P.L. 112-140, 6/29/2012, as detailed below:
   1. Sec. 40102(b)(2)(A) amended para. (c)(4), prior to amendment para. (c)(4) read as follows:
"(4) Taxable period. The term 'taxable period' means any year beginning before July 1, 2012, and the period which begins on July 1, 2012, and ends at the close of September 30, 2012."
   [Ed Note: The amendment made by Sec 40102(b)(2)(A) of P.L. 112-141 did not take into account the previous amendment made by Sec. 402(e) of P.L. 112-140 which read as follows: "(4) Taxable period.—The term 'taxable period' means any year beginning before July 1, 2013, and the period which begins on July 1, 2013, and ends at the close of September 30, 2013."
Effective Date (Sec. 40102(b)(2)(B), P.L. 112-141, 7/6/2012 and Sec 402(e), P.L. 112-140, 6/29/2012) effective 10/1/2011, as if included in the amendments made by Sec. 142 of the Surface Transportation Extension Act of 2011, Part II (P.L. 112-30).

   Code Sec. 4482(d) was amended by Sec. 40102(b)(1)(B), P.L. 112-141, 7/6/2012, as detailed below:
   2. Sec. 40102(b)(1)(B) substituted "2017" for "2013" after "September 30," in subsec. (d)
Effective Date (Sec. 40102(f), P.L. 112-141, 7/6/2012) effective 7/1/2012.

[¶ 3128]   Code Sec. 4483.   Exemptions.
   (a)   State and local governmental exemption. Under regulations prescribed by the Secretary, no tax shall be imposed by section 4481 on the use of any highway motor vehicle by any State or any political subdivision of a State.

* * * * * * * * * * * *

(c)   **Certain transit-type buses.** Under regulations prescribed by the Secretary, no tax shall be imposed by section 4481 on the use of any bus which is of the transit type (rather than of the intercity type) by a person who, for the last 3 months of the preceding year (or for such other period as the Secretary may by regulations prescribe for purposes of this subsection), met the 60-percent passenger fare revenue test set forth in section 6421(b)(2) (as in effect on the day before the date of the enactment [11/9/78] of the Energy Tax Act of 1978) as applied to the period prescribed for purposes of this subsection.

* * * * * * * * * * * *

(i)   **Termination of exemptions.** Subsections (a) and (c) shall not apply on and after [1]*October 1, 2017.*

[For Analysis, see ¶ 1805. For Committee Reports, see ¶ 5401.]

[Endnote Code Sec. 4483]

Code Sec. 4483(i) was amended by Sec. 40102(d)(2) of the Moving Ahead for Progress in the 21st Century Act, P.L. 112-141, 7/6/2012, after it was amended by Sec. 402(c), P.L. 112-140, 6/29/2012, as detailed below:

1. Sec. 40102(d)(2) substituted "October 1, 2017" for "July 1, 2012 [sic July 7, 2012]" in subsec. (i). [Ed. Note: The amendment made by Sec. 40102(d)(2) of this Act did not take into account the previous amendment made by Sec. 402(c) of P.L. 112-140, which substituted "July 7, 2012" for "July 1, 2012" in subsec. (i)]

Effective Date (Sec. 40102(f), P.L. 112-141, 7/6/2012 and Sec. 402(f)(1), P.L. 112-140, 6/29/2012), effective 7/1/2012.

[¶ 3129]   Code Sec. 4973.   Tax on excess contributions to certain tax-favored accounts and annuities.

* * * * * * * * * * * *

(b)   **Excess contributions.** For purposes of this section, in the case of individual retirement accounts, or individual retirement annuities, the term "excess contributions" means the sum of—

(1) the excess (if any) of—

(A) the amount contributed for the taxable year to the accounts or for the annuities (other than a contribution to a Roth IRA or a rollover contribution described in section 402(c), 403(a)(4), 403(b)(8), [1]*408(d)(3), or 457(e)(16)*), over

(B) the amount allowable as a deduction under section 219 for such contributions, and

* * * * * * * * * * * *

(e)   **Excess contributions to Coverdell education savings accounts.** For purposes of this section—

(1)   **In general.** In the case of Coverdell education savings accounts maintained for the benefit of any one beneficiary, the term "excess contributions" means the sum of—

(A) the amount by which the amount contributed for the taxable year to such accounts exceeds [2]*$2,000* (or, if less, the sum of the maximum amounts permitted to be contributed under section 530(c) by the contributors to such accounts for such year); [3]*and*

[4]*(B)* the amount determined under this subsection for the preceding taxable year, reduced by the sum of—

(i) the distributions out of the accounts for the taxable year (other than rollover distributions); and

(ii) the excess (if any) of the maximum amount which may be contributed to the accounts for the taxable year over the amount contributed to the accounts for the taxable year.

* * * * * * * * * * * *

[For Analysis, see ¶ 704.]

[Endnote Code Sec. 4973]
Sec. 101(a)(1) of the American Taxpayer Relief Act of 2012, P.L. 112-240, 1/2/2013, deleted Title IX [Sec. 901] of the Economic Growth and Tax Relief Reconciliation Act of 2001, P.L. 107-16, the effect of which is to eliminate the sunset of all provisions enacted by P.L. 107-16. Following are the amendments made to Code Sec. 4973, by P.L. 107-16.
Effective Date (Sec. 101(a)(3), P.L. 112-240, 1/2/2013) effective for taxable, plan, or limitation years beginning after 12/31/2012, and estates of decedents dying, gifts made, or generation skipping transfers after 12/31/2012.

Code Sec. 4973(b)(1)(A) was amended by Sec. 641(e)(11) of the Economic Growth and Tax Relief Reconciliation Act of 2001, P.L. 107-16, 6/7/2001. This amendment was made permanent by Sec. 811, P.L. 109-280, 8/17/2006.
　1. Sec. 641(e)(11) substituted "408(d)(3), or 457(e)(16)" for "or 408(d)(3)" in subpara. (b)(1)(A)
Effective Date (Sec. 641(f), P.L. 107-16, 6/7/2001) effective for distributions after 12/31/2001.

Code Sec. 4973(e)(1)(A), Code Sec. 4973(e)(1)(B) [as amended by Sec. 402(a)(4)(A) of this Act, made permanent by Sec. 1304(a), P.L. 109-280, 8/17/2006] and Code Sec. 4973(e)(1)(C) was amended by Sec. 401(a)(2) and (g)(2)(D), P.L. 107-16, 6/7/2001, as detailed below:
　2. Sec. 401(a)(2) substituted "$2,000" for "$500" in subpara. (e)(1)(A)
　3. Sec. 401(g)(2)(D) added "and" at the end of subpara. (e)(1)(A)
　4. Sec. 401(g)(2)(D) deleted subpara. (e)(1)(B) and redesignated subpara. (e)(1)(C) as (e)(1)(B). Prior to deletion, subpara. (e)(1)(B) read as follows:
　"(B) if any amount is contributed (other than a contribution described in section 530(b)(2)(B)) during such year to a qualified State tuition program for the benefit of such beneficiary, any amount contributed to such accounts for such taxable year; and"
Effective Date (Sec. 401(h), P.L. 107-16, 6/7/2001) effective for tax. yrs. begin. after 12/31/2001.

[¶ 3130]　Code Sec. 4980B.　Failure to satisfy continuation coverage requirements of group health plans.

* * * * * * * * * * * *

(f)　Continuation coverage requirements of group health plans.

(1)　In general. A group health plan meets the requirements of this subsection only if the coverage of the costs of pediatric vaccines (as defined under section 2162 of the Public Health Service Act) is not reduced below the coverage provided by the plan as of May 1, 1993, and only if each qualified beneficiary who would lose coverage under the plan as a result of a qualifying event is entitled to elect, within the election period, continuation coverage under the plan.

(2)　Continuation coverage. For purposes of paragraph (1), the term "continuation coverage" means coverage under the plan which meets the following requirements:

(A) Type of benefit coverage. The coverage must consist of coverage which, as of the time the coverage is being provided, is identical to the coverage provided under the plan to similarly situated beneficiaries under the plan with respect to whom a qualifying event has not occurred. If coverage under the plan is modified for any group of similarly situated beneficiaries, the coverage shall also be modified in the same manner for all individuals who are qualified beneficiaries under the plan pursuant to this subsection in connection with such group.

(B) Period of coverage. The coverage must extend for at least the period beginning on the date of the qualifying event and ending not earlier than the earliest of the following:

(i) Maximum required period.

(I) General rule for terminations and reduced hours. In the case of a qualifying event described in paragraph (3)(B), except as provided in subclause (II), the date which is 18 months after the date of the qualifying event.

(II) Special rule for multiple qualifying events. If a qualifying event (other than a qualifying event described in paragraph (3)(F)) occurs during the 18 months after the date of a qualifying event described in paragraph (3)(B), the date which is 36 months after the date of the qualifying event described in paragraph (3)(B).

(III) Special rule for certain bankruptcy proceedings. In the case of a qualifying event described in paragraph (3)(F) (relating to bankruptcy proceedings), the date of the death of the covered employee or qualified beneficiary (described in subsection (g)(1)(D)(iii)), or in the case of the surviving spouse or dependent children of the covered employee, 36 months after the date of the death of the covered employee.

(IV) General rule for other qualifying events. In the case of a qualifying event not described in paragraph (3)(B) or (3)(F), the date which is 36 months after the date of the qualifying event.

(V) Special rule for PBGC recipients. In the case of a qualifying event described in paragraph (3)(B) with respect to a covered employee who (as of such qualifying event) has a nonforfeitable right to a benefit any portion of which is to be paid by the Pension Benefit Guaranty Corporation under title IV of the Employee Retirement Income Security Act of 1974, notwithstanding subclause (I) or (II), the date of the death of the covered employee, or in the case of the surviving spouse or dependent children of the covered employee, 24 months after the date of the death of the covered employee. The preceding sentence shall not require any period of coverage to extend beyond [1]*January 1, 2014.*

(VI) Special rule for TAA-eligible individuals. In the case of a qualifying event described in paragraph (3)(B) with respect to a covered employee who is (as of the date that the period of coverage would, but for this subclause or subclause (VII), otherwise terminate under subclause (I) or (II)) a TAA-eligible individual (as defined in paragraph (5)(C)(iv)(II)), the period of coverage shall not terminate by reason of subclause (I) or (II), as the case may be, before the later of the date specified in such subclause or the date on which such individual ceases to be such a TAA-eligible individual. The preceding sentence shall not require any period of coverage to extend beyond [2]*January 1, 2014.*

(VII) Medicare entitlement followed by qualifying event. In the case of a qualifying event described in paragraph (3)(B) that occurs less than 18 months after the date the covered employee became entitled to benefits under title XVIII of the Social Security Act, the period of coverage for qualified beneficiaries other than the covered employee shall not terminate under this clause before the close of the 36-month period beginning on the date the covered employee became so entitled.

(VIII) Special rule for disability. In the case of a qualified beneficiary who is determined, under title II or XVI of the Social Security Act, to have been disabled at any time during the first 60 days of continuation coverage under this section, any reference in subclause (I) or (II) to 18 months is deemed a reference to 29 months (with respect to all qualified beneficiaries), but only if the qualified beneficiary has provided notice of such determination under paragraph (6)(C) before the end of such 18 months.

(ii) End of plan. The date on which the employer ceases to provide any group health plan to any employee.

(iii) Failure to pay premium. The date on which coverage ceases under the plan by reason of a failure to make timely payment of any premium required under the plan with respect to the qualified beneficiary. The payment of any premium (other than any payment referred to in the last sentence of subparagraph (C)) shall be considered to be timely if made within 30 days after the date due or within such longer period as applies to or under the plan.

(iv) Group health plan coverage or Medicare entitlement. The date on which the qualified beneficiary first becomes, after the date of the election—

(I) covered under any other group health plan (as an employee or otherwise), which does not contain any exclusion or limitation with respect to any preexisting condition of such beneficiary (other than such an exclusion or limitation which does not apply to (or is satisfied by) such beneficiary by reason of chapter 100 of this title, part 7 of subtitle B of title I of the Employee Retirement Income Security Act of 1974, or title XXVII of the Public Health Services Act), or

(II) in the case of a qualified beneficiary other than a qualified beneficiary described in subsection (g)(1)(D) entitled to benefits under title XVIII of the Social Security Act.

(v) Termination of extended coverage for disability. In the case of a qualified beneficiary who is disabled at any time during the first 60 days of continuation coverage under this section, the month that begins more than 30 days after the date of the final determination under title II or XVI of the Social Security Act that the qualified beneficiary is no longer disabled.

(C) Premium requirements. The plan may require payment of a premium for any period of continuation coverage, except that such premium—

(i) shall not exceed 102 percent of the applicable premium for such period, and

(ii) may, at the election of the payor, be made in monthly installments.

In no event may the plan require the payment of any premium before the day which is 45 days after the day on which the qualified beneficiary made the initial election for continuation coverage. In the case of an individual described in the last sentence of subparagraph (B)(i), any reference in clause (i) of this subparagraph to "102 percent" is deemed a reference to "150 percent" for any month after the 18th month of continuation coverage described in subclause (I) or (II) of subparagraph (B)(i).

(D) No requirement of insurability. The coverage may not be conditioned upon, or discriminate on the basis of lack of, evidence of insurability.

(E) Conversion option. In the case of a qualified beneficiary whose period of continuation coverage expires under subparagraph (B)(i), the plan must, during the 180-day period ending on such expiration date, provide to the qualified beneficiary the option of enrollment under a conversion health plan otherwise generally available under the plan.

(3) Qualifying event. For purposes of this subsection, the term "qualifying event" means, with respect to any covered employee, any of the following events which, but for the continuation coverage required under this subsection, would result in the loss of coverage of a qualified beneficiary—

(A) The death of the covered employee.

(B) The termination (other than by reason of such employee's gross misconduct), or reduction of hours, of the covered employee's employment.

(C) The divorce or legal separation of the covered employee from the employee's spouse.

(D) The covered employee becoming entitled to benefits under title XVIII of the Social Security Act.

(E) A dependent child ceasing to be a dependent child under the generally applicable requirements of the plan.

(F) A proceeding in a case under title 11, United States Code, commencing on or after July 1, 1986, with respect to the employer from whose employment the covered employee retired at any time.

In the case of an event described in subparagraph (F), a loss of coverage includes a substantial elimination of coverage with respect to a qualified beneficiary described in subsection (g)(1)(D) within one year before or after the date of commencement of the proceeding.

(4) Applicable premium. For purposes of this subsection—

(A) In general. The term "applicable premium" means, with respect to any period of continuation coverage of qualified beneficiaries, the cost to the plan for such period of the coverage for similarly situated beneficiaries with respect to whom a qualifying event has not occurred (without regard to whether such cost is paid by the employer or employee).

(B) Special rule for self-insured plans. To the extent that a plan is a self-insured plan—

(i) In general. Except as provided in clause (ii), the applicable premium for any period of continuation coverage of qualified beneficiaries shall be equal to a reasonable estimate of the cost of providing coverage for such period for similarly situated beneficiaries which—

(I) is determined on an actuarial basis, and

(II) takes into account such factors as the Secretary may prescribe in regulations.

(ii) Determination on basis of past cost. If a plan administrator elects to have this clause apply, the applicable premium for any period of continuation coverage of qualified beneficiaries shall be equal to—

(I) the cost to the plan for similarly situated beneficiaries for the same period occurring during the preceding determination period under subparagraph (C), adjusted by

(II) the percentage increase or decrease in the implicit price deflator of the gross national product (calculated by the Department of Commerce and published in the Survey of Current Business) for the 12-month period ending on the last day of the sixth month of such preceding determination period.

(iii) Clause (ii) not to apply where significant change. A plan administrator may not elect to have clause (ii) apply in any case in which there is any significant difference between the determination period and the preceding determination period, in coverage under or in employees covered by, the plan. The determination under the preceding sentence for any determination period shall be made at the same time as the determination under subparagraph (C).

(C) Determination period. The determination of any applicable premium shall be made for a period of 12 months and shall be made before the beginning of such period.

(5) **Election.** For purposes of this subsection

(A) Election period. The term "election period" means the period which—

(i) begins not later than the date on which coverage terminates under the plan by reason of a qualifying event,

(ii) is of at least 60 days' duration, and

(iii) ends not earlier than 60 days after the later of—

(I) the date described in clause (i), or

(II) in the case of any qualified beneficiary who receives notice under paragraph (6)(D), the date of such notice.

(B) Effect of election on other beneficiaries. Except as otherwise specified in an election, any election of continuation coverage by a qualified beneficiary described in subparagraph (A)(i) or (B) of subsection (g)(1) shall be deemed to include an election of continuation coverage on behalf of any other qualified beneficiary who would lose coverage under the plan by reason of the qualifying event. If there is a choice among types of coverage under the plan, each qualified beneficiary is entitled to make a separate selection among such types of coverage.

(C) Temporary extension of COBRA election period for certain individuals.

(i) In general. In the case of a nonelecting TAA-eligible individual and notwithstanding subparagraph (A), such individual may elect continuation coverage under this subsection during the 60-day period that begins on the first day of the month in which the individual becomes a TAA-eligible individual, but only if such election is made not later than 6 months after the date of the TAA-related loss of coverage.

(ii) Commencement of coverage; no reach-back. Any continuation coverage elected by a TAA-eligible individual under clause (i) shall commence at the beginning of the 60-day election period described in such paragraph and shall not include any period prior to such 60-day election period.

(iii) Preexisting conditions. With respect to an individual who elects continuation coverage pursuant to clause (i), the period—

(I) beginning on the date of the TAA-related loss of coverage, and

(II) ending on the first day of the 60-day election period described in clause (i),

shall be disregarded for purposes of determining the 63-day periods referred to in section 9801(c)(2), section 701(c)(2) of the Employee Retirement Income Security Act of 1974, and section 2701(c)(2) of the Public Health Service Act.

(iv) Definitions. For purposes of this subsection:

(I) Nonelecting TAA-eligible individual. The term "nonelecting TAA-eligible individual" means a TAA-eligible individual who has a TAA-related loss of coverage and did not elect continuation coverage under this subsection during the TAA-related election period.

(II) TAA-eligible individual. The term "TAA-eligible individual" means an eligible TAA recipient (as defined in paragraph (2) of section 35(c)) and an eligible alternative TAA recipient (as defined in paragraph (3) of such section).

(III) TAA-related election period. The term "TAA-related election period" means, with respect to a TAA-related loss of coverage, the 60-day election period under this subsection which is a direct consequence of such loss.

(IV) TAA-related loss of coverage. The term "TAA-related loss of coverage" means, with respect to an individual whose separation from employment gives rise to being an TAA-eligible individual, the loss of health benefits coverage associated with such separation.

(6) Notice requirement. In accordance with regulations prescribed by the Secretary—

(A) The group health plan shall provide, at the time of commencement of coverage under the plan, written notice to each covered employee and spouse of the employee (if any) of the rights provided under this subsection.

(B) The employer of an employee under a plan must notify the plan administrator of a qualifying event described in subparagraph (A), (B), (D), or (F) of paragraph (3) with respect to such employee within 30 days (or, in the case of a group health plan which is a multiemployer plan, such longer period of time as may be provided in the terms of the plan) of the date of the qualifying event.

(C) Each covered employee or qualified beneficiary is responsible for notifying the plan administrator of the occurrence of any qualifying event described in subparagraph (C) or (E) of paragraph (3) within 60 days after the date of the qualifying event and each qualified beneficiary who is determined, under title II or XVI of the Social Security Act, to have been disabled at any time during the first 60 days of continuation coverage under this section is responsible for notifying the plan administrator of such determination within 60 days after the date of the determination and for notifying the plan administrator within 30 days of the date of any final determination under such title or titles that the qualified beneficiary is no longer disabled.

(D) The plan administrator shall notify—

(i) in the case of a qualifying event described in subparagraph (A), (B), (D), or (F) of paragraph (3), any qualified beneficiary with respect to such event, and

(ii) in the case of a qualifying event described in subparagraph (C) or (E) of paragraph (3) where the covered employee notifies the plan administrator under subparagraph (C), any qualified beneficiary with respect to such event,

of such beneficiary's rights under this subsection.

The requirements of subparagraph (B) shall be considered satisfied in the case of a multiemployer plan in connection with a qualifying event described in paragraph (3)(B) if the plan provides that the determination of the occurrence of such qualifying event will be made by the plan administrator. For purposes of subparagraph (D), any notification shall be made within 14 days (or, in the case of a group health plan which is a multiemployer plan, such longer period of time as may be provided in the terms of the plan) of the date on which the plan administrator is notified under subparagraph (B) or (C), whichever is applicable, and any such notification to an individual who is a qualified beneficiary as the spouse of the covered employee shall be treated as notification to all other qualified beneficiaries residing with such spouse at the time such notification is made.

(7) Covered employee. For purposes of this subsection, the term "covered employee" means an individual who is (or was) provided coverage under a group health plan by virtue of the performance of services by the individual for 1 or more persons maintaining the plan (including as an employee defined in section 401(c)(1)).

(8) Optional extension of required periods. A group health plan shall not be treated as failing to meet the requirements of this subsection solely because the plan provides both—

(A) that the period of extended coverage referred to in paragraph (2)(B) commences with the date of the loss of coverage, and

(B) that the applicable notice period provided under paragraph (6)(B) commences with the date of the loss of coverage.

* * * * * * * * * * * *

[For Analysis, see ¶ 1612.]

[Endnote Code Sec. 4980B]
   Code Sec. 4980B(f)(2)(B)(i)(V) and Code Sec. 4980B(f)(2)(B)(i)(VI) was amended by Sec. 243(a)(3) and (4) of Trade Adjustment Assistance Extension Act of 2011, P.L. 112-40, 10/21/2011, as detailed below:
   1. Sec. 243(a)(3) substituted 'January 1, 2014' for 'February 12, 2011' in subcl. (f)(2)(B)(i)(V)
   2. Sec. 243(a)(4) substituted 'January 1, 2014' for 'February 12, 2011' in subcl. (f)(2)(B)(i)(VI)
Effective Date (Sec. 243(b), P.L. 112-40, 10/21/2011) effective for periods of coverage which would (without regard to the amendments made by this section) end on or after 11/20/2011.

[¶ 3131]   Code Sec. 4980H.   Shared responsibility for employers regarding health coverage.

* * * * * * * * * * * *

(b) Large employers offering coverage with employees who qualify for premium tax credits or cost-sharing reductions.

(1) In general. If—

(A) an applicable large employer offers to its full-time employees (and their dependents) the opportunity to enroll in minimum essential coverage under an eligible employer-sponsored plan (as defined in section 5000A(f)(2)) for any month, and

(B) 1 or more full-time employees of the applicable large employer has been certified to the employer under section 1411 of the Patient Protection and Affordable Care Act as having enrolled for such month in a qualified health plan with respect to which an applicable premium tax credit or cost-sharing reduction is allowed or paid with respect to the employee,
   then there is hereby imposed on the employer an assessable payment equal to the product of the number of full-time employees of the applicable large employer described in subparagraph (B) for such month and an amount equal to $1/12$ of $3,000.

(2) Overall limitation. The aggregate amount of tax determined under paragraph (1) with respect to all employees of an applicable large employer for any month shall not exceed the product of the applicable payment amount and the number of individuals employed by the employer as full-time employees during such month.

^{1}*(3) Repealed.*

* * * * * * * * * * * *

[For Analysis, see ¶ 1603.]

[Endnote Code Sec. 4980H]
   Code Sec. 4980H(b)(3) was deleted by Sec. 1858(b)(4) of the Department of Defense and Full-Year Continuing Appropriations Act, 2011, P.L. 112-10, 4/15/2011, as detailed below:
   1. Sec. 1858(b)(4) deleted para. (b)(3)
   Prior to deletion, para. (b)(3) read as follows:
"(3) Special rules for employers providing free choice vouchers. No assessable payment shall be imposed under paragraph (1) for any month with respect to any employee to whom the employer provides a free choice voucher under section 10108 of the Patient Protection and Affordable Care Act for such month."

Effective Date (Sec. 1858(d), P.L. 112-10, 4/15/2011) effective for months begin. after 12/31/2013, as if included in the provisions of Sec. 10108(i)(1)(A) of P.L. 111-148.

[¶ 3132]   Code Sec.[1] 6039H.   *Information with respect to Alaska Native Settlement Trusts and sponsoring Native Corporations.*

    (a)   Requirement. *The fiduciary of an electing Settlement Trust (as defined in section 646(h)(1)) shall include with the return of income of the trust a statement containing the information required under subsection (c).*

    (b)   Application with other requirements. *The filing of any statement under this section shall be in lieu of the reporting requirements under section 6034A to furnish any statement to a beneficiary regarding amounts distributed to such beneficiary (and such other reporting rules as the Secretary deems appropriate).*

    (c)   Required information. *The information required under this subsection shall include—*

        (1) the amount of distributions made during the taxable year to each beneficiary,

        (2) the treatment of such distribution under the applicable provision of section 646, including the amount that is excludable from the recipient beneficiary's gross income under section 646, and

        (3) the amount (if any) of any distribution during such year that is deemed to have been made by the sponsoring Native Corporation (as defined in section 646(h)(5)).

    (d)   Sponsoring Native Corporation.

        *(1)   **In general.** The electing Settlement Trust shall, on or before the date on which the statement under subsection (a) is required to be filed, furnish such statement to the sponsoring Native Corporation (as so defined).*

        *(2)   **Distributees.** The sponsoring Native Corporation shall furnish each recipient of a distribution described in section 646(e)(3) a statement containing the amount deemed to have been distributed to such recipient by such corporation for the taxable year.*

    [For Analysis, see ¶ 1503.]

[Endnote Code Sec. 6039H]

    Sec. 101(a)(1) of the American Taxpayer Relief Act of 2012, P.L. 112-240, 1/2/2013, deleted Title IX [Sec. 901] of the Economic Growth and Tax Relief Reconciliation Act of 2001, P.L. 107-16, the effect of which is to eliminate the sunset of all provisions enacted by P.L. 107-16. Following are the amendments made to Code Sec. 6039H, by P.L. 107-16.

Effective Date (Sec. 101(a)(3), P.L. 112-240, 1/2/2013) effective for taxable, plan, or limitation years beginning after 12/31/2012, and estates of decedents dying, gifts made, or generation skipping transfers after 12/31/2012.

    Code Sec. 6039H was added by Sec. 671(b) of the Economic Growth and Tax Relief Reconciliation Act of 2001, P.L. 107-16, 6/7/2001.

    1. Sec. 671(b) added Code Sec. 6039H

Effective Date (Sec. 671(d), P.L. 107-16, 6/7/2001) effective for tax. yrs. end. after 6/7/2001 and for contributions made to electing Settlement Trusts for such year or any subsequent year.

[¶ 3133]   Code Sec. 6041.   Information at source.

    (a)   Payments of $600 or more. All persons engaged in a trade or business and making payment in the course of such trade or business to another person, of rent, salaries, wages, [1]premiums, annuities, compensations, remunerations, emoluments, or other [2]fixed or determinable gains, profits, and income (other than payments to which section 6042(a)(1), 6044(a)(1), 6047(e), 6049(a), or 6050N(a) applies, and other than payments with respect to which a statement is required under the authority of section 6042(a)(2), 6044(a)(2), or 6045), of $600 or more in any taxable year, or, in the case of such payments made by the United States, the officers or employees of the United States having information as to such payments and required to make returns in regard thereto by the regulations hereinafter provided for, shall render a true and accurate return to the Secretary, under such regulations and in such form and manner and to such extent as may be prescribed by the Secretary, setting forth the amount of such [3]gains, profits, and income, and the name and address of the recipient of such payment.

* * * * * * * * * * * *

[4]*(h)   Repealed.*

[5]*(i)   Repealed.*

[6]*(j)   Repealed.*
[For Analysis, see ¶ 1905, ¶ 1906 and ¶ 1907. For Committee Reports, see ¶ 5901 and ¶ 5902.]

[Endnote Code Sec. 6041]
   Code Sec. 6041(a) was amended by 2(b)(1)-(2) of the Comprehensive 1099 Taxpayer Protection and Repayment of Exchange Subsidy Overpayments Act of 2011, P.L. 112-9, 4/14/2011, as detailed below:
   1. Sec. 2(b)(1) deleted "amounts in consideration for property," after "of rent, salaries, wages," in subsec. (a)
   2. Sec. (2)(b)(2) deleted "gross proceeds," after "emoluments, or other" in subsec. (a)
   3. Sec. (2)(b)(2) deleted "gross proceeds," after 'setting forth the amount of such" in subsec. (a)
Effective Date (Sec. 2(c), P.L. 112-9, 4/11/2011) effective for payments made after 12/31/2011.

   Code Sec. 6041(h) was deleted by Sec. 3(a), HR4, 4/11/2011, as detailed below:
   4. Sec. 3(a) deleted subsec. (h). Prior to deletion, subsec. (h) read as follows:
"(h) Treatment of rental property expense payments.
   "(1) In general. Solely for purposes of subsection (a) and except as provided in paragraph (2), a person receiving rental income from real estate shall be considered to be engaged in a trade or business of renting property.
   "(2) Exceptions. Paragraph (1) shall not apply to—
   "(A) any individual, including any individual who is an active member of the uniformed services or an employee of the intelligence community (as defined in section 121(d)(9)(C)(iv), if substantially all rental income is derived from renting the principal residence (within the meaning of section 121) of such individual on a temporary basis,
   "(B) any individual who receives rental income of not more than the minimal amount, as determined under regulations prescribed by the Secretary, and
   "(C) any other individual for whom the requirements of this section would cause hardship, as determined under regulations prescribed by the Secretary."
Effective Date (Sec. 3(b), P.L. 112-9, 4/11/2011) effective for payments made after 12/31/2010.

   Code Sec. 6041(i)-Code Sec. 6041(j) were deleted by Sec. 2(a), P.L. 112-9, 4/11/2011, as detailed below:
   5. Sec. 2(a) deleted subsec. (i). Prior to deletion subsec. (i) read as follows:
"(i) Application to corporations.
   "Notwithstanding any regulation prescribed by the Secretary before the date of the enactment of this subsection, for purposes of this section the term "person" includes any corporation that is not an organization exempt from tax under section 501(a)"
   6. Sec. 2(a) deleted subsec. (j). Prior to deletion subsec. (j) read as follows:
"(j) Regulations.
   "The Secretary may prescribe such regulations and other guidance as may be appropriate or necessary to carry out the purposes of this section, including rules to prevent duplicative reporting of transactions. "
Effective Date (Sec. 2(c), P.L. 112-9, 4/11/2011) effective for payments made after 12/31/2011.

[¶ 3134]   Code Sec. 6050S.   Returns relating to higher education tuition and re-lated expenses.

* * * * * * * * * * * *

   (e)   Definitions. For purposes of this section, the terms "eligible educational institution" and "qualified tuition and related expenses" have the meanings given such terms by section 25A (without regard to subsection (g)(2) thereof), and except as provided in regulations, the term "qualified education loan" has the meaning given such term by [1]*section 221(d)(1).*

* * * * * * * * * * * *

[Endnote Code Sec. 6050S]

Sec. 101(a)(1) of the American Taxpayer Relief Act of 2012, P.L. 112-240, 1/2/2013, deleted Title IX [Sec. 901] of the Economic Growth and Tax Relief Reconciliation Act of 2001, P.L. 107-16, the effect of which is to eliminate the sunset of all provisions enacted by P.L. 107-16. Following are the amendments made to Code Sec. 6050S, by P.L. 107-16.

Effective Date (Sec. 101(a)(3), P.L. 112-240, 1/2/2013) effective for taxable, plan, or limitation years beginning after 12/31/2012, and estates of decedents dying, gifts made, or generation skipping transfers after 12/31/2012.

Code Sec. 6050S(e) was amended by Sec. 412(a)(2) of the Economic Growth and Tax Relief Reconciliation Act of 2001, P.L. 107-16, 6/7/2001, as detailed below:

1. Sec. 412(a)(2) substituted "section 221(d)(1)" for "section 221(e)(1)" in subsec. (e)

Effective Date (Sec. 412(a)(3), P.L. 107-16, 6/7/2001) effective for loan interest paid after 12/31/2001, in tax. yrs. end. after 12/31/2001.

[¶ 3135]   Code Sec. 6056.   Certain employers required to report on health insurance coverage.

(a) In general. Every applicable large employer required to meet the requirements of section 4980H with respect to its full-time employees during a calendar year [1] shall, at such time as the Secretary may prescribe, make a return described in subsection (b).

(b) Form and manner of return. A return is described in this subsection if such return—

(1) is in such form as the Secretary may prescribe, and

(2) contains—

(A) the name, date, and employer identification number of the employer,

(B) a certification as to whether the employer offers to its full-time employees (and their dependents) the opportunity to enroll in minimum essential coverage under an eligible employer-sponsored plan (as defined in section 5000A(f)(2)),

(C) if the employer certifies that the employer did offer to its full-time employees (and their dependents) the opportunity to so enroll—

(i) [2] the length of any waiting period (as defined in section 2701(b)(4) of the Public Health Service Act) with respect to such coverage,

(ii) the months during the calendar year for which coverage under the plan was available,

(iii) the monthly premium for the lowest cost option in each of the enrollment categories under the plan, [3]*and*

(iv) the employer's share of the total allowed costs of benefits provided under the plan, [4]

[5]*(v) Repealed.*

(D) the number of full-time employees for each month during the calendar year,

(E) the name, address, and TIN of each full-time employee during the calendar year and the months (if any) during which such employee (and any dependents) were covered under any such health benefits plans, and

(F) such other information as the Secretary may require.

The Secretary shall have the authority to review the accuracy of the information provided under this subsection, including the applicable large employer's share under paragraph (2)(C)(iv).

(d) Coordination with other requirements. To the maximum extent feasible, the Secretary may provide that—

(1) any return or statement required to be provided under this section may be provided as part of any return or statement required under section 6051 or 6055, and

(2) in the case of an applicable large employer [6] offering health insurance coverage of a health insurance issuer, the employer may enter into an agreement with the issuer to in-

clude information required under this section with the return and statement required to be provided by the issuer under section 6055.

(e) Coverage provided by governmental units. In the case of any applicable large employer [7] which is a governmental unit or any agency or instrumentality thereof, the person appropriately designated for purposes of this section shall make the returns and statements required by this section.

[8]*(f)* *Definitions. For purposes of this section, any term used in this section which is also used in section 4980H shall have the meaning given such term by section 4980H.*
[For Analysis, see ¶ 1613.]

[Endnote Code Sec. 6056]

Code Sec. 6056 was added by Sec. 1858(b)(5)(A), (B)(i)-(iv), (C) and (D) of the Department of Defense and Full-Year Continuing Appropriations Act, 2011, P.L. 112-10, 4/15/2011, as detailed below:

1. Sec. 1858(b)(5)(A) deleted 'and every offering employer' after 'during a calendar year' in subsec. (a)

2. Sec. 1858(b)(5)(B)(i) deleted 'in the case of an applicable large employer,' before 'the length of any waiting period' in clause (b)(2)(C)(i)

3. Sec. 1858(b)(5)(B)(ii) added 'and' at the end of clause (b)(2)(C)(iii)

4. Sec. 1858(b)(5)(B)(iii) deleted 'and' at the end of clause (b)(2)(C)(iv)

5. Sec. 1858(b)(5)(B)(iv) deleted clause (b)(2)(C)(v)

Prior to deletion, clause (b)(2)(C)(v) read as follows:

"(v) in the case of an offering employer, the option for which the employer pays the largest portion of the cost of the plan and the portion of the cost paid by the employer in each of the enrollment categories under such option,"

6. Sec. 1858(b)(5)(C) deleted 'or offering employer' after 'applicable large employer' in para. (d)(2)

7. Sec. 1858(b)(5)(C) deleted 'or offering employer' after 'applicable large employer' in subsec. (e)

8. Sec. 1858(b)(5)(D) amended subsec. (f)

Prior to amendment, subsec. (f) read as follows:

"(f) Definitions. For purposes of this section—

"(1) Offering employer.

"(A) In general. The term 'offering employer' means any offering employer (as defined in section 10108(b) of the Patient Protection and Affordable Care Act) if the required contribution (within the meaning of section 5000A(e)(1)(B)(i)) of any employee exceeds 8 percent of the wages (as defined in section 3121(a)) paid to such employee by such employer.

"(B) Indexing. In the case of any calendar year beginning after 2014, the 8 percent under subparagraph (A) shall be adjusted for the calendar year to reflect the rate of premium growth between the preceding calendar year and 2013 over the rate of income growth for such period.

"(2) Other definitions. Any term used in this section which is also used in section 4980H shall have the meaning given such term by section 4980H."

Effective Date (Sec. 1858(d), P.L. 112-10, 4/15/2011) effective for periods begin. after 12/31/2013, as if included in the provisions of Sec. 10108(j) of P.L. 111-148.

[¶ 3136]   Code Sec. 6103.   Confidentiality and disclosure of returns and return information.

(a) General rule. Returns and return information shall be confidential, and except as authorized by this title—

(1) no officer or employee of the United States,

(2) no officer or employee of any State, any local law enforcement agency receiving information under subsection (i)(7)(A), any local child support enforcement agency, or any local agency administering a program listed in subsection (l)(7)(D) who has or had access to returns or return information under this section or section 6104(c), and

(3) no other person (or officer or employee thereof) who has or had access to returns or return information under subsection (e)(1)(D)(iii), [1]*subsection (k)(10)*, paragraph (6), (10), (12), (16), (19), (20) or (21) of subsection (l), paragraph (2) or (4)(B) of subsection (m), or subsection (n),

shall disclose any return or return information obtained by him in any manner in connection with his service as such an officer or an employee or otherwise or under the provisions of this section. For purposes of this subsection, the term "officer or employee" includes a former officer or employee.

* * * * * * * * * * * *

(k) **Disclosure of certain returns and return information for tax administration purposes.**

* * * * * * * * * * * *

(10)[2] *Disclosure of certain returns and return information to certain prison officials.*

(A) *In general.* Under such procedures as the Secretary may prescribe, the Secretary may disclose to officers and employees of the Federal Bureau of Prisons and of any State agency charged with the responsibility for administration of prisons any returns or return information with respect to individuals incarcerated in Federal or State prison systems whom the Secretary has determined may have filed or facilitated the filing of a false or fraudulent return to the extent that the Secretary determines that such disclosure is necessary to permit effective Federal tax administration.

(B) *Disclosure to contractor-run prisons.* Under such procedures as the Secretary may prescribe, the disclosures authorized by subparagraph (A) may be made to contractors responsible for the operation of a Federal or State prison on behalf of such Bureau or agency.

(C) *Restrictions on use of disclosed information.* Any return or return information received under this paragraph shall be used only for the purposes of and to the extent necessary in taking administrative action to prevent the filing of false and fraudulent returns, including administrative actions to address possible violations of administrative rules and regulations of the prison facility and in administrative and judicial proceedings arising from such administrative actions.

(D) *Restrictions on redisclosure and disclosure to legal representatives.* Notwithstanding subsection (h)

(i) *Restrictions on redisclosure.* Except as provided in clause (ii), any officer, employee, or contractor of the Federal Bureau of Prisons or of any State agency charged with the responsibility for administration of prisons shall not disclose any information obtained under this paragraph to any person other than an officer or employee or contractor of such Bureau or agency personally and directly engaged in the administration of prison facilities on behalf of such Bureau or agency.

(ii) *Disclosure to legal representatives.* The returns and return information disclosed under this paragraph may be disclosed to the duly authorized legal representative of the Federal Bureau of Prisons, State agency, or contractor charged with the responsibility for administration of prisons, or of the incarcerated individual accused of filing the false or fraudulent return who is a party to an action or proceeding described in subparagraph (C), solely in preparation for, or for use in, such action or proceeding.

* * * * * * * * * * * *

(p) **Procedure and recordkeeping.**

* * * * * * * * * * * *

(4) **Safeguards.** Any Federal agency described in subsection (h)(2), (h)(5), (i)(1), (2), (3), (5), or (7), (j)(1), (2), or (5), (k)(8) or (10), (l)(1), (2), (3), (5), (10), (11), (13), (14), (17), or (22) or (o)(1)(A), the Government Accountability Office, the Congressional Budget Office, or any agency, body, or commission described in subsection (d), (i)(3)(B)(i) or 7(A)(ii), or (k)(10), (l)(6), (7), (8), (9), (12), (15), or (16), any appropriate State officer (as defined in section 6104(c)), or any other person described in [3]*subsection (k)(10),* subsection (l)(10), (16), (18), (19), or (20) , or any entity described in subsection (l)(21), shall, as a condition for receiving returns or return information—

(A) establish and maintain, to the satisfaction of the Secretary, a permanent system of standardized records with respect to any request, the reason for such request, and the date of such request made by or of it and any disclosure of return or return information made by or to it;

(B) establish and maintain, to the satisfaction of the Secretary, a secure area or place in which such returns or return information shall be stored;

815

(C) restrict, to the satisfaction of the Secretary, access to the returns or return information only to persons whose duties or responsibilities require access and to whom disclosure may be made under the provisions of this title;

(D) provide such other safeguards which the Secretary determines (and which he prescribes in regulations) to be necessary or appropriate to protect the confidentiality of the returns or return information;

(E) furnish a report to the Secretary, at such time and containing such information as the Secretary may prescribe, which describes the procedures established and utilized by such agency, body, or commission, the Government Accountability Office, or the Congressional Budget Office for ensuring the confidentiality of returns and return information required by this paragraph; and

(F) upon completion of use of such returns or return information—

(i) in the case of an agency, body, or commission described in subsection (d), (i)(3)(B)(i), [4] *subsection (k)(10)*,or (l)(6), (7), (8), (9), or (16), any appropriate State officer (as defined in section 6104(c)), or any other person described in [5]*subsection (k)(10) or* subsection (l)(10), (16), (18), (19), or (20) return to the Secretary such returns or return information (along with any copies made therefrom) or make such returns or return information undisclosable in any manner and furnish a written report to the Secretary describing such manner,

(ii) in the case of an agency described in subsections (h)(2), (h)(5), (i)(1), (2), (3), (5) or (7), (j)(1), (2), or (5), (k)(8) or (10), (l)(1), (2), (3), (5), (10), (11), (12), (13), (14), (15), (17), or (22), or (o)(1)(A) or any entity described in subsection (l)(21), the Government Accountability Office, or the Congressional Budget Office, either—

(I) return to the Secretary such returns or return information (along with any copies made therefrom),

(II) otherwise make such returns or return information undisclosable, or

(III) to the extent not so returned or made undisclosable, ensure that the conditions of subparagraphs (A), (B), (C), (D), and (E) of this paragraph continue to be met with respect to such returns or return information, and

(iii) in the case of the Department of Health and Human Services for purposes of subsection (m)(6), destroy all such return information upon completion of its use in providing the notification for which the information was obtained, so as to make such information undisclosable;

except that the conditions of subparagraphs (A), (B), (C), (D), and (E) shall cease to apply with respect to any return or return information if, and to the extent that, such return or return information is disclosed in the course of any judicial or administrative proceeding and made a part of the public record thereof. If the Secretary determines that any such agency, body, or commission, including an agency, an appropriate State officer (as defined in section 6104(c)), or any other person described in [6]*subsection (k)(10) or* subsection (l)(10), (16), (18), (19), or (20) or any entity described in subsection (l)(21), or the Government Accountability Office or the Congressional Budget Office, has failed to, or does not, meet the requirements of this paragraph, he may, after any proceedings for review established under paragraph (7), take such actions as are necessary to ensure such requirements are met, including refusing to disclose returns or return information to such agency, body, or commission, including an agency, an appropriate State officer (as defined in section 6104(c)), or any other person described in [7]*subsection (k)(10) or* subsection (l)(10), (16), (18), (19), or (20) or any entity described in subsection (l)(21), or the Government Accountability Office or the Congressional Budget Office, until he determines that such requirements have been or will be met. In the case of any agency which receives any mailing address under paragraph (2), (4), (6), or (7) of subsection (m) and which discloses any such mailing address to any agent, or which receives any information under paragraph (6)(A), (10), (12)(B), or (16) of subsection (l) and which discloses any such information to any agent, or any person including an agent described in [8]*subsection (k)(10) or* subsection (l)(10) or (16), this paragraph shall apply to such agency and each such agent or other person (except that, in the case of an agent, or any person including an agent described in [9]*subsection (k)(10) or* subsection (l)(10) or (16), any report to the Secretary or other action with respect to the Secretary shall be made or taken through such agency). For purposes of applying this paragraph in any case to which subsection (m)(6) applies, the term "return information" includes related blood donor records (as defined in section 1141(h)(2) of the Social Security Act).

* * * * * * * * * * * *

[For Analysis, see ¶ 1505.]

[Endnote Code Sec. 6103]

  Code Sec. 6103(a)(3), Code Sec. 6103(k)(10), Code Sec. 6103(p)(4) and Code Sec. 6103(p)(4)(F)(i) were amended by Sec. 209(a), (b)(1), (b)(2)(A), (b)(2)(C), (b)(2)(B)(i) and (ii) of the American Taxpayer Relief Act of 2012, 1/2/2013, as detailed below:

  1. Sec. 209(b)(1) added "subsection (k)(10)" after "subsection (e)(l)(D)(iii)" in para. (a)(3)

  2. Prior to amendment, para. (k)(10) read as follows:

"DISCLOSURE OF CERTAIN RETURN INFORMATION TO CERTAIN PRISON OFFICIALS.

  "(A) In general. Under such procedures as the Secretary may prescribe, the Secretary may disclose to the head of the Federal Bureau of Prisons and the head of any State agency charged with the responsibility for administration of prisons any return information with respect to individuals incarcerated in Federal or State prison whom the Secretary has determined may have filed or facilitated the filing of a false return to the extent that the Secretary determines that such disclosure is necessary to permit effective Federal tax administration.

  "(B) Restriction on redisclosure. Notwithstanding subsection (n), the head of the Federal Bureau of Prisons and the head of any State agency charged with the responsibility for administration of prisons may not disclose any information obtained under subparagraph (A) to any person other than an officer or employee of such Bureau or agency.

  "(C) Restriction on use of disclosed information. Return information received under this paragraph shall be used only for purposes of and to the extent necessary in taking administrative action to prevent the filing of false and fraudulent returns, including administrative actions to address possible violations of administrative rules and regulations of the prison facility.

  "(D) Termination. No disclosure may be made under this paragraph after December 31, 2011."

  3. Sec. 209(b)(2)(A) added "subsection (k)(10)," before "subsection (l)(10)," in para. (p)(4)

  4. Sec. 209(b)(2)(B)(i) added "(k)(10)," before "or (l)(6)," in cl. (p)(4)(F)(i)

  5. Sec. 209(b)(2)(B)(ii) added "subsection (k)(10) or" before "subsection (l)(10)," in cl. (p)(4)(F)(i)

  6. Sec. 209(b)(2)(C) added "subsection (k)(10) or" before "subsection (1)(10)," where it appeared in para. (p)(4)

  7. Sec. 209(b)(2)(C) added "subsection (k)(10) or" before "subsection (1)(10)," where it appeared in para. (p)(4)

  8. Sec. 209(b)(2)(C) added "subsection (k)(10) or" before "subsection (1)(10)," where it appeared in para. (p)(4)

  9. Sec. 209(b)(2)(C) added "subsection (k)(10) or" before "subsection (1)(10)," where it appeared in para. (p)(4)

Effective Date (Sec. 209(c), P.L. 112-240, 1/2/2013) effective 1/2/2013.

[¶ 3137]   *Code Sec.*[1] *6116.*   **Requirement for prisons located in united states to provide information for tax administration.**

  (a) **In general.** *Not later than September 15, 2012, and annually thereafter, the head of the Federal Bureau of Prisons and the head of any State agency charged with the responsibility for administration of prisons shall provide to the Secretary in electronic format a list with the information described in subsection (b) of all the inmates incarcerated within the prison system for any part of the prior 2 calendar years or the current calendar year through August 31.*

  (b) **Information.** *The information with respect to each inmate is—*

  (1) first, middle, and last name,

  (2) date of birth,

  (3) institution of current incarceration or, for released inmates, most recent incarceration,

  (4) prison assigned inmate number,

  (5) the date of incarceration,

  (6) the date of release or anticipated date of release,

  (7) the date of work release,

  (8) taxpayer identification number and whether the prison has verified such number,

  (9) last known address, and

  (10) any additional information as the Secretary may request.

(c) Format. The Secretary shall determine the electronic format of the information described in subsection (b).
[For Analysis, see ¶ 1908. For Committee Reports, see ¶ 5802.]

[Endnote Code Sec. 6116]
Matter in *italics* in Code Sec. 6116 was redesignated by section 502(a) of the United States—Korea Free Trade Agreement Implementation Act, P.L. 112-41, 10/21/2011.
1. Sec. 502(a) "redesignated Code Sec. 6116 as 6117 and added a new Code Sec. 6116"
Effective Date (P.L. 112-41, 10/21/2011) effective 10/21/2011.

[¶ 3138]   Code Sec. 6331.   Levy and distraint.

* * * * * * * * * * * *

(h)   Continuing levy on certain payments.
(1)   In general. If the Secretary approves a levy under this subsection, the effect of such levy on specified payments to or received by a taxpayer shall be continuous from the date such levy is first made until such levy is released. Notwithstanding section 6334, such continuous levy shall attach to up to 15 percent of any specified payment due to the taxpayer.
(2)   Specified payment. For the purposes of paragraph (1), the term "specified payment" means—
(A) any Federal payment other than a payment for which eligibility is based on the income or assets (or both) of a payee,
(B) any payment described in paragraph (4), (7), (9), or (11) of section 6334(a), and
(C) any annuity or pension payment under the Railroad Retirement Act or benefit under the Railroad Unemployment Insurance Act.
(3)   Increase in levy for certain payments. Paragraph (1) shall be applied by substituting "100 percent" for "15 percent" in the case of any specified payment due to a vendor of [1]*property, goods, or services* sold or leased to the Federal Government.

* * * * * * * * * * * *

[For Analysis, see ¶ 1916.]

[Endnote Code Sec. 6331]
Code Sec. 6331(h)(3) was amended by Sec. 301(a) of an Act To amend the Internal Revenue Code of 1986 to repeal the imposition of 3 percent withholding on certain payments made to vendors by government entities, to modify the calculation of modified adjusted gross income for purposes of determining eligibility for certain healthcare-related programs, and for other purposes, P.L. 112-56, 11/21/2011, as detailed below.
1. Sec. 301(a) substituted "property, goods, or services" for "goods or services" in para. (h)(3)
Effective Date (Sec. 301(b), P.L. 112-56, 11/21/2011) effective for levies issued after 11/21/2011.

**[¶ 3139]   *Code Sec.*[1] *6409.   Refunds disregarded in the administration of federal programs and federally assisted programs.*
Notwithstanding any other provision of law, any refund (or advance payment with respect to a refundable credit) made to any individual under this title shall not be taken into account as income, and shall not be taken into account as resources for a period of 12 months from receipt, for purposes of determining the eligibility of such individual (or any other individual) for benefits or assistance (or the amount or extent of benefits or assistance) under any Federal program or under any State or local program financed in whole or in part with Federal funds.
[For Analysis, see ¶ 310.]

[Endnote Code Sec. 6409]
Code Sec. 6409 was amended by Sec. 103(d) of the American Taxpayer Relief Act of 2012, 1/2/2013, as detailed below:
1. Prior to amendment, Code Sec. 6409 read as follows:
"SEC. 6409 REFUNDS DISREGARDED IN THE ADMINISTRATION OF FEDERAL PROGRAMS AND FEDERALLY ASSISTED PROGRAMS.

"(a) In general.

"Notwithstanding any other provision of law, any refund (or advance payment with respect to a refundable credit) made to any individual under this title shall not be taken into account as income, and shall not be taken into account as resources for a period of 12 months from receipt, for purposes of determining the eligibility of such individual (or any other individual) for benefits or assistance (or the amount or extent of benefits or assistance) under any Federal program or under any State or local program financed in whole or in part with Federal funds.

"(b) Termination.

"Subsection (a) shall not apply to any amount received after December 31, 2012."

Effective Date (Sec. 103(e)(2), P.L. 112-240, 1/2/2013) effective for amounts received after 12/31/2012.

[¶ 3140]   Code Sec. 6412.   Floor stocks refunds.

(a) In general.

(1) Tires and taxable fuel. Where before [1]*October 1, 2016*, any article subject to the tax imposed by section 4071 or 4081 has been sold by the manufacturer, producer, or importer and on such date is held by a dealer and has not been used and is intended for sale, there shall be credited or refunded (without interest) to the manufacturer, producer, or importer an amount equal to the difference between the tax paid by such manufacturer, producer, or importer on his sale of the article and the amount of tax made applicable to such article on and after [2]*October 1, 2016*, if claim for such credit or refund is filed with the Secretary on or before [3]*March 31, 2017*, based upon a request submitted to the manufacturer, producer, or importer before [4]*January 1, 2017*, by the dealer who held the article in respect of which the credit or refund is claimed, and, on or before [5]*March 31, 2017*, reimbursement has been made to such dealer by such manufacturer, producer, or importer for the tax reduction on such article or written consent has been obtained from such dealer to allowance of such credit or refund. No credit or refund shall be allowable under this paragraph with respect to taxable fuel in retail stocks held at the place where intended to be sold at retail, nor with respect to taxable fuel held for sale by a producer or importer of taxable fuel.

(2) Definitions. For purposes of this section—

(A) The term "dealer" includes a wholesaler, jobber, distributor, or retailer.

(B) An article shall be considered as "held by a dealer" if title thereto has passed to such dealer (whether or not delivery to him has been made), and if for purposes of consumption title to such article or possession thereof has not at any time been transferred to any person other than a dealer.

* * * * * * * * * * * *

[For Analysis, see ¶ 1804. For Committee Reports, see ¶ 5401.]

[Endnote Code Sec. 6412]

Code Sec. 6412(a)(1) was amended by Secs. 40102(c)(1)-(3) of the Moving Ahead for Progress in the 21st Century Act, P.L. 112-141, 7/6/2012, after it was amended by Secs. 402(b)(1)-(3) of the Temporary Surface Transportation Extension Act of 2012, P.L. 112-140, 6/29/2012, as detailed below:

1. Sec. 40102(c)(1) substituted "October 1, 2016" for "July 1, 2012 [sic July 7, 2012]" in para. (a)(1). [Ed. Note: The amendment made by Sec. 40102(c)(1) of this Act did not take into account the previous amendment made by Sec. 402(b)(1) of P.L. 112-140, which substituted "July 7, 2012" for "July 1, 2012" in para. (a)(1)]

2. Sec. 40102(c)(1) substituted "October 1, 2016" for 'July 1, 2012 [sic July 7, 2012]" in para. (a)(1). [Ed. Note: The amendment made by Sec. 40102(c)(1) of this Act did not take into account the previous amendment made by Sec. 402(b)(1) of P.L. 112-140, which substituted "July 7, 2012" for "July 1, 2012" in para. (a)(1)]

3. Sec. 40102(c)(2) substituted "March 31, 2017" for "December 31, 2012 [sic January 6, 2013]" in para. (a)(1). [Ed. Note: The amendment made by Sec. 40102(c)(2) of this Act did not take into account the previous amendment made by Sec. 402(b)(2) of P.L. 112-140, which substituted "January 6, 2013" for "December 31, 2012" in para. (a)(1)]

4. Sec. 40102(c)(3) substituted "January 1, 2017" for "October 1, 2012 [sic October 7, 2012]" after "or importer before" in para. (a)(1). [Ed. Note: The amendment made by Sec. 40102(c)(3) of this Act did not take into account the previous amendment made by Sec. 402(b)(3) of P.L. 112-140, which substituted "October 7, 2012" for "October 1, 2012" in para. (a)(1)]

5. Sec. 40102(c)(2) substituted "March 31, 2017" for "December 31, 2012 [sic January 6, 2013]" in para. (a)(1). [Ed. Note: The amendment made by Sec. 40102(c)(2) of this Act did not take into account the previous amendment made by Sec. 402(b)(2) of P.L. 112-140, which substituted "January 6, 2013" for "December 31, 2012" in para. (a)(1)]

Effective Date (Sec. 40102(f), P.L. 112-141, 7/6/2012 and Sec. 402(f)(1), P.L. 112-140, 6/29/2012), effective 7/1/2012.

[¶ 3141]   Code Sec. 6426.   Credit for alcohol fuel, biodiesel and alternative fuel mixtures.

* * * * * * * * * * * *

(c) Biodiesel mixture credit.

(1) In general. For purposes of this section, the biodiesel mixture credit is the product of the applicable amount and the number of gallons of biodiesel used by the taxpayer in producing any biodiesel mixture for sale or use in a trade or business of the taxpayer.

(2) Applicable amount. For purposes of this subsection, the applicable amount is $1.00.

(3) Biodiesel mixture. For purposes of this section, the term "biodiesel mixture" means a mixture of biodiesel and diesel fuel (as defined in section 4083(a)(3)), determined without regard to any use of kerosene, which—

(A) is sold by the taxpayer producing such mixture to any person for use as a fuel, or

(B) is used as a fuel by the taxpayer producing such mixture.

(4) Certification for biodiesel. No credit shall be allowed under this subsection unless the taxpayer obtains a certification (in such form and manner as prescribed by the Secretary) from the producer of the biodiesel which identifies the product produced and the percentage of biodiesel and agri-biodiesel in the product.

(5) Other definitions. Any term used in this subsection which is also used in section 40A shall have the meaning given such term by section 40A.

(6) Termination. This subsection shall not apply to any sale, use, or removal for any period after [1]*December 31, 2013.*

(d) Alternative fuel credit.

(1) In general. For purposes of this section, the alternative fuel credit is the product of 50 cents and the number of gallons of an alternative fuel or gasoline gallon equivalents of a nonliquid alternative fuel sold by the taxpayer for use as a fuel in a motor vehicle or motorboat, sold by the taxpayer for use as a fuel in aviation, or so used by the taxpayer.

(2) Alternative fuel. For purposes of this section, the term "alternative fuel" means—

(A) liquefied petroleum gas,

(B) P Series Fuels (as defined by the Secretary of Energy under section 13211(2) of title 42, United States Code),

(C) compressed or liquefied natural gas,

(D) liquefied hydrogen,

(E) any liquid fuel which meets the requirements of paragraph (4) and which is derived from coal (including peat) through the Fischer-Tropsch process,

(F) compressed or liquefied gas derived from biomass (as defined in section 45K(c)(3)), and

(G) liquid fuel derived from biomass (as defined in section 45K(c)(3)).

Such term does not include ethanol, methanol, biodiesel, or any fuel (including lignin, wood residues, or spent pulping liquors) derived from the production of paper or pulp.

(3) Gasoline gallon equivalent. For purposes of this subsection, the term "gasoline gallon equivalent" means, with respect to any nonliquid alternative fuel, the amount of such fuel having a Btu content of 124,800 (higher heating value).

(4) Carbon capture requirement.

(A) In general. The requirements of this paragraph are met if the fuel is certified, under such procedures as required by the Secretary, as having been derived from coal produced at a gasification facility which separates and sequesters not less than the applicable percentage of such facility's total carbon dioxide emissions.

(B) Applicable percentage. For purposes of subparagraph (A), the applicable percentage is—

(i) 50 percent in the case of fuel produced after September 30, 2009, and on or before December 30, 2009, and

(ii) 75 percent in the case of fuel produced after December 30, 2009.

(5) Termination. This subsection shall not apply to any sale or use for any period after [2]*December 31, 2013* (September 30, 2014, in the case of any sale or use involving liquefied hydrogen).

(e) Alternative fuel mixture credit.

(1) In general. For purposes of this section, the alternative fuel mixture credit is the product of 50 cents and the number of gallons of alternative fuel used by the taxpayer in producing any alternative fuel mixture for sale or use in a trade or business of the taxpayer.

(2) Alternative fuel mixture. For purposes of this section, the term "alternative fuel mixture" means a mixture of alternative fuel and taxable fuel (as defined in subparagraph (A), (B), or (C) of section 4083(a)(1)) which—

(A) is sold by the taxpayer producing such mixture to any person for use as fuel, or

(B) is used as a fuel by the taxpayer producing such mixture.

(3) Termination. This subsection shall not apply to any sale or use for any period after [3]*December 31, 2011* (September 30, 2014, in the case of any sale or use involving liquefied hydrogen).

* * * * * * * * * * *

[For Analysis, see ¶ 1009 and ¶ 1010.]

[Endnote Code Sec. 6426]

Code Sec. 6426(c)(6), Code Sec. 6426(d)(5), and Code Sec. 6426(e)(3) were amended by Secs. 405(b)(1) and 412(a) of the American Taxpayer Relief Act of 2012, 1/2/2013, as detailed below:

1. Sec. 405(b)(1) substituted "December 31, 2013" for "December 31, 2011" in para. (c)(6)

Effective Date (Sec. 405(c), P.L. 112-240, 1/2/2013) effective for fuel sold or used after 12/31/2011.

2. Sec. 412(a) substituted "December 31, 2013" for "December 31, 2011" in paras. (d)(5) and (e)(3)

Effective Date (Sec. 412(c), P.L. 112-240, 1/2/2013) effective for fuel sold or used after 12/31/2011.

[¶ 3142]   Code Sec. 6427.   Fuels not used for taxable purposes.

* * * * * * * * * * *

(e) Alcohol, biodiesel, or alternative fuel. Except as provided in subsection (k)—

(1) Used to produce a mixture. If any person produces a mixture described in section 6426 in such person's trade or business, the Secretary shall pay (without interest) to such person an amount equal to the alcohol fuel mixture credit or the biodiesel mixture credit or the alternative fuel mixture credit with respect to such mixture.

(2) Alternative fuel. If any person sells or uses an alternative fuel (as defined in section 6426(d)(2)) for a purpose described in section 6426(d)(1) in such person's trade or business, the Secretary shall pay (without interest) to such person an amount equal to the alternative fuel credit with respect to such fuel.

(3) Coordination with other repayment provisions. No amount shall be payable under paragraph (1) or (2) with respect to any mixture or alternative fuel with respect to which an amount is allowed as a credit under section 6426.

(4) Registration requirement for alternative fuels. The Secretary shall not make any payment under this subsection to any person with respect to any alternative fuel credit or alternative fuel mixture credit unless the person is registered under section 4101.

(5) Limitation to fuels with connection to the United States. No amount shall be payable under paragraph (1) or (2) with respect to any mixture or alternative fuel if credit is not allowed with respect to such mixture or alternative fuel by reason of section 6426(i).

(6) Termination. This subsection shall not apply with respect to—

(A) any alcohol fuel mixture (as defined in section 6426(b)(3)) sold or used after December 31, 2011,

(B) any biodiesel mixture (as defined in section 6426(c)(3)) sold or used after [1]*December 31, 2013,*

(C) except as provided in subparagraph (D), any alternative fuel [2]*(as defined in section 6426(d)(2))* sold or used after [3]*December 31, 2013,* and

(D) any alternative fuel[4] (as so defined) involving liquefied hydrogen sold or used after September 30, 2014[5], *and*

[6]*(E) any alternative fuel mixture (as defined in section 6426(e)(2)) sold or used after December 31, 2011.*

* * * * * * * * * * * *

[For Analysis, see ¶ 1009 and ¶ 1010.]

[Endnote Code Sec. 6427]

Code Sec. 6427(e)(6)(B) was amended by Sec. 405(b)(2) of the American Taxpayer Relief Act of 2012, P.L. 112-240, 1/2/2013, as detailed below:

1. Sec. 405(b)(2) substituted "December 31, 2013" for "December 31, 2011" in subpara. (e)(6)(B)

Effective Date (Sec. 405(c), P.L. 112-240, 1/2/2013) effective for fuel sold or used after 12/31/2011.

Code Sec. 6427(e)(6)(C) - Code Sec. 6427(e)(6)(E) were amended by Secs. 412(b)(1)(A)-(B), 412(b)(2)(A)-(B), and 412(b)(3), P.L. 112-240, 1/2/2013, as detailed below:

2. Sec. 412(b)(1)(A) substituted "(as defined in section 6426(d)(2))" for "or alternative fuel mixture (as defined in subsection (d)(2) or (e)(3) of section 6426)" in subpara. (e)(6)(C)

3. Sec. 412(b)(1)(B) substituted "December 31, 2013," for "December 31, 2011, and" in subpara. (e)(6)(D)

4. Sec. 412(b)(2)(A) deleted "or alternative fuel mixture" after "any alternative fuel" in subpara. (e)(6)(D)

5. Sec. 412(b)(2)(B) substituted ", and" for the period at the end of subpara. (e)(6)(D)

6. Sec. 412(b)(3) added subpara. (e)(6)(E)

Effective Date (Sec. 412(c), P.L. 112-240, 1/2/2013) effective for fuel sold or used after 12/31/2011.

[¶ 3143]   Code Sec. 6655.   Failure by corporation to pay estimated income tax.

(a)   Addition to tax. Except as otherwise provided in this section, in the case of any underpayment of estimated tax by a corporation, there shall be added to the tax under chapter 1 for the taxable year an amount determined by applying—

(1) the underpayment rate established under section 6621,

(2) to the amount of the underpayment,

(3) for the period of the underpayment.

(b)   Amount of underpayment; period of underpayment. For purposes of subsection (a)—

(1)   Amount. The amount of the underpayment shall be the excess of—

(A) the required installment, over

(B) the amount (if any) of the installment paid on or before the due date for the installment.

(2)   Period of underpayment. The period of the underpayment shall run from the due date for the installment to whichever of the following dates is the earlier—

(A) the 15th day of the 3rd month following the close of the taxable year, or

(B) with respect to any portion of the underpayment, the date on which such portion is paid.

(3)   Order of crediting payments. For purposes of paragraph (2)(B), a payment of estimated tax shall be credited against unpaid required installments in the order in which such installments are required to be paid.

(c)   Number of required installments; due dates. For purposes of this section—

(1)   Payable in 4 installments. There shall be 4 required installments for each taxable year.

(2)   Time for payment of installments.

In the case of the following required installments:	The due date is:
1st	April 15

2nd	June 15
3rd	September 15
4th	December 15.

(d) Amount of required installments. For purposes of this section—

(1) Amount.

(A) In general. Except as otherwise provided in this section, the amount of any required installment shall be 25 percent of the required annual payment.

(B) Required annual payment. Except as otherwise provided in this subsection, the term "required annual payment" means the lesser of—

(i) 100 percent of the tax shown on the return for the taxable year (or, if no return is filed, 100 percent of the tax for such year), or

(ii) 100 percent of the tax shown on the return of the corporation for the preceding taxable year.

Clause (ii) shall not apply if the preceding taxable year was not a taxable year of 12 months, or the corporation did not file a return for such preceding taxable year showing a liability for tax.

(2) Large corporations required to pay 100 percent of current year tax.

(A) In general. Except as provided in subparagraph (B), clause (ii) of paragraph (1)(B) shall not apply in the case of a large corporation.

(B) May use last year's tax for 1st installment. Subparagraph (A) shall not apply for purposes of determining the amount of the 1st required installment for any taxable year. Any reduction in such 1st installment by reason of the preceding sentence shall be recaptured by increasing the amount of the next required installment determined under paragraph (1) by the amount of such reduction.

(e) Lower required installment where annualized income installment or adjusted seasonal installment is less than amount determined under Subsection (d).

(1) In general. In the case of any required installment, if the corporation establishes that the annualized income installment or the adjusted seasonal installment is less than the amount determined under subsection (d)(1) (as modified by paragraphs (2) and (3) of subsection (d))

(A) the amount of such required installment shall be the annualized income installment (or, if lesser, the adjusted seasonal installment), and

(B) any reduction in a required installment resulting from the application of this paragraph shall be recaptured by increasing the amount of the next required installment determined under subsection (d)(1) (as so modified) by the amount of such reduction (and by increasing subsequent required installments to the extent that the reduction has not previously been recaptured under this subparagraph).

(2) Determination of annualized income installment.

(A) In general. In the case of any required installment, the annualized income installment is the excess (if any) of—

(i) an amount equal to the applicable percentage of the tax for the taxable year computed by placing on an annualized basis the taxable income, alternative minimum taxable income, and modified alternative minimum taxable income—

(I) for the first 3 months of the taxable year, in the case of the 1st required installment,

(II) for the first 3 months of the taxable year, in the case of the 2nd required installment,

(III) for the first 6 months of the taxable year in the case of the 3rd required installment, and

(IV) for the first 9 months of the taxable year, in the case of the 4th required installment, over

(ii) the aggregate amount of any prior required installments for the taxable year.

(B) Special rules. For purposes of this paragraph—

823

(i) Annualization. The taxable income, alternative minimum taxable income, and modified alternative minimum taxable income shall be placed on an annualized basis under regulations prescribed by the Secretary.

(ii) Applicable percentage.

In the case of the following required installments:	The applicable percentage is:
1st	25
2nd	50
3rd	75
4th	100

(iii) Modified alternative minimum taxable income. The term "modified alternative minimum taxable income" has the meaning given to such term by section 59A(b).

(C) Election for different annualization periods.

(i) If the taxpayer makes an election under this clause—

(I) subclause (I) of subparagraph (A)(i) shall be applied by substituting "2 months" for "3 months",

(II) subclause (II) of subparagraph (A)(i) shall be applied by substituting "4 months" for "3 months",

(III) subclause (III) of subparagraph (A)(i) shall be applied by substituting "7 months" for "6 months", and

(IV) subclause (IV) of subparagraph (A)(i) shall be applied by substituting "10 months" for "9 months".

(ii) If the taxpayer makes an election under this clause—

(I) subclause (II) of subparagraph (A)(i) shall be applied by substituting "5 months" for "3 months",

(II) subclause (III) of subparagraph (A)(i) shall be applied by substituting "8 months" for "6 months", and

(III) subclause (IV) of subparagraph (A)(i) shall be applied by substituting "11 months" for "9 months".

(iii) An election under clause (i) or (ii) shall apply to the taxable year for which made and such an election shall be effective only if made on or before the date required for the payment of the first required installment for such taxable year.

(3) Determination of adjusted seasonal installment.

(A) In general. In the case of any required installment, the amount of the adjusted seasonal installment is the excess (if any) of—

(i) 100 percent of the amount determined under subparagraph (C), over

(ii) the aggregate amount of all prior required installments for the taxable year.

(B) Limitation on application of paragraph. This paragraph shall apply only if the base period percentage for any 6 consecutive months of the taxable year equals or exceeds 70 percent.

(C) Determination of amount. The amount determined under this subparagraph for any installment shall be determined in the following manner—

(i) take the taxable income for all months during the taxable year preceding the filing month,

(ii) divide such amount by the base period percentage for all months during the taxable year preceding the filing month,

(iii) determine the tax on the amount determined under clause (ii), and

(iv) multiply the tax computed under clause (iii) by the base period percentage for the filing month and all months during the taxable year preceding the filing month.

(D) Definitions and special rules. For purposes of this paragraph—

(i) Base period percentage. The base period percentage for any period of months shall be the average percent which the taxable income for the corresponding months in each of the 3 preceding taxable years bears to the taxable income for the 3 preceding taxable years.

(ii) Filing month. The term "filing month" means the month in which the installment is required to be paid.

(iii) Reorganization, etc. The Secretary may by regulations provide for the determination of the base period percentage in the case of reorganizations, new corporations, and other similar circumstances.

(4) Treatment of subpart F and section 936 income.

(A) In general. Any amounts required to be included in gross income under section 936(h) or 951(a) (and credits properly allocable thereto) shall be taken into account in computing any annualized income installment under paragraph (2) in a manner similar to the manner under which partnership income inclusions (and credits properly allocable thereto) are taken into account.

(B) Prior year safe harbor.

(i) In general. If a taxpayer elects to have this subparagraph apply for any taxable year—

(I) subparagraph (A) shall not apply, and

(II) for purposes of computing any annualized income installment for such taxable year, the taxpayer shall be treated as having received ratably during such taxable year items of income and credit described in subparagraph (A) in an amount equal to 115 percent of the amount of such items shown on the return of the taxpayer for the preceding taxable year (the second preceding taxable year in the case of the first and second required installments for such taxable year).

(ii) Special rule for noncontrolling shareholder.

(I) In general. If a taxpayer making the election under clause (i) is a noncontrolling shareholder of a corporation, clause (i)(II) shall be applied with respect to items of such corporation by substituting "100 percent" for "115 percent".

(II) Noncontrolling shareholder. For purposes of subclause (I), the term "noncontrolling shareholder" means, with respect to any corporation, a shareholder which (as of the beginning of the taxable year for which the installment is being made) does not own (within the meaning of section 958(a)), and is not treated as owning (within the meaning of section 958(b)), more than 50 percent (by vote or value) of the stock in the corporation.

(5) Treatment of certain REIT dividends.

(A) In general. Any dividend received from a closely held real estate investment trust by any person which owns (after application of subsection (d)(5) of section 856) 10 percent or more (by vote or value) of the stock or beneficial interests in the trust shall be taken into account in computing annualized income installments under paragraph (2) in a manner similar to the manner under which partnership income inclusions are taken into account.

(B) Closely held REIT. For purposes of subparagraph (A), the term "closely held real estate investment trust" means a real estate investment trust with respect to which 5 or fewer persons own (after application of subsection (d)(5) of section 856) 50 percent or more (by vote or value) of the stock or beneficial interests in the trust.

(f) Exception where tax is small amount. No addition to tax shall be imposed under subsection (a) for any taxable year if the tax shown on the return for such taxable year (or, if no return is filed, the tax) is less than $500.

(g) Definitions and special rules.

(1) Tax. For purposes of this section, the term "tax" means the excess of—

(A) the sum of—

(i) the tax imposed by section 11 or 1201(a), or subchapter L of chapter 1, whichever applies,

(ii) the tax imposed by section 55,

(iii) the tax imposed by section 59A, plus

(iv) the tax imposed by section 887, over

(B) the credits against tax provided by part IV of subchapter A of chapter 1.

For purposes of the preceding sentence, in the case of a foreign corporation subject to taxation under section 11 or 1201(a), or under subchapter L of chapter 1, the tax imposed by section 881 shall be treated as a tax imposed by section 11.

(2) Large corporation.

(A) In general. For purposes of this section, the term "large corporation" means any corporation if such corporation (or any predecessor corporation) had taxable income of $1,000,000 or more for any taxable year during the testing period.

(B) Rules for applying subparagraph (A).

(i) Testing period. For purposes of subparagraph (A), the term "testing period" means the 3 taxable years immediately preceding the taxable year involved.

(ii) Members of controlled group. For purposes of applying subparagraph (A) to any taxable year in the testing period with respect to corporations which are component members of a controlled group of corporations for such taxable year, the $1,000,000 amount specified in subparagraph (A) shall be divided among such members under rules similar to the rules of section 1561.

(iii) Certain carrybacks and carryovers not taken into account. For purposes of subparagraph (A), taxable income shall be determined without regard to any amount carried to the taxable year under section 172 or 1212(a).

(3) Certain tax-exempt organizations. For purposes of this section—

(A) Any organization subject to the tax imposed by section 511, and any private foundation, shall be treated as a corporation subject to tax under section 11.

(B) Any tax imposed by section 511, and any tax imposed by section 1 or 4940 on a private foundation, shall be treated as a tax imposed by section 11.

(C) Any reference to taxable income shall be treated as including a reference to unrelated business taxable income or net investment income (as the case may be).

In the case of any organization described in subparagraph (A), subsection (b)(2)(A) shall be applied by substituting "5th month" for "3rd month", subsection (e)(2)(A) shall be applied by substituting "2 months" for "3 months" in clause (i)(I), the election under clause (i) of subsection (e)(2)(C) may be made separately for each installment, and clause (ii) of subsection (e)(2)(C) shall not apply. In the case of a private foundation, subsection (c)(2) shall be applied by substituting "May 15" for "April 15".

(4) Application of section to certain taxes imposed on S corporations. In the case of an S corporation, for purposes of this section—

(A) The following taxes shall be treated as imposed by section 11:

(i) The tax imposed by section 1374(a) (or the corresponding provisions of prior law).

(ii) The tax imposed by section 1375(a).

(iii) Any tax for which the S corporation is liable by reason of section 1371(d)(2).

(B) Paragraph (2) of subsection (d) shall not apply.

(C) Clause (ii) of subsection (d)(1)(B) shall be applied as if it read as follows:

"(ii) the sum of—

"(I) the amount determined under clause (i) by only taking into account the taxes referred to in clauses (i) and (iii) of subsection (g)(4)(A), and

"(II) 100 percent of the tax imposed by section 1375(a) which was shown on the return of the corporation for the preceding taxable year."

(D) The requirement in the last sentence of subsection (d)(1)(B) that the return for the preceding taxable year show a liability for tax shall not apply.

(E) Any reference in subsection (e) to taxable income shall be treated as including a reference to the net recognized built-in gain or the excess passive income (as the case may be).

(h) Excessive adjustment under section 6425.

(1) Addition to tax. If the amount of an adjustment under section 6425 made before the 15th day of the 3rd month following the close of the taxable year is excessive, there shall be added to the tax under chapter 1 for the taxable year an amount determined at the underpayment rate established under section 6621 upon the excessive amount from the date on which the credit is allowed or the refund is paid to such 15th day.

(2) **Excessive amount.** For purposes of paragraph (1), the excessive amount is equal to the amount of the adjustment or (if smaller) the amount by which—

(A) the income tax liability (as defined in section 6425(c)) for the taxable year as shown on the return for the taxable year, exceeds

(B) the estimated income tax paid during the taxable year, reduced by the amount of the adjustment.

(i) **Fiscal years and short years.**

(1) **Fiscal years.** In applying this section to a taxable year beginning on any date other than January 1, there shall be substituted, for the months specified in this section, the months which correspond thereto.

(2) **Short taxable year.** This section shall be applied to taxable years of less than 12 months in accordance with regulations prescribed by the Secretary.

(j) **Regulations.** The Secretary shall prescribe such regulations as may be necessary to carry out the purposes of this section.

[For Analysis, see ¶ 1915.]

[Endnote Code Sec. 6655]

Sec. 4 of the African Growth and Opportunity Amendments, P.L. 112-63, 8/10/2012, relating to the time for payment of corporate estimated taxes, provides:

"Sec. 4. Time for payment of corporate estimated taxes. Notwithstanding section 6655 of the Internal Revenue Code of 1986—

"(1) in the case of a corporation with assets of not less than $1,000,000,000 (determined as of the end of the preceding taxable year), the amount of any required installment of corporate estimated tax which is otherwise due in July, August, or September of 2017 shall be 100.25 percent of such amount; and

"(2) the amount of the next required installment after an installment referred to in paragraph (1) shall be appropriately reduced to reflect the amount of the increase by reason of such paragraph."

[¶ 3144]   Code Sec. 6695.   Other assessable penalties with respect to the preparation of tax returns for other persons.

* * * * * * * * * * * *

(g) **Failure to be diligent in determining eligibility for earned income credit.** Any person who is a tax return preparer with respect to any return or claim for refund who fails to comply with due diligence requirements imposed by the Secretary by regulations with respect to determining eligibility for, or the amount of, the credit allowable by section 32 shall pay a penalty of [1]*$500* for each such failure.

[For Analysis, see ¶ 1912. For Committee Reports, see ¶ 5801.]

[Endnote Code Sec. 6695]

Matter in *italics* in Code Sec. 6695 was amended by Sec. 501(a) of the United States—Korea Free Trade Agreement Implementation Act, P.L. 112-41, 10/21/2011, which struck out:

1. Sec. 501(a) "$100"

Effective Date (P.L. 112-41, 10/21/2011) effective for returns required to be filed after 12/31/2011.

[¶ 3145]   Code Sec. 7213.   Unauthorized disclosure of information.

(a) **Returns and return information.**

(1) **Federal employees and other persons.** It shall be unlawful for any officer or employee of the United States or any person described in section 6103(n) (or an officer or employee of any such person), or any former officer or employee, willfully to disclose to any person, except as authorized in this title, any return or return information (as defined in section 6103(b)). Any violation of this paragraph shall be a felony punishable upon conviction by a fine in any amount not exceeding $5,000, or imprisonment of not more than 5

years, or both, together with the costs of prosecution, and if such offense is committed by any officer or employee of the United States, he shall, in addition to any other punishment, be dismissed from office or discharged from employment upon conviction for such offense.

(2) State and other employees. It shall be unlawful for any person (not described in paragraph (1)) willfully to disclose to any person, except as authorized in this title, any return or return information (as defined in section 6103(b)) acquired by him or another person under subsection (d), (i)(3)(B)(i) or (7)(A)(ii), [1]*(k)(10)*, (l)(6), (7), (8), (9), (10), (12), (15), (16), (19), (20) or (21), or (m)(2), (4), (5), (6), or (7) of section 6103 or under section 6104(c). Any violation of this paragraph shall be a felony punishable by a fine in any amount not exceeding $5,000, or imprisonment of not more than 5 years, or both, together with the costs of prosecution.

(3) Other persons. It shall be unlawful for any person to whom any return or return information (as defined in section 6103(b)) is disclosed in a manner unauthorized by this title thereafter willfully to print or publish in any manner not provided by law any such return or return information. Any violation of this paragraph shall be a felony punishable by a fine in any amount not exceeding $5,000, or imprisonment of not more than 5 years, or both, together with the costs of prosecution.

(4) Solicitation. It shall be unlawful for any person willfully to offer any item of material value in exchange for any return or return information (as defined in section 6103(b)) and to receive as a result of such solicitation any such return or return information. Any violation of this paragraph shall be a felony punishable by a fine in any amount not exceeding $5,000, or imprisonment of not more than 5 years, or both, together with the costs of prosecution.

(5) Shareholders. It shall be unlawful for any person to whom a return or return information (as defined in section 6103(b)) is disclosed pursuant to the provisions of section 6103(e)(1)(D)(iii) willfully to disclose such return or return information in any manner not provided by law. Any violation of this paragraph shall be a felony punishable by a fine in any amount not to exceed $5,000, or imprisonment of not more than 5 years, or both, together with the costs of prosecution.

* * * * * * * * * * * *

[Endnote Code Sec. 7213]

Code Sec. 7213(a)(2) was amended by Sec. 209(b)(3) of the American Taxpayer Relief Act of 2012, P.L. 112-240, 1/2/2013, as detailed below:

1. Sec. 209(b)(3) added "(k)(10)" before "(l)(6)" in para. (a)(2)

Effective Date (Sec. 209(c), P.L. 112-240, 1/2/2013) effective 1/2/2013.

[¶ 3146] Code Sec. 7275. Penalty for offenses relating to certain airline tickets and advertising.

* * * * * * * * * * * *

(c)[1] *Non-tax charges.*

(1) In general. In the case of transportation by air for which disclosure on the ticket or advertising for such transportation of the amounts paid for passenger taxes is required by subsection (a)(2) or (b)(1)(B), if such amounts are separately disclosed, it shall be unlawful for the disclosure of such amounts to include any amounts not attributable to such taxes.

(2) Inclusion in transportation cost. Nothing in this subsection shall prohibit the inclusion of amounts not attributable to the taxes imposed by subsection (a), (b), or (c) of section 4261 in the disclosure of the amount paid for transportation as required by subsection (a)(1) or (b)(1)(A), or in a separate disclosure of amounts not attributable to such taxes.

^{2}**(d)   Penalty.** Any person who violates any provision of ^{3}*subsection (a), (b), or (c)* is, for each violation, guilty of a misdemeanor, and upon conviction thereof shall be fined not more than $100.

[For Analysis, see ¶ 1911. For Committee Reports, see ¶ 5604.]

[Endnote Code Sec. 7275]
  Code Sec. 7275(c) and Code Sec. 7275(d) were amended by Sec. 1104(a)(1)-(3) of the FAA Modernization and Reform Act of 2012, P.L. 112-95, 2/14/2012, as detailed below:
  1. Sec 1104(a)(3) added new subsec. (c)
  2. Sec. 1104(a)(1) redesignated subsec. (c) as subsec. (d)
  3. Sec. 1104(a)(2) substituted "subsection (a), (b), or (c)" for "subsection (a) or (b)" in subsec. (d), as so redesignated.
Effective Date (Sec. 1104(b), P.L. 112-95, 2/14/2012) effective for taxable transportation provided after 3/31/2012.

[¶ 3147]   Code Sec. 7518.   Tax incentives relating to Merchant Marine capital construction funds.

* * * * * * * * * * * *

(g)   Tax treatment of nonqualified withdrawals.
  (1)   In general. Except as provided in subsection (h), any withdrawal from a capital construction fund which is not a qualified withdrawal shall be treated as a nonqualified withdrawal.
  (2)   Ordering rule. Any nonqualified withdrawal from a fund shall be treated—
    (A) first as made out of the ordinary income account,
    (B) second as made out of the capital gain account, and
    (C) third as made out of the capital account.
  For purposes of this section, items withdrawn from any account shall be treated as withdrawn on a first-in-first-out basis; except that (i) any nonqualified withdrawal for research, development, and design expenses incident to new and advanced ship design, machinery and equipment, and (ii) any amount treated as a nonqualified withdrawal under the second sentence of subsection (f)(4), shall be treated as withdrawn on a last-in-first-out basis.
  (3)   Operating rules. For purposes of this title—
    (A) any amount referred to in paragraph (2)(A) shall be included in income as an item of ordinary income for the taxable year in which the withdrawal is made,
    (B) any amount referred to in paragraph (2)(B) shall be included in income for the taxable year in which the withdrawal is made as an item of gain realized during such year from the disposition of an asset held for more than 6 months, and
    (C) for the period on or before the last date prescribed for payment of tax for the taxable year in which this withdrawal is made—
      (i) no interest shall be payable under section 6601 and no addition to the tax shall be payable under section 6651,
      (ii) interest on the amount of the additional tax attributable to any item referred to in subparagraph (A) or (B) shall be paid at the applicable rate (as defined in paragraph (4)) from the last date prescribed for payment of the tax for the taxable year for which such item was deposited in the fund, and
      (iii) no interest shall be payable on amounts referred to in clauses (i) and (ii) of paragraph (2) or in the case of any nonqualified withdrawal arising from the application of the recapture provision of section 606(5) of the Merchant Marine Act, 1936, as in effect on December 31, 1969.
  (4)   Interest rate. For purposes of paragraph (3)(C)(ii), the applicable rate of interest for any nonqualified withdrawal—
    (A) made in a taxable year beginning in 1970 or 1971 is 8 percent, or
    (B) made in a taxable year beginning after 1971, shall be determined and published jointly by the Secretary of the Treasury or his delegate and the applicable Secretary and shall bear a relationship to 8 percent which the Secretaries determine under joint regula-

tions to be comparable to the relationship which the money rates and investment yields for the calendar year immediately preceding the beginning of the taxable year bear to the money rates and investment yields for the calendar year 1970.

(5) Amount not withdrawn from fund after 25 years from deposit taxed as nonqualified withdrawal.

(A) In general. The applicable percentage of any amount which remains in a capital construction fund at the close of the 26th, 27th, 28th, 29th, or 30th taxable year following the taxable year for which such amount was deposited shall be treated as a nonqualified withdrawal in accordance with the following table:

If the amount remains in the fund at the close of the—	The applicable percentage is—
26th taxable year	20 percent
27th taxable year	40 percent
28th taxable year	60 percent
29th taxable year	80 percent
30th taxable year	100 percent.

(B) Earnings treated as deposits. The earnings of any capital construction fund for any taxable year (other than net gains) shall be treated for purposes of this paragraph as an amount deposited for such taxable year.

(C) Amounts committed treated as withdrawn. For purposes of subparagraph (A), an amount shall not be treated as remaining in a capital construction fund at the close of any taxable year to the extent there is a binding contract at the close of such year for a qualified withdrawal of such amount with respect to an identified item for which such withdrawal may be made.

(D) Authority to treat excess funds as withdrawn. If the Secretary determines that the balance in any capital construction fund exceeds the amount which is appropriate to meet the vessel construction program objectives of the person who established such fund, the amount of such excess shall be treated as a nonqualified withdrawal under subparagraph (A) unless such person develops appropriate program objectives within 3 years to dissipate such excess.

(E) Amounts in fund on January 1, 1987. For purposes of this paragraph, all amounts in a capital construction fund on January 1, 1987, shall be treated as deposited in such fund on such date.

(6) Nonqualified withdrawals taxed at highest marginal rate.

(A) In general. In the case of any taxable year for which there is a nonqualified withdrawal (including any amount so treated under paragraph (5)), the tax imposed by chapter 1 shall be determined—

(i) by excluding such withdrawal from gross income, and

(ii) by increasing the tax imposed by chapter 1 by the product of the amount of such withdrawal and the highest rate of tax specified in section 1 (section 11 in the case of a corporation).

With respect to the portion of any nonqualified withdrawal made out of the capital gain account during a taxable year to which section 1(h) or 1201(a) applies, the rate of tax taken into account under the preceding sentence shall not exceed [1]*20 percent* (34 percent in the case of a corporation).

(B) Tax benefit rule. If any portion of a nonqualified withdrawal is properly attributable to deposits (other than earnings on deposits) made by the taxpayer in any taxable year which did not reduce the taxpayer's liability for tax under chapter 1 for any taxable year preceding the taxable year in which such withdrawal occurs—

(i) such portion shall not be taken into account under subparagraph (A), and

(ii) an amount equal to such portion shall be treated as allowed as a deduction under section 172 for the taxable year in which such withdrawal occurs.

(C) Coordination with deduction for net operating losses. Any nonqualified withdrawal excluded from gross income under subparagraph (A) shall be excluded in determining taxable income under section 172(b)(2).

* * * * * * * * * * * * *

[For Analysis, see ¶ 210.] [For Analysis, see ¶ 210.]

[Endnote Code Sec. 7518]
Code Sec. 7518(g)(6)(A) was amended by Sec. 102(c)(1)(D) of the American Taxpayer Relief Act of 2012, P.L. 112-240, 1/2/2013, as detailed below:
1. Sec. 102(c)(1)(D) substituted "20 percent" for "15 percent" in subpara. (g)(6)(A)
Effective Date (Sec. 102(d)(1), P.L. 112-240, 1/2/2013) effective for taxable years ending after 12/31/2012.

Sec. 102(a), P.L. 112-240, 1/2/2013, deleted sec. 303, P.L. 108-27, the effect of which is to eliminate the sunset of all provisions enacted by Title III, P.L. 108-27. Sec. 301(a)(2)(D), P.L. 108-27 amended Code Sec. 7518 by subsituting "15 percent" for "20 percent" in subpara. (g)(6)(A), effective for tax. yrs. ending on or after 5/6/2003

[¶ 3148]   Code Sec. 7527.   Advance payment of credit for health insurance costs of eligible individuals.

* * * * * * * * * * * * *

(b)   Limitation on advance payments during any taxable year. The Secretary may make payments under subsection (a) only to the extent that the total amount of such payments made on behalf of any individual during the taxable year does not exceed [1]*72.5 percent* of the amount paid by the taxpayer for coverage of the taxpayer and qualifying family members under qualified health insurance for eligible coverage months beginning in the taxable year.

* * * * * * * * * * * * *

(d)   Qualified health insurance costs eligibility certificate.
   (1)   In general. For purposes of this section, the term "qualified health insurance costs eligibility certificate" means any written statement that an individual is an eligible individual (as defined in section 35(c)) if such statement provides such information as the Secretary may require for purposes of this section and—
      (A) in the case of an eligible TAA recipient (as defined in section 35(c)(2)) or an eligible alternative TAA recipient (as defined in section 35(c)(3)), is certified by the Secretary of Labor (or by any other person or entity designated by the Secretary), or
      (B) in the case of an eligible PBGC pension recipient (as defined in section 35(c)(4)), is certified by the Pension Benefit Guaranty Corporation (or by any other person or entity designated by the Secretary).
   (2)   Inclusion of certain information. In the case of any statement described in paragraph (1) [2], such statement shall not be treated as a qualified health insurance costs credit eligibility certificate unless such statement includes—
      (A) the name, address, and telephone number of the State office or offices responsible for providing the individual with assistance with enrollment in qualified health insurance (as defined in section 35(e)),
      (B) a list of the coverage options that are treated as qualified health insurance (as so defined) by the State in which the individual resides, and
      (C) in the case of a TAA-eligible individual (as defined in section 4980B(f)(5)(C)(iv)(II)), a statement informing the individual that the individual has 63 days from the date that is 7 days after the date of the issuance of such certificate to enroll in such insurance without a lapse in creditable coverage (as defined in section 9801(c)).
(e)   Payment for premiums due prior to commencement of advance payments.[3]
   (1)   In general. The program established under subsection (a) shall provide that the Secretary shall make 1 or more retroactive payments on behalf of a certified individual in

an aggregate amount equal to [4]*72.5 percent* of the premiums for coverage of the taxpayer and qualifying family members under qualified health insurance for eligible coverage months (as defined in section 35(b)) occurring prior to the first month for which an advance payment is made on behalf of such individual under subsection (a).

(2) Reduction of payment for amounts received under national emergency grants. The amount of any payment determined under paragraph (1) shall be reduced by the amount of any payment made to the taxpayer for the purchase of qualified health insurance under a national emergency grant pursuant to section 173(f) of the Workforce Investment Act of 1998 for a taxable year including the eligible coverage months described in paragraph (1).

[For Analysis, see ¶ 1605, ¶ 1606 and ¶ 1610.]

[Endnote Code Sec. 7527]

Code Sec. 7527(b) was amended by Sec. 241(b)(2)(A) of the Trade Adjustment Assistance Extension Act of 2011, P.L. 112-40, 10/21/2011, as detailed below:

1. Sec. 241(b)(2)(A) substituted "72.5 percent" for "65 percent (80 percent in the case of eligible coverage months beginning before February 13, 2011)" in subpara. (b)(2)(A)

Effective Date (Sec. 241(c)(1), P.L. 112-40, 10/21/2011) effective for coverage months beginning after 12/12/2011.

Code Sec. 7527(d)(2) was deleted by Sec. 241(d)(2), P.L. 112-40, 10/21/2011, as detailed below:

2. Sec. 241(b)(2)(B) deleted "which is issued before February 13, 2011" in para. (d)(2)

Effective Date (Sec. 241(c)(2)(A), P.L. 112-40, 10/21/2011) effective for certificates issued after the date which is 30 days after 10/21/2011.

Code Sec. 7527(e) was deleted by Sec. 241(b)(2)(C), P.L. 112-40, 10/21/2011, as detailed below:

3. Sec. 241(b)(2)(C) deleted "In the case of eligible coverage months beginning before February 13, 2011—" in subsec. (e)

Effective Date (Sec. 241(c)(1), P.L. 112-40, 10/21/2011) effective for coverage months beginning after 12/12/2011.

Code Sec. 7527(e) was amended by Sec. 241(b)(2)(D), P.L. 112-40, 10/21/2011, as detailed below:

4. Sec. 241(b)(2)(D) substituted "72.5 percent" for "80 percent" in subsec. (e)

Effective Date (Sec. 241(c)(2)(B), P.L. 112-40, 10/21/2011) effective for coverage months beginning after the date which is 30 days after 10/21/2011.

[¶ 3149]   Code Sec. 9801.   Increased portability through limitation on preexisting condition exclusions.

* * * * * * * * * * * *

(c) Rules relating to crediting previous coverage.

(1) Creditable coverage defined. For purposes of this part, the term "creditable coverage" means, with respect to an individual, coverage of the individual under any of the following:

(A) A group health plan.

(B) Health insurance coverage.

(C) Part A or part B of title XVIII of the Social Security Act.

(D) Title XIX of the Social Security Act, other than coverage consisting solely of benefits under section 1928.

(E) Chapter 55 of title 10, United States Code.

(F) A medical care program of the Indian Health Service or of a tribal organization.

(G) A State health benefits risk pool.

(H) A health plan offered under chapter 89 of title 5, United States Code.

(I) A public health plan (as defined in regulations).

(J) A health benefit plan under section 5(e) of the Peace Corps Act (22 U.S.C. 2504(e)).

Such term does not include coverage consisting solely of coverage of excepted benefits (as defined in section 9832(c)).

(2) Not counting periods before significant breaks in coverage.

(A) In general. A period of creditable coverage shall not be counted, with respect to enrollment of an individual under a group health plan, if, after such period and before the enrollment date, there was a 63-day period during all of which the individual was not covered under any creditable coverage.

(B) Waiting period not treated as a break in coverage. For purposes of subparagraph (A) and subsection (d)(4), any period that an individual is in a waiting period for any coverage under a group health plan or is in an affiliation period shall not be taken into account in determining the continuous period under subparagraph (A).

(C) Affiliation period.

(i) In general. For purposes of this section, the term "affiliation period" means a period which, under the terms of the health insurance coverage offered by the health maintenance organization, must expire before the health insurance coverage becomes effective. During such an affiliation period, the organization is not required to provide health care services or benefits and no premium shall be charged to the participant or beneficiary.

(ii) Beginning. Such period shall begin on the enrollment date.

(iii) Runs concurrently with waiting periods. Any such affiliation period shall run concurrently with any waiting period under the plan.

(D) TAA-eligible individuals. In the case of plan years beginning before [1]*January 1, 2014—*

(i) TAA pre-certification period rule. In the case of a TAA-eligible individual, the period beginning on the date the individual has a TAA-related loss of coverage and ending on the date which is 7 days after the date of the issuance by the Secretary (or by any person or entity designated by the Secretary) of a qualified health insurance costs credit eligibility certificate for such individual for purposes of section 7527 shall not be taken into account in determining the continuous period under subparagraph (A).

(ii) Definitions. The terms "TAA-eligible individual" and "TAA-related loss of coverage" have the meanings given such terms in section 4980B(f)(5)(C)(iv).

(3) Method of crediting coverage.

(A) Standard method. Except as otherwise provided under subparagraph (B), for purposes of applying subsection (a)(3), a group health plan shall count a period of creditable coverage without regard to the specific benefits for which coverage is offered during the period.

(B) Election of alternative method. A group health plan may elect to apply subsection (a)(3) based on coverage of any benefits within each of several classes or categories of benefits specified in regulations rather than as provided under subparagraph (A). Such election shall be made on a uniform basis for all participants and beneficiaries. Under such election a group health plan shall count a period of creditable coverage with respect to any class or category of benefits if any level of benefits is covered within such class or category.

(C) Plan notice. In the case of an election with respect to a group health plan under subparagraph (B), the plan shall—

(i) prominently state in any disclosure statements concerning the plan, and state to each enrollee at the time of enrollment under the plan, that the plan has made such election, and

(ii) include in such statements a description of the effect of this election.

(4) Establishment of period. Periods of creditable coverage with respect to an individual shall be established through presentation of certifications described in subsection (e) or in such other manner as may be specified in regulations.

* * * * * * * * * * * *

[For Analysis, see ¶ 1611.]

[Endnote Code Sec. 9801]

Code Sec. 9801(c)(2)(D) was amended by Sec. 242(a)(1) of the Trade Adjustment Assistance Extension Act of 2011, P.L. 112-40, 10/21/2011, as detailed below:

1. Sec. 242(a)(1) substituted "January 1, 2014" for "February 13, 2011" in subpara. (c)(2)(D)

Effective Date (Sec. 242(b)(1), P.L. 112-40, 10/21/2011) effective for plan yrs. begin. after 2/12/2011. Sec. 242(b)(2) of this Act, reads as follows:

"(2) Transitional rules.

"(A) Benefit determinations. Notwithstanding the amendments made by this section (and the provisions of law amended thereby), a plan shall not be required to modify benefit determinations for the period beginning on February 13, 2011, and ending 30 days after the date of the enactment of this Act, but a plan shall not fail to be qualified health insurance within the meaning of section 35(e) of the Internal Revenue Code of 1986 during this period merely due to such failure to modify benefit determinations.

"(B) Guidance concerning periods before 30 days after enactment. Except as provided in subparagraph (A), the Secretary of the Treasury (or his designee), in consultation with the Secretary of Health and Human Services and the Secretary of Labor, may issue regulations or other guidance regarding the scope of the application of the amendments made by this section to periods before the date which is 30 days after the date of the enactment of this Act.

"(C) Special rule relating to certain loss of coverage. In the case of a TAA-related loss of coverage (as defined in section 4980B(f)(5)(C)(iv) of the Internal Revenue Code of 1986) that occurs during the period beginning on February 13, 2011, and ending 30 days after the date of the enactment of this Act, the 7-day period described in section 9801(c)(2)(D) of the Internal Revenue Code of 1986, section 701(c)(2)(C) of the Employee Retirement Income Security Act of 1974, and section 2701(c)(2)(C) of the Public Health Service Act shall be extended until 30 days after such date of enactment."

[¶ 3500]   Code as Amended
This section reproduces ERISA Code as Amended by the Trade Adjustment Assistance Extension Act, PL 112-40, 10/21/2011 and the Highway Investment Act of 2012, PL 112-141. ERISA Sections appear in order, as amended, added or repealed. New matter is shown in italics. All changes and effective dates are shown in the endnotes.

[¶ 3501]
ERISA §101. [29 USC 1021] Duty of disclosure and reporting.

* * * * * * * * * * * *

(e) Notice of transfer of excess pension assets to health benefits accounts.

   (1) Notice to participants. Not later than 60 days before the date of a qualified transfer by an employee pension benefit plan of excess pension assets to a health benefits account [1]*or applicable life insurance account*, the administrator of the plan shall notify (in such manner as the Secretary may prescribe) each participant and beneficiary under the plan of such transfer. Such notice shall include information with respect to the amount of excess pension assets, the portion to be transferred, the amount of health benefits liabilities [2]*or applicable life insurance benefit liabilities* expected to be provided with the assets transferred, and the amount of pension benefits of the participant which will be nonforfeitable immediately after the transfer.

   (2) Notice to Secretaries, administrator, and employee organizations.

      (A) In general. Not later than 60 days before the date of any qualified transfer by an employee pension benefit plan of excess pension assets to a health benefits account [3]*or applicable life insurance account*, the employer maintaining the plan from which the transfer is made shall provide the Secretary, the Secretary of the Treasury, the administrator, and each employee organization representing participants in the plan a written notice of such transfer. A copy of any such notice shall be available for inspection in the principal office of the administrator.

      (B) Information relating to transfer. Such notice shall identify the plan from which the transfer is made, the amount of the transfer, a detailed accounting of assets projected to be held by the plan immediately before and immediately after the transfer, and the current liabilities under the plan at the time of the transfer.

      (C) Authority for additional reporting requirements. The Secretary may prescribe such additional reporting requirements as may be necessary to carry out the purposes of this section.

   (3) Definitions. For purposes of paragraph (1), any term used in such paragraph which is also used in section 420 of the Internal Revenue Code of 1986 [26 USC §420] (as in effect on the date of the enactment of the [4]*MAP-21*) shall have the same meaning as when used in such section.

(f) Defined benefit plan funding notices.

   (1) In general. The administrator of a defined benefit plan to which title IV applies shall for each plan year provide a plan funding notice to the Pension Benefit Guaranty Corporation, to each plan participant and beneficiary, to each labor organization representing such participants or beneficiaries, and, in the case of a multiemployer plan, to each employer that has an obligation to contribute to the plan.

   (2) Information contained in notices.

      (A) Identifying information. Each notice required under paragraph (1) shall contain identifying information, including the name of the plan, the address and phone number of the plan administrator and the plan's principal administrative officer, each plan sponsor's employer identification number, and the plan number of the plan.

901

(B) Specific information. A plan funding notice under paragraph (1) shall include—

(i) (I) in the case of a single-employer plan, a statement as to whether the plan's funding target attainment percentage (as defined in section 303(d)(2) [29 USC 1083(d)(2)]) for the plan year to which the notice relates, and for the 2 preceding plan years, is at least 100 percent (and, if not, the actual percentages), or

(II) in the case of a multiemployer plan, a statement as to whether the plan's funded percentage (as defined in section 305(i) [29 USC 1085(i)]) for the plan year to which the notice relates, and for the 2 preceding plan years, is at least 100 percent (and, if not, the actual percentages),

(ii) (I) in the case of a single-employer plan, a statement of—

(aa) the total assets (separately stating the prefunding balance and the funding standard carryover balance) and liabilities of the plan, determined in the same manner as under section 303 [29 USC 1083], for the plan year to which the notice relates and for the 2 preceding plan years, as reported in the annual report for each such plan year, and

(bb) the value of the plan's assets and liabilities for the plan year to which the notice relates as of the last day of the plan year to which the notice relates determined using the asset valuation under subclause (II) of section 4006(a)(3)(E)(iii) [29 USC 1306(a)(3)(E)(iii)] and the interest rate under section 4006(a)(3)(E)(iv) [29 USC 1306(a)(3)(E)(iv)], and

(II) in the case of a multiemployer plan, a statement, for the plan year to which the notice relates and the preceding 2 plan years, of the value of the plan assets (determined both in the same manner as under section 304 and under the rules of subclause (I)(bb)) and the value of the plan liabilities (determined in the same manner as under section 304 except that the method specified in section 305(i)(8) shall be used),

(iii) a statement of the number of participants who are—

(I) retired or separated from service and are receiving benefits,

(II) retired or separated participants entitled to future benefits, and

(III) active participants under the plan,

(iv) a statement setting forth the funding policy of the plan and the asset allocation of investments under the plan (expressed as percentages of total assets) as of the end of the plan year to which the notice relates,

(v) in the case of a multiemployer plan, whether the plan was in critical or endangered status under section 305 [29 USC 1085] for such plan year and, if so—

(I) a statement describing how a person may obtain a copy of the plan's funding improvement or rehabilitation plan, as appropriate, adopted under section 305 [29 USC 1085] and the actuarial and financial data that demonstrate any action taken by the plan toward fiscal improvement, and

(II) a summary of any funding improvement plan, rehabilitation plan, or modification thereof adopted under section 305 [29 USC 1085] during the plan year to which the notice relates,

(vi) in the case of any plan amendment, scheduled benefit increase or reduction, or other known event taking effect in the current plan year and having a material effect on plan liabilities or assets for the year (as defined in regulations by the Secretary), an explanation of the amendment, schedule increase or reduction, or event, and a projection to the end of such plan year of the effect of the amendment, scheduled increase or reduction, or event on plan liabilities,

(vii) (I) in the case of a single-employer plan, a summary of the rules governing termination of single-employer plans under subtitle C of title IV, or

(II) in the case of a multiemployer plan, a summary of the rules governing reorganization or insolvency, including the limitations on benefit payments,

(viii) a general description of the benefits under the plan which are eligible to be guaranteed by the Pension Benefit Guaranty Corporation, along with an explanation of the limitations on the guarantee and the circumstances under which such limitations apply,

(ix) a statement that a person may obtain a copy of the annual report of the plan filed under section 104(a) [29 U.S.C 1024(a)] upon request, through the Internet website of the Department of Labor, or through an Intranet website maintained by the applicable plan sponsor (or plan administrator on behalf of the plan sponsor), and

(x) if applicable, a statement that each contributing sponsor, and each member of the contributing sponsor's controlled group, of the single-employer plan was required to provide the information under section 4010 [29 USC 1310] for the plan year to which the notice relates.

(C) Other information. Each notice under paragraph (1) shall include—

(i) in the case of a multiemployer plan, a statement that the plan administrator shall provide, upon written request, to any labor organization representing plan participants and beneficiaries and any employer that has an obligation to contribute to the plan, a copy of the annual report filed with the Secretary under section 104(a) [29 USC 1024(a)], and

(ii) any additional information which the plan administrator elects to include to the extent not inconsistent with regulations prescribed by the Secretary.

[5]*(D) Effect of segment rate stabilization on plan funding.*

(i) In general. In the case of a single-employer plan for an applicable plan year, each notice under paragraph (1) shall include—

(I) a statement that the MAP-21 modified the method for determining the interest rates used to determine the actuarial value of benefits earned under the plan, providing for a 25-year average of interest rates to be taken into account in addition to a 2-year average,

(II) a statement that, as a result of the MAP-21, the plan sponsor may contribute less money to the plan when interest rates are at historical lows, and

(III) a table which shows (determined both with and without regard to section 303(h)(2)(C)(iv)) the funding target attainment percentage (as defined in section 303(d)(2)), the funding shortfall (as defined in section 303(c)(4)), and the minimum required contribution (as determined under section 303), for the applicable plan year and each of the 2 preceding plan years.

(ii) Applicable plan year. For purposes of this subparagraph, the term "applicable plan year" means any plan year beginning after December 31, 2011, and before January 1, 2015, for which—

(I) the funding target (as defined in section 303(d)(2)) is less than 95 percent of such funding target determined without regard to section 303(h)(2)(C)(iv),

(II) the plan has a funding shortfall (as defined in section 303(c)(4) and determined without regard to section 303(h)(2)(C)(iv)) greater than $500,000, and

(III) the plan had 50 or more participants on any day during the preceding plan year. For purposes of any determination under subclause (III), the aggregation rule under the last sentence of section 303(g)(2)(B) shall apply.

(iii) Special rule for plan years beginning before 2012. In the case of a preceding plan year referred to in clause (i)(III) which begins before January 1, 2012, the information described in such clause shall be provided only without regard to section 303(h)(2)(C)(iv).

(3) Time for providing notice.

(A) In general. Any notice under paragraph (1) shall be provided not later than 120 days after the end of the plan year to which the notice relates.

(B) Exception for small plans. In the case of a small plan (as such term is used under section 303(g)(2)(B) [29 USC 1083(g)(2)(B)]) any notice under paragraph (1) shall be provided upon filing of the annual report under section 104(a) [29 USC 1024(a)].

(4) Form and manner. Any notice under paragraph (1)—

(A) shall be provided in a form and manner prescribed in regulations of the Secretary,

(B) shall be written in a manner so as to be understood by the average plan participant, and

(C) may be provided in written, electronic, or other appropriate form to the extent such form is reasonably accessible to persons to whom the notice is required to be provided.

[For Analysis, see ¶ 1701, ¶ 1702 and ¶ 1703. For Committee Reports, see ¶ 5402, ¶ 5405.]

[Endnote ERISA §t29_1021]

29 USC §1021(e)(1), (2)(A) [ERISA Sec. 101] was amended by Sec. 40242(e)(14)(A)-(B) of the Moving Ahead for Progress in the 21st Century Act, P.L. 112-141, 7/6/2012, as detailed below:

1. Sec. 40242(e)(14)(A) added 'or applicable life insurance account' after 'health benefits account' in para. (e)(1)

2. Sec. 40242(e)(14)(B) added 'or applicable life insurance benefit liabilities' after 'health benefits liabilities' in para. (e)(1)

3. Sec. 40242(e)(14)(A) added 'or applicable life insurance account' after 'health benefits account' in para. (e)(2)(A)

Effective Date (Sec. 40242(h)(1) P.L. 112-141, 7/6/2012), effective for transfers made after 7/6/2012.

---

29 USC §1021(e)(3) [ERISA Sec. 101] was amended by Sec. 40241(b)(1), P.L. 112-141, 7/6/2012, as detailed below:

4. Sec. 40241(b)(1) substituted 'MAP-21' for 'Pension Protection Act of 2006' in para. (e)(3)

Effective Date (Sec. 40241(c) P.L. 112-141, 7/6/2012), effective 7/6/2012.

---

29 USC §1021(f)(2)(D) [ERISA Sec. 101] was amended by Sec. 40211(b)(2)(A), P.L. 112-141, 7/6/2012, as detailed below:

5. Sec. 40211(b)(2)(A) added subpara. (f)(2)(D)

Effective Date (Sec. 40211(c)(1), P.L. 112-141, 7/6/2012) effective with respect to plan yrs. begin. after 12/31/2011. Sec. 40211(c)(2) of this Act, provides:

"(2) Rules with respect to elections.

"(A) Adjusted funding target attainment percentage. A plan sponsor may elect not to have the amendments made by this section apply to any plan year beginning before January 1, 2013, either (as specified in the election)—

"(i) for all purposes for which such amendments apply, or

"(ii) solely for purposes of determining the adjusted funding target attainment percentage under sections 436 of the Internal Revenue Code of 1986 and 206(g) of the Employee Retirement Income Security Act of 1974 for such plan year.

"A plan shall not be treated as failing to meet the requirements of sections 204(g) of such Act and 411(d)(6) of such Code solely by reason of an election under this paragraph.

"(B) Opt out of existing elections. If, on the date of the enactment of this Act, an election is in effect with respect to any plan under sections 303(h)((2)(D)(ii) of the Employee Retirement Income Security Act of 1974 and 430(h)((2)(D)(ii) of the Internal Revenue Code of 1986, then, notwithstanding the last sentence of each such section, the plan sponsor may revoke such election without the consent of the Secretary of the Treasury. The plan sponsor may make such revocation at any time before the date which is 1 year after such date of enactment and such revocation shall be effective for the 1st plan year to which the amendments made by this section apply and all subsequent plan years. Nothing in this subparagraph shall preclude a plan sponsor from making a subsequent election in accordance with such sections."

[¶ 3502]

ERISA §205. [29 USC 1055] Requirement of joint and survivor annuity and preretirement survivor annuity.

* * * * * * * * * * * *

(g) Distribution of present value of annuity; written consent; determination of present value.

(1) A plan may provide that the present value of a qualified joint and survivor annuity or a qualified preretirement survivor annuity will be immediately distributed if such value does not exceed the amount that can be distributed without the participant's consent under section 203(e). No distribution may be made under the preceding sentence after the annuity starting date unless the participant and the spouse of the participant (or where the participant has died, the surviving spouse) consent in writing to such distribution.

(2) If—

(A) the present value of the qualified joint and survivor annuity or the qualified preretirement survivor annuity exceeds the amount that can be distributed without the participant's consent under section 203(e), and

(B) the participant and the spouse of the participant (or where the participant has died, the surviving spouse) consent in writing to the distribution,

the plan may immediately distribute the present value of such annuity.

(3) (A) For purposes of paragraphs (1) and (2), the present value shall not be less than the present value calculated by using the applicable mortality table and the applicable interest rate.

(B) For purposes of subparagraph (A)—

(i) The term "applicable mortality table" means a mortality table, modified as appropriate by the Secretary of the Treasury, based on the mortality table specified for the plan year under subparagraph (A) of section 303(h)(3) (without regard to subparagraph (C) or (D) of such section).

(ii) The term "applicable interest rate" means the adjusted first, second, and third segment rates applied under rules similar to the rules of [1]*section 303(h)(2)(C) (determined by not taking into account any adjustment under clause (iv) thereof)* for the month before the date of the distribution or such other time as the Secretary of the Treasury may by regulations prescribe.

(iii) For purposes of clause (ii), the adjusted first, second, and third segment rates are the first, second, and third segment rates which would be determined under [2]*section 303(h)(2)(C) (determined by not taking into account any adjustment under clause (iv) thereof)* if—

(I) section 303(h)(2)(D) were applied by substituting the average yields for the month described in clause (ii) for the average yields for the 24-month period described in such section,

(II) section 303(h)(2)(G)(i)(II) were applied by substituting "section 205(g)(3)(A)(ii)(II)" for "section 302(b)(5)(B)(ii)(II)", and

(III) the applicable percentage under section 303(h)(2)(G) were determined in accordance with the following table:

The applicable percentage is:	In the case of plan years beginning in:
2008	20 percent
2009	40 percent
2010	60 percent
2011	80 percent.

* * * * * * * * * * * *

[For Analysis, see ¶ 1701. For Committee Reports, see ¶ 5402.]

[Endnote ERISA §t29_1055]

29 USC §1055(g)(3)(B)(iii) [ERISA Sec. 205] was amended by Sec. 40211(b)(3)(B) of the Moving Ahead for Progress in the 21st Century Act, P.L. 112-141, 7/6/2012, as detailed below:

1. Sec. 40211(b)(3)(B) substituted 'section 303(h)(2)(C) (determined by not taking into account any adjustment under clause (iv) thereof)' for 'section 303(h)(2)(C)' in clause (g)(3)(B)(ii)

2. Sec. 40211(b)(3)(B) substituted 'section 303(h)(2)(C) (determined by not taking into account any adjustment under clause (iv) thereof)' for 'section 303(h)(2)(C)' in clause (g)(3)(B)(iii)

Effective Date (Sec. 40211(c)(1), P.L. 112-141, 7/6/2012) effective with respect to plan yrs. begin. after 12/31/2011. Sec. 40211(c)(2) of this Act, provides:

"(2) Rules with respect to elections.

"(A) Adjusted funding target attainment percentage. A plan sponsor may elect not to have the amendments made by this section apply to any plan year beginning before January 1, 2013, either (as specified in the election)—

"(i) for all purposes for which such amendments apply, or

"(ii) solely for purposes of determining the adjusted funding target attainment percentage under sections 436 of the Internal Revenue Code of 1986 and 206(g) of the Employee Retirement Income Security Act of 1974 for such plan year.

"A plan shall not be treated as failing to meet the requirements of sections 204(g) of such Act and 411(d)(6) of such Code solely by reason of an election under this paragraph.

"(B) Opt out of existing elections. If, on the date of the enactment of this Act, an election is in effect with respect to any plan under sections 303(h)((2)(D)(ii) of the Employee Retirement Income Security Act of 1974 and 430(h)((2)(D)(ii) of the Internal Revenue Code of 1986, then, notwithstanding the last sentence of each such section, the plan sponsor may revoke such election without the consent of the Secretary of the Treasury. The plan sponsor may make such revocation at any time before the date which is 1 year after such date of enactment and such revocation shall be effective for the 1st plan year to which the amendments made by this section apply and all subsequent plan years. Nothing in this subparagraph shall preclude a plan sponsor from making a subsequent election in accordance with such sections."

[¶ 3503]

ERISA §303. [29 USC 1083]   Minimum funding standards for single-employer defined benefit pension plans.

* * * * * * * * * * * *

(h) Actuarial assumptions and methods.

(1) In general. Subject to this subsection, the determination of any present value or other computation under this section shall be made on the basis of actuarial assumptions and methods—

(A) each of which is reasonable (taking into account the experience of the plan and reasonable expectations), and

(B) which, in combination, offer the actuary's best estimate of anticipated experience under the plan.

(2) Interest rates.

(A) Effective interest rate. For purposes of this section, the term "effective interest rate" means, with respect to any plan for any plan year, the single rate of interest which, if used to determine the present value of the plan's accrued or earned benefits referred to in subsection (d)(1), would result in an amount equal to the funding target of the plan for such plan year.

(B) Interest rates for determining funding target. For purposes of determining the funding target and normal cost of a plan for any plan year, the interest rate used in determining the present value of the benefits of the plan shall be—

(i) in the case of benefits reasonably determined to be payable during the 5-year period beginning on the first day of the plan year, the first segment rate with respect to the applicable month,

(ii) in the case of benefits reasonably determined to be payable during the 15-year period beginning at the end of the period described in clause (i), the second segment rate with respect to the applicable month, and

(iii) in the case of benefits reasonably determined to be payable after the period described in clause (ii), the third segment rate with respect to the applicable month.

(C) Segment rates. For purposes of this paragraph—

(i) First segment rate. The term "first segment rate" means, with respect to any month, the single rate of interest which shall be determined by the Secretary of the Treasury for such month on the basis of the corporate bond yield curve for such month, taking into account only that portion of such yield curve which is based on bonds maturing during the 5-year period commencing with such month.

(ii) Second segment rate. The term "second segment rate" means, with respect to any month, the single rate of interest which shall be determined by the Secretary of the Treasury for such month on the basis of the corporate bond yield curve for such month, taking into account only that portion of such yield curve which is based on bonds maturing during the 15-year period beginning at the end of the period described in clause (i).

(iii) Third segment rate— The term "third segment rate" means, with respect to any month, the single rate of interest which shall be determined by the Secretary of the Treasury for such month on the basis of the corporate bond yield curve for such month, taking into account only that portion of such yield curve which is based on bonds maturing during periods beginning after the period described in clause (ii).

[1]*(iv) Segment rate stabilization.*

(I) In general. If a segment rate described in clause (i), (ii), or (iii) with respect to any applicable month (determined without regard to this clause) is less than the

applicable minimum percentage, or more than the applicable maximum percentage, of the average of the segment rates described in such clause for years in the 25-year period ending with September 30 of the calendar year preceding the calendar year in which the plan year begins, then the segment rate described in such clause with respect to the applicable month shall be equal to the applicable minimum percentage or the applicable maximum percentage of such average, whichever is closest. The Secretary of the Treasury shall determine such average on an annual basis and may prescribe equivalent rates for years in any such 25-year period for which the rates described in any such clause are not available.

(II) Applicable minimum percentage; applicable maximum percentage. For purposes of subclause (I), the applicable minimum percentage and the applicable maximum percentage for a plan year beginning in a calendar year shall be determined in accordance with the following table:

(D) Corporate bond yield curve. For purposes of this paragraph—

(i) In general. The term "corporate bond yield curve" means, with respect to any month, a yield curve which is prescribed by the Secretary of the Treasury for such month and which reflects the average, for the 24-month period ending with the month preceding such month, of monthly yields on investment grade corporate bonds with varying maturities and that are in the top 3 quality levels available.

(ii) Election to use yield curve. Solely for purposes of determining the minimum required contribution under this section, the plan sponsor may, in lieu of the segment rates determined under subparagraph (C), elect to use interest rates under the corporate bond yield curve. For purposes of the preceding sentence such curve shall be determined without regard to the 24-month averaging described in clause (i). Such election, once made, may be revoked only with the consent of the Secretary of the Treasury.

(E) Applicable month. For purposes of this paragraph, the term "applicable month" means, with respect to any plan for any plan year, the month which includes the valuation date of such plan for such plan year or, at the election of the plan sponsor, any of the 4 months which precede such month. Any election made under this subparagraph shall apply to the plan year for which the election is made and all succeeding plan years, unless the election is revoked with the consent of the Secretary of the Treasury.

(F) Publication requirements. The Secretary of the Treasury shall publish for each month the corporate bond yield curve (and the corporate bond yield curve reflecting the modification described in section 205(g)(3)(B)(iii)(I)) for such month) and each of the rates determined under subparagraph (C) [2]and the averages determined under subparagraph (C)(iv) for such month. The Secretary of the Treasury shall also publish a description of the methodology used to determine such yield curve and such rates which is sufficiently detailed to enable plans to make reasonable projections regarding the yield curve and such rates for future months based on the plan's projection of future interest rates.

(G) Transition rule.

(i) In general. Notwithstanding the preceding provisions of this paragraph, for plan years beginning in 2008 or 2009, the first, second, or third segment rate for a plan with respect to any month shall be equal to the sum of—

(I) the product of such rate for such month determined without regard to this subparagraph, multiplied by the applicable percentage, and

(II) the product of the rate determined under the rules of section 302(b)(5)(B)(ii)(II) (as in effect for plan years beginning in 2007), multiplied by a percentage equal to 100 percent minus the applicable percentage.

(ii) Applicable percentage. For purposes of clause (i), the applicable percentage is $33^1/_3$ percent for plan years beginning in 2008 and $66^2/_3$ percent for plan years beginning in 2009.

(iii) New plans ineligible. Clause (i) shall not apply to any plan if the first plan year of the plan begins after December 31, 2007.

(iv) Election. The plan sponsor may elect not to have this subparagraph apply. Such election, once made, may be revoked only with the consent of the Secretary of the Treasury.

(3) Mortality tables.

(A) In general. Except as provided in subparagraph (C) or (D), the Secretary of the Treasury shall by regulation prescribe mortality tables to be used in determining any present value or making any computation under this section. Such tables shall be based on the actual experience of pension plans and projected trends in such experience. In prescribing such tables, the Secretary of the Treasury shall take into account results of available independent studies of mortality of individuals covered by pension plans.

(B) Periodic revision. The Secretary of the Treasury shall (at least every 10 years) make revisions in any table in effect under subparagraph (A) to reflect the actual experience of pension plans and projected trends in such experience.

(C) Substitute mortality table.

(i) In general. Upon request by the plan sponsor and approval by the Secretary of the Treasury, a mortality table which meets the requirements of clause (iii) shall be used in determining any present value or making any computation under this section during the period of consecutive plan years (not to exceed 10) specified in the request.

(ii) Early termination of period. Notwithstanding clause (i), a mortality table described in clause (i) shall cease to be in effect as of the earliest of—

(l) the date on which there is a significant change in the participants in the plan by reason of a plan spinoff or merger or otherwise, or

(ll) the date on which the plan actuary determines that such table does not meet the requirements of clause (iii).

(iii) Requirements. A mortality table meets the requirements of this clause if—

(l) there is a sufficient number of plan participants, and the pension plans have been maintained for a sufficient period of time, to have credible information necessary for purposes of subclause (II), and

(ll) such table reflects the actual experience of the pension plans maintained by the sponsor and projected trends in general mortality experience.

(iv) All plans in controlled group must use separate table. Except as provided by the Secretary of the Treasury, a plan sponsor may not use a mortality table under this subparagraph for any plan maintained by the plan sponsor unless—

(l) a separate mortality table is established and used under this subparagraph for each other plan maintained by the plan sponsor and if the plan sponsor is a member of a controlled group, each member of the controlled group, and

(ll) the requirements of clause (iii) are met separately with respect to the table so established for each such plan, determined by only taking into account the participants of such plan, the time such plan has been in existence, and the actual experience of such plan.

(v) Deadline for submission and disposition of application.

(l) Submission. The plan sponsor shall submit a mortality table to the Secretary of the Treasury for approval under this subparagraph at least 7 months before the 1st day of the period described in clause (i).

(ll) Disposition. Any mortality table submitted to the Secretary of the Treasury for approval under this subparagraph shall be treated as in effect as of the 1st day of the period described in clause (i) unless the Secretary of the Treasury, during the 180-day period beginning on the date of such submission, disapproves of such table and provides the reasons that such table fails to meet the requirements of clause (iii). The 180-day period shall be extended upon mutual agreement of the Secretary of the Treasury and the plan sponsor.

(D) Separate mortality tables for the disabled. Notwithstanding subparagraph (A)—

(i) In general. The Secretary of the Treasury shall establish mortality tables which may be used (in lieu of the tables under subparagraph (A)) under this subsection for individuals who are entitled to benefits under the plan on account of disability. The

Secretary of the Treasury shall establish separate tables for individuals whose disabilities occur in plan years beginning before January 1, 1995, and for individuals whose disabilities occur in plan years beginning on or after such date.

(ii) Special rule for disabilities occurring after 1994. In the case of disabilities occurring in plan years beginning after December 31, 1994, the tables under clause (i) shall apply only with respect to individuals described in such subclause who are disabled within the meaning of title II of the Social Security Act and the regulations thereunder.

(iii) Periodic revision. The Secretary of the Treasury shall (at least every 10 years) make revisions in any table in effect under clause (i) to reflect the actual experience of pension plans and projected trends in such experience.

(4) Probability of benefit payments in the form of lump sums or other optional forms. For purposes of determining any present value or making any computation under this section, there shall be taken into account—

(A) the probability that future benefit payments under the plan will be made in the form of optional forms of benefits provided under the plan (including lump sum distributions, determined on the basis of the plan's experience and other related assumptions), and

(B) any difference in the present value of such future benefit payments resulting from the use of actuarial assumptions, in determining benefit payments in any such optional form of benefits, which are different from those specified in this subsection.

(5) Approval of large changes in actuarial assumptions.

(A) In general. No actuarial assumption used to determine the funding target for a plan to which this paragraph applies may be changed without the approval of the Secretary of the Treasury.

(B) Plans to which paragraph applies. This paragraph shall apply to a plan only if—

(i) the plan is a single-employer plan to which title IV applies,

(ii) the aggregate unfunded vested benefits as of the close of the preceding plan year (as determined under section 4006(a)(3)(E)(iii)) of such plan and all other plans maintained by the contributing sponsors (as defined in section 4001(a)(13)) and members of such sponsors' controlled groups (as defined in section 4001(a)(14)) which are covered by title IV (disregarding plans with no unfunded vested benefits) exceed $50,000,000, and

(iii) the change in assumptions (determined after taking into account any changes in interest rate and mortality table) results in a decrease in the funding shortfall of the plan for the current plan year that exceeds $50,000,000, or that exceeds $5,000,000 and that is 5 percent or more of the funding target of the plan before such change.

* * * * * * * * * * * *

[For Analysis, see ¶ 1701. For Committee Reports, see ¶ 5402.]

[Endnote ERISA §t29_1083]

29 USC §1083(h)(2)(C)(iv), (F) [ERISA Sec. 303] was amended by Sec. 40211(b)(1), (3)(A) of the Moving Ahead for Progress in the 21st Century Act, P.L. 112-141, 7/6/2012, as detailed below:

1. Sec. 40211(b)(1) added clause (h)(2)(C)(iv)

2. Sec. 40211(b)(3)(A) added 'and the averages determined under subparagraph (C)(iv)' after 'subparagraph (C)' in subpara. (h)(2)(F)

Effective Date (Sec. 40211(b)(3)(A), P.L. 112-141, 7/6/2012) effective with respect to plan yrs. begin. after 12/31/2011. Sec. 40211(c)(2) of this Act, provides:

"(2) Rules with respect to elections.

"(A) Adjusted funding target attainment percentage. A plan sponsor may elect not to have the amendments made by this section apply to any plan year beginning before January 1, 2013, either (as specified in the election)—

"(i) for all purposes for which such amendments apply, or

"(ii) solely for purposes of determining the adjusted funding target attainment percentage under sections 436 of the Internal Revenue Code of 1986 and 206(g) of the Employee Retirement Income Security Act of 1974 for such plan year.

"A plan shall not be treated as failing to meet the requirements of sections 204(g) of such Act and 411(d)(6) of such Code solely by reason of an election under this paragraph.

"(B) Opt out of existing elections. If, on the date of the enactment of this Act, an election is in effect with respect to any plan under sections 303(h)((2)(D)(ii) of the Employee Retirement Income Security Act of 1974 and

430(h)((2)(D)(ii) of the Internal Revenue Code of 1986, then, notwithstanding the last sentence of each such section, the plan sponsor may revoke such election without the consent of the Secretary of the Treasury. The plan sponsor may make such revocation at any time before the date which is 1 year after such date of enactment and such revocation shall be effective for the 1st plan year to which the amendments made by this section apply and all subsequent plan years. Nothing in this subparagraph shall preclude a plan sponsor from making a subsequent election in accordance with such sections."

[¶ 3504]
ERISA §403. [29 USC 1103]   Establishment of trust.

* * * * * * * * * * * *

(c) Assets of plan not to inure to benefit of employer; allowable purposes of holding plan assets.

(1) Except as provided in paragraph (2), (3), or (4) or subsection (d), or under section 4042 [29 USC §1342] and 4044 [29 USC §1344] (relating to termination of insured plans), or under section 420 of the Internal Revenue Code of 1986 [26 USC §420] (as in effect on the date of the enactment of the ¹MAP-21), the assets of a plan shall never inure to the benefit of any employer and shall be held for the exclusive purposes of providing benefits to participants in the plan and their beneficiaries and defraying reasonable expenses of administering the plan.

(2)   (A) In the case of a contribution, or a payment of withdrawal liability under part 1 of subtitle E of Title IV—

(i) if such contribution or payment is made by an employer to a plan (other than a multiemployer plan) by a mistake of fact, paragraph (1) shall not prohibit the return of such contribution to the employer within one year after the payment of the contribution, and

(ii) if such contribution or payment is made by an employer to a multiemployer plan by a mistake of fact or law (other than a mistake relating to whether the plan is described in section 401(a) of the Internal Revenue Code of 1986 [26 USC §401(a)] or the trust which is part of such plan is exempt from taxation under section 501(a) of such Code [26 USC §501(a)]), paragraph (1) shall not prohibit the return of such contribution or payment to the employer within 6 months after the plan administrator determines that the contribution was made by such a mistake.

(B) If a contribution is conditioned on initial qualification of the plan under section 401 or 403(a) of the Internal Revenue Code of 1986, [26 USC §§401 or 403] and if the plan receives an adverse determination with respect to its initial qualification, then paragraph (1) shall not prohibit the return of such contribution to the employer within one year after such determination, but only if the application for the determination is made by the time prescribed by law for filing the employer's return for the taxable year in which such plan was adopted, or such later date as the Secretary of the Treasury may prescribe.

(C) If a contribution is conditioned upon the deductibility of the contribution under section 404 of the Internal Revenue Code of 1986 [26 USC §404], then, to the extent the deduction is disallowed, paragraph (1) shall not prohibit the return to the employer of such contribution (to the extent disallowed) within one year after the disallowance of the deduction.

(3) In the case of a withdrawal liability payment which has been determined to be an overpayment, paragraph (1) shall not prohibit the return of such payment to the employer within 6 months after the date of such determination.

* * * * * * * * * * * *

[For Analysis, see ¶ 1703. For Committee Reports, see ¶ 5405.]

[Endnote ERISA §t29_1103]
29 USC §1103(c)(1) [ERISA Sec. 403] was amended by Sec. 40241(b)(1) of the Moving Ahead for Progress in the 21st Century Act, P.L. 112-141, 7/6/2012, as detailed below:

1. Sec. 40241(b)(1) substituted 'MAP-21' for 'Pension Protection Act of 2006' in para. (c)(1)
Effective Date (Sec. 40241(c), P.L. 112-141, 7/6/2012) effective 7/6/2012.

[¶ 3505]
ERISA §408. [29 USC 1108] Exemptions from prohibited transactions.

* * * * * * * * * * * *

(b) **Enumeration of transactions exempted from 29 USC §1106 prohibitions.** The prohibitions provided in section 406 [29 USC §1106] shall not apply to any of the following transactions:

(1) Any loans made by the plan to parties in interest who are participants or beneficiaries of the plan if such loans (A) are available to all such participants and beneficiaries on a reasonably equivalent basis, (B) are not made available to highly compensated employees (within the meaning of section 414(q) of the Internal Revenue Code of 1986) in an amount greater than the amount made available to other employees, (C) are made in accordance with specific provisions regarding such loans set forth in the plan, (D) bear a reasonable rate of interest, and (E) are adequately secured. A loan made by a plan shall not fail to meet the requirements of the preceding sentence by reason of a loan repayment suspension described under section 414(u)(4) of the Internal Revenue Code of 1986.

(2) Contracting or making reasonable arrangements with a party in interest for office space, or legal, accounting, or other services necessary for the establishment or operation of the plan, if no more than reasonable compensation is paid therefor.

(3) A loan to an employee stock ownership plan (as defined in section 407(d)(6) [29 USC §1107(d)(6)]), if—

(A) such loan is primarily for the benefit of participants and beneficiaries of the plan, and

(B) such loan is at an interest rate which is not in excess of a reasonable rate.

If the plan gives collateral to a party in interest for such loan, such collateral may consist only of qualifying employer securities (as defined in section 407(d)(5) [29 USC §1107(d)(5)]).

(4) The investment of all or part of a plan's assets in deposits which bear a reasonable interest rate in a bank or similar financial institution supervised by the United States or a State, if such bank or other institution is a fiduciary of such plan and if—

(A) the plan covers only employees of such bank or other institution and employees of affiliates of such bank or other institution, or

(B) such investment is expressly authorized by a provision of the plan or by a fiduciary (other than such bank or institution or affiliate thereof) who is expressly empowered by the plan to so instruct the trustee with respect to such investment.

(5) Any contract for life insurance, health insurance, or annuities with one or more insurers which are qualified to do business in a State, if the plan pays no more than adequate consideration, and if each such insurer or insurers is—

(A) the employer maintaining the plan, or

(B) a party in interest which is wholly owned (directly or indirectly) by the employer maintaining the plan, or by any person which is a party in interest with respect to the plan, but only if the total premiums and annuity considerations written by such insurers for life insurance, health insurance, or annuities for all plans (and their employers) with respect to which such insurers are parties in interest (not including premiums or annuity considerations written by the employer maintaining the plan) do not exceed 5 percent of the total premiums and annuity considerations written for all lines of insurance in that year by such insurers (not including premiums or annuity considerations written by the employer maintaining the plan).

(6) The providing of any ancillary service by a bank or similar financial institution supervised by the United States or a State, if such bank or other institution is a fiduciary of such plan, and if—

(A) such bank or similar financial institution has adopted adequate internal safeguards which assure that the providing of such ancillary service is consistent with sound banking and financial practice, as determined by Federal or State supervisory authority, and

(B) the extent to which such ancillary service is provided is subject to specific guidelines issued by such bank or similar financial institution (as determined by the Secretary after consultation with Federal and State supervisory authority), and adherence to such guidelines would reasonably preclude such bank or similar financial institution from providing such ancillary service (i) in an excessive or unreasonable manner, and (ii) in a manner that would be inconsistent with the best interests of participants and beneficiaries of employee benefit plans.

Such ancillary services shall not be provided at more than reasonable compensation.

(7) The exercise of a privilege to convert securities, to the extent provided in regulations of the Secretary, but only if the plan receives no less than adequate consideration pursuant to such conversion.

(8) Any transaction between a plan and (i) a common or collective trust fund or pooled investment fund maintained by a party in interest which is a bank or trust company supervised by a State or Federal agency or (ii) a pooled investment fund of an insurance company qualified to do business in a State, if—

(A) the transaction is a sale or purchase of an interest in the fund,

(B) the bank, trust company, or insurance company receives not more than reasonable compensation, and

(C) such transaction is expressly permitted by the instrument under which the plan is maintained, or by a fiduciary (other than the bank, trust company, or insurance company. or an affiliate thereof) who has authority to manage and control the assets of the plan.

(9) The making by a fiduciary of a distribution of the assets of the plan in accordance with the terms of the plan if such assets are distributed in the same manner as provided under section 4044 of this Act [29 USC §1344] (relating to allocation of assets).

(10) Any transaction required or permitted under part 1 of subtitle E of title IV [29 USC §§1381 *et seq.*].

(11) A merger of multiemployer plans, or the transfer of assets or liabilities between multiemployer plans, determined by the Pension Benefit Guaranty Corporation to meet the requirements of section 4231 [29 USC §1411].

(12) The sale by a plan to a party in interest on or after December 18, 1987, or any stock, if—

(A) the requirements of paragraphs (1) and (2) of subsection (e) are met with respect to such stock,

(B) on the later of the date on which the stock was acquired by the plan, or January 1, 1975, such stock constituted a qualifying employer security (as defined in section 407(d)(5) [29 USC §1107(d)(5)] as then in effect), and

(C) such stock does not constitute a qualifying employer security (as defined in section 407(d)(5) [29 USC §1107(d)(5)] as in effect at the time of the sale).

(13) Any transfer made before [1]*January 1, 2022,* of excess pension assets from a defined benefit plan to a retiree health account in a qualified transfer permitted under section 420 of title 26 (as in effect on the date of the enactment of the [2]*MAP-21*).

(14) Any transaction in connection with the provision of investment advice described in section 3(21)(A)(ii) to a participant or beneficiary of an individual account plan that permits such participant or beneficiary to direct the investment of assets in their individual account, if—

(A) the transaction is—

(i) the provision of the investment advice to the participant or beneficiary of the plan with respect to a security or other property available as an investment under the plan,

(ii) the acquisition, holding, or sale of a security or other property available as an investment under the plan pursuant to the investment advice, or

(iii) the direct or indirect receipt of fees or other compensation by the fiduciary adviser or an affiliate thereof (or any employee, agent, or registered representative of the fiduciary adviser or affiliate) in connection with the provision of the advice or in connection with an acquisition, holding, or sale of a security or other property available as an investment under the plan pursuant to the investment advice; and

(B) the requirements of subsection (g) are met.

(15) (A) Any transaction involving the purchase or sale of securities, or other property (as determined by the Secretary), between a plan and a party in interest (other than a fiduciary described in section 3(21)(A)) with respect to a plan if—

(i) the transaction involves a block trade,

(ii) at the time of the transaction, the interest of the plan (together with the interests of any other plans maintained by the same plan sponsor), does not exceed 10 percent of the aggregate size of the block trade,

(iii) the terms of the transaction, including the price, are at least as favorable to the plan as an arm's length transaction, and

(iv) the compensation associated with the purchase and sale is not greater than the compensation associated with an arm's length transaction with an unrelated party.

(B) For purposes of this paragraph, the term "block trade" means any trade of at least 10,000 shares or with a market value of at least $200,000 which will be allocated across two or more unrelated client accounts of a fiduciary.

(16) Any transaction involving the purchase or sale of securities, or other property (as determined by the Secretary), between a plan and a party in interest if—

(A) the transaction is executed through an electronic communication network, alternative trading system, or similar execution system or trading venue subject to regulation and oversight by—

(i) the applicable Federal regulating entity, or

(ii) such foreign regulatory entity as the Secretary may determine by regulation,

(B) either—

(i) the transaction is effected pursuant to rules designed to match purchases and sales at the best price available through the execution system in accordance with applicable rules of the Securities and Exchange Commission or other relevant governmental authority, or

(ii) neither the execution system nor the parties to the transaction take into account the identity of the parties in the execution of trades,

(C) the price and compensation associated with the purchase and sale are not greater than the price and compensation associated with an arm's length transaction with an unrelated party,

(D) if the party in interest has an ownership interest in the system or venue described in subparagraph (A), the system or venue has been authorized by the plan sponsor or other independent fiduciary for transactions described in this paragraph, and

(E) not less than 30 days prior to the initial transaction described in this paragraph executed through any system or venue described in subparagraph (A), a plan fiduciary is provided written or electronic notice of the execution of such transaction through such system or venue.

(17) (A) Transactions described in subparagraphs (A), (B), and (D) of section 406(a)(1) between a plan and a person that is a party in interest other than a fiduciary (or an affiliate) who has or exercises any discretionary authority or control with respect to the investment of the plan assets involved in the transaction or renders investment advice (within the meaning of section 3(21)(A)(ii)) with respect to those assets, solely by reason of providing services to the plan or solely by reason of a relationship to such a service provider described in subparagraph (F), (G), (H), or (I) of section 3(14), or both, but only if in connection with such transaction the plan receives no less, nor pays no more, than adequate consideration.

(B) For purposes of this paragraph, the term "adequate consideration" means—

(i) in the case of a security for which there is a generally recognized market—

(I) the price of the security prevailing on a national securities exchange which is registered under section 6 of the Securities Exchange Act of 1934, taking into account factors such as the size of the transaction and marketability of the security, or

(II) if the security is not traded on such a national securities exchange, a price not less favorable to the plan than the offering price for the security as established by the current bid and asked prices quoted by persons independent of the issuer and of the party in interest, taking into account factors such as the size of the transaction and marketability of the security, and

(ii) in the case of an asset other than a security for which there is a generally recognized market, the fair market value of the asset as determined in good faith by a fiduciary or fiduciaries in accordance with regulations prescribed by the Secretary.

(18) Foreign exchange transactions. Any foreign exchange transactions, between a bank or broker-dealer (or any affiliate of either), and a plan (as defined in section 3(3)) with respect to which such bank or broker-dealer (or affiliate) is a trustee, custodian, fiduciary, or other party in interest, if—

(A) the transaction is in connection with the purchase, holding, or sale of securities or other investment assets (other than a foreign exchange transaction unrelated to any other investment in securities or other investment assets),

(B) at the time the foreign exchange transaction is entered into, the terms of the transaction are not less favorable to the plan than the terms generally available in comparable arm's length foreign exchange transactions between unrelated parties, or the terms afforded by the bank or broker-dealer (or any affiliate of either) in comparable arm's-length foreign exchange transactions involving unrelated parties,

(C) the exchange rate used by such bank or broker-dealer (or affiliate) for a particular foreign exchange transaction does not deviate by more than 3 percent from the interbank bid and asked rates for transactions of comparable size and maturity at the time of the transaction as displayed on an independent service that reports rates of exchange in the foreign currency market for such currency, and

(D) the bank or broker-dealer (or any affiliate of either) does not have investment discretion, or provide investment advice, with respect to the transaction.

(19) Cross trading. Any transaction described in sections 406(a)(1)(A) and 406(b)(2) involving the purchase and sale of a security between a plan and any other account managed by the same investment manager, if—

(A) the transaction is a purchase or sale, for no consideration other than cash payment against prompt delivery of a security for which market quotations are readily available,

(B) the transaction is effected at the independent current market price of the security (within the meaning of section 270.17a-7(b) of title 17, Code of Federal Regulations),

(C) no brokerage commission, fee (except for customary transfer fees, the fact of which is disclosed pursuant to subparagraph (D)), or other remuneration is paid in connection with the transaction,

(D) a fiduciary (other than the investment manager engaging in the cross-trades or any affiliate) for each plan participating in the transaction authorizes in advance of any crosstrades (in a document that is separate from any other written agreement of the parties) the investment manager to engage in cross trades at the investment manager's discretion, after such fiduciary has received disclosure regarding the conditions under which cross trades may take place (but only if such disclosure is separate from any other agreement or disclosure involving the asset management relationship), including the written policies and procedures of the investment manager described in subparagraph (H),

(E) each plan participating in the transaction has assets of at least $100,000,000, except that if the assets of a plan are invested in a master trust containing the assets of plans maintained by employers in the same controlled group (as defined in section 407(d)(7)), the master trust has assets of at least $100,000,000,

(F) the investment manager provides to the plan fiduciary who authorized cross trading under subparagraph (D) a quarterly report detailing all cross trades executed by the investment manager in which the plan participated during such quarter, including the following information, as applicable: (i) the identity of each security bought or sold; (ii) the number of shares or units traded, (iii) the parties involved in the cross-trade; and (iv) trade price and the method used to establish the trade price,

(G) the investment manager does not base its fee schedule on the plan's consent to cross trading, and no other service (other than the investment opportunities and cost savings available through a cross trade) is conditioned on the plan's consent to cross trading,

(H) the investment manager has adopted, and cross-trades are effected in accordance with, written cross-trading policies and procedures that are fair and equitable to all accounts participating in the cross-trading program, and that include a description of the manager's pricing policies and procedures, and the manager's policies and procedures for allocating cross trades in an objective manner among accounts participating in the cross-trading program, and

(I) the investment manager has designated an individual responsible for periodically reviewing such purchases and sales to ensure compliance with the written policies and procedures described in subparagraph (H), and following such review, the individual shall issue an annual written report no later than 90 days following the period to which it relates signed under penalty of perjury to the plan fiduciary who authorized cross trading under subparagraph (D) describing the steps performed during the course of the review, the level of compliance, and any specific instances of non-compliance.

The written report under subparagraph (I) shall also notify the plan fiduciary of the plan's right to terminate participation in the investment manager's cross-trading program at any time.

(20) (A) Except as provided in subparagraphs (B) and (C), a transaction described in section 406(a) in connection with the acquisition, holding, or disposition of any security or commodity, if the transaction is corrected before the end of the correction period.

(B) Subparagraph (A) does not apply to any transaction between a plan and a plan sponsor or its affiliates that involves the acquisition or sale of an employer security (as defined in section 407(d)(1)) or the acquisition, sale, or lease of employer real property (as defined in section 407(d)(2)).

(C) In the case of any fiduciary or other party in interest (or any other person knowingly participating in such transaction), subparagraph (A) does not apply to any transaction if, at the time the transaction occurs, such fiduciary or party in interest (or other person) knew (or reasonably should have known) that the transaction would (without regard to this paragraph) constitute a violation of section 406(a).

(D) For purposes of this paragraph, the term "correction period" means, in connection with a fiduciary or party in interest (or other person knowingly participating in the transaction), the 14-day period beginning on the date on which such fiduciary or party in interest (or other person) discovers, or reasonably should have discovered, that the transaction would (without regard to this paragraph) constitute a violation of section 406(a).

(E) For purposes of this paragraph—

(i) The term "security" has the meaning given such term by section 475(c)(2) of the Internal Revenue Code of 1986 (without regard to subparagraph (F)(iii) and the last sentence thereof).

(ii) The term "commodity" has the meaning given such term by section 475(e)(2) of such Code (without regard to subparagraph (D)(iii) thereof).

(iii) The term "correct" means, with respect to a transaction—

(I) to undo the transaction to the extent possible and in any case to make good to the plan or affected account any losses resulting from the transaction, and

(II) to restore to the plan or affected account any profits made through the use of assets of the plan.

* * * * * * * * * * * *

[For Analysis, see ¶ 1703. For Committee Reports, see ¶ 5405.]

[Endnote ERISA §t29_1108]

29 USC §1108(b)(13), (c)(1) [ERISA Sec. 408] was amended by Sec. 40241(b)(1)-(2) of the Moving Ahead for Progress in the 21st Century Act, P.L. 112-141, 7/6/2012, as detailed below:
  1. Sec. 40241(b)(2) substituted 'January 1, 2022' for 'January 1, 2014' in para. (b)(13)
  2. Sec. 40241(b)(1) substituted 'MAP-21' for 'Pension Protection Act of 2006' in para. (c)(1)
Effective Date (Sec. 40241(c), P.L. 112-141, 7/6/2012) effective 7/6/2012.

[¶ 3506]
ERISA §602. [29 USC 1162] Continuation coverage.
For purposes of section 601 [29 USC §1161], the term "continuation coverage" means coverage under the plan which meets the following requirements:

  (1) Type of benefit coverage. The coverage must consist of coverage which, as of the time the coverage is being provided, is identical to the coverage provided under the plan to similarly situated beneficiaries under the plan with respect to whom a qualifying event has not occurred. If coverage is modified under the plan for any group of similarly situated beneficiaries, such coverage shall also be modified in the same manner for all individuals who are qualified beneficiaries under the plan pursuant to this part [29 USC §§1161 et seq.] in connection with such group.

  (2) Period of coverage. The coverage must extend for at least the period beginning on the date of the qualifying event and ending not earlier than the earliest of the following:

    (A) Maximum required period.

      (i) General rule for terminations and reduced hours. In the case of a qualifying event described in section 603(2) [29 USC §1163(2)], except as provided in clause (ii), the date which is 18 months after the date of the qualifying event.

      (ii) Special rule for multiple qualifying events. If a qualifying event (other than a qualifying event described in section 603(6) [29 USC §1163(6)] occurs during the 18 months after the date of a qualifying event described in section 603(2) [29 USC §1163(2)], the date which is 36 months after the date of the qualifying event described in section 603(2) [29 USC §1163(2)].

      (iii) Special rule for certain bankruptcy proceedings. In the case of a qualifying event described in section 603(6) [29 USC §1163(6)] (relating to bankruptcy proceedings), the date of the death of the covered employee or qualified beneficiary (described in section 607(3)(C)(iii) [29 USC §1167(3)(C)(iii)]), or in the case of the surviving spouse or dependent children of the covered employee, 36 months after the date of the death of the covered employee.

      (iv) General rule for other qualifying events. In the case of a qualifying event not described in section 603(2) or 603(6) [29 USC §1163(2) or (6)], the date which is 36 months after the date of the qualifying event.

      (v) Special rule for PBGC recipients. In the case of a qualifying event described in section 603(2) with respect to a covered employee who (as of such qualifying event) has a nonforfeitable right to a benefit any portion of which is to be paid by the Pension Benefit Guaranty Corporation under title IV, notwithstanding clause (i) or (ii), the date of the death of the covered employee, or in the case of the surviving spouse or dependent children of the covered employee, 24 months after the date of the death of the covered employee. The preceding sentence shall not require any period of coverage to extend beyond ¹*January 1, 2014.*

      (vi) Special rule for TAA-eligible individuals. In the case of a qualifying event described in section 603(2) with respect to a covered employee who is (as of the date that the period of coverage would, but for this clause or clause (vii), otherwise terminate under clause (i) or (ii)) a TAA-eligible individual (as defined in section 605(b)(4)(B)), the period of coverage shall not terminate by reason of clause (i) or (ii), as the case may be, before the later of the date specified in such clause or the date on which such individual ceases to be such a TAA-eligible individual. The preceding sentence shall not require any period of coverage to extend beyond ²*January 1, 2014.*

(vii) Medicare entitlement followed by qualifying event. In the case of a qualifying event described in section 603(2) [29 USC §1163(2)] that occurs less than 18 months after the date the covered employee became entitled to benefits under title XVIII of the Social Security Act [42 USC §§1395 *et seq.*], the period of coverage for qualified beneficiaries other than the covered employee shall not terminate under this subparagraph before the close of the 36-month period beginning on the date the covered employee became so entitled.

(viii) Special rule for disability. In the case of a qualified beneficiary who is determined, under title II [29 USC §§401 *et seq.*] or XVI of the Social Security Act [42 USC §§1381 *et seq.*], to have been disabled at any time during the first 60 days of continuation coverage under this part, any reference in clause (i) or (ii) to 18 months is deemed a reference to 29 months (with respect to all qualified beneficiaries), but only if the qualified beneficiary has provided notice of such determination under section 606(3) [29 USC §1166(3)] before the end of such 18 months.

(B) End of plan. The date on which the employer ceases to provide any group health plan to any employee.

(C) Failure to pay premium. The date on which coverage ceases under the plan by reason of a failure to make timely payment of any premium required under the plan with respect to the qualified beneficiary. The payment of any premium (other than any payment referred to in the last sentence of paragraph (3)) shall be considered to be timely if made within 30 days after the date due or within such longer period as applies to or under the plan.

(D) Group health plan coverage or Medicare entitlement. The date on which the qualified beneficiary first becomes, after the date of the election—

(i) covered under any other group health plan (as an employee or otherwise) which does not contain any exclusion or limitation with respect to any preexisting condition of such beneficiary (other than such an exclusion or limitation which does not apply to (or is satisfied by) such beneficiary by reason of chapter 100 of the Internal Revenue Code of 1986 [26 USC §§9801 *et seq.*], part 7 of this subtitle [29 USC §§1181 *et seq.*], or title XXVII of the Public Health Service Act) [42 USC §§300gg *et seq.*], or

(ii) in the case of a qualified beneficiary other than a qualified beneficiary described in section 607(3)(C) [29 USC §1167(3)(C)], entitled to benefits under title XVIII of the Social Security Act [42 USC §§1395 *et seq.*].

(E) Termination of extended coverage for disability. In the case of a qualified beneficiary who is disabled at any time during the first 60 days of continuation coverage under this part [29 USC §§1161 *et seq.*], the month that begins more than 30 days after the date of the final determination under title II [29 USC §401 *et seq.*] or XVI of the Social Security Act [42 USC §1381 *et seq.*] that the qualified beneficiary is no longer disabled.

* * * * * * * * * * * *

[For Analysis, see ¶ 1612.]

[Endnote ERISA §t29_1162]
29 USC §1162(2)(A)(v)-(vi) [ERISA Sec. 602] was amended by Sec. 243(a)(1)-(2) of the Trade Adjustment Assistance Extension Act of 2011, P.L. 112-40, 10/21/2011, as detailed below:
1. Sec. 243(a)(1) substituted "January 1, 2014" for "February 12, 2011" in clause (2)(A)(v)
2. Sec. 243(a)(2) substituted "January 1, 2014" for "February 12, 2011" in clause (2)(A)(vi)
Effective Date (Sec. 243(b) P.L. 112-40, 10/21/2011) effective for periods of coverage which would (without regard to the amendments made by this section) end on or after 11/20/2011.

[¶ 3507]
ERISA §701. [29 USC 1181] Increased portability through limitation on preexisting condition exclusions.

* * * * * * * * * * * *

(c) Rules relating to crediting previous coverage.

(1) Creditable coverage defined. For purposes of this part, the term "creditable coverage" means, with respect to an individual, coverage of the individual under any of the following:

(A) A group health plan.

(B) Health insurance coverage.

(C) Part A [42 USC §§1395c *et seq.*] or part B [42 USC §§1395j *et seq.*] of title XVIII of the Social Security Act.

(D) Title XIX of the Social Security Act [42 USC §§1396 *et seq.*], other than coverage consisting solely of benefits under section 1928.

(E) Chapter 55 of title 10, United States Code [10 USC §§1071 *et seq.*]..

(F) A medical care program of the Indian Health Service or of a tribal organization.

(G) A State health benefits risk pool.

(H) A health plan offered under chapter 89 of title 5, United States Code [5 USC §§8901 *et seq.*].

(I) A public health plan (as defined in regulations).

(J) A health benefit plan under section 5(e) of the Peace Corps Act (22 USC 2504(e)).

Such term does not include coverage consisting solely of coverage of excepted benefits (as defined in section 733(c) [29 USC §1191b(c)]).

(2) Not counting periods before significant breaks in coverage.

(A) In general. A period of creditable coverage shall not be counted, with respect to enrollment of an individual under a group health plan, if, after such period and before the enrollment date, there was a 63-day period during all of which the individual was not covered under any creditable coverage.

(B) Waiting period not treated as a break in coverage. For purposes of subparagraph (A) and subsection (d)(4), any period that an individual is in a waiting period for any coverage under a group health plan (or for group health insurance coverage) or is in an affiliation period (as defined in subsection (g)(2)) shall not be taken into account in determining the continuous period under subparagraph (A).

(C) TAA-eligible individuals. In the case of plan years beginning before [1]*January 1, 2014—*

(i) TAA pre-certification period rule. In the case of a TAA-eligible individual, the period beginning on the date the individual has a TAA-related loss of coverage and ending on the date that is 7 days after the date of the issuance by the Secretary (or by any person or entity designated by the Secretary) of a qualified health insurance costs credit eligibility certificate for such individual for purposes of section 7527 of the Internal Revenue Code of 1986 shall not be taken into account in determining the continuous period under subparagraph (A).

(ii) Definitions. The terms "TAA eligible individual" and "TAA-related loss of coverage" have the meanings given such terms in section 605(b)(4).

(3) Method of crediting coverage.

(A) Standard method. Except as otherwise provided under subparagraph (B), for purposes of applying subsection (a)(3), a group health plan, and a health insurance issuer offering group health insurance coverage, shall count a period of creditable coverage without regard to the specific benefits covered during the period.

(B) Election of alternative method. A group health plan, or a health insurance issuer offering group health insurance coverage, may elect to apply subsection (a)(3) based on coverage of benefits within each of several classes or categories of benefits specified in regulations rather than as provided under subparagraph (A). Such election shall be made on a uniform basis for all participants and beneficiaries. Under such election a group health plan or issuer shall count a period of creditable coverage with respect to any class or category of benefits if any level of benefits is covered within such class or category.

(C) Plan notice. In the case of an election with respect to a group health plan under subparagraph (B) (whether or not health insurance coverage is provided in connection with such plan), the plan shall—

(i) prominently state in any disclosure statements concerning the plan, and state to each enrollee at the time of enrollment under the plan, that the plan has made such election, and

(ii) include in such statements a description of the effect of this election.

(4) Establishment of period. Periods of creditable coverage with respect to an individual shall be established through presentation of certifications described in subsection (e) or in such other manner as may be specified in regulations.

* * * * * * * * * * * *

[For Analysis, see ¶ 1611.]

[Endnote ERISA §t29_1181]
29 USC §1181(c)(2)(C) [ERISA Sec. 701] was amended by Sec. 242(a)(2) of the Trade Adjustment Assistance Extension Act of 2011, P.L. 112-40, 10/21/2011, as detailed below:
1. Sec. 242(a)(2) substituted "January 1, 2014" for "February 13, 2011" in subpara. (c)(2)(C)
Effective Date (Sec. 242(b)(1) P.L. 112-40, 10/21/2011) effective for plan yrs. begin. after 2/12/2011.Sec. 242(b)(2) of this Act, reads as follows:
"(2) Transitional rules.
"(A) Benefit determinations. Notwithstanding the amendments made by this section (and the provisions of law amended thereby), a plan shall not be required to modify benefit determinations for the period beginning on February 13, 2011, and ending 30 days after the date of the enactment of this Act, but a plan shall not fail to be qualified health insurance within the meaning of section 35(e) of the Internal Revenue Code of 1986 during this period merely due to such failure to modify benefit determinations.
"(B) Guidance concerning periods before 30 days after enactment. Except as provided in subparagraph (A), the Secretary of the Treasury (or his designee), in consultation with the Secretary of Health and Human Services and the Secretary of Labor, may issue regulations or other guidance regarding the scope of the application of the amendments made by this section to periods before the date which is 30 days after the date of the enactment of this Act.
"(C) Special rule relating to certain loss of coverage. In the case of a TAA-related loss of coverage (as defined in section 4980B(f)(5)(C)(iv) of the Internal Revenue Code of 1986) that occurs during the period beginning on February 13, 2011, and ending 30 days after the date of the enactment of this Act, the 7-day period described in section 9801(c)(2)(D) of the Internal Revenue Code of 1986, section 701(c)(2)(C) of the Employee Retirement Income Security Act of 1974, and section 2701(c)(2)(C) of the Public Health Service Act shall be extended until 30 days after such date of enactment."

[¶ 3508]
ERISA §4002. [29 USC 1302] Pension Benefit Guaranty Corporation.

* * * * * * * * * * * *

[1]*(c) The Director shall be accountable to the board of directors. The Director shall serve for a term of 5 years unless removed by the President or the board of directors before the expiration of such 5-year term.*

(d) Board of directors; compensation; reimbursement for expenses.

[2]*(1) The board of directors* of the corporation consists of the Secretary of the Treasury, the Secretary of Labor, and the Secretary of Commerce. Members of the board shall serve without compensation, but shall be reimbursed for travel, subsistence, and other necessary expenses incurred in the performance of their duties as members of the board. The Secretary of Labor is the chairman of the board of directors.

[3]*(2) A majority of the members of the board of directors in office shall constitute a quorum for the transaction of business. The vote of the majority of the members present and voting at a meeting at which a quorum is present shall be the act of the board of directors.*

(3) Each member of the board of directors shall designate in writing an official, not below the level of Assistant Secretary, to serve as the voting representative of such member on the board. Such designation shall be effective until revoked or until a date or event specified therein. Any such representative may refer for board action any matter under con-

sideration by the designating board member, but such representative shall not count toward establishment of a quorum as described under paragraph (2).

(4) The Inspector General of the corporation shall report to the board of directors, and not less than twice a year, shall attend a meeting of the board of directors to provide a report on the activities and findings of the Inspector General, including with respect to monitoring and review of the operations of the corporation.

(5) The General Counsel of the corporation shall—

(A) serve as the secretary to the board of directors, and advise such board as needed; and

(B) have overall responsibility for all legal matters affecting the corporation and provide the corporation with legal advice and opinions on all matters of law affecting the corporation, except that the authority of the General Counsel shall not extend to the Office of Inspector General and the independent legal counsel of such Office.

(6) Notwithstanding any other provision of this Act, the Office of Inspector General and the legal counsel of such Office are independent of the management of the corporation and the General Counsel of the corporation.

(7) The board of directors may appoint and fix the compensation of employees as may be required to enable the board of directors to perform its duties. The board of directors shall determine the qualifications and duties of such employees and may appoint and fix the compensation of experts and consultants in accordance with the provisions of section 3109 of title 5, United States Code.

(e) Meetings.

[4](1) The board of directors shall meet at the call of its chairman, or as otherwise provided by the bylaws of [5]the corporation, but in no case less than 4 times a year with not fewer than 2 members present. Not less than 1 meeting of the board of directors during each year shall be a joint meeting with the advisory committee under subsection (h).

[6](2) (A) Except as provided in subparagraph (B), the chairman of the board of directors shall make available to the public the minutes from each meeting of the board of directors.

(B) The minutes of a meeting of the board of directors, or a portion thereof, shall not be subject to disclosure under subparagraph (A) if the chairman reasonably determines that such minutes, or portion thereof, contain confidential employer information including information obtained under section 4010, information about the investment activities of the corporation, or information regarding personnel decisions of the corporation.

(C) The minutes of a meeting, or portion of thereof, exempt from disclosure pursuant to subparagraph (B) shall be exempt from disclosure under section 552(b) of title 5, United States Code. For purposes of such section 552, this subparagraph shall be considered a statute described in subsection (b)(3) of such section 552.

(f) Adoption of bylaws; amendment; alteration; publication in the Federal Register. As soon as practicable, but not later than 180 days after the date of enactment of this Act [enacted Sept. 2, 1974], the board of directors shall adopt initial bylaws and rules relating to the conduct of the business of the corporation. Thereafter, the board of directors may alter, supplement, or repeal any existing bylaw or rule, and may adopt additional bylaws and rules from time to time as may be necessary. The chairman of the board shall cause a copy of the bylaws of the corporation to be published in the Federal Register not less often than once each year.

(g) Exemption from taxation.

(1) The corporation, its property, its franchise, capital, reserves, surplus, and its income (including, but not limited to, any income of any fund established under section 4005 [29 USC §1305]), shall be exempt from all taxation now or hereafter imposed by the United States (other than taxes imposed under chapter 21 of the Internal Revenue Code of 1986, relating to Federal Insurance Contributions Act [26 USC §§3101 et seq.], and chapter 23 of such Code, relating to Federal Unemployment Tax Act [26 USC §§3301 et seq.]), or by any State or local taxing authority, except that any real property and any tangible personal property (other than cash and securities) of the corporation shall be subject to State and lo-

cal taxation to the same extent according to its value as other real and tangible personal property is taxed.

(2) The receipts and disbursements of the corporation in the discharge of its functions shall be included in the totals of the budget of the United States Government. The United States is not liable for any obligation or liability incurred by the corporation.

(3) [Omitted]

(h) Advisory committee to corporation.

(1) There is established an advisory committee to the corporation, for the purpose of advising the corporation as to its policies and procedures relating to (A) the appointment of trustees in termination proceedings, (B) investment of moneys, (C) whether plans being terminated should be liquidated immediately or continued in operation under a trustee[7], *(D) such other issues as the corporation may request from* [8]*time to time, and (E) other issues as determined appropriate by the advisory committee.* The advisory committee may also recommend persons for appointment as trustees in termination proceedings, make recommendations with respect to the investment of moneys in the funds, and advise the corporation as to whether a plan subject to being terminated should be liquidated immediately or continued in operation under a trustee. [9]*In the event of a vacancy or impending vacancy in the office of the Participant and Plan Sponsor Advocate established under section 4004, the Advisory Committee shall, in consultation with the Director of the corporation and participant and plan sponsor advocacy groups, nominate at least two but no more than three individuals to serve as the Participant and Plan Sponsor Advocate.*

(2) The advisory committee consists of seven members appointed, from among individuals recommended by the board of directors, by the President. Of the seven members, two shall represent the interests of employee organizations, two shall represent the interests of employers who maintain pension plans, and three shall represent the interests of the general public. The President shall designate one member as chairman at the time of the appointment of that member.

(3) Members shall serve for terms of 3 years each, except that, of the members first appointed, one of the members representing the interests of employee organizations, one of the members representing the interests of employers, and one of the members representing the interests of the general public shall be appointed for terms of 2 years each, one of the members representing the interests of the general public shall be appointed for a term of 1 year, and the other members shall be appointed to full 3-year terms. The advisory committee shall meet at least six times each year and at such other times as may be determined by the chairman or requested by any three members of the advisory committee. [10]*Not less than 1 meeting of the advisory committee during each year shall be a joint meeting with the board of directors under subsection (e).*

(4) Members shall be chosen on the basis of their experience with employee organizations, with employers who maintain pension plans, with the administration of pension plans, or otherwise on account of outstanding demonstrated ability in related fields. Of the members serving on the advisory committee at any time, no more than four shall be affiliated with the same political party.

(5) An individual appointed to fill a vacancy occurring other than by the expiration of a term of office shall be appointed only for the unexpired term of the member he succeeds. Any vacancy occurring in the office of a member of the advisory committee shall be filled in the manner in which that office was originally filled.

(6) The advisory committee shall appoint and fix the compensation of such employees as it determines necessary to discharge its duties, including experts and consultants in accordance with the provisions of section 3109 of title 5, United States Code [5 USC §3109]. The corporation shall furnish to the advisory committee such professional, secretarial, and other services as the committee may request.

(7) Members of the advisory committee shall, for each day (including traveltime) during which they are attending meetings or conferences of the committee or otherwise engaged in the business of the committee, be compensated at a rate fixed by the corporation which is not in excess of the daily equivalent of the annual rate of basic pay in effect for grade

GS-18 of the General Schedule [5 USC §5332], and while away from their homes or regular places of business they may be allowed travel expenses, including per diem in lieu of subsistence, as authorized by section 5703 of title 5, United States Code [5 USC §5703].

(8) The Federal Advisory Committee Act [5 USC Appx. §§1 *et seq.*] does not apply to the advisory committee established by this subsection.

(i) Special rules regarding disasters, etc. In the case of a pension or other employee benefit plan, or any sponsor, administrator, participant, beneficiary, or other person with respect to such plan, affected by a Presidentially declared disaster (as defined in section 1033(h)(3) of the Internal Revenue Code of 1986) or a terroristic or military action (as defined in section 692(c)(2) of such Code), the corporation may, notwithstanding any other provision of law, prescribe, by notice or otherwise, a period of up to 1 year which may be disregarded in determining the date by which any action is required or permitted to be completed under this Act. No plan shall be treated as failing to be operated in accordance with the terms of the plan solely as the result of disregarding any period by reason of the preceding sentence.

[11]*(j)* **Conflicts of interest.**

(1) **In general.** *The Director of the corporation and each member of the board of directors shall not participate in a decision of the corporation in which the Director or such member has a direct financial interest. The Director of the corporation shall not participate in any activities that would present a potential conflict of interest or appearance of a conflict of interest without approval of the board of directors.*

(2) **Establishment of policy.** *The board of directors shall establish a policy that will inform the identification of potential conflicts of interests of the members of the board of directors and mitigate perceived conflicts of interest of such members and the Director of the corporation.*

[12]*(k)* **Risk management officer.** *The corporation shall have a risk management officer whose duties include evaluating and mitigating the risk that the corporation might experience. The individual in such position shall coordinate the risk management efforts of the corporation, explain risks and controls to senior management and the board of directors of the corporation, and make recommendations.*

[For Analysis, see ¶ 1709, ¶ 1710, ¶ 1711 and ¶ 1712. For Committee Reports, see ¶ 5402.]

[Endnote ERISA §t29_1302]

29 USC §1302(c), (d), (e)(1)-(2) and (h)(1) [ERISA Sec. 4002] was amended by Sec. 40231(a)(1)-(3)(A)(ii) of the Moving Ahead for Progress in the 21st Century Act, P.L. 112-141, 7/6/2012, as detailed below:

1. Sec. 40231(d) added subsec. (c)

2. Sec. 40231(a)(1)(A) substituted '(d)(1) The board of directors' for '(d) The board of directors' in subsec. (d) [Ed. Note: We believe that the intention of Congress was to have the amendment read 'substituted "(d) Board of directors; compensation; reimbursement for expenses. (1) The board of directors" for "(d) Board of directors; compensation; reimbursement for expenses. The board of directors" in subsec. (d)';

3. Sec. 40231(a)(1)(B) added paras. (d)(2)-(7)

4. Sec. 40231(a)(2)(A) substituted '(1) The board' for 'The board' in subsec. (e)

5. Sec. 40231(a)(2)(B) substituted 'the corporation, but in no case less than 4 times a year with not fewer than 2 members present. Not less than 1 meeting of the board of directors during each year shall be a joint meeting with the advisory committee under subsection (h).' for 'the corporation.' in para. (e)(1) [as redesignated by Sec. 40231(a)(2)(A) of this Act, see above];

6. Sec. 40231(a)(2)(C) added para. (e)(2)

7. Sec. 40231(a)(3)(A)(i) substituted ', (D)' for ', and (D)' in para. (h)(1)

8. Sec. 40231(a)(3)(A)(ii) substituted 'time to time, and (E) other issues as determined appropriate by the advisory committee.' for 'time to time.' in para. (h)(1)

Effective Date Effective 7/6/2012

---

29 USC §1302(h)(1) [ERISA Sec. 4002] was amended by Sec. 40232(b), P.L. 112-141, 7/6/2012, as detailed below:

9. Sec. 40232(b) added the sentence at the end of para. (h)(1)

Effective Date Effective 7/6/2012.

---

29 USC §1302(h)(3), (j) and (k) [ERISA Sec. 4002] were amended by Sec. 40231(a)(3)(B), (b), (c), P.L. 112-141, 7/6/2012, as detailed below:

10. Sec. 40231(a)(3)(B) added the sentence at the end of para. (h)(3)

11. Sec. 40231(b) added subsec. (j)

12. Sec. 40231(c) added subsec. (k)

Effective Date Effective 7/6/2012. Sec. 40231(e) of this Act, provides:

"(e) Senses of Congress.

"(1) Formation of committees. It is the sense of Congress that the board of directors of the Pension Benefit Guaranty Corporation established under section 4002 of the Employee Retirement Income Security Act of 1974 (29 U.S.C. 1302), as amended by this section, should form committees, including an audit committee and an investment committee composed of not less than 2 members, to enhance the overall effectiveness of the board of directors.

"(2) Advisory committee. It is the sense of Congress that the advisory committee to the Pension Benefit Guaranty Corporation established under section 4002 of the Employee Retirement Income Security Act of 1974 (29 U.S.C. 1302), as amended by this section, should provide to the board of directors of such corporation policy recommendations regarding changes to the law that would be beneficial to the corporation or the voluntary private pension system."

[¶ 3509]

ERISA §4004. [29 USC 1304] Participant and plan sponsor advocate.

(a) **In general.** The board of directors of the corporation shall select a Participant and Plan Sponsor Advocate from the candidates nominated by the advisory committee to the corporation under section 4002(h)(1) and without regard to the provisions of title 5, United States Code, relating to appointments in the competitive service or Senior Executive Service.

(b) **Duties.** The Participant and Plan Sponsor Advocate shall—

(1) act as a liaison between the corporation, sponsors of defined benefit pension plans insured by the corporation, and participants in pension plans trusteed by the corporation;

(2) advocate for the full attainment of the rights of participants in plans trusteed by the corporation;

(3) assist pension plan sponsors and participants in resolving disputes with the corporation;

(4) identify areas in which participants and plan sponsors have persistent problems in dealings with the corporation;

(5) to the extent possible, propose changes in the administrative practices of the corporation to mitigate problems;

(6) identify potential legislative changes which may be appropriate to mitigate problems; and

(7) refer instances of fraud, waste, and abuse, and violations of law to the Office of the Inspector General of the corporation.

(c) **Removal.** If the Participant and Plan Sponsor Advocate is removed from office or is transferred to another position or location within the corporation or the Department of Labor, the board of the directors of the corporation shall communicate in writing the reasons for any such removal or transfer to Congress not less than 30 days before the removal or transfer. Nothing in this subsection shall prohibit a personnel action otherwise authorized by law, other than transfer or removal.

(d) **Compensation.** The annual rate of basic pay for the Participant and Plan Sponsor Advocate shall be the same rate as the highest rate of basic pay established for the Senior Executive Service under section 5382 of title 5, United States Code, or, if the board of directors of the corporation so determines, at a rate fixed under section 9503 of such title.

(e) **Annual report.**

(1) **In general.** Not later than December 31 of each calendar year, the Participant and Plan Sponsor Advocate shall report to the Health, Education, Labor, and Pensions Committee of the Senate, the Committee on Finance of the Senate, the Committee on Education and the Workforce of the House of Representatives, and the Committee on Ways and Means of the House of Representatives on the activities of the Office of the Participant and Plan Sponsor Advocate during the fiscal year ending during such calendar year.

(2) **Content.** Each report submitted under paragraph (1) shall—

(A) summarize the assistance requests received from participants and plan sponsors and describe the activities, and evaluate the effectiveness, of the Participant and Plan Sponsor Advocate during the preceding year;

(B) identify significant problems the Participant and Plan Sponsor Advocate has identified;

(C) include specific legislative and regulatory changes to address the problems; and

(D) identify any actions taken to correct problems identified in any previous report.

(3) Concurrent submission. The Participant and Plan Sponsor Advocate shall submit a copy of each report to the Secretary of Labor, the Director of the corporation, and any other appropriate official at the same time such report is submitted to the committees of Congress under paragraph (1).

[For Analysis, see ¶ 1701. For Committee Reports, see ¶ 5404.]

[Endnote ERISA §t29_1304]

29 USC §1304 [ERISA Sec. 4004] was added by Sec. 40232(a) of the Moving Ahead for Progress in the 21st Century Act, P.L. 112-141, 7/6/2012, as detailed below:

1. Sec. 40232(a) added 29 USC 1304 [ERISA Sec. 4004]

Effective Date Effective 7/6/2012.

[¶ 3510]
ERISA §4005. [29 USC 1305] Pension benefit guaranty funds.

* * * * * * * * * * * *

(b) Credits to funds; availability of funds; investment of moneys in excess of current needs.

(1) Each fund established under this section shall be credited with the appropriate portion of—

[1]*(A)* premiums, penalties, interest, and charges collected under this title,

[2]*(B)* the value of the assets of a plan administered under section 4042 [29 USC §1342] by a trustee to the extent that they exceed the liabilities of such plan,

(C) the amount of any employer liability payments under subtitle D, to the extent that such payments exceed liabilities of the plan (taking into account all other plan assets),

(D) earnings on investments of the fund or on assets credited to the fund under this subsection,

(E) attorney's fees awarded to the corporation, and

(F) receipts from any other operations under this title.

(2) Subject to the provisions of subsection (a), each fund shall be available—

(A) for making such payments as the corporation determines are necessary to pay benefits guaranteed under section 4022 or 4022A [29 USC §§1322 or 1322a] or benefits payable under section 4050 [29 USC §1350],

(B) to purchase assets from a plan being terminated by the corporation when the corporation determines such purchase will best protect the interests of the corporation, participants in the plan being terminated, and other insured plans,

[3]*(C)* to pay the operational and administrative expenses of the corporation, including reimbursement of the expenses incurred by the Department of the Treasury in maintaining the funds, and the Comptroller General in auditing the corporation, and

[4]*(D)* to pay to participants and beneficiaries the estimated amount of benefits which are guaranteed by the corporation under this title and the estimated amount of other benefits to which plan assets are allocated under section 4044 [29 USC §1344], under single-employer plans which are unable to pay benefits when due or which are abandoned.

(3) Whenever the corporation determines that the moneys of any fund are in excess of current needs, it may request the investment of such amounts as it determines advisable by the Secretary of the Treasury in obligations issued or guaranteed by the United States[5].

924

[6](c) *[Repealed.]*

(d) Establishment of fifth fund; purpose, availability, etc.

(1) A fifth fund shall be established for the reimbursement of uncollectible withdrawal liability under section 4222 [29 USC §1322], and shall be credited with the appropriate—

(A) premiums, penalties, and interest charges collected under this title, and

(B) earnings on investments of the fund or on assets credited to the fund.

The fund shall be available to make payments pursuant to the supplemental program established under section 4222 [29 USC §1322], including those expenses and other charges determined to be appropriate by the corporation.

(2) The corporation may invest amounts of the fund in such obligations as the corporation considers appropriate.

(e) Establishment of sixth fund; purpose, availability, etc.

(1) A sixth fund shall be established for the supplemental benefit guarantee program provided under section 4022A(g)(2) [29 USC §1322a(g)(2)].

(2) Such fund shall be credited with the appropriate—

(A) premiums, penalties, and interest charges collected under section 4022A(g)(2) [29 USC §1322a(g)(2)], and

(B) earnings on investments of the fund or on assets credited to the fund.

The fund shall be available for making payments pursuant to the supplemental benefit guarantee program established under section 4022A(g)(2) [29 USC §1322a(g)(2)] including those expenses and other charges determined to be appropriate by the corporation.

(3) The corporation may invest amounts of the fund in such obligations as the corporation considers appropriate.

(f) Deposit of premiums into separate revolving fund.

(1) A seventh fund shall be established and credited with

(A) premiums, penalties, and interest charges collected under section 4006(a)(3)(A)(i) [29 USC §1306(a)(3)(A)(i)] (not described in subparagraph (B)) to the extent attributable to the amount of the premium in excess of $8.50,

(B) premiums, penalties, and interest charges collected under section 4006(a)(3)(E) [29 USC §1306(a)(3)(E)], and

(C) earnings on investments of the fund or on assets credited to the fund.

(2) Amounts in the fund shall be available for transfer to other funds established under this section with respect to a single-employer plan but shall not be available to pay—

(A) administrative costs of the corporation, or

(B) benefits under any plan which was terminated before October 1, 1988, unless no other amounts are available for such payment.

(3) The corporation may invest amounts of the fund in such obligations as the corporation considers appropriate.

(g) Other use of funds; deposits of repayments.

(1) Amounts in any fund established under this section may be used only for the purposes for which such fund was established and may not be used to make loans to (or on behalf of) any other fund or to finance any other activity of the corporation.

[7]*(2)* Any repayment to the corporation of any amount paid out of any fund in connection with a multiemployer plan shall be deposited in such fund.

(h) Voting by corporation of stock paid as liability. Any stock in a person liable to the corporation under this title which is paid to the corporation by such person or a member of such person's controlled group in satisfaction of such person's liability under this title may be voted only by the custodial trustees or outside money managers of the corporation.

[For Analysis, see ¶ 1715. For Committee Reports, see ¶ 5404.]

[Endnote ERISA §t29_1305]

29 USC §1305(b)(1)(A)-(G), (2)(C)-(E) (3), (c) and (g)(2)-(3) [ERISA Sec. 4005] was amended by Sec. 40234(a)-(b)(1) of the Moving Ahead for Progress in the 21st Century Act, P.L. 112-141, 7/6/2012, as detailed below:

1. Sec. 40234(b)(1)(A)(i)(I) deleted subpara. (b)(1)(A) Prior to deletion, subpara. (b)(1)(A) read as follows: "(A) funds borrowed under subsection (c),"

2. Sec. 40234(b)(1)(A)(i)(II) redesignated subparas. (b)(1)(B)-(G) as subparas. (b)(1)(A)-(F), respectively

3. Sec. 40234(b)(1)(A)(ii)(I) deleted subpara. (b)(2)(C) Prior to deletion, subpara. (b)(2)(C) read as follows: (C) to re-pay to the Secretary of the Treasury such sums as may be borrowed (together with interest thereon) under subsection (c),"

4. Sec. 40234(b)(1)(A)(ii)(II) redesignated subparas. (b)(2)(D)-(E) as subparas. (b)(2)(C)-(D), respectively

5. Sec. 40234(b)(1)(A)(iii) substituted a period for 'but, until all borrowings under subsection (c) have been repaid, the obligations in which such excess moneys are invested may not yield a rate of return in excess of the rate of interest payable on such borrowings.' at the end of para. (b)(3)

6. Sec. 40234(a) deleted subsec. (c) Prior to deletion, subsec. (c) read as follows: "(c) Authority to issue notes or other obligations; purchase by Secretary of the Treasury as public debt transaction. The corporation is authorized to is-sue to the Secretary of the Treasury notes or other obligations in an aggregate amount of not to exceed $100,000,000, in such forms and denominations, bearing such maturities, and subject to such terms and conditions as may be prescribed by the Secretary of the Treasury. Such notes or other obligations shall bear interest at a rate determined by the Secretary of the Treasury, taking into consideration the current average market yield on outstanding marketable obligations of the United States of comparable maturities during the month preceding the issuance of such notes or other obligations of the corporation. The Secretary of the Treasury is authorized and directed to purchase any notes or other obligations issued by the corporation under this subsection, and for that purpose he is authorized to use as a public debt transaction the proceeds from the sale of any securities issued under the Second Liberty Bond Act, as amended, and the purposes for which securities may be issued under that Act, as amended, are extended to include any purchase of such notes and ob-ligations. The Secretary of the Treasury may at any time sell any of the notes or other obligations acquired by him under this subsection. All redemptions, purchases, and sales by the Secretary of the Treasury of such notes or other obli-gations shall be treated as public debt transactions of the United States."

7. Sec. 40234(b)(1)(B)(i)-(ii) deleted para. (g)(2) and redesignated para. (g)(3) as para. (g)(2) Prior to deletion, para. (g)(2) read as follows: (2) None of the funds borrowed under subsection (c) may be used to make loans to (or on behalf of) any fund other than a fund described in the second sentence of subsection (a)."

Effective Date Effective 7/6/2012.

[¶ 3511]
ERISA §4006. [29 USC 1306] Premium rates.

(a) **Schedules for premium rates and bases for application; establishment, coverage, etc.**

(1) The corporation shall prescribe such schedules of premium rates and bases for the application of those rates as may be necessary to provide sufficient revenue to the fund for the corporation to carry out its functions under this title. The premium rates charged by the corporation for any period shall be uniform for all plans, other than multiemployer plans, insured by the corporation with respect to basic benefits guaranteed by it under section 4022 [29 USC §1322], and shall be uniform for all multiemployer plans with respect to ba-sic benefits guaranteed by it under section 4022A [29 USC §1322a].

(2) The corporation shall maintain separate schedules of premium rates, and bases for the application of those rates, for—

(A) basic benefits guaranteed by it under section 4022 [29 USC §1322] for sin-gle-employer plans,

(B) basic benefits guaranteed by it under section 4022A [29 USC §1322a] for mul-tiemployer plans,

(C) nonbasic benefits guaranteed by it under section 4022 [29 USC §1322] for sin-gle-employer plans,

(D) nonbasic benefits guaranteed by it under section 4022A [29 USC §1322a] for multiemployer plans, and

(E) reimbursements of uncollectible withdrawal liability under section 4222 [29 USC §1402]. The corporation may revise such schedules whenever it determines that revised schedules are necessary. Except as provided in section 4022A(f) [29 USC §1322a(f)], in order to place a revised schedule described in subparagraph (A) or (B) in effect, the cor-poration shall proceed in accordance with subsection (b)(1), and such schedule shall ap-ply only to plan years beginning more than 30 days after the date on which a joint reso-lution approving such revised schedule is enacted.

(3) (A) Except as provided in subparagraph (C), the annual premium rate payable to the corporation by all plans for basic benefits guaranteed under this title is—

[1](i) in the case of a single-employer plan, an amount for each individual who is a participant in such plan during the plan year equal to the sum of the additional premium (if any) determined under subparagraph (E) and—

   (I) for plan years beginning after December 31, 2005, and before January 1, 2013, $30;

   (II) for plan years beginning after December 31, 2012, and before January 1, 2014, $42; and

   (III) for plan years beginning after December 31, 2013, $49.

(ii) in the case of a multiemployer plan, for the plan year within which the date of enactment of the Multiemployer Pension Plan Amendments Act of 1980 [enacted Sept. 26, 1980] falls, an amount for each individual who is a participant in such plan for such plan year equal to the sum of—

   (I) 50 cents, multiplied by a fraction the numerator of which is the number of months in such year ending on or before such date and the denominator of which is 12, and

   (II) $1.00, multiplied by a fraction equal to 1 minus the fraction determined under clause (i),

(iii) in the case of a multiemployer plan, for plan years beginning after the date of enactment of the Multiemployer Pension Plan Amendments Act of 1980 [enacted Sept. 26, 1980], and before January 1, 2006, an amount equal to—

   (I) $1.40 for each participant, for the first, second, third, and fourth plan years,

   (II) $1.80 for each participant, for the fifth and sixth plan years,

   (III) $2.20 for each participant, for the seventh and eighth plan years, and

   (IV) $2.60 for each participant, for the ninth plan year, and for each succeeding plan year, [2]

(iv) in the case of a multiemployer plan, for plan years beginning after December 31, 2005, [3]and before January 1, 2013, $8.00 for each individual who is a participant in such plan during the applicable plan year[4], or

[5](v) in the case of a multiemployer plan, for plan years beginning after December 31, 2012, $12.00 for each individual who is a participant in such plan during the applicable plan year.

(B) The corporation may prescribe by regulation the extent to which the rate described in clause (iii) or (iv) of subparagraph (A) applies more than once for any plan year to an individual participating in more than one plan maintained by the same employer, and the corporation may prescribe regulations under which the rate described in subparagraph (A)(iii) will not apply to the same participant in any multiemployer plan more than once for any plan year.

(C)   (i) If the sum of—

   (I) the amounts in any fund for basic benefits guaranteed for multiemployer plans, and

   (II) the value of any assets held by the corporation for payment of basic benefits guaranteed for multiemployer plans,

   is for any calendar year less than 2 times the amount of basic benefits guaranteed by the corporation under this title for multiemployer plans which were paid out of any such fund or assets during the preceding calendar year, the annual premium rates under subparagraph (A) shall be increased to the next highest premium level necessary to insure that such sum will be at least 2 times greater than such amount during the following calendar year.

   (ii) If the board of directors of the corporation determines that an increase in the premium rates under subparagraph (A) is necessary to provide assistance to plans which are receiving assistance under section 4261 [29 USC §1431] and to plans the board finds are reasonably likely to require such assistance, the board may order such increase in the premium rates.

   (iii) The maximum annual premium rate which may be established under this subparagraph is $2.60 for each participant.

(iv) The provisions of this subparagraph shall not apply if the annual premium rate is increased to a level in excess of $2.60 per participant under any other provisions of this title.

(D) (i) Not later than 120 days before the date on which an increase under subparagraph (C)(ii) is to become effective, the corporation shall publish in the Federal Register a notice of the determination described in subparagraph (C)(ii), the basis for the determination, the amount of the increase in the premium, and the anticipated increase in premium income that would result from the increase in the premium rate. The notice shall invite public comment, and shall provide for a public hearing if one is requested. Any such hearing shall be commenced not later than 60 days before the date on which the increase is to become effective.

(ii) The board of directors shall review the hearing record established under clause (i) and shall, not later than 30 days before the date on which the increase is to become effective, determine (after consideration of the comments received) whether the amount of the increase should be changed and shall publish its determination in the Federal Register.

(E) (i) Except as provided in subparagraph (H), the additional premium determined under this subparagraph with respect to any plan [6]*for any plan year*—

(I) shall be an amount equal to the amount determined under clause (ii) divided by the number of participants in such plan as of the close of the preceding plan year; and

(II) in the case of plan years beginning in a calendar year after 2012, shall not exceed $400.

(ii) The amount determined under this clause for any plan year shall be an amount equal to [7]the applicable dollar amount under paragraph (8) for each $1,000 (or fraction thereof) of unfunded vested benefits under the plan as of the close of the preceding plan year.

(iii) For purposes of clause (ii), the term "unfunded vested benefits" means, for a plan year, the excess (if any) of—

(I) the funding target of the plan as determined under section 303(d) for the plan year by only taking into account vested benefits and by using the interest rate described in clause (iv), over

(II) the fair market value of plan assets for the plan year which are held by the plan on the valuation date.

(iv) The interest rate used in valuing benefits for purposes of subclause (I) of clause (iii) shall be equal to the first, second, or third segment rate for the month preceding the month in which the plan year begins, which would be determined under [8]*section 303(h)(2)(C) (notwithstanding any regulations issued by the corporation, determined by not taking into account any adjustment under clause (iv) thereof)* if section 303(h)(2)(D) were applied by using the monthly yields for the month preceding the month in which the plan year begins on investment grade corporate bonds with varying maturities and in the top 3 quality levels rather than the average of such yields for a 24-month period.

(F) For each plan year beginning in a calendar year after 2006, there shall be substituted for the premium rate specified in clause (i) of subparagraph (A) an amount equal to the greater of—

(i) the product derived by multiplying the premium rate specified in clause (i) of subparagraph (A) by the ratio of—

(I) the national average wage index (as defined in section 209(k)(1) of the Social Security Act) for the first of the 2 calendar years preceding the calendar year in which such plan year begins, to

(II) the national average wage index (as so defined) for 2004 [9]*(2012 in the case of plan years beginning after calendar year 2014)*; and

(ii) the premium rate in effect under clause (i) of subparagraph (A) for plan years beginning in the preceding calendar year.

If the amount determined under this subparagraph is not a multiple of $1, such product shall be rounded to the nearest multiple of $1. [10]*This subparagraph shall not apply to plan years beginning in 2013 or 2014.*

(G) For each plan year beginning in a calendar year after 2006, there shall be substituted for the premium rate specified in clause (iv) of subparagraph (A) an amount equal to the greater of—

(i) the product derived by multiplying the premium rate specified in clause (iv) of subparagraph (A) by the ratio of—

(I) the national average wage index (as defined in section 209(k)(1) of the Social Security Act) for the first of the 2 calendar years preceding the calendar year in which such plan year begins, to

(II) the national average wage index (as so defined) for 2004; and

(ii) the premium rate in effect under clause (iv) of subparagraph (A) for plan years beginning in the preceding calendar year.

If the amount determined under this subparagraph is not a multiple of $1, such product shall be rounded to the nearest multiple of $1.

(H) (i) In the case of an employer who has 25 or fewer employees on the first day of the plan year, the additional premium determined under subparagraph (E) for each participant shall not exceed $5 multiplied by the number of participants in the plan as of the close of the preceding plan year.

(ii) For purposes of clause (i), whether an employer has 25-or-fewer-employees on the first day of the plan year is determined by taking into consideration all of the employees of all members of the contributing sponsor's controlled group. In the case of a plan maintained by two or more contributing sponsors, the employees of all contributing sponsors and their controlled groups shall be aggregated for purposes of determining whether the 25-or fewer-employees limitation has been satisfied.

[11]*(I) For each plan year beginning in a calendar year after 2013, there shall be substituted for the premium rate specified in clause (v) of subparagraph (A) an amount equal to the greater of—*

(i) the product derived by multiplying the premium rate specified in clause (v) of subparagraph (A) by the ratio of—

(I) the national average wage index (as defined in section 209(k)(1) of the Social Security Act [42 USC §409(k)(1)]) for the first of the 2 calendar years preceding the calendar year in which such plan year begins, to

(II) the national average wage index (as so defined) for 2011; and

(ii) the premium rate in effect under clause (v) of subparagraph (A) for plan years beginning in the preceding calendar year.

If the amount determined under this subparagraph is not a multiple of $1, such product shall be rounded to the nearest multiple of $1.

[12]*(J) For each plan year beginning in a calendar year after 2013, there shall be substituted for the dollar amount specified in subclause (II) of subparagraph (E)(i) an amount equal to the greater of—*

(i) the product derived by multiplying such dollar amount by the ratio of—

(I) the national average wage index (as defined in section 209(k)(1) of the Social Security Act [42 USC §409(k)(1)]) for the first of the 2 calendar years preceding the calendar year in which such plan year begins, to

(II) the national average wage index (as so defined) for 2011; and

(ii) such dollar amount for plan years beginning in the preceding calendar year.

If the amount determined under this subparagraph is not a multiple of $1, such product shall be rounded to the nearest multiple of $1.

(4) The corporation may prescribe, subject to the enactment of a joint resolution in accordance with this section or section 4022A(f) [29 USC §1322a(f)], alternative schedules of premium rates, and bases for the application of those rates, for basic benefits guaranteed by it under sections 4022 and 4022A [29 USC §§1322 and 1322a] based, in whole or in part, on the risks insured by the corporation in each plan.

(5) (A) In carrying out its authority under paragraph (1) to establish schedules of premium rates, and bases for the application of those rates, for nonbasic benefits guaranteed under sections 4022 and 4022A [29 USC §§1322 and 1322a], the premium rates charged by the corporation for any period for nonbasic benefits guaranteed shall—

(i) be uniform by category of nonbasic benefits guaranteed,

(ii) be based on the risks insured in each category, and

(iii) reflect the experience of the corporation (including experience which may be reasonably anticipated) in guaranteeing such benefits.

(B) Notwithstanding subparagraph (A), premium rates charged to any multiemployer plan by the corporation for any period for supplemental guarantees under section 4022A(g)(2) [29 USC §1322a(g)(2)] may reflect any reasonable considerations which the corporation determines to be appropriate.

(6) (A) In carrying out its authority under paragraph (1) to establish premium rates and bases for basic benefits guaranteed under section 4022 [29 USC §1322] with respect to single-employer plans, the corporation shall establish such rates and bases in coverage schedules in accordance with the provisions of this paragraph.

(B) The corporation may establish annual premiums for single-employer plans composed of the sum of—

(i) a charge based on a rate applicable to the excess, if any, of the present value of the basic benefits of the plan which are guaranteed over the value of the assets of the plan, not in excess of 0.1 percent, and

(ii) an additional charge based on a rate applicable to the present value of the basic benefits of the plan which are guaranteed.

The rate for the additional charge referred to in clause (ii) shall be set by the corporation for every year at a level which the corporation estimates will yield total revenue approximately equal to the total revenue to be derived by the corporation from the charges referred to in clause (i) of this subparagraph.

(C) The corporation may establish annual premiums for single-employer plans based on—

(i) the number of participants in a plan, but such premium rates shall not exceed the rates described in paragraph (3),

(ii) unfunded basic benefits guaranteed under this title, but such premium rates shall not exceed the limitations applicable to charges referred to in subparagraph (B)(i), or

(iii) total guaranteed basic benefits, but such premium rates shall not exceed the rates for additional charges referred to in subparagraph (B)(ii).

If the corporation uses two or more of the rate bases described in this subparagraph, the premium rates shall be designed to produce approximately equal amounts of aggregate premium revenue from each of the rate bases used.

(D) For purposes of this paragraph, the corporation shall by regulation define the terms "value of assets" and "present value of the benefits of the plan which are guaranteed" in a manner consistent with the purposes of this title and the provisions of this section.

(7) Premium rate for certain terminated single-employer plans.

(A) In general. If there is a termination of a single-employer plan under clause (ii) or (iii) of section 4041(c)(2)(B) or section 4042, there shall be payable to the corporation, with respect to each applicable 12-month period, a premium at a rate equal to $1,250 multiplied by the number of individuals who were participants in the plan immediately before the termination date. Such premium shall be in addition to any other premium under this section.

(B) Special rule for plans terminated in bankruptcy reorganization. In the case of a single-employer plan terminated under section 4041(c)(2)(B)(ii) or under section 4042 during pendency of any bankruptcy reorganization proceeding under chapter 11 of title 11, United States Code, or under any similar law of a State or a political subdivision of a State (or a case described in section 4041(c)(2)(B)(i) filed by or against such person has been converted, as of such date, to such a case in which reorganization is sought), subparagraph (A) shall not apply to such plan until the date of the discharge or dismissal of such person in such case.

(C) Applicable 12-month period. For purposes of subparagraph (A)—

    (i) In general. The term "applicable 12-month period" means—

        (I) the 12-month period beginning with the first month following the month in which the termination date occurs, and

        (II) each of the first two 12-month periods immediately following the period described in subclause (I).

    (ii) Plans terminated in bankruptcy reorganization. In any case in which the requirements of subparagraph (B) are met in connection with the termination of the plan with respect to 1 or more persons described in such subparagraph, the 12-month period described in clause (i)(I) shall be the 12-month period beginning with the first month following the month which includes the earliest date as of which each such person is discharged or dismissed in the case described in such clause in connection with such person.

(D) Coordination with section 4007.

    (i) Notwithstanding section 4007—

        (I) premiums under this paragraph shall be due within 30 days after the beginning of any applicable 12-month period, and

        (II) the designated payor shall be the person who is the contributing sponsor as of immediately before the termination date.

    (ii) The fifth sentence of section 4007(a) shall not apply in connection with premiums determined under this paragraph.

(E) Repealed.

[13] *(8)* **Applicable dollar amount for variable rate premium.** *For purposes of paragraph (3)(E)(ii)—*

    (A) In general. Except as provided in subparagraphs (B) and (C), the applicable dollar amount shall be—

        (i) $9 for plan years beginning in a calendar year before 2015;

        (ii) for plan years beginning in calendar year 2015, the amount in effect for plan years beginning in 2014 (determined after application of subparagraph (C)); and

        (iii) for plan years beginning after calendar year 2015, the amount in effect for plan years beginning in 2015 (determined after application of subparagraph (C)).

    (B) Adjustment for inflation. For each plan year beginning in a calendar year after 2012, there shall be substituted for the applicable dollar amount specified under subparagraph (A) an amount equal to the greater of—

        (i) the product derived by multiplying such applicable dollar amount for plan years beginning in that calendar year by the ratio of—

            (I) the national average wage index (as defined in section 209(k)(1) of the Social Security Act [42 USC §409(k)(1)]) for the first of the 2 calendar years preceding the calendar year in which such plan year begins, to

            (II) the national average wage index (as so defined) for the base year; and

        (ii) such applicable dollar amount in effect for plan years beginning in the preceding calendar year.

    If the amount determined under this subparagraph is not a multiple of $1, such product shall be rounded to the nearest multiple of $1.

    (C) Additional increase in 2014 and 2015. The applicable dollar amount determined under subparagraph (A) (after the application of subparagraph (B)) shall be increased—

        (i) in the case of plan years beginning in calendar year 2014, by $4; and

        (ii) in the case of plan years beginning in calendar year 2015, by $5.

    (D) Base year. For purposes of subparagraph (B), the base year is—

        (i) 2010, in the case of plan years beginning in calendar year 2013 or 2014;

        (ii) 2012, in the case of plan years beginning in calendar year 2015; and

(iii) 2013, in the case of plan years beginning after calendar year 2015.

* * * * * * * * * * * *

[For Analysis, see ¶ 1701, ¶ 1706, ¶ 1707 and ¶ 1708. For Committee Reports, see ¶ 5402 and comrep vol='2013-01' n='5403'>.]

[Endnote ERISA §t29_1306]

29 USC §1306(a)(3)(A)(i) [ERISA Sec. 4004] was amended by Sec. 40221(a)(1) of the Moving Ahead for Progress in the 21st Century Act, P.L. 112-141, 7/6/2012, as detailed below:

1. Sec. 40221(a)(1) amended clause (a)(3)(A)(i) Prior to amendment, clause (a)(3)(A)(i) read as follows: "(i) in the case of a single-employer plan, for plan years beginning after December 31, 2005, an amount equal to the sum of $30 plus the additional premium (if any) determined under subparagraph (E) for each individual who is a participant in such plan during the plan year;"

Effective Date Effective 7/6/2012.

---

29 USC §1306(a)(3)(A)(iii)-(v) [ERISA Sec. 4004] was amended by Sec. 40222(a)(1)-(4), P.L. 112-141, 7/6/2012, as detailed below:

2. Sec. 40222(a)(2) deleted 'or' at the end of sbcl. (a)(3)(A)(iii)(IV)
3. Sec. 40222(a)(1) added 'and before January 1, 2013,' after 'December 31, 2005,' in clause (a)(3)(A)(iv)
4. Sec. 40222(a)(3) substituted ', or' for the period at the end of clause (a)(3)(A)(iv)
5. Sec. 40222(a)(4) added clause (a)(3)(A)(v)

29 USC §1306(a)(3)(E)(i)-(ii) [ERISA Sec. 4004] was amended by Sec. 40221(b)(1)-(3)(A), P.L. 112-141, 7/6/2012, as detailed below:

6. Sec. 40221(b)(3)(A) substituted 'for any plan year-(I) shall be an amount equal to the amount determined under clause (ii) divided by the number of participants in such plan as of the close of the preceding plan year; and (II) in the case of plan years beginning in a calendar year after 2012, shall not exceed $400.' for 'for any plan year shall be an amount equal to the amount determined under clause (ii) divided by the number of participants in such plan as of the close of the preceding plan year.' in clause (a)(3)(E)(i)
7. Sec. 40221(b)(1) substituted 'the applicable dollar amount under paragraph (8)' for '$9.00' in clause (a)(3)(E)(ii)

Effective Date Effective 7/6/2012.

---

29 USC §1306(a)(3)(E)(iv) [ERISA Sec. 4004] was amended by Sec. 40211(b)(3)(C), P.L. 112-141, 7/6/2012, as detailed below:

8. Sec. 40211(b)(3)(C) substituted 'section 303(h)(2)(C) (notwithstanding any regulations issued by the corporation, determined by not taking into account any adjustment under clause (iv) thereof)' for 'section 303(h)(2)(C)' in clause (a)(3)(E)(iv)

Effective Date (Sec. 40211(c)(1), P.L. 112-141, 7/6/2012) effective with respect to plan yrs. begin. after 12/31/2011. Sec. 40211(c)(2) of this Act, provides:

"(2) Rules with respect to elections.

"(A) Adjusted funding target attainment percentage. A plan sponsor may elect not to have the amendments made by this section apply to any plan year beginning before January 1, 2013, either (as specified in the election)—

"(i) for all purposes for which such amendments apply, or

"(ii) solely for purposes of determining the adjusted funding target attainment percentage under sections 436 of the Internal Revenue Code of 1986 and 206(g) of the Employee Retirement Income Security Act of 1974 for such plan year.

"A plan shall not be treated as failing to meet the requirements of sections 204(g) of such Act and 411(d)(6) of such Code solely by reason of an election under this paragraph.

"(B) Opt out of existing elections. If, on the date of the enactment of this Act, an election is in effect with respect to any plan under sections 303(h)((2)(D)(ii) of the Employee Retirement Income Security Act of 1974 and 430(h)((2)(D)(ii) of the Internal Revenue Code of 1986, then, notwithstanding the last sentence of each such section, the plan sponsor may revoke such election without the consent of the Secretary of the Treasury. The plan sponsor may make such revocation at any time before the date which is 1 year after such date of enactment and such revocation shall be effective for the 1st plan year to which the amendments made by this section apply and all subsequent plan years. Nothing in this subparagraph shall preclude a plan sponsor from making a subsequent election in accordance with such sections."

---

29 USC §1306(a)(3)(F) [ERISA Sec. 4004] was amended by Sec. 40221(a)(2)(A)-(B), P.L. 112-141, 7/6/2012, as detailed below:

9. Sec. 40221(a)(2)(A) added '(2012 in the case of plan years beginning after calendar year 2014)' after '2004' in sbcl. (a)(3)(F)(i)(II)
10. Sec. 40221(a)(2)(B) added the last sentence at the end of subpara. (a)(3)(F)

Effective Date Effective 7/6/2012.

---

29 USC §1306(a)(3)(I) [ERISA Sec. 4004] was added by Sec. 40222(b), P.L. 112-141, 7/6/2012, as detailed below:

11. Sec. 40222(b) added subpara. (a)(3)(I)

Effective Date Effective 7/6/2012.

---

29 USC §1306(a)(3)(J) and (8) [ERISA Sec. 4004] were added by Sec. 40221(b)(2) and (3)(B), P.L. 112-141, 7/6/2012, as detailed below:

12. Sec. 40221(b)(3)(B) added subpara. (a)(3)(J)
13. Sec. 40221(b)(2) added para. (a)(8)
Effective Date Effective 7/6/2012.

[¶ 3512]
ERISA §4010. [29 USC 1310] Authority to require certain information.

* * * * * * * * * * * *

(d) Additional information required.

(1) In general. The information submitted to the corporation under subsection (a) shall include—

(A) the amount of benefit liabilities under the plan determined using the assumptions used by the corporation in determining liabilities;

(B) the funding target of the plan determined as if the plan has been in at-risk status for at least 5 plan years; and

(C) the funding target attainment percentage of the plan.

(2) Definitions. For purposes of this subsection:

(A) Funding target. The term "funding target" has the meaning provided under section 303(d)(1).

(B) Funding target attainment percentage. The term "funding target attainment percentage" has the meaning provided under section 303(d)(2).

(C) At-risk status. The term "at-risk status" has the meaning provided in section 303(i)(4).

[1]*(3) Pension stabilization disregarded. For purposes of this section, the segment rates used in determining the funding target and funding target attainment percentage shall be determined by not taking into account any adjustment under section 302(h)((2)(C)(iv).*

* * * * * * * * * * * *

[For Analysis, see ¶ 1701. For Committee Reports, see ¶ 5402.]

[Endnote ERISA §t29_1310]

29 USC §1310(d)(3) [ERISA Sec. 4010] was added by Sec. 40211(b)(3)(D) of the Moving Ahead for Progress in the 21st Century Act, P.L. 112-141, 7/6/2012, as detailed below:

1. Sec. 40211(b)(3)(D) added para. (d)(3)

Effective Date (Sec. 40211(c)(1), P.L. 112-141, 7/6/2012) effective with respect to plan yrs. begin. after 12/31/2011. Sec. 40211(c)(2) of this Act, provides:

"(2) Rules with respect to elections.

"(A) Adjusted funding target attainment percentage. A plan sponsor may elect not to have the amendments made by this section apply to any plan year beginning before January 1, 2013, either (as specified in the election)—

"(i) for all purposes for which such amendments apply, or

"(ii) solely for purposes of determining the adjusted funding target attainment percentage under sections 436 of the Internal Revenue Code of 1986 and 206(g) of the Employee Retirement Income Security Act of 1974 for such plan year.

"A plan shall not be treated as failing to meet the requirements of sections 204(g) of such Act and 411(d)(6) of such Code solely by reason of an election under this paragraph.

"(B) Opt out of existing elections. If, on the date of the enactment of this Act, an election is in effect with respect to any plan under sections 303(h)((2)(D)(ii) of the Employee Retirement Income Security Act of 1974 and 430(h)((2)(D)(ii) of the Internal Revenue Code of 1986, then, notwithstanding the last sentence of each such section, the plan sponsor may revoke such election without the consent of the Secretary of the Treasury. The plan sponsor may make such revocation at any time before the date which is 1 year after such date of enactment and such revocation shall be effective for the 1st plan year to which the amendments made by this section apply and all subsequent plan years. Nothing in this subparagraph shall preclude a plan sponsor from making a subsequent election in accordance with such sections."

American Taxpayer Relief Act of 2012 [P.L. 112-240, 1/2/2013]

[¶ 4000] In the Senate of the United States, January 1 (legislative day, December 30, 2012), 2013.

Resolved, That the bill from the House of Representatives (H.R. 8) entitled "An Act to extend certain tax relief provisions enacted in 2001 and 2003, and to provide for expedited consideration of a bill providing for comprehensive tax reform, and for other purposes.", do pass with the following

Amendments:

Strike all after the enacting clause and insert the following:

[¶ 4001] **Sec. 1. Short title, etc.**

(a) Short Title. This Act may be cited as the "American Taxpayer Relief Act of 2012".

(b) Amendment of 1986 Code. Except as otherwise expressly provided, whenever in this Act an amendment or repeal is expressed in terms of an amendment to, or repeal of, a section or other provision, the reference shall be considered to be made to a section or other provision of the Internal Revenue Code of 1986.

* * * * * * * * * * *

TITLE I— General extensions

[¶ 4002] **Sec. 101. Permanent extension and modification of 2001 tax relief.**

(a) Permanent Extension.
     * * * * * * * * * * *

     (3) Effective date. The amendments made by this subsection shall apply to taxable, plan, or limitation years beginning after December 31, 2012, and estates of decedents dying, gifts made, or generation skipping transfers after December 31, 2012.

(b) Application of Income Tax to Certain High-Income Taxpayers.
     * * * * * * * * * * *

     (3) Effective date. The amendments made by this subsection shall apply to taxable years beginning after December 31, 2012.

(c) Modifications of Estate Tax.
     * * * * * * * * * * *

     (3) Effective dates.
         (A) In general. Except as otherwise provided by in this paragraph, the amendments made by this subsection shall apply to estates of decedents dying, generation-skipping transfers, and gifts made, after December 31, 2012.
         (B) Technical correction. The amendment made by paragraph (2) shall take effect as if included in the amendments made by section 303 of the Tax Relief, Unemployment Insurance Reauthorization, and Job Creation Act of 2010.

[¶ 4003] **Sec. 102. Permanent extension and modification of 2003 tax relief.**
     * * * * * * * * * * *

(d) Effective dates.
     (1) In general. Except as otherwise provided, the amendments made by subsections (b) and (c) shall apply to taxable years beginning after December 31, 2012.
     (2) Withholding. The amendments made by paragraphs (1)(C) and (3) of subsection (c) shall apply to amounts paid on or after January 1, 2013.

[¶ 4004] Sec. 103. Extension of 2009 tax relief.
* * * * * * * * * * * *

(e) Effective dates.
   (1) In general. Except as provided in paragraph (2), the amendments made by this section shall apply to taxable years beginning after December 31, 2012.
   (2) Rule regarding disregard of refunds. The amendment made by subsection (d) shall apply to amounts received after December 31, 2012.

[¶ 4005] Sec. 104. Permanent alternative minimum tax relief.
* * * * * * * * * * * *

(d) Effective date. The amendments made by this section shall apply to taxable years beginning after December 31, 2011.

TITLE II— Individual tax extenders

[¶ 4006] Sec. 201. Extension of deduction for certain expenses of elementary and secondary school teachers.
* * * * * * * * * * * *

(b) Effective date. The amendment made by this section shall apply to taxable years beginning after December 31, 2011.

[¶ 4007] Sec. 202. Extension of exclusion from gross income of discharge of qualified principal residence indebtedness.
* * * * * * * * * * * *

(b) Effective date. The amendment made by this section shall apply to indebtedness discharged after December 31, 2012.

[¶ 4008] Sec. 203. Extension of parity for exclusion from income for employer-provided mass transit and parking benefits.
* * * * * * * * * * * *

(b) Effective date. The amendment made by this section shall apply to months after December 31, 2011.

[¶ 4009] Sec. 204. Extension of mortgage insurance premiums treated as qualified residence interest.
* * * * * * * * * * * *

(c) Effective date. The amendments made by this section shall apply to amounts paid or accrued after December 31, 2011.

[¶ 4010] Sec. 205. Extension of deduction of state and local general sales taxes.
* * * * * * * * * * * *

(b) Effective date. The amendment made by this section shall apply to taxable years beginning after December 31, 2011.

[¶ 4011] Sec. 206. Extension of special rule for contributions of capital gain real property made for conservationPURPOSES.
* * * * * * * * * * * *

(c) Effective date. The amendments made by this section shall apply to contributions made in taxable years beginning after December 31, 2011.

[¶ 4012] Sec. 207. Extension of above-the-line deduction for qualified tuition and related expenses.
* * * * * * * * * * *

(b) Effective date. The amendment made by this section shall apply to taxable years beginning after December 31, 2011.

[¶ 4013] Sec. 208. Extension of tax-free distributions from individual retirement plans for charitable purposes.
* * * * * * * * * * *

(b) Effective Date; Special Rule.
  (1) Effective date. The amendment made by this section shall apply to distributions made in taxable years beginning after December 31, 2011.
  (2) Special rules. For purposes of subsections (a)(6), (b)(3), and (d)(8) of section 408 of the Internal Revenue Code of 1986, at the election of the taxpayer (at such time and in such manner as prescribed by the Secretary of the Treasury)—
    (A) any qualified charitable distribution made after December 31, 2012, and before February 1, 2013, shall be deemed to have been made on December 31, 2012, and
    (B) any portion of a distribution from an individual retirement account to the taxpayer after November 30, 2012, and before January 1, 2013, may be treated as a qualified charitable distribution to the extent that—
      (i) such portion is transferred in cash after the distribution to an organization described in section 408(d)(8)(B)(i) before February 1, 2013, and
      (ii) such portion is part of a distribution that would meet the requirements of section 408(d)(8) but for the fact that the distribution was not transferred directly to an organization described in section 408(d)(8)(B)(i).

[¶ 4014] Sec. 209. Improve and make permanent the provision authorizing the Internal Revenue Service to disclose certain return and return information to certain prison officials.
* * * * * * * * * * *

(c) Effective date. The amendments made by this section shall take effect on the date of the enactment of this Act.

TITLE III— Business tax extenders

[¶ 4015] Sec. 301. Extension and modification of research credit.
* * * * * * * * * * *

(d) Effective date.
  (1) Extension. The amendments made by subsection (a) shall apply to amounts paid or incurred after December 31, 2011.
  (2) Modifications. The amendments made by subsections (b) and (c) shall apply to taxable years beginning after December 31, 2011.

[¶ 4016] Sec. 302. Extension of temporary minimum low-incometax credit rate for non-federally subsidized new buildings.
* * * * * * * * * * *

(b) Effective date. The amendment made by this section shall take effect on the date of the enactment of this Act.

[¶ 4017] Sec. 303. Extension of housing allowance exclusion for determining area median gross income for qualified residential rental project exempt facility bonds.
* * * * * * * * * * *

(b) Effective date. The amendment made by this section shall take effect as if included in the enactment of section 3005 of the Housing Assistance Tax Act of 2008.

[¶ 4018] Sec. 304. Extension of Indian employment tax credit.
* * * * * * * * * * * *

(b) Effective date. The amendment made by this section shall apply to taxable years beginning after December 31, 2011.
* * * * * * * * * * * *

[¶ 4019] Sec. 305. Extension of new markets tax credit.
* * * * * * * * * * * *

(c) Effective date. The amendments made by this section shall apply to calendar years beginning after December 31, 2011.

[¶ 4020] Sec. 306. Extension of railroad track maintenance credit.
* * * * * * * * * * * *

(b) Effective date. The amendment made by this section shall apply to expenditures paid or incurred in taxable years beginning after December 31, 2011.

[¶ 4021] Sec. 307. Extension of mine rescue team training credit.
* * * * * * * * * * * *

(b) Effective date. The amendment made by this section shall apply to taxable years beginning after December 31, 2011.

[¶ 4022] Sec. 308. Extension of employer wage credit for employees who are active duty members of the uniformed services.
* * * * * * * * * * * *

(b) Effective date. The amendment made by this section shall apply to payments made after December 31, 2011.

[¶ 4023] Sec. 309. Extension of work opportunity tax credit.
* * * * * * * * * * * *

(b) Effective date. The amendment made by this section shall apply to individuals who begin work for the employer after December 31, 2011.

[¶ 4024] Sec. 310. Extension of qualified zone academy bonds.
* * * * * * * * * * * *

(b) Effective date. The amendments made by this section shall apply to obligations issued after December 31, 2011.

[¶ 4025] Sec. 311. Extension of 15-Year straight-line cost recovery for qualified leasehold improvements, qualified restaurant buildings and improvements, and qualified retail improvements.
* * * * * * * * * * * *

(b) Effective date. The amendments made by this section shall apply to property placed in service after December 31, 2011.

[¶ 4026] Sec. 312. Extension of 7-year recovery period for motorsports entertainment complexes.

(b) Effective date. The amendment made by this section shall apply to property placed in service after December 31, 2011.

[¶ 4027] Sec. 313. Extension of accelerated depreciation for business property on an Indian reservation.

* * * * * * * * * * *

(b) Effective Date. The amendment made by this section shall apply to property placed in service after December 31, 2011.

[¶ 4028] Sec. 314. Extension of enhanced charitable deduction for contributions of food inventory.

* * * * * * * * * * *

(b) Effective date. The amendment made by this section shall apply to contributions made after December 31, 2011.

[¶ 4029] Sec. 315. Extension of increased expensing limitations and treatment of certain real property as section 179 property.

* * * * * * * * * * *

(e) Effective Date. The amendments made by this section shall apply to taxable years beginning after December 31, 2011.

[¶ 4030] Sec. 316. Extension of election to expense mine safety equipment.

* * * * * * * * * * *

(b) Effective date. The amendment made by this section shall apply to property placed in service after December 31, 2011.

[¶ 4031] Sec. 317. Extension of special expensing rules for certain film and television productions.

* * * * * * * * * * *

(b) Effective date. The amendment made by this section shall apply to productions commencing after December 31, 2011.

[¶ 4032] Sec. 318. Extension of deduction allowable with respect to income attributable to domestic production activities in Puerto Rico.

* * * * * * * * * * *

(b) Effective date. The amendments made by this section shall apply to taxable years beginning after December 31, 2011.

[¶ 4033] Sec. 319. Extension of modification of tax treatment of certain payments to controlling exempt organizations.

* * * * * * * * * * *

(b) Effective date. The amendment made by this section shall apply to payments received or accrued after December 31, 2011.

[¶ 4034] Sec. 320. Extension of treatment of certain dividends of regulated investment companies.

* * * * * * * * * * *

(b) Effective date. The amendments made by this section shall apply to taxable years beginning after December 31, 2011.

[¶ 4035] Sec. 321. Extension of RIC qualified investment entity treatment under FIRPTA.
* * * * * * * * * * * *

(b) Effective date.
(1) In general. The amendment made by subsection (a) shall take effect on January 1, 2012. Notwithstanding the preceding sentence, such amendment shall not apply with respect to the withholding requirement under section 1445 of the Internal Revenue Code of 1986 for any payment made before the date of the enactment of this Act.
(2) Amounts withheld on or before date of enactment. In the case of a regulated investment company—
(A) which makes a distribution after December 31, 2011, and before the date of the enactment of this Act; and
(B) which would (but for the second sentence of paragraph (1)) have been required to withhold with respect to such distribution under section 1445 of such Code,
such investment company shall not be liable to any person to whom such distribution was made for any amount so withheld and paid over to the Secretary of the Treasury.

[¶ 4036] Sec. 322. Extension of Subpart F exception for active financing income.
* * * * * * * * * * * *

(c) Effective date. The amendments made by this section shall apply to taxable years of foreign corporations beginning after December 31, 2011, and to taxable years of United States shareholders with or within which any such taxable year of such foreign corporation ends.

[¶ 4037] Sec. 323. Extension of look-thru treatment of payments between related controlled foreign corporations under foreign PERSONAL HOLDING COMPANY RULES.
* * * * * * * * * * * *

(b) Effective date. The amendment made by this section shall apply to taxable years of foreign corporations beginning after December 31, 2011, and to taxable years of United States shareholders with or within which such taxable years of foreign corporations end.

[¶ 4038] Sec. 324. Extension of temporary exclusion of 100 percent of gain on certain small business stock.
* * * * * * * * * * * *

(c) Effective dates.
(1) In general. The amendments made by subsection (a) shall apply to stock acquired after December 31, 2011.
(2) Subsection (b)(1). The amendment made by subsection (b)(1) shall take effect as if included in section 1241(a) of division B of the American Recovery and Reinvestment Act of 2009.
(3) Subsection (b)(2). The amendment made by subsection (b)(2) shall take effect as if included in section 2011(a) of the Creating Small Business Jobs Act of 2010.

[¶ 4039] Sec. 325. Extension of basis adjustment to stock of S corporations making charitable contributions of property.
* * * * * * * * * * * *

(b) Effective date. The amendment made by this section shall apply to contributions made in taxable years beginning after December 31, 2011.

[¶ 4040] Sec. 326. Extension of reduction in s-corporation recognition period for built-in gains tax.
* * * * * * * * * * * *

(c) Effective date. The amendments made by this section shall apply to taxable years beginning after December 31, 2011.

[¶ 4041] Sec. 327. Extension of empowerment zone tax incentives.
   * * * * * * * * * * *

(c) Treatment of Certain Termination Dates Specified in Nominations. In the case of a designation of an empowerment zone the nomination for which included a termination date which is contemporaneous with the date specified in subparagraph (A)(i) of section 1391(d)(1) of the Internal Revenue Code of 1986 (as in effect before the enactment of this Act), subparagraph (B) of such section shall not apply with respect to such designation if, after the date of the enactment of this section, the entity which made such nomination amends the nomination to provide for a new termination date in such manner as the Secretary of the Treasury (or the Secretary's designee) may provide.

(d) Effective date. The amendments made by this section shall apply to periods after December 31, 2011.

[¶ 4042] Sec. 328. Extension of tax-exempt financing for New York liberty zone.
   * * * * * * * * * * *

(b) Effective date. The amendment made by this section shall apply to bonds issued after December 31, 2011.

[¶ 4043] Sec. 329. Extension of temporary increase in limit on cover over of rum excise taxes to Puerto Rico and the Virgin Islands
   * * * * * * * * * * *

(b) Effective date. The amendment made by this section shall apply to distilled spirits brought into the United States after December 31, 2011.

[¶ 4044] Sec. 330. Modification and extension of American Samoa economic development credit.

(a) Modification.
    (1) In general. Subsection (a) of section 119 of division A of the Tax Relief and Health Care Act of 2006 is amended by striking "if such corporation" and all that follows and inserting "if—
    "(1) in the case of a taxable year beginning before January 1, 2012, such corporation—
    "(A) is an existing credit claimant with respect to American Samoa, and
    "(B) elected the application of section 936 of the Internal Revenue Code of 1986 for its last taxable year beginning before January 1, 2006, and
    "(2) in the case of a taxable year beginning after December 31, 2011, such corporation meets the requirements of subsection (e).".
    (2) Requirements. Section 119 of division A of such Act is amended by adding at the end the following new subsection:
    "(e) Qualified Production Activities Income Requirement- A corporation meets the requirement of this subsection if such corporation has qualified production activities income, as defined in subsection (c) of section 199 of the Internal Revenue Code of 1986, determined by substituting "American Samoa" for "the United States" each place it appears in paragraphs (3), (4), and (6) of such subsection (c), for the taxable year.".

(b) Extension. Subsection (d) of section 119 of division A of the Tax Relief and Health Care Act of 2006 is amended by striking "shall apply" and all that follows and inserting "shall apply—

"(1) in the case of a corporation that meets the requirements of subparagraphs (A) and (B) of subsection (a)(1), to the first 8 taxable years of such corporation which begin after December 31, 2006, and before January 1, 2014, and

"(2) in the case of a corporation that does not meet the requirements of subparagraphs (A) and (B) of subsection (a)(1), to the first 2 taxable years of such corporation which begin after December 31, 2011, and before January 1, 2014.".

(c) Effective date. The amendments made by this section shall apply to taxable years beginning after December 31, 2011.

[¶ 4045] Sec. 331. Extension and modification of bonus depreciation.
* * * * * * * * * * *

(f) Effective date. The amendments made by this section shall apply to property placed in service after December 31, 2012, in taxable years ending after such date.

TITLE IV— Energy tax extenders

[¶ 4046] Sec. 401. Extension of credit for energy-efficient existing homes.

(b) Effective date. The amendment made by this section shall apply to property placed in service after December 31, 2011.

[¶ 4047] Sec. 402. Extension of credit for alternative fuel vehicle refueling property.
* * * * * * * * * * *

(b) Effective date. The amendment made by this section shall apply to property placed in service after December 31, 2011.

[¶ 4048] Sec. 403. Extension of credit for 2- or 3-wheeled plug-in electric vehicles.
* * * * * * * * * * *

(c) Effective date. The amendments made by this section shall apply to vehicles acquired after December 31, 2011.

[¶ 4049] Sec. 404. Extension and modification of cellulosic biofuel producer credit.

(a) Extension.
* * * * * * * * * * *
(3) Effective date. The amendments made by this subsection shall take effect as if included in section 15321(b) of the Heartland, Habitat, and Horticulture Act of 2008.

(b) Algae Treated as a Qualified Feedstock.
* * * * * * * * * * *
(4) Effective date. The amendments made by this subsection shall apply to fuels sold or used after the date of the enactment of this Act.

[¶ 4050] Sec. 405. Extension of incentives for biodiesel and renewable diesel.

(b) Excise Tax Credits and Outlay Payments for Biodiesel and Renewable Diesel Fuel Mixtures.
* * * * * * * * * * *

(c) Effective date. The amendments made by this section shall apply to fuel sold or used after December 31, 2011.

[¶ 4051] Sec. 406. Extension of production credit for Indian coal facilities placed in service before 2009.

* * * * * * * * * * * *

(b) Effective date. The amendment made by this section shall apply to coal produced after December 31, 2012.

[¶ 4052] Sec. 407. Extension and modification of credits with respect to facilities producing energy from certain renewable resources.

(d) Effective dates.

    (1) In general. Except as provided in paragraphs (2) and (3), the amendments made by this section shall take effect on the date of the enactment of this Act.

    (2) Modification to definition of municipal solid waste. The amendments made by subsection (a)(2) shall apply to electricity produced and sold after the date of the enactment of this Act, in taxable years ending after such date.

    (3) Technical corrections. The amendments made by subsection (c) shall apply as if included in the enactment of the provisions of the American Recovery and Reinvestment Act of 2009 to which they relate.

[¶ 4053] Sec. 408. Extension of credit for energy-efficient new homes.
    * * * * * * * * * * * *

(c) Effective date. The amendments made by this section shall apply to homes acquired after December 31, 2011.

[¶ 4054] Sec. 409. Extension of credit for energy-efficient appliances.
    * * * * * * * * * * * *

(b) Provisions Specified. The provisions of section 45M(b) specified in this subsection are subparagraph (C) of paragraph (1) and subparagraph (E) of paragraph (2).

(c) Effective date. The amendments made by this section shall apply to appliances produced after December 31, 2011.

[¶ 4055] Sec. 410. Extension and modification of special allowance for cellulosic biofuel plant property.

(a) Extension/
    * * * * * * * * * * * *

    (2) Effective date. The amendment made by this subsection shall apply to property placed in service after December 31, 2012.

(b) Algae Treated as a Qualified Feedstock for Purposes of Bonus Depreciation for Biofuel Plant Property—
    * * * * * * * * * * * *

    (3) Effective date. The amendments made by this subsection shall apply to property placed in service after the date of the enactment of this Act.

[¶ 4056] Sec. 411. Extension of special rule for sales or dispositions to implement FERC or state electric restructuring policy for qualified electric utilities.

(b) Effective date. The amendment made by this section shall apply to dispositions after December 31, 2011.

[¶ 4057] Sec. 412. Extension of alternative fuels excise tax credits.
    * * * * * * * * * * * *

(c) Effective date. The amendments made by this section shall apply to fuel sold or used after December 31, 2011.

TITLE V— Unemployment

[¶ 4058] Sec. 501. Extension of emergency unemployment compensation program.

(a) Extension. Section 4007(a)(2) of the Supplemental Appropriations Act, 2008 (Public Law 110-252; 26 U.S.C. 3304 note) is amended by striking "January 2, 2013" and inserting "January 1, 2014".

(b) Funding. Section 4004(e)(1) of the Supplemental Appropriations Act, 2008 (Public Law 110-252; 26 U.S.C. 3304 note) is amended—

    (1) in subparagraph (H), by striking "and" at the end; and

    (2) by inserting after subparagraph (I) the following:

"(J) the amendments made by section 501(a) of the American Taxpayer Relief Act of 2012;".

(c) Effective date. The amendments made by this section shall take effect as if included in the enactment of the Unemployment Benefits Extension Act of 2012 (Public Law 112-96)

[¶ 4059] Sec. 502. Temporary extension of extended benefit provisions.

(a) In General. Section 2005 of the Assistance for Unemployed Workers and Struggling Families Act, as contained in Public Law 111-5 (26 U.S.C. 3304 note), is amended—

    (1) by striking "December 31, 2012" each place it appears and inserting "December 31, 2013"; and

    (2) in subsection (c), by striking "June 30, 2013" and inserting "June 30, 2014".

(b) Extension of Matching for States With no Waiting Week. Section 5 of the Unemployment Compensation Extension Act of 2008 (Public Law 110-449; 26 U.S.C. 3304 note) is amended by striking "June 30, 2013" and inserting "June 30, 2014".

(c) Extension of Modification of Indicators Under the Extended Benefit Program. Section 203 of the Federal-State Extended Unemployment Compensation Act of 1970 (26 U.S.C. 3304 note) is amended—

    (1) in subsection (d), by striking "December 31, 2012" and inserting "December 31, 2013"; and

    (2) in subsection (f)(2), by striking "December 31, 2012" and inserting "December 31, 2013".

(d) Effective date. The amendments made by this section shall take effect as if included in the enactment of the Unemployment Benefits Extension Act of 2012 (Public Law 112-96).

[¶ 4060] Sec. 503. Extension of funding for reemployment services and reemployment and eligibility assessment activities.

(a) In General. Section 4004(c)(2)(A) of the Supplemental Appropriations Act, 2008 (Public Law 110-252; 26 U.S.C. 3304 note) is amended by striking "through fiscal year 2013" and inserting "through fiscal year 2014".

(b) Effective date. The amendments made by this section shall take effect as if included in the enactment of the Unemployment Benefits Extension Act of 2012 (Public Law 112-96).

[¶ 4061] Sec. 504. Additional extended unemployment benefits under the Railroad Unemployment Insurance Act.

(a) **Extension.** Section 2(c)(2)(D)(iii) of the Railroad Unemployment Insurance Act, as added by section 2006 of the American Recovery and Reinvestment Act of 2009 (Public Law 111-5) and as amended by section 9 of the Worker, Homeownership, and Business Assistance Act of 2009 (Public Law 111-92), section 505 of the Tax Relief, Unemployment Insurance Reauthorization, and Job Creation Act of 2010 (Public Law 111-312), section 202 of the Temporary Payroll Tax Cut Continuation Act of 2011 (Public Law 112-78), and section 2124 of the Unemployment Benefits Extension Act of 2012 (Public Law 112-96), is amended—

　(1) by striking "June 30, 2012" and inserting "June 30, 2013"; and

　(2) by striking "December 31, 2012" and inserting "December 31, 2013".

(b) **Clarification on Authority to Use Funds.** Funds appropriated under either the first or second sentence of clause (iv) of section 2(c)(2)(D) of the Railroad Unemployment Insurance Act shall be available to cover the cost of additional extended unemployment benefits provided under such section 2(c)(2)(D) by reason of the amendments made by subsection (a) as well as to cover the cost of such benefits provided under such section 2(c)(2)(D), as in effect on the day before the date of enactment of this Act.

(c) **Funding for Administration.** Out of any funds in the Treasury not otherwise appropriated, there are appropriated to the Railroad Retirement Board $250,000 for administrative expenses associated with the payment of additional extended unemployment benefits provided under section 2(c)(2)(D) of the Railroad Unemployment Insurance Act by reason of the amendments made by subsection (a), to remain available until expended.

* * * * * * * * * * * *

TITLE IX— Budget provisions

Subtitle A— Modifications of Sequestration

[¶ 4062] Sec. 901. Treatment of sequester.

(a) **Adjustment.** Section 251A(3) of the Balanced Budget and Emergency Deficit Control Act of 1985 is amended—

　(1) in subparagraph (C), by striking "and" after the semicolon;

　(2) in subparagraph (D), by striking the period and inserting" ; and"; and

　(3) by inserting at the end the following:

"(E) for fiscal year 2013, reducing the amount calculated under subparagraphs (A) through (D) by $24,000,000,000.".

(b) **After Session Sequester.** Notwithstanding any other provision of law, the fiscal year 2013 spending reductions required by section 251(a)(1) of the Balanced Budget and Emergency Deficit Control Act of 1985 shall be evaluated and implemented on March 27, 2013.

(c) **Postponement of Budget Control Act Sequester for Fiscal Year 2013.** Section 251A of the Balanced Budget and Emergency Deficit Control Act of 1985 is amended—

　(1) in paragraph (4), by striking "January 2, 2013" and inserting "March 1, 2013"; and

　(2) in paragraph (7)(A), by striking "January 2, 2013" and inserting "March 1, 2013".

(d) Additional Adjustments—

　(1) **Section 251.** Paragraphs (2) and (3) of section 251(c) of the Balanced Budget and Emergency Deficit Control Act of 1985 are amended to read as follows:

"(2) for fiscal year 2013—

"(A) for the security category, as defined in section 250(c)(4)(B), $684,000,000,000 in budget authority; and

"(B) for the nonsecurity category, as defined in section 250(c)(4)(A), $359,000,000,000 in budget authority;

"(3) for fiscal year 2014—
"(A) for the security category, $552,000,000,000 in budget authority; and
"(B) for the nonsecurity category, $506,000,000,000 in budget authority;".

(e) 2013 Sequester. On March 1, 2013, the President shall order a sequestration for fiscal year 2013 pursuant to section 251A of the Balanced Budget and Emergency Deficit Control Act of 1985, as amended by this section, pursuant to which, only for the purposes of the calculation in sections 251A(5)(A), 251A(6)(A), and 251A(7)(A), section 251(c)(2) shall be applied as if it read as follows:
"(2) For fiscal year 2013—
"(A) for the security category, $544,000,000,000 in budget authority; and
"(B) for the nonsecurity category, $499,000,000,000 in budget authority;".

[¶ 4063] Sec. 902. Amounts in APPLICABLE retirement plans may be transferred to designated roth accounts without distribution.

(b) Effective date. The amendment made by this section shall apply to transfers after December 31, 2012, in taxable years ending after such date.

Subtitle B— Budgetary Effects

[¶ 4064] Sec. 911. Budgetary effects.

(a) PAYGO Scorecard. The budgetary effects of this Act shall not be entered on either PAYGO scorecard maintained pursuant to section 4(d) of the Statutory Pay-As-You-Go Act of 2010.

(b) Senate PAYGO Scorecard. The budgetary effects of this Act shall not be entered on any PAYGO scorecard maintained for purposes of section 201 of S. Con. Res. 21 (110th Congress).

Amend the title so as to read: "An Act entitled the "American Taxpayer Relief Act of 2012".

Attest:
Secretary.
112th CONGRESS
2d Session
H.R. 8
AMENDMENTS

To amend the African Growth and Opportunity Act to extend the third-country fabric program and to add South Sudan to the list of countries eligible for designation under that Act, to make technical corrections to the Harmonized Tariff Schedule of the United States relating to the textile and apparel rules of origin for the Dominican Republic-Central America-United States Free Trade Agreement, to approve the renewal of import restrictions contained in the Burmese Freedom and Democracy Act of 2003, and for other purposes. [PL112-163, 8/2/2012]

[¶ 4065] One Hundred Twelfth Congress 2d Session

AN ACT

To amend the African Growth and Opportunity Act to extend the third-country fabric program and to add South Sudan to the list of countries eligible for designation under that Act, to make technical corrections to the Harmonized Tariff Schedule of the United States relating to the textile and apparel rules of origin for the Dominican Republic-Central America-United States Free Trade Agreement, to approve the renewal of import restrictions contained in the Burmese Freedom and Democracy Act of 2003, and for other purposes.

Be it enacted by the Senate and House of Representatives of the United States of America in Congress assembled,

* * * * * * * * * * *

[¶ 4066] **Sec. 4. TIME FOR PAYMENT OF CORPORATE ESTIMATED TAXES.** Notwithstanding section 6655 of the Internal Revenue Code of 1986—

(1) in the case of a corporation with assets of not less than $1,000,000,000 (determined as of the end of the preceding taxable year), the amount of any required installment of corporate estimated tax which is otherwise due in July, August, or September of 2017 shall be 100.25 percent of such amount; and

(2) the amount of the next required installment after an installment referred to in paragraph (1) shall be appropriately reduced to reflect the amount of the increase by reason of such paragraph.

* * * * * * * * * * *

Passed the House of Representatives August 2, 2012.

* * * * * * * * * * *

Moving Ahead for Progress in the 21st Century Act [PL112-141, 6/29/2012]

[¶ 4067] One Hundred Twelfth Congress of the
United States of America

AT THE SECOND SESSION

Begun and held at the City of Washington on Tuesday,
the third day of January, two thousand and twelve

An Act

To authorize funds for Federal-aid highways, highway safety programs, and transit programs, and for other purposes.

Be it enacted by the Senate and House of Representatives of the United States of America in Congress assembled,

DIVISION D— FINANCE [§§40001—40251]

[¶ 4068] **Sec. 40001. SHORT TITLE.** This division may be cited as the "Highway Investment, Job Creation, and Economic Growth Act of 2012".

TITLE I— EXTENSION OF HIGHWAY TRUST FUND EXPENDITURE AUTHORITY AND RELATED TAXES [§§40101—40102]

[¶ 4069] **Sec. 40101. EXTENSION OF TRUST FUND EXPENDITURE AUTHORITY.**
* * * * * * * * * * * *

(d) Effective Date- The amendments made by this section shall take effect on July 1, 2012.

[¶ 4070] **Sec. 40102. EXTENSION OF HIGHWAY-RELATED TAXES.**
* * * * * * * * * * * *

(f) Effective Date- Except as otherwise provided in this section, the amendments made by this section shall take effect on July 1, 2012.

TITLE II— REVENUE PROVISIONS [§§40201—40251]

Subtitle A— Leaking Underground Storage Tank Trust Fund [§40201]

[¶ 4071] **Sec. 40201. TRANSFER FROM LEAKING UNDERGROUND STORAGE TANK TRUST FUND TO HIGHWAY TRUST FUND.**
* * * * * * * * * * * *

Subtitle B— Pension Provisions [§§40211—40242]

PART I— PENSION FUNDING STABILIZATION [§40211]

[¶ 4072] **Sec. 40211. PENSION FUNDING STABILIZATION.**
* * * * * * * * * * * *

(c) Effective Date—
(1) IN GENERAL- The amendments made by this section shall apply with respect to plan years beginning after December 31, 2011.
(2) RULES WITH RESPECT TO ELECTIONS—
(A) ADJUSTED FUNDING TARGET ATTAINMENT PERCENTAGE- A plan sponsor may elect not to have the amendments made by this section apply to any plan year beginning before January 1, 2013, either (as specified in the election)—
(i) for all purposes for which such amendments apply, or

(ii) solely for purposes of determining the adjusted funding target attainment percentage under sections 436 of the Internal Revenue Code of 1986 and 206(g) of the Employee Retirement Income Security Act of 1974 for such plan year.

A plan shall not be treated as failing to meet the requirements of sections 204(g) of such Act and 411(d)(6) of such Code solely by reason of an election under this paragraph.

(B) OPT OUT OF EXISTING ELECTIONS- If, on the date of the enactment of this Act, an election is in effect with respect to any plan under sections 303(h)((2)(D)(ii) of the Employee Retirement Income Security Act of 1974 and 430(h)((2)(D)(ii) of the Internal Revenue Code of 1986, then, notwithstanding the last sentence of each such section, the plan sponsor may revoke such election without the consent of the Secretary of the Treasury. The plan sponsor may make such revocation at any time before the date which is 1 year after such date of enactment and such revocation shall be effective for the 1st plan year to which the amendments made by this section apply and all subsequent plan years. Nothing in this subparagraph shall preclude a plan sponsor from making a subsequent election in accordance with such sections.

PART II— PBGC PREMIUMS [§§40221—40222]

[¶ 4073] Sec. 40221. SINGLE EMPLOYER PLAN ANNUAL PREMIUM RATES.
* * * * * * * * * * *

[¶ 4074] Sec. 40222. MULTIEMPLOYER ANNUAL PREMIUM RATES.
* * * * * * * * * * *

PART III— IMPROVEMENTS OF PBGC [§§40231—40234]

[¶ 4075] Sec. 40231. PENSION BENEFIT GUARANTY CORPORATION GOVERNANCE IMPROVEMENT.

(a) Board of Directors of the Pension Benefit Guaranty Corporation—
* * * * * * * * * * *

(e) Senses of Congress—
(1) FORMATION OF COMMITTEES- It is the sense of Congress that the board of directors of the Pension Benefit Guaranty Corporation established under section 4002 of the Employee Retirement Income Security Act of 1974 (29 U.S.C. 1302), as amended by this section, should form committees, including an audit committee and an investment committee composed of not less than 2 members, to enhance the overall effectiveness of the board of directors.
(2) ADVISORY COMMITTEE- It is the sense of Congress that the advisory committee to the Pension Benefit Guaranty Corporation established under section 4002 of the Employee Retirement Income Security Act of 1974 (29 U.S.C. 1302), as amended by this section, should provide to the board of directors of such corporation policy recommendations regarding changes to the law that would be beneficial to the corporation or the voluntary private pension system.

(f) Study Regarding Governance Structures—
(1) IN GENERAL- Not later than 90 days after the date of enactment of this Act, the Pension Benefit Guaranty Corporation shall enter into a contract with the National Academy of Public Administration to conduct the study described in paragraph (2) with respect to the Pension Benefit Guaranty Corporation.
(2) CONTENT OF STUDY- The study conducted under paragraph (1) shall include—
(A) a review of the governance structures of governmental and nongovernmental organizations that are analogous to the Pension Benefit Guaranty Corporation; and
(B) recommendations regarding (i) the ideal size and composition of the board of directors of the Pension Benefit Guaranty Corporation;

(ii) procedures to select and remove members of such board;

(iii) qualifications and term lengths of members of such board; and

(iv) policies necessary to enhance Congressional oversight and transparency of such board and to mitigate potential conflicts of interest of the members of such board.

(3) SUBMISSION TO CONGRESS- Not later than 1 year after the initiation of the study under paragraph (1), the National Academy of Public Administration shall submit the results of the study to the Committees on Health, Education, Labor, and Pensions and Finance of the Senate and the Committees on Education and the Workforce and Ways and Means of the House of Representatives.

[¶ 4076] Sec. 40232. PARTICIPANT AND PLAN SPONSOR ADVOCATE.
* * * * * * * * * * * *

[¶ 4077] Sec. 40233. QUALITY CONTROL PROCEDURES FOR THE PENSION BENEFIT GUARANTY CORPORATION.

(a) Annual Peer Review of Insurance Modeling Systems- The Pension Benefit Guaranty Corporation shall contract with a capable agency or organization that is independent from the Corporation, such as the Social Security Administration, to conduct an annual peer review of the Corporation's Single-Employer Pension Insurance Modeling System and the Corporation's Multiemployer Pension Insurance Modeling System. The board of directors of the Corporation shall designate the agency or organization with which any such contract is entered into. The first of such annual peer reviews shall be initiated no later than 3 months after the date of enactment of this Act.

(b) Policies and Procedures Relating to the Policy, Research, and Analysis Department- The Pension Benefit Guaranty Corporation shall—

(1) develop written quality review policies and procedures for all modeling and actuarial work performed by the Corporation's Policy, Research, and Analysis Department; and

(2) conduct a record management review of such Department to determine what records must be retained as Federal records.

(c) Report Relating to OIG Recommendations- Not later than 2 months after the date of enactment of this Act, the Pension Benefit Guaranty Corporation shall submit to Congress a report, approved by the board of directors of the Corporation, setting forth a timetable for addressing the outstanding recommendations of the Office of the Inspector General relating to the Policy, Research, and Analysis Department and the Benefits Administration and Payment Department.

[¶ 4078] Sec. 40234. LINE OF CREDIT REPEAL.
* * * * * * * * * * * *

PART IV— TRANSFERS OF EXCESS PENSION ASSETS [§§40241—40242]

[¶ 4079] Sec. 40241. EXTENSION FOR TRANSFERS OF EXCESS PENSION ASSETS TO RETIREE HEALTH ACCOUNTS.
* * * * * * * * * * * *

(c) Effective Date- The amendments made by this Act shall take effect on the date of the enactment of this Act.

[¶ 4080] Sec. 40242. TRANSFER OF EXCESS PENSION ASSETS TO RETIREE GROUP TERM LIFE INSURANCE ACCOUNTS.
* * * * * * * * * * * *

(h) Effective Date—

(1) IN GENERAL- The amendments made by this section shall apply to transfers made after the date of the enactment of this Act.

(2) CONFORMING AMENDMENTS RELATING TO PENSION PROTECTION ACT- The amendments made by subsections (b)(3)(B) and (f) shall take effect as if included in the amendments made by section 841(a) of the Pension Protection Act of 2006.

Subtitle C— Additional Transfers to Highway Trust Fund [§40251]

[¶ 4081] Sec. 40251. ADDITIONAL TRANSFERS TO HIGHWAY TRUST FUND.

* * * * * * * * * * * *

DIVISION F— MISCELLANEOUS [§§100101—100302]

TITLE I— REAUTHORIZATION OF CERTAIN PROGRAMS [§§100101—100125]

Subtitle A— Secure Rural Schools and Community Self-determination Program [§100101]

[¶ 4082] Sec. 100101. SECURE RURAL SCHOOLS AND COMMUNITY SELF-DETERMINATION PROGRAM.

(a) Amendments- The Secure Rural Schools and Community Self-Determination Act of 2000 (16 U.S.C. 7101 et seq.) is amended—

  (1) in section 3(11)

  (A) in subparagraph (A), by striking "and" after the semicolon at the end;

  (B)in subparagraph (B)(i) by striking "fiscal year 2009 and each fiscal year thereafter" and inserting "each of fiscal years 2009 through 2011"; and

  (ii) by striking the period at the end and inserting "; and"; and

  (C) by adding at the end the following:

"(C) for fiscal year 2012 and each fiscal year thereafter, the amount that is equal to 95 percent of the full funding amount for the preceding fiscal year.";

  (2) in sections 101, 102, 203, 207, 208, 304, and 402, by striking "2011" each place it appears and inserting "2012";

  (3) in section 102

  (A) by striking "2008" each place it appears and inserting "2012";

  (B) in subsection (b)(2)(B), by inserting "in 2012" before ", the election"; and

  (C)in subsection (d)(i) in paragraph (1)(A), by striking "paragraph (3)(B)" and inserting "subparagraph (D)"; and

  (ii) in paragraph (3)—

    (I) by striking subparagraph (A) and inserting the following:

"(A) NOTIFICATION- The Governor of each eligible State shall notify the Secretary concerned of an election by an eligible county under this subsection not later than September 30, 2012, and each September 30 thereafter for each succeeding fiscal year.";

    (II) by redesignating subparagraph (B) as subparagraph (D) and moving the subparagraph so as to appear at the end of paragraph (1) of subsection (d); and

    (III) by inserting after subparagraph (A) the following:

"(B) FAILURE TO ELECT- If the Governor of an eligible State fails to notify the Secretary concerned of the election for an eligible county by the date specified in subparagraph (A)—

"(i) the eligible county shall be considered to have elected to expend 80 percent of the funds in accordance with paragraph (1)(A); and

"(ii) the remainder shall be available to the Secretary concerned to carry out projects in the eligible county to further the purpose described in section 202(b).";

  (4) in section 103(d)(2), by striking "fiscal year 2011" and inserting "each of fiscal years 2011 and 2012";

(5) in section 202, by adding at the end the following:

"(c) Administrative Expenses- A resource advisory committee may, in accordance with section 203, propose to use not more than 10 percent of the project funds of an eligible county for any fiscal year for administrative expenses associated with operating the resource advisory committee under this title.";

    (6) in section 204(e)(3)(B)(iii), by striking "and 2011" and inserting "through 2012";

    (7) in section 205(a)(4), by striking "2006" each place it appears and inserting "2011";

    (8) in section 208(b), by striking "2012" and inserting "2013";

    (9) in section 302(a)(2)(A), by inserting "and" after the semicolon; and

    (10) in section 304(b), by striking "2012" and inserting "2013".

(b) Failure To Make Election- For each county that failed to make an election for fiscal year 2011 in accordance with section 102(d)(3)(A) of the Secure Rural Schools and Community Self-Determination Act of 2000 (16 U.S.C. 7112(d)(3)(A)), there shall be available to the Secretary of Agriculture to carry out projects to further the purpose described in section 202(b) of that Act (16 U.S.C. 7122(b)), from amounts in the Treasury not otherwise appropriated, the amount that is equal to 15 percent of the total share of the State payment that otherwise would have been made to the county under that Act for fiscal year 2011.

Subtitle B— Payment in Lieu of Taxes Program [§100111]

[¶ 4083] Sec. 100111. PAYMENTS IN LIEU OF TAXES. Section 6906 of title 31, United States Code, is amended by striking "2012" and inserting "2013".

Subtitle C— Offsets [§§100121—100125]

[¶ 4084] Sec. 100121. PHASED RETIREMENT AUTHORITY.

(a) CSRS- Chapter 83 of title 5, United States Code, is amended—

    (1) in section 8331

        (A) in paragraph (30) by striking "and" at the end;

        (B) in paragraph (31) by striking the period at the end and inserting "; and"; and

        (C) by adding at the end the following:

"(32) "Director" means the Director of the Office of Personnel Management.";

    (2) by inserting after section 8336 the following:

"Sec. 8336a. Phased retirement

"(a) For the purposes of this section—

"(1) the term "composite retirement annuity" means the annuity computed when a phased retiree attains full retirement status;

"(2) the term "full retirement status" means that a phased retiree has ceased employment and is entitled, upon application, to a composite retirement annuity;

"(3) the term "phased employment" means the less-than-full-time employment of a phased retiree;

"(4) the term "phased retiree" means a retirement-eligible employee who—

"(A) makes an election under subsection (b); and

"(B) has not entered full retirement status;

"(5) the term "phased retirement annuity" means the annuity payable under this section before full retirement;

"(6) the term "phased retirement percentage" means the percentage which, when added to the working percentage for a phased retiree, produces a sum of 100 percent;

"(7) the term "phased retirement period" means the period beginning on the date on which an individual becomes entitled to receive a phased retirement annuity and ending on the date on which the individual dies or separates from phased employment;

"(8) the term "phased retirement status" means that a phased retiree is concurrently employed in phased employment and eligible to receive a phased retirement annuity;

"(9) the term "retirement-eligible employee"—

"(A) means an individual who, if the individual separated from the service, would meet the requirements for retirement under subsection (a) or (b) of section 8336; but

"(B) does not include an employee described in section 8335 after the date on which the employee is required to be separated from the service by reason of such section; and

"(10) the term "working percentage" means the percentage of full-time employment equal to the quotient obtained by dividing—

"(A) the number of hours per pay period to be worked by a phased retiree, as scheduled in accordance with subsection (b)(2); by

"(B) the number of hours per pay period to be worked by an employee serving in a comparable position on a full-time basis.

"(b)(1) With the concurrence of the head of the employing agency, and under regulations promulgated by the Director, a retirement-eligible employee who has been employed on a full-time basis for not less than the 3-year period ending on the date on which the retirement-eligible employee makes an election under this subsection may elect to enter phased retirement status.

"(2)(A) Subject to subparagraph (B), at the time of entering phased retirement status, a phased retiree shall be appointed to a position for which the working percentage is 50 percent.

"(B) The Director may, by regulation, provide for working percentages different from the percentage specified under subparagraph (A), which shall be not less than 20 percent and not more than 80 percent.

"(C) The working percentage for a phased retiree may not be changed during the phased retiree's phased retirement period.

"(D)(i) Not less than 20 percent of the hours to be worked by a phased retiree shall consist of mentoring.

"(ii) The Director may, by regulation, provide for exceptions to the requirement under clause (i).

"(iii) Clause (i) shall not apply to a phased retiree serving in the United States Postal Service. Nothing in this clause shall prevent the application of clause (i) or (ii) with respect to a phased retiree serving in the Postal Regulatory Commission.

"(3) A phased retiree—

"(A) may not be employed in more than one position at any time; and

"(B) may transfer to another position in the same or a different agency, only if the transfer does not result in a change in the working percentage.

"(4) A retirement-eligible employee may make not more than one election under this subsection during the retirement-eligible employee's lifetime.

"(5) A retirement-eligible employee who makes an election under this subsection may not make an election under section 8343a.

"(c)(1) Except as otherwise provided under this subsection, the phased retirement annuity for a phased retiree is the product obtained by multiplying—

"(A) the amount of an annuity computed under section 8339 that would have been payable to the phased retiree if, on the date on which the phased retiree enters phased retirement status, the phased retiree had separated from service and retired under section 8336(a) or (b); by

"(B) the phased retirement percentage for the phased retiree.

"(2) A phased retirement annuity shall be paid in addition to the basic pay for the position to which a phased retiree is appointed during phased employment.

"(3) A phased retirement annuity shall be adjusted in accordance with section 8340.

"(4)(A) A phased retirement annuity shall not be subject to reduction for any form of survivor annuity, shall not serve as the basis of the computation of any survivor annuity, and shall not be subject to any court order requiring a survivor annuity to be provided to any individual.

"(B) A phased retirement annuity shall be subject to a court order providing for division, allotment, assignment, execution, levy, attachment, garnishment, or other legal process on the same basis as other annuities.

"(5) Any reduction of a phased retirement annuity based on an election under section 8334(d)(2) shall be applied to the phased retirement annuity after computation under paragraph (1).

"(6)(A) Any deposit, or election of an actuarial annuity reduction in lieu of a deposit, for military service or for creditable civilian service for which retirement deductions were not made or refunded shall be made by a retirement-eligible employee at or before the time the retirement-eligible employee enters phased retirement status. No such deposit may be made, or actuarial adjustment in lieu thereof elected, at the time a phased retiree enters full retirement status.

"(B) Notwithstanding subparagraph (A), if a phased retiree does not make such a deposit and dies in service as a phased retiree, a survivor of the phased retiree shall have the same right to make such deposit as would have been available had the employee not entered phased retirement status and died in service.

"(C) If a phased retiree makes an election for an actuarial annuity reduction under section 8334(d)(2) and dies in service as a phased retiree, the amount of any deposit upon which such actuarial reduction shall have been based shall be deemed to have been fully paid.

"(7) A phased retirement annuity shall commence on the date on which a phased retiree enters phased employment.

"(8) No unused sick leave credit may be used in the computation of the phased retirement annuity.

"(d) All basic pay not in excess of the full-time rate of pay for the position to which a phased retiree is appointed shall be deemed to be basic pay for purposes of section 8334.

"(e) Under such procedures as the Director may prescribe, a phased retiree may elect to enter full retirement status at any time. Upon making such an election, a phased retiree shall be entitled to a composite retirement annuity.

"(f)(1) Except as provided otherwise under this subsection, a composite retirement annuity is a single annuity computed under regulations prescribed by the Director, equal to the sum of—

"(A) the amount of the phased retirement annuity as of the date of full retirement, before any reduction based on an election under section 8334(d)(2), and including any adjustments made under section 8340; and

"(B) the product obtained by multiplying—

"(i) the amount of an annuity computed under section 8339 that would have been payable at the time of full retirement if the individual had not elected a phased retirement and as if the individual was employed on a full-time basis in the position occupied during the phased retirement period and before any reduction for survivor annuity or reduction based on an election under section 8334(d)(2); by

"(ii) the working percentage.

"(2) After computing a composite retirement annuity under paragraph (1), the Director shall adjust the amount of the annuity for any applicable reductions for a survivor annuity and any previously elected actuarial reduction under section 8334(d)(2).

"(3) A composite retirement annuity shall be adjusted in accordance with section 8340, except that subsection (c)(1) of that section shall not apply.

"(4) In computing a composite retirement annuity under paragraph (1)(B)(i), the unused sick leave to the credit of a phased retiree at the time of entry into full retirement status shall be adjusted by dividing the number of hours of unused sick leave by the working percentage.

"(g)(1) Under such procedures and conditions as the Director may provide, and with the concurrence of the head of the employing agency, a phased retiree may elect to terminate phased retirement status and return to a full-time work schedule.

"(2) Upon entering a full-time work schedule based upon an election under paragraph (1), the phased retirement annuity of a phased retiree shall terminate.

"(3) After the termination of a phased retirement annuity under this subsection, the individual's rights under this subchapter shall be determined based on the law in effect at the time of any subsequent separation from service. For purposes of this subchapter or chapter 84, at time of the subsequent separation from service, the phased retirement period shall be treated as if it had been a period of part-time employment with the work schedule described in subsection (b)(2).

"(h) For purposes of section 8341—

"(1) the death of a phased retiree shall be deemed to be the death in service of an employee; and

"(2) the phased retirement period shall be deemed to have been a period of part-time employment with the work schedule described in subsection (b)(2).

"(i) Employment of a phased retiree shall not be deemed to be part-time career employment, as defined in section 3401(2).

"(j) A phased retiree is not eligible to apply for an annuity under section 8337.

"(k) For purposes of section 8341(h)(4), retirement shall be deemed to occur on the date on which a phased retiree enters into full retirement status.

"(l) For purposes of sections 8343 and 8351, and subchapter III of chapter 84, a phased retiree shall be deemed to be an employee.

"(m) A phased retiree is not subject to section 8344.

"(n) For purposes of chapter 87, a phased retiree shall be deemed to be receiving basic pay at the rate of a full-time employee in the position to which the phased retiree is appointed."; and

(3) in the table of sections by inserting after the item relating to section 8336 the following:

"8336a. Phased retirement.".

(b) FERS- Chapter 84 of title 5, United States Code, is amended—

(1) by inserting after section 8412 the following new section:

"Sec. 8412a. Phased retirement

"(a) For the purposes of this section—

"(1) the term "composite retirement annuity" means the annuity computed when a phased retiree attains full retirement status;

"(2) the term "full retirement status" means that a phased retiree has ceased employment and is entitled, upon application, to a composite retirement annuity;

"(3) the term "phased employment" means the less-than-full-time employment of a phased retiree;

"(4) the term "phased retiree" means a retirement-eligible employee who—

"(A) makes an election under subsection (b); and

"(B) has not entered full retirement status;

"(5) the term "phased retirement annuity" means the annuity payable under this section before full retirement;

"(6) the term "phased retirement percentage" means the percentage which, when added to the working percentage for a phased retiree, produces a sum of 100 percent;

"(7) the term "phased retirement period" means the period beginning on the date on which an individual becomes entitled to receive a phased retirement annuity and ending on the date on which the individual dies or separates from phased employment;

"(8) the term "phased retirement status" means that a phased retiree is concurrently employed in phased employment and eligible to receive a phased retirement annuity;

"(9) the term "retirement-eligible employee"—

"(A) means an individual who, if the individual separated from the service, would meet the requirements for retirement under subsection (a) or (b) of section 8412; and

"(B) does not include—

"(i) an individual who, if the individual separated from the service, would meet the requirements for retirement under subsection (d) or (e) of section 8412; but

"(ii) does not include an employee described in section 8425 after the date on which the employee is required to be separated from the service by reason of such section; and

"(10) the term "working percentage" means the percentage of full-time employment equal to the quotient obtained by dividing—

"(A) the number of hours per pay period to be worked by a phased retiree, as scheduled in accordance with subsection (b)(2); by

"(B) the number of hours per pay period to be worked by an employee serving in a comparable position on a full-time basis.

"(b)(1) With the concurrence of the head of the employing agency, and under regulations promulgated by the Director, a retirement-eligible employee who has been employed on a full-time basis for not less than the 3-year period ending on the date on which the retirement-eligible employee makes an election under this subsection may elect to enter phased retirement status.

"(2)(A) Subject to subparagraph (B), at the time of entering phased retirement status, a phased retiree shall be appointed to a position for which the working percentage is 50 percent.

"(B) The Director may, by regulation, provide for working percentages different from the percentage specified under subparagraph (A), which shall be not less than 20 percent and not more than 80 percent.

"(C) The working percentage for a phased retiree may not be changed during the phased retiree's phased retirement period.

"(D)(i) Not less than 20 percent of the hours to be worked by a phased retiree shall consist of mentoring.

"(ii) The Director may, by regulation, provide for exceptions to the requirement under clause (i).

"(iii) Clause (i) shall not apply to a phased retiree serving in the United States Postal Service. Nothing in this clause shall prevent the application of clause (i) or (ii) with respect to a phased retiree serving in the Postal Regulatory Commission.

"(3) A phased retiree—

"(A) may not be employed in more than one position at any time; and

"(B) may transfer to another position in the same or a different agency, only if the transfer does not result in a change in the working percentage.

"(4) A retirement-eligible employee may make not more than one election under this subsection during the retirement-eligible employee's lifetime.

"(5) A retirement-eligible employee who makes an election under this subsection may not make an election under section 8420a.

"(c)(1) Except as otherwise provided under this subsection, the phased retirement annuity for a phased retiree is the product obtained by multiplying—

"(A) the amount of an annuity computed under section 8415 that would have been payable to the phased retiree if, on the date on which the phased retiree enters phased retirement status, the phased retiree had separated from service and retired under section 8412 (a) or (b); by

"(B) the phased retirement percentage for the phased retiree.

"(2) A phased retirement annuity shall be paid in addition to the basic pay for the position to which a phased retiree is appointed during the phased employment.

"(3) A phased retirement annuity shall be adjusted in accordance with section 8462.

"(4)(A) A phased retirement annuity shall not be subject to reduction for any form of survivor annuity, shall not serve as the basis of the computation of any survivor annuity, and shall not be subject to any court order requiring a survivor annuity to be provided to any individual.

"(B) A phased retirement annuity shall be subject to a court order providing for division, allotment, assignment, execution, levy, attachment, garnishment, or other legal process on the same basis as other annuities.

"(5)(A) Any deposit, or election of an actuarial annuity reduction in lieu of a deposit, for military service or for creditable civilian service for which retirement deductions were not made or refunded, shall be made by a retirement-eligible employee at or before the time the retirement-eligible employee enters phased retirement status. No such deposit may be made, or actuarial adjustment in lieu thereof elected, at the time a phased retiree enters full retirement status.

"(B) Notwithstanding subparagraph (A), if a phased retiree does not make such a deposit and dies in service as a phased retiree, a survivor of the phased retiree shall have the same right to make such deposit as would have been available had the employee not entered phased retirement status and died in service.

"(6) A phased retirement annuity shall commence on the date on which a phased retiree enters phased employment.

"(7) No unused sick leave credit may be used in the computation of the phased retirement annuity.

"(d) All basic pay not in excess of the full-time rate of pay for the position to which a phased retiree is appointed shall be deemed to be basic pay for purposes of sections 8422 and 8423.

"(e) Under such procedures as the Director may prescribe, a phased retiree may elect to enter full retirement status at any time. Upon making such an election, a phased retiree shall be entitled to a composite retirement annuity.

"(f)(1) Except as provided otherwise under this subsection, a composite retirement annuity is a single annuity computed under regulations prescribed by the Director, equal to the sum of—

"(A) the amount of the phased retirement annuity as of the date of full retirement, including any adjustments made under section 8462; and

"(B) the product obtained by multiplying—

"(i) the amount of an annuity computed under section 8412 that would have been payable at the time of full retirement if the individual had not elected a phased retirement and as if the individual was employed on a full-time basis in the position occupied during the phased retirement period and before any adjustment to provide for a survivor annuity; by

"(ii) the working percentage.

"(2) After computing a composite retirement annuity under paragraph (1), the Director shall adjust the amount of the annuity for any applicable reductions for a survivor annuity.

"(3) A composite retirement annuity shall be adjusted in accordance with section 8462, except that subsection (c)(1) of that section shall not apply.

"(4) In computing a composite retirement annuity under paragraph (1)(B)(i), the unused sick leave to the credit of a phased retiree at the time of entry into full retirement status shall be adjusted by dividing the number of hours of unused sick leave by the working percentage.

"(g)(1) Under such procedures and conditions as the Director may provide, and with the concurrence of the head of employing agency, a phased retiree may elect to terminate phased retirement status and return to a full-time work schedule.

"(2) Upon entering a full-time work schedule based on an election under paragraph (1), the phased retirement annuity of a phased retiree shall terminate.

"(3) After termination of the phased retirement annuity under this subsection, the individual's rights under this chapter shall be determined based on the law in effect at the time of any subsequent separation from service. For purposes of this chapter, at the time of the subsequent separation from service, the phased retirement period shall be treated as if it had been a period of part-time employment with the work schedule described in subsection (b)(2).

"(h) For purposes of subchapter IV—

"(1) the death of a phased retiree shall be deemed to be the death in service of an employee;

"(2) except for purposes of section 8442(b)(1)(A)(i), the phased retirement period shall be deemed to have been a period of part-time employment with the work schedule described in subsection (b)(2) of this section; and

"(3) for purposes of section 8442(b)(1)(A)(i), the phased retiree shall be deemed to have been at the full-time rate of pay for the position occupied.

"(i) Employment of a phased retiree shall not be deemed to be part-time career employment, as defined in section 3401(2).

"(j) A phased retiree is not eligible to receive an annuity supplement under section 8421.

"(k) For purposes of subchapter III, a phased retiree shall be deemed to be an employee.

"(l) For purposes of section 8445(d), retirement shall be deemed to occur on the date on which a phased retiree enters into full retirement status.

"(m) A phased retiree is not eligible to apply for an annuity under subchapter V.

"(n) A phased retiree is not subject to section 8468.

"(o) For purposes of chapter 87, a phased retiree shall be deemed to be receiving basic pay at the rate of a full-time employee in the position to which the phased retiree is appointed."; and

(2) in the table of sections by inserting after the item relating to section 8412 the following:

"8412a. Phased retirement.".

.* * * * * * * * * * * *

(d) Effective Date- The amendments made by subsections (a) and (b) shall take effect on the effective date of the implementing regulations issued by the Director of the Office of Personnel Management.

[¶ 4085] Sec. 100122. ROLL-YOUR-OWN CIGARETTE MACHINES.

* * * * * * * * * * * *

(b) Effective Date- The amendment made by this section shall apply to articles removed after the date of the enactment of this Act.

* * * * * * * * * * * *

Middle Class Tax Relief and Job Creation Act of 2012 [PL112-96, 2/22/2012]

[¶ 4086] One Hundred Twelfth Congress of the
United States of America

AT THE SECOND SESSION

Begun and held at the City of Washington on Tuesday,
the third day of January, two thousand and twelve
An Act
To provide incentives for the creation of jobs, and for other purposes.
Be it enacted by the Senate and House of Representatives of the United States of America in Congress assembled,
* * * * * * * * * * *

TITLE II— UNEMPLOYMENT BENEFIT CONTINUATION AND PROGRAM IMPROVEMENT [§§2001—2184]

[¶ 4087] Sec. 2103. IMPROVING PROGRAM INTEGRITY BY BETTER RECOVERY OF OVERPAYMENTS.
* * * * * * * * * * *

(c) Effective Date- The amendments made by this section shall apply to weeks beginning after the end of the first session of the State legislature which begins after the date of enactment of this Act.
* * * * * * * * * * *

[¶ 4088] Sec. 2161. TREATMENT OF SHORT-TIME COMPENSATION PROGRAMS.
* * * * * * * * * * *

(a) Definition.
* * * * * * * * * * *

(2) EFFECTIVE DATE. Subject to paragraph (3), the amendment made by paragraph (1) shall take effect on the date of the enactment of this Act.

(3) TRANSITION PERIOD FOR EXISTING PROGRAMS- In the case of a State that is administering a short-time compensation program as of the date of the enactment of this Act and the State law cannot be administered consistent with the amendment made by paragraph (1), such amendment shall take effect on the earlier of—

(A) the date the State changes its State law in order to be consistent with such amendment; or

(B) the date that is 2 years and 6 months after the date of the enactment of this Act.
* * * * * * * * * * *

FAA Air Transportation Modernization and Safety Improvement Act [PL112-95, 2/6/2012]

[¶ 4089] One Hundred Twelfth Congress of the United States of America

AT THE SECOND SESSION

Begun and held at the City of Washington on Tuesday,

the third day of January, two thousand and twelve

An Act

To amend title 49, United States Code, to authorize appropriations for the Federal Aviation Administration for fiscal years 2011 through 2014, to streamline programs, create efficiencies, reduce waste, and improve aviation safety and capacity, to provide stable funding for the national aviation system, and for other purposes.

Be it enacted by the Senate and House of Representatives of the United States of America in Congress assembled,

[¶ 4090] **Sec. 1. SHORT TITLE; TABLE OF CONTENTS.**

(a) Short Title- This Act may be cited as the "FAA Modernization and Reform Act of 2012".

* * * * * * * * * * *

TITLE XI— AIRPORT AND AIRWAY TRUST FUND PROVISIONS AND RE-LATED TAXES [§§1100—1108]

[¶ 4091] **Sec. 1100. AMENDMENT OF 1986 CODE.** Except as otherwise expressly provided, whenever in this title an amendment or repeal is expressed in terms of an amendment to, or repeal of, a section or other provision, the reference shall be considered to be made to a section or other provision of the Internal Revenue Code of 1986.

[¶ 4092] **Sec. 1101. EXTENSION OF TAXES FUNDING AIRPORT AND AIRWAY TRUST FUND.**

* * * * * * * * * * *

(c) Effective Date- The amendments made by this section shall take effect on February 18, 2012.

[¶ 4093] **Sec. 1102. EXTENSION OF AIRPORT AND AIRWAY TRUST FUND EXPENDITURE AUTHORITY.**

* * * * * * * * * * *

(c) Effective Date- The amendments made by this section shall take effect on February 18, 2012.

[¶ 4094] **Sec. 1103. TREATMENT OF FRACTIONAL AIRCRAFT OWNERSHIP PROGRAMS.**

* * * * * * * * * * *

(d) Effective Dates—

(1) SUBSECTION (a)- The amendments made by subsection (a) shall apply to fuel used after March 31, 2012.

(2) SUBSECTION (b)- The amendment made by subsection (b) shall apply to uses of aircraft after March 31, 2012.

(3) SUBSECTION (c)- The amendments made by subsection (c) shall apply to taxable transportation provided after March 31, 2012.

[¶ 4095] Sec. 1104. TRANSPARENCY IN PASSENGER TAX DISCLOSURES.

* * * * * * * * * * *

(b) Effective Date- The amendments made by this section shall apply to taxable transportation provided after March 31, 2012.

[¶ 4096] Sec. 1105. TAX-EXEMPT BOND FINANCING FOR FIXED-WING EMERGENCY MEDICAL AIRCRAFT.

* * * * * * * * * * *

(b) Effective Date- The amendment made by this section shall apply to obligations issued after the date of the enactment of this Act.

* * * * * * * * * * * *

[¶ 4097] Sec. 1107. TERMINATION OF EXEMPTION FOR SMALL JET AIRCRAFT ON NONESTABLISHED LINES.

* * * * * * * * * * *

(b) Effective Date- The amendment made by this section shall apply to taxable transportation provided after March 31, 2012.

[¶ 4098] Sec. 1108. MODIFICATION OF CONTROL DEFINITION FOR PURPOSES OF SECTION 249.

* * * * * * * * * * *

[¶ 4099] Sec. 1108. MODIFICATION OF CONTROL DEFINITION FOR PURPOSES OF SECTION 249.

* * * * * * * * * * *

(c) Effective Date- The amendments made by this section shall apply to repurchases after the date of the enactment of this Act.

TITLE XII— COMPLIANCE WITH STATUTORY PAY-AS-YOU-GO ACT OF 2010
[§1201]

[¶ 4100] Sec. 1201. COMPLIANCE PROVISION. The budgetary effects of this Act, for the purpose of complying with the Statutory Pay-As-You-Go Act of 2010, shall be determined by reference to the latest statement titled "Budgetary Effects of PAYGO Legislation" for this Act, jointly submitted for printing in the Congressional Record by the Chairmen of the House and Senate Budget Committees, provided that such statement has been submitted prior to the vote on passage in the House acting first on this conference report or amendment between the Houses.

* * * * * * * * * * *

Airport and Airway Extension Act of 2012 [PL112-91, 1/26/2012]

[¶ 4101] One Hundred Twelfth Congress of the
United States of America

AT THE SECOND SESSION

Begun and held at the City of Washington on Tuesday,
the third day of January, two thousand and twelve

An Act

To amend the Internal Revenue Code of 1986 to extend the funding and expenditure authority of the Airport and Airway Trust Fund, to amend title 49, United States Code, to extend authorizations for the airport improvement program, and for other purposes.

Be it enacted by the Senate and House of Representatives of the United States of America in Congress assembled,

* * * * * * * * * * *

[¶ 4102] Sec. 2. EXTENSION OF TAXES FUNDING AIRPORT AND AIRWAY TRUST FUND.

* * * * * * * * * * * *

(c) Effective Date- The amendments made by this section shall take effect on February 1, 2012.

[¶ 4103] Sec. 3. EXTENSION OF AIRPORT AND AIRWAY TRUST FUND EXPENDITURE AUTHORITY.

* * * * * * * * * * * *

(c) Effective Date- The amendments made by this section shall take effect on February 1, 2012.

* * * * * * * * * * * *

Temporary Payroll Tax Cut Continuation Act of 2011 [PL112-78, 12/23/2011]

[¶ 4104] 112th CONGRESS 1st Session

AN ACT

To extend the payroll tax holiday, unemployment compensation, Medicare physician payment, provide for the consideration of the Keystone XL pipeline, and for other purposes.

Be it enacted by the Senate and House of Representatives of the United States of America in Congress assembled,

[¶ 4105] Sec. 1. SHORT TITLE; TABLE OF CONTENTS.

(a) Short Title. This Act may be cited as the "Temporary Payroll Tax Cut Continuation Act of 2011".

(b) Table of Contents. The table of contents of this Act is as follows:

TITLE I— TEMPORARY PAYROLL TAX RELIEF [§101]

[¶ 4106] Sec. 101. EXTENSION OF PAYROLL TAX HOLIDAY.

(a) In General. Subsection (c) of section 601 of the Tax Relief, Unemployment Insurance Reauthorization, and Job Creation Act of 2010 (26 U.S.C. 1401 note) is amended to read as follows:

"(c) Payroll Tax Holiday Period- The term "payroll tax holiday period" means—

"(1) in the case of the tax described in subsection (a)(1), calendar years 2011 and 2012, and

"(2) in the case of the taxes described in subsection (a)(2), the period beginning January 1, 2011, and ending February 29, 2012.".

(b) Special Rules for 2012. Section 601 of such Act (26 U.S.C. 1401 note) is amended by adding at the end the following new subsection:

"(f) Special Rules for 2012—

"(1) LIMITATION ON SELF-EMPLOYMENT INCOME- In the case of any taxable year beginning in 2012, subsection (a)(1) shall only apply with respect to so much of the taxpayer's self-employment income (as defined in section 1402(b) of the Internal Revenue Code of 1986) as does not exceed the excess (if any) of—

"(A) $18,350, over

"(B) the amount of wages and compensation received during the portion of the payroll tax holiday period occurring during 2012 subject to tax under section 3101(a) of such Code or section 3201(a) of such Code.

"(2) COORDINATION WITH DEDUCTION FOR EMPLOYMENT TAXES- In the case of a taxable year beginning in 2012, subparagraph (A) of subsection (b)(2) shall be applied as if it read as follows:

"(A) the sum of—

"(i) 59.6 percent of the portion of such taxes attributable to the tax imposed by section 1401(a) of such Code (determined after the application of this section) on so much of self-employment income (as defined in section 1402(b) of such Code) as does not exceed the amount of self-employment income described in paragraph (1), plus

"(ii) one-half of the portion of such taxes attributable to the tax imposed by section 1401(a) of such Code (determined without regard to this section) on self-employment income (as so defined) in excess of such amount, plus".".

(c) Recapture of Excess Benefit. Section 601 of such Act (26 U.S.C. 1401 note), as amended by subsection (b), is further amended by adding at the end the following new subsection:

"(g) Recapture of Excess Benefit—

"(1) IN GENERAL- There is hereby imposed on the income of every individual a tax equal to 2 percent of the sum of wages (within the meaning of section 3121(a)(1) of the Internal Revenue Code of 1986) and compensation (to which section 3201(a) of such Code applies) received during the period beginning January 1, 2012, and ending February 29, 2012, to the extent the amount of such sum exceeds $18,350.

"(2) REGULATIONS- The Secretary of the Treasury or the Secretary's delegate shall prescribe such regulations or other guidance as may be necessary or appropriate to carry out this subsection, including guidance for payment by the employee of the tax imposed by paragraph (1).".

(d) Technical Amendments. Paragraph (2) of section 601(b) of such Act (26 U.S.C. 1401 note) is amended—

(1) by inserting "of such Code" after "164(f)";

(2) by inserting "of such Code" after "1401(a)" in subparagraph (A); and

(3) by inserting "of such Code" after "1401(b)" in subparagraph (B).

(e) Effective Dates.

(1) IN GENERAL. Except as provided in paragraph (2), the amendments made by this section shall apply to remuneration received, and taxable years beginning, after December 31, 2011.

(2) TECHNICAL AMENDMENTS. The amendments made by subsection (d) shall take effect as if included in the enactment of section 601 of the Tax Relief, Unemployment Insurance Reauthorization, and Job Creation Act of 2010.

TITLE II— TEMPORARY EXTENSION OF UNEMPLOYMENT COMPENSATION PROVISIONS [§§201—202]

[¶ 4107] Sec. 201. TEMPORARY EXTENSION OF UNEMPLOYMENT COMPENSATION PROVISIONS.

(a) In General.

(1) Section 4007 of the Supplemental Appropriations Act, 2008 (Public Law 110-252; 26 U.S.C. 3304 note) is amended—

(A) by striking "January 3, 2012" each place it appears and inserting "March 6, 2012";

(B) in the heading for subsection (b)(2), by striking "JANUARY 3, 2012" and inserting "MARCH 6, 2012"; and

(C) in subsection (b)(3), by striking "June 9, 2012" and inserting "August 15, 2012".

(2) Section 2005 of the Assistance for Unemployed Workers and Struggling Families Act, as contained in Public Law 111-5 (26 U.S.C. 3304 note; 123 Stat. 444), is amended—

(A) by striking "January 4, 2012" each place it appears and inserting "March 7, 2012"; and

(B) in subsection (c), by striking "June 11, 2012" and inserting "August 15, 2012".

(3) Section 5 of the Unemployment Compensation Extension Act of 2008 (Public Law 110-449; 26 U.S.C. 3304 note) is amended by striking "June 10, 2012" and inserting "August 15, 2012".

(4) Section 203 of the Federal-State Extended Unemployment Compensation Act of 1970 (26 U.S.C. 3304 note) is amended—

　(A) in subsection (d), in the second sentence of the flush matter following paragraph (2), by striking "December 31, 2011" and inserting "February 29, 2012"; and

　(B) in subsection (f)(2), by striking "December 31, 2011" and inserting "February 29, 2012".

(b) Funding. Section 4004(e)(1) of the Supplemental Appropriations Act, 2008 (Public Law 110-252; 26 U.S.C. 3304 note) is amended—

　(1) in subparagraph (F), by striking "and" at the end; and

　(2) by inserting after subparagraph (G) the following:

　"(H) the amendments made by section 201(a)(1) of the Temporary Payroll Tax Cut Continuation Act of 2011; and".

(c) Effective Date. The amendments made by this section shall take effect as if included in the enactment of the Tax Relief, Unemployment Insurance Reauthorization, and Job Creation Act of 2010 (Public Law 111-312).

* * * * * * * * * * * *

Passed the House of Representatives December 23, 2011.

Attest:

Clerk.

112th CONGRESS

1st Session

PL112-78

AN ACT

To extend the payroll tax holiday, unemployment compensation, Medicare physician payment, provide for the consideration of the Keystone XL pipeline, and for other purposes.

**To amend the Internal Revenue Code of 1986 to repeal the impo-
sition of 3 percent withholding on certain payments made to vendors by government entities, to modify the calculation of modified adjusted gross income for purposes of determining eligibility
for certain healthcare-related programs, and for other purposes.
[P.L. 112-56, 11/21/2011]**

[¶ 4108] One Hundred Twelfth Congress of the
United States of America

AT THE FIRST SESSION

Begun and held at the City of Washington on Wednesday,
the fifth day of January, two thousand and eleven

An Act

To amend the Internal Revenue Code of 1986 to repeal the imposition of 3 percent withholding on certain payments made to vendors by government entities, to modify the calculation of modified adjusted gross income for purposes of determining eligibility for certain
healthcare-related programs, and for other purposes.

Be it enacted by the Senate and House of Representatives of the United States of America
in Congress assembled,

TITLE I— THREE PERCENT WITHHOLDING REPEAL AND JOB CREATION ACT [§§101—102]

[¶ 4109] **Sec. 101. 9 SHORT TITLE.** This title may be cited as the "3% Withholding Repeal and Job Creation Act".

[¶ 4110] **Sec. 102. REPEAL OF IMPOSITION OF 3 PERCENT WITHHOLDING ON
CERTAIN PAYMENTS MADE TO VENDORS BY GOVERNMENT ENTITIES.**

* * * * * * * * * * *

(b) Effective Date- The amendment made by this section shall apply to payments made after
December 31, 2011.

TITLE II— VOW TO HIRE HEROES [§§201—265]

[¶ 4111] **Sec. 201. SHORT TITLE.** This title may be cited as the "VOW to Hire Heroes
Act of 2011".

* * * * * * * * * * *

Subtitle E— Other Matters [§§261—265]

[¶ 4112] **Sec. 261. RETURNING HEROES AND WOUNDED WARRIORS WORK OP-
PORTUNITY TAX CREDITS.**

* * * * * * * * * * *

(e) Credit Made Available to Tax-exempt Organizations in Certain Circumstances—

* * * * * * * * * * *

(3) TRANSFERS TO FEDERAL OLD-AGE AND SURVIVORS INSURANCE TRUST
FUND- There are hereby appropriated to the Federal Old-Age and Survivors Trust Fund
and the Federal Disability Insurance Trust Fund established under section 201 of the Social
Security Act (42 U.S.C. 401) amounts equal to the reduction in revenues to the Treasury
by reason of the amendments made by paragraphs (1) and (2). Amounts appropriated by
the preceding sentence shall be transferred from the general fund at such times and in such
manner as to replicate to the extent possible the transfers which would have occurred to
such Trust Fund had such amendments not been enacted.

(f) Treatment of Possessions—

  (1) PAYMENTS TO POSSESSIONS—

    (A) MIRROR CODE POSSESSIONS- The Secretary of the Treasury shall pay to each possession of the United States with a mirror code tax system amounts equal to the loss to that possession by reason of the amendments made by this section. Such amounts shall be determined by the Secretary of the Treasury based on information provided by the government of the respective possession of the United States.

    (B) OTHER POSSESSIONS- The Secretary of the Treasury shall pay to each possession of the United States which does not have a mirror code tax system the amount estimated by the Secretary of the Treasury as being equal to the loss to that possession that would have occurred by reason of the amendments made by this section if a mirror code tax system had been in effect in such possession. The preceding sentence shall not apply with respect to any possession of the United States unless such possession establishes to the satisfaction of the Secretary that the possession has implemented (or, at the discretion of the Secretary, will implement) an income tax benefit which is substantially equivalent to the income tax credit in effect after the amendments made by this section.

  (2) COORDINATION WITH CREDIT ALLOWED AGAINST UNITED STATES INCOME TAXES- The credit allowed against United States income taxes for any taxable year under the amendments made by this section to section 51 of the Internal Revenue Code of 1986 to any person with respect to any qualified veteran shall be reduced by the amount of any credit (or other tax benefit described in paragraph (1)(B)) allowed to such person against income taxes imposed by the possession of the United States by reason of this subsection with respect to such qualified veteran for such taxable year.

  (3) DEFINITIONS AND SPECIAL RULES—

    (A) POSSESSION OF THE UNITED STATES- For purposes of this subsection, the term "possession of the United States" includes American Samoa, Guam, the Commonwealth of the Northern Mariana Islands, the Commonwealth of Puerto Rico, and the United States Virgin Islands.

    (B) MIRROR CODE TAX SYSTEM- For purposes of this subsection, the term "mirror code tax system" means, with respect to any possession of the United States, the income tax system of such possession if the income tax liability of the residents of such possession under such system is determined by reference to the income tax laws of the United States as if such possession were the United States.

    (C) TREATMENT OF PAYMENTS- For purposes of section 1324(b)(2) of title 31, United States Code, the payments under this subsection shall be treated in the same manner as a refund due from credit provisions described in such section.

* * * * * * * * * * *

(g) Effective Date- The amendments made by this section shall apply to individuals who begin work for the employer after the date of the enactment of this Act.

* * * * * * * * * * *

TITLE III— OTHER PROVISIONS RELATING TO FEDERAL VENDORS [§§301—302]

[¶ 4113] Sec. 301. ONE HUNDRED PERCENT LEVY FOR PAYMENTS TO FEDERAL VENDORS RELATING TO PROPERTY.

* * * * * * * * * * *

(b) Effective Date- The amendment made by this section shall apply to levies issued after the date of the enactment of this Act.

* * * * * * * * * * *

TITLE IV— MODIFICATION OF CALCULATION OF MODIFIED ADJUSTED GROSS INCOME FOR DETERMINING CERTAIN HEALTHCARE PROGRAM ELIGIBILITY [§401]

[¶ 4114] Sec. 401. MODIFICATION OF CALCULATION OF MODIFIED ADJUSTED GROSS INCOME FOR DETERMINING CERTAIN HEALTHCARE PROGRAM ELIGIBILITY.

* * * * * * * * * * * *

(b) Effective Date- The amendments made by this section shall take effect on the date of the enactment of this Act.

(c) No Impact on Social Security Trust Funds—

  (1) ESTIMATE OF SECRETARY- The Secretary of the Treasury, or the Secretary's delegate, shall annually estimate the impact that the amendments made by subsection (a) have on the income and balances of the trust funds established under section 201 of the Social Security Act (42 U.S.C. 401).

  (2) TRANSFER OF FUNDS- If, under paragraph (1), the Secretary of the Treasury or the Secretary's delegate estimates that such amendments have a negative impact on the income and balances of such trust funds, the Secretary shall transfer, not less frequently than quarterly, from the general fund an amount sufficient so as to ensure that the income and balances of such trust funds are not reduced as a result of such amendments.

* * * * * * * * * * * *

United States-Korea Free Trade Agreement Implementation Act
[PL112-41, 10/3/2011]

[¶ 4115] 112th CONGRESS 1st Session

To implement the United States-Korea Free Trade Agreement.

IN THE HOUSE OF REPRESENTATIVES

October 3, 2011

Mr. CANTOR (for himself and Mr. LEVIN) (both by request) introduced the following bill; which was referred to the Committee on Ways and Means

A BILL

To implement the United States-Korea Free Trade Agreement.

Be it enacted by the Senate and House of Representatives of the United States of America in Congress assembled,

[¶ 4116] Sec. 1. SHORT TITLE.

(a) Short Title- This Act may be cited as the "United States-Korea Free Trade Agreement Implementation Act".

* * * * * * * * * * *

TITLE V— OFFSETS [§§501—505]

[¶ 4117] Sec. 501. INCREASE IN PENALTY ON PAID PREPARERS WHO FAIL TO COMPLY WITH EARNED INCOME TAX CREDIT DUE DILIGENCE REQUIRE-MENTS.

* * * * * * * * * * *

(b) Effective Date- The amendment made by this section shall apply to returns required to be filed after December 31, 2011.

* * * * * * * * * * *

To extend the Generalized System of Preferences, and for other purposes. [PL112-40, 10/13/2011]

[¶ 4118] One Hundred Twelfth Congress of the
United States of America

AT THE FIRST SESSION

Begun and held at the City of Washington on Wednesday,
the fifth day of January, two thousand and eleven
An Act

To extend the Generalized System of Preferences, and for other purposes.

Be it enacted by the Senate and House of Representatives of the United States of America in Congress assembled,

* * * * * * * * * * *

TITLE II— TRADE ADJUSTMENT ASSISTANCE [§§200—263]

[¶ 4119] Sec. 200. SHORT TITLE; TABLE OF CONTENTS.

(a) Short Title- This title may be cited as the "Trade Adjustment Assistance Extension Act of 2011".

* * * * * * * * * * *

Subtitle B— Health Coverage Improvement [§§241—243]

[¶ 4120] Sec. 241. HEALTH CARE TAX CREDIT.

* * * * * * * * * * *

(c) Effective Dates—
   (1) IN GENERAL- Except as otherwise provided in this subsection, the amendments made by this section shall apply to coverage months beginning after February 12, 2011.
   (2) ADVANCE PAYMENT PROVISIONS—
      (A) The amendment made by subsection (b)(2)(B) shall apply to certificates issued after the date which is 30 days after the date of the enactment of this Act.
      (B) The amendment made by subsection (b)(2)(D) shall apply to coverage months beginning after the date which is 30 days after the date of the enactment of this Act.

[¶ 4121] Sec. 242. TAA PRE-CERTIFICATION PERIOD RULE FOR PURPOSES OF DETERMINING WHETHER THERE IS A 63-DAY LAPSE IN CREDITABLE COVERAGE.

* * * * * * * * * * *

(b) Effective Date—
   (1) IN GENERAL- The amendments made by this section shall apply to plan years beginning after February 12, 2011.
   (2) TRANSITIONAL RULES—
      (A) BENEFIT DETERMINATIONS- Notwithstanding the amendments made by this section (and the provisions of law amended thereby), a plan shall not be required to modify benefit determinations for the period beginning on February 13, 2011, and ending 30 days after the date of the enactment of this Act, but a plan shall not fail to be qualified health insurance within the meaning of section 35(e) of the Internal Revenue Code of 1986 during this period merely due to such failure to modify benefit determinations.
      (B) GUIDANCE CONCERNING PERIODS BEFORE 30 DAYS AFTER ENACTMENT- Except as provided in subparagraph (A), the Secretary of the Treasury (or his designee), in consultation with the Secretary of Health and Human Services and the Sec-

retary of Labor, may issue regulations or other guidance regarding the scope of the application of the amendments made by this section to periods before the date which is 30 days after the date of the enactment of this Act.

(C) SPECIAL RULE RELATING TO CERTAIN LOSS OF COVERAGE- In the case of a TAA-related loss of coverage (as defined in section 4980B(f)(5)(C)(iv) of the Internal Revenue Code of 1986) that occurs during the period beginning on February 13, 2011, and ending 30 days after the date of the enactment of this Act, the 7-day period described in section 9801(c)(2)(D) of the Internal Revenue Code of 1986, section 701(c)(2)(C) of the Employee Retirement Income Security Act of 1974, and section 2701(c)(2)(C) of the Public Health Service Act shall be extended until 30 days after such date of enactment.

[¶ 4122] Sec. 243. EXTENSION OF COBRA BENEFITS FOR CERTAIN TAA-ELIGIBLE INDIVIDUALS AND PBGC RECIPIENTS.

* * * * * * * * * * *

(b) Effective Date- The amendments made by this section shall apply to periods of coverage which would (without regard to the amendments made by this section) end on or after the date which is 30 days after the date of the enactment of this Act.

Subtitle C— Offsets [§§251—263]

PART I— UNEMPLOYMENT COMPENSATION PROGRAM INTEGRITY [§§251—253]

[¶ 4123] Sec. 251. MANDATORY PENALTY ASSESSMENT ON FRAUD CLAIMS.

* * * * * * * * * * *

[¶ 4124] Sec. 252. PROHIBITION ON NONCHARGING DUE TO EMPLOYER FAULT.

* * * * * * * * * * *

(b) Effective Date—

(1) IN GENERAL- Except as provided in paragraph (2), the amendments made by this section shall apply to erroneous payments established after the end of the 2-year period beginning on the date of the enactment of this Act.

(2) AUTHORITY- A State may amend its State law to apply such amendments to erroneous payments established prior to the end of the period described in paragraph (1).

* * * * * * * * * * *

Department of Defense and Full-Year Continuing Appropriations Act, 2011 [P.L. 112-10, 4/11/2011]

[¶ 4125] One Hundred Twelfth Congress of the
United States of America
AT THE FIRST SESSION
Begun and held at the City of Washington on Wednesday,
the fifth day of January, two thousand and eleven
An Act

Making appropriations for the Department of Defense and the other departments and agencies of the Government for the fiscal year ending September 30, 2011, and for other purposes.

Be it enacted by the Senate and House of Representatives of the United States of America in Congress assembled,

[¶ 4126] **Sec. 1. SHORT TITLE.** This Act may be cited as the "Department of Defense and Full-Year Continuing Appropriations Act, 2011".

* * * * * * * * * * * *

FREE CHOICE VOUCHERS

[¶ 4127] **Sec. 1858.**

(a) In General- Subsections (a), (b), (c), (d), and (e) of section 10108 of the Patient Protection and Affordable Care Act are repealed.

* * * * * * * * * * * *

(c) Other Conforming Change- Section 18B(a)(3) of the Fair Labor Standards Act of 1938 (29 U.S.C. 218B) is amended by striking "and the employer does not offer a free choice voucher".

(d) Effective Date- The amendments made by this section shall take effect as if included in the provisions of, and the amendments made by, the provisions of the Patient Protection and Affordable Care Act to which they relate.

* * * * * * * * * * * *

Comprehensive 1099 Taxpayer Protection and Repayment of Exchange Subsidy Overpayments Act of 2011 [PL112-9, 4/6/2011]

[¶ 4128] One Hundred Twelfth Congress of the
United States of America

AT THE FIRST SESSION

Begun and held at the City of Washington on Wednesday,
the fifth day of January, two thousand and eleven
An Act
To repeal the expansion of information reporting requirements for payments of $600 or more to corporations, and for other purposes.

Be it enacted by the Senate and House of Representatives of the United States of America in Congress assembled,

[¶ 4129] Sec. 1. SHORT TITLE. This Act may be cited as the "Comprehensive 1099 Taxpayer Protection and Repayment of Exchange Subsidy Overpayments Act of 2011".

[¶ 4130] Sec. 2. REPEAL OF EXPANSION OF INFORMATION REPORTING REQUIREMENTS TO PAYMENTS MADE TO CORPORATIONS AND TO PAYMENTS FOR PROPERTY AND OTHER GROSS PROCEEDS.
* * * * * * * * * * * *

(b) Payments for Property and Other Gross Proceeds- Subsection (a) of section 6041 of such Code is amended—

(c) Effective Date- The amendments made by this section shall apply to payments made after December 31, 2011.

[¶ 4131] Sec. 3. REPEAL OF EXPANSION OF INFORMATION REPORTING REQUIREMENTS FOR RENTAL PROPERTY EXPENSE PAYMENTS.
* * * * * * * * * * * *

(b) Effective Date- The amendment made by this section shall apply to payments made after December 31, 2010.

[¶ 4132] Sec. 4. INCREASE IN AMOUNT OF OVERPAYMENT OF HEALTH CARE CREDIT WHICH IS SUBJECT TO RECAPTURE.
* * * * * * * * * * * *

(b) Effective Date- The amendment made by this section shall apply to taxable years ending after December 31, 2013.
Speaker of the House of Representatives.
Vice President of the United States and
President of the Senate.

[¶ 5000] Congressional Committee Reports Accompanying the American Taxpayer Relief Act of 2012

No committee reports have been issued to accompany the American Taxpayer Relief Act of 2012 (P.L. 112-240, 1/2/2013).

[¶ 5400] Conference Report Accompanying the Highway Investment Act of 2012

This section, in ¶ 5401 through ¶ 5405, reproduces all relevant parts of the Conference Report (Conf. Rept. 112-557, 6/28/2012) accompanying the Highway Investment Act of 2012 (P.L. 112-141, 7/6/2012).

[¶ 5401]   Section 40102.   Extension of highway-related taxes.

(Code Sec. 4041, 4051, 4071, 4081, 4221, 4481, 4482, 4483, 6412, 9503)[1]

[Conference Report]

Present Law Highway Trust Fund Excise Taxes

In general

Six separate excise taxes are imposed to finance the Federal Highway Trust Fund program. Three of these taxes are imposed on highway motor fuels. The remaining three are a retail sales tax on heavy highway vehicles, a manufacturers' excise tax on heavy vehicle tires, and an annual use tax on heavy vehicles. A substantial majority of the revenues produced by the Highway Trust Fund excise taxes are derived from the taxes on motor fuels. The annual use tax on heavy vehicles expires October 1, 2013. Except for 4.3 cents per gallon of the Highway Trust Fund fuels tax rates, the remaining taxes are scheduled to expire after June 30, 2012. The 4.3-cents-per-gallon portion of the fuels tax rates is permanent.[2] The six taxes are summarized below.

Highway motor fuels taxes

The Highway Trust Fund motor fuels tax rates are as follows:[3]

Gasoline	18.3 cents per gallon
Diesel fuel and kerosene	24.3 cents per gallon
Alternative fuels	18.3 or 24.3 cents per gallon generally[4]

Non-fuel highway trust fund excise taxes

In addition to the highway motor fuels excise tax revenues, the Highway Trust Fund receives revenues produced by three excise taxes imposed exclusively on heavy highway vehicles or tires. These taxes are:

(1) A 12-percent excise tax imposed on the first retail sale of heavy highway vehicles, tractors, and trailers (generally, trucks having a gross vehicle weight in excess of 33,000 pounds and trailers having such a weight in excess of 26,000 pounds);[5]

(2) An excise tax imposed on highway tires with a rated load capacity exceeding 3,500 pounds, generally at a rate of 0.945 cents per 10 pounds of excess;[6] and

---

1. Except where otherwise stated, all section references are to the Internal Revenue Code of 1986, as amended (the "Code").
2. This portion of the tax rates was enacted as a deficit reduction measure in 1993. Receipts from it were retained in the General Fund until 1997 legislation provided for their transfer to the Highway Trust Fund.
3. Secs. 4081(a)(2)(A)(i), 4081(a)(2)(A)(iii), 4041(a)(2), 4041(a)(3), and 4041(m). Some of these fuels also are subject to an additional 0.1-cent-per-gallon excise tax to fund the Leaking Underground Storage Tank Trust Fund (secs. 4041(d) and 4081(a)(2)(B)).
4. See secs. 4041(a)(2), 4041(a)(3), and 4041(m).
5. Sec. 4051.
6. Sec. 4071.

(3) An annual use tax imposed on highway vehicles having a taxable gross weight of 55,000 pounds or more.[7] (The maximum rate for this tax is $550 per year, imposed on vehicles having a taxable gross weight over 75,000 pounds.)

The taxable year for the annual use tax is from July 1st through June 30th of the following year. For the period July 1, 2013, through September 30, 2013, the amount of the annual use tax is reduced by 75 percent.[8]

Present Law Highway Trust Fund Expenditure Provisions

In general

Under present law, revenues from the highway excise taxes, as imposed through June 30, 2012, generally are dedicated to the Highway Trust Fund. Dedication of excise tax revenues to the Highway Trust Fund and expenditures from the Highway Trust Fund are governed by the Code.[9] The Code authorizes expenditures (subject to appropriations) from the Highway Trust Fund through June 30, 2012, for the purposes provided in authorizing legislation, as such legislation was in effect on the date of enactment of the Surface Transportation Extension Act of 2012.

Highway Trust Fund expenditure purposes

The Highway Trust Fund has a separate account for mass transit, the Mass Transit Account.[10] The Highway Trust Fund and the Mass Transit Account are funding sources for specific programs.

Highway Trust Fund expenditure purposes have been revised with each authorization Act enacted since establishment of the Highway Trust Fund in 1956. In general, expenditures authorized under those Acts (as the Acts were in effect on the date of enactment of the most recent such authorizing Act) are specified by the Code as Highway Trust Fund expenditure purposes.[11] The Code provides that the authority to make expenditures from the Highway Trust Fund expires after June 30, 2012. Thus, no Highway Trust Fund expenditures may occur after June 30, 2012, without an amendment to the Code.

As noted above, section 9503 appropriates to the Highway Trust Fund amounts equivalent to the taxes received from the following: the taxes on diesel, gasoline, kerosene and special motor fuel, the tax on tires, the annual heavy vehicle use tax, and the tax on the retail sale of heavy trucks and trailers.[12] Section 9601 provides that amounts appropriated to a trust fund pursuant to sections 9501 through 9511, are to be transferred at least monthly from the General Fund of the Treasury to such trust fund on the basis of estimates made by the Secretary of the Treasury of the amounts referred to in the Code section appropriating the amounts to such trust fund. The Code requires that proper adjustments be made in amounts subsequently transferred to the extent prior estimates were in excess of, or less than, the amounts required to be transferred.

---

7. Sec. 4481.
8. Sec. 4482(c)(4) and (d).
9. Sec. 9503. The Highway Trust Fund statutory provisions were placed in the Internal Revenue Code in 1982.
10. Sec. 9503(e)(1).
11. The authorizing Acts that currently are referenced in the Highway Trust Fund provisions of the Code are: the Highway Revenue Act of 1956; Titles I and II of the Surface Transportation Assistance Act of 1982; the Surface Transportation and Uniform Relocation Act of 1987; the Intermodal Surface Transportation Efficiency Act of 1991; the Transportation Equity Act for the 21st Century, the Surface Transportation Extension Act of 2003, the Surface Transportation Extension Act of 2004; the Surface Transportation Extension Act of 2004, Part II; the Surface Transportation Extension Act of 2004, Part III; the Surface Transportation Extension Act of 2004, Part IV; the Surface Transportation Extension Act of 2004, Part V; the Safe, Accountable, Flexible, Efficient Transportation Equity Act: A Legacy for Users; the SAFETEA-LU Technical Corrections Act of 2008; the Surface Transportation Extension Act of 2010; the Surface Transportation Extension Act of 2010, Part II; the Surface Transportation Extension Act of 2011; the Surface Transportation Extension Act of 2011, Part II, and the Surface Transportation Extension Act of 2012.
12. Sec. 9503(b)(1).

House Bill

Present-law expenditure authority and taxes are extended for an additional three months, through September 30, 2012.

Senate Amendment

The expenditure authority for the Highway Trust Fund is extended through September 30, 2013. The Code provisions governing the purposes for which monies in the Highway Trust Fund may be spent are updated to include the reauthorization bill, Moving Ahead for Progress for the 21st Century (MAP-21).[13]

The provision extends the motor fuel taxes, and all three nonfuel excise taxes at their current rates through September 30, 2015.[14] The provision resolves the projected deficit in the Highway Trust Fund, assures a cushion of $2.8 billion in each account of the Highway Trust Fund, and creates a solvency account available for use by either highways or mass transit. Specifically, the Secretary of the Treasury is to transfer the excess of (1) any amount appropriated to the Highway Trust Fund before October 1, 2013, by reason of the provisions of this bill, over (2) the amount necessary to meet the required expenditures from the Highway Trust Fund as authorized in section 9503(c) of the Code (which provides expenditure authority from the Highway Trust Fund) for the period ending before October 1, 2013. Amounts in the solvency account are available for transfers to the Highway Account and the Mass Transit Account in such amounts as determined necessary by the Secretary to ensure that each account has a surplus balance of $2.8 billion on September 30, 2013. The solvency account terminates on September 30, 2013 and any remainder in the solvency account remains in the Highway Trust Fund. The Committee expects that the Secretary of the Treasury will consult with the Secretary of Transportation in making determinations concerning amounts necessary to meet required expenditures and amounts necessary to ensure the cushion of $2.8 billion.

Conference Agreement

The conference agreement provides for expenditure authority through September 30, 2014. The Code provisions governing the purposes for which monies in the Highway Trust Fund may be spent are updated to include the conference agreement bill, MAP-21. Cross-references to the reauthorization bill in the Code provisions governing the Sport Fish Restoration and Boating Trust Fund are also updated to include the conference agreement bill. In general, the provision extends the taxes dedicated to the Highway Trust Fund at their present law rates through September 30, 2016, and for the heavy vehicle use tax, through September 30, 2017.[15]

Effective Date

The provision is effective on July 1, 2012.

---

13. The provision also replaces cross-references to the Surface Transportation Extension Act of 2011, Part II, with MAP-21, and replaces April 1, 2012 references with October 1, 2013 in the Code provisions governing the Leaking Underground Storage Tank Trust Fund, and the Sport Fish Restoration and Boating Trust Fund.
14. The Leaking Underground Storage Tank Trust Fund financing rate of 0.1 cent per gallon also is extended through September 30, 2015.
15. The Leaking Underground Storage Tank Trust Fund financing rate also is extended through September 30, 2016. The provision also corrects a potential drafting ambiguity regarding the taxable period as reflected in prior legislation. The provision is effective as if included in section 142 of the Surface Transportation Extension Act of 2011, Part II.

[¶ 5402]   Section 40211.   Pension funding stabilization.

(Code Sec. 430)

[Conference Report]

Present Law

Minimum funding rules

Defined benefit plans generally are subject to minimum funding rules that require the sponsoring employer generally to make a contribution for each plan year to fund plan benefits.[20] Parallel rules apply under the Employee Retirement Income Security Act of 1974 ("ERISA"), which is generally in the jurisdiction of the Department of Labor.[21] The minimum funding rules for single-employer defined benefit plans were substantially revised by the Pension Protection Act of 2006 ("PPA").[22]

Minimum required contributions

In general

The minimum required contribution for a plan year for a single-employer defined benefit plan generally depends on a comparison of the value of the plan's assets, reduced by any prefunding balance or funding standard carryover balance ("net value of plan assets"),[23] with the plan's funding target and target normal cost. The plan's funding target for a plan year is the present value of all benefits accrued or earned as of the beginning of the plan year. A plan's target normal cost for a plan year is generally the present value of benefits expected to accrue or to be earned during the plan year.

If the net value of plan assets is less than the plan's funding target, so that the plan has a funding shortfall (discussed further below), the minimum required contribution is the sum of the plan's target normal cost and the shortfall amortization charge for the plan year (determined as described below).[24] If the net value of plan assets is equal to or exceeds the plan's funding target, the minimum required contribution is the plan's target normal cost, reduced by the amount, if any, by which the net value of plan assets exceeds the plan's funding target.

Shortfall amortization charge

The shortfall amortization charge for a plan year is the sum of the annual shortfall amortization installments attributable to the shortfall bases for that plan year and the six previous plan years. Generally, if a plan has a funding shortfall for the plan year, a

---

20. Sec. 412. A number of exceptions to the minimum funding rules apply. For example, governmental plans (within the meaning of section 414(d) and church plans (within the meaning of section 414(e)) are generally not subject to the minimum funding rules. Under section 4971, an excise tax applies to an employer maintaining a single-employer plan if the minimum funding requirements are not satisfied.
21. Sec. 302 of ERISA.
22. Pub. L. No. 109-280. The PPA minimum funding rules for single-employer plans are generally effective for plan years beginning after December 31, 2007. Delayed effective dates apply to single-employer plans sponsored by certain large defense contractors, multiple-employer plans of some rural cooperatives, eligible charity plans, and single-employer plans affected by settlement agreements with the Pension Benefit Guaranty Corporation. Subsequent changes to the single-employer plan and multiemployer plan funding rules (including temporary funding relief) were made by the Worker, Retiree, and Employer Recovery Act of 2008 ("WRERA"), Pub. L. No. 110-458, and the Preservation of Access to Care for Medicare Beneficiaries and Pension Relief Act of 2010 ("PRA 2010"), Public Law 111-192.
23. The value of plan assets is generally reduced by any prefunding balance or funding standard carryover balance in determining minimum required contributions, including for this purpose. A prefunding balance results from contributions to a plan that exceed the minimum required contributions. A funding standard carryover balance results from a positive balance in the funding standard account that applied under the funding requirements in effect before PPA. Subject to certain conditions, a prefunding balance or funding standard carryover balance may be credited against the minimum required contribution for a year, reducing the amount that must be contributed.
24. If the plan has obtained a waiver of the minimum required contribution (a funding waiver) within the past five years, the minimum required contribution also includes the related waiver amortization charge, that is, the annual installment needed to amortize the waived amount in level installments over the five years following the year of the waiver.

shortfall amortization base must be established for the plan year.[25] A plan's funding shortfall is the amount by which the plan's funding target exceeds the net value of plan assets. The shortfall amortization base for a plan year is: (1) the plan's funding shortfall, minus (2) the present value, determined using the segment interest rates (discussed below), of the aggregate total of the shortfall amortization installments that have been determined for the plan year and any succeeding plan year with respect to any shortfall amortization bases for the six previous plan years. The shortfall amortization base is amortized in level annual installments ("shortfall amortization installments") over a seven-year period beginning with the current plan year and using the segment interest rates (discussed below).[26]

The shortfall amortization base for a plan year may be positive or negative, depending on whether the present value of remaining installments with respect to amortization bases for previous years is more or less than the plan's funding shortfall. If the shortfall amortization base is positive (that is, the funding shortfall exceeds the present value of the remaining installments), the related shortfall amortization installments are positive. If the shortfall amortization base is negative, the related shortfall amortization installments are negative. The positive and negative shortfall amortization installments for a particular plan year are netted when adding them up in determining the shortfall amortization charge for the plan year, but the resulting shortfall amortization charge cannot be less than zero (i.e., negative amortization installments may not offset normal cost).

If the net value of plan assets for a plan year is at least equal to the plan's funding target for the year, so the plan has no funding shortfall, any shortfall amortization bases and related shortfall amortization installments are eliminated.[27] As indicated above, if the net value of plan assets exceeds the plan's funding target, the excess is applied against target normal cost in determining the minimum required contribution.

Interest rate used to determine target normal cost and funding target

The minimum funding rules for single-employer plans specify the interest rates and other actuarial assumptions that must be used in determining the present value of benefits for purposes of a plan's target normal cost and funding target.

Present value is determined using three interest rates ("segment" rates), each of which applies to benefit payments expected to be made from the plan during a certain period. The first segment rate applies to benefits reasonably determined to be payable during the five-year period beginning on the first day of the plan year; the second segment rate applies to benefits reasonably determined to be payable during the 15-year period following the initial five-year period; and the third segment rate applies to benefits reasonably determined to be payable at the end of the 15-year period. Each segment rate is a single interest rate determined monthly by the Secretary of the Treasury ("Secretary") on the basis of a corporate bond yield curve, taking into account only the portion of the yield curve based on corporate bonds maturing during the particular segment rate period. The corporate bond yield curve used for this purpose reflects the average, for the 24-month period ending with the preceding month, of yields on investment grade corporate bonds with varying maturities and that are in the top three quality levels available. The Internal Revenue Service (IRS) publishes the segment rates each month.

---

25. If the value of plan assets, reduced only by any prefunding balance if the employer elects to apply the prefunding balance against the required contribution for the plan year, is at least equal to the plan's funding target, no shortfall amortization base is established for the year.
26. Under PRA 2010, employers were permitted to elect to use one of two alternative extended amortization schedules for up to two "eligible" plan years during the period 2008-2011. The use of an extended amortization schedule has the effect of reducing the amount of the shortfall amortization installments attributable to the shortfall amortization base for the eligible plan year. However, the shortfall amortization installments attributable to an eligible plan year may be increased by an additional amount, an "installment acceleration amount," in the case of employee compensation exceeding $1 million, extraordinary dividends, or stock redemptions within a certain period of the eligible plan year.
27. Any amortization base relating to a funding waiver for a previous year is also eliminated.

The present value of liabilities under a plan is determined using the segment rates for the "applicable month" for the plan year. The applicable month is the month that includes the plan's valuation date for the plan year, or, at the election of the employer, any of the four months preceding the month that includes the valuation date.

Solely for purposes of determining minimum required contributions, in lieu of the segment rates described above, an employer may elect to use interest rates on a yield curve based on the yields on investment grade corporate bonds for the month preceding the month in which the plan year begins (i.e., without regard to the 24-month averaging described above) ("monthly yield curve"). If an election to use a monthly yield curve is made, it cannot be revoked without IRS approval.

Use of segment rates for other purposes

In general

In addition to being used to determine a plan's funding target and target normal cost, the segment rates are used also for other purposes, either directly because the segment rates themselves are specifically cross-referenced or indirectly because funding target, target normal cost, or some other concept, such as funding target attainment percentage (discussed below) in which funding target or target normal cost is an element, is cross-referenced elsewhere.

Funding target attainment percentage

A plan's funding target attainment percentage for a plan year is the ratio, expressed as a percentage, that the net value of plan assets bears to the plan's funding target for the year. Special rules may apply to a plan if its funding target attainment percentage is below a certain level. For example, funding target attainment percentage is used to determine whether a plan is in "at-risk" status, so that special actuarial assumptions ("at-risk assumptions") must be used in determining the plan's funding target and target normal cost.[28] A plan is in at risk status for a plan year if, for the preceding year: (1) the plan's funding target attainment percentage, determined without regard to the at-risk assumptions, was less than 80 percent, and (2) the plan's funding target attainment percentage, determined using the at-risk assumptions (without regard to whether the plan was in at-risk status for the preceding year), was less than 70 percent.[29] In addition, special reporting to the Pension Benefit Guaranty Corporation ("PBGC") may be required if a plan's funding target attainment percentage is less than 80 percent.[30]

Restrictions on benefit increases, certain types of benefits and benefit accruals (collectively referred to as "benefit restrictions") may apply to a plan if the plan's adjusted funding target attainment percentage is below a certain level.[31] Adjusted funding target attainment percentage is determined in the same way as funding target attainment percentage, except that the net value of plan assets and the plan's funding target are both increased by the aggregate amount of purchases of annuities for employees, other than highly compensated employees, made by the plan during the two preceding plan years. Although anti-cutback rules generally prohibit reductions in benefits that have already been earned under a plan,[32] reductions required to comply with the benefit restrictions are permitted.

---

28. If a plan is in at-risk status, under section 409A(b)(3), limitations apply on the employer's ability to set aside assets to provide benefits under a nonqualified deferred compensation plan.
29. A similar test applies in order for an employer to be permitted to apply a prefunding balance against its required contribution, that is, for the preceding year, the ratio of the value of plan assets (reduced by any prefunding balance) must be at least 80 percent of the plan's funding target (determined without regard to the at-risk rules).
30. ERISA sec. 4010.
31. Code sec. 436 and ERISA sec. 206(g).
32. Code sec. 411(d)(6) and ERISA sec. 204(g).

Minimum and maximum lump sums, limits on deductible contributions, retiree health

Defined benefit plans commonly allow a participant to choose among various forms of benefit offered under the plan, such as a lump-sum distribution. These optional forms of benefit generally must be actuarially equivalent to the life annuity benefit payable to the participant at normal retirement age. For certain forms of benefit, such as lump sums, the benefit amount cannot be less than the amount determined using the segment rates and a specified mortality table.[33] For this purpose, however, the segment rates are determined on a monthly basis, rather than using a 24-month average of corporate bond rates.

The amount of benefits under a defined benefit plan are subject to certain limits.[34] The segment rates used in determining minimum lump sums (and certain other forms of benefit) are also used in applying the benefit limits to lump sums (and the certain other forms of benefit).

Limits apply to the amount of plan contributions that may be deducted by an employer.[35] In the case of a single-employer defined benefit plan, the plan's funding target and target normal cost, determined using the segment rates that apply for funding purposes, are taken into account in calculating the limit on deductible contributions.

Subject to various conditions, a qualified transfer of excess assets of a single-employer defined benefit plan to a retiree medical account within the plan may be made in order to fund retiree health benefits.[36] For this purpose, excess assets generally means the excess, if any, of the value of the plan's assets over 125 percent of the sum of the plan's funding target and target normal cost for the plan year.

PBGC premiums and 4010 reporting

PBGC premiums apply with respect to defined benefit plans covered by ERISA.[37] In the case of a single-employer defined benefit plan, flat-rate premiums apply at a rate of $35.00 per participant for 2012.[38] If a single-employer defined benefit plan has unfunded vested benefits, variable-rate premiums also apply at a rate of $9 per $1,000 of unfunded vested benefits divided by the number of participants. For purposes of determining variable-rate premiums, unfunded vested benefits are equal to the excess (if any) of (1) the plan's funding target for the year determined as under the minimum funding rules, but taking into account only vested benefits, over (2) the fair market value of plan assets. In determining the plan's funding target for this purpose, the interest rates used are segment rates determined as under the minimum funding rules, but determined on a monthly basis, rather than using a 24-month average of corporate bond rates.

In certain circumstances, the contributing sponsor of a singleemployer plan defined benefit pension plan covered by the PBGC (and members of the contributing sponsor's controlled group) must provide certain information to the PBGC (referred to as "section 4010 reporting").[39] This information includes actuarial information with respect to single-employer plans maintained by the contributing sponsor (and controlled group members). Section 4010 reporting is required if: (1) the funding target attainment percentage at the end of the preceding plan year of a plan maintained by the contributing sponsor or any member of its controlled group is less than 80 percent; (2) the conditions for imposition of a lien (i.e., required contributions totaling more than $1 million have not been made) have occurred with respect to a plan maintained by the contributing sponsor or

---

33. Code sec. 417(e) and ERISA sec. 205(g).
34. Sec. 415(b).
35. Sec. 404.
36. Sec. 420. Under present law, a qualified transfer is not permitted after December 31, 2013.
37. ERISA sec. 4006.
38. Flat-rate premiums apply also to multiemployer defined benefit plans at a rate of $9.00 per participant. Single-employer and multiemployer flat-rate premium rates are indexed for inflation. The rate of variable-rate premiums is not indexed.
39. ERISA sec. 4010

any member of its controlled group; or (3) minimum funding waivers in excess of $1 million have been granted with respect to a plan maintained by the contributing sponsor or any member of its controlled group and any portion of the waived amount is still outstanding.

Annual funding notice

The plan administrator of a defined benefit plan must provide an annual funding notice to: (1) each participant and beneficiary; (2) each labor organization representing such participants or beneficiaries; and (4) the PBGC.[40]

In addition to the information required to be provided in all funding notices, certain information must be provided in the case of a single-employer defined benefit plan, including:

a statement as to whether the plan's funding target attainment percentage (as defined under the minimum funding rules) for the plan year to which the notice relates and the two preceding plan years, is at least 100 percent (and, if not, the actual percentages); and

a statement of (a) the total assets (separately stating any funding standard carryover or prefunding balance) and the plan's liabilities for the plan year and the two preceding years, determined in the same manner as under the funding rules, and (b) the value of the plan's assets and liabilities as of the last day of the plan year to which the notice relates, determined using fair market value and the interest rate used in determining variable rate premiums.

A funding notice may also include any additional information that the plan administrator elects to include to the extent not inconsistent with regulations. The notice must be written so as to be understood by the average plan participant. As required under PPA, the Secretary of Labor has issued a model funding notice that can be used to satisfy the notice requirement.

House Bill

No provision.

Senate Amendment

The Senate amendment revises the rules for determining the segment rates under the single-employer plan funding rules by adjusting a segment rate if the rate determined under the regular rules is outside a specified range of the average of the segment rates for the preceding 25-year period ("average" segment rates). In particular, if a segment rate determined for an applicable month under the regular rules is less than the applicable minimum percentage, the segment rate is adjusted upward to match that percentage. If a segment rate determined for an applicable month under the regular rules is more than the applicable maximum percentage, the segment rate is adjusted downward to match that percentage. For this purpose, the average segment rate is the average of the segment rates determined under the regular rules for the 25-year period ending September 30 of the calendar year preceding the calendar year in which the plan year begins. The Secretary is to determine average segment rates on an annual basis and may prescribe equivalent rates for any years in the 25-year period for which segment rates determined under the regular rules are not available. The Secretary is directed to publish the average segment rates each month.

The applicable minimum percentage and the applicable maximum percentage depend on the calendar year in which the plan year begins as shown by the following table:

---

40. ERISA sec. 101(f). In the case of a multiemployer plan, the notice must also be sent to each employer that has an obligation to contribute under the plan;

If the calendar year is:	The applicable minimum percentage is:	The applicable maximum percentage is:
2012	90 percent	110 percent
2013	85 percent	115 percent
2014	80 percent	120 percent
2015	75 percent	125 percent
2016 or later	70 percent	130 percent

Thus, for example, if the first segment rate determined for an applicable month under the regular rules for a plan year beginning in 2012 is less than 90 percent of the average of the first segment rates determined under the regular rules for the 25-year period ending September 30, 2011, the segment rate is adjusted to 90 percent of the 25-year average.

The change in the method of determining segment rates generally applies for the purposes for which segment rates are used under present law, except for purposes of determining minimum and maximum lump-sum benefits,[41] limits on deductible contributions to single-employer defined benefit plans, and PBGC variablerate premiums.

Effective Date

The provision in the Senate Amendment is generally effective for plan years beginning after December 31, 2011. Under a special rule, an employer may elect, for any plan year beginning on or before the date of enactment and solely for purposes of determining the plan's adjusted funding target attainment percentage (used in applying the benefit restrictions) for that year, not to have the provision apply. A plan is not treated as failing to meet the requirements of the anti-cutback rules solely by reason of an election under the special rule.

Conference Agreement

The conference agreement follows the Senate amendment with several modifications.

Average segment rates

The change in the method of determining segment rates generally applies for the purposes for which segment rates are used under present law, except for purposes of minimum and maximum lump-sum benefits,[42] limits on deductible contributions to singleemployer defined benefit plans, qualified transfers of excess pension assets to retiree medical accounts,[43] PBGC variable-rate premiums,[44] and 4010 reporting to the PBGC.

The special effective date rule is modified under the conference agreement so that an employer may elect, for any plan year beginning before January 1, 2013, not to have the provision apply either (1) for all purposes for which the provision would otherwise apply, or (2) solely for purposes of determining the plan's adjusted funding target attainment percentage (used in applying the benefit restrictions) for that year. A plan is not treated as failing to meet the requirements of the anti-cutback rules solely by reason of an election under the special rule.

Under the conference agreement, if, as of the date of enactment, an employer election is in effect to use a monthly yield curve in determining minimum required contributions, rather than segment rates, the employer may revoke the election (and use segment rates, as modified by the conference agreement provision) without obtaining IRS approval.

---

41. The provision does not provide a specific exception for determining maximum lump sum benefits. However, the exception for minimum lump sum benefits applies by cross-reference.
42. The provision does not provide a specific exception for determining maximum lump sum benefits. However, the exception for minimum lump sum benefits applies by cross-reference.
43. Another provision of the conference agreement extends to December 31, 2021, the ability to make a qualified transfer. In addition, another provision of the conference agreement allows qualified transfers to be made to provide group-term life insurance benefits.
44. Another provision of the conference agreement increases PBGC flat-rate and variable-rate premiums.

The revocation must be made at any time before the date that is one year after the date of enactment, and the revocation will be effective for the first plan year to which the amendments made by the provision apply and all subsequent plan years. The employer is not precluded from making a subsequent election to use a monthly yield curve in determining minimum required contributions in accordance with present law.

Annual funding notice

The conference agreement requires additional information to be included in the annual funding notice in the case of an applicable plan year. For this purpose, an applicable plan year is any plan year beginning after December 31, 2011, and before January 1, 2015, for which (1) the plan's funding target, determined using segment rates as adjusted to reflect average segment rates ("adjusted" segment rates), is less than 95 percent of the funding target determined without regard to adjusted segment rates (that is, determined as under present law), (2) the plan has a funding shortfall, determined without regard to adjusted segment rates, greater than $500,000 and (3) the plan had 50 or more participants on any day during the preceding plan year.

The additional information that must be provided is:

a statement that MAP-21 modified the method for determining the interest rates used to determine the actuarial value of benefits earned under the plan, providing for a 25-year average of interest rates to be taken into account in addition to a 2-year average;

a statement that, as a result of MAP-21, the plan sponsor may contribute less money to the plan when interest rates are at historical lows, and

a table showing, for the applicable plan year and each of the two preceding plan years, the plan's funding target attainment percentage, funding shortfall, and the employer's minimum required contribution, each determined both using adjusted segment rates and without regard to adjusted segment rates (that is, as under present law). In the case of a preceding plan year beginning before January 1, 2012, the plan's funding target attainment percentage, funding shortfall, and the employer's minimum required contribution provided are determined only without regard to adjusted segment rates (that is, as under present law).

As under present law, a funding notice may also include any additional information that the plan administrator elects to include to the extent not inconsistent with regulations. For example, a funding notice may include a statement of the amount of the employer's actual or planned contributions to the plan.

The Secretary of Labor is directed to modify the model funding notice required so that the model includes the additional information in a prominent manner, for example, on a separate first page before the remainder of the notice.

[¶ 5403] Section 40221; 40222. Single employer plan annual premium rates; Multiemployer annual premium rates.

(Code Sec. None)

[Conference Report]

Present Law

Defined benefit plans subject to ERISA are covered by the Pension Benefit Guaranty Corporation ("PBGC") insurance program and related premium requirements.

In the case of a single-employer defined benefit plan, flat-rate premiums apply at a rate of $35.00 per participant for 2012. Single-employer flat-rate premium rates are indexed for inflation.

If a single-employer defined benefit plan has unfunded vested benefits, variable-rate premiums also apply at a rate of $9 per $1,000 of unfunded vested benefits divided by the number of participants. Variable-rate premiums are not indexed for inflation. For purposes of determining variable-rate premiums, unfunded vested benefits are equal to the excess (if any) of (1) the plan's funding target for the year, as determined under the minimum funding rules, but taking into account only vested benefits, over (2) the fair market value of plan assets. In determining the plan's funding target for this purpose, the interest rates used are segment rates determined as under the minimum funding rules, but determined on a monthly basis, rather than using a 24-month average of corporate bond rates.

In the case of a multiemployer defined benefit plan, flat-rate premiums apply at a rate of $9.00 per participant for 2012. Multiemployer flat-rate premium rates are indexed for inflation and are expected to increase to $10 for 2013.

House Bill

No provision.

Senate Amendment

No provision.

Conference Agreement

The conference agreement increases PBGC premiums for single-employer plans and multiemployer plans.

Single-employer plan flat-rate premiums are increased to $42 per participant for 2013 and $49 per participant for 2014 with indexing thereafter.

For plan years beginning after 2012, the rate for variable-rate premiums ($9 per $1,000 of unfunded vested benefits) is indexed and the per-participant variable-rate premium is subject to a limit. The limit is $400 for 2013 with indexing thereafter. In addition, the rate for variable-rate premiums per $1,000 of unfunded vested benefits is increased by $4 for 2014 and another $5 for 2015. These increases are applied to the rate applicable for the preceding year (that is, $9 as indexed for the preceding year per $1,000 of unfunded vested benefits) and indexing continues to apply thereafter.

Multiemployer plan flat-rate premiums are increased by $2 per participant for 2013.

[¶ 5404]   Section 40231; 40232; 40233; 40234.   Pension Benefit Guaranty Corporation Governance Improvement; Participant and plan sponsor advocate; Quality control procedures for the Pension Benefit Guaranty Corporation; Line of credit repeal.

(Code Sec. None)

[Conference Report]

Present Law

The Pension Benefit Guaranty Corporation ("PBGC"), which was created by the Employee Retirement Income Security Act of 1974 ("ERISA"), insures benefits provided under defined benefit plans covered by ERISA, collects premiums with respect to such plans, and manages assets and pays benefits with respect to certain terminated plans. PBGC's purposes are to encourage the continuation and maintenance of voluntary private defined benefit plans, provide timely and uninterrupted payment of pension benefits to participants and beneficiaries, and maintain premiums at the lowest level consistent with carrying out its obligations under ERISA.[149]

---

149. ERISA sec. 4002(a).

PBGC is administered by a director, who is appointed by the President with the advice and consent of the Senate. PBGC's board of directors consists of the Secretary of the Treasury, the Secretary of Labor, and the Secretary of Commerce, with the Secretary of Labor serving as chair. An advisory committee has been established for the purpose of advising the PBGC as to various policies and procedures. ERISA contains general provisions as to the board of directors and advisory committee.

House Bill

No provision.

Senate Amendment

No provision.

Conference Agreement

PBGC governance improvement

The conference agreement expands the ERISA provisions relating to the PBGC board of directors, advisory committee, director and other PBGC officials.

With respect to the board of directors, the conference agreement addresses timing and procedures for meetings (including a joint meeting with the advisory committee). It also ensures that the PBGC inspector general has direct access to the board, clarifies the role of the General Counsel, and provides authority to the board to hire its own employees, experts and consultants as may be required to enable the board to perform its duties. The conference agreement includes specific rules on conflicts of interest with respect to the board of directors and the director of PBGC and provides for the PBGC to have a risk management officer. It further clarifies that the PBGC board of directors is ultimately responsible for overseeing PBGC and that the director is directly accountable to the board of directors and can be removed by the board of directors or the president. It also sets the director's term at five years unless removed before the expiration of the term by the President or the board of directors.

The conference agreement states the sense of Congress that (1) the board of directors should form committees, including an audit committee and an investment committee composed of at least two members, to enhance the overall effectiveness of the board, and (2) the advisory committee should provide the board with policy recommendations regarding changes to the law that would be beneficial to the PBGC or the voluntary private pension system.

The conference agreement also directs the PBGC, not later than 90 days after enactment, to contract with the National Academy of Public Administration to conduct a study of the PBGC to include (1) a review of governance structures of organizations (governmental and nongovernmental) that are analogous to the PBGC and (2) recommendations with respect to various topics relating to the board of directors, such as composition, procedures, and policies to enhance Congressional oversight. The results of the study are to be reported within a year of initiation of the study to the Committee on Health, Education, Labor, and Pensions and Committee on Finance of the Senate and the Committee on Education and the Workforce and Committee on Ways and Means of the House of Representatives.

Participant and plan sponsor advocate

The conference agreement establishes a new Participant and Plan Sponsor Advocate. The Advocate is chosen by the Board of Directors from the candidates nominated by the advisory committee. This individual will act as a liaison between the corporation and participants in terminated pension plans. The Advocate will ensure that participants receive everything they are entitled to under the law. The Advocate will also provide plan sponsors with assistance in resolving disputes with the corporation. Each year, the Advocate will provide a report on their activities to the Committee on Health, Education, Labor, and Pensions and Committee on Finance of the Senate, the Committee on Education and the Workforce of the House of Representatives, and the Committee on Ways and Means of the House of Representatives summarizing the issues raised by participants and plan sponsors and making recommendations for changes to improve the system.

Quality control procedures for the PBGC

The conference agreement states that the PBGC will contract with an outside agency (such as the Social Security Administration) to conduct an annual review of the Corporation's Single-Employer and Multiemployer Pension Insurance Modeling Systems ("PIMS"). The first reviews will be initiated no later than 3 months after the enactment of this Act.

The conference agreement also states that the PBGC will make its own efforts to develop review policies to examine actuarial work, management, and record keeping. Finally, the conference agreement instructs the PBGC to provide a specific report addressing outstanding recommendations made by the Office of the Inspector General ("OIG") relating to the Policy, Research, and Analysis Department and the Benefits Administration and Payment Department.

Line of credit repeal

The conference agreement repeals section 4005(c) of ERISA, which provides authority for the PBGC to issue notes or other obligations in an amount up to $100,000,000.

[¶ 5405]　Section 40241; 40242.　Extension for transfers of excess pension assets to retiree health accounts;　Transfer of excess pension assets to retiree group term life insurance accounts.

(Code Sec. 420)

[Conference Report]

Present Law

Defined benefit pension plan reversions

Defined benefit plan assets generally may not revert to an employer prior to termination of the plan and satisfaction of all plan liabilities.[45] Upon plan termination, the accrued benefits of all plan participants are required to be 100-percent vested. A reversion prior to plan termination may constitute a prohibited transaction and may result in plan disqualification. Any assets that revert to the employer upon plan termination are includible in the gross income of the employer and subject to an excise tax. The excise tax rate is 20 percent if the employer maintains a replacement plan or makes certain benefit increases in connection with the termination; if not, the excise tax rate is 50 percent. Medical benefits and life insurance benefits provided under a pension plan.

Retiree medical accounts

A pension plan may provide medical benefits to retired employees through a separate account that is part of a defined benefit plan ("retiree medical accounts").[46] Medical benefits provided through a retiree medical account are generally not includible in the retired employee's gross income.[47]

---

45. In addition, a reversion may occur only if the terms of the plan so provide.
46. Sec. 401(h) and Treas. Reg. sec. 1.401-1(b).
47. Treas. Reg. sec. 1.72-15(h).

Transfers of excess pension assets

In general

A qualified transfer of excess assets of a defined benefit plan, including a multiemployer plan,[48] to a retiree medical account within the plan may be made in order to fund retiree health benefits.[49] A qualified transfer does not result in plan disqualification, is not a prohibited transaction, and is not treated as a reversion. Thus, transferred assets are not includible in the gross income of the employer and are not subject to the excise tax on reversions. No more than one qualified transfer may be made in any taxable year. No qualified transfer may be made after December 31, 2013.

Excess assets generally means the excess, if any, of the value of the plan's assets[50] over 125 percent of the sum of the plan's funding target and target normal cost for the plan year. In addition, excess assets transferred in a qualified transfer may not exceed the amount reasonably estimated to be the amount that the employer will pay out of such account during the taxable year of the transfer for qualified current retiree health liabilities. No deduction is allowed to the employer for (1) a qualified transfer, or (2) the payment of qualified current retiree health liabilities out of transferred funds (and any income thereon). In addition, no deduction is allowed for amounts paid other than from transferred funds for qualified current retiree health liabilities to the extent such amounts are not greater than the excess of (1) the amount transferred (and any income thereon), over (2) qualified current retiree thereon). An employer may not contribute any amount to a health benefits account or welfare benefit fund with respect to qualified current retiree health liabilities for which transferred assets are required to be used.

Transferred assets (and any income thereon) must be used to pay qualified current retiree health liabilities for the taxable year of the transfer. Transferred amounts generally must benefit pension plan participants, other than key employees, who are entitled upon retirement to receive retiree medical benefits through the separate account. Retiree health benefits of key employees may not be paid out of transferred assets.

Amounts not used to pay qualified current retiree health liabilities for the taxable year of the transfer are to be returned to the general assets of the plan. These amounts are not includible in the gross income of the employer, but are treated as an employer reversion and are subject to a 20-percent excise tax.

In order for the transfer to be qualified, accrued retirement benefits under the pension plan generally must be 100-percent vested as if the plan terminated immediately before the transfer (or in the case of a participant who separated in the one-year period ending on the date of the transfer, immediately before the separation).

In order for a transfer to be qualified, there is maintenance of effort requirement under which, the employer generally must maintain retiree health benefits at the same level for the taxable year of the transfer and the following four years.

In addition, the Employee Retirement Income Security Act of 1974 ("ERISA")[51] provides that, at least 60 days before the date of a qualified transfer, the employer must notify the Secretary of Labor, the Secretary of the Treasury, employee representatives, and the plan administrator of the transfer, and the plan administrator must notify each plan participant and beneficiary of the transfer.[52]

---

48. The Pension Protection Act of 2006 ("PPA"), Pub. L. No. 109-280, extended the application of the rules for qualified transfers to multiemployer plans with respect to transfers made in taxable years beginning after December 31, 2006. However, the rules for qualified future transfers and collectively bargained transfers do not apply to multiemployer plans.
49. Sec. 420.
50. The value of plan assets for this purpose is the lesser of fair market value or actuarial value.
51. Pub. L. No. 93-406.
52. ERISA sec. 101(e). ERISA also provides that a qualified transfer is not a prohibited transaction under ERISA or a prohibited reversion.

Qualified future transfers and collectively bargained transfers

If certain requirements are satisfied, transfers of excess pension assets under a single-employer plan to retiree medical accounts to fund the expected cost of retiree medical benefits are permitted for the current and future years (a "qualified future transfer") and such transfers are also allowed in the case of benefits provided under a collective bargaining agreement (a "collectively bargained transfer").[53] Transfers must be made for at least a two-year period. An employer can elect to make a qualified future transfer or a collectively bargained transfer rather than a qualified transfer. A qualified future transfer or collectively bargained transfer must meet the requirements applicable to qualified transfers, except that the provision modifies the rules relating to: (1) the determination of excess pension assets; (2) the limitation on the amount transferred; and (3) the maintenance of effort requirement. The general sunset applicable to qualified transfer applies (i.e., no transfers can be made after December 31, 2013).

Qualified future transfers and collectively bargained transfers can be made to the extent that plan assets exceed 120 percent of the sum of the plan's funding target and the normal cost for the plan year. During the transfer period, the plan's funded status must be maintained at the minimum level required to make transfers. If the minimum level is not maintained, the employer must make contributions to the plan to meet the minimum level or an amount required to meet the minimum level must be transferred from the health benefits account. The transfer period is the period not to exceed a total of ten consecutive taxable years beginning with the taxable year of the transfer. As previously discussed, the period must be not less than two consecutive years.

Employer provided group-term life insurance

Group-term life insurance coverage provided under a policy carried by an employer is includible in the gross income of an employee (including a former employee) but only to the extent that the cost exceeds the sum of the cost of $50,000 of such insurance plus the amount, if any, paid by the employee toward the purchase of such insurance.[54] Special rules apply for determining the cost of group-term life insurance that is includible in gross income under a discriminatory group-term life insurance plan.

A pension plan may provide life insurance benefits for employees (including retirees) but only to the extent that the benefits are incidental to the retirement benefits provided under the plan.[55] The cost of term life insurance provided through a pension plan is includible in the employee's gross income.[56]

House Bill

No provision.

Senate Amendment

Extension of existing provisions

The provision allows qualified transfers, qualified future transfers, and collectively bargained transfers to retiree medical accounts to be made through December 31, 2021. No transfers are permitted after that date.

Transfers to fund retiree group-term life insurance permitted

The provision allows qualified transfers, qualified future transfers, and collectively bargained transfers to be made to fund the purchase of retiree group-term life insurance. The assets transferred for the purchase of group-term life insurance must be maintained

---

53. The rules for qualified transfers and collectively bargained transfers were added by the PPA and apply to transfers after the date of enactment (August 17, 2006).
54. Sec. 79.
55. Treas. Reg. sec. 1.401-1(b).
56. Secs. 72(m)(3) and 79(b)(3).

in a separate account within the plan ("retiree life insurance account"), which must be separate both from the assets in the retiree medical account and from the other assets in the defined benefit plan.

Under the provision, the general rule that the cost of groupterm life insurance coverage provided under a defined benefit plan is includable in gross income of the participant does not apply to group-term life insurance provided through a retiree life insurance account. Instead, the general rule for determining the amount of employer-provided group-term life insurance that is includible in gross income applies. However, group-term life insurance coverage is permitted to be provided through a retiree life insurance account only to the extent that it is not includible in gross income. Thus, generally, only group-term life insurance not in excess of $50,000 may be purchased with such transferred assets.

Generally, the present law rules for transfers of excess pension assets to retiree medical accounts to fund retiree health benefits also apply to transfers to retiree life insurance accounts to fund retiree group-term life. However, generally, the rules are applied separately. Thus, for example, the one-transfer-a-year rule generally applies separately to transfers to retiree life insurance accounts and transfers to retiree medical accounts. Further, the maintenance of effort requirement for qualified transfers applies separately to life insurance benefits and health benefits. Similarly, for qualified future transfers and collectively bargained transfers for retiree group-term life insurance, the maintenance of effort and other special rules are applied separately to transfers to retiree life insurance accounts and retiree medical accounts.

Reflecting the inherent differences between life insurance coverage and health coverage, certain rules are not applied to transfers to retiree life insurance accounts, such as the special rules allowing the employer to elect to determine the applicable employer cost for health coverage during the cost maintenance period separately for retirees eligible for Medicare and retirees not eligible for Medicare. However, a separate test is allowed for the cost of retiree group-term life insurance for retirees under age 65 and those retirees who have reached age 65.

The provision makes other technical and conforming changes to the rules for transfers to fund retiree health benefits and removes certain obsolete ("deadwood") rules.

The same sunset applicable to qualified transfers, qualified future transfers, and collectively bargained transfers to retiree medical accounts applies to transfers to retiree life insurance accounts (i.e., no transfers can be made after December 31, 2021).

Effective Date

The provision applies to transfers made after the date of enactment.

Conference Agreement

The conference agreement includes the Senate amendment provision.

[¶ 5500] Conference Report Accompanying the Middle Class Tax Relief and Job Creation Act of 2012

This section, in ¶ 5501, reproduces all relevant parts of the Conference Report (Conf. Rept. 112-399, 2/16/2012) accompanying the Middle Class Tax Relief and Job Creation Act of 2012 (P.L. 112-96, 2/22/2012).

[¶ 5501]   **Section 1001.**   **Extension of payroll tax reduction.**

(Code Sec. 1401)

[Conference Report]

Present Law

Federal Insurance Contributions Act ("FICA") tax

The FICA tax applies to employers based on the amount of covered wages paid to an employee during the year.[1] Generally, covered Sec. 3111 wages means all remuneration for employment, including the cash value of all remuneration paid in any medium other than cash.[2] Certain exceptions from covered wages are also provided. The tax imposed is composed of two parts: (1) the old age, survivors, and disability insurance ("OASDI") tax equal to 6.2 percent of covered wages up to the taxable wage base ($106,800 for 2011 and $110,100 for 2012); and (2) the Medicare hospital insurance ("HI") tax amount equal to 1.45 percent of covered wages.

In addition to the tax on employers, each employee is generally subject to FICA taxes equal to the amount of tax imposed on the employer (the "employee portion").[3] The employee portion of FICA taxes generally must be withheld and remitted to the Federal government by the employer.

Self-Employment Contributions Act ("SECA") Tax

As a parallel to FICA taxes, the SECA tax applies to the selfemployment income of self-employed individuals.[4] The rate of the OASDI portion of SECA taxes is generally 12.4 percent, which is equal to the combined employee and employer OASDI FICA tax rates, and applies to self-employment income up to the FICA taxable wage base. Similarly, the rate of the HI portion of SECA tax is 2.9 percent, the same as the combined employer and employee HI rates under the FICA tax, and there is no cap on the amount of self-employment income to which the rate applies.[5]

An individual may deduct, in determining net earnings from self-employment under the SECA tax, the amount of the net earnings from self-employment (determined without regard to this deduction) for the taxable year multiplied by one half of the combined OASDI and HI rates.[6]

Additionally, a deduction, for purposes of computing the income tax of an individual, is allowed for one-half of the amount of the SECA tax imposed on the individual's self-employment income for the taxable year.[7]

---

1. Sec. 3111.
2. Sec. 3121(a).
3. Sec. 3101. For taxable years beginning after 2012, an additional HI tax applies to certain employees.
4. Sec. 1401.
5. For taxable years beginning after 2012, an additional HI tax applies to certain self-employed individuals.
6. Sec. 1402(a)(12).
7. Sec. 164(f).

Railroad retirement tax

Instead of FICA taxes, railroad employers and employees are subject, under the Railroad Retirement Tax Act ("RRTA"), to taxes equivalent to the OASDI and HI taxes under FICA.[8] The employee portion of RRTA taxes generally must be withheld and remitted to the Federal government by the employer.

Temporary reduced OASDI rates

Under the Tax Relief, Unemployment Insurance Reauthorization, and Job Creation Act of 2010,[9] for 2011, the OASDI rate for the employee portion of the FICA tax, and the equivalent employee portion of the RRTA tax, is reduced by two percentage points to percent. Similarly, for taxable years beginning in 2011, the OASDI rate for a self-employed individual is reduced by two percentage points to 10.4 percent.

Special rules coordinate the SECA tax rate reduction with a self-employed individual's deduction in determining net earnings from self-employment under the SECA tax and the income tax deduction for one-half of the SECA tax. The rate reduction is not taken into account in determining the SECA tax deduction allowed for determining the amount of the net earnings from self-employment for the taxable year. The income tax deduction allowed for the SECA tax for taxable years beginning in 2011 is 59.6 percent of the OASDI portion of the SECA tax imposed for the taxable year plus one-half of the HI portion of the SECA tax imposed for the taxable year.[10]

The Federal Old-Age and Survivors Trust Fund, the Federal Disability Insurance Trust Fund and the Social Security Equivalent Benefit Account established under the Railroad Retirement Act of 1974[11] receive transfers from the General Fund of the United States Treasury equal to any reduction in payroll taxes attributable to the rate reduction for 2011. The amounts are transferred from the General Fund at such times and in such a manner as to replicate to the extent possible the transfers which would have occurred to the Trust Funds or Benefit Account had the provision not been enacted.

For purposes of applying any provision of Federal law other than the provisions of the Internal Revenue Code of 1986, the employee rate of OASDI tax is determined without regard to the reduced rate for 2011.

Under the Temporary Payroll Tax Cut Continuation Act of 2011,[12] the reduced employee OASDI tax rate of 4.2 percent under the FICA tax, and the equivalent employee portion of the RRTA tax, is extended to apply to covered wages paid in the first two months of 2012. A recapture applies for any benefit a taxpayer may have received from the reduction in the OASDI tax rate, and the equivalent employee portion of the RRTA tax, for remuneration received during the first two months of 2012 in excess of $18,350.[13] The recapture is accomplished by a tax equal to two percent of the amount of wages (and railroad compensation) received during the first two months of 2012 that exceed $18,350. The Secretary of the Treasury (or the Secretary's delegate) is to prescribe regulations or other guidance that is necessary and appropriate to carry out this provision.

In addition, for taxable years beginning in 2012, the OASDI rate for a self-employed individual is reduced to 10.4 percent, for self-employment income of up to $18,350 (reduced by wages subject to the lower OASDI rate for 2012). Related rules for 2011 con-

---

8. Secs. 3201(a) and 3211(a).
9. Pub. L. No. 111-312.
10. This percentage replaces the rate of one half (50 percent) otherwise allowed for this portion of the deduction. The percentage is necessary to allow the self-employed individual to deduct the full amount of the employer portion of SECA taxes. The employer OASDI tax rate remains at 6.2 percent, while the employee portion falls to 4.2 percent. Thus, the employer share of total OASDI taxes is 6.2 divided by 10.4, or 59.6 percent of the OASDI portion of SECA taxes.
11. 45 U.S.C. 231n-1(a).
12. Pub. L. No. 112-78, enacted after passage of H.R. 3630 by the House of Representatives and the Senate.
13. $18,350 is ⅙ of the 2012 taxable wage base of $110,100.

cerning coordination of a self-employed individual's deductions in determining net earnings from self-employment and income tax also apply for 2012, except that the income tax deduction allowed for the OASDI portion of SECA tax imposed for taxable years beginning in 2012 is computed at the rate of 59.6 percent[14] of the OASDI portion of the SECA tax imposed on self-employment income of up to $18,350. For self-employment income in excess of this amount, the deduction is equal to half of the OASDI portion of the SECA tax.

Rules related to the OASDI rate reduction for 2011 concerning (1) transfers to the Federal Old-Age and Survivors Trust Fund, the Federal Disability Insurance Trust Fund and the Social Security Equivalent Benefit Account established under the Railroad Retirement Act of 1974, and (2) determining the employee rate of OASDI tax in applying provisions of Federal law other than the Code also apply for 2012.

House Bill[15]

Under the House bill, the reduced employee OASDI tax rate of 4.2 percent under the FICA tax, and the equivalent portion of the RRTA tax, is extended to apply for 2012. Similarly, a reduced OASDI tax rate of 10.4 percent under the SECA tax, is extended to apply for taxable years beginning in 2012.

Related rules concerning (1) coordination of a self-employed individual's deductions in determining net earnings from self-employment and income tax, (2) transfers to the Federal Old-Age and Survivors Trust Fund, the Federal Disability Insurance Trust Fund and the Social Security Equivalent Benefit Account established under the Railroad Retirement Act of 1974, and (3) determining the employee rate of OASDI tax in applying provisions of Federal law other than the Code also apply for 2012.

Senate Amendment[16]

Under the Senate amendment, the reduced employee OASDI tax rate of 4.2 percent under the FICA tax, and the equivalent employee portion of the RRTA tax, applies to covered wages paid up to $18,350 in the first two months of 2012.[17]

In addition, for taxable years beginning in 2012, the Senate amendment provides that the OASDI rate for a self-employed individual is reduced to 10.4 percent, for self-employment income of up to $18,350 (reduced by wages subject to the lower OASDI rate for 2012). Related rules for 2011 concerning coordination of a self-employed individual's deductions in determining net earnings from self-employment and income tax also apply for 2012, except that the income tax deduction allowed for the OASDI portion of SECA tax imposed for taxable years beginning in 2012 is computed at the rate of 59.6 percent[18] of the OASDI portion of the SECA tax imposed on self-employment income of up to $18,350. For self-employment income in excess of this amount, the deduction is equal to half of the OASDI portion of the SECA tax.

The Senate amendment also contains rules related to the OASDI rate reduction for 2011 concerning (1) transfers to the Federal Old-Age and Survivors Trust Fund, the Federal Disability Insurance Trust Fund and the Social Security Equivalent Benefit Account established under the Railroad Retirement Act of 1974, and (2) determining the

---

14. This percentage used with respect to the first $18,350 of self-employment income is necessary to continue to allow the self-employed taxpayer to deduct the full amount of the employer portion of SECA taxes. The employer OASDI tax rate remains at 6.2 percent, while the employee portion falls to a 4.2 percent rate for the first $18,350 of self-employment income. Thus, the employer share of total OASDI taxes is 6.2 divided by 10.4, or 59.6 percent of the OASDI portion of SECA taxes, for the first $18,350 of self-employment income
15. The House bill passed prior to the enactment of the"Temporary Payroll Tax Cut Continuation Act of 2011", Pub. L. No. 112-78, described above.
16. The Senate amendment passed prior to the enactment of the'Temporary Payroll Tax Cut Continuation Act of 2011', Pub. L. No. 112-78, described above.
17. $18,350 is 1/6 of the 2012 taxable wage base of $110,100.
18. See footnote 14.

employee rate of OASDI tax in applying provisions of Federal law other than the Code also apply for 2012.

Conference Agreement

The conference agreement follows the House bill, providing for a reduced employee OASDI tax rate of 4.2 percent under the FICA tax, and the equivalent potion of the RRTA tax, through 2012. Similarly, a reduced OASDI tax rate of 10.4 percent under the SECA tax applies for taxable years beginning in 2012.

As in the House bill and Senate amendment, related rules concerning (1) coordination of a self-employed individual's deductions in determining net earnings from self-employment and income tax, (2) transfers to the Federal Old-Age and Survivors Trust Fund, the Federal Disability Insurance Trust Fund and the Social Security Equivalent Benefit Account established under the Railroad Retirement Act of 1974, and (3) determining the employee rate of OASDI tax in applying provisions of Federal law other than the Code also apply for 2012.

The conference agreement repeals the present-law recapture provision applicable to a taxpayer who receives the reduced OASDI rate with respect to more than $18,350 of wages (or railroad compensation) received during the first two months of 2012, and removes the $18,350 limitation on self-employment income subject to the lower rate for taxable years beginning in 2012.

Effective Date

The provision applies to remuneration received, and taxable years beginning, after December 31, 2011.

[¶ 5600] Conference Report Accompanying the FAA Modernization and Reform Act of 2012

This section, in ¶ 5601 through ¶ 5608, reproduces all relevant parts of the Conference Report (Conf. Rept. 112-381, 2/1/2012) accompanying the FAA Modernization and Reform Act of 2012 (P.L. 112-95, 2/14/2012).

[¶ 5601]   Section 1101.   Extension of taxes funding airport and airway trust fund.

(Code Sec. 4081, 4261, 4271)

[Conference Report]

Present Law

Overview

Excise taxes are imposed on amounts paid for commercial air passenger and freight transportation and on fuels used in commercial aviation and noncommercial aviation (i.e., transportation that is not "for hire") to fund the Airport and Airway Trust Fund. The present aviation excise taxes are as follows:

Tax (and Code section)	Tax Rates
Domestic air passengers (sec. 4261)	7.5 percent of fare, plus $3.80 (2012) per domestic flight segment generally[1]
International travel facilities tax (sec. 4261)	$16.70 (2012) per arrival or departure[2]
Amounts paid for right to award free or reduced rate passenger air transportation (sec. 4261).	7.5 percent of amount paid
Air cargo (freight) transportation (sec. 4271)	6.25 percent of amount charged for domestic transportation; no tax on international cargo transportation
Aviation fuels (sec. 4081):[3]	
1. Commercial aviation	4.3 cents per gallon
2. Non-commercial (general) aviation: . . .	
Aviation gasoline	19.3 cents per gallon
Jet fuel	21.8 cents per gallon

All Airport and Airway Trust Fund excise taxes, except for 4.3 cents per gallon of the taxes on aviation fuels, are scheduled to expire after February 17, 2012. The 4.3-cents-per-gallon fuels tax rate is permanent.

Taxes on transportation of persons by air

Domestic air passenger excise tax

Domestic air passenger transportation generally is subject to a two-part excise tax. The first component is an ad valorem tax imposed at the rate of 7.5 percent of the amount paid for the transportation. The second component is a flight segment tax. For

---

1. The domestic flight segment portion of the tax is adjusted annually (effective each January 1) for inflation (adjustments based on the changes in the consumer price index (the "CPI")).
2. The international travel facilities tax rate is adjusted annually for inflation (measured by changes in the CPI).
3. Like most other taxable motor fuels, aviation fuels are subject to an additional 0.1-cent-per-gallon excise tax to fund the Leaking Underground Storage Tank Trust Fund.

2012, the flight segment tax rate is $3.80.[4] A flight segment is defined as transportation involving a single take-off and a single landing. For example, travel from New York to San Francisco, with an intermediate stop in Chicago, consists of two flight segments (without regard to whether the passenger changes aircraft in Chicago).

The flight segment component of the tax does not apply to segments to or from qualified "rural airports." For any calendar year, a rural airport is defined as an airport that in the second preceding calendar year had fewer than 100,000 commercial passenger departures, and meets one of the following three additional requirements: (1) the airport is not located within 75 miles of another airport that had more than 100,000 such departures in that year; (2) the airport is receiving payments under the Federal "essential air service" program; or (3) the airport is not connected by paved roads to another airport.[5]

The domestic air passenger excise tax applies to "taxable transportation." Taxable transportation means transportation by air that begins in the United States or in the portion of Canada or Mexico that is not more than 225 miles from the nearest point in the continental United States and ends in the United States or in such 225-mile zone. If the domestic transportation is paid for outside of the United States, it is taxable only if it begins and ends in the United States.

For purposes of the domestic air passenger excise tax, taxable transportation does not include "uninterrupted international air transportation." Uninterrupted international air transportation is any transportation that does not both begin and end in the United States or within the 225-mile zone and does not have a layover time of more than 12 hours. The tax on international air passenger transportation is discussed below.

International travel facilities tax

For 2012, international air passenger transportation is subject to a tax of $16.70 per arrival or departure in lieu of the taxes imposed on domestic air passenger transportation if the transportation begins or ends in the United States.[6] The definition of international transportation includes certain purely domestic transportation that is associated with an international journey. Under these rules, a passenger traveling on separate domestic segments integral to international travel is exempt from the domestic passenger taxes on those segments if the stopover time at any point within the United States does not exceed 12 hours.

In the case of a domestic segment beginning or ending in Alaska or Hawaii, the tax applies to departures only and is $8.40 for calendar year 2012.

"Free" travel

Both the domestic air passenger tax and the use of international air facilities tax apply only to transportation for which an amount is paid. Thus, free travel, such as that awarded in "frequent flyer" programs and nonrevenue travel by airline industry employees, is not subject to tax. However, amounts paid to air carriers (in cash or in kind) for the right to award free or reduced-fare transportation are treated as amounts paid for taxable air transportation and are subject to the 7.5 percent ad valorem tax (but not the flight segment tax or the use of international air facilities tax). Examples of such payments are purchases of miles by credit card companies and affiliates (including airline affiliates) for use as "rewards" to cardholders.

---

4. Sec. 4261(b)(1) and 4261(d)(4). Unless otherwise stated, all section references are to the Internal Revenue Code of 1986, as amended (the "Code"). The Code provides for a $3 tax indexed annually for inflation, effective each January 1, resulting in the current rate of $3.80.
5. In the case of an airport qualifying as "rural" because it is not connected by paved roads to another airport, only departures for flight segments of 100 miles or more are considered in calculating whether the airport has fewer than 100,000 commercial passenger departures. The Department of Transportation has published a list of airports that meet the definition of rural airports. See Rev. Proc. 2005-45.
6. Secs. 4261(c) and 4261(d)(4). The international air facilities tax rate of $12 is indexed annually for inflation, effective each January 1, resulting in the current rate of $16.70.

Disclosure of air passenger transportation taxes on tickets and in advertising

Transportation providers are subject to special penalties relating to the disclosure of the amount of the passenger taxes on tickets and in advertising. The ticket is required to show the total amount paid for such transportation and the tax. The same requirements apply to advertisements. In addition, if the advertising separately states the amount to be paid for the transportation or the amount of taxes, the total shall be stated at least as prominently as the more prominently stated of the tax or the amount paid for transportation. Failure to satisfy these disclosure requirements is a misdemeanor, upon conviction of which the guilty party is fined not more than $100 per violation.[7]

Tax on transportation of property (cargo) by air

Amounts equivalent to the taxes received from the transportation of property by air are transferred to the Airport and Airway Trust Fund. Domestic air cargo transportation is subject to a 6.25 percent ad valorem excise tax on the amount paid for the transportation.[8] The tax applies only to transportation that both begins and ends in the United States. There is no disclosure requirement for the air cargo tax.

Aviation fuel taxes

The Code imposes excise taxes on gasoline used in commercial aviation (4.3 cents per gallon) and noncommercial aviation (19.3 cents per gallon), and on jet fuel (kerosene) and other aviation fuels used in commercial aviation (4.3 cents per gallon) and noncommercial aviation (21.8 cents per gallon).[9] Amounts equivalent to these taxes are transferred to the Airport and Airway Trust Fund.

House Bill

The provision extends the present-law Airport and Airway Trust Fund excise taxes through September 30, 2014.

Senate Amendment

The provision extends the present-law Airport and Airway Trust Fund excise taxes through September 30, 2013.

Conference Agreement

The conference agreement extends the present-law Airport and Airway Trust Fund excise taxes through September 30, 2015.

Effective Date

The provision takes effect on February 18, 2012.

[¶ 5602]   Section 1102.   Extension of airport and airway trust fund expenditure authority.

(Code Sec. 9502)

[Conference Report]

Present Law

In general

The Airport and Airway Trust Fund was created in 1970 to finance a major portion of Federal expenditures on national aviation programs. Operation of the Airport and Air-

---

7. Sec. 7275.
8. Sec. 4271.
9. These fuels are also subject to an additional 0.1 cent per gallon for the Leaking Underground Storage Tank Trust Fund. If there was not a taxable sale of the fuel pursuant to section 4081of the Code, a backup tax exists under section 4041(c) for such fuel that is subsequently sold or used in aviation.

way Trust Fund is governed by the Internal Revenue Code (the "Code")[10] and authorizing statutes. The Code provisions govern deposit of revenues into the trust fund and approve the use of trust fund money (as provided by appropriation acts) for expenditure purposes in authorizing statutes as in effect on the date of enactment of the latest authorizing Act. The authorizing acts provide specific trust fund expenditure programs and purposes.

Authorized expenditures from the Airport and Airway Trust Fund include the following principal programs:

(1.) Airport Improvement Program (airport planning, construction, noise compatibility programs, and safety projects);

(2.) Facilities and Equipment program (costs of acquiring, establishing, and improving the air traffic control facilities);

(3.) Research, Engineering, and Development program (Federal Aviation Administration ("FAA") research and development activities);

(4.) FAA Operations and Maintenance ("O&M") programs; and 10 Unless otherwise stated, all section references are to the Internal Revenue Code of 1986, as amended.

(5.) Certain other aviation-related programs specified in authorizing acts.

Part of the O&M programs is financed from General Fund monies as well.[11]

Limits on Airport and Airway Trust Fund expenditures

No expenditures are currently permitted to be made from the Airport and Airway Trust Fund after February 17, 2012. Because the purposes for which Airport and Airway Trust Fund monies are permitted to be expended are fixed as of the date of enactment of the Airport and Airway Extension Act of 2012, the Code must be amended to authorize new Airport and Airway Trust Fund expenditure purposes. In addition, the Code contains a specific enforcement provision to prevent expenditure of Airport and Airway Trust Fund monies for purposes not authorized under section 9502. Should such unapproved expenditures occur, no further aviation excise tax receipts will be transferred to the Airport and Airway Trust Fund. Rather, the aviation taxes would continue to be imposed, but the receipts would be retained in the General Fund.

House Bill

The provision authorizes expenditures from the Airport and Airway Trust Fund through September 30, 2014, and revises the purposes for which money from the Airport and Airway Trust Fund funds are permitted to be expended to include those obligations authorized under the reauthorization legislation of 2011 (i.e., the "FAA Reauthorization and Reform Act of 2011," which sets forth aviation program expenditure purposes through September 30, 2014).

Senate Amendment

The provision authorizes expenditures from the Airport and Airway Trust Fund through September 30, 2013. The provision also amends the list of authorizing statutes to include the "FAA Air Transportation Modernization and Safety Improvement Act," which sets forth aviation program expenditure purposes through September 30, 2013.

---

10. Unless otherwise stated, all section references are to the Internal Revenue Code of 1986, as amended.
11. According to the Government Accountability Office, for FY 2000 through FY 2010 the contribution of general revenues has increased to cover a larger share of the FAA's operation expenditures. United States Government Accountability Office, Airport and Airway Trust Fund: Declining Balance Raises Concerns Over Ability to Meet Future Demands, Statement of Gerald Dillingham, Director Physical Infrastructure Before the Committee on Finance, U.S. Senate (GAO-11-358T), February 3, 2011, p. 5, Fig. 2. Congressional Budget Office, Financing Federal Aviation Programs: Statement of Robert A. Sunshine before the House Committee on Ways and Means, May 7, 2009, p. 3.

Conference Agreement

The conference agreement authorizes expenditures from the Airport and Airway Trust Fund through September 30, 2015. The provision also amends the list of authorizing statutes to include the "FAA Modernization and Reform Act of 2012," which sets forth aviation program expenditure purposes through September 30, 2015.

Effective Date

The provision takes effect on February 18, 2012.

[¶ 5603]   Section 1103.   Treatment of fractional aircraft ownership programs.

(Code Sec. 4043)

[Conference Report]

Present Law

For excise tax purposes, fractional ownership aircraft flights are treated as commercial aviation. As commercial aviation, for 2012, such flights are subject to the ad valorem tax of 7.5 percent of the amount paid for the transportation, a $3.80 segment tax, and tax of 4.4 cents per gallon on fuel. For international flights, fractional ownership flights pay the $16.70 international travel facilities tax.

For purposes of the FAA safety regulations, fractional ownership aircraft programs are treated as a special category of general aviation.[29] Under those FAA regulations, a "fractional ownership program" is defined as any system of aircraft ownership and exchange that consists of all of the following elements: (i) the provision for fractional ownership program management services by a single fractional ownership program manager on behalf of the fractional owners; (ii) two or more airworthy aircraft; (iii) one or more fractional owners per program aircraft, with at least one program aircraft having more than one owner; (iv) possession of at least a minimum fractional ownership interest in one or more program aircraft by each fractional owner; (v) a dry-lease aircraft exchange arrangement among all of the fractional owners; and (vi) multi-year program agreements covering the fractional ownership, fractional ownership program management services, and dry-lease aircraft exchange aspects of the program.

House Bill

No provision.

Senate Amendment

Under the provision, transportation as part of a fractional ownership aircraft program is not classified as commercial aviation for Federal excise tax purposes. Instead, such flights would be subject to the increased Airport and Airway Trust Fund fuel tax rate for non-commercial aviation and an additional fuel surtax of 14.1 cents per gallon. For this purpose, a "fractional ownership aircraft program" is defined as a program in which:

• A single fractional ownership program manager provides fractional ownership program management services on behalf of the fractional owners;

• Two or more airworthy aircraft are part of the program;

• There are one or more fractional owners per program aircraft, with at least one program aircraft having more than one owner;

---

29. 14 CFR Part 91, subpart k.

• Each fractional owner possesses at least a minimum fractional ownership interest in one or more program aircraft;[30]

• There exists a dry-lease aircraft exchange arrangement among all of the fractional owners;[31] and

• There are multi-year program agreements covering the fractional ownership, fractional ownership program management services, and dry-lease aircraft exchange aspects of the program.

The fuel taxes are dedicated to the Airport and Airway Trust Fund. Consistent with the general extension of the taxes dedicated to the Airport and Airway Trust Fund, the provision sunsets September 30, 2013.

Conference Agreement

The conference agreement provides an exemption, through September 30, 2015, from the commercial aviation taxes (secs. 4261, 4271 and the 4.4 cents-per-gallon tax on fuel) for certain fractional aircraft program flights. In place of the commercial aviation taxes, the conference agreement applies a fuel surtax to certain flights made as part of a fractional ownership program.

Through September 30, 2015, these flights are treated as noncommercial aviation, subject to the fuel surtax and the base fuel tax for fuel used in noncommercial aviation.[32] Specifically, the additional fuel surtax of 14.1 cents per gallon will apply to fuel used in a fractional program aircraft (1) for the transportation of a qualified fractional owner with respect to the fractional aircraft program of which such aircraft is a part, and (2) with respect to the use of such aircraft on the account of such a qualified owner. Such use includes positioning flights (flights in deadhead service).[33] Through September 30, 2015, the commercial aviation taxes do not apply to fractional program aircraft uses subject to the fuel surtax. Under the conference agreement, flight demonstration, maintenance,and crew training flights by a fractional program aircraft are excluded from the fuel surtax and are subject to the noncommercial aviation fuel tax only.[34] The fuel surtax of 14.1 cents per gallon sunsets September 30, 2021.

A "fractional program aircraft" means, with respect to any fractional ownership aircraft program, any aircraft which is listed as a fractional program aircraft in the management specifications issued to the manager of such program by the Federal Aviation Administration under subpart K of part 91 of title 14, Code of Federal Regulations and is registered in the United States.

A "fractional ownership aircraft program" is a program under which:

• A single fractional ownership program manager provides fractional ownership program management services on behalf of the fractional owners;

• There are one or more fractional owners per program aircraft, with at least one program aircraft having more than one owner;

---

30. A "minimum fractional ownership interest" means: (1) A fractional ownership interest equal to or greater than one-sixteenth ($^1/_{16}$) of at least one subsonic, fixed wing or powered lift programaircraft; or (2) a fractional ownership interest equal to or greater than one-thirty-second ($^1/_{32}$) of at least one rotorcraft program aircraft. A "fractional ownership interest" is (1) the ownership interest in a program aircraft; (2) the holding of a multi-year leasehold interest in a program aircraft; or (3) the holding or a multi-year leasehold interest that is convertible into an ownership interest in a program aircraft.
31. A "dry-lease aircraft exchange" means an arrangement, documented by the written program agreements, under which the program aircraft are available, on an as-needed basis withoutcrew, to each fractional owner.
32. No inference is intended as to the treatment of these flights as noncommercial aviation under present law.
33. A flight in deadhead service is presumed subject to the fuel surtax unless the costs for such flight are separately billed to a person other than a qualified owner. For example, if the costs associated with a positioning flight of a fractional program aircraft are separately billed to a person chartering the aircraft, that positioning flight is treated as commercial aviation.
34. It is the understanding of the conferees that a prospective purchaser does not pay any amount for transportation by demonstration flights, and that if an amount were paid for the flight, the flight would be subject to the commercial aviation taxes and not treated as non-commercial aviation.

• With respect to at least two fractional program aircraft, none of the ownership interests in such aircraft can be less than the minimum fractional ownership interest, or held by the program manager;

• There exists a dry-lease aircraft exchange arrangement among all of the fractional owners; and

• There are multi-year program agreements covering the fractional ownership, fractional ownership program management services, and dry-lease aircraft exchange aspects of the program.

The term "qualified fractional owner" means any fractional owner that has a minimum fractional ownership interest in at least one fractional program aircraft. A "minimum fractional ownership interest" means: (1) A fractional ownership interest equal to or greater than one-sixteenth ($1/16$) of at least one subsonic, fixed wing or powered lift program aircraft; or (2) a fractional ownership interest equal to or greater than one-thirty-second ($1/32$) of at least one rotorcraft program aircraft. A "fractional ownership interest" is (1) the ownership interest in a program aircraft; (2) the holding of a multi-year leasehold interest in a program aircraft; or (3) the holding or a multi-year leasehold interest that is convertible into an ownership interest in a program aircraft. A "fractional owner" means a person owning any interest (including the entire interest) in a fractional program aircraft.

Amounts equivalent to the revenues from the fuel surtax are dedicated to the Airport and Airway Trust Fund.

Effective Date

The provision is effective for taxable transportation provided after, uses of aircraft after, and fuel used after, March 31, 2012.

[¶ 5604]   Section 1104.   Transparency in passenger tax disclosures.

(Code Sec. 7275)

[Conference Report]

Present Law

Transportation providers are subject to special penalties relating to the disclosure of the amount of the passenger taxes on tickets and in advertising. The ticket is required to show the total amount paid for such transportation and the tax. The same requirements apply to advertisements. In addition, if the advertising separately states the amount to be paid for the transportation or the amount of taxes, the total shall be stated at least as prominently as the more prominently stated of the tax or the amount paid for transportation. Failure to satisfy these disclosure requirements is a misdemeanor, upon conviction of which the guilty party is fined not more than $100 per violation.[35]

There is no prohibition against airlines including other charges in the required passenger taxes disclosure (e.g., fuel surcharges retained by the commercial airline). In practice, some but not all airlines include such other charges in the required passenger taxes disclosure.

House Bill

No provision.

Senate Amendment

The provision prohibits all transportation providers from including amounts other than the passenger taxes imposed by section 4261 in the required disclosure of passenger

---

35. Sec. 7275.

taxes on tickets and in advertising when the amount of such tax is separately stated. Disclosure elsewhere on tickets and in advertising (e.g., as an amount paid for transportation) of non-tax charges is allowed.

Conference Agreement

The conference agreement follows the Senate amendment, except the Effective date is for transportation provided after March 31, 2012.

[¶ 5605]   Section 5605.   Tax-exempt bond financing for fixed-wing emergency medical aircraft.

(Code Sec. 147)

[Conference Report]

Present Law

Interest on bonds issued by State and local governments generally is excluded from gross income for Federal income tax purposes.[36] Bonds issued by State and local governments may be classified as either governmental bonds or private activity bonds. Governmental bonds are bonds the proceeds of which are primarily used to finance governmental functions or which are repaid with governmental funds. In general, private activity bonds are bonds in which the State or local government serves as a conduit providing financing to nongovernmental persons (e.g., private businesses or individuals).[37] The exclusion from income for State and local bonds does not apply to private activity bonds, unless the bonds are issued for certain permitted purposes ("qualified bonds") and other Code requirements are met.[38]

Section 147(e) of the Code provides, in part, that a private activity bond is not a qualified bond if issued as part of an issue and any portion of the proceeds of such issue is used for airplanes.[39] The IRS has ruled that a helicopter is not an "airplane" for purposes of section 147(e).[40]

A fixed-wing aircraft providing air transportation for emergency medical services and that is equipped for, and exclusively dedicated on that flight to, acute care emergency medical services is exempt from the air transportation excise taxes imposed by sections 4261 and 4271.[41]

House Bill

No provision.

Senate Amendment

The provision amends section 147(e) so that the prohibition on the use of proceeds for airplanes does not apply to any fixed-wing aircraft equipped for, and exclusively dedicated to, providing acute care emergency medical services (within the meaning of section 4261(g)(2)).

Effective Date

The provision is effective for obligations issued after the date of enactment.

---

36. Sec. 103(a).
37. See sec. 141 defining "private activity bond."
38. See sec. 103(b) and sec. 141(e).
39. Other prohibited facilities include any skybox, or other private luxury box, health club facility, facility primarily used for gambling, or store the principal business of which is the sale of alcoholic beverages for consumption off premises. Sec. 147(e).
40. Rev. Rul. 2003-116, 2003-46 I.R.B. 1083, 2003-2 C.B. 1083, November 17, 2003, (released: October 29, 2003).
41. Sec. 4261(g)(2).

Conference Agreement

The conference agreement follows the Senate amendment.

[¶ 5606]   Section 1106.   Rollover of amounts received in airline carrier bankruptcy.

(Code Sec. None)

[Conference Report]

Present Law

The Code provides for two types of individual retirement arrangements ("IRAs"): traditional IRAs and Roth IRAs.[43] In general, contributions (other than a rollover contribution) to a traditional IRA may be deductible from gross income, and distributions from a traditional IRA are includible in gross income to the extent not attributable to a return of nondeductible contributions. In contrast, contributions to a Roth IRA are not deductible, and qualified distributions from a Roth IRA are excludable from gross income. Distributions from a Roth IRA that are not qualified distributions are includible in gross income to the extent attributable to earnings. In general, a qualified distribution is a distribution that (1) is made after the five taxable year period beginning with the first taxable year for which the individual first made a contribution to a Roth IRA, and (2) is made on or after the individual attains age $59\frac{1}{2}$, death, or disability or which is a qualified special purpose distribution.

The total amount that an individual may contribute to one or more IRAs for a year is generally limited to the lesser of: (1) a dollar amount ($5,000 for 2012); or (2) the amount of the individual's compensation that is includible in gross income for the year.[44] As under the rules relating to traditional IRAs, a contribution of up to the dollar limit for each spouse may be made to a Roth IRA provided the combined compensation of the spouses is at least equal to the contributed amount.

If an individual makes a contribution to an IRA (traditional or Roth) for a taxable year, the individual is permitted to recharacterize (in a trustee-to-trustee transfer) the amount of that contribution as a contribution to the other type of IRA (traditional or Roth) before the due date for the individual's income tax return for that year.[45] In the case of a recharacterization, the contribution will be treated as having been made to the transferee plan. The amount transferred must be accompanied by any net income allocable to the contribution and no deduction is allowed with respect to the contribution to the transferor plan. Both regular contributions and conversion contributions to a Roth IRA can be recharacterized as having been made to a traditional IRA. However, Treasury regulations limit the number of times a contribution for a taxable year may be recharacterized.[46]

Taxpayers generally may convert a traditional IRA into a Roth IRA.[47] The amount converted is includible in income as if a withdrawal had been made, except that the early distribution tax (discussed below) does not apply. However, the early distribution tax is applied if the taxpayer withdraws the amount within five years of the conversion.

If certain requirements are satisfied, a participant in an employer-sponsored qualified plan (which includes a tax-qualified retirement plan described in section 401(a), an employee retirement annuity described in section 403(a), a tax-sheltered annuity described

---

43. Traditional IRAs are described in section 408, and Roth IRAs are described in section 408A.
44. The maximum contribution amount is increased for individuals 50 years of age or older.
45. Sec. 408A(d)(6).
46. Treas. Reg. sec. 1.408A-5.
47. For taxable years beginning prior to January 1, 2010, taxpayers with modified AGI in excess of $100,000, and married taxpayers filing separate returns, were generally not permitted to convert a traditional IRA into a Roth IRA. Under the Tax Increase Prevention and Reconciliation Act of 2005, Pub. L. No. 109-222, these limits on conversion are repealed for taxable years beginning after December 31, 2009.

in section 403(b), and a governmental section 457(b) plan) or a traditional IRA may roll over distributions from the plan, annuity or IRA into another plan, annuity or IRA. For distributions after December 31, 2007, certain taxpayers also are permitted to make roll-over contributions into a Roth IRA (subject to inclusion in gross income of any amount that would be includible were it not part of the rollover contribution).

Under section 125 of the Worker, Retiree, and Employer Recovery Act of 2008 ("WRERA"),[48] a "qualified airline employee" may contribute any portion of an "airline payment amount" to a Roth IRA within 180 days of receipt of such amount (or, if later, within 180 days of enactment of the provision). Such a contribution is treated as a qualified rollover contribution to the Roth IRA. Thus, the portion of the airline payment amount contributed to the Roth IRA is includible in gross income to the extent that such payment would be includible were it not part of the rollover contribution.

A qualified airline employee is an employee or former employee of a commercial passenger airline carrier who was a participant in a defined benefit plan maintained by the carrier which: (1) is qualified under section 401(a); and (2) was terminated or became subject to the benefit accrual and other restrictions applicable to plans maintained by commercial passenger airlines pursuant to section 402(b) of the Pension Protection Act of 2006 ("PPA").

An airline payment amount is any payment of any money or other property payable by a commercial passenger airline to a qualified airline employee: (1) under the approval of an order of a Federal bankruptcy court in a case filed after September 11, 2001, and before January 1, 2007; and (2) in respect of the qualified air-line employee's interest in a bankruptcy claim against the airline carrier, any note of the carrier (or amount paid in lieu of a note being issued), or any other fixed obligation of the carrier to pay a lump sum amount. An airline payment amount does not include any amount payable on the basis of the carrier's future earnings or profits. The amount that may be contributed to a Roth IRA is the gross amount of the payment; any reduction in the airline payment amount on account of employment tax withholding is disregarded.

House Bill

No provision.

Senate Amendment

The amendment expands the choices for recipients of airline payment amounts by allowing qualified airline employees to contribute airline payment amounts to a traditional IRA as a rollover contribution. An individual making such a rollover contribution may exclude the contributed airline payment amount from gross income in the taxable year in which the airline payment amount was paid.

Qualified airline employees who made a qualified rollover contribution of an airline payment amount to a Roth IRA pursuant to WRERA are permitted to recharacterize all or a portion of the qualified rollover contribution as a rollover contribution to a traditional IRA by transferring, in a trustee-to-trustee transfer, the contribution (or a portion thereof) plus attributable earnings (or losses) from the Roth IRA. As in the case of a recharacterization under present law, the airline payment amount so transferred (with attributable earnings) is deemed to have been contributed to the traditional IRA at the time of the initial rollover contribution into the Roth IRA. The trustee-to-trustee transfer to a traditional IRA must be made within 180 days of the amendment's enactment.

If an amount contributed to a Roth IRA as a rollover contribution is recharacterized as a rollover contribution to a traditional IRA, the amount so recharacterized may not be contributed to a Roth IRA as a qualified rollover contribution (i.e., reconverted to a

48. Pub. L. No. 110-455.

Roth IRA) during the five taxable years immediately following the taxable year in which the transfer to the traditional IRA was made.

Qualified airline employees who were eligible to make a qualified rollover to a Roth IRA under WRERA, but declined to do so, are now permitted to roll over the airline payment amount to a traditional IRA within 180 days of the receipt of the amount (or, if later, within 180 days of enactment of the amendment). As mentioned above, any portion of an airline payment amount recharacterized as a rollover contribution to a traditional IRA pursuant to the amendment is excluded from gross income in the taxable year in which the airline payment amount was paid to the qualified airline employee by the commercial passenger airline carrier. Individuals recharacterizing such contributions may file a claim for a refund until the later of: (1) the period of limitations under section 6511(a) (generally, three years from the time the return was filed or two years from the time the tax was paid, whichever period expires later); or (2) April 15, 2012.

An airline payment amount does not fail to be treated as wages for purposes of Social Security and Medicare taxes under the Federal Insurance Contributions Act[49] and section 209 of the Social Security Act, merely because the amount is excluded from gross income because it is rolled over into a traditional IRA pursuant to the amendment.

Surviving spouses of qualified airline employees are granted the same rights as qualified airline employees under section 125 of WRERA and under the amendment.

Effective Date

Effective for all transfers (made after date of enactment) of qualified airline payment amounts received before, on, or after date of enactment.

Conference Agreement

The conference agreement follows the Senate amendment with three modifications. First, a qualified airline employee is not permitted to contribute (using either a rollover or recharacterization) an airline payment amount to a traditional IRA for a taxable year if, before the end of the taxable year, the employee was at any time a covered employee, as defined in section 162(m)(3),[50] of the commercial passenger airline carrier making the qualified airline payment. Second, a qualified airline employee who was not at any time a covered employee may only roll over, or recharacterize, into a traditional IRA 90 percent of the aggregate amount of airline payment amounts received before the end of the taxable year. Third, individuals recharacterizing their contributions may file a claim for a refund until the later of: (1) the period of limitations under section 6511(a) (generally, three years from the time the return was filed or two years from the time the tax was paid, whichever period expires later); or (2) April 15, 2013.

---

49. Chapter 21 of the Code.
50. Section 162(m) defines a covered employee as (1) the chief executive officer of the corporation (or an individual acting in such capacity) as of the close of the taxable year and (2) the four most highly compensated officers for the taxable year (other than the chief executive officer). Treas. Reg. sec. 1.162-27(c)(2) provides that whether an employee is the chief executive officer or among the four most highly compensated officers should be determined pursuant to the executive compensation disclosure rules promulgated under the Securities Exchange Act of 1934. Notice 2007-49, 2007-25 I.R.B. 1429 provides that "covered employee" means any employee who is (1) the principal executive officer (or an individual acting in such capacity) defined in reference to the Exchange Act, or (2) among the three most highly compensated officers for the taxable year (other than the principal executive officer) to reflect the 2006 change by the Securities and Exchange Commission to its rules.

[¶ 5607]   Section 1107.   Termination of exemption for small jet aircraft on nonestablished lines.

(Code Sec. 4281)

[Conference Report]

Present Law

Under present law, transportation by aircraft with a certificated maximum takeoff weight of 6,000 pounds or less is exempt from the excise taxes imposed on the transportation of persons by air and the transportation of cargo by air when operating on a non-established line. Similarly, when such aircraft are operating on a flight for the sole purpose of sightseeing, the taxes imposed on the transportation or persons or cargo by air do not apply.

House Bill

No provision.

Senate Amendment

The provision repeals the exemption as it applies to turbine engine powered aircraft (jet aircraft).

Conference Agreement

The conference agreement follows the Senate amendment provision, repealing the exemption as it applies to jet aircraft, effective for transportation provided after March 31, 2012.

[¶ 5608]   Section 1108.   Modification of control definition for purposes of section 249.

(Code Sec. 249)

[Conference Report]

Present Law

In general, where a corporation repurchases its indebtedness for a price in excess of the adjusted issue price, the excess of the repurchase price over the adjusted issue price (the "repurchase premium") is deductible as interest.[60] However, in the case of indebtedness that is convertible into the stock of (1) the issuing corporation, (2) a corporation in control of the issuing corporation, or (3) a corporation controlled by the issuing corporation, section 249 provides that any repurchase premium is not deductible to the extent it exceeds "a normal call premium on bonds or other evidences of indebtedness which are not convertible."[61]

For purposes of section 249, the term "control" has the meaning assigned to such term by section 368(c). Section 368(c) defines "control" as "ownership of stock possessing at least 80 percent of the total combined voting power of all classes of stock entitled to vote and at least 80 percent of the total number of shares of all other classes of stock of the corporation." Thus, section 249 can apply to debt convertible into the stock of the issuer, the parent of the issuer, or a first-tier subsidiary of the issuer.

---

60. See Treas. Reg. sec. 1.163-7(c).
61. Regulations under section 249 provide that "[f]or a convertible obligation repurchased on or after March 2, 1998, a call premium specified in dollars under the terms of the obligation is considered to be a normal call premium on a nonconvertible obligation if the call premium applicable when the obligation is repurchased does not exceed an amount equal to the interest (including original issue discount) that otherwise would be deductible for the taxable year of repurchase (determined as if the obligation were not repurchased)." Treas. Reg. sec. 1.249-1(d)(2). Where a repurchase premium exceeds a normal call premium, the repurchase premium is still deductible to the extent that it is attributable to the cost of borrowing (e.g., a change in prevailing yields or the issuer's creditworthiness) and not attributable to the conversion feature. See Treas. Reg. sec. 1.249-1(e).

House Bill

No provision.

Senate Amendment

The provision modifies the definition of "control" in section 249(b)(2) to incorporate indirect control relationships of the nature described in section 1563(a)(1). Section 1563(a)(1) defines a parent-subsidiary controlled group as one or more chains of corporations connected through stock ownership with a common parent corporation if (1) stock possessing at least 80 percent of the total combined voting power of all classes of stock entitled to vote or at least 80 percent of the total value of shares of all classes of stock of each of the corporations, except the common parent corporation, is owned (within the meaning of subsection (d)(1)) by one or more of the other corporations; and (2) the common parent corporation owns (within the meaning of subsection (d)(1)) stock possessing at least 80 percent of the total combined voting power of all classes of stock entitled to vote or at least 80 percent of the total value of shares of all classes of stock of at least one of the other corporations, excluding, in computing such voting power or value, stock owned directly by such other corporations.

Effective Date

The provision is effective for repurchases after the date of enactment.

Conference Agreement

The conference agreement follows the Senate amendment provision.

[¶ 5700] Congressional Committee Reports Accompanying the Job Creation Act of 2011

This section, in ¶ 5701, reproduces all relevant parts of the House Report (H. Rept. 112-253, 10/18/2011) accompanying the Job Creation Act of 2011 (P.L. 112-56, 11/21/2011).

[¶ 5701]   Section 102.   Repeal of imposition of 3 percent withholding on certain payments made to vendors by government entities.

(Code Sec. 3402)

[House Report]

Present Law

In general

Wages paid to employees, including wages and salaries of employees or elected officials of Federal, State, and local government units, are subject to withholding of income tax, which employers are required to collect and remit to the government. Withholding rates vary depending on the amount of wages paid, the length of the payroll period, and the number of withholding allowances claimed by the employee. The withholding amount is allowed as a credit against the individual taxpayer's income tax liability. It may be refunded if it is determined, when a tax return is filed, that the taxpayer's liability is less than the tax withheld, or additional tax may be due if it is determined that the taxpayer's liability is more than the tax withheld.

Certain nonwage payments also may be subject to withholding. Such payments include pensions,[3] gambling proceeds,[4] Social Security and other specified Federal payments,[5] unemployment compensation benefits,[6] and reportable payments such as dividends and interest.[7]

Nonbusiness income received by foreign persons from U.S. sources is generally subject to tax on a gross basis at a rate of 30 percent (14 percent for certain items of income), which is collected by withholding at the source of the payment.[8] The categories of income subject to the 30-percent tax and the categories for which withholding is required are generally coextensive, such that determination of the withholding tax liability determines the substantive liability.

Nonwage payments by governmental entities

Other than as described above, tax is not currently required to be withheld from payments made by government entities. Effective for payments made after December 31,

---

3. Payors of pensions are required to withhold from payments made to payees, unless the payee elects no withholding. Withholding from periodic payments is at variable rates, parallel to income tax withholding from wages, whereas withholding from nonperiodic payments is at a flat 10-percent rate. Sec. 3405(a), (b). Withholding at a rate of 20 percent is required in the case of an eligible rollover distribution that is not directly rolled over. Sec. 3405(c).
4. Certain gambling proceeds are subject to withholding obligations which vary depending on the form of wager or game. Sec. 3402(q)(3). Withholding is at a flat rate based on the third lowest rate of tax applicable to single taxpayers. As a general rule, every person making payment of gambling winnings from a wagering transaction subject to withholding must withhold 25 percent of such payment. Sec. 3402(q)(1). If the winnings are payable to a non-resident alien individual or a foreign corporation, the extent to which the payment is subject to withholding is determined under the withholding regime generally applicable to foreigners. Sec. 3402(q)(2).
5. Voluntary withholding applies to specified Federal payments which include Social Security payments, certain payments received as a result of destruction or damage to crops, certain amounts received as loans from the Commodity Credit Corporation, and other payments.
6. Withholding is at a flat 10-percent rate. Sec. 3402(p)(2).
7. A variety of payments (such as interest and dividends) are subject to backup withholding if the payee has not provided a valid taxpayer identification number ("TIN"). Withholding is at a flat rate based on the fourth lowest rate of tax applicable to single taxpayers. Sec. 3406.
8. Secs. 1441 and 1442.

2011,[9] new withholding requirements apply to certain government payments for goods and services. Specifically, government entities must withhold three percent of certain payments to persons providing property or services.[10] Government entities include the government of the United States, every State, every political subdivision thereof, and every instrumentality of the foregoing (including multistate agencies). The withholding requirement applies regardless of whether the government entity making such payment is the recipient of the property or services. Political subdivisions of States (or any instrumentality thereof) with less than $100 million of annual expenditures for property or services that would otherwise be subject to withholding under this provision are exempt from the withholding requirement.

Payments subject to three-percent withholding include any payment made in connection with a government voucher or certificate program which functions as a payment for property or services. For example, payments to a commodity producer under a government commodity support program are subject to the withholding requirement.

Withholding is not required with respect to government payments made through Federal, State, or local government public assistance or public welfare programs for which eligibility is determined by a needs or income test. For example, payments under government programs providing food vouchers or medical assistance to low-income individuals are not subject to withholding under the provision. However, payments under government programs to provide health care or other services that are not based on the needs or income of the recipients are subject to withholding, including programs where eligibility is based on the age of the beneficiary.

Three-percent withholding is not required with respect to payments of wages or any other payment with respect to which mandatory (e.g., U.S.-source income of foreign taxpayers) or voluntary (e.g., unemployment benefits) withholding applies under present law. In addition, if taxes are actually withheld from payments under the backup withholding rules, the three-percent withholding provision is not applicable.

Three-percent withholding also does not apply to the following: payments of interest; payments for real property; payments to tax-exempt entities or foreign governments; intra-governmental payments; payments made pursuant to a classified or confidential contract (as defined in section 6050M(e)(3)); and payments to government employees that are not otherwise excludable from this withholding provision with respect to the employees' services as employees.

Under final regulations issued by the Secretary of Treasury, the withholding (and accompanying reporting) requirements apply to payments by government entities to any person providing property or services made after December 31, 2012.[11] Under these rules, a payment is subject to withholding if it is $10,000 or more on a payment-by-payment basis. Multiple payments by a government entity generally will not be aggregated in applying this $10,000 limit.

---

9. Sec. 3402(t), which was added by section 511 of TIPRA. Pub. L. No. 109-222. As originally enacted, its provisions were to be effective for payments made after December 31, 2010. Section 1511 of ARRA delayed the effective date until payments made after December 31, 2011. Pub. L. No. 111-5. The regulations, as discussed infra, deferred the effective date an additional year.

10. Amounts withheld from any payment under section 3402(t) are creditable against the income taxes of the payee. Treas. Reg. sec. 31.3402(t)-6(a). Thus, for calendar year taxpayers, taxes due on March 15 (for corporations) and April 15 (for individuals) will be reduced by amounts withheld under section 3402. For taxpayers making estimated tax payments, tax withheld under section 3402(t) and allowed as a credit may be taken into account in determining estimated tax liability. For calendar year taxpayers, section 3402(t) withholding generally would be treated as a payment of estimated tax for the same calendar year and liability for other payments of estimated tax for that year would be reduced. Treas. Reg. sec. 31.3402(t)-6(c).

11. Treas. Reg. sec. 31.3402(t)-1(d)(1). The final regulations provide an exception to the section 3402(t) withholding rules for payments made under a written binding contract (as defined) that was in effect on December 31, 2012, and is not materially modified. However, if an existing contract is materially modified (i.e., the contract is changed such that it materially affects either the payment terms of the contract or the services or property to be provided under the contract) after December 31, 2012, payments under the contract become subject to section 3402(t) withholding. Treas. Reg. sec. 31.3402(t)-1(d)(2).

Reasons for Change

The Committee understands that poor tax compliance by some government contractors has been identified as a contributing factor to the tax gap, or difference between the amount of tax owed by taxpayers and the amount voluntarily paid to the IRS. The Committee recognizes that withholding and information reporting requirements can improve taxpayer compliance, but is concerned that the requirement of three-percent withholding on certain payments made to vendors by government entities is an overly broad remedy to this tax gap problem. The Committee believes that this withholding requirement would reduce the cash flow to many cashstrapped employers that contract with governmental entities, undermining job creation. The Committee further believes that the looming implementation of this requirement is contributing to the severe uncertainty facing employers during this challenging economic time. Moreover, the Committee believes that the withholding requirement imposes substantial costs on Federal, State, and local governmental agencies required to withhold payments, including costs to acquire new software or pay for additional accounting services. In addition to direct costs of implementation, the possibility that three-percent withholding will result in increased procurement costs at all levels of government, as small businesses contracting with governmental entities adjust their prices to address the changes in their cash flows, also concerns the Committee. The Committee believes these burdens are disproportionate when compared to the resulting improvement in tax compliance and therefore believes that the three-percent withholding requirement should be repealed.

Explanation of Provision

Under the proposal, section 3402(t) enacted under section 511 of TIPRA, is repealed.

Effective Date

The proposal is effective for payments made after December 31, 2011.

[¶ 5800] **Congressional Committee Reports Accompanying the U.S.-Korea Free Trade Agreement Implementation Act of 2011**

This section, in ¶ 5801 through ¶ 5802, reproduces all relevant parts of the House Report (H. Rept. 112-239, 10/6/2011) accompanying the U.S.-Korea Free Trade Agreement Implementation Act of 2011 (P.L. 112-41, 10/21/2011).

[¶ 5801]   **Section 501.   Increase in penalty on paid preparers who fail to comply with earned income tax credit due diligence requirements.**

(Code Sec. 6695)

[House Report]

Present Law

Under Section 6695(g) of the Internal Revenue Code of 1986, paid preparers who fail to comply with earned income tax credit due diligence requirements are fined $100 per return.

Explanation of Provision

Section 501 increases the penalty for paid preparers who fail to comply with earned income tax credit due diligence requirements from $100 to $500 per return. The increased penalty applies to returns required to be filed after December 31, 2011.

Reasons for Change

The Committee believes it is appropriate to increase the penalty for paid preparers who fail to comply with earned income tax credit due diligence requirements to deter non-compliance and for budgetary offset purposes.

[¶ 5802]   **Section 502.   Requirement for prisons located in the United States to provide information for tax administration.**

(Code Sec. 6116)

[House Report]

Present Law

No provision.

Explanation of Provision

Section 502 requires the head of the Federal Bureau of Prisons and the head of any State agency that administers prisons to provide certain information regarding inmates incarcerated, in electronic format, to the Secretary of the Treasury. The information must be filed no later than September 15, 2012, and annually thereafter.

Reasons for Change

The information provided will assist in detecting and deterring fraudulent tax return filings from inmates. The Committee believes it is appropriate to identify inmates who are filing fraudulent tax returns and for budgetary offset purposes.

[¶ 5900] Congressional Committee Reports Accompanying the Taxpayer Protection Act of 2011

This section, in ¶ 5901 through ¶ 5903, reproduces all relevant parts of the House Report (H. Rept. 112-15, 2/22/2011) and Joint Committee on Taxation Report (JCX-9-11, 2/14/2011) accompanying the Taxpayer Protection Act of 2011 (P.L. 112-9, 4/14/2011).

[¶ 5901]   Section 2.   Repeal of expansion of information reporting requirements to payments made to corporations and to payments for property and other gross proceeds.

(Code Sec. 6041)

[House Report]

Present Law

A variety of information reporting requirements apply under present law.[1] The primary provision governing information reporting by payors requires an information return by every person en-gaged in a trade or business who makes payments to any one payee aggregating $600 or more in any taxable year in the course of that payor's trade or business.[2] Reportable payments include compensation for both goods and services, and may include gross proceeds. Certain enumerated types of payments that are subject to other specific reporting requirements are carved out of reporting under this general rule by regulation.[3] Another carveout excepts payments to corporations from reporting requirements.[4]

For payments made after December 31, 2011, the class of payments subject to reporting was expanded in two ways.[5] First, the regulatory carveout for payments to corporations was expressly overridden by the addition of section 6041(i). In addition, information reporting requirements were expanded to include gross proceeds paid in consideration for any type of property. The payor is required to provide the recipient of the payment with an annual statement showing the aggregate payments made and contact information for the payor.[6] The regulations generally except from reporting payments to exempt organizations, governmental entities, international organizations, or retirement plans.

Additionally, the requirement that businesses report certain payments is generally not applicable to payments by persons engaged in a passive investment activity. However, beginning in 2011, recipients of rental income from real estate generally are subject to the same information reporting requirements as taxpayers engaged in a trade or business.[7] In particular, rental income recipients making payments of $600 or more to a ser-

---

1. Secs. 6031 through 6060.
2. Sec. 6041(a). Information returns are generally submitted electronically on Forms 1096 and Forms 1099, although certain payments to beneficiaries or employees may require use of Forms W-3 and W-2, respectively. Treas. Reg. sec. 1.6041-1(a)(2).
3. Sec. 6041(a) requires reporting of payments "other than payments to which section 6042(a)(1), 6044(a)(1), 6047(c), 6049(a), or 6050N(a) applies and other than payments with respect to which a statement is required under authority of section 6042(a), 6044(a)(2) or 6045[.]" The payments thus excepted include most interest, royalties, and dividends.
4. Treas. Reg. sec. 1.6041-3(p).
5. The Patient Protection and Affordable Care Act, Pub. L. No. 111-148, sec. 9006 (March 23, 2010).
6. Sec. 6041(d). Specifically, the recipient of the payment is required to provide a Form W-9 to the payor, which enables the payee to provide the recipient of the payment with an annual statement showing the aggregate payments made and contact information for the payor. If a Form W-9 is not provided, the payor is required to "backup withhold" tax at a rate of 28 percent of the gross amount of the payment unless the payee has otherwise established that the income is exempt from backup withholding. The backup withholding tax may be credited by the payee against regular income tax liability, i.e., it is effectively an advance payment of tax, similar to the withholding of tax from wages.
7. Sec. 6041(h); Small Business Jobs Act of 2010, Pub. L. No. 111-240, sec. 2101 ept. 27, 2010).

vice provider (such as a plumber, painter, or accountant) in the course of earning rental income are required to provide an information return (typically Form 1099-MISC) to the IRS and to the service provider. Exceptions to this reporting requirement are made for (i) individuals who rent their principal residence on a temporary basis, including members of the military or employees of the intelligence community (as defined in section 121(d)(9)), (ii) individuals who receive only minimal amounts of rental income, as determined by the Secretary in accordance with regulations, and (iii) individuals for whom the requirements would cause hardship, as determined by the Secretary in accordance with regulations.[8]

Detailed rules are provided for the reporting of various types of investment income, including interest, dividends, and gross proceeds from brokered transactions (such as a sale of stock).[9] In general, the requirement to file Form 1099 applies with respect to amounts paid to U.S. persons and is linked to the backup withholding rules of section 3406. Thus, a payor of interest, dividends or gross proceeds generally must request that a U.S. payee (other than certain exempt recipients) furnish a Form W-9 providing that person's name and taxpayer identification number.[10] That information is then used to complete the Form 1099.

Failure to comply with the information reporting requirements results in penalties, which may include a penalty for failure to file the information return,[11] a penalty for failure to furnish payee statements,[12] or failure to comply with other various reporting requirements.[13]

Reasons for Change

The Committee understands that there is a significant tax gap, or difference between the amount of tax owed by taxpayers and the amount voluntarily paid to the IRS, that must be addressed. The Committee also recognizes that information reporting requirements generally improve taxpayer compliance. However, the Committee is concerned that the expansion of the information reporting requirements imposes a substantial tax compliance burden on small businesses, including costs to acquire new software or pay for additional accounting services. The Committee believes this burden is disproportionate as compared with any resulting improvement in tax compliance and therefore believes that these requirements should be repealed in their entirety. The Committee will continue to explore other potential solutions to the tax gap problem.

Explanation of Provision

Under the provision, the changes to section 6041 enacted under section 9006 of the Patient Protection and Affordable Care Act that provide rules for payments to corporations, provide additional regulatory authority and impose a reporting requirement with respect to gross proceeds from property, are repealed in their entirety.

Effective Date

This provision is effective for payments made after December 31, 2011.

---

8. Treasury has not promulgated regulations defining these "minimal amounts of rental income" or "hardship" cases.
9. Secs. 6042 (dividends), 6045 (broker reporting) and 6049 (interest), as well as the Treasury regulations thereunder.
10. See Treas. Reg. sec. 31.3406(h)-3.
11. Sec. 6721.
12. Sec. 6722.
13. Sec. 6723.

[¶ 5902]   Section 3.   Repeal of expansion of information reporting requirements for rental property expense payments.

(Code Sec. 6041)

[Joint Committee on Taxation Report [JCX-9-11]]

Present Law

A variety of information reporting requirements apply under present law.[15] The primary provision governing information reporting by payors requires an information return by every person engaged in a trade or business who makes payments to any one payee aggregating $600 or more in any taxable year in the course of that payor's trade or business.[16] Reportable payments include compensation for both goods and services, and may include gross proceeds. Certain enumerated types of payments that are subject to other specific reporting requirements are carved out of reporting under this general rule by regulation.[17] Another carveout excepts payments to corporations from reporting requirements.[18]

For payments made after December 31, 2011, the class of payments subject to reporting was expanded in two ways.[19] First, the regulatory carveout for payments to corporations was expressly overridden by the addition of section 6041(i). In addition, information reporting requirements were expanded to include gross proceeds paid in consideration for any type of property. The payor is required to provide the recipient of the payment with an annual statement showing the aggregate payments made and contact information for the payor.[20] The regulations generally except from reporting payments to exempt organizations, governmental entities, international organizations, or retirement plans.

Additionally, the requirement that businesses report certain payments is generally not applicable to payments by persons engaged in a passive investment activity. However, beginning in 2011, recipients of rental income from real estate generally are subject to the same information reporting requirements as taxpayers engaged in a trade or business.[21] In particular, rental income recipients making payments of $600 or more to a service provider (such as a plumber, painter, or accountant) in the course of earning rental income are required to provide an information return (typically Form 1099-MISC) to the IRS and to the service provider. Exceptions to this reporting requirement are made for (i) individuals who rent their principal residence on a temporary basis, including members of the military or employees of the intelligence community (as defined in section 121(d)(9)), (ii) individuals who receive only minimal amounts of rental income, as determined by the Secretary in accordance with regulations, and (iii) individuals for whom the requirements would cause hardship, as determined by the Secretary in accordance with regulations.[22]

---

15. Secs. 6031 through 6060.
16. Sec. 6041(a). Information returns are generally submitted electronically on Forms 1096 and Forms 1099, although certain payments to beneficiaries or employees may require use of Forms W-3 and W-2, respectively. Treas. Reg. sec. 1.6041-1(a)(2).
17. Sec. 6041(a) requires reporting of payments "other than payments to which section 6042(a)(1), 6044(a)(1), 6047(c), 6049(a) or 6050N(a) applies and other than payments with respect to which a statement is required under authority of section 6042(a), 6044(a)(2) or 6045[.]" The payments thus excepted include most interest, royalties, and dividends.
18. Treas. Reg. sec. 1.6041-3(p).
19. The Patient Protection and Affordable Care Act, Pub. L. No. 111-148, sec. 9006 (March 23, 2010).
20. Sec. 6041(d). Specifically, the recipient of the payment is required to provide a Form W-9 to the payor, which enables the payee to provide the recipient of the payment with an annual statement showing the aggregate payments made and contact information for the payor. If a Form W-9 is not provided, the payor is required to "backup withhold" tax at a rate of 28 percent of the gross amount of the payment unless the payee has otherwise established that the income is exempt from backup withholding. The backup withholding tax may be credited by the payee against regular income tax liability, i.e., it is effectively an advance payment of tax, similar to the withholding of tax from wages.
21. Sec. 6041(h); Small Business Jobs Act of 2010, Pub. L. No. 111-240, sec. 2101 (Sept. 27, 2010).
22. Treasury has not promulgated regulations defining these "minimal amounts of rental income" or "hardship" cases.

Detailed rules are provided for the reporting of various types of investment income, including interest, dividends, and gross proceeds from brokered transactions (such as a sale of stock).[23] In general, the requirement to file Form 1099 applies with respect to amounts paid to U.S. persons and is linked to the backup withholding rules of section 3406. Thus, a payor of interest, dividends or gross proceeds generally must request that a U.S. payee (other than certain exempt recipients) furnish a Form W-9 providing that person's name and taxpayer identification number.[24] That information is then used to complete the Form 1099.

Failure to comply with the information reporting requirements results in penalties, which may include a penalty for failure to file the information return,[25] and a penalty for failure to furnish payee statements[26] or failure to comply with other various reporting requirements.[27]

Explanation of Provision

Under the provision, recipients of rental income from real estate who are not otherwise considered to be engaged in a trade or business of renting property are not subject to the same information reporting requirements as taxpayers who are considered to be engaged in a trade or business. As a result, rental income recipients making payments of $600 or more to a service provider (such as a plumber, painter, or accountant) in the course of earning rental income are not required to provide an information return (typically Form 1099-MISC) to the IRS and to the service provider.

Effective Date

The provision is effective for payments made after December 31, 2010.

[¶ 5903]   Section 4.   Increase in amount of overpayment of health care credit which is subject to recapture.

(Code Sec. 36B)

[Joint Committee on Taxation Report [JCX-9-11]]

Present Law

Premium assistance credit

For taxable years ending after December 31, 2013, section 36B provides a refundable tax credit (the "premium assistance credit") for eligible individuals and families who purchase health insurance through an exchange.[28] The premium assistance credit, which is refundable and payable in advance directly to the insurer, subsidizes the purchase of certain health insurance plans through an exchange.

To become entitled to an advance premium assistance credit under section 36B, an eligible individual enrolls in a plan offered through an exchange and reports his or her income to the exchange.[29] Based on the information provided to the exchange, the indi-

---

23. Secs. 6042 (dividends), 6045 (broker reporting) and 6049 (interest), as well as the Treasury regulations thereunder.
24. See Treas. Reg. sec. 31.3406(h)-3.
25. Sec. 6721. The penalty for failure to file an information return generally is $50 for each return for which such failure occurs. The total penalty imposed on a person for all failures during a calendar year cannot exceed $250,000. Additionally, special rules apply to reduce the per-failure and maximum penalties where the failure is corrected within a specified period.
26. Sec. 6722. The penalty for failure to provide a correct payee statement is $50 for each statement with respect to which such failure occurs, with the total penalty for a calendar year not to exceed $100,000. Special rules apply that increase the per-statement and total penalties where there is intentional disregard of the requirement to furnish a payee statement.
27. Sec. 6723. The penalty for failure to timely comply with a specified information reporting requirement is $50 per failure, not to exceed $100,000 for a calendar year.
28. Individuals enrolled in multistate plans, pursuant to section 1334 of the Patient Protection and Affordable Care Act, Pub. L. No. 111-148, are also eligible for the credit.
29. Sec. 1412 of the Patient Protection and Affordable Care Act, Pub. L. No. 111-148, describes the program for advance payment of the premium assistance credit.

vidual receives an advance premium assistance credit based on income and the Treasury pays the premium assistance credit amount directly to the insurance plan in which the individual is enrolled. The individual then pays to the plan in which he or she is enrolled the dollar difference between the premium assistance credit amount and the total premium charged for the plan.[30] Individuals who fail to pay all or part of the remaining premium amount are given a mandatory three-month grace period prior to an involuntary termination of their participation in the plan. Eligibility for the advance premium assistance credit is generally based on the individual's income for the taxable year ending two years prior to the enrollment period.

The premium assistance credit is available for individuals (single or joint filers) with household incomes between 100 and 400 percent of the Federal poverty level ("FPL") for the family size involved who do not receive health insurance through an employer or a spouse's employer.[31] Household income is defined as the sum of: (1) the taxpayer's modified adjusted gross income, plus (2) the aggregate modified adjusted gross incomes of all other individuals taken into account in determining that taxpayer's family size (but only if such individuals are required to file a tax return for the taxable year). Modified adjusted gross income is defined as adjusted gross income increased by: (1) the amount (if any) normally excluded by section 911(the exclusion from gross income for citizens or residents living abroad), plus (2) any tax-exempt interest received or accrued during the tax year. To be eligible for the premium assistance credit, taxpayers who are married (within the meaning of section 7703) must file a joint return. Individuals who are listed as dependents on a return are ineligible for the premium assistance credit.

As described in Table 1 below, premium assistance credits are available on a sliding scale basis for individuals and families with household incomes between 100 and 400 percent of FPL to help offset the cost of private health insurance premiums. The premium assistance credit amount is determined based on the percentage of income the cost of premiums represents, rising from two percent of income for those at 100 percent of FPL for the family size involved to 9.5 percent of income for those at 400 percent of FPL for the family size involved. Beginning in 2014, the percentages of income are indexed to the excess of premium growth over income growth for the preceding calendar year. Beginning in 2018, if the aggregate amount of premium assistance credits and cost-sharing reductions[32] exceeds 0.504 percent of the gross domestic product for that year, the percentage of income is also adjusted to reflect the excess (if any) of premium growth over the rate of growth in the consumer price index for the preceding calendar year. For purposes of calculating household size, individuals who are in the country illegally are not included.

Premium assistance credits, or any amounts that are attributable to them, cannot be used to pay for abortions for which federal funding is prohibited. Premium assistance credits are not available for months in which an individual has a free choice voucher under section 139A.

The low income premium credit phase-out

The premium assistance credit increases, on a sliding scale in a linear manner, as shown in the table below.

---

30. Although the credit is generally payable in advance directly to the insurer, individuals may elect to purchase health insurance out-of-pocket and apply to the IRS for the credit at the end of the taxable year. The amount of the reduction in premium as a result of the assistance credit is required to be included with each bill sent to the individual.
31. Individuals who are lawfully present in the United States but are not eligible for Medicaid because of their immigration status are treated as having a household income equal to 100 percent of FPL (and thus eligible for the premium assistance credit) as long as their household income does not actually exceed 100 percent of FPL.
32. As described in section 1402 of the Patient Protection and Affordable Care Act, Pub. L. No. 111-148.

TABLE 1

Household Income (expressed as a percent of FPL)	Initial Premium (percentage)	Final Premium (percentage)
100% up to 133%	2.0	2.0
133% up to 150%	3.0	4.0
150% up to 200%	4.0	6.3
200% up to 250%	6.3	8.05
250% up to 300%	8.05	9.5
300% up to 400%	9.5	9.5

The premium assistance credit amount is tied to the cost of the second lowest-cost silver plan (adjusted for age) which: (1) is in the rating area where the individual resides, (2) is offered through an exchange in the area in which the individual resides, and (3) provides self-only coverage in the case of an individual who purchases self-only coverage, or family coverage in the case of any other individual. If the plan in which the individual enrolls offers benefits in addition to essential health benefits,[33] even if the State in which the individual resides requires such additional benefits, the portion of the premium that is allocable to those additional benefits is disregarded in determining the premium assistance credit amount.[34] Premium assistance credits may be used for any plan purchased through an exchange, including bronze, silver, gold and platinum level plans and, for those eligible,[35] catastrophic plans.

Minimum essential coverage and employer offer of health insurance coverage

Generally, if an employee is offered minimum essential coverage[36] in the group market, including employer-provided health insurance coverage, the individual is ineligible for the premium assistance credit for health insurance purchased through a State exchange.

If an employee is offered unaffordable coverage by his or her employer or the plan's share of provided benefits is less than 60 percent, the employee can be eligible for the premium assistance credit, but only if the employee declines to enroll in the coverage and satisfies the conditions for receiving a tax credit through an exchange. Unaffordable is defined as coverage with a premium required to be paid by the employee that is more than 9.5 percent of the employee's household income, based on self-only coverage.[37] The percentage of income that is considered unaffordable is indexed in the same manner as the percentage of income is indexed for purposes of determining eligibility for the credit (as discussed above). The Secretary of the Treasury is informed of the name and employer identification number of every employer that has one or more employees receiving a premium assistance credit.

Procedures for determining eligibility

For purposes of the premium assistance credit, during the open enrollment period for coverage during the next calendar year, exchange participants must provide information from their tax return from two years prior. For example, if during the 2013 open enrollment period an individual applies for a premium assistance credit for 2014, the individual must provide his or her tax return from 2012. The IRS is authorized to disclose to the Department of Health and Human Services limited tax return information to verify a

---

33. As defined in section 1302(b) of the Patient Protection and Affordable Care Act, Pub. L. No. 111-148.
34. A similar rule applies to additional benefits that are offered in multi-State plans, under section 1334 of the Patient Protection and Affordable Care Act, Pub. L. No. 111-148.
35. Those eligible to purchase catastrophic plans either must have not reached the age of 30 before the beginning of the plan year, or have certification of an affordability or hardship exemption from the individual responsibility payment, as described in sections 5000A(e)(1) and 5000A(e)(5), respectively.
36. As defined in section 5000A(f).
37. The 9.5 percent amount is indexed for calendar years beginning after 2014.

taxpayer's income based on the most recent return information available to establish eligibility for the premium assistance credit. Existing privacy and safeguard requirements apply. Individuals who do not qualify for the premium assistance credit on the basis of their prior year income may apply for the premium assistance credit based on specified changes in circumstances. For individuals and families who did not file a tax return in the prior tax year, the Secretary of Health and Human Services is directed to establish alternative income documentation that may be provided to determine income eligibility for the premium assistance credit.

Reconciliation

If the premium assistance credit received through advance payment exceeds the amount of premium assistance credit to which the taxpayer is entitled for the taxable year, the liability for the excess advance payment must be reflected on the taxpayer's income tax return for the taxable year subject to a limitation on the amount of such liability. For persons with household income below 500 percent of FPL, the liability for the excess payment for a taxable year is limited to a specific dollar amount (the "applicable dollar amount") as shown in Table 2 below (one half of the applicable dollar amount shown in Table 2 for unmarried individuals who are not surviving spouses or filing as heads of households).[38]

TABLE 2

Household Income (expressed as a percent of FPL)	Applicable Dollar Amount
Less than 200%	$600
At least 200% but less than 250%	$1,000
At least 250% but less than 300%	$1,500
At least 300% but less than 350%	$2,000
At least 350% but less than 400%	$2,500
At least 400% but less than 450%	$3,000
At least 450% but less than 500%	$3,500

If the premium assistance credit for a taxable year received through advance payment is less than the amount of the credit to which the taxpayer is entitled for the year, the shortfall in the credit is also reflected on the taxpayer's tax return for the year.

The eligibility for and amount of the advance premium assistance credit is generally determined in advance of the coverage year, on the basis of household income and family size shown on the taxpayer's return for the taxable year from two years prior, and the monthly premiums for qualified health plans in the individual market in which the taxpayer, spouse and any dependent enroll in an exchange. Any advance premium assistance credit is paid during the year for which coverage is provided by the exchange. In the subsequent year, the amount of advance premium assistance credit is required to be reconciled with the allowable refundable premium assistance credit for the year of coverage. Generally, this reconciliation is to be accomplished on the tax return filed for the year of coverage, based on that year's actual household income, family size, and premiums.

Separately, the provision requires that the exchange, or any person with whom it contracts to administer the insurance program, must report to the Secretary with respect to any taxpayer's participation in the health plan offered by the Exchange. The information to be reported is information necessary to determine whether a person has received ex-

---

38. Medicare and Medicaid Extenders Act of 2010, Pub. L. No. 111-309, sec. 208. Prior to the Medicare and Medicaid Extenders Act of 2010, for persons whose household income was below 400 percent of the FPL, the amount of the increase in tax was limited to $400 ($250 for unmarried individuals who are not surviving spouses or filing as heads of households).

cess advance payments, identifying information about the taxpayer (such as name, taxpayer identification number, months of coverage) and any other person covered by that policy; the level of coverage purchased by the taxpayer; the total premium charged for the coverage, as well as the aggregate advance payments credited to that taxpayer; and information provided to the exchange for the purpose of establishing eligibility for the program, including changes of circumstances of the taxpayer since first purchasing the coverage. Finally, the party submitting the report must provide a copy to the taxpayer whose information is the subject of the report.

Explanation of Provision

Under the provision, the applicable dollar amount with respect to any excess advance payment of a taxpayer's allowable premium assistance credit for a taxable year is revised as shown in Table 3 below (one half of the applicable dollar amount shown in Table 3 for unmarried individuals who are not surviving spouses or filing as heads of households).

TABLE 3

Household Income (expressed as a percent of poverty line)	Applicable Dollar Amount
Less than 200%	$600
At least 200% but less than 300%	$1,500
At least 300% but less than 400%	$2,500

Persons with household incomes of 400 percent of FPL and above must repay the full amount of the premium assistance credit received through an advance payment.

Effective Date

The provision is effective for taxable years beginning after December 31, 2013.

¶ 6000. Act Section Cross Reference Table

Act § cites are to the 2012 Taxpayer Relief Act unless otherwise indicated.

* denotes 2012 Highway Investment Act
† denotes 2012 FAA Modernization Act
** denotes 2012 Middle Class Tax Relief Act
*** denotes 2012 African Growth Act
✓ denotes 2012 Aviation Extension Act
+ denotes 2011 Appropriations Act
~ denotes 2011 Job Creation Act
• denotes 2011 Taxpayer Protection Act
‡ denotes 2011 Temporary Payroll Act
++ denotes 2011 U.S.-Korea Trade Act
≈ denotes 2011 Trade Extension Act

Act §	Code §	Topic	Effective Date	Analy-sis ¶	Com Rep ¶
2(a)•	6041(i)	Expanded information reporting requirement for post-2011 payments of $600 or more to non-tax-exempt corporations is repealed	Payments made after Dec. 31, 2011	1905	5901
2(a)•	6041(j)	Expanded information reporting requirement for post-2011 payments of $600 or more to non-tax-exempt corporations is repealed	Payments made after Dec. 31, 2011	1905	5901
2(b)(1)•	6041(a)	Expanded information reporting for post-2011 payments of $600 or more of gross proceeds or amounts in consideration for property is repealed	Payments made after Dec. 31, 2011	1906	5901
2(b)(2)•	6041(a)	Expanded information reporting for post-2011 payments of $600 or more of gross proceeds or amounts in consideration for property is repealed	Payments made after Dec. 31, 2011	1906	5901
3(a)•	6041(h)	Information reporting for certain recipients of rental income for payments of $600 or more to service providers is retroactively repealed	Payments made after Dec. 31, 2010	1907	5902

Act §	Code §	Topic	Effective Date	Analy-sis ¶	Com Rep ¶
4(1) ***	6655	Certain 2017 estimated taxes for corporations with assets of $1 billion or more increase to 100.25%	Aug. 10, 2012	1915	None
4(2) ***	6655	Certain 2017 estimated taxes for corporations with assets of $1 billion or more increase to 100.25%	Aug. 10, 2012	1915	None
4(a) •	36B(f)(2)(B)(i)	Simplified payback caps on excess advance premium assistance credits apply to taxpayers below 400% of poverty line	Tax years ending after Dec. 31, 2013	1602	5903
101	None	Additional increase in arbitrage rebate exception for government bonds used to finance education facilities made permanent	Tax, plan or limitation years beginning after Dec. 31, 2012	1404	None
101(a)	142(a)(13)	Tax-exempt status of public educational facility bonds is made permanent	Tax years beginning after Dec. 31, 2012	1403	None
101(a)	142(k)	Tax-exempt status of public educational facility bonds is made permanent	Tax years beginning after Dec. 31, 2012	1403	None
101(a)	148(f)(4)(D)(vii)	Additional increase in arbitrage rebate exception for government bonds used to finance education facilities made permanent	Tax, plan or limitation years beginning after Dec. 31, 2012	1404	None
101(a) ‡	1401(a)	Reduced 10.4% OASDI rate applied for 2012 to self-employment income up to $110,100 ceiling	Remuneration received, and tax years beginning, after, Dec. 31, 2011	1901	5501
101(a) ‡	3101(a)	Reduced 4.2% employee social security tax rate applied for 2012 under payroll tax holiday	Remuneration received, and tax years beginning, after Dec. 31, 2011	1902	5501

Act §	Code §	Topic	Effective Date	Analysis ¶	Com Rep ¶
101(a)	None	2012 estate, gift and GST tax rules made permanent, but top rate increases from 35% to 40%	After 2012	501	None
101(a)	None	Tax-exempt status of public educational facility bonds is made permanent	Tax years beginning after Dec. 31, 2012	1403	None
101(a)(1)	1(f)(2)(A)	Expansion of marrieds-filing-jointly 15% rate bracket to provide marriage penalty relief is extended permanently	Tax years beginning after Dec. 31, 2012	102	None
101(a)(1)	1(f)(8)	Expansion of marrieds-filing-jointly 15% rate bracket to provide marriage penalty relief is extended permanently	Tax years beginning after Dec. 31, 2012	102	None
101(a)(1)	1(g)(7)(B)(ii)(II)	Reduced rates for kiddie tax and some withholding (each tied to the reduced individual rates) are permanently extended	For tax years beginning after Dec. 31, 2012	103	None
101(a)(1)	21	EGTRRA-expanded dependent care credit permanently extended	Tax years beginning after Dec. 31, 2012	603	None
101(a)(1)	24(a)	$1,000 per child amount and expanded refundability of child tax credit are permanently extended	Tax years beginning after Dec. 31, 2012.	601	None
101(a)(1)	23	Expanded adoption credit rules (but not refundability) made permanent	Tax years beginning after Dec. 31, 2012	604	None
101(a)(1)	24(b)(3)	Child tax credit can permanently offset AMT	Tax years beginning after Dec. 31, 2012	404	None
101(a)(1)	24(d)(1)	$1,000 per child amount and expanded refundability of child tax credit are permanently extended	Tax years beginning after Dec. 31, 2012.	601	None

Act §	Code §	Topic	Effective Date	Analy-sis ¶	Com Rep ¶
101(a)(1)	25A(e)	Increased $2,000 contribution limit and other EGTRRA enhancements to Coverdell ESAs are made permanent	For tax years beginning after Dec. 31, 2012	704	None
101(a)(1)	26(a)(1)	Child tax credit can permanently offset AMT	Tax years beginning after Dec. 31, 2012	404	None
101(a)(1)	32(a)(2)(B)	EIC simplification made permanent	Tax years beginning after Dec. 31, 2012	605	None
101(a)(1)	32(b)(2)	$5,000 increase in EIC phaseout threshold for joint filers is extended through 2017	Tax years beginning after Dec. 31, 2012	606	None
101(a)(1)	32(c)	EIC simplification made permanent	Tax years beginning after Dec. 31, 2012	605	None
101(a)(1)	32(c)(1)(C)	EIC simplification made permanent	Tax years beginning after Dec. 31, 2012	605	None
101(a)(1)	32(c)(2)(A)(i)	EIC simplification made permanent	Tax years beginning after Dec. 31, 2012	605	None
101(a)(1)	32(h)	EIC simplification made permanent	Tax years beginning after Dec. 31, 2012	605	None
101(a)(1)	32(j)	$5,000 increase in EIC phaseout threshold for joint filers is extended through 2017	Tax years beginning after Dec. 31, 2012	606	None
101(a)(1)	32(n)	$1,000 per child amount and expanded refundability of child tax credit are permanently extended	Tax years beginning after Dec. 31, 2012.	601	None
101(a)(1)	38(b)(15)	Employer-provided child care credit is extended permanently	Tax years beginning after 2012	903	None
101(a)(1)	45F	Employer-provided child care credit is extended permanently	Tax years beginning after 2012	903	None
101(a)(1)	63(c)(2)	Standard deduction marriage penalty relief is made permanent	Tax years beginning after Dec. 31, 2012	304	None

Act §	Code §	Topic	Effective Date	Analy-sis ¶	Com Rep ¶
101(a)(1)	117(c)(2)	Income exclusion for awards under the National Health Service Corps and Armed Forces Health Professions programs made permanent	For taxable years beginning after Dec. 31, 2012	706	None
101(a)(1)	127	Exclusion for employer-provided educational assistance, and restoration of the exclusion for graduate-level courses, made permanent	Tax years beginning after 2012	705	None
101(a)(1)	137	Adoption assistance exclusion is made permanent	Tax years beginning after 2012	309	None
101(a)(1)	221	EGTRRA changes to student loan deduction rules are made permanent	Tax years beginning after Dec. 31, 2012	703	None
101(a)(1)	221(b)(2)(B)	EGTRRA changes to student loan deduction rules are made permanent	Tax years beginning after Dec. 31, 2012	703	None
101(a)(1)	221(f)	EGTRRA changes to student loan deduction rules are made permanent	Tax years beginning after Dec. 31, 2012	703	None
101(a)(1)	530(b)(1)	Increased $2,000 contribution limit and other EGTRRA enhancements to Coverdell ESAs are made permanent	For tax years beginning after Dec. 31, 2012	704	None
101(a)(1)	530(b)(1)(A)(iii)	Increased $2,000 contribution limit and other EGTRRA enhancements to Coverdell ESAs are made permanent	For tax years beginning after Dec. 31, 2012	704	None
101(a)(1)	530(b)(2)	Increased $2,000 contribution limit and other EGTRRA enhancements to Coverdell ESAs are made permanent	For tax years beginning after Dec. 31, 2012	704	None

Act §	Code §	Topic	Effective Date	Analy-sis ¶	Com Rep ¶
101(a)(1)	530(b)(4)	Increased $2,000 contribution limit and other EGTRRA enhancements to Coverdell ESAs are made permanent	For tax years beginning after Dec. 31, 2012	704	None
101(a)(1)	530(b)(5)	Increased $2,000 contribution limit and other EGTRRA enhancements to Coverdell ESAs are made permanent	For tax years beginning after Dec. 31, 2012	704	None
101(a)(1)	530(c)(1)	Increased $2,000 contribution limit and other EGTRRA enhancements to Coverdell ESAs are made permanent	For tax years beginning after Dec. 31, 2012	704	None
101(a)(1)	530(d)(2)	Increased $2,000 contribution limit and other EGTRRA enhancements to Coverdell ESAs are made permanent	For tax years beginning after Dec. 31, 2012	704	None
101(a)(1)	530(d)(2)(C)	Increased $2,000 contribution limit and other EGTRRA enhancements to Coverdell ESAs are made permanent	For tax years beginning after Dec. 31, 2012	704	None
101(a)(1)	530(d)(2)(D)	Increased $2,000 contribution limit and other EGTRRA enhancements to Coverdell ESAs are made permanent	For tax years beginning after Dec. 31, 2012	704	None
101(a)(1)	530(d)(4)(C)(i)	Increased $2,000 contribution limit and other EGTRRA enhancements to Coverdell ESAs are made permanent	For tax years beginning after Dec. 31, 2012	704	None
101(a)(1)	646	Favorable income tax treatment for Alaska Native Settlement Trusts and their beneficiaries is made permanent	Tax years beginning after 2012	1503	None
101(a)(1)	1016(a)(28)	Employer-provided child care credit is extended permanently	Tax years beginning after 2012	903	None

Act §	Code §	Topic	Effective Date	Analy-sis ¶	Com Rep ¶
101(a)(1)	3402(p)(1)(B)	Reduced rates for kiddie tax and some withholding (each tied to the reduced individual rates) are permanently extended	For tax years beginning after Dec. 31, 2012	103	None
101(a)(1)	3402(p)(2)	Reduced rates for kiddie tax and some withholding (each tied to the reduced individual rates) are permanently extended	For tax years beginning after Dec. 31, 2012	103	None
101(a)(1)	3402(q)(1)	Reduced rates for kiddie tax and some withholding (each tied to the reduced individual rates) are permanently extended	For tax years beginning after Dec. 31, 2012	103	None
101(a)(1)	3402(r)(3)	Reduced rates for kiddie tax and some withholding (each tied to the reduced individual rates) are permanently extended	For tax years beginning after Dec. 31, 2012	103	None
101(a)(1)	3406(a)(1)	Reduced rates for kiddie tax and some withholding (each tied to the reduced individual rates) are permanently extended	For tax years beginning after Dec. 31, 2012	103	None
101(a)(1)	4973(e)(1)(A)	Increased $2,000 contribution limit and other EGTRRA enhancements to Coverdell ESAs are made permanent	For tax years beginning after Dec. 31, 2012	704	None
101(a)(1)	4973(e)(1)(B)	Increased $2,000 contribution limit and other EGTRRA enhancements to Coverdell ESAs are made permanent	For tax years beginning after Dec. 31, 2012	704	None
101(a)(1)	6039H	Favorable income tax treatment for Alaska Native Settlement Trusts and their beneficiaries is made permanent	Tax years beginning after 2012	1503	None

Act §	Code §	Topic	Effective Date	Analy-sis ¶	Com Rep ¶
101(a)(1)	None	Personal exemption phaseout (PEP) applies when AGI exceeds $300,000 (joint returns) and $250,000 (single filers) for tax years beginning after Dec. 31, 2012	Tax years beginning after Dec. 31, 2012	301	None
101(a)(1)	None	$1,000 per child amount and expanded refundability of child tax credit are permanently extended	Tax years beginning after Dec. 31, 2012.	601	None
101(a)(1)	None	$5,000 increase in EIC phaseout threshold for joint filers is extended through 2017	Tax years beginning after Dec. 31, 2012	606	None
101(a)(1)	None	25%, 28%, and 33% trust and estate income tax rates are permanently extended, top rate increases to 39.6% after 2012	Tax years beginning after Dec. 31, 2012	104	None
101(a)(1)	None	Child tax credit can permanently offset AMT	Tax years beginning after Dec. 31, 2012	404	None
101(a)(1)	None	EGTRRA-expanded dependent care credit permanently extended	Tax years beginning after Dec. 31, 2012	603	None
101(a)(1)	None	EIC simplification made permanent	Tax years beginning after Dec. 31, 2012	605	None
101(a)(1)	None	Expanded adoption credit rules (but not refundability) made permanent	Tax years beginning after Dec. 31, 2012	604	None
101(a)(1)	None	Expansion of marrieds-filing-jointly 15% rate bracket to provide marriage penalty relief is extended permanently	Tax years beginning after Dec. 31, 2012	102	None
101(a)(1)	None	Increased $2,000 contribution limit and other EGTRRA enhancements to Coverdell ESAs are made permanent	For tax years beginning after Dec. 31, 2012	704	None

Act §	Code §	Topic	Effective Date	Analy-sis ¶	Com Rep ¶
101(a)(1)	None	Individuals' 10%, 25%, 28%, 33%, and 35% tax brackets are made permanent; high-income taxpayers taxed at 39.6% rate after 2012	Tax years beginning after Dec. 31, 2012	101	None
101(a)(1)	None	Overall limitation on itemized deductions is restored, applies when AGI exceeds $300,000 (joint returns) and $250,000 (single filers)	Tax years beginning after Dec. 31, 2012	302	None
101(a)(1)	None	Reduced rates for kiddie tax and some withholding (each tied to the reduced individual rates) are permanently extended	For tax years beginning after Dec. 31, 2012	103	None
101(a)(1)	None	Standard deduction marriage penalty relief is made permanent	Tax years beginning after Dec. 31, 2012	304	None
101(a)(1)	None	Adoption assistance exclusion is made permanent	Tax years beginning after 2012	309	None
101(b) ‡	164(f)	Reduced 10.4% OASDI rate applied for 2012 to self-employment income up to $110,100 ceiling	Remuneration received, and tax years beginning, after, Dec. 31, 2011	1901	5501
101(b) ‡	1401(a)	Reduced 10.4% OASDI rate applied for 2012 to self-employment income up to $110,100 ceiling	Remuneration received, and tax years beginning, after, Dec. 31, 2011	1901	5501
101(b)(1)(A)	1(i)(2)	25%, 28%, and 33% trust and estate income tax rates are permanently extended, top rate increases to 39.6% after 2012	Tax years beginning after Dec. 31, 2012	104	None
101(b)(1)(A)	1(i)(2)	Individuals' 10%, 25%, 28%, 33%, and 35% tax brackets are made permanent; high-income taxpayers taxed at 39.6% rate after 2012	Tax years beginning after Dec. 31, 2012	101	None

Act §	Code §	Topic	Effective Date	Analysis ¶	Com Rep ¶
101(b)(1)(B)	1(i)(3)	Individuals' 10%, 25%, 28%, 33%, and 35% tax brackets are made permanent; high-income taxpayers taxed at 39.6% rate after 2012	Tax years beginning after Dec. 31, 2012	101	None
101(b)(2)(A)(i)	68(b)	Overall limitation on itemized deductions is restored, applies when AGI exceeds $300,000 (joint returns) and $250,000 (single filers)	Tax years beginning after Dec. 31, 2012	302	None
101(b)(2)(A)(ii)	68(g)	Overall limitation on itemized deductions is restored, applies when AGI exceeds $300,000 (joint returns) and $250,000 (single filers)	Tax years beginning after Dec. 31, 2012	302	None
101(b)(2)(B)(i)	151(d)(3)	Personal exemption phaseout (PEP) applies when AGI exceeds $300,000 (joint returns) and $250,000 (single filers) for tax years beginning after Dec. 31, 2012	Tax years beginning after Dec. 31, 2012	301	None
101(b)(2)(B)(ii)	151(d)(4)	Personal exemption phaseout (PEP) applies when AGI exceeds $300,000 (joint returns) and $250,000 (single filers) for tax years beginning after Dec. 31, 2012	Tax years beginning after Dec. 31, 2012	301	None
101(c)‡	3121(a)(1)	Reduced 4.2% employee social security tax rate applied for 2012 under payroll tax holiday	Remuneration received, and tax years beginning, after Dec. 31, 2011	1902	5501
101(c)(1)	2001(c)	2012 estate, gift and GST tax rules made permanent, but top rate increases from 35% to 40%	After 2012	501	None
101(c)(2)	2010(c)(4)(B)(i)	2012 estate, gift and GST tax rules made permanent, but top rate increases from 35% to 40%	After 2012	501	None

Act §	Code §	Topic	Effective Date	Analy-sis ¶	Com Rep ¶
102(a)	1(h)(1)	0% and 15% capital gain rates are made permanent; 20% rate is added for high-income taxpayers after 2012	Tax years beginning after Dec. 31, 2012	201	None
102(a)	1(h)(1)(D)(i)	Qualified dividends are taxed at 0%, 15%, and 20% rates after 2012	Tax years beginning after Dec. 31, 2012	202	None
102(a)	1(h)(2)	Election to include qualified dividends in investment income for purposes of investment interest deduction is made permanent	Tax years beginning after Dec. 31, 2012	208	None
102(a)	1(h)(3)(B)	Qualified dividends are taxed at 0%, 15%, and 20% rates after 2012	Tax years beginning after Dec. 31, 2012	202	None
102(a)	1(h)(11)	Qualified dividends are taxed at 0%, 15%, and 20% rates after 2012	Tax years beginning after Dec. 31, 2012	202	None
102(a)	1(h)(11)(D)(i)	Election to include qualified dividends in investment income for purposes of investment interest deduction is made permanent	Tax years beginning after Dec. 31, 2012	208	None
102(a)	1(h)(11)(D)(ii)	Long-term capital loss treatment on stock to extent extraordinary dividends were taxed as capital gain is made permanent	Tax years beginning after Dec. 31, 2012	204	None
102(a)	55(b)(3)	AMT rates on capital gain and qualified dividends are 0%, 15%, and 20% after 2012	Tax years beginning after Dec. 31, 2012	402	None
102(a)	57(a)(7)	7% AMT preference for excluded gain on qualified small business stock is permanently extended	Tax years beginning after Dec. 31, 2012	405	None
102(a)	163(d)(4)(B)	Election to include qualified dividends in investment income for purposes of investment interest deduction is made permanent	Tax years beginning after Dec. 31, 2012	208	None

Act §	Code §	Topic	Effective Date	Analy-sis ¶	Com Rep ¶
102(a)	306(a)(1)(D)	Qualified dividend income treatment for ordinary income on disposition of Code Sec. 306 stock made permanent	Tax years beginning after Dec. 31, 2012	212	None
102(a)	341	Repeal of collapsible corporation provision is made permanent	Tax years beginning after Dec. 31, 2012.	1504	None
102(a)	584(c)	Passthrough of qualified dividend income by common trust funds is made permanent	Tax years beginning after 2012	207	None
102(a)	691(c)(4)	Inclusion of qualified dividend income in prohibition on IRD double benefit is made permanent	Tax years beginning after 2012	211	None
102(a)	702(a)(5)	Passthrough of qualified dividend income by partnerships is made permanent	Tax years beginning after Dec. 31, 2012	205	None
102(a)	854(a)	Passthrough of qualified dividend income by RICs and REITs is made permanent	Tax years beginning after Dec. 31, 2012	206	None
102(a)	854(b)(1)(B)	Passthrough of qualified dividend income by RICs and REITs is made permanent	Tax years beginning after Dec. 31, 2012	206	None
102(a)	854(b)(1)(C)	Passthrough of qualified dividend income by RICs and REITs is made permanent	Tax years beginning after Dec. 31, 2012	206	None
102(a)	854(b)(4)	Passthrough of qualified dividend income by RICs and REITs is made permanent	Tax years beginning after Dec. 31, 2012	206	None
102(a)	857(c)(2)	Passthrough of qualified dividend income by RICs and REITs is made permanent	Tax years beginning after Dec. 31, 2012	206	None

Act §	Code §	Topic	Effective Date	Analy-sis ¶	Com Rep ¶
102(a) ~	3402(t)	Mandatory 3% withholding on payments to government contractors was repealed prospectively	For payments made after 2011	1909	5701
102(a)	7518(g)(6)(A)	Tax rate on individuals' nonqualifying capital gain withdrawals from CCFs is increased from 15% to 20% after 2012	Tax years beginning after Dec. 31, 2012	210	None
102(a)	None	7% AMT preference for excluded gain on qualified small business stock is permanently extended	Tax years beginning after Dec. 31, 2012	405	None
102(a)	None	Accumulated earnings tax rate and personal holding company tax rate of 20% (up from 15%)	Tax years beginning after Dec. 31, 2012	203	None
102(a)	None	IRS may impose 20% withholding rate (up from 15%) on USRPI gains passed through to foreign persons by U.S. partnerships, trusts or estates	Amounts paid after Dec. 31, 2012	1203	None
102(a)	None	Long-term capital loss treatment on stock to extent extraordinary dividends were taxed as capital gain is made permanent	Tax years beginning after Dec. 31, 2012	204	None
102(a)	None	Passthrough of qualified dividend income by RICs and REITs is made permanent	Tax years beginning after Dec. 31, 2012	206	None
102(a)	None	Passthrough of qualified dividend income by partnerships is made permanent	Tax years beginning after Dec. 31, 2012	205	None
102(a)	None	Qualified dividend income treatment for ordinary income on disposition of Code Sec. 306 stock made permanent	Tax years beginning after Dec. 31, 2012	212	None

Act §	Code §	Topic	Effective Date	Analysis ¶	Com Rep ¶
102(a)	None	Repeal of collapsible corporation provision is made permanent	Tax years beginning after Dec. 31, 2012.	1504	None
102(b)(1)	1(h)(1)(C)	0% and 15% capital gain rates are made permanent; 20% rate is added for high-income taxpayers after 2012	Tax years beginning after Dec. 31, 2012	201	None
102(b)(1)	1(h)(1)(D)	0% and 15% capital gain rates are made permanent; 20% rate is added for high-income taxpayers after 2012	Tax years beginning after Dec. 31, 2012	201	None
102(b)(2)	55(b)(3)(C)	AMT rates on capital gain and qualified dividends are 0%, 15%, and 20% after 2012	Tax years beginning after Dec. 31, 2012	402	None
102(b)(2)	55(b)(3)(D)	AMT rates on capital gain and qualified dividends are 0%, 15%, and 20% after 2012	Tax years beginning after Dec. 31, 2012	402	None
102(c)(1)(A)	531	Accumulated earnings tax rate and personal holding company tax rate of 20% (up from 15%)	Tax years beginning after Dec. 31, 2012	203	None
102(c)(1)(B)	541	Accumulated earnings tax rate and personal holding company tax rate of 20% (up from 15%)	Tax years beginning after Dec. 31, 2012	203	None
102(c)(1)(D)	7518(g)(6)(A)	Tax rate on individuals' nonqualifying capital gain withdrawals from CCFs is increased from 15% to 20% after 2012	Tax years beginning after Dec. 31, 2012	210	None
102(c)(1)(E)	None	Tax rate on individuals' nonqualifying capital gain withdrawals from CCFs is increased from 15% to 20% after 2012	Tax years beginning after Dec. 31, 2012	210	None

Act §	Code §	Topic	Effective Date	Analy-sis ¶	Com Rep ¶
102(c)(2)	1(h)(1)(B)	0% and 15% capital gain rates are made permanent; 20% rate is added for high-income taxpayers after 2012	Tax years beginning after Dec. 31, 2012	201	None
102(c)(2)	55(b)(3)(B)	AMT rates on capital gain and qualified dividends are 0%, 15%, and 20% after 2012	Tax years beginning after Dec. 31, 2012	402	None
102(c)(1)(C)	1445(e)(1)	IRS may impose 20% withholding rate (up from 15%) on USRPI gains passed through to foreign persons by U.S. partnerships, trusts or estates	Amounts paid after Dec. 31, 2012	1203	None
103(a)(1)	25A(i)	American Opportunity Tax Credit (AOTC) for higher education expenses is extended five years, through 2017	Tax years beginning after Dec. 31, 2012 and before Jan. 1, 2018	701	None
103(a)(2)	None	American Opportunity Tax Credit (AOTC) for higher education expenses is extended five years, through 2017	Tax years beginning after Dec. 31, 2012 and before Jan. 1, 2018	701	None
103(b)(2)	24(d)(4)	Increase in refundable portion of child tax credit is extended through 2017	Tax years beginning after Dec 31, 2012 and before Jan. 1, 2018	602	None
103(c)(2)	32(b)(3)	$5,000 increase in EIC phaseout threshold for joint filers is extended through 2017	Tax years beginning after Dec. 31, 2012	606	None
103(c)(2)	32(b)(3)	Increased EIC for families with three or more qualifying children is extended for five years	Tax years beginning after Dec. 31, 2012 and before 2018	607	None
103(d)	6409	Tax refunds won't affect eligibility for federal benefit programs	Amounts received after Dec. 31, 2012	310	None

Act §	Code §	Topic	Effective Date	Analy-sis ¶	Com Rep ¶
104(a)(1)(A)	55(d)(1)(A)	AMT exemption amounts are increased to $50,600 for unmarrieds and $78,750 for joint filers for 2012 and are indexed for inflation after 2012	Tax years beginning after Dec. 31, 2011	401	None
104(a)(1)(B)	55(d)(1)(B)	AMT exemption amounts are increased to $50,600 for unmarrieds and $78,750 for joint filers for 2012 and are indexed for inflation after 2012	Tax years beginning after Dec. 31, 2011	401	None
104(b)(1)	55(d)(4)	AMT exemption amounts are increased to $50,600 for unmarrieds and $78,750 for joint filers for 2012 and are indexed for inflation after 2012	Tax years beginning after Dec. 31, 2011	401	None
104(b)(2)(A)	55(b)(1)(A)(iii)	AMT exemption amounts are increased to $50,600 for unmarrieds and $78,750 for joint filers for 2012 and are indexed for inflation after 2012	Tax years beginning after Dec. 31, 2011	401	None
104(b)(2)(B)	55(d)(3)	AMT exemption amounts are increased to $50,600 for unmarrieds and $78,750 for joint filers for 2012 and are indexed for inflation after 2012	Tax years beginning after Dec. 31, 2011	401	None
104(c)(1)	26(a)	Nonrefundable personal credits can offset AMT and regular tax for all tax years beginning after Dec. 31, 2011	Tax years beginning after Dec. 31, 2011.	403	None
104(c)(2)	23(b)(4)	Nonrefundable personal credits can offset AMT and regular tax for all tax years beginning after Dec. 31, 2011	Tax years beginning after Dec. 31, 2011.	403	None

Act §	Code §	Topic	Effective Date	Analy-sis ¶	Com Rep ¶
104(c)(2)	24(b)(3)	Nonrefundable personal credits can offset AMT and regular tax for all tax years beginning after Dec. 31, 2011	Tax years beginning after Dec. 31, 2011.	403	None
104(c)(2)	25(e)(1)(C)	Nonrefundable personal credits can offset AMT and regular tax for all tax years beginning after Dec. 31, 2011	Tax years beginning after Dec. 31, 2011.	403	None
104(c)(2)	25A(i)(5)	Nonrefundable personal credits can offset AMT and regular tax for all tax years beginning after Dec. 31, 2011	Tax years beginning after Dec. 31, 2011.	403	None
104(c)(2)	25B(g)	Nonrefundable personal credits can offset AMT and regular tax for all tax years beginning after Dec. 31, 2011	Tax years beginning after Dec. 31, 2011.	403	None
104(c)(2)	25D(c)	Nonrefundable personal credits can offset AMT and regular tax for all tax years beginning after Dec. 31, 2011	Tax years beginning after Dec. 31, 2011.	403	None
104(c)(2)	26(a)(1)	Nonrefundable personal credits can offset AMT and regular tax for all tax years beginning after Dec. 31, 2011	Tax years beginning after Dec. 31, 2011.	403	None
104(c)(2)	30(c)(2)	Nonrefundable personal credits can offset AMT and regular tax for all tax years beginning after Dec. 31, 2011	Tax years beginning after Dec. 31, 2011.	403	None
104(c)(2)	30B(g)(2)	Nonrefundable personal credits can offset AMT and regular tax for all tax years beginning after Dec. 31, 2011	Tax years beginning after Dec. 31, 2011.	403	None

Act §	Code §	Topic	Effective Date	Analy-sis ¶	Com Rep ¶
104(c)(2)	30D(c)(2)	Nonrefundable personal credits can offset AMT and regular tax for all tax years beginning after Dec. 31, 2011	Tax years beginning after Dec. 31, 2011.	403	None
104(c)(2)	904(i)	Nonrefundable personal credits can offset AMT and regular tax for all tax years beginning after Dec. 31, 2011	Tax years beginning after Dec. 31, 2011.	403	None
104(c)(2)	1400C(d)	Nonrefundable personal credits can offset AMT and regular tax for all tax years beginning after Dec. 31, 2011	Tax years beginning after Dec. 31, 2011.	403	None
201(a)	62(a)(2)(D)	Up-to-$250 above-the-line deduction for teachers' out-of-pocket classroom-related expenses is retroactively extended through 2013	Tax years beginning after Dec. 31, 2011 and before Jan. 1, 2014	308	None
202(a)	108(a)(1)(E)	Exclusion for debt discharge income from home mortgage forgiveness is extended for one year until the end of 2013	Discharges of indebtedness after Dec. 31, 2012, and before Jan. 1, 2014	306	None
203(a)	132(f)(2)	Parity extended through 2013 for employer-provided mass transit and parking benefits	For months in 2012 and 2013	307	None
204(a)	163(h)(3)(E)(iv)	Interest deduction for mortgage insurance premiums is extended to amounts paid or accrued before 2014	Amounts paid or accrued after Dec. 31, 2011 and before Jan. 1, 2014	305	None
205(a)	164(b)(5)(I)	Election to claim itemized deduction for state/local sales taxes is extended through 2013	Tax years beginning after Dec. 31, 2011 and before Jan. 1, 2014	303	None

Act §	Code §	Topic	Effective Date	Analysis ¶	Com Rep ¶
206(a)	170(b)(1)(E)(vi)	Special rules are retroactively extended for qualified conservation easements contributed by individuals (including ranchers and farmers) before 2014	Contributions made in tax years beginning after Dec. 31, 2011 and before Jan. 1, 2014	1102	None
206(b)	170(b)(2)(B)(iii)	For qualified conservation easements contributed by corporate farmers or ranchers in tax years beginning before 2014, special rules are retroactively extended	Contributions made in tax years beginning after Dec. 31, 2011 and before Jan. 1, 2014	1103	None
207(a)	222(e)	Qualified tuition deduction is retroactively extended through 2013	Tax years beginning after Dec. 31, 2011 and before Jan. 1, 2014	702	None
208(a)	408(d)(8)(F)	Rule allowing tax-free IRA distributions of up to $100,000 if donated to charity, is retroactively extended through 2013	For IRA distributions made during 2012 and 2013	1101	None
209(a)	6103(k)(10)	Provision authorizing IRS to disclose certain returns and return information to certain prison officials is improved and made permanent	Jan. 2, 2013	1505	None
241(a)≈	35(a)	HCTC and percentage limit on advance HCTC payments are retroactively increased to 72.5% (from 65%) for post-Feb. 2011 coverage months	Coverage months beginning after Feb. 12, 2011	1606	None
241(b)(1)≈	7527(b)	HCTC and percentage limit on advance HCTC payments are retroactively increased to 72.5% (from 65%) for post-Feb. 2011 coverage months	Coverage months beginning after Feb. 12, 2011	1606	None

Act §	Code §	Topic	Effective Date	Analy-sis ¶	Com Rep ¶
241(b)(1)(B)≈	35(a)	Health coverage tax credit (HCTC) for health insurance costs of trade-displaced workers and PBGC pension recipients won't be allowed after 2013	Coverage months beginning after Feb. 12, 2011	1604	None
241(b)(2)(B)≈	7527(d)(2)	HCTC eligibility certificates issued after Nov. 20, 2011 must include information on qualified health insurance and enrollment procedures	Certificates issued after Nov. 20, 2011	1610	None
241(b)(2)(C)≈	7527(e)	Requirement that IRS make retroactive HCTC payments is reinstated for coverage months beginning after Nov. 20, 2011	Coverage months beginning after Nov. 20, 2011	1605	None
241(b)(2)(D)≈	7527(e)	Requirement that IRS make retroactive HCTC payments is reinstated for coverage months beginning after Nov. 20, 2011	Coverage months beginning after Nov. 20, 2011	1605	None
241(b)(3)(A)≈	35(c)(2)(B)	HCTC eligibility for individuals not enrolled in training programs was extended retroactively to coverage periods beginning after Feb. 12, 2011	Coverage months beginning after Feb. 12, 2011	1608	None
241(b)(3)(B)≈	35(e)(1)(K)	Allowance of HCTC for VEBA coverage was extended	Coverage months beginning after Feb. 12, 2011	1607	None
241(b)(3)(C)≈	35(g)(9)	Continued HCTC eligibility of family members after certain events was extended retroactively to coverage months beginning after Feb. 12, 2011	Coverage months beginning after Feb. 12, 2011	1609	None

Act §	Code §	Topic	Effective Date	Analy-sis ¶	Com Rep ¶
242(a)(1)≈	9801(c)(2)(D)	Rule under which a period after a TAA-related loss of health coverage is not counted in determining a HIPAA 63-day lapse in creditable coverage—extended to plan years beginning before Jan. 1, 2014	Plan years beginning after Feb. 12, 2011 and before Jan. 1, 2014	1611	None
243(a)≈	4980B(f)(2)(B)(i)	Eligibility for COBRA continuation coverage extended from Nov. 20, 2011 through Jan. 1, 2014 for PBGC recipients and TAA-eligible individuals who lose employment or work hours	Coverage periods that would otherwise end on or after Nov. 20, 2011 and through Jan. 1, 2014	1612	None
252(a)(2)≈	3303(f)	To qualify for additional FUTA tax credit, state unemployment programs must charge employers for payments caused by employer's failure to respond	Erroneous payments established after Oct. 20, 2013	1903	None
261(a)~	51(b)(3)	Work opportunity credit as applied to qualified veterans was extended through 2012 and modified	Individuals who begin work for the employer after Nov. 21, 2011 and before Jan. 1, 2013	1910	None
261(b)(3)~	51(d)(3)(A)	Work opportunity credit as applied to qualified veterans was extended through 2012 and modified	Individuals who begin work for the employer after Nov. 21, 2011 and before Jan. 1, 2013	1910	None
261(c)~	51(d)(13)(D)	Work opportunity credit as applied to qualified veterans was extended through 2012 and modified	Individuals who begin work for the employer after Nov. 21, 2011 and before Jan. 1, 2013	1910	None
261(d)~	51(c)(4)(B)	Work opportunity credit as applied to qualified veterans was extended through 2012 and modified	Individuals who begin work for the employer after Nov. 21, 2011 and before Jan. 1, 2013	1910	None

Act §	Code §	Topic	Effective Date	Analy-sis ¶	Com Rep ¶
261(e)(1)~	52(c)	Work opportunity credit as applied to qualified veterans was extended through 2012 and modified	Individuals who begin work for the employer after Nov. 21, 2011 and before Jan. 1, 2013	1910	None
261(e)(2)~	3111(e)	Tax-exempt employers get FICA tax credit for hiring qualified veterans	Individuals who begin work for an employer after Nov. 21, 2011	1904	None
261(f)~	51	Work opportunity credit as applied to qualified veterans was extended through 2012 and modified	Individuals who begin work for the employer after Nov. 21, 2011 and before Jan. 1, 2013	1910	None
301(a)~	6331(h)(3)	100% maximum rate for continuous levy expanded to include governmental payments to vendors from the sale or lease of property	Levies issued after Nov. 21, 2011	1916	None
301(a)(1)	41(h)(1)(B)	Research credit is retroactively extended, with modifications, to apply to amounts paid or incurred before Jan. 1, 2014	Amounts paid or incurred after Dec. 31, 2011 (for credit modifications, tax years beginning after Dec. 31, 2011)	901	None
301(a)(2)	45C(b)(1)(D)	Research credit is retroactively extended, with modifications, to apply to amounts paid or incurred before Jan. 1, 2014	Amounts paid or incurred after Dec. 31, 2011 (for credit modifications, tax years beginning after Dec. 31, 2011)	901	None
301(b)(1)	41(f)(3)(A)	Research credit is retroactively extended, with modifications, to apply to amounts paid or incurred before Jan. 1, 2014	Amounts paid or incurred after Dec. 31, 2011 (for credit modifications, tax years beginning after Dec. 31, 2011)	901	None

Act §	Code §	Topic	Effective Date	Analysis ¶	Com Rep ¶
301(b)(2)	41(f)(3)(B)	Research credit is retroactively extended, with modifications, to apply to amounts paid or incurred before Jan. 1, 2014	Amounts paid or incurred after Dec. 31, 2011 (for credit modifications, tax years beginning after Dec. 31, 2011)	901	None
301(c)(1)	41(f)(1)(A)	Research credit is retroactively extended, with modifications, to apply to amounts paid or incurred before Jan. 1, 2014	Amounts paid or incurred after Dec. 31, 2011 (for credit modifications, tax years beginning after Dec. 31, 2011)	901	None
301(c)(2)	41(f)(1)(B)	Research credit is retroactively extended, with modifications, to apply to amounts paid or incurred before Jan. 1, 2014	Amounts paid or incurred after Dec. 31, 2011 (for credit modifications, tax years beginning after Dec. 31, 2011)	901	None
302(a)	42(b)(2)	Temporary minimum low-income housing credit rate of 9% applies to new non-federally subsidized buildings with respect to housing credit dollar amount allocations made before Jan. 1, 2014	Jan. 2, 2013	906	None
303(a)	42(g)(4)	The military housing allowance exclusion for tax-exempt bond financing and the low-income housing credit is extended until 2014	Income determinations made after July 30, 2008 and before 2014	1408	None
303(a)	142(d)(2)(B)(ii)	The military housing allowance exclusion for tax-exempt bond financing and the low-income housing credit is extended until 2014	Income determinations made after July 30, 2008 and before 2014	1408	None
304(a)	45A(f)	Indian employment credit for wages paid to qualified Native Americans is extended through Dec. 31, 2013	Tax years starting after Dec. 31, 2011 and before Jan. 1, 2014	907	None

Act §	Code §	Topic	Effective Date	Analy-sis ¶	Com Rep ¶
305(a)	45D(f)(1)(G)	New markets tax credit is extended through calendar year 2013	Calendar years starting after 2011 and before 2014	1401	None
305(b)	45D(f)(3)	New markets tax credit is extended through calendar year 2013	Calendar years starting after 2011 and before 2014	1401	None
306(a)	45G(f)	Railroad track maintenance credit for qualified expenditures is extended to include qualified expenditures paid or incurred during tax years beginning in 2012 and 2013	Expenditures paid or incurred during tax years beginning after Dec. 31, 2011 and before Jan. 1 2014	908	None
307(a)	45N(e)	Mine rescue team training credit is retroactively restored and extended to tax years beginning before Jan. 1, 2014	Tax years beginning after Dec. 31, 2011 and before Jan. 1, 2014	905	None
308(a)	45P(f)	Differential wage payment credit is retroactively restored and extended to apply to payments made before Jan. 1, 2014	Payments made after Dec. 31, 2011 and before Jan. 1, 2014	904	None
309(a)	51(c)(4)(B)	Work opportunity credit is retroactively extended to apply to all individuals who begin work for an employer through Dec. 31, 2013	Individuals who begin work for the employer after Dec. 31, 2011 and before Jan. 1, 2014	902	None
310(a)	54E(c)(1)	QZAB program is extended through 2013	Bonds issued after Dec. 31, 2011 and before Jan. 1, 2014	1402	None
311(a)	168(e)(3)(E)(iv)	15-year MACRS depreciation for certain building improvements and restaurants is extended to apply to property placed in service before Jan. 1, 2014	Property placed in service after Dec. 31, 2011 and before Jan. 1, 2014	807	None

Act §	Code §	Topic	Effective Date	Analy-sis ¶	Com Rep ¶
311(a)	168(e)(3)(E)(v)	15-year MACRS depreciation for certain building improvements and restaurants is extended to apply to property placed in service before Jan. 1, 2014	Property placed in service after Dec. 31, 2011 and before Jan. 1, 2014	807	None
311(a)	168(e)(3)(E)(ix)	15-year MACRS depreciation for certain building improvements and restaurants is extended to apply to property placed in service before Jan. 1, 2014	Property placed in service after Dec. 31, 2011 and before Jan. 1, 2014	807	None
312(a)	168(i)(15)(D)	7-year recovery period for motorsports entertainment complexes extended to facilities placed in service through 2013	Property placed in service after Dec. 31, 2011 and before Jan. 1, 2014	809	None
313(a)	168(j)(8)	Depreciation tax breaks for Indian reservation property are extended to property placed in service through 2013	Property placed in service after Dec. 31, 2011 and before Jan. 1, 2014	810	None
314(a)	170(e)(3)(C)(iv)	Above-basis deduction rules are retroactively extended for charitable contributions of food inventory made through 2013	Contributions made after Dec. 31, 2011 and before Jan. 1, 2014	1104	None
315(a)(1)	179(b)(1)(D)	Increased 2010 and 2011 Code 179 dollar limitation and phase-out threshold, and 2010 and 2011 treatment of qualified real property as section 179 property, are extended to 2012 and 2013	Tax years beginning after Dec. 31, 2011 and before Jan. 1, 2014	801	None
315(a)(1)(A)	179(b)(1)(B)	Increased 2010 and 2011 Code 179 dollar limitation and phase-out threshold, and 2010 and 2011 treatment of qualified real property as section 179 property, are extended to 2012 and 2013	Tax years beginning after Dec. 31, 2011 and before Jan. 1, 2014	801	None

Act §	Code §	Topic	Effective Date	Analy-sis ¶	Com Rep ¶
315(a)(1)(B)	179(b)(1)(C)	Increased 2010 and 2011 Code 179 dollar limitation and phase-out threshold, and 2010 and 2011 treatment of qualified real property as section 179 property, are extended to 2012 and 2013	Tax years beginning after Dec. 31, 2011 and before Jan. 1, 2014	801	None
315(a)(2)(A)	179(b)(2)(B)	Increased 2010 and 2011 Code 179 dollar limitation and phase-out threshold, and 2010 and 2011 treatment of qualified real property as section 179 property, are extended to 2012 and 2013	Tax years beginning after Dec. 31, 2011 and before Jan. 1, 2014	801	None
315(a)(2)	179(b)(2)(D)	Increased 2010 and 2011 Code 179 dollar limitation and phase-out threshold, and 2010 and 2011 treatment of qualified real property as section 179 property, are extended to 2012 and 2013	Tax years beginning after Dec. 31, 2011 and before Jan. 1, 2014	801	None
315(a)(2)(B)	179(b)(2)(C)	Increased 2010 and 2011 Code 179 dollar limitation and phase-out threshold, and 2010 and 2011 treatment of qualified real property as section 179 property, are extended to 2012 and 2013	Tax years beginning after Dec. 31, 2011 and before Jan. 1, 2014	801	None
315(a)(3)	179(b)(6)	Increased 2010 and 2011 Code 179 dollar limitation and phase-out threshold, and 2010 and 2011 treatment of qualified real property as section 179 property, are extended to 2012 and 2013	Tax years beginning after Dec. 31, 2011 and before Jan. 1, 2014	801	None

Act §	Code §	Topic	Effective Date	Analy-sis ¶	Com Rep ¶
315(b)	179(d)(1)(A)(ii)	Revocation of Code Sec. 179 election without IRS consent, and eligibility of software for election, are extended to include tax years beginning in 2013	Tax years beginning after Dec. 31, 2011 and before Jan. 1, 2014	803	None
315(c)	179(c)(2)	Revocation of Code Sec. 179 election without IRS consent, and eligibility of software for election, are extended to include tax years beginning in 2013	Tax years beginning after Dec. 31, 2011 and before Jan. 1, 2014	803	None
315(d)(1)	179(f)(1)	Increased 2010 and 2011 Code 179 dollar limitation and phase-out threshold, and 2010 and 2011 treatment of qualified real property as section 179 property, are extended to 2012 and 2013	Tax years beginning after Dec. 31, 2011 and before Jan. 1, 2014	801	None
315(d)(2)(A)	179(f)(4)	Increased 2010 and 2011 Code 179 dollar limitation and phase-out threshold, and 2010 and 2011 treatment of qualified real property as section 179 property, are extended to 2012 and 2013	Tax years beginning after Dec. 31, 2011 and before Jan. 1, 2014	801	None
315(d)(2)(B)(ii)	179(f)(4)(D)	Increased 2010 and 2011 Code 179 dollar limitation and phase-out threshold, and 2010 and 2011 treatment of qualified real property as section 179 property, are extended to 2012 and 2013	Tax years beginning after Dec. 31, 2011 and before Jan. 1, 2014	801	None
316(a)	179E(g)	Election to expense cost of qualified advanced mine safety equipment property is extended two years to property placed in service through 2013	Property placed in service after Dec. 31, 2011 and before Jan. 1, 2014	811	None

Act §	Code §	Topic	Effective Date	Analy-sis ¶	Com Rep ¶
317(a)	181(f)	Expensing rules for qualified film and television productions are retroactively extended for two years to productions beginning before Jan. 1, 2014	Productions beginning after Dec. 31, 2011 and before Jan. 1, 2014	808	None
318(a)	199(d)(8)(C)	Allowance of Code Sec. 199 deduction for Puerto Rico activities is retroactively extended two years to taxpayer's first eight tax years beginning after 2005	Tax years beginning after Dec. 31, 2011 and before Jan. 1, 2014	909	None
319(a)	512(b)(13)(E)(iv)	Rule mitigating tax-exempt parent's UBTI "specified payments" received from a controlled entity, is retroactively extended through 2013	Payments received or accrued in 2012 and 2013	1502	None
320(a)	871(k)(1)(C)	Withholding tax exemption for RIC interest-related dividends and short-term capital gains dividends paid to foreign persons is extended for tax years beginning in 2012 and 2013	Tax years beginning after Dec. 31, 2011 and before Jan. 1, 2014	1205	None
320(a)	871(k)(2)(C)	Withholding tax exemption for RIC interest-related dividends and short-term capital gains dividends paid to foreign persons is extended for tax years beginning in 2012 and 2013	Tax years beginning after Dec. 31, 2011 and before Jan. 1, 2014	1205	None
321(a)	897(h)(4)(A)(ii)	Inclusion of RICs in the definition of qualified investment entity is extended for certain FIRPTA purposes through 2013	Jan. 1, 2012 through Dec. 31, 2013	1204	None
322(a)	953(e)(10)	Subpart F exception for active financing income extended through tax years beginning before 2014	Tax Years beginning after Dec. 31, 2011 and before Jan. 1, 2014	1201	None

Act §	Code §	Topic	Effective Date	Analy-sis ¶	Com Rep ¶
322(b)	954(h)(9)	Subpart F exception for active financing income extended through tax years beginning before 2014	Tax Years beginning after Dec. 31, 2011 and before Jan. 1, 2014	1201	None
323(a)	954(c)(6)(C)	Look-through treatment for payments between related CFCs under foreign personal holding company income rules extended through 2013	Tax years of foreign corporations beginning after Dec. 31, 2011 and before Jan. 1, 2014	1202	None
324(a)(1)	1202(a)(4)	Acquisition date defined for qualified small business stock (QSBS) qualifying for the 100% exclusion	Stock acquired after Dec. 31, 2011 and before Jan. 1, 2014	209	None
324(b)(1)	1202(a)(3)	Acquisition date defined for qualified small business stock (QSBS) qualifying for the 75% exclusion	Stock acquired after Feb. 17, 2009 and before Sept. 28, 2010	209	None
324(b)(2)	1202(a)(4)	100% gain exclusion for qualified small business stock (QSBS) is retroactively restored and extended through Dec. 31, 2013	Stock acquired after Sept. 27, 2010	209	None
325(a)	1367(a)(2)	Rule that S corporation's charitable contribution of property reduces shareholder's basis only by contributed property's basis is extended for tax years beginning in 2012 and 2013	Contributions made in tax years beginning after Dec. 31, 2011 and before Jan. 1, 2014.	1105	None
326(a)	1374(d)(7)	Shortened S Corp built-in gains holding period extended for 2012 and 2013 and application of built-in gains tax clarified	Tax years beginning after Dec. 31, 2011	1501	None
326(b)	1374(d)(2)(B)	Shortened S Corp built-in gains holding period extended for 2012 and 2013 and application of built-in gains tax clarified	Tax years beginning after Dec. 31, 2011	1501	None

Act §	Code §	Topic	Effective Date	Analysis ¶	Com Rep ¶
327(a)	1391(d)(1)(A)(i)	Round I empowerment zone designation period is retroactively extended through the end of 2013	Periods after Dec. 31, 2011 and before Jan. 1, 2014	1406	None
327(b)	1202(a)(2)(C)	Partial exclusion of gain from the sale or exchange of certain QSBS in empowerment zone C corporations is extended through the end of 2018	Periods after Dec. 31, 2011 and before Jan. 1, 2019	1407	None
327(c)	1391(d)(1)(B)	Round I empowerment zone designation period is retroactively extended through the end of 2013	Periods after Dec. 31, 2011 and before Jan. 1, 2014	1406	None
328(a)	1400L(d)(2)(D)	Period for issuance of qualified New York Liberty Bonds is retroactively restored and extended to bonds issued before Jan. 1, 2014	Bonds issued after Dec. 31, 2011 and before Jan. 1, 2014	1405	None
330	30A	Possessions tax credit for American Samoa extended through 2013 with an American Samoa production requirement	Tax years beginning after Dec. 31, 2011 and before Jan. 1, 2014	1206	None
330	936	Possessions tax credit for American Samoa extended through 2013 with an American Samoa production requirement	Tax years beginning after Dec. 31, 2011 and before Jan. 1, 2014	1206	None
331(a)	168(k)(2)(A)(iv)	Additional round of trading bonus and accelerated depreciation for deferred credits is provided	Property placed in service after Dec. 31, 2012 and before Jan. 1, 2014	805	None
331(a)	168(k)(2)(A)(iv)	Increase in first-year depreciation cap for cars that are "qualified property" is extended through Dec. 31, 2013	Property placed in service after Dec. 31, 2012 and before Jan. 1, 2014	802	None

Act §	Code §	Topic	Effective Date	Analy-sis ¶	Com Rep ¶
331(a)(1)	168(k)(2)(A)(iv)	Bonus depreciation and AMT depreciation relief are extended for certain aircraft and long-production period property placed in service through Dec. 31, 2014	Property placed in service after Dec. 31, 2012 and before Jan. 1, 2015	804	None
331(a)(2)	168(k)(2)(A)(iii)	Bonus depreciation and AMT depreciation relief are extended for qualified property placed in service through, generally, Dec. 31, 2013	Property placed in service after Dec. 31, 2012 and before Jan. 1, 2014	804	None
331(a)(2)	168(k)(2)(A)(iv)	Bonus depreciation and AMT depreciation relief are extended for qualified property placed in service through, generally, Dec. 31, 2013	Property placed in service after Dec. 31, 2012 and before Jan. 1, 2014	804	None
331(a)(2)	168(k)(2)(B)(ii)	Bonus depreciation and AMT depreciation relief are extended for qualified property placed in service through, generally, Dec. 31, 2013	Property placed in service after Dec. 31, 2012 and before Jan. 1, 2014	804	None
331(a)(2)	168(k)(2)(E)(i)	Bonus depreciation and AMT depreciation relief are extended for qualified property placed in service through, generally, Dec. 31, 2013	Property placed in service after Dec. 31, 2012 and before Jan. 1, 2014	804	None
331(b)	460(c)(6)(B)(ii)	Disregard of certain bonus depreciation in applying the percentage of completion method is allowed for an additional time period	Property placed in service after Dec. 31, 2012 and before Jan. 1, 2014	806	None
331(c)(1)	168(k)(4)(D)(iii)(II)	Additional round of trading bonus and accelerated depreciation for deferred credits is provided	Property placed in service after Dec. 31, 2012 and before Jan. 1, 2014	805	None

Act §	Code §	Topic	Effective Date	Analy-sis ¶	Com Rep ¶
331(c)(2)	168(k)(4)(J)	Additional round of trading bonus and accelerated depreciation for deferred credits is provided	Property placed in service after Dec. 31, 2012 and before Jan. 1, 2014	805	None
331(d)	168(i)(9)(A)(ii)	MACRS elections must be taken into account under normalization accounting for public utility property	Property placed in service after Dec. 31, 2012	812	None
401(a)	25C(g)(2)	Nonbusiness energy property credit is retroactively reinstated and extended through 2013	Property placed in service after Dec. 31, 2011 and before Jan. 1, 2014	1004	None
401(a) ~	36B(d)(2)(B)(iii)	Modified AGI for determining eligibility for and amount of post-2013 premium tax credit will include nontaxable social security income	Nov. 21, 2011	1601	None
402(a)	30C(g)(2)	Non-hydrogen QAFV refueling property credit is retroactively restored and extended to property placed in service before Jan. 1, 2014	Property placed in service after Dec. 31, 2011 and before Jan. 1, 2014	1008	None
403(a)	30D(g)	Credit for 2- or 3-wheeled plug-in electric vehicles is retroactively extended two years to apply to vehicles acquired before Jan. 1, 2014	Vehicles acquired after Dec. 31, 2011 and before Jan. 1, 2014	1006	None
404(a)(1)	40(b)(6)(H)	Cellulosic biofuel producer credit is retroactively restored and extended through Dec. 31, 2013	Fuel produced after Dec. 31, 2008 and before Jan. 1, 2014	1015	None
403(b)(1)	30D(f)(2)	Credit for 2- or 3-wheeled plug-in electric vehicles is retroactively extended two years to apply to vehicles acquired before Jan. 1, 2014	Vehicles acquired after Dec. 31, 2011 and before Jan. 1, 2014	1006	None

Act §	Code §	Topic	Effective Date	Analysis ¶	Com Rep ¶
404(b)(1)	40(b)(6)(E)(i)(I)	Algae is treated as a qualified feedstock for purposes of the cellulose biofuel producer credit	Fuels sold or used after Jan. 2, 2013.	1016	None
403(b)(2)	30D(f)(7)	Credit for 2- or 3-wheeled plug-in electric vehicles is retroactively extended two years to apply to vehicles acquired before Jan. 1, 2014	Vehicles acquired after Dec. 31, 2011 and before Jan. 1, 2014	1006	None
404(b)(2)	40(b)(6)(F)	Algae is treated as a qualified feedstock for purposes of the cellulose biofuel producer credit	Fuels sold or used after Jan. 2, 2013.	1016	None
404(b)(2)	40(b)(6)(G)	Algae is treated as a qualified feedstock for purposes of the cellulose biofuel producer credit	Fuels sold or used after Jan. 2, 2013.	1016	None
404(b)(3)(A)(ii)	40(b)(6)	Algae is treated as a qualified feedstock for purposes of the cellulose biofuel producer credit	Fuels sold or used after Jan. 2, 2013.	1016	None
404(b)(3)(C)	4101(a)	Algae is treated as a qualified feedstock for purposes of the cellulose biofuel producer credit	Fuels sold or used after Jan. 2, 2013.	1016	None
405(a)	40A(g)	Income and excise tax credits/refunds for biodiesel and renewable diesel are extended retroactively through 2013	Fuel sold or used after Dec. 31, 2011 and before Jan. 1, 2014	1009	None
405(b)(1)	6426(c)(6)	Income and excise tax credits/refunds for biodiesel and renewable diesel are extended retroactively through 2013	Fuel sold or used after Dec. 31, 2011 and before Jan. 1, 2014	1009	None
405(b)(2)	6427(e)(6)(B)	Income and excise tax credits/refunds for biodiesel and renewable diesel are extended retroactively through 2013	Fuel sold or used after Dec. 31, 2011 and before Jan. 1, 2014	1009	None

Act §	Code §	Topic	Effective Date	Analysis ¶	Com Rep ¶
406(a)	45(e)(10)	Period of credit for Indian coal produced by taxpayer at Indian coal facilities extended to eight-year period beginning Jan. 1, 2006	Coal produced after Dec. 31, 2012	1007	None
407(a)(1)	45(d)(1)	Credits with respect to facilities producing energy from certain renewable resources are extended and modified	Jan. 2, 2013	1005	None
407(a)(2)	45(c)(6)	Definition of municipal solid waste does not include paper that is commonly recycled and segregated from other solid waste	Electricity produced and sold after Jan. 2, 2013, in tax years ending after Jan. 2, 2013	1011	None
407(a)(3)(A)(i)	45(d)(1)	Credits with respect to facilities producing energy from certain renewable resources are extended and modified	Jan. 2, 2013	1005	None
407(a)(3)(A)(ii)	45(d)(2)(A)(i)	Credits with respect to facilities producing energy from certain renewable resources are extended and modified	Jan. 2, 2013	1005	None
407(a)(3)(A)(iii)	45(d)(3)(A)(i)(I)	Credits with respect to facilities producing energy from certain renewable resources are extended and modified	Jan. 2, 2013	1005	None
407(a)(3)(A)(iv)	45(d)(6)	Credits with respect to facilities producing energy from certain renewable resources are extended and modified	Jan. 2, 2013	1005	None
407(a)(3)(A)(v)	45(d)(7)	Credits with respect to facilities producing energy from certain renewable resources are extended and modified	Jan. 2, 2013	1005	None

Act §	Code §	Topic	Effective Date	Analy-sis ¶	Com Rep ¶
407(a)(3)(A)(vi)	45(d)(9)(B)	Credits with respect to facilities producing energy from certain renewable resources are extended and modified	Jan. 2, 2013	1005	None
407(a)(3)(A)(vii)	45(d)(11)(B)	Credits with respect to facilities producing energy from certain renewable resources are extended and modified	Jan. 2, 2013	1005	None
407(a)(3)(B)	45(d)(2)(A)	Credits with respect to facilities producing energy from certain renewable resources are extended and modified	Jan. 2, 2013	1005	None
407(a)(3)(C)	45(d)(3)(A)(ii)	Credits with respect to facilities producing energy from certain renewable resources are extended and modified	Jan. 2, 2013	1005	None
407(a)(3)(D)(i)	45(d)(4)	Credits with respect to facilities producing energy from certain renewable resources are extended and modified	Jan. 2, 2013	1005	None
407(a)(3)(E)(iv)	45(d)(9)(C)	Credits with respect to facilities producing energy from certain renewable resources are extended and modified	Jan. 2, 2013	1005	None
407(c)(1)(C)	48(a)(5)(D)	Definition of qualified property for purposes of the election to take a 30% energy credit instead of the electricity production credit is retroactively clarified	Facilities placed in service after Dec. 31, 2008	1012	None
408(a)	45L(g)	New energy efficient home credit for eligible contractors is retroactively restored and extended through Dec. 31, 2013	Homes acquired after Dec. 31, 2011 and before Jan. 1, 2014	1002	None

Act §	Code §	Topic	Effective Date	Analysis ¶	Com Rep ¶
408(b)	45L(c)(1)(A)(i)	Construction standards for the qualified new energy efficient home credit are modified	Homes acquired after Dec. 31, 2011	1003	None
409(a)	45M(b)(1)(D)	Energy efficient appliance credit is extended for certain appliances manufactured in 2012 or 2013	Appliances produced after Dec. 31, 2011 and before Jan. 1, 2014	1001	None
409(a)	45M(b)(1)(E)	Energy efficient appliance credit is extended for certain appliances manufactured in 2012 or 2013	Appliances produced after Dec. 31, 2011 and before Jan. 1, 2014	1001	None
409(a)	45M(b)(2)(F)	Energy efficient appliance credit is extended for certain appliances manufactured in 2012 or 2013	Appliances produced after Dec. 31, 2011 and before Jan. 1, 2014	1001	None
409(a)	45M(b)(3)(E)	Energy efficient appliance credit is extended for certain appliances manufactured in 2012 or 2013	Appliances produced after Dec. 31, 2011 and before Jan. 1, 2014	1001	None
409(a)	45M(b)(3)(F)	Energy efficient appliance credit is extended for certain appliances manufactured in 2012 or 2013	Appliances produced after Dec. 31, 2011 and before Jan. 1, 2014	1001	None
410(a)(1)	168(l)(2)(D)	Bonus depreciation and AMT depreciation relief for certain biofuel plant property is extended one year through Dec. 31, 2013 and expanded	Property placed in service after Dec. 31, 2012 (after Jan. 2, 2013 for qualified second generation biofuel plant property) and before Jan. 1, 2014	1013	None

Act §	Code §	Topic	Effective Date	Analy-sis ¶	Com Rep ¶
410(b)(1)	168(l)(2)(A)	Bonus depreciation and AMT depreciation relief for certain biofuel plant property is extended one year through Dec. 31, 2013 and expanded	Property placed in service after Dec. 31, 2012 (after Jan. 2, 2013 for qualified second generation biofuel plant property) and before Jan. 1, 2014	1013	None
410(b)(2)(A)	168(l)	Bonus depreciation and AMT depreciation relief for certain biofuel plant property is extended one year through Dec. 31, 2013 and expanded	Property placed in service after Dec. 31, 2012 (after Jan. 2, 2013 for qualified second generation biofuel plant property) and before Jan. 1, 2014	1013	None
411(a)	451(i)(3)	Gain deferral election on qualifying electric transmission transactions is retroactively restored and extended to dispositions before Jan. 1, 2014	Dispositions after Dec. 31, 2011 and before Jan. 1, 2014	1014	None
412(a)	6426(d)(5)	Alternative fuels and alternative fuel mixture excise tax credit, and alternative fuels excise tax refund rules, are retroactively extended through 2013	Fuel sold or used after Dec. 31, 2011 and before Jan. 1, 2014	1010	None
412(a)	6426(e)(3)	Alternative fuels and alternative fuel mixture excise tax credit, and alternative fuels excise tax refund rules, are retroactively extended through 2013	Fuel sold or used after Dec. 31, 2011 and before Jan. 1, 2014	1010	None
412(b)(1)	6427(e)(6)(C)	Alternative fuels and alternative fuel mixture excise tax credit, and alternative fuels excise tax refund rules, are retroactively extended through 2013	Fuel sold or used after Dec. 31, 2011 and before Jan. 1, 2014	1010	None

Act §	Code §	Topic	Effective Date	Analy-sis ¶	Com Rep ¶
412(b)(2)	6427(e)(6)(D)	Alternative fuels and alternative fuel mixture excise tax credit, and alternative fuels excise tax refund rules, are retroactively extended through 2013	Fuel sold or used after Dec. 31, 2011 and before Jan. 1, 2014	1010	None
412(b)(3)	6427(e)(6)(E)	Alternative fuels and alternative fuel mixture excise tax credit, and alternative fuels excise tax refund rules, are retroactively extended through 2013	Fuel sold or used after Dec. 31, 2011 and before Jan. 1, 2014	1010	None
501(a)++	6695(g)	Penalty on Paid Preparers for Noncompliance with Due Diligence Rules Increased from $100 to $500	Returns required to be filed after Dec. 31, 2011.	1912	5801
502(a)++	6116	Principal administrators of U.S. prisons have to provide IRS with certain information about inmates each year	Oct. 21, 2011	1908	5802
902(a)	402A(c)(4)(E)	Distribution restrictions eased for "in-plan Roth rollovers"	Transfers to designated Roth accounts made after Dec. 31, 2012	1301	None
1001(a)**	1401(a)	Reduced 10.4% OASDI rate applied for 2012 to self-employment income up to $110,100 ceiling	Remuneration received, and tax years beginning, after, Dec. 31, 2011	1901	5501
1001(a)**	3101(a)	Reduced 4.2% employee social security tax rate applied for 2012 under payroll tax holiday	Remuneration received, and tax years beginning, after Dec. 31, 2011	1902	5501
1001(a)**	3201(a)	Reduced 4.2% employee social security tax rate applied for 2012 under payroll tax holiday	Remuneration received, and tax years beginning, after Dec. 31, 2011	1902	5501
1001(a)**	3211(a)	Reduced 4.2% employee social security tax rate applied for 2012 under payroll tax holiday	Remuneration received, and tax years beginning, after Dec. 31, 2011	1902	5501

Act §	Code §	Topic	Effective Date	Analy-sis ¶	Com Rep ¶
1001(b)**	164(f)	Reduced 10.4% OASDI rate applied for 2012 to self-employment income up to $110,100 ceiling	Remuneration received, and tax years beginning, after, Dec. 31, 2011	1901	5501
1001(b)**	3101(a)	Reduced 4.2% employee social security tax rate applied for 2012 under payroll tax holiday	Remuneration received, and tax years beginning, after Dec. 31, 2011	1902	5501
1101(a)†	4081(d)(2)(B)	Airport and airway trust fund excise taxes are extended through Sept. 30, 2015	Feb. 18, 2012	1806	5601
1101(b)(1)†	4261(j)(1)(A)(ii)	Airport and airway trust fund excise taxes are extended through Sept. 30, 2015	Feb. 18, 2012	1806	5601
1101(b)(2)†	4271(d)(1)(A)(ii)	Airport and airway trust fund excise taxes are extended through Sept. 30, 2015	Feb. 18, 2012	1806	5601
1103(a)(1)†	4043	14.1¢-per-gallon surtax is imposed on fuel used in fractional ownership aircraft flights; flights are also taxed as noncommercial aviation, but exempted from air transportation taxes	Taxable transportation provided, and aircraft and fuel used, after Mar. 31, 2012	1808	5603
1103(a)(2)†	4082(e)	14.1¢-per-gallon surtax is imposed on fuel used in fractional ownership aircraft flights; flights are also taxed as noncommercial aviation, but exempted from air transportation taxes	Taxable transportation provided, and aircraft and fuel used, after Mar. 31, 2012	1808	5603
1103(b)†	4083(b)	14.1¢-per-gallon surtax is imposed on fuel used in fractional ownership aircraft flights; flights are also taxed as noncommercial aviation, but exempted from air transportation taxes	Taxable transportation provided, and aircraft and fuel used, after Mar. 31, 2012	1808	5603

Act §	Code §	Topic	Effective Date	Analysis ¶	Com Rep ¶
1103(c) †	4261(j)	14.1¢-per-gallon surtax is imposed on fuel used in fractional ownership aircraft flights; flights are also taxed as noncommercial aviation, but exempted from air transportation taxes	Taxable transportation provided, and aircraft and fuel used, after Mar. 31, 2012	1808	5603
1103(c) †	4261(j)	Airport and airway trust fund excise taxes are extended through Sept. 30, 2015	Feb. 18, 2012	1806	5601
1104(a) †	7275(c)	Penalty imposed for lack of transparency in airline passenger tax disclosures	Taxable transportation provided after Mar. 31, 2012.	1911	5604
1105(a) †	147(e)	Tax-exempt qualified bonds can be used to finance fixed-wing emergency medical aircraft	Bonds issued after Feb. 14, 2012	1913	5605
1106 †	402	Rollovers to traditional IRAs allowed for amounts received from airlines that filed for bankruptcy after Sept. 11, 2001 and before Jan. 1, 2007	For amounts paid before, on, or after Feb. 14, 2012	1705	5606
1107(a) †	4281	Exemption from air transportation excise taxes for small jet aircraft operated on nonestablished lines is eliminated	For taxable transportation provided after Mar. 31, 2012	1807	5607
1108(a) †	249(a)	Repurchase bond premium deduction limitation extended to debt convertible to controlled group stock	For repurchases after Feb. 14, 2012	1914	5608
1108(b) †	249(b)	Repurchase bond premium deduction limitation extended to debt convertible to controlled group stock	For repurchases after Feb. 14, 2012	1914	5608
1858(a) +	None	Employers won't have to provide free choice vouchers to employees, as post-2013 rules are repealed	For vouchers that would have been provided after 2013	1603	None

Act §	Code §	Topic	Effective Date	Analysis ¶	Com Rep ¶
1858(b)(1)+	36B(c)(2)	Employers won't have to provide free choice vouchers to employees, as post-2013 rules are repealed	For vouchers that would have been provided after 2013	1603	None
1858(b)(2)(A)+	139D	Employers won't have to provide free choice vouchers to employees, as post-2013 rules are repealed	For vouchers that would have been provided after 2013	1603	None
1858(b)(3)+	162(a)	Employers won't have to provide free choice vouchers to employees, as post-2013 rules are repealed	For vouchers that would have been provided after 2013	1603	None
1858(b)(4)+	4980H(b)(3)	Employers won't have to provide free choice vouchers to employees, as post-2013 rules are repealed	For vouchers that would have been provided after 2013	1603	None
1858(b)(5)(A)+	6056(a)	Post-2013 health insurance coverage information reporting and related statement requirements for "offering employers" are repealed	Periods beginning after Dec. 31, 2013	1613	None
1858(b)(5)(B)(i)+	6056(b)(2)(C)(i)	Post-2013 health insurance coverage information reporting and related statement requirements for "offering employers" are repealed	Periods beginning after Dec. 31, 2013	1613	None
1858(b)(5)(B)(iv)+	6056(b)(2)(C)(v)	Post-2013 health insurance coverage information reporting and related statement requirements for "offering employers" are repealed	Periods beginning after Dec. 31, 2013	1613	None
1858(b)(5)(C)+	6056(d)(2)	Post-2013 health insurance coverage information reporting and related statement requirements for "offering employers" are repealed	Periods beginning after Dec. 31, 2013	1613	None

Act §	Code §	Topic	Effective Date	Analy- sis ¶	Com Rep ¶
1858(b)(5)(C)+	6056(e)	Post-2013 health insurance coverage information reporting and related statement requirements for "offering employers" are repealed	Periods beginning after Dec. 31, 2013	1613	None
1858(b)(5)(D)+	6056(f)	Post-2013 health insurance coverage information reporting and related statement requirements for "offering employers" are repealed	Periods beginning after Dec. 31, 2013	1613	None
100121(c)*	72(t)(2)	Additional 10% tax on early withdrawals from qualified retirement plans will not apply to federal phased retirement program payments	July 6, 2012	1704	None
40102(a)(1)(A)*	4041(a)(1)(C)(iii)(I)	Reduction of various fuel excise tax rates is delayed until after Sept. 30, 2016	July 1, 2012	1801	5401
40102(a)(1)(B)*	4041(m)(1)(B)	Reduction of various fuel excise tax rates is delayed until after Sept. 30, 2016	July 1, 2012	1801	5401
40102(a)(1)(C)*	4081(d)(1)	Reduction of various fuel excise tax rates is delayed until after Sept. 30, 2016	July 1, 2012	1801	5401
40102(a)(2)(A)*	4041(m)(1)(A)	Reduction of various fuel excise tax rates is delayed until after Sept. 30, 2016	July 1, 2012	1801	5401
40102(a)(2)(B)*	4051(c)	Retail truck and manufacturer's tire excise taxes, and certain exemptions, are extended through Sept. 30, 2016	July 1, 2012	1803	5401
40102(a)(2)(C)*	4071(d)	Retail truck and manufacturer's tire excise taxes, and certain exemptions, are extended through Sept. 30, 2016	July 1, 2012	1803	5401

Act §	Code §	Topic	Effective Date	Analy-sis ¶	Com Rep ¶
40102(a)(2)(D)*	4081(d)(3)	Leaking Underground Storage Tank (LUST) Trust Fund 0.1¢-per-gallon tax is extended through Sept. 30, 2016	July 1, 2012	1802	5401
40102(b)(1)(A)*	4481(f)	Highway use tax, and certain highway use tax exemptions, are extended through Sept. 30, 2017	July 1, 2012	1805	5401
40102(b)(1)(B)*	4482(d)	Highway use tax, and certain highway use tax exemptions, are extended through Sept. 30, 2017	July 1, 2012	1805	5401
40102(b)(2)(A)*	4482(c)(4)	Highway use tax, and certain highway use tax exemptions, are extended through Sept. 30, 2017	July 1, 2012	1805	5401
40102(b)(2)(B)*	4482(c)(4)	Highway use tax, and certain highway use tax exemptions, are extended through Sept. 30, 2017	July 1, 2012	1805	5401
40102(c)*	6412(a)(1)	Floor stocks credit, or refund for tire tax and removal-at-terminal fuel tax, is to apply to tires or fuel held by dealers on Oct. 1, 2016	July 1, 2012	1804	5401
40102(d)(1)*	4221(a)	Retail truck and manufacturer's tire excise taxes, and certain exemptions, are extended through Sept. 30, 2016	July 1, 2012	1803	5401
40102(d)(2)*	4483(i)	Highway use tax, and certain highway use tax exemptions, are extended through Sept. 30, 2017	July 1, 2012	1805	5401
40211(a)(1)*	430(h)(2)(C)(iv)	Plans can use interest rate smoothing over a 25-year period to determine liabilities	Plan years beginning after Dec. 31, 2011	1701	5402
40211(a)(2)(A)*	404(o)(6)	Plans can use interest rate smoothing over a 25-year period to determine liabilities	Plan years beginning after Dec. 31, 2011	1701	5402

Act §	Code §	Topic	Effective Date	Analy-sis ¶	Com Rep ¶
40211(a)(2)(B)*	430(h)(2)(F)	Plans can use interest rate smoothing over a 25-year period to determine liabilities	Plan years beginning after Dec. 31, 2011	1701	5402
40211(a)(2)(C)*	417(e)(3)(C)	Plans can use interest rate smoothing over a 25-year period to determine liabilities	Plan years beginning after Dec. 31, 2011	1701	5402
40211(a)(2)(C)*	417(e)(3)(D)	Plans can use interest rate smoothing over a 25-year period to determine liabilities	Plan years beginning after Dec. 31, 2011	1701	5402
40211(a)(2)(D)*	420(g)	Plans can use interest rate smoothing over a 25-year period to determine liabilities	Plan years beginning after Dec. 31, 2011	1701	5402
40241(a)*	420(b)(5)	Rules permitting transfer of excess defined benefit plan assets to retiree health accounts are extended through 2021	July 6, 2012	1703	5405
40242(a)*	420(a)	Excess pension plan assets may be used to fund retiree group-term life insurance	Transfers made after July 6, 2012	1702	5405
40242(b)(1)*	420(e)(4)	Excess pension plan assets may be used to fund retiree group-term life insurance	Transfers made after July 6, 2012	1702	5405
40242(b)(2)*	420(e)(1)(D)	Excess pension plan assets may be used to fund retiree group-term life insurance	Transfers made after July 6, 2012	1702	5405
40242(b)(3)(A)*	420(f)(6)(D)	Excess pension plan assets may be used to fund retiree group-term life insurance	Transfers made after July 6, 2012	1702	5405
40242(b)(3)(B)(i)*	420(e)(1)(C)	Excess pension plan assets may be used to fund retiree group-term life insurance	Transfers made after July 6, 2012	1702	5405
40242(b)(3)(B)(ii)*	420(f)(6)(C)	Excess pension plan assets may be used to fund retiree group-term life insurance	Transfers made after July 6, 2012	1702	5405

Act §	Code §	Topic	Effective Date	Analy-sis ¶	Com Rep ¶
40242(c)(1)*	420(c)(3)(A)	Excess pension plan assets may be used to fund retiree group-term life insurance	Transfers made after July 6, 2012	1702	5405
40242(c)(2)(A)(i)*	420(c)(3)(B)(i)(I)	Excess pension plan assets may be used to fund retiree group-term life insurance	Transfers made after July 6, 2012	1702	5405
40242(c)(2)(A)(ii)*	420(c)(3)(B)(ii)	Excess pension plan assets may be used to fund retiree group-term life insurance	Transfers made after July 6, 2012	1702	5405
40242(c)(2)(B)*	420(c)(3)(C)	Excess pension plan assets may be used to fund retiree group-term life insurance	Transfers made after July 6, 2012	1702	5405
40242(c)(2)(E)*	420(f)(2)(D)(i)(II)	Excess pension plan assets may be used to fund retiree group-term life insurance	Transfers made after July 6, 2012	1702	5405
40242(c)(2)(F)*	420(f)(2)(D)(ii)	Excess pension plan assets may be used to fund retiree group-term life insurance	Transfers made after July 6, 2012	1702	5405
40242(d)*	79(f)	Excess pension plan assets may be used to fund retiree group-term life insurance	Transfers made after July 6, 2012	1702	5405
40242(e)(2)*	420(d)(1)(A)	Excess pension plan assets may be used to fund retiree group-term life insurance	Transfers made after July 6, 2012	1702	5405
40242(e)(3)*	420(b)(2)	Excess pension plan assets may be used to fund retiree group-term life insurance	Transfers made after July 6, 2012	1702	5405
40242(e)(5)(A)*	420(e)(1)(A)	Excess pension plan assets may be used to fund retiree group-term life insurance	Transfers made after July 6, 2012	1702	5405

Act §	Code §	Topic	Effective Date	Analy- sis ¶	Com Rep ¶
40242(e)(6)(A)*	420(e)(1)(B)	Excess pension plan assets may be used to fund retiree group-term life insurance	Transfers made after July 6, 2012	1702	5405
40242(f)*	420(f)(6)(B)	Excess pension plan assets may be used to fund retiree group-term life insurance	Transfers made after July 6, 2012	1702	5405
40242(g)(2)*	420(b)(4)	Excess pension plan assets may be used to fund retiree group-term life insurance	Transfers made after July 6, 2012	1702	5405
40242(g)(4)(A)*	420(c)(2)(B)	Excess pension plan assets may be used to fund retiree group-term life insurance	Transfers made after July 6, 2012	1702	5405

¶ 6001. Code Section Cross Reference Table

Act § cites are to the 2012 Taxpayer Relief Act unless otherwise indicated.
* denotes 2012 Highway Investment Act
† denotes 2012 FAA Modernization Act
** denotes 2012 Middle Class Tax Relief Act
*** denotes 2012 African Growth Act
✓ denotes 2012 Aviation Extension Act
+ denotes 2011 Appropriations Act
~ denotes 2011 Job Creation Act
• denotes 2011 Taxpayer Protection Act
‡ denotes 2011 Temporary Payroll Act
++ denotes 2011 U.S.-Korea Trade Act
≈ denotes 2011 Trade Extension Act

Code §	Act §	Topic	Effective Date	Analysis ¶	Com Rep ¶
1(f)(2)(A)	101(a)(1)	Expansion of marrieds-filing-jointly 15% rate bracket to provide marriage penalty relief is extended permanently	Tax years beginning after Dec. 31, 2012	102	None
1(f)(8)	101(a)(1)	Expansion of marrieds-filing-jointly 15% rate bracket to provide marriage penalty relief is extended permanently	Tax years beginning after Dec. 31, 2012	102	None
1(g)(7)(B)(ii)(II)	101(a)(1)	Reduced rates for kiddie tax and some withholding (each tied to the reduced individual rates) are permanently extended	For tax years beginning after Dec. 31, 2012	103	None
1(h)(1)	102(a)	0% and 15% capital gain rates are made permanent; 20% rate is added for high-income taxpayers after 2012	Tax years beginning after Dec. 31, 2012	201	None
1(h)(1)(B)	102(c)(2)	0% and 15% capital gain rates are made permanent; 20% rate is added for high-income taxpayers after 2012	Tax years beginning after Dec. 31, 2012	201	None
1(h)(1)(C)	102(b)(1)	0% and 15% capital gain rates are made permanent; 20% rate is added for high-income taxpayers after 2012	Tax years beginning after Dec. 31, 2012	201	None

Code §	Act §	Topic	Effective Date	Analysis ¶	Com Rep ¶
1(h)(1)(D)	102(b)(1)	0% and 15% capital gain rates are made permanent; 20% rate is added for high-income taxpayers after 2012	Tax years beginning after Dec. 31, 2012	201	None
1(h)(1)(D)(i)	102(a)	Qualified dividends are taxed at 0%, 15%, and 20% rates after 2012	Tax years beginning after Dec. 31, 2012	202	None
1(h)(2)	102(a)	Election to include qualified dividends in investment income for purposes of investment interest deduction is made permanent	Tax years beginning after Dec. 31, 2012	208	None
1(h)(3)(B)	102(a)	Qualified dividends are taxed at 0%, 15%, and 20% rates after 2012	Tax years beginning after Dec. 31, 2012	202	None
1(h)(11)	102(a)	Qualified dividends are taxed at 0%, 15%, and 20% rates after 2012	Tax years beginning after Dec. 31, 2012	202	None
1(h)(11)(D)(i)	102(a)	Election to include qualified dividends in investment income for purposes of investment interest deduction is made permanent	Tax years beginning after Dec. 31, 2012	208	None
1(h)(11)(D)(ii)	102(a)	Long-term capital loss treatment on stock to extent extraordinary dividends were taxed as capital gain is made permanent	Tax years beginning after Dec. 31, 2012	204	None
1(i)(2)	101(b)(1)(A)	25%, 28%, and 33% trust and estate income tax rates are permanently extended, top rate increases to 39.6% after 2012	Tax years beginning after Dec. 31, 2012	104	None
1(i)(2)	101(b)(1)(A)	Individuals' 10%, 25%, 28%, 33%, and 35% tax brackets are made permanent; high-income taxpayers taxed at 39.6% rate after 2012	Tax years beginning after Dec. 31, 2012	101	None

Code §	Act §	Topic	Effective Date	Analysis ¶	Com Rep ¶
1(i)(3)	101(b)(1)(B)	Individuals' 10%, 25%, 28%, 33%, and 35% tax brackets are made permanent; high-income taxpayers taxed at 39.6% rate after 2012	Tax years beginning after Dec. 31, 2012	101	None
21	101(a)(1)	EGTRRA-expanded dependent care credit permanently extended	Tax years beginning after Dec. 31, 2012	603	None
23	101(a)(1)	Expanded adoption credit rules (but not refundability) made permanent	Tax years beginning after Dec. 31, 2012	604	None
23(b)(4)	104(c)(2)	Nonrefundable personal credits can offset AMT and regular tax for all tax years beginning after Dec. 31, 2011	Tax years beginning after Dec. 31, 2011.	403	None
24(a)	101(a)(1)	$1,000 per child amount and expanded refundability of child tax credit are permanently extended	Tax years beginning after Dec. 31, 2012.	601	None
24(b)(3)	101(a)(1)	Child tax credit can permanently offset AMT	Tax years beginning after Dec. 31, 2012	404	None
24(b)(3)	104(c)(2)	Nonrefundable personal credits can offset AMT and regular tax for all tax years beginning after Dec. 31, 2011	Tax years beginning after Dec. 31, 2011.	403	None
24(d)(1)	101(a)(1)	$1,000 per child amount and expanded refundability of child tax credit are permanently extended	Tax years beginning after Dec. 31, 2012.	601	None
24(d)(4)	103(b)(2)	Increase in refundable portion of child tax credit is extended through 2017	Tax years beginning after Dec 31, 2012 and before Jan. 1, 2018	602	None
25(e)(1)(C)	104(c)(2)	Nonrefundable personal credits can offset AMT and regular tax for all tax years beginning after Dec. 31, 2011	Tax years beginning after Dec. 31, 2011.	403	None

Code §	Act §	Topic	Effective Date	Analysis ¶	Com Rep ¶
25A(e)	101(a)(1)	Increased $2,000 contribution limit and other EGTRRA enhancements to Coverdell ESAs are made permanent	For tax years beginning after Dec. 31, 2012	704	None
25A(i)	103(a)(1)	American Opportunity Tax Credit (AOTC) for higher education expenses is extended five years, through 2017	Tax years beginning after Dec. 31, 2012 and before Jan. 1, 2018	701	None
25A(i)(5)	104(c)(2)	Nonrefundable personal credits can offset AMT and regular tax for all tax years beginning after Dec. 31, 2011	Tax years beginning after Dec. 31, 2011.	403	None
25B(g)	104(c)(2)	Nonrefundable personal credits can offset AMT and regular tax for all tax years beginning after Dec. 31, 2011	Tax years beginning after Dec. 31, 2011.	403	None
25C(g)(2)	401(a)	Nonbusiness energy property credit is retroactively reinstated and extended through 2013	Property placed in service after Dec. 31, 2011 and before Jan. 1, 2014	1004	None
25D(c)	104(c)(2)	Nonrefundable personal credits can offset AMT and regular tax for all tax years beginning after Dec. 31, 2011	Tax years beginning after Dec. 31, 2011.	403	None
26(a)	104(c)(1)	Nonrefundable personal credits can offset AMT and regular tax for all tax years beginning after Dec. 31, 2011	Tax years beginning after Dec. 31, 2011.	403	None
26(a)(1)	101(a)(1)	Child tax credit can permanently offset AMT	Tax years beginning after Dec. 31, 2012	404	None
26(a)(1)	104(c)(2)	Nonrefundable personal credits can offset AMT and regular tax for all tax years beginning after Dec. 31, 2011	Tax years beginning after Dec. 31, 2011.	403	None

Code §	Act §	Topic	Effective Date	Analy-sis ¶	Com Rep ¶
30(c)(2)	104(c)(2)	Nonrefundable personal credits can offset AMT and regular tax for all tax years beginning after Dec. 31, 2011	Tax years beginning after Dec. 31, 2011.	403	None
30A	330	Possessions tax credit for American Samoa extended through 2013 with an American Samoa production requirement	Tax years beginning after Dec. 31, 2011 and before Jan. 1, 2014	1206	None
30B(g)(2)	104(c)(2)	Nonrefundable personal credits can offset AMT and regular tax for all tax years beginning after Dec. 31, 2011	Tax years beginning after Dec. 31, 2011.	403	None
30C(g)(2)	402(a)	Non-hydrogen QAFV refueling property credit is retroactively restored and extended to property placed in service before Jan. 1, 2014	Property placed in service after Dec. 31, 2011 and before Jan. 1, 2014	1008	None
30D(c)(2)	104(c)(2)	Nonrefundable personal credits can offset AMT and regular tax for all tax years beginning after Dec. 31, 2011	Tax years beginning after Dec. 31, 2011.	403	None
30D(g)	403(a)	Credit for 2- or 3-wheeled plug-in electric vehicles is retroactively extended two years to apply to vehicles acquired before Jan. 1, 2014	Vehicles acquired after Dec. 31, 2011 and before Jan. 1, 2014	1006	None
30D(f)(2)	403(b)(1)	Credit for 2- or 3-wheeled plug-in electric vehicles is retroactively extended two years to apply to vehicles acquired before Jan. 1, 2014	Vehicles acquired after Dec. 31, 2011 and before Jan. 1, 2014	1006	None
30D(f)(7)	403(b)(2)	Credit for 2- or 3-wheeled plug-in electric vehicles is retroactively extended two years to apply to vehicles acquired before Jan. 1, 2014	Vehicles acquired after Dec. 31, 2011 and before Jan. 1, 2014	1006	None

Code §	Act §	Topic	Effective Date	Analy- sis ¶	Com Rep ¶
32(a)(2)(B)	101(a)(1)	EIC simplification made permanent	Tax years beginning after Dec. 31, 2012	605	None
32(b)(2)	101(a)(1)	$5,000 increase in EIC phaseout threshold for joint filers is extended through 2017	Tax years beginning after Dec. 31, 2012	606	None
32(b)(3)	103(c)(2)	$5,000 increase in EIC phaseout threshold for joint filers is extended through 2017	Tax years beginning after Dec. 31, 2012	606	None
32(b)(3)	103(c)(2)	Increased EIC for families with three or more qualifying children is extended for five years	Tax years beginning after Dec. 31, 2012 and before 2018	607	None
32(c)	101(a)(1)	EIC simplification made permanent	Tax years beginning after Dec. 31, 2012	605	None
32(c)(1)(C)	101(a)(1)	EIC simplification made permanent	Tax years beginning after Dec. 31, 2012	605	None
32(c)(2)(A)(i)	101(a)(1)	EIC simplification made permanent	Tax years beginning after Dec. 31, 2012	605	None
32(h)	101(a)(1)	EIC simplification made permanent	Tax years beginning after Dec. 31, 2012	605	None
32(j)	101(a)(1)	$5,000 increase in EIC phaseout threshold for joint filers is extended through 2017	Tax years beginning after Dec. 31, 2012	606	None
32(n)	101(a)(1)	$1,000 per child amount and expanded refundability of child tax credit are permanently extended	Tax years beginning after Dec. 31, 2012.	601	None
35(a)	241(a)≈	HCTC and percentage limit on advance HCTC payments are retroactively increased to 72.5% (from 65%) for post-Feb. 2011 coverage months	Coverage months beginning after Feb. 12, 2011	1606	None

Code §	Act §	Topic	Effective Date	Analy-sis ¶	Com Rep ¶
35(a)	241(b)(1)(B)≈	Health coverage tax credit (HCTC) for health insurance costs of trade-displaced workers and PBGC pension recipients won't be allowed after 2013	Coverage months beginning after Feb. 12, 2011	1604	None
35(c)(2)(B)	241(b)(3)(A)≈	HCTC eligibility for individuals not enrolled in training programs was extended retroactively to coverage periods beginning after Feb. 12, 2011	Coverage months beginning after Feb. 12, 2011	1608	None
35(e)(1)(K)	241(b)(3)(B)≈	Allowance of HCTC for VEBA coverage was extended	Coverage months beginning after Feb. 12, 2011	1607	None
35(g)(9)	241(b)(3)(C)≈	Continued HCTC eligibility of family members after certain events was extended retroactively to coverage months beginning after Feb. 12, 2011	Coverage months beginning after Feb. 12, 2011	1609	None
36B(c)(2)	1858(b)(1)+	Employers won't have to provide free choice vouchers to employees, as post-2013 rules are repealed	For vouchers that would have been provided after 2013	1603	None
36B(d)(2)(B)(iii)	401(a)~	Modified AGI for determining eligibility for and amount of post-2013 premium tax credit will include nontaxable social security income	Nov. 21, 2011	1601	None
36B(f)(2)(B)(i)	4(a)•	Simplified payback caps on excess advance premium assistance credits apply to taxpayers below 400% of poverty line	Tax years ending after Dec. 31, 2013	1602	5903
36C	101(a)(1)	Expanded adoption credit rules (but not refundability) made permanent	Tax years beginning after Dec. 31, 2012	604	None

Code §	Act §	Topic	Effective Date	Analysis ¶	Com Rep ¶
38(b)(15)	101(a)(1)	Employer-provided child care credit is extended permanently	Tax years beginning after 2012	903	None
40(b)(6)	404(b)(3)(A)(ii)	Algae is treated as a qualified feedstock for purposes of the cellulose biofuel producer credit	Fuels sold or used after Jan. 2, 2013.	1016	None
40(b)(6)(E)(i)(I)	404(b)(1)	Algae is treated as a qualified feedstock for purposes of the cellulose biofuel producer credit	Fuels sold or used after Jan. 2, 2013.	1016	None
40(b)(6)(F)	404(b)(2)	Algae is treated as a qualified feedstock for purposes of the cellulose biofuel producer credit	Fuels sold or used after Jan. 2, 2013.	1016	None
40(b)(6)(G)	404(b)(2)	Algae is treated as a qualified feedstock for purposes of the cellulose biofuel producer credit	Fuels sold or used after Jan. 2, 2013.	1016	None
40(b)(6)(H)	404(a)(1)	Cellulosic biofuel producer credit is retroactively restored and extended through Dec. 31, 2013	Fuel produced after Dec. 31, 2008 and before Jan. 1, 2014	1015	None
40A(g)	405(a)	Income and excise tax credits/refunds for biodiesel and renewable diesel are extended retroactively through 2013	Fuel sold or used after Dec. 31, 2011 and before Jan. 1, 2014	1009	None
41(f)(1)(A)	301(c)(1)	Research credit is retroactively extended, with modifications, to apply to amounts paid or incurred before Jan. 1, 2014	Amounts paid or incurred after Dec. 31, 2011 (for credit modifications, tax years beginning after Dec. 31, 2011)	901	None
41(f)(1)(B)	301(c)(2)	Research credit is retroactively extended, with modifications, to apply to amounts paid or incurred before Jan. 1, 2014	Amounts paid or incurred after Dec. 31, 2011 (for credit modifications, tax years beginning after Dec. 31, 2011)	901	None

Code §	Act §	Topic	Effective Date	Analy- sis ¶	Com Rep ¶
41(f)(3)(A)	301(b)(1)	Research credit is retroactively extended, with modifications, to apply to amounts paid or incurred before Jan. 1, 2014	Amounts paid or incurred after Dec. 31, 2011 (for credit modifications, tax years beginning after Dec. 31, 2011)	901	None
41(f)(3)(B)	301(b)(2)	Research credit is retroactively extended, with modifications, to apply to amounts paid or incurred before Jan. 1, 2014	Amounts paid or incurred after Dec. 31, 2011 (for credit modifications, tax years beginning after Dec. 31, 2011)	901	None
41(h)(1)(B)	301(a)(1)	Research credit is retroactively extended, with modifications, to apply to amounts paid or incurred before Jan. 1, 2014	Amounts paid or incurred after Dec. 31, 2011 (for credit modifications, tax years beginning after Dec. 31, 2011)	901	None
42(b)(2)	302(a)	Temporary minimum low-income housing credit rate of 9% applies to new non-federally subsidized buildings with respect to housing credit dollar amount allocations made before Jan. 1, 2014	Jan. 2, 2013	906	None
42(g)(4)	303(a)	The military housing allowance exclusion for tax-exempt bond financing and the low-income housing credit is extended until 2014	Income determinations made after July 30, 2008 and before 2014	1408	None
45(c)(6)	407(a)(2)	Definition of municipal solid waste does not include paper that is commonly recycled and segregated from other solid waste	Electricity produced and sold after Jan. 2, 2013, in tax years ending after Jan. 2, 2013	1011	None

Code §	Act §	Topic	Effective Date	Analysis ¶	Com Rep ¶
45(d)(1)	407(a)(1)	Credits with respect to facilities producing energy from certain renewable resources are extended and modified	Jan. 2, 2013	1005	None
45(d)(1)	407(a)(3)(A)(i)	Credits with respect to facilities producing energy from certain renewable resources are extended and modified	Jan. 2, 2013	1005	None
45(d)(2)(A)	407(a)(3)(B)	Credits with respect to facilities producing energy from certain renewable resources are extended and modified	Jan. 2, 2013	1005	None
45(d)(2)(A)(i)	407(a)(3)(A)(ii)	Credits with respect to facilities producing energy from certain renewable resources are extended and modified	Jan. 2, 2013	1005	None
45(d)(3)(A)(i)(I)	407(a)(3)(A)(iii)	Credits with respect to facilities producing energy from certain renewable resources are extended and modified	Jan. 2, 2013	1005	None
45(d)(3)(A)(ii)	407(a)(3)(C)	Credits with respect to facilities producing energy from certain renewable resources are extended and modified	Jan. 2, 2013	1005	None
45(d)(4)	407(a)(3)(D)(i)	Credits with respect to facilities producing energy from certain renewable resources are extended and modified	Jan. 2, 2013	1005	None
45(d)(6)	407(a)(3)(A)(iv)	Credits with respect to facilities producing energy from certain renewable resources are extended and modified	Jan. 2, 2013	1005	None

Code §	Act §	Topic	Effective Date	Analy-sis ¶	Com Rep ¶
45(d)(7)	407(a)(3)(A)(v)	Credits with respect to facilities producing energy from certain renewable resources are extended and modified	Jan. 2, 2013	1005	None
45(d)(9)(C)	407(a)(3)(E)(iv)	Credits with respect to facilities producing energy from certain renewable resources are extended and modified	Jan. 2, 2013	1005	None
45(d)(9)(B)	407(a)(3)(A)(vi)	Credits with respect to facilities producing energy from certain renewable resources are extended and modified	Jan. 2, 2013	1005	None
45(d)(11)(B)	407(a)(3)(A)(vii)	Credits with respect to facilities producing energy from certain renewable resources are extended and modified	Jan. 2, 2013	1005	None
45(e)(10)	406(a)	Period of credit for Indian coal produced by taxpayer at Indian coal facilities extended to eight-year period beginning Jan. 1, 2006	Coal produced after Dec. 31, 2012	1007	None
45A(f)	304(a)	Indian employment credit for wages paid to qualified Native Americans is extended through Dec. 31, 2013	Tax years starting after Dec. 31, 2011 and before Jan. 1, 2014	907	None
45C(b)(1)(D)	301(a)(2)	Research credit is retroactively extended, with modifications, to apply to amounts paid or incurred before Jan. 1, 2014	Amounts paid or incurred after Dec. 31, 2011 (for credit modifications, tax years beginning after Dec. 31, 2011)	901	None
45D(f)(1)(G)	305(a)	New markets tax credit is extended through calendar year 2013	Calendar years starting after 2011 and before 2014	1401	None
45D(f)(3)	305(b)	New markets tax credit is extended through calendar year 2013	Calendar years starting after 2011 and before 2014	1401	None

Code §	Act §	Topic	Effective Date	Analy-sis ¶	Com Rep ¶
45F	101(a)(1)	Employer-provided child care credit is extended permanently	Tax years beginning after 2012	903	None
45G(f)	306(a)	Railroad track maintenance credit for qualified expenditures is extended to include qualified expenditures paid or incurred during tax years beginning in 2012 and 2013	Expenditures paid or incurred during tax years beginning after Dec. 31, 2011 and before Jan. 1 2014	908	None
45L(c)(1)(A)(i)	408(b)	Construction standards for the qualified new energy efficient home credit are modified	Homes acquired after Dec. 31, 2011	1003	None
45L(g)	408(a)	New energy efficient home credit for eligible contractors is retroactively restored and extended through Dec. 31, 2013	Homes acquired after Dec. 31, 2011 and before Jan. 1, 2014	1002	None
45M(b)(1)(D)	409(a)	Energy efficient appliance credit is extended for certain appliances manufactured in 2012 or 2013	Appliances produced after Dec. 31, 2011 and before Jan. 1, 2014	1001	None
45M(b)(1)(E)	409(a)	Energy efficient appliance credit is extended for certain appliances manufactured in 2012 or 2013	Appliances produced after Dec. 31, 2011 and before Jan. 1, 2014	1001	None
45M(b)(2)(F)	409(a)	Energy efficient appliance credit is extended for certain appliances manufactured in 2012 or 2013	Appliances produced after Dec. 31, 2011 and before Jan. 1, 2014	1001	None
45M(b)(3)(E)	409(a)	Energy efficient appliance credit is extended for certain appliances manufactured in 2012 or 2013	Appliances produced after Dec. 31, 2011 and before Jan. 1, 2014	1001	None
45M(b)(3)(F)	409(a)	Energy efficient appliance credit is extended for certain appliances manufactured in 2012 or 2013	Appliances produced after Dec. 31, 2011 and before Jan. 1, 2014	1001	None

Code §	Act §	Topic	Effective Date	Analy-sis ¶	Com Rep ¶
45N(e)	307(a)	Mine rescue team training credit is retroactively restored and extended to tax years beginning before Jan. 1, 2014	Tax years beginning after Dec. 31, 2011 and before Jan. 1, 2014	905	None
45P(f)	308(a)	Differential wage payment credit is retroactively restored and extended to apply to payments made before Jan. 1, 2014	Payments made after Dec. 31, 2011 and before Jan. 1, 2014	904	None
48(a)(5)(D)	407(c)(1)(C)	Definition of qualified property for purposes of the election to take a 30% energy credit instead of the electricity production credit is retroactively clarified	Facilities placed in service after Dec. 31, 2008	1012	None
51	261(f)~	Work opportunity credit as applied to qualified veterans was extended through 2012 and modified	Individuals who begin work for the employer after Nov. 21, 2011 and before Jan. 1, 2013	1910	None
51(b)(3)	261(a)~	Work opportunity credit as applied to qualified veterans was extended through 2012 and modified	Individuals who begin work for the employer after Nov. 21, 2011 and before Jan. 1, 2013	1910	None
51(c)(4)(B)	309(a)	Work opportunity credit is retroactively extended to apply to all individuals who begin work for an employer through Dec. 31, 2013	Individuals who begin work for the employer after Dec. 31, 2011 and before Jan. 1, 2014	902	None
51(c)(4)(B)	261(d)~	Work opportunity credit as applied to qualified veterans was extended through 2012 and modified	Individuals who begin work for the employer after Nov. 21, 2011 and before Jan. 1, 2013	1910	None
51(d)(3)(A)	261(b)(3)~	Work opportunity credit as applied to qualified veterans was extended through 2012 and modified	Individuals who begin work for the employer after Nov. 21, 2011 and before Jan. 1, 2013	1910	None

Code §	Act §	Topic	Effective Date	Analy-sis ¶	Com Rep ¶
51(d)(13)(D)	261(c) ~	Work opportunity credit as applied to qualified veterans was extended through 2012 and modified	Individuals who begin work for the employer after Nov. 21, 2011 and before Jan. 1, 2013	1910	None
52(c)	261(e)(1) ~	Work opportunity credit as applied to qualified veterans was extended through 2012 and modified	Individuals who begin work for the employer after Nov. 21, 2011 and before Jan. 1, 2013	1910	None
54E(c)(1)	310(a)	QZAB program is extended through 2013	Bonds issued after Dec. 31, 2011 and before Jan. 1, 2014	1402	None
55(b)(1)(A)(iii)	104(b)(2)(A)	AMT exemption amounts are increased to $50,600 for unmarrieds and $78,750 for joint filers for 2012 and are indexed for inflation after 2012	Tax years beginning after Dec. 31, 2011	401	None
55(b)(3)	102(a)	AMT rates on capital gain and qualified dividends are 0%, 15%, and 20% after 2012	Tax years beginning after Dec. 31, 2012	402	None
55(b)(3)(B)	102(c)(2)	AMT rates on capital gain and qualified dividends are 0%, 15%, and 20% after 2012	Tax years beginning after Dec. 31, 2012	402	None
55(b)(3)(C)	102(b)(2)	AMT rates on capital gain and qualified dividends are 0%, 15%, and 20% after 2012	Tax years beginning after Dec. 31, 2012	402	None
55(b)(3)(D)	102(b)(2)	AMT rates on capital gain and qualified dividends are 0%, 15%, and 20% after 2012	Tax years beginning after Dec. 31, 2012	402	None
55(d)(1)(A)	104(a)(1)(A)	AMT exemption amounts are increased to $50,600 for unmarrieds and $78,750 for joint filers for 2012 and are indexed for inflation after 2012	Tax years beginning after Dec. 31, 2011	401	None

Code §	Act §	Topic	Effective Date	Analysis ¶	Com Rep ¶
55(d)(1)(B)	104(a)(1)(B)	AMT exemption amounts are increased to $50,600 for unmarrieds and $78,750 for joint filers for 2012 and are indexed for inflation after 2012	Tax years beginning after Dec. 31, 2011	401	None
55(d)(3)	104(b)(2)(B)	AMT exemption amounts are increased to $50,600 for unmarrieds and $78,750 for joint filers for 2012 and are indexed for inflation after 2012	Tax years beginning after Dec. 31, 2011	401	None
55(d)(4)	104(b)(1)	AMT exemption amounts are increased to $50,600 for unmarrieds and $78,750 for joint filers for 2012 and are indexed for inflation after 2012	Tax years beginning after Dec. 31, 2011	401	None
57(a)(7)	102(a)	7% AMT preference for excluded gain on qualified small business stock is permanently extended	Tax years beginning after Dec. 31, 2012	405	None
62(a)(2)(D)	201(a)	Up-to-$250 above-the-line deduction for teachers' out-of-pocket classroom-related expenses is retroactively extended through 2013	Tax years beginning after Dec. 31, 2011 and before Jan. 1, 2014	308	None
63(c)(2)	101(a)(1)	Standard deduction marriage penalty relief is made permanent	Tax years beginning after Dec. 31, 2012	304	None
68(b)	101(b)(2)(A)(i)	Overall limitation on itemized deductions is restored, applies when AGI exceeds $300,000 (joint returns) and $250,000 (single filers)	Tax years beginning after Dec. 31, 2012	302	None
68(b)	101(b)(2)(A)(ii)	Overall limitation on itemized deductions is restored, applies when AGI exceeds $300,000 (joint returns) and $250,000 (single filers)	Tax years beginning after Dec. 31, 2012	302	None

Code §	Act §	Topic	Effective Date	Analy-sis ¶	Com Rep ¶
68(g)	101(b)(2)(A)(i)	Overall limitation on itemized deductions is restored, applies when AGI exceeds $300,000 (joint returns) and $250,000 (single filers)	Tax years beginning after Dec. 31, 2012	302	None
72(t)(2)	100121(c)*	Additional 10% tax on early withdrawals from qualified retirement plans will not apply to federal phased retirement program payments	July 6, 2012	1704	None
79(f)	40242(d)*	Excess pension plan assets may be used to fund retiree group-term life insurance	Transfers made after July 6, 2012	1702	5405
108(a)(1)(E)	202(a)	Exclusion for debt discharge income from home mortgage forgiveness is extended for one year until the end of 2013	Discharges of indebtedness after Dec. 31, 2012, and before Jan. 1, 2014	306	None
117(c)(2)	101(a)(1)	Income exclusion for awards under the National Health Service Corps and Armed Forces Health Professions programs made permanent	For taxable years beginning after Dec. 31, 2012	706	None
127	101(a)(1)	Exclusion for employer-provided educational assistance, and restoration of the exclusion for graduate-level courses, made permanent	Tax years beginning after 2012	705	None
132(f)(2)	203(a)	Parity extended through 2013 for employer-provided mass transit and parking benefits	For months in 2012 and 2013	307	None
137	101(a)(1)	Adoption assistance exclusion is made permanent	Tax years beginning after 2012	309	None
139D	1858(b)(2)(A)+	Employers won't have to provide free choice vouchers to employees, as post-2013 rules are repealed	For vouchers that would have been provided after 2013	1603	None

Code §	Act §	Topic	Effective Date	Analy-sis ¶	Com Rep ¶
142(a)(13)	101(a)	Tax-exempt status of public educational facility bonds is made permanent	Tax years beginning after Dec. 31, 2012	1403	None
142(d)(2)(B)(ii)	303(a)	The military housing allowance exclusion for tax-exempt bond financing and the low-income housing credit is extended until 2014	Income determinations made after July 30, 2008 and before 2014	1408	None
142(k)	101(a)	Tax-exempt status of public educational facility bonds is made permanent	Tax years beginning after Dec. 31, 2012	1403	None
147(e)	1105(a) †	Tax-exempt qualified bonds can be used to finance fixed-wing emergency medical aircraft	Bonds issued after Feb. 14, 2012	1913	5605
148(f)(4)(D)(vii)	101(a)	Additional increase in arbitrage rebate exception for government bonds used to finance education facilities made permanent	Tax, plan or limitation years beginning after Dec. 31, 2012	1404	None
151(d)(3)	101(b)(2)(B)(i)	Personal exemption phaseout (PEP) applies when AGI exceeds $300,000 (joint returns) and $250,000 (single filers) for tax years beginning after Dec. 31, 2012	Tax years beginning after Dec. 31, 2012	301	None
151(d)(4)	101(b)(2)(B)(ii)	Personal exemption phaseout (PEP) applies when AGI exceeds $300,000 (joint returns) and $250,000 (single filers) for tax years beginning after Dec. 31, 2012	Tax years beginning after Dec. 31, 2012	301	None
162(a)	1858(b)(3) +	Employers won't have to provide free choice vouchers to employees, as post-2013 rules are repealed	For vouchers that would have been provided after 2013	1603	None

Code §	Act §	Topic	Effective Date	Analy-sis ¶	Com Rep ¶
163(d)(4)(B)	102(a)	Election to include qualified dividends in investment income for purposes of investment interest deduction is made permanent	Tax years beginning after Dec. 31, 2012	208	None
163(h)(3)(E)(iv)	204(a)	Interest deduction for mortgage insurance premiums is extended to amounts paid or accrued before 2014	Amounts paid or accrued after Dec. 31, 2011 and before Jan. 1, 2014	305	None
164(b)(5)(I)	205(a)	Election to claim itemized deduction for state/local sales taxes is extended through 2013	Tax years beginning after Dec. 31, 2011 and before Jan. 1, 2014	303	None
164(f)	101(b)‡	Reduced 10.4% OASDI rate applied for 2012 to self-employment income up to $110,100 ceiling	Remuneration received, and tax years beginning, after, Dec. 31, 2011	1901	5501
164(f)	1001(b)**	Reduced 10.4% OASDI rate applied for 2012 to self-employment income up to $110,100 ceiling	Remuneration received, and tax years beginning, after, Dec. 31, 2011	1901	5501
168(e)(3)(E)(iv)	311(a)	15-year MACRS depreciation for certain building improvements and restaurants is extended to apply to property placed in service before Jan. 1, 2014	Property placed in service after Dec. 31, 2011 and before Jan. 1, 2014	807	None
168(e)(3)(E)(v)	311(a)	15-year MACRS depreciation for certain building improvements and restaurants is extended to apply to property placed in service before Jan. 1, 2014	Property placed in service after Dec. 31, 2011 and before Jan. 1, 2014	807	None
168(e)(3)(E)(ix)	311(a)	15-year MACRS depreciation for certain building improvements and restaurants is extended to apply to property placed in service before Jan. 1, 2014	Property placed in service after Dec. 31, 2011 and before Jan. 1, 2014	807	None

Code §	Act §	Topic	Effective Date	Analy-sis ¶	Com Rep ¶
168(i)(9)(A)(ii)	331(d)	MACRS elections must be taken into account under normalization accounting for public utility property	Property placed in service after Dec. 31, 2012	812	None
168(i)(15)(D)	312(a)	7-year recovery period for motorsports entertainment complexes extended to facilities placed in service through 2013	Property placed in service after Dec. 31, 2011 and before Jan. 1, 2014	809	None
168(j)(8)	313(a)	Depreciation tax breaks for Indian reservation property are extended to property placed in service through 2013	Property placed in service after Dec. 31, 2011 and before Jan. 1, 2014	810	None
168(k)(2)(A)(iii)	331(a)(2)	Bonus depreciation and AMT depreciation relief are extended for qualified property placed in service through, generally, Dec. 31, 2013	Property placed in service after Dec. 31, 2012 and before Jan. 1, 2014	804	None
168(k)(2)(A)(iv)	331(a)	Additional round of trading bonus and accelerated depreciation for deferred credits is provided	Property placed in service after Dec. 31, 2012 and before Jan. 1, 2014	805	None
168(k)(2)(A)(iv)	331(a)	Increase in first-year depreciation cap for cars that are "qualified property" is extended through Dec. 31, 2013	Property placed in service after Dec. 31, 2012 and before Jan. 1, 2014	802	None
168(k)(2)(A)(iv)	331(a)(1)	Bonus depreciation and AMT depreciation relief are extended for certain aircraft and long-production-period property placed in service through Dec. 31, 2014	Property placed in service after Dec. 31, 2012 and before Jan. 1, 2015	804	None
168(k)(2)(A)(iv)	331(a)(2)	Bonus depreciation and AMT depreciation relief are extended for qualified property placed in service through, generally, Dec. 31, 2013	Property placed in service after Dec. 31, 2012 and before Jan. 1, 2014	804	None

Code §	Act §	Topic	Effective Date	Analy-sis ¶	Com Rep ¶
168(k)(2)(B)(ii)	331(a)(2)	Bonus depreciation and AMT depreciation relief are extended for qualified property placed in service through, generally, Dec. 31, 2013	Property placed in service after Dec. 31, 2012 and before Jan. 1, 2014	804	None
168(k)(2)(E)(i)	331(a)(2)	Bonus depreciation and AMT depreciation relief are extended for qualified property placed in service through, generally, Dec. 31, 2013	Property placed in service after Dec. 31, 2012 and before Jan. 1, 2014	804	None
168(k)(4)(D)(iii)(II)	331(c)(1)	Additional round of trading bonus and accelerated depreciation for deferred credits is provided	Property placed in service after Dec. 31, 2012 and before Jan. 1, 2014	805	None
168(k)(4)(J)	331(c)(2)	Additional round of trading bonus and accelerated depreciation for deferred credits is provided	Property placed in service after Dec. 31, 2012 and before Jan. 1, 2014	805	None
168(l)	410(b)(2)(A)	Bonus depreciation and AMT depreciation relief for certain biofuel plant property is extended one year through Dec. 31, 2013 and expanded	Property placed in service after Dec. 31, 2012 (after Jan. 2, 2013 for qualified second generation biofuel plant property) and before Jan. 1, 2014	1013	None
168(l)(2)(A)	410(b)(1)	Bonus depreciation and AMT depreciation relief for certain biofuel plant property is extended one year through Dec. 31, 2013 and expanded	Property placed in service after Dec. 31, 2012 (after Jan. 2, 2013 for qualified second generation biofuel plant property) and before Jan. 1, 2014	1013	None

Code §	Act §	Topic	Effective Date	Analy-sis ¶	Com Rep ¶
168(l)(2)(D)	410(a)(1)	Bonus depreciation and AMT depreciation relief for certain biofuel plant property is extended one year through Dec. 31, 2013 and expanded	Property placed in service after Dec. 31, 2012 (after Jan. 2, 2013 for qualified second generation biofuel plant property) and before Jan. 1, 2014	1013	None
170(b)(1)(E)(vi)	206(a)	Special rules are retroactively extended for qualified conservation easements contributed by individuals (including ranchers and farmers) before 2014	Contributions made in tax years beginning after Dec. 31, 2011 and before Jan. 1, 2014	1102	None
170(b)(2)(B)(iii)	206(b)	For qualified conservation easements contributed by corporate farmers or ranchers in tax years beginning before 2014, special rules are retroactively extended	Contributions made in tax years beginning after Dec. 31, 2011 and before Jan. 1, 2014	1103	None
170(e)(3)(C)(iv)	314(a)	Above-basis deduction rules are retroactively extended for charitable contributions of food inventory made through 2013	Contributions made after Dec. 31, 2011 and before Jan. 1, 2014	1104	None
179(b)(1)(B)	315(a)(1)(A)	Increased 2010 and 2011 Code 179 dollar limitation and phase-out threshold, and 2010 and 2011 treatment of qualified real property as section 179 property, are extended to 2012 and 2013	Tax years beginning after Dec. 31, 2011 and before Jan. 1, 2014	801	None
179(b)(1)(C)	315(a)(1)(B)	Increased 2010 and 2011 Code 179 dollar limitation and phase-out threshold, and 2010 and 2011 treatment of qualified real property as section 179 property, are extended to 2012 and 2013	Tax years beginning after Dec. 31, 2011 and before Jan. 1, 2014	801	None

Code §	Act §	Topic	Effective Date	Analysis ¶	Com Rep ¶
179(b)(1)(D)	315(a)(1)	Increased 2010 and 2011 Code 179 dollar limitation and phase-out threshold, and 2010 and 2011 treatment of qualified real property as section 179 property, are extended to 2012 and 2013	Tax years beginning after Dec. 31, 2011 and before Jan. 1, 2014	801	None
179(b)(2)(B)	315(a)(2)(A)	Increased 2010 and 2011 Code 179 dollar limitation and phase-out threshold, and 2010 and 2011 treatment of qualified real property as section 179 property, are extended to 2012 and 2013	Tax years beginning after Dec. 31, 2011 and before Jan. 1, 2014	801	None
179(b)(2)(C)	315(a)(2)(B)	Increased 2010 and 2011 Code 179 dollar limitation and phase-out threshold, and 2010 and 2011 treatment of qualified real property as section 179 property, are extended to 2012 and 2013	Tax years beginning after Dec. 31, 2011 and before Jan. 1, 2014	801	None
179(b)(2)(D)	315(a)(2)	Increased 2010 and 2011 Code 179 dollar limitation and phase-out threshold, and 2010 and 2011 treatment of qualified real property as section 179 property, are extended to 2012 and 2013	Tax years beginning after Dec. 31, 2011 and before Jan. 1, 2014	801	None
179(b)(6)	315(a)(3)	Increased 2010 and 2011 Code 179 dollar limitation and phase-out threshold, and 2010 and 2011 treatment of qualified real property as section 179 property, are extended to 2012 and 2013	Tax years beginning after Dec. 31, 2011 and before Jan. 1, 2014	801	None

Code §	Act §	Topic	Effective Date	Analy-sis ¶	Com Rep ¶
179(c)(2)	315(c)	Revocation of Code Sec. 179 election without IRS consent, and eligibility of software for election, are extended to include tax years beginning in 2013	Tax years beginning after Dec. 31, 2011 and before Jan. 1, 2014	803	None
179(d)(1)(A)(ii)	315(b)	Revocation of Code Sec. 179 election without IRS consent, and eligibility of software for election, are extended to include tax years beginning in 2013	Tax years beginning after Dec. 31, 2011 and before Jan. 1, 2014	803	None
179(f)(1)	315(d)(1)	Increased 2010 and 2011 Code 179 dollar limitation and phase-out threshold, and 2010 and 2011 treatment of qualified real property as section 179 property, are extended to 2012 and 2013	Tax years beginning after Dec. 31, 2011 and before Jan. 1, 2014	801	None
179(f)(4)	315(d)(2)(A)	Increased 2010 and 2011 Code 179 dollar limitation and phase-out threshold, and 2010 and 2011 treatment of qualified real property as section 179 property, are extended to 2012 and 2013	Tax years beginning after Dec. 31, 2011 and before Jan. 1, 2014	801	None
179(f)(4)(D)	315(d)(2)(B)(ii)	Increased 2010 and 2011 Code 179 dollar limitation and phase-out threshold, and 2010 and 2011 treatment of qualified real property as section 179 property, are extended to 2012 and 2013	Tax years beginning after Dec. 31, 2011 and before Jan. 1, 2014	801	None
179E(g)	316(a)	Election to expense cost of qualified advanced mine safety equipment property is extended two years to property placed in service through 2013	Property placed in service after Dec. 31, 2011 and before Jan. 1, 2014	811	None

Code §	Act §	Topic	Effective Date	Analysis ¶	Com Rep ¶
181(f)	317(a)	Expensing rules for qualified film and television productions are retroactively extended for two years to productions beginning before Jan. 1, 2014	Productions beginning after Dec. 31, 2011 and before Jan. 1, 2014	808	None
199(d)(8)(C)	318(a)	Allowance of Code Sec. 199 deduction for Puerto Rico activities is retroactively extended two years to taxpayer's first eight tax years beginning after 2005	Tax years beginning after Dec. 31, 2011 and before Jan. 1, 2014	909	None
221	101(a)(1)	EGTRRA changes to student loan deduction rules are made permanent	Tax years beginning after Dec. 31, 2012	703	None
221(b)(2)(B)	101(a)(1)	EGTRRA changes to student loan deduction rules are made permanent	Tax years beginning after Dec. 31, 2012	703	None
221(f)	101(a)(1)	EGTRRA changes to student loan deduction rules are made permanent	Tax years beginning after Dec. 31, 2012	703	None
222(e)	207(a)	Qualified tuition deduction is retroactively extended through 2013	Tax years beginning after Dec. 31, 2011 and before Jan. 1, 2014	702	None
249(a)	1108(a)†	Repurchase bond premium deduction limitation extended to debt convertible to controlled group stock	For repurchases after Feb. 14, 2012	1914	5608
249(b)	1108(b)†	Repurchase bond premium deduction limitation extended to debt convertible to controlled group stock	For repurchases after Feb. 14, 2012	1914	5608
306(a)(1)(D)	102(a)	Qualified dividend income treatment for ordinary income on disposition of Code Sec. 306 stock made permanent	Tax years beginning after Dec. 31, 2012	212	None
341	102(a)	Repeal of collapsible corporation provision is made permanent	Tax years beginning after Dec. 31, 2012.	1504	None

Code §	Act §	Topic	Effective Date	Analy-sis ¶	Com Rep ¶
402	1106†	Rollovers to traditional IRAs allowed for amounts received from airlines that filed for bankruptcy after Sept. 11, 2001 and before Jan. 1, 2007	For amounts paid before, on, or after Feb. 14, 2012	1705	5606
402A(c)(4)(E)	902(a)	Distribution restrictions eased for "in-plan Roth rollovers"	Transfers to designated Roth accounts made after Dec. 31, 2012	1301	None
404(o)(6)	40211(a)(2)(A)*	Plans can use interest rate smoothing over a 25-year period to determine liabilities	Plan years beginning after Dec. 31, 2011	1701	5402
408(d)(8)(F)	208(a)	Rule allowing tax-free IRA distributions of up to $100,000 if donated to charity, is retroactively extended through 2013	For IRA distributions made during 2012 and 2013	1101	None
417(e)(3)(C)	40211(a)(2)(C)*	Plans can use interest rate smoothing over a 25-year period to determine liabilities	Plan years beginning after Dec. 31, 2011	1701	5402
417(e)(3)(D)	40211(a)(2)(C)*	Plans can use interest rate smoothing over a 25-year period to determine liabilities	Plan years beginning after Dec. 31, 2011	1701	5402
420(a)	40242(a)*	Excess pension plan assets may be used to fund retiree group-term life insurance	Transfers made after July 6, 2012	1702	5405
420(b)(2)	40242(e)(3)*	Excess pension plan assets may be used to fund retiree group-term life insurance	Transfers made after July 6, 2012	1702	5405
420(b)(4)	40242(g)(2)*	Excess pension plan assets may be used to fund retiree group-term life insurance	Transfers made after July 6, 2012	1702	5405
420(b)(5)	40241(a)*	Rules permitting transfer of excess defined benefit plan assets to retiree health accounts are extended through 2021	July 6, 2012	1703	5405

Code §	Act §	Topic	Effective Date	Analy-sis ¶	Com Rep ¶
420(c)(2)(B)	40242(g)(4)(A)*	Excess pension plan assets may be used to fund retiree group-term life insurance	Transfers made after July 6, 2012	1702	5405
420(c)(3)(A)	40242(c)(1)*	Excess pension plan assets may be used to fund retiree group-term life insurance	Transfers made after July 6, 2012	1702	5405
420(c)(3)(B)(i)(I)	40242(c)(2)(A)(i)*	Excess pension plan assets may be used to fund retiree group-term life insurance	Transfers made after July 6, 2012	1702	5405
420(c)(3)(B)(ii)	40242(c)(2)(A)(ii)*	Excess pension plan assets may be used to fund retiree group-term life insurance	Transfers made after July 6, 2012	1702	5405
420(c)(3)(C)	40242(c)(2)(B)*	Excess pension plan assets may be used to fund retiree group-term life insurance	Transfers made after July 6, 2012	1702	5405
420(d)(1)(A)	40242(e)(2)*	Excess pension plan assets may be used to fund retiree group-term life insurance	Transfers made after July 6, 2012	1702	5405
420(e)(1)(A)	40242(e)(5)(A)*	Excess pension plan assets may be used to fund retiree group-term life insurance	Transfers made after July 6, 2012	1702	5405
420(e)(1)(B)	40242(e)(6)(A)*	Excess pension plan assets may be used to fund retiree group-term life insurance	Transfers made after July 6, 2012	1702	5405
420(e)(1)(C)	40242(b)(3)(B)(i)*	Excess pension plan assets may be used to fund retiree group-term life insurance	Transfers made after July 6, 2012	1702	5405
420(e)(1)(D)	40242(b)(2)*	Excess pension plan assets may be used to fund retiree group-term life insurance	Transfers made after July 6, 2012	1702	5405

Code §	Act §	Topic	Effective Date	Analy-sis ¶	Com Rep ¶
420(e)(4)	40242(b)(1)*	Excess pension plan assets may be used to fund retiree group-term life insurance	Transfers made after July 6, 2012	1702	5405
420(f)(2)(D)(i)(II)	40242(c)(2)(E)*	Excess pension plan assets may be used to fund retiree group-term life insurance	Transfers made after July 6, 2012	1702	5405
420(f)(2)(D)(ii)	40242(c)(2)(F)*	Excess pension plan assets may be used to fund retiree group-term life insurance	Transfers made after July 6, 2012	1702	5405
420(f)(6)(B)	40242(f)*	Excess pension plan assets may be used to fund retiree group-term life insurance	Transfers made after July 6, 2012	1702	5405
420(f)(6)(C)	40242(b)(3)(B)(ii)*	Excess pension plan assets may be used to fund retiree group-term life insurance	Transfers made after July 6, 2012	1702	5405
420(f)(6)(D)	40242(b)(3)(A)*	Excess pension plan assets may be used to fund retiree group-term life insurance	Transfers made after July 6, 2012	1702	5405
420(g)	40211(a)(2)(D)*	Plans can use interest rate smoothing over a 25-year period to determine liabilities	Plan years beginning after Dec. 31, 2011	1701	5402
430(h)(2)(C)(iv)	40211(a)(1)*	Plans can use interest rate smoothing over a 25-year period to determine liabilities	Plan years beginning after Dec. 31, 2011	1701	5402
430(h)(2)(F)	40211(a)(2)(B)*	Plans can use interest rate smoothing over a 25-year period to determine liabilities	Plan years beginning after Dec. 31, 2011	1701	5402
451(i)(3)	411(a)	Gain deferral election on qualifying electric transmission transactions is retroactively restored and extended to dispositions before Jan. 1, 2014	Dispositions after Dec. 31, 2011 and before Jan. 1, 2014	1014	None

Code §	Act §	Topic	Effective Date	Analy-sis ¶	Com Rep ¶
460(c)(6)(B)(ii)	331(b)	Disregard of certain bonus depreciation in applying the percentage of completion method is allowed for an additional time period	Property placed in service after Dec. 31, 2012 and before Jan. 1, 2014	806	None
512(b)(13)(E)(iv)	319(a)	Rule mitigating tax-exempt parent's UBTI "specified payments" received from a controlled entity, is retroactively extended through 2013	Payments received or accrued in 2012 and 2013	1502	None
530(b)(1)	101(a)(1)	Increased $2,000 contribution limit and other EGTRRA enhancements to Coverdell ESAs are made permanent	For tax years beginning after Dec. 31, 2012	704	None
530(b)(1)(A)(iii)	101(a)(1)	Increased $2,000 contribution limit and other EGTRRA enhancements to Coverdell ESAs are made permanent	For tax years beginning after Dec. 31, 2012	704	None
530(b)(2)	101(a)(1)	Increased $2,000 contribution limit and other EGTRRA enhancements to Coverdell ESAs are made permanent	For tax years beginning after Dec. 31, 2012	704	None
530(b)(4)	101(a)(1)	Increased $2,000 contribution limit and other EGTRRA enhancements to Coverdell ESAs are made permanent	For tax years beginning after Dec. 31, 2012	704	None
530(b)(5)	101(a)(1)	Increased $2,000 contribution limit and other EGTRRA enhancements to Coverdell ESAs are made permanent	For tax years beginning after Dec. 31, 2012	704	None
530(c)(1)	101(a)(1)	Increased $2,000 contribution limit and other EGTRRA enhancements to Coverdell ESAs are made permanent	For tax years beginning after Dec. 31, 2012	704	None

Code §	Act §	Topic	Effective Date	Analy-sis ¶	Com Rep ¶
530(d)(2)	101(a)(1)	Increased $2,000 contribution limit and other EGTRRA enhancements to Coverdell ESAs are made permanent	For tax years beginning after Dec. 31, 2012	704	None
530(d)(2)(C)	101(a)(1)	Increased $2,000 contribution limit and other EGTRRA enhancements to Coverdell ESAs are made permanent	For tax years beginning after Dec. 31, 2012	704	None
530(d)(2)(D)	101(a)(1)	Increased $2,000 contribution limit and other EGTRRA enhancements to Coverdell ESAs are made permanent	For tax years beginning after Dec. 31, 2012	704	None
530(d)(4)(C)(i)	101(a)(1)	Increased $2,000 contribution limit and other EGTRRA enhancements to Coverdell ESAs are made permanent	For tax years beginning after Dec. 31, 2012	704	None
531	102(c)(1)(A)	Accumulated earnings tax rate and personal holding company tax rate of 20% (up from 15%)	Tax years beginning after Dec. 31, 2012	203	None
541	102(c)(1)(B)	Accumulated earnings tax rate and personal holding company tax rate of 20% (up from 15%)	Tax years beginning after Dec. 31, 2012	203	None
584(c)	102(a)	Passthrough of qualified dividend income by common trust funds is made permanent	Tax years beginning after 2012	207	None
646	101(a)(1)	Favorable income tax treatment for Alaska Native Settlement Trusts and their beneficiaries is made permanent	Tax years beginning after 2012	1503	None
691(c)(4)	102(a)	Inclusion of qualified dividend income in prohibition on IRD double benefit is made permanent	Tax years beginning after 2012	211	None

Code §	Act §	Topic	Effective Date	Analy- sis ¶	Com Rep ¶
702(a)(5)	102(a)	Passthrough of qualified dividend income by partnerships is made permanent	Tax years beginning after Dec. 31, 2012	205	None
854(a)	102(a)	Passthrough of qualified dividend income by RICs and REITs is made permanent	Tax years beginning after Dec. 31, 2012	206	None
854(b)(1)(B)	102(a)	Passthrough of qualified dividend income by RICs and REITs is made permanent	Tax years beginning after Dec. 31, 2012	206	None
854(b)(1)(C)	102(a)	Passthrough of qualified dividend income by RICs and REITs is made permanent	Tax years beginning after Dec. 31, 2012	206	None
854(b)(4)	102(a)	Passthrough of qualified dividend income by RICs and REITs is made permanent	Tax years beginning after Dec. 31, 2012	206	None
857(c)(2)	102(a)	Passthrough of qualified dividend income by RICs and REITs is made permanent	Tax years beginning after Dec. 31, 2012	206	None
871(k)(1)(C)	320(a)	Withholding tax exemption for RIC interest-related dividends and short-term capital gains dividends paid to foreign persons is extended for tax years beginning in 2012 and 2013	Tax years beginning after Dec. 31, 2011 and before Jan. 1, 2014	1205	None
871(k)(2)(C)	320(a)	Withholding tax exemption for RIC interest-related dividends and short-term capital gains dividends paid to foreign persons is extended for tax years beginning in 2012 and 2013	Tax years beginning after Dec. 31, 2011 and before Jan. 1, 2014	1205	None

Code §	Act §	Topic	Effective Date	Analy-sis ¶	Com Rep ¶
897(h)(4)(A)(ii)	321(a)	Inclusion of RICs in the definition of qualified investment entity is extended for certain FIRPTA purposes through 2013	Jan. 1, 2012 through Dec. 31, 2013	1204	None
904(i)	104(c)(2)	Nonrefundable personal credits can offset AMT and regular tax for all tax years beginning after Dec. 31, 2011	Tax years beginning after Dec. 31, 2011.	403	None
936	330	Possessions tax credit for American Samoa extended through 2013 with an American Samoa production requirement	Tax years beginning after Dec. 31, 2011 and before Jan. 1, 2014	1206	None
953(e)(10)	322(a)	Subpart F exception for active financing income extended through tax years beginning before 2014	Tax Years beginning after Dec. 31, 2011 and before Jan. 1, 2014	1201	None
954(c)(6)(C)	323(a)	Look-through treatment for payments between related CFCs under foreign personal holding company income rules extended through 2013	Tax years of foreign corporations beginning after Dec. 31, 2011 and before Jan. 1, 2014	1202	None
954(h)(9)	322(b)	Subpart F exception for active financing income extended through tax years beginning before 2014	Tax Years beginning after Dec. 31, 2011 and before Jan. 1, 2014	1201	None
1016(a)(28)	101(a)(1)	Employer-provided child care credit is extended permanently	Tax years beginning after 2012	903	None
1202(a)(2)(C)	327(b)	Partial exclusion of gain from the sale or exchange of certain QSBS in empowerment zone C corporations is extended through the end of 2018	Periods after Dec. 31, 2011 and before Jan. 1, 2019	1407	None
1202(a)(3)	324(b)(1)	Acquisition date defined for qualified small business stock (QSBS) qualifying for the 75% exclusion	Stock acquired after Feb. 17, 2009 and before Sept. 28, 2010	209	None

Code §	Act §	Topic	Effective Date	Analysis ¶	Com Rep ¶
1202(a)(4)	324(a)(1)	Acquisition date defined for qualified small business stock (QSBS) qualifying for the 100% exclusion	Stock acquired after Sept. 27, 2010	209	None
1202(a)(4)	324(b)(2)	100% gain exclusion for qualified small business stock (QSBS) is retroactively restored and extended through Dec. 31, 2013	Stock acquired after Dec. 31, 2011 and before Jan. 1, 2014	209	None
1367(a)(2)	325(a)	Rule that S corporation's charitable contribution of property reduces shareholder's basis only by contributed property's basis is extended for tax years beginning in 2012 and 2013	Contributions made in tax years beginning after Dec. 31, 2011 and before Jan. 1, 2014.	1105	None
1374(d)(2)(B)	326(b)	Shortened S Corp built-in gains holding period extended for 2012 and 2013 and application of built-in gains tax clarified	Tax years beginning after Dec. 31, 2011	1501	None
1374(d)(7)	326(a)	Shortened S Corp built-in gains holding period extended for 2012 and 2013 and application of built-in gains tax clarified	Tax years beginning after Dec. 31, 2011	1501	None
1391(d)(1)(A)(i)	327(a)	Round I empowerment zone designation period is retroactively extended through the end of 2013	Periods after Dec. 31, 2011 and before Jan. 1, 2014	1406	None
1391(d)(1)(B)	327(c)	Round I empowerment zone designation period is retroactively extended through the end of 2013	Periods after Dec. 31, 2011 and before Jan. 1, 2014	1406	None
1400C(d)	104(c)(2)	Nonrefundable personal credits can offset AMT and regular tax for all tax years beginning after Dec. 31, 2011	Tax years beginning after Dec. 31, 2011.	403	None

Code §	Act §	Topic	Effective Date	Analysis ¶	Com Rep ¶
1400L(d)(2)(D)	328(a)	Period for issuance of qualified New York Liberty Bonds is retroactively restored and extended to bonds issued before Jan. 1, 2014	Bonds issued after Dec. 31, 2011 and before Jan. 1, 2014	1405	None
1401(a)	101(a)‡	Reduced 10.4% OASDI rate applied for 2012 to self-employment income up to $110,100 ceiling	Remuneration received, and tax years beginning, after, Dec. 31, 2011	1901	5501
1401(a)	101(b)‡	Reduced 10.4% OASDI rate applied for 2012 to self-employment income up to $110,100 ceiling	Remuneration received, and tax years beginning, after, Dec. 31, 2011	1901	5501
1401(a)	1001(a)**	Reduced 10.4% OASDI rate applied for 2012 to self-employment income up to $110,100 ceiling	Remuneration received, and tax years beginning, after, Dec. 31, 2011	1901	5501
1445(e)(1)	102(c)(1)(C)	IRS may impose 20% withholding rate (up from 15%) on USRPI gains passed through to foreign persons by U.S. partnerships, trusts or estates	Amounts paid after Dec. 31, 2012	1203	None
2001(c)	101(c)(1)	2012 estate, gift and GST tax rules made permanent, but top rate increases from 35% to 40%	After 2012	501	None
2010(c)(4)(B)(i)	101(c)(2)	2012 estate, gift and GST tax rules made permanent, but top rate increases from 35% to 40%	After 2012	501	None
3101(a)	101(a)‡	Reduced 4.2% employee social security tax rate applied for 2012 under payroll tax holiday	Remuneration received, and tax years beginning, after Dec. 31, 2011	1902	5501
3101(a)	1001(a)**	Reduced 4.2% employee social security tax rate applied for 2012 under payroll tax holiday	Remuneration received, and tax years beginning, after Dec. 31, 2011	1902	5501

Code §	Act §	Topic	Effective Date	Analysis ¶	Com Rep ¶
3101(a)	1001(b) **	Reduced 4.2% employee social security tax rate applied for 2012 under payroll tax holiday	Remuneration received, and tax years beginning, after Dec. 31, 2011	1902	5501
3111(e)	261(e)(2) ~	Tax-exempt employers get FICA tax credit for hiring qualified veterans	Individuals who begin work for an employer after Nov. 21, 2011	1904	None
3121(a)(1)	101(c) ‡	Reduced 4.2% employee social security tax rate applied for 2012 under payroll tax holiday	Remuneration received, and tax years beginning, after Dec. 31, 2011	1902	5501
3201(a)	1001(a) **	Reduced 4.2% employee social security tax rate applied for 2012 under payroll tax holiday	Remuneration received, and tax years beginning, after Dec. 31, 2011	1902	5501
3211(a)	1001(a) **	Reduced 4.2% employee social security tax rate applied for 2012 under payroll tax holiday	Remuneration received, and tax years beginning, after Dec. 31, 2011	1902	5501
3303(f)	252(a)(2) ≈	To qualify for additional FUTA tax credit, state unemployment programs must charge employers for payments caused by employer's failure to respond	Erroneous payments established after Oct. 20, 2013	1903	None
3402(p)(1)(B)	101(a)(1)	Reduced rates for kiddie tax and some withholding (each tied to the reduced individual rates) are permanently extended	For tax years beginning after Dec. 31, 2012	103	None
3402(p)(2)	101(a)(1)	Reduced rates for kiddie tax and some withholding (each tied to the reduced individual rates) are permanently extended	For tax years beginning after Dec. 31, 2012	103	None
3402(q)(1)	101(a)(1)	Reduced rates for kiddie tax and some withholding (each tied to the reduced individual rates) are permanently extended	For tax years beginning after Dec. 31, 2012	103	None

Code §	Act §	Topic	Effective Date	Analysis ¶	Com Rep ¶
3402(r)(3)	101(a)(1)	Reduced rates for kiddie tax and some withholding (each tied to the reduced individual rates) are permanently extended	For tax years beginning after Dec. 31, 2012	103	None
3402(t)	102(a)~	Mandatory 3% withholding on payments to government contractors was repealed prospectively	For payments made after 2011	1909	5701
3406(a)(1)	101(a)(1)	Reduced rates for kiddie tax and some withholding (each tied to the reduced individual rates) are permanently extended	For tax years beginning after Dec. 31, 2012	103	None
4041(a)(1)(C)(iii)(I)	40102(a)(1)(A)*	Reduction of various fuel excise tax rates is delayed until after Sept. 30, 2016	July 1, 2012	1801	5401
4041(m)(1)(A)	40102(a)(2)(A)*	Reduction of various fuel excise tax rates is delayed until after Sept. 30, 2016	July 1, 2012	1801	5401
4041(m)(1)(B)	40102(a)(1)(B)*	Reduction of various fuel excise tax rates is delayed until after Sept. 30, 2016	July 1, 2012	1801	5401
4043	1103(a)(1)†	14.1¢-per-gallon surtax is imposed on fuel used in fractional ownership aircraft flights; flights are also taxed as noncommercial aviation, but exempted from air transportation taxes	Taxable transportation provided, and aircraft and fuel used, after Mar. 31, 2012	1808	5603
4051(c)	40102(a)(2)(B)*	Retail truck and manufacturer's tire excise taxes, and certain exemptions, are extended through Sept. 30, 2016	July 1, 2012	1803	5401
4071(d)	40102(a)(2)(C)*	Retail truck and manufacturer's tire excise taxes, and certain exemptions, are extended through Sept. 30, 2016	July 1, 2012	1803	5401

Code §	Act §	Topic	Effective Date	Analy-sis ¶	Com Rep ¶
4081(d)(1)	40102(a)(1)(C)*	Reduction of various fuel excise tax rates is delayed until after Sept. 30, 2016	July 1, 2012	1801	5401
4081(d)(2)(B)	1101(a)†	Airport and airway trust fund excise taxes are extended through Sept. 30, 2015	Feb. 18, 2012	1806	5601
4081(d)(3)	40102(a)(2)(D)*	Leaking Underground Storage Tank (LUST) Trust Fund 0.1¢-per-gallon tax is extended through Sept. 30, 2016	July 1, 2012	1802	5401
4082(e)	1103(a)(2)†	14.1¢-per-gallon surtax is imposed on fuel used in fractional ownership aircraft flights; flights are also taxed as noncommercial aviation, but exempted from air transportation taxes	Taxable transportation provided, and aircraft and fuel used, after Mar. 31, 2012	1808	5603
4083(b)	1103(b)†	14.1¢-per-gallon surtax is imposed on fuel used in fractional ownership aircraft flights; flights are also taxed as noncommercial aviation, but exempted from air transportation taxes	Taxable transportation provided, and aircraft and fuel used, after Mar. 31, 2012	1808	5603
4101(a)	404(b)(3)(C)	Algae is treated as a qualified feedstock for purposes of the cellulose biofuel producer credit	Fuels sold or used after Jan. 2, 2013.	1016	None
4221(a)	40102(d)(1)*	Retail truck and manufacturer's tire excise taxes, and certain exemptions, are extended through Sept. 30, 2016	July 1, 2012	1803	5401

Code §	Act §	Topic	Effective Date	Analy-sis ¶	Com Rep ¶
4261(j)	1103(c) †	14.1¢-per-gallon surtax is imposed on fuel used in fractional ownership aircraft flights; flights are also taxed as noncommercial aviation, but exempted from air transportation taxes	Taxable transportation provided, and aircraft and fuel used, after Mar. 31, 2012	1808	5603
4261(j)	1103(c) †	14.1¢-per-gallon surtax is imposed on fuel used in fractional ownership aircraft flights; flights are also taxed as noncommercial aviation, but exempted from air transportation taxes	Taxable transportation provided, and aircraft and fuel used, after Mar. 31, 2012	1808	5603
4261(j)	1103(c) †	Airport and airway trust fund excise taxes are extended through Sept. 30, 2015	Feb. 18, 2012	1806	5601
4261(j)(1)(A)(ii)	1101(b)(1) †	Airport and airway trust fund excise taxes are extended through Sept. 30, 2015	Feb. 18, 2012	1806	5601
4271(d)(1)(A)(ii)	1101(b)(2) †	Airport and airway trust fund excise taxes are extended through Sept. 30, 2015	Feb. 18, 2012	1806	5601
4281	1107(a) †	Exemption from air transportation excise taxes for small jet aircraft operated on nonestablished lines is eliminated	For taxable transportation provided after Mar. 31, 2012	1807	5607
4481(f)	40102(b)(1)(A) *	Highway use tax, and certain highway use tax exemptions, are extended through Sept. 30, 2017	July 1, 2012	1805	5401
4482(c)(4)	40102(b)(2)(A) *	Highway use tax, and certain highway use tax exemptions, are extended through Sept. 30, 2017	July 1, 2012	1805	5401
4482(c)(4)	40102(b)(2)(B) *	Highway use tax, and certain highway use tax exemptions, are extended through Sept. 30, 2017	July 1, 2012	1805	5401

Code §	Act §	Topic	Effective Date	Analy-sis ¶	Com Rep ¶
4482(d)	40102(b)(1)(B)*	Highway use tax, and certain highway use tax exemptions, are extended through Sept. 30, 2017	July 1, 2012	1805	5401
4483(i)	40102(d)(2)*	Highway use tax, and certain highway use tax exemptions, are extended through Sept. 30, 2017	July 1, 2012	1805	5401
4973(e)(1)(A)	101(a)(1)	Increased $2,000 contribution limit and other EGTRRA enhancements to Coverdell ESAs are made permanent	For tax years beginning after Dec. 31, 2012	704	None
4973(e)(1)(B)	101(a)(1)	Increased $2,000 contribution limit and other EGTRRA enhancements to Coverdell ESAs are made permanent	For tax years beginning after Dec. 31, 2012	704	None
4980B(f)(2)(B)(i)	243(a)≈	Eligibility for COBRA continuation coverage extended from Nov. 20, 2011 through Jan. 1, 2014 for PBGC recipients and TAA-eligible individuals who lose employment or work hours	Coverage periods that would otherwise end on or after Nov. 20, 2011 and through Jan. 1, 2014	1612	None
4980H(b)(3)	1858(b)(4)+	Employers won't have to provide free choice vouchers to employees, as post-2013 rules are repealed	For vouchers that would have been provided after 2013	1603	None
6039H	101(a)(1)	Favorable income tax treatment for Alaska Native Settlement Trusts and their beneficiaries is made permanent	Tax years beginning after 2012	1503	None
6041(a)	2(b)(1)•	Expanded information reporting for post-2011 payments of $600 or more of gross proceeds or amounts in consideration for property is repealed	Payments made after Dec. 31, 2011	1906	5901

Code §	Act §	Topic	Effective Date	Analy-sis ¶	Com Rep ¶
6041(a)	2(b)(2)•	Expanded information reporting for post-2011 payments of $600 or more of gross proceeds or amounts in consideration for property is repealed	Payments made after Dec. 31, 2011	1906	5901
6041(h)	3(a)•	Information reporting for certain recipients of rental income for payments of $600 or more to service providers is retroactively repealed	Payments made after Dec. 31, 2010	1907	5902
6041(i)	2(a)•	Expanded information reporting requirement for post-2011 payments of $600 or more to non-tax-exempt corporations is repealed	Payments made after Dec. 31, 2011	1905	5901
6041(j)	2(a)•	Expanded information reporting requirement for post-2011 payments of $600 or more to non-tax-exempt corporations is repealed	Payments made after Dec. 31, 2011	1905	5901
6056(a)	1858(b)(5)(A)+	Post-2013 health insurance coverage information reporting and related statement requirements for "offering employers" are repealed	Periods beginning after Dec. 31, 2013	1613	None
6056(b)(2)(C)(i)	1858(b)(5)(B)(i)+	Post-2013 health insurance coverage information reporting and related statement requirements for "offering employers" are repealed	Periods beginning after Dec. 31, 2013	1613	None
6056(b)(2)(C)(v)	1858(b)(5)(B)(iv)+	Post-2013 health insurance coverage information reporting and related statement requirements for "offering employers" are repealed	Periods beginning after Dec. 31, 2013	1613	None

Code §	Act §	Topic	Effective Date	Analysis ¶	Com Rep ¶
6056(d)(2)	1858(b)(5)(C)+	Post-2013 health insurance coverage information reporting and related statement requirements for "offering employers" are repealed	Periods beginning after Dec. 31, 2013	1613	None
6056(e)	1858(b)(5)(C)+	Post-2013 health insurance coverage information reporting and related statement requirements for "offering employers" are repealed	Periods beginning after Dec. 31, 2013	1613	None
6056(f)	1858(b)(5)(D)+	Post-2013 health insurance coverage information reporting and related statement requirements for "offering employers" are repealed	Periods beginning after Dec. 31, 2013	1613	None
6103(k)(10)	209(a)	Provision authorizing IRS to disclose certain returns and return information to certain prison officials is improved and made permanent	Jan. 2, 2013	1505	None
6116	502(a)++	Principal administrators of U.S. prisons have to provide IRS with certain information about inmates each year	Oct. 21, 2011	1908	5802
6331(h)(3)	301(a)~	100% maximum rate for continuous levy expanded to include governmental payments to vendors from the sale or lease of property	Levies issued after Nov. 21, 2011	1916	None
6409	103(d)	Tax refunds won't affect eligibility for federal benefit programs	Amounts received after Dec. 31, 2012	310	None
6412(a)(1)	40102(c)*	Floor stocks credit, or refund for tire tax and removal-at-terminal fuel tax, is to apply to tires or fuel held by dealers on Oct. 1, 2016	July 1, 2012	1804	5401

Code §	Act §	Topic	Effective Date	Analy-sis ¶	Com Rep ¶
6426(c)(6)	405(b)(1)	Income and excise tax credits/refunds for biodiesel and renewable diesel are extended retroactively through 2013	Fuel sold or used after Dec. 31, 2011 and before Jan. 1, 2014	1009	None
6426(d)(5)	412(a)	Alternative fuels and alternative fuel mixture excise tax credit, and alternative fuels excise tax refund rules, are retroactively extended through 2013	Fuel sold or used after Dec. 31, 2011 and before Jan. 1, 2014	1010	None
6426(e)(3)	412(a)	Alternative fuels and alternative fuel mixture excise tax credit, and alternative fuels excise tax refund rules, are retroactively extended through 2013	Fuel sold or used after Dec. 31, 2011 and before Jan. 1, 2014	1010	None
6427(e)(6)(B)	405(b)(2)	Income and excise tax credits/refunds for biodiesel and renewable diesel are extended retroactively through 2013	Fuel sold or used after Dec. 31, 2011 and before Jan. 1, 2014	1009	None
6427(e)(6)(C)	412(b)(1)	Alternative fuels and alternative fuel mixture excise tax credit, and alternative fuels excise tax refund rules, are retroactively extended through 2013	Fuel sold or used after Dec. 31, 2011 and before Jan. 1, 2014	1010	None
6427(e)(6)(D)	412(b)(2)	Alternative fuels and alternative fuel mixture excise tax credit, and alternative fuels excise tax refund rules, are retroactively extended through 2013	Fuel sold or used after Dec. 31, 2011 and before Jan. 1, 2014	1010	None
6427(e)(6)(E)	412(b)(3)	Alternative fuels and alternative fuel mixture excise tax credit, and alternative fuels excise tax refund rules, are retroactively extended through 2013	Fuel sold or used after Dec. 31, 2011 and before Jan. 1, 2014	1010	None
6655	4(1)***	Certain 2017 estimated taxes for corporations with assets of $1 billion or more increase to 100.25%	Aug. 10, 2012	1915	None

Code §	Act §	Topic	Effective Date	Analy-sis ¶	Com Rep ¶
6655	4(2)***	Certain 2017 estimated taxes for corporations with assets of $1 billion or more increase to 100.25%	Aug. 10, 2012	1915	None
6695(g)	501(a)++	Penalty on Paid Preparers for Noncompliance with Due Diligence Rules Increased from $100 to $500	Returns required to be filed after Dec. 31, 2011.	1912	5801
7275(c)	1104(a)†	Penalty imposed for lack of transparency in airline passenger tax disclosures	Taxable transportation provided after Mar. 31, 2012.	1911	5604
7518(g)(6)(A)	102(a)	Tax rate on individuals' nonqualifying capital gain withdrawals from CCFs is increased from 15% to 20% after 2012	Tax years beginning after Dec. 31, 2012	210	None
7518(g)(6)(A)	102(c)(1)(D)	Tax rate on individuals' nonqualifying capital gain withdrawals from CCFs is increased from 15% to 20% after 2012	Tax years beginning after Dec. 31, 2012	210	None
7527(b)	241(b)(1)≈	HCTC and percentage limit on advance HCTC payments are retroactively increased to 72.5% (from 65%) for post-Feb. 2011 coverage months	Coverage months beginning after Feb. 12, 2011	1606	None
7527(d)(2)	241(b)(2)(B)≈	HCTC eligibility certificates issued after Nov. 20, 2011 must include information on qualified health insurance and enrollment procedures	Certificates issued after Nov. 20, 2011	1610	None
7527(e)	241(b)(2)(C)≈	Requirement that IRS make retroactive HCTC payments is reinstated for coverage months beginning after Nov. 20, 2011	Coverage months beginning after Nov. 20, 2011	1605	None

Code §	Act §	Topic	Effective Date	Analysis ¶	Com Rep ¶
7527(e)	241(b)(2)(D)≈	Requirement that IRS make retroactive HCTC payments is reinstated for coverage months beginning after Nov. 20, 2011	Coverage months beginning after Nov. 20, 2011	1605	None
9801(c)(2)(D)	242(a)(1)≈	Rule under which a period after a TAA-related loss of health coverage is not counted in determining a HIPAA 63-day lapse in creditable coverage—extended to plan years beginning before Jan. 1, 2014	Plan years beginning after Feb. 12, 2011 and before Jan. 1, 2014	1611	None
None	101(a)(1)	Personal exemption phaseout (PEP) applies when AGI exceeds $300,000 (joint returns) and $250,000 (single filers) for tax years beginning after Dec. 31, 2012	Tax years beginning after Dec. 31, 2012	301	None
None	101	Additional increase in arbitrage rebate exception for government bonds used to finance education facilities made permanent	Tax, plan or limitation years beginning after Dec. 31, 2012	1404	None
None	101(a)	2012 estate, gift and GST tax rules made permanent, but top rate increases from 35% to 40%	After 2012	501	None
None	101(a)	Tax-exempt status of public educational facility bonds is made permanent	Tax years beginning after Dec. 31, 2012	1403	None
None	101(a)(1)	$1,000 per child amount and expanded refundability of child tax credit are permanently extended	Tax years beginning after Dec. 31, 2012.	601	None
None	101(a)(1)	$5,000 increase in EIC phaseout threshold for joint filers is extended through 2017	Tax years beginning after Dec. 31, 2012	606	None

Code §	Act §	Topic	Effective Date	Analysis ¶	Com Rep ¶
None	101(a)(1)	25%, 28%, and 33% trust and estate income tax rates are permanently extended, top rate increases to 39.6% after 2012	Tax years beginning after Dec. 31, 2012	104	None
None	101(a)(1)	Child tax credit can permanently offset AMT	Tax years beginning after Dec. 31, 2012	404	None
None	101(a)(1)	EGTRRA-expanded dependent care credit permanently extended	Tax years beginning after Dec. 31, 2012	603	None
None	101(a)(1)	EIC simplification made permanent	Tax years beginning after Dec. 31, 2012	605	None
None	101(a)(1)	Expanded adoption credit rules (but not refundability) made permanent	Tax years beginning after Dec. 31, 2012	604	None
None	101(a)(1)	Expansion of marrieds-filing-jointly 15% rate bracket to provide marriage penalty relief is extended permanently	Tax years beginning after Dec. 31, 2012	102	None
None	101(a)(1)	Increased $2,000 contribution limit and other EGTRRA enhancements to Coverdell ESAs are made permanent	For tax years beginning after Dec. 31, 2012	704	None
None	101(a)(1)	Individuals' 10%, 25%, 28%, 33%, and 35% tax brackets are made permanent; high-income taxpayers taxed at 39.6% rate after 2012	Tax years beginning after Dec. 31, 2012	101	None
None	101(a)(1)	Overall limitation on itemized deductions is restored, applies when AGI exceeds $300,000 (joint returns) and $250,000 (single filers)	Tax years beginning after Dec. 31, 2012	302	None
None	101(a)(1)	Reduced rates for kiddie tax and some withholding (each tied to the reduced individual rates) are permanently extended	For tax years beginning after Dec. 31, 2012	103	None

Code §	Act §	Topic	Effective Date	Analy-sis ¶	Com Rep ¶
None	101(a)(1)	Standard deduction marriage penalty relief is made permanent	Tax years beginning after Dec. 31, 2012	304	None
None	101(a)(1)	Adoption assistance exclusion is made permanent	Tax years beginning after 2012	309	None
None	102(a)	7% AMT preference for excluded gain on qualified small business stock is permanently extended	Tax years beginning after Dec. 31, 2012	405	None
None	102(a)	Accumulated earnings tax rate and personal holding company tax rate of 20% (up from 15%)	Tax years beginning after Dec. 31, 2012	203	None
None	102(a)	IRS may impose 20% withholding rate (up from 15%) on USRPI gains passed through to foreign persons by U.S. partnerships, trusts or estates	Amounts paid after Dec. 31, 2012	1203	None
None	102(a)	Long-term capital loss treatment on stock to extent extraordinary dividends were taxed as capital gain is made permanent	Tax years beginning after Dec. 31, 2012	204	None
None	102(a)	Passthrough of qualified dividend income by RICs and REITs is made permanent	Tax years beginning after Dec. 31, 2012	206	None
None	102(a)	Passthrough of qualified dividend income by partnerships is made permanent	Tax years beginning after Dec. 31, 2012	205	None
None	102(a)	Qualified dividend income treatment for ordinary income on disposition of Code Sec. 306 stock made permanent	Tax years beginning after Dec. 31, 2012	212	None
None	102(a)	Repeal of collapsible corporation provision is made permanent	Tax years beginning after Dec. 31, 2012.	1504	None

Code §	Act §	Topic	Effective Date	Analysis ¶	Com Rep ¶
None	102(c)(1)(E)	Tax rate on individuals' nonqualifying capital gain withdrawals from CCFs is increased from 15% to 20% after 2012	Tax years beginning after Dec. 31, 2012	210	None
None	103(a)(2)	American Opportunity Tax Credit (AOTC) for higher education expenses is extended five years, through 2017	Tax years beginning after Dec. 31, 2012 and before Jan. 1, 2018	701	None
None	1858(a)+	Employers won't have to provide free choice vouchers to employees, as post-2013 rules are repealed	For vouchers that would have been provided after 2013	1603	None

¶ 6002. Act Section ERISA Cross Reference Table

Act § cites are to the 2012 Taxpayer Relief Act unless otherwise indicated.

* denotes 2012 Highway Investment Act

† denotes 2012 FAA Modernization Act

** denotes 2012 Middle Class Tax Relief Act

*** denotes 2012 African Growth Act

✓ denotes 2012 Aviation Extension Act

\+ denotes 2011 Appropriations Act

~ denotes 2011 Job Creation Act

• denotes 2011 Taxpayer Protection Act

‡ denotes 2011 Temporary Payroll Act

++ denotes 2011 U.S.-Korea Trade Act

≈ denotes 2011 Trade Extension Act

Act §	ERISA §	Topic	Effective Date	Analy-sis ¶	Com Rep ¶
242(a)(2)≈	701(c)(2)(C)	Rule under which a period after a TAA-related loss of health coverage is not counted in determining a HIPAA 63-day lapse in creditable coverage—extended to plan years beginning before Jan. 1, 2014	Plan years beginning after Feb. 12, 2011 and before Jan. 1, 2014	1611	None
243(a)≈	602(2)(A)	Eligibility for COBRA continuation coverage extended from Nov. 20, 2011 through Jan. 1, 2014 for PBGC recipients and TAA-eligible individuals who lose employment or work hours	Coverage periods that would otherwise end on or after Nov. 20, 2011 and through Jan. 1, 2014	1612	None
40211(b)(1)*	303(h)(2)(C)(iv)	Plans can use interest rate smoothing over a 25-year period to determine liabilities	Plan years beginning after Dec. 31, 2011	1701	5402
40211(b)(2)(A)*	101(f)(2)(D)	Plans can use interest rate smoothing over a 25-year period to determine liabilities	Plan years beginning after Dec. 31, 2011	1701	5402
40211(b)(2)(B)*	None	Plans can use interest rate smoothing over a 25-year period to determine liabilities	Plan years beginning after Dec. 31, 2011	1701	5402

Act §	ERISA §	Topic	Effective Date	Analysis ¶	Com Rep ¶
40211(b)(3)(A)*	303(h)(2)(F)	Plans can use interest rate smoothing over a 25-year period to determine liabilities	Plan years beginning after Dec. 31, 2011	1701	5402
40211(b)(3)(B)*	205(g)(3)(B)(ii)	Plans can use interest rate smoothing over a 25-year period to determine liabilities	Plan years beginning after Dec. 31, 2011	1701	5402
40211(b)(3)(B)*	205(g)(3)(B)(iii)	Plans can use interest rate smoothing over a 25-year period to determine liabilities	Plan years beginning after Dec. 31, 2011	1701	5402
40211(b)(3)(C)*	4006(a)(3)(E)(iv)	Plans can use interest rate smoothing over a 25-year period to determine liabilities	Plan years beginning after Dec. 31, 2011	1701	5402
40211(b)(3)(D)*	4010(d)(3)	Plans can use interest rate smoothing over a 25-year period to determine liabilities	Plan years beginning after Dec. 31, 2011	1701	5402
40221(a)(1)*	4006(a)(3)(A)(i)	PBGC flat-rate premiums for single-employer defined benefit plans are increased from $35 per participant to $42 for 2013, to $49 for 2014, and indexed for inflation after 2014	July 6, 2012	1706	5403
40221(a)(2)*	4006(a)(3)(F)	PBGC flat-rate premiums for single-employer defined benefit plans are increased from $35 per participant to $42 for 2013, to $49 for 2014, and indexed for inflation after 2014	July 6, 2012	1706	5403
40221(b)(1)*	4006(a)(3)(E)(ii)	PBGC variable-rate premiums for single-employer defined benefit plans are indexed for inflation after 2012 plan years; increased by $4 for 2014 and by another $5 for 2015; and capped at $400 per participant, as indexed for inflation	July 6, 2012	1707	5403

Act §	ERISA §	Topic	Effective Date	Analysis ¶	Com Rep ¶
40221(b)(2)*	4006(a)(8)	PBGC variable-rate premiums for single-employer defined benefit plans are indexed for inflation after 2012 plan years; increased by $4 for 2014 and by another $5 for 2015; and capped at $400 per participant, as indexed for inflation	July 6, 2012	1707	5403
40221(b)(3)(A)*	4006(a)(3)(E)(i)	PBGC variable-rate premiums for single-employer defined benefit plans are indexed for inflation after 2012 plan years; increased by $4 for 2014 and by another $5 for 2015; and capped at $400 per participant, as indexed for inflation	July 6, 2012	1707	5403
40221(b)(3)(B)*	4006(a)(3)(J)	PBGC variable-rate premiums for single-employer defined benefit plans are indexed for inflation after 2012 plan years; increased by $4 for 2014 and by another $5 for 2015; and capped at $400 per participant, as indexed for inflation	July 6, 2012	1707	5403
40222(a)(1)*	4006(a)(3)(A)(iv)	PBGC premium rates for multiemployer defined benefit plans are raised from $9 per participant to $12 after 2012, indexed for inflation for post-2013 plan years	July 6, 2012	1708	5403
40222(a)(4)*	4006(a)(3)(A)(v)	PBGC premium rates for multiemployer defined benefit plans are raised from $9 per participant to $12 after 2012, indexed for inflation for post-2013 plan years	July 6, 2012	1708	5403

Act §	ERISA §	Topic	Effective Date	Analy-sis ¶	Com Rep ¶
40222(b)*	4006(a)(3)(I)	PBGC premium rates for multiemployer defined benefit plans are raised from $9 per participant to $12 after 2012, indexed for inflation for post-2013 plan years	July 6, 2012	1708	5403
40231(a)(1)*	4002(d)(2)	ERISA Adds Rules Governing PBGC Board of Directors' Meetings, Actions, and Minutes of Meetings	July 6, 2012	1709	5404
40231(a)(1)*	4002(d)(3)	ERISA Adds Rules Governing PBGC Board of Directors' Meetings, Actions, and Minutes of Meetings	July 6, 2012	1709	5404
40231(a)(1)*	4002(d)(4)	Responsibilities of PBGC Inspector General and General Counsel, and the independence of each office, are established in ERISA	July 6, 2012	1711	5404
40231(a)(1)*	4002(d)(5)	Responsibilities of PBGC Inspector General and General Counsel, and the independence of each office, are established in ERISA	July 6, 2012	1711	5404
40231(a)(1)*	4002(d)(6)	Responsibilities of PBGC Inspector General and General Counsel, and the independence of each office, are established in ERISA	July 6, 2012	1711	5404
40231(a)(1)*	4002(d)(7)	ERISA is amended to establish: the position of PBGC Risk Management Officer, the term and accountability of the PBGC Director, and the PBGC Board of Directors' hiring responsibilities	July 6, 2012	1712	5404

Act §	ERISA §	Topic	Effective Date	Analysis ¶	Com Rep ¶
40231(a)(2)(B)*	4002(e)(1)	ERISA Adds Rules Governing PBGC Board of Directors' Meetings, Actions, and Minutes of Meetings	July 6, 2012	1709	5404
40231(a)(2)(C)*	4002(e)(2)	ERISA Adds Rules Governing PBGC Board of Directors' Meetings, Actions, and Minutes of Meetings	July 6, 2012	1709	5404
40231(a)(3)(B)*	4002(h)(3)	ERISA Adds Rules Governing PBGC Board of Directors' Meetings, Actions, and Minutes of Meetings	July 6, 2012	1709	5404
40231(b)*	4002(j)	Conflict of interest rules established for PBGC Director and Board of Directors	July 6, 2012	1710	5404
40231(c)*	4002(k)	ERISA is amended to establish: the position of PBGC Risk Management Officer, the term and accountability of the PBGC Director, and the PBGC Board of Directors' hiring responsibilities	July 6, 2012	1712	5404
40231(d)*	4002(c)	ERISA is amended to establish: the position of PBGC Risk Management Officer, the term and accountability of the PBGC Director, and the PBGC Board of Directors' hiring responsibilities	July 6, 2012	1712	5404
40232(a)*	4004	PBGC must establish "Participant and Plan Sponsor Advocate" position	July 6, 2012	1713	5404
40232(b)*	4002(h)(1)	PBGC must establish "Participant and Plan Sponsor Advocate" position	July 6, 2012	1713	5404
40233*	None	PBGC must adopt specified quality control procedures	July 6, 2012	1714	5404

Act §	ERISA §	Topic	Effective Date	Analy-sis ¶	Com Rep ¶
40234(a)*	4005(c)	PBGC's authority to borrow up to $100 million from the U.S. Treasury is repealed	July 6, 2012	1715	5404
40241(b)(1)*	101(e)(3)	Rules permitting transfer of excess defined benefit plan assets to retiree health accounts are extended through 2021	July 6, 2012	1703	5405
40241(b)(1)*	403(c)(1)	Rules permitting transfer of excess defined benefit plan assets to retiree health accounts are extended through 2021	July 6, 2012	1703	5405
40241(b)(1)*	408(b)(13)	Rules permitting transfer of excess defined benefit plan assets to retiree health accounts are extended through 2021	July 6, 2012	1703	5405
40241(b)(2)*	408(b)(13)	Rules permitting transfer of excess defined benefit plan assets to retiree health accounts are extended through 2021	July 6, 2012	1703	5405
40242(e)(14)*	101(e)	Excess pension plan assets may be used to fund retiree group-term life insurance	Transfers made after July 6, 2012	1702	5405

¶ 6003. ERISA Section Cross Reference Table

Act § cites are to the 2012 Taxpayer Relief Act unless otherwise indicated.
* denotes 2012 Highway Investment Act
† denotes 2012 FAA Modernization Act
** denotes 2012 Middle Class Tax Relief Act
*** denotes 2012 African Growth Act
✓ denotes 2012 Aviation Extension Act
+ denotes 2011 Appropriations Act
~ denotes 2011 Job Creation Act
• denotes 2011 Taxpayer Protection Act
‡ denotes 2011 Temporary Payroll Act
++ denotes 2011 U.S.-Korea Trade Act
≈ denotes 2011 Trade Extension Act

ERISA §	Act §	Topic	Effective Date	Analysis ¶	Com Rep ¶
101(e)	40242(e)(14)*	Excess pension plan assets may be used to fund retiree group-term life insurance	Transfers made after July 6, 2012	1702	5405
101(e)(3)	40241(b)(1)*	Rules permitting transfer of excess defined benefit plan assets to retiree health accounts are extended through 2021	July 6, 2012	1703	5405
101(f)(2)(D)	40211(b)(2)(A)*	Plans can use interest rate smoothing over a 25-year period to determine liabilities	Plan years beginning after Dec. 31, 2011	1701	5402
205(g)(3)(B)(ii)	40211(b)(3)(B)*	Plans can use interest rate smoothing over a 25-year period to determine liabilities	Plan years beginning after Dec. 31, 2011	1701	5402
205(g)(3)(B)(iii)	40211(b)(3)(B)*	Plans can use interest rate smoothing over a 25-year period to determine liabilities	Plan years beginning after Dec. 31, 2011	1701	5402
303(h)(2)(C)(iv)	40211(b)(1)*	Plans can use interest rate smoothing over a 25-year period to determine liabilities	Plan years beginning after Dec. 31, 2011	1701	5402
303(h)(2)(F)	40211(b)(3)(A)*	Plans can use interest rate smoothing over a 25-year period to determine liabilities	Plan years beginning after Dec. 31, 2011	1701	5402

ERISA §	Act §	Topic	Effective Date	Analy-sis ¶	Com Rep ¶
403(c)(1)	40241(b)(1)*	Rules permitting transfer of excess defined benefit plan assets to retiree health accounts are extended through 2021	July 6, 2012	1703	5405
408(b)(13)	40241(b)(1)*	Rules permitting transfer of excess defined benefit plan assets to retiree health accounts are extended through 2021	July 6, 2012	1703	5405
408(b)(13)	40241(b)(2)*	Rules permitting transfer of excess defined benefit plan assets to retiree health accounts are extended through 2021	July 6, 2012	1703	5405
602(2)(A)	243(a)≈	Eligibility for COBRA continuation coverage extended from Nov. 20, 2011 through Jan. 1, 2014 for PBGC recipients and TAA-eligible individuals who lose employment or work hours	Coverage periods that would otherwise end on or after Nov. 20, 2011 and through Jan. 1, 2014	1612	None
701(c)(2)(C)	242(a)(2)≈	Rule under which a period after a TAA-related loss of health coverage is not counted in determining a HIPAA 63-day lapse in creditable coverage—extended to plan years beginning before Jan. 1, 2014	Plan years beginning after Feb. 12, 2011 and before Jan. 1, 2014	1611	None
4002(c)	40231(d)*	ERISA is amended to establish: the position of PBGC Risk Management Officer, the term and accountability of the PBGC Director, and the PBGC Board of Directors' hiring responsibilities	July 6, 2012	1712	5404
4002(d)(2)	40231(a)(1)*	ERISA Adds Rules Governing PBGC Board of Directors' Meetings, Actions, and Minutes of Meetings	July 6, 2012	1709	5404

1,500

ERISA §	Act §	Topic	Effective Date	Analy-sis ¶	Com Rep ¶
4002(d)(3)	40231(a)(1)*	ERISA Adds Rules Governing PBGC Board of Directors' Meetings, Actions, and Minutes of Meetings	July 6, 2012	1709	5404
4002(d)(4)	40231(a)(1)*	Responsibilities of PBGC Inspector General and General Counsel, and the independence of each office, are established in ERISA	July 6, 2012	1711	5404
4002(d)(5)	40231(a)(1)*	Responsibilities of PBGC Inspector General and General Counsel, and the independence of each office, are established in ERISA	July 6, 2012	1711	5404
4002(d)(6)	40231(a)(1)*	Responsibilities of PBGC Inspector General and General Counsel, and the independence of each office, are established in ERISA	July 6, 2012	1711	5404
4002(d)(7)	40231(a)(1)*	ERISA is amended to establish: the position of PBGC Risk Management Officer, the term and accountability of the PBGC Director, and the PBGC Board of Directors' hiring responsibilities	July 6, 2012	1712	5404
4002(e)(1)	40231(a)(2)(B)*	ERISA Adds Rules Governing PBGC Board of Directors' Meetings, Actions, and Minutes of Meetings	July 6, 2012	1709	5404
4002(e)(2)	40231(a)(2)(C)*	ERISA Adds Rules Governing PBGC Board of Directors' Meetings, Actions, and Minutes of Meetings	July 6, 2012	1709	5404
4002(h)(1)	40232(b)*	PBGC must establish "Participant and Plan Sponsor Advocate" position	July 6, 2012	1713	5404

ERISA §	Act §	Topic	Effective Date	Analy-sis ¶	Com Rep ¶
4002(h)(3)	40231(a)(3)(B) *	ERISA Adds Rules Governing PBGC Board of Directors' Meetings, Actions, and Minutes of Meetings	July 6, 2012	1709	5404
4002(j)	40231(b) *	Conflict of interest rules established for PBGC Director and Board of Directors	July 6, 2012	1710	5404
4002(k)	40231(c) *	ERISA is amended to establish: the position of PBGC Risk Management Officer, the term and accountability of the PBGC Director, and the PBGC Board of Directors' hiring responsibilities	July 6, 2012	1712	5404
4004	40232(a) *	PBGC must establish "Participant and Plan Sponsor Advocate" position	July 6, 2012	1713	5404
4005(c)	40234(a) *	PBGC's authority to borrow up to $100 million from the U.S. Treasury is repealed	July 6, 2012	1715	5404
4006(a)(3)(A)(i)	40221(a)(1) *	PBGC flat-rate premiums for single-employer defined benefit plans are increased from $35 per participant to $42 for 2013, to $49 for 2014, and indexed for inflation after 2014	July 6, 2012	1706	5403
4006(a)(3)(A)(iv)	40222(a)(1) *	PBGC premium rates for multiemployer defined benefit plans are raised from $9 per participant to $12 after 2012, indexed for inflation for post-2013 plan years	July 6, 2012	1708	5403
4006(a)(3)(A)(v)	40222(a)(4) *	PBGC premium rates for multiemployer defined benefit plans are raised from $9 per participant to $12 after 2012, indexed for inflation for post-2013 plan years	July 6, 2012	1708	5403

ERISA §	Act §	Topic	Effective Date	Analy-sis ¶	Com Rep ¶
4006(a)(3)(E)(i)	40221(b)(3)(A)*	PBGC variable-rate premiums for single-employer defined benefit plans are indexed for inflation after 2012 plan years; increased by $4 for 2014 and by another $5 for 2015; and capped at $400 per participant, as indexed for inflation	July 6, 2012	1707	5403
4006(a)(3)(E)(ii)	40221(b)(1)*	PBGC variable-rate premiums for single-employer defined benefit plans are indexed for inflation after 2012 plan years; increased by $4 for 2014 and by another $5 for 2015; and capped at $400 per participant, as indexed for inflation	July 6, 2012	1707	5403
4006(a)(3)(E)(iv)	40211(b)(3)(C)*	Plans can use interest rate smoothing over a 25-year period to determine liabilities	Plan years beginning after Dec. 31, 2011	1701	5402
4006(a)(3)(F)	40221(a)(2)*	PBGC flat-rate premiums for single-employer defined benefit plans are increased from $35 per participant to $42 for 2013, to $49 for 2014, and indexed for inflation after 2014	July 6, 2012	1706	5403
4006(a)(3)(I)	40222(b)*	PBGC premium rates for multiemployer defined benefit plans are raised from $9 per participant to $12 after 2012, indexed for inflation for post-2013 plan years	July 6, 2012	1708	5403

ERISA §	Act §	Topic	Effective Date	Analy- sis ¶	Com Rep ¶
4006(a)(3)(J)	40221(b)(3)(B)*	PBGC variable-rate premiums for single-employer defined benefit plans are indexed for inflation after 2012 plan years; increased by $4 for 2014 and by another $5 for 2015; and capped at $400 per participant, as indexed for inflation	July 6, 2012	1707	5403
4006(a)(8)	40221(b)(2)*	PBGC variable-rate premiums for single-employer defined benefit plans are indexed for inflation after 2012 plan years; increased by $4 for 2014 and by another $5 for 2015; and capped at $400 per participant, as indexed for inflation	July 6, 2012	1707	5403
4010(d)(3)	40211(b)(3)(D)*	Plans can use interest rate smoothing over a 25-year period to determine liabilities	Plan years beginning after Dec. 31, 2011	1701	5402
None	40211(b)(2)(B)*	Plans can use interest rate smoothing over a 25-year period to determine liabilities	Plan years beginning after Dec. 31, 2011	1701	5402
None	40233*	PBGC must adopt specified quality control procedures	July 6, 2012	1714	5404

¶ 6004. Code Sections Amended by Acts

Act § cites are to the 2012 Taxpayer Relief Act unless otherwise indicated.
* denotes 2012 Highway Investment Act
† denotes 2012 FAA Modernization Act
** denotes 2012 Middle Class Tax Relief Act
*** denotes 2012 African Growth Act
✓ denotes 2012 Aviation Extension Act
+ denotes 2011 Appropriations Act
~ denotes 2011 Job Creation Act
• denotes 2011 Taxpayer Protection Act
‡ denotes 2011 Temporary Payroll Act
++ denotes 2011 U.S.-Korea Trade Act
≈ denotes 2011 Trade Extension Act

Code §	Act §	Code §	Act §
1(h)(1)(B)	102(c)(2)	35(g)(9)	241(b)(3)(C)≈
1(h)(1)(C)	102(b)(1)	36B(c)(2)(D)	1858(b)(1)+
1(h)(1)(D)	102(b)(1)	36B(d)(2)(B)(i)	401(a)~
1(h)(1)(E)	102(b)(1)	36B(d)(2)(B)(ii)	401(a)~
1(h)(1)(F)	102(b)(1)	36B(d)(2)(B)(iii)	401(a)~
1(i)(2)	101(b)(1)(A)	36B(f)(2)(B)(i)	4(a)•
1(i)(3)	101(b)(1)(B)	40	404(b)(3)(A)(i)
1(i)(3)	101(b)(1)(B)	40(b)(6)	404(b)(3)(A)(ii)
1(i)(4)	101(b)(1)(B)	40(b)(6)(C)	404(b)(3)(A)(iii)
23(b)(4)	104(c)(2)(A)(i)	40(b)(6)(D)	404(b)(3)(A)(iii)
23(c)(1)	104(c)(2)(A)(ii)	40(b)(6)(E)	404(b)(3)(A)(ii)
23(c)(2)	104(c)(2)(A)(ii)	40(b)(6)(E)(i)(I)	404(b)(1)
23(c)(3)	104(c)(2)(A)(iii)	40(b)(6)(E)(ii)	404(b)(3)(B)
24(b)(3)	104(c)(2)(B)(i)	40(b)(6)(F)	404(b)(2)
24(d)(1)	104(c)(2)(B)(ii)(II)	40(b)(6)(G)	404(b)(2)
24(d)(1)(A)	104(c)(2)(B)(ii)(I)	40(b)(6)(H)	404(a)(1)
24(d)(1)(B)	104(c)(2)(B)(ii)(I)	40(b)(6)(H)	404(b)(2)
24(d)(4)	103(b)(1)	40(b)(6)(H)	404(b)(3)(A)(iii)
24(d)(4)	103(b)(2)	40(b)(6)(I)	404(b)(2)
25(e)(1)(C)	104(c)(2)(C)	40(b)(6)(J)	404(b)(2)
25A(i)	103(a)(1)	40(d)(3)(D)	404(b)(3)(A)(ii)
25A(i)(5)	104(c)(2)(D)(ii)	40(d)(6)	404(b)(3)(A)(iii)
25A(i)(5)	104(c)(2)(D)(i)	40(e)(2)	404(a)(2)
25A(i)(6)	104(c)(2)(D)(i)	40(e)(3)	404(b)(3)(A)(iii)
25A(i)(7)	104(c)(2)(D)(i)	40A(g)	405(a)
25B(g)	104(c)(2)(E)	41(f)(1)	301(c)(1)
25C(g)(2)	401(a)	41(f)(1)	301(c)(2)
25D(c)	104(c)(2)(F)	41(f)(3)(A)	301(b)(1)
26(a)	104(c)(1)	41(f)(3)(B)	301(b)(2)
30(c)(2)	104(c)(2)(G)	41(h)(1)(B)	301(a)(1)
30B(g)(2)	104(c)(2)(H)	42(b)(2)(A)	302(a)
30C(g)(2)	402(a)	45(c)(6)	407(a)(2)
30D(c)(2)	104(c)(2)(I)	45(d)(1)	407(a)(1)
30D(f)(2)	403(b)(1)(A)	45(d)(1)	407(a)(3)(A)(i)
30D(f)(2)	403(b)(1)(B)	45(d)(11)(B)	407(a)(3)(A)(vii)
30D(f)(7)	403(b)(2)	45(d)(2)(A)	407(a)(3)(B)
30D(g)	403(a)	45(d)(2)(A)(i)	407(a)(3)(A)(ii)
32(b)(3)	103(c)(1)	45(d)(3)(A)(i)(I)	407(a)(3)(A)(iii)
32(b)(3)	103(c)(2)	45(d)(3)(A)(ii)	407(a)(3)(C)
35(a)	241(b)(1)≈	45(d)(4)	407(a)(3)(D)(i)[sic]
35(b)(1)(B)	241(a)≈	45(d)(6)	407(a)(3)(A)(iv)
35(c)(2)(B)	241(b)(3)(A)≈	45(d)(7)	407(a)(3)(A)(v)
35(e)(1)(K)	241(b)(3)(B)≈	45(d)(9)	407(a)(3)(E)(ii)

Code §	Act §	Code §	Act §
45(d)(9)(A)(i)	407(a)(3)(E)(i)	151(d)(3)(D)	101(b)(2)(B)(i)(II)
45(d)(9)(A)(ii)	407(a)(3)(E)(i)	151(d)(3)(E)	101(b)(2)(B)(i)(III)
45(d)(9)(B)	407(a)(3)(E)(i)	151(d)(3)(F)	101(b)(2)(B)(i)(III)
45(d)(9)(B)	407(a)(3)(A)(vi)	151(d)(4)	101(b)(2)(B)(ii)(III)
45(d)(9)(B)	407(a)(3)(E)(iii)	151(d)(4)(A)	101(b)(2)(B)(ii)(II)
45(d)(9)(C)	407(a)(3)(E)(iii)	151(d)(4)(A)(i)	101(b)(2)(B)(ii)(II)
45(d)(9)(C)	407(a)(3)(E)(iv)	151(d)(4)(A)(ii)	101(b)(2)(B)(ii)(II)
45(e)(10)(A)	406(a)	151(d)(4)(B)	101(b)(2)(B)(ii)(II)
45A(f)	304(a)	151(d)(4)(B)	101(b)(2)(B)(ii)(I)
45C(b)(1)(D)	301(a)(2)	162(a)	1858(b)(3)+
45D(f)(1)(G)	305(a)	163(h)(3)(E)(iv)(I)	204(a)
45D(f)(3)	305(b)	163(h)(4)(E)(i)	204(b)(1)
45G(f)	306(a)	163(h)(4)(E)(i)	204(b)(2)
45L(c)(1)(A)(i)	408(b)	164(b)(5)(I)	205(a)
45L(g)	408(a)	168(e)(3)(E)(iv)	311(a)
45M(b)	409(a)	168(e)(3)(E)(ix)	311(a)
45N(e)	307(a)	168(e)(3)(E)(v)	311(a)
45P(f)	308(a)	168(i)(15)(D)	312(a)
48(a)(5)(C)	407(b)	168(i)(9)(A)(ii)	331(d)
48(a)(5)(D)(i)(II)	407(c)(1)(A)	168(j)(8)	313(a)
49	103(d)	168(k)	331(e)(1)
51(b)(3)	261(a)~	168(k)(2)	331(a)(2)
51(c)(4)(B)	261(d)~	168(k)(2)(A)(iv)	331(a)(1)
51(d)(13)(D)	261(c)~	168(k)(2)(B)(ii)	331(e)(2)
51(d)(3)(A)(i)	261(b)(1)~	168(k)(4)(D)(iii)(II)	331(c)(1)
51(d)(3)(A)(ii)(II)	261(b)(2)~	168(k)(4)(J)	331(c)(2)
51(d)(3)(A)(iii)	261(b)(3)~	168(l)	410(b)(2)(A)
51(d)(3)(A)(iv)	261(b)(3)~	168(l)	410(b)(2)(C)
51(c)(4)(B)	309(a)	168(l)(2)	410(b)(2)(D)
54E(c)(1)	310(a)	168(l)(2)(A)	410(b)(1)
55(b)(1)(A)(iii)	104(b)(2)(A)	168(l)(2)(D)	410(a)(1)
55(b)(3)(B)	102(c)(2)	168(l)(3)	410(b)(2)(B)
55(b)(3)(C)	102(b)(2)	168(l)(4)	410(b)(2)(B)
55(b)(3)(D)	102(b)(2)	168(l)(5)	410(b)(2)(B)
55(b)(3)(E)	102(b)(2)	168(l)(6)	410(b)(2)(B)
55(c)(3)	104(c)(2)(J)	168(l)(7)	410(b)(2)(B)
55(d)(1)(A)	104(a)(1)(A)	168(l)(8)	410(b)(2)(B)
55(d)(1)(B)	104(a)(1)(B)	168(n)(2)(C)	331(e)(3)
55(d)(1)(C)	104(a)(1)(C)	170(b)(1)(E)(vi)	206(a)
55(d)(3)(A)	104(b)(2)(B)(i)	170(b)(2)(B)(iii)	206(b)
55(d)(3)(B)	104(b)(2)(B)(ii)	170(e)(3)(C)(iv)	314(a)
55(d)(3)(C)	104(b)(2)(B)(iii)	179(b)(1)(B)	315(a)(1)(A)
55(d)(3)(D)	104(b)(2)(B)(iii)	179(b)(1)(C)	315(a)(1)(B)
55(d)(4)	104(b)(1)	179(b)(1)(C)	315(a)(1)(D)
62(a)(2)(D)	201(a)	179(b)(1)(D)	315(a)(1)(C)
68(b)	101(b)(2)(A)(i)	179(b)(2)(B)	315(a)(2)(A)
68(f)	101(b)(2)(A)(ii)	179(b)(2)(C)	315(a)(2)(B)
68(g)	101(b)(2)(A)(ii)	179(b)(2)(C)	315(a)(2)(D)
72(t)(2)(A)(vi)	100121(c)*	179(b)(2)(D)	315(a)(2)(C)
72(t)(2)(A)(vii)	100121(c)*	179(b)(6)	315(a)(3)
72(t)(2)(A)(viii)	100121(c)*	179(c)(2)	315(c)
79(f)	40242(d)*	179(d)(1)(A)(ii)	315(b)
108(a)(1)(E)	202(a)	179(f)(1)	315(d)(1)
132(f)(2)	203(a)	179(f)(4)	315(d)(2)(A)
139D	1858(b)(2)(A)+	179(f)(4)(C)	315(d)(2)(B)(i)
147(e)	1105(a)†	179(f)(4)(C)	315(d)(2)(B)(ii)
151(d)(3)(A)	101(b)(2)(B)(i)(I)	179E(g)	316(a)
151(d)(3)(B)	101(b)(2)(B)(i)(I)	181(f)	317(a)
151(d)(3)(C)	101(b)(2)(B)(i)(II)	199(d)(8)(C)	318(a)(1)

Code §	Act §	Code §	Act §
199(d)(8)(C)	318(a)(2)	420(f)(2)(D)(i)(II)	40242(c)(2)(E)(iii) *
222(e)	207(a)	420(f)(2)(D)(i)(II)	40242(c)(2)(E)(iv) *
249(a)	1108(a) †	420(f)(2)(D)(ii)	40242(c)(2)(F)(i) *
249(b)(1)	1108(b)(1) †	420(f)(2)(D)(ii)	40242(c)(2)(F)(ii) *
249(b)(2)	1108(b)(2) †	420(f)(2)(D)(iii)	40242(c)(2)(G)(i) *
404(o)(6)	40211(a)(2)(A) *	420(f)(2)(D)(iii)	40242(c)(2)(G)(ii) *
408(a)(5)(D)(ii)	407(c)(1)(B)	420(f)(2)(E)(i)(III)	40242(e)(9)(A) *
408(a)(5)(D)(iii)	407(c)(1)(C)	420(f)(2)(E)(i)(III)	40242(e)(9)(B) *
408(a)(5)(D)(iv)	407(c)(1)(C)	420(f)(2)(E)(ii)	40242(e)(2) *
408(d)(8)(F)	208(a)	420(f)(6)	40242(e)(10) *
417(e)(3)(C)	40211(a)(2)(C) *	420(f)(6)(A)(i)	40242(e)(11)(A) *
417(e)(3)(D)	40211(a)(2)(C) *	420(f)(6)(A)(ii)	40242(e)(11)(A) *
420	40242(e)(1) *	420(f)(6)(A)(ii)	40242(e)(11)(B) *
420(a)	40242(a) *	420(f)(6)(B)	40242(e)(12)(C) *
420(b)(4)	40242(g)(2) *	420(f)(6)(B)(i)	40242(e)(12)(A) *
420(b)(1)(A)	40242(e)(2) *	420(f)(6)(B)(ii)	40242(e)(12)(B)(ii) *
420(b)(1)(A)	40242(f) *	420(f)(6)(C)	40242(b)(3)(B)(ii)(I) *
420(b)(1)(A)	40242(g)(1) *	420(f)(6)(C)	40242(b)(3)(B)(ii)(IV) *
420(b)(2)	40242(g)(3)(B) *	420(f)(6)(C)(i)	40242(b)(3)(B)(ii)(II) *
420(b)(2)(A)	40242(e)(3)(A) *	420(f)(6)(C)(i)	40242(b)(3)(B)(ii)(III) *
420(b)(2)(B)	40242(g)(3)(A) *	420(f)(6)(D)	40242(b)(3)(A) *
420(b)(3)	40242(e)(3)(B) *	420(f)(6)(E)	40242(b)(3)(A) *
420(b)(5)	40241(a) *	420(f)(6)(E)	40242(e)(13)(A) *
420(b)(5)	40242(g)(2) *	420(f)(6)(E)	40242(e)(13)(B) *
420(c)(1)(A)	40242(e)(2) *	420(f)(6)(E)	40242(e)(13)(C) *
420(c)(1)(B)	40242(e)(4) *	420(f)(6)(B)(ii)	40242(e)(12)(B)(i) *
420(c)(1)(B)(i)	40242(e)(2) *	420(g)	40211(a)(2)(D) *
420(c)(1)(C)	40242(e)(2) *	430(h)(2)(C)(iv)	40211(a)(1) *
420(c)(2)(A)	40242(g)(4)(B) *	430(h)(2)(F)	40211(a)(2)(B) *
420(c)(2)(A)	40242(g)(4)(C) *	451(i)(3)	411(a)
420(c)(2)(B)	40242(g)(4)(A) *	460(c)(6)(B)(ii)	331(b)
420(c)(3)	40242(c)(1) *	512(b)(13)(E)(iv)	319(a)
420(c)(3)(B)	40242(c)(2)(A)(ii) *	531	102(c)(1)(A)
420(c)(3)(B)(i)(I)	40242(c)(2)(A)(i) *	541	102(c)(1)(B)
420(c)(3)(B)(i)(II)	40242(c)(2)(A)(i) *	871(k)(1)(C)(v)	320(a)
420(c)(3)(B)(i)(III)	40242(c)(2)(A)(i) *	871(k)(2)(C)(v)	320(a)
420(c)(3)(C)	40242(c)(2)(B)(i) *	897(h)(4)(A)(ii)	321(a)
420(c)(3)(C)	40242(c)(2)(B)(ii) *	904(i)	104(c)(2)(K)
420(c)(3)(E)(i)	40242(c)(2)(C)(i) *	904(j)	104(c)(2)(K)
420(c)(3)(E)(ii)	40242(c)(2)(C)(ii) *	904(k)	104(c)(2)(K)
420(c)(3)(E)(ii)(II)	40242(c)(2)(C)(iii) *	904(l)	104(c)(2)(K)
420(d)(1)(A)	40242(e)(2) *	953(e)(10)	322(a)(1)
420(e)(4)	40242(b)(1) *	953(e)(10)	322(a)(2)
420(e)(1)	40242(e)(5)(B) *	954(c)(6)(C)	323(a)
420(e)(1)(A)	40242(e)(5)(A) *	954(h)(9)	322(b)
420(e)(1)(B)(i)	40242(e)(6)(A) *	1202(a)(2)(C)	327(b)(1)
420(e)(1)(B)(i)	40242(e)(6)(B) *	1202(a)(2)(C)	327(b)(2)
420(e)(1)(B)(i)	40242(e)(6)(C) *	1202(a)(3)	324(b)(1)
420(e)(1)(C)(i)	40242(b)(3)(B)(i) *	1202(a)(4)	324(a)(1)
420(e)(1)(D)	40242(b)(2) *	1202(a)(4)	324(a)(2)
420(e)(1)(E)	40242(b)(2) *	1202(a)(4)	324(b)(2)
420(e)(5)	40242(b)(1) *	1367(a)(2)	325(a)
420(e)(6)	40242(b)(1) *	1374(d)(2)(B)	326(b)
420(f)	40242(e)(7) *	1374(d)(7)(C)	326(a)(1)
420(f)(4)	40242(e)(10) *	1374(d)(7)(C)	326(a)(2)
420(f)(2)	40242(c)(2)(D) *	1374(d)(7)(D)	326(a)(1)
420(f)(2)(B)(ii)(II)	40242(e)(8) *	1374(d)(7)(E)	326(a)(3)
420(f)(2)(D)(i)(I)	40242(c)(2)(E)(i) *	1391(d)(1)(A)(i)	327(a)
420(f)(2)(D)(i)(I)	40242(c)(2)(E)(ii) *	1400C(d)	104(c)(2)(L)

Code §	Act §	Code §	Act §
1400L(d)(2)(D)	328(a)	6331(h)(3)	301(a) ~
1400L(b)(2)(D)	331(e)(4)	6412(a)(1)	40102(c)(1) *
1400N(d)(3)(B)	331(e)(5)	6412(a)(1)	40102(c)(2) *
1445(e)(1)	102(c)(1)(C)	6412(a)(1)	40102(c)(3) *
1445(e)(6)	102(c)(3)	6426(c)(6)	405(b)(1)
2010(c)(4)(B)	101(c)(2)	6426(d)(5)	412(a)
3303(f)	252(a)(1) ≈	6426(e)(3)	412(a)
3303(f)	252(a)(2) ≈	6427(e)(6)(B)	405(b)(2)
3303(g)	252(a)(1) ≈	6427(e)(6)(C)	412(b)(1)(A)
3402(t)	102(a) ~	6427(e)(6)(C)	412(b)(1)(B)
4041(a)(1)(C)(iii)(I)	40102(a)(1)(A) *	6427(e)(6)(D)	412(b)(2)(A)
4041(m)(1)(A)	40102(a)(2)(A) *	6427(e)(6)(D)	412(b)(2)(B)
4041(m)(1)(B)	40102(a)(1)(B) *	6427(e)(6)(E)	412(b)(3)
4043	1103(a)(1) †	6655	4 ***
4051(c)	40102(a)(2)(B) *	6695(g)	501(a) ++
4071(d)	40102(a)(2)(C) *	7213(a)(2)	209(b)(3)
4081(d)(2)(B)	1101(a) †	7275(c)	1104(a)(1) †
4081(d)(2)(B)	2(a) ✔	7275(d)	1104(a)(1) †
4082(e)	1103(a)(2) †	7518(g)(6)(A)	102(c)(1)(D)
4083(b)	1103(b) †	7527(b)	241(b)(2)(A) ≈
4101(a)(1)	404(b)(3)(C)	7527(d)(2)	241(b)(2)(B) ≈
4261(j)	1103(c) †	7527(d)(2)	241(b)(2)(C) ≈
4261(j)(1)(A)(ii)	1101(b)(1) †	7527(e)	241(b)(2)(D) ≈
4261(j)(1)(A)(ii)	2(b)(1) ✔	7652(f)(1)	329(a)
4261(k)	1103(c) †	9502(b)(1)(B)	1103(a)(3) †
4271(d)(1)(A)(ii)	1101(b)(2) †	9502(b)(1)(C)	1103(a)(3) †
4271(d)(1)(A)(ii)	2(b)(2) ✔	9502(b)(1)(D)	1103(a)(3) †
4281	1107(a) †	9502(d)(1)	1102(a)(1) †
4481(f)	40102(b)(1)(A) *	9502(d)(1)	3(a)(1) ✔
4482(c)(4)	40102(b)(2)(A) *	9502(d)(1)	3(a)(2) ✔
4482(c)(4)	40102(b)(2)(A) *	9502(d)(1)(A)	1102(a)(2) †
4482(d)	40102(b)(1)(B) *	9502(e)(2)	1102(b) †
4483(i)	40102(d)(3) *	9502(e)(2)	3(b) ✔
4980B(f)(2)(B)(i)(V)	243(a)(3) ≈	9503(b)(1)	40102(e)(1)(A)(i) *
4980B(f)(2)(B)(i)(VI)	243(a)(4) ≈	9503(b)(2)	40102(e)(1)(A)(i) *
4980H(b)(3)	1858(b)(4) +	9503(b)(2)	40102(e)(1)(A)(ii) *
6041(a)	2(b)(1) •	9503(b)(2)	40102(e)(1)(A)(iii) *
6041(a)	2(b)(2) •	9503(b)(2)	40102(e)(1)(A)(i) *
6041(h)	3(a) •	9503(b)(6)(B)	40101(a)(1) *
6041(i)	2(a) •	9503(c)(1)	40101(a)(1) *
6041(j)	2(a) •	9503(c)(1)	40101(a)(2) *
6056(a)	1858(b)(5)(A) +	9503(c)(2)	40102(e)(1)(B) *
6056(b)(2)(C)(i)	1858(b)(5)(B)(i) +	9503(c)(3)(A)(i)	40102(e)(2)(A) *
6056(b)(2)(C)(iii)	1858(b)(5)(B)(ii) +	9503(c)(4)(A)	40102(e)(2)(A) *
6056(b)(2)(C)(iv)	1858(b)(5)(B)(iii) +	9503(e)(3)	40101(a)(1) *
6056(b)(2)(C)(v)	1858(b)(5)(B)(iv) +	9503(f)(3)	40201(b)(1) *
6056(d)(2)	1858(b)(5)(C) +	9503(f)(4)	40201(b)(2)(A) *
6056(e)	1858(b)(5)(C) +	9503(f)(4)	40201(b)(2)(B) *
6056(f)	1858(b)(5)(D) +	9503(f)(4)	40251 *
6103(a)(3)	209(b)(1)	9503(f)(5)	40251 *
6103(k)(10)	209(a)	9504(b)(2)	40101(b)(1) *
6103(p)(4)	209(b)(2)(A)	9504(d)(2)	40101(b)(2) *
6103(p)(4)	209(b)(2)(C)	9508(c)	40201(a)(1) *
6103(p)(4)(F)(i)	209(b)(2)(B)(i)	9508(c)(2)	40201(a)(2) *
6103(p)(4)(F)(i)	209(b)(2)(B)(ii)	9508(e)(2)	40101(c) *
6116	502(a) ++	9801(c)(2)(D)	242(a)(1) ≈

¶ 6005. Act Sections Amending Code

Act § cites are to the 2012 Taxpayer Relief Act unless otherwise indicated.

* denotes 2012 Highway Investment Act
† denotes 2012 FAA Modernization Act
** denotes 2012 Middle Class Tax Relief Act
*** denotes 2012 African Growth Act
✓ denotes 2012 Aviation Extension Act
+ denotes 2011 Appropriations Act
~ denotes 2011 Job Creation Act
• denotes 2011 Taxpayer Protection Act
‡ denotes 2011 Temporary Payroll Act
++ denotes 2011 U.S.-Korea Trade Act
≈ denotes 2011 Trade Extension Act

Act §	Code §	Act §	Code §
4(a)•	36B(f)(2)(B)(i)	2(b)(2)✓	4271(d)(1)(A)(ii)
2(b)(1)•	6041(a)	3(a)(1)✓	9502(d)(1)
2(b)(2)•	6041(a)	3(a)(2)✓	9502(d)(1)
3(a)•	6041(h)	3(b)✓	9502(e)(2)
2(a)•	6041(i)	1105(a)†	147(e)
2(a)•	6041(j)	1108(a)†	249(a)
1858(b)(5)(B)(ii)+	6056(b)(2)(C)(iii)	1108(b)(1)†	249(b)(1)
1858(b)(5)(B)(iii)+	6056(b)(2)(C)(iv)	1108(b)(2)†	249(b)(2)
1858(b)(5)(B)(iv)+	6056(b)(2)(C)(v)	1103(a)(1)†	4043
1858(b)(5)(C)+	6056(d)(2)	1101(a)†	4081(d)(2)(B)
1858(b)(5)(C)+	6056(e)	1103(a)(2)†	4082(e)
1858(b)(5)(D)+	6056(f)	1103(b)†	4083(b)
241(b)(1)≈	35(a)	1103(c)†	4261(j)
241(a)≈	35(b)(1)(B)	1101(b)(1)†	4261(j)(1)(A)(ii)
241(b)(3)(A)≈	35(c)(2)(B)	1103(c)†	4261(k)
241(b)(3)(B)≈	35(e)(1)(K)	1101(b)(2)†	4271(d)(1)(A)(ii)
241(b)(3)(C)≈	35(g)(9)	1107(a)†	4281
252(a)(1)≈	3303(f)	1104(a)(1)†	7275(c)
252(a)(2)≈	3303(f)	1104(a)(1)†	7275(d)
252(a)(1)≈	3303(g)	1103(a)(3)†	9502(b)(1)(B)
243(a)(3)≈	4980B(f)(2)(B)(i)(V)	1103(a)(3)†	9502(b)(1)(C)
243(a)(4)≈	4980B(f)(2)(B)(i)(VI)	1103(a)(3)†	9502(b)(1)(D)
241(b)(2)(A)≈	7527(b)	1102(a)(1)†	9502(d)(1)
241(b)(2)(B)≈	7527(d)(2)	1102(a)(2)†	9502(d)(1)(A)
241(b)(2)(C)≈	7527(d)(2)	1102(b)†	9502(e)(2)
241(b)(2)(D)≈	7527(e)	40242(e)(2)*	420(f)(2)(E)(ii)
242(a)(1)≈	9801(c)(2)(D)	40242(e)(10)*	420(f)(6)
502(a)++	6116	40242(e)(11)(A)*	420(f)(6)(A)(i)
501(a)++	6695(g)	40242(e)(11)(A)*	420(f)(6)(A)(ii)
401(a)~	36B(d)(2)(B)(i)	40242(e)(11)(B)*	420(f)(6)(A)(ii)
401(a)~	36B(d)(2)(B)(ii)	40242(e)(12)(C)*	420(f)(6)(B)
401(a)~	36B(d)(2)(B)(iii)	40242(e)(12)(A)*	420(f)(6)(B)(i)
261(a)~	51(b)(3)	40242(e)(12)(B)(ii)*	420(f)(6)(B)(ii)
261(d)~	51(c)(4)(B)	40242(b)(3)(B)(ii)(I)*	420(f)(6)(C)
261(c)~	51(d)(13)(D)	40242(b)(3)(B)(ii)(IV)*	420(f)(6)(C)
261(b)(1)~	51(d)(3)(A)(i)	40242(b)(3)(B)(ii)(II)*	420(f)(6)(C)(i)
261(b)(2)~	51(d)(3)(A)(ii)(II)	40242(b)(3)(B)(ii)(III)*	420(f)(6)(C)(i)
261(b)(3)~	51(d)(3)(A)(iii)	40242(b)(3)(A)*	420(f)(6)(D)
261(b)(3)~	51(d)(3)(A)(iv)	40242(b)(3)(A)*	420(f)(6)(E)
102(a)~	3402(t)	40242(e)(13)(A)*	420(f)(6)(E)
301(a)~	6331(h)(3)	40242(e)(13)(B)*	420(f)(6)(E)
2(a)✓	4081(d)(2)(B)	40242(e)(13)(C)*	420(f)(6)(E)
2(b)(1)✓	4261(j)(1)(A)(ii)	40242(e)(12)(B)(i)*	420(f)(6)(B)(ii)

Act §	Code §	Act §	Code §
40211(a)(2)(D) *	420(g)	103(a)(1)	25A(i)
40211(a)(1) *	430(h)(2)(C)(iv)	104(c)(2)(D)(ii)	25A(i)(5)
40211(a)(2)(B) *	430(h)(2)(F)	104(c)(2)(D)(i)	25A(i)(5)
40102(a)(1)(A) *	4041(a)(1)(C)(iii)(I)	104(c)(2)(D)(i)	25A(i)(6)
40102(a)(2)(A) *	4041(m)(1)(A)	104(c)(2)(D)(i)	25A(i)(7)
40102(a)(1)(B) *	4041(m)(1)(B)	104(c)(2)(E)	25B(g)
40102(a)(2)(B) *	4051(c)	401(a)	25C(g)(2)
40102(a)(2)(C) *	4071(d)	104(c)(2)(F)	25D(c)
40102(b)(1)(A) *	4481(f)	104(c)(1)	26(a)
40102(b)(2)(A) *	4482(c)(4)	104(c)(2)(G)	30(c)(2)
40102(b)(2)(A) *	4482(c)(4)	104(c)(2)(H)	30B(g)(2)
40102(b)(1)(B) *	4482(d)	402(a)	30C(g)(2)
40102(d)(3) *	4483(i)	104(c)(2)(I)	30D(c)(2)
40102(c)(1) *	6412(a)(1)	403(b)(1)(A)	30D(f)(2)
40102(c)(2) *	6412(a)(1)	403(b)(1)(B)	30D(f)(2)
40102(c)(3) *	6412(a)(1)	403(b)(2)	30D(f)(7)
40102(e)(1)(A)(i) *	9503(b)(1)	403(a)	30D(g)
40102(e)(1)(A)(i) *	9503(b)(2)	103(c)(1)	32(b)(3)
40102(e)(1)(A)(ii) *	9503(b)(2)	103(c)(2)	32(b)(3)
40102(e)(1)(A)(iii) *	9503(b)(2)	404(b)(3)(A)(i)	40
40102(e)(1)(A)(i) *	9503(b)(2)	404(b)(3)(A)(ii)	40(b)(6)
40101(a)(1) *	9503(b)(6)(B)	404(b)(3)(A)(iii)	40(b)(6)(C)
40101(a)(1) *	9503(c)(1)	404(b)(3)(A)(iii)	40(b)(6)(D)
40101(a)(2) *	9503(c)(1)	404(b)(3)(A)(ii)	40(b)(6)(E)
40102(e)(1)(B) *	9503(c)(2)	404(b)(1)	40(b)(6)(E)(i)(I)
40102(e)(2)(A) *	9503(c)(3)(A)(i)	404(b)(3)(B)	40(b)(6)(E)(ii)
40102(e)(2)(A) *	9503(c)(4)(A)	404(b)(2)	40(b)(6)(F)
40101(a)(1) *	9503(e)(3)	404(b)(2)	40(b)(6)(G)
40201(b)(1) *	9503(f)(3)	404(a)(1)	40(b)(6)(H)
40201(b)(2)(A) *	9503(f)(4)	404(b)(2)	40(b)(6)(H)
40201(b)(2)(B) *	9503(f)(4)	404(b)(3)(A)(iii)	40(b)(6)(H)
40251 *	9503(f)(4)	404(b)(2)	40(b)(6)(I)
40251 *	9503(f)(5)	404(b)(2)	40(b)(6)(J)
40101(b)(1) *	9504(b)(2)	404(b)(3)(A)(ii)	40(d)(3)(D)
40101(b)(2) *	9504(d)(2)	404(b)(3)(A)(iii)	40(d)(6)
40201(a)(1) *	9508(c)	404(a)(2)	40(e)(2)
40201(a)(2) *	9508(c)(2)	404(b)(3)(A)(iii)	40(e)(3)
40101(c) *	9508(e)(2)	405(a)	40A(g)
4 ***	6655	301(c)(1)	41(f)(1)
102(c)(2)	1(h)(1)(B)	301(c)(2)	41(f)(1)
102(b)(1)	1(h)(1)(C)	301(b)(1)	41(f)(3)(A)
102(b)(1)	1(h)(1)(D)	301(b)(2)	41(f)(3)(B)
102(b)(1)	1(h)(1)(E)	301(a)(1)	41(h)(1)(B)
102(b)(1)	1(h)(1)(F)	302(a)	42(b)(2)(A)
101(b)(1)(A)	1(i)(2)	407(a)(2)	45(c)(6)
101(b)(1)(B)	1(i)(3)	407(a)(1)	45(d)(1)
101(b)(1)(B)	1(i)(3)	407(a)(3)(A)(i)	45(d)(1)
101(b)(1)(B)	1(i)(4)	407(a)(3)(A)(vii)	45(d)(11)(B)
104(c)(2)(A)(i)	23(b)(4)	407(a)(3)(B)	45(d)(2)(A)
104(c)(2)(A)(ii)	23(c)(1)	407(a)(3)(A)(ii)	45(d)(2)(A)(i)
104(c)(2)(A)(ii)	23(c)(2)	407(a)(3)(A)(iii)	45(d)(3)(A)(i)(I)
104(c)(2)(A)(iii)	23(c)(3)	407(a)(3)(C)	45(d)(3)(A)(ii)
104(c)(2)(B)(i)	24(b)(3)	407(a)(3)(D)(i)[sic]	45(d)(4)
104(c)(2)(B)(ii)(II)	24(d)(1)	407(a)(3)(A)(iv)	45(d)(6)
104(c)(2)(B)(ii)(I)	24(d)(1)(A)	407(a)(3)(A)(v)	45(d)(7)
104(c)(2)(B)(ii)(I)	24(d)(1)(B)	407(a)(3)(E)(ii)	45(d)(9)
103(b)(1)	24(d)(4)	407(a)(3)(E)(i)	45(d)(9)(A)(i)
103(b)(2)	24(d)(4)	407(a)(3)(E)(i)	45(d)(9)(A)(ii)
104(c)(2)(C)	25(e)(1)(C)	407(a)(3)(E)(i)	45(d)(9)(B)

Act §	Code §	Act §	Code §
407(a)(3)(A)(vi)	45(d)(9)(B)	312(a)	168(i)(15)(D)
407(a)(3)(E)(iii)	45(d)(9)(B)	331(d)	168(i)(9)(A)(ii)
407(a)(3)(E)(iii)	45(d)(9)(C)	313(a)	168(j)(8)
407(a)(3)(E)(iv)	45(d)(9)(C)	331(e)(1)	168(k)
406(a)	45(e)(10)(A)	331(a)(2)	168(k)(2)
304(a)	45A(f)	331(a)(1)	168(k)(2)(A)(iv)
301(a)(2)	45C(b)(1)(D)	331(e)(2)	168(k)(2)(B)(ii)
305(a)	45D(f)(1)(G)	331(c)(1)	168(k)(4)(D)(iii)(II)
305(b)	45D(f)(3)	331(c)(2)	168(k)(4)(J)
306(a)	45G(f)	410(b)(2)(A)	168(l)
408(b)	45L(c)(1)(A)(i)	410(b)(2)(C)	168(l)
408(a)	45L(g)	410(b)(2)(D)	168(l)(2)
409(a)	45M(b)	410(b)(1)	168(l)(2)(A)
307(a)	45N(e)	410(a)(1)	168(l)(2)(D)
308(a)	45P(f)	410(b)(2)(B)	168(l)(3)
407(b)	48(a)(5)(C)	410(b)(2)(B)	168(l)(4)
407(c)(1)(A)	48(a)(5)(D)(i)(II)	410(b)(2)(B)	168(l)(5)
103(d)	49	410(b)(2)(B)	168(l)(6)
309(a)	51(c)(4)(B)	410(b)(2)(B)	168(l)(7)
310(a)	54E(c)(1)	410(b)(2)(B)	168(l)(8)
104(b)(2)(A)	55(b)(1)(A)(iii)	331(e)(3)	168(n)(2)(C)
102(c)(2)	55(b)(3)(B)	206(a)	170(b)(1)(E)(vi)
102(b)(2)	55(b)(3)(C)	206(b)	170(b)(2)(B)(iii)
102(b)(2)	55(b)(3)(D)	314(a)	170(e)(3)(C)(iv)
102(b)(2)	55(b)(3)(E)	315(a)(1)(A)	179(b)(1)(B)
104(c)(2)(J)	55(c)(3)	315(a)(1)(B)	179(b)(1)(C)
104(a)(1)(A)	55(d)(1)(A)	315(a)(1)(D)	179(b)(1)(C)
104(a)(1)(B)	55(d)(1)(B)	315(a)(1)(C)	179(b)(1)(D)
104(a)(1)(C)	55(d)(1)(C)	315(a)(2)(A)	179(b)(2)(B)
104(b)(2)(B)(i)	55(d)(3)(A)	315(a)(2)(B)	179(b)(2)(C)
104(b)(2)(B)(ii)	55(d)(3)(B)	315(a)(2)(D)	179(b)(2)(C)
104(b)(2)(B)(iii)	55(d)(3)(C)	315(a)(2)(C)	179(b)(2)(D)
104(b)(2)(B)(iii)	55(d)(3)(D)	315(a)(3)	179(b)(6)
104(b)(1)	55(d)(4)	315(c)	179(c)(2)
201(a)	62(a)(2)(D)	315(b)	179(d)(1)(A)(ii)
101(b)(2)(A)(i)	68(b)	315(d)(1)	179(f)(1)
101(b)(2)(A)(ii)	68(f)	315(d)(2)(A)	179(f)(4)
101(b)(2)(A)(ii)	68(g)	315(d)(2)(B)(i)	179(f)(4)(C)
202(a)	108(a)(1)(E)	315(d)(2)(B)(ii)	179(f)(4)(C)
203(a)	132(f)(2)	316(a)	179E(g)
101(b)(2)(B)(i)(I)	151(d)(3)(A)	317(a)	181(f)
101(b)(2)(B)(i)(I)	151(d)(3)(B)	318(a)(1)	199(d)(8)(C)
101(b)(2)(B)(i)(II)	151(d)(3)(C)	318(a)(2)	199(d)(8)(C)
101(b)(2)(B)(i)(II)	151(d)(3)(D)	207(a)	222(e)
101(b)(2)(B)(i)(III)	151(d)(3)(E)	407(c)(1)(B)	408(a)(5)(D)(ii)
101(b)(2)(B)(i)(III)	151(d)(3)(F)	407(c)(1)(C)	408(a)(5)(D)(iii)
101(b)(2)(B)(ii)(III)	151(d)(4)	407(c)(1)(C)	408(a)(5)(D)(iv)
101(b)(2)(B)(ii)(II)	151(d)(4)(A)	208(a)	408(d)(8)(F)
101(b)(2)(B)(ii)(II)	151(d)(4)(A)(i)	411(a)	451(i)(3)
101(b)(2)(B)(ii)(II)	151(d)(4)(A)(ii)	331(b)	460(c)(6)(B)(ii)
101(b)(2)(B)(ii)(II)	151(d)(4)(B)	319(a)	512(b)(13)(E)(iv)
101(b)(2)(B)(ii)(I)	151(d)(4)(B)	102(c)(1)(A)	531
204(a)	163(h)(3)(E)(iv)(I)	102(c)(1)(B)	541
204(b)(1)	163(h)(4)(E)(i)	320(a)	871(k)(1)(C)(v)
204(b)(2)	163(h)(4)(E)(i)	320(a)	871(k)(2)(C)(v)
205(a)	164(b)(5)(I)	321(a)	897(h)(4)(A)(ii)
311(a)	168(e)(3)(E)(iv)	104(c)(2)(K)	904(i)
311(a)	168(e)(3)(E)(ix)	104(c)(2)(K)	904(j)
311(a)	168(e)(3)(E)(v)	104(c)(2)(K)	904(k)

Act §	Code §	Act §	Code §
104(c)(2)(K)	904(l)	102(c)(1)(C)	1445(e)(1)
322(a)(1)	953(e)(10)	102(c)(3)	1445(e)(6)
322(a)(2)	953(e)(10)	101(c)(2)	2010(c)(4)(B)
323(a)	954(c)(6)(C)	404(b)(3)(C)	4101(a)(1)
322(b)	954(h)(9)	209(b)(1)	6103(a)(3)
327(b)(1)	1202(a)(2)(C)	209(a)	6103(k)(10)
327(b)(2)	1202(a)(2)(C)	209(b)(2)(A)	6103(p)(4)
324(b)(1)	1202(a)(3)	209(b)(2)(C)	6103(p)(4)
324(a)(1)	1202(a)(4)	209(b)(2)(B)(i)	6103(p)(4)(F)(i)
324(a)(2)	1202(a)(4)	209(b)(2)(B)(ii)	6103(p)(4)(F)(i)
324(b)(2)	1202(a)(4)	405(b)(1)	6426(c)(6)
325(a)	1367(a)(2)	412(a)	6426(d)(5)
326(b)	1374(d)(2)(B)	412(a)	6426(e)(3)
326(a)(1)	1374(d)(7)(C)	405(b)(2)	6427(e)(6)(B)
326(a)(2)	1374(d)(7)(C)	412(b)(1)(A)	6427(e)(6)(C)
326(a)(1)	1374(d)(7)(D)	412(b)(1)(B)	6427(e)(6)(C)
326(a)(3)	1374(d)(7)(E)	412(b)(2)(A)	6427(e)(6)(D)
327(a)	1391(d)(1)(A)(i)	412(b)(2)(B)	6427(e)(6)(D)
104(c)(2)(L)	1400C(d)	412(b)(3)	6427(e)(6)(E)
328(a)	1400L(d)(2)(D)	209(b)(3)	7213(a)(2)
331(e)(4)	1400L(b)(2)(D)	102(c)(1)(D)	7518(g)(6)(A)
331(e)(5)	1400N(d)(3)(B)	329(a)	7652(f)(1)

¶ 6006. ERISA Sections Amended by Acts

Act § cites are to the 2012 Taxpayer Relief Act unless otherwise indicated.

* denotes 2012 Highway Investment Act
† denotes 2012 FAA Modernization Act
** denotes 2012 Middle Class Tax Relief Act
*** denotes 2012 African Growth Act
✓ denotes 2012 Aviation Extension Act
+ denotes 2011 Appropriations Act
~ denotes 2011 Job Creation Act
• denotes 2011 Taxpayer Protection Act
‡ denotes 2011 Temporary Payroll Act
++ denotes 2011 U.S.-Korea Trade Act
≈ denotes 2011 Trade Extension Act

ERISA §	Act §	ERISA §	Act §
101(e)	40242(e)(14) *	4002(e)(1)	40231(a)(2)(B) *
101(e)(3)	40241(b)(1) *	4002(e)(2)	40231(a)(2)(C) *
101(f)(2)(D)	40211(b)(2)(A) *	4002(h)(1)	40232(b) *
205(g)(3)(B)(ii)	40211(b)(3)(B) *	4002(h)(3)	40231(a)(3)(B) *
205(g)(3)(B)(iii)	40211(b)(3)(B) *	4002(j)	40231(b) *
303(h)(2)(C)(iv)	40211(b)(1) *	4002(k)	40231(c) *
303(h)(2)(F)	40211(b)(3)(A) *	4004	40232(a) *
403(c)(1)	40241(b)(1) *	4005(c)	40234(a) *
408(b)(13)	40241(b)(1) *	4006(a)(3)(A)(i)	40221(a)(1) *
408(b)(13)	40241(b)(2) *	4006(a)(3)(A)(iv)	40222(a)(1) *
602(2)(A)	243(a) ≈	4006(a)(3)(A)(v)	40222(a)(4) *
701(c)(2)(C)	242(a)(2) ≈	4006(a)(3)(E)(i)	40221(b)(3)(A) *
4002(c)	40231(d) *	4006(a)(3)(E)(ii)	40221(b)(1) *
4002(d)(2)	40231(a)(1) *	4006(a)(3)(E)(iv)	40211(b)(3)(C) *
4002(d)(3)	40231(a)(1) *	4006(a)(3)(F)	40221(a)(2) *
4002(d)(4)	40231(a)(1) *	4006(a)(3)(I)	40222(b) *
4002(d)(5)	40231(a)(1) *	4006(a)(3)(J)	40221(b)(3)(B) *
4002(d)(6)	40231(a)(1) *	4006(a)(8)	40221(b)(2) *
4002(d)(7)	40231(a)(1) *	4010(d)(3)	40211(b)(3)(D) *

¶ 6007. Act Sections Amending ERISA

Act § cites are to the 2012 Taxpayer Relief Act unless otherwise indicated.

* denotes 2012 Highway Investment Act
† denotes 2012 FAA Modernization Act
** denotes 2012 Middle Class Tax Relief Act
*** denotes 2012 African Growth Act
✓ denotes 2012 Aviation Extension Act
+ denotes 2011 Appropriations Act
~ denotes 2011 Job Creation Act
• denotes 2011 Taxpayer Protection Act
‡ denotes 2011 Temporary Payroll Act
++ denotes 2011 U.S.-Korea Trade Act
≈ denotes 2011 Trade Extension Act

Act §	ERISA §	Act §	ERISA §
242(a)(2)≈	701(c)(2)(C)	40231(a)(1)*	4002(d)(3)
243(a)≈	602(2)(A)	40231(a)(1)*	4002(d)(4)
40211(b)(1)*	303(h)(2)(C)(iv)	40231(a)(1)*	4002(d)(5)
40211(b)(2)(A)*	101(f)(2)(D)	40231(a)(1)*	4002(d)(6)
40211(b)(3)(A)*	303(h)(2)(F)	40231(a)(1)*	4002(d)(7)
40211(b)(3)(B)*	205(g)(3)(B)(ii)	40231(a)(2)(B)*	4002(e)(1)
40211(b)(3)(B)*	205(g)(3)(B)(iii)	40231(a)(2)(C)*	4002(e)(2)
40211(b)(3)(C)*	4006(a)(3)(E)(iv)	40231(a)(3)(B)*	4002(h)(3)
40211(b)(3)(D)*	4010(d)(3)	40231(b)*	4002(j)
40221(a)(1)*	4006(a)(3)(A)(i)	40231(c)*	4002(k)
40221(a)(2)*	4006(a)(3)(F)	40231(d)*	4002(c)
40221(b)(1)*	4006(a)(3)(E)(ii)	40232(a)*	4004
40221(b)(2)*	4006(a)(8)	40232(b)*	4002(h)(1)
40221(b)(3)(A)*	4006(a)(3)(E)(i)	40234(a)*	4005(c)
40221(b)(3)(B)*	4006(a)(3)(J)	40241(b)(1)*	101(e)(3)
40222(a)(1)*	4006(a)(3)(A)(iv)	40241(b)(1)*	403(c)(1)
40222(a)(4)*	4006(a)(3)(A)(v)	40241(b)(1)*	408(b)(13)
40222(b)*	4006(a)(3)(I)	40241(b)(2)*	408(b)(13)
40231(a)(1)*	4002(d)(2)	40242(e)(14)*	101(e)

¶ 6008. FTC 2nd ¶ s Affected by Acts

FTC 2d ¶	Analysis ¶	FTC 2d ¶	Analysis ¶	FTC 2d ¶	Analysis ¶
A-1100	101, 102	A-4500	403, 701	B-1900	205
A-1100.1	102	A-4501	701	B-1903	205
A-1101	101	A-4517	701	C-1000	104, 1503
A-1102	101	A-4523	701	C-1003	104
A-1103	101, 102	A-4525.1	403, 701	C-1005	104
A-1104	101	A-4525.2	701	C-1026	1503
A-1113	101	A-4530	701	C-7000	104
A-1114	102	A-4533	701	C-7002	104
A-1325	103	A-4537	701	C-7004	104
A-1325.1	103	A-4600	704	C-9550	211
A-1330	103	A-4601	704	C-9563	211
A-2601	308	A-4602	704	D-1640	1501
A-2611.2	308	A-4603	704	D-1643	1501
A-2730	302	A-4604	704	D-1644,	1501
A-2731	302	A-4606	704	D-1645	
A-2800	304	A-4607	704	D-1655	1501
A-2803	304	A-4608	704	D-1760	1105
A-3500	301	A-4610	704	D-1775	1105
A-3502	301	A-4611	704	D-1860	1105
A-4010	403	A-4613	704	D-1865	1105
A-4050	403, 601, 602	A-4614	704	D-2600	203
A-4050.1	404	A-4615	704	D-2601	203
A-4051	601	A-4616	704	D-3200	203
A-4054	403	A-4617	704	D-3202	203
A-4055	601, 602	A-4618	704	D-6900	1502
A-4200	601, 605, 606, 607	A-4619	704	D-6913.2	1502
		A-4620	704	E-3600	207
A-4201	605, 606, 607	A-4625	704	E-3602	207
A-4202	605, 606	A-4750	1004	E-6150	206
A-4203	605	A-4751	1004	E-6163.1	206
A-4209	605	A-4780	403	E-6600	206
A-4211	605	A-4781.1	403	E-6619.1	206
A-4212	605	A-4870	1605, 1606,	F-12100	212
A-4216	605		1610	F-12101	212
A-4222	605	A-4871	1606	F-15000	1504
A-4230	1604, 1606,	A-4873	1605	F-15001	1504
	1607, 1608,	A-4875	1610	G-3143	806
	1609	A-4900	403	H-1250	1612
A-4231	1606	A-4901	403, 701	H-1296.4A	1612
A-4232	1608	A-4902	701	H-1296.4B	1612
A-4234.1	1604	A-4903	403	H-1325	1611
A-4235.3	1609	A-6000	1901	H-1325.6	1611
A-4236	1607	A-6001.1	1901	H-1450	309
A-4240	1601, 1602	A-6100	1901	H-1451	309
A-4247.1	1601	A-6114	1901	H-1453	309
A-4248.1	1602	A-8102	402	H-1518	1702
A-4255	403	A-8160	401	H-2050	705
A-4300	603	A-8162	401	H-2064	705
A-4301	603	A-8163	401	H-2065	705
A-4302	603	A-8221	1013	H-2200	307
A-4400	403	A-8300	209, 402, 403,	H-2217	307
A-4405	403		405	H-4475	103
A-4406	403	A-8300.1	405	H-4483	103
A-4450	403	A-8304	209, 405	H-4483.1	103
A-4455	403	A-8304.1	209	H-4530	103
A-4470	702	A-8304.2	209	H-4541	103
A-4471	702	A-8320	403	H-4542	103

FTC 2d ¶	Analysis ¶	FTC 2d ¶	Analysis ¶	FTC 2d ¶	Analysis ¶
H-4685	1902	J-3164	1403	L-9315	804
H-4687	1902	J-3196	1913	L-9316	802, 804, 805
H-4870	1610	J-3200	1403, 1408	L-9316.1	804, 805
H-4875	1610	J-3210	1408	L-9356	1013
H-4805	1903	J-3216	1408	L-9357	1013
H-7600	1701	J-3242	1403	L-9400	807
H-7751.1	1701	J-3325	1405	L-9403	807
H-7754	1701	J-3326	1405	L-9900	801, 803
H-7754.3	1701	J-3382	1406	L-9901.1	801
H-7755	1701	J-3554	1404	L-9907	801
H-7756	1701	J-3599.12	1404	L-9907.3	801
H-7756.1	1701	J-7417	306	L-9907.1	801
H-8100	1702	J-8600	103	L-9917.1	801
H-8162	1701	J-8600.1	103	L-9922	803
H-8163	1702, 1703	J-8602	103	L-9922.1	801
H-8167	1701	J-9000	103	L-9933	803
H-8168	1702	J-9000.1	103	L-9940,	811
H-8173	1702	J-9001	103	L-9941	
H-8180	1702	K-3200	1104	L-10000	802
H-8182	1702	K-3201.1	1104	L-10004	802
H-8701	1701	K-3501	1102	L-10004.1A	802
H-8703	1701	K-3670	1102	L-15200	805
H-10101	1701	K-3694.1	1102	L-15213	805
H-10106	1701	K-3694.2	1102	L-15213.3	805
H-11100	1704	K-3701.1	1102	L-15213.4	805
H-11102	1704	K-3830	1103	L-15216.1	805
H-12200	1101	K-3831.1	1103	L-15300	901
H-12253.2	1101	K-4400	1901	L-15301	901
H-12290.19B	1705	K-4401	1901	L-15580	1402
H-12295	1301	K-4500	303	L-15586	1402
H-12295.3	1301	K-4510	303	L-15615	901
H-12295.5D	1301	K-4570	305	L-15624	901
H-12295.5E	1301	K-5318.1	208	L-15670	907
H-12295.5K	1301	K-5493	305	L-15671	907
H-12295.10	1301	K-5500	703	L-15673	907
I-2600	1014	K-5501	703	L-15675	904
I-2622	1014	K-5502	703	L-15676	904
I-4522	1907	K-5682	1914	L-15700	906
I-4528.4A	1907	K-5683	1914	L-15713	906
I-5100	201, 204, 205	K-5684	1914	L-15714	906
I-5100.1	205	K-5685	1914	L-15714.1	906
I-5104.1	204	K-5749	1914	L-15718	906
I-5107	201	L-3140	808	L-15800	1408
I-5110	201	L-3141	808	L-15804	1408
I-5110.7	202	L-4325	909	L-16401.2	1012
I-5110.10	201	L-4336.2	909	L-16440	1012
I-5115	202	L-4387.4	909	L-17516.1	1015
I-5115.1	208	L-8200	807, 809	L-17516.3	1016
I-5115.2	202	L-8206	809	L-17516.5	1016
I-9100	209, 1407	L-8206.3	809	L-17516.8	1016
I-9100.1	209, 1407	L-8208	807	L-17570	1009
I-9100.1A	209	L-8208.1	807	L-17571	1009
I-9100.1B	209	L-8208.2	807	L-17585	1009
I-9100.1C	209, 1407	L-8208.5	807	L-17585.1	1009
J-1230	706	L-8800	810	L-17750	1005, 1007
J-1258.1	706	L-8806	810	L-17771	1005
J-1360	210	L-9304	812	L-17771.1B	1005
J-3100	1913	L-9310	802, 804, 805	L-17771.2	1005
J-3150	1403	L-9312	802, 804, 805	L-17771.4	1005, 1011

FTC 2d ¶	Analysis ¶	FTC 2d ¶	Analysis ¶	FTC 2d ¶	Analysis ¶
L-17771.5	1005	O-10734.2	1204	T-11051.4	404
L-17771.6	1005	O-10753	1204	T-11051.5	404
L-17771.8	1007	O-10771	1204	T-11054	604
L-17775	902	O-13000	1203, 1204	T-11060	203, 205, 206,
L-17779.2	1910	O-13001	1204		211, 601
L-17784.1	1910	O-13035	1203	T-11061	101, 102, 104,
L-17785.1	1910	Q-8003.1	501		304, 601
L-17789A	1904, 1910	R-1000.1	501	T-11062	201, 202, 203,
L-17870	903	R-4500	501		205, 206, 207,
L-17871	903	R-4501	501		208, 210, 402,
L-17920	1401	R-4700	501		405, 1203
L-17927	1401	R-4708	501	T-11062.1	202, 206, 211
L-17940,	1002	R-6900	501	T-11070	404, 601
L-17941		R-6901	501	T-11071	101, 304, 404,
L-17940	1003	R-7006	501		601, 704
L-17947	1003	R-7101	501	V-2630	1912
L-17952	1001	R-7200	501	V-2677.1	1912
L-17953	1001	R-7200.1	501	V-5200	1916
L-17954	1001	R-9500	501	V-5216	1916
L-18020	403	R-9522	501	W-1500	1009, 1010,
L-18022.1	403	R-9550	501		1806, 1808
L-18030	403	R-9551	501	W-1501	1801, 1802,
L-18034.1	403	R-9552	501		1806
L-18035	403, 1006	R-9554.1	501	W-1501.1	1801, 1802,
L-18037	1006	R-9562	501		1806, 1808
L-18039.1	403	R-9563	501	W-1515.1B	1808
L-18040	1008	R-9570	501	W-1515.2C	1808
L-18041	1008	R-9584	501	W-1518	1009, 1010
L-18050	908	S-2000	1503	W-1519	1009, 1010
L-18051	908	S-2009.5	1503	W-1519.1	1010
L-18200	905	S-3330	1613	W-1527	1016
L-18205	905	S-3331	1613	W-1570	1804
O-1500	1206	S-3332	1613	W-1571	1804
O-1500.1	1206	S-3334	1613	W-1700	1010, 1808
O-2500	1201	S-3335	1613	W-1707	1801
O-2508	1201	S-3655	1905, 1906,	W-1711	1801
O-2509	1201		1907	W-1713	1808
O-2530	1201, 1202	S-3656	1905, 1906,	W-1720	1802
O-2550	1202		1907	W-1726	1801
O-2553	1202	S-5320	1915	W-1737.1	1010
O-2554	1202	S-5324.1	1915	W-1737.2	1010
O-2555	1202	S-6000	501	W-1737.3	1010
O-2558	1201	S-6013	501	W-2227	1803
O-2584	1201	S-6030.1	501	W-2240	1803
O-2585	1201	S-6037	501	W-2601	1803
O-2589	1201	S-6360.2	1505	W-2621	1804
O-2591	1201	T-11050	404, 601, 604,	W-3101	1803
O-2592	1201		706, 903,	W-3201	1802
O-2650	1201		1403, 1404	W-5100	1806, 1807,
O-2651	1201	T-11051	101, 102, 103,		1808, 1911
O-4401	403		104, 301, 302,	W-5101	1806, 1808
O-10200	1205		304, 404, 601,	W-5103	1806, 1808
O-10230.2	1205		703, 704, 705,	W-5139	1807
O-10230.3	1205		706, 903,	W-5140	1807
O-10230.4	1205		1403, 1404,	W-5140.1	1807
O-10700	1204		1503	W-5148.1	1911
O-10701	1204	T-11051.1A	404	W-5200	1806, 1807,
O-10734	1204	T-11051.2	404		1808
O-10734.1	1204	T-11051.3	404	W-5201	1806, 1808

FTC 2d ¶	Analysis ¶	FTC 2d ¶	Analysis ¶	FTC 2d ¶	Analysis ¶
W-5204.1	1807	W-6438	1805	W-6451	1805
W-6401	1805				

¶ 6009. USTR ¶ s Affected by Acts

USTR ¶	Analysis ¶	USTR ¶	Analysis ¶	USTR ¶	Analysis ¶
14	101	514	902, 1904,	3414	1504
14.08	101, 102, 201,		1910	402A4	1301
	202	514.002	1910	4044.02	1701
14.11	103	54E4.01	1402	4084.03	1101
14.13	104	554.01	401, 402	408A4	1301, 1705
14.085	202, 205, 206,	574	209, 405	4124	1701
	208, 211	594	401	4204	1702, 1703
14.087	204	624	308	4204.01	1702
214	603	624.02	308	4204.02	1702
214.04	603	634	304	4204.03	1701, 1702
234	403	684	302	4204.04	1702
244	601	724.22	1704	4304.01	1701
244.01	403	794.03	1702	4304.017	1701
244.02	601, 602	1084.01	306	4514.200	1014
254.01	403	1174.05	706	4604.001	806
25A4	701	1214	1907	5124	1502
25A4.02	701	1274	705	5304	704
25A4.03	403, 701	1274.01	705	5304.01	704
25A4.04	701	1324.08	307	5324.01	203
25A4.07	701	1374	309	5414	203
25B4	403	1424.02	1408	5844	207
25C4	1004	1424.13	1403	6464	1503
25D4	403	1474.01	1913	6914.07	211
264	403, 701	1484.04	1404	7024.01	205
304	1006	1514	301	8524.02	206
304.01	1006	1634.052	305	8574.02	206
304.06	403	1634.053	208	8714.02	1205
30B4	403	1644.03	303	8974	1204
30C4	1008	1644.07	1901	8974.02	1204
30D4.07	403	1684.01	809, 810, 812	9044.01	403
324.01	605, 606, 607	1684.02	807	9314.06	1206
324.02	605	1684.03	807	9534.01	1201
324.05	605	1684.08	1013	9544.02	1201, 1202
354	1604, 1606,	1684.025	804	9544.035	1201, 1202
	1607, 1608,	1684.026	802, 804, 805	12,024	209, 1407
	1609	1684.027	802, 804, 805	12,024.05	209
36B4.01	1601, 1602	1684.081	1013	13,664	1105
404.07	1015, 1016	1684.0281	802	13,674	1105
40A4	1009	1684.0293	805	13,744.01	1501
40A4.05	1009	1704.11	1102, 1103	13,914	1406
414	901	1704.13	1102	14,00C4	403
424.10	906	1704.14	1103	14,00L4.30	1405
454	1007	1704.42	1104	14,014	1901
454.09	1005	1704.45	1102	14,024	1901
454.13	1011	1794.01	801	14,414.02	1205
454.14	1005	1794.02	801, 803	14,414.05	1205
45A4	907	1794.04	803	14,454	1204
45C4	901	179E4	811	14,454.02	1203
45D4	1401	1814	808	20,014	501
45F4	903	1994.002	909	22,104	501
45G4	908	1994.050	909	26,644	501
45L4	1002, 1003	2214	703	31,114	1902
45M4	1001	2224	702	34,024.13	103
45N4	905	2224.01	702	34,024.25	103
45P4	904	2494	1914	34,024.26	103
484	1012	280F4	802	34,064	103
484.02	1012	3064.02	212		

USTR ¶	Analysis ¶	USTR ¶	Analysis ¶	USTR ¶	Analysis ¶
40,414	1801, 1802, 1808	60,39H4	1503	75,184	210
40,424	1802	60,414	1905, 1906, 1907	75,274	1605, 1606, 1610
40,514	1803	60,414.035	1905	79,006	601
40,714	1803	60,564.01	1613	79,006.86	101, 102, 103, 104, 203, 301, 302, 304, 404, 604, 703, 704, 705, 706, 903, 1403, 1404, 1503
40,814	1801, 1802, 1806, 1808	60,564.02	1613		
40,824	1808	60,564.04	1613		
41,014	1016	60,564.05	1613		
42,214	1803	61,034.052	1505		
42,614.01	1806, 1808	63,314.03	1916		
42,714	1806, 1808	64,124	1804		
42,814.01	1807	64,264	1009, 1010	79,006.87	201, 202, 206, 207, 210, 212, 402, 405, 601
44,814	1805	64,274	1009, 1010		
44,814.01	1805	66,554	1915		
49,734	704	66,954.01	1912	79,006.88	404, 601
49,80B4.07	1612	72,094	1911	98,014	1611

¶ 6010. Tax Desk ¶ s Affected by Acts

Tax Desk ¶	Analysis ¶	Tax Desk ¶	Analysis ¶	Tax Desk ¶	Analysis ¶
133,603	309	268,411.01	801	397,143	403
133,605	309	268,411.02	801	397,170	1006
134,591	307	268,420.1	801	397,177	1006
136,525	705	268,424	803	397,180	403
137,007	1702	268,424.1	801	397,201	1008
143,003.2	1101	268,450,	811	528,933	701
147,105	705	268,451		538,053	103
147,201	704	269,341	804	538,054	103
147,202	704	269,342	802, 804, 805	538,518	103
147,203	704	269,345	804	538,519	103
147,204	704	269,346	802, 804, 805	541,002	1902
147,206	704	269,346.1	804, 805	550,505	1903
147,207	704	269,451	808	554,001	103
147,208	704	314,105	703	554,013	103
147,210	704	314,519.1	305	554,501	103
147,211	704	315,018.1	208	560,706.1	308
147,213	704	326,002	1901	561,801	302
147,214	704	326,019	303	562,002	304
147,215	704	331,625	1102	564,401	301
147,216	704	331,702	1104	568,201	101
147,217	704	333,021.1	1102, 1103	568,202	101
147,218	704	333,021.2	1102	568,203	101, 102
147,219	704	333,022.1	1103	568,213	101
147,220	704	333,302.2	1102	568,214	102
147,225	704	352,000	702	568,405	103
158,013	1404	352,001	702	568,805	403
173,002.1	206	380,501	908	568,901	701
173,009	206	380,502	403	568,917	701
188,029	306	380,511	805	568,923	701
193,517	706	380,512	805	568,925	403
222,413	1014	380,513	805	568,925.1	403, 701
223,304.1	204	380,520	805	568,925.2	701
223,307	201	380,700	902, 1904,	568,930	701
223,312	201		1910	568,933	701
223,319.1	202	380,702.2	1910	568,937	701
223,319.4	201	380,708	1910	569,001	605, 606, 607
223,345	202	380,711	1910	569,002	605, 606
223,346	208	381,601.2	1012	569,003	605
223,347	202	381,608	1012	569,009	605
225,702	1907	382,101	903	569,010	605
225,708.3A	1907	382,213	1015, 1016	569,011	605
244,401	212	382,401	1009	569,012	605
246,600	209	382,409	1009	569,016	605
246,600.1	209, 1407	383,001	906	569,023	605
246,601	209	383,006	906	569,100	601
246,602	209, 1407	384,001	901	569,104	403
266,206	809	384,020	1406	569,105	602
266,208	807	384,028	1005	569,205	403
266,208.1	807	384,039	907	569,301	603
266,208.2	807	384,054	1005	569,302	603
266,208.5	807	384,054.1	1005, 1011	569,401	1604, 1606,
267,007	810	384,062	905		1608
267,503	807	384,711	1401	569,404.1	1609
267,602.2	802	393,001	403	569,405	1607
268,401.1	801	394,500.1	1206	569,408	1606
268,409	803	397,102.1	403	569,410	1605
268,411	801	397,103	403	569,412	1610

Tax Desk ¶	Analysis ¶	Tax Desk ¶	Analysis ¶	Tax Desk ¶	Analysis ¶
569,473	1601	617,001	1105	814,001	1905, 1906,
569,478	1602	643,015	1204		1907
569,505	403	643,016	1204	854,851	904
569,506	403	644,019	1203	867,017	1912
569,551	1004	651,003	104	880,011	101, 102, 103,
569,561.1	403	651,004	104		104, 301, 302,
569,571	1002	657,304	207		304, 404, 601,
569,575	1003	661,003	104		703, 704, 706,
569,582	1001	661,004	104		903, 1403,
569,583	1001	691,002	402		1404, 1503
569,584	1001	691,302	401	880,011.2	404
569,601	403, 701	691,303	401	880,011.3	404
569,602	701	697,004	209, 405	880,011.4	404
569,603	403	697,004.1	209	880,011.5	404
575,501	1901	744,003.1	501	880,013	601
576,025	1901	751,000.1	501	880,014	201, 202, 204,
579,012	211	761,200.1	501		205, 206, 207,
584,003	205	773,408	501		208, 210, 212,
601,001	203	779,001	501		402, 405,
601,501	203	780,506	501		1203
609,201	1915	782,001	501	880,014.1	202, 206, 211
614,716	1105	784,002	501	880,015	404, 601
615,003,	1501	791,004	501	880,017	604
615,005		814,000	1907	902,216	1916
615,014	1501				

¶ 6011. Pension Analysis ¶ s Affected by Acts

PCA ¶	Analysis ¶	PCA ¶	Analysis ¶	PCA ¶	Analysis ¶
25,601	1701	30,202	1701	56,620	1701
25,752.1	1701	30,207	1701	58,101	1714
25,755	1701	32,203	1704	58,106	1709
25,755.3	1701	35,154.2	1101	58,107	1709
25,756	1701	35,220B	1705	58,107.1	1709, 1710
25,757	1701	35,251	1301	58,108	1713
25,757.1	1701	35,251.3	1301	58,112	1715
26,514	1702, 1703	35,251.5D	1301	58,304	1706
26,518	1701	35,251.10	1301	58,305	1707
26,519	1702	56,411	1702	58,307.1	1701
26,524	1702	56,456.1	1702	58,335	1708
26,531	1702	56,456.2	1701	60,708	1703
26,533	1702				

¶ 6012. Pension & Benefits Explanations ¶ s Affected by Acts

PBE ¶	Analysis ¶	PBE ¶	Analysis ¶	PBE ¶	Analysis ¶
79-4.03	1702	420-4.01	1702	ER408-4.14	1703
127-4	705	420-4.02	1702	ER4002-4	1709, 1710,
127-4.01	705	420-4.03	1701, 1702		1713, 1714
132-4.08	307	420-4.04	1702	ER4005-4	1715
402A-4	1301	430-4.01	1701	ER4006-4.01	1701, 1706,
404-4.02	1701	430-4.017	1701		1707
408A-4	1301, 1705	7900-6.86	705	ER4006-4.02	1708
412-4	1701	ER101-4.01	1702	ER4010-4.02	1701
420-4	1702, 1703	ER101-4.022	1701		

¶ 6013. Benefits Explanation ¶ s Affected by Acts

BCA ¶	Analysis ¶	BCA ¶	Analysis ¶	BCA ¶	Analysis ¶
119,210	705	127,511	307	132,309	307
119,211	705				

¶ 6014. Estate Planning Analysis ¶ s Affected by Acts

EP ¶	Analysis ¶	EP ¶	Analysis ¶	EP ¶	Analysis ¶
43,051.1	501	46,053	501	46,175	501
43,872	501	46,092	501	46,177	501
43,900.3	501	46,093	501	83,214	501
44,892	501	46,095.1	501	83,231.1	501
44,907	501	46,103	501	83,238	501
45,151.1	501	46,104	501	85,027	1503
46,031.1	501				

¶ 6015. Appendix

Senate Finance Committee Staff Summary of the 2012 Taxpayer Relief Act

SUMMARY OF PROVISIONS IN
The American Taxpayer Relief Act of 2012
PRELIMINARY

Title I. General Extensions

Permanent extension of 2001 tax relief

Permanently extend the 10% bracket. Under current law, the 10% individual income tax bracket expires at the end of 2012. Upon expiration, the lowest tax rate will be 15%. The bill extends the 10% individual income tax bracket for taxable years beginning after December 31, 2012.
This provision is estimated to cost[1] $442.641 billion over ten years.

Permanently extend the 25%, 28%, and 33% income tax rates for certain taxpayers. Under current law, the 25%, 28%, 33%, and 35% individual income tax brackets expire at the end of 2012. Upon expiration, the rates become 28%, 31%, 36%, and 39.6% respectively. The bill extends the 25%, 28%, 33% rates on income at or below $400,000 (individual filers), $425,000 (heads of households) and $450,000 (married filing jointly) for taxable years beginning after December 31, 2012.
This provision is estimated to cost $319.711 billion over ten years.[2]

Permanently repeal the Personal Exemption Phaseout for certain taxpayers. Personal exemptions allow a certain amount per person to be exempt from tax. Due to the Personal Exemption Phase-out ("PEP"), the exemptions are phased out for taxpayers with AGI above a certain level. The *Economic Growth and Tax Relief Reconciliation Act of 2001* (EGTRRA) repealed PEP for 2010. The *Tax Relief, Unemployment Insurance Reauthorization and Job Creation Act of 2010* (TRUIRJCA) extended the repeal through 2012. The bill extends the repeal of PEP on income at or below $250,000 (individual filers), $275,000 (heads of households) and $300,000 (married filing jointly) for taxable years beginning after December 31, 2012.
The combined cost of this provision and the one described below is estimated to be $10.514 billion over ten years.[3]

Permanently repeal the itemized deduction limitation for certain taxpayers. Generally, taxpayers itemize deductions if the total deductions are more than the standard deduction amount. Since 1991, the amount of itemized deductions that a taxpayer may claim has been reduced, to the extent the taxpayer's AGI is above a certain amount. This limitation is generally known as the "Pease limitation." The EGTRRA repealed the Pease limitation on itemized deductions for 2010. The TRUIRJCA extended the repeal through 2012. The bill extends the repeal of the Pease limitation on income at or below

---

[1] The Joint Committee on Taxation estimates the budgetary cost of tax provisions – reflecting both the revenue loss and outlay effects associated with those provisions – relative to current law. Where applicable, savings relative to current policy (extension of tax laws in effect during 2012) are noted in footnotes.

[2] The provision raises $396.889 billion relative to current policy.

[3] The provisions raise $152.186 billion relative to current policy.

1

$250,000 (individual filers), $275,000 (heads of households) and $300,000 (married filing jointly) for taxable years beginning after December 31, 2012.

The combined cost of this provision and the one described above is estimated to be $10.514 billion over ten years.[4]

Permanently extend the 2001 modifications to the child tax credit. Generally, taxpayers with income below certain threshold amounts may claim the child tax credit to reduce federal income tax for each qualifying child under the age of 17. The EGTRRA increased the credit from $500 to $1,000 and expanded refundability. The amount that may be claimed as a refund was 15% of earnings above $10,000. The bill extends this provision for taxable years beginning after December 31, 2012.

This provision is estimated to cost $354.493 billion over ten years.

Permanently extend marriage penalty relief. The bill extends the marriage penalty relief for the standard deduction, the 15% bracket, and the EITC for taxable years beginning after December 31, 2012.

This provision is estimated to cost $84.630 billion over ten years.

Permanently extend expanded Coverdell Accounts. Coverdell Education Savings Accounts are tax-exempt savings accounts used to pay the higher education expenses of a designated beneficiary. The EGTRRA increased the annual contribution amount from $500 to $2,000 and expanded the definition of education expenses to include elementary and secondary school expenses. The bill extends the changes to Coverdell accounts for taxable years beginning after December 31, 2012.

This provision is estimated to cost $271 million over ten years.

Permanently extend the expanded exclusion for employer-provided educational assistance. An employee may exclude from gross income up to $5,250 for income and employment tax purposes per year of employer-provided education assistance. Prior to 2001, this incentive was temporary and only applied to undergraduate courses. The EGTRRA expanded this provision to graduate education and extended the provision for undergraduate and graduate education. The bill extends the changes to this provision for taxable years beginning after December 31, 2012.

This provision is estimated to cost $11.477 billion over ten years.

Permanently extend the expanded student loan interest deduction. Certain individuals who have paid interest on qualified education loans may claim an above-the-line deduction for such interest expenses up to $2,500. Prior to 2001, this benefit was only allowed for 60 months and phased-out for taxpayers with income between $40,000 and $55,000 ($60,000 and $75,000 for joint filers). The EGTRRA eliminated the 60-month rule and increased the income phase-out to $55,000 to $70,000 ($110,000 and $140,000 for joint filers). The bill extends the changes to this provision for taxable years beginning after December 31, 2012.

This provision is estimated to cost $9.676 billion over ten years.

Permanently extend the exclusion from income of amounts received under certain scholarship programs. Scholarships for qualified tuition and related expenses are excludible from income.

---

[4] The provisions raise $152.186 billion relative to current policy.

2

Qualified tuition reductions for certain education provided to employees are also excluded. Generally, this exclusion does not apply to qualified scholarships or tuition reductions that represent payment for teaching, research, or other services. The National Health Service Corps Scholarship Program and the F. Edward Hebert Armed Forces Health Professions Scholarship and Financial Assistance Program provide education awards to participants on the condition that the participants perform certain services. The EGTRRA allowed the scholarship exclusion to apply to these programs. The bill extends the changes to this provision for taxable years beginning after December 31, 2012.

This provision is estimated to cost $1.501 billion over ten years.

Arbitrage rebate exception for school construction bonds. Under current law, issuers of tax-exempt bonds must rebate to the U.S. Treasury arbitrage (excess interest income) earned from the investment of tax-exempt bond proceeds in higher-yielding taxable securities. The calculation of excess interest income can be complex, and as a result, many governments incur large costs to comply with the requirements. To ease the burden on small issuers, the federal tax code exempts governments that issue a relatively small number of tax-exempt bonds in a given year from the requirement. In general, the small issuer rebate exception can only be used by state and local governments that issue less than $5 million in governmental and 501(c)(3) bonds annually. This exception is $10 million for bonds issued for qualified educational facilities. The EGTRRA increased the small-issuer arbitrage rebate exception for school construction from $10 million to $15 million. The bill extends the $15 million arbitrage rebate exception for school construction for taxable years beginning after December 31, 2012.

This provision is estimated to cost $72 million over ten years.

Tax-exempt private activity bonds for qualified education facilities. Under current law, proceeds from private activity bonds issued by a state or local government qualify as tax-exempt if 95% or more of the net bond proceeds are used for a qualified purpose as defined by the Internal Revenue Code. The EGTRRA expanded the definition of a private activity for which tax-exempt bonds may be issued to include bonds for qualified public educational facilities. Bonds issued for qualified educational facilities are not counted against a state's private-activity volume cap. Instead, these bonds have their own volume capacity limit equal to the lesser of $10 per resident or $5 million. The bill extends the allowance to issue tax-exempt private activity bonds for public school facilities for taxable years beginning after December 31, 2012.

This provision is estimated to cost $152 million over ten years.

Permanently extend the expanded dependent care credit. The dependent care credit allows a taxpayer a credit for an applicable percentage of child care expenses for children under 13 and disabled dependents. The EGTRRA increased the amount of eligible expenses from $2,400 for one child and $4,800 for two or more children to $3,000 and $6,000, respectively. The EGTRRA also increased the applicable percentage from 30% to 35%. The bill extends the changes to the dependent care credit made by EGTRRA for taxable years beginning after December 31, 2012.

This provision is estimated to cost $1.791 billion over ten years.

Permanently extend the increased adoption tax credit and the adoption assistance programs exclusion. Taxpayers that adopt children can receive a tax credit for qualified adoption expenses. A taxpayer may also exclude from income adoption expenses paid by an employer. The EGTRRA increased the credit from $5,000 ($6,000 for a special needs child) to $10,000, and provided a $10,000

3

income exclusion for employer-assistance programs. The Patient Protection and Affordable Care Act of 2010 extended these benefits to 2011 and made the credit refundable. The bill extends for taxable years beginning after December 31, 2012, the increased adoption credit amount and the exclusion for employer-assistance programs as enacted in EGTRRA.

This provision is estimated to cost $5.580 billion over ten years.

Permanently extend the credit for employer expenses for child care assistance. The EGTRRA provided employers with a credit of up to $150,000 for acquiring, constructing, rehabilitating or expanding property which is used for a child care facility. The bill extends this provision for taxable years beginning after December 31, 2012.

This provision is estimated to cost $209 million over ten years.

Permanently extend tax relief for Alaska settlement funds. The EGTRRA allowed an election in which Alaska Native settlement trusts can elect to pay tax at the same rate as the lowest individual marginal rate, rather than the higher rates that generally apply to trusts. Beneficiaries of the trust do not pay tax on the distributions of an electing trust's taxable income. Finally, contributions by an Alaska Native corporation to an electing trust will not be deemed distributions to the corporation's shareholders. The bill extends the elective tax treatment for Alaska Native settlement trusts for taxable years beginning after December 31, 2012.

This provision is estimated to cost $46 million over ten years.

Permanent estate, gift and generation skipping transfer tax relief. The EGTRRA phased-out the estate and generation-skipping transfer taxes so that they were fully repealed in 2010, and lowered the gift tax rate to 35 percent and increased the gift tax exemption to $1 million for 2010. In 2010, the TRUIRJCA set the exemption at $5 million per person with a top tax rate of 35 percent for the estate, gift, and generation skipping transfer taxes for two years, through 2012. The exemption amount was indexed beginning in 2012. The bill makes permanent the indexed TRUIRJCA exclusion amount and indexes that amount for inflation going forward, but sets the top tax rate to 40 percent for estates of decedents dying after December 31, 2012.

This provision is scored in combination with the two provisions below. Together these provisions are estimated to cost $396.068 billion over ten years.[5]

Portability of unused exemption. The TRUIRJCA allowed the executor of a deceased spouse's estate to transfer any unused exemption to the surviving spouse for estates of decedents dying after December 31, 2010 and before December 31 2012. The bill makes permanent this provision and is effective for estates for decedents dying after December 31, 2012.

Reunification. Prior to the EGTRRA, the estate and gift taxes were unified, creating a single graduated rate schedule for both. That single lifetime exemption could be used for gifts and/or bequests. The EGTRRA decoupled these systems. The TRUIRJCA reunified the estate and gift taxes. The bill permanently extends unification and is effective for gifts made after December 31, 2012.

---

[5] These provisions save $19.132 billion relative to current policy.

4

Permanent extension of 2003 tax relief

Permanently extend the capital gains and dividend rates. Under current law, the capital gains and dividend rates for taxpayers below the 25% bracket is equal to zero percent. For those in the 25% bracket and above, the capital gains and dividend rates are currently 15%. These rates expire at the end of 2012. Upon expiration, the rates for capital gains become 10% and 20%, respectively, and dividends are subject to the ordinary income rates. The bill extends the current capital gains and dividends rates on income at or below $400,000 (individual filers), $425,000 (heads of households) and $450,000 (married filing jointly) for taxable years beginning after December 31, 2012. For income in excess of $400,000 (individual filers), $425,000 (heads of households) and $450,000 (married filing jointly), the rate for both capital gains and dividends will be 20%.

This provision is estimated to cost $289.920 billion over ten years.[6]

Extension of 2009 tax relief

Temporarily extend the American Opportunity Tax Credit. Created under the ARRA, the American Opportunity Tax Credit is available for up to $2,500 of the cost of tuition and related expenses paid during the taxable year. Under this tax credit, taxpayers receive a tax credit based on 100% of the first $2,000 of tuition and related expenses (including course materials) paid during the taxable year and 25% of the next $2,000 of tuition and related expenses paid during the taxable year. Forty percent of the credit is refundable. This tax credit is subject to a phase-out for taxpayers with adjusted gross income in excess of $80,000 ($160,000 for married couples filing jointly). The bill extends the American Opportunity Tax Credit for five additional years, through 2017.

This provision is estimated to cost $67.280 billion over ten years.

Temporarily extend the 2009 modifications to the child tax credit. The *American Recovery and Reinvestment Act of 2009* (ARRA) provided that earnings above $3,000 would count towards refundability. The bill extends the ARRA child tax credit expansion for five additional years, through 2017.

This provision is estimated to cost $50.518 billion over ten years.

Temporarily extend third-child EITC. Under current law, working families with two or more children currently qualify for an earned income tax credit equal to 40% of the family's first $12,570 of earned income. The ARRA increased the earned income tax credit to 45% for families with three or more children and increased the beginning point of the phase-out range for all married couples filing a joint return (regardless of the number of children) to lessen the marriage penalty. The bill extends for five additional years, through 2017, the ARRA expansions that increased the EITC for families with three or more children and increased the phase-out range for all married couples filing a joint return.

This provision is estimated to cost $16.446 billion over ten years.

Permanently extend refund and tax credit disregard for means-tested programs
Current law ensures that the refundable components of the EITC and the Child Tax Credit do not make households ineligible for means-tested benefit programs and includes provisions stating that these tax credits do not count as income in determining eligibility (and benefit levels) in means-tested benefit

---

[6] The provision raises $56.180 billion relative to current policy.

5

programs, and also do not count as assets for specified periods of time. Without them, the receipt of a tax credit would put a substantial number of families over the income limits for these programs in the month that the tax refund is received. A provision enacted as part of the TRUIRJCA, disregarded all refundable tax credits and refunds as income for means-tested programs through 2012. The bill permanently extends the provision for any amount received after December 31, 2012.

A score for this provision will be provided by the Congressional Budget Office.

Permanent individual Alternative Minimum Tax (AMT) relief

Permanent AMT patch. Currently, a taxpayer receives an exemption of $33,750 (individuals) and $45,000 (married filing jointly) under the AMT. Current law also does not allow nonrefundable personal credits against the AMT. The bill increases the exemption amounts for 2012 to $50,600 (individuals) and $78,750 (married filing jointly) and indexes the exemption and phaseout amounts thereafter. The bill also allows the nonrefundable personal credits against the AMT. The bill is effective for taxable years beginning after December 31, 2011.

This provision is estimated to cost $1,815.6 billion over ten years.

Title II. Individual Tax Extenders

Deduction for certain expenses of elementary and secondary school teachers. The bill extends for two years the $250 above-the-line tax deduction for teachers and other school professionals for expenses paid or incurred for books, supplies (other than non-athletic supplies for courses of instruction in health or physical education), computer equipment (including related software and service), other equipment, and supplementary materials used by the educator in the classroom.

This provision is estimated to cost $406 million over ten years.

Mortgage Debt Relief. Under current law, taxpayers who have mortgage debt canceled or forgiven after 2012 may be required to pay taxes on that amount as taxable income. Under this provision, up to $2 million of forgiven debt is eligible to be excluded from income ($1 million if married filing separately) through tax year 2013. This provision was created in the Mortgage Debt Relief Act of 2007 to prevent the taxation of so-called "shadow income" from foreclosures and cancelled debts through 2010. It was extended through 2012 by the Emergency Economic Stabilization Act of 2008.

This provision is estimated to cost $1.327 billion over ten years.

Parity for exclusion from income for employer-provided mass transit and parking benefits. This provision would extend through 2013 the increase in the monthly exclusion for employer-provided transit and vanpool benefits from $125 to $240, so that it would be the same as the exclusion for employer-provided parking benefits.

This provision is estimated to cost $220 million over ten years.

Premiums for mortgage insurance deductible as interest that is qualified residence interest. The provision extends the ability to deduct the cost of mortgage insurance on a qualified personal residence. The deduction is phased-out ratably by 10% for each $1,000 by which the taxpayer's AGI

6

exceeds $100,000. Thus, the deduction is unavailable for a taxpayer with an AGI in excess of $110,000. The bill extends this provision for two additional years, through 2013.

This provision is estimated to cost $1.297 billion over ten years.

Deduction for state and local general sales taxes. The bill extends for two years the election to take an itemized deduction for State and local general sales taxes in lieu of the itemized deduction permitted for State and local income taxes.

This provision is estimated to cost $5.538 billion over ten years.

Special rules for contributions of capital gain real property made for conservation purposes. The bill extends for two years the increased contribution limits and carryforward period for contributions of appreciated real property (including partial interests in real property) for conservation purposes.

This provision is estimated to cost $254 million over ten years.

Above-the-line deduction for qualified tuition related expenses. The Economic Growth and Tax Relief Reconciliation Act (EGTRRA) created an above-the-line tax deduction for qualified higher education expenses. The maximum deduction was $4,000 for taxpayers with AGI of $65,000 or less ($130,000 for joint returns) or $2,000 for taxpayers with AGI of $80,000 or less ($160,000 for joint returns). The proposal extends the deduction to the end of 2013.

This provision is estimated to cost $1.706 billion over ten years.

Tax-free distributions from individual retirement plan for charitable purposes. The bill extends for two years the provision that permits tax-free distributions to charity from an Individual Retirement Arrangement (IRA) held by someone age 70½ or older of up to $100,000 per taxpayer, per taxable year. The provision contains a transition rule under which an individual can make a rollover during January of 2013 and have it count as a 2012 rollover. Also, individuals who took a distribution in December of 2012 will be able to contribute that amount to a charity and count as an eligible charitable rollover to the extent it otherwise meets the requirements for an eligible charitable rollover.

This provision is estimated to cost $1.280 billion over ten years.

Disclosure of prisoner return information to certain prison officials. The IRS is authorized to disclose certain limited return information about tax violations identified by the IRS, so that prison officials could punish and deter the prisoner's conduct through administrative sanctions. The provision expired on December 31, 2011. The proposal would make the provision permanent. It would also modify and expand the provision to permit disclosure of the actual tax return as well as tax return information, allow disclosure to prison officials directly, expand disclosure to include private contractors administering prisons, and provide disclosure to representatives of the prisoners. The proposal would make the provision permanent.

This provision is estimated to raise $12 million over ten years.

7

Title III. Business Tax Extenders

Tax credit for research and experimentation expenses. The bill extends for two years, through 2013, the research tax credit equal to 20 percent of the amount by which a taxpayer's qualified research expenses for a taxable year exceed its base amount for that year and provides an alternative simplified credit of 14 percent. The bill also modifies rules for taxpayers under common control and rules for computing the credit when a portion of a trade or business changes hands.

This provision is estimated to cost $14.324 billion over ten years.

9% Credit Rate Freeze for the Low-Income Housing Tax Credit Program. The low-income housing tax credit program provides a tax credit over a period of ten years after the housing facility is placed-in-service. The credit provided each year is determined by present-value formula based on the federal cost of borrowing. Over the past few years, as the federal cost of borrowing has declined, so has the amount of tax credits that can be used to build a LIHTC project. To deal with this, in 2008, Congress adjusted the formula and set a minimum credit amount of 9%, which is based on the original credit rate when the program was created. The provision is effective for facilities placed-in-service before December 31, 2013. This proposal would extend the expiration date by changing the deadline to projects that have received an allocation before January 1, 2014.

This provision is estimated to cost $8 million over ten years.

Treatment of military basic housing allowances under low-income housing credit. The bill extends a provision whereby a member of the military's basic housing allowance is not considered income for purposes of calculating whether the individual qualifies as a low-income tenant for the low income housing tax credit program. The provision expired at the end of 2011. The current proposal would continue this treatment for two additional years.

This provision is estimated to cost $37 million over ten years.

Indian employment tax credit. The bill extends for two years, through 2013, the business tax credit for employers of qualified employees that work and live on or near an Indian reservation. The amount of the credit is 20 percent of the excess of wages and health insurance costs paid to qualified employees (up to $20,000 per employee) in the current year over the amount paid in 1993.

This provision is estimated to cost $119 million over ten years.

New Markets Tax Credit. Through the New Markets Tax Credit (NMTC) program, the federal government is able to leverage federal tax credits to encourage significant private investment in businesses in low-income communities. The program provides a 39 percent tax credit spread over 7 years. The bill extends for two years the new markets tax credit, permitting a maximum annual amount of qualified equity investments of $3.5 billion each year.

This provision is estimated to cost $1.794 billion over ten years.

Credit for certain expenditures for maintaining railroad tracks. The bill extends for two years, through 2013, the railroad maintenance credit that provides Class II and Class III railroads (generally, short-line and regional railroads) with a tax credit equal to 50 percent of gross expenditures for maintaining railroad tracks that they own or lease. This credit is allowable against the AMT.

This provision is estimated to cost $331 million over ten years.

8

Mine rescue team training credit. The bill extends for two years, through 2013, a credit of up to $10,000 for the training of mine rescue team members.
This provision is estimated to cost $5 million over ten years.

Employer wage credit for activated military reservists. The bill extends for two years, through 2013, the provision that provides eligible small business employers with a credit against the employer's income tax liability for a taxable year in an amount equal to 20 percent of the sum of differential wage payments to activated military reservists.
This provision is estimated to cost $7 million over ten years.

Work opportunity tax credit. This bill extends for two years, through 2013, the provision that allows businesses to claim a work opportunity tax credit equal to 40 percent of the first $6,000 of wages paid to new hires of one of eight targeted groups. These groups include members of families receiving benefits under the Temporary Assistance to Needy Families (TANF) program, qualified ex-felons, designated community residents, vocational rehabilitation referrals, qualified summer youth employees, qualified food and nutrition recipients, qualified SSI recipients, and long-term family assistance recipients.
This provision is estimated to cost $1.773 billion over ten years.

Returning Heroes and Wounded Warriors Work Opportunity Tax Credits. Currently businesses are allowed to claim a work opportunity tax credit (WOTC) for hiring qualified veterans in the following targeted groups and up to the following credit amounts:

- Veterans in a family receiving supplemental nutrition assistance: $2,400
- Short-term unemployed veterans: $2,400
- Service-related disabled veterans discharged from active duty within a year: $4,800
- Long-term unemployed veterans: $5,600
- Long-term unemployed service-related disabled veterans: $9,600

A credit against Social Security taxes is also available to tax-exempt employers. Transfers are made from general revenues to make the Social Security trust fund whole. The provision expires on December 31, 2012. The proposal would extend these credits for an additional year, though 2013.
This provision is estimated to cost $125 million over ten years.

Qualified zone academy bonds (QZABs) - allocation of bond limitation. QZABs are a form of tax credit bond which offer the holder a Federal tax credit instead of interest. QZABs can be used to finance renovations, equipment purchases, developing course material, and training teachers and personnel at a qualified zone academy. In general, a qualified zone academy is any public school (or academic program within a public school) below college level that is located in an empowerment zone or enterprise community and is designed to cooperate with businesses to enhance the academic curriculum and increase graduation and employment rates. The provision extends the QZAB program for 2012 and 2013 providing $400 million in bond volume per year.
This provision is estimated to cost $235 million over ten years.

9

15-year straight-line cost recovery for qualified leasehold improvements, qualified restaurant buildings and improvements, and qualified retail improvements. The bill extends for two years, through 2013, the temporary 15-year cost recovery period for certain leasehold, restaurant, and retail improvements, and new restaurant buildings, which are placed in service before January 1, 2014. The extension is effective for qualified property placed in service after December 31, 2011.
This provision is estimated to cost $3.717 billion over ten years.

Seven-year recovery period for motorsports entertainment complexes. The bill extends for two years, through 2013, the special seven year cost recovery period for property used for land improvements and support facilities at motorsports entertainment complexes.
This provision is estimated to cost $78 million over ten years.

Accelerated depreciation for business property on Indian reservation. The bill extends for two years, through 2013, the placed-in-service date for the special depreciation recovery period for qualified Indian reservation property. In general, qualified Indian reservation property is property used predominantly in the active conduct of a trade or business within an Indian reservation, which is not used outside the reservation on a regular basis and was not acquired from a related person.
This provision is estimated to cost $222 million over ten years.

Enhanced charitable deduction for contributions of food inventory. The bill extends for two years the provision allowing businesses to claim an enhanced deduction for the contribution of food inventory.
This provision is estimated to cost $314 million over ten years.

Temporarily extend increase in the maximum amount and phase-out threshold under section 179. Under current law, a taxpayer with a sufficiently small amount of annual investment may elect to deduct the cost of certain property placed in service for the year rather than depreciate those costs over time. The 2003 tax cuts temporarily increased the maximum dollar amount that may be deducted from $25,000 to $100,000. The tax cuts also increased the phase-out amount from $200,000 to $400,000. These amounts have been further modified and extended several times on a temporary basis, increasing up to a high of $500,000 and $2 million respectively for taxable years beginning in 2010 and 2011, and then to $125,000 and $500,000 respectively for taxable years beginning in 2012, before reverting to the permanent amounts of $25,000 and $200,000 respectively for taxable years beginning in 2013 and thereafter. The modified proposal would increase the maximum amount and phase-out threshold in 2012 and 2013 to the levels in effect in 2010 and 2011 ($500,000 and $2 million respectively). Within those thresholds, the proposal would also allow a taxpayer to expense up to $250,000 of the cost of qualified leasehold improvement property, qualified restaurant property, and qualified retail improvement property. This proposal expires at the end of 2013 and the amounts revert to $25,000 and $200,000, respectively.
This provision is estimated to cost $2.352 billion over ten years.

Election to expense advanced mine safety equipment. The bill extends for two years, through 2013, the provision that allows a 50 percent immediate expensing for the following advanced underground mine safety equipment: (1) communications technology enabling miners to remain in constant contact with individuals above ground; (2) electronic tracking devices that enable individuals above ground to locate miners in the mine at all times; (3) self-rescue emergency breathing apparatuses

10

carried by the miners and additional oxygen supplies stored in the mine; and (4) mine atmospheric monitoring equipment to measure levels of carbon monoxide, methane, and oxygen in the mine.

This provision is estimated to have a negligible cost over ten years.

Special expensing rules for certain film and television productions. The bill extends for two years, through 2013, the provision that allows film and television producers to expense the first $15 million of production costs incurred in the United States ($20 million if the costs are incurred in economically depressed areas in the United States).

This provision is estimated to cost $248 million over ten years.

Deduction allowable with respect to income attributable to domestic production activities in Puerto Rico. The bill extends for two years the provision extending the section 199 domestic production activities deduction to activities in Puerto Rico.

This provision is estimated to cost $358 million over ten years.

Modification of tax treatment of certain payments to controlling exempt organizations. In general, interest, rent, royalties, and annuities paid to a tax–exempt organization from a controlled entity are treated as unrelated business income of the tax-exempt organization. The Pension Protection Act (PPA) provided that if a payment to a tax-exempt organization by a controlled entity is no more than fair market value, then the payment is excludable from the tax-exempt organization's unrelated business income. The bill extends the provision two years to the end of 2013.

This provision is estimated to cost $40 million over ten years.

Treatment of certain dividends of regulated investment companies (RIC's). The bill extends a provision allowing a RIC, under certain circumstances, to designate all or a portion of a dividend as an "interest-related dividend," by written notice mailed to its shareholders not later than 60 days after the close of its taxable year. In addition, an interest-related dividend received by a foreign person generally is exempt from U.S. gross-basis tax under sections 871(a), 881, 1441 and 1442 of the Code. The proposal extends the treatment of interest-related dividends and short-term capital gain dividends received from a RIC to taxable years of the RIC beginning before January 1, 2014.

This provision is estimated to cost $151 million over ten years.

RIC qualified investment entity treatment under FIRPTA. The bill extends the inclusion of a RIC within the definition of a "qualified investment entity" under section 897 of the Tax Code through December 31, 2013.

This provision is estimated to cost $60 million over ten years.

Exceptions under subpart F for active financing income. The U.S. parent of a foreign subsidiary engaged in a banking, financing, or similar business is eligible for deferral of tax on such subsidiary's earnings if the subsidiary is predominantly engaged in such business and conducts substantial activity with respect to such business. The subsidiary must pass an entity level income test to demonstrate that the income is active income and not passive income. The proposal extends the provision to the end of 2013.

This provision is estimated to cost $11.225 billion over ten years.

11

Look-through treatment of payments between related controlled foreign corporations under the foreign personal holding company rules. The bill allows deferral for certain payments (interest, dividends, rents and royalties) between commonly controlled foreign corporations (CFC). This provision allows U.S. taxpayers to deploy capital from one CFC to another without triggering U.S. tax. The proposal extends present law to the end of 2013. The proposal is effective for tax years beginning after December 31, 2011.

This provision is estimated to cost $1.503 billion over ten years.

Special rules for qualified small business stock. Generally, non-corporate taxpayers may exclude 50 percent of the gain from the sale of certain small business stock acquired at original issue and held for more than five years. For stock acquired after February 17, 2009 and on or before September 27, 2010, the exclusion is increased to 75 percent. For stock acquired after September 27, 2010 and before January 1, 2012, the exclusion is 100 percent and the AMT preference item attributable for the sale is eliminated. Qualifying small business stock is from a C corporation whose gross assets do not exceed $50 million (including the proceeds received from the issuance of the stock) and who meets a specific active business requirement. The amount of gain eligible for the exclusion is limited to the greater of ten times the taxpayer's basis in the stock or $10 million of gain from stock in that corporation. The provision extends the 100 percent exclusion of the gain from the sale of qualifying small business stock that is acquired before January 1, 2014 and held for more than five years. The bill also clarifies that in the case of stock acquired after February 17, 2009, and before January 1, 2014, the date of acquisition for purposes of determining the percentage exclusion is the date the holding period for the stock begins.

This provision is estimated to cost $954 million over ten years.

Basis adjustment to stock of S corporations making charitable contributions of property. The bill extends for two years the provision allowing S corporation shareholders to take into account their pro rata share of charitable deductions even if such deductions would exceed such shareholder's adjusted basis in the S corporation.

This provision is estimated to cost $225 million over ten years.

Reduction in S corporation recognition period for built-in gains tax. If a taxable corporation converts into an S corporation, the conversion is not a taxable event. However, following such a conversion, an S corporation must hold its assets for a certain period in order to avoid a tax on any built-in gains that existed at the time of the conversion. The American Recovery and Reinvestment Act reduced that period from 10 years to 7 years for sales of assets in 2009 and 2010. The Small Business Jobs Act reduced that period to 5 years for sales of assets in 2011. The bill extends the reduced 5-year holding period for sales occurring in 2012 and 2013. In addition, this bill clarifies rules for carryforwards and installment sales.

This provision is estimated to cost $256 million over ten years.

Empowerment zone tax incentives. The bill extends for two years the designation of certain economically depressed census tracts as Empowerment Zones. Businesses and individual residents within Empowerment Zones are eligible for special tax incentives.

This provision is estimated to cost $450 million over ten years.

12

Extension of tax incentives for the New York Liberty Zone. The bill extends through 2013 the time for issuing New York Liberty Zone bonds effective for bonds issued after December 31, 2009.

This provision is estimated to have no cost over ten years.

Temporary increase in limit on cover over of rum excise tax revenues (from $10.50 to $13.25 per proof gallon) to Puerto Rico and the Virgin Islands. The bill extends for two years the provision providing for payment of $13.25 per gallon to cover over a $13.50 per proof gallon excise tax on distilled spirits produced in or imported into the United States.

This provision is estimated to cost $222 million over ten years.

American Samoa economic development credit. Certain domestic corporations operating in American Samoa are eligible for a possessions tax credit, which offsets their U.S. tax liability on income earned in American Samoa from active business operations, sales of assets used in a business, or certain investments in American Samoa. Further, the credit is subject to an economic activity-based limitation, and is based on the taxpayers', depreciation, and American Samoa income taxes. The bill extends the provision two years to the end of 2013 and modifies the credit to make it available to all qualifying manufacturing businesses operating in American Samoa.

This provision is estimated to cost $62 million over ten years.

Bonus depreciation. Under current law, businesses are allowed to recover the cost of capital expenditures over time according to a depreciation schedule. For 2008 through 2010, Congress allowed businesses to take an additional depreciation deduction allowance equal to 50 percent of the cost of the depreciable property. The TRUIRJCA expanded this provision to allow 100 percent bonus depreciation for investments placed in service after September 8, 2010 and before 2012 and 50 percent bonus depreciation for investments placed in service during 2012. This provision would extend the current 50 percent expensing provision for qualifying property purchased and placed in service before January 1, 2014 (before January 1, 2015 for certain longer-lived and transportation assets) and also allow taxpayers to elect to accelerate some AMT credits in lieu of bonus depreciation. This provision also decouples bonus deprecation from allocation of contract costs under the percentage of completion accounting method rules for assets with a depreciable life of seven years or less that are placed in service in 2013. For regulated utilities, the provision clarifies that it is a violation of the normalization rules to assume a bonus depreciation benefit for ratemaking purposes when a utility has elected not to take bonus depreciation.

This provision is estimated to cost $4.956 billion over ten years.

Title IV. Energy Tax Extenders

Credit for certain nonbusiness energy property (25C). The bill extends for two years, through 2013, the credit under Section 25C of the Code for energy-efficient improvements to existing homes, reinstating the credit as it existed before passage of the American Recovery and Reinvestment Act. Standards for property eligible under 25C are updated to reflect improvements in energy efficiency. The provision also updates the energy efficiency requirements from the 2003 International Energy Conservation Code to the 2006 International Energy Conservation Code.

This provision is estimated to cost $2.446 billion over ten years.

13

Alternative fuel vehicle refueling property (non-hydrogen refueling property). The bill extends for two years, through 2013, the 30% investment tax credit for alternative vehicle refueling property. *This provision is estimated to cost $44 million over ten years.*

Plug-in electric motorcycles and highway vehicles. The provision reforms and extends for two years, through 2013, the individual income tax credit for highway-capable plug-in motorcycles and 3-wheeled vehicles. This proposal replaces a 10 percent tax credit that expired at the end of 2011 for plug-in electric motorcycles, three-wheeled vehicles and low-speed vehicles. Thus it repeals the ability for golf carts and other low-speed vehicles to qualify for the credit. *This provision is estimated to cost $7 million over ten years.*

Cellulosic biofuels producer tax credit. Under current law, facilities producing cellulosic biofuel can claim a $1.01 per gallon production tax credit on fuel produced before the end of 2012. This provision was created in the 2008 Farm Bill. The provision would extend this production tax credit for one additional year, for cellulosic biofuel produced through 2013. The proposal also expands the definition of qualified cellulosic biofuel production to include algae-based fuel. *This provision is estimated to cost $59 million over ten years.*

Incentives for biodiesel and renewable diesel. The bill extends for two years, through 2013, the $1.00 per gallon tax credit for biodiesel, as well as the small agri-biodiesel producer credit of 10 cents per gallon. The bill also extends through 2013 the $1.00 per gallon tax credit for diesel fuel created from biomass. *This provision is estimated to cost $2.181 billion over ten years.*

Indian country coal production tax credit. Under the 2005 Energy Policy Act, coal produced on land owned by an Indian tribe qualifies for a production tax credit equivalent to $2 per ton through 2012. This provision would extend the tax credit through 2013. *This provision is estimated to cost $1 million over ten years.*

Extension and modification of incentives for renewable electricity property wind production tax credit and modification of other renewable energy credits. Under current law, taxpayers can claim a 2.2 cent per kilowatt hour tax credit for wind electricity produced for a 10-year period from a wind facility placed-in-service by the end of 2012 (the wind production tax credit). The bill extends through 2013 the production tax credit for wind. The provision also modifies section 45 to allow renewable energy facilities that begin construction before the end of 2013 to claim the 10-year credit, and amends section 45 to clarify that commonly recycled paper is excluded from qualifying from the production tax credit. *This provision is estimated to have a net of cost $12.109 billion over ten years.*

Investment tax credit in lieu of production tax credit. Under current law, facilities that produce electricity from solar facilities are eligible to take a thirty percent (30%) investment tax credit in the year that the facility is placed-in-service. Facilities that produce electricity from wind, closed-loop biomass, open-loop biomass, geothermal, small irrigation, hydropower, landfill gas, waste-to-energy, and marine renewable facilities are eligible for a production tax credit for electricity produced over a ten-year period. The investment tax credit is better for small and offshore wind facilities. The bill

14

would allow facilities qualifying for the production tax credit to elect to take the investment tax credit in lieu of the production tax credit for facilities that begin construction by the end of 2013.

This provision is estimated to cost $135 million over ten years.

Credit for construction of new energy efficient homes. The bill extends for two years, through 2013, the credit for the construction of energy-efficient new homes that achieve a 30% or 50% reduction in heating and cooling energy consumption relative to a comparable dwelling constructed per the standards of the 2003 International Energy Conservation Code (including supplements).

This provision is estimated to cost $154 million over ten years.

Credit for energy efficient appliances. The bill extends for two years, through 2013, the tax credit for US-based manufacturers of energy-efficient clothes washers, dishwashers and refrigerators.

This provision is estimated to cost $650 million over ten years.

Cellulosic biofuels bonus depreciation. Under current law, facilities producing cellulosic biofuel can expense 50 percent of their eligible capital costs in the first year for facilities placed-in-service by the end of 2012. This provision was created in the 2008 Farm Bill. The provision would extend this bonus depreciation for one additional year for facilities placed-in-service before the end of 2013. The proposal also expands the definition of qualified cellulosic biofuel production to include algae-based fuel.

This provision is estimated to cost less than $500,000 over ten years.

Special rule for sales or dispositions to implement Federal Energy Regulatory Commission or State electric restructuring policy. The bill extends for two years, for sales prior to January 1, 2014, the present law deferral of gain on sales of transmission property by vertically integrated electric utilities to FERC-approved independent transmission companies. Rather than recognizing the full amount of gain in the year of sale, this provision would allow gain on such sales to be recognized ratably over an eight-year period.

This provision has a negligible cost over ten years.

Incentives for alternative fuel and alternative fuel mixtures (other than liquefied hydrogen). The bill extends through 2013 the $0.50 per gallon alternative fuel tax credit and alternative fuel mixture tax credit. This credit can be claimed as a nonrefundable excise tax credit or a refundable income tax credit. Due to claims of abuse in the alternative mixture tax credit, the Committee adopted an amendment denying taxpayers from claiming the refundable portion of the alternative fuel mixture tax credit.

This provision is estimated to cost $360 million over ten years.

Title V. Unemployment

Extension of Emergency Unemployment Compensation Program and Extended Benefit Provisions. This provision extends for one year the availability of benefits in all tiers of Federal Emergency Unemployment Compensation (EUC). In addition , this provision continues for one year the extended benefits (EB) program with a 3-year look-back.

15

This provision is scored in combination with the two provisions below. Together these provisions are estimated to cost $30 billion over ten years.

Extension of Funding for Reemployment Services and Reemployment and Eligibility Assessment Activities. This provision continues reassessments of unemployment eligibility for the long term unemployed preventing needless overpayments while ensuring that individuals receive the benefits they have earned. Furthermore, the provision continues reemployment services to individuals in order to get people back to work more quickly.

Extended Unemployment Benefits Under the Railroad Unemployment Insurance Act. This provision permits for a continuation of benefits for railroad workers for one year.

Title VI. Medicare and Other Health Extensions

Medicare extensions

Medicare Physician Payment Update. This provision guarantees seniors have continued access to their doctors by fixing the Sustainable Growth Rate (SGR) through the end of 2013. Medicare physician payment rates are scheduled to be reduced by 26.5 percent on December 31, 2012. This provision would avoid that reduction and extend current Medicare payment rates through December 31, 2013.
A score for this provision will be provided by the Congressional Budget Office

Work Geographic Adjustment. Under current law, the Medicare fee schedule is adjusted geographically for three factors to reflect differences in the cost of resources needed to produce physician services: physician work, practice expense, and medical malpractice insurance. This provision extends the existing 1.0 floor on the "physician work" index through December 31, 2013.
A score for this provision will be provided by the Congressional Budget Office

Payment for Outpatient Therapy Services. Current law places annual per beneficiary payment limits of $1,880 for all outpatient therapy services provided by non-hospital providers, but includes an exceptions process for cases in which the provision of additional therapy services is determined to be medically necessary. This provision extends the exception process through December 31, 2013. The provision also extends the cap to services received in hospital outpatient departments only through December 31, 2013.
A score for this provision will be provided by the Congressional Budget Office

Ambulance Add-On Payments. Under current law, ground ambulance transports receive add-on to their base rate payments of 2% for urban providers, 3% for rural providers, and 22.6% for super-rural providers. The air ambulance temporary payment policy maintains rural designation for application of rural air ambulance add-on for areas reclassified as urban by OMB in 2006. This provision extends the add-on payment for ground including in super rural areas, through December 31, 2013, and the air ambulance add-on until June 30, 2013.
A score for this provision will be provided by the Congressional Budget Office

16

Extension of Medicare inpatient hospital payment adjustment for low-volume hospitals. Qualifying low-volume hospitals receive add-on payments based on the number of Medicare discharges. To qualify, the hospital must have less than 1,600 Medicare discharges and be 15 miles or greater from the nearest like hospital. This provision extends the payment adjustment until December 31, 2013.
A score for this provision will be provided by the Congressional Budget Office

Extension of the Medicare-Dependent hospital (MDH) program. The Medicare Dependent Hospital (MDH) program provides enhanced reimbursement to support rural health infrastructure and to support small rural hospitals for which Medicare patients make up a significant percentage of inpatient days or discharges. This greater dependence on Medicare may make these hospitals more financially vulnerable to prospective payment, and the MDH designation is designed to reduce this risk. This provision extends the MDH program until October 1, 2013.
A score for this provision will be provided by the Congressional Budget Office

Extension for specialized Medicare Advantage plans for special needs individuals. Extends the authority of specialize plans to target enrollment to certain populations through 2015.
A score for this provision will be provided by the Congressional Budget Office

Extension of Medicare Reasonable Cost Contracts. This provision allows Medicare cost plans to continue to operate through 2014 in an area where at least two Medicare Advantage coordinated care plans operate.
A score for this provision will be provided by the Congressional Budget Office

Performance Improvement. Under the Medicare Improvement for Patients and Providers Act of 2008, HHS entered into a five year contract with a consensus-based entity for certain activities relating to health care performance. This provision continues this funding through 2013. This provision also requires HHS to develop a strategy for providing data on performance improvement in a timely manner.
A score for this provision will be provided by the Congressional Budget Office

Extension of funding outreach and assistance for low-income programs. This provision extends the funding for one year for State Health Insurance Counseling Programs (SHIPs), Area Agencies on Aging (AAAs), Aging and Disability Resource Centers (ADRCs), and The National Center for Benefits Outreach and Enrollment.
A score for this provision will be provided by the Congressional Budget Office

Other health provisions

Extension of the Qualifying Individual Program. The Qualifying Individual (QI) program allows Medicaid to pay the Medicare Part B premiums for low-income Medicare beneficiaries with incomes between 120 percent and 135 percent of poverty. Under current law, QI expires December 31, 2012. This provision extends the QI program until December 31, 2013.
A score for this provision will be provided by the Congressional Budget Office

Extension of Transitional Medical Assistance. Transitional Medical Assistance (TMA) allows low-income families to maintain their Medicaid coverage as they transition into employment and increase

17

1,549

their earnings. Under current law, TMA expires December 31, 2012. This provision extends TMA until December 31, 2013.

A score for this provision will be provided by the Congressional Budget Office

Extension of Medicaid and CHIP Express Lane option. The CHIP Reauthorization Act of 2009 created a new option that allows state Medicaid and CHIP offices to rely on data from other state offices, like SNAP and school lunch programs, in making income eligibility determinations for children, called Express Lane Eligibility (ELE). The authority to use ELE expires on September 30, 2013. This provision would extend ELE authority through September 30, 2014.

A score for this provision will be provided by the Congressional Budget Office

Extension of Family-to-Family Health Information Centers. This provision continues the Family to Family Health Information Centers (F2F HIC) to assist families of children/youth with special health care needs in making informed choices about health care in order to promote good treatment decisions, cost-effectiveness and improved health outcomes. This provision will help families navigate the health care system so that their children can get the care and benefits they need through Medicaid, SCHIP, SSI, early intervention services, private insurance and other programs. In addition, F2F HICs provide leadership and training for health care providers and policymakers to promote family-centered "medical home" for every child. There is one F2F HIC in every state and the District of Columbia. The total cost of this provision is $5 million per year.

A score for this provision will be provided by the Congressional Budget Office

Extension of Special Diabetes Program for Type 1 diabetes and for Indians. Funds research for type I diabetes and supports diabetes treatment and prevention initiatives for American Indians and Alaska Natives. The Special Diabetes Program (SDP) expires at the end of 2013, but early reauthorization is critical to the continuation of the existing research initiatives. This provision would extend the SDP for one year.

A score for this provision will be provided by the Congressional Budget Office

Title VII. Extension of Agricultural Programs

Farm Bill. The 2008 Farm Bill is extended until September 30, 2013 for all currently funded programs.

A score for this provision will be provided by the Congressional Budget Office

Title IX. Miscellaneous Provisions

Strategic Delivery Systems.

A score for this provision will be provided by the Congressional Budget Office

Pay Freeze for Members of Congress. This provision clarifies that no cost of living adjustment is made for the salaries of Members of Congress for fiscal year 2013.

A score for this provision will be provided by the Congressional Budget Office

18

Title X. Budget Provisions

Sequestration. This proposal would delay by two months automatic across-the-board cuts set to take effect January 2.

Roth conversions for retirement plans. Under current law, a deferral plan under section 401(k) (including the Thrift Savings Plan), 403(b) or 457(b) governmental plan can have Roth accounts that allow participants to save on a Roth basis. That is, they can make after-tax contributions to the plan and all the principal and earnings are tax-free when distributed. Plans can currently allow participants to convert their pre-tax accounts to Roth accounts, but only with respect to money they have a right to take out of the plan, usually because they have reached age 59½ or separated from service. This proposal would allow any amount in a non-Roth account to be converted to a Roth account in the same plan, whether or not the amount is distributable. The amount converted would be subject to regular income tax.

This provision is estimated to raise $12.186 billion over ten year.

19

OVERVIEW OF THE FEDERAL TAX SYSTEM
AS IN EFFECT FOR 2013

Prepared by the Staff
of the
JOINT COMMITTEE ON TAXATION

January 8, 2013
JCX-2-13R

¶ 6015. Appendix

CONTENTS

i

INTRODUCTION

This document,[1] prepared by the staff of the Joint Committee on Taxation ("Joint Committee Staff"), provides a summary of the present-law Federal tax system as in effect for 2013.

The current Federal tax system has four main elements: (1) an income tax on individuals and corporations (which consists of both a "regular" income tax and an alternative minimum tax); (2) payroll taxes on wages (and corresponding taxes on self-employment income) to finance certain social insurance programs; (3) estate, gift, and generation-skipping taxes, and (4) excise taxes on selected goods and services. This document provides a broad overview of each of these elements.[2]

A number of aspects of the Federal tax laws are subject to change over time. For example, some dollar amounts and income thresholds are indexed for inflation. The standard deduction, tax rate brackets, and the annual gift tax exclusion are examples of amounts that are indexed for inflation. In general, the Internal Revenue Service adjusts these numbers annually and publishes the inflation-adjusted amounts in effect for a tax year prior to the beginning of that year. Where applicable, this document generally includes dollar amounts in effect for 2013 and notes whether dollar amounts are indexed for inflation. A number of the inflation indexed 2013 values have not yet been published by the Internal Revenue Service. In these cases, the referenced figures were calculated by the Joint Committee Staff in accordance with the governing statute and published Consumer Price Index values.

In addition, a number of the provisions in the Federal tax laws have been enacted on a temporary basis or have parameters that vary by statute from year to year. For simplicity, this document describes the Federal tax laws in effect for 2013 and generally does not include references to provisions as they may be in effect for future years or to termination dates for expiring provisions.

---

[1] This document may be cited as follows: Joint Committee on Taxation, *Overview of the Federal Tax System as in Effect for 2013* (JCX-2-13R), January 8, 2013.

[2] If certain requirements are met, certain entities or organizations are exempt from Federal income tax. A description of such organizations is beyond the scope of this document.

1

I. SUMMARY OF PRESENT-LAW FEDERAL TAX SYSTEM

A. Individual Income Tax

In general

A United States citizen or resident alien generally is subject to the U.S. individual income tax on his or her worldwide taxable income.[3] Taxable income equals the taxpayer's total gross income less certain exclusions, exemptions, and deductions. Graduated tax rates are then applied to a taxpayer's taxable income to determine his or her individual income tax liability. A taxpayer may face additional liability if the alternative minimum tax applies. A taxpayer may reduce his or her income tax liability by any applicable tax credits.

Adjusted gross income

Under the Internal Revenue Code of 1986 (the "Code"), gross income means "income from whatever source derived" except for certain items specifically exempt or excluded by statute. Sources of income include compensation for services, interest, dividends, capital gains, rents, royalties, alimony and separate maintenance payments, annuities, income from life insurance and endowment contracts (other than certain death benefits), pensions, gross profits from a trade or business, income in respect of a decedent, and income from S corporations, partnerships,[4] trusts or estates.[5] Statutory exclusions from gross income include death benefits payable under a life insurance contract, interest on certain State and local bonds, employer-provided health insurance, employer-provided pension contributions, and certain other employer-provided benefits.

An individual's adjusted gross income ("AGI") is determined by subtracting certain "above-the-line" deductions from gross income. These deductions include trade or business expenses, capital losses, contributions to a qualified retirement plan by a self-employed individual, contributions to individual retirement arrangements ("IRAs"), certain moving expenses, certain education-related expenses, and alimony payments.

---

[3] Foreign tax credits generally are available against U.S. income tax imposed on foreign source income to the extent of foreign income taxes paid on that income. A nonresident alien generally is subject to the U.S. individual income tax only on income with a sufficient nexus to the United States.

[4] In general, partnerships and S corporations are treated as pass-through entities for Federal income tax purposes. Thus, no Federal income tax is imposed at the entity level. Rather, income of such entities is passed through and taxed to the owners at the individual level. A business entity organized as a limited liability company ("LLC") under applicable State law generally is treated as a partnership for Federal income tax purposes.

[5] In general, estates and most trusts pay tax on income at the entity level, unless the income is distributed or required to be distributed under governing law or under the terms of the governing instrument. Such entities determine their tax liability using a special tax rate schedule and are subject to the alternative minimum tax. Certain trusts, however, do not pay Federal income tax at the trust level. For example, certain trusts that distribute all income currently to beneficiaries are treated as pass-through or conduit entities (similar to a partnership). Other trusts are treated as being owned by grantors in whole or in part for tax purposes; in such cases, the grantors are taxed on the income of the trust.

2

Taxable income

To determine taxable income, an individual reduces AGI by any personal exemption deductions and either the applicable standard deduction or his or her itemized deductions. Personal exemptions generally are allowed for the taxpayer, his or her spouse, and any dependents. For 2013, the amount deductible for each personal exemption is $3,900. This amount is indexed annually for inflation. Additionally, the personal exemption phase-out ("PEP") reduces a taxpayer's personal exemptions by two percent for each $2,500 ($1,250 for married filing separately), or fraction thereof, by which the taxpayer's AGI exceeds $250,000 (single), $275,000 (head-of-household), $300,000 (married filing jointly) and $150,000 (married filing separately).[6] These threshold amounts are indexed for inflation.

A taxpayer also may reduce AGI by the amount of the applicable standard deduction. The basic standard deduction varies depending upon a taxpayer's filing status. For 2013, the amount of the standard deduction is $6,100 for single individuals and married individuals filing separate returns, $8,950 for heads of households, and $12,200 for married individuals filing a joint return and surviving spouses. An additional standard deduction is allowed with respect to any individual who is elderly or blind.[7] The amounts of the basic standard deduction and the additional standard deductions are indexed annually for inflation.

In lieu of taking the applicable standard deductions, an individual may elect to itemize deductions. The deductions that may be itemized include State and local income taxes (or, in lieu of income, sales taxes), real property and certain personal property taxes, home mortgage interest, charitable contributions, certain investment interest, medical expenses (in excess of 10 percent of AGI), casualty and theft losses (in excess of 10 percent of AGI and in excess of $100 per loss), and certain miscellaneous expenses (in excess of two percent of AGI). Additionally, the total amount of itemized deductions allowed is reduced by $0.03 for each dollar of AGI in excess of $250,000 (single), $275,000 (head-of-household), $300,000 (married filing jointly) and $150,000 (married filing separately).[8] These threshold amounts are indexed for inflation.

---

[6] A taxpayer thus has all personal exemptions completely phased out at incomes of $372, 501 (single), $397,501 (head-of-household), $422,501 (married filing jointly) and $211,251 (married filing separately).

[7] For 2013, the additional amount is $1,200 for married taxpayers (for each spouse meeting the applicable criterion) and surviving spouses. The additional amount for single individuals and heads of households is $1,500. If an individual is both blind and aged, the individual is entitled to two additional standard deductions, for a total additional amount (for 2013) of $2,400 or $3,000, as applicable.

[8] This rule is sometimes referred to as the "Pease limitation." A taxpayer may not lose more than 80 percent of his or her deductions as a result of this provision.

3

Table 1.–2013 Standard Deduction and Personal Exemption Values

Standard Deduction	
Married Filing Jointly	$12,200
Head of Household	$8,950
Single and Married Filing Separately	$6,100
Personal Exemptions	$3,900

Tax liability

In general

A taxpayer's net income tax liability is the greater of (1) regular individual income tax liability reduced by credits allowed against the regular tax, or (2) tentative minimum tax reduced by credits allowed against the minimum tax. The amount of income subject to tax is determined differently under the regular tax and the alternative minimum tax, and separate rate schedules apply. Lower rates apply for long-term capital gains; those rates apply for both the regular tax and the alternative minimum tax.

Regular tax liability

To determine regular tax liability, a taxpayer generally must apply the tax rate schedules (or the tax tables) to his or her regular taxable income. The rate schedules are broken into several ranges of income, known as income brackets, and the marginal tax rate increases as a taxpayer's income increases. Separate rate schedules apply based on an individual's filing status. For 2013, the regular individual income tax rate schedules are as follows:

4

Table 2.–Federal Individual Income Tax Rates for 2013

If taxable income is:	Then income tax equals:
Single Individuals	
Not over $8,925..	10% of the taxable income
Over $8,925 but not over $36,250....................................	$892.50 plus 15% of the excess over $8,925
Over $36,250 but not over $87,850..................................	$4,991.25 plus 25% of the excess over $36,250
Over $87,850 but not over $183,250................................	$17,891.25 plus 28% of the excess over $87,850
Over $183,250 but not over $398,350	$44,603.25 plus 33% of the excess over $183,250
Over $398,350 but not over $400,000	$115,586.25 plus 35% of the excess over $398,350
Over $400,000...	$116,163.75 plus 39.6% of the excess over $400,000
Heads of Households	
Not over $12,750..	10% of the taxable income
Over $12,750 but not over $48,600..................................	$1,275 plus 15% of the excess over $12,750
Over $48,600 but not over $125,450................................	$6,652.50 plus 25% of the excess over $48,600
Over $125,450 but not over $203,150..............................	$25,865 plus 28% of the excess over $125,450
Over $203,150 but not over $398,350..............................	$47,621 plus 33% of the excess over $203,150
Over $398,350 but not over $425,000	$112,037 plus 35% of the excess over $398,350
Over $425,000...	$121,364.50 plus 39.6% of the excess over $425,000
Married Individuals Filing Joint Returns and Surviving Spouses	
Not over $17,850..	10% of the taxable income
Over $17,850 but not over $72,500..................................	$1,785 plus 15% of the excess over $17,850
Over $72,500 but not over $146,400................................	$9,982.50 plus 25% of the excess over $72,500
Over $146,400 but not over $223,050..............................	$28,457.50 plus 28% of the excess over $146,400

5

Over $223,050 but not over $398,350	$49,919.50 plus 33% of the excess over $223,050
Over $398,350 but not over $450,000	$107,768.50 plus 35% of the excess over $398,350
Over $450,000	$125,846 plus 39.6% of the excess over $450,000

Married Individuals Filing Separate Returns

Not over $8,925	10% of the taxable income
Over $8,925 but not over $36,250	$892.50 plus 15% of the excess over $8,925
Over $36,250 but not over $73,200	$4,991.25 plus 25% of the excess over $36,250
Over $73,200 but not over $111,525	$14,228.75 plus 28% of the excess over $73,200
Over $111,525 but not over $199,175	$24,959.75 plus 33% of the excess over $111,525
Over $199,175 but not over $225,000	$53,884.25 plus 35% of the excess over $199,175
Over $225,000	$62,923 plus 39.6% of the excess over $225,000

An individual's marginal tax rate may be reduced by the allowance of a deduction equal to a percentage of income from certain domestic manufacturing activities.[9]

Alternative minimum tax liability

An alternative minimum tax is imposed on an individual, estate, or trust in an amount by which the tentative minimum tax exceeds the regular income tax for the taxable year. For 2013, the tentative minimum tax is the sum of (1) 26 percent of so much of the taxable excess as does not exceed $179,500 ($89,750 in the case of a married individual filing a separate return) and (2) 28 percent of the remaining taxable excess. The taxable excess is so much of the alternative minimum taxable income ("AMTI") as exceeds the exemption amount. The breakpoint between the 26-percent and 28-percent bracket is indexed for inflation. The maximum tax rates on net capital gain and dividends used in computing the regular tax are used in computing the tentative minimum tax. AMTI is the taxpayer's taxable income increased by the taxpayer's tax preferences and adjusted by determining the tax treatment of certain items in a manner that negates the deferral of income resulting from the regular tax treatment of those items.

The exemption amounts for 2013 are: (1) $80,800 in the case of married individuals filing a joint return and surviving spouses; (2) $51,900 in the case of other unmarried individuals; (3) $40,400 in the case of married individuals filing separate returns; and

---

[9] This deduction is described in more detail below in the summary of the tax rules applicable to corporations.

6

(4) $23,100 in the case of an estate or trust. The exemption amounts are phased out by an amount equal to 25 percent of the amount by which the individual's AMTI exceeds (1) $153,900 in the case of married individuals filing a joint return and surviving spouses, (2) $115,400 in the case of other unmarried individuals, and (3) $76,950 in the case of married individuals filing separate returns or an estate or a trust. These amounts are indexed for inflation.

Among the preferences and adjustments applicable to the individual alternative minimum tax are accelerated depreciation on certain property used in a trade or business, circulation expenditures, research and experimental expenditures, certain expenses and allowances related to oil and gas and mining exploration and development, certain tax-exempt interest income, and a portion of the amount of gain excluded with respect to the sale or disposition of certain small business stock. In addition, personal exemptions, the standard deduction, and certain itemized deductions, such as State and local taxes and miscellaneous deductions, are not allowed to reduce AMTI.

<u>Special capital gains and dividends rates</u>

In general, gain or loss reflected in the value of an asset is not recognized for income tax purposes until a taxpayer disposes of the asset. On the sale or exchange of a capital asset, any gain generally is included in income. Any net capital gain of an individual is taxed at maximum rates lower than the rates applicable to ordinary income. Net capital gain is the excess of the net long-term capital gain for the taxable year over the net short-term capital loss for the year. Gain or loss is treated as long-term if the asset is held for more than one year.

Capital losses generally are deductible in full against capital gains. In addition, individual taxpayers may deduct capital losses against up to $3,000 of ordinary income in each year. Any remaining unused capital losses may be carried forward indefinitely to another taxable year.

A maximum rate applies to capital gains and dividends. For 2013, the maximum rate of tax on the adjusted net capital gain of an individual is 20 percent on any amount of gain that otherwise would be taxed at a 39.6 rate. In addition, any adjusted net capital gain otherwise taxed at a 10- or 15-percent rate is taxed at a zero-percent rate. Adjusted net capital gain otherwise taxed at rates greater than 15-percent but less than 39.6 percent is taxed at a 15 percent rate. These rates apply for purposes of both the regular tax and the alternative minimum tax. Dividends are generally taxed at the same rate as capital gains.

<u>Credits against tax</u>

An individual may reduce his or her tax liability by any available tax credits. In some instances, a permissible credit is "refundable", *i.e.*, it may result in a refund in excess of any credits for withheld taxes or estimated tax payments available to the individual. Two major credits are the child tax credit and the earned income credit.

7

An individual may claim a tax credit for each qualifying child under the age of 17. The amount of the credit per child is $1,000.[10] The aggregate amount of child credits that may be claimed is phased out for individuals with income over certain threshold amounts. Specifically, the otherwise allowable child tax credit is reduced by $50 for each $1,000 (or fraction thereof) of modified adjusted gross income over $75,000 for single individuals or heads of households, $110,000 for married individuals filing joint returns, and $55,000 for married individuals filing separate returns. To the extent the child credit exceeds the taxpayer's tax liability, the taxpayer is eligible for a refundable credit[11] (the additional child tax credit) equal to 15 percent of earned income in excess of $3,000.[12]

A refundable earned income tax credit ("EITC") is available to low-income workers who satisfy certain requirements. The amount of the EITC varies depending upon the taxpayer's earned income and whether the taxpayer has one, two, more than two, or no qualifying children. In 2013, the maximum EITC is $6,044 for taxpayers with more than two qualifying children, $5,372 for taxpayers with two qualifying children, $3,250 for taxpayers with one qualifying child, and $487 for taxpayers with no qualifying children. The credit amount begins to phaseout at an income level of $17,530 ($7,970 for taxpayers with no qualifying children). The phaseout percentages are 15.98 for taxpayers with one qualifying child, 17.68 for two or more qualifying children, and 7.65 for no qualifying children.

Tax credits are also allowed for certain business expenditures, certain foreign income taxes paid or accrued, certain education expenditures, certain child care expenditures, and for certain elderly or disabled individuals. Credits allowed against the regular tax are allowed against the alternative minimum tax.

Tax on net investment income

For taxable years beginning after December 31, 2012, a tax is imposed on net investment income in the case of an individual, estate, or trust. In the case of an individual, the tax is 3.8 percent of the lesser of net investment income or the excess of modified adjusted gross income over the threshold amount.[13] The threshold amount is $250,000 in the case of a joint return or surviving spouse, $125,000 in the case of a married individual filing a separate return, and $200,000 in any other case.[14]

---

[10] A child who is not a citizen, national, or resident of the United States cannot be a qualifying child.

[11] The refundable credit may not exceed the maximum credit per child of $1,000.

[12] Families with three or more children may determine the additional child tax credit using an alternative formula, if this results in a larger credit than determined under the earned income formula. Under the alternative formula, the additional child tax credit equals the amount by which the taxpayer's social security taxes exceed the taxpayer's earned income tax credit.

[13] The tax is subject to the individual estimated tax provisions. The tax is not deductible in computing any tax imposed by subtitle A of the Code (relating to income taxes).

[14] These amounts are not indexed for inflation.

8

Net investment income is the excess of (1) the sum of (a) gross income from interest, dividends, annuities, royalties, and rents, other than such income which is derived in the ordinary course of a trade or business that is not a passive activity with respect to the taxpayer or a trade or business of trading in financial instruments or commodities, and (b) net gain (to the extent taken into account in computing taxable income) attributable to the disposition of property other than property held in the active conduct of a trade or business that is not in the trade or business of trading in financial instruments or commodities, over (2) deductions properly allocable to such gross income or net gain.

For purposes of this tax, modified adjusted gross income is AGI increased by the amount excluded from income as foreign earned income under section 911(a)(1) (net of the deductions and exclusions disallowed with respect to the foreign earned income).

In the case of an estate or trust, the tax is 3.8 percent of the lesser of undistributed net investment income or the excess of adjusted gross income (as defined in section 67(e)) over the dollar amount at which the highest income tax bracket applicable to an estate or trust begins.[15]

---

[15] The tax does not apply to a nonresident alien or to a trust in which all the unexpired interests are devoted to charitable purposes. The tax also does not apply to a trust that is exempt from tax under section 501 or a charitable remainder trust exempt from tax under section 664.

9

B. Corporate Income Tax

Taxable income

Corporations organized under the laws of any of the 50 States (and the District of Columbia) generally are subject to the U.S. corporate income tax on their worldwide taxable income.[16]

The taxable income of a corporation generally is comprised of gross income less allowable deductions. Gross income generally is income derived from any source, including gross profit from the sale of goods and services to customers, rents, royalties, interest (other than interest from certain indebtedness issued by State and local governments), dividends, gains from the sale of business and investment assets, and other income.

Allowable deductions include ordinary and necessary business expenditures, such as salaries, wages, contributions to profit-sharing and pension plans and other employee benefit programs, repairs, bad debts, taxes (other than Federal income taxes), contributions to charitable organizations (subject to an income limitation), advertising, interest expense, certain losses, selling expenses, and other expenses. Expenditures that produce benefits in future taxable years to a taxpayer's business or income-producing activities (such as the purchase of plant and equipment) generally are capitalized and recovered over time through depreciation, amortization or depletion allowances. A net operating loss incurred in one taxable year may be carried back two years or carried forward 20 years. Deductions are also allowed for certain amounts despite the lack of a direct expenditure by the taxpayer. For example, a deduction is allowed for all or a portion of the amount of dividends received by a corporation from another corporation (provided certain ownership requirements are satisfied). Moreover, a deduction is allowed for a portion of the amount of income attributable to certain manufacturing activities.

The Code also specifies certain expenditures that may not be deducted, such as dividends paid to shareholders, expenses associated with earning tax-exempt income,[17] certain entertainment expenditures, certain executive compensation in excess of $1,000,000 per year, a portion of the interest on certain high-yield debt obligations that resemble equity, as well as fines, penalties, bribes, kickbacks and illegal payments.

---

[16] Foreign tax credits generally are available against U.S. income tax imposed on foreign source income to the extent of foreign income taxes paid on that income. A foreign corporation generally is subject to the U.S. corporate income tax only on income with a sufficient nexus to the United States.

Under subchapter S of the Code, a qualified small business corporation may elect not to be subject to the corporate income tax. If an S corporation election is made, the income of the corporation will flow through to the shareholders and be taxable directly to the shareholders.

[17] For example, the carrying costs of tax-exempt State and local obligations and the premiums on certain life insurance policies are not deductible.

10

Tax liability

A corporation's regular income tax liability generally is determined by applying the following tax rate schedule to its taxable income.

Table 3.–Federal Corporate Income Tax Rates

If taxable income is:	Then the income tax rate is:
$0-$50,000	15 percent of taxable income
$50,001-$75,000	25 percent of taxable income
$75,001-$10,000,000	34 percent of taxable income
Over $10,000,000	35 percent of taxable income

The first two graduated rates described above are phased out for corporations with taxable income between $100,000 and $335,000. As a result, a corporation with taxable income between $335,000 and $10,000,000 effectively is subject to a flat tax rate of 34 percent. Also, the application of the 34-percent rate is gradually phased out for corporations with taxable income between $15,000,000 and $18,333,333, such that a corporation with taxable income of $18,333,333 or more effectively is subject to a flat rate of 35 percent.

In contrast to the treatment of capital gains in the individual income tax, no separate rate structure exists for corporate capital gains. Thus, the maximum rate of tax on the net capital gains of a corporation is 35 percent. A corporation may not deduct the amount of capital losses in excess of capital gains for any taxable year. Disallowed capital losses may be carried back three years or carried forward five years.

Corporations are taxed at lower rates on income from certain domestic production activities. This rate reduction is effected by the allowance of a deduction equal to a percentage of qualifying domestic production activities income. The deduction is equal to nine percent of the income from manufacturing, construction, and certain other activities specified in the Code.[18]

Like individuals, corporations may reduce their tax liability by any applicable tax credits. Tax credits applicable to businesses include credits for biofuels and renewable power, investment tax credits (applicable to investment in certain renewable energy property and the rehabilitation of certain real property), the research credit, the low-income housing credit

---

[18] With a nine percent deduction, a corporation is taxed at a rate of 35 percent on only 91 percent of qualifying income, resulting in an effective tax rate of 0.91 * 35, or 31.85 percent. A similar reduction applies to the graduated rates applicable to individuals with qualifying domestic production activities income.

11

(applicable to investment in certain low-income housing projects), the empowerment zone employment credit (applicable to wages paid to certain residents of, or employees in, empowerment zones), the work opportunity credit (applicable to wages paid to individuals from certain targeted groups), and the disabled access credit (applicable to expenditures by certain small businesses to make the businesses accessible to disabled individuals). Unused credits generally may be carried back one year and carried forward twenty years.

A foreign tax credit is available, subject to limitations, for certain foreign income taxes paid or accrued. Foreign income taxes limited in a tax year may be carried back one year or forward ten years.

Affiliated group

Domestic corporations that are affiliated through 80 percent or more corporate ownership may elect to file a consolidated return in lieu of filing separate returns. Corporations filing a consolidated return generally are treated as a single corporation; thus, the losses of one corporation can offset the income (and thus reduce the otherwise applicable tax) of other affiliated corporations.

Minimum tax

A corporation is subject to an alternative minimum tax that is payable, in addition to all other tax liabilities, to the extent that it exceeds the corporation's regular income tax liability. The tax is imposed at a flat rate of 20 percent on alternative minimum taxable income in excess of a $40,000 exemption amount.[19] Credits that are allowed to offset a corporation's regular tax liability generally are not allowed to offset its minimum tax liability. If a corporation pays the alternative minimum tax, the amount of the tax paid is allowed as a credit against the regular tax in future years.

Alternative minimum taxable income is the corporation's taxable income increased by the corporation's tax preferences and adjusted by determining the tax treatment of certain items in a manner that negates the deferral of income resulting from the regular tax treatment of those items. Among the preferences and adjustments applicable to the corporate alternative minimum tax are accelerated depreciation on certain property, certain expenses and allowances related to oil and gas and mining exploration and development, certain amortization expenses related to pollution control facilities, and certain tax-exempt interest income. In addition, corporate alternative minimum taxable income is increased by 75 percent of the amount by which the corporation's "adjusted current earnings" exceed its alternative minimum taxable income (determined without regard to this adjustment). Adjusted current earnings generally are determined with reference to the rules that apply in determining a corporation's earnings and profits.

---

[19] The exemption amount is phased out for corporations with income above certain threshold, and is completely phased out for corporations with alternative minimum taxable income of $310,000 or more.

12

Treatment of corporate distributions

The taxation of a corporation generally is separate and distinct from the taxation of its shareholders. A distribution by a corporation to one of its shareholders generally is taxable as a dividend to the shareholder to the extent of the corporation's current or accumulated earnings and profits.[20] Thus, the amount of a corporate dividend generally is taxed twice: once when the income is earned by the corporation and again when the dividend is distributed to the shareholder.[21] Conversely, amounts paid as interest to the debtholders of a corporation generally are subject to only one level of tax (at the recipient level) since the corporation generally is allowed a deduction for the amount of interest expense paid or accrued.

Amounts received by a shareholder in complete liquidation of a corporation generally are treated as full payment in exchange for the shareholder's stock. A liquidating corporation recognizes gain or loss on the distributed property as if such property were sold to the distributee for its fair market value. However, if a corporation liquidates a subsidiary corporation of which it has 80 percent or more control, no gain or loss generally is recognized by either the parent corporation or the subsidiary corporation.

Accumulated earnings and personal holding company taxes

Taxes at a rate of 20 percent (the top rate generally applicable to dividend income of individuals) may be imposed upon the accumulated earnings or personal holding company income of a corporation. The accumulated earnings tax may be imposed if a corporation retains earnings in excess of reasonable business needs. The personal holding company tax may be imposed upon the excessive passive income of a closely held corporation. The accumulated earnings tax and the personal holding company tax, when they apply, in effect impose the shareholder level tax in addition to the corporate level tax on accumulated earnings or undistributed personal holding company income.

---

[20] A distribution in excess of the earnings and profits of a corporation generally is a tax-free return of capital to the shareholder to the extent of the shareholder's adjusted basis (generally, cost) in the stock of the corporation; such distribution is a capital gain if in excess of basis. A distribution of property other than cash generally is treated as a taxable sale of such property by the corporation and is taken into account by the shareholder at the property's fair market value. A distribution of stock of the corporation generally is not a taxable event to either the corporation or the shareholder.

[21] This double taxation is mitigated by a reduced tax rate generally applicable to dividend income of individuals.

13

C. Estate, Gift and Generation-Skipping Transfer Taxes

The United States generally imposes a gift tax on any transfer of property by gift made by a U.S. citizen or resident, whether made directly or indirectly and whether made in trust or otherwise. Nonresident aliens are subject to the gift tax with respect to transfers of tangible real or personal property where the property is located in the United States at the time of the gift. The gift tax is imposed on the donor and is based on the fair market value of the property transferred. Deductions are allowed for certain gifts to spouses and to charities. Annual gifts of $14,000 (for 2013) or less per donor and per donee generally are not subject to tax.

An estate tax also is imposed on the taxable estate of any person who was a citizen or resident of the United States at the time of death, and on certain property belonging to a nonresident of the United States that is located in the United States at the time of death. The estate tax is imposed on the estate of the decedent and generally is based on the fair market value of the property passing at death.[22] The taxable estate generally equals the worldwide gross estate less certain allowable deductions, including a marital deduction for certain bequests to the surviving spouse of the decedent and a deduction for certain bequests to charities.

The gift and estate taxes are unified such that a single graduated rate schedule and effective exemption amount apply to an individual's cumulative taxable gifts and bequests. The unified estate and gift tax rates begin at 18 percent on the first $10,000 in cumulative taxable transfers and reach 40 percent on cumulative taxable transfers over $1,000,000. A unified credit of $2,045,800 (for 2013) is available with respect to taxable transfers by gift or at death. This credit effectively exempts a total of $5.25 million[23] (for 2013) in cumulative taxable transfers from the gift tax or the estate tax. The unified credit thus generally also has the effect of rendering the marginal rates below 40 percent inapplicable. Unused exemption as of the death of a spouse generally is available for use by the surviving spouse; this feature of the law sometimes is referred to as exemption portability.

A separate transfer tax is imposed on generation-skipping transfers in addition to any estate or gift tax that is normally imposed on such transfers. This tax generally is imposed on transfers, either directly or through a trust or similar arrangement, to a beneficiary in more than

---

[22] In addition to interests in property owned by the decedent at the time of death, the Federal estate tax also is imposed on (1) life insurance that was either payable to the decedent's estate or in which the decedent had an incident of ownership at death, (2) property over which the decedent had a general power of appointment at death, (3) annuities purchased by the decedent or his employer that were payable to the decedent before death, (4) property held by the decedents as joint tenants, (5) property transferred by the decedent before death in which the decedent retained a life estate or over which the decedent had the power to designate who will possess or enjoy the property, (6) property revocably transferred by the decedent before death, and (7) certain transfers taking effect at the death of the decedent.

[23] The Tax Relief, Unemployment Insurance Reauthorization, and Job Creation Act of 2010, Pub. L. No. 111-312, establishes an exemption amount of $5 million for 2010 and 2011 and indexes this amount for inflation for years after 2011. The American Taxpayer Relief Act of 2012 makes permanent the exemption provisions of the 2010 Act.

14

one generation below that of the transferor. For 2013, the generation-skipping transfer tax is imposed at a flat rate of 40 percent on generation-skipping transfers in excess of $5.25 million.

15

D. Social Insurance Taxes

In general

Social Security benefits and certain Medicare benefits are financed primarily by payroll taxes on covered wages. The Federal Insurance Contributions Act ("FICA") imposes tax on employers based on the amount of wages paid to an employee during the year. The tax imposed is composed of two parts: (1) the old age, survivors, and disability insurance ("OASDI") tax equal to 6.2 percent of covered wages up to the taxable wage base ($113,700 in 2013); and (2) the Medicare hospital insurance ("HI") tax amount equal to 1.45 percent of covered wages.[24] In addition to the tax on employers, each employee is subject to FICA taxes equal to the amount of tax imposed on the employer. The employee level tax generally must be withheld and remitted to the Federal government by the employer.

As a parallel to FICA taxes, the Self-Employment Contributions Act ("SECA") imposes taxes on the net income from self-employment of self-employed individuals. The rate of the OASDI portion of SECA taxes is equal to the combined employee and employer OASDI FICA tax rates and applies to self-employment income up to the FICA taxable wage base. Similarly, the rate of the HI portion is the same as the combined employer and employee HI rates and there is no cap on the amount of self-employment income to which the rate applies.[25]

In addition to FICA taxes, employers are subject to a Federal unemployment insurance payroll tax equal to 6 percent of the total wages of each employee (up to $7,000) on covered employment. Employers are eligible for a Federal credit equal to 5.4 percent for State unemployment taxes, yielding a 0.6 percent effective tax rate. Federal unemployment insurance payroll taxes are used to fund programs maintained by the States for the benefit of unemployed workers.

Additional hospital insurance tax on certain high-income individuals

For remuneration received in taxable years beginning after December 31, 2012, the employee portion of the HI tax is increased by an additional tax of 0.9 percent on wages received in excess of a specific threshold amount.[26] However, unlike the general 1.45 percent HI tax on wages, this additional tax is on the combined wages of the employee and the employee's spouse, in the case of a joint return. The threshold amount is $250,000 in the case of a joint return,

---

[24] Since 1994, the HI payroll tax has not been subject to a wage cap.

[25] For purposes of computing net earnings from self-employment, taxpayers are permitted a deduction equal to the product of the taxpayer's earnings (determined without regard to this deduction) and one-half of the sum of the rates for OASDI (12.4 percent) and HI (2.9 percent), *i.e.*, 7.65 percent of net earnings. This deduction reflects the fact that the FICA rates apply to an employee's wages, which do not include FICA taxes paid by the employer, whereas a self-employed individual's net earnings are economically equivalent to an employee's wages plus the employer share of FICA taxes.

[26] Sec. 3101(b), as amended by the Patient Protection and Affordable Care Act ("PPACA"), Pub. L. No. 111-148.

16

$125,000 in the case of a married individual filing a separate return, and $200,000 in any other case (unmarried individual, head of household or surviving spouse).[27]

The same additional HI tax applies to the HI portion of SECA tax on self-employment income in excess of the threshold amount. Thus, an additional tax of 0.9 percent is imposed on every self-employed individual on self-employment income in excess of the threshold amount.[28]

---

[27] These threshold amounts are not indexed for inflation.

[28] Sec. 1402(b).

17

E. Major Excise Taxes

The Federal tax system imposes excise taxes on selected goods and services. Generally, excise taxes are taxes imposed on a per unit or ad valorem (*i.e.*, percentage of price) basis on the production, importation, or sale of a specific good or service. Among the goods and services subject to U.S. excise taxes are motor fuels, alcoholic beverages, tobacco products, firearms, air and ship transportation, certain environmentally hazardous products (*e.g.*, the tax on ozone depleting chemicals, and a tax on crude oil and certain petroleum products to fund the Oil Spill Liability Trust Fund), coal, certain telephone communications (*e.g.* local service), certain wagers, certain medical devices, indoor tanning services, and vehicles lacking in fuel efficiency.[29] Additionally, an annual fee is imposed on certain manufacturers and importers of branded prescription drugs pursuant to specified government programs. The largest excise taxes in terms of revenue (for fiscal year 2010) are those for gasoline motor fuel ($25.1 billion), domestic cigarettes ($14.9 billion), diesel motor fuel ($8.6 billion), and domestic air tickets ($7.6 billion).[30]

Revenues from certain Federal excise taxes are dedicated to trust funds (*e.g.*, the Highway Trust Fund) for designated expenditure programs, and revenues from other excise taxes (*e.g.*, alcoholic beverages) go to the General Fund for general purpose expenditures.

Table 4.–2013 Federal Excise Tax Rates for Selected Taxed Products or Services

Gasoline Motor Fuel	18.3 cents per gallon
Diesel Motor Fuel	24.3 cents per gallon
Domestic Cigarettes	$50.33 per thousand small cigarettes; $105.69 per thousand large cigarettes.
Domestic Air Tickets	7.5 percent of fare, plus $3.90 (2013) per domestic flight segment generally.

---

[29] See Joint Committee on Taxation, *Present Law and Background Information on Federal Excise Taxes* (JCX-1-11), January 2011, for a description the various Federal excise taxes.

[30] Internal Revenue Service, *Statistics of Income Bulletin*, Historical Table 20, "Federal Excise Taxes Reported to or Collected By the Internal Revenue Service, Alcohol and Tobacco Tax and Trade Bureau, and Customs Service, By Type of Excise Tax, Fiscal Years 1999-2010," http://www.irs.gov/pub/irs-soi/histab20.xls (2011).

18

Rev Proc 2013-15

Part III

Administrative, Procedural, and Miscellaneous

26 CFR 601.602: Tax forms and instructions.
(Also Part I, §§ 1, 23, 24, 25A, 32, 55, 63, 68, 132, 137, 151, 221, 2010)

Rev. Proc. 2013-15

Table of Contents

SECTION 1. PURPOSE

SECTION 2. 2013 ADJUSTED ITEMS

- 2 -

SECTION 3. MODIFICATION OF REV. PROC. 2011-52

SECTION 4. EFFECT ON OTHER REVENUE PROCEDURES

SECTION 5. EFFECTIVE DATE

SECTION 6. DRAFTING INFORMATION

SECTION 1. PURPOSE

This revenue procedure sets forth inflation adjusted items for 2013. It also includes some items whose values for 2013 are specified in the American Taxpayer Relief Act of 2012, Pub. L. No. 112-240, 126 Stat. 2313 (ATRA): the beginning of the new 39.6 percent income brackets; the beginning income levels for the limitation on certain itemized deductions; and the beginning income levels for the phaseout of personal exemptions. This revenue procedure also modifies and supersedes section 3.12 of Rev. Proc. 2011-52, 2011-45 I.R.B. 701 to reflect a statutory amendment to § 132(f)(2) made by ATRA. Other inflation adjusted items for 2013 are set forth in Rev. Proc. 2012-41, 2012-45 I.R.B. 539 (dated November 5, 2012).

SECTION 2. 2013 ADJUSTED ITEMS

.01 Tax Rate Tables. For taxable years beginning in 2013, the tax rate tables under § 1 are as follows:

TABLE 1 - Section 1(a) - Married Individuals Filing Joint Returns and Surviving Spouses

If Taxable Income Is:	The Tax Is:
Not over $17,850	10% of the taxable income
Over $17,850 but not over $72,500	$1,785 plus 15% of the excess over $17,850
Over $72,500 but not over $146,400	$9,982.50 plus 25% of the excess over $72,500
Over $146,400 but not over $223,050	$28,457.50 plus 28% of the excess over $146,400
Over $223,050 but not over $398,350	$49,919.50 plus 33% of the excess over $223,050
Over $398,350 but not over $450,000	$107,768 plus 35% of the excess over $398,350
Over $450,000	$125,846 plus 39.6% of the excess over $450,000

TABLE 2 - Section 1(b) – Heads of Households

If Taxable Income Is:	The Tax Is:
Not over $12,750	10% of the taxable income
Over $12,750 but not over $48,600	$1,275 plus 15% of the excess over $12,750
Over $48,600 but not over $125,450	$6,652.50 plus 25% of the excess over $48,600
Over $125,450 but not over $203,150	$25,865 plus 28% of the excess over $125,450
Over $203,150 but not over $398,350	$47,621 plus 33% of the excess over $203,150
Over $398,350	$112,037 plus 35% of

- 4 -

| not over $425,000 | the excess over $398,350 |
| Over $425,000 | $121,394.50 plus 39.6% of the excess over $425,000 |

TABLE 3 - Section 1(c) – Unmarried Individuals (other than Surviving Spouses and Heads of Households)

If Taxable Income Is:	The Tax Is:
Not over $8,925	10% of the taxable income
Over $8,925 but not over $36,250	$892.50 plus 15% of the excess over $8,925
Over $36,250 but not over $87,850	$4,991.25 plus 25% of the excess over $36,250
Over $87,850 but not over $183,250	$17,891.25 plus 28% of the excess over $87,850
Over $183,250 but not over $398,350	$44,603.25 plus 33% of the excess over $183,250
Over $398,350 not over $400,000	$115,586.25 plus 35% of the excess over $398,350
Over $400,000	$116,163.75 plus 39.6% of the excess over $400,000

TABLE 4 - Section 1(d) – Married Individuals Filing Separate Returns

If Taxable Income Is:	The Tax Is:
Not over $8,925	10% of the taxable income
Over $8,925 but not over $36,250	$892.5 plus 15% of the excess over $8,925
Over $36,250 but not over $73,200	$4,991.25 plus 25% of the excess over $36,250
Over $73,200 but not over $111,525	$14,228.75 plus 28% of the excess over $73,200

Over $111,525 but not over $199,175	$24,959.75 plus 33% of the excess over $111,525
Over $199,175 not over $225,000	$53,884.25 plus 35% of the excess over $199,175
Over $225,000	$62,923 plus 39.6% of the excess over $225,000

TABLE 5 - Section 1(e) – Estates and Trusts

If Taxable Income Is:	The Tax Is:
Not over $2,450	15% of the taxable income
Over $2,450 but not over $5,700	$367.50 plus 25% of the excess over $2,450
Over $5,700 but not over $8,750	$1,180 plus 28% of the excess over $5,700
Over $8,750 but not over $11,950	$2,034 plus 33% of the excess over $8,750
Over $11,950	$3,090 plus 39.6% of the excess over $11,950

.02 Adoption Credit. For taxable years beginning in 2013, under § 23(a)(3) the credit allowed for an adoption of a child with special needs is $12,970. For taxable years beginning in 2013, under § 23(b)(1) the maximum credit allowed for other adoptions is the amount of qualified adoption expenses up to $12,970. The available adoption credit begins to phase out under § 23(b)(2)(A) for taxpayers with modified adjusted gross income in excess of $194,580 and is completely phased out for taxpayers with modified adjusted gross income of $234,580 or more. (See section 3.10 of this revenue procedure for the adjusted items relating to adoption assistance programs.)

.03 Child Tax Credit. For taxable years beginning in 2013, the value used in

- 6 -

§ 24(d)(1)(B)(i) to determine the amount of credit under § 24 that may be refundable is $3,000.

.04 Hope Scholarship, American Opportunity, and Lifetime Learning Credits.

(1) For taxable years beginning in 2013, the Hope Scholarship Credit under § 25A(b)(1), as increased under § 25A(i) (the American Opportunity Tax Credit), is an amount equal to 100 percent of qualified tuition and related expenses not in excess of $2,000 plus 25 percent of those expenses in excess of $2,000, but not in excess of $4,000. Accordingly, the maximum Hope Scholarship Credit allowable under § 25A(b)(1) for taxable years beginning in 2013 is $2,500.

(2) For taxable years beginning in 2013, a taxpayer's modified adjusted gross income in excess of $80,000 ($160,000 for a joint return) is used to determine the reduction under § 25A(d)(2) in the amount of the Hope Scholarship Credit otherwise allowable under § 25A(a)(1). For taxable years beginning in 2013, a taxpayer's modified adjusted gross income in excess of $53,000 ($107,000 for a joint return) is used to determine the reduction under § 25A(d)(2) in the amount of the Lifetime Learning Credit otherwise allowable under § 25A(a)(2).

.05 Earned Income Credit.

(1) In general. For taxable years beginning in 2013, the following amounts are used to determine the earned income credit under § 32(b). The "earned income amount" is the amount of earned income at or above which the maximum amount of the earned income credit is allowed. The "threshold phaseout amount" is the amount of adjusted gross income (or, if greater, earned income) above which the maximum amount of the

credit begins to phase out. The "completed phaseout amount" is the amount of adjusted gross income (or, if greater, earned income) at or above which no credit is allowed. The threshold phaseout amounts and the completed phaseout amounts shown in the table below for married taxpayers filing a joint return include the increase provided in § 32(b)(3)(B)(i), as adjusted for inflation for taxable years beginning in 2013.

	Number of Qualifying Children			
Item	One	Two	Three or More	None
Earned Income Amount	$9,560	$13,430	$13,430	$6,370
Maximum Amount of Credit	$3,250	$5,372	$6,044	$487
Threshold Phaseout Amount (Single, Surviving Spouse, or Head of Household)	$17,530	$17,530	$17,530	$7,970
Completed Phaseout Amount (Single, Surviving Spouse, or Head of Household)	$37,870	$43,038	$46,227	$14,340
Threshold Phaseout Amount (Married Filing Jointly)	$22,870	$22,870	$22,870	$13,310
Completed Phaseout Amount (Married Filing Jointly)	$43,210	$48,378	$51,567	$19,680

The instructions for the Form 1040 series provide tables showing the amount of the earned income credit for each type of taxpayer.

   (2) Excessive Investment Income. For taxable years beginning in 2013, the earned

income tax credit is not allowed under § 32(i) if the aggregate amount of certain

investment income exceeds $3,300.

.06 <u>Exemption Amounts for Alternative Minimum Tax</u>. For taxable years beginning in

2013, the exemption amounts under § 55(d)(1) are:

Joint Returns or Surviving Spouses	$80,800
Unmarried Individuals (other than Surviving Spouses)	$51,900
Married Individuals Filing Separate Returns	$40,400
Estates and Trusts	$23,100

For taxable years beginning in 2013, under § 55(b)(1), the excess taxable income

above which the 28 percent tax rate applies is:

Married Individuals Filing Separate Returns	$89,750
Joint Returns, Unmarried Individuals (other than surviving spouses), and Estates and Trusts	$179,500

For taxable years beginning in 2013, the amounts used under § 55(d)(3) to determine

the phaseout of the exemption amounts are:

Joint Returns or a Surviving Spouses	$153,900
Unmarried Individuals (other than Surviving Spouses)	$115,400
Married Individuals Filing Separate Returns and Estates and Trusts	$76,950

.07 <u>Standard Deduction</u>.

(1) <u>In general</u>. For taxable years beginning in 2013, the standard deduction amounts under § 63(c)(2) are as follows:

Filing Status	Standard Deduction
Married Individuals Filing Joint Returns and Surviving Spouses (§ 1(a))	$12,200
Heads of Households (§ 1(b))	$8,950
Unmarried Individuals (other than Surviving Spouses and Heads of Households) (§ 1(c))	$6,100
Married Individuals Filing Separate Returns (§ 1(d))	$6,100

(2) <u>Dependent</u>. For taxable years beginning in 2013, the standard deduction amount under § 63(c)(5) for an individual who may be claimed as a dependent by another taxpayer cannot exceed the greater of (1) $1,000, or (2) the sum of $350 and the individual's earned income.

(3) <u>Aged or blind</u>. For taxable years beginning in 2013, the additional standard deduction amount under § 63(f) for the aged or the blind is $1,200. The additional standard deduction amount is increased to $1,500 if the individual is also unmarried and not a surviving spouse.

.08 <u>Overall Limitation on Itemized Deductions</u>. For taxable years beginning in 2013, the applicable amounts under § 68(b) are $300,000 in the case of a joint return or a surviving spouse, $275,000 in the case of a head of household, $250,000 in the case of an individual who is not married and who is not a surviving spouse or head of household, $150,000 in the case of a married individual filing a separate return.

.09 <u>Qualified Transportation Fringe Benefit</u>. For taxable years beginning in 2013, the monthly limitation under § 132(f)(2)(A) regarding the aggregate fringe benefit exclusion amount for transportation in a commuter highway vehicle and any transit pass is $245. The monthly limitation under § 132(f)(2)(B) regarding the fringe benefit exclusion amount for qualified parking is $245.

.10 Adoption Assistance Programs. For taxable years beginning in 2013, under § 137(a)(2) the amount that can be excluded from an employee's gross income for the adoption of a child with special needs is $12,970. For taxable years beginning in 2013, under § 137(b)(1) the maximum amount that can be excluded from an employee's gross income for the amounts paid or expenses incurred by an employer for qualified adoption expenses furnished pursuant to an adoption assistance program for other adoptions by the employee is $12,970. The amount excludable from an employee's gross income begins to phase out under § 137(b)(2)(A) for taxpayers with modified adjusted gross income in excess of $194,580 and is completely phased out for taxpayers with modified adjusted gross income of $234,580 or more. (See section 3.02 of this revenue procedure for the adjusted items relating to the adoption credit.)

.11 Personal Exemption.

(1) For taxable years beginning in 2013, the personal exemption amount under § 151(d) is $3,900.

(2) Phaseout. For taxable years beginning in 2013, the personal exemption phases out for taxpayers with the following adjusted gross income amounts:

Filing Status	AGI – Beginning of Phaseout	AGI – Completed Phaseout
Married Individuals Filing Joint Returns and	$300,000	$422,500

Surviving Spouses (§ 1(a))		
Heads of Households (§ 1(b))	$275,000	$397,500
Unmarried Individuals (other than Surviving Spouses and Heads of Households) (§ 1(c))	$250,000	$372,500
Married Individuals Filing Separate Returns (§ 1(d))	$150,000	$211,250

.12 <u>Interest on Education Loans</u>. For taxable years beginning in 2013, the $2,500 maximum deduction for interest paid on qualified education loans under § 221 begins to phase out under § 221(b)(2)(B) for taxpayers with modified adjusted gross income in excess of $60,000 ($125,000 for joint returns), and is completely phased out for taxpayers with modified adjusted gross income of $75,000 or more ($155,000 or more for joint returns).

.13 <u>Unified Credit Against Estate Tax</u>. For an estate of any decedent dying during calendar year 2013, the basic exclusion amount is $5,250,000 for determining the amount of the unified credit against estate tax under § 2010.

SECTION 3. MODIFICATION OF REV. PROC. 2011-52

To reflect a statutory amendment made by ATRA to § 132(f)(2), section 3.12 of Rev. Proc. 2011-52 is modified to read as follows:

.12 <u>Qualified Transportation Fringe Benefit</u>. For taxable years beginning in 2012, the monthly limitation under § 132(f)(2)(A) regarding the aggregate fringe benefit exclusion amount for transportation in a commuter highway vehicle and any transit pass is $240. The monthly limitation under § 132(f)(2)(B) regarding the fringe benefit exclusion amount for qualified parking is $240 for 2012.

SECTION 4. EFFECT ON OTHER REVENUE PROCEDURES

This revenue procedure modifies and supersedes section 3.12 of Rev. Proc. 2011-52.

SECTION 5. EFFECTIVE DATE

Except for section 3, this revenue procedure applies to taxable years beginning in 2013. Section 3 of this revenue procedure applies to taxable years beginning in 2012.

SECTION 6. DRAFTING INFORMATION

The principal author of this revenue procedure is William Ruane of the Office of Associate Chief Counsel (Income Tax & Accounting). For further information regarding this revenue procedure, contact Mr. Ruane at (202) 622-4920 (not a toll-free call).

IR-2013-4

IRS 🦅 News Release

INTERNAL REVENUE SERVICE

Media Relations Office | Washington, D.C. | Media Contact: 202.622.4000
www.IRS.gov/newsroom | | Public Contact: 800.829.1040

Annual Inflation Adjustments for 2013

IR-2013-4, Jan. 11, 2013

WASHINGTON — The Internal Revenue Service announced today annual inflation adjustments for tax year 2013, including the tax rate schedules, and other tax changes from the recently passed American Taxpayer Relief Act of 2012.

The tax items for 2013 of greatest interest to most taxpayers include the following changes.

- Beginning in tax year 2013 (generally for tax returns filed in 2014), a new tax rate of 39.6 percent has been added for individuals whose income exceeds $400,000 ($450,000 for married taxpayers filing a joint return). The other marginal rates — 10, 15, 25, 28, 33 and 35 percent — remain the same as in prior years. The guidance contains the taxable income thresholds for each of the marginal rates.

- The standard deduction rises to $6,100 ($12,200 for married couples filing jointly), up from $5,950 ($11,900 for married couples filing jointly) for tax year 2012.

- The American Taxpayer Relief Act of 2012 added a limitation for itemized deductions claimed on 2013 returns of individuals with incomes of $250,000 or more ($300,000 for married couples filing jointly).

- The personal exemption rises to $3,900, up from the 2012 exemption of $3,800. However beginning in 2013, the exemption is subject to a phase-out that begins with adjusted gross incomes of $150,000 ($300,000 for married couples filing jointly). It phases out completely at $211,250 ($422,500 for married couples filing jointly.)

- The Alternative Minimum Tax exemption amount for tax year 2013 is $51,900 ($80,800, for married couples filing jointly), set by the American Taxpayer Relief Act of 2012, which indexes future amounts for inflation. The 2012 exemption amount was $50,600 ($78,750 for married couples filing jointly).

- The maximum Earned Income Credit amount is $6,044 for taxpayers filing jointly who have 3 or more qualifying children, up from a total of $5,891 for tax year 2012.

- Estates of decedents who die during 2013 have a basic exclusion amount of $5,250,000, up from a total of $5,120,000 for estates of decedents who died in 2012.

- For tax year 2013, the monthly limitation regarding the aggregate fringe benefit exclusion amount for transit passes and transportation in a commuter highway vehicle is $245, up from $240 for tax year 2012 (the legislation provided a retroactive increase from the $125 limit that had been in place).

Details on these inflation adjustments and others are contained in Revenue Procedure 2013-15, which will be published in Internal Revenue Bulletin 2013-5 on Jan.28, 2013. Other inflation adjusted items were published in October 2012 in Revenue Procedure 2012-41.

—30—

INDEX

References are to paragraph numbers

Farmers